Yearbook on
International
Communist Affairs
1982

Yearbook on International Communist Affairs

1982

Parties and Revolutionary Movements

EDITOR: Richard F. Staar

MANAGING EDITOR: Robert Wesson

ASSOCIATE AREA EDITORS

Africa and the Middle East	•	*Thomas H. Henriksen*
The Americas	•	*Robert Wesson*
Asia and the Pacific	•	*William E. Ratliff*
Western Europe	•	*Dennis L. Bark*
Eastern Europe and the Soviet Union	•	*Milorad M. Drachkovitch*

HOOVER INSTITUTION PRESS
Stanford University, Stanford, California

Hoover Press Publication 272

Contents

ASIA AND THE PACIFIC

WESTERN EUROPE

EASTERN EUROPE AND THE SOVIET UNION

Preface

The *Yearbook on International Communist Affairs* was inaugurated in 1966. Since 1969, Dr. Richard F. Staar, associate director and senior fellow of the Hoover Institution, has served as its editor and is responsible for its national and international reputation as a major reference work. In October 1981, Dr. Staar was appointed ambassador of the United States to the Mutual and Balanced Force Reduction negotiations being conducted in Vienna, Austria. While Dr. Staar is on leave from the Hoover Institution to serve in this capacity, responsibility for the editorial management of the *Yearbook* has been assumed by the undersigned.

The general structure of this sixteenth edition, as of previous editions, was designed by Dr. Staar, and it was he who selected the contributors to this volume in collaboration with the respective area editors. Dr. Staar is not responsible for the content of the profiles contained in this edition. A major debt of gratitude is, however, due him for the time and effort he devoted to this and previous editions.

Staff members and several of the associate editors were responsible for some of the writing and research and most of the data-collecting effort that produced this *Yearbook*. Profiles were contributed by 73 scholars, many of whom prepared more than one. Names and affiliations appear at the end of individual essays. Mrs. Margit Grigory assisted in the processing and filing of research materials, the assembling of some of the data, and much of the final typing. Mrs. Grigory also handled most of the correspondence with the contributors. Special appreciation for the bibliography and for their response to emergency requests is due to the curators, the staff, and the members of the readers' services department at the Hoover Institution. John Ziemer heroically performed the task of ably and carefully copy-editing the entire volume in a compressed period.

Robert Wesson
Managing Editor

*   *   *

The following abbreviations are used for frequently cited publications and news agencies:

CSM	*Christian Science Monitor*
FBIS	*Foreign Broadcast Information Service*
IB	*Information Bulletin* (of the *WMR*)
JPRS	*Joint Publications Research Service*
NYT	*New York Times*
WMR	*World Marxist Review*
WP	*Washington Post*
YICA	*Yearbook on International Communist Affairs*

ACAN	Agencia Centro Americano Noticias
ADN	Allgemeiner Deutscher Nachrichtendienst
AFP	Agence France-Presse
ANSA	Agenzia Nazionale Stampa Associata
AP	Associated Press
BTA	Bulgarska telegrafna agentsiya
ČETEKA	Ceskoslovenská tisková kancelár
DPA	Deutsche Presse Agentur
KPL	Khaosan Pathet Lao
MENA	Middle East News Agency
MTI	Magyar Távirati Iroda
NCNA	New China News Agency
PAP	Polska Agencja Prasowa
UPI	United Press International
VNA	Vietnam News Agency

Introduction

The purpose of the 1982 *Yearbook on International Communist Affairs* is to provide data on the organization, leadership, policies, activities, and international relations of communist or Marxist-Leninist parties throughout the world during calendar year 1981. Much of the information comes from primary sources in the native languages and from local broadcasts as reported by the U.S. Foreign Broadcast Information Service (FBIS). It is the policy of the *Yearbook* to cover major communist parties wherever they are known to exist; those of 96 countries are included.* Nigeria and Saudi Arabia have been omitted for insufficiency of data.

Like previous *Yearbooks*, this edition differs from its predecessors in several, for the most part, minor ways. Two should be mentioned. More space than previously is devoted to the past year, less to antecedents. It represents less of an updated encyclopedia on communist parties and more an almanac of developments within these movements and communist-ruled states. The reader desirous of more information regarding events prior to 1981 must refer to previous editions.

The other change involves a modest broadening of scope, as indicated by the subtitle: *Parties and Revolutionary Movements*. This edition includes for the first time a discussion of the ruling parties in several countries not formally designated as communist, namely Afghanistan, Angola, Ethiopia, Grenada, Mozambique, and South Yemen; the ruling party of Nicaragua was included in preceding volumes. Adherence of these regimes to Marxism-Leninism, ideological rhetoric, political and economic structures, and association with communist-ruled countries and causes suggest that it would be unrealistic to exclude them from the community in which the Soviet Union, East Germany, and Cuba are prominent members. It is significant that Angola, Ethiopia, Grenada, Mozambique, and South Yemen were the only officially noncommunist states that voted with the Soviet Union against the U.N. resolution on Afghanistan in both 1980 and 1981. A number of other ruling parties might conceivably have been included by virtue of their association with communist parties. For example, the following additional ruling parties attended party congresses in the Soviet Union, Bulgaria, and East Germany during 1981: the African Party for the Independence of Guinea and the Cape Verde Islands, the Benin People's Revolutionary Party, the Congolese Labor Party, the Algerian National Liberation Front, the Democratic Party of Guinea, the Congress Party for Malagasy Independence (member of a ruling coalition), the Baathist Arab Socialist Renaissance Party of Syria, and the Revolutionary Party of Tanzania. Representatives of many of these had the honor of the podium in Moscow at the Twenty-Sixth Congress of the CPSU during February–March 1981. A list of all congresses held during the year follows this introduction.

It is even more difficult to classify many other radical parties and organizations. The general

---

*At the Twenty-Sixth CPSU Congress on 23 February 1981, Brezhnev announced the existence of communist parties in 94 countries. Since that time, the movement in Kampuchea has been resurrected and the Communist Party of Suriname has been founded.

criteria for inclusion as communist are the following: (1) adherence to the ideology of Marxism-Leninism, (2) declared objective of revolution and socialization of the economy, (3) support for communist causes in general, and (4) participation in communist meetings and organizations. However, there have been splits and divisions almost from the day of the Bolshevik Revolution. Not only pro-Soviet but also pro-Chinese, pro-Albanian, and Trotskyite movements, as well as other rival, mostly nationalistic, groups consider themselves communist and are discussed here in the *Yearbook* to a limited extent. The confusion is compounded by the fact that many pro-Moscow groups call themselves "workers' " or "people's" parties, while many of the movements named "communist" are usually more radical than the pro-Moscow parties.

It is impractical to attempt to cover all leftist-revolutionary movements, radical-socialist parties, and national liberation fronts. They may look to the Soviet Union or other communist-ruled countries for support, maintain close relationships with communist organizations, attend party congresses, join with the USSR on international issues, participate in Soviet front organizations (e.g., the World Peace Council) and even be recognized by Moscow as "revolutionary democratic" or "socialist" in the sense of "scientific socialism." The largest number in this general category not covered by the *Yearbook* are in the African and Near Eastern regions, such as the African National Congress, the Bahrain National Liberation Front, and the South-West African People's Organization (SWAPO). Numerous terrorist organizations, such as the Red Brigades in Italy and the Japanese Red Army, also seemed inappropriate for *Yearbook* coverage.

Because of the salience of the U.S.-USSR confrontation throughout the world, there is special interest in the pro-Soviet movements. For this reason, a checklist of parties and their affiliations follows this introduction. A large number of the major communist parties of the world are pro-Moscow, probably because the Soviet Union can offer much more economic and political support than can its communist rivals. Many of the other groups, especially the Chinese- or Albanian-oriented, are violently hostile to the USSR and its allies. Despite internecine differences, however, the various Marxist parties are all collectivist in philosophy, anticapitalist, and opposed in general outlook to the West, particularly to the United States. They may identify America and the Soviet Union as imperialist powers, but in actions they are certainly more inimical to the former. An exception is the case of the People's Republic of China, where antagonism toward Moscow outweighs dislike for Washington. It would seem that the reason for a communist orientation is not usually admiration for the Soviet example (or that of China or Albania) but antipathy for what is generally called "American imperialism" and the prevalent world economic order. Except in the Islamic regions of North Africa and the Near East, where Muslim fundamentalism inspires many radical parties, to be desirous of violent change often seems equivalent to adoption of Marxism-Leninism and something like a communist orientation in politics.

The Balance in 1981. By far the most significant developments for the world communist movement were in Poland, although the net effect had not become clear at year's end. During most of 1981, the Soviet bloc was disconcerted by the spectacle of a communist regime unable to check a workers' movement that went from victory to growing strength after the successful strikes and regime concessions after August 1980. The position of the free trade unions seemed to become more solidified as the impotence of the state increased. However, the economy continued to deteriorate and tensions mounted. The government seemed to be trying to retract some of its concessions, while many leaders of Solidarity, impatient with the moderation of Lech Walesa, began demanding free elections, that is, an end to communist rule. In October, Gen. Wojciech Jaruzelski became head of both party and government; and on 13 December he led the first military coup in a communist-ruled state, decreeing martial law and placing a military junta in power. Repression came swiftly. Although resistance spread into many areas, it was difficult to see how military rule could possibly be shaken without precipitating a Soviet occupation.

The USSR relieved itself (insofar as the coup had been prompted by Moscow) of a major concern by having the military of Poland in effect occupy their own country as Soviet surrogates. This represented, however, a confession of moral and political weakness that communism had to resort to Bonapartism. Broadly speaking, regimes were not thriving in the Soviet bloc. The economic performance of the USSR was poor. Yet another bad harvest forced large grain imports. Industrial output, according to official statistics, remained dismal. The country faced a decline in its standard of living. The economic prospects for East European states were likewise generally bad, and they also suffered from political stagnation.

The Twenty-Sixth Congress of the CPSU made history by what it failed to do, that is, to make any changes at all in the steadily aging Politburo and Secretariat, the first time a congress had not injected new blood into the ruling organs. It seems clear that the succession to Brezhnev will be traumatic, although it may be delayed, as the president and secretary general appeared more vigorous than in the recent past. In the East European countries (except Poland), leadership also remained remarkably static. The coherence of the Soviet bloc seemed somewhat dubious, however, as Hungary moved farther from the Soviet economic model and Romania endorsed President Reagan's proposals regarding withdrawal of missiles from the European theater.

In Western Europe, somewhat ironically, the greatest gain of any communist movement came through the victory of the rather anti-Soviet Socialist party in France. Although suffering a sharp electoral setback, the French Communists received four, mostly minor, positions in the cabinet. This involved the first appearance of Communists in the national government of a major European power since 1947. There were speculations that it might serve as a precedent for other Communists to gain similar status, especially in Italy.

Elsewhere in Western Europe, the total strength of communist parties did not change much during the year. The Spanish and Italian parties, along with the French (the strongest in the region), continued to criticize Soviet policies, especially in Afghanistan and Poland. Elsewhere, for the most part, the movements remained ineffective splinters. They contributed, however, to a massive upsurge of antiwar, antinuclear, and to a considerable extent anti-American sentiment, manifested in many large rallies. These demonstrations seemed far more useful to the USSR than anything the communist parties, obedient or independent Eurocommunist, could achieve by themselves. The pacifist tide diminished on 18 November after President Reagan's disarmament proposals and the shock at the heavy-handed crackdown in Poland in December. Overall, Soviet prestige seemed to have declined toward the end of the year.

During 1981, the CPSU actively developed its relations with communist parties and a variety of radical or revolutionary movements in the Near East and North Africa, especially by championing the Arab cause against Israel and by giving diplomatic recognition and promising arms to the PLO. Moscow seemed to have some success in eroding the negative impression caused by its invasion of Afghanistan. It appeared to increase its influence in Iran and several Arab countries, although it is perhaps remarkable that this agitated region did not become subject to more communist penetration. The Soviet-Cuban military presence in South Yemen and Ethiopia was strengthened, and USSR cooperation with Libya was intensified.

The communist parties had little to celebrate in Asia during 1981. China, the apparent near-superpower of Maoist times, turned increasingly inward toward economic, political, and educational reconstruction under the leadership of Deng Xiaoping. Maoism seemed largely discarded, and little remained of its revolutionary aspirations. Pro-Chinese parties consequently tended to decline around the world, except in the immediate vicinity of the Mainland; several of them turned to Albania.

China's policy continued to be preoccupied with its antagonism toward the Soviet Union and the latter's ally, Vietnam. A corollary involved Chinese help for anti-Vietnamese guerrillas in Kampuchea.

In Asia, communism was embarrassed by guerrilla war in both Kampuchea and Afghanistan. The pro-Soviet Vietnamese in the former and USSR armed forces in the latter made little or no progress against the insurgents. As far as free Asia is concerned, only in Japan and India did communist parties seem capable of playing a consequential political role; elsewhere, they remained insignificant.

In Latin America, 1981 saw a heightening of tensions, at least in the Central American-Caribbean area. Leftist guerrillas extended their activities throughout Guatemala, although in El Salvador their victory seemed farther away than during the previous year, as civil war turned into a sporadic terrorist campaign. The most important development involved the leftward slide of the Sandinista revolution in Nicaragua, bringing the country nearer, although not yet approximating, Cuban-style totalitarianism. Elsewhere communist movements generally continued fragmented and impotent, and Cuba suffered diplomatic reverses. South America stayed relatively tranquil, and the main Soviet activity on that continent included courting economically the military governments of Argentina and Brazil.

In sum, ruling communist parties did not prosper much, and their attractiveness as models continued to decline. What successes they enjoyed, based primarily on military force, mostly were confined to the Third World. The principal appeals of Marxism-Leninism in Europe centered on the fear of war and Soviet military power, and in the Third World on the resentment of the poor and weak nations against the rich and powerful, appeals that paradoxically bore no direct relationship to the theories of Karl Marx.

Richard F. Staar
Editor

Communist Party Congresses

Country	Occasion	Date
Israel (RAKAH)	19th	11–14 February
USSR	26th	23 February–3 March
Mexico	19th and 20th	9–14 March; 15 October
	National Unification Assembly	5–7 November
Réunion	Special	29 March
Bulgaria	12th	31 March–4 April
Czechoslovakia	16th	6–10 April
East Germany (SED)	10th	11–16 April
West Berlin (SEW)	6th	15–17 May
Finland	19th	22–24 May
Kampuchea (KPRP)	4th (CP resurrected)	26–29 May
Mongolia (MPRP)	18th	26–31 May
West Germany	6th	29–31 May
Argentina	9th National Conference*	June
Nicaragua (PSN)	12th	3 July
Poland (PUWP)	9th Extraordinary	14–20 July
Suriname	Founding	24 July
Spain	10th	28–31 July
Senegal (PIT)	Constituent	ca. 8 August
Australia (SPA)	4th	2 October
Albania (APL)	8th	1–8 November
Guinea-Bissau (PAIGC)	1st	8–14 November
Great Britain	37th	14–17 November
Iceland (AB)	Convention	20–22 November
Sweden (VPK)	26th	20–24 November
Ecuador	10th	26–29 November
Norway	17th	4–6 December
Jamaica (WPJ)	2d	18–21 December

*"Tantamount to a congress," according to *WMR* (London), December 1981, p. 27.

Checklist of Communist Parties and Front Organizations

AFRICA AND THE MIDDLE EAST (17)

	Mid–1981 Population (est.)	Communist Party Membership	Percentage of Vote; Seats in Legislature	Status	Orientation
Algeria (PAGS)	19,422,000	450 est.	—	proscribed	pro-Moscow
Egypt	43,300,000	500 est.	—	proscribed	pro-Moscow
Iran (Tudeh)	39,958,000	1,500 est.	— (1980); none	legal	pro-Moscow
Iraq	13,575,000	2,000 est.	— (1980); none	legal	pro-Moscow
Israel (RAKAH)	3,948,000	1,500 est.	3.4 (1981); 4 of 120	legal	pro-Moscow
Jordan	3,443,000	500 est.	—	proscribed	pro-Moscow
Lebanon	3,097,000[1]	2,500 est.	— (1972); none	legal	pro-Moscow
Lesotho	1,365,000	negligible	—	proscribed	pro-Moscow
Morocco (PPS)	21,590,000	2,750 est.	— (1977); 1 of 264	legal	pro-Moscow
Nigeria (SWPP)	79,682,000	unknown	—	proscribed	pro-Moscow
Réunion	518,000	2,000 est.	— (1981); none	legal	pro-Moscow
Saudi Arabia	9,686,000	negligible	—	proscribed	pro-Moscow
Senegal (PIT)	5,834,000	1,000 est.[2]	0.32 (1978); none	legal	pro-Moscow
South Africa	29,313,000	unknown	—	proscribed	pro-Moscow
Sudan	19,312,000	1,500 est.	—	proscribed	pro-Moscow
Syria	9,107,000	5,000 est.	3.0 (1981); none	legal	pro-Moscow
Tunisia	6,663,000	100 est.	2.1 (1981); none	legal	pro-Moscow
Total	309,813,000	21,300			

THE AMERICAS (27)

	Mid–1981 Population (est.)	Communist Party Membership	Percentage of Vote; Seats in Legislature	Status	Orientation
Argentina	28,130,000	80,000 claim	—	proscribed	pro-Moscow
Bolivia	5,490,000	500 est.[3]	—	proscribed	pro-Moscow
Brazil	124,800,000	6,000 est.	—	proscribed	pro-Moscow
Canada (CPC)	24,200,000	5,000 est.	0.05 (1980); none	legal	pro-Moscow
(CPC-ML)		for all groups	0.13 (1980); none	legal	pro-Beijing
Chile	11,162,000	20,000 est.	—	proscribed	pro-Moscow
Colombia	25,217,000	12,000 est.	1.9 (1978); 3 of 311	legal	pro-Moscow
Costa Rica (PVP)	2,322,000	3,200 est.	2.7 (1978); 3 of 57	legal	pro-Moscow
Cuba	9,800,000	434,000 claim	— (1981); all 499	in power	pro-Moscow
Dominican Republic	5,855,000	4,500 est.[4]	— (1978); none	legal	pro-Moscow
Ecuador	8,275,000	1,000 est.	3.2 (1979); 1 of 69[5]	legal	pro-Moscow
El Salvador	4,610,000	800 est.[6]	—	proscribed	pro-Moscow
Guadeloupe	304,000	3,000 est.	38.6 (1981); 1 of 3	legal	pro-Moscow
Guatemala (PGT)	7,310,000	750 est.	—	proscribed	pro-Moscow
Guyana (PPP)	857,000	unknown	20.4 (1980); 10 of 65	legal	pro-Moscow
Haiti (PUCH)	5,923,000	350 est.	—	proscribed	pro-Moscow
Honduras	3,940,000	1,500 est.	—	proscribed	pro-Moscow
Jamaica (WPJ)	2,268,000	unknown	— (1980); none	legal	pro-Moscow
Martinique	302,000	1,000 est.	6.4 (1981); none	legal	pro-Moscow
Mexico (PUSM)	69,100,000	112,000 claim	5.4 (1979); 19 of 400	legal	independent
Nicaragua (PSN)[7]	2,559,000	250 est.	—	legal	pro-Moscow
Panama (PPP)	1,928,000	550 est.	— (1978); none	legal	pro-Moscow
Paraguay	3,268,000	3,500 est.	—	proscribed	pro-Moscow
Peru	18,119,000	3,000 est.[8]	2.8 (1980); 4 of 60	legal	pro-Moscow
Puerto Rico (PSP)[9]	3,258,000	125 est.	0.3 (1980); none	legal	pro-Moscow
United States	229,700,000	11,000 est.	0.01 (1980); none	legal	pro-Moscow
Uruguay	2,944,000	7,000 est.	—	proscribed	pro-Moscow
Venezuela	17,913,000	4,500 est.	9.0 (1978); 22 of 195	legal	pro-Moscow
Total	619,554,000	715,525			

ASIA AND THE PACIFIC (19)

	Mid–1981 Population (est.)	Communist Party Membership	Percentage of Vote; Seats in Legislature	Status	Orientation
Australia (CPA)	14,800,000	2,000 est.	— (1980); none	legal	independent
(SPA)		1,500 est.	— (1980); none	legal	pro–Moscow
Bangladesh	90,680,000	2,500 est.	— (1979); 1 of 300	legal	pro–Moscow
Burma (BCP–White Flag)	35,289,000	3,000 claim	—	proscribed	pro–Beijing
China	1,041,500,000	39,000,000 claim	(1981); all 3,202	in power	pro–Beijing
India (CPI)	692,400,000	150,000 est.[10]	2.6 (1980); 11 of 525	legal	pro–Moscow
(CPM)		100,000 est.	6.2 (1980); 36 of 525	legal	neutral
Indonesia (PKI-Moscow)	154,300,000	50 est.	—	proscribed	pro–Moscow
(PKI-Beijing)		250 est.	—	proscribed	pro–Beijing
Japan	117,700,000	440,000 claim	10.4 (1980); 29 of 511	legal	independent
Kampuchea (KPRP)[11]	5,774,000	5,000 est.	99.0 (1981); all 117	in power	pro–Moscow
Korea (North)	19,000,000	2,000,000 claim	100.0 (1977); all 579	in power	neutral
Laos (LPRP)	3,700,000	15,000 claim	no legislature	in power	pro–Moscow
Malaysia (CPM)	14,330,000	3,000 est.[12]	—	proscribed	pro–Beijing
(NKCP)		200 est.	—	proscribed	pro–Beijing
Mongolia	1,700,000	76,000 claim	99.0 (1977); all 354	in power	pro–Moscow
Nepal	15,338,000	1,500 est.[13]	— (1981); none	legal	pro–Moscow
New Zealand (CPNZ)	3,117,000	under 100	— (1981); none	legal	independent
(SUP)		200 claim	0.5 (1981); none	legal	pro–Moscow
Pakistan	90,439,000	a few hundred	—	proscribed	pro–Moscow
Philippines (PKP)	50,100,000	200 est.	—	proscribed	pro–Moscow
(CPP-ML)		3,000 est.	—	proscribed	pro–Beijing
Sri Lanka	15,172,000	6,000 est.	1.9 (1977); none[14]	legal	pro–Moscow
Thailand	48,787,000	1,000 est.[15]	—	proscribed	pro–Beijing
Vietnam	55,100,000	1,480,000 est.	97.9 (1981); all 538	in power	pro–Moscow
Total	2,469,226,000	43,290,500			

WESTERN EUROPE (23)

	Mid–1981 Population (est.)	Communist Party Membership	Percentage of Vote; Seats in Legislature	Status	Orientation
Austria	7,509,000	25,000 est.	0.96 (1979); none	legal	pro-Moscow
Belgium	9,900,000	10,000 est.	2.3 (1981); 2 of 212	legal	independent
Cyprus (AKEL)	636,000	12,000 est.	32.8 (1981); 12 of 35	legal	pro-Moscow
Denmark	5,100,000	9,000 est.	1.1 (1981); none	legal	pro-Moscow
Finland	4,784,000	47,000 est.	17.9 (1979); 35 of 200	legal	independent
France	54,000,000	700,000 claim	16.2 (1981); 44 of 491	legal	pro-Moscow
Great Britain	56,000,000	18,500 claim	0.05 (1979); none	legal	independent
Greece (KKE-Exterior)	9,671,000	33,500 est.[16]	10.9 (1981); 13 of 300	legal	pro-Moscow
Iceland (AB)[17]	229,000	2,200 est.	19.7 (1979); 11 of 60	legal	isolationist
Ireland	3,400,000	500 est.	— (1981); none	legal	pro-Moscow
Italy	57,200,000	1,715,890 claim	30.4 (1979); 201 of 630	legal	independent
Luxembourg	365,000	600 est.	5.0 (1979); 2 of 59	legal	pro-Moscow
Malta	370,000	150 est.	— (1981); none	legal	pro-Moscow
Netherlands	14,200,000	13,000 est.	2.1 (1981); 3 of 150	legal	independent
Norway (NKP) (SV)[18]	4,100,000	500 est. 2,000 est.	— (1981); none 4.9 (1981); 4 of 155	legal	pro-Moscow pro-Moscow
Portugal	9,996,000	187,000 claim	16.7 (1980); 41 of 250	legal	pro-Moscow
San Marino	22,000	300 est.	25.0 (1978); 16 of 60	legal	independent
Spain	37,700,000	140,000 est.	10.6 (1979); 23 of 350	legal	independent
Sweden (VPK)	8,324,000	18,000 claim	5.6 (1979); 23 of 349	legal	independent
Switzerland (PdA)	6,390,000	5,000 est.	1.5 (1979); 3 of 200	legal	pro-Moscow
Turkey	46,700,000	negligible	—	proscribed	pro-Moscow
West Germany	61,666,000	48,856 claim	0.2 (1980); none	legal	pro-Moscow
West Berlin (SEW)[19]	1,894,000	7,000 est.	0.7 (1981); none	legal	pro-Moscow
Total	400,156,000	2,995,796			

EASTERN EUROPE AND THE SOVIET UNION (9)

	Mid–1981 Population (est.)	Communist Party Membership	Percentage of Vote; Seats in Legislature	Status	Orientation
Albania (APL)	2,700,000	122,600 claim	99.9 (1978); all 250 Democratic Front	in power	independent
Bulgaria	8,900,000	825,876 claim	99.9 (1976); all 400 Fatherland Front	in power	pro-Moscow
Czechoslovakia	15,300,000	1,538,179 claim	99.9 (1981); all 350 National Front	in power	pro-Moscow
East Germany (SED)	16,700,000	2,172,110 claim	99.9 (1981); all 500 National Front	in power	pro-Moscow
Hungary (HSWP)	10,700,000	812,000 claim	99.3 (1980); all 352 Patriotic People's Front	in power	pro-Moscow
Poland (PUWP)	35,700,000	2,734,000 claim	99.5 (1980); all 460 National Unity Front	in power	pro-Moscow
Romania	22,400,000	3,004,336 claim	98.5 (1980); all 369 Socialist Unity Front	in power	independent
USSR	266,750,000	17,480,000 claim	99.9 (1979); all 1,500 CPSU approved	in power	pro-Moscow
Yugoslavia (LCY)	22,352,000	2,199,444 claim	— (1978); all 308 Socialist Alliance	in power	independent
Total	401,502,000	30,888,545			
Grand Total[20]	4,200,251,000	77,911,666			

INTERNATIONAL COMMUNIST FRONT ORGANIZATIONS (10)

	Year Founded	Headquarters	Claimed Membership[21]	Affiliates	Countries
Afro-Asian Peoples' Solidarity Organization	1957	Cairo	no data	87	
Christian Peace Conference	1958	Prague	no data		at least 80
International Association of Democratic Lawyers	1946	Brussels	ca. 25,000		nearly 80
International Organization of Journalists	1946	Prague	over 180,000		120 plus
International Union of Students	1946	Prague	over 10,000,000	ca. 118	
Women's International Democratic Federation	1945	East Berlin	over 200,000,000	129	114
World Federation of Democratic Youth	1945	Budapest	over 150,000,000	over 250	100 plus
World Federation of Scientific Workers	1946	Paris	ca. 450,000	ca. 33	
World Federation of Trade Unions	1945	Prague	ca. 200,000,000	ca. 71	
World Peace Council	1949	Helsinki	no data	over 135	

NOTES TO CHECKLIST OF COMMUNIST PARTIES AND FRONT ORGANIZATIONS

1. Not accounting for possible impact of civil war.

2. This figure excludes an estimated 2,000 members in a legal branch of PIT not recognized by Moscow.

3. Communist Party of Bolivia (PCB). Other leftist organizations include PCB–Marxist-Leninist, Movement of the Revolutionary Left (MIR), Revolutionary Party of Bolivian Workers, and Trotskyist groupings.

4. Includes about a dozen Marxist groups, the Dominican Communist Party being pro-Moscow and pro-Havana.

5. The one deputy represents the Maoist MPD, not the Communist Party of Ecuador (PCE).

6. Estimate is for the combined political and guerrilla forces of the PCES.

7. This socialist party is restricted to domestic activities. The Sandinist National Liberation Front (FSLN) sent a delegation to the Twenty-Sixth CPSU Congress in Moscow. The pro-Beijing CPN claims 1,200 members.

8. The pro-Beijing groups probably total about 1,500 members. In addition, other Marxist-Leninist and Trotskyist parties exist.

9. The Puerto Rican Communist Party (PCP) also is pro-Moscow and has about 125 members.

10. The CPI claimed a highly inflated membership of 466,483 as of September 1981 (*WMR*, December 1981, p. 46).

11. Kampuchean People's Revolutionary Party, established in May 1981 and the ninety-fifth communist movement recognized by Moscow.

12. Combined total for party members and guerrillas.

13. Total of all factions in the CPN.

14. In a January 1981 by-election, the SLCP won one seat in the 168-member parliament.

15. This does not include an estimated 10,000 insurgents of the Thai People's Liberation Armed Forces.

16. This estimate does not include the smaller KKE-Interior, which remains independent, leans toward Eurocommunism, and claims about 4,800 members.

17. People's Alliance.

18. The Socialist Left Party is the strongest among three Marxist movements, the others being the (pro-Chinese) Workers' Communist Party and the Norwegian Communist Party, the weakest of all.

19. The SEW is considered a subsidiary of the ruling movement in East Germany.

20. According to Boris Vesnin, "The Communists and Peace, Detente, Disarmament," *New Times*, Moscow, no. 49 (December 1981), p. 10, communist parties exist in 94 countries, with a total membership of more than 77 million. This figure obviously includes the Chinese movement, which claims 39 million members.

21. Figures for CPC, IADL, IOJ, WIDF, and WFDY from *WMR*, December 1981, pp. 121–22. In the case of countries, figures also include individual members and not affiliated associations.

Editor's Note: Parties included in the Checklist are affiliated or were formerly affiliated with the Soviet-led Marxist-Leninist movement.

AFRICA AND THE MIDDLE EAST

Introduction

Despite setbacks and preoccupations in Afghanistan and Poland, Moscow continued to exploit opportunities and to consolidate gains in Africa and the Middle East. This year's Twenty-Sixth Congress of the Communist Party of the Soviet Union (CPSU) afforded the Soviets a publicity forum to strengthen fraternal ties and to receive public endorsements for Moscow's policies. Thirteen nonruling communist parties of Africa and the Middle East sent representatives to the Congress (Egypt, Iraq, Israel, Jordan, Lebanon, Lesotho, Réunion, South Africa, Sudan, Syria, Tunisia, the Party of Progress and Socialism of Morocco, and the African Independence Party of Senegal). Three parties did not attend: Algeria's Socialist Vanguard Party, Iran's Tudeh Party, and the Communist Party of Saudi Arabia. Additionally, seven ruling parties or movements, which consider themselves "Marxist-Leninist," "vanguard" or "scientific socialist" in orientation, dispatched delegates to Moscow. Because of the commitment to social, political, and economic restructuring of their societies by four of them, the *Yearbook* editorial staff decided to include profiles on Angola, Mozambique, Ethiopia, and the People's Democratic Republic of Yemen (PDRY). (Profiles on Benin, Guinea-Bissau, and the People's Republic of the Congo were not included because their ruling movements lacked the commitment of the others.) Five parties from the region with a "revolutionary democratic" character also were represented at the Soviet congress: Algerian Liberation Front, Democratic Front of Guinea, African Party for the Independence of Guinea and the Cape Verde Islands, Arab Socialist Renaissance Party of Syria, and the Revolutionary Party of Tanzania. Two African liberation movements were also present: the South-West African People's Organization (SWAPO) and the African National Congress (ANC). Two liberation movements not represented were the Popular Front for the Liberation of Oman and the Frente Popular para la Liberacion de Saguia El-Hamra y de Rio de Oro (POLISARIO) of the Western Sahara. The Palestine Liberation Organization (PLO), a united front, was also represented. In addition to those already mentioned, the congress was attended by delegates from a number of ruling and nonruling parties in Africa and the Middle East. One socialist party was the Progressive Socialist Party of Lebanon. Other ruling parties that attended were Burundi's Unity and National Progress Party, the General People's Congress of the Socialist People's Libyan Arab Jamahiriyah, the Democratic Union of the Mali People, the Movement for the Liberation of São Tome and Principe, All People's Congress of Sierra Leone, and Zambia's United National Independence Party.

Moscow followed up its invitations to the congress with a diplomatic offensive in the Middle East. First, it signed an agreement with the PLO to supply "SAM-6, SAM-9, and long-range missiles" (*Akhbar al-Usbu,* 5 October; *FBIS,* 6 October). Then it granted the PLO mission in the Soviet capital embassy status. Yassir Arafat, head of the PLO, described the elevation of the mission to diplomatic status a "very important signal" to the world that the Soviet Union supported the PLO's struggle for an independent Palestinian state (Kuwait News Agency, 21 October; *FBIS,* 22 October). Salah Khalaf, a member of the Central Committee of Al Fatah, a Palestinian organization, stated that the Soviet Union is "extending its hand to the Arabs" to counter the U.S.-Israeli alliance (Voice of Palestine, 21 October; *FBIS,* 22 October). Soviet actions were also calculated to offset the USSR's perceived anti-Muslim posture in Afghanistan.

This year witnessed a pattern of stepped-up meetings among communist parties and left-wing movements of the Middle East, which began with a gathering of "the Arab parties and organizations attending the 26th CPSU Congress at the PLO office in Moscow" (Radio Damascus, 28 February; *FBIS/USSR,* 4 March). Eleven Arab and communist workers' parties next met in Beirut and issued a joint statement on 9 May. In attendance were the communist parties of Saudi Arabia, Tunisia, Jordan, Sudan, Syria, Iraq, Lebanon, and Egypt, plus the Moroccan Party of Progress and Socialism, the Algerian Socialist Vanguard Party, and the National Liberation Front of Bahrain (*al-Nida,* 10 May). Their statement condemned American imperialism, supported the Soviet Union's policy of coexistence, backed popular liberation struggles, welcomed the revolutionary successes in Angola, Afghanistan, Ethiopia, and Mozambique, gave cautious support to the Iranian revolution, praised the consolidation of the progressive regime in the PDRY, and lauded the growth of the Palestinian resistance movement. It went on to censor the Camp David agreement, American designs for securing a sphere of influence in the Persian Gulf, and American-Omani collaboration. The statement also regretted the war between Iran and Iraq, the ongoing imperialist offensive against Syria, and "machinations" of Zionism. The statement additionally called for an anti-imperialist national-democratic front comprising a variety of anti-imperialist classes and strata. It envisioned the working class having "the chief role to play in the achievement of such alliances." An Arab national-liberation movement would have to be allied with the Soviet Union as "a necessity which has a profound objective basis" (*IB,* August, pp. 12–19).

A preliminary meeting in June at an unidentified location brought together the communist parties of Cyprus, Egypt, Greece, Jordan, Iraq, Israel, Saudi Arabia, Sudan, Syria, and Turkey as well as the National Liberation Front of Bahrain, the People's Democratic Party of Afghanistan, and the Commission to Organize the Party of the Working People of Ethiopia (*Rizospastis,* 8 July; *Zo Ha-Derekh,* 29 July). The subsequent meeting "somewhere in Europe" in September was attended by all those participating in the June preliminary conference along with the Tudeh Party of Iran (*Jerusalem Post,* 16 October). The meeting's declaration was distributed in Athens (Tass, Athens, 28 September; *FBIS/USSR,* 2 October). No explanation was provided for the absence of the Communist Party of Lebanon. In a lengthy report, the Somali Communist Party stated that it was unable to attend the conference because of the "difficult struggle Somali communists are waging in their country" (*Rizospastis,* 28 October; *FBIS,* 30 October). Juxtaposed alongside this expanded frequency of meetings among Mid Eastern communist parties is their continuing lack of success. In Syria, for example, the communist party lost all its seats in the November parliamentary elections. Likewise, the Tunisian Communists polled only 0.78 percent of the vote (they claimed 20 percent) in the November parliamentary elections.

Throughout recent years, Moscow has offered examples of its ability to project its power into the Middle Eastern arena. Massive amounts of Soviet military equipment and advisers accompanied by Cuban troops were interjected into Ethiopia to save it from a Somali invasion of Ogaden province in 1977–1978. This followed the Soviet-Cuban intrusion into the Angolan civil war of 1975–1976. The regimes in both countries remain dependent on the Soviet bloc for security against internal and external foes.

In January 1980, dozens of Soviet generals and hundreds of Cuban troops flew into South Yemen and Ethiopia. In February, according to Egyptian sources, a thousand Cubans sailed through the Suez

Canal to the PDRY. South Yemen, already hosting the advance elements of a Soviet parachute brigade, may now have an estimated eight thousand Cubans and seven thousand East Germans. Two American experts suggested that the Soviet Union has achieved the capacity to airlift "two fully equipped elite armies" into the area within 30 to 72 hours in its version of a rapid deployment force (Peter Vanneman and Martin James, "Moscow Has a 'Rapid Deployment Force,' Too," *CSM,* 27 January). This year, the Eastern Mediterranean saw the joint participation of Soviet and Syrian armed forces in combined military maneuvers. A representative of the Eritrean Liberation Front–Forces of Popular Liberation stated that the Soviet Union has built three new bases in the northern Ethiopia province of Eritrea: a missile base on Mount Moussa, 20 km from the port of Assab; a communication base in an evacuated town along the Eritrean coast; and a base on the archipelago of Dahlak, north of the port of Massawa (AFP, 6 November, *FBIS,* 19 November).

Other causes for Western concern remain the lingering instability in Iran and the looming possibility of upheaval in Egypt. The Khomeini regime in Iran continued to lead a precarious existence. It was beset with a no-win border war against Iraq and with the growing militancy of opposition groups, the most important of which, the Mojahedin-e Khalq, strives to blend Marxism and Islam. A more recent sign of uncertainty developed with the assassination of Egyptian President Anwar Sadat. The West relied on his policies of peace with Israel and opposition to Soviet expansionism. Before his death, Sadat expelled several hundred Soviet officials and technicians for espionage (MENA, 14 and 17 January; *FBIS,* 16 and 19 January).

Moscow expected the assassination, perpetrated by Islamic fundamentalists, to lead to a shift in Cairo toward an anti-American stance and an Islamic viewpoint ("Soviets See US Losing in Mid-East," *WP,* 14 October). This interpretation could well turn out to be valid in light of events in Iran. Arab communist parties in the last decade have been driven underground or to the political wilderness. But Islamic fundamentalism is—and has been—on the rise. This movement shapes and reflects mass opinion, which simplistically blames U.S. and Western "exploitation" for Middle Eastern misery and underdevelopment. The attack on the "capitalist" path of development can work to the advantage of politicians and movements that promise "noncapitalist" economic development and an "Islamic way of life" (Arnold Hottinger, "Arab Communism at Low Ebb," *Problems of Communism,* 30, no. 4, July–August, 1981, p. 32). The new Egyptian government of Muhammed Hosni Mubarak soon incurred verbal attack by fundamentalist groups and those that see it as a representative of "parasitic capitalism" (Voice of the Egyptian People, 10 October; *FBIS,* 14 October).

Islamic revivalism, poverty, and the removal of Sadat's stabilizing influence also signaled trouble for the Sudanese government of Ja'far Numayri. The Sudan's hostile neighbor, Libya, under the capricious leadership of Colonel Moammar Khadafy, invaded Chad early in the year and threatened the Sudan in the last quarter of 1981. The voluntary withdrawal of Libyan forces from Chad in November failed to lessen tensions in the northeast corner of Africa. Numayri placed his armed forces on alert for a possible invasion from Libya. An alternative danger to the Numayri government existed from Libyan-backed internal groups, two of which issued death threats to Numayri from Tripoli (for the statements of the Sudanese Socialist Popular Front and the statement of the United Sudanese National Front, see Jamahiriya News Agency, 10 and 20 October; *FBIS,* 13 and 21 October). Military exercises code named Bright Star and involving elements of the United States' Rapid Deployment Force in Egypt in November were interpreted as an effort to reassure both the Sudan and Egypt of Washington's commitment and capability.

To the south and east, two of the Sudan's neighbors—Ethiopia and the PDRY—entered into a cooperation treaty with Libya committing the signatories to "further strengthen their anti-imperialist, antireactionary, anti-Zionist and antiracist stance" (the complete public text was aired by Addis Ababa Domestic Service, 1 September; *FBIS,* 2 September). Their cooperation extended to "political, economic and other fields." Somalia, which shares a border with Ethiopia and looks across the Gulf of Aden at the PDRY, stated that the Libyan presence introduced a new element of uncertainty into the area (Alan Cowell, "Qaddafi Is New Chip in Horn of Africa Poker Game," *NYT,* 21 September).

Further south, the Soviet Union reinforced its footing in the Indian Ocean and on the east African coast by stationing warships in Mozambique's Maputo harbor. The positioning of Soviet combat ships was justified by Moscow as a means of supporting Mozambique's granting of staging bases to South African guerrillas and to defend Mozambique against Pretoria's retaliatory strikes on the bases. Yet the projection of Soviet naval power on a permanent basis into the southern Indian Ocean served to underline the view of Moscow's successive advances into the vital seaway between Africa and India and across the Persian Gulf oil route to the West and Japan. It will intensify the race for naval facilities and anchorages in the Indian Ocean (Michael T. Kaufman, "Ports and Oil Spur Naval Buildups by U.S. and Soviet," *NYT,* 20 April). Another sign of Soviet consolidation in Mozambique came with the arrival of a floating dock and workshop in Maputo in late October (Maputo Domestic Service, 27 October; *FBIS,* 30 October).

The increased raids within South Africa by Mozambican-based guerrillas of the ANC underscored the building tensions at the foot of the continent. Celebrating its sixtieth anniversary, the oldest party in the continent, the South African Communist Party, continued its alliance with the ANC; both seek to undermine by guerrilla warfare and subversion the present government in Pretoria (Toussaint, "In Retrospect: 60 Years On," *African Communist,* no. 84, 3rd Quarter, 1981, pp. 43–45).

On the other side of the continent, South Africa escalated the scope of its forays into Angola from South-West Africa, a territory it has administered since the conclusion of World War I. A large-scale sweep into southern Angola in August to uproot SWAPO bases resulted in the killing of several Soviet soldiers and the capturing of a noncommissioned officer (Humphrey Tyler, "S. Africa Savors News of Russian Involvement in Angola," *CSM,* 4 September). This irrefutable evidence of Soviet involvement was significant since Moscow has never publicly admitted the deployment of ground forces in Angola.

Elsewhere in Africa an abortive left-wing coup in Gambia, one of Africa's smallest countries, paved the way for the formation of a new political entity. The attempted coup, launched on 30 July, left about eight hundred dead in ten days of fighting before crack troops from Senegal suppressed the insurrection. Instability and the presence of Senegalese forces contributed to the decision by Gambian President Dawda Jawana to unite Gambia in confederation with Senegal; the new confederation is known as Senegambia. (The *Yearbook* does not reflect this name change in the title of its profile on Senegal because the coverage of communist and left-wing parties belongs to Senegal and because the confederation itself allows for separate identification.)

In the neighboring states of Mali and Guinea-Bissau, developments this year pointed away from socialist policies. Mali, once ruled by stridently Marxist Modibo Keita, has drifted further this year from its faith in socialism. The government of Moussa Traore announced that it will close or sell to private interests 20 of the 31 state corporations within the next four years. The government took this action despite its representation at the CPSU congress and a visit by a CPSU delegation in June (Bamako Domestic Service, 29 June, 8 July; *FBIS,* 1 and 9 July). In nearby Guinea-Bissau, the coup of 14 November 1980 that replaced President Luis Cabral with João Bernardo Viera, has led to further decline in revolutionary fervor within the ruling Partido Africano de Independência de Guiné e Cabo Verde (PAIGC). Under Amilcar Cabral, the PAIGC was once acknowledged as the most successful guerrilla movement opposing Portuguese rule and the most devoted to revamping of the social order along Marxist lines.

Other developments on the continent witnessed the arrival of one hundred North Korean military advisers in Zimbabwe to train a brigade (Jay Ross, "N. Korean Advisers to Train Force in Zimbabwe," *WP,* 11 August); the visit of a Soviet delegation to Benin at the invitation of the country's ruling People's Revolutionary Party (Cotonou Domestic Service, 28 August; *FBIS*, 1 September); the legalization of the Communist Party of Ghana under the leadership of N. A. K. Latsu (Accra Domestic Service, 16 June; *FBIS*, 19 June); and the legal recognition of seven parties in Senegal espousing varying degrees of Marxism. The People's Revolutionary Republic of Guinea signed a protocol for cultural and scientific cooperation with the Soviet Union (Conakry Domestic Service, 14 July; *FBIS*, 15 July). The Socialist Unity Party of East Germany sent a delegation to the People's Republic of the Congo at the invitation of the governing Congolese Labor Party (Brazzaville Domestic Service, 20 October; *FBIS*, 22 October). The dispatch of a Soviet parliamentary delegation to Zaire in May to discuss economic development represents one sign of an increased wooing of the staunchly anticommunist country (Kinshasa Domestic Service, 21 May; *FBIS*, 22 May). Other signs are the expanded trade with countries in the Council for Mutual Economic Assistance (CMEA) and the proposed air link between Kinshasa and Moscow. Further up the coast, the Cape Verde Islands and the Soviet Union signed an agreement in the field of posts and telecommunications (AFP, 21 April; *FBIS*, 22 April).

This step-up in diplomatic and economic activity by the Soviet bloc in West Africa indicates a departure from the policy of recent years. In the past half decade, Soviet attention has focused on strategically important southern Africa and the Horn. But almost unnoticed, the Soviets and their CMEA partners have laid the foundation for a new trading empire in much of the developing world (Peter O'Neill, "Soviet Drive for Third-World Raw Materials Gathers Steam," *CSM*, 10 June). Using Western multinational-style operations, they have discreetly established companies to gain access to strategic raw materials and minerals in Africa. (For more information on and analysis of communist states in Africa, see Thomas H. Henriksen, ed., *Communist Powers and Sub-Saharan Africa*, Stanford: Hoover Institution Press, 1981.) This places the Soviet bloc in direct competition with the West and Japan, which also seek the wherewithal to fuel their industries into the next century.

Hoover Institution   Thomas H. Henriksen

Algeria

The Algerian Communist Party (Parti communiste algerien; PCA) was founded in 1920 as an extension of the French Communist Party. It has existed independently since 1936. Following Algerian independence in 1962, dissident left-wing elements of the legal National Liberation Front (NLF) joined with Communists from the outlawed PCA to form the Popular Resistance Organization. In January 1966, this group was renamed the Socialist Vanguard Party (Parti de l'avant-garde socialiste; PAGS), which is recognized in the communist world as the official Algerian communist party. Membership is now estimated to be four hundred to five hundred. The population of Algeria is just over nineteen million.

Leadership and Party Affairs. Sadiq Hadjeres is first secretary of the party. Other prominent members of the party in recent years are believed to include former PCA Secretary General Larbi Bukhali, Bashir Hadj 'Ali, Ahmad Karim, and 'Ali Malki.

Political Climate. Algerian President Chadli Benjedid continued to consolidate his position in 1981 by removing from power leading figures on both extremes of the political spectrum. The highlight of this process was the 30 June to 2 July meeting of the Central Committee of the ruling NLF, Algeria's only government-approved political party. The Central Committee dropped both Abdelaziz Bouteflika and Mohamed Salah Yahiaoui from the NLF Politburo. Bouteflika, who served as Algerian foreign minister from 1964 to 1979, favored economic liberalism and closer relations with the West, whereas Yahiaoui, former NLF secretary general and party coordinator, favored doctrinaire socialism and strong ties with the USSR. The exclusion of these two figures from positions of political influence marked a transition point in the Algerian power structure—a movement away from a ruling group formed by the previous leader, Houari Boumediene, who dominated Algeria from 1965 until his death in 1978, and toward a governing elite handpicked by President Benjedid.

Algeria's new ruling group is composed almost entirely of civilians. At the political level, the composition of the new and enlarged NLF Politburo reflects Benjedid's determination to pursue pragmatic policies—a middle road between a radical and Marxist socialism on one side, and a militant Arabism on the other. The latter option is the tendency of the Islamic fundamentalists in Algeria who favor economic liberalism. Of special note was the election to the Politburo of Mohamed Cherif Messaadia, secretary general of the NLF Central Committee. In the months leading up to the summer meeting of the Central Committee, Messaadia worked to eliminate positions of responsibility within Algeria's mass organizations, especially the labor unions, whose membership includes Marxists who do not belong to the NLF. The effect of this government-backed effort was felt most heavily by PAGS militants.

In this hostile climate, the PAGS prudently opted to refrain from taking any public positions of note on either domestic or international issues and perhaps began to reconsider the policy of "critical support" that the party has followed toward the regime since 1971. At the same time, the PAGS placed cells in factories to compete with the units of the General Union of Algerian Workers, the government-sanctioned labor union that is one of the NLF's five mass organizations.

Publications. At infrequent intervals the PAGS issued the clandestine journal *Sawt al-Sha'b* (Voice of the people).

Portland State University   John Damis

Angola

Angola, located in southwest Africa, has a land area as large as Alaska and a population of 6.9 million divided among nine ethnolinguistic groups. The population of Luanda, its capital, is estimated at 460,000. Both capital and countryside are mere reflections of their former prosperous state. Angola became independent in 1975 after fourteen years of guerrilla war. It has since endured a massive exodus of whites, as 400,000 Portuguese fled, draining the country of managerial talent, financial capital, and equipment.

Independence also led to civil war, as three insurgent armies fought for power. The National Front for the Liberation of Angola (FNLA), led by Holden Roberto, and the National Union for the Total Independence of Angola (UNITA), led by Jonas Savimbi, acquired limited funds and weapons from the United States. They were opposed, however, by the increasingly Marxist-oriented Popular Movement for the Liberation of Angola (MPLA), which used Russian military equipment and Cuban troops to establish political authority in Luanda and throughout most of the country by 1976. The FNLA dissolved; UNITA survives in Angola's southern provinces in active opposition.

Leadership and the Organization of State Authority. The only legal political party is the MPLA, now known as the Popular Liberation Movement of Angola–Labor Party (MPLA–PT). It wields power through a Central Committee, elected by a People's Assembly. The Central Committee in turn selects the president, currently José Eduardo dos Santos. In 1980–1981, much of the underlying support for this political structure was established. In September 1980, the Central Committee approved a constitutional change that replaced the appointed Council of the Revolution with the elected People's Assembly as the supreme legislative body. Members were elected from among deputies to eighteen provincial assemblies. These, in turn, were chosen by electoral colleges, whose members were to be nominated at workplaces and areas of residence. At this level, every Angolan over eighteen could vote.

Elections began under this system as early as August, when members of the electoral colleges were chosen. These selected nominees to the provincial assemblies in October. The latter designated deputies to the People's Assembly in November, with President dos Santos in the chair.

The Extraordinary Congress. The MPLA convened an extraordinary congress on 17–23 December 1980. Its initial act was to confirm dos Santos in the presidency, a post he had held only on an interim basis since the death of Agostinho Neto. The congress also elected twelve new members to the Central Committee, a move intended to "bring worker and peasant blood" into the leading ranks (*Zezi*, 1981, p. 11). The new members included Jacinto João Antonio Francisco, Paulo (Massengo Ukentir), Carlos (Kangulo) Domingos, Filipe (Chinguengo Madiola), Domingos Francisco Bartolomeu (Chitaka Ecassundo Afaneto), João Batista (Panzo), Luís Sebastiao Mateus, Artur Videl Gomes (Fundi Dizabo), and José Carlos (Ilenga Explosivo). The congress also urged the party to adhere to the concepts of "democratic centralism . . . criticism and self-criticism" in making vital decisions, as well as the fight against "such incorrect modes of behavior as liberalism, protectionism, elitism, regionalism, racism, sectionalism . . . and other bourgeois practices" (*Southern Africa*, 3, December 1980).

Mass Organizations. These are directed by party members in leading positions within the movements themselves. The youth movement, Angolan Pioneers, was formed in 1963. The Organization of Angolan Women was founded in 1963 by MPLA female militants in exile in Kinshasha. Both are structured along Soviet lines. The National Union of Angolan Workers, originally independent of the MPLA, came under its control in the early 1960s. All three organizations form primary links between the MPLA leadership and its constituents.

Domestic Affairs. The extraordinary congress took formal notice of the country's serious economic problems. Angola has great economic potential. Its economy, however, has not yet recovered from the devastation of the 1970s and is beset by several major problems. Perhaps the least solvable of these is drought and the consequent shortage of food. Corn-producing regions were particularly stricken. In 1973 (before independence) 700,000 tons were produced. War, white flight, and UNITA activities combined to drop production to 198,000 tons in 1978. In 1981, however, production fell to 17,740 tons.

Drought has also affected meat supplies. The minister of agriculture, speaking in December 1980, declared that meat has "become a luxury product" (*Quarterly Economic Review* [QER], no. 1, p. 12). Fish had also become scarce, although for different reasons. To repay Russia for its military aid, the MPLA has permitted Soviet vessels to fish its coastal waters. In response, Russian "fishing factories" vacuum the waters clean, leaving few fish to feed Angolans.

The scarcity of food, as well as many consumer goods, has encouraged the growth of a black market. The need to queue outside shops and markets has created a whole new class of professional "line-standers," who wait as long as needed and then resell the goods on the black market. Black marketeers, in turn, have driven up urban food prices past the possibility of purchase. Urbanites have been forced back to the countryside in search of food, causing widespread absenteeism. The MPLA, at its December conference, took special note of these practices, attacking line-standing, black marketeering, and speculative sale of food and goods as inimical to socialism.

Cash crop production, most notably in cotton and coffee, was mixed during this period. Cotton production dropped from 79,281 tons before independence (1973) to approximately 1,000 tons in 1981. Before independence, coffee was grown on Portuguese plantations, sustained by a migrant work force of Ovimbundu. The war caused both groups to flee, and neither has returned. Despite this, production has gradually been restored, reaching 1.6 million bags this year, half of pre-independence levels. Part of the crop is promised to Cuba, in part payment for military aid (*WP*, 25 July). The balance will go to Algeria and the Soviet bloc, producing an estimated U.S. $300 million in revenues (*QER*, no. 1, p. 2).

The mining sector of the economy appears more favorable. A state diamond company has been established to represent Angola in Diamang, the mixed company that controls diamond operations. Diamond extraction began in 1913, becoming of commercial importance in the 1920s. An average of two million carats was extracted annually prior to independence. Production reached 1.5 million carats in 1981 and is expected to equal pre-independence levels by 1983, bringing in an estimated $500 million in revenues (ibid., no. 2, p. 1).

Oil production has also expanded, rising from 8 million tons in 1980 to 15 million tons in 1981. Expansion should continue as the Essungo oil field in Angola's lower Congo basin enters production and production in Cabinda increases. Gulf, Texaco, Marathon, Mobil, City Service, and United Texas Petroleum are active in these areas, as are several European firms. The continuous rise in oil prices assures Angola substantial revenues, estimated at almost U.S. $2.2 billion for 1980, and more for 1981 (ibid.). "Asked what happens to Angola's oil revenue, Petroleum Minister Jorge August de Morais said, 'There is a war. Most of the profit is eaten up by the war.' " (*WP*, 22 September.)

Plans to restore Angola's iron production are also complete. Austro-mineral, a subsidiary of the

Austrian Steel consortium VOEST-Alpine, is to reopen the Cassinga mines, closed since 1975, in the southern province of Cuando-Cubango. Before independence, Cassinga produced 5.6 million tons per year. The MPLA claims that it will resume production in 1983, with an initial capacity of one million tons per year (*QER*, no. 2, p. 14). The claim is disputed, however, by Jonas Savimbi, who asserts that the mines lie within the area held by his troops. Western analysts place them on its fringe. UNITA may lack the power to seize the mines, but it may well be able to disrupt future production.

UNITA's disruptive capacity is also evident in the area of transportation. Angola's Benguela Railway serves as a transit route for Zambia's copper and Zaire's manganese. Before independence, the railway handled 2.6 million tons of freight annually. It was shut down during the war and is currently subject to track cutting and derailment by UNITA. In consequence, it handles only a fraction of its former capacity. In September 1980, for example, only eighteen wagons reached Lobito, Angola, from Zaire and none from Zambia. None left Lobito for either inland destination. Those wagons that rolled took two months to make the journey, due to delays for track repair. It once took three days.

The MPLA has responded in three ways. Having initially decided to nationalize the Benguela Railway in 1979, it subsequently reversed the decision, permitting the line to remain in private hands. It has also asked the Southern African Development Coordination Conference to assist in establishing three north-south railway links to supplement the three existing east-west lines. Existing track now runs from Lobito to Zaire (Benguela Railway), Luanda to Malange, and Moçamedes to Menongue. The government would like to supplement these with a 640-km link between the Benguela and Luanda railways, a 240-km link between the Benguela and Moçamedes railways, and a 250-km branch line between Mbanza and the new port of Soya on the Zaire River (ibid., no. 1, p. 17).

Angola has, finally, appealed to several nations for material aid in running the Benguela Railway, which is also vital to Zaire and Zambia. Thus far, Western and Arab sources have responded with offers of easily transported bridging material and additional rolling stock.

Foreign sources have also assisted in overcoming shipping problems. Before independence, the ports of Luanda and Lobito handled 1.2–2.5 million tons of freight annually. Currently, the volume of trade through both facilities has declined sharply. Congestion is particularly serious at Luanda, where backlogs of "at least 50 ships" wait to unload at any time (*WP*, 22 September). Unloading takes three months, while demurrage charges run to $200,000 per day per ship. Expansion of the Lobito facility has been undertaken by a Dutch corporation.

The government has also moved to resolve problems in manufacturing. The massive Portuguese withdrawal after 1975, accompanied by widespread industrial sabotage and theft, left many manufacturing concerns paralyzed. The MPLA recently nationalized several firms, in order to reconstruct their operation. In October 1980, 39 small manufacturing concerns and three fishing companies were nationalized on the grounds that their former owners had abandoned them (*QER*, no. 1, p. 3). President dos Santos stated in an address marking Angola's sixth anniversary of independence that the country will adopt greater austerity measures. He noted that funds were needlessly spent for foreign goods that could be produced by Angolans. To combat vandalism, subversion, and banditry, he called for the establishment of vigilante brigades in which the party and people would play a dominant role. (AN-GOP, 11 November; *FBIS*, 12 November.)

Foreign Aid, East and West. In 1980–1981, Angola sought to broaden relations with the West, thereby diminishing its dependence on the Soviet bloc. Of the seventeen current foreign aid projects, eleven are Western and two are Yugoslavian. Portugal now plays a significant role in these projects, having contributed over eight hundred economic advisers, with more expected (*WP*, 20 September). Angola has also turned to Brazil. It will soon open an embassy in Brasilia, and Brazil is considering meeting part of Angola's need for public housing.

Contacts have also been established with Western Europe. An Angolan embassy will soon open in

London, and a Belgian delegation is investigating the rebuilding of Angola's palm oil industry. Two French oil companies (Elf-Acquitaine and Total) have signed exploration agreements with the government, and a third firm, Creuse Loire, has completed a textile factory in Benguela. A fourth French firm, Dupez, has signed a contract to build two factories capable of producing 4,000 prefabricated houses in three years (*QER*, no. 2, p. 7).

Angola's largest trading partner, however, is the United States. General Electric, Bechtel, Boeing, and the six major U.S. oil companies previously cited have invested substantially. Gulf, for example, has just agreed to add $116 million to its current investment of $416 million, making this the largest investment by a U.S. company in a country not recognized by the U.S. government. Funds are also expected from the U.S. Export-Import Bank, which recently approved an $85 million loan to increase productivity in offshore wells. An accompanying $50 million is to be arranged by the Morgan Guaranty Trust Company (*WP*, 23 September). In brief, Angola depends on Western nations for 70 percent of its export income.

Soviet bloc nations contributed relatively little economic aid during this period. A Soviet delegation visited Angola at the end of 1980 to study the feasibility of restoring production in wheat and cotton. The Soviets have also renegotiated the treaty permitting them access to Angola's fishing waters. Militarily, Russia has provided approximately a thousand advisers, used chiefly in training and logistical roles. They have been joined by an undetermined number of East Germans, who are believed responsible for military intelligence and security.

Substantially greater economic aid is contributed by Cuba. Western analysts believe there are 4,500 Cuban civilians in Angola (ibid., 23 September). The MPLA claims 1,500, mostly in education. Before independence, 90 percent of Angola's people were illiterate. Since then, 2.4 million children have entered primary school, and 759,000 adults have entered literacy classes. The Cubans have provided both "teaching" and "teachers." In March 1980, President dos Santos visited Cuba for one week. Accompanied by Cuban President Fidel Castro, he toured four camps where three thousand Angolans had been brought for education and training (*YICA*, 1981, p. 67; *San Francisco Examiner*, 6 December 1980). In February, 370 Cuban teachers arrived in Angola to begin a seven-month teaching stint. They replaced 411 others, who had taught about 70,000 pupils over the preceding two years. Cubans also predominate in apartment construction in Luanda. Large blocks of housing have been built by all-Cuban construction teams.

The Angolan Defence Force (FAPLA). The Angolan army is primarily occupied with containing the UNITA insurgency. Cuban forces not occupied with training are primarily used in garrison duties, thereby releasing FAPLA units to seek out and engage UNITA. The official government position is that the UNITA force has been reduced to the level of bandits. Lieutenant Colonel Foguetao, Angolan commander for the southern regions, told visiting U.S. congressmen in July that UNITA "practically does not exist" (*WP*, 21 September).

In contrast, two *Washington Post* journalists who visited UNITA forces in July and September found an organized, highly trained, and moderately well-equipped force, estimated by its own leadership at 15,000 men. UNITA controlled at least one town (Mavinga) in its Cuando-Cubangu stronghold and claimed control over the Benguela Railway, Cassinga mines, and 40 percent of Angolan territory, claims neither journalist was able to assess.

The FAPLA has become increasingly aggressive during the past year, displaying a growing willingness to engage both UNITA and South African troops. One reason for this combativeness is the intensive training received from Cuban and Soviet advisers by more and more units. A second may be the continuous increase in military equipment received from Soviet bloc nations, including Star-class trucks, T-55 heavy trucks, amphibious vehicles, and MiG-21 jets. On the other hand, the FAPLA has yet to demonstrate the capacity to dislodge UNITA forces from known bases in Cuando-Cubango.

International Relations. Angola's international relations are dominated by events in South Africa and South-West Africa (Namibia), as well as by shifting attitudes in the United States. Portugal's collapse in the mid-1970s was of great concern to South Africa. Encouraged by U.S. support for UNITA, it entered the struggle, repeatedly sending troops and planes across the Namibian border into southern Angola. Its intent was to destroy the insurgent forces of the South-West African People's Organization (SWAPO), a paramilitary force seeking independence for Namibia. In the process, however, South African forces destroyed some of Angola's economic infrastructure, thereby aligning themselves with the purposes of UNITA. This informal alliance was strengthened as Pretoria began to provide Savimbi's forces with military supplies.

South Africa withdrew its initial force in 1976. Since then, however, the continued failure of the Namibian peace talks has led to the resumption of both aid to UNITA and cross-border raids. In January 1981, for example, South African forces attacked Cumato, in Cunene province, and claimed to have killed 36 SWAPO guerrillas. In three raids in February, South African forces occupied Mulemba, destroyed a railway bridge, and attacked five other villages in Cunene province. In August, 4,500–5,000 troops crossed the border in a major ten-day operation. In October, operations were extended westward from Cunene to Moçamedes province. A three-week sweep in November was said to have "destroyed" SWAPO central headquarters. (*QER*, no. 2, p. 8; *San Francisco Chronicle*, 7 December.)

South Africa has reportedly used a predominantly African mercenary force known as the 32d Battalion (the Buffalo regiment). Its existence was confirmed by a senior South African staff officer, speaking to foreign journalists in Namibia. It is said to contain 1,100 men, of whom 80 percent are Portuguese-speaking Africans. Most are former FNLA soldiers who took refuge in Namibia after the MPLA victory and then joined the South African Army. Most of the white members are former Rhodesian soldiers. The unit's primarily African membership, however, suggests that its actions inside Angola may be frequently confused with those of UNITA (*QER*, no 2, p. 9).

This pattern of raiding has led South Africa to maintain a relatively permanent presence in Angola's south. Analysts suggest that its ultimate intent is to install UNITA in a "southern salient" extending westward from its current base in Cuando-Cubango into Cunene province and beyond. Ideally, UNITA would then serve as a buffer between Namibia and the MPLA. It would also isolate SWAPO within its present narrow stronghold, thereby facilitating its elimination. This, in turn, would allow South Africa to legitimize the multiracial government it has installed despite U.N. demands for internationally supervised elections.

Paulo Jorge, Angolan foreign minister, has declared that the Cuban military presence is the direct result of South African raids. Once these cease, the need for Cuban troops to counter them will disappear, so the argument runs. South Africa's actions, in turn, depend on those of SWAPO. In theory, resolution of the Namibian conflict would end the need for SWAPO's insurgency. This would permit a South African withdrawal, ending its support for UNITA. Thus deprived, UNITA would make terms and bring peace to the region. This may be wishful thinking, however, since Pretoria could continue to supply Savimbi's "southern salient," if only to preoccupy and destabilize the MPLA.

Angola's relations with the Soviet bloc have remained close since Soviet and East European aid assured an MPLA victory in the civil war. To consolidate its ties with Moscow, the MPLA signed a twenty-year treaty of friendship and cooperation with the Soviet party in 1976, the significance of which lies in the fact that the connection is between parties rather than between states. The MPLA still depends heavily on the Cubans, East Germans, and Soviets for security. President dos Santos was quoted this year as saying: "In the field of internationalism we will continue to strengthen our international friendship with the socialist countries, particularly the USSR and the Republic of Cuba . . . We will support the liberation struggles of the peoples still dominated by colonialism, neocolonialism and imperialism, particularly the peoples of Namibia, the Saharan Democratic Arab Republic, East

Timor, South Africa, Palestine and El Salvador" (*Southern Africa*, 31 March). The MPLA sent a delegation to the Soviet party congress in February–March.

Publications. All media are controlled by the government. One major daily is published in Angola—*Jornal de Angola*.

Eastern Michigan University   Jeffrey A. Fadiman

Egypt

The small Egyptian Communist Party, founded in 1921 but illegal virtually continuously since then, reportedly held its first congress on Egyptian territory in September 1980. This was noted in a number of sources, but details of the congress have not been published.

The program adopted by the party congress focuses on the Arab-Israeli conflict (*IB*, March, pp. 21–25). "Liberation of the whole Arab homeland from imperialism and Zionism is indispensable for Egypt to attain, assert and preserve its political and economic independence." It castigates "Israel's aggressive policy" and notes that "the Palestinian people's legitimate national rights are being ignored and denied." The Palestinian movement is "a liberation struggle, which is an integral part of the international struggle against imperialism." The program accuses Israel of being "a bridgehead of world imperialism," "an aggressive base," "a racist colonialist entity," and "a hotbed of war, a direct and constant threat to international peace and security." Peace can be achieved through "the Arab liberation struggle, in which the Palestine Liberation Organization plays the major role, and its merging with the struggle of other anti-imperialist and anti-Zionist forces in Israel itself and on the occupied Arab territories, led by the Palestinian Communist Organization in the West Bank and the Gaza Strip and the RAKAH Party [Israel's communist party], which are carrying on a heroic and consistent struggle against Zionism and its aggressive policy."

National Progressive Unionist Party. Leftist activity centers around the National Progressive Unionist Party (NPUP), under the leadership of Khalid Muhyi al-Din, one of the original Free Officers of the 1952 revolution and long associated with Marxist-oriented elements in Egypt. The NPUP has links with the various communist groupings in Egypt and continues to serve as a focal point of legal left opposition to the regime's policies.

The party continues to focus its attention on the need to change the government of Egypt and to adopt a new economic program. Muhyi al-Din has noted his dissatisfaction with the government's domination of all aspects of Egyptian life, especially since economic and social difficulties are increasing and government promises have not been fulfilled. He believes that "the future belongs to the Egyptian opposition" and "there is no doubt that the opposition is gaining new ground and the Egyptian government is losing more ground every day." (*as-Siyasah*, Kuwait, 2 April; *FBIS*, 9 April.)

As for the foreign policy of the Sadat government, Muhyi al-Din emphasized NPUP opposition to the Camp David accords and noted that "foreign policy is completely pro-U.S. Egypt has become part of American strategy." He suggested an alternative solution "in which all parties were to participate," as expressed in the U.S.-Soviet joint statement of 1977. He reiterated this theme on various occasions. In late August he condemned imperialism's intrigues in the Middle East and indicated further support for Brezhnev's proposal for a zone of peace and security in the Persian Gulf. He denounced "a new military alliance [that] has been formed by the parties to the Camp David agreements" and suggested that a just solution to the Arab-Israeli conflict had been included in the program of the First NPUP Congress (April 1980). He noted that the conflict could be solved by complete withdrawal of Israeli forces from all occupied Arab territories and "the full implementation of the inalienable national rights of the Palestinian people." (*Pravda*, 30 August; *FBIS*, 3 September.)

Representation at the Soviet Party Congress. In a message to the Soviet party congress, Michel Kamil, a member of the Egyptian Communist Party Politburo, voiced opposition to American imperialism and the Camp David process. "The Camp David agreements and the Israeli-Egyptian separate treaty clearly confirmed the Egyptian regime's role in implementing the American plans." He noted that the Egyptian Communist Party preferred, and expressed its "full support" for, Brezhnev's initiative to create a security system in the Persian Gulf region. (*Pravda*, 4 March; *FBIS*, 10 March.)

Muhyi al-Din led an NPUP delegation to the congress. "I went to Moscow by invitation to attend the Twenty Sixth Congress," he said later. "No contacts took place between me and the Soviet leaders because they were preoccupied with the congress. We went there as one of the participating delegations. We delivered a speech of greetings at the congress. I believe that the speech Brezhnev delivered at the congress was the most important speech delivered recently." (*as-Siyasah*, 2 April; *FBIS*, 9 April.) In his address of greetings, he noted that the NPUP had emerged when the achievements secured by the 1952 revolution under Nasser were challenged. "Our party unites in its ranks all the leftwing forces in Egyptian society which emerged in and passed through the crucible of the 23 July 1952 revolution. It unites an-Nasirist, Marxist, religious enlightenment, Arab patriotic, socialist and democratic currents." He described its program as strict observance of the principles of the 1952 revolution and further development of that revolution. "Our Party wages an unflagging struggle against imperialism, colonialism and Zionism" and sees "the importance of cooperation and solidarity among the forces of the world national liberation movement . . . and also the significance of solidarity with the socialist countries, especially the Soviet Union." He saw Egypt as a part of the Arab world and the achievement of Arab unity as a major principle. The NPUP opposes the Camp David accords. "Our party fully supports and shares the opinion voiced in Comrade L. I. Brezhnev's report to the effect that the Camp David agreements are aimed at splitting the Arab world, have produced another deterioration in the situation in the region and have been a setback to a Near East settlement." He also welcomed the program for the demilitarization of the Persian Gulf put forward by Brezhnev. (*Pravda*, 4 March; *FBIS*, 9 March.)

Domestic Dissent and Opposition. Much of the recent opposition to the Egyptian regime has come from the right, particularly from Muslim fundamentalists seeking to increase the role of Islam in Egypt and opposing Sadat's policy of peace and normalization with Israel. Sectarian clashes and other violence erupted on occasion.

On 22 June Sadat blamed the Socialist Labor Party and the Communists for sectarian clashes in Cairo in which ten were killed and 55 were injured. Sadat noted that a disagreement between Christians and Muslims in Zawiyah Hamra had been intensified by "agitators" like those who had "incited" the food riots of January 1977, which Sadat had blamed on the Communists and other regime opponents. Sadat criticized the Socialist Labor Party, noting that some of its members "sat together with the Communists who tried to make the agitation of thieves into the agitation of the people." This was a continuation of attacks on the Socialist Labor Party that he had begun in May. (*NYT*, 23 June.)

In late June Sadat said that "Communists, reactionaries and opportunists" had sought to exploit the Egyptian Bar Association's governing board. He called the small group "stooges of the Soviet Union—those full of bitterness and grudges." A group of some two hundred people stormed the association's headquarters, and a no-confidence vote in the association's leadership was passed. Sadat claimed that lawyers loyal to government policy had foiled the board's efforts "because it made decisions absolutely alien to the will of this country." The head of the association, Ahmed al-Khawaga, said that Sadat's supporters were trying to dismember the association's governing council because it opposed Sadat's peace treaty with Israel. (Ibid., 28 June.)

Following Sadat's assassination, former Egyptian Chief of Staff Gen. Saadeddin Shazli, leader of the Egyptian National Front (ENF), an opposition, nonfundamentalist exile group, shifted his headquarters to Libya and noted that his work would continue. Although Shazli contended that his ENF was supported by a variety of "steadfast Arab powers," it appeared that Moammar Khadafy provided not only a base but also financial assistance. "We will use violence to topple [Sadat's successor, Muhammad Hosni] Mubarak. We will continue . . . until we topple that regime and establish democracy." (*WP*, 14 October.) Shazli opposed Sadat's policy on the Arab-Israeli conflict because "the political aspect of the Camp David agreement has been to eliminate Egypt from all other Arab countries . . . to weaken her militarily, and to force her to go with the West. Then Israel can defeat other Arab countries and then return eventually to defeat Egypt and to dominate the area." His precise program for achieving democracy in Egypt remained unclear. In June an Egyptian government prosecutor had charged that Shazli and eighteen other opponents of the regime living in exile had plotted to overthrow Sadat and that they had received $2.8 million in funding from Libya. (*NYT*, 8 June.)

In early September Sadat launched an extensive crackdown on critics of his regime and its policies, the most sweeping in his eleven-year (1970–1981) tenure in office. Police broke up demonstrations in mosques and arrested 1,536 people. Among those arrested were Muslim fundamentalists, Coptic clergymen, politicians, academicians, lawyers, and journalists, including such prominent Egyptians as Mohammed Hassanein Heikal (a confidant of Nasser and critic of Sadat) and Pope Shenouda III, leader of Egypt's Coptic Christians. The main target was the right—the Islamic fundamentalists, particularly the Muslim Brotherhood, which has been banned since 1954. Sadat announced his efforts in a lengthy speech accusing Muslim religious leaders of engaging in political activity. He closed newspapers and shifted journalists to new, less sensitive positions. He at first justified it as a roundup of those who had been involved in Christian-Muslim fighting in Cairo in June. But those arrested included many critics of the regime and its policies. Several publications were closed, including the newspaper of the opposition Socialist Labor Party. Ibrahim Shukry, leader of the Socialist Labor Party, was among those arrested, as were most of the leaders of the party. The government closed the headquarters of the NPUP and put it under armed guard. Khalid Muhyi al-Din said in an interview that "the Sadat government was using the religious issue as a 'cover' to strike against its political opponents of both the left and right." (*FBIS*, 16 September.)

Sadat accused the Muslim Brotherhood of being an "illegitimate" entity that he had erroneously allowed to function and that "jeopardizes the sovereignty and security of this nation" (*NYT*, 6 September). Ultimately, Muslim fundamentalists were identified as Sadat's assassins. His successor, Hosni Mubarak, noted that some extremist Muslim fanatics planned to assassinate him and much of the leadership and then declare an Islamic revolution. Members of Takfir Wal Hijira, an underground Muslim fundamentalist group, were named as the culprits. No leftist complicity was identified by the Egyptian government.

In early November the government arrested 65 members of the Egyptian Communist Party and the Egyptian Workers' Communist Party. According to the Interior Ministry, its security organs noticed that members of the communist organizations had begun increasing their activities "in the belief that the security organs were occupied with liquidating the terrorist organization and in pursuing its remnants" (MENA, 9 November; *FBIS*, 9 November). The activities included a propaganda campaign to foment sectarian sedition by distributing antigovernment leaflets.

Relations with the Soviet Union. On 15 September Sadat expelled Soviet Ambassador Vladimir P. Polyakov and six members of his staff, two Soviet journalists (Konstantin Kapitonov, a correspondent for *Trud*, and Aleksandr Sourikov, a correspondent for Tass), and more than a thousand Soviet technicians working on various projects in Egypt. He ordered the Soviet military bureau closed, cut the number of embassy employees allowed, and abrogated all existing contracts between Egypt and the Soviet Union. In addition, one Hungarian diplomat was expelled. (*FBIS*, 16 and 17 September.) Polyakov had served in Egypt since 1974. The stated reason for the expulsion order was that the Soviet Union had attempted to undermine the Sadat regime and had tried to recruit dissidents to subvert "Egypt's national unity." An Eyptian cabinet statement accused the Soviet Union of trying to "cause troubles on the internal front, distort democracy and incite sedition and conflicts among Egyptians through the activities of Soviet intelligence and elements in the Soviet Embassy. The aim was to carry out a hostile plot against the regime, Egypt's national unity and its social security." (*NYT*, 16 September.)

In a speech discussing the crackdown on regime opponents, Sadat noted that of those arrested a dozen had been conniving with the Russians to destabilize the government by exploiting sectarian religious differences among Egyptians (*FBIS*, 16 September). In part the Soviet Union was a convenient scapegoat for criticism of his arrest of so many critics of the regime. Sadat insisted that there was overwhelming evidence of widespread Soviet interference in Egyptian affairs. The press (under tight government "supervision") recounted various tales of plots linked to Soviet agents. The press claimed that the most serious involved Soviet agents led by former Deputy Prime Minister Muhammad 'Abd as-Salam az-Zayyat, who maintained close contacts with the Russian embassy and with Soviet agents and traveled to the Soviet Union. *May*, the weekly organ of Sadat's National Democratic Party, reported (14 September) that after a three-year surveillance the Egyptian intelligence service had uncoverd a group called the Swamp, "who attempted to undermine national unity, to spread sedition and rumors, and to incite the workers and farmers to undermine the internal front." The group included as-Salam az-Zayyat, some former ministers, and a number of university professors and journalists. The Swamp reportedly included "some elements who pretended to be Nasserites, members of the leftist National Progressive Unionist Grouping, and a number of Marxists. Members of the Swamp contacted the Muslim Brotherhood group to disguise their true colors and to deceive the Egyptian people, who hate communism." *May* reported "what it called details of a communist plan to incite sectarian sedition in Egypt." It was drawn up in Moscow to foment sedition among Muslims and Copts. "Soviet strategy aimed at bringing about the downfall of the Egyptian regime, considering that it was the main obstacle standing in the way of Soviet hegemony in the Arab area. Members of Soviet and Hungarian intelligence, under diplomatic and press cover, contacted a number of members of the opposition in Egypt, including Dr. Hilmi Murad. They also arranged meetings with leaders of the leftist National Progessive Unionist Grouping. All these schemes have been uncovered by Egyptian security men." (MENA, 13 September; *FBIS*, 14 September.)

Ambassador Polyakov left on 17 September and was soon followed by other Soviet diplomats, journalists, and technicians. Some experts were to remain, many of them working in steel and aluminum plants. The departure of Polyakov and the other Russians reduced the Soviet presence in Egypt to its lowest point since before the Soviet arms deal with Nasser's regime in 1955. The NPUP charged that the expulsion was a propaganda stunt to justify the internal crackdown by asserting that opposition parties were involved in a conspiracy with the Soviet Union. (*NYT*, 18 and 22 September.)

Following Sadat's assassination, the Soviet Union initiated tentative efforts to improve relations with Egypt. Its first reaction was cautious—it sent a correct but cool message to Cairo. Later, Leonid Brezhnev sent a message to Mubarak suggesting that the Soviet Union would look favorably on Egyptian moves to improve relations. While congratulating Mubarak on his election as president (seen as an overture to Mubarak), Brezhnev said: "You can be assured that readiness on your part to improve relations between Egypt and the Soviet Union . . . will always meet with understanding and support from the Soviet side." (Ibid., 16 October.) The message suggested that the initiative should come from Egypt. No immediate Egyptian response was reported.

George Washington University   Bernard Reich

Ethiopia

On 20 December 1974 Ethiopia declared itself a socialist state based on the principles of Marx and Lenin. Although there is no communist party in Ethiopia (in fact, no political parties exist), in June 1980 the First Congress of the Commission to Organize the Party of the Working People of Ethiopia (COPWE) met to begin the process of creating a vanguard political party. The top echelon of COPWE is made up largely of the military personnel who overthrew Emperor Haile Selassie in 1974 and then established the Provisional Military Administrative Committee (PMAC), a political-military structure through which Ethiopia is led. "Of the COPWE Central Committee members . . . two-thirds are military" (*Swiss Review of World Affairs*, May). According to COPWE representative Legesse Asfaw, "the resolutions approved [in June 1980] and the strategy for action have speeded up the development of the incipient [communist] party, which will soon emerge" (*Granma*, Havana, 4 June). Mengistu Haile Mariam, chairman of COPWE and PMAC, articulated the position of COPWE with precision: "Though not a party, [COPWE] is currently playing the role of a workers' party. Thus the formation of tomorrow's workers' party is inseparably linked with today's COPWE." (Addis Ababa Domestic Service, 1 May.) A primary organ of COPWE is its newspaper *Serto Ader* (Working people). Its role is the "political education of the masses, the reconstruction of public life [and] educating the masses . . . on Marxist-Leninist propaganda" (*Pravda*, 19 June). Although COPWE is structured from the provincial to the central level, decision making primarily revolves around Mengistu Haile Mariam.

Domestic Activities. The Second Congress of COPWE was held 9–13 February. Fifteen hundred delegates from urban organizations, peasant cooperatives, and government and the 123 Central Committee members attended. The purpose of the congress appeared to be to foster closer ideological connections to the Soviet Union. The congress was held just prior to Mengistu's departure for Moscow to attend the Twenty-Sixth Congress of the Soviet party.

The 16,000 troops Cuba sent to Ethiopia in 1977–1978 to aid it in its war with Somalia over the Ogaden region of Ethiopia played a large role in defeating the then invading Somalian army. In 1981

Cuba continued to develop its growing relationship with Ethiopia. In May it signed a Scientific Cooperation Agreement with Ethiopia. The agreement commits Cuba's Pedro Kouri Tropical Medicine Institute to send biological materials to Ethiopia and to train Ethiopian scientific personnel (Havana Domestic Service, 23 May). In July a joint Cuban-Ethiopian commission signed an agreement to strengthen cooperation in the fields of health, construction equipment, education, and livestock (Addis Ababa Domestic Service, 5 July). In the Ogaden, Ethiopian and Cuban troops fought sporadic battles with the Western Somali Liberation Front, which is an Ogaden-based movement attempting to wrest the Ogaden from Ethiopia. Somalia claimed on 13 June that 30 people were killed in Ethiopian air raids over Somalia (*NYT*, 14 June).

Since 1962 Ethiopia has been battling secessionist forces in its northern province of Eritrea. With Soviet and Cuban help, Ethiopia has succeeded in limiting the effectiveness of the Muslim-oriented Eritrean Liberation Front (ELF) and the Marxist Eritrean People's Liberation Front. In July, the ELF declared its willingness to hold a dialogue with Ethiopia through representatives from the United Nations, the Arab League, and the Organization of African Unity in order to ensure the independence and self-determination of Eritrea (Qatar News Agency, Doha, 12 July). The Ethiopian government, which never responds to such overtures, refused to comment. COPWE and PMAC have steadfastly adhered to a nationalist policy of attempting to defeat the secessionists militarily because of the importance to Ethiopia of its Eritrean ports on the Red Sea.

International Affairs. In 1977 the Soviet Union signed a Treaty of Friendship and Cooperation with Ethiopia and since that time has been a strong supporter of socialist Ethiopia. Some 1,500 Soviet military advisers and over $1 billion in Soviet weaponry have been sent to Ethiopia to shore up the government and to support Ethiopia in the Ogaden and Eritrea (*NYT*, 10 March 1978). In 1981 the Soviet Navy developed an anchorage in the Dahlak Islands of Ethiopia on the Red Sea and was reported to be constructing a naval base in the islands (ibid., 19 April). A Treaty of Friendship, Cooperation, and Consular Convention between Bulgaria and Ethiopia was signed 11 July in Addis Ababa. An attempt to improve bilateral relations between Yugoslavia and Ethiopia was made in April when Yugoslav head of state Cvijetin Mijatović visited Addis Ababa to meet with Mengistu Haile Mariam.

Three pro-Soviet states, Libya, South Yemen, and Ethiopia, signed a Treaty of Friendship and Cooperation on 19 August. President 'Ali Nasir Muhammad al-Hassani of South Yemen stated that the new group would be "a material force taking action on the path of joint struggle against all forms of conspiracy and aggression which threaten the peoples of these three countries." He went on to say that peace and security were endangered "by action centers and aggressive imperialist bases located . . . in Israel, Egypt, Somalia, Oman and the Indian Ocean." (Ibid., 20 August.)

Publications. The government controls all media. The COPWE publishes the weekly *Serto Ader.* The *Negarit Gezeta* is the official government organ and publishes the documents passed by the PMAC. Two daily newspapers are printed—the English-language *Ethiopian Herald* and the Amharic-language *Addis Zemea.*

State University of New York   Peter Schwab
College at Purchase

Biography. *Mengistu Haile Mariam.* Born in 1941 in Addis Ababa, Lt. Col. Mengistu Haile Mariam came from humble origins and a minor ethnic community, the Shankella. His mother worked as a servant for an aristocratic Amhara family. Her apparent mistreatment in this position possibly accounts for Mengistu's hatred of the Amhara, who ruled Ethiopia for centuries. At the age of seventeen, he became a cadet at the Holeta military center, graduating as a second lieutenant in 1959. After serving a short tour in the Ethiopian Army, he briefly studied industrial economics at the University of Maryland in the United States. In December 1960, Mengistu took part in an abortive coup staged by Haile Selassie's Imperial Guard. The emperor spared him for his political activities. This pardon was every bit as fatal to Haile Selassie's regime as was the tsar's leniency toward some Bolshevik leaders to imperial rule in Russia.

A feudal state in its political and social systems, Ethiopia experienced serious civil disturbances in early 1974 when unemployment, inflation, and famine destabilized Haile Selassie's regime. Junior officers called for an increase in pay, land reform, and dismissal of the government. The military organized the Dergue, a 120-man coordinating committee, to oppose the emperor's government. During the remainder of 1974 and early the following year, liberal elements in the Dergue lost out to self-professed Marxists led ultimately by Mengistu. Colonel Mengistu purged the Dergue of his opponents, as he crushed political opposition throughout the country. At the same time, the Dergue abolished the monarchy and moved to implement a Marxist state. But Mengistu still retains many of the imperial trappings of the former regime, presiding over official functions in an imitation Louis XV chair. His portrait is as ubiquitous in government offices as was Haile Selassie's.

Mengistu moved the country into the Soviet orbit, and the Soviet bloc responded with massive aid to shore up the new Marxist government from internal enemies and to defend it against Somalia's invasion and rebels in Eritrea in the late 1970s. Since then, Mengistu has loyally supported Moscow's political line by, for example, endorsing its intervention in Afghanistan and campaigning against Western investment in Africa. In 1980, Leonid Brezhnev decorated Mengistu with the Order of the October Revolution and put on an impressive program for him in Alma-Ata, a region similar to Ethiopia, which could serve as model for the east African state.

Mengistu's present positions are commander in chief of the armed forces, head of state, and chairman of COPWE.

Hoover Institution   Thomas H. Henriksen

Iran

The chaos and upheaval that have characterized life in Iran since the downfall of the Shah in 1978 continued. Iran is now involved in several great struggles. First, the Islamic Republican Party (IRP) and Ayatollah Ruhollah Khomeini are battling both leftist and rightist challenges to their regime, as well as separatist movements in Kurdestan, Azerbaijan, Baluchestan, and Khuzestan (or Arabestan). Second, the economy is in a shambles and will probably become worse. There has been negative growth since the revolution, inflation is now believed to be well over 50 percent and still rising, and unemployment is staggering. Finally, the nation is involved in a costly war with Iraq, a war neither side seems able to win. In the midst of these troubles stand Marxist groups of various shades—the Maoist Marxists (the Peykar and Razmandegan groups), the Islamic Marxists (the Fedayin-e Khalq, the Mojahedin-e Khalq, and others), and the Moscow Marxists (the Tudeh Party).

The roots of communism in Iran date to the Red Army's invasion of parts of the Caspian littoral in 1917–1918 and the short-lived Gilan Republic of 1920–1921 in the same area. Throughout the 1930s, the illegal Communist Party of Iran (Hezb-e Komunist-e Iran) operated clandestinely. Following the Soviet occupation of northern Iran in 1941, the movement reappeared as the Tudeh Party (Hezb-e Tudeh-ye Iran), or the "party of the masses." This regenerated group increased in strength until in 1944 the party claimed a membership of 25,000. Under Soviet aegis, independent and pro-Soviet republics were created in Azerbaijan and Kurdestan. At this time the Tudeh Party was represented by three cabinet members in the Tehran government. With the pullout of Soviet troops in 1946 and the collapse of these republics, the power of the Tudeh Party began to decline. In February 1949 the Pahlavi government formally outlawed the Tudeh Party. During the oil crisis of 1951–1953, the party's strength again rose, and it supported Prime Minister Mohammad Mossadegh's National Front government. The proroyalist coup of August 1953 ended not only the Mossadegh regime, but also the growing influence of the Tudeh Party. From 1953 until 1979 the Tudeh Party was centered in East Germany. Its leaders there consisted of exiled party figures, such as Dr. Iraj Eskandari, longtime party secretary.

The events of late 1978 and early 1979 that deposed the Pahlavi dynasty also led to the Tudeh Party's return to Iran. After 26 years in exile, the party returned as the only communist organization recognized and allowed to operate openly by the new Islamic Republic.

On 1 October, the fortieth anniversary of the founding of the Tudeh Party, congratulatory messages were received from the communist parties of Bulgaria, Czechoslovakia, East Germany, Hungary, and Romania (*FBIS*, 1–7 October).

The present situation of the Tudeh Party is difficult to determine due to the constant fluctuations in Iran. During the past year a number of appraisals have come out. The British Foreign and Commonwealth Office stated in its July 1981 *Background Brief* that the Tudeh Party "is well organized and funded but lacks popular appeal and is numerically small. In contrast with other left-wing groups, it has consistently supported Khomeini and the Islamic Republican Party and, though its officials and premises have periodically been the target of popular hostility against the Soviet Union, it has suffered less than other groups from official purges of the Left." According to Agence France Presse, "Iranian communists in the staunchly pro-Khomeini Tudeh Party have spent the past nine months in a political limbo; although their organization is authorized, their operations are semi-clandestine. The party no longer has official offices. Its Tehran headquarters has been occupied since July 1980 by Hezbollahi religious extremists. Nor does it hold rallies or demonstrations. Yet, its leadership believes that the Tudeh Party enjoys more freedom now than it ever did in the days of Prime Minister Mohammad Mossadegh." (Ibid., 5 May.) The Paris journal *Le Point* (2 March) said that "Ayatollah Kianuri" and his Tudeh Party were in the best position and best graces since the Mossadegh era and could even criticize then President Abolhassan Bani-Sadr himself with impunity, obviously with the backing of some fundamentalist circles. Most important was the statement of Nureddin Kianuri, secretary general of the Tudeh, that "the relatively small number of Tudeh militants kept a low profile to avoid provocations." But he stressed that the party line, faithfully reflected in Tudeh publications, consisted of creating a popular front in league with pro-Khomeini religious revolutionaries. "The best guarantee for the party's future," its leader said, "was Ayatollah Ruhollah Khomeini, whose role as guide of Iran's Islamic revolution was accepted by the Tudeh for its main qualities, anti-imperialist, anti-despotic, and supportive of freedom and democracy." Tudeh officials decline to speculate on their prospects in post-Khomeini Iran, but they say conditions are now right for the creation of a major Iranian communist party. (*FBIS*, 5 May.) Kianuri later said that the "Tudeh has political influence which is growing every day" and that "the group should soon be given the right to hold meetings" (ibid., 29 July). The reports are somewhat conflicting, but all agree that the Tudeh is in the strongest position it has known since the early 1950s.

In July the clandestine radio Free Voice of Iran claimed that captured documents showed that Ayatollah Mohammad Beheshti had negotiated with the Tudehis and had promised to appoint three procommunist ministers in return for Soviet support. The radio said that the documents also referred to the purchase of $3 billion worth of obsolete Soviet arms from Libya and Syria. (Ibid., 20 July.) In August another clandestine broadcast claimed that there were three communist members in Mohammad Javad Bahonar's cabinet: the defense minister, the executive minister, and the minister for planning and budget. Since the appointment of the three, the propaganda techniques of Khomeini's government had changed; for example, editorials from the Tudeh newspaper, *Mardom*, were now cited officially. (Ibid., 25 August.) In April, former Foreign Minister Sadegh Qotbzadeh, now in exile in Paris, warned "that the communists are planning to take over power in Tehran and they are trying to reach such a target by controlling the Islamic Republican Party, which controls most of the government machinery." He went on to say that "the communists are exploiting the IRP for a purpose. They have a detailed plan, and the role being played by the IRP is nothing but part of a wider plan. In Tehran alone the communists are spending $700,000 weekly, which comes from outside Iran." He did not say from where. (Ibid., 14 April; *Wall Street Journal*, 22 April.) According to a correspondent of the clandestine radio Voice of Iran, the "Tudeh and other leftists have been working lately in Baluchestan." Although they seem to have had little success with the inhabitants, "in a few border areas . . . direct contacts between Tudeh Party members and Soviet agents, who are among the so-called Afghan refugees, have been noticed." (*FBIS*, 27 May.)

Many in the higher echelons of the present Iranian government seem unconcerned about any communist threat. For example, Ali Khamene'i, who has since become president of Iran, said in April that "world radio reports of the dangers of communism in Iran are aimed at causing Muslims in the region to become pessimistic about Iran's Islamic revolution and at giving imperialists an excuse to launch an attack in the region . . . the United States is Iran's real foe and communism is weak and insignificant in Iran." (Ibid., 6 April.)

Not all the Tudeh Party's efforts have met with success. In February, Khomeini said that "the Tudeh Party killed great numbers of people after the revolution" and that "the danger of communism is as great as Western capitalism" (ibid., 9 and 12 February). In March, the Iranian government prevented a Tudeh delegation from attending the Soviet party congress (ibid., 11 March). *Mardom* was banned from June until September for "engaging in a creeping plot against the Islamic Republic" (ibid., 8 June). In July, Nureddin Kianuri and another Tudeh official were declared ineligible as candidates for Majles (parliament) by-elections (ibid., 20 July).

Due to its publicly professed total support for Khomenini and the Islamic Republic, the Tudeh Party has been forced to serve them. In a verbal message to officials of the party, Mehdi Chamran, a member of Khomeini's security organization, SAVAMA, stated that the continuation of the political life of the Tudeh Party depended on its regular cooperation in the field of information. The strike by employees of the Tehran bus union is among the cases where information gathered by Tudeh Party members was placed at the Tehran regime's disposal. This information led to the arrest, imprisonment, and torture of a large number of workers. This cooperation also extends beyond Iran's borders. (Ibid., 23 April.) Reaction of other groups to such Tudeh activities has been vehement. For example, Mas'ud Rajavi, the exiled leader of the Mojahedin-e Khalq, denounced the Tudeh as a "dirty opportunistic group that is doing the work of SAVAK [the Shah's secret police] for Khomeini by informing on Mojahedin members" (*Wall Street Journal*, 23 September). The Free Voice of Iran complained that everyone had suffered blows during Khomeini's regime; the nationalists, the revolutionary groups, the conservatives, and even the mullahs. "In the midst of all this the only group that has not been harmed is the Tudeh Party. Khomeini's Islamic Republic . . . is removing the obstacles in front of the Tudehis and is paving the ground for their advancement and infiltration." (*FBIS*, 15 October.)

Organization and Leadership. There has been no important change in the Tudeh organization since 1979 when longtime First Secretary Iraj Eskandari was replaced by his deputy, Nureddin Kianuri, due to the former's total misreading of the overthrow of the Shah. Soon after assuming power, Kianuri arrived in Iran.

The current membership of the Tudeh Party is unknown, although in 1976 it was thought to have something less than a thousand members. It seems clear, however, that the party has gained strength as a result of the Islamic Revolution and probably now has 1,500 to 2,000 regular members. In November 1979 Tudeh candidates to the constituent assembly drew 50,000 votes in Tehran. In the parliamentary elections of March 1980, the party earned 60,000 votes. Mid-1981 estimates of *Mardom* readership hovered at about 60,000. (*Radio Liberty Bulletin*, 1 September.) The party receives support from Soviet and East European sources. Little is published or known about internal party affairs.

In March 1981 the Tudeh Central Committee held its seventeenth (enlarged) plenum in Iran. Its published communiqué stressed the "party's policy of support for Imam Khomeini's anti-imperialist and popular line, the line of consistent struggle against imperialism, Zionism and counterrevolution, and also against liberalism." The new party program drafted at the meeting stated that "the central question is that of ways for the country's economic, social, political and cultural development after the revolution, the renewal of society in accordance with the people's interests, and also ways to ensure the country's independence, prosperity and development and the people's happiness and well-being." (*IB*, June.)

Domestic Issues. The Soviet Union's policy toward Iran is said to have three major objectives: (1) to gain influence in the country by supporting Khomeini; (2) to foster anti-American and anti-Western sentiment in Iran; and (3) to bolster the position of its surrogate in Iran, the Tudeh Party (*Radio Liberty Bulletin*, 1 September). The Tudeh Party's domestic policy closely follows this line. The party staunchly supports Khomeini and the Islamic Revolution (*WMR*, July). According to Kianuri "we supported Prime Minister Ali Raja'i in the presidential election because he was the universal candidate of all Iranian anti-imperialist forces. The orientations of revolutionary Islam coincide with the communist program." (*FBIS*, 29 July.) Amir Khosravi, a member of the Tudeh Central Committee, said that "Bani-Sadr and Mas'ud Rajavi [in Paris] still represent an important political force." He also said that "the main danger for the Islamic Republic would be if it failed to solve Iran's economic and social problems." (Ibid., 21 August.)

One change in Tudeh domestic policy from a year ago is its cessation of support for the various national separatist movements in Iran. In February, *Mardom* reported that a Baluchestan liberation front had been formed in the southeast border province. The communist newspaper said that the front was led by "feudal elements" that had supported the Shah's regime and had contacts with former Prime Minister Shahpur Bakhtiar and Omani Sultan Qabus ibn Sa'id. (Ibid., 2 February.)

In April Abdorrahman Qasemlu, leader of the Iranian Kurdish Democratic Party (KDP), said that his group was not cooperating with the Tudeh Party (ibid., 7 April). In a 7 May statement, supporters "warned that the activities of the Qasemlu gang were directed toward the creation of strife between Sunnis and Shi'ites and declared their readiness to defend the revolution and the Islamic Republic and to confront counterrevolutionary plots" (ibid., 5 June).

The Tudeh Party has shown no support for other leftist groups and is evidently content to watch the Khomeini regime eliminate its competition on the left. In an interview Nureddin Kianuri said, "Revolutionaries of the entire world do not care what the bourgeois world thinks about the 250 executions of the fundamentalists' political opponents since the 20th of July. The leaders of the counterrevolutionary groups are murderers and they deserve the death penalty." (Ibid., 29 July.) Most of those executed were members of the Marxist-oriented Mojahedin-e Khalq.

Foreign Policy. The Tudeh Party's foreign policy continues to feature the same three main tenets as in the past—anti-Americanism, anti-imperialism, and anti-Zionism. This trinity is still blamed for most of Iran's problems, external and internal, as well as for attacks on the Tudeh Party by other Iranian groups and political parties. The Tudeh's foreign policy was quite well summed up in an editorial in the 13 April issue of *Mardom*. "The three pillars of support constructed by American-led imperialism to preserve its interests in the Middle East . . . Israel, Egypt and Imperial Iran . . . are now tottering. Without rebuilding the third pillar America cannot maintain its balance in the region . . . Imperialist diplomacy is trying first to contain the Iranian revolution by means of the reactionary forces of the region, to isolate and weaken it, and then to deliver a final blow . . . On the basis of its hostility to the Islamic Republic of Iran, America is striving to form a single front out of the reactionary puppet Arab countries, especially Jordan, Egypt and Saudi Arabia, to be used to pressure the Islamic Republic of Iran and to oppose progressive states such as Libya, Syria, Algeria, Afghanistan, the PDRY [South Yemen] and the PLO [Palestine Liberation Organization]. The principal nucleus of this front will be the Rapid Deployment Force." (Ibid., 24 April.)

Other Marxist Organizations. Since the 1960s, several Marxist-oriented organizations of various shades have emerged in Iran. Some of them, such as the Communist Union of Iran, developed from splits within the Tudeh Party because of its pro-Moscow stance. Others arose more or less spontaneously and were indigenous to the Iranian revolutionary spirit. Besides the traditional Tudeh Party, major Marxist parties include three Trotskyist parties: the Socialist Workers' Party (Hezb-e Kargaran-e Sosialist; HKS), the Revolutionary Workers' Party (Hezb-e Kargaran-e Enqelabi; HKE), and the Workers' Unity Party (Hezb-e Vahdat-e Kargaran; HVK). All three belong the the Fourth International. Two other militant, paramilitary organizations are Marxist in orientation, but cannot be called political parties in the usual sense: the Fedayin-e Khalq and the Mojahedin-e Khalq. The latter has been particularly successful and has drawn many more supporters than has the Tudeh Party.

The HKE was formed in Tehran in 1978 and has grown rapidly. The party has a militant Trotskyist revolutionary policy. Headed by its theoretician Babak Zahraie, the HKE consists largely of intelligentsia and university students. The party platform calls for a workers' and peasants' government, equality for women, self-determination for ethnic minorities, and separation of church and state. This last item has made it difficult for the party to attract mass support.

The HKS differs from the HKE over minor points and approaches. The HKS is smaller and newer than the HKE. One point of contention between the two parties arose in mid-1980 when the militant Islamic councils took over Iran's universities and launched an educational cultural revolution. The effect on political organizing on the campuses was substantial. The HKS, along with the Tudeh Party, the Fedayin, and the Mojahedin, opposed this takeover, but the HKE supported the Islamic councils for eliminating imperialist influences at the universities.

The HVK, like the HKS and the HKE, is a militant Trotskyist revolutionary organization. It has demanded an end to executions of opposition groups, supported autonomy for the Kurds, Turkomans, Baluchis, and others, and called for the implementation of the Land Reform Law and equality for women.

The Marxist-Leninist Fedayin-e Khalq is a militant, paramilitary group of some five thousand members, founded in 1971. From its inception until the revolution, it was very active in guerrilla operations, accounting for numerous bombings and political murders. Once the largest of the left-wing groups, it split in mid-1980. This led to the formation of a majority faction very close to the Tudeh Party. One of the Fedayin's better-known leaders, the prominent playwright Said Sultanpur, was among the first group of those executed following violent protests on 20 June against the Majles's decision to impeach Bani-Sadr. The Fedayin's minority wing has remained violently opposed to the present government and has participated in the armed struggle of the Kurds against government forces and Revolutionary Guards in the hills of northwest Iran. It also has links with the radical Maoist groups.

The Mojahedin-e Khalq is also a paramilitary, guerrilla organization that fought the Shah's regime until the revolution. It continued to suffer large numbers of casualties after the revolution in battles with fundamentalist Muslim groups, such as the Hezbollahis. The Mojahedin are a tightly knit and well-armed unit of revolutionaries, led by Mas'ud Rajavi (now in exile in Paris) and Mohsen Reza'i. The group is ready to die for its beliefs. "The Mojahedin believe that the practice of Islam (not its fundamental principles) must be updated so as to fit the needs of contemporary Iran and bring about a more truly just and classless society" (*San Francisco Examiner*, 21 August 1980). They consider themselves Marxist and Islamic, but not Marxist-Leninist. They feel they are Iran's only true hope left because they are devoted to Islam and in tune with the broad popular base of the Iranian revolution.

During the past year the Mojahedin have continued to battle the Hezbollahi fundamentalists, but they have suffered much more from the government's all-out effort to eliminate them. They have fought the Revolutionary Guards in Tehran and in all parts of the country, even distant Baluchestan (*FBIS*, 28 September). They claimed responsibility for the bombing that killed Ali Raja'i, Mohammad Bahonar, and Mohammad Beheshti in Tehran and attacks on Iranian diplomatic posts around the world (*Los Angeles Times*, 5 August). Recently, the IRP's newspaper, *Jomhuri-ye Eslami*, claimed that more than 1,700 people have been put to death on charges of antigovernment activities and that 4,000 have been arrested since Bani-Sadr was deposed in June (*NYT*, 24 October). The great majority of these were Mojahedin. Still the group claims to have an organized following of up to 100,000 (ibid., 24 October). The Mojahedin have given strong support to ex-President Bani-Sadr and to Kurdish and Baluchi minorities fighting for autonomy. Abdorrahman Qasemlu said in an interview with the journal *al-Hawadith* that the KDP has been cooperating for several months with the banned Mojahedin-e Khalq and that the two organizations are in the process of establishing a "broad democratic front" (*FBIS*, 7 April).

In addition to these major leftist opposition groups, there are a number of smaller groups. For example, there is the Communist Union of Iran, a splinter group that broke from the Tudeh over its ties with Moscow. On 4 July, Revolutionary Guards raided a Communist Union center in Shiraz. Two days later Farnush Vakilzadeh, a leader of the group, was executed "for having and distributing communist propapanda, having printing equipment, being an infidel, waging war against God, and for being corrupt on earth" (ibid., 9 July). Other small groups include the Maoist organizations Peykar and Razmandegan, which appear to have small-scale, but organized support in Tehran and other urban centers (*U.K. Foreign and Commonwealth Office, Background Brief*, July).

Altogether the Marxist groups in Iran probably include over 200,000 dedicated followers and active sympathizers, enough to make a difference in the outcome of happenings in Iran.

Publications. Iran's Marxist factions publish a number of newspapers. The Tudeh Party publishes the daily *Mardom* (The people) and the weekly *Donya* (The world). The HKE puts out the weekly *Kargar* (The worker), the HKS the fortnightly *Che Bayad Kard?* (What is to be done?), and the HVK the weekly *Hemmat* (Aspiration). The Maoist group, Peykar, publishes a paper called *Edalat* (Justice). All of these appear more or less regularly in Tehran, except for periods when the Iranian government temporarily suspends publication of one or another of them. The Mojahedin distribute many pamphlets, and their vendors are frequently attacked and their stocks destroyed by fundamentalist Muslims. The Fedayin-e Khalq has no regular publication, but issues occasional tracts and handbills.

Hoover Institution   Jospeh D. Dwyer

Iraq

The communist movement in Iraq was in worse shape at the end of 1981 than at the end of 1980. The monolithic Baath regime leaves no room for the Iraqi Communist Party (ICP) to function. Draconian laws and regulations that prohibit political activity outside the Baath framework have excluded Communists from the armed forces, the assembly, and government departments. Party leaders, including Secretary General Aziz Muhammad, live in exile in Eastern Europe.

Domestic Attitudes and Activities. The war between Iraq and Iran, which began in September 1980, has given the ICP its only significant opportunity to engage in political activity. It is doing so in collaboration with Kurdish political organizations, and it is, for all practical purposes, only in Iraqi Kurdistan that the ICP functions. The Central Committee had decided in mid-1979 to work for the establishment of a democratic, national front. Its efforts met with success, albeit limited, at the end of November 1980. On 28 November, the Democratic Party of Kurdistan/Iraq (DPK/I), the ICP, and the Unified Socialist Party of Kurdistan signed the charter of the Democratic Iraqi Front. The charter admitted that "this rapprochement among our parties is only one of the efforts now being undertaken by the various national and progressive Iraqi parties and powers" and that it was not "a substitute for the inspired comprehensive alliance" that the Iraqi situation required. The charter called for the overthrow of the Baathist regime and its replacement by a national coalition government, a peaceful solution to the Kurdish issue under a form of autonomy, "a large-scale and comprehensive purge of the corrupt reactionary and chauvinistic elements" in the armed forces and police, a progressive economic policy that would "terminate Iraq's ties with the world capitalist market," participation in the Arab nations' battle against imperialism, Zionism, and reaction, and an independent foreign policy that consolidated "the ties of friendship and cooperation with the socialist countries." (Voice of Iraqi Kurdistan, 1 December 1980; *FBIS*, 3 December 1980.)

Of the three members of the front, the DPK/I is the strongest and the Unified Socialist Party the weakest. The DPK/I has a clandestine radio transmitter, through which the ICP's views and attitudes are communicated to the people of northeast Iraq.

Two weeks before the charter was signed, groups that the ICP had hoped would join a broad opposition grouping established the National Pan-Arab Democratic Front with the support of the Syrian government. Among its members are the Patriotic Union of Kurdistan (PUK), a bitter enemy of the DPK/I, a group of dissident Iraqi Communists, and a Syrian-supported organization of dissident Iraqi Baathists. The DPK/I and the ICP have continued to call for a broad national front, but so far no progress has been made. Nor has the Iranian-supported Shia Muslim organization, al-Da'wah (The Call), been willing to collaborate with the Democratic Iraqi Front.

The demands of the war with Iran have caused the Iraqi government to draw on the forces it customarily stations in Kurdistan. While the central government is still in control of the northeast, this development has given the opposition forces more freedom to maneuver. The DPK/I gets some help from the government of Iran, even though that government is trying to crush Iranian Kurds. ICP guerrillas undertake operations against Iraqi government installations in collaboration with larger DPK/I forces.

The shift in the ICP's activity to Kurdistan has had two consequences for the party. First, it involves the ICP in fratricidal struggles among the Kurds. The DPK/I and the PUK fight each other as well as the Kurdish Revolutionary Party, which is allied with Baghdad. In a statement broadcast by DPK/I radio, the ICP deplored "the tragic fratricide which prevails in Kurdistan" and noted that even "some comrades of our party have been dragged into it" (Voice of Iraqi Kurdistan, 27 September; *FBIS*, 9 October). Second, due to the shifting of the ICP's activity to Kurdistan, it is becoming a heavily Kurdish party, in a way analogous to the ascendancy of Kurds in the ICP in the early 1950s.

International Views. The ICP continued throughout 1981 to take strong exception to Iraq's war with Iran. In a speech to the Soviet party congress, Aziz Muhammad said: "It is well known that the Iraqi people have no national interest in the involvement of our army and country in the destructive military adventure which serves only imperialist, Zionist aggression, and the reactionary forces . . . Our party condemns the continuation of this bloody massacre . . . and demands that it should be halted immediately." (*Pravda* 2 March; *FBIS*, 10 March.)

The Baath Party of Iraq did not send an official delegation to the Soviet congress, although it had to the previous congress. In the late fall of 1980, an Iraqi spokesman attempted to distinguish between the ICP's opposition to the war and the Soviet Union's neutral position, but in fact the USSR had for some months indicated its disapproval of the Iraqi stand by refusing to supply Baghdad with war material that the latter needed. By the fall of 1981, relations on a state-to-state level had improved. Several new agreements for cooperation in economic and technical fields had been signed, and the USSR presided over the sixth session of the Iraq–Council for Mutual Economic Assistance joint committee in October. This improvement has not been reflected in the ICP's view of Baghdad. The party is still in opposition and still critical of Iraqi treatment of the population in the northeast and of those not supporting the government.

In its published statements, the ICP has maintained its traditional opposition to Zionism and its support for the more extreme of the Arab states confronting Israel. The November 1980 charter supported the Steadfastness and Confrontation Front, which consists of Syria, Libya, the Palestine Liberation Organization (PLO), Algeria, and the People's Democratic Republic of Yemen.

Relations with Other Parties. The ICP receives guidance and support from the Soviet party. From the limited data on its relations with other communist parties, the ICP appears to be on conventionally good terms with pro-Moscow parties in the Middle East. Following a joint meeting with the Syrian Communist Party in November 1980, the two parties issued a statement supporting Syria's external policies and advocating the PLO as "sole legitimate representative of the Arab Palestinian people" (Radio Damascus, 26 November 1980; *FBIS*, 26 November 1980).

Publications. The ICP continues to publish the monthly *Tariq al-Sha'b* (People's road). Distributed clandestinely, it may not appear as regularly as in the past.

Swarthmore, Pennsylvania   John F. Devlin

Israel

The communist movement in Palestine began in 1920. Two years later, a Palestine Communist Party (Palestinische kommunistische Partei; PKP) was established; it joined the Comintern in 1924. Following the periodic appearance of factional divisions, the PKP split along ethnic lines in 1943. In October 1948, with the new state of Israel gaining control of most of Palestine, both groups reunited to form the Israeli Communist Party (Miflaga Kommunistit Isra'elit; MAKI).

The movement split again in 1965, partly along ethnic lines. The New Communist List (Reshima Kommunistit Hadasha; RAKAH)—pro-Moscow, strongly anti-Zionist, and primarily Arabic in membership—gained international recognition as the Communist Party of Israel (CPI). The party usually calls itself the "CPI," especially on the international level, but "RAKAH" continues to be the more common designation within Israel. It eclipsed the MAKI, which became an almost completely Jewish organization and moderate in its opposition to government policies. In 1975, the MAKI disappeared as a separate organization after merging with the MOKED (Focus), a Zionist socialist organization moderate in attitude toward the Arabs. In 1977, the MOKED united with other noncommunist groups in the "peace camp" to form Peace for Israel (Shalom le-Israel; SHELLI). By this time, some former (post–1965) MAKI members had joined or at least supported the RAKAH as the country's only communist party.

In keeping with Israel's competitive political party system, Communists generally have been free to organize and participate in public life. The prevailing system of proportional representation has facilitated election of candidates from small parties, including communist ones, to the Knesset (parliament).

Although CPI membership is about 80 percent Arab, many of its leaders (including a majority on top party organs) are Jewish. A pattern recently has emerged in which a Jewish general secretary is balanced by an Arab deputy general secretary. The party presents itself as a model for Arab-Jewish cooperation. Its membership—up about 25 percent since 1978, according to a party official—is estimated at about 1,500 out of an Israeli population (not including occupied territories) of four million (*Jerusalem Post,* 4–10 October).

However, the CPI is isolated from the mainstream of Israeli politics. No communist party has ever participated in the cabinet. In the June 1981 elections, the CPI-led coalition, the Democratic Front for Peace and Equality (DFPE) obtained four seats in the Knesset, compared with five between 1977 and 1981. The less radical SHELLI, whose two members in the Knesset sometimes had voted with the DFPE, failed to get enough votes to win representation. The DFPE dominates local politics in Arab towns. A member of the CPI, Tawfiq Zayyad, has been mayor of Nazareth, the largest Arab town, since 1975.

Leadership and Organization. The Nineteenth Congress of the CPI met in Haifa during 11–14 February and elected the Central Committee and the Central Control Commission. The first plenary meeting of the new Central Committee met later that same month in Tel Aviv and elected a Political

Bureau of nine members and four alternate members, as well as a seven-member Secretariat. The Central Committee also re-elected Meir Vilner as general secretary and Tawfiq Toubi as deputy general secretary. A meeting of the Central Control Commission again designated W. Erlich as its chairman and R. Khuri as deputy chairman. Five additional plenary meetings were held between March and July.

Auxiliary and Mass Organizations. The CPI dominates the DFPE—which includes two noncommunist coalition partners, the Black Panthers (an Afro-Asian, or Oriental, Jewish group protesting alleged discrimination by Jews of European origin) and the Arab Local Council Heads. The CPI sponsors the active Young Pioneer children's movement and a youth organization, the Young Communist League. The CPI also participates in the Democratic Women's Movement, the Israeli Association of Anti-Fascist Fighters and Victims of Nazism, and the Israeli-USSR Friendship Movement.

Domestic Attitudes and Activities. CPI statements during 1981 emphasized the adverse impact of "militarism" on Israel. Vilner told the Soviet party congress that this "has led to aggravation of the economic, social and moral crisis in Israel" (Tass, 2 March; *FBIS,* 3 March). The Central Committee condemned the Likud government for its "anti-people's and anti-workers' policy" (Tass, 25 March; *FBIS,* 26 March). The "theses" for the CPI congress stated that "Zionist ideology and practices . . . express capitalist interests and are in conflict with the interests of the working class, of the masses" (quoted by Tawfiq Toubi, *WMR,* July, p. 37). Toubi characterized the "Likud government . . . as a direct representative of capital," which had raised "military spending to a level unknown before" and created "unprecedented capitalist perfidy while the social rights and interests of the working class and middle strata were severely damaged." He pointed to the 133 percent inflation rate, the $20 billion foreign debt, an internal debt of nearly $70 billion, and decreases in consumption, social services, real wages, and employment." The CPI congress called for a decreased military budget, "nationalizing the banks, insurance companies, and foreign trade, taxing capital profits . . . and reducing the taxes on wages and salaries," as well as increases in real wages, "subsidies for essential commodities and services," and increased spending for social purposes. It declared "that the assumption of power by the rightist government had aggravated the danger of fascism," exemplified in "anti-democratic laws affecting freedom of speech and organization." Other CPI statements deplored the formation of a new Likud government and warned of a new move to the right. The party continued to deplore "the stepped-up anti-democratic, racist measures against the Arab population," citing as examples "laws and measures aimed at wider expropriation of Arab-owned land, such as the draconian law on the confiscation of land owned by the Arab bedouin population of the Negev or the setting up of military outposts in Galilee." Other statements "directed the party's attention to the burning issue of discrimination against the Oriental communities among the Jewish population," among which "the overwhelming majority of the poor . . . are to be found." (Ibid., pp. 38–39.)

The CPI continued to dominate the annual Day of the Land (30 March), celebrated by Arabs in Israel (and now also in the West Bank) since 1976. Vilner, Zayyad, and others spoke to a crowd of four thousand in Nazareth, while other CPI representatives spoke to demonstrators in Tayyibah and Beersheba. The Nazareth crowd chanted: "In blood and spirit we shall redeem Galilee" (*NYT,* 31 March).

Other CPI-led activities were banned. Applying an emergency regulation enacted by the British in 1945, the government issued a restraining order preventing a National Congress of the Arab Population—expected to deal with anti-Arab discrimination and to urge negotiations with the Palestine Liberation Organization (PLO)—from being held in Nazareth on 6 December 1980. Toubi declared this ban a "black day" and "dangerous to the whole of Israeli society and to democracy" (ibid., 2 December 1980). Citing alleged support for the PLO, the Israeli government banned the National

Coordinating Committee established by Israeli Arabs belonging to various groups, including the CPI, in February.

The DFPE's loss of one seat in the Knesset as a result of the June elections came as a surprise to pollsters. It polled 64,918 votes, or 3.35 percent of the total (*Jerusalem Post,* 12–18 July). As always, its percentage of the Jewish vote was insignificant. It got 53 percent of the vote in Nazareth but only 37 percent of the nationwide non-Jewish vote (including only about 10 percent of the bedouin vote and few from among the Druze, who are officially labeled non-Arab in Israel). Excluding the Druze, it got 45 percent of the Arab vote, down from 50 percent in 1977 (ibid., 18–24 October). The Arab defections went primarily to the Labor Alignment, seemingly because of a distaste for the Likud that dictated voting for the lesser evil. Some analysts attributed the loss to various factors, including a high rate of Arab abstention, the DFPE's alleged excessive concern with international issues rather than the immediate problems of Arab voters, and even to government patronage that gained Likud a few Arab votes. Other Israeli analysts saw the DFPE's drop as an indication of a decline in the Arab population's militance, although some Arabs reject the DFPE as too moderate on the Palestine question.

International Activity and Contacts. Vilner headed a CPI delegation to the Twenty-Sixth Congress of the Communist Party of the Soviet Union (CPSU) in March. The delegation met with representatives of the PLO while in Moscow. Twenty other communist parties—including those of Hungary, East Germany, the USSR, Poland, Greece, Bulgaria, Italy, Romania, and Mongolia—and also the *World Marxist Review* sent delegations to the CPI congress in February. Political Bureau member and secretary David Khenin met with Bulgarian party leaders in June in Sofia.

International Views and Policies. The CPI is closely aligned with Moscow. The Nineteenth Congress condemned "the virulent, trouble-making anti-Soviet campaign conducted by the Israeli government and international Zionism"; it went on to call "the attitude toward the Soviet Union and the CPSU an important criterion of loyalty to the cause of socialism and the anti-imperialist struggle" (Toubi, *WMR,* July, p. 40). According to Vilner, "To come out against the Soviet Union and to fight for peace at the same time is incompatible. Peace and the Soviet Union are indivisible" (Tass, 2 March; *FBIS,* 3 March). Beijing's policy was described as "nationalist, hegemonist, and anti-Soviet" and as "increasingly outspoken in seeking a strategic alliance with imperialism" (Toubi, *WMR,* July, p. 40). Joint statements with Hungarian, East German, and Bulgarian parties stressed "fraternal" ties and solidarity. A plenary meeting adopted a resolution entitled "Stop Israeli Aid to the Fascist Junta in El Salvador," demanding an end to Israeli military aid to dictatorships (Tass, 25 March; *FBIS,* 26 March).

The CPI continued to call for negotiations with the PLO, withdrawal of Israeli forces from all occupied territories, removal of Israeli settlements, the creation of a Palestinian state, and continued Israeli independence within the pre-1967 lines. Vilner told the CPSU congress that he supported Leonid Brezhnev's proposal for a special international conference to bring about a comprehensive settlement of the Arab-Israeli conflict (Tass, 2 March; *FBIS,* 3 March). Toubi spoke of his party's "opposition to the policy of aggression pursued by [Israel's] Zionist rulers," who are "preventing peace" and "pursuing a pro-imperialist policy against the Arab national liberation movement, and trampling the legitimate rights of the Palestinian Arab people." He called the Camp David agreements a hindrance to "genuine and all-inclusive peace" and "a military alliance between the reactionary pro-imperialist ruling circles of Israel and Egypt under U.S. aegis." (WMR, July, p. 37.) The CPI congress opposed "land expropriation and colonization" and "harassment and terroristic measures" in the occupied territories (ibid., p. 38). Vilner denounced Israeli attacks on Palestinian refugee camps and on Lebanon as "barbarous" (Tass, 2 March; *FBIS,* 3 March).

Publications. The CPI newspaper, *al-Ittihad* (Union), is an Arabic biweekly published in Haifa, edited by Toubi and Emile Habibi. A Hebrew weekly, *Zo Ha-Derekh* (This is the way), is edited by Vilner in Tel Aviv. Other party publications are *al-Jadid* (The new), a monthly literary and cultural magazine published in Haifa by Samih al-Qasim; *al-Ghad* (Tomorrow), a youth magazine; the Yiddish *Der Weg* (The way), published weekly by Vilner in Tel Aviv; the Bulgarian *Tovaye Putnam* (This is the way), published every two weeks in Jaffa; the theoretical *Arakim: Be'ayot ha-Shalom ve-ha-Soatziyalizm* (Values: Problems of Peace and Socialism), published six times a year in Tel Aviv; and the sporadic *Information Bulletin, Communist Party of Israel,* published in Tel Aviv by the Foreign Relations Department of the Central Committee.

Other Organizations. Several other Marxist groups exist in Israel, but as a political force none is comparable to the CPI. Each consists of a handful of members, originally mostly young Jews but now including some Arabs as well. None offers its own list of electoral candidates.

The most radical trend is represented by the Israeli Socialist Organization (Irgun Sotziyalisti Israeli; ISO), formed by a group expelled in 1962 from the MAKI. Widely known by the name of its monthly Hebrew publication, *Matzpen* (Compass), issued from Tel Aviv, the ISO condemns establishment of Israel at the expense of Palestinian Arabs and its "open alliance with . . . imperialism and collusion with the most reactionary forces in the Arab world." The ISO recognizes the continued existence of a Hebrew nation in Palestine but calls for "de-Zionification" and a "socialist revolution," as well as "integration into a unified, socialist Middle East." It criticizes the USSR's policy of "peaceful coexistence," Soviet "bureaucracy," and the CPI's acceptance of the Soviet line. It also has censured Beijing's policies. The Matzpen viewpoint has received more attention outside Israel.

Several splits in Matzpen occurred during the early 1970s. Breakaway groups included the Revolutionary Communist League (Brit Kommunistit Mahapkhanit), which is the Israeli section of the Fourth (Trotskyist) International; the Workers' League (Brit ha-Po'alim), also Trotskyist (Lambertist section), which publishes *Avant-garde* and tends to emphasize opposition to capitalism more than opposition to Zionism; and the Maoist-oriented Revolutionary Communist Alliance (Brit Kommunistit Mahapkhanit), which publishes *Ma'avak* (Struggle).

The Israeli New Left (Smol Yisrael Chadish; SIAH, or "Dialogue") was launched in 1968. It consisted of a few loosely organized youths, mainly students, previously associated with the MAKI and the United Workers' Party. The SIAH, which identifies with the radical student movement in Europe, professes devotion to Marxism and, in the case of the group in Tel Aviv but not the more radical Jerusalem branch, to Zionism. It calls for the creation of an independent Palestinian state to exist alongside Israel. Its publications include *Siah* (published irregularly in Hebrew) and *Israleft,* a biweekly English newsletter that disseminates statements by various leftist and peace groups.

Indiana State University   Glenn E. Perry

Jordan

The Communist Party of Jordan (al-Hizb al-Shuyu'i al-Urdunni; CPJ) was officially established in June 1951 and has operated under the guise of various popular front organizations since that time. Its work has centered on the West Bank, where it has drawn support from students, teachers, professional workers, and the lower middle class.

The CPJ has been illegal since 1957, although the government's normally repressive measures have been relaxed on occasion. At present, communist party membership is punishable by jail sentences from three to fifteen years. Israeli sources report that Jordan has promised the Soviet Union that it will permit the CPJ to operate openly, although not under its own name, within the framework of the Jordanian-USSR Friendship Committee (*FBIS,* 2 July). Few other radical organizations are active in Jordan; however, various Palestinian groups, such as the Marxist-oriented Popular Front for the Liberation of Palestine (embittered by "repression" of the Palestinians during 1970–1971), urge the overthrow of King Hussein. They appear to have little overt influence in Jordan. Beginning in 1972, Israel clamped down on the party in the West Bank because it had engaged in terrorist activities. During the late 1970s, West Bank Communists reportedly returned to more conventional political action, perhaps in preparation for Israel's implementation of an autonomy plan for the West Bank.

The CPJ has perhaps no more than five hundred members, mostly Palestinians. Jordan's population of about 3.2 million includes roughly 835,000 in Israeli-occupied East Jerusalem and the West Bank.

Leadership and Organization. The CPJ is said to be a tightly organized, well-disciplined network of small cells. (For details regarding party leaders, see *YICA,* 1979, p. 413.) There are two West Bank communist factions. The Palestine Communist Organization, an establishment-oriented group headed by Bashir Barghuti, is reportedly the larger of the two. The Palestine Communist Party is a small, militant organization affiliated with the Leninist Lodge, which seceded from the CPJ in the early 1970s because of ideological and personal differences. Both factions engage in organizational and propaganda activity and recruit from the five small West Bank colleges. They have made their influence felt by penetrating municipalities, professional associations, trade unions, and welfare organizations. They have become more open about their Marxist orientation. The Communists are among the few groups with a political organization operating throughout the West Bank.

Auxiliary and Mass Organizations. The Palestine National Front (PNF) is composed of professional and labor union representatives and "patriotic personalities." It was established in August 1973 on the West Bank, evidently on CPJ initiative, by Muhammad Abu Mayzar. A small organization with an estimated strength of 100–500 men, it is a resistance group reportedly containing communist exiles from Jordan, Syria, Iraq, and Lebanon and apparently is based in Lebanon. The PNF follows the Palestine Liberation Organization (PLO) line and advocates an independent Palestinian state comprising the West Bank and the Gaza Strip. Its program includes mass political struggle and armed resistance in the occupied territories. The PNF's precise relation to the CPJ is unknown. According to a report of the CPJ Central Committee in 1980, the Palestinians of the occupied territories are heroically resisting Israel and the plans for administrative autonomy. The Palestine Communist Organization of the West Bank is playing an "outstanding" role in this struggle. Other "militant mass organizations" are continually being established. (*IB*, 1980, nos. 19–20.)

Party Internal Affairs. The CPJ has been described officially as the working-class party of two fraternal peoples—Jordanian and Palestinian. Despite its support of Palestinian statehood, the CPJ remains somewhat suspicious of the PLO, an attitude the PLO reciprocates.

Domestic Attitudes and Activities. The CPJ's leaders have consistently denounced the "reactionary regime" in Amman and its links with "imperialism." For example, the 1980 Central Committee report accused Jordan of being "linked politically, financially and militarily to the forces that are prodding for a cold war," in particular, the United States. According to the report, Jordan's "economic weakness is used by the regime as a pretext for prolonging its ties with imperialism, Arab and world reaction." Government policy has led to "a swollen state bureaucracy, expanded privileges for top officials and growing reliance on 'foreign support.' " The bureaucracy is characterized by "widespread corruption and indifference," while top officials and contractors involved in economic projects are being enriched through "pilfering, machinations, mismanagement, wastefulness, speculation and embezzlement." (Ibid.)

The Central Committee declares that the key to Jordan's progress is the creation of a popularly supported "national democratic regime." Such a regime would stress democratic freedoms and release all political prisoners, hold "free and just elections," struggle against monopolies, and undertake efforts to reduce the high cost of living and raise living standards for the masses of people. The Central Committee calls attention to Jordan's "unprecedented" lag in agricultural output and emphasizes the importance of "effective measures for building an independent national economy . . . [which would] insure that all the country's manpower resources are used for social production." It urges the establishment of a "sound domestic front to mobilize the people in defense of their interests." (Ibid.)

The Palestine issue has vexed the party since its inception. As a generally pro-Soviet organization, the CPJ evidently has not been entirely free to take an independent stand. Consequently it has lost support to more committed and radical Palestinian liberation groups. The party recognizes the PLO as the sole representative of the Palestinian people and has urged all Palestinians to rally round the PLO against "renegades and traitors" (*WMR*, November 1978). It "advocates the establishment of an independent Palestinian state on the West Bank of the Jordan, in the Gaza Strip and in the Arab section of Jerusalem" (ibid., July 1979). The Palestine Communist Organization has taken a similar position. It "vigorously rejects the 'conspiratorial' Camp David agreements," opposes an "autonomous administration" on the West Bank, and supports creation of an independent Palestinian state on the West Bank and the Gaza Strip based on the 4 June 1967 borders (*IB*, 1978, no. 23).

The 1980 Central Committee report accuses the Jordanian government of intending to revive the United Arab Kingdom plan for the East and West Banks and the Gaza Strip. Jordan's "ambiguous and contradictory" policy allows Israel "an opportunity to trample the rights of the Palestinian people." Strengthened resistance to the Israeli occupation is necessary to ensure the "inalienable rights of the Arab people of Palestine." The Palestinian national struggle requires greater unity within the PLO as well as structural reorganization of that body, including the elimination of all "corrupt elements." The report argues that efforts are being made to weaken the role of national progressive forces within the PLO, especially the Communists, in order to make the organization internationally "acceptable." In particular, "certain influential circles" within the PLO are under the "illusion" that a dialogue with the United States could induce U.S. imperialism to renounce the conspiracy against Palestinian national rights. Israel, the report notes, is stepping up its repression of the Palestinians as part of the "conspiracy of U.S. imperialism and Zionism." (Ibid., 1980, nos. 19–20.)

International Activities and Attitudes. In a recording broadcast over Moscow Radio Peace and Progress in February, CPJ Secretary General Fa'iq Warrad declared that the United States and other imperialist, Zionist, and reactionary circles are attempting to weaken the Arab-Soviet alliance. He noted that the imperialists have had some success through the Camp David accords, splitting Egypt away from the unified Arab position and leading to Egypt's alliance with the United States. However, the Soviet Union continues firmly to support the just struggle of the Arabs, particularly the Palestinians. (*FBIS,* 26 February.) Warrad praised Soviet peace policy in an interview with a Moscow reporter, declaring that it "represents not just the ambitions of the Soviet people but also the conscience of noble people the world over." He termed Camp David a "dead end," the only achievement of which was to subject Egypt to "American imperialist domination and policy." Moreover, Camp David permitted Israel "more freedom to launch attacks and expand in the region." Warrad supported the Brezhnev proposal for an international conference, including PLO representatives, to deal with the Palestinian question. He warned that U.S. power was being amassed in the Persian Gulf region on the pretext of meeting a Soviet threat to the oil fields but in reality to prevent progress and development. (Ibid., 3 March.)

A CPJ statement circulating in Moscow in July urged the Arab states to end their political, economic, financial, and military relations with the United States. According to the statement, Arab reactionary regimes serve U.S. interests, thereby encouraging Tel Aviv, along with its U.S. patrons, to new large-scale aggression. Israel's "aggression" against Lebanon, the bombing of the Iraqi nuclear reactor, and threats against Syria were denounced as "brazen violations of international law." (Ibid., 3 August.) The Central Committee's 1980 report also stressed anti-imperialist themes: the need for a vigorous policy of resistance against Zionism and the United States, promotion of relations with the Soviet Union, strengthened pan-Arab solidarity, and vigilance against Arab reaction. It denounced "the apostate Chinese leadership, which has become a direct accomplice of U.S. imperialism." (*IB,* 1980, nos. 19–20.)

Publications. The CPJ publishes *al-Jamahir* (Masses) and an underground newspaper, *al-Watan* (Homeland); both appear once or twice a month, the former in Jordan and the latter on the West Bank. The party also issues a political and theoretical magazine *al-Haqiqah* (Truth), distributed in Jordan and the West Bank. These publications are circulated clandestinely on both sides of the Jordan River, except for *al-Watan,* which is restricted mainly to the West Bank. In early 1978, *al-Taliyah* (Vanguard), an Arabic weekly published in East Jerusalem with the knowledge of Israeli authorities, appeared on the West Bank. Its editor-in-chief and founder is Elias Nasralla, a member of the Communist Party of Israel; senior editor is Bashir Barghuti. Shortly after its appearance, Israeli military authorities ordered *al-Taliyah* to cease publication because it did not have a permit. Another CPJ organ, *al-Shaab* (The people), appeared in 1978. The PNF publishes its own newspaper, *Filastin* (Palestine). News of CPJ activities also appears in the organs of the Lebanese Communist Party, *al-Akhbar* and *al-Nida'.* Many communists and communist-inspired pamphlets have appeared recently on the West Bank.

U.S. Department of State   Norman F. Howard
Washington, D.C.

(Note: Views expressed in this article are the author's own and do not represent those of the State Department.)

Lebanon .

The roots of the Lebanese Communist Party (al-Hizb al-Shuyu'i al-Lubnani; LCP) are traceable to the establishment of the Lebanese People's Party in October 1924 by intellectuals and workers. The LCP's First Congress was held in December 1943–January 1944. Initially unresponsive to Arab nationalism, the party adopted a more sympathetic stance at its Second Congress in July 1968. According to ICP Secretary General George Hawi, the party's membership remained stable at about two thousand in the late 1960s but has increased seven to eight times since then (*Monday Morning,* Beirut, 8–14 June; *FBIS,* 17 June). The greatest influx of new members took place in 1974 when the membership allegedly increased more than 60 percent—all of them under age 25. Membership doubled during the 1975–76 civil war, when the party was said to have about five thousand volunteers under arms. The Communists traditionally have drawn much of their support from the Greek Orthodox community, although Shia Muslims are increasingly active in the party. The population of Lebanon is about three million (the demographic impact of the civil war and subsequent internal strife cannot be determined accurately).

Leadership and Organization. The Congress, which is supposed to be convened every four years, is the supreme LCP organ. Owing to the instability in Lebanon, the Fourth Congress was not held until 1979 and was characterized by complete secrecy. During the congress, Niqula al-Shawi was elected to the new post of party president, an honorary position created for the longtime LCP leader. George Hawi, the effective leader of the party, was elected secretary general. (For a listing of Central Committee members, see *YICA,* 1981, p. 14.)

Domestic Views and Activities. The LCP has taken an active role in Lebanese affiars. It belongs to the National Movement, a coalition of leftist parties, and its secretary general is described variously as "vice-president" of the National Movement or simply "member" of the executive office of the movement's Politburo (*FBIS,* 27 February, 17 June). The party advocates a "unified, independent Lebanon with territorial integrity and the sovereignty of the legitimate authorities" (ibid., 3 June). It favors the efforts of President Elias Sarkis, supported by Syria, to reach a national accord and normalize the situation in Lebanon (ibid., 28 May).

A statement by the party's Central Committee attributed worsening violence in Lebanon in the spring of 1981 to the provocations of U.S. imperialists, Israel, and Israel's agents in Lebanon, whose purpose was to weaken Syria and the Palestinian revolution and to "undermine the sovereignty of the lawful Lebanese authorities" (ibid., 4 June). Right-wing Christians reportedly were attempting to make Zahlah a base and were intensifying provocations against the Syrian Arab Deterrent Force. George Hawi has accused the Phalangists of attempting to establish "a racist, sectarian regime over all the Lebanese territories" (ibid., 27 February). In particular, the rightists are trying to create "a racist denominational statelet" in parts of Mt. Lebanon and Beirut that would be linked to Maj. Saad Haddad's "midget state" in south Lebanon (ibid., 2 July).

To confront these activities, the secretary general claims that the LCP is active everywhere in the country, including Haddad's border strip. The party reportedly has more than one training camp in each Lebanese governorate, and in the late spring of 1981 it established two additional camps. Young party members under age 30 were directed to report for military training "immediately"; the goal was to recruit a 3,000-man regular military force in summer 1981, to be supplemented by 5,000 irregulars. Despite obvious antipathy toward the right, Secretary General Hawi has stated that the LCP and the National Movement are ready to begin a dialogue with Phalangist leader Bashir al-Jumayyil as soon as the latter severs his ties to Israel. Surprisingly, Hawi has suggested that left and right "will have no differences on Lebanon's future economic system and even its political system." (Ibid., 17 June.)

During the civil war, the LCP may have lost as many as two hundred fighters. In 1981, frequent battles between communist groups and the Shia militia, Amal, were reported in Beirut and southern Lebanon. However, rivalries within the Shia community were perhaps more important than ideological differences in triggering these clashes.

The LCP and the Arab World. The LCP supports the Palestinian revolution and statehood for the Palestinian people. It believes that Israeli aggression against southern Lebanon is directed at the Palestinian revolution and the Lebanese National Movement. Israel's purpose is to achieve control over Lebanon (ibid., 27 February). In a visit to South Yemen, Central Committee member Nadim 'Abd al-Samad praised the decision of the People's Democratic Republic of Yemen (PDRY) to send token forces to Syria to assist in the battle against the Zionists and thanked PDRY leaders for their understanding of the situation in Lebanon (ibid., 8 June). George Hawi has called the presence of Libyan volunteers in Lebanon fully justified because of Israeli military activities and Israel's "surrogate fighters" in Lebanon. However, the LCP and the National Movement would ask for the evacuation of all non-Lebanese fighters if Israel and its allies removed their troops and if agreement were reached on the status of the Palestinian resistance in Lebanon (ibid., 17 June).

Secretary Hawi has affirmed that relations between the Lebanese state and the Palestinian revolution must be based on trust. The Palestinians must not be allowed to revert to their former status as refugees. Hawi believes that the conspiracy to disperse the Palestinians and "demilitarize" their revolution would also harm the Lebanese people, including the Christian community. (*IB*, August.)

Several Arab states have provided support to the LCP. According to Hawi, the party obtains financial support from Iraq and Libya and also receives funds from Iraq, Libya, and Algeria allotted to the LCP because of its membership in the National Movement. The party reportedly obtains weapons from the Palestine Liberation Organization, Syria, Libya, Iraq, Kuwait, Saudi Arabia, and others, but not from the Soviet Union (ibid.).

International Views and Activities. The LCP has maintained a consistently pro-Soviet posture. George Hawi attended the Twenty-Sixth Congress of the Soviet party in Moscow in February. An LCP statement circulated in Moscow termed the congress "an outstanding event of great significance." The statement noted that the LCP would work "tirelessly" to strengthen Soviet-Lebanese friendship. (Ibid., 30 March.) An LCP delegation led by Hawi also met with Soviet officials in May; the delegation supported the Soviet call for an international conference to settle the Arab-Israeli conflict on a just basis (ibid., 28 May). In an interview in June, Hawi declared that Soviet-Lebanese relations "can be model relations in which the big does not dominate the small," noting that the policies of the LCP are not dictated by Moscow. He also stated that a Soviet-Lebanese treaty of friendship was not a direct goal of the LCP and that such a treaty could be signed only if a majority of the Lebanese people supported it (ibid., 17 June). According to Hawi, about two thousand Lebanese students are in the Soviet Union at Soviet expense, supported by scholarships distributed by the LCP, the Lebanese-Soviet association, the Lebanese government, and other Lebanese parties.

LCP delegations visited Bulgaria on at least two occasions, from 26 December 1980 to 4 January 1981 and again in August (ibid., 9 January, 17 August).

In March, Shafik Handal, secretary general of the Communist Party of El Salvador, visited Lebanon, meeting with Palestinian leaders and with the Executive Committee of the National Movement. LCP Central Committee member Shawi, speaking on behalf of the movement, declared its support for the revolution in El Salvador and termed U.S. intervention there a threat to world peace (ibid., 25 March). Despite the LCP's anti-U.S. stance, Secretary General Hawi has taken a "realistic" view of U.S.-Lebanese relations. The party does not ask the Lebanese government to "draw away from the U.S. We . . . recognize the nature of American-Lebanese relations." (Ibid., 17 June.) However, the LCP does ask the Lebanese government to be firmer with the United States on the subject of Israeli attacks against Lebanon.

In a statement circulated in Beirut, the LCP Politburo declared that the United States was interested in using Egypt and Sudan as "springboards for aggression against progressive Arab states" as well as the socialist countries, especially the USSR (ibid, 19 October). In particular, the United States was accused of attempting to intimidate the people of Egypt to ensure that the new government of Muhammed Hosni Mubarak adheres to Sadat's policy. The statement charged the White House with an effort to impose a pro-American course on the Arab world, including the liquidation of the National Front of Steadfastness and Confrontation, beginning with Libya and Moammur Khadafy. All progressive forces were encouraged to support the Libyan leader.

Publications. The party publishes a daily newspaper, *al-Nida'* (The call), which celebrated its twentieth anniversary in 1979. Other LCP publications, distributed with varying degrees of regularity during the Lebanese crisis, are the weekly magazine *al-Akhbar* (The news) and the literary and ideological monthly *al-Tariq* (The road). These organs also serve as general information media for illegal communist parties in the Middle East.

The Organization of Communist Action (OCAL). The OCAL, composed mostly of students, was formed in May 1970 and held its first congress in 1971. Like the LCP, it has drawn recruits from Shia migrants in Beirut. About 75 of its members reportedly were killed during the civil war. Its secretary general is Muhsin Ibrahim, who is also secretary general of the National Movement. The OCAL has consistently supported the Palestinian resistance and maintains close ties with the Democratic Front for the Liberation of Palestine (DFLP). Since its first congress, the OCAL has moderated its strong support for China in the Sino-Soviet conflict; at present it rejects loyalty either to Moscow or Beijing. In recent years, the OCAL and the LCP have drawn closer. In early October, the OCAL held a press conference to review alleged plots by the Phalange and Lebanese Army intelligence to assassinate Muhsin Ibrahim; the recent "detonation" of the organization's central warehouse also was discussed (*FBIS*, 8 October). The OCAL publishes the weekly journal *al-Hurriya* in cooperation with the DFLP.

U.S. Department of State   Norman F. Howard
Washington, D.C.

(Note: Views expressed in this article are the author's own and do not represent those of the State Department.)

Morocco

The Moroccan Communist Party (Parti communiste moracain), founded in 1943 as a branch of the French Communist Party, was banned by the French protectorate in 1952. After three years of open operations in independent Morocco, it was banned in 1959. Renamed the Party of Progress and Socialism (Parti du progrès et du socialisme; PPS), it was granted legal status in 1974. In the 1976 municipal elections, the party secured a modest representation on the city council of Casablanca. The PPS participated in the Moroccan national elections in the spring of 1977 and won one seat in parliament. The PPS has 825 active cell members, and estimates of total party membership range from 1,500 to 4,000. Morocco's population is about 21 million.

Leadership and Organization. The PPS's Second Congress (February 1979) re-elected 'Ali Yata as secretary general and elected a seven-member Secretariat (see *YICA,* 1980, p. 425).

Domestic Issues. The view of the PPS toward the country's economic crisis and social tensions remains substantially unchanged (see ibid., 1981, p. 18). The PPS's immediate goals are more efficient management of the existing economic system to strengthen the internal front against neighboring Algeria and more equitable distribution of the benefits of the economic system.

The PPS abstained from the 8 May communal council elections held at Dakhla in the southern Sahara and several by-elections held the same day at various towns in the northern Sahara and southern Morocco. The party cited insufficient campaign time as the reason for its decision not to participate. When the government announced massive price increases on staple products on 28 May, the PPS joined other political parties in Morocco in denouncing the decision.

Following violent riots in Casablanca on 20–21 June, the PPS daily journal *al-Bayane* was banned for the second time in less than six months. On 14 July, the journal was allowed to resume publication, although the ban on the publications of Morocco's major left-wing opposition party, the Socialist Union of Popular Forces (USFP), was not lifted. In the first issue after resuming publication, *al-Bayane* carried a declaration from the PPS Politburo blaming the government for the Casablanca riots. After citing the widespread unemployment, bad housing, the baneful effects of Morocco's worst drought in nearly fifty years, and the high failure rate of students taking their final exams, the declaration concluded that "the government assumes the entire responsibility for the explosive situation created." The Politburo then called for the replacement of the present government coalition by a "representative government" that included the Moroccan left, that is, the PPS and the USFP.

On 15 July, after publishing only two editions, *al-Bayane* was suppressed again. Although no official explanation was given for the renewed ban, the move probably resulted from the journal's forthright account of the trials in Casablanca of members of the USFP-aligned labor union, the Democratic Confederation of Labor.

International Issues. PPS Secretary General 'Ali Yata, the party's sole member of parliament and editor of *al-Bayane,* accompanied King Hassan II to the Organization of African Unity summit meeting in Nairobi in late June. This action was intended to show that the PPS, while opposed to the government on domestic policy, strongly supported the government's nationalist campaign to "recover" the Western Sahara. Despite this show of support, when 'Ali Yata wanted to travel abroad on 5 July, his passport was seized without explanation. This move by the government may have been linked to Yata's refusal in May to accompany an emissary of King Hassan to Moscow and other East European capitals to protest against the Libyan threat in northwest Africa.

Earlier in the year, Yata had visited Moscow to attend the Soviet party congress. In his greetings to the congress, Yata deplored the "artificially created tension" in north Africa. He urged that both "Morocco and Algeria ought to achieve through negotiation a harmonious political solution taking into account the rights and national interests of both states; this would restore peace, stability and the fraternal solidarity of the Maghreb's peoples." (*Pravda,* 2 March; *FBIS,* 9 March.)

Publications. The PPS publishes two daily newspapers, *al-Bayane* (The bulletin) in French and *al-Makafih* (The fighter) in Arabic.

Portland State University   John Damis

Mozambique

Opponents of Portugal's colonial rule in Mozambique formed the Frente de Libertação de Moçambique (Front for the Liberation of Mozambique; FRELIMO) in 1962. Made up of three small exile parties meeting in Dar es Salaam, Tanzania, FRELIMO held its First Congress in September 1962, barely three months after its formation. Its initial platform called for consolidation and promotion of a mass movement to achieve independence rather than an integrated ideology for a planned economy, scientific revolution, or proletarian internationalism. The early aims of the party paid scant attention to post-independence objectives except for improvement of educational and health services for Mozambicans.

Following the First Congress, FRELIMO prepared for guerrilla war with Lisbon, which began in 1964. Revolutionaries in Portugal's two other mainland African colonies of Angola and Guinea-Bissau preceded the Mozambicans in launching their own "wars of national liberation." FRELIMO made poor progress in the northern districts of the country, but its unexpected shift of irregular warfare to the west and central regions contributed to the general deterioration of Portugal's military situation in the three colonial struggles. Partly in reaction to an apparent breakthrough into the "waist" of Mozambique, Portuguese officers overthrew the Marcelo Caetano government in Lisbon in 1974, bringing the wars to an end. After a nine-month transition, an independent People's Republic of Mozambique was proclaimed on 25 June 1975.

Organization and Leadership. During the war, significant developments that ensured the present Marxist orientation of the FRELIMO government took place. Military assistance, guerrilla warfare doctrine, organizational structure, and ideological outlook came from the communist world, with the Soviet Union the principal purveyor. The increasing radicalization of elements of the leadership determined the adoption by the Second Congress in 1968 of standard communist party form, including cell structure, democratic centralism, self-criticism sessions, and a pervasive Marxian phraseology. This revolutionizing process helped to trigger bloody internal fights. The most notable of several assassinations was the bombing death of President Eduardo Mondlane, who some believed held moderate views. When the six-month triumvirate that ruled in Mondlane's place dissolved, Samora Machel, the commander of the guerrilla army, assumed the presidency as well.

The Third Congress in 1977 approved the transformation of FRELIMO into a "Marxist-Leninist vanguard party." As such, the party is the "leading force of society and state" and "must guide, mobilise and organise the broad masses in the task of building a People's Democracy." (Mozambique, Angola and Guinea Information Centre, *Central Committee Report to the Third Congress of FRELIMO,* p. 33.) No exact figures on the size of the party have been released. A campaign to widen the party's base among the population in 1978 stated that it entailed the "admission of tens of thousands of new members to the party" (*People's Power,* no. 12, p. 41).

In the years since independence, FRELIMO has sought to erect the conventional structures of a communist party in power. Because of the sudden collapse of the Portuguese role, FRELIMO first strove to fill the political vacuum with hastily formed "dynamizing groups" at the lowest level of the political apparatus. The original plans called for the universal elevation of these groups to the level of party committees at some future date. But experience showed that the groups, which often functioned without model or direction, were staffed by opportunists, incompetents, or the misinformed. FRELIMO purged the groups and formed party committees only from the most politically committed members of the groups and other organizations.

At the apex of FRELIMO's organizational scheme is the Congress; three have been convened since the formation of FRELIMO. Official figures state that at the Third Party Congress, 40 percent of the delegates were classified as working class, 27 percent as peasants, and 33 percent as belonging to the white-collar sector, the army, and so on. The Third Congress expanded the membership of the Central Committee, which is to implement the policy adopted by the congresses, to 67 members. Central Committee meetings are called to maintain continuity. Between meetings the Central Committee depends on the Permanent Political Committee, a type of political bureau, whose ten-member composition was determined by the last congress. This committee has wide powers because it is the policymaking body of FRELIMO. Most of the committee's members also hold ministerial positions in the government and sit on the Council of Ministers, the cabinet of the government.

The Permanent Political Committee constitutes Mozambique's supreme political authority. Its members are Samora Moises Machel, Marcelino dos Santos, Joaquim Alberto Chissano, Alberto Joaquim Chipande, Armando Emilio Guebuza, Jorge Rebelo, Mariano Matsinha, Sebastião João Marcos Mabote, Jacinto Soares Veloso, and Mário de Graca Machungo. All except Machungo have been members of FRELIMO since its inception.

Mozambique's constitution, which was approved by the Central Committee in 1977, accorded FRELIMO the status of a state institution since the "People's Republic of Mozambique is guided by the political line laid down by FRELIMO" (Constitution, Article 3). It is the case in Mozambique, as in long-established communist states, that the most prominent party members hold important posts in the government. The constitution provides that the president has the power to make many appointments. President Samora Machel, who is also president of FRELIMO, is empowered to appoint provincial governors and members of the Council of Ministers, among others. His power reaches to annulling decisions of the provincial assemblies. The office of vice-president no longer exists; the congress scrapped it. Each of the country's ten provincial governors is held responsible to the party and the Council of Ministers.

When FRELIMO reorganized the guerrilla army in 1980 to create a formal officer corps, it conferred high military rank on leading party officials and ministers. President Machel took the title of field marshal. The three military members of the Permanent Political Committee received the rank of lieutenant general: Defense Minister Alberto Chipande, Vice Minister for Defense Sebastião Mabote, and Political Commissar for the People's Forces for the Liberation of Mozambique Armando Guebuza. Appointments to the rank of major general included Minister of Foreign Affairs Joaquim Chissano, Minister of the Interior Mariano Matsinha, and Ministers of Security Jacinto Veloso, Jorge Rebelo, and Marcelino dos Santos. The year before, dos Santos and Rebelo had been removed from the ministeries of planning and information, respectively. Presently, dos Santos is secretary of economic policy in the party, and Rebelo is in charge of ideological work in the party's Secretariat. The cabinet reshuffles were interpreted as a move away from heavy party control in the economy and as a movement toward greater allowance for the free market in small economic enterprises (*Africa,* no. 105, May 1980, p. 16). Official criticism has been voiced since 1980 about incompetence and disorganization in a number of state organizations. The cabinet changes can also be interpreted as a reflection of these failures (Maputo Domestic Service, 25 September; *FBIS,* 26 September).

The People's National Assembly is regarded by the constitution as the highest legislative organ. FRELIMO organized elections for it in 1977 by presenting lists of candidates to the voters, who could publicly question them, according to official statements. Rather than direct elections of representatives to each central assembly, FRELIMO implemented an indirect election process. Eligible at eighteen years old, Mozambicans voted publicly (so as to overcome illiteracy, official statements explained) for representatives to their local assemblies, which selected delegates from their membership to a district electoral conference. This body in turn elected deputies to the district assembly. The district assemblies then met to choose deputies for the provincial assembly. The ten provincial assemblies met individually to vote on the membership of the National Assembly; the Central Committee proposed a list of candidates. The National Assembly also includes members of the Council of Ministers and the ten provincial governors. FRELIMO instituted this elaborate election process partially as a mobilization technique. As such, it shares this aim with mass organizations.

Mass Organizations. FRELIMO has not yet instituted a full range of professional, cultural, and mass organizations. Despite the impetus given to their formation by the Third Congress, FRELIMO's other goals have absorbed its attention. In the course of the guerrilla struggle with Portugal, FRELIMO made appeals to various groups, one of which was women. As a result, FRELIMO organized the League of Mozambican Women. Later in the war it changed the name to Organization of Mozambican Women (OMM). The OMM held its first conference in Tanzania in 1973 and its second in Mozambique in 1976. In addition to publicizing and implementing the party line, the OMM seeks to liberate women from their traditional views and increase their economic and political opportunities.

Another movement begun early in the war involved youth. FRELIMO originally formed an organization for Mozambican students studying abroad. When many of the students refused to return for military duty or used the organization to launch criticism of FRELIMO leaders, the front suspended the student group in the early 1970s. Not until the Third Congress did FRELIMO establish the Mozambique Youth Organization (OJM); its goals are international education for youth, literacy campaigns, and construction projects. Mozambicans between the ages of 14 and 30 are eligible for membership. As in the case of OMM, membership figures of the OJM are unknown to observers.

In order to raise productivity and mobilize workers, FRELIMO has formed hundreds of workers' production councils for factories, mills, and foundries (*People's Power,* no. 10, p. 21). The party also established a national organization for journalists and has moved to set up organizations for artists and peasants who live in cooperatives. In some localities, the provincial governments have organized people's vigilance groups that will cooperate with the army "to detect and neutralize enemy activity."

The People's Forces for the Liberation of Mozambique (FPLM). The Machel government views the FPLM as both a defense and a mobilizing force. This perception is an outgrowth of the struggle with Portugal when the guerrilla army numbered 10,000–12,000 fighters with about 10,000 men (and a few women) in the militia or undergoing some form of military training. Since independence, Maputo has moved to turn the FPLM into a conventional force with the importation of Soviet tanks, heavy artillery, and jet aircraft. Although the party still cherishes the guerrilla ideals of an army self-sufficient in food and focusing on political training, it has introduced military ranks into the FPLM. This stratification of the FPLM into ranks resulted in part from a mutiny that rocked the capital in December 1975. Army detachments in Maputo demanded ranks and pay as compensation for the privileges gained by FRELIMO personnel who transferred to government positions. Because the party viewed the mutiny seriously, it granted the FPLM's demands. Another sign of FRELIMO's concern surfaced during the following six months as the party purged dissidents from the armed forces. Today the 15,000-man FPLM remains an institutionalized and powerful organization in Mozambique.

International Positions. Independent Mozambique has theoretically adopted a policy of nonalignment. As with many Third World nations, professed nonalignment means a search for diverse international relations so as to attract aid and trade. At the Third Congress, President Machel, however, stated that Mozambique considers "the socialist countries and the Marxist-Leninist Parties" its "natural allies" (*Africa Contemporary Record, 1976–1977*, p. B297). This compatibility with socialist states and Marxist-Leninist parties stems from the political orientation of the ruling FRELIMO party.

During the war FRELIMO relied almost totally on communist countries for military aid. Nonmilitary assistance came from international organizations and some Western countries. Because FRELIMO received sustained aid from both the Soviet Union and the People's Republic of China, it generally kept aloof from the Sino-Soviet controversy. Many observers concluded that FRELIMO stood closer to Beijing than to Moscow since Chinese cadres in southern Tanzania trained Mozambican recruits in Mao Zedong's politics as well as in military tactics.

After independence Mozambique moved closer to the Soviet camp. At least two factors contributed to a realignment of FRELIMO's former evenhanded policy. First, Beijing backed not only the losing side in the Angolan civil war of 1975–1976 but also the side supported by South Africa and opposed by the Soviet Union. China's assistance to the faction supported by Pretoria, whose apartheid policies are anathema in Black Africa, tarnished its image on the continent. Thus, FRELIMO pulled away from Beijing. The other main explanation of FRELIMO's altered policy toward the two communist superpowers lies in the Soviet bloc's ability to supply more industrial and technical aid than Beijing can offer. As a result, Mozambique signed a twenty-year cooperation and friendship treaty with the Soviet Union in 1977—one of four such treaties in Africa.

After the signing of economic and technical accords with Moscow, Maputo dispatched a high-level delegation to China, resulting in the signing of economic and technical accords with Beijing. FRELIMO also permitted Chinese cadres to instruct Robert Mugabe's guerrillas in the war against Rhodesia. Yet Mozambique's relations remain closer to the Soviet bloc than to China. Both during the U.N. votes and afterward, Maputo has endorsed the Soviet-backed Vietnamese invasion of Kampuchea and the Soviet occupation of Afghanistan. The number of delegations to and from the Warsaw Pact countries and Cuba are much more extensive than those to and from the People's Republic of China. In 1981 Mozambique joined the Council for Mutual Economic Assistance. On 27 February, Marcelino dos Santos conveyed "proletarian greetings from the communists and working people of

Mozambique and from our Marxist-Leninist FRELIMO party" to the Twenty-Sixth Congress of the Soviet party (*Izvestiia*, 1 March; *FBIS*, 3 March). In Moscow in May, the first session of the Soviet-Mozambique intergovernmental commission for economic and technical cooperation and trade signed a program of economic trade and cooperation between the USSR and Mozambique for the period 1981–1990. A protocol on Soviet assistance promised aid for developing agriculture and training national cadres for Mozambique (*Pravda*, 21 May; *FBIS*, 29 May). In 1981, Moscow began stationing warships in Mozambican harbors in support of FRELIMO's granting of bases to South African guerrillas and in defense of Mozambique against Pretoria's retaliatory strikes on the bases.

Mozambique's relations with all its neighbors except South Africa are friendly now that white rule in Rhodesia has given way to the black-ruled state of Zimbabwe. In spite of its animosity toward South Africa, Mozambique depends on its southern neighbor for the fees it generates by using Maputo harbor. This reliance does not restrain Mozambique's press from bitterly attacking South Africa. The FRELIMO-controlled press is also critical of the United States and Western institutions.

Domestic Affairs. Economic and political problems have accompanied the independence of Mozambique. The nationalization of foreign-owned enterprises and the flight of Portuguese settlers left the country deficient in capital and skills. The closing of the border with Rhodesia to apply U.N. sanctions and the hot-pursuit raids of Rhodesian forces against Zimbabwean sanctuaries were disastrous for the Mozambican economy. The end of the Rhodesian war saw the cessation of the cross-border raids but not the final conclusion of fighting in Mozambique's western borderlands. Today the Resistência Nacional Moçambicana (RNM), a legacy of the Rhodesian war, operates almost at will against FRELIMO forces. The RNM disrupts development and threatens Zimbabwean trade across the country to the port of Beira.

Concern for internal security was the reason given by the Machel government for expelling four American diplomats (and two of their wives) from the country in March. It stated that the embassy officially engaged in "espionage, conducted subversive activities, interfered in the country's internal affairs" (Maputo Domestic Service, 4 March; *FBIS*, 5 March).

A doctrinaire Marxist-Leninist approach to the economy resulted in tumbling production, bottlenecks, inefficiencies, graft, and maldistribution of goods between the capital and the rest of the country. Early in 1980, Machel announced in a marathon speech: "We declare war on the enemy within." He signaled a new direction by declaring that the state apparatus was not suited to organizing small retail trade. "The state does not sell matches." (*People's Power*, no. 16, p. 31.) To deal with shortages in foodstuffs and consumer goods, the government issued ration cards and proposed to move the capital's surplus population into nearby "green zones." FRELIMO also turned over the "people's shops" to private hands or consumer cooperatives. Government officials began unannounced visits to warehouses, ports, and factories to weed out corruption, incompetence, and inefficiency. In addition, the government looked more kindly on foreign investment as means to development (*Wall Street Journal*, 30 December 1980). This year witnessed a quieter continuation of these efforts and a clarification of their degree. The changes affect only the lowest level of the economy and mark no significant departure from FRELIMO's commitment to application of "scientific socialism" to develop the country and reorder society.

Publications. The government controls all the media. Since independence, FRELIMO has relied on two main publications to carry its messages to the populace: the daily paper *Noticias* and the weekly magazine *O Tempo*. In September the appearance of two more national circulation newspapers emphasized the government's efforts to improve the popular appeal of the media. *Diario de Moçambique* appears in Beira, Mozambique's second city. A new weekly, *Domingo*, is released on Sundays. Both seek to reach the population by carrying material on culture, photos, and interaction with readers. On 25 September, the FPLM published the first issue of its own newspaper, *O Combate,* to celebrate the beginning of the guerrilla war with Portugal seventeen years before. Earlier in 1981, the government created a weekly cinema "newsreel" as part of an effort to reach viewers in a country with a 75 percent illiteracy rate.

Biography. *Samora Moises Machel.* Samora Moises Machel is president of the People's Republic of Mozambique and of FRELIMO and field marshal of the FPLM. Born in 1933 in the southern province of Gaza, Machel obtained some Western education in missionary schools. The blocking of his academic career because of his non-Catholic religious adherence may account in part for his hostility toward the Catholic church once in power. He also feels that the church aligned itself with Portuguese colonialism against the interests of the Mozambican people. As a youth, he worked for a time as a male nurse before joining the opposition to Portugal's rule. His seemingly meager education was not without some distinction in colonial Mozambique, where education was not widespread.

Machel was among the first 250 recruits sent to Algeria in 1963 for training before the guerrilla war began. He rose through the ranks to become secretary of defense and commander in chief of the FPLM in 1966, when the incumbent was killed. From this base of power, Machel assumed the presidency of FRELIMO when Eduardo Mondlane was assassinated in 1969. FRELIMO's Central Commitee officially conferred the presidency on him in 1970. He was invested as president of independent Mozambique in 1975.

His rise to power was marked by a move of FRELIMO to the political left. In retrospect he claimed that FRELIMO was a Marxist-Leninist party by 1973, a year before the war with Portugal ended. During the war, FRELIMO had the reputation of being Maoist in orientation, perhaps because it employed many Chinese guerrilla warfare tactics. Under his leadership, FRELIMO has moved closer to the Soviet Union since independence. He has made several visits to China and to the Soviet Union, where he received the Lenin Centenary Medal in 1971 and the Order of Friendship of Peoples in 1980. Machel often wears military uniforms especially fatigues, even on state visits. Ordinary Mozambicans refer to him by his first name, and he enjoys charismatic appeal in many parts of the country. Machel is considered a clever guerrilla tactician and has been sometimes called the Vo Nguyen Giap of Mozambique.

Hoover Institution   Thomas H. Henriksen

Réunion

The island of Réunion is a French overseas department with a population of approximately 500,000 inhabitants. The Réunion Communist Party (Parti communiste réunionnaise; PCR), a legal political party, was organized in 1959 when the Réunion federation of the French Communist Party became autonomous. Réunion is administered by a Paris-appointed prefect and an elected general council.

The Department of Réunion is represented by three deputies and two senators in the French parliament. Following the election of François Mitterrand as president of France, legislative elections were held in Réunion on 21 June. The PCR claimed electoral fraud after the left suffered a setback in second-round balloting (*Témoignages,* 3 July). Two incumbent deputies of the French Democratic Union–Rally for the Republic were re-elected by a small majority. The third seat was won by Wilfrid Berthile, first secretary of the Socialist Party federation. Paul Vergès, secretary general of the PCR and a member of the European Parliament since 1979, lost his seat in France's parliament to Socialist Jean Fontaine. PCR Central Committee member Bruny Payet lost his parliamentary bid to Michel Debre, one of the island's representatives for many years. An appeal by Vergès to the Constitutional Council in Paris asking for an annulment of the elections was denied.

Vergès is mayor of Le Port; Payet is head of the General Federation of Réunion Workers and a member of the World Peace Council and the General Council of the World Federation of Trade Unions. Other prominent members of the PCR are Elie Hoarau, Jean-Baptiste Ponama, Julien Ramin, Ary Yee Chong Tchi-kan, Gervais Barret, Roger Hoarau, Hippolite Piot, Laurence Vergès, Daniel Lallemand, and Lucet Langenier.

Party Organization and Leadership. The PCR's conventional communist party organizational base of cells is grouped into nineteen sections. The Central Committee has 32 members, the Politburo 12, and the Secretariat 5. The party claimed 10,000 members as of September 1981. Names of party officers were not released under the previous government. An extraordinary party congress is scheduled for 1982, at which time the names of officers and members of the leadership organs will probably be released.

The PCR also coordinates the activities of the allied groups of the communist left on the island: the Réunion Front of Autonomous Youth, the General Confederation of Réunion Workers, the General Confederation of Réunion Farmers and Cattlemen, the Union of Réunion Women, and the Christian Witness Union. The Anticolonialist Front for Réunion Autonomy was created in 1979 to incorporate a united force of these organizations in their struggle for the island's autonomy.

Domestic Policies and Activities. The presidential and legislative elections were the focus of PCR domestic activity this year. The PCR is dedicated to the struggle for democratic and popular autonomy within the framework of the French republic. A proposal to create two departments in Réunion, termed an economic and administrative error by the PCR, continues to fuel political agitation (ibid., 13 August).

Since the major problem for Réunion is economic development, the party continues to strive for a more balanced economy and means of redressing the inequalities between social benefits in France and on the island. A special party congress, with over 1,400 delegates, chaired by Lucet Langenier, was held on 29 March. After presenting what was termed a "negative balance sheet resulting from 35 years of departmentalization," the congress adopted resolutions to promote *Témoignages* (the party organ), to strengthen the party membership campaign, to support the autonomy plan, to develop a new emigration policy, and to protect sugar production (ibid., 30 March).

International Activities. Members of the PCR participate regularly in various international conferences and communist party activities. In October 1980, Paul Vergès addressed the International Scientific Conference in Berlin organized by the Socialist Unity Party of Germany. Réunion was also represented by Marcel Soubou, president of the General Union of Réunionese Workers in France. The secretary general led a PCR delegation to the Cuban party congress in December 1980 and attended the Soviet party congress in March 1981. As a member of a European Parliament delegation to Japan, Vergès visited the Japanese Communist Party headquarters in Tokyo. The PCR delegation to the East German congress in April 1981 was led by Daniel Lallemand.

The PCR supports the liberation struggles of South Africa and Namibia, endorses the Palestine Liberation Organization, and approves the Soviet occupation of Afghanistan. The party favors the creation of a zone of peace in the Indian Ocean and has repeatedly called for the removal of all foreign military forces in the region.

Publications. *Témoignages,* the PCR's daily newspaper, has a circulation of about ten thousand. It was scheduled to expand from 16 to 24 pages in November 1981. The General Confederation of Réunion Workers publishes the semimonthly *Travailleur réunionnais.*

Senegal

The transfer of the Senegalese presidency from Léopold Senghor to Abdou Diouf on 1 January was followed shortly by the lifting of restrictions on the number of parties that could legally exist in Senegal. In the past, legal political activity was restricted to four parties whose orientations were prescribed by statute as conservative, liberal, socialist, and Marxist. But on 24 April, the National Assembly approved a measure abolishing the old restrictions and allowing an unlimited number of parties. By autumn, the number of registered parties had expanded to eleven; of these seven espouse varying degrees of Marxism. This widening of the political system has thus far further fragmented the communist movement in Senegal. In a departure from the efforts of the past several years to unify Marxist-Leninist groups, factions are now breaking off from the traditional movements in the belief that they can successfully compete in future elections. In an attempt to improve their voter appeal, several of the established movements have changed their names by adding the appellation *travail* ("labor") to their title. Some of the parties are also downplaying their Marxist-Leninist orientation in hopes of attracting support from noncommunists.

Majmout Diop's wing of the African Independence Party (Parti africain de l'indépendance; PAI), which had been the only legal communist movement in Senegal, may be the organization most adversely affected by the recent liberalization, as its estimated two thousand members find that they now have other legal Marxist alternatives. The Democratic League (Ligue démocratique), which associated itself with the legal PAI in 1979, has already defected. This group was registered as a legal party on 9 July under the title Democratic League–Labor Party Movement (Ligue démocratique–Mouvement pour le parti du travail). It is expected to draw support from students and the militant Sole and Democratic Trade Union of Senegalese Teachers (Syndicat unique et démocratique d'enseignants sénégalais). This union, whose secretary general, Mamadou Ndoye, is an influential member of the league (*Le Soleil*, 10 July), organized several strikes over the past few years. The pro-Soviet clandestine wing of the PAI, which was the best known of the clandestine communist organizations, reacted to the new party system by renaming itself the Independence and Labor Party (Parti de l'indépendance et du travail; PIT). The strength of this group, estimated earlier at one thousand (*YICA*, 1980, p. 429), has probably been weakened by the defection of its principal spokesman, former Prime Minister Mamadou Dia. Dia, together with several other old-time nationalist figures such as former Interior Minister Valdiodio N'Diaye, has organized the Popular Democratic Movement (Mouvement démocratique populaire; MDP), which espouses a doctrine of self-management socialism.

Three Marxist-influenced movements that did not directly evolve from either the legal or the clandestine branch of the PAI have also been granted legal status. Cheikh Anta Diop's National Democratic Rally (Rassemblement national démocratique; RND), which has unsuccessfully been trying to gain legal status since its formation in 1976, is expected to have the largest following among all the newly legalized parties. Diop has refused to adopt a socialist or a Marxist label, arguing that the RND is to be a rallying point for a broad spectrum of political philosophies ranging from traditional elements to Marxists of various tendencies. According to Diop, the common base of the RND will be a blend of nationalism with pan-Africanism. (*FBIS*, 19 June.) The pro-Chinese Karebi-And-Jëf group formed the party And-Jëf-Revolutionary Movement for the New Democracy (And-Jëf-Mouvement revolutionnaire pour la démocratie nouvelle; And-Jëf-MRDN). ("And-Jëf" is a Wolof expression meaning "to unite for a purpose.") The Proletarian Democratic Organization (Organisation démocratique prolétarienne), headed by former Minister Abdoulaye Ly, rallied to the And-Jëf banner earlier this year, bringing with it almost all its members. And-Jëf hopes this action will induce others who were associated with Abdoulaye Ly in the former African Realignment Party (Parti du regroupement africain) to join their organization (*Jaay Doole Bi*, 15 June). In an attempt probably designed to attract more supporters by softening And-Jëf's Marxist reputation, the party had the influential Senegelese newspaper *Le Soleil* (6 August) print a letter informing its readers that the new party was not communist, although it admitted many of its members were Marxist-Leninists. The last of the newly formed communist parties is the Union for People's Democracy (Union pour la démocratie populaire; UDP) headed by Hamedine Racine Guisse. The pro-Albanian UDP had earlier split from the And-Jëf organization. Guisse's party, whose membership is quite small, claims to be an organization of workers, peasants, and revolutionary intellectuals (*Le Continent*, 31 July).

Party Organization and Internal Affairs. The principal activity of the new parties in 1981 was to document their bid for recognition by the Ministry of Interior and then to transform themselves into organizations that can be competitive in forthcoming elections. In most cases the organizational outlines of, and scope of support for, the transformed parties are still unclear.

And-Jëf-MRDN is led by Secretary General Landing Savanne, a statistician and publisher of the opposition newspaper *Jaay Doole Bi* (The proletarian). Savanne was publications director of the review *Le Communist*, which was banned in 1980. Although the group portrays itself as a party of working peasants and revolutionary intellectuals, the composition of its National Executive Committee shows that its leadership is drawn from a wide range of middle-class occupations. Under party rules promulgated in June, the General Council is the party's highest leadership organ. The council, which meets at least twice annually, selects from among its own members the secretary general, his two deputies (currently Alioune Sene and Mamadou Diop), and the 25-member National Executive Committee. Party congresses are to be convoked every two years by the council to define policies and elect the council. Below the national level, the party's structure ranges from rank-and-file committees (ranging from 5 to 50 members) through sectional, federation, and regional units. (*Jaay Doole Bi*, 30 August.)

The MDP is led by former Prime Minister Mamadou Dia, who holds the party's title of first *mawdo*. Under Dia's leadership in 1960, Senegal adopted its first development plan, which introduced socialization, rural development, and agricultural cooperatives. From 1962 to 1974, Dia was imprisoned for his alleged role in an abortive coup attempt. The MDP and its policy of self-management socialism seem to draw support largely from intellectual circles. The party appears to have gained temporarily at least one seat in the Senegalese National Assembly when Pape Demba Diallo resigned from the opposition Senegalese Democratic Party (Parti démocratique senegalais; PDS) and joined the MDP. (*Le Soleil*, 29 June.)

The RND is headed by Cheikh Anta Diop, a prominent Egyptologist. The party had tried unsuccessfully since its founding in 1976 to win legal recognition. In 1980, the party brought suit in the Supreme Court against the government for its refusal to register the RND, but lost the case on procedural grounds (*FBIS*, 19 June). Subsequently the government on 3 December 1980 had Cheikh Anta Diop brought to trial for heading a "forbidden league." The court's decision, scheduled to be announced on 7 April, was, however, made moot by a government amnesty for all political and publication offenses committed between 31 December 1975 and 31 December 1980.

Domestic Policies and Activities. Cheikh Anta Diop's RND is expected to emerge as the largest of the recently formed parties and may over time replace the noncommunist PDS as the prime opposition to the ruling Socialist Party (Parti socialist). With its long battle for recognition now behind it, the RND appears to be moderating its policies in hopes of building a broad base of support. Diop has broken ranks with other leftist Senegalese parties by supporting the government's proposed merger of Senegal and Gambia. One long-term RND objective is the gradual substitution of Senegal's several national languages for French in government operations. (*Taxaw*, March.)

In contrast, And-Jëf-MRDN still maintains the group's earlier confrontational stance toward political life in Senegal. In a recent statement of party aims, And-Jëf-MRDN declared that it seeks to organize the vast popular masses for a "new democracy." Since the party's foundation rests with the working peasants and revolutionary intellectuals, its greatest immediate challenge is to have the masses assimilate its program, which it describes as a fight against the Senegalese neocolonial bourgeoisie, French imperialism, and their local allies. (*Jaay Doole Bi*, 30 June.)

The PIT is maintaining continuity with its PAI predecessor by opposing France's neocolonial influence in Senegal. At the conclusion of the party's constituent assembly in August, Seydou Cissoko, secretary general of the PIT, called for the removal of all French forces from Senegal and the renegotiation of all Franco-Senegalese agreements. According to Cissoko, the inclusion of communist ministers in the new government of François Mitterrand now makes successful negotiations possible.

Publications. Several times a year, the RND publishes the review *Taxaw*, which is written in

French as well as Wolof. The Wolof section is written in Arabic characters in contrast to the government's policy of transliterating Wolof in the roman alphabet. The And-Jëf-MRDN publishes the newspaper *Jaay Doole Bi* approximately every other week. An interview with Seydou Cissoko, secretary general of the PIT, appeared in the *African Communist* (no. 84).

U.S. Department of State   Dennis Linskey
Washington, D.C.

(Note: Views expressed in this article are the author's own and do not represent those of the State Department.)

South Africa

Celebrating the sixtieth anniversary of its founding, the South African Communist Party continued to operate in exile and clandestinely within the country. Since its inception, the party has been regarded by successive South African governments as a focal point of a Marxist threat to the established racial and political order.

With roots reaching into the militant white workers' movements of the early twentieth century, the Communist Party of South Africa came into existence as an overwhelmingly white party of several hundred members in Cape Town on 30 July 1921. As the continent's first communist party and the country's first nonracial party, it initially led a tenuous existence, periodically subject to government pressure and convulsed by its own internal disputes in the late 1920s and early 1930s. Only in the late 1930s and 1940s did the tiny party strike roots in the emerging black trade union movement and in Indian and African nationalist groups. The party also engaged in electoral politics, unsuccessfully presenting candidates for local council and parliamentary seats chosen by the predominantly white electorate and in the late 1940s successfully getting a white member elected to parliament as a representative of African voters then enfranchised on a separate roll. Faced with proscription under Nationalist government legislation in 1950, the multiracial leadership of the highly visible and hitherto legal party, numbering several thousand members drawn from all racial groups, voted the party's dissolution.

In 1953 leading cadres of the defunct party reversed the 1950 decision and reconstituted themselves into the underground South African Communist Party (SACP). Within the formidable constraints posed by tightening government legislation, SACP members strove to strengthen the clandestine party while simultaneously participating actively in the mainly racially based and then legal political and trade organizations, the African National Congress (ANC), the South African Indian Congress, the Coloured Peoples' Congress, the Congress of Democrats (for whites), and the multiracial South African Congress of Trade Unions (SACTU), which together made up the Congress

Alliance. When the ANC was banned in 1960, the SACP joined with it to form Umkhonto we Sizwe, a separate military body that instigated a campaign of selected sabotage in late 1961, marking a radical departure for the party and the ANC, which had both previously eschewed the use of violence. The response of the South African government was thorough and effective: "A ferocity of reprisal which almost decimated the movement, which smashed the Party headquarters and penetrated deeply into its membership cells; and which finally made the retreat of the Party and the ANC leadership into temporary exile abroad essential if anything was to be saved for rebuilding" (*African Communist,* no. 86, p. 44). With many of its prominent leaders as well as more recently recruited members imprisoned, key remaining longtime party activists took up residence in friendly African countries and in Europe from where both the SACP and the ANC undertook to fashion new structures appropriate to the changed situation and to re-establish an effective presence within South Africa. Despite internal differences and unrelenting government efforts to eliminate all radical opposition, the SACP and its allies have succeeded in reconstituting underground structures within South Africa. From the mid-1970s onward, they have been confronting the government directly with renewed sabotage and attacks on selected police and military installations while extending clandestine efforts at political mobilization in all sectors of South African society.

Under present conditions it is impossible to determine the size or racial composition of the SACP. It appears that the bulk of the membership of the Central Committee lives and works outside the country, and undoubtedly there are concentrations of party members in the dispersed African and European centers of exile activity. "Many of the new generation of Communists which has emerged since the Soweto upsurge in 1976 have joined Umkhonto we Sizwe and some have already died on the field of battle" (ibid., p. 6); other centers of party membership are most likely in allied trade union and political bodies in major South African cities as well as in exile.

Organization and Leadership. The two senior posts in the SACP are occupied by nonwhites. Both have a record of party activity stretching back to the pre-1950 legal period, but have been in exile since the early 1960s. The party chairman, Dr. Yusef Dadoo, a 72-year-old Indian medical practitioner, has headed the SACP since 1972; Moses Mabhida, a 58-year-old African trade unionist who had been engaged full-time in the work of Umkhonto we Sizwe since 1963, was elected general secretary only this year, filling the post left vacant in 1978 by the death of Moses Kotane, who had held the position since 1939. Other members of the Political Bureau and the Central Committee have not been publicly named; most contributors to the party press use a nom de plume.

The SACP continues to consider itself "a vital part of the liberation forces headed by the African National Congress" (ibid., p. 7). From its establishment in 1912 as the first countrywide African nationalist organization, the ANC has encompassed a broad spectrum of African opinion. With the exception of a brief period in the 1930s, its ranks have been open to African Communists, and they have participated at all levels of ANC activity. Common persecution after 1950 strengthened ties between many noncommunist ANC leaders and African and non-African members of the clandestine SACP. With the outlawing of the ANC in 1960 and the shift of its headquarters, the leaderships of the ANC and the SACP were thrown even closer together both underground and in exile. Since the opening of ANC membership in 1969 to all South Africans, regardless of race, prominent non-African SACP members have joined African SACP members and noncommunist ANC leaders in important ANC councils. In the words of Oliver Tambo, president of the ANC, "the relationship between the ANC and the SACP is not an accident of history, nor is it a natural and inevitable development. For, as we can see, similar relationships have not emerged in the course of liberation struggles in other parts of Africa ... our alliance is a living organism that has grown out of struggle. We have built it out of our separate and common experiences ... Our organizations have been able to agree on fundamental strategies and tactical positions while retaining our separate identities ... Within our revolutionary alliance each organization has a distinct and vital role to play. A correct understanding of these roles, and respect for their boundaries, has ensured the survival and consolidation of our cooperation and unity." (*Sechaba,* September, pp. 4–5.) For its part, the SACP sees itself as having "an independent role to play not only as a constituent part of the alliance, but also as the political vanguard of the proletariat whose special historical role as the grave-digger of capitalism and the builder of socialism we have always safeguarded" (*African Communist,* no. 80, p. 37).

Domestic Activities and Attitudes. Party leaders have consistently adhered to the party program adopted in 1962 at an underground meeting inside South Africa, more recently extensively rearticulated at an augmented meeting of the Central Committee held in November 1979 and reaffirmed in a Central Committee statement of September 1980, with a further brief statement from the Central Committee on the sixtieth anniversary of the party in July. In the eyes of the SACP, "all sections and classes amongst the oppressed and other truly democratic forces" must be brought together in alliance "for a revolution to destroy white domination. This revolution, whose main context is the national liberation of the African and other black oppressed groups, must put an end to race discrimination in all its forms, restore the land and wealth of our country to the people and guarantee democracy, freedom and equality of rights and opportunities to all"; yet the "immediate struggle to destroy racist colonialism and to win national freedom is an essential part of the struggle for a future socialist South Africa" in which "the key force has always been, and will continue to be, the black working class in alliance with the masses of the landless rural people. It is this class which finds its most staunch champions in our South African Communist Party." (Ibid., no. 86, pp. 7–8.)

Surveying developments within South Africa, the SACP remains heartened by mounting resistance "on all fronts." Growing worker militancy among blacks is expressing itself through strikes and advances in trade union organization. Black students continue to defy and challenge governmental authorities throughout the country, and women's organizations are showing new initiative. Black churches are more determinedly rejecting the "worst features of racism." In the face of "unending intimidation, harassment and bannings, the people are ever finding new ways of setting up popular legal and semi-legal forms of mass organization" (ibid., p. 8). The increasingly sophisticated armed actions of Umkhonto we Sizwe provide inspiration and demonstration of an improved capacity to challenge authority. Although the question of the nature and role of black consciousness continues to be debated (ibid., no. 83, pp. 86–93, no. 86, pp. 104–9), the Central Committee of the SACP has confidently asserted that "the ANC and its allies stand today as the unchallenged leaders of mass resistance and the struggle for people's power" (ibid., no. 86, p. 8). The characterization of the Central Committee that "amongst all strata of our oppressed people a renewed sense of anticipation and a mood of revolutionary fervour were emerging" seems validated for the SACP; in the estimate of the Political Bureau, "that mood has already begun to express itself on a wide front" (ibid., no. 84, p. 31).

Yet greater militancy and willingness to act signifies not immediate victory, but rather the imperative for further efforts in mass political mobilization and the strengthening of underground political structures. "At the moment the outbursts of resistance are gaining in momentum and present a serious challenge to the enemy. But they still lack the necessary level of coordination and the quality of united offensive of the whole people. It is only our liberation front which has the understanding and the leadership qualities to channel and coordinate the people's militancy and to raise it to even higher levels." "Mass political action combined with escalating *armed blows against the enemy*" is seen as the route to "the destruction of racist rule and the seizure of people's power." (Ibid., pp. 34–35.)

Particular attention must be devoted to achieving "unity in action between all oppressed black communities" with a special focus on the further mobilization and organization of the black working class, as well as renewed efforts among the rural population to galvanize their struggle against Bantustan "independence," a struggle that "continues to occupy one of the most important sectors of the immediate battles we face." In this context, the "continuing positive opposition" of Gatsha Buthelezi of KwaZulu to the idea of Bantustan independence is recognized at the same time that he is explicitly attacked for "his harmful and dangerous role in the present upsurge"—a reference to Buthelezi's opposition to student boycotts and other ANC-supported mass actions. In the assessment of the SACP, a prime concern of the liberation front must be organizational: "We must work more urgently than ever to strengthen our capacity to lead the people on the ground, and to strengthen our underground apparatus to the point where it will be capable of responding to and taking initiatives, not only from day to day, but also from hour to hour. Internal collective underground leadership at all levels—national, regional and local—must be reinforced and strengthened with all possible speed." (Ibid., pp. 35–36.)

From the perspective of the SACP, the task of internal party building is even more daunting: "Once again, as in 1921 at its founding, the Party's task is to build up amongst the working people inside the country a Marxist-Leninist party, based on the very highest standards of discipline and understanding—a party proving itself not by what positions it manages to seize but by how it mobilizes the fighting spirit and unity of the masses." Prospects in the 1980s are extremely promising because "the Party today marches in the midst of a fraternity of our people, in the heart of an alliance with the national movements of all the people, and above all the black majority represented by the ANC," in contrast to the 1920s when the party members had "tenuous roots amongst the native population, black and white, with little experience to guide them." (Ibid., no. 86, pp. 44–45.)

Events elsewhere in southern Africa also remain encouraging. The demise of white minority rule in Zimbabwe and the intensification of the South-West African People's Organization's armed struggle in Namibia are seen as eliminating buffer states around South Africa. "South African Communists, whose party 60 years ago was the first to raise the red flag of Marxism-Leninism on our continent, are especially inspired by the newly born states of Mozambique and Angola led by liberation movements which have transformed themselves into Marxist-Leninist vanguards of their working people and are engaged in the continuing revolution to create conditions for the building of socialism in their countries" (ibid., p. 9).

International Views and Activities. The visible focus of the SACP's international activities have been on relations with the ruling communist parties of the Soviet Union and East European states. Both the party chairman and general secretary enthusiastically attended the Soviet party congress and subsequently traveled to Bulgaria, Czechoslovakia, and the German Democratic Republic to attend congresses of the ruling parties of those countries. In the estimation of the SACP, "the reports of the respective Central Committees delivered by comrades Zhivkov, Husák and Honecker were models of Marxist-Leninist thinking on the most pressing issues facing humanity today . . . the experience of these countries shows clearly that it is not possible to build socialism without the closest fraternal revolutionary alliance with the Soviet Union." The extent of the SACP's identification with the Soviet Union and its closest East European allies was underlined by the SACP's full support for "efforts to defeat the plans of imperialism, local counter-revolutionary and anti-socialist forces to destabilize Poland. Poland was, is and remains an organic part of the socialist community." (Ibid., p. 55.) Not surprisingly, the SACP has also reiterated its condemnation of the "adventurism of the Chinese hegemonists" and has opened the pages of its journal to a Vietnamese attack upon Mao Zedong and Chinese policy (ibid., no. 85, pp. 98–109).

Upon the African continent it is almost certain that the SACP has maintained, if not expanded, links with African radical and socialist bodies in keeping with "A Communist Call to Africa," the document issued by the 1978 conference of "communist and workers' parties of Africa" (ibid., no. 75, pp. 5–33); such contacts have not, however, been reported in the party press.

Publications. The SACP's quarterly journal, *African Communist,* offers not only analysis of the South African situation, but coverage of developments elsewhere on the continent as well as within pro-Moscow parties throughout the world in line with its stated goal of providing "a forum for Marxist-Leninist thought throughout our Continent" and furthering "the interests of African solidarity." Published since 1959, the *African Communist* is printed in the German Democratic Republic but distributed from an office in London, which also sells other public party documents. Within South Africa the SACP circulates the *African Communist* clandestinely along with Marxist-Leninist classics and internally produced party publications. The party's allies, the ANC and SACTU, also publish externally. The ANC's major journal is the monthly *Sechaba*; SACTU distributes *Workers' Unity*. Umkhonto we Sizwe issues the journal *Dawn,* primarily directed at its own cadres.

Within South Africa the ANC and SACTU both produce underground literature; through state-owned radio stations in Angola, Madagascar, Tanzania, and Zambia, "Radio Freedom, Voice of the African National Congress and the People's Army, Umkhonto we Sizwe" is beamed via shortwave at South Africa for several hours daily, both in the morning and in the evening.

Duke University   Sheridan Johns

Sudan

The Sudanese Communist party (al-Hizb al Shuyu'i al-Sudani; SCP) traces its origins to 1946. After being implicated in an attempted coup in 1971, the party was banned. Its most prominent leaders were executed; many more were driven into exile. At present, the party is illegal and operates mainly abroad. (For its leaders and organization, see *YICA*, 1980, p. 434.) The party maintains underground cadres in Sudan, where its influence among intellectuals and railway workers is considerable. Communists are also said to be active among the several hundred thousand refugees in Sudan from Ethiopia; Sudanese and Ethiopian agents have reportedly infiltrated some of the refugee camps, where poor conditions have led to rampant discontent.

Domestic Issues. According to a major policy statement, the SCP believes that Sudan faces economic collapse. Internally, the regime of President Ja'far Numayri depends on an alliance of the army, civil service technocrats, and the new "administrative bourgeoisie"; these three groups together dominate the country. The new ruling group derives mainly from those petit-bourgeois strata who sided with leftist forces during the 1960s and some of whom even belonged to the SCP. The SCP argues that the new administrative bourgeoisie has turned state power both into an instrument of primitive capitalist accumulation and into a means of personal enrichment. The administrative bourgeoisie now prospers at the expense of the "old" bourgeoisie, but the expansion of the state sector ultimately benefits the capitalist class as a whole, as well as foreign investors. The administrative bourgeoisie has succeeded only in worsening the condition of the masses, and Sudan now faces unsolvable contradictions that the regime cannot handle. (*WMR*, June 1980.)

The SCP looks to a "national democratic revolution as a stepping-stone to socialism." The "national democratic revolution" should derive from a union of the working class; the working peasantry; the small and middle bourgeoisie in industry, trade, and handicrafts; and the patriotically minded intelligentsia. (Ibid.) These groups should join a national democratic front dedicated to the overthrow of the present military dictatorship, to land reform, to the democratization of the state apparatus, and to independence from foreign monopoly capital.

This year, the Numayri government was placed under threat of military invasion from Libya or destabilizing pressures from Libyan strongman Col. Moammar Khadafy. Libyan warplanes carried out over 25 strikes on Sudanese territory in retaliation for Sudan's support of guerrilla forces from Chad. Libya's military occupation of Chad caused refugees to flee that country into the Sudan, from where a guerrilla force operated. The Chadian front Frolinat Fundamental opposed the Libyan forces. The SCP's efforts to rally support among Sudanese armed forces not only offered a new field for communist activity but also menaced a country dependent on its military for external and internal security. The party sympathizes with a new movement called the People's Armed Forces for the Salvation of the Homeland. In June, the London office of this organization issued a statement that accused the existing government of having handed over Sudan to an American occupation army, of having wrecked the country's economy, and bartered away its independence. The organization called on intellectuals, soldiers, workers, students, businessmen, and peasants to "reject the tricks of this dubious regime and to prepare . . . for the day of deliverance." (*FBIS*, 19 June.)

International Views. The SCP supports Soviet foreign policy worldwide. According to the SCP, the Soviet invasion of Afghanistan was a justified response to ward off external aggression. The SCP condemns what it regards as the menacing U.S. military buildup in Egypt, Somalia, Kenya, and Oman. The SCP equally decries the intervention of French troops in the Central African Republic and the pro-Zionist and pro-U.S. policies pursued by President Anwar Sadat of Egypt. The SCP has generally sided with the Soviet Union in the Sino-Soviet dispute, but has tended to downplay this issue and concentrate on what it regards as more immediate perils arising from supposed American, Egyptian, and Zionist machinations. The SCP was represented at the Soviet party congress in February and at the East German congress in April.

Publications. The SCP, as an illegal organization, lacks a regular organ in the Sudan, but publishes and distributes leaflets clandestinely.

Hoover Institution   L. H. Gann

Syria

The Syrian Communist Party (al-Hizb al-Shuyu'i al-Suri; SCP) is an offshoot of the Lebanese Communist Party, which was founded in 1924. Cooperation between the SCP and the Syrian government began shortly after the Baath coup d'etat of 8 March 1963. The SCP has held several nonsensitive cabinet posts since 1971. In March 1972 the party gained de facto legality through its participation in the Baathist-led National Progressive Front (NFP), composed of the Baath Party, the SCP, and other nationalist forces. There are at least two dissident SCP factions, one led by Riyad al-Turki, who left the party in 1973, and another created in 1980 by expelled Central Committee member Murad Yusuf. Neither is represented in the cabinet. Membership in the SCP is estimated at less than five thousand, with a possible ten thousand sympathizers.

Leadership and Organization. Khalid Bakhdash, a Syrian Kurd, was re-elected secretary general of the SCP at its Fifth Congress (May 1980). Yusuf Faisal is deputy secretary general. The Politburo consists of Bakhdash, Ibrahim Bakr, Khalid Hammami, Maurice Salibi, Dahir 'Abd al-Samad, Ramu Shaikhu, and 'Umar Sibai, who is minister of state in the Syrian cabinet. Danilel Ni'mah, another member of the Politburo in 1980, is reported to have broken away over his support for Iraq in its war with Iran. Bakhdash is the SCP representative in the NFP. In the general elections of 1977 (Syria's last), six SCP members were elected to the 195-seat Syrian legislature. The November parliamentary elections resulted in the loss of all SCP seats (*NYT,* 12 November).

Domestic Activities. In obedience to Soviet directives, the SCP is a strong advocate of and participant in the NFP, which is dominated by the Baath Party led by President Hafiz al-Asad. In a speech at the Fifth SCP Congress, Bakhdash advocated the strengthening of the state sector of the economy and support of the Baath in its struggle against the reactionary Muslim Brotherhood, as well as the general goals of the Baath Party. He went on to lend SCP support to the regime in its efforts to "ensure a further rise in the economy and living standards of the country's population." The SCP backs the regime's opposition to the Camp David peace settlement between Egypt and Israel, characterizing it as an attempt by the United States to "impose its will on the Arab peoples and to draw them into the orbit of reactionary policy." (*FBIS,* 9 July.) Furthermore, the SCP supports Syrian policy toward Lebanon, which is viewed as advocating national concord founded on Lebanon's independence, the integrity of its territory, and preservation of its unity. The SCP also attacked "bankrupt" Eurocommunism.

International Views. The SCP regards the Egyptian-Israeli treaty as a "capitulationist" peace with an aggressor (Israel) and a betrayal of the true interests of the Egyptian people and the Arabs in general. Egyptian-U.S. cooperation is viewed as a plot to weaken the influence of the Soviet Union in the Arab world. It attacked Egyptian President Anwar Sadat personally, alleging that he had little support among the Egyptian people. The SCP, along with the rest of the Syrian regime, gloated over

Sadat's assassination. The Baathist regime in Iraq is criticized by the SCP for its bloody repression of the Communists and its effort to eliminate Kurdish autonomy. (*IB*, October 1979.)

Bakhdash attended the Soviet party congress in late February. Here he declaimed that actions of "national liberation movements" were not terrorism behind which was the hand of Moscow, but manifestations of the "march of history." Furthermore, he supported Brezhnev's proposals, made on a visit to India, for a "neutral" Persian Gulf area and "guarantees of security" for this area. After the congress, Bakhdash visited and met with the leaders of Bulgaria and Czechoslovakia. During 1980–81, Bakhdash received in Damascus leaders of a number of communist parties, including those of South Yemen, Bulgaria, Romania, and East Germany. The SCP fully backs the Soviet intervention in Afghanistan and the pro-Soviet regimes in Kampuchea, Vietnam, and Laos.

The Syrian Baathist regime closely parallels the SCP in its support of Moscow's goals, especially those in the Middle East. Baathist leaders regularly visit the Eastern bloc countries, and delegations from them are sent to Damascus regularly. Soviet Vice-President Vasili V. Kuznetsov visited Damascus in December 1980. In an unusual step in the fall of 1980, Asad visited Moscow and signed a twenty-year friendship treaty with the Soviet Union, after years of refusing to do so. The Soviet Union is Syria's main arms supplier, and Syria has received some of Moscow's most up-to-date arms; as a consequence there is a feeling of deep gratitude to the Soviet Union among Syrians. There are over 3,500 Soviet and Eastern bloc military advisers in the country, and Moscow has on more than one occasion seriously threatened to intervene militarily in support of Syria against Israel. However, despite Moscow's heavy investment in the country, Syria cannot be considered a Soviet puppet.

The SCP calls for a comprehensive Middle East settlement based on Israel's total withdrawal from the occupied territories and the securing of the legitimate rights of the Palestinians, including an independent national state. As for the European socialist parties, Bakhdash has accused them of a lack of concern for the welfare of the peoples of the developing countries and has stated that the Socialist International is being used by imperialism to deradicalize and "pacify" progressive forces.

Bethesda, Maryland   Gordon Torrey

Tunisia

The Tunisian Communist Party (Parti communiste tunisien; PCT) was founded in 1920 as a branch of the French Communist Party and became independent in 1934. The banning of the PCT in 1963 formalized a single-party state under the direction of the Destourian Socialist Party. On 18 July, the government lifted the ban on the PCT, ending the party's eighteen-year period of clandestine existence. Membership in the PCT is estimated to be about one hundred. The population of Tunisia is around 6.4 million.

Leadership. Muhammad Harmel is the secretary general of the PCT. Leading members of the party include 'Abd al-Hamid ben Mustafa, Tahar 'Ali, and K. Tahar.

Domestic Issues. In April, President Habib Bourguiba announced that he would allow all political factions to campaign for votes. On 18 July, Bourguiba recognized the legality of the PCT and received Harmel, the first meeting between a Tunisian head of state and a PCT leader. Bourguiba also decided to permit the publication of a PCT journal, *al-Tariq al-Jadid.*

In early September, the PCT announced that it planned to participate in Tunisia's 1 November parliamentary elections, its first participation in an election since 1962. In his first press conference since the government decision to legalize the party, Harmel deplored the inability of Tunisia's opposition movements to present united lists of candidates to challenge those of the ruling Destourian Socialist Party. He also called for a progressive overall policy that focused on agricultural reform. (*Le Monde,* 11 September.)

The PCT claimed that it had won as much as 20 percent of the vote in the 1 November elections, in which all 136 seats in parliament were officially taken by a government coalition between the Destourian Socialist Party and the country's largest trade union. In the first multiparty elections in 25 years, the government announced that the PCT polled only 0.78 percent of the vote nationwide. The Communists challenged the official results and charged the government with irregularities at the polling stations. (AFP, 5 November; *FBIS,* 5 November.)

International Views. Harmel attended the Soviet party congress in Moscow, where he gave an interview to Radio Moscow. In his first visit to the USSR in ten years, Harmel supported the Brezhnev proposal of an international conference to deal with the Arab-Israeli issue. He blamed the United States and the Camp David accords for the lack of progress in reaching a comprehensive settlement in the Middle East. In addition, Harmel was highly critical of Chinese foreign policy. (Radio Moscow, in Arabic to North Africa, 6 March; *FBIS,* 9 March.) At his September press conference in Tunis, Harmel deplored the Tunisian government's frequent support of Western positions and called for a genuinely nonaligned Tunisian foreign policy (*Le Monde,* 11 September).

Publications. In July, the PCT received government authorization to publish an official organ, *al-Tariq al-Jadid* (The new path). The party had not issued any publication since its proscription in January 1963.

Portland State University   John Damis

Yemen:
People's Democratic Republic of Yemen

The People's Democratic Republic of Yemen (PDRY) has been governed by a militant, Marxist-oriented regime since June 1969. Although a local communist party, the People's Democratic Union (PDU), has existed for two decades, the party has never been the dominant power in South Yemeni (PDRY) politics. Throughout the 1970s, the PDU's status and role in national affairs have been highly circumscribed by the practical necessity, both legal and political, for it to operate in close association with a substantially larger organization.

In 1981, the PDU enjoyed official status in the prevailing, larger organization, the Yemen Socialist Party (YSP). PDU members held one of five posts in the YSP's Politburo—both the YSP's and the government's highest policymaking body—and several seats on the YSP's 47-member Central Committee. In addition, PDU representatives sat in the nonparty 111-member Supreme People's Council (SPC), which served as a consultative body and debating forum for the government. These positions, in addition to other, less formal ones within the national power structure, have accorded the PDU a degree of influence in PDRY politics far beyond what its limited membership (estimated at less than five hundred) would suggest.

Evolution of the Communist Party. The PDU's headquarters, both before and since national independence in late 1967, has always been in the South Yemen capital of Aden. It has always been led by one of three sons of the Ba Dhib family, which comes from the Hadramawt region in eastern PDRY. The party's rank-and-file membership, moreover, has long come from the poorest and most politically disenfranchised elements of the working class. Yet many of these elements have their roots not so much in Aden or in the tribal-oriented regions of the country's interior as in the villages of the neighboring Yemen Arab Republic (North Yemen). These distinguishing characteristics have from time to time been the cause of difficulties between the PDU and some of the more nationally oriented, indigenous organizations. Similarly, the party's perennially close identification with youth and student groups has been at times a source of strength, certainly in terms of the social importance accorded those two constituencies, just as, at the level of real power, it has often been a source of weakness.

The PDU was officially founded in October 1961 by 'Abdallah bin 'Abd al-Razzaq Ba Dhib—the first Communist in Yemen and eventually the foremost Communist in all Arabia. Regarded from the outset as a communist organization, the PDU supported a variety of groups that sought to cater to the needs of laborers and students. Given the severe restrictions placed on trade union organizations by British colonial authorities a year prior to the PDU's establishment, the party chose to establish a youth group instead: the Shabiba (Youth).

In October 1975, the ruling National Front Party (NF), in a major reform, aligned itself with both the Shabiba and al-Tali'ah (Vanguard), a comparatively small, pro-Syrian, Baathist group. With the NF retaining its position as the predominant group, they formed a new, much larger party, the United

Political Organization of the National Front (UPONF). Shabiba retained, as it had since the constitution of 1971, official status alongside the NF and al-Tali'ah in the SPC. In addition, its members were permitted to retain previously held portfolios—the Ministry of Education, the Ministry of Information, and/or the Ministry of Culture and Tourism—in the government's Council of Ministers. 'Abdallah Ba Dhib held such portfolios at different times in the 1970s, providing the Shabiba a degree of visibility and respectability that was highly valued by party members. As PDU leader and as a journalist, poet, administrator, and teacher, his numerous cultural and educational contributions would leave their mark on other PDRY citizens as well.

After his untimely death on 16 August 1976, the PDU leadership passed, in accordance with a previous agreement, to his younger brother and party cofounder, 'Ali Ba Dhib. Involved in PDU affairs from the beginning and long identified with the Shabiba, 'Ali Ba Dhib brought his own impressive credentials to the post of party leader. He was, in addition, a high-ranking PDRY government official in his own right.

During the next four years, 'Ali Ba Dhib headed the Shabiba during a period of deepening Soviet influence in the country. The period was also one when, largely because of that influence, a temporary rapprochement with Saudi Arabia, which had begun in 1976, lost momentum; when UPONF Secretary General 'Abd al-Fattah Isma'il increased the frequency of contacts between the Communist Party of the Soviet Union and the UPONF; and when a Treaty of Friendship and Cooperation between the USSR and PDRY was signed on 25 October 1979 at the end of an official visit by Isma'il to Moscow.

Of even greater significance, however, were events on the domestic front. In October 1978, for example, Isma'il and his supporters oriented the UPONF more directly along the path of "scientific socialism." At its First Congress, the UPONF changed its name to Yemen Socialist Party and reorganized itself along lines of Soviet-style Marxist-Leninist organizations found elsewhere. Moreover, the YSP constitution adopted at the congress accorded Shabiba members official status in the YSP's Politburo and Central Committee.

A significant Shabiba achievement was the election of its new secretary general, 'Ali Ba Dhib, to the YSP's powerful, eight-man Politburo. In addition, Ba Dhib was appointed to two other important posts: secretary of the Ideology Department of the Secretariat of the YSP's 47-member Central Committee, and deputy prime minister (one of three) in the government's Council of Ministers. These achievements, the high point of official communist influence in PDRY politics, were short-lived, however. Indeed, they lasted only until April 1980, when Isma'il, longtime collaborator with the Shabiba on ideological, cultural, and foreign policy matters, was ousted from his positions as YSP secretary general and head of state and replaced by Prime Minister 'Ali Nasir Muhammad al-Hasani.

The Post-Isma'il Balance of Power. The transition from the Isma'il era to that of 'Ali Nasir has been swift, far reaching, and, as of late 1981, ongoing. The process itself was facilitated by 'Ali Nasir's use of his posts as de facto head of state, prime minister, member and chairman of the YSP's Politburo and Central Committee, and chairman of the SPC's eleven-man Presidium to convene an extraordinary congress of the YSP in October 1980. Elections for a new Presidium confirmed 'Ali Nasir in the YSP positions he had assumed upon the ouster of Isma'il.

One other revelation of the 1980 election was a substantial decline in popularity for Ba Dhib and other Shabiba stalwarts, largely due to their previous close association with Isma'il. 'Ali Ba Dhib has since remained active as a senior government official, YSP member, and lecturer at the PDU-dominated Higher Institute for Scientific Socialism in Aden (also known as the Party School), but in recognition of the electoral results, he was dropped from the YSP Politburo.

Abu Bakr Ba Dhib, 'Ali Ba Dhib's younger brother and an adviser to 'Ali Nasir, was appointed in his place. Some observers viewed this shake-up among the PDRY's political elites as a major setback for the pro-Soviet and pro–North Yemen factions in PDRY politics. Others, however, viewed the departure of the pro-Isma'il faction as having been offset by the appointment to what would henceforth be only a five-man YSP Politburo of two other (non-PDU) Marxists—one as a full member, the other as an alternate. Hence, depending on the issue before the Politburo and on which members were present, it remained theoretically possible that positions originating with the Shabiba representative could become government policy.

Balanced against such a potential combination, however, were other Politburo members who placed less emphasis on ideological or pro-Soviet considerations than on personal, regional, and factional variables. Thus, although the two founding members of the PDU were no longer in the forefront, members of Shabiba, and a number of other prominent leftists previously unassociated with Isma'il, retained an important measure of influence within the state's ruling councils. (See Arnold Hottinger, "Arab Communism at Low Ebb," *Problems of Communism,* July–August.)

The Role of the Communist Party. Besides the several reasons already mentioned, three other attributes explain the party's limited role in the PDRY: the party's less than fully nationalist credentials, owing to its consistently pro-Soviet orientation; its exceptionally small membership; and its geographic base, which, being centered mainly on Aden, compares poorly with the countrywide breadth and depth of the YSP. In 1981, as the PDU marked its twentieth anniversary, these characteristics continued to constrain the PDU in terms of its overall acceptance and effectiveness in PDRY society.

Another factor dates from the pre-independence period. Many YSP members have remarked that it is difficult for them, in policy matters, to accord Shabiba leaders and members the kind of respect that others receive for the roles they played in liberating Aden from colonial rule. Many Shabiba members, to be sure, are too young to have participated in the independence movement. Others, however, are considered to have deliberately avoided the armed struggle that, from 1963 to 1967, was waged against the British and other groups in Aden and against the traditional, tribal-oriented rulers in the interior.

Although local and Arab nationalist leaders urged Yemenis to side with one or another of the several guerrilla groups, the vast majority of Shabiba members remained in urban Aden and refused to join forces, either there or in the more rugged regions of the interior, with anyone. The Shabiba leadership, although never eschewing violence as an appropriate revolutionary tactic, thus produced few practitioners of violence within its own ranks and, in comparison with most other groups, suffered few casualties.

In their defense, Shabiba leaders have explained that the revolutionary situation in the early to mid-1960s was one that called for tactical flexibility and a division of labor. Their strength, they emphasize, has never been in numbers but, rather, in their organizational and journalistic skills, in their role as liaison with kindred organizations abroad, and in their proven ability to provide an ideological orientation for a given objective. It has been primarily these attributes, among others, that have earned the PDU its official status, its relative autonomy, and its influence over policy matters and government activities.

In education and culture, as in national political life, Shabiba has wielded a degree of influence far in excess of its numbers. As an example, PDU lecturers at the Higher Institute for Scientific Socialism in Aden have provided doctrinal and organizational training in accordance with Marxist-Leninist principles for many YSP members. In an effort to limit the role of Soviet bloc instructors at the institute, they have used their connections with other communist parties in the Sudan and Iraq to recruit lecturers who are Arabs.

Not the least of the PDU's roles, however, have been those of obtaining scholarships for South Yemeni students seeking further training abroad and in obtaining medical help from socialist bloc countries for government and other PDRY leaders. The PDU, in short, has played the role of agent and broker—material, ideological, cultural, educational, political—for both the Soviet Union and for an important segment of the South Yemeni people.

Whether the PDU's new leader, Abu Bakr Ba Dhib, can match, let alone surpass, the influence and political longevity of his two older brothers is impossible to predict. It is significant, however, that he, like his predecessors, has become the leading Communist in both the party and the government. Even so, the nature and extent of his role in the period ahead will depend, just as much as his brothers' did, on the personal relationships he and the Shabiba as a group can establish with the far more numerous, and at times quite differently oriented, members of the YSP mainstream.

The Johns Hopkins Foreign   John Duke Anthony
Policy Institute in Washington

THE AMERICAS

Introduction

More than at any time since 1973, when the radical government of Salvador Allende in Chile was cut down by the armed forces, Latin America in 1981 was the scene of ideological warfare. The atmosphere of confrontation grew heated, not only in rhetoric but in violence and threats of possible violent action to contain violence. Tensions rose markedly, and communism or something akin to communism became a bigger issue than it has been for many years.

Stormy weather descended, however, only on the Central American–Caribbean area. There was no hemispheric upsurge of radicalism. In Canada and the United States, the communist, pro-Moscow, Trotskyite, or independent groups were perhaps even more than previously a tiny fringe outside normal politics. In Mexico, the radical left seemed to have an opportunity to become a substantial force as a tolerated critical opposition when half a dozen groups, led by the communist party, agreed in August to unite. This amalgam fell apart in November, however (*NYT*, 8 November, p. 8), and it seemed unlikely that the Communists could raise themselves from the condition of leftist gadfly to become major participants in the national political scene—much less to become serious challengers of the monopoly of office of the venerable Institutional Revolutionary Party.

In no country of South America is a communist party—or any radical party—a serious contender for power, and the ideological temperature is nowhere very feverish. In a number of countries, including Bolivia, Paraguay, Uruguay, and Chile, the communist party is quite effectively repressed and consists mostly of small exile bands. So far as leftist groups can operate, they are plagued by the old divisiveness, split into splinters with varying degrees of dedication to violence. In Argentina, for example, the largest group is the Moscow-aligned party, which enjoys at least the backing of the superpower. It is generally supportive of the military dictatorship because this cooperates economically with the Soviet Union. It has thereby gained a degree of tolerance from the regime and may figure in any future redemocratization of Argentina. To the left of the traditional Communists, there are several more activist, anti-Soviet, and antiregime groups, merging into terrorist or formerly terrorist organizations.

In Brazil, the once sizable and influential Brazilian Communist Party exists on the margin of legality, free to organize and publish but unable to present candidates for office in its own name. In an effort to gain legal status, the party has de-emphasized revolution and sought accommodation with the military-dominated government. It has also sought cooperation with larger recognized parties, although efforts to work with one cause hostility with others. The communist party hopes to participate in the elections scheduled for late 1982, with candidates under labels of admitted parties if not in its own name. This policy has its evil cost, including a dispute between the Central Committee majority and the longtime boss of the party, Luis Carlos Prestes. The latter was followed out of the party by many supporters. The dynamics of revolution, however, seem to fall largely to the formerly pro-Beijing, now pro-Albanian Communist Party of Brazil, which organized well-publicized squatter occupations to make itself spokesman of the poor.

In the countries of Latin South America with elected governments—Peru, Ecuador, Colombia, and Venezuela—communist parties participated under their own banner. Insurrectional forces were able to continue to harass the government of Colombia during 1981, as they had since 1948, but they seemed no nearer to success than for years past, and the constitutional order appeared much more threatened by a rightist military coup than by a leftist assault on the establishment. The Communist Party of Colombia sought to dissociate itself from the guerrilla group, the Revolutionary Armed Forces, generally considered to be its illegal arm. As in other Latin American countries, the old-line pro-Moscow party was subject to the competition of sundry, more activist organizations, including the M-19. This received support from Cuba, a circumstance that led to Colombia's breaking relations with Castro.

In Venezuela, the radical left was split into more than two dozen groups. The left was more impressive electorally than in any other country of Latin America, apparently holding the loyalty of 10–20 percent of the voters as shown by recent elections. There have been various efforts to form coalitions or new unity parties, but they have had little success. Much the most important leftist organization is the Movement Toward Socialism, which has taken a strongly anti-Soviet stance and has been moderately accommodating toward U.S. interests.

Exceptionally, in Guyana the ruling party is strongly leftist and has quite friendly relations with both Cuba and the Soviet Union, while the chief opposition party is fully Marxist-Leninist and Soviet-aligned. But Guyana has very little influence on Latin America. Generally speaking, South America remains as it has been for the most part since 1973, tranquil by the standards of its tumultuous history. The influence of the United States has declined in most places, but governments are generally desirous of friendship with that country, with which there are no serious quarrels. There are no heated controversies over foreign (mostly U.S.) investment, no hostile nationalizations, and no strong party that makes anti-U.S. sentiment its big theme.

The situation is, of course, quite different in the Central American and Caribbean area, which has become in 1981 the focus of major tensions, local and, to some extent, global. Marxist-Leninist or communist forces, with the support of Cuba and indirectly of the Soviet Union, have assaulted the traditional order on a scale quite new to the region and without precedent since the overthrow of the leftist regime of Jacobo Arbenz in Guatemala in 1954. This is not true everywhere, of course. In Panama, the communist party has rather lost ground since the canal treaties were ratified in 1978, although the demise of Omar Torrijos brought uncertainty, as yet undissipated. The Communists remained a minor force in democratic Costa Rica, although grave economic troubles raised questions about the future.

In the Caribbean, the Dominican Republic and Haiti seemed little affected by the regional turbulence. In the former, the left was split into numerous, bitterly contending factions, the total weight of which remained minor. The Haitian dictatorship seemed unthreatened by the repressed communist party. In Jamaica, the two communist parties were insignificant; of much more import was the decisive electoral victory in 1980 of Edward Seaga over the pro-Castro although noncommunist Michael Manley. Seaga undertook in 1981 to turn the Jamaican economy from a socialist to a free enterprise basis; if successful, his effort might be expected to be broadly influential in the region. Many smaller islands continued on the customary path of elected governments and open market economies; Grenada, however, affirmed its ties to the communist world, especially to Cuba. Cuba, enjoying leadership of the nonaligned bloc, emerged as an increasingly important champion of communist or simply anti-U.S. ("anti-imperialist") causes in the Third World. Cuba suffered setbacks, as several hemispheric countries, including Colombia, Costa Rica, Ecuador, Venezuela, and Jamaica, broke or downgraded diplomatic relations; Castro seemed to be sacrificing his long effort to secure respectability in the hemisphere to revolutionary activities. However, Cuban prestige, in the standoff against the United States, recovered somewhat from the low in 1980 at the time of the mass exodus of Cubans by boat to Florida.

Whether because of internal failures or in reaction to the sterner anticommunist policies of the Reagan administration, Cuba underwent ideological tightening, reaffirmed its revolutionary mission, and in effect declared a state of siege. The Soviet Union assisted by furnishing Cuba much larger amounts of armaments than in years past; and in the latter part of the year, Castro mobilized his forces, as though in a fortress awaiting attack (*CSM*, 18 November, p. 1).

The major developments in Marxist-Leninist politics in the hemisphere came, however, on the mainland of Central America north of Costa Rica. Least affected was Honduras, which held apparently free and honest elections in November, in which a mild liberal was elected president and the radical-leftist coalition candidate received an insignificant number of votes. Nonetheless, Honduras was somewhat involved in the civil struggle in El Salvador—many thousand refugees and guerrillas crowded the border—and there were fears that the Salvadoran violence might spread to Honduras.

The prime scene of guerrilla combat or civil war was, as in the previous year, El Salvador. The leftist forces, having somewhat miraculously united with the help of Cuban mediation, made a strong effort, around the turn of the year, to gain control of the country before the Reagan administration could come to the rescue of the government of José Napoléon Duarte. The "final offensive," however, did not receive general popular support, and it failed to capture and hold any important centers. The guerrillas were forced to withdraw to their hideouts in the mountains. They did not give up, however, but rearmed and reorganized; and in subsequent months, they resumed a war of attrition, aimed mostly at destroying the economic capacity of the government. They turned to hit-and-run actions, attacking a town or garrison here and there and then pulling back, blocking highways, blowing up bridges, cutting power transmission lines, and harassing production in many ways. This caused great difficulties, but it seemed unlikely to lead to victory as long as the U.S. government was determined to provide sufficient economic and military aid to shore up the government. On the other hand, the Salvadoran Army, despite many offensive sweeps, seemed incapable of routing the guerrillas, who ranged fairly freely over a large part of the country. At the same time, unofficial murder, attributed mostly to right-wing forces not controlled by the Duarte government, continued at a high level, costing over 10,000 civilian lives in the first ten months of 1981 (*NYT*, 15 November, p. 4E). There was no end in view to the woes of the tortured country.

If guerrillas in El Salvador had to be satisfied with a standoff at best, in Guatemala it appeared that the scattered actions of revolutionary violence familiar for years might be approaching civil war, potentially endangering the basically conservative order that has prevailed, with some changes but no interruption, since the overthrow of Arbenz in 1954. Unlike their fellows in El Salvador, the Guatemalan radicals were still unable to unite. As in El Salvador, no early end to the torment seemed likely, as the military-dominated government was unbending, unofficial terrorism on both sides was unremittent, and elections scheduled for 1982 were unlikely to be more than a charade to anoint another unpopular general as the new president.

In both El Salvador and Guatemala, the strength of the radicals owed much to the moral and material support of the victorious Sandinistas in Nicaragua. The most notable development of 1981 for the communist or radical cause in the hemisphere was the hardening of the Nicaraguan regime in a Marxist-Leninist mold. Probably the chief reason for this was the inherent dynamics of revolutions. The overthrow of Somoza was brought about by a broad coalition, in which business leaders, professionals, the church, labor, and peasants who wanted freedom, especially release from the old Somoza dictatorship, joined forces with the radicals who wanted a socialist transformation of Nicaraguan society under their control. From the moment of victory, the coalition began to be strained, and it largely broke up in 1980, with the most determined and best-organized group, that is, the Sandinistas, emerging on top. The process was virtually completed during 1981, as moderates were practically eliminated from official positions and opposition organizations and expressions of opinion were severely limited. An additional factor for the tightening of the regime was the severe economic depression. In the face of shortages and hardships, the revolutionary leadership was not disposed to admit having made mistakes and to allow more freedom to the private sector. Instead, it blamed capitalists for removing capital from production and (so far as they could) from the country, nationalized many more enterprises, and decreed a state of emergency.

The Nicaraguan revolution was also hardened by confrontation with the Reagan administration, which turned away from the more accommodationist approach of the Carter administration. The Sandinistas blamed their troubles on "imperialism," saw elements of the old regime—or at least opponents of the new—mobilizing across the border in Honduras, and heard hints of possible intervention from U.S. Secretary of State Alexander Haig, especially in the latter part of the year. The dangers they perceived to their revolution were reason or excuse enough to mobilize the Nicaraguan people in a more totalitarian fashion than any other regime in the Americas except that of Castro, and Nicaragua was converted into something of an armed camp. The Army, which had numbered about 7,000 under Somoza, was expanded to several times that number, as many as 50,000 by some estimates (*Newsweek*, 4 December, p. 45), with 30 Soviet tanks and some dozens of MiG fighter planes, pilots for which were training in Bulgaria. This constituted a military buildup quite novel in the politics of Central America. In addition, there was a militia force of perhaps 100,000, and the controls of the party-state were extended by neighborhood Committees for the Defense of Sandinism, maintaining household surveillance like that exercised by the Cuban Committees for the Defense of the Revolution.

The Sandinista leadership used strong revolutionary Marxist-Leninist rhetoric, claiming the right to act on behalf of the people and the proletariat against the bourgeoisie and the imperialists; and it may be assumed that they would have liked to institute a thoroughly Leninist or Castroite-style state. They moved in this direction during 1981, but held back from completion of their revolution. One opposition paper, *La Prensa*, which had carried the banner of the fight against Somoza, was permitted to publish, although it was frequently suspended for short periods. Spokesmen of the democratic movement were occasionally allowed to speak on the government-controlled radio, although some were arrested for criticizing the government. Most important, over half of the economy and perhaps 80 percent of production remained in the private sector (*NYT*, 30 November, p. 3). Sandinista leaders continued to espouse pluralism and to disavow the idea of creating a Cuban-style state. This was realistic. They were not organized to administer the entire economy and badly needed the cooperation of private enterprise—as the Soviet Union itself had needed it in the first years in power. Geography is unfavorable; Nicaragua cannot disregard its neighbors as the island nation of Cuba can. There was also an apparent realization that Nicaragua could not really afford to defy the power of the United States, and there was not much indication that the Soviet Union was willing and able to come to the rescue.

Consequently, Nicaragua suffered a certain ambivalence. It relied heavily on Cuban teachers, military advisers, and even administrators, partly to replace Nicaraguans who had fled the country. The Cubans were supported by a growing crowd of Soviet, East German, Libyan, and miscellaneous nationals doing their part to help the Nicaraguan revolution on its way. The radical revolutionary regime spoke of the total evil of capitalism, imperialism, and the United States and called for a solidarity with the international revolutionary cause, especially the guerrillas of El Salvador. The state promoted a siege mentality as the answer to material hardships. Yet it expressed a desire to mend relations with the United States, promised eventual free elections, and tolerated some freedom of opposition. Extremists of the Nicaraguan Communist Party, who wanted a fully communist social order, were jailed along with the leader of the business community (*FBIS*, 20 and 22 October; *NYT*, 17 November, p. 6). With per capita real income down by at least one-third and a ballooning foreign debt, despite assistance from Mexico, Libya, and the Soviet Union, options were limited.

Much depended on the still uncertain outcome of the Nicaraguan revolution. It was this event more than anything else that charged up the forces of change in a region long suffering from the gross inequality, poverty, and frustrations of much of the Third World, from feudal economic relations and narrow dictatorships hardly tempered by democratic facades. The fall of the Somoza regime was due mostly to its weakness and corruption, but the fact that it fell and was replaced by a socialistic Marxist-Leninist state was evidence enough for the discontented of Central America that persistent violence could bring victory. A crucial catalyst was the fact that Castro was prepared to offer encouragement and a modicum of material support where a few guns might suffice to keep a guerrilla movement alive. But the condition of El Salvador and Guatemala is not the same as that of Nicaragua in the latter times of the Somoza dynasty. In the former countries, the people are not solidly opposed to the regime but indifferent or divided, while elites are more capable and more determined to resist.

Latin America is subject to revolutionary volcanism, but it seemed in 1981 that the volcanos were more likely to smolder than to erupt.

Hoover Institution   Robert Wesson

Argentina

The Communist Party of Argentina (Partido Comunista de Argentina; PCA) originated from the Internationalist Socialist Party, a splinter from the Socialist Party. It was established in 1918 and took its present name in 1920. Presently, the PCA represents the pro-Soviet wing of international communism in Argentina.

Since all parties are illegal in Argentina, PCA membership is unascertainable. In its most recent period of legality (1973–1976), it claimed more than 125,000 members, although noncommunist sources put its membership at a considerably lower figure. One U.S. government source estimated PCA membership in 1978 at 70,000, and there is no indication that it has risen substantially since then. A majority of PCA members are manual workers, although the leaders are principally middle class. In July 1980, PCA Secretary General Athos Fava noted that "a study of the class composition of those who have joined the party in the last few years shows that about 70 percent are wage earners" (*Convicción*, 31 July 1980).

Other communist parties in Argentina include the Revolutionary Communist Party (Partido Comunista Revolucionario), the Communist Vanguard (Vanguardia Comunista), and the Marxist-Leninist Communist Party (Partido Comunista Marxista Leninista de Argentina), all of which are anti-Soviet. Trotskyism is represented by several rival groups, one of which resorted to guerrilla activities in the early 1970s and was largely liquidated by the military regime after 1976. The armed forces have also succeeded in largely exterminating or dispersing the extremist Peronista groups, which had resorted to guerrilla activities in the late 1960s and early 1970s; the most significant of these was the Montoneros.

Leadership and Organization. After the death in June 1980 of PCA Secretary General Gerónimo Arnedo Alvarez, Athos Fava, a member of the party Secretariat, was named to replace him. Unlike his predecessors, Fava is a veteran trade unionist. Other party leaders include Rodolfo Ghioldi, Rubens Iscaro, Pedro Tadioli, Jorge Pereyra, Irene Rodríguez, Fernando Nadra, and Oscar Arévalo. (*IB*, 1980, nos. 19–20.) The PCA is organized pyramidally in cells, neighborhood committees, local committees, provincial committees, the Central Committee, the Executive Committee, and the Secretariat.

All Argentine parties have been officially forbidden to function since the military coup of 1976. However, the PCA was "only suspended by the regime, when parties farther to the left were banned outright" (*NYT*, 26 April). Its headquarters remain open, and its newspaper, *Qué Pasa*, appears regularly and openly (ibid., 12 July). In May, however, Athos Fava claimed that "during the past five years thousands of communists have been imprisoned, 30 have been killed, and 105 have been (and still are) listed missing" (*WMR*, May).

Organization of the PCA youth movement, the Communist Youth Federation (Federación Juvenil Comunista), parallels that of the party. Before illegalization, it claimed some 40,000 members and in 1973 sent 50 of the 510 delegates to the PCA's last legal congress. In December 1980, it was reported that federal police had arrested 49 people during a meeting organized by the Communist Youth Federation in Buenos Aires (*FBIS*, 18 December 1980).

The PCA is still weak in the labor movement despite the presence of party units in many unions. During the year, there was no evidence that communist unionists played any appreciable role in the moves to re-establish the General Confederation of Labor, which had been outlawed by the military government. Leadership of all factions involved in that effort was Peronista, not communist.

Domestic Attitudes and Activities. Relatively friendly relations between the PCA and the military regime apparently continued during the year. "The junta tolerates the party largely because it is handy for maintaining relations with the Soviet Union; Argentine Communists are often the middlemen in trade . . . The Argentine Communist newspaper is generally supportive of leftist guerrillas in El Salvador and Guatemala, but it makes no connection between Central American struggles and possible revolution further south. On domestic issues, the party is critical of the junta but not strident like the Peronists." (*NYT*, 12 July.)

A key element in relations between the PCA and the military government has been the great growth in commercial and economic relations between Argentina and the Soviet Union. In 1980, some 60 percent of Argentine grain sales were to the USSR, and in 1981 sales were destined to rise from 7 million to 12 million tons (*Buenos Aires Herald*, 10 January). The Argentina ambassador to the USSR noted that "Argentina purchases from the USSR machinery, equipment, and transportation equipment" (*FBIS*, 24 December 1980). He might have added that the Argentines had bought atomic materials and were discussing arms purchases.

The clearest official statement of the PCA's position was made by Athos Fava in the May issue of *World Marxist Review*. According to Fava, the military includes "not only Pinochetists, agents of the imperialist monopolies and the finance-landowner oligarchy, but also moderates: representatives of currents that may be characterized as liberal-conservative and popular-nationalist, proponents of military professionalism and the growth of the national industrial potential." Fava argued that "the Pinochetists failed to impose their will on the government, which remains a conglomerate of conflicting groups." He added that "this contradictoriness also affects foreign policy. For example, despite pressure from imperialism and the local reactionaries linked to imperialism ... Argentina continues to promote relations with the USSR and other socialist countries. It has refused to join in the wheat boycott demanded by the USA and has signed a new five-year agreement for the sale of cereals to the Soviet Union. In spite of pressure and blackmail, Argentina remains a member of the non-aligned movement ... Nothing has come of the plans to form an aggressive military bloc in the South Atlantic."

The communist leader's statement argued that "the working class and the entire people of Argentina now face two main obstacles, namely, the absence of democratic rights and the anti-people, anti-national economic policy. Both factors are crucial to the present regime, which has brought about an aggravation of the crisis in the economy, politics, education and all other spheres of society's life." It went on to claim that "the dissatisfaction of the majority of the Argentine people is becoming increasingly evident. They are demanding the lifting of the state of emergency, the release of political prisoners, information about the thousands of missing persons, the normalization of the work of the trade unions on a democratic basis, the lifting of the ban on political parties, a return to constitutional order, and a fundamental change of the economic policy."

Fava argued that "since unity is the logical imperative of the times, the movement for democracy in Argentina is inconceivable without a broad popular front against the oligarchy and imperialism. It is also obviously a part of the class struggle waged by the Argentine proletariat." The secretary general insisted that "the mass democratic movement is influencing the army, which, as in many other Latin American countries, is the force that holds real power and takes part in the solution of socio-economic problems. Our stand is that we reject the concept of a 'neutral' army and differentiate between the various currents among the military. It is extremely important to draw thinking soldiers and officers into the people's struggle for democracy, in defense of national sovereignty ... in and outside the government and the army there are people who recognize that there is an impasse."

The PCA put into practice its advocacy of unity among the opposition parties. In August a coalition of the Justicialista (Peronist), Radicals, Christian Democrats, and Developmentalist and Intransigent parties entered into discussions with other groups, including the PCA. Four PCA leaders met with this so-called Multiparty Group and expressed themselves in "total agreement" with the "general guidelines" of the coalition, which the PCA representatives described as aimed at "attaining broad democratic opening, lifting the state of siege and the political and union ban, and reinstating the full validity of the national constitution and human rights" (*FBIS*, 25 August).

International Views and Contacts. During the year, the PCA remained fervently loyal to the Soviet Union and the Communist Party of the Soviet Union (CPSU). In March, Athos Fava headed the party's delegation to the Twenty-Sixth Congress of the CPSU. In a speech to the meeting, he asserted that "the decisions of your congress will serve as stimulus for all those who are struggling for social progress and durable peace. We, Argentinian communists, waging a difficult struggle for the country's democratic renovation, striving to unite all forces in the name of the true democratic revival of the nation, are inspired by the achievements of the USSR and other socialist countries." (Ibid., 3 March.) Several months later, Fava made another trip to Eastern Europe, where he was received and conferred with, among others, János Kádár, leader of the Hungarian party, and Romanian party chief Nicolae Ceauşescu.

Other Groups. The other far-left groups attracted little public attention during the year. However, in October 1980, arrests were announced in Asunción, Paraguay, of members of the People's Revolutionary Army (Ejército Revolucionario del Pueblo), who were allegedly involved in the assassination of exiled Nicaraguan dictator Anastasio Somoza (*Hoy*, Asunción, 12 October 1980). In December 1980, Jorge Abelardo Ramos of the pro-Peronista Trotskyist group, the Popular Leftist Front (Frente Izquierdista Popular), announced the arrest in Tucumán of regional leaders of his group (*FBIS*, 18 December 1980).

In July, Mario Firmenich, head of the principal Peronista extremist group, the Montoneros, was interviewed in Havana. He analyzed the various elements opposed to the military regime and indicated his organization's desire to encourage all of them. There was no indication during the year that the Montoneros had sufficient strength to influence the political situation.

Rutgers University   Robert J. Alexander

Bolivia

Virtually all of the far-left parties and tendencies in Bolivia originated in one of five original groups: (1) the pro-Stalinist Party of the Revolutionary Left (Partido de Izquierda Revolucionaria), established in 1940, whose heirs include the pro-Moscow Communist Party of Bolivia (Partido Comunista de Bolivia; PCB) and the pro-Beijing Marxist-Leninist Communist Party of Bolivia (Partido Comunista de Bolivia Marxista-Leninista; PCB-ML); (2) the Trotskyist Revolutionary Workers' Party (Partido Obrero Revolucionario; POR), also organized in 1940, the ancestor of many other parties, most still using the name POR: (3) the National Liberation Army (Ejercito de Liberacion Nacional), a guerrilla group organized by Ernesto "Che" Guevara in 1966, which in 1975 established the Revolutionary Party of Bolivian Workers (Partido Revolucionario de los Trabajadores de Bolivia); (4) the middle-of-the-road Christian Democratic Party, which gave birth to the Movement of the Revolutionary Left (Movimiento de Izquierda Revolucionaria; MIR) in 1971; and (5) the center-left Nationalist Revolutionary Movement (Movimiento Nacionalista Revolucionario), which gave rise to a dissident left-wing group that formed the Socialist Party (Partido Socialista de Bolivia) in the early 1970s. The total membership of these factions does not exceed two or three thousand.

The military dictatorship that seized power in July 1980, the most tyrannical regime the country has experienced for many decades, remained in power throughout the year. The ouster of President Luís García Meza in August did not fundamentally change the nature of the regime. The dictatorship drove all political parties and groups underground during the year. As a result, their activities gained little public attention.

Most leaders of the far left were either arrested and deported after the July 1980 coup or succeeded in leaving the country surreptitiously. However, in April, Jorge Kolle Cueto, secretary general of the PCB, tried to return clandestinely, but was captured at the Peruvian frontier. He was subsequently deported to Switzerland (*FBIS*, 4 May). Several months earlier, Peruvian authorities arrested Oscar Zamora, secretary general of the PCB-ML, when he secretly crossed the frontier (ibid., 17 November 1980).

The principal representative in Europe of the PCB was Simón Reyes, a member of the PCB Political Commission and a leader of the Miners' Federation and the Labor Federation. In February he reported to Hermann Axen, a member of the Politburo of the East German Socialist Unity Party, on "the courageous resistance of the Bolivian communists and all democratic and patriotic forces to the antipeople dictatorship of the military junta" (ibid., 19 February).

Among the leftist parties, the most grievously hurt by the military dictatorship was the MIR. In mid-January a police raid on a house in La Paz where the underground leadership of the MIR was meeting left nine party members dead, including Artemio Carmargo, head of the miners' union at the Siglo XX mine. At about the same time, several Trotskyist leaders of the POR-Combate and POR-Masas groups were reportedly arrested. (*Intercontinental Press*, 16 February).

In spite of the decimation of its underground leadership, the MIR continued to be active both inside the country and in exile. In May, its exile leadership proposed a "national convergence" accord of all groups opposed to the dictatorship (*FBIS*, 3 June). On 8 September, it published a paid advertisement, signed by Oscar Eid Franco, Alfonso Camacho Pena, and Gaston Encinas Valverde, in the La Paz daily *Hoy* in commemoration of the tenth anniversary of its founding. "All MIR members and the current members of the board," it said, "renew their commitment to the struggle and confirm their loyalty to the principles which have been and are the bases of the party: collective leadership, constant MIR presence in the territory of the nation, its unquestionable and definitive unity" (ibid., 9 September).

Rutgers University   Robert J. Alexander

Brazil

The original Communist Party of Brazil (Partido Comunista do Brasil; (PDdoB), founded in March 1922, remains the most important Marxist-Leninist organization in the nation. Several small groups that broke away or were expelled from the party in its first decade formed a Trotskyist movement that subsequently split into several factions. At least two of these still remain. In 1960, the original pro-Soviet party changed its name to Brazilian Communist Party (Partido Comunista Brasileiro; PCB). A pro-Chinese element broke away the following year and in February 1962 adopted the original party name, PCdoB. This group has since abandoned allegiance to China and become pro-Albanian. After the establishment of the military dictatorship in 1964, several far-left groups were formed, most of them by PCB dissidents, which advocated and practiced various kinds of guerrilla warfare.

All Marxist-Leninist parties and groups functioned more or less freely during 1981. However, none obtained legal recognition under the new political parties law enacted by the government of President João Baptista Figueiredo.

Organization and Leadership. For the first time since the military coup of 1964, the PCB was able in 1980 and 1981 to establish an organizational structure at virtually all levels. At the national level, the party has a Central Committee and an Executive Board, led by Secretary General Giocondo Gervasi Dias, with Salomão Malina, Teodoro Mello, Luiz Tenório de Lima, and Givaldo Siqueira as its other members (*Jornal do Brasil*, 24 July 1980). In most states the party was able to reorganize state committees, as well as municipal committees in many cities and towns. It publishes a national weekly, *Voz da Unidade*.

Domestic Activities. Much of the PCB leaders' time and propaganda was spent on attempts to obtain legal recognition. In December 1980, President Figueiredo's press secretary announced that "if it were up to President Figueiredo," he would legalize the PCB (*FBIS*, 16 December 1980). However, the party did not gain legal status. When, in May, party leaders announced the date of the forthcoming party congress, they stressed that that event would be a major contribution to gaining legalization.

Preparations for the party's Seventh Congress constituted another major activity of the PCB leaders. Although originally planned for sometime in early 1981, this date proved impossible. It was finally announced in May that the meeting would take place on the sixtieth anniversary of the party, 25 March 1982. An extensive draft document presenting the PCB position on party, national, and international issues to be considered by the congress was published. Secretary General Dias announced that for four months all party members were free to send in criticisms of the program, after which there would be discussions for five months by district, municipal, and state committees of the party. During this second period, delegates to the congress would be chosen. (*Jornal do Brasil*, 7 May.)

Although not yet legal, the PCB actively planned to participate in the promised 1982 elections. It advocated unity of all opposition parties and planned to support several gubernatorial candidates, particularly members of the major opposition group, the Brazilian Democratic Movement Party (PMDB). In July it announced its favorites for the races in São Paulo, Pernambuco, Amazonas, and Goiás (*O Estado de São Paulo*, 2 July).

PCB militants returned to extensive activity in the organized labor movement. Attention of communist unionists particularly centered on the first National Conference of the Working Class, which was held in August. Attended by 5,247 delegates from some 1,800 local unions, this meeting was reportedly organized by PCB unionists and those under the influence of the Ministry of Labor. The principal opposition in the session came from unionists associated with the Workers' Party (PT) of São Paulo metalworkers' leader, Luis Inácio da Silva ("Lula"). When a national committee was elected, the PCB and their allies had a minority of its members. (*Intercontinental Press*, 28 September.)

Relations between the PCB and Lula varied during the year. In April he met with Dias to discuss unemployment problems; the two men reportedly spoke "very little" about politics (*Jornal do Brasil*, 1 May). The following month, however, Lula attacked the PCB for trying to undermine his efforts to build up the trade union–based PT, a charge the Communists denied (*FBIS*, 30 June), although the PCB's announced desire to work with the PMDB lends credence to the accusation.

On several occasions during the year, the PCB declared that the labor movement should not be "politicized." In the discussion document for the forthcoming Seventh Congress, the PCB argued that "politicization has worsened divisions within the union sector. Most of the forces that seek to politicize the union sector insist on taking control of the unions and on using them to the benefit of their political-party interests." (*Jornal do Brasil*, 7 May.)

Factional Struggle with Luis Carlos Prestes. One of the most persistent themes in the PCB during the year was the factional dispute with Luis Carlos Prestes, who was deposed as secretary general in May 1980. Prestes criticized the party's acceptance of President Figueiredo's efforts to democratize the political system, as well as its support for a proposed constituent assembly. He continued to attack his successors publicly, accusing them late in December 1980 of "a betrayal of the working class" and of making statements that were "dangerously close to those of the party of the dictatorship" (ibid., 27 December 1980). In February 1981, he summed up his differences with party leaders by saying that "he [had] fought for a revolutionary, reformist, Marxist-Leninist, internationalist party, against monopolies and large landholdings . . . while the present Central Committee is thinking about the implantation of a national and democratic government because it believes there can be a capitalism that is not savage. In his opinion this is utopian because capitalism is always savage." (*Correio Braziliense*, 15 February.) Prestes launched the newspaper *Voz Operária* to disseminate his views.

In a document submitted by the Central Committee in preparation for the 1982 party congress, current PCB leaders claimed that "Comrade Prestes scored the use of self-criticism, and in a letter to Communists, which has been answered by the collective leadership . . . he denied the PCB's revolutionary nature and its political outlines, and he scored the collective leadership and the party, promoting factionalism and liquidation. He continued to disseminate his personal guidelines . . . and stimulating the creation of another organization while trying to obtain the political support of the communist parties of other countries." The Central Committee added that "his activities are being rejected by the Communists . . . the collective leadership continues to invite him to debate his disagreements, in accordance with communist principles, but all it encounters are refusals with the excuse that he is a minority." (*Jornal do Brasil*, 7 May.)

Early in January Prestes was honored by his followers with a large party celebrating his eighty-third birthday. Organized by Oscar Niemeyer, the architect, it was attended by friends, labor leaders from several states, and politicians, but not by members of the PCB Central Committee. At this party, Prestes's daughter, Anita Leocadia, claimed that "the vast majority of communist militants still consider Prestes the secretary general of the party." (Ibid., 4 January.) In November, however, Prestes reportedly joined the PT.

Principles and Program of the PCB. The most complete statement of the current position of the PCB was the document submitted for discussion at the forthcoming Seventh Congress. It started by proclaiming that "considering the current situation in Brazil and in the world, the revolution has real possibilities of reaching its objectives through means that may exclude armed struggle, insurrection, and civil war . . . The working classes are struggling for their deepest interests, namely the conquest of political democracy . . . as a condition that will favor, among other essential aspects of their struggle, revolutionary changes through nonviolent means." The party also claimed that "within the framework of a democratic society, military participation in the political life of a country is a positive fact."

The party statement stressed the importance of promised elections in late 1982 for state governments and the national congress. It argued that "the two conditions that the opposition should meet to achieve victory are (1) the maneuvers concocted by the dictatorship to influence electoral results must be overcome, and (2) opposition parties should unite in major elections."

As for the future of the PCB itself, the document foresaw it becoming "a democratic party of the masses that will be capable of absorbing every type of class and social level struggling for democratic freedom . . . as a path toward achieving socialism in Brazil." It will be "profoundly nationalist, democratic, and internationalist . . . a party that, in view of the type of its relations with other political organizations within and without our national borders, is autonomous and independent. In sum, a party that adopts Marxism-Leninism as an instrument for the analysis of reality."

The statement indirectly attacked Prestes, saying that "the PCB that we need must be built upon a system of organizations, but not around people or those who support the 'personality cult' of the tradition of the *caudillo* that exists in the country . . . It must be managed on the basis of a collective directorate." Furthermore, it will be "a party that will give priority to the creation of worker cadres in order to reverse the historical predominance within the Central Committee and the intermediate leadership that comes from the middle class ... and one that is capable of stopping *caudillos* and the personalism of the petite bourgeoisie to flourish within its ranks." (Ibid., 7 May.)

International Views and Contacts. Both the new Central Committee and Prestes and his faction agreed on the PCB's alignment with the Soviet Union. At the January party in his honor, Prestes said that "the first duty of every citizen is to work for peace in the world and to understand the historical role of the great Soviet Union (ibid., 4 January). Dias, who headed the PCB delegation to the Twenty-Sixth Congress of the Soviet party (CPSU) in March, said in an interview in Moscow that "the experience of the Soviet people and the CPSU is a lodestar for all progressive mankind" (*FBIS*, 19 March).

However, in June, when rumors of a possible Soviet invasion of Poland were widespread, the Central Committee of the PCB was reported ready to "repudiate a possible Soviet intervention in Poland." The committee supported the position of Polish party leader Stanislaw Kania, which was then being attacked in Moscow, saying that "to overcome the crisis the only sensible alternative is the policy of renovation" (*Jornal do Brasil*, 14 June).

Communist Party of Brazil. Like the PCB, the PCdoB continued the task of restructuring on a more or less open base. Although not repudiating its former guerrilla tactics and speculating on the possibility of resuming them at some time in the future, its "main watchword" was "a single and broad opposition front" (*O Estado de São Paulo*, 20 November 1980). However, the PCdoB strongly rejected any rapprochement with the government of President Figueiredo. Its leaders ridiculed the PCB's acceptance of the president's offer of "outstretched hands" to all Brazilian political elements (ibid., 4 September). The PCdoB was apparently the strongest of the groups to the left of the PCB. *O Estado de São Paulo* reported on 20 November 1980 that military observers thought that the PCdoB had a "truly strong structure, even well established among students, the press, and the clergy, which translates into a substantial increase of its mobilization capability and the expansion of its sphere of influence." The PCdoB continued throughout the year to be aligned internationally with the Albanian Communists. It publishes the periodical *Tribuna da Luta Operaria*.

Other Organizations. Other far-left groups that had returned to open activity in 1980 did not gain much public attention in 1981. These include the Revolutionary Communist Party and the MR-8 Revolutionary Movement, which broke from the PCB during the late 1960s, and at least two Trotskyist groups, Socialist Convergence (associated with the United Secretariat of the Fourth International) and the International Socialist Organization. The MR-8 publishes the periodical *Hora do Povo*, and Socialist Convergence *Convergencia Socialista*. Apparently Socialist Convergence carried out most of its organizational and political work within the PT of Luis Inacio da Silva.

Rutgers University

Robert J. Alexander

Canada

Several Marxist-Leninist parties and groups operate legally in Canada. The oldest and largest is the Communist Party of Canada (CPC). Since its founding in 1921, the CPC has been consistently pro-Moscow in alignment. The Workers Communist Party (Marxist-Leninist) (WCP) is pro-Beijing. The Communist Party of Canada (Marxist-Leninist) (CPC-ML), founded in 1970, is pro-Albanian. The Marxist-Leninist Organization of Canada–In Struggle (MLOC), founded in 1972, has no formal international affiliation. Several Trotskyist groups exist, including the Revolutionary Workers League (RWL), Group socialiste des travailleurs (GST), Trotskyist League (TL), and Forward Readers Group (FRG).

In the last federal election (1980), the combined vote for all communist parties was less than 0.2 percent of the vote (*YICA*, 1981, pp. 42–46). Communist candidates ran in the 1981 provincial elections in Quebec, Ontario, and Manitoba. No candidates were elected. The parties have been active in several cities, notably Vancouver, Winnipeg, and Toronto.

The 20 May Quebec referendum on sovereignty-association and the re-election of the Parti Quebecois (PQ) in the 13 April Quebec provincial elections continued to dominate political events. Prime Minister Pierre Trudeau's attempt to bypass the stalled federal-provincial first ministers' conference to "patriate" and rewrite the Canadian constitution led to significant opposition by eight of the ten provincial governments. The Supreme Court ruling that constitutional change without substantial provincial consent was unconstitutional was a catalyst for the historic first ministers' conference of 2–5 November that drafted a new Canadian constitution. All but Quebec agreed.

For much of the year, energy policy disagreements exacerbated federal-provincial relations. The Canadian economy continued to deteriorate. High interest rates, inflation, unemployment, the decline of the Canadian dollar, and cutbacks in government social services led to a renewed high level of strike activity, culminating in the 100,000-person Canadian Labour Congress demonstration in Ottawa on 21 November.

Communist Party of Canada. Headquartered in Toronto, with an estimated 2,500 members, the CPC ran 18 candidates in the Ontario provincial elections (a decline from 33 in 1977), 10 in Quebec, and 2 in Manitoba (*Forge*, 13 March). None were elected. Among the leadership changes, Gordon Massie was elected party leader in Saskatchewan and Paula Fletcher was chosen in Manitoba to replace the ailing William Ross, who had served more than thirty years in the post (*Canadian Tribune*, 13 and 27 April). After a successful half-million dollar fund drive, the rebuilt Tim Buck–Norman Bethune Educational Centre opened on 14 October. The year 1982 promises to be eventful: the CPC will celebrate its sixtieth anniversary during its Twenty-Fifth Convention on 13–15 February in Toronto. The long-awaited *History of the Communist Party of Canada, 1921–1976* will be published, and changes are also anticipated in the party's program, *The Road to Socialism in Canada*. Municipal politics is now seen as fertile ground for communist activity (*Communist Viewpoint*, May). On women's affairs, the CPC concedes that it has not "sufficiently measured up" and calls for the creation of women's commissions and the recruitment of more women into the party (ibid., March). Most important, party leader William Kashtan observed that at a recent Central Committee meeting, "questions were sometimes argued sharply." He warned that "sectarian aloofness" and underestimation of the "potential to unite all varied anti-monopoly movements . . . would be nothing short of criminal" (*Canadian Tribune*, 26 October). It seems that some in the CPC continue to question the proposed strategies of an elected "anti-monopoly bloc" with the New Democratic Party (NDP) and "unity with individual left NDPers around specific issues" (ibid., 2 and 16 March).

Summing up the current domestic situation, the CPC declares that "Canada faces a critical period; its very survival is at stake" (*Communist Viewpoint*, March). Opposed to the fragmentation of Canada, the CPC accuses the eight dissident provincial premiers of attempting to break Canada into principalities (*Canadian Tribune*, 27 April). While opposing separation, the CPC preferred the re-election of the PQ to the election of the Quebec Liberals (ibid., 23 March). Seeking to scrap the Binational Act, the CPC proposes a new republican constitution that would recognize the binational makeup of Canada (ibid., 9 February, 2 March). Western Canadian separatism is believed to be fostered by U.S. oil monopolies wishing to gain greater control over resource-rich territories (ibid., 2 February). At a 1 February meeting of Western Canadian CPC leaders, the CPC demanded a new deal for the west to mollify legitimate Western grievances (ibid., 16 February; *Communist Viewpoint*, March). Joint federal-provincial crown corporations are deemed the most appropriate forms for an equitable distribution of oil revenues (*Canadian Tribune*, 2 February). An all-Canadian gas and oil pipeline is also advocated (ibid., 9 March). Suggesting that the closings of U.S. branch-plants are "de-industrializing" Canada, the CPC calls for a government takeover of Chrysler and the establishment of a Canadian auto industry (ibid., 16 February, 2 March, 4 May). Canada's economic woes are said to be largely caused by its inordinate expenditures on defense (ibid., 11 May).

An 18 June joint statement of the CPC, the Communist Party, U.S.A., and the Mexican Communist Party suggested that U.S. imperialism was on the offensive (*Combat*, August; *Canadian Tribune*, 22 June). Greatly concerned by Reagan's efforts to return to the confrontational tactics of the cold war, to accelerate the arms race with ghastly new weapons such as the neutron bomb, to seek nuclear superiority, and to shift to a nuclear first-strike strategy, the CPC warns that peace is not inevitable and suggests that the most urgent task is to mobilize people against nuclear catastrophe and into support for détente and disarmament (*Canadian Tribune*, 27 April, 15 June, 17 August, 26 October; *IB*, March). The Canadian Peace Congress, a CPC-front organization established in 1948, has sought one million signatures on a peace petition calling for the U.S. to sign the Strategic Arms Limitation Treaty, a dissolution of all military alliances, and the convening of a European conference on détente and disarmament (*Canadian Tribune*, 9 February, 20 April). The NDP is seen as one of the key forces in a people's peace coalition (ibid., 20 July). The CPC advises that Canada's military budget should be cut in half (ibid., 2 March). The CPC continues to echo Soviet positions in foreign affairs. Accordingly, Kashtan and provincial leaders William Stewart (Ontario) and Sam Walsh (Quebec) attended the Soviet party congress in February and March (ibid., 16 March).

Workers Communist Party. Headquartered in Montreal, with an estimated membership of 1,500, the WCP ran 33 candidates and received 5,005 votes in the party's first entry into Quebec provincial elections (*Forge*, 17 April). It also ran one candidate, Judy Darcy, in the Ontario provincial elections. The party has grown in strength in the last few years and placed ahead of most other Marxist parties in the Quebec elections (ibid., 6 February, 3 and 17 April). In 1981, it opened up a new office in Quebec City, bought radio advertising time, and successfully raised $176,700 in funds (ibid., 13 and 20 February, 17 April). Strongest in Quebec, as evidenced by a Montreal election rally of six hundred, the party claims that half of its membership is proletarian and that it is successfully recruiting immigrants (ibid., 20 March, 16 April, 12 June). However, the party acknowledges that chauvinism exists within party ranks and has adopted special measures to promote women to leadership roles (ibid., 20 February). Believing that socialism ultimately will triumph only through "armed revolution," the party resists efforts to downplay Leninist organizational principles and notes how easily the left was vulnerable to the repressive War Measures Act during the October 1970 Quebec crisis (ibid., 30 January, 6 February; *October*, Summer). The WCP states that it is engaged in clandestine work (*Forge*, 30 January).

Portraying Canada as a "prison of nationalities," the WCP favors regional autonomy for the Acadians, Quebec's equality with English Canada, Quebec's right of self-determination as a nation, and extension of French-language rights across Canada (ibid., 23 January, 13 and 20 March, 29 May). Skeptical that Quebec workers alone could make socialist gains, the WCP calls for multinational unity in the struggle for socialism in Canada (ibid., 12 June). The party criticized the content and procedure of Trudeau's constitutional reforms (ibid., 6 February).

While not seeing a swing to the new right among workers in Canada, the WCP does perceive a tough new offensive against workers by means of government cutbacks in social services, tax increases, layoffs, and falling wages (ibid., 13 February, 1 and 29 May). The WCP took a high profile in defending the right of government workers to strike (ibid., 13 February). In this regard, it is highly critical of the PQ as being yet another bourgeois party (ibid., 5 June). To combat unemployment, the WCP called for public works projects, six months notice of and compensation for layoffs, and a guaranteed income (ibid., 23 January, 13 February). Arguing that U.S. multinational corporations "have been robbing Canada blind for decades," the WCP demands nationalization of all foreign oil monopolies and Chrysler—"without any compensation" (ibid., 13 February, 20 March, 19 June). It does, however, warn that nationalization is not a panacea. The WCP favors scrapping the U.S.-Canada Auto Pact and establishing an independent Canadian auto industry (ibid., 22 May). The party also stresses the struggle for independent Canadian unions and encourages the unity of Canadian labor federations (ibid., 30 January, 5 June). The anti-U.S. theme is mitigated somewhat by the WCP postulate that U.S. control over the Canadian economy is weakening and that Canada's bourgeoisie increasingly controls the Canadian state (ibid., 14 August; *October*, Autumn 1980). Canada, therefore, should be classified as a "secondary imperialist power" (*October*, Autumn 1980).

To end the growing danger of war, the WCP calls for the total destruction of nuclear weapons and the dismantling of all foreign bases. Canada should leave NATO and the North American defense system (ibid., 19 June). The USSR, now a degenerate "social fascist" state (*Forge–Tribune Debate*, 1981), has created "the biggest war machine ever seen" and is on the "military, political and ideological offensive" (*Forge*, 13 February; *October*, Spring). The WPC condemned the invasion of Afghanistan (*Forge*, 23 January). While Vietnam is criticized for its expansionism and Albania for its anti-Maoism, even China is criticized for its current "confusion, uncertainty," and "erroneous" policies (ibid., 13 February, 5 June; *October*, Spring). The WCP opposes Chinese efforts at negating the Cultural Revolution and deplores China's moves toward decentralization, use of profit incentives, and reduced emphasis on planning (*Forge*, 9 and 23 January). The WCP has concluded that very serious problems, particularly right opportunism, exist in the world Marxist-Leninist movement (ibid., 5 June; *October*, Spring). The strongest Marxist-Leninist parties are now perceived to be in the Third World, particularly in Southeast Asia. In January, party leader Roger Rashi attended the founding of the Dominican Workers' Party (*October*, Spring).

Communist Party of Canada (Marxist-Leninist). Headquartered in Montreal, with an estimated membership of five hundred to a thousand, the CPC-ML ran 40 candidates and received 3,481 votes in the 1981 Quebec provincial elections. Believing that the "capitalist-revisionist world" is deep in crisis and that the Canadian economy is in the worst condition in forty years, the CPC-ML warns that members must "resist the shifting of the burden of the economic crisis onto the backs of the working class" (*People's Canada Daily News*, 21 and 23 July, 4 August). Observing a growing tendency toward fascism in Canada, the CPC-ML believes that racism is encouraged by government officials and the police (ibid., 21 August, 25 June). One example is the government's new restrictions on immigration (ibid., 25 July). The CPC-ML resolutely calls for a banning of the Ku Klux Klan and militant self-defense against racist assaults (ibid., 18 and 22 July). Not surprisingly, the CPC-ML has been associated with acts of violence either instigated by the party (*Toronto Globe and Mail*, 15 January, 28 October), or by attacks against it (*People's Canada Daily News*, 22 July). The WCP has even suggested that the CPC-ML is composed of "thugs" and "agents provocateurs" (*Forge*, 9 October).

In its analysis of international affairs, the CPC-ML warns that the danger of war is increasing (*People's Canada Daily News*, 27 July). While suggesting that the United States and the USSR are "equally aggressive and dangerous," the party sees the USSR as the "most dangerous superpower" (ibid., 6 July, 3 August). Nevertheless, President Reagan is criticized for escalating the arms race and the propaganda war (ibid., 22 August). The CPC-ML calls for an end to war preparations and a withdrawal from NATO and the North American defense system (ibid., 28 July, 27 August). The Strategic Arms Limitation Talks are dismissed as deceptions (ibid., 29 August). Emphasis is placed on defending the purity of Marxist-Leninism against revisionism (ibid., 4 April, 27 August). Critical of China, the party sees Albania as the only state pursuing a proper course of action. Events in Poland are criticized as moving in a revisionist path a la Yugoslavia.

The party has established numerous front organizations, the most significant being the People's Front Against Racist and Fascist Violence (founded 27 November 1980), the Central Council of the Revolutionary Trade Union Opposition (founded 27 December 1980), the Democratic Women's Union of Canada (founded 8 March), and the East Indian Defence Committee, an organization in existence for several years. The most ambitious activity of the party was its eleven-city All-Canada March (19 July–3 August) protesting imperialism, social imperialism, racism, fascism, and war.

Marxist-Leninist Organization of Canada–In Struggle. The MLOC, with an estimated core membership of four hundred, eschews electoral politics and advises its members to spoil their ballots. While rejecting dogmatism (*Proletarian Unity*, January 1980 [1981]; *In Struggle*, 14 April), the MLOC concedes that it is "beset with serious problems" (*In Struggle*, 13 October). Democratic centralism has been applied too rigidly (ibid., 19 May). Insufficient attention has been given to legitimate women's questions and women are underrepresented in leadership positions. The result is "oppression" within the MLOC itself (ibid., 19 May). Newspaper circulation has dropped, some members are "burned out," and women are resigning (ibid., 19 May, 13 October). In short, the MLOC is "not a viable alternative," and radical changes must be made at next year's Fourth Congress (ibid., 13 October). The proposals include suspending the current constitution, shifting power from leadership ranks to base units, reducing full-time staff, easier membership criteria, representative bodies for women, greater opportunities for discussion, and a mandate to unite with other leftists on a minimal political platform of anti-imperialism and self-determination for Quebec and other oppressed nationalities (ibid., 13 October). Despite these problems, the MLOC raised $175,000, of which 75 percent came from Quebec (ibid., 10 February, 19 May).

Domestically, the MLOC perceives the Canadian imperialist bourgeoisie as the main enemy (*International Forum*, February). The growth of the extreme right is mitigated somewhat by the loss of illusions among workers about the PQ and NDP (*In Struggle*, 11 and 18 August). Still the MLOC acknowledges that revolution is not imminent (ibid., 13 October). The MLOC calls for a unity of Quebec and English Canadian workers.

Internationally, the Marxist-Leninist movement is in an "ideological and political crisis" (*International Forum*, August), particularly in the imperialist countries (*In Struggle*, 13 October). Nationalism and Chinese revisionism are cited as significant factors causing revisionism's rise (*International*

Forum, April 1980, February and August 1981). While claiming neutrality in the Maoist versus Hoxha-Stalinist debate, the 1980 inaugural issue of *International Forum* was decidedly pro-Albanian (see also *Proletarian Unity*, January). The MLOC criticizes Soviet aggressiveness. International capitalism is in its worst slump in fifty years, and no short-term solution is apparent (*In Struggle*, 11 and 18 August).

Revolutionary Workers League. The RWL, active in five cities, belongs to the Trotskyist Fourth International and has several hundred members. The Young Socialist Organizing Committee is its youth wing. While on the whole supporting the reformist NDP, the RWL is nevertheless critical of NDP failure to fully support Quebec's right to self-determination (*Socialist Voice*, 23 March). The RWL calls for the NDP to take a more left-wing and working-class orientation (ibid., 29 June). While conceding that the PQ heads the nationalist movement in Quebec, the RWL criticizes the PQ's repressive antilabor laws and calls for the formation of a labor party in Quebec (ibid., 9 February). It ran one candidate in the Quebec elections (ibid., 20 April). It is critical of U.S. imperialism in Latin America and supports Cuba as a revolutionary regime (ibid., 9 March). Last year's shift in policy on the Quebec referendum and Latin America caused the emergence of a splinter group—the Socialist Challenge Organization–Organization combat socialiste.

Groupe Socialiste des Travailleurs. The GST, affiliated with the Fourth International (International Committee), is estimated to be the second-largest Trotskyist organization. It presented ten candidates in the Quebec elections. The GST favors Quebec independence and the creation of a workers' party in Quebec.

Trotskyist League. The TL denies that the RWL is revolutionary, noting that the RWL is unwilling to use violence and supports the reformist NDP (*Sparticist Canada*, March). While critical of the Stalinist degeneration of the USSR, the TL claims that while the Soviet leadership is a parasitic caste, the USSR and Cuba, nevertheless, should be defended from attacks (ibid., May, September). It calls for a military victory in El Salvador (ibid., July).

Forward Readers Group. The FRG chooses to operate within the NDP. Despite the deficiencies of the NDP, the FRG sees the NDP as the only mass labor vehicle capable of coming to power (*Forward*, February). Attempting to follow the example of a left-wing shift in the British Labour Party, the FRG suggests that the growing malaise in the NDP is an indication of rank-and-file discontent with NDP leaders' attempts to push the party into a rightist electoral stance. The FRG calls on the Left Caucus of the NDP to become bolder in its commitment to socialism and opposition to Canada's military treaties.

Publications. Among CPC publications are the weekly *Canadian Tribune* (Toronto) and *Pacific Tribune* (Vancouver); the semimonthly French-language *Combat*; the bimonthly theoretical *Communist Viewpoint* and the irregular *Le Communist*; and the bimonthly youth magazines *New Horizons* and *Jeunesse militante*. The CPC publishes the North American editions of the Prague-based *World Marxist Review* and *Information Bulletin* in Toronto. A French-language version of the former entitled *Nouvelle revue internationale* also appears. The CPC-ML publishes daily and weekly versions of *People's Canada Daily News* and *Le Quotidien du Canada populaire*. Publication of the theoretical journal *Road of the Party* is temporarily suspended. The WCP publishes the weekly newspapers *Forge* and *La Forge*, as well as the theoretical journals *October* and *Octobre*. The MLOC publishes the bilingual weekly newspaper *In Struggle/En Lutte* and the quarterly theoretical journal *Proletarian Unity*. The latter is to change its name. In April, *International Forum* began publishing English, French and Spanish editions. *Socialist Voice* and *Lutte ouvrière* are the two sister bimonthly publications of the RWL. Following the split in the RWL, *Combat socialiste* is now published by a splinter group, the Socialist Challenge Organization. The GST publishes *Tribune Ouvrière*. The TL publishes the monthly *Sparticist Canada*. Other revolutionary left-wing publications include *Forward* (FRG), *Leftwords* (Marxist Socialist Organizing Committee), and *Workers Action* (International Socialists).

Royal Military College of Canada   Alan Whitehorn

Chile

The Communist Party of Chile (Partido Comunista de Chile; PCCh) traces its roots to the establishment of the Socialist Workers' Party of Chile in 1912. Illegal between 1948 and 1958, since the mid-1950s it has worked in close cooperation with the Chilean Socialist Party. In 1970, it was largely as a result of the PCCh's efforts that Salvador Allende, a Socialist, was nominated as the presidential candidate of the Popular Unity coalition of six leftist parties and subsequently gained a narrow victory (36.9 percent of the popular vote in a three-way race).

During the Allende period, the Communists continued to uphold the *via pacifica* ("peaceful road to power"), which they had endorsed at the time the party had been legalized. They supported Allende against more militant tendencies in his own party and extremist revolutionary groups outside the coalition, such as the Movement of the Revolutionary Left (MIR). The escalation of violence on the part of left and right during the last year of the Allende presidency, combined with the virtual collapse of the Chilean economy, was the major reason for the overthrow of Allende by the Chilean armed forces on 11 September 1973.

The PCCh did not engage in armed resistance to the coup, but concentrated on keeping its organizational structure intact. Along with the other leftist parties, it was outlawed by the military government of Gen. Augusto Pinochet, its headquarters was burned, and its secretary general, Luís Corvalán, was imprisoned. In 1976, Corvalán was allowed to leave the country for the Soviet Union in exchange for the release of a leading Soviet dissident. Most well-known PCCh leaders have fled or been expelled from Chile and forbidden to return, but the underground structure of the party is believed to be intact, especially in areas where the party's influence in organized labor has been strong.

In August 1980 General Pinochet announced a plebiscite on a new Constitution of Liberty, which would give him an eight-year presidential term with the possibility of re-election by plebiscite for an additional eight years. Initially the PCCh favored abstention in the plebiscite, but later they supported a negative vote and attempted to use the campaign against the constitution to establish closer links with the centrist Christian Democratic Party, which was leading the public opposition. The Pinochet government, in turn, used the leftist opposition to the constitution to argue that a no vote would mean a return to the chaos and violence of the Allende years. The resulting 67 percent vote in favor of the constitution was a considerable psychological blow to Pinochet's opponents, and it has reinforced the Christian Democrats' determination to avoid any association with the PCCh or other Popular Unity parties.

In 1981, PCCh leaders seem to have concentrated on bringing together the divided left in exile. This has meant working with the leaders of the two sectors of the Socialist Party, which split in 1979, as well as with three small splinter groups that left the Christian Democratic Party in 1969 and 1971. The most important development has been the improvement of relations between the PCCh and the MIR, which in the past was often attacked by the party because of its commitment to violence. In January the leaders of eight Chilean leftist groups, including the MIR, signed a joint communiqué calling for coordinated action against Pinochet, while Corvalán, in a press interview in Lima, seemed to endorse the *via violenta:* "The only road left is that of confrontation all along the line . . . using every means of combat to overthrow [Pinochet]" (AFP, 11 January). In March Radio Moscow quoted Corvalán in support of "the sacred right of rebellion of the people."

In fact, terrorist actions within Chile declined during 1981 in comparison with 1980—although a discotheque was bombed in February, a radio station was briefly taken over in April, and a bank and two police stations were attacked in June. Chilean authorities, including the National Intelligence Center, were reported to have "detained" a total of 724 persons suspected of antigovernment activities between May 1980 and April 1981. Of these 557 were subsequently released, 29 were later acquitted, fourteen were sentenced to prison, and the rest were exiled. (*Qué Pasa,* 28 May.) In May seven underground communist leaders were charged with violation of the internal security law and the law on unlawful political associations, and in July the leaders of an unrecognized "solidarity"-type labor movement, the National Trade Union Coordination, were arrested. A month later, four leading political figures, a former Christian Democratic cabinet minister and three prominent members of the Allende coalition were expelled from the country for supporting the union organization.

For the expulsions Pinochet used Article 24 of the transitional provisions of the new constitution, which authorizes the president to expel from the country and prohibit the re-entry of anyone who propagates subversive doctrines "or has the reputation of being an activist in favor of such doctrines, as well as those who act contrary to the interests of Chile or constitute a threat to internal peace." The same article also allows the president to censor new publications, forbid public meetings, detain suspects for five days with the possibility of a fifteen-day extension, and send "specified persons" into three months of internal exile.

The legitimation and legalization of plebiscitary dictatorship in the new constitution has demoralized the internal opposition and radicalized the Communists. Radio Moscow announced in March 1981 that the antigovernment disturbances at the February Music Festival in Viña del Mar were organized by the Manuel Rodríguez Patriotic Command, which seems to be attempting to compete with the MIR in carrying out terrorist acts. The Christian Democrats have attacked the Communists for their endorsement of violence, and the two groups now seem to be farther apart than at any time since the coup.

If the twenty-point party program broadcast in September 1981 by Radio Moscow is any indication, the PCCh is becoming increasingly isolated from contemporary events in Chile. The program calls for nationalization of banking and expropriation of the holdings of major financial groups, redistribution of large landholdings and state control of agricultural inputs and marketing, repeal of the foreign investment law, review of the status of state enterprises sold to the private sector, repeal of the new labor law, and elections for an assembly to write a new constitution.

The Pinochet government is now engaged in the decentralization of the Chilean economy and society in areas such as education, medicine, and in the (distant) future local and regional electoral structures, so that the rapid takeover of large sectors of the country under Allende can never be repeated. The new labor law promoting plant unions and forbidding industry-wide labor organizations and strikes is also aimed at destroying one of the main bases of the PCCh's power—organized labor.

The recent evolution of the party, now publicly committed to the use of violence for the first time in many years, has given credence to the Pinochet government's blanket characterization of the left as terrorist in nature. The party's dependence on Moscow is increasing as its internal base declines, and unless it can devise a convincing answer to the Pinochet government's claims to success in lessening inflation and expanding the economy, it may become increasingly irrelevant to the future of Chile.

Princeton University Paul E. Sigmund

Colombia

The communist movement in Colombia has undergone various transformations in both name and organization since the party's initial formation in December 1926. The Communist Party of Columbia (Partido Comunista de Colombia; PCC) was publicly proclaimed on 17 July 1930. In July 1965 a schism within the PCC between pro-Soviet and pro-Chinese factions resulted in the latter's becoming the Communist Party of Columbia, Marxist-Leninist (PCC-ML). Only the PCC has legal status. It has been allowed to participate in elections under its own banner since 1972. According to U.S. intelligence estimates, the PCC has 12,000 members. Although the party contends that its ranks have increased in recent years, the 1978 elections suggest that the party's growth has been less than its leaders had hoped, especially in the larger cities. The PCC exercises only marginal influence in national affairs.

The general secretary of the PCC is Gilberto Vieira. A major source of the party's influence is its control of the Trade Union Confederation of Workers of Colombia (CSTC), which claims a membership of 300,000 and is a member of the World Federation of Trade Unions. The PCC attempts to influence the CSTC through the National Federation of Agrarian Syndicates, which functions as a part of the CSTC.

The PCC's youth organization, the Communist Youth of Columbia, has an estimated membership of two thousand.

Guerrilla Warfare. Although not a serious threat to the government, guerrilla warfare has been a feature of Colombian life since the late 1940s; the current wave began in 1964. The four main guerrilla organizations are the Revolutionary Armed Forces of Colombia (FARC), long controlled by the PCC; the M-19, a guerrilla organization that claims to be the armed hand of the National Popular Alliance (ANAPO); the pro-Chinese People's Liberation Army (EPL), which is the guerrilla arm of the PCC-ML; and the Castroite National Liberation Army (ELN). A fifth group, the Trotskyist-oriented Workers' Self-Defense Movement, claimed no credit for guerrilla actions in 1981.

On 22 January, the military launched an antiguerrilla offensive against FARC and M-19 forces responsible for four kidnappings and seventeen murders in southwestern Colombia (*El Tiempo*, 23 January). In March the army captured 75 guerrillas and killed 19 when two M-19 columns "invaded" the Putumayo region near Ecuador. Alleged Cuban involvement in the training and transportation of the guerrillas prompted President Julio Turbay Ayala to break diplomatic relations with Cuba on 23 March. The army's decisive victory led Colombia's defense minister, Gen. Luís Carlos Camacho Leyva, to proclaim that the insurgents were "virtually annihilated." However, guerrillas inflicted heavy losses on army troops in various parts of the country in July and August, leading Camacho to report a "communist guerrilla resurgence" (AFP, 13 July).

In November, the government announced the formation of a peace commission to initiate a dialogue with guerrilla leaders (ibid., 6 November). The M-19 announced its support for the government's initiative, claiming that it had proposed such a dialogue "many times" in its "search for peace." For its part, the FARC said that it would suspend guerrilla actions from 1 November 1981 until 1 June 1982 "to guarantee the normal development of the electoral process" (ibid., 3 November). Despite the possibility of a reduction in the level of guerrilla activity, it is unlikely that the state of siege will be rescinded as long as guerrilla forces retain the capacity to disrupt public order.

According to intelligence estimates, the FARC has expanded its areas of influence in recent years to include portions of the departments of Huila, Caquetá, Tolima, Cauca, Boyacá, Santander, Antioquia, Valle, Meta, Cundinamarca, and the intendency of Arauca. In 1981 the FARC concentrated its actions in the middle Magdalena region and in vast areas of Huila, Meta, and Caquetá. Carlos Romero, a member of the Central Committee of the PCC, reported in July that the FARC had some three thousand men divided into twelve rural and urban fronts (ibid., 15 July). FARC activities are directed by a fifteen-member command, headed by Mario Marulanda, Jacobo Arenas, and Martín Villa (*El Siglo*, 18 December 1980). The FARC's general headquarters is located somewhere in the border zone between Caquetá and Huila. Each FARC unit (or squad) consists of a minimum of twelve men. Two units comprise a guerrilla cell. Four units, with an equal number of replacements, make up a column. Each of the FARC's rural fronts is composed of two columns, numbering about two hundred men. The leadership mechanisms and general policy of the FARC are determined by the PCC's bylaws and political resolutions emitted at various congresses and plenums and presumably transmitted to the various fronts through Marulanda's directives.

In June, military authorities announced the discovery of a FARC plan to intensify guerrilla action in rural areas and increase mass agitation in the cities. According to documents allegedly confiscated from guerrillas, Marulanda instructed FARC commanders to be prepared to wage "an all-out war" in the countryside to coincide with the increase of military activity by the M-19 forces that entered Colombia in March (ibid., 4 June). In preparation for the guerrilla offensive, FARC intensified its recruitment efforts early in the year, especially in the areas of El Pato, middle Magdalena, and Uraba. In response to the increase in FARC activity, the military undertook large-scale counterguerrilla operations in April. Army Commander Gen. Landazábal Reyes told the press that two thousand troops were involved in a campaign against traditional FARC strongholds in Meta and Caquetá (*El Espectador*, 28 April). Armed clashes in the middle Magdalena region in April and May resulted in the deaths of 21 guerrillas and the capture of 18.

Several FARC leaders were killed during the year, including Palmenio Rojas, one of the movement's top commanders in Santander, and Jorge Linares, regarded by army intelligence as one of the FARC's most important urban strategists (AFP, 11 October). FARC units continued through October to occupy towns, ambush army patrols, kidnap wealthy ranchers for ransom, and execute peasants for collaborating with military forces.

Domestic Attitudes and Activities. The PCC recognizes the experience of the Communist Party of the Soviet Union (CPSU) as an ideological source, but it also takes "maximum account of the national characteristics and revolutionary and democratic traditions of the Colombian people." This has enabled the party to devise its own tactics, which combine diverse forms of mass struggle ranging from electoral campaigns to guerrilla warfare.

The Thirteenth Congress (November 1980) reaffirmed the party's commitment to the creation of a broad antimonopoly and anti-imperialist front. As a basis for forming this front, the party approved a program aimed at combating inflation, increasing wages, nationalizing oil and coal resources, and providing free health, education, and social assistance programs. Political demands call for lifting the state of siege, repeal of the 1978 security statute, and a general amnesty for political prisoners. The party also supports the withdrawal of North American military missions, the cessation of armed operations against peasants, and the implementation of agrarian reform. (*Voz Proletaria*, 13 November 1980; *El Espectador*, 7 June 1981.)

Gilberto Vieira announced in May that opposition groups had been contacted to present a common candidate for the 1982 presidential elections. The Executive Committee declared in June that it would not submit PCC precandidates for the legislative elections "for the sake of popular unity" (*Voz Proletaria*, 11 June). The PCC officially opened its election campaign on 21 June with a mass meeting in Bogotá. Speakers representing various left-wing groups emphasized the need to form "a genuine democratic front" to participate in the March 1982 legislative elections (*El Espectador*, 22 June). Vieira said in July that the PCC would not back the nomination of M-19 commander Jaime Bateman Cayón for president "because he cannot represent all leftist groups." He added that the PCC was "leaning toward" Gerardo Molina, former National University rector and founder of the FIRMES movement (*Voz Proletaria*, 30 July). The PCC subsequently endorsed Molina's nomination at the convention of leftist opposition parties in November (AFP, 29 November).

On 29 July, two bombs exploded at the PCC's headquarters in Bogotá. causing some damage but no casualties. In a message to the interior minister, Vieira demanded guarantees for all normal party activities, including the right to participate in elections. He cited "growing anxiety" caused by the "campaign of persecution and slander" against the party by "certain military circles in Colombia" (*El Tiempo*, 31 July).

International Views and Positions. The PCC faithfully follows the Soviet line in its international positions. In a report to the Thirteenth Congress, Vieira described the international situation as "complicated and dangerous" due to the "more belligerent policy of imperialism." He accused the United States of opposing détente and creating a policy of confrontation with the USSR (*Voz Proletaria*, 13 November 1980). According to Vieira, the Soviet Union is "an inspiring example for the working people of the bourgeois countries." As "patriots and internationalists," Colombian Communists unreservedly support the Soviets' achievements. (*Pravda*, 2 March.) In the Western Hemisphere, the PCC condemned Colombia's decision to break diplomatic relations with Cuba. Vieira accused the government of making false accusations against Cuba in order to conceal "the real intervention of U.S. imperialism in Colombia's domestic affairs" (*Voz Proletaria*, 26 March). The PCC continues to support the "socialist orientation" of the Nicaraguan revolutionary council and the "popular movements" active in El Salvador and Guatemala.

Party Contacts. A PCC delegation headed by Gilberto Vieira attended the Twenty-Sixth Congress of the CPSU in February. The CPSU Central Committee sent congratulations to Vieira on his seventieth birthday, acknowledging his many years of service in the party's "struggle against imperialism in the interests of Colombia's working class"(*Pravda*, 5 April).

Publications. The PCC publishes the weekly newspaper *Voz Proletaria* (reported circulation 40,000), the theoretical journal *Documentos Políticos* (5,000), and the Colombian edition of *World Marxist Review* (7,500). The FARC publishes the clandestine bulletin *Resistencia*.

The Maoists. The PCC-ML is firmly pro-Chinese. Its present leadership hierarchy is not clearly known, although in 1977 the Chinese press cited Arturo Acero as the political secretary of a group referred to as the Marxist-Leninist League of Colombia. The PCC-ML has an estimated membership of one thousand. Unlike the PCC, it has not attempted to obtain legal status, and its impact in terms of national political life is insignificant. Its official news organ is *Revolución*. The Marxist-Leninist League of Colombia publishes the monthly *Nueva Democracia*. PCC-ML statements are sometimes found in Chinese publications and those of pro-Chinese parties in Europe and Latin America.

The PCC-ML's guerrilla arm, the EPL, was the first to attempt a revolutionary "people's war" in Latin America. The EPL has conducted only limited operations, primarily in urban areas, since 1975, although several rural attacks in Córdoba and Antioquia were attributed to the group in 1981.

The Independent Revolutionary Workers' Movement (MOIR) has aspired since 1971 to become the first mass-based Maoist party in Latin America. Its leadership and organization are independent from those of the PCC-ML. General secretary is Francisco Mosquera. The MOIR has been unable to strengthen its political position since its poor showing in the 1978 elections.

The M-19. The M-19, which first appeared in January 1974 as the self-proclaimed armed branch of ANAPO, takes its name from the contested presidential election of 19 April 1970. Since 1976, the M-19 has been actively involved in Colombia's guerrilla movement, pursuing "a popular revolution of national liberation aimed toward socialism." Intelligence sources have identified former law student Jaime Bateman Cayón as the M-19's top leader, with ex-ANAPO Congressman Carlos Toledo Plata and Iván Marino Ospina among the more prominent members of the movement's supreme command.

Ideologically, the M-19 is a heterogeneous group embracing revolutionary principles ranging from Castroism to Trotskyism. Differences of opinion exist among the movement's leaders regarding operational tactics and future strategy. The division deepened in January when the faction headed by Bateman denounced the kidnapping of Charles Allen Bitterman, an American affiliated with the Summer Institute of Linguistics. Bitterman's body was found on 7 March, allegedly the victim of a dissident M-19 command that calls itself the National Cadre Coordination Board.

The M-19's most noteworthy operation in 1981 was the abortive "invasion" of Putumayo in March. Among the leaders captured during the attack were Carlos Toledo Plata and Rosenberg Pabón, the leader of an assault on the Dominican Embassy in Bogotá in February 1980. Toledo assumed full blame for the guerrillas' failure but denied that M-19 militants had been trained in Cuba (*El Tiempo*, 10 April). According to Toledo, the M-19 has five fronts, each made up of several columns. An army spokesman estimated the movement's armed potential at two thousand men, significantly higher than figures provided by the military in 1980 (see *YICA*, 1981, p. 55). In September the Defense Ministry reported the capture of Iván Almarales, head of the M-19's youth organization (*El Espectador*, 20 September). The M-19 also admitted the death in combat of another leader, Elmer Marín, leaving Jaime Bateman and Iván Marino as the movement's principal coordinators.

The M-19 announced in October that it was prepared to engage in a "peace dialogue" with the government on the condition that Bateman be accepted as a presidential candidate for the 1982 elections. The M-19 indicated that the country could be pacified if the government agreed to lift the state of siege, grant an unconditional amnesty to political prisoners and guerrilla activists, and allow M-19 participation in the peace commission formed by the government (ibid., 28 October). On 5 November the movement announced its support for the peace commission appointed by President Turbay. In view of the government's proposal of limited amnesty, which covers only those guerrillas who are not facing trial or have not been convicted of criminal activities, it is unlikely that the M-19 will agree, or be allowed, to compete for public support as a political party.

The National Liberation Army. The ELN was formed in Santander in 1964 under the inspiration of the Cuban revolution. It undertook its first military action in January 1965.

Once recognized as the largest and most militant of the guerrilla forces operating in Colombia, the ELN has never recovered from the toll exacted on its leadership and urban network in recent years by government forces, including the defection in 1976 of its principal founder and maximum leader, Fabio Vásquez Castaño. Eleven of the ELN's top leaders have been killed in its seventeen years of existence, resulting in the dismemberment of the movement into viciously feuding local groups.

Since late 1979 ELN operations have been limited to the middle Magdalena region. According to a spokesman for the Defense Ministry, the ELN has fewer than forty members. Although several minor actions were attributed to the ELN in October, the group was virtually inoperative for most of the year. Like the EPL, the ELN no longer appears to be relevant to the future course of guerrilla activity in Colombia.

Washington College   Daniel L. Premo

Costa Rica

The Communist Party of Costa Rica (Partido Comunista de Costa Rica) was founded in 1931, under the leadership of Manuel Mora Valverde, still its secretary general. It was accepted as a full member of the Comintern in 1935. In 1943, in conformity with the Browderite policy accepted by several Latin American communist parties, it changed its name to the Popular Vanguard Party (Partido Vanguardia Popular; PVP). It remains the country's pro-Moscow communist party. The PVP is estimated to have about 3,200 members but is able to mobilize several thousand more sympathizers through its control of the Unitary Confederation of Workers (Confederación Unitaria de Trabajadores; CUT) and peasant, student, and public employee groups. In late March, the PVP Central Committee announced a goal of increasing the circulation of *Libertad*, its weekly newspaper, to 7,000 by the time of the party's anniversary, 16 June (*Libertad*, San José, 27 March–2 April).

Since 1974, the PVP has participated in a coalition with two other far-left parties (see below) under the name of the United People's Coalition (Coalición Pueblo Unido; PU). In 1980, the PU selected its nominee for president in the 1978 elections, Rodrigo Gutiérrez Sáenz, as its candidate for president in the 7 February 1982 elections. The three most important presidential candidates are Luís Alberto Monge of the National Liberation Party, a party affiliated with the democratic Socialist International; Rafael Angel Calderón Fournier of the Unity Coalition, the coalition of incumbent President Rodrigo Carazo Odio, for whom Calderón was foreign minister from 1978 to 1980; and Mario Echandi Jiménez, candidate of the Movimiento Nacional and president of Costa Rica, 1958–1962. Monge is expected to win the election over the two conservatives, Calderón and Echandi, whose groups could not agree on a unified candidate. The PVP is among eighteen registered parties nominating candidates for the nation's two vice-presidential positions, all 57 seats in the Legislative Assembly, and positions in municipal government in Costa Rica's 81 *municipios*.

The other important leftist party is the Revolutionary Movement of the People (Movimiento Revolucionario del Pueblo; MRP), headed by Sergio Frick Ardón. Although the MRP advocated violent revolution between 1978 and 1980, in June and July party leaders disclaimed responsibility for various terrorist acts probably aimed at embroiling Costa Rica further in the turmoil of El Salvador, Guatemala, and Nicaragua. After police had announced the arrest of four persons involved in a shoot-out in San José and the discovery of several safe houses in San José, Ardón indicated that terrorist actions can be explained but not justified: "Those kids . . . do not know if they are being used for unknown purposes or if they are really fighting certain injustices from which Costa Rica has not escaped. But even if their reasons are well grounded, the MRP feels that popular struggles can still be waged here . . . without the unjust violence of terrorist actions." (Radio Reloj, 25 June; *FBIS*, 26 June.)

On 1 May, the Judicial Investigation Organization (OIJ) of the Costa Rican government disclosed that it had discovered evidence of a new leftist-extremist group, the Carlos Aguero Echeverría Command, as a consequence of the arrest of four men at a San José safe house (Radio Reloj, 1 May; *FBIS*, 4 May). On 17 July, an OIJ spokesman said that his organization had discovered another abandoned safe house belonging to the group but he was not sure if the command—named after a Costa Rican who died fighting with the Sandinista movement—was an autonomous group or linked to some other group because of a complex structure linking only one member of each cell with one member of another cell.

The Carlos Aguero Command had claimed credit for a 17 March bazooka attack against a U.S. Embassy car carrying three Marine guards and a bomb explosion near the Honduran Embassy and Consulate in San José (Radio Reloj, 17 March; *FBIS*, 18 March). The PVP issued an official communiqué the same day "energetically condemning the terrorist attack against the U.S. Embassy personnel . . . Such acts benefit only the extreme rightist forces interested in dragging our country into a climate of violence that would enable the 'far right' to eradicate the democratic system in which we live" (Radio Reloj, 17 March; *FBIS*, 18 March). The bazooka attack and bombing came the same day a U.S. missile cruiser and an accompanying landing dock and cargo ship were scheduled to visit Puerto Límon on the Caribbean coast—a visit that PVP deputies in the Legislative Assembly stopped by securing postponement of voting the necessary permission until the vessel had proceeded to Cartegena, Colombia.

On 23 June, OIJ officials disclosed that police had arrested 23 persons after raiding several safe houses in San José. OIJ officials said that one group of terrorists claimed to be linked to the Central American Vanguard Forces (Fuerzas Avanzadas de Centro América) or the Central American Armed Front (Frente Armado de Centro América), which allegedly also included the Honduran Cinchonero People's Liberation Movement, the Guatemalan Ernesto Guevara Guerrilla Front, and the Salvadoran Farabundo Martí National Liberation Front (Radio Reloj, 16 and 22 June; *FBIS*, 18 and 23 June). On 11 July, the OIJ said the recently disbanded group had collected 1 million *colones* (approximately U.S. $60,000) for its operations from member contributions and business robberies in San José.

The three other small Marxist parties did not make headlines in 1981. The Socialist Action Party (Partido de Acción Socialista; PS) is a communist splinter group led by Dr. Licamaco Leiva. The Workers' Party (Partido Obrero) is a radical group reportedly linked to the Nicaraguan Sandinista Liberation Front. The Costa Rican Socialist Party (PSC) is a pro-Cuban party headed by Alberto Salom. There is also an anti-Soviet far-left group, the Costa Rican People's Front (Frente Popular Costarricense).

Leadership and Organization of the PVP. In addition to its 71-year-old secretary general, Manuel Mora Valverde, important PVP leaders include Deputy Secretary General Eduardo Mora Valverde, Manuel's brother; Arnaldo Ferreto Segura, 70-year-old secretary of organization and member of the Secretariat and Political Commission; and Humberto Vargas Carbonell, head of the three-member PVP bloc in the Legislative Assembly. These four men make most of the "urgent daily decisions" of the party. (For the names of other members of the Political Commission, see *YICA*, 1981, p. 57.)

Since the 1930s, the PVP has had a strong base in the unions of banana workers of Costa Rican subsidiaries of United Fruit Company and Standard Fruit Company/Castle and Cooke, who have been organized into the United Agricultural and Plantation Workers (FENTAP) and the Union of Golfito Workers (UTG). On 21 November 1980, FENTAP, UTG, and General Confederation of Workers (CGT) leaders joined delegates of the National Federation of Municipal Workers and White-Collar Employees, the National Peasant Federation—all led by PVP members—and delegates from unions of dockworkers, railroaders, and university groups to form the CUT. The PVP claims the new union represents more than 50,000 workers. The CUT—and its CGT predecessor—generally have been superior in financial strength and organizational work outside of San José to the noncommunist Confederation of Democratic Workers (CCTD), which is affiliated with the Inter-American Regional Organization of Workers to which the AFL-CIO and most democratic socialist federations in the hemisphere belong. In 1978, the CGT was said to have an annual income of more than U.S. $90,000, a sum that permitted the CGT to maintain a staff of 32 well-trained activists and thirteen lawyers, many of whom play an active role in the PVP and the PS.

In 1981, the CCTD initiated an effort to reduce UTG and PVP control of unions in banana-growing areas. A union organized in Golfito rapidly grew to at least 500 members by August 1981 and planned to challenge the UTG over the right to bargain collectively on behalf of Standard Fruit workers in April 1982.

Labor-management problems, especially within multinational corporations, inflation, the declining value of Costa Rican currency, increases in bank interest rates, and organization of neighborhood committees to defend neighborhoods against alleged wrongdoing by municipal or national authorities are principal themes in the pages of *Libertad*, the weekly PVP newspaper edited by Eduardo Mora Valverde, and *El Trabajador*, the MRP weekly, both of which were sold on San José streets for one *colon* (U.S. 11.5¢).

The Juventud Vanguardista Costarricense (JVC) is one of several Marxist-Leninist groups active among university students. The JVC is probably the best organized, with some fourteen regional organizations. It is headed by César Solano, a voting member of the PVP Central Committee. The JVC was one of many student groups demanding that the Legislative Assembly create a permanent fund for higher education in the amount of 12 percent of the national budget.

Leadership and Organization of the MRP and PSC. Much less is known about the organization and structure of the MRP. Its top leaders include Sergio Frick Ardón, Rolando V. Barrantes, and J. Araya. On 16 July, Ardón accused the conservative San José newspaper *La Nación* of publishing false rumors and characterized articles linking the MRP to different guerrilla groups as "fantasies" and "alarmistic." In a MRP communiqué, Ardón said *La Nación* sought to make the MRP illegal as part of a "repressive offensive" against the MRP and the PU coalition. Ardón charged that the Costa Rican bourgeoisie (*la gran burgesía*) and its allies in Central America and the United States "were worried about the ascendancy of the MRP in popular struggles . . . and feared the PU would obtain a high vote in the forthcoming elections and elect an important number of deputies" (*La Nación*, 17 July). One day later, Otto Castro, possibly a leader of the MRP-affiliated Union of Small Agriculturalists of the Atlantic, sarcastically charged two other newspapers, *La República* and *La Prensa*, of joining *La Nación* in "informing" Costa Ricans that "peasants in different places . . . were being organized to promote armed violence." In reality, Castro and the MRP were struggling against low wages paid by large landowners and seeking parcels of land for marginalized peasants from the Costa Rican Institute of Land and Colonization. (Ibid., 18 July.)

On 18 March, PSC leader Salom protested a raid by eight armed OIJ officers on PSC headquarters the previous afternoon as an "irresponsible provocation" and an attempt to link the PSC with the "criminal attacks" on the American Embassy car and the Honduran Embassy (Radio Reloj, 18 March; *FBIS*, 19 March).

Controversy Over Radio Station. Costa Rica's relatively free society was the setting of a controversy lasting from late 1979 to March 1981 over the broadcasting activities of a 50-kilowatt clear-channel station, Radio Noticias del Continente, which seldom carried commercials and was difficult to hear within Costa Rica. The radio station's newscasts, which could be heard in other parts of Central and South America, reportedly contained "subversive" messages aimed at undermining the governments of El Salvador, Guatemala, Argentina, Chile, and Uruguay. The transmitter, located in the municipio of Grecia, was attacked three times in 1980, including a December 1980 attempt during which a Costa Rican policeman was killed. The station's broadcasts were suspended by President Carazo on 7 March after a late February police raid confiscated a cache of automatic weapons, two pistols, ammunition, uniforms, and other items at the station and a nearby house. Station director Ana Lorena Cartín told the PVP's *Libertad* that she felt the arms had been planted and hoped the police would find the organizers of this "farce" (*Libertad*, 20–26 February; Radio Reloj, 16 March; *FBIS*, 17 March). On 6 March, Cartín announced the founding of an International Solidarity Network during the San José station's suspension that would include Radio México International, Radio Sandino of Nicaragua, Radio Centre Viole of Montreal, Radio Exterior of Spain, Radio ABC of Panama, Radio Cuzco and Radio Corporación of Peru, Radio Popular of Santo Domingo, and the Voice of Germany, reportedly the official station of the Federal Republic of Germany. On 10 March, Cartín announced that various Mexican and Central American newspapers would carry the station's material until its suspension was lifted. (AFP, Paris, 7 March; Editorial Report, Radio Sandino, Managua, 10 March; Radio Reloj, 10 March; *FBIS*, 9 and 12 March.) Finally, in late March, a Grecia judge discovered that the station's equipment and transmitters had been removed (Radio Reloj, 26 March; *FBIS*, 27 March).

International Activities and Contacts. Manuel Mora Valverde, Arnaldo Ferreto Segura, and *Libertad* writer José Merino del Rio attended the Twenty-Sixth Congress of the Communist Party of the Soviet Union, which met in Moscow on 23 February. In an address to the congress, Mora Valverde denounced "North American imperialism as [being] representative of the most reactionary and most inhumane forces seeking to terrorize humanity with threats of atomic war." Mora Valverde lauded Leonid Brezhnev as a "symbol of socialism" that ought to be emulated in the fields of economics, science, culture, and art. Later, Ferreto Segura and Eduardo Mora Valverde, speaking at the Costa Rican–Soviet Cultural Institute, praised the USSR's new five-year plan (*Libertad*, 20–26 February, 13–19 March).

On 22 April, Maj. Luís Alvarado Saravia, a Salvadoran guerrilla who had defected, told San José's Radio Reloj that many Costa Ricans were being trained in four-month training courses in Cuba, along with guerrillas from El Salvador, Chileans from the Movement of the Revolutionary Left, Colombians of the 19th of April Movement (M-19 April), and Guatemalans of the People's Revolutionary Army (*FBIS*, 23 April).

In April Costa Rica formally renounced an October 1977 Technical and Economic Cooperation Agreement with the Soviet Union and in May closed its consulate in Havana (Radio Monumental, 8 May; Radio Reloj, 22 April; *FBIS*, 23 April). According to Costa Rica's foreign minister, the consulate was closed because of the "offensive tone" of a Cuban note "violating the framework of mutual respect between the countries." The action also came after several Costa Rican Ministry of Security officials were indicted for embezzlement, bribery, and illegal enrichment for issuing visas permitting Cubans to enter Costa Rica en route to the United States; other officials of the ministry reportedly sold Cuban arms to Salvadoran leftists that had been part of Cuban shipments to the Sandinistas "stockpiled" in Costa Rica for "police use" in case Somoza's National Guard invaded Costa Rica in retaliation for the Carazo regime's granting of safe-havens to the Sandinistas (AFP, Paris, 18 May; Radio Reloj, 22 April; *FBIS*, 23 April, 18 May). Costa Rica was also unhappy with Cuban and Nicaraguan opposition to Costa Rica's candidacy for a two-year term on the U.N. Security Council in October–November 1980—a seat ultimately won by Panama. Nor was Costa Rica happy with Cuba's financing and arming of M-19 April guerrillas trying to topple the Turbay Ayala government in Colombia. Probably contributing to the renunciation of the Costa Rican–Soviet agreement was the involvement of three Cubans, one Russian, one Yugoslav, and one Bulgarian—all of whom were expelled—in a December 1979–January 1980 strike on banana plantations (the agreement provided for training in the Soviet Union of Costa Ricans in labor relations).

On 19 August, a colonel in the Costa Rican National Security Agency revealed that four women and one man carrying Sandinista People's Army identity cards had been captured just after they had crossed the Nicaraguan border into Liberia in Guanacaste province. The commando group had received military training in Havana and planned to assault the Guatemalan Embassy in San José as part of a plan to obtain the release of ten Guatemalan political prisoners and 50 million *colones* (approximately $2.5 million) (*La Prensa*, San Pedro Sula, Honduras, 19 August).

On 14 June, an estimated three thousand persons from different parts of the country celebrated the fiftieth anniversary of the PVP in San José. The rally was attended by delegates from the German Democratic Republic, Cuba, Nicaragua, Panama, and El Salvador (Radio Reloj, 15 June; *FBIS*, 16 June).

Texas Tech University   Neale J. Pearson

Cuba

The Communist Party of Cuba (Partido Comunista de Cuba; PCC), the ruling and only legal party in the country under its 1976 constitution, increased its roster to 434,143 members and candidates for membership in 1981. The educational level of the membership is said to be improving: in 1975 some 60 percent of members and candidates had primary education only; in 1981, 80.7 percent had completed the eighth grade. (*WMR*, July.) According to Fidel Castro, PCC first secretary and Cuba's president, party membership is becoming more proletarian, the number of workers having tripled. Castro also indicated that party members constitute most of those sent abroad, especially to Africa.

More than 100,000 communist combatants have "fulfilled international missions," he said. (*Granma*, 28 December 1980.)

The top leadership of the PCC, its Political Bureau, Secretariat, and Central Committee remained virtually unchanged in 1981, and there were no claims that the party has been effective in assuaging the country's endemic economic and social problems. "Counterrevolution survives, also the lumpen and antisocial elements," said Castro in October, warning Cubans that they would have to tighten their belts again. A July plenum of the PCC Central Committee urged the party's rank and file to work harder under the slogan of "defense and economy."

Mass Organizations. The membership and functions of the Cuban mass organizations remained virtually unchanged in 1981. The principal organizations, the Federation of Cuban Women (Federación de Mujeres Cubanas) and the Committees for the Defense of the Revolution (Comités de Defensa de la Revolución), appeared to be operating in a lifeless fashion, and no special tasks were required of them by the Castro regime.

The Revolutionary Armed Forces. Cuba's military involvement abroad in 1981 was maintained at the level of 1980. About 20,000 troops and military and security advisers were stationed in Angola, some 16,000 in Ethiopia, and thousands more in scores of countries from South Yemen to Nicaragua. The Cubans appeared not to be involved in fighting in Angola, and "many Angolans consider the Cubans a costly and sometimes disruptive presence in their country," according to Portuguese Foreign Minister Andre Gonçalves Pereira. The Portuguese official said that the Cubans, who had been deliberately isolated from the rest of the population because "a certain number of frictions came up," represent a financial drain on Angola because their presence costs $250 million a year. (*NYT*, 3 October.)

Preparing for what Cuban propaganda called "the eventuality of a total war" with the United States, the government continued to build up the territorial militias and, with Soviet assistance, to overhaul the armament of its regular forces. According to Castro, the militias are to replace regular armed forces units in combatting enemy paratroop landing and fifth columnists, protecting factories, bridges, and railways, and "carrying out irregular war missions in the case of occupied territories." (Radio Havana, 20 January; *FBIS*, 21 January.) The militias were being built up to a total strength of one million. Cuban regular forces are believed to number 190,000 and are augmented by a reserve of 200,000. In 1981, these units, according to U.S. Secretary of State Alexander Haig, received more Soviet arms shipments than in any year since 1962, the year of the Cuban missile crisis. (*Los Angeles Times*, 31 July.) Washington has also charged that the Soviet arms buildup exceeds Cuba's legitimate needs and that Moscow was stockpiling arms on the island for clandestine shipment to Nicaragua and to guerrilla groups in Latin America, especially in El Salvador. State Department officials said that between January and August Cuba received approximately 46,000 tons of Soviet military equipment, whereas in all of 1980 Moscow had sent only 20,000 tons. In addition, the Soviet Union delivered to Cuba a modern 2,300-ton frigate of the Koni class, now the largest ship in the Cuban Navy, which consists mostly of torpedo boats and patrol craft. (*WP*, 4 August.) The military and naval facility at Cienfuegos was being enlarged, as was the San Antonio de los Baños air base, home for Soviet TU-95D Bear long-range reconnaissance planes. There were no indications that the strength of the 5,000-man Soviet brigade in Cuba had changed.

International Positions. Cuban international initiatives were limited in 1981, and the government appeared to be on the defensive internally as well as externally. The failure of the January offensive by leftist guerrillas in El Salvador was a blow to Castro, whose propaganda had indicated a Nicaragua-like denouement was possible there. Late in the summer, Havana ordered a nationwide mobilization of the military forces, ostensibly to prepare for an imminent U.S. attack. Cuba did not complain to any international body, however, and insisted, as Politburo member Carlos Rafael Rodríguez Rodríguez said, that "our preparation is not motivated by paranoia—by an excess of precautions, but it is a demonstration that we are ready to confront any eventuality that presents itself." (*Miami Herald*, *Washington Post* Service, 27 September.) The prestige of Fidel Castro was affected when Mexican President José López Portillo, the host of the Cancún conference, decided to uninvite the Cuban president to permit the presence at Cancún of President Reagan, who agreed to attend only on condition that Castro not be present.

Relations with the United States. Since its inauguration, the Reagan administration has adopted a hard-line approach toward Cuba, entertaining no notion of a rapprochement with the Castro government. Secretary of State Haig accused the Castro government of being partly responsible for a "terrorist network" aimed at taking over all of Central America and implied that drastic action against Castro might be taken. Soon, relations reached the lowest ebb since the April 1961 Bay of Pigs invasion. In February, presidential adviser Edwin Meese said that the United States would take "the necessary steps" to stop the arms flow from Cuba to El Salvador. A few weeks later, Walter J. Stoessel, under secretary of state for political affairs, stated that the "use of force against Cuba over Salvador arms [shipment] was an option." (*NYT*, 23 February, 19 March.) Cuba responded by accusing Washington of supporting the Salvadoran regime and being responsible for what it called genocide there. In April, Castro reportedly told West German Social Democratic Party leader Hans-Jürgen Wischnewski that Cuba had shipped arms to insurgents in El Salvador but the shipments had ended. Castro added that the Soviet Union had not been involved in that traffic. (Ibid., 25 April.) For the next three months, the U.S.-Cuban controversy appeared to quieten. But it was resumed with new bitterness on 26 July when Castro publicly suggested that the United States might have been responsible for the introduction into Cuba of dengue fever, which affected some 350,000 persons and killed about 150. Dengue fever, which is transmitted by mosquitoes, has been sweeping much of the Caribbean. But Castro said that the mosquitoes "could have been introduced into Cuba by the CIA." One day later, the State Department called Castro's charge "totally without foundation" and said that the Castro government "has always tried to blame the United States for its failures and its internal problems." (On 17 July, Washington had approved a request from the Panamerican Health Organization for the immediate shipment to Cuba of 300 tons of U.S.-manufactured pesticide to combat the dengue-carrying mosquitoes. Officials believed that dengue could have been brought to Cuba by soldiers returning from Africa or Asia, where the disease is common.) (Ibid., 5 September.)

After July, there were reports that the Reagan administration had again elevated Cuba to a higher priority on its international agenda. Haig repeatedly stated that the only way to end the fighting in El Salvador was to "go to the source" of the arms shipments—Cuba. The White House announced plans to create a radio station, similar to Radio Free Europe, that would broadcast to Cuba "to tell the truth to the Cuban people." Haig, referring to reports about policy options toward the Castro regime, declared in October that "extensive studies" had been completed about ways to thwart what he identified as increasing Cuban subversion and terrorism in the Western Hemisphere "in order to make the risks [to Cuba] seem to be more costly than the advantages." Trying to keep pressure on Cuba, Assistant Secretary of State Thomas Enders said at the same time: "Our policy toward Cuba is under active consideration. You have not heard the last of it yet." (*Miami Herald*, *Los Angeles Times* Service, 28 November.) Simultaneously, U.S. naval forces in the Caribbean were strengthened, and combined sea-air exercises were held in the area. Also in November, the Pentagon announced the formation of a new military command for the Caribbean in Key West, Florida, upgrading somewhat a small task force established there in 1979 by President Carter.

With his troops mobilized, Castro accused the United States of "setting the stage" for aggressive actions against Cuba. In a letter to various American newspapers, the Cuban president said that a "campaign" under way for several weeks accusing Cuba of shipping new arms to El Salvador was "totally false." (*NYT*, 12 November.)

On 10 November, President Reagan, asked at a news conference about reports of U.S. military actions in the Caribbean, said: "We have no plans for putting Americans in combat any place in the world, and our goal is peace" (ibid., 11 November). While Reagan did not comment on the policy options that his administration is considering against Cuba, they included (1) an invasion of Cuba, regarded as unrealistic and an action that would certainly produce a serious confrontation with the Soviet Union; (2) a naval blockade of Cuba, similar to that ordered by President Kennedy in October 1962, which also could lead to a direct confrontation with Moscow; (3) a limited naval blockade in the Gulf of Mexico aimed at stopping Cuban shipments to Nicaragua and Salvadoran guerrillas, whose effectiveness cannot be predicted; and (4) new economic sanctions against Cuba, which would produce only marginal results since a trade embargo already exists against the island (ibid., 17 November). The only positive result of the pressure applied on Castro appears to be Cuba's growing isolation in Latin America and a higher cost to the Soviet Union of maintaining Cuba, whose military mobilization has affected industrial and agricultural production.

Relations with Latin America and the Caribbean. Cuba, which in the 1970s normalized relations with several Latin American and Caribbean nations, suffered a series of diplomatic setbacks in 1981. The turnaround began in 1980 when Peru and Venezuela froze relations with Cuba. In February 1981, Ecuador recalled its ambassador over the storming of the Ecuadoran Embassy in Havana by Cuban security forces. In March, Colombia broke off relations with Havana, charging that some eighty guerrillas, captured after landing on the Colombian coast, had been trained and armed in Cuba. In May, Costa Rica suspended relations with Cuba. In October, Jamaica broke diplomatic relations with the Castro government and ordered the Cuban embassy in Kingston closed. Jamaican Prime Minister Edward Seaga said that diplomatic ties, established in 1962 when Jamaica became independent, were cut because Cuba had refused to return three men wanted in Jamaica on murder charges. According to Havana, the break was carried out on Washington's orders. Even Cuban-Panamanian relations, once very close, became strained over El Salvador and Nicaragua. Nicaragua and Grenada maintained very close ties with Havana, as did Mexico, whose president tried to act as an intermediary between Washington and Havana. Ironically, Cuban relations with the right-wing military regime of Argentina were cordial and commercial relations were thriving.

Relations with Other Countries. There were fewer anti-Chinese diatribes in 1981 than in the previous years, as Cuba continued to trade with China. In the Middle East, Cuba was particularly friendly with Libya and the Palestine Liberation Organization. The Palestinians, said Castro, "are a vivid example of sacrifice and patriotism, living symbols of the most terrible crime of our era" (*Granma*, 5 July). Cuba continued its modest trade with Western Europe, principally with Spain and France. In July, Havana announced the purchase of a 330,000 kw power plant from a French company.

Domestic Affairs. After two bad years, the Castro government tried to rebound economically in 1981. The president claimed that the production of sugar, the country's principal product, was close to eight million tons, one million more than in 1980. (American officials thought the sugar harvest was no higher than seven million tons.) But lower sugar prices on the world market (an average of 13 cents a pound in 1981 compared with 30 cents in 1980) meant that Cuba actually got less money for its good sugar harvest in 1981 than for the 6.8 million tons harvested in 1980. To obtain dollars, badly needed to pay its foreign currency obligations, Cuba, for the first time, sought partnerships with foreign corporations, especially to develop beach resorts on the island. But at the same time, the Havana government, for political reasons, made it harder and more expensive for exiles to visit their relatives, losing an estimated $80 million of the $120 million it earned from "family visits" in 1980.

While some harvests, such as tobacco, were better than before, others, notably rice, were considerably lower. As a result, strict rationing continued in the country, which was dependent on imports for most of its manufactured goods, raw materials, and key food items, such as grain and lard.

In 1981, Cuba's hard-currency debt reached $3 billion, of which $2 billion was to private Western banks and the rest to international export-import institutions. Havana was fulfilling its financial obligations despite its problems, regarding repayment of debts as its prime commitment. According to a published report based on "reliable sources," Havana's eagerness to obtain hard currency has led it to understate production figures to Moscow, which receives the bulk of Cuban production, so that undeclared surpluses could be sold for cash in the West (*NYT*, 25 June).

Cuba continued to be heavily subsidized by Moscow. Soviet economic aid was estimated at well over $3 billion, and judging by the fragmentary data of the 1981–1985 plan, this dependence will increase.

International Contacts. At the end of February, Fidel Castro attended the Soviet party congress in Moscow, where he effusively praised Leonid Brezhnev and pledged eternal friendship and gratitude to the Soviet leadership. "Cuban-Soviet relations have passed the test of the first twenty years and surely will pass the test of centuries," said Castro. "We are proud of our relations with the Soviet Union . . . we are and always will be faithful friends of the generous and heroic people who helped us so much. We will never harbor ingratitude, opportunism, and betrayal." (*Granma*, 3 March.)

Also in February Cuba signed an agreement with the German Democratic Republic covering cooperation between the two countries through 1985. Other agreements signed during 1981 included economic cooperation agreements with Algeria and Mozambique (June) and a technical cooperation agreement with Grenada (September).

Several visits were exchanged with Mexico. In March the head of the Mexican Navy was in Havana. In June, Miguel de la Madrid, then minister of planning and finance and later in the year named the presidential candidate of Mexico's ruling party (which assures that he will become president), visited Havana to sign an agreement on technical cooperation and economic planning. Shortly afterward, the PCC Politburo member in charge of foreign relations, Carlos Rafael Rodríguez, met with Mexican President López Portillo in Mexico. In August, Castro flew to Mexico for discussions with the Mexican president. He apparently expressed his disappointment at being excluded from the Cancún conference. Also in August, a Mexican training ship paid a call to Havana. The Cuban press portrayed her three-day stay as a new sign of Cuban-Mexican friendship.

Cuba's one attempt to play the role of international peacemaker failed. In January and February Cuban Foreign Minister Isidoro Malmierca Peoli traveled to several Asian and Middle Eastern countries in an unsuccessful attempt to mediate the Iraqi-Iranian conflict.

Prominent visitors to Havana during the year included ex–Prime Minister Edward Heath of Great Britain, Soviet Chief of Staff Marshal Nikolai V. Ogarkov, ex–Prime Minister Michael Manley of Jamaica, ex–Prime Minister Adolfo Súarez of Spain, two leaders of the Sandinista government of Nicaragua, Daniel and Humberto Ortega, East German leader Erich Honecker, Maurice Bishop of Grenada, Italian Communist Party leader Enrico Berlinguer, and Laotian Foreign Minister Phoun Sipaseut.

A number of international groups held meetings in Cuba in 1981, including the Interparliamentary Conference; Intellectuals for the Sovereignty of the Peoples of America; Seminar on Palestine; the World Peace Council; Nonaligned Countries Meeting on Cooperation in Fishing; and the International Seminar in Solidarity with Vietnam, Laos, and Kampuchea. Cuba now has an International Conference Center in Havana.

Publications. Strong criticism of the Cuban media expressed in 1980 and at the Second Congress of the PCC in December 1980 did not result in any improvement of its quality. The media continued as monotonous, repetitious, and obsequious as ever. The official organ of the PCC Central Committee is *Granma*, a Havana newspaper published six days a week with a circulation of some 600,000. Central Committee member Jorge Enrique Mendoza is its publisher and editor, although Fidel Castro is known to have intervened occasionally in its front-page makeup and content. Spanish, English, and French international weekly editions of *Granma* are distributed free of charge to some 100,000 readers abroad. In July, the U.S. Treasury Department, citing a 1917 law that bars trade with certain foreign countries in the event of a national emergency, ordered U.S. Customs officers to block the delivery of some 30,000 copies of *Granma* and other Cuban publications, mostly sent free of charge to libraries, news organizations, universities, and schools. The Customs Service required recipients of Cuban publications to obtain an import license. The legality of the Treasury measure is being contested, and the action was criticized editorially by a number of American newspapers. Other Cuban publications are the Havana daily *Juventud Rebelde*, organ of the Union of Young Communists, with a circulation of 200,000; *Bohemia*, a general news weekly magazine, which has a print run of 300,000 copies; and the weekly *Verde Olivo*, the organ of the Revolutionary Armed Forces. Prensa Latina, the Cuban news agency, has 34 offices abroad and access to two satellite communication channels to Moscow. Cuba has 40 radio stations of considerable power and twenty television stations. Radio Havana Cuba broadcasts in eight languages on several shortwave frequencies for a total of 50 hours weekly.

The PCC and the Future. Although concerned about the current state of the economy, and painting its future in bleak colors, or at best in terms of cyclical ups and downs, Castro seemed to be dedicating more of his time to foreign affairs. But Cuban media made few comments about the situation in Poland. It was as if Havana recognized that many socioeconomic factors that initiated the disarray of the Polish communist party exist in Cuba today. Cuban Communists were barely muddling through. No new vision, new ideas, or new faces appeared on the Cuban political scene. The PCC structure was rigidly bureaucratic, the party's highest organs being mere rubberstamps for Castro and his cronies. Castro, 54 in 1981, has not admitted new blood into the top party and government echelons, producing fossilization on its intermediate levels and ennui among the populace.

PCC leaders are said to be increasingly perceived by working Cubans as a privileged class. In the 1960s, Castro made a concerted effort to convince the population and the world that an egalitarian society was being created in Cuba and that becoming a member of the communist party implied making sacrifices rather than receiving perquisites. The party, very small then, consisted, according to Castro, of idealistic individuals selflessly working for common good. By 1981, puritanism had been totally forgotten. Egalitarian austerity was for working Cubans. The communist elite, unaffected by scarcities, was a class by itself, and the difference was growing.

Under a wage and price reform, Cubans were paying more for virtually all products, and Castro conceded that the present standard of living would decline. "This [reform] goes together with the restrictive measures we will have to take, and we will have to sacrifice some programs and plans, some investments and possibly standards of living." (Ibid., 1 November.) There were no indications that the PCC was ready to confront this admittedly deteriorating socioeconomic situation. Indicative of the government's task was a speech by Politburo member and Minister of Interior Ramiro Valdés: "Repression for us is not a goal but a means to preserve the people's interests and to contribute to the formation of the socialist awareness of all our population . . . We cannot depend on spontaneity . . . In recent times, there have been manifestations of economic-type crimes, both on large and small scales. Crimes against property, robbery and theft have continued to occur and we do not always act with the necessary energy and adopt realistic and coherent measures to combat these criminal manifestations." (Radio Havana, 6 June; *FBIS*, 7 June.)

University of Miami   George Volsky

Dominican Republic

The political left in the Dominican Republic continued in 1981 to be split in many factions. Despite occasional calls for unity, these groupings maintained their separate identities. The main Marxist group was the Dominican Communist Party (Partido Comunista Dominicano; PCD), pro-Soviet and pro-Cuban, whose general secretary was the 38-year-old Narciso Isa Conde. The Communist Party of the Dominican Republic (Partido Comunista de la República Dominicana) and the New Republic Revolutionary Movement (Movimiento Revolucionario Nueva República) were the two pro-Chinese groups, led, respectively, by Luís (Pin) Montas and Rafael Gamudy Cordero. Another pro-Beijing group, the Dominican People's Movement (Movimiento Popular Dominicano) consisted of two mini-factions, one headed by Onelio Espaillat and Jorge Puello Soriano and the other by Rafael Chaljub Mejía. Other leftist groupings were the Nucleus of Communist Workers (Núcleo de los Trabajadores Comunistas), led by Rafael (Fafa) Tavares; the Dominican Liberation Party (Partido de Liberación Dominicana), a pro-Cuban group whose leader was former President Juan Bosch; the Patriotic Anti-Imperialist Union (Unión Patriótica Anti-Imperialista), headed by Franklin Franco; the Camilo Torres Revolutionary Committee (Comité Revolucionario Camilo Torres); the Marxist-Leninist Path (Vía Marxista-Leninista), presided over by Fidelio Despradel; the Dominican Liberation Movement (Movimiento de Liberación Dominicana), led by Agustín Alvarez; the Trinitarian National Liberation Movement (Movimiento de Liberación Nacional de los Trinitarios), led by Lorenzo Mejía Frías; and the Popular Socialist Party (Partido Socialista Popular), led by Felipe Servio Cucoundray. A newer pro-Chinese group was the Dominican Workers' Party (Partido de Trabajadores Dominicanos), which resulted from the 1979 merger of two small organizations. Also created in 1979 was a Guevarista group called the Revolutionary Leftist Movement (Movimiento de Izquierda Revolucionaria), whose leaders were Fernando Paniagua and Enrique Cabrera Vázquez (El Mellizo). A new leftist group founded in April 1981 was the Socialist Party (Partido Socialista), whose president was Max Puig and secretary general Arístides Santana.

The combined membership of these and possibly a few other minuscule leftist groups was estimated at less than five thousand, although before the 1978 election the PCD collected 127,000 signatures, more than the 111,000 necessary to qualify a candidate for the presidential ballot. The next presidential election is scheduled for 16 May 1982. The PCD has decided to participate and must submit a list of 117,000 supporters. In 1981, leaders of several leftist groupings called for a unity election slate, but Isa Conde indicated the unity had to be achieved on his terms and rejected rapprochement with, among others, former President Bosch. "Many of those in the Dominican Republic who claim to be on the left belong to Maoist groups and pursue a policy of alliance with the bourgeoisie, which is dependent on foreign imperialism. They slander the Soviet Union, the Cuban Revolution and the whole socialist community. It goes without saying that we cannot join them," wrote Isa Conde. (*WMR*, March, pp. 62–65.)

The two main contenders in the May 1982 elections will be the candidates of the ruling Dominican Revolutionary Party (Partido Revolucionario Dominicano; PRD), whose leader, José Francisco Peña Gómez, is secretary of the Socialist International's Latin American Bureau; and the Reformist Party (Partido Reformista), a centrist party headed by former President Joaquín Balaguer, who will run again. President Antonio Guzmán, when he took office in 1978, promised that he would serve only a single term, and the PRD elected Senator Salvador Jorge Blanco as its candidate. Both major parties promised to conduct an orderly campaign and to refrain from personal attacks that could lead to violence.

Under the constitution, all leftist groupings can operate legally in the country. Isa Conde travels frequently to various Latin American and Soviet bloc countries and regularly to conferences in Havana.

University of Miami   George Volsky

Ecuador

Politically 1981 was an eventful year in Ecuador. In January and February, a renewal of hostilities over the long-unresolved border conflict with Peru erupted. An eventual truce failed to eliminate the two countries' disagreement over the Cordillera del Cóndor boundary. On 24 May, President Jaime Roldós Aguilera was killed in a plane crash near the region under dispute. Constitutional continuity was maintained through the succession of Vice-President Osvaldo Hurtado Larrea, but the civilian regime continued to meet opposition in its effort to implement a modestly reformist program. In all of this, however, the role and the influence of Ecuador's Marxist sector were minimal.

The Communist Party of Ecuador (Partido Comunista del Ecuador; PCE) and its electoral arm, the Popular Democratic Union (Unión Democrática Popular), continued to support civilian government while sharply criticizing official policies. The PCE joined the nationalistic outcry against Peru at the time of the border fighting and supported the continuation of constitutionality in the replacement of Roldós by Hurtado. Otherwise, it attacked the administration for alleged ties with "classically reactionary and pro-fascist" business elements (*El Comercio*, 23 August). The only Marxist in the 69-member National Chamber of Representatives, Jorge Chiriboga Guerrero, did not always obey party directives, sometimes voting in support of administration policies.

Domestic Activities. After a lapse of eight years, despite a rule calling for congresses every two years, the PCE's Tenth Congress met in Guayaquil on 27–29 November. The longtime dictatorial rule of party founder Pedro Antonio Saad was overthrown, and former presidential candidate René Mauge was elected the new secretary general (*FBIS*, 4 December). Other members of the new PCE Executive Committee were José Solís Castro, Efraín Alvarez Fiallo, Milton Jijón Saavedra, Bolivar Bolanos Sánchez, Ghandi Burbano Burbano, Exavier Garaycoa Ortiz, Alfredo Castillo, and Freddy Almeidau (*El Tiempo*, 30 November 1981).

During the year, the PCE had difficulties in its attempts to hold together the Broad Front of the Left (Frente Amplio de la Izquierda; FADI), a coalition originally created for electoral purposes in 1979. The PCE devoted less time to congressional politics than to organized labor. It continues to control the Confederation of Ecuadorian Workers (Confederación de Trabajadores Ecuatorianos; CTE), which it founded in 1945. On 13 May, the CTE joined the other two national labor federations in calling a nationwide strike. Their coalition, the United Labor Front (Frente Unido de Trabajadores; FUT), presented three major demands: a rollback of consumer prices; higher income tax deductions; and a 75 percent increase in the minimum wage. Marxist labor leader Emilio Velasco declared on May Day that the "national government must announce whether it accepts all FUT demands since we shall not accept anything less from the regime" (*Expreso*, 3 May).

Approximately half of the industrial labor force observed the strike, but participation in other sectors was lower. The government termed the work stoppage illegal but did not employ force to prevent it. The FUT's demands were not met, and the labor movement remained fragmented. Of Ecuador's estimated economically active population of 2.8 million, only 1.1 million belong to the national federations, each of which suffers from internal divisions. The CTE continues to have problems with its affiliate in the capital province, the Pichincha Workers' Federation (Federación de Trabajadores de Pichincha), which is dominated by Maoists. Much the same is true of the National Union of Educators (Unión Nacional de Educadores), which generally stands closer to the Maoists' Democratic Popular Movement (Movimiento Popular Democrático; MPD).

The Federation of Ecuadorian University Students (Federación de Estudiantes Universitarios del Ecuador; FEUE) played only a minor role. It, too, was subject to Maoist influences, which affected its disunited leadership. Rubén Andrade, FEUE president, told interviewers during a May visit to Cuba that FEUE membership in the FUT was crucial, yet this was questionable at best. Pro-PCE student leaders sought to strengthen ties with pro-Moscow forces, and the FEUE joined the Continental Organization of Latin American Students (Organización Continental Latinoamericana de Estudiantes). In addition, Andrade pledged to "avail ourselves of this occasion to convey to Cuban students and youth the greeting of the Ecuadorian youth, who are in solidarity with their heroic anti-imperialist struggle" (*FBIS*, 6 May).

International Views. The PCE continued to support Soviet policies. During the Twenty-Sixth Congress of the Soviet party in Moscow, Pedro Antonio Saad reiterated PCE approval of Leonid Brezhnev's "brilliant report." Furthermore, "one cannot fail to note the profound sense of self-criticism and frankness in the speeches by the delegates when they point to the shortcomings and difficulties which still exist . . . Lenin's heirs are talking about the need to overcome them and at the same time are expressing faith in the Soviet people, who were the pathfinders of the building of a communist society" (ibid., 27 February).

The PCE, also a champion of the Castro regime, was perplexed by the dispute between Cuba and Ecuador. On 13 February, a group of Cubans seized Ecuador's Embassy in Havana, demanding treatment as political refugees. After the release of Ecuadorian hostages on 19 February, Cuban forces attacked with tear gas and occupied the building. Ecuador protested the action as a violation of its diplomatic immunity, and nationalistic sentiment was aroused in Quito. After complicated negotiations, the dispute was defused and the crisis passed (*Weekly Analysis*, 27 March). The PCE's comments were brief and ambiguous, given the anti-Cuban views provoked in Ecuador by the episode. Similarly, it made little comment on the government's decision to maintain relations with Havana only at the subambassadorial level.

There was less uncertainty in the PCE's reaction to the M-19 border affair. In March, 48 members of Colombia's M-19 guerrilla movement crossed the border into Ecuador, where they were captured by the Ecuadorian Army. M-19 spokesmen immediately threatened reprisals if the guerrillas were turned over to Colombian forces. A leaflet distributed to the press attacked government officials "who seek to distort the nature of our organization to justify the turning over of our companions to torture and death" (*FBIS*, 20 March). Without a "radical change" in Ecuador's attitude, government officials would "have to face the consequences." It was later reported that the M-19 group had split, with some of its members still at large in northern Ecuador. The government in Quito nonetheless promptly returned the captives to Colombian authorities. Ignoring criticism from domestic opponents, including the PCE, the administration promised to defend national territorial sovereignty and integrity in the event of another incursion (ibid., 26 March).

Other Marxist Parties. Competition and recrimination continued to mark relations between the PCE and the MPD. In addition, there were sporadic outbursts of ideological and doctrinal conflict from the two rival factions of the tiny Ecuadorian Revolutionary Socialist Party (Partido Socialista Revolucionario Ecuatoriano). Overall, 1981 demonstrated the continuing weakness and fragmentation of Ecuadorian Marxists. There are few indications that their role or influence can be expected to increase significantly in the near future.

The Pennsylvania State University   John D. Martz

El Salvador

In 1981 El Salvador faced grave political and economic problems growing out of the civil war between the civilian-military revolutionary junta, backed by the United States, and Marxist rebels, backed by Cuba and, indirectly, the Soviet Union. The war interfered with every aspect of life and destroyed the already shaky economy of the country. The gross national product, down 10 percent in 1980, was expected to fall even more rapidly in 1981. Actual starvation was the lot of many. The junta, at war with the left, was also menaced by the threat of a rightist coup. Right-wing death squads operated almost openly throughout government-occupied areas. Urged by the United States, the junta sought to bolster its position by scheduling elections to a constituent assembly for March 1982. It called on the legal parties of the left to participate, but they have, so far, refused, demanding that the junta step down and that guarantees of personal safety be given their candidates. In the ongoing climate of violence, it is difficult to see how meaningful elections can be held.

Marxist Movements. The oldest Marxist-Leninist movement in El Salvador is the Moscow-oriented Communist Party of El Salvador (Partido Comunista de El Salvador; PCES), whose secretary general is Shafik Jorge Handal. Since January 1980, the PCES has been the military arm of the movement; the political arm is the National Democratic Union (Unión Nacional Democrática; UDN), a frequent participant in past elections but now part of the forces opposed to the junta headed by Christian Democrat José Napoleón Duarte. The secretary general of the UDN is Mario Aguiñada Carranza. The largest of the Marxist-Leninist movements is the Popular Revolutionary Bloc (Bloque Popular Revolucionario; BPR) under Facundo Guardado y Guardado. Its military arm is the Popular Liberation Forces (Fuerzas Populares de Liberación; FPL) headed by Salvador Cayetano Carpio, a former secretary general of the PCES. Another large Marxist-Leninist movement is the Unified Popular Action Front (Frente Acción Popular Unificada; FAPU), led by Alberto Ramos; its military arm is the Armed Forces of National Resistence (Fuerzas Armadas de Resistencia Nacional; FARN) under the command of Fermán Cienfuegos. Other movements are the Popular Leagues of 28 February (Ligas Populares 28 de Febrero; LP-28) led by José Leoncio Pichinte, which is linked with the People's Revolutionary Arm (Ejército Popular Revolucionario; ERP) of Joaquín Villalobos, and the Popular Liberation Movement (Movimiento de Liberación Popular; MLP) under Fabio Castillo, whose military arm is the Central American Revolutionary Workers' Party (Partido Revolucionario de Trabajadores Centroamericanos; PRTC) commanded by Roberto Roca.

Since November 1980, the UDN, BPR, FAPU, LP-28, and MLP have been part of the umbrella group known as Revolutionary Coordination of the Masses (Coordinadora Revolucionaria de Masas; CRM). The CRM, in turn, is part of the larger opposition movement known as the Democratic Revolutionary Front (Frente Democrático Revolucionario; FDR), which includes non-Marxist elements as well. The FDR was founded on 16 April 1980. One element of the FDR is the small social democratic party known as the National Revolutionary Movement (Movimiento Nacional Revolucionario; MNR) led by Guillermo Manuel Ungo. A breakaway group from the ruling Christian Democratic Party, the Popular Social Christian Movement (Movimiento Popular Social Cristiano; MPSC), and a number of labor unions and civic groups also participate in the FDR. The president of the FDR is Guillermo Manuel Ungo, and the vice-president is Eduardo Calles. The most important body of the FDR is the Political Diplomatic Commission, a virtual government in exile headquartered in Mexico City. The chairman of the commission is Dr. Ungo; other members include Mario Aguiñada (UDN), Salvador Samayoa (BPR), José Napoleón Rodríguez Ruiz (FAPU), Rubén Ignacio Zamora Rivas (MPSC), Ana Guadalupe Martínez (LP-28), and Fabio Castillo (MLP).

The five military arms of the parties in the CRM (PCES, FPL, FARN, ERP, and PRTC) are under the command of the Unified Revolutionary Directorate (Directorio Revolucionario Unificada; DRU), composed of the heads of the five movements, plus additional members from each. The DRU was formed on 22 May 1980, but it did not embrace all of these movements until November of that year. The coordinator of the DRU is Salvador Cayetano Carpio. In November, DRU forces began to style themselves the Farabundo Martí National Liberation Front (Frente Farabundo Martí de Liberación Nacional; FMLN), named for the martyred leader of the 1932 communist revolt. The FMLN is currently engaged in a civil war against the anti-Marxist civilian-military revolutionary junta, which overthrew the last constitutional government in October 1979.

The Civil War. The civil war in El Salvador grew out of clashes between the military and the various guerrilla movements that now form the FMLN. It began on a large scale in May 1980. Over 30,000 persons, more than half noncombatants, have been killed, and the economy of the country has been devastated. In organizing for the conflict, the FMLN divided itself into four commands, each named for a geographical section and for a fallen hero of earlier revolts. The commands and the departments covered are: Western "Feliciano Ama" Front (Ahuachapán, Santa Ana, and Sonsonate departments), Central "Modesto Ramírez" Front (San Salvador, La Libertad, Chalatenango, and Cuscatlán), Near Central "Anastasio Aquino" Front (Cabañas, San Vicente, and La Paz), and Eastern "Francisco Sánchez" Front (Usulután, San Miguel, Morazán, and La Unión). Although the FMLN has not succeeded in permanently holding any major center of population, many municipalities have frequently changed hands. These include Cinquera and Victoria in Cabañas; La Luguna, Arcatao, and Las Vueltas in Chalatenango; Perquín, Torola, and Rosario in Morazán; and San Lorenzo in San Vicente. Those areas from which the military have been unable to dislodge the FMLN include El Cucurucho hill in Chalatenango, Guazapa volcano in Cuscatlán, Siguatepeque hill in San Vicente, and Conchagua volcano in La Unión.

During the last part of 1980, the FMLN contented itself with hit-and-run raids, while it consolidated its mountainous positions and built up a supply of arms; but on 10 January 1981, it launched what it billed as its "final offensive" and called for a general strike to begin in government-held regions on 12 January. The object of the assault, as Fermán Cienfuegos of the FARN explained it, was "not to take the big cities, but to surround them, just as happened to Saigon" (*NYT*, 27 December 1980). The strength of the offensive took the Salvadoran army by surprise, and casualties ran high. The Defense Ministry announced that 142 soldiers had been killed in the first nine days of the fighting (AFP, Paris, 19 January; *FBIS*, 21 January). The FMLN seized Suchitoto in Cuscatlán and held San Francisco Gotera, the capital of Morazán, for four days. Under Capt. Francisco Mena Sandoval, the leader of the October 1979 coup, the garrison of Santa Ana, the nation's second largest city, revolted, destroyed the military installation, and joined the rebels. The city of Chalatenango, while not taken, was under FMLN siege for several days. On 14 January, Duarte announced that "at least one hundred foreign guerrillas" had landed on Cuco beach in San Miguel, presumably from Nicaragua. The FDR denied the report, as did the government of Nicaragua. (AFP, Paris, 14 January; *FBIS*, 15 January.) The army eventually beat back all the FMLN assaults; the general strike failed, although it did tie up some sectors of the economy temporarily. "We have not succeeded in carrying out sufficiently large-scale military actions to make a general strike possible," admitted Shafik Handal of the PCES (*L'Humanité*, Paris, 29 January).

The fact that this had been billed as the "final offensive" made its failure all the more embarrassing to the FMLN, which quickly changed the title to the "January offensive." Shafik Handal stated that the FMLN had been able to gain important military experience, wiped out some junta garrisons, contracted the junta's territory, and convinced the world that the FMLN was serious (*Horizont*, East Berlin, no. 13). Nevertheless, the FMLN found diplomatic support ebbing in the wake of this failure and was reported to be short of arms (*NYT*, 16 and 22 January). On the other hand, the government's amnesty program, which ran to 11 March, failed to convince many to lay down their arms.

In early February, the government forces went over to the offensive, with Col. Jaime Abdul Gutiérrez, the vice-president of the junta and commander in chief of the armed forces, promising "a more aggressive search and destroy type of war" (*News Gazette*, San Salvador, 15 February). But most observers, including the Pentagon, considered the regular military forces ill prepared and poorly trained and agreed that they had little hope of overcoming the rebels (*NYT*, 21 February; *CSM*, 16 March). In fact, the army's drive into Morazán stalled when troops were unable to fight their way across the Sapo river. Attempts to take the Guazapa volcano region were equally unsuccessful. (*Granma*, Havana, 12 and 19 April.)

The forces of the FMLN spent the spring regrouping. Each military command now had three distinct types of personnel; commando strike forces or shock troops for regular combat, self-defense militias for holding the "liberated" areas, and guerrilla-terrorist bands for operating within enemy-held territory. The last went on a rampage of violence, designed to destroy the fragile communications and power structures of the country. Bridges were dynamited, buses were destroyed, power lines downed, and generators smashed. On 19 July the FMLN launched its rainy season offensive, a much better prepared attack than the January offensive. The municipality of Perquín in Morazán was overrun and 24 of its garrison captured on 10 August. Not until 18 August did the government recover the city (*La Prensa Gráfica*, San Salvador, 18 August).

In subsequent months, guerrilla activity consisted of scattered raids, ambushes, bombings, and the like, especially of power lines and bridges. Large parts of the country were blacked out for considerable periods, and traffic to many places was impeded; an important blow was the destruction on 15 October of the principal bridge over the Lempa river dividing the country. On the same day, the curfew was lifted.

The U.S. government, in a White Paper issued in February, charged that El Salvador represented a classic case of indirect communist aggression. The major point of the document was the quantity of arms supplied to the FMLN from the Soviet bloc. Although the FMLN purchases arms on the international market and often seizes government weapons, a major supply appeared to be coming from Cuba through Nicaragua. The capture of two planes in January appeared to bear this out, although the FMLN and the Nicaraguan government both steadfastly denied such reports. (*WP*, 1 March.) The United States' pressure on Nicaragua appeared to diminish the flow from that source, but by April a new route had been opened up through Honduras (*NYT*, 30 April).

International Contacts. The leaders of both the FDR and the FMLN traveled extensively during 1981 seeking international support. One of the most tireless was Shafik Handal, who flew to several Eastern European capitals, including Budapest and East Berlin, during the January offensive. In March he met with Yassir Arafat in Lebanon; Handal, himself of Palestinian origin, received a pledge of Palestinian solidarity with the people of El Salvador. Marisol Galindo of the FMLN received similar pledges of solidarity from Col. Moammar Khadafy of Libya. Rubén Zamora of the FDR traveled to India in February and presented the rebels' case before a conference of nonaligned nations. In September he traveled to South American capitals. A number of leaders, including Guillermo Ungo himself, attended a meeting of the Socialist International, to which the MNR belongs, in Panama in March. The most significant diplomatic coup of the FDR was the joint Mexican-French declaration in August that the two powers "recognize that the alliance between the FMLN and the FDR is a representative political force ready to assume the obligations and exercise the rights that derive from that representation" (*NOTIMEX*, Mexico City, 28 August; *FBIS*, 31 August). Efforts were then launched to get other countries to adhere to this declaration, but by November they had borne little fruit. Led by Venezuela, over a dozen Latin American countries protested the French-Mexican démarche as interference in El Salvador's internal affairs.

Eastern Connecticut State College   Thomas P. Anderson

Grenada

Led by Maurice Bishop, the left-wing New Jewel Movement (NJM) seized power on 13 March 1979. In a nearly bloodless coup d'etat, it overthrew the government of Sir Eric Gairy, who had dominated local politics for much of the previous 25 years and who had engineered Grenada's independence in 1974. Gairy had come to power initially through the support of his Grenada United Labour Party (GULP), formed in 1952. He continued to lead the country through GULP, but increasingly ties of loyalty to himself became more important than party goals and ideals.

The extreme aspects of personalist leadership under Gairy set the scene for the 1979 coup. He was removed from office in 1962, for example, for excessive and unauthorized expenditures of public funds. Upon re-election to office in 1967, Gairy began to consolidate his control through a combination of patronage and strong-arm tactics, notably through the "mongoose men." His campaign for independence, moreover, met with stiff opposition, including from Bishop and the NJM, out of concern that Gairy would curtail human rights and freedoms. Intense political, social, and industrial tensions accompanied the move toward independence in 1974, with the NJM leading much of the opposition, a setting that produced riots, shootings, and the imprisonment of opposition leaders. Independence did not reduce the conflict between Gairy and his opposition, and the 1979 coup occurred when Gairy was in New York to attend a U.N. meeting. It was the first left-wing coup in the Caribbean since the Cuban revolution of 1959.

The New Jewel Movement. The NJM resulted in 1973 from the merger of two opposition groups formed in 1972. The first, Joint Effort for Welfare, Education, and Liberation (JEWEL), emphasized ties with agricultural workers, and the core of its program was an agricultural cooperative. It hoped to pressure the government to change its one-man operation, and it displayed a distinctly Marxist bent, stressing Marx's concept of property held in common. The second group, the Movement for the Assemblies of the People (MAP), was led by two lawyers, Bishop and Kendrick Radix. This organization tended toward socialism but was reluctant to identify publicly with "scientific socialism." The merger brought together various disaffected urban and rural middle-class elements united under Bishop's leadership in opposition to Gairy.

The NJM's 1973 manifesto is both socialist and nationalist, committed to destruction of class relationships in Grenadian society through a number of changes, including democratization of the political and economic systems through the establishment of "people's assemblies" and the nationalization of all foreign-owned hotels, banks, and insurance companies. There appears to have been some internal ambivalence toward the socialist aspects of the manifesto since its publication, owing to the recognized need for support from the business community in Grenada. The NJM, moreover, includes some businessmen as well as Roman Catholics, which tends to produce a conservative influence in Grenada. Finally, some members early expressed reservations about the impact of a full commitment to "scientific socialism" on a mass following since Gairy referred to the NJM as "communists" before the coup and continued to do so afterwards.

Leadership and Organization. Following the 1979 coup, a People's Revolutionary Government (PRG) was established. Its leadership reflected the previous merger of JEWEL with MAP. Bishop assumed the premiership of the PRG, as well as the foreign affairs, national security, home affairs, information, and culture portfolios. Radix became minister of legal affairs. Members of JEWEL included in the new PRG were Unison Whitman (minister of agriculture, tourism, and fisheries) and Selwyn Strachan (minister of communications, works, and labor). Bernard Coard, formerly a university lecturer, became minister of trade, finance, industry, and planning. Other members were drawn from the rural working class, which is not surprising in light of the strong emphasis placed on improved food production in the NJM manifesto.

Domestic Attitudes and Activities. In the period following these appointments, Grenada's governmental organization increasingly mirrored characteristics found in Cuba as the revolution evolved in that country. Given the close links formed between Cuba and Grenada after diplomatic relations were established in April 1979, it seems likely that either Cuban advisers played a major role in this evolution or that Cuba's governmental and mass organizations served as a model for Bishop's PRG. The National Youth Organization, which Bishop described as the "vanguard organization for youth," became a member of the Socialist International in September 1980 (*Intercontinental Press*, 7 September). The National Women's Organization is the leading mass organization for women in Grenada. Grenada's NJM Young Pioneers group, which unites children in an effort to instill in them specific virtues deemed necessary to keep the revolution on track—discipline, confidence, commitment, leadership, and patriotism—is strikingly similar to Cuba's children's organization. Grenada's "agro-proletariat" was forged into the Agricultural and General Workers Union; many of its members have been cited for their work on Sundays in community work brigades, akin to the voluntary work groups found in Cuba.

The NJM also became active in organizing fund-raising events and participating in seminars, education courses, and other activities aimed at raising the political consciousness of the population. In still another change reflecting the Cuban model, the NJM linked itself to the new National Community Development Committees, which monitor the benefits coming to each village in Grenada. They appear somewhat akin to the Committees for the Defense of the Revolution in Cuba, but without the degree of interpersonal monitoring found there. The NJM, not surprisingly, is known in Grenada as the "vanguard party" (*El Dia*, Mexico City, 12 June).

Grenada's Economic Difficulties. The NJM faced serious economic strains once it assumed power. The Gairy government's poor performance in economic development was one of the major points of NJM opposition. At the time of the 1979 coup, for example, over 16,000 people, or some 50 percent of the island's workforce, were unemployed. The country was running a serious trade deficit, the national debt had grown to EC $60 million (one East Caribbean dollar equaled U.S. $0.38 in October 1981), and real per capita income had fallen approximately 3 percent per year throughout the 1970s. Most food was imported at high prices, hospitals were poorly equipped, schools were reportedly on the verge of collapse and without sufficient textbooks, while corruption and waste appeared widespread throughout the Gairy government.

Behind this bleak picture lie certain constants of Grenada's economy. As an island of 133 square miles with a population of approximately 111,000, it does not boast a large internal market. Its small size, moreover, is matched by a lack of natural resources. Per capita income in 1975 of U.S. $390 made it one of the poorest countries in the Western Hemisphere. With no industries to speak of, it is essentially an agricultural exporting country, chiefly bananas, cocoa, and spices. Yet it must import food to feed its population. Tourism, which had expanded in the 1960s, virtually collapsed in 1974 during the political instability surrounding independence. Between 1974 and 1979, the tourist industry recovered somewhat, but not to the levels of the 1960s.

Bishop's PRG sought to implement development plans in order to address these conditions, not only through new grass-roots mass political organizations following the Cuban model, but also through other domestic and international policies.

NJM Economic Policies. After the 1979 coup, the NJM defined the first stage of its revolution as the "anti-imperialist, national, democratic phrase" (ibid.). This definition meant in essence a transition toward greatly expanded state control over Grenada's economy, yet certainly not the total demise of the private sector. In pursuit of an enlarged role for the state, the Bishop government began to concentrate on agriculture, fishing, and tourism. By June 1981, 31 state farms comprised approximately one-third of the land cultivated in Grenada, most of it previously owned by Gairy. The government also opened a coffee-processing plant, an agro-industrial plant producing nectars and juices, and a fish-processing plant—all under state auspices. As for tourism, the NJM envisioned a new kind in which the type of tourist attracted to Grenada would no longer be predominantly white, well-endowed Americans and Europeans, but rather nonwhite, lower-income travelers interested in Grenada's culture, cuisine, and development activities. This "work tourism" would be integrated into the local economy, with the food, entertainment, and direction being strictly Grenadian.

The NJM's economic plans called for massive changes in education and training, again reminiscent of events in neighboring Cuba, especially since some of these changes occurred with Cuban support. The PRG launched a literacy campaign through the new People's Education Center, which was aimed at teaching everyone to read, with subsequent emphasis on language arts and mathematics. Other training schools were opened for the newly established people's militia, the agricultural and agroindustrial training school was enlarged significantly, and an in-service teacher-training school to increase the number of teachers and to strengthen the individual and collective consciousness of Grenada's masses was established. Indeed, as educational reorganization proceeded, the PRG predicted an increase in the masses' unity and political awareness.

These social and economic changes were linked to new objectives in the international economic field. The PRG government's attempt to secure new loans abroad met with some success, including U.S. $1.5 million from the Caribbean Development Bank for a water project; $1 million from the Organization of Petroleum Exporting Countries to initiate a national bus service; and $650,000 from the International Monetary Fund (IMF) to support the government's 1980 financial program. Syria and Libya gave EC $10 million for various development projects. After joining the Nonaligned Movement during its 1979 summit meeting in Havana, Grenada began to press for the objectives of the New International Economic Order. The PRG also signed agreements with Venezuela on energy, tourism, education, and construction of a new international airport.

Despite these efforts, the PRG faced severe economic strains after the 1979 coup. The world cocoa price dropped 55 percent during 1981, while nutmeg and mace exports fell off sharply due to recession in the industrialized countries. Foul weather had meanwhile reduced the cocoa and banana crops in 1981, following unseasonal, heavy rain in 1980. The United States also blocked a PRG request to the IMF for $7.6 million in special drawing rights, contending that the PRG's balance of payments situation did not warrant the loan. These conditions led to new economic efforts in 1981, including cabinet changes to increase efficiency and output, despite what Bishop characterized as "U.S. imperialist plans at isolating the Grenada revolution, destabilizing the situation in Grenada and overthrowing the people's power" (*FBIS*, 1 September).

Civil Discontent. Labor problems did not make life easier for the PRG. The Public Workers Union's strike in March 1981, for example, followed other labor unrest by unions, such as the teachers, who had been demanding better salaries since December 1980. Counterdemonstrations were organized by "thousands of Grenadians" protesting against the action of teachers and other public servants. (Ibid., 6 March.) In apparently unrelated incidents in November 1980, five members of the PRG's security forces were killed by "terrorist" groups.

Considerable concern exists elsewhere in the Caribbean about Grenada's lack of a constitution and the absence of elections. In defending his decision to suspend the constitution, Bishop described the old one as a "farce" and a "sham" that did not guarantee the rights it was supposed to. By late 1981 Bishop had not given any timetable for introducing a new constitution.

New Military Orientations. Following the lead of Cuba, the PRG completely disbanded the old Gairy army and began to build a new one based on "the people," comprising, to a large extent, unemployed youth. At the same time, the PRG formed a people's militia strongly resembling Cuba's new Territorial Militia, which also began to take shape during the same period. These military reorganizations on the Cuban model were not unusual since Bishop not only established formal and very close ties with Cuba after the 1979 coup, but also characterized his coup as "a successful Moncada," referring to Castro's unsuccessful 1953 assault on a Cuban army barracks that marked the spiritual beginning of the Cuban revolution. By August 1981, Bishop was urging the strengthening of the people's militia in order that Grenadians might continue to increase their consciousness, as well as their level of training and discipline, in order to protect their homeland and "the revolution." In February 1981, combined army, militia, police, coast guard and fire-fighting units held the first joint military maneuvers since the 1979 coup. These exercises simulated the repelling of an attack on the island. In July, the island was placed on a war footing, based on the PRG's claim that the United States was preparing for military action against the country during military exercises on the island of Vieques off Puerto Rico. In September, thousands of Grenadians took part in another military maneuver as part of the effort to respond to alleged U.S. plans of "aggression." (Ibid., 21 August, 10 September.)

International Views and Positions. The outstanding characteristic of the PRG's foreign relations is its close ties with Cuba. Following the establishment of diplomatic relations one month after the 1979 coup, lines of cooperation and communication between the two countries were solidified. Grenada, to illustrate the point, was the only Latin American or Caribbean country to vote with Cuba against the January 1980 U.N. resolution deploring the Soviet intervention in Afghanistan. Among the frequent visits of leading government officials between Havana and St. George's were Maurice Bishop's attendance at the Sixth Nonaligned Countries Conference in 1979 and the Second Congress of the Communist Party of Cuba in December 1980 and the arrival in March 1981 of a delegation headed by Sergio del Valle Jiménez, a member of the Politburo of the Communist Party of Cuba, to attend the second anniversary celebrations of the PRG's revolution. By January 1981 Cuba and the PRG had established weekly flights between the two countries by Air Cubana. The two governments also decided to abandon the use of visas in their bilateral relations.

These ties produced a significant Cuban involvement in Grenada's economy, politics, and society. Cuba began to assist the PRG in health, education, and fishing. An estimated fifteen doctors, dentists, and technicians served in Grenada for a year during 1980–81. The Cubans donated eleven fishing boats to Grenada and helped to establish a fishing school and a fish-processing plant. Such aid is, in one sense, a kind of Soviet technology transfer program to Grenada; the USSR provided substantial fisheries aid and training to Cuba, which that country has begun to use in its own foreign aid program to other Caribbean islands, including Grenada.

The Cubans provided political indoctrination to Grenada's newly formed militia, and by 1980 approximately a hundred Cuban military advisers had arrived in Grenada to assist in training a 2,000-person army. Havana's help in expanding the PRG's radio station, Radio Free Grenada, will make its

75-kilowatt transmitter the most powerful radio facility in the eastern Caribbean. Cuba is expected to use Radio Free Grenada to relay news, commentaries, and cultural programs to a wide audience in the southern Caribbean and in Latin America.

Cuban involvement in the construction of Grenada's new international airport attracted the most attention. The airport is designed to accommodate aircraft as large as Boeing 747s and will replace a dilapidated landing strip serving only small planes. The PRG argues that the airport project will alleviate widespread unemployment and boost a slackening tourist industry, one of the pillars of the PRG's economic recovery program. The number of Cuban construction workers reached, by some accounts, an estimated thousand by 1980. This project raised the suspicion of Western observers, who envisioned the airport as a military air base available to Cuba and giving it a strong position at each end of the Caribbean. Critics of the project also argued that Grenada simply does not have the tourist infrastructure to accommodate the large numbers of tourists that the airport is capable of serving. The international debate over Grenada's airport continued during 1980 and 1981, with Cuba contributing building materials and teams of construction workers. Cuba's own economic difficulties have, however, limited the amount of support. The project was far from completed as 1981 progressed.

The presence of Cubans in Grenada and the help provided by Havana are highly praised by Bishop's PRG. In December 1980, Bishop lauded the Cubans, for example, stating that "Cuba has been a beacon for us in Grenada . . . It has reminded us of the central role of the party in building the revolution . . . of the critical importance of being the genuine vanguard of the people . . . of building and maintaining close links with the people through the mass organizations." He went on to state that "there can be absolutely no doubt that without the leadership and guidance of the Communist Party of Cuba, the heroic vanguard of the Cuban people, there would not have been such a dramatic improvement in health, education, economic development and diversification, the raising of political and class consciousness and the deep-rooted development of a genuine spirit of proletarian internationalism." (Ibid., 24 December 1980.)

Relations with the Soviet Union and East European countries proceeded parallel with those with Cuba. The PRG established direct trade links with the USSR, following talks on economic cooperation in St. George's with a visiting Soviet delegation in January 1980. Subsequent trade agreements with Moscow covered the purchase of nutmeg, one of Grenada's chief exports, and an agreement to give the PRG agricultural equipment worth U.S. $1 million. More limited aid goes to the fishing industry. Moscow also delivered new police cars to the PRG. In September 1981, Bishop cited the PRG's "very warm relations with the USSR" and averred that Moscow "marches in the vanguard of the struggle for peace, security, for relaxation of international tension and social progress—the struggle to enable every people to have the right to independent development" (ibid., 1 September). The PRG meanwhile expanded diplomatic relations with Bulgaria and Poland during 1980. By December 1980, about two hundred students were studying abroad on scholarships in Cuba and in Hungary and other East European countries.

Relations with the United States, in contrast, began to deteriorate dramatically from the early days of the revolution. The United States, for its part, deplored the close Cuban-PRG ties, the growing number of Cubans in Grenada, and especially the efforts of Cubans in connection with the airport and the strategic implications suggested by Havana's distinct presence. PRG leaders, in return, accused the United States of a wide range of acts that, in the perception of the new revolutionary government, constituted major threats to the PRG's survival. Among the acts most sharply criticized were (1) late recognition of the PRG; (2) warnings against establishment of close ties with Cuba; (3) an alleged Central Intelligence Agency plan to undermine the PRG through propaganda, economic sabotage, terrorism, and counterrevolutionary activity; (4) the failure to extradite Gairy to Grenada; (5) blocking of the PRG's efforts to secure European Economic Community aid for its international airport; (6)

general "economic imperialism" in the Caribbean and Central America; and (7) alleged preparations for military action against Grenada in July–September 1981.

As 1981 progressed, U.S. "imperialism" increasingly became the focus of Grenada's foreign policy. Bishop stressed the U.S. "threat" to the Nonaligned Movement, depicting the United States as viewing the movement as a "mortal enemy," and accused the United States of trying to be the "policeman of the world." During a cabinet reshuffle in July 1981 to meet the alleged U.S. "threat," the PRG formed a new Ministry of National Mobilization to ensure that the program and policies of the PRG and the revolution are executed effectively. (Ibid., 7 May, 30 July, 10 September.)

The PRG began to support other left-wing groups and governments in the Caribbean and Central America soon after its coup. It gave its fullest support to the left-wing guerrilla movement in El Salvador, emphasizing that the majority of Salvadorans—"patriots, democrats, progressives, socialists, and Communists"—were fighting against "a small minority backed by the military, U.S. imperialism, and certain Christian Democrats in the region" (*Intercontinental Press*, 2 February). The PRG also sided strongly with the Sandinistas and the Government of National Reconstruction in Nicaragua. During Sandino Day observances in February 1980 in Managua, Bishop spoke at a mass rally. He visited Nicaragua again in July to mark the first anniversary of the Sandinista overthrow of Anastasio Somoza. Bishop has said that Grenada's relations with the Nicaraguan revolution started one month before the Sandinista victory, when the Provisional Government of Nicaragua was established. Since then, Grenada has sent teachers to Nicaragua to aid in the literacy campaign among the English-speaking population along the Atlantic coast. (*Granma Weekly Review*, Havana, 11 January.)

The PRG has extended its sense of proletarian internationalism into the Caribbean and Central America in other ways. It hosted a major three-day conference on Caribbean affairs in January 1981, attended by representatives of a substantial number of nationalist, radical, democratic socialist, and Marxist-Leninist parties in the region as well as trade unions and other "progressive" groups. The conference concluded with pledges of solidarity in opposing attempts to "destabilize" the revolutions in Cuba, Nicaragua, and Grenada; to prevent a "people's victory" in El Salvador, and to thwart "progressive" changes elsewhere in the region. As might be expected, U.S. "imperialism" was a key focus during this conference. (*Caribbean Contact*, February.) The PRG has emphasized that its foreign policy indeed is based, like Cuba's, on a spirit of "internationalism," and it especially stresses the importance of "internationalism" to Caribbean revolutionaries who looked "forward to a change in the world." Bishop argues that internationalism in the early 1980s means ensuring "the victory of the people of El Salvador" and the success of "other revolutions and other revolutionary people around the world fighting for their own liberation." (*FBIS*, 13 January.) Toward this end, the PRG has contributed EC $50,000 to the Nonaligned Movement's Namibia Liberation Fund out of a sense of "internationalist responsibility" and joined the Socialist International.

Not all Caribbean governments were sympathetic to the left-wing forces released with the 1979 coup. In November 1980, Barbadan Prime Minister Tom Adams, for example, called on the PRG to hold general elections, as promised soon after the 1979 coup. Bishop reacted by accusing the Barbadan government of interfering in the PRG's internal affairs and dubbed Adams an Uncle Tom to the then incoming Reagan administration (ibid., 25 November 1980). This conflict had escalated by early 1981, with the PRG accusing Barbados of complicity with the Western powers in preparing for war in the Caribbean. Several Caribbean newspapers have demonstrated distinct opposition to the PRG, including the Trinidad *Express*, the Jamaica *Gleaner*, and the Barbadan *Advocate* and *Nation* (ibid., 31 July).

Publications. The PRG claims that the press is not restricted in any way in Grenada. Yet the opposition paper, *Torchlight*, was closed in 1979 under the justification that it had begun to incite the

Rastafarian movement to counterrevolutionary activity. The PRG's positions are expressed in its own newspaper, the *Free West Indian*. The PRG asserts that the paper is frequently confiscated or destroyed on arrival in other Caribbean countries.

Biography. *Maurice Rupert Bishop.* Bishop was born on 29 May 1944, the son of Rupert Bishop and Alimenta Marie Bishop. Educated in Grenada, he was awarded a gold medal in 1962 for general achievement. He studied law in England, where he obtained the LL.B. degree from the University of London in 1966 and his professional qualification from Gray's Inn in 1966.

While in England, Bishop was president of the West Indian Students Society at his college and a leading member of the campaign against racial discrimination and of the Standing Conference of West Indian Organizations. In addition, he was cofounder of a legal aid clinic in London and was responsible for the establishment of the Assembly of Youth After Truth, an organization of young people concerned with major economic, political, and social issues in Grenada.

When Bishop returned to Grenada in March 1970, he immediately became involved in political life. He founded the New Jewel Movement, which challenged Eric Gairy's ruling Grenada Labour Party. He became leader of the opposition in the Grenada House of Representatives in 1976. The New Jewel Movement overthrew the Gairy government in March 1979.

Bishop is married to Angela Redhead and has a son and a daughter.

Hoover Institution   W. Raymond Duncan

Guatemala

The communist party in Guatemala, renamed the Guatemalan Party of Labor (Partido Guatemalteco del Trabajo; PGT) in 1952, originated in the predominantly communist-controlled Socialist Labor Unification founded in 1921. The PGT operated legally between 1951 and 1954, playing an active role in the administration of Guatemalan President Jacobo Arbenz. Outlawed in 1954 following the overthrow of Arbenz, it has since operated underground. Although the party has some influence among students, intellectuals, and workers, its role in national affairs is insignificant. According to U.S. intelligence sources, the PGT has about 750 members.

Guerrilla and General Violence. Although military and press reports do not always distinguish among them, four guerrilla groups have been active in Guatemala in recent years. The Revolutionary Armed Forces, which is the military arm of the PGT, and the Rebel Armed Forces (Fuerzas Armadas Rebeldes; FAR), some of whose members have claimed affiliation with the PGT, are relatively inactive. The FAR probably has fewer than one hundred members, plus several hundred sympathizers. A FAR communiqué in September claimed that its forces had inflicted 330 casualties on the

Guatemalan Army and occupied four villages in El Petén in the previous four months. including the archeological center at Tikal (Havana International Service, 29 September). Apart from these sporadic operations in El Petén, the FAR did not figure prominently in Guatemala's guerrilla activity in 1981.

A third guerrilla organization is the Armed People's Organization (Organización del Pueblo en Armas; ORPA), which announced the beginning of military actions in September 1979. Based on information published in its clandestine newspaper, *Erupción*, and communiqués distributed to the Guatemalan press, ORPA continued to increase the scope and intensity of its military operations in 1981.

The most active and largest of Guatemala's guerrilla organizations is the Guerrilla Army of the Poor (Ejército Guerrillero de los Pobres; EGP), which is believed to contain remnants of leftist guerrilla groups that succumbed to the effective counterinsurgency tactics of the Guatemalan military during the late 1960s and the "law and order" administration of Gen. Carlos Arana Osorio (1970–1974). The EGP does not claim direct affiliation with the PGT, nor is there any compelling evidence for such an inference.

Although not a guerrilla organization, the 31 January People's Front (FP-31) was created in 1981 "to combat the government at the political level." Taking its name from the occupation of the Spanish Embassy in 1980, the FP-31 is composed of student, worker, and peasant organizations, including the Robín García Student Front, the Felipe Antonio García Revolutionary Workers' Nuclei, and the Committee for Peasant Unity. During a visit to Havana in June, a member of its Coordinating Committee claimed that the front was active in 10 of the country's 22 departments (ibid., 25 June). The FP-31 operates underground, with a secret organizational structure. Its activities in 1981 included the explosion of propaganda bombs, the disruption of traffic, popular mobilizations, and acts of sabotage intended to weaken the economy (*El Imparcial*, 19 January; *Prensa Libre*, 11 May; AFP, 14 September). FP-31 leaders claimed in August to have consolidated the front's organization and increased its popular support. The front has assumed certain aspects of the internal work of the Democratic Front Against Repression (Frente Democrática Contra la Represión; FDCR), many of whose leaders are now in exile (*Barricada*, Managua, 10 August).

According to documents allegedly captured from the EGP, the major guerrilla movements met in late 1980 to consider unification. Guerrilla leaders issued a joint communiqué in January calling for ideological and tactical agreement (AFP, 29 January). Despite periodic statements of solidarity, the guerrillas have been unable to resolve their differences satisfactorily. In July, the ORPA accused the EGP of attempting to take over the leadership of the revolutionary movement. The ORPA also blamed the EGP for the disclosure of some thirty guerrilla camps and urban hideouts, which allowed security forces to recover large quantities of weapons and ammunition (ACAN, 23 July; AFP, 14 September). A Jesuit priest, Luís Pellecer, introduced at a government press conference in October as a "high-ranking leader of the EGP," confirmed that "ideological and basic differences" continue to exist among the principal guerrilla groups (*El Imparcial*, 10 October).

Military officials reported an increase in guerrilla activity early in the year, especially in the departments of El Quiché, Sololá, Huehuetenango, Quezaltenango, Alta Verapaz, and Chimaltenango. Guatemala's defense minister, Gen. Aníbal Guevara, reported in April that guerrilla groups were trying to upset the national economy by damaging oil installations (*Prensa Libre*, 29 April). By June guerrilla sources claimed to be operating in nineteen departments. President Romeo Lucas García accused Cuba of encouraging the intensification of guerrilla actions and providing training for Guatemalan guerrillas. He further charged that the Soviet Union was behind Cuba's attempt to overthrow the governments of Central America (*Diario el Gráfico*, 3 June). The president also maintained that the Soviet Union "has always seen Guatemala as a strategic area for an attack on the United States," with Cuba and Nicaragua being used to serve this plan (*Prensa Libre*, 14 July).

According to information disclosed by Pellecer, guerrilla forces planned to implement a "final offensive" in late 1981 or early 1982. Chief of Staff Gen. Benedicto Lucas García charged that Cuban President Fidel Castro had ordered Guatemala's guerrilla organizations to unite but had lost contact with them after security forces dismantled numerous hideouts. Lucas estimated the EGP to be the strongest guerrilla branch, with some 1,200 potential combatants (ibid., 10 October). According to the U.S. State Department, Guatemala's combined guerrilla forces total about two thousand (*NYT*, 10 May). The Guatemalan Army announced that it was "fully prepared" to face a guerrilla offensive. Infantry units supported by helicopters staged their own offensive in October against guerrilla groups operating in the mountains of El Quiché, Huehuetenango, and San Marcos. General Lucas said that the antiguerrilla campaign would continue "until all guerrilla groups are eradicated." He claimed that guerrilla forces had been reduced by "20 to 30 percent" as a result of desertions and casualties inflicted by military units (ACAN, 26 October).

Press reports indicate that Indians continued to join the guerrilla movement in 1981, although their numbers are difficult to determine. The ORPA appears to be the most active group in the recruitment of Indians, who make up approximately half the country's population. Neither the government nor the guerrillas seem capable of any decisive military action at this time. The guerrillas have operated more successfully in the countryside than in the cities, although the number of mobile, well-trained forces is still limited. As yet, they do not appear to have the capacity to launch a major coordinated offensive, although EGP units reportedly carried out simultaneous attacks on the cities of Sololá, Mazatenango, and Escuintla in late October (*El Imparcial*, 30 October). Military authorities reported in December that the Army had thwarted a guerrilla plan to take over several western departments and establish a provisional government (ACAN, 2 December).

Politically motivated killings involving leftist groups and right-wing paramilitary organizations have been a common feature of Guatemalan daily life since the mid-1960s. Many observers date the origin of the present violence to the 1954 coup in which Arbenz was deposed. Others point to guerrilla movements dating from the early 1960s and revived in 1975 following charges of electoral fraud. Political life has become increasingly violent since President Lucas García assumed power in July 1978. Spokesmen for the FDCR claim that 3,700 people have been killed for political reasons during his presidency, not to mention the large number of missing persons (ibid., 10 March). Other sources place the number of deaths in excess of five thousand (*Pravda*, 22 March; *NYT*, 3 May). For the period since 1966, the death toll is numbered at 30,000.

Right-wing terror is carried out primarily by the clandestine Secret Anticommunist Army (ESA) and self-proclaimed death squads, evidently the successors of similar right-wing paramilitary organizations dating back to the 1960s. In recent years, the systematic assassination of people in opinion-making positions has decimated university faculties, student associations, rural cooperatives, trade unions, peasant leagues, and the leadership of moderate and left-of-center political organizations, such as the Social Democratic and Christian Democratic parties. Guatemala's alarming rate of political violence continued in 1981, but security forces responsible for public order made no arrests or investigations. In a two-week period in Chimaltenango in March, 171 people were killed and 43 others "disappeared" after being kidnapped (*NYT*, 9 May). According to reports, the number of deaths increased by 50 percent during August in El Quiché, Huehuetenango, San Marcos, and Suchitepéquez. Although accurate data are difficult to obtain, authorities reported that over forty persons were killed as a result of political violence during the last weekend in August (ACAN, 31 August). The ESA reappeared in southern Guatemala in August, expressing its commitment to fighting communism. Some forty people were threatened, a number of whom reportedly fled the country or left for other departments (*El Imparcial*, 22 August).

The threatening positions adopted by both the extreme left and the extreme right have led to a growing polarization that may eventually lead to armed confrontation. While the guerrillas do not yet appear strong enough to pose an immediate threat to the government, the military's willingness to condone repressive measures against peasants and independently minded professionals seems likely to work in the long run to the guerrillas' advantage by drawing public sympathy to them at a time when they do not enjoy widespread support.

Leadership and Organization. Little information is available on PGT leaders or structure. Since 1972, two general secretaries and nineteen ranking members of the Central Committee have "disappeared," apparently the victims of assassination. The current general secretary is Carlos González. Other prominent members of the Central Committee are Antonio Castro, Daniel Ríos, José Cardoza Aguilar, Otto Sánchez, Jorge Muñoz, A. Bauer País, Antonio Fuentes, Pedro González Torres, and Pablo Hernández.

The PGT has a youth auxiliary, the Patriotic Youth of Labor (Juventud Patriótica del Trabajo; JPT). Student agitators are active at the secondary and university levels but disclaim direct affiliation with the PGT. Student leaders supported by the PGT have been unsuccessful in recent years in gaining control of the influential Association of University Students (AEU), although the AEU's statements on domestic issues tend to be strongly critical of the government and its inability to control right-wing extremists. Members of the JPT are believed to be active in the Robín García Student Front and other student organizations involved with the FP-31. In April, treasury police seized a printing firm in Guatemala City for allegedly printing propaganda pamphlets for the JPT (*Prensa Libre*, 11 April). University students, professors, and administrators have been prime targets for kidnapping and murder in recent years. So many members of Guatemala's academic community are currently in exile in Costa Rica that serious consideration has been given to establishing a "branch" of San Carlos University there.

The PGT also controls the clandestine Guatemalan Autonomous Federation of Trade Unions, a small and relatively unimportant labor organization. The federation affiliated with the communist-front World Federation of Trade Unions in October 1974. The National Committee for Labor Unity, which includes some seventy unions, has become the most important voice for organized labor in Guatemala. Some observers believe that its militant activities in recent years have resulted from increasing PGT influence within its ranks.

Domestic Attitudes and Activities. It is difficult to determine whether the PGT's Central Committee met on a regular basis during 1981. Similarly, there are few sources that reveal the content of any political resolutions that may have been adopted. In order to characterize the PGT's attitudes on domestic and foreign issues, it is necessary to rely on statements of party leaders made in foreign publications or in occasional interviews. Clandestine bulletins attributed to the PGT appear occasionally in Guatemala, but their authenticity is questionable.

For over 25 of the party's 31 years of existence, it has been forced to work underground and subjected to varying levels of persecution. Despite such adverse conditions, the party claims a steady increase in influence among the masses, especially among workers, peasants, and other sectors of the population that it says are "suffering from capitalist oppression and exploitation."

Since the Fourth Congress in 1969, the PGT has adhered to the position that the revolution can triumph only through the use of force. In an article in the *World Marxist Review* (March), Antonio Castro, a member of the Central Committee's Political Commission, affirmed that "only an armed mass movement will determine the final outcome." The party does not believe, however, that legal opportunities are totally closed and is prepared to adopt various forms of struggle depending upon conditions.

The party believes that the task of the revolutionary organizations is to channel popular discontent and to intensify the people's urge for unity in combating Guatemala's "fascist dictatorship."

Although the party is convinced that further escalation of repression is inevitable, it does not believe that all organizations should go underground "to prevent the annihilation of their leaders." In Castro's view, "there is a need to use and develop any opportunity, however insignificant, for open action." According to Committee member Daniel Ríos, armed revolutionary struggle is "the only road" to obtain the urgent economic and social changes needed by Guatemala. During a press conference in Mexico City in May, he announced the formation of "a people's revolutionary army" made up primarily of PGT members. He described the military participation of the PGT as a "tactical shift," stating that efforts would be made to incorporate other leftist organizations. Although in recent years the party has expanded its organizational efforts to increase the political awareness of the masses, Ríos admitted that the PGT had experienced a setback in its military operations because of "ideological weaknesses." He disclosed a program of party demands that included the right for labor, peasant, and popular groups to organize; a general wage increase and a policy to protect workers against the high cost of living; implementation of an effective agrarian reform; and a halt to terrorist repression by the Guatemalan government. (AFP, 31 May.)

The party claimed responsibility for two political murders in Guatemala City, although it denied involvement in the deaths of three others for which it was blamed (*El Imparcial*, 3 March). Party militants detonated propaganda bombs in March to commemorate the party's founding. Leaflets denouncing U.S. intervention in Central America were distributed in Quezaltenango and the capital. The PGT also celebrated the second anniversary of the Sandinista revolution by setting off several bombs and painting communist slogans on the walls of several buildings in the capital (ACAN, 17 July). In June, Pablo Hernández, a member of the Political Commission, called for a boycott of the 1982 elections "in order to isolate a process that the government is trying to use demagogically for its repressive plans against the people" (Havana International Service, 29 June). According to a communiqué attributed to the PGT, the party announced in August that it had dissociated itself from the alleged guerrilla alliance formed in 1980 with the EGP, the ORPA, and the FAR (*Prensa Libre*, 11 August).

International Positions and Contacts. The PGT's positions on international issues follow those of the USSR closely. According to Otto Sánchez, Guatemalan Communists view strengthening the party's solidarity with the Soviet Union and other socialist countries as their primary international duty. The party maintains that by steadfastly supporting the USSR, the international working class "strengthens its solidarity with all the peoples fighting for political emancipation, economic independence, democracy, peace and socialism" (*WMR*, April 1979). The PGT firmly opposes the "aggression" and "Maoist subversion" of Chinese leaders. The party believes that Guatemala's growing dependence on imperialism and its subordination to foreign interests are the key problems facing the country (ibid., March).

José Cardoza Aguilar headed a delegation of the PGT to the congress of the Communist Party of Cuba in December 1980. Carlos González headed the party's delegation to the Soviet party congress in February (*Pravda*, 3 March).

Publications. The party's clandestine newspaper, *Verdad*, appears irregularly.

Armed People's Organization. Little is known of the ORPA's leaders, membership, or political orientation, although according to Guatemalan intelligence sources, its principal leader is Gaspar Ilón (ACAN, 2 December). The movement proposes to seize power through armed struggle and is thought to be especially effective in recruiting among Guatemala's Indian population.

The ORPA reported in March that it had staged about eighty armed actions in six departments during the first two months of the year, inflicting 413 casualties. The report added that units had taken over 47 farms and temporarily occupied six villages (Havana International Service, 10 March). Casualty figures reported by the guerrillas and the Guatemalan military are frequently contradictory. An ORPA communiqué dated 20 March indicated that guerrillas had ambushed a military convoy in Suchitepéquez, inflicting 127 casualties. According to the Army's official report of the incident, three guerrillas and only one soldier were killed (AFP, 1 April).

According to *Erupción*, continuous pressure by guerrilla forces had created a "panic spiral" among the oligarchy by midyear, leading to "serious doubts" about the army's ability to maintain control in the countryside (Radio Sandino, Managua, 4 June). ORPA guerrillas operating in groups of up to two hundred occupied towns in San Marcos, Retalhuleu, and Huehuetenango in June, conducting propaganda rallies and seizing arms from the local police stations (*Prensa Libre*, 2 June, 27 June). Two ORPA guerrillas captured in June claimed to have received training in Cuba, adding that "at least twenty other Guatemalan leftists" had also been training in Cuba while they were there (*Diario de Centro America*, 26 June). Police reported that one Cuban and two Spanish priests, identified as ORPA commanders, were killed in the capital (*Diario el Gráfico*, 27 July). According to official reports, combined army and police forces dismantled nine guerrilla centers during a two-week period in July. Heavy shooting was reported on three occasions, resulting in the death of 55 guerrillas purportedly belonging to the ORPA. In addition, security forces reported that the names of 800 leftist guerrillas were obtained from general files discovered in one of the hideouts located in Guatemala City (ACAN, 23 July).

Despite frequent assurances by military authorities that subversive forces operating in the capital and in the interior were "under control," ORPA units have remained highly operational. Guerrillas occupied two towns in Suchitepéquez and Quezaltenango in September, stealing weapons, burning government buildings, and distributing propaganda (AFP, 18 September). In November, ORPA guerrillas reportedly killed sixteen troops in attacks on army forces in the southern part of the country (Havana International Service, 17 November).

Guerrilla Army of the Poor. The EGP made its initial appearance in November 1975. Its forces are believed to have increased in number from an initial 300 to an estimated 1,200 in 1981. Four independent commands operate in the countryside and one in Guatemala City. The formation of a fifth guerrilla front was announced in July to increase harassment against the oil installations located in Alta Verapaz (*Granma*, Havana, 26 July). The movement's rural fronts were most active in the mountainous regions of El Quiché and Huehuetenango in northwestern Guatemala; in Chimaltenango and Sololá in the central highlands; near Escuintla, along the tropical Pacific coast; and to a lesser extent, in the department of Zacapa, where the guerrillas had their strongest support a decade ago. The EGP's principal leader is César Montes, a member of the Revolutionary Armed Forces until that group was crushed with U.S. assistance in the late 1960s. Ricardo Ramírez de León represented the EGP at a summit meeting of guerrilla leaders reportedly held in September 1980 (Guatemala Domestic Service, 6 March).

American and Guatemalan officials agree that the guerrillas are not under the direct command of the PGT, although a large percentage of urban guerrillas are believed to be party members. César Montes reportedly resigned from the PGT's Central Committee in 1968 to protest the party's failure to support the guerrilla movement fully.

In a communiqué issued jointly with the PGT in March, the two guerrilla movements claimed credit for ten ambushes of army columns, thirteen harassment attacks, 74 invasions of ranches and villages, 47 propaganda operations, seven sabotage operations, and the assassination of 23 "repressive officials" in actions carried out over a period of several months in the departments of El Quiché, Huehuetenango, Chimaltenango, and Escuintla (*Prensa Libre*, 21 March). The EGP claimed to have inflicted more than two hundred casualties on government troops during operations in April and May, including one hundred soldiers killed on 30 April in an attack on a town in El Quiché (Havana International Service, 10 June).

In early July, the EGP attacked the Guatemalan offices of Eastern Airlines and the U.S. Chamber of Commerce. The movement affirmed that it would continue armed actions against companies and individuals who actively support the Lucas García government economically and become "accomplices of Washington's warmongering policy in Central America" (ibid., 24 July). The EGP claimed responsibility for the death of 86 persons in various parts of the country during August because they cooperated with security forces (*Prensa Libre*, 1 September).

Guatemala's new defense minister, Gen. René Mendoza Palomo, reported in October that the army was prepared to "meet effectively" any guerrilla attempt to undertake a "final offensive." According to information revealed by former EGP militant Luís Pellecer, "the EGP, with a force of 8,000 men, intends to assume power late this year or early in 1982" (ibid., 7 October). On 29 October, approximately three hundred guerrillas attacked the provincial capital of Sololá, killing the civilian governor and the deputy chief of police. EGP units simultaneously attacked the cities of Mazatenango and Escuintla in what some observers considered the first coordinated guerrilla offensive conducted in the interior (*El Imparcial*, 30 October; ACAN, 1 November). EGP guerrillas continued to attack police substations and occupy towns in Huehuetenango, Chimaltenango, and El Quiché in November, causing considerable property damage and killing municipal officials (*Diario el Gráfico*, 4 November; ACAN, 17 November).

Guatemala's armed forces have thus far proven incapable of preventing the occupation of towns, the seizure of farms, the kidnapping of landowners, the murder of local officials and peasant informers, and similar operations by EGP and ORPA guerrillas. Although the Army succeeded in dismantling numerous guerrilla camps and urban hideouts, occasionally inflicting substantial casualties in the process, the guerrillas continue to pose a dilemma for the government. Despite military assurances that "the country is calm," Guatemalan officials have reason to be concerned about the intensification of guerrilla activity in 1981. On 23 November, Gen. Lucas García reportedly told correspondents of international news agencies that the government has offered to bring to the capital guerrilla leaders who want to discuss the search for a peaceful solution to Guatemala's political violence (Guatemala Domestic Service, 23 November). The country confronts its most serious guerrilla threat since the late 1960s.

Washington College   Daniel L. Premo

Guyana

The People's Progressive Party (PPP), founded in 1950, represents mostly Guyanans of East Indian background. In 1969, party leader Cheddi Jagan aligned the PPP unequivocally with the Soviet Union, and in turn, Soviet leaders recognized the PPP as a communist party. Party leaders say that the transformation of the PPP into a Leninist party began in 1969.

The PPP is a legal organization and the main opposition to the ruling People's National Congress (PNC), which represents mostly Guyanans of African background. The PNC is led by Forbes Burnham, onetime PPP member and present Guyanese president. Burnham was elected to a third term as prime minister in 1973 and became president with the adoption of a new national constitution in October 1980. In the December 1980 elections, the PPP won 10 seats in the National Assembly (as against 41 for the PNC and 2 for the right-wing United Force [UF]) and 35 seats in local governments (as against 169 for the PNC and 1 for the UF). PPP leaders say their party lost the 1968, 1973, and 1980 elections because of widespread fraud (*Mirror*, 20 September) and claim that in honest elections, the PPP and the other important leftist party, the Working People's Alliance (WPA), would win 75–80 percent of the vote (*WMR*, January). The WPA was formally established as a party in 1979.

The membership of the PPP is unknown, although the number of active and influential Marxist-Leninists probably is no more than five hundred. In the past few years, a number of blacks have joined the PPP, while some East Indians have drifted into the PNC, thus diminishing the racial orientation of the parties. The WPA has grown fairly rapidly since its registration as a party, particularly among Guyanese intellectuals and professionals, although several of its top leaders, including founder Walter Rodney, have been assassinated.

Leadership and Organization. At its Twentieth Congress in August 1979, the PPP elected a Politburo, Secretariat, and a 32-member Central Committee. The Politburo (Executive Committee) consists of Cheddi Jagan (general secretary), Janet Jagan (secretary for international affairs), Ram Karran (secretary for labor), Feroze Mohamed (secretary for education), Pariag Sukhai (secretary for mass organizations), Clinton Collymore (secretary for propaganda), Narbada Persaud (secretary for finance), Isahak Basir, Rohit Persaud, Cyril Belgrave, Reepu Daman Persaud, and Harry Persaud Nokta. The nine PPP leaders elected to the Guyanan parliament in 1980 were Cheddi Jagan, Janet Jagan, Collymore, Mohamed, Basir, Belgrave, Karran, Rohit Persaud, and Narbada Persaud.

The PPP Central Committee decided in early September to "agitate on all fronts around the slogan of '*Organize and Resist*'" (*Mirror*, 6 September, emphasis in original).

The PPP mass organizations are the Progressive Youth Organization (PYO), the Guyana Agricultural and General Workers' Union (GAWU), and the Women's Progressive Organization (WPO). The PYO, traditionally a strong source of personal support for Cheddi Jagan, is headed by First Secretary Navin Chandarpal, a member of the Central Committee of the PPP. The PYO sent a delegation to Jamaica in January for the founding congress of the Young Communist League, which is an arm of the Workers' Party of Jamaica, and hosted a delegation from the Soviet Komsomol in September. The

PYO is a member of the Executive Committee of the Soviet-front World Federation of Democratic Youth (WFDY) and sent its secretary for education, Mike Persaud, to a consultative meeting of the WFDY in Nicaragua in October. Like the PYO, The WPO, which is headed by Janet Jagan, Gail Teixeira, and Indra Chandarpal, devoted particular attention to the problem of employment.

The GAWU, based in the sugar industry, claims some 20,000 members. During the year, GAWU President Ram Karran frequently cooperated with three other leaders of self-proclaimed "militant" unions—including the WPA's University of Guyana Staff Association (UGSA)—which claim to represent some 40 percent of Guyana's organized workers (ibid., 27 September). The GAWU frequently protested that the Guyana Trade Union Congress (TUC) failed to stand up for the rights and needs of Guyanese workers (ibid., 26 July, 13, 20, and 27 September).

Domestic and International Policies. The PPP Central Committee commented in September on "the deepening of the political, economic and social crisis engulfing the nation and the inability of the ruling party to solve the most vital questions." The inability, according to the PPP, "stems from the nature of the petty bourgeois, nationalist regime, which seeks only to keep itself in power contrary to the wishes of the vast majority of the people." PNC austerity, unemployment, development, social justice, housing, health, and education programs are all a farce, according to the PPP. Democracy is manipulated, the judicial system is corrupt, and the People's Militia is a PNC preserve. (Ibid., 6 September; see also ibid., 30 August, 13 and 20 September, 4, 11, and 18 October, 8 November.) The PNC "has become an obstacle to progress," the Central Committee proclaimed, "and must therefore be removed." The PPP itself, said Cheddi Jagan, "is prepared to share power with all the democratic and progressive political and social forces operating in the country ... We stand for a multiparty government." However, Jagan protested, the PNC "refused to support the PPP's call for the establishment of a National Patriotic Front government" based on democracy, anti-imperialism, and socialism. (Ibid., 6 September; *WMR*, January.)

The PPP charges that the United States and the International Monetary Fund (IMF) dictate domestic policy to the Burnham government. "The aggressiveness of the Reagan administration has led ... to the reintroduction of cold-war and big-stick methods in fighting against national liberation and socialism under the pretext of combatting 'Soviet terrorism.' The escalating arms race, taking the world to the brink of nuclear confrontation, seems to be the cornerstone of the United States' adventurism." (*Mirror*, 6 September.) The United States' policies in Central America and the Caribbean are marked by a particularly high level of adventurism, according to PPP leaders (*IB*, August; *Daily World*, New York, 16 October). The much-heralded heads of state summit at Cancún, Mexico, held in October, was "a waste of time and energy." The only way for Third World countries to solve their problems, according to a commentary in the *Mirror* (25 October), is to break away from "pro-imperialist policies," work to end the "world-wide imperialist-inspired arms race," "enhance global security and détente," and invest in economic development projects. The aggravation of the border dispute with Venezuela, according to Jagan, is the responsibility of the Georgetown government; Burnham hopes to divert attention from pressures imposed by the International Monetary Fund and other economic issues, generate support for his government in the country, and improve the PNC's image abroad (*Mirror*, 19 July).

The PPP considers the November Revolution in Russia "the most important event in the history of mankind" (ibid., 1 November). Cheddi Jagan and other PPP leaders travel to the Soviet Union and Soviet bloc countries and participate in the activities of Soviet front organizations. But the PPP's relationship with the Soviet bloc is complicated somewhat by Soviet and Cuban ties to the PNC government. The Soviet Union sent a delegate to the Fourth PNC Congress in August and discussed increased cooperation between the two governments. Cuba offered Guyana credits during the year and was rumored to have 15,000 troops stationed in Guyana (AFP, 19 August). The PNC congress also was attended by a high-ranking member of the International Liaison Department of the People's Republic of China, Zhu Liang.

Publications. The PPP suffered seriously from a government-imposed shortage of newsprint during the first half of 1981; after midyear the four-page weekly edition of the party organ, *Mirror*, appeared in somewhat increased numbers. The PPP theoretical journal is *Thunder*. Party statements are carried by publications of pro-Soviet parties around the world.

The Working People's Alliance. The WPA pledges to use Marxism-Leninism to create a classless society in Guyana. It disclaims any international links, but has strong ties to Cuba and to other revolutionary parties and governments in the Caribbean. The WPA is led by Clive Thomas, president of the UGSA, and Eusi Kwayana. On 29 May, a Guyanese court dismissed arson charges the government had filed against three WPA members, one of them the previously assassinated Rodney. A WPA street demonstration was broken up with considerable force on 17 September and, along with other incidents of "systematic harassment" of party members—as alleged by the Guyana Human Rights Association—led to WPA discussions of the best strategy to follow in Guyana at this time. A few members proposed the adoption of armed struggle, but the WPA paper, *Dayclean*, evidently speaking for the majority of party members, proposed a more moderate line of civil disobedience.

Hoover Institution   William E. Ratliff

Haiti

The United Party of Haitian Communists (Parti unifié des communistes Haitiens; PUCH) was formed in 1968 by the merger of several small leftist parties. In April 1969 a Haitian law declared all forms of communist activity crimes against the state, punishable by confiscation of property and death. During 1981 the Haitian government alleged communist involvement in domestic subversion and warned that communism will become a greater threat if the United States does not provide aid to the region (*Latin America Regional Report: Caribbean*, 21 August). Membership in PUCH in 1981 was estimated at approximately 350 persons, all of whom were in jail, working underground in Haiti, or active among other exiles in Europe, the Soviet Union, and the Americas, particularly Cuba. In 1980 the main PUCH spokesman was René Theodore, identified by Cuban sources as the party's general secretary; in 1979 Jacques Dorcilien was reportedly elected PUCH general secretary. Gerald Pierre Charles was PUCH representative at the Second Congress of the Communist Party of Cuba in Havana in December 1980.

Domestic and International Positions. Just before the Haitian government crackdown on dissidents in November 1980, Theodore stated that the labor union movement was gaining importance in Haiti and that peasants were becoming more critical of the government. "It is absolutely necessary," Theodore stated in *Trabajadores* (Havana, 12 August 1980), that all citizens "combine their efforts to form a large, united anti-Duvalier force able to overcome the dictatorship." The most important step toward that end came in September 1981 when a number of Haitian groups attended the First Continental Conference of Solidarity with Haiti, held in Panama with the active support of the PUCH. The conference delegates described the Duvalier government as "a regime of terror." They also condemned the United States for its alleged discrimination against black Haitians seeking asylum in the United States and for its plans to set up a military base in Le Mole de St. Nicolas, "which would give Yankee imperialism another instrument for aggression against Central America and the Caribbean" (*Granma*, Havana, English ed., 28 September). More than two hundred delegates from various countries and "most Haitian revolutionary, progressive, and democratic organizations" were represented. According to a report from Cuba, Haitian exiles living in the United States, Costa Rica, France, Mexico, Canada, Cuba, Venezuela, and other countries, together with Haitians in the homeland, resolved to "consult all opposition sectors with a view to setting up a work committee to study ways and means to establish a base of political cooperation to accelerate the process of national liberation" (ibid., 18 October).

The PUCH maintained its support for the objectives of the Soviet Union, its opposition to anti-Soviet policies, and its condemnations of "imperialism's efforts to unleash the arms race once again" (Theodore on Radio Moscow, 26 February).

Hoover Institution   William E. Ratliff

Honduras

The Communist Party of Honduras (Partido Comunista de Honduras; PCH) was organized in 1927, destroyed in 1932, and reorganized in 1954. A dispute over strategy and tactics in 1967 led to the expulsion of one group and the division of the PCH into rival factions. Since 1971, a self-proclaimed pro-Chinese Communist Party of Honduras/Marxist-Leninist (PCH-ML) has functioned, but it did little until May–June 1980, when it publicly complained of persecution by the Directorate of National Investigations, which confiscated its printing equipment and tortured several of its members.

The PCH has been illegal since 1957 but has operated openly in varying degrees under recent governments. The prospects for legal status are doubtful; few knowledgeable observers feel the PCH could muster the 10,000 authenticated signatures required for registration as a national party under the 1978 electoral law. In addition, PCH leaders would probably be reluctant to reveal the names and addresses of PCH members even if they could obtain the necessary signatures. Neither the PCH nor the Honduran Patriotic Front, a coalition of 30 groups of varying size and organizational structure, was able to participate in the national elections of 29 November.

Nothing more has been reported of the Trotskyist Revolutionary Party of Central American Workers (PRTC) since police announced on 23 April 1980 that they had broken up a PRTC plot to hinder the 20 April 1980 elections for a constituent assembly.

On 17 September, San Pedro Sula police announced the capture of two members of the Morazanista Front for the Liberation of Honduras (FMLH) who were part of a small group planning to kidnap a well-known businessman and coffee plantation owner as well as the commander of the 12th Infantry Battalion (Radio America, Tegucigalpa, 17 September; *FBIS*, 21 September). The FMLH—apparently formed by a group of PCH-members whose links with PCH Secretary General Rigoberto Padilla Rush are not fully known—has engaged in kidnapping since it announced in February 1980 that it was going to start "armed action to assume power" after the 20 April 1980 constituent assembly elections. On 30 October, the FMLH claimed responsibility for several shots fired at the U.S. Embassy in Tegucigalpa. In November 1980, the FMLH began smearing the walls of buildings in several cities as well as rocks along the Pan American Highway with slogans and propaganda.

Another group linked to the PCH and the FMLH is the Lorenzo Zelaya Popular Revolutionary Command, which claimed responsibility for the 23 September shooting of two U.S. military advisers near the Honduran Air Force base at Tegucigalpa's international airport (*NYT*, 24 and 25 September). The 7:30 A.M. shooting preceeded a peaceful march by an estimated 60,000 Hondurans through Tegucigalpa to protest "repression" by Honduran security forces of different groups and individuals, as well as the Honduran Army's involvement in the Salvadoran conflict.

Another group of left-wing militants linked to the PCH, the People's Revolutionary Union (Unión Revolucionaria del Pueblo; URP) may have been weakened irreparably when Fidel Martínez, its secretary general, was killed and URP President Tomás Nativi, a well-known PCH professor at the National Autonomous University of Honduras (UNAH), disappeared in the wake of an 11 June assault on his home in Tegucigalpa (*FBIS*, 16 June). Subsequently, conflicting stories circulated that Nativi had been kidnapped or killed, or had sought refuge in Nicaragua and Cuba (ibid., 2 July; visits with Honduran journalists, 20–26 August).

On 27 March, members of a group calling itself the Movimiento Popular de Liberación Cinchonero hijacked a Honduran airliner en route to San Pedro Sula and the United States from Tegucigalpa. After forcing the plane to fly to Managua, Nicaragua, the hijackers released 30 of its 81 passengers—mostly women and children. They released the rest in Panama in return for the release of fifteen Salvadorans and Hondurans in police custody in Honduras, including Facundo Guardado, ex–secretary general of the Salvadoran Popular Revolutionary Bloc (*FBIS*, 30 March; *Granma*, Havana, 12 April). Among the several kidnappings in the past fourteen months, the most spectacular was the 18 December 1980 abduction of Paul Vinelli, president of the Banco Atlantida, a Chase Manhattan subsidiary, who was released on 4 March 1981. Although his captors were never identified, it was reported in March that Vinelli had been kidnapped by Salvadoran guerrillas with the help of FMLN members and released only after payment of a large ransom of over $100,000 (*Tiempo*, San Pedro Sula, 4 March; Radio America, 19 March; *FBIS*, 20 March).

Leadership and Organization. Rigoberto Padilla Rush has been PCH secretary general since late 1978. Other important PCH leaders are Longino Becerra, director of the PCH weekly, *Patria*; Mario Sosa Navarro, a longtime member of the Political Commission and point of contact with other Honduran party leaders; and Milton Rene Paredes, secretary of the Central Committee.

Membership in the PCH is around 1,500. Membership in the PCH-ML, FMLH, and URP is estimated at less than a hundred persons each, although the last two groups can muster several hundred additional sympathizers from UNAH.

The party has been active in recruiting and organizing university and secondary students as well as workers. The PCH sponsors the Socialist Student Front (FES) and the Federation of Secondary

Students (FESE). Both groups have been active since late 1979 in organizing street parades and demonstrations on UNAH campuses in Tegucigalpa, San Pedro Sula, and La Ceiba in support of revolutionary groups in other Central American countries. On several occasions in 1981, FESE students occupied private school buildings (*colegios*) and offices of the Ministry of Education in different cities to pressure the ministry to take over private schools and thus provide more funding for salaries, equipment, and other needs, which would reduce secondary school tuition and guarantee the national accreditation for graduates that many of the poorer *colegios* have been unable to provide in recent years (*Tiempo*, 4 March; *FBIS*, 8 September). Fifteen FESE members occupied the Tegucigalpa offices of U.N. representative Anton Kruiderink on 8–9 August in support of demands that the Honduran government end the "repression, persecution, and imprisonment" of current and former FESE leaders working at UNAH and that the Education Ministry officially take over some fifty private *colegios* (*FBIS*, 9 September).

The FES and other left-wing groups suffered a major defeat in August elections for officers and school represenatives of the Honduran University Student Federation (FEUH). The United University Democratic Front (FUUD)—linked to the National Party and conservative businessmen and lawyers—won a plurality of votes for the first time in ten years to gain the presidency and four positions on the FEUH Executive Committee. The FUUD obtained 3,027 votes, the University Reform Front 2,938 votes and four seats, and the United Revolutionary Front 2,170 votes. (*La Prensa*, San Pedro Sula, 19, 21, and 29 August; *El Heraldo*, Tegucigalpa, 1 September.)

The PCH has been active in selected urban industrial and agricultural firms, especially subsidiaries of American multinational corporations such as United Fruit, Standard Fruit/Castle and Cooke, and Coca-Cola. PCH influence was reduced in one important sector of the trade union movement when the slate of candidates of the Democratic Forces, headed by Desiderio Elvir Carbajal for president and Armando Galdámez for secretary general, swept the 28 August elections of the Sixteenth Ordinary Congress of the Sindicato of Workers of the Tela Railroad Company, a United Fruit subsidiary. The Elvir-Galdámez ticket ousted Evaristo Euceda, the Maoist-oriented secretary of organization, and two other known leftists. (*El Heraldo*, 22 August; *La Tribuna*, Tegucigalpa, 29 August.)

The PCH continued its efforts in the central part of the country and especially in the beverage industry and among telegraph and telephone workers. Napoleón Acevedo Granados, a former labor leader linked to the PCH who headed the Sindicato of Workers of the Standard Fruit Company before his 1977 ouster by Democratic Forces linked to the Inter-American Regional Organization of Workers (ORIT), was the reported PCH mastermind behind the effort to combine the Comité de Unidad Sindical (CUS), the Frente Sindical Independiente (FSI), and the Comité de Unidad Intersindical into the Unitary Federation of Honduran Workers (*Latin America Weekly Report*, London, 22 May). CUS, FSI, and PCH members made inroads into various groups affiliated with the Christian Democratic–oriented Central General de Trabajadores and the Sindicato de Bebidas y Similares, the nationwide union of employees in the beverage industry (*La Tribuna*, 29 August).

Domestic Events and Views. Most political activity in Honduras in 1981 centered around the 29 November national elections for president, the National Congress, and 283 mayors. With over 80 percent of registered voters going to the polls, Roberto Suazo Cordova of the Liberal Party was elected president with 633,365 votes (54.1 percent of the total valid votes cast), compared with 486,092 votes (41.5 percent) for Ricardo Zúñiga Agustinius of the National Party, 29,133 votes (2.4 percent) for Miguel Andonie Fernández of the Party of Innovation and Unity, and 18,785 votes (1.6 percent) for Dr. Hernan Corrales Padilla of the Christian Democratic Party. Another 3,938 votes (0.34 percent) were cast for Marco Virgilio Carias of the Honduran Socialist Party and two "independent" candidates of the Honduran Patriotic Front—a coalition of the Socialist Party, the PCH, the PCH-ML—and other individuals.

During the year, the PCH, PCH-ML, and Socialist Party joined dissident members of the ALIPO faction of the Liberal Party in denouncing rumors of a coup to be led by Gen. Mario Chinchilla Carcamo, chief of the Military High Command, who said he would fight "terrorists" and the "Attilas of the twentieth century." The presidential press secretary and President Policarpo Paz García repeatedly denied rumors that a group of twelve colonels would take over the government before the elections or shortly thereafter, using as pretexts the stagnant economy, events in Nicaragua or El Salvador, or any combination of these (*FBIS*, 15 April; conversations with political party leaders in Tegucigalpa, 20–26 August).

International Activities and Contacts. There is no evidence that PCH or PCH-ML leaders visited Eastern Europe, the USSR, or the Chinese People's Republic as in previous years or attended the Second Congress of the Communist Party of Cuba in December 1980. After returning from second anniversary celebrations in honor of the Sandinista victory in Managua, Nicaragua, PCH Secretary General Rigoberto Padilla said that the Nicaraguan people were giving "unrestricted support" to the policies of the Government of National Reconstruction and the Sandinista movement. In May, Padilla told a Havana radio interviewer that U.S. military aid was aimed at making Honduras a "launching pad for U.S. aggression in the area" against Nicaragua or the Salvadoran revolution. (*FBIS*, 30 July.) In late December 1980, the PCH Central Committee, the PCH–ML, and the Honduran Socialist Party announced their "militant unity" and opposition to the peace treaty signed between Honduras and El Salvador, saying that the "treaty's main purpose [was] to reunify the [Central American] region's reactionary forces to repress the desires for liberation of the Central American peoples" (ibid., 29 December 1980).

The PCH was undoubtedly involved in the work of the Honduran Coordinating Board of Solidarity with the Salvadoran People, a member of the World Anti-Interventionist Movement. The board published newspaper advertisements and sponsored several public meetings accusing the Honduran Army of collaborating with the Salvadoran Army by pursuing innocent Salvadoran refugees fleeing into Honduras, of pursuing Salvadoran groups into El Salvador in order to take hostages, and of permitting the kidnapping and arrest of Salvadorans resident in Tegucigalpa and other Honduran cities (*Tiempo*, 22 August 1981).

Publications. *Patria*, the PCH weekly newspaper, was not distributed as openly in 1981 as in 1980. Party statements are occasionally published in Honduran newspapers, the *World Marxist Review*, or that journal's *International Bulletin*.

Texas Tech University   Neale J. Pearson

Jamaica

Jamaica has two communist parties: the small and insignificant Jamaican Communist Party (JCP) and the more active and influential Workers' Party of Jamaica (WPJ). The JCP, founded in 1975, is led by its general secretary, Chris Lawrence. It operates within the Independent Trade Union Action Council, a federation of small unions affiliated with a Soviet front organization, the World Federation of Trade Unions. The JCP gave critical support to People's National Party (PNP) leader Michael Manley in his 1980 race against Jamaican Labor Party (JLP) leader Edward Seaga. (In the election, Seaga received 59 percent of the vote to Manley's 41 percent, and the JLP took 51 seats in parliament against 9 for the PNP.)

The WPJ was founded in 1978 when the Workers' Liberation League (formed by a number of small discussion and agitation groups in 1974) transformed itself into the WPJ at a founding conference. Trevor Munroe was elected general secretary and continued to hold that position during 1981. The WPJ also gave critical support to the PNP during the 1980 elections.

Leadership and Internal Affairs. Besides Munroe, prominent WPJ leaders include Central Committee members Barry Chevannes, Tony Harriott, Percy Thompson, and Rupert Lewis (editor of the WPJ paper, *Struggle*). No membership figures have been released, although Munroe claims that 100,-000 voters in the last election (12 percent of the total) are "definitely pro-communist, people who, while not agreeing with everything we say or do, are objectively marching with us in the class struggle" (*Marxism Today*, London, May). Subscriptions to the party organ have reportedly leveled off at 17,000. The WPJ ran two candidates in rural areas (Lucea and Georges Plain) for local governmental positions in March. These candidates received 12.5 and 15 percent of the vote, more than any other third-party candidate in Jamaican history (ibid.; a *Struggle* editorial on 13 March claimed 12.9 and 16 percent, respectively). Toward the end of 1981, the WPJ claimed that two of every five poor youths and two of every ten workers support communism (*Struggle*, 11 September). Citing figures like these, the party denies charges that it has no local roots: "Communist political organization in Jamaica is not something imported from abroad, is not something which is in the head of a few university intellectuals, but is a movement, a party, and a force that grows out of the conditions of the Jamaican poor, of the Jamaican workers and farmers, and therefore has its roots in Jamaica" (ibid., 27 February).

At a meeting shortly after the October 1980 elections, the WPJ revised its goals and tactics: "For the immediate future, our main emphasis is going to be on mass work to strengthen the party's links with, first and foremost, the unionised working class, with the working people as consumers and with the young unemployed. True, our tactics are defensive now, but there's a difference between defensive tactics of retreat ... and defensive tactics designed to hold the line at the point you've reached to engage the enemy as he advances and to accumulate the forces to resume the offensive. Those are our tactics—defensive leading to offensive." (*Marxism Today*, May.) This policy, party leaders assure WPJ members, follows directly along lines carried out by Lenin in 1905 (Lewis, *WMR*, June). The shift to a more defensive line reportedly alienated some party members, but it drew in at least an equal number of new members (*Marxism Today*, May).

Munroe claims that the Seaga government has concentrated on weakening the WPJ since "imperialism and reaction recognise that our party is going to be playing a bigger role and therefore needs to be crushed immediately." As far as possible, the WPJ general secretary says, the JLP attack will be carried out within constitutional means. This line of attack includes (1) efforts by the government-controlled *Daily News*, which prints *Struggle*, to silence the paper by raising printing fees drastically and requiring a $50,000 bond in case of libel actions against the WPJ paper; (2) trumping up charges against party leaders to discredit or convict them; (3) identifying and firing WPJ members from the state apparatus; and (4) planting guns on party members so they can be arrested. If this fails to break up the party, Munroe concludes, "and it will fail," then the government "will try more repressive measures, such as proscription of our trade union work and selected assassination." (Ibid.)

At midyear, Munroe emphasized the importance of WPJ ties with the "national democratic" PNP, despite differences between the two parties. The relationship between the two parties had "taken a dip" since the 1980 elections, but cooperation continued "at all levels." (Ibid.) *Struggle* editor Lewis wrote (*WMR*, June) that the WPJ rejects the view that the "progressive front" suffered a "decisive defeat" in the 1980 elections. "The electoral setback has caused no split in the vanguard, that is, a split between the Marxist left in the PNP and the WPJ." Shortly thereafter, Manley told the Executive Committee of the PNP that allegations of ties with the WPJ had contributed more than any other single factor to the party's electoral defeat in 1980 and the PNP disavowed any ties to the WPJ (*Latin America Regional Report: Caribbean*, 29 May, 12 June). Nonetheless, Jamaican Security Minister Winston Spaulding charged in late September that threats to the national government had their genesis in an "unholy alliance" between the WPJ and the PNP established when the latter controlled the government (CANA, Bridgetown, 30 September; *FBIS*, 10 October; *Latin America Regional Report: Caribbean*, 9 October). The Communist Party of the Soviet Union maintains ties with the PNP and sent a representative to the October conference of the PNP (*Pravda*, 8 October; *FBIS*, 15 October).

In mid-December, the WPJ held its Second Congress.

Mass Organizations. The main WPJ-led mass organizations are the Young Communist League (YCL), the Committee of Women for Progress (CWP), the University and Allied Workers Union (UAWU), and the National Union of Democratic Teachers. The YCL was formed on 18 January following the decision of the Jamaican Union of Democratic Youth to transform itself into the youth arm of the WPJ. More than two hundred delegates at the congress elected a Central Committee, headed by General Secretary Arthur Newland, and voted on a constitution and program of action. The founding congress was attended by delegations from Cuba, Guyana, Grenada, and the Soviet Union. The main focuses of YCL activists were declared to be education and programs for unemployed young people. (*Struggle*, 19 January, 8 May, 28 August.)

The CWP, described as "a democratic organization led by Communists and revolutionary democratic women," was founded in October 1976. Its objectives are to build up the consciousness of women and lead them in struggles for their rights (ibid., 9 October).

The UAWU was founded in 1971 and reportedly is active in thirty-odd plants (ibid., 23 October). Its general secretary is Trevor Munroe. According to Munroe, evidence of increasing WPJ influence in the life of the nation is shown most of all in the trade unions, where the UAWU is drawing more workers than ever before from the manufacturing and sugar industries (*Marxism Today*, May). The UAWU's Sixth Congress met on 8 November.

Domestic and International Policies. The JLP won the 1980 elections, according to *Struggle* editor Lewis, by the application of tactics "based on economic destabilization and psychological warfare, especially through the media . . . In an atmosphere of growing tensions, centrist-minded social sections shifted to the right, feeling uncertain concerning the capability of the PNP to achieve economic recovery and stop violence." Since taking office, the Seaga government's economic policy has been "geared above all else to encouraging private enterprise, reducing the public sector, giving foreign investors access to the nation's resources, keeping down the price of labor and hence limiting the working people's incomes." (*WMR*, June; see also *Marxism Today*, May.)

The WPJ condemned the "deliverance politics" of the Seaga government and urged laborers to work together, regardless of political affiliation, to their mutual benefit (*Struggle*, 27 March, 11 and 25 September). At times after midyear, party leaders attacked the "democratic socialist politics" of the PNP and contrasted their ineffectiveness with the achievements of the "communist working class policies" of the WPJ (ibid., 31 July). Throughout the year the WPJ charged that the Seaga government engaged in scapegoat politics: "Today, Seaga and Spaulding, faced with the total failure of deliverance to bring anything but more hardship for the small people, are now blaming 'highly educated terrorists' for frustrating the government, trying to put up the police and the people to support persecution of WPJ and of anybody who stands for change of the imperialist system in Jamaica" (ibid., 9 October).

WPJ policy to counter the Seaga government involved (1) strengthening the alliance between revolutionary democracy and Communists at the top and the bottom, nationally and internationally; (2) exposing the aims of the Seaga government's economic policy; and (3) changing its tactics should the regime and its apparatus resort to fascist-type violence. The WPJ continually links the policies of the Seaga and the U.S. governments, finding the former merely an extension of the latter. This was reflected at the end of October when Jamaica broke relations with Cuba in what the WPJ called "a move designed to curry favor from the U.S. Government in its undeclared war against Cuba" (*Granma*, Havana, English ed., 15 November). The WPJ also condemns any Jamaican contacts with the International Monetary Fund.

Hoover Institution   William E. Ratliff

Mexico

The Mexican Communist Party (Partido Comunista Mexicano; PCM) is one of the world's oldest, having been founded in November 1919 and using its present name since 1920. It long remained barred from electoral politics, however, by laws restricting the registration of small parties. A 1977 reform permitted several additional parties, including the PCM and the Socialist Workers' Party, to present candidates and obtain seats in the Chamber of Deputies under provisions for proportional representation.

In the 1979 elections, a leftist coalition led by the PCM outpolled other leftist tickets, receiving 5.4 percent of the vote and 18 of the 300 seats in the Chamber of Deputies. The PCM thereby gained a national forum and was able to make itself a significant spokesman for the leftist opposition to the effectively one-party state. With a membership estimated at 100,000 in 1981, and considerable strength in universities, the PCM could claim to be an important force. It sought to make itself a national party on the Eurocommunist model, dissociating itself from the Soviet Union, condemning the invasion of Afghanistan, and supporting the demands of the Polish workers—positions that were attacked by the Popular Socialist Party (Partido Popular Socialista; PPS), a minor Moscow-line party that normally works with the governing Institutional Revolutionary Party (Partido Revolucionario Institucional; PRI), by the Socialist Revolutionary Party (Partido Socialista Revolucionario; PRS), and by other radical splinter groups.

In January 1981, the PCM sought changes in Mexico's constitution to give more power in choosing administrative appointments to the Chamber of Deputies, in which the PCM and its ally, the PSR, control 29 seats. This proposal failed for lack of broad support, however, and leftist leaders urged increased political action to win more seats in the legislature. José Luís Moreno Borbolla, leader of the Socialist Group of the Valley of Mexico (Grupo Socialista del Valle de México), announced that the Mexican left "will soon launch an offensive to gain ground in the country" (*El Sol de Mexico*, 22 February).

In March, the PCM held its Nineteenth Congress. This meeting renamed the party's Executive Commission and confirmed Secretary General Arnaldo Martínez Verdugo, Marcos Leonel Posadas Segura, Samuel Meléndez Luevano, Eduardo Montes Manzano, and Jesús Sosa Castro as key members. All five are members of the party's Secretariat. The congress also moved to unify the radical left.

Efforts to Unite the Left. Mexico's small but vocal Marxist and near-Marxist parties have long quarreled violently. Dozens of leftist groups have been formed during the past decade, many with as few as ten members, and these new groupings have tended to dissipate PCM strength and membership rolls. But in mid-August, a long-sought merger of the parties took place, and for a few weeks it began to look as if unity might finally become a reality. Five political groups, headed by the PCM, signed a document on 15 August agreeing to set up a single party apparatus before the year was over. The PCM's Twentieth Congress (15–17 October) formally approved the merger with the smaller radical parties. Two smaller parties joined in October and November.

Their unity was tenuous, however. Even before the new political force formally came into being, it was riven with dispute and dissension. The Mexican Workers' Party (Partido Mexicano de los Trabajadores; PMT), headed by Heberto Castillo, the country's best-known and most highly respected opposition leader, withdrew. Castillo argued that the Communists were trying to impose their ideology and structure on the new party. Martínez responded by calling Castillo "sectarian and bureaucratic." (*NYT*, 9 November.) The leftist weekly *Proceso* (4 November) greeted the withdrawal of Castillo from the new organization with the headline "Defeated Before It Began." Mexican observers asserted that Castillo's action resulted from a personal feud between the two leaders and had little to do with ideology.

The PCM proceeded, however, to press for the formation of the new, united party without the PMT; and the leftist amalgam was consummated at the National Unification Assembly on 5–6 November. Six parties dismantled their separate organizations and united under one banner, the United Socialist Party of Mexico (Partido Socialista Unido de México; PSUM). The new unit brought together the PCM, the PSR, the Mexican People's Party (Partido Popular Mexicano), the Socialist Action and Unity Movement (Movimiento de Acción y Unidad Socialista), the Popular Action Movement (Movimiento de Acción Popular), and the Left Communist Unity (Unidad de Izquierda Comunista). Of these only the PMC and the PSR had been legally registered.

The PSUM proceeded to nominate Martínez as its candidate for the July 1982 presidential election. No leftist candidate had any chance of defeating the PRI nominee, Miguel de la Madrid Hurtado, but the division between Martínez and Castillo—generally considered the more popular—removed any likelihood that the radical left would make an impressive showing. If the proposed coalition had held together, it might have emerged as Mexico's second largest political force.

International Relations. Expressions of unity with the PCM were made by several dozen visiting delegations from the Soviet Union, Cuba, and other socialist bloc countries. Many of them took up the theme of El Salvador, calling on the United States to withdraw its support of the military-civilian junta of government in the Central American country. Through Valentín Campa, a member of the party's Secretariat, the PCM argued that the "socialist world must strengthen itself daily to support solidarity with the Salvadoran people and to thwart the American interventionists' plans." The same words were used by PCM Deputy Pablo Gómez Alvarado in a meeting of Mexican congressional committees. (*Oposición*, 3 March.)

The PCM, the PPS, and the PSR joined in March to condemn the Reagan administration's proposal to open the borders of the United States to Mexican workers, arguing that the United States will use the undocumented workers as an instrument to pressure the Mexican government on energy policies. "What is evident is that U.S. farmers need the Mexican work force. If an open door is proposed only when they need that work force and they expel it when they no longer need it, they should also grant them all the rights that are appropriate to their status as workers," stated PCM Deputy Gerardo Unzueta Lorenzana in March (*Excélsior*, 6 March). In August, the PCM and the PPS joined in calling on the Mexican government to withdraw from the U.S.-supported Caribbean aid program, arguing that Mexico should not serve the United States in its Caribbean and Central American activities.

In October, Enrico Berlinguer, the Italian Communist Party's secretary general, visited Mexico to confer with Mexican President José López Portillo. He also met with PCM officials, headed by Secretary General Martínez, and attended the PCM's Twentieth Congress. They took a joint stand in opposition to the U.S. role in El Salvador, expressing "complete solidarity" with the Democratic Revolutionary Front–Farabundo Martí National Liberation Front in that country (*FBIS*, 29 October).

Also in October, a PCM delegation, led by Samuel Meléndez Luevano, visited Hungary where the PCM and the Hungarian party expressed solidarity with El Salvador's "enslaved masses" and expressed opposition to U.S. machinations in Central America" (ibid., 9 October).

Christian Science Monitor   James Nelson Goodsell

Nicaragua

Throughout 1981, Nicaragua slipped steadily toward Marxist-Leninist totalitarianism. The Sandinist National Liberation Front (Frente Sandinista de Liberación Nacional; FSLN), which dominates the government that came to power in the wake of the 1978–1979 civil war, appeared to abandon its proclaimed goals of a pluralistic political system and a mixed economy. Personal rivalries among the top Sandinista commanders, serious economic turmoil, and growing bureaucratic confusion were all part of the picture. A significant and widespread opposition movement headed by former allies of the Sandinistas and including key elements in the Roman Catholic church also developed. But such signs of discontent did not appear to slow, much less halt, the movement toward totalitarianism.

Ultimate authority in Nicaragua remained with the nine-member Sandinista Directorate, a group of former guerrillas, all claiming to be Marxists, who coalesced in 1978 to bring about the final military triumph of the Sandinistas over the government of Gen. Anastasio Somoza Debayle and the 45-year-old Somoza dynasty. While all nine are supposed to be equal, evidence emerged in 1981 that several of the group are more equal than others. The Ortega brothers—Daniel Ortega Saavedra and Humberto Ortega Saavedra—appear to have more power than some others, including Minister of the Interior Tomás Borge Martínez, the only surviving founder of the FSLN. Whether this trend will continue remains to be seen, but with Daniel Ortega serving as the government's coordinator because of his role on the Directorate and in the scaled-down three-man junta of government and Humberto serving on the Directorate, as head of the Army, and as minister of defense, their positions appear increasingly solid. Moreover, Jaime Wheelock Román, Directorate member and head of the powerful Ministry of Agrarian Reform, was thought to have thrown his support to the Ortega brothers.

The FSLN came to dominate Nicaraguan life in 1981. Founded in 1961, it was essentially a small guerrilla group opposed to General Somoza until early 1978, when its ranks were swelled by thousands of anti-Somoza Nicaraguans. Although the FSLN leadership was essentially Marxist, thousands of Sandinista supporters were swayed not so much by ideology as by an anti-Somoza stance.

There are three other leftist parties, all of which support in some measure the Sandinista government and movement. But they are relatively minor in importance. The Socialist Party of Nicaragua (Partido Socialista Nicaraguense; PSN) is a pro-Soviet group founded in 1937. It was declared illegal a year later and was a clandestine organization until the Sandinista triumph in 1979. Its membership is estimated at 250, some of whom have links with the Sandinista movement. The Communist Party of Nicaragua (Partido Comunista Nicaraguense; PCN) is an anti-Soviet group founded in 1967, when an internal struggle within the PSN resulted in the expulsion of six party leaders. These six established the PCN, but they have had limited success in attracting supporters to their cause. The PCN's present membership is estimated at two hundred despite massive enrollment efforts that continued into 1981. The party claims to have 1,500 members. A third group, the Popular Action Movement (Movimiento de Acción Popular; MAP), emerged in 1967, declaring itself a Maoist organization. Its sharply leftist Marxist-Leninist philosophy put it at the far left of the political spectrum in Nicaragua, and the MAP ran afoul of Sandinista leadership on several occasions during 1981. Its newspaper, *El Pueblo*, remained closed for much of the year. The MAP's membership was thought to be less than 250, although *El Pueblo*, when published, had a larger circulation.

The Crisis. The heady enthusiasm in Nicaragua over the end of the Somoza dynasty, so evident in late 1979 and throughout much of 1980, dissipated during 1981. Many of the original supporters of the FSLN defected either publicly or privately. Groups that had entered into an uneasy alliance with the FSLN in forming the government grew increasingly critical of the Sandinistas. As the economy turned sour with production slowing, unemployment soaring, and debts rising, the word "crisis" began to be used more frequently, even by leaders of the FSLN. In an October speech, Daniel Ortega admitted there was a crisis, but put much of the blame on world economic conditions and on "economic aggression, threats, pressure, and a policy of blackmail" carried out by the United States (*FBIS*, 23 October).

Earlier, a private memorandum circulated among top Sandinista commanders admitted that inexperience, ineptitude, and lack of coordination by the top arms of government were also responsible. Moreover, as the economic situation worsened during the year, the government imposed new political and social controls on the nation. A series of Sandinista decrees in September made it a crime to voice public opposition to the government. Daniel Ortega, in announcing the moves, said that "the FSLN National Directorate and the junta of the Government of National Reconstruction have decided to impose respect for the revolutionary laws and not to allow actions that go against the efforts that the working people and the small, medium, and large-scale producers and businessmen, professionals and technicians are making in favor of the nation's reconstruction in line with the state of economic and special emergency" (ibid., 22 September). Earlier, the government had issued a state of emergency decree that specifically banned "the dissemination of false news that might lead to the alteration of prices, salaries, food supplies, or currency" (ibid., 10 September).

Within weeks, five businessmen who had accused the Sandinistas of leading Nicaragua to Marxism and "preparing a new genocide" were arrested; eventually three were given prison terms of nine months to a year for violating the emergency decree. At the same time, the government arrested 22 members of the PCN for a similar offense. The PCN had accused the government of not moving fast enough toward a Marxist economic structure, "which has to be the goal of all right-thinking Nicaraguans." The group also accused the government of not being hard enough in dealing with its opponents "on the right." (Ibid., 20 and 22 October.)

Daniel Ortega emphasized that opponents of the government from both the right and the left had been arrested—repression apparently being more pardonable if it is broad—and other government officials pointed out that while only three of the businessmen had been imprisoned, 22 members of the PCN were in jail. But this effort could not mask the general impression in Nicaragua that the government was drawing battle lines with the private sector and non-Sandinista political moderates. Indeed, earlier Sandinista decisions in connection with the Roman Catholic church tended to support this view. Beginning in early July, the government refused to permit Archbishop Miguel Obando y Bravo, the country's leading Roman Catholic clergyman, to speak on television as he had done since 1974, even during the height of the Somoza years when he often criticized General Somoza.

The archbishop has been critical of the government. "We are not in agreement with this style of spurious socialism," he said in an interview in July. "We cannot accept the elevation of the revolution to the status of a god. Nor can we accept totalitarianism and exhortation to class warfare." (*CSM*, 3 August.)

Late in 1980 and early in 1981, the Nicaraguan National Bishops Conference, headed by Archbishop Obando y Bravo, sought unsuccessfully to get four priests in high government positions to relinquish their government jobs and return to active pastoral roles. The four included Foreign Minister Miguel d'Escoto Brockmann, a Maryknoll father. The move provoked angry reactions not only from the four priests involved, but also from other government officials who accused the church of interfering in "matters that should not concern it" (*FBIS*, 10 February).

Nicaragua's leading newspaper, *La Prensa*, was shut down five times during the last half of 1981 for defying a government ban on "alarmist" news. The first time, *La Prensa* reported that junta followers had torn down church posters. On another occasion, the paper was closed down for three days because it had suggested in an ironic commentary that the government should send a book by revolutionary hero Carlos Fonseca Amador, founder of the FSLN, as a wedding gift to the Prince of Wales and Lady Diana. "National security," the government said, "is endangered by such comments." In a speech two days later, while *La Prensa*'s presses were still idled, Daniel Ortega said "the force of the revolution" will be used against the "reactionary and counterrevolutionary *La Prensa*."

This war of words and bitter denunciations did not mask the growing disarray in Sandinista Nicaragua. Inflation topped 25 percent for the year; foreign debts were increasing (the government refused to release figures); the nation's balance of payments was in deficit to the tune of $500 million for the year; production fell by 1 percent during 1981; unemployment was officially reported to be 17.5 percent. Private sources insisted the situation was even worse than the government admitted.

A private government memorandum in July blamed the problem on "lack of coordination and failure to communicate." That charge seemed corroborated by evidence that many members of the Sandinista Directorate, including Borge, simply run their own offices and pay little attention to integrating the activities of their ministries into the national picture. A leading critic of the government told foreign journalists in July that "each has his own fiefdom and doesn't care what is happening elsewhere." This situation, which is akin to the way Sandinista commanders ran guerrilla operations before uniting in January 1978, apparently was encouraged by the emergence of Daniel and Humberto Ortega as the key members of the government. With Borge being nudged aside, it was not surprising that he would try to run his own show as minister of the interior without much regard for the others in the Sandinista Directorate. Businessmen, particularly members of the Higher Council of Private Enterprise (COSEP), were critical throughout the year of the operation of government ministries—with the surprising exception of Wheelock's Ministry of Agrarian Reform. Wheelock was given high marks for efficiency and an understanding of the private sector's needs in agriculture, although his ministry often was unable to deliver on promises of seed, fertilizer, and credits.

Aggravating the poor economic showing was the flight of thousands of managers, technicians, and professionals, whose skills are badly needed. It was estimated that some 10 percent of the population, perhaps as many as 250,000 people, have left since the Sandinistas came to power in July 1979, in a flight that resembles the mass exodus of Cubans in the first two or three years of Fidel Castro's rule.

During 1981, in an effort to deal with this emigration, much of it clandestine, and other local economic and social problems such as hoarding and theft, the Sandinista Directorate encouraged the development of Committees for the Defense of Sandinism (Comités para la Defensa de Sandinismo). Originally set up in late 1979, they had been allowed to languish. These committees, patterned after the neighborhood networks established by Castro in Cuba in the early 1960s, began maintaining block-by-block watches for dissidents. Denunciations were frequent, and as many as 10,000 Nicaraguans were brought in for questioning as a result. Streets in Managua were patrolled by troops armed with submachine guns; and automobile and personal body checks were increasingly frequent as the year ended.

These crackdowns, together with the totalitarian drift of the Sandinista movement, led to the departure during 1981 of numerous heroes of the struggle against General Somoza. Edén Pastora Gómez, the noted Commandante Cero of the struggle against General Somoza, left the country mysteriously at the end of July along with a number of other commanders. He went first to Costa Rica, then to Panama, and subsequently disappeared. He was known to have been unhappy with the secondary roles assigned him in the government, but his family thought he broke with the government on ideological grounds.

Relations with the United States. Those ideological considerations were key factors in Sandinista relations with the United States. In early 1981, the outgoing Carter administration suspended distribution of $15 million that was still on hand from an economic development loan of $75 million granted to Nicaragua in 1980. The suspension was formally on the technical grounds that the United States needed to verify the proper use of previous disbursements, but was actually a protest over the direction of the Sandinista movement and alleged arms shipments through Nicaragua from Cuba to El Salvador's leftist guerrillas. In February, as reports of an arms conduit through Nicaragua increased, the Reagan administration held up the sale of $9.6 million worth of U.S. wheat. Subsequently, the new administration also announced the continuation of the suspension of aid, which meant that in addition to the $15 million held up by the Carter administration, another $60 million was being sidetracked. Daniel Ortega responded in late February with a charge that the U.S. move "violates the human rights of all Nicaraguans." The pro-government newspaper *Barricada* called the wheat cutoff "a criminal aggression" and warned that "it is only a step from economic war to military aggression." (*Intercontinental Press*, 2 March.)

As the year went on, the United States and Nicaragua traded verbal blows. The FSLN command said in April that "the criminal U.S. conspiracy to bring us to our knees is nothing more than a ruthless capitalist venture that will not work because it is evil." The U.S. State Department, for its part, accused Nicaragua of a massive arms buildup and of totalitarian abuses. The arms buildup included Soviet T-54 and T-55 tanks. In June, U.S. intelligence officials characterized them as the largest weapons ever imported into Central America. The FSLN at first refused to admit the presence of the tanks, but later confirmed their existence. At about the same time, it was disclosed that Sandinista Directorate member Bayardo Arce Castaño had been active in arms shipments through Nicaragua to El Salvador. FSLN sources privately admitted his involvement, and Sandinista officials told the United States that the transfer of arms through Nicaragua would stop.

For a time during July and August, it appeared that U.S.-Nicaragua relations might improve. But disclosures that Nicaragua was acquiring Russian-built MiGs and that Nicaraguans had gone to Cuba and, perhaps, Bulgaria for training in their use led to a further deterioration in relations. A joint U.S.-Honduran military exercise was seen in Managua as evidence "that the United States is not interested in improving relations" (*Barricada*, 15 October). Two weeks later, the pro-Sandinista newspaper *El Nuevo Diario* published the names of thirteen people who it said were Central Intelligence Agency members attached to the U.S. embassy in Managua. The Reagan administration protested the publication and noted that the list included "half a dozen" names of people not in the embassy.

At the United Nations, Daniel Ortega spent more than half of his two-hour speech in October criticizing the United States for "aggression, interference, pressures, and blackmail." The same words were used in the speeches of eight other ranking Sandinista Directorate members, a sign the U.S. State Department viewed as evidence of a coordinated anti-U.S. attack.

As the year ended, the United States indicated that it had not ruled out military action against Nicaragua in light of the totalitarian nature of the Sandinista government and the role Nicaragua was playing "in destabilizing all of Central America."

Relations with Socialist Bloc Nations. The FSLN strengthened its ties with socialist bloc countries throughout the year. Typical of this trend were visits in July by Sandinista Directorate member Henry Ruiz Hernández to East Germany, by labor official Dennis Meléndez to Czechoslovakia, and Nicaraguan Peace Committee President Doris Tijerino to the Soviet Union. Newspapers in Eastern Europe regularly interviewed Nicaraguan leaders—Budapest's *Magyar Hirlap* carried a two-page interview with Borge in August entitled "We Are Building a New Nicaragua." In September, Arce participated in a meeting of the Socialist International's Politburo in Paris and then visited both Sweden and Spain.

FSLN connections with the Arab world grew in 1981. In August, for example, Libya donated $20,000 to the Agencia Nueva Nicaragua, the government news agency. In October, Ernesto Aloma, chief of the Department of Nonaligned Countries and the Middle East in the Nicaraguan Foreign Ministry, commenting on the death of Egyptian President Anwar Sadat, said that Sadat had "betrayed the Arab people" and added that his assassination was "something that was expected" (*FBIS*, 8 October).

Other Parties. The PCN and PSN carried on activities as usual during 1981, but the MAP kept a low profile because of government attacks.

PCN leader Eli Altamirano Pérez claimed in August that the death of Panama's Gen. Omar Torrijos Herrera was "a criminal action by international reaction, part of a vast, aggressive, and cruel plan sponsored by the Reagan government." He did not further elaborate. Earlier, in February, the PCN newspaper, *Avance*, had begun challenging the FSLN to take more aggressive action against the United States. It argued that the mixed economy and pluralistic society promised by the FSLN was "harmful" to the country. *Avance* said it hoped that the FSLN "will change its policy." During the year, Altamirano made similar accusations. In October, he, along with 21 members of the PCN, was arrested by the Interior Ministry for violating the state of emergency and criticizing the government. The ministry spoke of the PCN's "aggressive campaign against our revolution" (ibid., 22 October).

The PSN held its annual congress in July, agreeing that the FSLN was "in the vanguard of our struggle against the forces of aggression, oppression, and imperialism." PSN leader Luís Sánchez spoke of the Sandinista revolution as "this true revolution that has defects but is loaded with virtue, that has limitations but is outstanding because of its greatness, and that has difficulties but is opening great possibilities for a definite social change." The PSN's milder criticism of the Sandinista government appeared to make its role smoother than that of the PCN, which openly criticized the government. PSN leaders, such as Gustavo Tablada, its secretary general, were sent on missions for the FSLN during the year; Tablada led a delegation to Hungary in September. Tablada is also secretary general of the Revolutionary Patriotic Front of Nicaragua (Frente Revolucionario Patriótico de Nicaragua), which is an umbrella group seeking to unite pro-government parties in Nicaragua. It includes the FSLN, the PSN, the Independent Liberal Party (Partido Liberal Independiente), and the Christian Social Populist Party (Partido Populista Social Cristiana).

Biographies: *Tomás Borge Martínez.* The only surviving founder of the FSLN, Tomás Borge Martínez has been a revolutionary for most of his life. As a youth leader at the University of Nicaragua, where he studied law, he flirted with Marxism. He readily joined Carlos Fonseca Amador in setting up the Sandinista movement in 1961.

As the other founders, including Fonseca, were killed in the Sandinista struggles against the Somoza government in the 1960s and 1970s, Borge came to personify the movement and helped give it a strong Marxist overtone. Nicknamed "El Viejo" (The Old Man), he kept the Sandinista cause alive during moments when its fortunes were at low ebb. In 1968, he told an interviewer, "If we can just hold together long enough, the Somoza tyranny will crumble." But there were times when it appeared that he might not live to see the day. He was imprisoned by General Somoza's National Guard on several occasions. By early 1978, it was thought that he had died in prison, but he emerged when political prisoners were ransomed in August 1978.

When the Sandinistas came to power in July 1979, he took over the key Ministry of Interior post, charged with internal security, and there were suggestions that he would emerge as the strong-man in the new government. But after more than two years of Sandinista rule, it is clear that Borge is only one of nine members of the Sandinista Directorate—and not as powerful as some of the others, such as Daniel and Humberto Ortega Saavedra.

At the same time, he remains a symbol of the movement. Born in Matagalpa more than fifty years ago ("the actual date," he says, "is a state secret"), Borge is a short man who is often swallowed up in the crowds of Nicaraguans who surround him as he walks through the streets of Managua. But the adulation that surrounded Borge immediately after the Sandinistas came to power in July 1979 is dissipating. He now appears increasingly as the odd man out in the movement. Still revered as the movement's founder, his importance in the government has declined decidedly.

Daniel and Humberto Ortega. Emerging as the most powerful men in Sandinista Nicaragua, Daniel Ortega Saavedra and Humberto Ortega Saavedra control much of the political and military apparatus of the government. Both are members of the nine-member Sandinista Directorate; Daniel is also one of the three members of the junta of government, and Humberto heads the new, enlarged Sandinista Army as minister of defense.

The sons of a former associate of Gen. Augusto César Sandino, after whom the FSLN was named, they and a third brother, who was killed in the struggle against the Somoza government, were part of the popular *tercerista* ("third") tendency of the Sandinista movement at the time of the fighting (see *YICA*, 1980, p. 378). They eventually came to dominate this tendency. When victory over General Somoza came in July 1979, they were in place to move toward control of the government formed in the wake of Somoza's departure.

Born in Managua, Daniel was 38 and Humberto 33 in 1981. Both studied law, but are not intellectuals. They embraced Marxism and the Sandinista movement in the late 1960s. Both were imprisoned during subsequent years, Daniel serving seven years in jail on bank robbery charges. The two have traveled frequently to Cuba and are regarded as the closest of all Sandinista commanders to Fidel Castro. Since coming to power, both have visited Cuba on several occasions. Daniel Ortega has also been in the United States and met with President Jimmy Carter during one visit.

Daniel has assumed the role of coordinator of the Sandinista movement, serving on both the Sandinista Directorate and in the junta of government. More fiery than his brother, it was assumed very early in the Sandinista government that Humberto was the moderating influence in the family. But Humberto's statements (including a vow in September 1981 to draw up lists of government enemies and to have them "hanged along the highway") are leading to a reassessment.

What seems certain at this moment is that the two brothers have assumed increasing control of the Sandinista movement and the Nicaraguan government since July 1979. During the latter half of 1981, more than two-thirds of all policy statements issued by the government came from either Daniel or Humberto.

Jaime Wheelock Román. A graduate in political science and onetime law professor at the University of Nicaragua, Jaime Wheelock Román is easily the most intellectual figure in the Sandinista leadership. One of nine members of the Sandinista Directorate, the ultimate authority in Sandinista Nicaragua, he is also minister of agrarian reform, charged with bringing order to Nicaragua's agriculture, the mainstay of the economy.

Descended from English settlers who arrived in Nicaragua at the end of the last century, Wheelock was born in Managua and spent some of his formative years in Mexico. He has traveled widely, including an important two-week visit to the United States in late 1979. He has also visited many parts of the Western Hemisphere, including Cuba and Chile. Accused of killing a National Guard officer in 1972, he took refuge in the Chilean Embassy and eventually fled to Chile, where he studied agricultural law at the University of Chile. When the government of President Salvador Allende was overthrown, Wheelock returned to Nicaragua and went underground, emerging as one of the top Sandinista guerrilla commanders in the civil war against General Somoza's government. He eventually came to head the urban faction within the Sandinista movement. During this time, he also wrote a number of scholarly articles and two monographs on Marxist themes, published in Mexico in 1975 and 1976. These books established Wheelock as something of a Marxist thinker.

Wheelock often quarreled with other Sandinista commanders, including Tomás Borge Martínez, during the struggle against the Somoza dynasty. At one point, Borge sought to drum Wheelock out of the Sandinista movement. The Wheelock-Borge feud has been downplayed since the Sandinista victory in July 1979, but insiders say it remains a major irritant within the Sandinista command.

Although Wheelock keeps to himself and is something of a private person, he has a wide personal following among Nicaraguans. His work as head of agrarian reform puts him in close contact with Nicaragua's peasants. A handsome man of 38, he also commands a loyal following of former Sandinista guerrillas who appear as committed to him as they are to the Sandinista cause.

Christian Science Monitor   James Nelson Goodsell

Panama

The pro-Soviet communist People's Party of Panama (PPP) was founded in 1930 and was banned from 1953 until 1968. In that year, however, Gen. Omar Torrijos took power by military coup, and the PPP came to his support. In return, members of the PPP received high positions, and the party was tolerated, although not formally recognized. In 1978, Torrijos opened the political system to participation of parties; the PPP shared in the process and was rewarded by formal recognition.

In that same year, however, the fortunes of the PPP declined. From 1968 to 1978, it was an important support for the somewhat isolated regime. After 1978, with the canal treaties ratified, the government shifted toward more conservative policies. A new official party, the Democratic Revolutionary Party, was founded, and the Communists were marginalized. The PPP was allowed to present candidates for elections in September 1980 only as independents since it was unable to secure the required number of signatures for registration. Subsequently, the party became increasingly critical of the government over such issues as hospitality for the Shah of Iran, support for leftist movements in El Salvador and Guatemala, and the Soviet invasion of Afghanistan.

In the spring of 1981, however, the PPP qualified for participation in the 1984 presidential elections. (*Latin American Regional Report: Mexico and Central America*, 19 July). This event represented the continuation of the process begun in 1978 when Torrijos and the National Guard "returned to the barracks" and gradually began to allow traditional parties to participate in the political process. At a meeting convened to celebrate the party's successful registration drive, Secretary General Rubén Darío Souza commented that it had thereby gained the right to speak for the Panamanian left (*FBIS*, 23 July).

On 31 July, a light plane carrying General Torrijos crashed into a mountain in the western part of the Isthmus of Panama. Despite deteriorating relations in recent years, the death of Torrijos dealt a serious blow to the party, which had gained status and recognition in the early 1970s as a key component in his political coalition. Reacting to Torrijos's death, the party's Political Bureau requested that members "express their grief and sorrow by attending all the public demonstrations and rallies that seek to confirm the unity of the forces of the process and the decision to continue onward." The bureau added that "General Torrijos struggled for the elimination of the colonial enclave of the Canal Zone, which was recovered with the signing and approval of the Torrijos-Carter treaties—an achievement of the greatest value in the Panamanian people's long anti-imperialist struggle, a struggle that must continue and culminate in the country's total liberation." (*Critica*, 3 August.) A PPP representative in the National Assembly of Representatives claimed that the Central Intelligence Agency was responsible for the plane accident (*La Prensa*, 18 August).

International Relations. Relations with the Chinese Communist Party remained hostile. In May, the Central Committee accused the Chinese of provocative acts along the Vietnamese border and of threatening the peace in Southeast Asia (*FBIS*, 1 June). However, when Panamanian President Arístides Royo conducted talks in June with a representative of the People's Republic of China, the government-controlled press speculated that formal relations might be established soon (*Critica*, 4 June). Party relations with Cuba remained friendly, although Torrijos and the Panamanian government took an increasingly hostile stance. Castro had not kept Torrijos informed about details of the January "final offensive" in El Salvador at a time when Torrijos was working toward a negotiated solution. In March, five members of the Panamanian Student Federation were captured by the Colombian armed forces as they attempted to join M-19 guerrillas in that country. Panama blamed Castro for arming and training the students and announced that it would review its relations with Cuba. (*Latin American Weekly Report*, 3 April.)

The PPP continued to play a rather conservative international role during 1981, while other groups on the left were more active. Not only did some Panamanian students attempt to join the M-19 guerrillas in Colombia, but members of Panama's Victoriano Lorenzo Brigade, which had fought with the Sandinistas in Nicaragua, discussed similar participation in El Salvador. Hugo Spadafora, a former vice-minister of health who fought in both Guinea-Bissau and Nicaragua, met in Panama with Sandinista leader Edén Pastora Gómez after Pastora left Nicaragua in July. There was speculation that the two guerrilla leaders wished to join Col. Adolfo Majano (a former member of the Salvadoran junta) in assembling a new international brigade. The ideological motivation was presumably social democracy and Simón Bolívar's dream of a united Latin America. (*La Republica*, 15 July.)

The Panamanian government's rift with Cuba coupled with the death of Omar Torrijos put the PPP in a difficult exposed position; it has reacted by calling for unity of the left. It is still too early to tell what impact Torrijos's death will have on the party's political future. This will probably depend on the coalition-building tactics adopted by the small group of colonels that aspire to leadership of the National Guard. Already, some have been courting elements of the left in an effort to gain the upper hand in coming power struggles. (*Diálogo Social*, November–December.)

New Mexico State University   Steven C. Ropp

Paraguay

The Paraguayan Communist Party (PCP), founded in 1928, has been illegal during most of its history. Most of its membership, estimated at around 3,500, lives in exile. Nevertheless, the PCP's newspaper, *Adelante*, circulates clandestinely inside Paraguay, and Communists continue trying to infiltrate labor unions and student organizations. Periodic arrests of communist agents by the Paraguayan police attest to the existence of an active underground movement. One of the more spectacular arrests was in 1977, when the PCP's first secretary, Miguel Angel Soler, Jr., was surprised in his Asunción hideout by the police. His fate is still unknown.

During 1981, the PCP spent most of its time trying to secure the release of Soler's successor, Antonio Maidana, who is thought to be a prisoner in Paraguay also. Maidana and a friend, Emilio Roa, were arrested by Argentine police in Buenos Aires on 27 August 1980. Since then, their families and friends have been unable to discover their whereabouts, although Maidana's wife has appealed to Argentina's president for help. Argentine authorities disclaim any knowledge about the affair, however, saying only that the case is being investigated.

Several theories, each claiming some "evidence," are circulating about Maidana's fate. Whatever the real facts, the PCP has used the incident as effective propaganda for mobilizing world opinion against the regime of Alfredo Stroessner. Human rights groups, like Amnesty International, have petioned the Argentine government, the United Nations Commission on Human Rights, and the International Commission of the Red Cross to investigate the affair. Since the PCP is a Moscow-oriented party, it has received the support of the Communist Party of Cuba for an international investigation (*Granma*, Havana, 4 January). In an interview with the Mexican newspaper *El Heraldo*, Stroessner accused the Communists of leading an international terrorist movement aimed at destabilizing the legitimate governments of Latin America. He specifically accused "Marxists-Leninists" of the assassination of Anastasio Somoza in Paraguay last year, but added that after the initial uproar, the killing had helped to unite the people against the terrorists. (*International Affairs*, Moscow, 12 November 1980.)

In August 1980, the PCP added its voice of protest to that of other opposition parties over Paraguay's proposed new electoral law, which prohibits political parties from joining international associations, instructing their members to cast blank ballots, or advocating abstention from voting. The PCP said that the new law was part of the regime's plan to stay in power (*NYT*, 20 September; *Latin America Regional Report: Southern Cone*, 4 September). Despite the PCP's support of the opposition, it has been unable to gain entry into the National Accord, the anti-Stroessner front composed of Liberals, Febreristas, dissident Colorados, and Christian Democrats. The PCP suffered another leadership crisis in April when its second secretary, Alfredo Alcorta, disappeared in Buenos Aires. Alcorta, who had led the party since Maidana was abducted, has not been heard of since (*World Affairs Report*, 11, no. 1).

Tulane University   Paul H. Lewis

Peru

The Peruvian Communist Party has been illegal most of the time since its founding in 1928. However, the return of civilian rule to Peru in July 1980 after a twelve-year hiatus ushered in a period of new opportunities and challenges for the country's many Marxist-Leninist political parties and labor organizations. Most of the "responsible" left formed a working coalition of political parties, which had considerable success in the November 1980 municipal elections and held together through 1981 to become, in the view of some observers, "the only presently operating clear-cut opposition" (*Expreso,* 13 July). A pioneering effort by this coalition to open and operate a new daily newspaper, *El Diario de Marka,* met with substantial initial success but subsequently fell into severe internal disagreements. Marxist-oriented labor unions and workers' federations actively pursued efforts to restore some of the wages lost to inflation and repression over the past several years by strike activity at a level almost unprecedented in Peru. Almost simultaneously with the inauguration of the new civilian president, Fernando Belaúnde Terry, elements of the irresponsible left began a campaign of bombings of public and foreign buildings and facilities that ebbed and flowed during 1981 with growing violence and increased popular concern. Relations with Cuba recuperated slightly from the damage suffered in the incidents accompanying the "occupation" of the Peruvian Embassy in Havana by some ten thousand Cubans in April 1980. The substantial economic, commercial, and military ties built between Peru and the Soviet Union during the Revolutionary Military Government (1968–1980) continued at a relatively high level.

Political Parties. It is estimated that Peru has between 40 and 50 political parties, of which 34 participated in the 1980 presidential and congressional elections; of these, 24 were of Marxist-Leninist orientation. The major divisions on the left revolve around ideology, leadership, and violence or non-violence as the way to socialism. The Marxist-Leninist parties taking part in the 1980 presidential and congressional elections gained 19 percent of the presidential vote (divided among five candidates). Seven of the parties or alliances of parties picked up 10 Senate seats (of 60) and 14 Chamber of Deputies seats (of 180). (*Latin America Regional Report [LARR],* 20 June 1980, p. 2; *Latin America Weekly Report [LAWR],* 30 May 1980, p. 7.) Although this level of support and representation seems substantial, it was quite disappointing to the left when compared with earlier successes. Together the various leftist parties had garnered over 34 percent of the vote for delegates to the constituent assembly in 1978. Further contributing to their disappointment was the collapse of the left's efforts to form a united front for the 1980 elections, the ill-fated Revolutionary Left Alliance. Each party then decided to fend for itself or in smaller alliances, with predictable results.

The national electoral debacle led to new efforts by the left to form a common front for the November 1980 municipal elections. This initiative was considerably more successful. The United Left (IU) took 27 percent of the total vote in Lima and pluralities in 6 of 23 department capitals, to become the "second party" of the country behind President Belaúnde's Popular Action (AP), which received 36 percent of the Lima vote and pluralities in 11 department capitals (*LARR,* 12 December

1980, p. 2). The IU's success spurred efforts by leftist leaders to make permanent their temporary electoral alliance; the result was the formalization of the IU with Alfonso Barrantes Lingan of the Communist Party of Peru (PCP) installed as president. Except for the Trotskyists, the IU included the major parties of the left: the Popular Democratic Union (UDP), the National Union of the Revolutionary Left (UNIR), the PCP, the Revolutionary Socialist Party (PSR), the Revolutionary Working Class Communist Party (PCR-CO), the Students', Peasants', and Workers' Popular Front (FOCEP), and, at times, the regional-based (Puno) National Workers' and Peasants' Front. (Ibid., 23 January, p. 3.) The Trotskyist parties—the Revolutionary Workers' Party, the Socialist Workers' Party (PST), the Trotskyist Revolutionary Labor Party, and the Marxist Revolutionary Workers' Party (POMR)—retained their independent position even though they lost most of the ground in the 1980 national and local elections that they had gained in the 1978 constituent assembly vote.

During 1981, the IU worked to establish itself as a viable opposition force to the Belaúnde government. Although its key members were willing to meet with the president in June and July to discuss his invitation to form a broad political pact to work together to solve a number of pressing social problems, they quickly rejected any formal collaboration. The position of the left was that Peru's real problems were economic, not social, and the government's conservative economic policy was making things worse (*FBIS,* 6 July). Nevertheless, as Barrantes pointed out, this was "the first time in Peruvian history that a president of Peru will hold talks with the left" (*Oiga,* 29 June, p. 29). The IU Executive Committee met with President Belaúnde for three hours on 2 July. It was made up of Barrantes, Genaro Ledesma (FOCEP), Jorge del Prado (PCP), Manuel Dammert (PCR-CO), Alfredo Filomeno (PSR), Edmundo Murrugarra and Luís Benítez (UDP), and Jorge Hurtado and Juan Sánchez (UNIR). The committee felt that the meeting added to the IU's legitimacy, although it rejected the president's initiatives and took advantage of the occasion to present its own document, "Proposals to the Country." Among the most important goals stressed were the need for general wage increases, a price freeze on staples, improvements in marketing, readjustment of salaries in advance of inflation, opposition to executive decree laws, repeal of the March terrorist law and amnesty for those imprisoned under it, respect for congressional and municipal immunity, reinstatement of dismissed workers, and the right to strike. (*Marka,* 3 July, pp. 12–14.) Subsequently, del Prado and Dammert distanced the left still further from the Belaúnde administration by arguing that the constitutional government was being converted into "a virtual civilian-military dictatorship by the actions of the AP, which has deceived the voters" (*El Comercio,* 23 July, p. A4).

Jorge del Prado agreed that the new organization was not yet ready to enter the government and exercise power. "With more work with the masses and the growing momentum of the class struggle," however, he believed that "we will create a single party" (*Marka,* 11 June; *FBIS,* 15 July). As Alfonso Barrantes put it, the IU wanted to organize and legitimate itself sufficiently so that it could "indulge in the luxury of winning the 1985 elections." As he interpreted the political dynamics of Peru, the strongest non-Marxist party with a well-organized mass base, the American Popular Revolutionary Alliance (APRA), "is collapsing, and the task of guiding the masses is shifting to leftist hands. (*Oiga,* 29 June, p. 31.) Whatever the ideological and personality differences that distinguish the left parties within the IU, they share a common perception that a historic opportunity is present in Peru that could enable them to advance toward socialism through elections. As one commentary put it, "all left-wing parties represented in congress have dropped their underground operations, with Red Fatherland [PCP-PR, part of FOCEP] the last to resurface. Apart from its traditional hold over the main union confederation, the General Confederation of Peruvian Workers [CGTP], the legal left is now well represented in local government and congress, and clearly feels that this is an inopportune moment to launch into armed struggle." (*LARR,* 23 January, p. 3.)

The Trotskyist parties are the most ambivalent on the issue of violence to gain their objectives. While they did participate in the 1980 elections, winning five seats in congress, they oppose a dialogue with the government because "it lends legitimacy to the bourgeoisie"; they look askance at violent acts against the government, not because they oppose violence per se, but because "objective conditions are not yet ready." Senator Ricardo Napurí Shapiro (POMR) articulated the Trotskyist position: "Our objective is to make every popular organization and its members become fighting forces, to boycott the enemy, and to strive for the formation of a mass organization." As a step toward the advancement of this position, Napurí announced the merging of POMR and the PST, led by Enrique Fernández Chacón, in late July. (*Caretas,* 6 July, pp. 34–39.)

The leftist groups most prepared to argue that the time was propitious for "launching a prolonged popular war in Peru" were Shining Path (PCP-SL), Red Town, and the Victoria Navarro group of the Revolutionary Left Movement (*LARR,* 23 January, p. 2). These organizations, particularly the PCP-SL, were most often accused by the media and the government of being responsible for most of the seven hundred acts of bombing public buildings or equipment and assaults against public authority recorded between July 1980 and March 1981 (*NYT,* 13 May).

Although these attacks posed no serious threat to the government, they were unsettling. During the year, they became more violent, with at least six deaths recorded between February and October (*LAWR,* 6 February, p. 12, 23 October, p. 7, 30 October, p. 12; *FBIS,* 16 August). One result of the escalation was the declaration of a state of emergency in October in five of the seven provinces of the department of Ayacucho, where four of the deaths had occurred. Another was the resignation of the minister of the interior, José María de la Jara, later in the month after a student died in Cuzco while in Civil Guard custody. (*LAWR,* 6 November, p. 8.) In Lima, where the first bombings occurred in December 1980 (*FBIS,* 16 December 1980), targets included embassies and official residences, including those of the United States, offices of foreign companies, and brief occupations of radio stations. In the provinces, particularly the Ayacucho area, power stations, high-tension pylons, and communications networks were bombed, and several police stations were assaulted by armed groups.

In March 1980, top PCP-SL members decided in a secret meeting that "conditions existed for launching a prolonged popular war in Peru, spreading from the countryside to the towns" (*LARR,* 23 January, p. 2). Through early 1981, the documented bombings had occurred primarily in Ayacucho. The PCP-SL had its major center here, at the University of San Cristóbal de Huamanga, since its founding in 1970 in an ideological split with the Maoist PCP-PR. Known leaders of the PCP-SL arrested on different occasions during the year included Luís Kawata Makabe (*El Comercio,* 25 February), Nicolás Matayoshi (*FBIS,* 4 June), Mario Cárdenas (*LAWR,* 23 October, p. 7), and original founder and ranking head Abimael Guzmán (ibid., 6 November, p. 8). In addition, several training camps were discovered in Apurímac, Ayacucho, and Lima. The August attack on a Civil Guard post in Quinua in which a sergeant was killed and a policeman wounded coincided with new wall paintings of PCP-SL slogans in nearby Ayacucho (*FBIS,* 16 August). The geographical spread of attacks outside the PCP-SL's known areas of strength in Ayacucho, Andahuaylas, and Cajamarca is believed in part to result from coordination with the Red Town group (ibid., 12 January).

The government responded by decreeing a tough new antiterrorist law in March (Decree Law 46) giving terms of up to twenty years for assaults or advocacy of violence. Although as of October no convictions had been obtained under the statute (*LAWR,* 23 October, p. 7), several hundred arrests were made, and a specialized Civil Guard antiterrorist brigade, the Sinchis, actively pursued bombers and assaulters in Ayacucho. Although considerable success was claimed, the groups presumably responsible for the attacks had also achieved part of their goal of sowing uncertainty and fear. The leftist parties represented in IU, however, were equally vigorous in their denunciations of both the government and the advocates of violence. They strenuously argued for the repeal of Decree Law 46 and alleged government torture, a position also supported by the church (*LARR,* 28 August, p. 7). IU leader Alfonso Barrantes also declared his group's opposition to terrorist acts: "We are neither terrorists nor anarchists. We are followers of [PCP founder José Carlos] Mariátegui" (*FBIS,* 15 July).

Through investigations and arrests during the year, high government officials were eventually prepared to document their long-standing suspicion that the PCP-SL was behind many incidents (ibid., 18 December).

Union Activity. In the absence of extensive union-organizing activity by the ruling AP, and with the weakening of the historically dominant labor movement of APRA, the Confederation of Peruvian Workers, the CGTP continued to dominate much of organized labor (about 10 percent of the workforce). At the January congress of the union, Moscow-line PCP leaders Isidoro Gamarra and Eduardo Sánchez Castillo were re-elected president and secretary general. (*LARR,* 27 February, p. 5.) At the same meeting, the radical 100,000-strong teachers' union, Sole Union of Peruvian Workers in Education, historically tied to the Maoist PCP-PR, was elected to membership. In addition, for the first time in CGTP history, the labor minister was invited to attend. This reflected in part appreciation of his ability to bring unions, the government, and management together into a Tripartite Commission to handle labor disputes, most particularly the issue of reinstatement of some two thousand workers fired during the last years of the military government (1968–1980), a priority of the CGTP.

The CGTP was less successful in gaining worker adherence to repeated calls or threats to call general strikes. A 15 January initiative to protest government price increases was only 30 percent effective (*LAWR,* 23 January, p. 6); a 22 September effort against the antistrike law, even less so. Threats of stoppages in April and August were "postponed" in the face of worker reluctance. Such lack of success was not the result of labor quiescence, however. In 1980, almost eighteen million man-hours were lost in 739 strikes; this high rate was exceeded in 1981 as workers continued to try to regain real wages lost between 1975 and 1979 (*Los Angeles Times,* 19 August). The problem for CGTP was that its calls for general strikes were perceived as intended to accomplish political goals during a period in which most workers were concerned about economic ones.

Foreign Relations. Peru retained under civilian rule the range of diplomatic missions to the communist bloc established under the military government between 1968 and 1980. Fairly strong economic and commercial ties developed between Peru and Romania, Czechoslovakia, and Hungary in particular, including economic assistance projects. Major arms purchases from the Soviet Union in 1976 and 1977 exceeded $800 million and included training for over four hundred Peruvian officers and enlisted personnel into 1981 as well as a contingent of about one hundred Soviet officers in Peru for training and support purposes during the year. Soviet commitments to various economic projects were reaffirmed, although the status of a major Soviet contribution to a proposed hydroelectric project at Olmos was still uncertain. The executive branch did not act on congress's approval of the project in principle in May. Senior Soviet Air Force officers visited Lima in June, and Supreme Soviet Deputy Chairman Antanas Barjauskas in November.

After a difficult period of relations with Cuba following the "invasion" of the Peruvian Embassy in Havana in April 1980 by an estimated ten thousand Cubans seeking to leave their country, slow improvement was noted. In September long and arduous secret negotiations enabled 19 of the 32 Cuban refugees remaining in the Embassy to return home (*LAWR,* 11 September, p. 12). There were some indications of interest by the Peruvian government in sending an ambassador to Cuba once again, but no firm timetable.

In a symbolic action, fifteen leftist deputies and senators declared the new U.S. ambassador to Peru, Frank Ortiz, persona non grata in October on the grounds of an unproven accusation by the military government in 1969 that Ortiz was an agent of the Central Intelligence Agency.

Publications. In a major publishing initiative, Peru's left-wing parties bought shares in a holding company to establish a new paper, *El Diario de Marka,* in May 1980. Party members were appointed to the staff and a distinguished intellectual, Guillermo Thorndike, became editor. From an initial press run of 5,000, the total increased to 75,000 by January 1981 (*LARR,* 23 January, p. 4). With Trotskyists running the accounting department, the Maoist-oriented UDP the editorial department, and the Moscow-line PCP the union, problems were bound to arise. In April, Guillermo Thorndike resigned. In June, Jorge del Prado (PCP) complained that the Chinese-oriented UDP's positions and initiatives were given more coverage than those of other left parties (*Marka,* 11 June, p. 20). In July, the chairman of the board, Jorge Flores Lamas, also left, withdrawing the services of the press that had been printing the paper. Although the IU and the union were able to work out an agreement to keep the paper going, the united left publishing effort clearly had stumbled badly.

Foreign Service Institute   David Scott Palmer

Puerto Rico

The Puerto Rican Socialist Party (Partido Socialista Puertorriqueño; PSP) is the main legal leftist group in the island. The PSP is a Marxist, pro-Moscow, and strongly pro-Cuban organization, which follows closely a Castroite line and reportedly is helped financially by Havana. Its secretary general, Juan Marí Bras, frequently visits Havana, where he is presented as a close friend and follower of Fidel Castro. To add to his stature, his invitations to Cuba are issued in the name of the Central Committee of the Communist Party of Cuba. Marí Bras often states his group's policies while in the Cuban capital. In May, he attacked President Reagan and said that the Reagan White House views Puerto Rico "as a strategic and geopolitical base in the Caribbean which should be led toward annexation in accordance with U.S. geopolitical purposes . . . This represents greater danger for the survival of our nationality and behooved us Puerto Ricans to make greater effort aimed at unity and militancy in order to oppose that aim." (Radio Havana, 13 May; *FBIS*, 14 May.) This view was similar to that of the Havana government. "Puerto Rico plays a key role in the global and regional military plan of imperialism," stated a Havana magazine in January. "Among other factors, it [Puerto Rico] is considered part of the defense system for the Panama Canal and its maritime accesses, a base of operations that facilitates possible military intervention in the Caribbean region and helps intimidate neighboring people, a center of naval activities and protection of maritime routes in the South Atlantic" (*Tricontinental*, January, pp. 74–75, 87, 100). The PSP maintains a permanent office in Havana, headed by Felipe Cirino, a member of the PSP Central Committee. According to Fidel Castro, Cuba's support for Puerto Rico's independence and for the PSP "is a historic and moral duty as well as an inescapable need because as long as there is a single Puerto Rican to defend the cause of independence our solidarity would go out to him" (Radio Havana, 24 September; *FBIS*, 25 September).

Organization and Leadership. Following the Soviet pattern, the PSP has a Political Bureau, its highest organ, a Secretariat, and a Central Committee. The last PSP congress was in 1979, when Marí Bras was elected secretary general. Carlos Callisá is president of the PSP. In the 4 November 1980 elections for governor, the highest elected office in Puerto Rico, PSP candidate Luís Lansell Hernández received 0.3 percent of the vote. The PSP publishes the daily newspaper *Claridad* in San Juan. Party membership is estimated at under 150.

Other Leftist Groups. The Puerto Rican Communist Party (Partido Comunista Puertorriqueño) is a pro-Moscow and anti-Beijing group that has had close and long ties with the Communist Party, U.S.A. Founded in 1934, dissolved in 1944, and revived in 1946, it has under 125 members. It publishes *El Pueblo* and *El Proletario*. There are other, illegal terrorist leftist groups that operate both on the island and among Puerto Rican communities in the continental United States. Among them are the Macheteros ("machete wielders"), also known as the Borícua Popular Army (Ejército Popular Borícua; the Armed Forces of Popular Resistance (Fuerzas Armadas de la Resistencia Popular); the Organization of Volunteers for the Puerto Rican Revolution; the Armed Forces of Puerto Rican National Liberation (Fuerzas Armadas de Liberación Nacional Puertorriqueña; FALN); and the Armed Forces of Popular Resistance (Fuerzas Armadas de la Resistencia Popular). The International Workers' League (Liga Internacional de Trabajadores) is said to be associated with the Fourth (Trotskyist) International. The Puerto Rican Socialist League (Liga Socialista Puertorriqueña; LSP), founded in 1964, is reported to have ties with the Progressive Labor Party of the United States. The LSP is led by Secretary General Juan Antonio Corretjei, a former aide to the late Pedro Albizú Campo, leader of the independence movement. All seven, whose total membership is believed to be about 150, advocate independence and a Marxist government in Puerto Rico.

Increase in Terrorism. Although tiny, the first five underground groups mentioned above, according to federal law enforcement officials, pose a real threat to Puerto Rican society because they are becoming more daring and sophisticated and more willing to kill. They are said to be difficult to penetrate because their recruitment is slow and selective. Officials say that Puerto Rican terrorist groups are organized in tight, clandestine cells of four or five people who do not know the members of other cells. This year, the terrorist groups concentrated on attacking military personnel, recruiting stations, and defense contractors in the island. On the mainland, they have been placing bombs in public places for years. The most serious incident was at Fraunces Tavern in lower Manhattan in 1975, where a FALN action killed four persons and injured 53. Early in January 1981, the Macheteros claimed responsibility for the destruction of half of the Air National Guard unit's complement of twenty airplanes, used primarily for training. In July, a FALN group in Chicago, according to court testimony, planned to kidnap a high-ranking government official or President Reagan's son Ron, who lives in New York, to seek release of eleven of its members sentenced to prison on terrorism charges. In November, the Macheteros took responsibility for a bomb explosion that damaged power lines to San Juan's main tourist district. Several other terrorist incidents were reported late in 1981 in various places on the island. Marí Bras and other PSP leaders praised the planning and execution of some of the terrorist actions, saying that they are not really terrorist attacks but demonstrations intended to show that Puerto Rico is a country occupied militarily by the United States. The overwhelming majority of Puerto Ricans, who consistently have voted against independence, repudiate violence as means of solving political issues.

Political Life. The 4 November 1980 gubernatorial, legislative, and municipal elections were the closest in the island's history. Only several months later, after many recounts, was the narrow victory (by some three thousand votes) of incumbent Governor Carlos Romero Barceló confirmed. For Romero Barceló, the leader of the pro-statehood New Progressive Party (Partido Nuevo Progresista; PNP), it was less than a convincing victory. He had predicted a margin of 10 to 20 percent over his opponent, former Governor Rafael Hernández Colón, who heads the Popular Democratic Party (Partido Popular Democrático; PPD) and supports the island's present political status as a commonwealth, or "free associated state" of the United States. Romero Barceló, had he won by a large margin, planned to hold a plebiscite on the statehood issue. The plebiscite was postponed indefinitely. In the gubernatorial race, Romero Barceló obtained 47.2 percent of the vote and Hernández Colón 47.1 percent. (About 5 percent of the electorate cast ballots for parties favoring independence, but only a handful chose the Puerto Rican Independence Party [Partido Independentista Puertorriqueño], which, in contrast to the PSP and the clandestine groups, favors peaceful transition to independence negotiated with Washington's approval.) Hernández Colón's PPD won a slim 26- to 25-seat margin over the PNP in the House of Representatives. But the PPD's one-seat advantage could be lost if the U.S. Supreme Court decides in January 1982 to order a new election in the disputed Caguas district, where the original PPD victor subsequently died. Winners in six mayoral seats were also involved in a dispute thirteen months after the elections. The PPD victories, its majority in the upper house of the state legislature, its control of most of the city halls, and its temporary control of the lower house have placed Hernández Colón in a good position for another try at the governorship in 1984. The platform of the PPD calls, within the framework of the Commonwealth, for more autonomy for Puerto Rico in immigration, customs, offshore exploration rights, foreign commercial representation, and other gubernatorial functions. There are two tendencies within the PPD. One stresses "permanent union" with the United States and shuns any contacts with Puerto Rico's various independence factions. The other emphasizes the "free association statehood" status implicit in the commonwealth arrangement, which would leave open the possibility that in the future Puerto Rico could choose to be "associated" with the United States. Hernández Colón appears to oscillate between the two views.

University of Miami   George Volsky

Suriname

With a population estimated at 388,000, Suriname became independent in 1975. A July 1980 military coup overthrew the moderate government of Henck Arron, installed at the time of independence, and established a "socialist republic," recently under the leadership of Lt. Col. Daysi Bouterse. There were several very small radical groups on the fringes of politics, including the People's Party, the Revolutionary People's Party, and one calling itself the Communist Party of Suriname. The last, however, was not really organized as a party until a founding congress on 24 July 1981.

The new party merged with Revolutionary Liberation Movement of Suriname, which had existed for two and a half years. Bram Behr was made its legal spokesman, and it began publication of a party organ, *Red Seri*. The party program calls for an "anti-imperialist revolution" to lead to a socialist revolution and a socialist Suriname, under the leadership of the proletariat allied with the poor peasants (*JPRS*, 78906, 3 September; *De Ware Tijd*, 10 July).

Hoover Institution   Robert Wesson

United States

The largest Marxist-Leninist organization in the United States is the Communist Party, U.S.A. (CPUSA). Formed in 1919, it also has been known as the Workers Party and the Communist Political Association. The CPUSA does not publish membership figures. However, its general secretary has claimed that the party has 20,000 members and that 300,000 others "consider themselves communists" but do not dare to join the party (*NYT*, 6 January). It is one of the most unreservedly pro-Soviet parties in the world.

There are several Trotskyist parties in the United States. The largest is the Socialist Workers Party (SWP), which claims about two thousand members. It traces its origins back to 1928 when James Cannon was expelled from the CPUSA for criticizing Stalin. The SWP was founded in 1938 as a member of the Fourth (Trotskyist) International, although since 1940 it has claimed to be legally disaffiliated from that organization because of the Voorhis Act. Nevertheless, the SWP is one of the largest parties playing an active role in the operations of the United Secretariat of the Fourth International.

Party Leadership and Internal Affairs. There were few changes in CPUSA leadership during 1981. Prominent officials during the year were Gus Hall (general secretary), Henry Winston (national chairman), Arnold Bechetti (national secretary), James Jackson (education director), Victor Perlo (chairman, Economics Section), and Michael Zagarell (editor, *Daily World*).

Shortly after the 1980 national elections in the United States, Hall told a plenary session of the Central Committee that campaign reports from party members indicated that "the party's influence is much greater" than before. These reports reflected a new respect for the party across the country, he said, and showed that "we have established new relationships with leaders of mass organizations." Hall also mentioned that in recent years "we have had a new kind of in-migration of people" into the party. Large numbers of Italian, Greek, Arabic, and Spanish speakers have joined the CPUSA, he said, and should be encouraged to conduct party meetings in their own language. (*IB*, March.)

The CPUSA won a major victory in a federal court decision in late September. After the 1976 national elections, the U.S. Federal Election Commission had filed a suit against the CPUSA because it refused to submit the names and addresses of persons who had contributed $50 or more to its campaign. In dismissing the case, the court noted that "the record plainly reflects an extensive history of governmental harassment . . . directed at the Party and its members and supporters." Party Election Committee attorney John Abt called the decision "a gain for all democratic people against the enemies of the Bill of Rights." (*Daily World*, 29 September; *Guardian*, New York, 14 October.)

Much of the CPUSA's limited influence in the United States comes from a network of organizations that are dominated by, though not officially tied to, the party. These include the Young Workers Liberation League (YWLL), which serves as the CPUSA's youth wing. The YWLL held its fifth national convention in New York City from 26 to 29 June. Some six hundred delegates attended from a membership of about four thousand. The YWLL national chairman is James Steele; its paper is *Young Worker*. Among the CPUSA's united front organizations are the National Alliance Against Racist and Political Repression, whose members include Angela Davis and onetime CPUSA presidential candidate Charlene Mitchell, who serves as executive director of the alliance; the Committee for Trade Union Action and Democracy; the National Council on American-Soviet Friendship; the Chile Solidarity Committee; the National Anti-Imperialist Movement in Solidarity with African Liberation; the Committee for a Just Peace in the Middle East; and Women for Racial and Economic Equality.

Domestic Attitudes and Activities. For the CPUSA, U.S. President Ronald Reagan represents everything that is wrong with capitalism and that "sick and violent society" he governs. "Emperor Reagan" is a servant of the monopolies, and his economic programs benefit only the rich. Thus the big issue in the 3 November elections was "Reaganomics." In carrying out their program, the Reaganites have launched a relentless antipeople offensive aimed particularly at labor. According to the editors of *Daily World*, "the most anti-labor, skinflint, sweatshop boss would find it hard to outdo President Reagan." The air traffic controllers' affair was regarded as an especially flagrant example of brutal strikebreaking and should serve as "a lesson to millions of other federal workers." In fact, the CPUSA charges, Reagan has put the government "into the strikebreaking and scab business." The aim of the Labor Department is "to destroy the barricades of protections labor has erected against employers." Thus the CPUSA strongly supported such unified labor demonstrations as the rally of the National Council of Senior Citizens in Washington on 21 July and the Solidarity Day called for 19 September by the AFL-CIO. (*Daily World*, 16 and 24 July, 4, 8, 12, 24, and 27 August, 3 and 11 September.)

Daily World editorialized (14 August) that Reagan has launched a "blitzkrieg against the people," which the president calls a campaign for "law and order," in order to support his repressive policies. Civil, minority, and other rights have been slashed, and under the guise of "getting the government off the backs of the people," Reagan has made it possible for the FBI, CIA, and other government agencies to further "disrupt and destroy the lives of innocent citizens" (ibid., 28 August, 8 October).

President Reagan was not the only government leader to draw criticism from the CPUSA. Indeed, passage of measures by Congress demonstrated clearly that the Democrats were allies of the Republicans. Just after the 1980 elections, Hall pointed out that 7.5 million Americans had expressed their displeasure with both major parties by voting for independents (*Political Affairs*, January). So "Why not a new party?" asked a *Daily World* editorial on 17 September. CPUSA leaders recognize some of the problems inherent in the formation of such a party, however, not least the "anti-Sovietism" that they find threatens not only leftist-labor unity but the international peace movement and our very chance for survival (*Daily World*, 6 August).

International Views and Activities. The CPUSA describes the world in terms virtually indistinguishable from those used by the Communist Party of the Soviet Union (CPSU). As a foundation for this allegiance to the Soviet Union and its positions, major CPUSA speeches and articles laud conditions in the USSR and assert the superiority of the government of the Soviet Union to that of the

United States (Hall, "A Tale of Two Systems," *Political Affairs*, June). This is accompanied by repeated assertions, as the title of one of Hall's articles puts it, that "peace and disarmament are supreme goals of the Soviet Union" (*IB*, August; the article is Hall's foreword to the English edition of Brezhnev's report to the Twenty-Sixth Congress of the CPSU). *Daily World* editorials and articles repeatedly adduce 120 or more Soviet efforts to ensure peace and disarmament, all of which have been rejected by recent U.S. presidents (*Daily World*, 20 June, 1 August, 13 August). One "big lie" of the United States is that the Soviet Union uses chemical weapons, when in fact it is the Americans who do so (ibid., 19 September). President Reagan's "scorecard," according to *Daily World* (21 August), is "0 for humanism and 100 percent for cold-war inhumanity."

The United States' foreign policy, according to editorials in *Daily World*, is governed by "anti-Sovietism and anti–national liberationism" (26 August) and is manifested in brinkmanship (20 August), new Vietnam-type involvements (3 October), feeding fires in the Middle East, particularly by aiding Israel, Egypt, and Saudi Arabia (23 June, 27 August, 14 October), and by promoting terrorism around the world (17 April). Among the most cynical of U.S. policies is America's effort to destroy socialism in Poland by supporting anti-Soviet elements in the Solidarity movement (Hall, *Neues Deutschland*, East Berlin, 9 July; *Daily World*, 5 August).

Hall and other CPUSA leaders made several trips to Soviet bloc countries during the year. In March Hall received the Georgi Dimitrov Order in Bulgaria in recognition of his "struggle for peace, democracy, and social progress" (Radio Sofia, 9 March).

Publications. *Daily World*, the CPUSA organ, appears five times a week in New York. *Political Affairs*, a monthly, is the party's theoretical journal. Other party-linked publications include *People's World*, published in San Francisco.

Socialist Workers Party. *Leadership and Internal Affairs.* The SWP is led by National Secretary Jack Barnes and National Co-chairperson Mary-Alice Waters (see also *YICA*, 1981, p. 107). The major leadership change during the year was the resignation from the party of national field organizer Peter Camejo at midyear for unspecified reasons.

The SWP held its Thirty-First National Convention in Oberlin, Ohio, in early August. The meeting reportedly was attended by more than 1,300 people, including members of the SWP and the party's youth support group, the Young Socialist Alliance (YSA), as well as other supporters and international visitors (*Militant*, 4 September, 20 October). At the convention, the SWP decided that all SWP members aged 29 or younger should become active members of the YSA (which has chapters in 60 cities).

The SWP reportedly has been shaken by internal policy differences over the majority's adoption of a positive attitude toward non-Trotskyist "revolutionary" organizations and governments around the world, such as those in Cuba, Nicaragua, and Grenada. The dispute, which is similar to one that occurred two decades ago after Fidel Castro first took power in Cuba, left the majority calling the minority "ultra-left" and the minority charging that the SWP was abandoning Trotskyism. Also at issue was the efficacy of YSA and SWP activities in the labor movement. (*Guardian*, September.)

One of the most important and time-consuming activities of the SWP during 1981 was the party's $40 million suit (originally filed in 1973) against the U.S. government. The nonjury trial began on 2 April in the Federal District Court in New York City. Testimony concluded on 25 June, although legal maneuverings continued into the fall. No decision was expected until early 1982. The SWP charged that the FBI, the CIA, and other U.S. government agencies have systematically spied on and harassed party members and then argued that SWP views and activities should be fully protected by the First Amendment of the Constitution. But the SWP went on to claim greater significance for the trial, asserting that it proved "the existence of a true conspiracy to subvert the Bill of Rights." The SWP sought to "force out the truth," while the government, it charged, tried to "obscure the truth." (*Militant*, 7 August.) Midway in the testimony, after the Immigration and Naturalization Service had begun to examine whether SWP members could be deported, the *Militant* (8 May) editorialized: "The trial is spotlighting outright crimes, challenging thought-control legislation, and exposing the claim that the president can order the investigation of anyone he deems a 'subversive,' even if they have done nothing illegal." A defense document argued: "The issue is whether the government has a right to keep itself informed of the activities of groups that openly advocate revolutionary change in the structure and leadership of the government of the U.S., even if such advocacy might be within the letter of the law" (*Guardian*, 15 April).

Domestic and International Positions. The SWP charged that the Reagan government, with the assistance of the Democrats, was trying to "turn the clock back" to the 1930s by discarding labor safeguards, the rights of minorities, and the interests of "the people" (*Militant*, 27 February, 3 April, 10 July). As the *Militant* (2 October) editorialized: "Today, American capitalists can safeguard their profits only by taking more and more out of the hides of working people in this country and around the world. They have to drive down real wages, cut back on hard won conditions, scrap health and safety controls, restrict democratic rights, and increase the military budget." On numerous occasions SWP leaders criticized the American "labor bureaucracy" (ibid., 22 May) and called for the formation of an American Labor Party that would draw the votes of minorities, women, and "all those who are targets of the capitalists' attack" (ibid., 4 and 25 September, 2 October; *International Socialist Review*, September).

The SWP condemned U.S. foreign policy, paying particular attention to the Middle East and Latin America. The party argued that Solidarity and its allies in Poland have advanced union democracy and various worker rights and benefits by rejecting Stalinism and securing a true socialist system (*Militant*, 24 July).

The SWP publishes the weekly *Militant*, the monthly *Young Socialist*, and, for the United Secretariat of the Fourth International, the weekly *Intercontinental Press*. The party also publishes several discussion bulletins that circulate only within the party.

Other Groups. Among the other numerous Marxist-Leninist organizations in the United States are two Trotskyist groups: the Workers World Party, under chairman Sam Marcy, and the Sparticist League. Other parties include the Communist Workers' Party, under General Secretary Jerry Tung, which has fractured into the Line of March and the Theoretical Review groups; the unstable Communist Party (Marxist-Leninist); and the Revolutionary Communist Party. (See also *YICA*, 1981, p. 105.)

Hoover Institution   William E. Ratliff

Uruguay

Since the 1973 military coup, pressures have mounted for a return to constitutional democracy, even though all political party activity remains proscribed. An attempt was made in November 1980 to ratify the Uruguayan military government's political transition plan, or *cronograma,* which would eventually have restored civilian government but with a guaranteed watchdog role for the military. The plebiscite failed to win popular approval, and in 1981 the Aparicio Méndez government prepared to carry out its own transition plan without a popular mandate. In August, the incumbent government appointed a Council of State and named retired General Gregorio Alvarez to head a transitional regime from 1 September 1981 until 1 March 1985, when popular elections were scheduled. None of these political innovations called for the participation of Uruguay's legal political parties, not to mention the illegal parties of the left, the Broad Front (Frente Amplio) and the Uruguayan Communist Party (PCU). There was little reported activity on the political left from *within* Uruguay during 1981.

In November, the transitional government announced a scheme for eventual political participation of organized parties that required a party to have at least eight thousand declared members to be recognized. Such parties could propose a limit of three presidential candidates each, with the winning candidate on each ticket getting all the votes for that party. The Blanco, Colorado, and Unión Cívica (a minor conservative group) were the only parties to which the plan was presented by the Political Affairs Commission of the Armed Forces. (*La Prensa*, Buenos Aires, 15 November.) A party-list system for electing legislators was also announced. There was no mention of including either the Broad Front or the PCU in the planned "normalization" of Uruguayan political life.

The Uruguayan Communist Party. During 1981, there were few PCU activities except occasional statements from exiled party members. PCU membership is estimated at over seven thousand. The population of Uruguay is three million.

Rodney Arismendi continued as first secretary of the PCU from exile. In the July issue of *World Marxist Review*, he wrote of the "discovery" of classified American documents, allegedly prepared for the Council for Inter-American Security, Inc., detailing the Reagan administration's plan for world hegemony using Latin America and the Caribbean as both a protective shield and a resource exploitation base. He argued that there was no alternative to détente and accused the United States of plotting to seize the Panama Canal and preparing to intervene in Nicaragua militarily. Arismendi told the French party daily *L'Humanité* (8 September) that the transitional government in Uruguay had to free some eight thousand political prisoners and restore political rights for all trade unions and parties of the left before meaningful political change could occur.

From Cuba, former Uruguayan Senator Enrique Rodríguez denounced the death of Gerardo Cuesta, a member of the PCU Politburo, in an Uruguayan prison, where he had been held since the military coup of 1973. Cuesta was also a member of the Secretariat of the National Confederation of Workers, also proscribed by military decree.

Other Opposition Groups. Radio Havana (24 July) broadcast a statement of Hugo Villar, exiled secretary general of the Broad Front, on the occasion of the second anniversary of the Nicaraguan Revolution on 19 July. Villar said that the Broad Front had joined an experimental coalition of exiles called the Democratic Convergence in Uruguay (Convergencia Democrática en Uruguay; CDU), which sought to unite exiled representatives of the traditional Blanco and Colorado parties and the PCU. He contended that, given "virtually half a million exiles cut off from the national life, and in the absence of a free press," it was imperative for onetime enemies to put aside their rancors in a spirit of national salvation (*IB*, June).

In June, Juan Ferreira, the president (in exile) of the CDU, told a symposium in Washington, D.C., that his organization represented the entire spectrum of Uruguayan social and political life and that its goals were to raise international support for the restoration of democracy in Uruguay. Ferreira cited pledges of support from European Socialist and Christian Democratic movements and analyzed the impact of revolutionary processes in Nicaragua and Central America on the reassessment of the status quo throughout Latin America. Another symposium participant, ex-Captain Gerónimo Cardozo of the Uruguayan Air Force, claimed that growing domestic support for the CDU included the Catholic church and the Rural Association (an agricultural interest group), which were pressuring Uruguay's military governors to accept the popular will. He argued that Brazil's democratization process had forced the Uruguayan generals to do likewise and supplied evidence of the torture of political prisoners in Uruguayan prisons. (*Uruguay After the Plebiscite: Prospects for Democracy*, Washington, D.C.: American University, 1981). Continued revelations in the international media of human rights abuses in Uruguay provided the PCU and other left-wing groups with a basis for their attacks on the legitimacy of the transitional government.

University of Missouri–St. Louis   Kenneth F. Johnson

Venezuela

In 1980, a Caracas newspaper listed no fewer than 27 distinct groups that originated in left-wing splits from the two major populist political parties, Democratic Action (AD) and the COPEI–Christian Democratic Party; the fragmentation of the Venezuelan Communist Party (PCV); and other sources (*El Diario de Caracas*, 26 August 1980). Only four of these groups are open political parties that satisfied requirements for continued representation on the Multiparty Supreme Council (CSE) by winning at least 1 percent of the vote in the 1978 general elections. One, Red Flag (Bandera Roja), appears to maintain itself as a guerrilla operation and is alleged to have been involved in some isolated acts of politically inspired violence. Given the many nuances in Marxism and the bitter clashes of personalities and institutional ambitions, the reader is cautioned to appreciate the limit of this and any other effort to classify systematically even the more significant elements of the Venezuelan left.

In 1981 these disparate groups seriously attempted to coalesce behind a single unity candidate for the 1983 general elections. The success the leftist unity slate had in the 1979 municipal elections (18.5 percent of the vote compared with the 1978 presidential elections in which four competing leftist candidates divided a paltry 7.8 percent of the vote) has been the prime reason for this unity effort.

After extensive negotiations, which started in 1979 following the municipal elections, eight political parties and groups organized the National Coordinating Entity of the Left (La Coordinadora de la Izquierda). With assistance from the official CSE, it hopes to organize in early 1982 Venezuela's first multiparty primary elections. This primary is designed to involve the grass roots in selecting a leftist unity candidate. By October 1981, eight groups had coalesced around three primary candidates: the PCV, Vanguard, Revolutionary Left Movement–Moises Moleiro faction, The People Advance (EPA), Revolutionary Action Group (GAR), and Socialist League (LS) support José Vicente Rangel of the New Alternative Party; the Movement Toward Socialism (MAS) supports its leader, Teodoro Petkoff; and the People's Electoral Movement (MEP) supports one of its leaders, Salom Mesa Espinoza.

A number of other groups such as the Party of the Venezuelan Revolution (PRV-Ruptura) and Radical Cause (Causa R) have explicitly rejected participation in the effort to find a unity candidate. There is considerable skepticism in Venezuela that these disparate groups will succeed in achieving the elusive electoral unity. As one journalistic account suggested, the selection of one presidential candidate of the left may be an insurmountable obstacle for these parties, given the personal enmity between Rangel and Petkoff.

Venezuelan Communist Party. An interview with Héctor Mujica, the PCV's 1978 presidential candidate, published in *El Diario de Caracas* (8 February) illustrated much of the party's 1981 political strategy, the repudiation of the increasingly anti-Soviet "socialism" of the MAS. After insisting that the PCV was not headed for extinction, Mujica declared that "not everyone in MAS thinks like Teodoro [Petkoff]." According to Mujica, Petkoff's increasingly anti-Soviet and pro-U.S. statements represent his personal opinions and are not the policy of MAS.

The reason for this fury was a May 1981 international symposium organized by MAS called "From the Existing Socialism to a New Socialism." With representatives from 28 nations, including Cuba, in attendance, Petkoff and other speakers severely attacked both the Soviet and Cuban models of socialism. Internal repression in the Soviet Union came under special scrutiny, and Petkoff alledgedly asserted that socialism did not exist in the Soviet Union. The PCV furiously attacked the pretense of what it called a "fantasy of a new socialism that sought to abolish and eradicate the existing socialism" (*El Nacional*, 29 May). On 21 April, the Central Committee of the PCV implemented its "stop Teodoro" policy by formally endorsing Dr. José Vicente Rangel as its presidential candidate for the primary (*Tribuna Popular*, 24–30 April). In July the PCV convoked its own conference on "true socialism." According to the PCV, following the example of Lenin is the best way to achieve socialism.

On the international scene, the PCV remains an orthodox Stalinist party in terms of its unswerving adherence to the Soviet line. Politburo member Pedro Ortega Díaz wrote in *World Marxist Review* (March) that due to its "ideological strength" the party was an important component of the prospective leftist unity in Venezuela despite its relatively small size. The PCV had been a primary mover in the effort "to achieve a common candidate of all democratic and left-wing forces." Despite differences, according to Ortega Díaz, the parties of the left "have a common platform" against the economic program of the government and oppose the support "rendered to the criminal, pro-imperialist junta in El Salvador."

In March, the Soviet party sent its "close fraternal greetings" to the PCV on its fiftieth anniversary (*Pravda*, 5 March; *FBIS*, 12 March). In July, the PCV Central Committee publicly celebrated the twentieth-eighth anniversary of Fidel Castro's attack on the Moncada garrison and expressed its "full support and solidarity with Cuba" (Havana Domestic Service, 23 July; *FBIS*, 27 July). In September 1981, PCV Foreign Affairs Director Eduardo Gallegos and Deputy Radamés Larraźabal publicly declared that they have proof that 30 Venezuelan "military men" are in El Salvador advising the junta despite the Venezuelan government's denial that it had provided any military aid (*NYT*, 18 September).

The New Alternative (La Nueva Alternativa). In November 1980, José Vicente Rangel announced the launching of a new "centrist" political party. The centrist quality of the party might be greeted with skepticism, given the PCV's endorsement of Rangel. Rangel's intent, according to a Venezuelan press account, was "to organize a broad-based coalition able to beat MAS and Petkoff in the prospective [1982] primary elections" (*El Diario de Caracas*, 2 August).

In his new role, Rangel refused to be provoked into making strident statements. His comment on the prospective purchase of F-16s from the United States, for example, was "if the F-16s are necessary for the country's security and defense, then we must buy the planes." Rangel indicated that he was inclined to accept the military's judgment on the need for the aircraft. (Caracas Radio Continente Network, 6 July.) While he seemed to want to avoid confronting the armed forces command, the July 1981 imprisonment of a reporter, María Eugenia Díaz, by the military for "revealing national security secrets" concerning recent military manuevers forced Rangel to protest this attack on the constitutional rights of a reporter.

Territorial disputes with both Colombia and Guyana have caused something of a "national security" scare in Venezuela. There is a special concern regarding possible Cuban involvement in Guyana. While Venezuelan officials have attacked some hysterical accounts of Cuban soldiers in the disputed territory, reliable reports of MiG-23s flying over Guyana have been published. (*El Diario de Caracas*, 3 May, 12 July.) Rangel would not want to become overly identified with a potential Cuban adversary.

The news that leaders of the Association of Military Officers are seriously considering launching their own political party and may present a "military candidate" for president in 1983 caused some commotion among Venezuela's left. Rangel reacted with apparent serenity to this prospect and suggested in his regular column in *El Diario de Caracas* (9 April) that both in Venezuelan and world history, fine and decent military men have assumed the office of presidency, for example, Eleazar López Contreras and Isaías Medina Angarita in Venezuela and de Gaulle in France and Lázaro Cárdenas in Mexico. A military candidate of that quality would be a good "test" for the political parties, according to Rangel.

In part, Rangel's serenity may be based on 1980 Gallup poll interviews showing that he had greater voter recognition and appeal than Petkoff. Rangel was noticeably less serene when a *Washington Star* news story stated that he and other leftist leaders have financial ties with Libya. Rangel stated in a radio interview that "what the *Washington Star* reported belongs to the 'world of speculation' " (Radio Madrid, 14 May; *FBIS*, 15 May).

Movement Toward Socialism. The target of the concern and furious political action on the part of the PCV and the New Alternative has been MAS and its youthful president, Teodoro Petkoff. In October 1980 (see *YICA* 1981, p. 114), Petkoff made a determined bid to secure his own ascendancy in MAS by getting elected to the party's newly created office of party president and by projecting a MAS hegemony over the left in general. Key to the apparent Petkoff strategy was the October 1980 decision of MAS to nominate one of its own leaders as its 1983 presidential candidate in place of Rangel. In a sense, the creation of the New Alternative was Rangel's response to Petkoff's manuevers.

Petkoff's ascendancy produced a new "socialist" image for MAS, an image that earned the party a 25 August *New York Times* article as a "Venezuelan surprise"—"friendly Marxists," understanding of legitimate U.S. security concerns in the Western Hemisphere and of the need to maintain a friendly dialogue between Washington and Caracas. The leadership of MAS, according to the *New York Times*, "outdoes the European Communist parties in denouncing the Soviet Union for internal repression and excursions into Afghanistan and other countries."

Petkoff has become something of a celebrity among those in the United States who focus on Latin America. The *New York Times* (25 November 1980) featured an extensive article on Petkoff, "Sign of Venezuela's Maturity: Guerrilla in Congress." This article featured both a complimentary photograph of the MAS leader in the beautiful courtyard of the Venezuelan Congress and the following description of MAS's program: "Nonviolent transition to a socialism that respects democratic pluralism . . . The Venezuelan left must recognize the political reality that the country is within the sphere of influence of the United States."

Petkoff was one of the Venezuelan guests at a late November 1980 seminar on U.S.-Venezuelan relations held at the Woodrow Wilson Institute on International Affairs. At that seminar, he had the opportunity to meet some members of the Reagan transition team. During one of his recent trips to the United States, Petkoff joined with Eduardo Fernández, COPEI chairperson, and Enrique Tejera Paris, AD foreign policy adviser, in presenting a Georgetown University forum on Venezuelan foreign policy. MAS has strenuously resisted the label of "Eurocommunist," insisting that it is instead an independent socialist party.

The competition between MAS and the New Alternative became quite bitter in 1981 and caused much personal enmity between Petkoff and Rangel. In late 1980, one MAS leader, Germán Lairet, head of its parliamentary bloc, publicly expressed his "disgust" at Vicente Rangel for creating the New Alternative (Radio Madrid, 12 November; *FBIS*, 14 November).

In July, Petkoff was formally designated the MAS precandidate for the prospective 1982 multiparty primary. By August, Petkoff was accusing Vicente Rangel of "breaking the climate of courtesy" that marked the internal debate within the left and of "malicious" slander and verbal aggression against MAS (*El Diario de Caracas*, 2 August). The personal enmity of Petkoff and Vicente Rangel and the bitterness between MAS and the New Alternative seems to lend credence to those who are predicting a breakdown of the efforts to achieve a leftist unity candidate for 1983.

By mid-1981, there were ample signs that MAS's interests were no longer Marxist-Leninist. Starting in June, Petkoff responded positively to a call by former Venezuelan President Carlos Andrés Pérez of the AD for a "synchronization of the opposition." Petkoff stated that both the AD and the MAS have "coincided" in questions of economic policy and the Sixth National Plan. Simón Antonio Pavan, secretary general of the once important Democratic Republican Union, which has been reduced to the status of a minor party, also expressed his interest in this potential synchronization (ibid., 7 June).

The ongoing civil war in El Salvador and the joint diplomatic initiatives undertaken by France and Mexico in August 1981 have greatly increased the possibility of cooperation between the AD and the MAS. The incumbent COPEI administration strongly supports its fellow Christian Democrats in El Salvador and a democratic "coincidence" with the United States regarding the turbulence in Central America. The AD and the Socialist International, which is chaired by Willy Brandt, have become strong advocates of a negotiated political solution and of the Franco-Mexican initiative. (Ibid., 1 March; *NYT*, 27 September.) The 27 September death of Rómulo Betancourt, founder of the AD, may have removed one critical obstacle to the growing coincidence between the AD and the MAS.

This MAS-AD rapprochement has been encouraged by the work in Venezuela of the West German Social Democratic–affiliated Friedrich Ebert Foundation, which maintains a large office in Caracas and collaborates in publishing the Spanish-language *Nueva Sociedad*, which advocates a broad democratic convergence of socialists, Christian socialists, and Eurocommunists. Another influence has been the activist "socialist" foreign policy of the Mitterrand administration in France. The convergence of MAS into Venezuela's democratic establishment has also been facilitated by the close relationship that party has developed with the radical elements of the Catholic clergy.

The Jesuit Center's magazine, *SIC* (Interdiocesan Seminary of Caracas), has contained several articles favorable to MAS. The Center's director and the editor of *SIC*, Arturo A. Sosa, S.J., attended the MAS-sponsored New Socialism conference and authored a highly favorable account of MAS's vision of a socialism appropriate to Venezuela. Sosa contended that in addition to a heterodox Marxist stance, MAS's philosophy includes that of "Christian socialism" (*SIC*, July–August).

The MAS has been less sanguine about the future of democracy in Venezuela than has José Vicente Rangel. In response to the news that retired military officers were contemplating the formation of a political party, Petkoff was quoted as saying that there was a "real danger of a military takeover" (*Diario las Americas*, Miami, 21 May).

One MAS leader, Secretary General Pompeyo Márquez, was also mentioned in the *Washington Star* article as having received financial support from Libya. In a vehement denial of this allegation, Marquez suggested that this "false accusation . . . corresponds to President Reagan's aggressive and threatening policy against the government of Cuba." Márquez, however, insisted that MAS is completely independent of all "world powers."

People's Electoral Movement. The late 1980 elections of the Venezuelan Confederation of Labor confirmed that MEP was the strongest party of the left in the labor movement. Despite its relatively poor showing in both the 1978 and 1979 elections, this labor union connection has enabled the MEP to maintain itself as an independent "third force" between MAS's Teodoro Petkoff and the coalition supporting Vicente Rangel.

In May 1981, MEP leaders nominated Deputy Salom Mesa Espinoza as its candidate in the prospective 1982 primary. Salom Mesa Espinoza had been imprisoned by the former AD administration of Carlos Andrés Pérez because of alleged involvement in the Niehaus kidnapping affair (see *YICA*, 1979, pp. 400–401). In accepting the nomination, Salom Mesa discussed the reasons for the ambivalent relationship between MEP, which "comes from social democracy" (the 1967 division of AD), and MAS, the result of a revulsion (in 1970) in the PCV against the invasion of Czechoslovakia and the revelations of Nikita Khrushchev concerning Stalin's crimes (*El Nacional*, 29 May). In a sense, because of their Stalinist derivation, MAS leaders have assumed a strident anti-Soviet stance; because of their former strident anticommunism, MEP leaders such as Salom Mesa are now acknowledging the "positive contributions of Lenin."

In an article in the respected weekly magazine *Resumen* (31 May), MEP Secretary General Jesús Angel Paz Galarraga hinted that MEP would be the logical keystone of successful leftist unity. Paz Galarraga argued that at a time when the election of Ronald Reagan could herald a "reactionary wave in South America," Venezuela's left must find an acceptable unity candidate. The victory of Mitterrand, according to Paz, demonstrated the advantages of such an electoral unity.

Other Parties. Four minor parties also made news in 1981. The LS of Julio Escalona announced its support of Vicente Rangel in the prospective 1982 primary elections. Escalona, who had supported the policy of maintaining "a people's war" throughout most of the 1970s, was also mentioned in the *Washington Star* report of Libyan financial aid to Venezuela's left. Two parties of Catholic derivation, GAR and EPA have also announced their support of Rangel. The GAR's Rafael Irribarren was at one time a member of COPEI. The EPA, led by Edwin Zambrano, comes from a radical faction of students and faculty associated with the Andrés Bello Catholic University. The Revolutionary Communist Vanguard of Guillermo García Ponce and Eduardo Machado, which split from the PCV in the mid-1970s, has also announced its support of Rangel.

Douglas Bravo, one of the most famous guerrillas of the 1960s and leader of the PRV-Ruptura, has, as indicated above, refused to participate in the Coordinating Entity of the Left. In July 1981, he was reported to "have publicly stated" that he would have no objection to supporting one of the potential military candidates (retired Generals Arnaldo Castro Hurtado or Luís Enrique Rangel Bourgoin) if their nationalist formulations are sincere (*Diario las Americas*, 10 July). This writer has been informed that because of the resentment generated by the alleged public remarks, Bravo has denied making them. Causa R, led by Alfredo Maneiro, had also stayed out of the Coordinating Entity of the Left as of late September 1981. Causa R has targeted its work in only two industrial areas. There were press reports that during a visit to Mexico in August 1981, Douglas Bravo was detained by the police. Both Bravo's motives for being in Mexico and the quality of the treatment he received while in custody have been the subject of journalistic speculation.

Guerrilla Communism. In 1981 Venezuela experienced one of the lowest incidences of politically inspired violence in years. In January, Gabriel Puerta Aponte, spokesperson for the América Silva Guerrilla Front of Red Flag, announced the renewal of guerrilla activities and explicitly and "harshly criticized" those leftists engaged in the electoral alternative to power (*El Nacional*, 14 January). Despite the rhetoric of the January communiqué, there has been little evidence of a renewed guerrilla struggle. The Red Flag group has been called the "only guerrilla movement" refusing to take advantage of the government's pacification policy (Radio Madrid, 6 September; *FBIS*, 9 September).

In January there were violent riots in the Catia neighborhood of Caracas and the 23 de Enero housing project. In responding to the clashes, which left three dead, Caracas police stated that they found evidence that the Red Flag and Punto Cero groups were involved (AFP, Paris, 28 January; *FBIS*, 30 January). Arrests were made, including two alleged members of Red Flag. The gunmen who executed a spectacular hijacking of three Venezuelan airliners on 7 December belonged to the Red Flag group (*NYT*, 10 December).

A Venezuelan official cautioned this writer that reports of guerrilla activities are often exaggerated. In some cases, people being dismissed from public jobs for other causes may unfortunately be accused of "alleged" ties to subversives. In similar fashion, bank robbers properly disguised with "stocking caps over their faces" may also leave the misinformation that their endeavor was a Red Flag operation.

The willingness of Venezuela's left to focus on the electoral road to influencing the future course of their nation is proof of the democratic climate in Venezuela. In the 28 July issue of the *Washington Report on the Hemisphere* (1, no. 21), published by the liberal Council on Hemispheric Affairs, the human rights situation in Venezuela during 1980–1981 was called "exemplary." "Venezuela ranks in the forefront of hemispheric nations as an active supporter of human rights practices in Latin America and sets an example for others as a society where the respect for personal liberties continues to increase."

Biography. *Teodoro Petkoff.* President of MAS and its candidate for the 1982 elections for president. In the early 1960s, he and his older brother, Luben Petkoff, were radical communist youth leaders who insisted that the PCV join with the pro-Castro MIR in an armed struggle against the elected government of Rómulo Betancourt. His brother assumed the leadership of the FALN in the mid-1960s. Luben has since left politics and is now a wealthy businessman. Teodoro remained a guerrilla, was captured, and escaped from prison only to accept "pacification" in 1967. He was elected to the Venezuelan legislature on the PCV front Union for Advance ticket. In 1968, he formally protested the Soviet invasion of Czechoslovakia and was expelled from the PCV at the insistence of the Soviet Union. He and Pompeyo Márquez created the MAS in early 1971. In the 1970s, Petkoff was a fre-

ASIA AND THE PACIFIC

Introduction

Communist parties and movements control or play a major role in the lives of nearly 2.5 billion people in Asia. They rule without legal opposition in the People's Republic of China (PRC), Vietnam, Kampuchea, Laos, North Korea, Mongolia, and Afghanistan, although in Kampuchea and Afghanistan they face substantial armed resistance by communist and anticommunist groups, respectively. Furthermore, communist parties play a significant part in the political systems of India and Japan. Government counterinsurgency action against pro-Chinese communist movements in Burma, Malaysia, Thailand, and the Philippines contributed to varying degrees of suppression of the population as a whole. As in recent years, Asian Communists were notably active across national boundaries.

The Soviet Union continued to play an active role in the region, most directly in Afghanistan. Soviet civilian advisers attempted to revamp the nation's disastrous economy, while Soviet military advisers, backed up by some 85,000 troops, sought unsuccessfully to rebuild the Afghan Army and defeat—or even contain—the nationwide resistance movement. Soviet and Afghan troops launched periodic military offensives into the countryside, with heavy aerial support. Babrak Karmal, secretary general of the ruling People's Democratic Party of Afghanistan (PDPA), as well as the Soviet Union and his other international allies, charged that the Afghan resistance movement, which now controls 75 to 90 percent of the country, was the creature of the United States, the People's Republic of China, and Pakistan. Besides trying to improve its international image, the Karmal government tried to expand its base within the country—the PDPA has from 10,000 to 20,000 members in a population of 12.5 million (discounting the approximately 3 million Afghanis who have sought refuge in Pakistan and Iran). The launching of a National Fatherland Front in June did little to bring popular support to the PDPA, and reforms within the ruling party failed to bring together the feuding Parcham and Khalq factions while strengthening the more openly pro-Soviet Parcham group.

Vietnamese Communist Party (VCP) reliance on the Soviet Union continued during 1981, despite some indications of Soviet disenchantment. Vietnam depends on the USSR for food, energy, arms, and, at times, advice. Some one hundred Soviet aid projects are under way and forty more in the planning stages. Soviet assistance is an essential element in the continued Vietnamese involvement in neighboring countries, most importantly Kampuchea. An estimated 200,000 Vietnamese troops remain in Kampuchea, although redeployments during the year suggest less aggressive policies in the immediate future. American intelligence estimates that there are still 20,000 Vietnamese troops in Laos; the PRC puts the number at 60,000. The VCP conflict with China continued, with border incidents and verbal attacks. Vietnamese relations with the Association of Southeast Asian Nations continued to fluctuate. Domestically, the Vietnamese government was substantially reformed, but the VCP—its Fifth Party Congress twice postponed and now scheduled for early 1982—remained intact, with the average age of Politburo members now 67. A new constitution established a National Assembly, headed by Nguyen Huu Tho, who has no significant power, and a Council of State. The council, which functions as a legislative body permanently in session, is headed by Truong Chinh, 76. A new Council of Ministers is under the leadership of Pham Van Dong, 75; parallel to that body is the National Defense Council, chaired by Truong Chinh. Clearly VCP members dominate the new government positions.

The Kampuchea People's Revolutionary Council transformed itself into the Kampuchean People's Revolutionary Party (KPRP) in May and thereby openly acknowledged that a communist party, still with fewer than five thousand members, controlled the country. The KPRP government continued to try to ally itself with prominent Khmer personalities to legitimize its rule even as it maintained its civil war against the Chinese-supported Khmer Communist Party (KCP) of Pol Pot, Khieu Samphan, and Ieng Sary. Pen Sovan continued his rise in power during the first eleven months of 1981. He traveled to the Soviet Union immediately before and after his selection as secretary general of the KPRP and his appointment as prime minister, both in May, thereby replacing Heng Samrin as the country's foremost political leader. However, in December, Pen Sovan resigned his positions, officially on grounds of poor health, but possibly because his increasingly open pro-Soviet statements offended the Vietnamese. Heng Samrin, who has been more pro-Vietnamese in his positions, returned to the top party position on Pen Sovan's departure. The Phnom Penh government still depends heavily on Vietnam for general economic and military assistance, as well as for advice and training. The KCP announced its dissolution in December, perhaps as a first move toward setting up an anti-Vietnamese front with noncommunist Khmer leaders, including Prince Norodom Sihanouk.

Chinese Communist Party (CCP) Vice-Chairman Deng Xiaoping consolidated his position as the PRC's most powerful leader during 1981, though not without concessions to other forces in the party. In June, the CCP Central Committee accused Hua Guofeng of opposition to Deng's policies, uncritical adherence to Mao Zedong's ideas, and precipitousness in the early stages of the national economic development program. Hua was replaced as party chairman by Hu Yaobang, a protégé of Deng, and removed from the chairmanship of the Military Commission of the Central Committee in favor of Deng. The Central Committee session also approved a document officially assessing the history of the CCP in recent decades, which recognized some mistakes, including the Cultural Revolution—a "comprehensive, long drawn out and grave blunder." The overthrow of the Gang of Four was a turning point in modern history and ushered in major changes. The document proclaimed that Mao's contributions to the Chinese Revolution, though marred by errors in his later years, "far outweigh his mistakes." Mao Zedong Thought will remain a guide for party action, but must not be applied dogmatically. (*Beijing Review*, 6 July.)

The party and government cracked down on intellectual and cultural critics, enforced additional limitations on contacts with foreigners in China and warned the foreign press to keep out of Chinese affairs. In January, a special court sentenced members of the Gang of Four and Clique of Six. The most important, Jiang Qing and Zhang Chunqiao, were sentenced to death with a two-year reprieve and permanent deprivation of political rights. In December, Premier Zhao Ziyang predicted five more years of economic retrenchment and indicated that during that period the government would stress development of energy, construction, transportation, communications, and light industry.

PRC criticism of the Soviet Union continued, but did not escalate, during the year, and a few contacts were initiated, including an exchange of proposals on border talks. Sino-American relations continued fairly good, although they suffered from PRC concern over U.S. ties to Taiwan. Tensions remained in relations with Vietnam, and China continued to support KCP forces in Kampuchea.

The Lao People's Revolutionary Party maintained close relations with Vietnam and supported Vienamese military actions in both Laos and Kampuchea. The Laotian conflict with the PRC continued.

The Korean Workers' Party (KWP), which maintained its neutrality between the Soviet Union and China, turned down several calls by the new government of South Korea for a Seoul-Pyongyang summit to discuss reunification of the peninsula. Indeed, confrontations continued along the 1953 armistice line, and the KWP repeatedly condemned what the party organ *Nodong Sinmun* called "the master and his faithful hound" (the U.S. and South Korean governments) in international forums. The Democratic People's Republic of Korea hosted many international visits, including one by Yassir Arafat of the Palestine Liberation Organization, which was rumored to have received weapons from the Koreans. Local people's assembly elections were held, which may signal the election of the Seventh Supreme People's Assembly and governmental rearrangement in 1982. It is speculated that Kim Chong-il, KWP leader Kim Il-song's 40-year-old son, increasingly promoted by propaganda organs, will be made vice-president.

The most important nonruling communist parties were those in Japan and India. The Japanese Communist Party (JCP), with a claimed membership of some 440,000 in 1981, was the third largest nonruling party in the world. It holds 29 (of 511) seats in the House of Representatives and 12 (of 252) in the House of Councillors. Party leaders, who focused much of their attention during the year on talk of rearming Japan, seemed to be pushing the party toward a more independent position in order to draw those Japanese who now feel unrepresented by the political system. The most important events of the year for the JCP were local elections in January, in which the party won 18 seats—a gain of 2— and the Tokyo Metropolitan Assembly elections in June. In the latter, the JCP won 16 (of 127) seats, a gain of 5. Thus, in Tokyo, where the governor is sponsored by three parties, the JCP is the largest opposition party. The Japanese Communists still protest Soviet activities in Afghanistan and the occupation of small islands north of Japan.

In India, no political groups are more efficiently organized in several states than the Communist Party–Marxist (CPM) and the Communist Party of India (CPI). Together they claim about 750,000 members and a following of millions of workers, farmers, and students. The Communists were strongest in the states of Kerala and West Bengal. In 1981, the two parties worked for unity against the ruling Congress (I) Party of Indira Gandhi. The cooperation was apparent in the elections in West Bengal, CPM acceptance of the CPI as a partner in the leftist government of that province, and in periodic meetings between leaders of the two parties. The main points of contention between the CPM and the CPI were the former's cooperation with the Bharatiya Janata Party, the main noncommunist opposition to Gandhi, and policy toward the PRC. Dissension continued within each party; the CPI split early in the year, with the newly formed All India Communist Party taking an undetermined number of members from the CPI.

The Burmese Communist Party (BCP), long one of the most militant Maoist organizations in the world, has initiated a major shift in its relations with the Burmese government. The BCP has begun to question the role of armed struggle in the seizure of power and to recognize that it is not the only group in Burma interested in revolution. The BCP explains that the need for an end to the civil war and the desirability of a multiparty system derive from the necessity to defend the country against "domination and hegemonistic policies of Soviet imperialism." The party warned against the danger posed by "small hegemonist Vietnam, which wants to hold sway over Southeast Asia." (*FBIS,* 17 June.) The BCP's decision to enter into peace talks with the government coincided with a reduction in military activity by BCP guerrillas, most of whom are active in northeastern border areas.

The most important communist activities in the Philippines during 1981 were those of the four thousand–member New People's Army (NPA), the guerrilla arm of the pro-Chinese Communist Party of the Philippines/Marxist-Leninist (CPP/ML). According to a CPP/ML statement in December 1980, the NPA had 27 "guerrilla fronts" in 43 provinces (*Philippine Liberation Courier*, June). The NPA claims to be drawing an increasing number of members from the Catholic clergy and to be working more effectively and more often with the stronger Moro National Liberation Front in the southern section of the country. The CPP/ML is believed to dominate the ten thousand–member National Democratic Front. The recently formed Catholic Liberation Army, which many consider a splinter of the rural-based NPA, seems to seek unification of urban guerrillas opposing the Marcos government. The pro-Soviet Philippine Communist Party continues to follow a more moderate policy of infiltrating unions, the bureaucracy, and other centers of power.

The Communist Party of Thailand (CPT) continued to decline in strength and effectiveness during 1981. In the first six months of the year alone, eight hundred of some ten thousand party members reportedly defected for reasons ranging from disillusionment with revolutionary politics to disappointment over the decline in external support for the CPT guerrilla campaign. The Thai government launched an offensive against the CPT in several areas and dealt the party serious setbacks. By the end of 1981, the CPT still maintained from three to six thousand guerrillas in the north and some three thousand in the south. The CCP withdrew more of its support from the CPT effort early in 1981 when it announced that it would not allow CCP ties with the CPT to interfere with Beijing's relations with Bangkok. The CPT has reportedly entered into an alliance with a Muslim separatist organization, the Barisan Revolutionary National Front. The CPT again postponed its Fourth Party Congress because of internal differences and the difficulty of finding a secure meeting place. A so-called New Party, thought to consist of CPT defectors, was formed in Laos at midyear; its relationship to another splinter group, the Northeast Thai Liberation Movement, is not clear.

The main communist activities in Malaya are those of the Communist Party of Malaya along the Thai-Malaysian border and those of the North Kalimantan Communist Party in Sarawak in eastern Malaysia, the latter at a lower level than the year before. The terrorists of al-Zulfikar in Pakistan, led by a son of executed Pakistani President Zulfikar Ali Bhutto, hijacked an airplane and were warmly received when they landed in Kabul. The Sri Lanka Communist Party won a seat in the national legislature for the first time since 1977.

Hoover Institution   William E. Ratliff

Afghanistan

The People's Democratic Party of Afghanistan (PDPA), which has transformed Afghanistan into a puppet of the Soviet Union, continues to be designated a "national democratic" rather than a communist party, a formulation thought to be more acceptable to Afghanistan's conservative Islamic society. Also, as a noncommunist state, Afghanistan can retain its membership in the nonaligned movement, an important consideration to the Soviets.

But the Marxist-Leninist orientation of the PDPA, apparent since its founding by Nur Mohammad Taraki in 1965, is clearly perceived in Afghanistan. Semantics and political strategy have, to date, failed to help the party broaden its base. The nationwide resistance to PDPA rule, which began almost immediately after the April 1978 coup brought the party to power and gained overwhelming popular support after the Soviets invaded Afghanistan in December 1979 to save "the revolution," continued unabated throughout 1981.

There is no reliable information about the size of the PDPA. A high party official claimed in February that party membership had increased by 25 percent in the preceding six months (PAP, Warsaw, 23 February; *FBIS*, 25 February), and Babrak Karmal, PDPA secretary general, told the fifth party plenum in March that the character of the party was changing and that 25–30 percent of new members were workers or farmers (Radio Kabul, 18 March; *FBIS*, 19 March). At the sixth party plenum in June, Karmal stated that "thousands of the best representatives of workers, peasants, craftsmen, employees, intelligentsias, students and other social strata have been admitted to the party [as] probationary members" (Bakhtar News Agency, Kabul, 14 June; *FBIS*, 15 June). According to an Indian journalist, Karmal claimed in August that party membership had grown to 60,000 (*Far Eastern Economic Review*, 31 July), but the absence of an official statement on the size of the party suggests that these figures are inflated and membership remains embarrassingly small.

Educated guesses put party membership at 10,000–20,000 out of a current population of approximately 12.5 million (3 million Afghans have fled to Pakistan or Iran). This membership figure, however, includes the numerically larger Khalq faction, which has become increasingly estranged from the minority Parcham faction, led by Karmal, who is both head of the party and president of the Democratic Republic of Afghanistan (DRA). Parcham loyalists may number only a few thousand.

The Soviets have tried persistently to neutralize the deep-seated feud that has plagued the PDPA since it split into the Khalq and Parcham factions in 1968, three years after it was founded. Parchamis, who suffered exile, imprisonment, and worse during the period of Khalq supremacy under Taraki and Hafizullah Amin from April 1978–December 1979, had hoped for revenge when the Soviets installed their leader in power in December 1979. But the Soviets, aware of the risks of further alienating the Khalqis, who are entrenched in the armed forces, have stressed reconciliation. They have managed to contrive a semblance of balance and unity at the upper levels of the party, but have been unable to prevent considerable purging of Khalqis at lower levels. Continuing reports of Khalq collaboration with the resistance movement indicate that the problem is still critical.

During 1981, the Parchamis attempted to reduce Khalq influence by bringing more workers into the party. Workers and peasants have been conspicuously absent in the past. The Parcham faction previously drew its membership primarily from the urban intelligentsia, the Khalqis from the military and the provincial bureaucracy. The new worker and farmer members, to the extent that they actually exist, have probably come primarily from state enterprises, where the government has some leverage. Also, the regime tries to lure potential members with Soviet-supplied food and consumer goods, which are available at special prices in return for political loyalty.

There are, however, many factors militating against a mass influx into the party, despite the inducements. Most important, the area of the country under government control has been steadily reduced. A former government official, who attended a secret meeting of provincial state and party officials in June, said, after his defection in August, that the assessment of the meeting was that the resistance controlled 90 percent of the country (AP, August 15). A U.S. State Department report put the figure at around 75 percent (Special Report no. 79, February). The party's recruiting opportunities are in effect limited to Kabul and its immediate suburbs and, to a lesser extent, to other major towns. Kabul, however, is now the scene of nightly gun battles despite heavy Soviet security and house-to-house searches, and in Kandahar and Herat, government authority has been seriously challenged throughout 1981.

Another factor impeding party recruitment is the danger associated with party membership. Parchamis continue to be almost daily victims of *mujahidin* (freedom fighter) assassins in Kabul and other towns. Young party loyalists are expected to join the Defense of the Revolution battalions, which serve as a special militia force. The high casualty rate among these units deters party membership as did the May 1981 order that all party members in the government should report for military duty at the "hot fronts."

Organization and Leadership. Like its model, the Communist Party of the Soviet Union (CPSU), the PDPA's structure parallels that of the state. There are primary organizations, district organizations, city committees, and provincial committees. In addition, a Central Committee member coordinates party, state, and defense matters in each of the DRA's eight zones.

According to an early constitution of the PDPA, the highest party authority is the party congress, which is to meet once every four years. Among other duties, the congress is to elect full and alternate members to the Central Committee. In practice, Central Committee plenums have constituted the highest authority, and Central Committee members have been selected by the top party leadership. A party congress would only reveal how small and narrowly based the party is. Furthermore, the current Parcham leadership could not run the risk of a congress dominated by the majority Khalq faction.

There has been a succession of Central Committee plenums since April 1978, including the fourth in November 1980, the fifth in March 1981, and the sixth in June 1981. The November 1980 plenum followed Karmal's state visit to Moscow in October and was devoted primarily to problems of party unity. Attention also focused on the security situation, the main preoccupation of the third plenum the preceding July, and on the importance to the Afghans of Soviet friendship. It was clear that during Karmal's visit, the Soviets had emphasized the harmful effects of the Khalq-Parcham split. Karmal's speech at the plenum established new criteria for party loyalty: henceforth only those who participated actively in the fight against counterrevolutionaries and worked for solidarity with the CPSU would be eligible for membership in the PDPA. Karmal stated that authorities were investigating high-level party officials who had abused their position. He also criticized Afghan officials who shirked their responsibilities, thus obliging their Soviet advisers to do all the work. (Radio Kabul, 14 November 1980; *FBIS*, 17 November 1980.)

Karmal's remarks were clearly aimed at the Khalqis; they coincided with increasing reports that the Khalqis were opposed to the continuing Soviet presence and were collaborating with the mujahidin. But the obliquely threatened purge of high-level Khalqis never materialized—undoubtedly because of Soviet influence.

The fifth plenum in March 1981 followed Karmal's second official trip to the USSR—this time to attend the Twenty-Sixth Congress of the Soviet party. At the time, Moscow and Kabul were focusing on legitimizing the Karmal regime. Internationally, this involved enticing the governments of Pakistan and Iran into negotiations with the Karmal government aimed at a political settlement of the Afghan problem. Domestically, it involved a campaign to lure all elements of Afghan society into joining the PDPA in the broad National Fatherland Front (NFF). Karmal's keynote address to the plenum took a conciliatory tone toward neighboring states and stressed the reasonableness of the regime. He emphasized the national democratic character of the present stage of the revolution, the regime's respect for Islam and tribal customs, and its positive achievements, particularly improvements in the life of the working class. He specifically mentioned that wages had been raised by an average of 26.6 percent and that the raise would amount to 40–50 percent for low-income workers. (Radio Kabul, 18 March; *FBIS*, 19 March.)

The sixth plenum in June 1981 was a major event for the PDPA. Called to make important organizational changes, it was preceded by weeks of intense wrangling between the Khalq and Parcham factions. Indeed, the inability of the Khalqis and Parchamis to agree on the proposed changes caused the plenum to be postponed from 13 May to 11 June. The sixth plenum preceded the much heralded congress of the NFF by a few days; the NFF congress had been postponed for several months for lack of a sufficient number of credible participants.

The changes in party and government organization announced at the June plenum and at simultaneous meetings of the Revolutionary Council—the highest government authority—centered on naming a prime minister. Until June, Karmal had served as prime minister as well as president of the republic and secretary general of the party. But on the occasion of the anniversary of the revolution on 27 April, in the course of a rather gloomy speech emphasizing "difficult conditions" and "unsolved problems," Karmal had stated that a "premier must be appointed to chair the Council of Ministers" (Radio Kabul, 26 April; *FBIS*, 27 April).

This announcement may have reflected a Soviet decision to start the process of gradually de-emphasizing Babrak's role in order to broaden the base of the party. Indeed, the Soviets may have hoped to prevail on the Parchamis to accept a Khalqi as prime minister to halt further alienation of the numerically superior faction. Certainly the Khalqis took this opening as an opportunity to recoup their lost political influence. Asadullah Sarwari, who headed the Khalq faction until he was sent in August 1980 into diplomatic exile as ambassador to Mongolia, is believed to have returned to Kabul during this period to participate in the negotiations over government changes.

Compromise proved impossible, however, and the Khalqis failed to improve their position. When forced to make a choice, the Soviets stuck by the Parchamis. Sultan Ali Keshtmand, then the Parchami deputy prime minister and vice-president of the republic, was named prime minister. Other changes improved the position of the Parchamis; all party (and government) organizations were enlarged and Parchamis outnumbered Khalqis in the new appointments. The Politburo was enlarged from seven to nine full members; two Parchamis were added (Mohammad Rafi and Dr. Najibullah), while the one new Khalqi (Mohammad Aslam Watanjar) replaced a former Khalq member (Asadullah Sarwari), who was dropped. The overall ratio in the Politburo in favor of the Parchamis shifted from 4–3 to 6–3. The six Parchamis are Babrak Karmal (PDPA secretary general; president, Revolutionary Council), Anahita Ratebzad (chairperson, Peace, Solidarity, and Friendship Organization; chairperson, Afghanistan Women's Organization; member, Revolutionary Council Presidium), Sultan Ali Keshtmand (chairman, Council of Ministers), Nur Ahmad Nur (PDPA secretary; member, Revolutionary Council Presidium), Mohammad Rafi (minister of defense), and Dr. Najibullah (director, Intelligence and Security Service). The three Khalqis are Saleh Mohammad Ziray (PDPA secretary; chairman, National Fatherland Front; member, Revolutionary Council Presidium), Ghulam Dastagir Panjshiri (chairman, PDPA Control Commission), and Mohammad Aslam Watanjar (minister of communications). In addition, the Politburo has two alternate members: Mohammad Ismail Danesh (a Khalqi and minister of mines and industries) and Karmal's brother, Mahmud Barialay (a Parchami and chairman, PDPA International Affairs Department). Both men were appointed at the June plenum. The Secretariat consists of Karmal, Ziray, Nur, Barialay, and Niaz Mohammad Mohmand (factional attachment unknown). Barialay and Mohmand joined the Secretariat in June.

In addition to enlarging the Politburo and the Secretariat, the plenum added seven new full members and ten new alternate members to the Central Committee to the original 36 full members and eight alternate members. In announcing the additions, Karmal stressed the importance of broadening the composition of party and state organizations; left unstated was the added advantage of reducing Khalq influence. (Bakhtar News Agency, Kabul, 14 June; *FBIS*, 15 June.)

Although some top Khalqis may have made peace with the Parchamis, others remained unreconciled to their weakened political position. The June reorganization did not settle the feud; it exacerbated it. In a speech to party activists in mid-August, Karmal once more lashed out against factionalism, which was obstructing efforts to put down the resistance. In late November, there were reports of a renewed power struggle within the leadership; these reports were reinforced by Keshtmand's two-month stay in Moscow, ostensibly for health reasons (Reuters, Moscow, 2 December). Keshtmand's prolonged absence from Kabul may also be related to factional splits within the Parcham faction and reported differences between Keshtmand and Karmal (U.S. Department of State, Special

Report no. 86, August). Given the deteriorating security situation and the obvious failures of party and government policies, it is not surprising that the beleaguered leadership is wracked by mutual recriminations.

The other important business before the Central Committee at the sixth plenum was to approve a written application from the PDPA to the preparatory commission of the founding congress of the NFF. The PDPA applied to join the NFF as the "guiding and organizing force" (Bakhtar News Agency, Kabul, 14 June; *FBIS*, 15 June).

Auxiliary and Mass Organizations. The campaign to establish the NFF was launched with a conference on 27 December 1980—the first anniversary of the Karmal regime. The conference appointed a committee to organize a founding congress to be held on 21 March, the Afghan New Year. The projected congress was intended to demonstrate broad support for Karmal and to legitimize his government. Despite an extraordinary effort to mobilize support, the congress had to be postponed repeatedly. It was finally held on 15 June.

On paper, the NFF sounds like a truly representative organization. The twelve founding member-organizations are the PDPA, Trade Union of Afghanistan, Union of Agricultural Cooperatives of the DRA, Democratic Organization of Youth of Afghanistan, Democratic Organization of Women of Afghanistan, Union of Poets and Writers of the DRA, Union of Journalists of the DRA, Union of Artists of the DRA, Peace, Solidarity, and Friendship Organization of Afghanistan, Economic Consultative Council of the DRA, Council of Scholars and Clergymen of Afghanistan, and High Jirga of Tribal Representatives. The superficiality of these organizations is clear, however, from the fact that many of them were either formed or held their first national conference after the 27 December 1980 conference. The greatest challenge to the regime was to create the High Jirga of Tribal Representatives. Observers have reported that tribal delegates to this assembly on 20 May and subsequently to the NFF congress in June, were, in fact, party and government functionaries dressed in tribal attire (U.S. Department of State, Special Report no. 86, August).

The constitution of the NFF emphasizes the organization's responsibility to explain and promote PDPA and DRA policies and to mobilize the people behind them. It also is charged with acquainting the people with the "gains and the historical achievements" of "friendly" countries, especially of the Soviet Union. In his "fundamental statement" to the NFF congress, Karmal claimed that the formation of the NFF was evidence of the normalization of the situation in Afghanistan, the unified support of all patriotic forces for PDPA principles, the fraternity of all of Afghanistan's social classes and ethnic groups, and the ability of the regime to solve difficult problems and create a new society. Throughout his statement, Karmal stressed the importance of unity: "One of the main political lessons of our history is that the patriots of Afghanistan have achieved victory arriving at their desired targets only when united." (Bakhtar News Agency, Kabul, 17 June; *FBIS*, 19 June.)

Much preliminary fanfare heralded the congress as a momentous occasion. It was portrayed as a contemporary version of Loga Jirga—the traditional assembly of Afghanistan's tribal chieftains called to make historic decisions. When it finally met, however, security considerations caused the proceedings to be curtailed to one day. It was generally recognized as a sham, and relatively little has been heard of the NFF since it was created. A resistance campaign to assassinate leading participants may have dampened enthusiasm. Indeed it was not until 1 November that a NFF provincial committee was formed in Kabul province (Radio Kabul, 1 November; *FBIS*, 3 November).

Domestic Affairs. Throughout 1981, the main preoccupations of the PDPA and the DRA have been the related political and military goals of establishing the legitimacy of the Babrak government and defeating the mujahidin forces of the resistance.

Political Policy. The cornerstone of the political policy was the creation of the NFF and its charter organizations. The objectives of the NFF are also reflected in the regime's tribal and nationality policy, which was institutionalized in late May in the creation of a Ministry of Nationalities and Tribal Affairs to replace the old Ministry of Border and Tribal Affairs. Closely resembling Soviet nationality policy, the DRA policy seeks to win the loyalty of individual tribal and ethnic groups by emphasizing their uniqueness. It is, in effect, a policy of divide and rule.

The regime has also reformulated land reform policy to rectify the damage done during the Taraki period. While the new measures are designed to appeal to farmers, who constitute over 70 percent of Afghanistan's population, a long list of exemptions is intended to gain support for the government from religious leaders, tribal leaders, military officers, and indeed any landowner who will openly support the regime. (Radio Kabul, 21 June, 10 August; *FBIS*, 25 June, 20 August.)

A new law on local organs of state power and administration, approved by the Presidium of the Revolutionary Council on 21 September, imposes the familiar Soviet principle of "democratic centralism" on Afghanistan's administrative structure of local councils, which are being portrayed as traditional jirgas. The Karmal regime claims the new law will democratize Afghanistan's social system. It will, however, have the opposite effect since power to nominate candidates for election to the local councils rests with the PDPA-controlled auxiliary organizations. (*Izvestiia*, 1 October.)

The Revolutionary Council also approved, on 23 September, a new DRA Council of Ministers law, apparently for the purpose of strengthening and expanding the role of the state in Afghan society. In March, a new law had reorganized the judicial system. All of these measures have been part of a comprehensive program to remake the Afghan government in the Soviet image.

Defense Policy. While civilian Soviet advisers have been overhauling Afghanistan's administrative machinery, military advisers, supplemented by some 85,000 troops, have been trying to rebuild the Afghanistan Army and combat the resistance movement. Because there are very few volunteer draftees to offset the steady stream of deserters and defectors, the regime must rely on joint Soviet/Afghan military sweeps to round up recruits. The Army is reportedly down to about 30,000 from a normal complement of 100,000. (U.S. Department of State, Special Report no. 79, February.)

A new draft law, enacted in January 1981, lowered the draft age, extended the obligatory tour of duty, and offered various incentives to join and/or stay in the security forces. The failure of these measures to improve the situation drove the DRA, in September, to the extreme measure of calling up almost all reservists up to age 35. Because of Afghanistan's mandatory service laws, this mobilization covered virtually the entire male population in the stipulated age bracket. The announcement provoked antigovernment student demonstrations, while eligible males took off for the hills, leaving government and business offices empty. The regime backtracked immediately and announced a number of exemptions. As the year ended, the results of the call-up continued to be disappointing, and as before, the government had to rely on military dragnet operations to try to enforce the directive.

The September call-up highlighted growing attention to the deteriorating security situation. In mid-August, the DRA established new defense councils at the national, provincial, and district levels to concentrate all aspects of defense under strict PDPA control. Announcing the formation of the new councils at a meeting of armed forces party activists, Babrak Karmal spoke of "troublesome and difficult conditions" and "increasing armed actions by counterrevolutionary elements." It was imperative for all forces to go on the offensive. Karmal again lashed out at party factionalism, which was hindering efforts to strengthen military effectiveness. (Radio Kabul, 16 and 17 August; *FBIS*, 17 and 18 August.) Recent articles in the Soviet press have also begun to give a more realistic picture of the Afghan war.

There are no indications that the Soviets and the regime have, as yet, made any headway in achieving their military objectives. Journalists who traveled in Afghanistan with the mujahidin during the summer and early fall described an aggressive resistance movement of increasingly confident free-dom fighters. They were able to move freely in many places even in the daytime. In strategic areas, where the mujahidin pose a threat to key cities such as Kabul, Kandahar, Herat, and Jalalabad, or to major transportation routes, Soviet and Afghan forces conduct periodic military offensives supplemented by intense aerial bombardments. Yet the Soviets have been unable, to date, to dislodge the mujahidin from their strongholds permanently. One frequently fought-over area, which has received much publicity, is Paghman, a hill town only twelve miles from Kabul.

The Economy. Afghanistan's economy continues to be a major casualty of the ongoing civil war. With much of the country in resistance hands, the government is unable to collect revenues. This fact was underscored by a DRA attempt to win the support of farmers in May by waiving some U.S. $16 million of fines previously imposed on farmers who had failed to pay their taxes from 1978 through 1980 (*Kabul New Times*, 20 May). Furthermore, the war has caused a drop in the production of agricultural products, which are normally foreign exchange earners.

Most official pronouncements on the economy are optimistic. The report on the 1981 budget, delivered in March by then Deputy Prime Minister Keshtmand, painted a relatively rosy picture, as did his economic report to the Revolutionary Council in September. But Keshtmand's speech to a seminar for local government officials in August revealed the economic paralysis caused by the fighting. He indicated major concern about the breakdown in the transportation system, the closing of many factories and mines, and inflation, which has risen sharply due to growing shortages. (Radio Kabul, 25 August; *FBIS*, 26 and 27 August.)

Afghanistan has become increasingly dependent on the USSR both for economic assistance and as a trading partner. In November 1980, Karmal stated that Moscow was supplying 80 percent of the DRA's foreign aid (Radio Kabul, 14 November 1980; *FBIS*, 17 November 1980). An article in the *Kabul New Times* (1 March) described "great changes" in Soviet-Afghan trade relations since December 1979 and listed a number of products now being supplied by the Soviets to Afghanistan including wheat and sugar, which have periodically been in short supply.

Afghanistan's trade with the USSR is on a barter basis. DRA earnings from its exports to the USSR, primarily from natural gas, are used to repay past debts incurred from Moscow's $2.5 billion economic and military programs begun in the 1950s. The Soviets recently tripled the price for Afghan gas (to $3.26 per thousand cubic feet) but the price is still well below that the Soviets charge West Europeans for natural gas from Siberia.

Foreign Affairs. The primary objective of DRA foreign policy has been to obtain international recognition of the Karmal regime (and by extension of the Soviet presence required to keep the regime in power). The policy was formalized in proposals put forth on 14 May 1980 and modified on 24 August 1981. It is based on the contention that the resistance movement is a creation of outside powers: the United States, Pakistan, China, and Egypt. Both sets of proposals require the cessation of all resistance as a precondition for the withdrawal of Soviet troops.

The DRA and the Soviets have used the bait of a political settlement to try to lure the government of Pakistan into negotiating directly with the Karmal government, that is, into a de facto recognition of that government. Pakistan has stood firm, agreeing to meet only with representatives of the party (PDPA) as opposed to government (DRA) officials and then only in the form of tripartite talks with Iran under the aegis of the United Nations. The formula for tripartite talks dates to the May 1980 Islamic Foreign Ministers Conference in Islamabad, which gave Pakistan and Iran a joint mandate to seek a political solution to the Afghan question. Iran has refused to participate in talks that do not include representatives of the resistance movement, thereby effectively blocking any talks for the present.

In February 1981, U.N. Secretary General Kurt Waldheim appointed then Under Secretary General Javier Pérez de Cuellar of Peru as his personal representative to seek a political settlement. Pérez traveled to Kabul and Islamabad in April and again in early August. Following the August visit, the DRA announced on 24 August a modification of its procedural conditions; it agreed to trilateral talks and to U.N. participation. Previously it had insisted on separate bilateral talks with Pakistan and Iran and had not publicly accepted an active role for the United Nations. Subsequently, during the autumn U.N. session, Waldheim and Pérez met separately with the foreign ministers of Pakistan and Afghanistan and their representatives in New York.

The DRA's 24 August proposals also dealt with the plan of the European Economic Community (EEC), which had been presented to Moscow on 6 July. This initiative called for an international conference to settle the Afghan question. The Soviets and the DRA rejected the EEC proposals because they excluded the DRA from the proposed conference. The DRA's 24 August proposals entertained the possibility of an international conference, but one with DRA participation. There were no indications, however, that the USSR or the DRA was willing to make concessions on the key issue— the withdrawal of Soviet troops.

Meanwhile, the regime, guided by its Soviet sponsors, has made a great effort to portray itself as a legitimate government empowered to participate in normal international activity, such as attending international congresses or conventions. In effect, this activity has been primarily limited to relations with the Soviets and countries within their sphere of influence.

The warm reception that Moscow gave Karmal during his state visit in October 1980 was clearly designed to enhance his international stature. Karmal's state visit to Czechoslovakia in June 1981 had a similar purpose, all the more obvious since it followed the founding congress of the NFF, which had been expected to demonstrate conclusively Karmal's claim to popular support in Afghanistan. Karmal also attended the Twenty-Sixth CPSU Congress in February–March and was received by Brezhnev in the Crimea in July.

Soviet bloc countries have also been expected to help enhance the prestige of the PDPA and the DRA. During April and May, PDPA delegations attended the Bulgarian, Czechoslovak, East German, and Mongolian party congresses. In September, a PDPA delegation went to Prague to attend a conference of "workers' parties" from Europe and Asia, and in October, a government delegation attended the thirteen hundredth anniversary celebrations of the Bulgarian state.

A more critical problem for the regime has been to demonstrate that conditions in Afghanistan are sufficiently settled to allow foreign delegates to attend conferences in Kabul safely. Afghan media coverage of the first DRA trade union congress on 7–8 March, therefore, focused heavily on the presence of foreign delegations. There were, however, no foreign well-wishers at the first congress of the DRA Peace, Friendship, and Solidarity Organization eight days later. Nor did foreign dignitaries participate in this year's celebrations of the anniversary of the 27 April coup, whereas in 1980 a number of guests from friendly countries came for this event.

At the end of the year, the regime staged a major propaganda event by hosting the Tenth Conference of the Presidium of the Afro-Asian Peoples' Solidarity Organization (AAPSO) in Kabul on 18–20 November. Although the delegates to the AAPSO conference demonstrated full support for their hosts, the extremely heavy security measures surrounding their visit may have made them a bit uneasy. Furthermore, in spite of the security, the mujahidin managed to fire off several rockets at the Intercontinental Hotel, the site of the conference; there were no direct hits, but some damage was done.

Afghanistan's close relations with the Soviet Union have produced, throughout the year, frequent delegations in both directions related to trade and technical assistance agreements. The Soviets have also sent numerous educational and cultural representatives, including Soviet Muslims from the neighboring Central Asian republics. Numerous Afghan groups have gone to the USSR to study the Soviet system. Fifteen hundred Afghan students were to enroll in Soviet institutions by October 1980.

In addition to overall trade and technical assistance agreements, the DRA and the USSR signed a number of separate contracts during the year covering the purchase by the DRA from the USSR of petroleum products, grain, tractors, tools, and sugar and agreements covering proposed development projects, including a copper complex and irrigation systems.

On 16 June, Moscow and Kabul signed a border treaty, delineating a section of the northeast boundary of the Wakhan corridor. The treaty was denounced by the People's Republic of China on the grounds that since the USSR holds territory north of the Wakhan that historically belongs to China, Moscow had no authority to enter into the treaty.

East European countries also signed new technical assistance and cooperation agreements with the DRA in 1981, but their involvement appears limited. East Germany agreed to help with an electrical system in Kabul and to equip and expand DRA radio and television studios. Czechoslovakia is to assist with transportation and will provide generators for outlying districts. These arrangements all involve credit on easy terms. Hungary gave 70 trucks as grant-in-aid and agreed to exchange information. All gave relief aid in the form of medicines, blankets, childrens' clothes, food, and stationery. The bloc countries do not appear to be making a major effort to help the Soviets in Afghanistan.

Media. In March, Radio Afghanistan announced that it was starting a new half-hour broadcast in Pashai, one of several Nuristani languages spoken in northeast Afghanistan. The announcement stated this was in accord with DRA policy of developing the culture of Afghanistan's diverse nationalities and observed that Radio Afghanistan already broadcast in Uzbek, Turkman, Baluchi and Nuristani minority languages. In keeping with the same policy, in April, the regime announced a new publication, *Bamian*, for the Hazara population in the central uplands. In September, another new magazine appeared, an illustrated bimonthly, *International Affairs*.

U.S. Department of State   Eliza Van Hollen
Washington, D.C.

(Note: Views expressed in this article are the author's own and do not represent those of the State Department.)

Australia

Most adherents of communism in Australia belong to one of three factions. The largest and oldest is the Communist Party of Australia (CPA), which was formed in 1920. It maintains a generally independent, Eurocommunist orientation. In 1964, several hundred militants broke away to form a pro-Beijing faction—the Communist Party of Australia/Marxist-Leninist (CPA/ML). In 1971, after another split in the party, the pro-Soviet Socialist Party of Australia (SPA) was founded.

In 1980, the CPA and the SPA made an attempt at leftist unity to challenge Prime Minister Malcolm Fraser's re-election. They issued a joint statement in May, and in August, leftists, including the CPA/ML faction (estranged for sixteen years), convened a Communist and Labour Movement History Conference in Melbourne. However, the poor showing of the left in the October 1980 elections ended what little leftist unity had been achieved.

Leadership. Judy Mundey has been CPA national president since her election in June 1979 at the party's Twenty-Sixth Congress. Eric Aarons and Bernie Taft serve as joint national secretaries. Rob Durbridge and Mark Taft were promoted from joint national assistant secretaries to joint national secretaries in April. The CPA/ML is headed by Edward Hill. Pat Clancy is president, Peter Symon is general secretary, and Alan Miller is deputy general secretary of the SPA.

Domestic Activities. In the 1980 parliamentary elections, the vote for leftist candidates remained much as it had been for years. No left-wing party won a seat. Leftist voters may have shifted to the Australian Labor Party in the expectation that Labor could win, but Prime Minister Fraser's governing Liberal Party–National Country Party coalition won by a comfortable margin. In several seats, leftists ran against each other, competing for the small left-wing vote. CPA President Judy Mundey was the most successful of the leftist candidates, polling 4 percent of the vote in Sydney. In addition to the CPA and SPA, smaller leftist parties, notably the Socialist Workers Party and the Socialist Labour League, ran candidates, who garnered 2–4 percent of the vote. The overall poor showing for the left demonstrates that its appeal to the Australian electorate is still very limited. (*Tribune*, 22 October 1980.)

In 1981, CPA attention focused on wages and the workweek. In January, CPA union officials and job activists from different states met in Sydney to discuss the party's policy on wages and hours. The CPA National Committee called the meeting to address the ongoing wage debate and to develop tactics for the 35-hour workweek campaign. The CPA seeks "an overall 'wage solidarity' package" that "links the leverage which skilled workers can exert with the relatively unorganized and low-paid majority." Moreover, "full automatic compensation paid quarterly for price hikes and inflation, in full [that is, after taxes], remains the cornerstone of socialist policy." (Ibid., 11 February.) The CPA meeting felt that the campaign for a shorter workweek was imperative and recommended that unions "should pursue gains by collective bargaining and direct negotiation based on industrial action" (ibid., 4 February).

In April, the CPA's National Committee met to discuss the impact of Australia's resources boom on particular states and the shift of the economy toward mining and related projects. The National Committee decided to publish a four-page broadsheet on living standards, wages, and taxes and to produce two pages of the CPA's weekly organ, *Tribune*, in a number of immigrant languages once a month. (ibid., 22 April.) (Australia's industrial work force consists largely of first- or second-generation immigrants.)

SPA activity in 1981 focused on preparations for the party's Fourth Congress, held in October in Sydney. General Secretary Peter Symon presented the Central Committee's report, and debate centered on global campaigns for peace, democracy, and socialism. Over four hundred people attended, with many representatives from socialist states. (*New Zealand Tribune*, 2 November.)

According to Deputy General Secretary Alan Miller, the SPA is "concentrating on forming Party organisations at industrial enterprises, mainly big facilities," to give the party a "larger role and influence in the labour movement, in the trade unions." The party is concerned about working-class unity and is seeking broader cooperation with the Australian Labor Party. It also hopes to bring together different segments of society—youth, women, intellectuals, small businessmen, and farmers—to work toward a "democratic, anti-monopoly government." (*WMR*, June.)

International Policies. The CPA issued a statement on Poland, reaffirming its support for independent trade unions and warning against Soviet interference in the internal affairs of that nation. The statement noted that "repression of the [Solidarity] movement could only strengthen anti-Socialist forces in Poland, make the long term problems of Poland and its neighbours worse, escalate the present trend to adopt military solutions to problems and inflict further damage on socialists everywhere" (*Tribune*, 8 April). The CPA's National Committee voted to invite a Solidarity trade union representative to visit Australia.

The SPA adheres to the general concerns of pro-Soviet communist parties, advocating world peace, détente, and an end to the arms race and opposing "Australia's use as a springboard for U.S. militarism" (*WMR*, June). The CPA/ML made direct contact with Chinese Communist Party (CCP) leaders in 1981. During a four-day visit to China in April, Chairman Edward Hill met with leaders of the CCP Central Committee, including Li Xiannian, vice-chairman of the CCP Central Committee, Ji Pengfei, head of the International Liaison Department of the CCP Central Committee, and Ji's deputy, Ou Tangliang (*FBIS*, 16 and 20 April).

Washington, D.C.   Roberta L. Chew

Bangladesh

Politics in Bangladesh is characterized by divisiveness and factionalism, and the communist movement is no exception. The major disagreement concerns the Sino-Soviet split. Within these two camps are further divisions, usually personality conflicts disguised as disputes over ideological purity. Indeed, few of the parties have a clear ideological perspective. During 1981, none of the communist parties played a significant role in the momentous political events that tested the political institutions of the country.

President Ziaur Rahman was assassinated by a few disgruntled military officers in Chittagong on 30 May. The abortive coup was quickly put down by Army Chief of Staff Lt. Gen. E. M. Ershad. The nation had to prepare for new presidential elections while a provisional government filled in for the charismatic Zia. The new constitutional system worked relatively well. Vice-President Abdus Sattar became acting president, and he demonstrated considerable skill in ending a strike among bank clerks and in persuading the opposition parties to participate in the 15 November elections. The Zia assassination probe ended with the execution of twelve officers on 23 September. The issue aroused remarkably little rancor during the sensitive transition period between presidents.

To get opposition participation, Sattar agreed to delay the poll from 31 September to 15 November. There were 29 candidates for the presidency. Sattar, the ruling Bangladesh Nationalist Party (BNP)'s candidate, won a large majority of the vote in fair elections, thus guaranteeing the continuation of a moderate government that would follow Zia's domestic and foreign policies.

None of the communist parties has significant popular support, and none had any impact on the elections. Communists exert some influence within university student unions and among some segments of the trade union movement. Leftist views get a more effective hearing in larger centrist parties. There is a substantial leftist faction in the Awami League (AL), the largest and best-organized political party, as well as in the Jatiya Samajtantrik Dal. Moderates have strengthened their hold on the AL during the past year. They are backed by Sheikh Hasina Wazed (daughter of late Prime Minister Sheikh Mujibur Rahman), who arrived from India on 17 May to take control of the AL.

The more active of the communist parties are the pro-Chinese United People's Party, Sammyabadi Dal, and Ganotantrik Party and the pro-Soviet Workers' Party, National Awami Party (Muzaffer), Jatiya Ekata Party, and Communist Party of Bangladesh (CPB). The Sammyabadi Dal has fraternal relations with the Chinese Communist Party and the CPB has party-to-party ties with the Communist Party of the Soviet Union.

Communist Activities. The Supreme Court released Mohammed Farhad, general secretary of the pro-Moscow CPB on 27 July, some two months after the assassination of President Zia. He and 38 other Communists had been arrested in April 1980 for voicing support of an Afghan-style revolution in Bangladesh. The others had been released earlier. While the government has not dropped its charges (no date has yet been set for a trial), the release of Farhad does suggest increased self-confidence on its part.

Anil Mukherji, a member of the CPB Central Committee, wrote an article in mid-1981 outlining the direction of CPB strategy (*WMR*, June). Mukherji argued that the party failed to implement the principal of "unity and struggle" correctly and weakened itself by united front tactics. The CPB overemphasized aligning with other "patriotic" forces and underemphasized the "limitations" of these groups and the notion of "struggle." The party, he maintained, must develop a more militant stand and must protect its organizational separateness.

He specifically repudiated the party's close links between 1972 and 1975 with the late Prime Minister Mujibur Rahman, whose "petty-bourgeois" limitations were not correctly understood. He further maintained that the AL, now led by Rahman's daughter, is no longer a militant organization. He appeared to be saying that the CPB should not repeat its mistakes. Moderates in the AL soon demonstrated their dominance by nominating Kamal Hossein for the presidency.

The CPB has abandoned its effort to unite the pro-Soviet parties or link up with one of the larger centrist parties on a united front platform. It apparently has decided to focus attention on its labor and student front groups and use them to build up mass support, as well to lobby for the foreign policy stands of the Soviet Union. Its Trade Union Center (TUC) has tried, so far with little success, to bring other trade unions under its umbrella. However, the TUC has won control of unions that represent private bus, railway, and some government workers. Chatra, its student wing, is small but active on the Dacca University campus.

There are recurrent rumors that the various pro-Chinese groups will unite, but the only movement in this direction in 1981 was the amalgamation of several minuscule pro-Chinese Marxist-Leninist groups into the Ganotantrik Party. Its chairman is Nurul Huda Mirza. However, the Sammyabadi Dal, the only pro-Chinese party with fraternal links with the Chinese Communist Party, remained aloof from these unity efforts.

Relations with Communist Countries. The Zia government maintained correct, but cool, relations with the USSR. Bangladesh refused to attend the Moscow Olympics in 1980 as a protest against the Soviet invasion of Afghanistan. In 1981, it voted in the United Nations against the continued Soviet occupation of Afghanistan and against seating the delegation of the Vietnamese-backed Heng Samrin regime in Kampuchea. In late June, the Soviet embassy was involved in an embarrassing episode. When it tried to bring electronic equipment marked as building materials into the country, there was a nasty scene at the airport involving Soviet embassy personnel, which aroused a storm of public protest against the USSR. A strong protest was delivered to the Soviet ambassador; two Soviet diplomats were expelled from the country; and the equipment was flown out on 29 June.

Nevertheless, Bangladesh tries to maintain a nonaligned, "equidistant" foreign policy. Soviet Deputy Minister for Foreign Trade Ivan T. Grishin visited Bangladesh in mid-February and signed an agreement for a substantially increased barter trade arrangement and for a major expansion of the Soviet-built Ghorasal power plant.

The government extols its relationship with the People's Republic of China (PRC), although the relationship is longer on rhetoric than substance. The PRC is Bangladesh's leading supplier of military equipment and a major importer of its products. Premier Zhao Ziyang visited Bangladesh on 7–8 June, soon after the assassination of President Zia, to demonstrate continuing support of the PRC. In return, Mirza Gholam Hafiz, speaker of the Bangladesh Parliament, visited the PRC in July.

Arlington, Virginia   Walter K. Andersen

Burma

The Burmese Communist Party (BCP), founded on 15 August 1939, was a leading part of the nationalist coalition that led the struggle for Burmese independence. The BCP split with the noncommunist nationalists in March 1948, three months after Burma gained independence. Outlawed, the party has been in insurrection against the central government ever since. From its inception, the BCP has been plagued by factionalism; some of the early Burmese Communists defected from the party and eventually became influential figures in the military-socialist government that has ruled Burma since 1962. Since the early 1960s, the BCP has been avowedly pro-Chinese, characterizing itself as a party guided by Marxism–Leninism–Mao Zedong Thought. Pro-Soviet Communists were purged from the party in a paroxysm of ideological infighting in the mid-1960s.

Leadership and Organization. The party is led by Central Committee Chairman Thakin Ba Thein Tin, a 72-year-old veteran of the communist movement. He is believed to reside in Beijing, where he evidently met with Burmese President U Ne Win during the latter's visit to China on 20–24 October 1980. Ba Thein Tin was reported to have attended the opening of a party school in northeastern Burma in mid-1981 (Voice of the People of Burma [VOPB], 25 October; FBIS, 28 October). The Central Committee, reconstituted in 1975, is composed of at least twenty members, of whom the following were identified during 1981: Vice-Chairman Pe Tint, Ye Tun, and Fran Gan Dee (VOPB, 14 June; FBIS, 17 June). Other commentary mentioned Tin Yee and Myo Myint (Asiaweek, 29 May).

In 1979, the BCP claimed some three thousand members, including candidate members. The party is organized in military-administrative regions, the largest of which is the Northeast Military Region along the Chinese border in Burma's Shan state. Also important is the 815th Military Region, south of the Northeast Military Region along Burma's border with China and Laos. Much smaller party units have been identified in Arakan state, Tenasserim division, and the Northwest division, which BCP commentary appears to identify with Magwe division (VOPB, 1 January 1980; FBIS, 4 January 1980). Estimates of the size of the BCP's guerrilla force, a loose organization of units up to battalion-size, range from 8,000 to 15,000 men operating generally east of the Salween River in the mountainous area of northeastern Burma bordering China's Yunnan province. (Burmese Defense Ministry estimates of 21,500 men reported in the 29 May issue of Far Eastern Economic Review [FEER] are probably exaggerations.)

Party Internal Affairs. The BCP's decision to enter into peace talks with the Burmese government had far-ranging implications both for party organization and for the evolution of its ideology. Although the prolonged negotiations with Rangoon were ultimately unsuccessful, positions taken by the party in justification of the negotiations mark a significant shift in its political and military doctrines. If the BCP remains committed to these new ideological interpretations of the "road to power," it could mean a fundamental break with the Maoist revolutionary line adopted by the party in 1964.

Consistent with the political line laid down at the November 1979 party conference (see YICA,

1981, pp. 129–30), the BCP continued to characterize the Ne Win government as embodying the "three evil systems"—"imperialism, feudal landlordism, and bureaucrat capitalism" (VOPB, 29 March, 16 August; *FBIS*, 1 April, 25 August). In commentary criticizing Ne Win's 8 August speech announcing his retirement from the presidency, VOPB (16 August) predicted that the government's reliance on the "three evil systems" and "its obstinate continuation of the civil war against the people [would] only hasten its downfall and disintegration" (*FBIS*, 25 August). The party also continued to maintain that the tool "to eradicate exploitation and oppression is a people's democratic dictatorship." Similarly, it reaffirmed its commitment "to firmly grasp the revolutionary spirit of 28 March [1948]— that is, the spirit to wage revolution to the end through self-reliance and arduous struggle in the interests of the party, revolution, and the people." (VOPB, 29 March; *FBIS*, 1 April.)

In a long statement on the collapse of the peace negotiations with Rangoon, however, the BCP appears to have abandoned or modified substantially two ideological tenets that have historically been fundamental to the BCP (VOPB, 14 June; *FBIS*, 17 June). First, the party has seriously questioned the role of "armed struggle" in the revolutionary road to power. While neither the party's general statement on the peace talks nor the accompanying address by Ba Thein Tin explicitly rejects "armed struggle," the concept now appears to relate more to the defense of the party than to the seizure of the state. The party statement speaks of confronting "the military government's reactionary civil war" with "our revolutionary civil war in accordance with the *principles of self-preservation*" (emphasis added). Likewise, "the BCP will resolutely and militarily continue to defend and attack in defensive warfare to protect the base areas and the people." Rather than emphasizing the goal of toppling the Ne Win government, the statement concludes with the pronouncement that the struggle will continue under "the three banners—the banner of ending civil war and establishing peace in the country, the banner of democracy, and the banner of national unity."

Second, the statement strongly implies that the BCP no longer maintains its ideological claim to a monopoly on political organization in making the revolution. In challenging the one-party rule of the government's Burma Socialist Program Party (BSPP), the statement explicitly recognizes the need for the BCP to share power with other parties, presumably including the BSPP.

> Today, Burmese society has many classes and strata. As long as such classes and strata exist, there will definitely be political parties, organizations and groupings which represent the classes and strata. As there is the vanguard of the proletariat in Burma—the BCP—so will there also be political parties and groupings politically representing the other classes and strata.

Subsequently, the party chairman emphasized that

> members of the military government delegation said . . . that from experience in Burma and the world, a multiparty system could only give rise to bad consequences. Is it really true? From what we have studied and learned from history we find it quite opposite. In the socialist countries the world over today, a multiparty system does exist. This does not give rise to bad consequences; on the contrary, good consequences result.
>
> After we have seized power nationally, we will certainly set up the dictatorship of the proletariat. This differs from the one-party dictatorship system. In fact it is vastly different. After we have seized power nationally, our BCP will have to grant the right to the democrats and to all the classes which support and desire our socialist revolution and socialist construction to set up their own respective parties. This means that the BCP will join hands with a broad, united multiparty front in successfully carrying out the socialist revolution and socialist construction.
>
> If a multiparty system is essential in the period of socialist revolution, Burma today needs a multiparty system even more. Nationwide unity can never be achieved under the one-party dictatorship system introduced by the military government.

Whether these shifts are a temporary tactical move or a longer-term adjustment of position will become clearer over time. It is still uncertain how much the goal of "socialist revolution" has been subordinated to anti-Soviet foreign policy considerations of China, the BCP's longtime ideological mentor and patron. Elsewhere in the peace-talk statement, the argument was made that resolution of the civil war and the creation of a multiparty system are essential for forging "national unity" in Burma, which, in turn, is necessary for defending the country against the "domination and hegemonistic policies of Soviet social-imperialism" and the "small hegemonist, Vietnam, which wants to hold sway over Southeast Asia." At the same time, the party has taken the tack that in pursuing national unity it will hold open the possibility of a peaceful reconciliation with the Ne Win government. Although the BCP has not stopped criticizing Ne Win, recent commentary on the government has been remarkably free from the harsh cant of the past. (See, for example, "The Military Is to Be Blamed for the Oil Shortage in the Country," VOPB, 11 November; FBIS, 12 November.)

In other party matters, the perennial problems of organization and weak leadership and cadres, detailed at length in the political report to the 1979 party conference (see YICA, 1981, pp. 129–31), continue to plague the BCP. A VOPB statement (17 May) on BCP efforts in Arakan state said the party's Arakan organization is "temporarily facing great hardships and difficulties" (FBIS, 28 May). Highlighted were the efforts of the Akyab and Kyaukoyu district organizations, which "resisted with all available forces" recent government efforts to reduce them. But the statement also criticized those who had surrendered to the government in Arakan and Northwest divisions in 1958 and 1980. In 1958, "the People's Independence Party and the People's Comrade Party surrendered en masse" along with a "major group" of BCP members "who had been deceived by the opportunists who took advantage of the revolution." In 1980, following the government's May amnesty offer, "the Arakan Communist Party and the Arakan Independence Army" surrendered. Following a subsequent government offensive, "the forces in the Northwest Command and Minbu District who had no courage to face hardship and who were afraid to die surrendered."

A 25 October VOPB broadcast marked the opening of a party training school in the Northeast Military Region (FBIS, 28 October). The school is apparently an effort to strengthen the notoriously weak grasp of party doctrine by many BCP military commanders, even senior military commanders. VOPB noted that "most of the trainees are old" and that "some of the trainees are leading officials at the regimental and divisional levels." Some of these "have served the revolution for more than 20 or 30 years."

While there were no concrete signs of factionalism during 1980, one commentary noted that the BCP's official move into the opium trade "could well precipitate geographic fragmentation and territorial rivalries" and quoted a diplomatic source that "it's already possible that some BCP officers are active in the opium trade on their own" (Asiaweek, 29 May). There were rumors of a pro-Soviet faction operating out of northwest Laos in late 1980, but these have not been given much weight (ibid., 5 December 1980).

Domestic Activities. For the third time since the beginning of the BCP's insurrection, negotiations were held in 1980–1981 between the government and the BCP. In contrast to the 1963 talks, these discussions were held secretly. The first public announcement came in Ne Win's 14 May speech to the BSPP Central Committee, which revealed that the negotiations had failed (Rangoon Domestic Service, 14 May; FBIS, 14 May). Ne Win announced that the BCP had insisted on three basic conditions: that the government recognize the existence of the BCP, that the BCP army remain intact, and that the BCP continue in possession of its border base area. These BCP demands could not be met, Ne Win declared, and the negotiations were called off. Further information on the failed talks was provided in a detailed and apparently accurate statement by Ba Thein Tin on 14 June (VOPB, 14 June; FBIS, 17

June). According to Ba Thein Tin, a BCP proposal for talks, characterized as an imperative for checking Soviet hegemonism, was delivered to the Burmese government on 25 September 1980. The first round of talks was held in 1980 between a government delegation led by Ne Win and including Foreign Minister U Lay Maung and BSPP Secretary U Than Hlaing, and a BCP group headed by Ba Thein Tin, which included BCP Central Committee Vice-Chairman Pe Tint and Central Committee member Ye Tun. Circumstances indicate that these discussions were most likely held in Beijing during Ne Win's official visit. There are reports that the Chinese leaders at that time pressed Ne Win to open talks with the BCP (*Economist*, 20 June). The second round of talks took place in government territory in Burma in 1981, between a government delegation led by BSPP Central Executive Committe member Lt. Gen. Aye Ko and a BCP delegation led by Central Committee Vice-Chairman Pe Tint (VOPB, 14 June; *FBIS*, 17 June). These talks were terminated on 9 May, and the BCP delegation returned to its own territory (VOPB, 29 June; *FBIS*, 30 June). Ba Thein Tin declared that at the government's insistence, a cease-fire was not part of these negotiations (unlike 1963), although fighting appears to have been lighter than normal in any case. This last point was confirmed in Ne Win's statement, which also indicated that the government considered the negotiation attempt confined to the Aye Ko–Pe Tint exchange. The government has not confirmed face-to-face contact between Ne Win and Ba Thein Tin. Subsequently, the BCP denounced the government's position during the talks as a "surrender demand" and particularly attacked an offer to let BCP members join the BSPP as trying to get a "stately white elephant" to "pass through a gate meant for dogs" (VOPB, 10 July; *FBIS*, 14 July).

On 10 July, VOPB broadcast a 12 June statement by the Kachin Independence Organization announcing the breakdown of talks between Kachin nationalists and the government. (The Kachins and the BCP have been allied since 1976; see *YICA*, 1981, p. 131.) According to this statement, more than ten rounds of discussions were held between the Kachins, the BSPP, and a "mediating group of honorable gentlemen" between August 1980 and 31 May 1981. The first round was held in Rangoon between Kachin leader Brang Seng and Ne Win. Later rounds were held in Myitkyina between a Kachin group, a delegation from the BSPP Kachin state regional party committee, and the mediators. These talks were broken off by the Burmese on 2 June, according to the statement (VOPB, 10 July; *FBIS*, 14 July). The Burmese government has not made a statement regarding any talks with the Kachin nationalists.

Commentary during the first half of 1981 indicated that BCP military activity had decreased noticeably. The *Far Eastern Economic Review* (29 May) noted there had been no major BCP operation as of that date and attributed the lull to China's desire to improve relations with Burma, as well as to signs of Burmese military success over the BCP. Regular combat reports over VOPB continued to announce military engagements, mostly small scale, until 7 March, when these reports ceased. Reporting resumed with two engagements in southern Shan state on 14 October (*FBIS*, 28 October). The significance of the reporting hiatus is unclear, although it appears likely to have been connected with the negotiations. A combat news review of 16 April noted that 120 engagements took place in eastern, northern, and northeastern Burma during the first three months of the year (VOPB, 16 April; *FBIS*, 16 April).

A 29 March VOPB commentary declared that the BCP had crushed the government's Operation King Conquerer, which began in November 1979 (*FBIS*, 1 April). The government reported that 118 BCP members had surrendered from January to March, including an acting regimental commander (*Working People's Daily*, 25 March). On 17 November, the *Guardian* and *Working People's Daily* reported the surrender of Ye Tun, described as secretary of the Arakan BCP from February to August 1980 and a candidate member of the BCP Central Committee.

BCP efforts to attract allies among the various disaffected ethnic minorities of Burma continued. Their greatest success apparently continues to be with the Kachin Independence Organization. On 9

August, the VOPB broadcast a joint BCP-Kachin Independence Organization statement that the two groups, in fighting the "common enemy," would "strengthen bilateral relations on the basis of the equality which exists among revolutionary forces, render mutual assistance and continue to extend friendly cooperation for the complete liberation of the people of all nationalities" (*FBIS*, 14 August). The VOPB broadcast several combat reports for the Shan State Nationalities Liberation Organization and the Kayah New Land Revolution Council, both small groups and perhaps breakaways from better-known insurgent groups representing the Shan and Kayah minorities (VOPB, 1 and 4 March; *FBIS*, 4 March). In contrast, the 1974 Shan State Army pact with the BCP reportedly degenerated into open fighting by October 1980, with a consequent cutoff of weapons assistance formerly funneled through the BCP, bringing the future of the Shan State Army into doubt (*Asiaweek*, 29 May). Significant new ties may be forming with the pseudo-nationalist opium-trafficking group, the Shan United Army of warlord Zhang Jifu. The Shan United Army now controls 75 percent of the opium traffic from BCP-held zones to the Thai border, according to one report (ibid., 29 May). BCP contacts with the Shan United Army and other opium traffickers are evidently motivated by the need to make up for reduced aid from China (ibid., 5 December 1980) and follow the decision several years ago to repeal the party's long ban on opium cultivation in its territory (*CSM*, 26 February; *YICA*, 1981, p. 131).

The unsuccessful outcome of the peace talks, the mixed results of attempts to repair or forge new alliances, and continuing problems of organization and resource shortages have apparently left the party with a sense of embattlement. In an unusual formulation, a 15 August VOPB editorial commemorating the forty-second anniversary of the BCP's formation described the party's situation as "surrounded by the enemy and constantly under attack from it." It is the darkest characterization of the party's situation yet broadcast over the VOPB. Nevertheless, the party is not resigned to its plight, but will "bravely confront the situations as they arise." (*FBIS*, 25 August.)

International Views and Contacts. Despite continued reports of cutbacks in Chinese aid, the BCP's world view showed little change during 1980, although some evolution was noticeable, probably due to continued Chinese antagonism toward Vietnam and the failed peace talks with the government. According to Ba Thein Tin, "it is the policy of our party to oppose the two hegemonists—U.S. imperialism and Soviet social-imperialism--particularly Soviet social-imperialism in the international sphere and the small hegemonist—Vietnam—in Southeast Asia" (VOPB, 14 June; *FBIS*, 17 June). In view of the invasions of Afghanistan and Kampuchea, "it is essential to be prepared to mobilize the entire nation for defense" (VOPB, 29 March; *FBIS*, 1 April).

Chinese Premier Zhao Ziyang's early 1981 statements limiting Chinese support to Southeast Asian communist parties to "political and spiritual" aid attracted attention in connection with reports that support to the BCP continues to fall. The BCP still stresses self-reliance (VOPB, 25 October; *FBIS*, 28 October), and reports emerged that the Chinese had cut off an annual cash grant of over U.S. $7 million (*Asiaweek*, 29 May; *FEER*, 29 May). Regardless of such cuts, Burmese government suspicion of China continues; Burmese officials assert continued Chinese supply of both weapons and money to the BCP (*CSM*, 26 February; *FEER*, 29 May). As part of the effort to cut the China-BCP tie, Rangoon is reportedly pushing for Chinese Communist Party (CCP) recognition of the BSPP (*Asiaweek*, 5 December 1980). The reduction in Chinese aid may be forcing the BCP to develop greater independence, in sharp contrast to its position in the years immediately following the 1968–1969 establishment of its current base area (ibid., 29 May). Regardless of aid reductions, the rhetoric of the BCP-CCP relationship has not diminished. "The BCP and the CCP have always supported each other and established a revolutionary friendship which is friendly and close," declared the BCP in its sixtieth anniversary greeting to the CCP. This "militant solidarity" is "based on Marxism–Leninism–Mao Zedong Thought and proletarian internationalism" (VOPB, 1 July; *FBIS*, 2 July). Clashes may be in prospect between the BCP and Laos; the BCP may be training Laotian guerrillas opposing the

Vietnamese presence in Laos (*Asiaweek*, 29 May; *Economist*, 20 June). Although given less credence, rumors of BCP factions seeking Vietnamese assistance or operating out of northwest Laos into Burma continues (*Asiaweek*, 5 December 1980; *FEER,* 29 May). Attracting some attention in Bangkok were reports of BCP movements toward the Thai border at Tachilek and possible BCP contacts with the Communist Party of Thailand (CPT), although Chinese-Thai relations are regarded as making substantial ties between the BCP and the CPT unlikely (*Asiaweek*, 29 May).

Publications. Burmese communist propaganda is primarily disseminated over the VOPB, which has broadcast since 1971 from a facility in Yunnan province in China. The VOPB broadcasts daily two-hour shortwave programs in Burmese, Mandarin, Shan, Karen, and possibly Kachin.

U.S. Department of State   Jon A. Wiant
Washington, D.C.   Charles B. Smith

(Note: Views expressed in this article are the authors' own and do not represent those of the State Department.)

China

The Chinese Communist Party (Zhongguo gongchan dang; CCP), founded in July 1921, is the largest communist party in the world. The CCP claimed 39 million members in mid-1981 (NCNA, Beijing, 1 July). As the only legal party, the CCP provides "absolute leadership" for all other organizations in the People's Republic of China (PRC).

Leadership and Organization. The Eleventh Central Committee (elected in August 1977) originally had 201 full members and 132 alternate members (the sixth plenum in June 1981 was attended by 195 members and 114 alternate members). The committee is dominated by older, experienced cadres, a great many of whom were purged or criticized in the Cultural Revolution. The first secretaries of all 29 of China's major administrative divisions—provinces, autonomous regions, and municipalities—are full members. There is a strong military presence.

The officers of the Eleventh Politburo are Chairman Hu Yaobang (replaced Hua Guofeng, 29 June 1981) and Vice-Chairmen Ye Jianying, Deng Xiaoping, Li Xiannian, Chen Yun, Zhao Ziyang (added June 1981), and Hua Guofeng (added June 1981). The Standing Committee of the Politburo consists of these seven men. Other members of the Politburo are Wei Guoqing, Ulanfu, Fang Yi, Liu Bocheng, Xu Shiyou, Su Zhenhua, Li Desheng, Yu Qiuli, Zhang Tingfa, Chen Yonggui, Geng Biao, Nie Rongzhen, Ni Zhifu, Xu Xiangqian, Peng Chong, Deng Yingchao, Wang Zhen, Peng Zhen, Ji Dengkui, and Wu De. Chen Muhua and Saifudin are alternate members.

Hu Yaobang was named general secretary of the re-established Secretariat of the Central Committee in February 1980. Since Hu was made party chairman in June 1981, it is unclear who the present general secretary is. The Secretariat consists of Wan Li, Wang Renzhong, Fang Yi, Gu Mu, Song Renqiong, Yu Qiuli, Yang Dezhi, Hu Qiaomu, Yao Yilin, and Peng Chong.

Below the Central Committee and its Politburo and Secretariat extends a network of party committees at the provincial, special district, county, and municipal levels. A similar network exists within the People's Liberation Army (PLA), from the level of the military region down to that of the regiment.

According to the state constitution adopted 5 March 1978, the highest organ of state power in the PRC is the National People's Congress (NPC). The NPC is elected for a term of five years and holds one session each year, although both of these stipulations are subject to alteration. The first session of the Fifth NPC was held 24 February to 8 March 1978; the fourth session met from 30 November to 13 December 1981.

The People's Political Consultative Conference (CPPCC) is the official united front organization. The Fifth National Committee of the CPPCC held its fourth session 28 November–13 December 1981, concurrently with the Fifth NPC's fourth session. The CPPCC's National Committee (the Fifth National Committee at its fourth session had 2,054 members, 1,586 of whom attended the opening ceremony) holds plenary sessions and elects the Standing Committee. Deng Xiaoping is chairman of the CPPCC's National Committee. The CPPCC also has local committees at the provincial, autonomous region, municipal, and other levels.

The PLA, which includes the Chinese Navy and Air Force, has over 3.9 million members. According to the 1978 state constitution, the command of this military organization is the responsibility of the chairman of the CCP. However, in June 1981, Deng Xiaoping was formally made chairman of the Military Affairs Commission of the Central Committee, a position he had actually assumed sometime earlier. The chief of the general staff is Yang Dezhi, who replaced Deng Xiaoping in February 1980. The defense minister is Geng Biao, who replaced 79-year-old Xu Xiangqian on 6 March (*NYT*, 7 March).

Mass organizations have played an important role in the organizational life of China, although they have at times fallen into desuetude. Such was the case during the Great Proletarian Cultural Revolution. However, in 1978 all three of the major mass organizations were reactivated. The All-China Women's Federation, founded in 1949, held its Fourth National Women's Congress in September 1978, its first since 1957. The Communist Youth League of China (CYL), which has 48 million members selected from the more than 300 million children of the country, held its Tenth National Congress in October 1978. The second plenary session of the Tenth Congress was held in February 1980. Central Committee member Han Ying is first secretary of the CYL's Tenth Central Committee. The All-China Federation of Trade Unions (ACFTU) held its Ninth National Trade Union Congress in October 1978. The present Ninth Executive Committee of the ACFTU has 278 members. Politburo member Ni Zhifu is president of the ACFTU.

Domestic Party Affairs. The year 1981 saw further significant consolidation of the power of party Vice-Chairman Deng Xiaoping, although opposition to him or his policies also continued. The sixth plenary session of the Eleventh Central Committee, held in June, was one of the most important party meetings ever. It approved the formal replacement of Hua Guofeng by Hu Yaobang as party chairman. The session also approved an important document officially assessing both the history of the PRC and the late Chairman Mao Zedong's contributions and mistakes. Controls over the expression of dissenting views continued to be tightened. Restrictions on relationships between Chinese and foreigners were also enforced, even as new policies encouraged appetites for foreign technology, commodities, and ways. The fourth session of the Fifth NPC was held from 30 November to 13 December. The Twelfth Party Congress, originally expected to be held in 1981, was deferred until 1982.

On 23 January, the special court that tried the so-called Gang of Four and Clique of Six pronounced its judgment. Jiang Qing and Zhang Chunqiao were sentenced to death with a two-year reprieve and permanent deprivation of political rights. Yao Wenyuan was sentenced to twenty years imprisonment and deprivation of political rights for five years. Wang Hongwen received life imprisonment and permanent deprivation of political rights. Chen Boda, Huang Yongsheng, and Jiang Tengjiao received eighteen-year sentences and deprivation of political rights for five years each. Wu Faxian and Li Zuopeng received sentences of seventeen years and deprivation of political rights for five years. Qiu Huizuo received a sentence of sixteen years and deprivation of political rights for five years. (*Beijing Review*, 2 February.) Public resentment at the high-handedness of the trial was tempered by the general unpopularity of the Gang of Four. Subsequently, Wu Faxian was released on medical grounds (*Far Eastern Economic Review*, 20 November).

The Standing Committee of the NPC met in Beijing from 25 February through 6 March. Yao Yilin, vice-premier and minister in charge of the State Planning Commission, reported on the readjustment of the 1981 national economic plan and state revenues and expenditures. Yao pointed to successive large financial deficits requiring further readjustment of the economic plan. Cheng Zihua, minister of civil affairs, reported on direct elections at the county level, and Jiang Hua, president of the Supreme People's Court and of the special court, reported on the recently concluded trial of the Gang of Four. Ji Pengfei explained the establishment of the Commission for Cultural Relations with Foreign Countries and the State Family Planning Commission. Also examined was a proposal to establish advisers to the State Council. The meeting also decided on several new personnel appointments and removals. (*Beijing Review*, 16 March.)

Mao Dun (Shen Yanbing), vice-chairman of the Fifth National Committee of the CPPCC and chairman of the Chinese Writers' Association, died at age 85 on 27 March in Beijing. On 11 April, a large memorial meeting was held for him in the Great Hall of the People, attended by then Chairman Hua Guofeng and Vice-Chairmen Deng Xiaoping and Li Xiannian, among other prominent leaders, as well as two thousand people. Ba Jin, aged 77, another prolific and popular writer, was subsequently elected acting chairman of the Chinese Writers' Association. (Ibid., 20 April, 11 May.)

On 29 May, Soong Ching Ling, widow of Sun Yat-sen, passed away at the age of 90. A memorial meeting, attended by ten thousand people and presided over by Hu Yaobang and Deng Xiaoping, was held in the Great Hall of the People on 3 June. Just prior to her death, Madame Sun had been admitted to the party and made honorary chairman of the PRC.

The nineteenth meeting of the Fifth NPC Standing Committee was held in Beijing on 4–10 June. The meeting adopted five resolutions ostensibly to improve socialist democracy and the socialist legal system: (1) Decisions on Approving the Death Sentence; (2) Decisions on Handling Escapees and Recidivists Who Are Under Reform Through Labor or Re-education Through Labor; (3) Regulations Governing the Elections of Deputies to the NPC and Local People's Congresses at Various Levels Among the PLA; (4) Provisional Regulations of the PRC on Punishing Army Men Who Commit Offenses Against Their Duties; and (5) Resolution on Strengthening the Work of Legal Interpretation. The meeting also accepted the resignation of Peng Zhen as director of the Commission for Legal Affairs and appointed Xi Zhongxun in his place. (Ibid., 22 June.)

From 27 to 29 June, a particularly important party meeting was held. The sixth plenum of the Eleventh Central Committee was attended by 195 members and 114 alternate members of the Central Committee and 53 nonvoting participants. The plenum elected Hu Yaobang the new chairman of the CCP, and Zhao Ziyang and Hua Guofeng vice-chairmen. Deng Xiaoping was elected chairman of the Military Commission of the Central Committee. The session decided that the Politburo's Standing

Committee will consist of the chairman and the vice-chairmen of the Central Committee. Xi Zhongxun was elected a member of the Secretariat of the Central Committee.

Thus was Hua Guofeng eased out of the chairmanship both of the party and of the Military Commission—his resignation from both was approved unanimously. This action, the result of determined maneuvering by Deng Xiaoping, had been predicted for months. Deng was undoubtedly compelled to allow Hua to remain a vice-chairman in the new political structure. Hua was accused of having opposed Deng's policy of "seeking truth from the facts," of having favored a mechanistic application of Mao's ideas, and of having impetuously started the grandiose and subsequently reduced 1978 economic program.

Hu Yaobang, aged 65, is a longtime associate and bridge partner of Deng Xiaoping, whose political fortune has long been linked with Deng. Like his mentor, Hu is a pragmatic politician who has had a hand in formulating current policies. He has not had extensive military experience and hence does not have a constituency in the PLA. However, as leader of the CYL during the 1950s and 1960s, he met many of the younger party leaders. He was an early outspoken critic of the Cultural Revolution and of Mao's role in it.

The sixth plenum adopted the Resolution on Certain Questions in the History of Our Party Since the Founding of the People's Republic of China, probably one of the most important documents ever produced by the CCP (for text, see ibid., 6 July). The resolution is the end result of a call made in September 1979 by Ye Jianying, chairman of the NPC Standing Committee, for a formal summation of recent party history. A committee to do this was established a month later, and the initial drafting began in March 1980. Seven discussion meetings bringing together different groups of cadres and others met in the course of the drafting and revising. The final document probably reflects the views of Deng Xiaoping more than of Ye Jianying, although various compromises were undoubtedly made. The resolution purports to analyze scientifically the rights and wrongs in the party's guiding ideology over the previous 32 years and the subjective factors and social causes that gave rise to mistakes. It also "realistically" evaluates the historical role of the late Chairman Mao and attempts to elaborate the "great significance" of Mao Zedong Thought as the guiding ideology of the party.

The resolution acknowledged the basic successes achieved by the party over the years, but soberly conceded that "New China has not been in existence for very long, and our successes are still preliminary." Before the Cultural Revolution, mistakes were made in enlarging the scope of class struggle and the economic program exhibited impetuosity and rashness. The Cultural Revolution itself was a "comprehensive, long-drawn out and grave blunder." However, the overthrow of the Gang of Four was a great turning point in history, and China then entered a new period of development. The "scientific principles of Mao Zedong Thought and the correct policies of the Party have been revived and developed under new conditions and all aspects of Party and government work have been flourishing again since the Third Plenary Session of the 11th Central Committee" (December 1978). As for Mao specifically, it is true that he made "gross mistakes" during the Cultural Revolution, but when his activities as a whole are considered, his contributions to the Chinese revolution "far outweigh his mistakes." Mao "was a great Marxist and a great proletarian revolutionary, strategist and theorist." Mao Zedong Thought, the assessment concludes, is "an original theory which has enriched and developed Marxism-Leninism" in several respects. "Mao Zedong Thought is the valuable spiritual asset of our Party . . . It will be our guide to action for a long time to come." On the other hand, it is "entirely wrong to adopt a dogmatic attitude towards the sayings of Comrade Mao Zedong, to regard whatever he said as the immutable truth which must be mechanically applied everywhere, and to be unwilling to admit honestly that he made mistakes in his later years, and even try to stick to them in our new activities."

The sixth plenum appears to have marked a further consolidation of Deng Xiaoping's power, but it was not an overwhelming success in this respect. Chen Yonggui, of the much-criticized campaign to emulate Dazhai, remained in the Politburo, despite recent media criticism and speculation that he was likely to be removed. No mention was made of the "senior advisory group" that Deng had been advocating for months. Nor was anything said about plans for the Twelfth Party Congress and draft revisions to the party constitution. (The fifth plenum in February 1980 had decided to convene the congress early and discussed draft revisions to the constitution.)

The sixtieth anniversary of the CCP was celebrated in the Great Hall of the People on 1 July by a meeting attended by ten thousand persons. Newly elected party Chairman Hu Yaobang gave the principal speech on the occasion (for text, see ibid., 13 July).

The fifty-fourth anniversary of the PLA was celebrated on 1 August. Apparently a special effort was made in connection with the anniversary to revive flagging morale in the PLA, where unease has been reported because of new policies promoted by Deng Xiaoping and because of budget cuts (see *Far Eastern Economic Review*, 17 April; *WP*, 3 August). Large military parades—the first since 1959—were staged for several days in eleven cities, including Beijing (NCNA, Beijing, 1 August; *FBIS*, 3 August).

Cultural developments and their social and political ramifications in the new era of foreign contact and relative liberalization were matters of increasing concern. There were reports of critical wall posters; one at Nankai University in Tianjin reportedly criticized the role of the party (*NYT*, 4 May). Party leaders incensed at the new "literature of the wounded" provoked a meeting in August of cadres working in the ideological and cultural fields. Convened by the Central Committee's Propaganda Department, the meeting heard demands for tougher resistance to further liberalization. Party Chairman Hu Yaobang specifically referred to the controversial film *Bitter Love*, saying that it was bad and should be criticized, although he conceded that its author, Bai Hua, has "written some good works" (*Far Eastern Economic Review*, 4 September). Writers associated with unofficial publications continued to be arrested during the year. Some dissidents reportedly had been calling for another Cultural Revolution (*NYT*, 19 February). The occasion of the centennial of writer Lu Xun's birth on 29 September was used to warn writers and artists that opposition to party rule and criticism of its policies would not be permitted. Chairman Hu, addressing six thousand cultural workers in the Great Hall of the People, railed against "bourgeois liberalism" and "pernicious writing" that cast doubt on the supreme virtues of communism and socialism. Hu said that writers with an "engrained hatred for new China, socialism and our party" must be punished "by law for their counterrevolutionary activities." (Ibid., 30 September.) On 1 November, authorities banned demonstrations and propaganda materials from Tian An Men Square, the scene of much protest activity in the past (AP, Beijing, 1 November; *NYT*, 2 November).

Chinese authorities also repeatedly imposed restrictions on meetings or fraternization between Chinese and foreigners during the year. In March, a U.S. correspondent wrote of a confidential bulletin circulating among Chinese officials that accused foreigners of gathering information illegally about the country's political, economic, and social developments, implying that such activities often amounted to espionage. It was said that the only proper relationship between a foreigner and a Chinese "is one undertaken with the approval of the citizen's organization, and that approval must be secured to borrow a book, see a movie, attend a reception or discuss anything more than the weather." "A foreigner, however innocent and friendly he seems, should never be trusted." (*Los Angeles Times*, 26 March.) In May, it was reported that barriers that had seemed to be coming down were being put back in place (*CSM*, 11 May). The arrest of a Chinese woman engaged to a French diplomat may have been another example of official efforts to curtail unauthorized contacts with foreigners (ibid., 25 September).

Foreign journalists also felt the effects of the tightening of controls and restricting of contacts. A Dutch correspondent was expelled in June for "behaving inappropriately" (*NYT*, 2 June). On 1 September, foreign correspondents were warned by Deputy Foreign Minister Zhong Xidong not to become involved in illegal activities. Apparently, he was referring to contacts with dissidents. (Ibid., 2 September.) On 21 September, the Ministry of Foreign Affairs accused Michael Weisskopf of the *Washington Post* of defying official regulations in his report on a dissident's purported account of his imprisonment in a Beijing jail and a provincial labor camp. Weisskopf was warned of unspecified future consequences if "things of a similar nature happen again in the future." (Ibid., 22 September.) The offending report was based on a 196-page handwritten document smuggled out of prison and said to be written by Liu Qing, who was active in the democracy movement of 1978–1979 and was arrested in November 1979. The author attacked China's political and legal systems and made charges of prison brutality. (Reuters, Beijing, 17 September; *NYT*, 18 September.)

On 30 September, Ye Jianying, chairman of the NPC Standing Committee, elaborated on the reunification of Taiwan and mainland China, a subject that received considerable media attention in 1981. Ye proposed that talks be held between the CCP and the Nationalist Party "so that the two parties will cooperate for the third time to accomplish the great cause of reunification." He proposed that both sides make arrangements "to facilitate the exchange of mails, trade, air and shipping services, family reunions and visits by relatives and tourists as well as academic, cultural and sports exchanges." After reunification, "Taiwan can enjoy a high degree of autonomy as a special administrative region and it can retain its armed forces." Ye promised that the "Central Government will not interfere with local affairs on Taiwan" and that "Taiwan's current socioeconomic system will remain unchanged, so will its way of life and its economic and cultural relations with foreign countries." Furthermore, "there will be no encroachment on the proprietary rights and lawful right of inheritance over private property, houses, land and enterprises, or on foreign investments." Leaders in Taiwan may take up posts of leadership in the PRC. Also, "when Taiwan's local finance is in difficulty, the Central Government may subsidize it as is fit for the circumstances." People who wished to do so would be allowed to come and settle on the mainland, and industrialists and businessmen on Taiwan "are welcome to invest and engage in various economic undertakings on the mainland." (*Beijing Review*, 5 October.)

The reunification theme was continued with fanfare on 10 October, the seventieth anniversary of the 1911 Revolution. The occasion was marked by another grand rally at the Great Hall of the People in Beijing, attended by ten thousand people. Chairman Hu Yaobang gave the principal address, during which he invited Nationalist leader Chiang Ching-kuo and other prominent leaders and personalities in Taiwan "to visit the mainland and their natal places" (ibid., 19 October).

At the fourth session of the Fifth NPC, which met in Beijing from 30 November to 13 December, Premier Zhao Ziyang delivered a major report on China's economy. His comments were basically optimistic, although he predicted continued economic retrenchment for the next five years. Zhao said that the budget deficit was expected to be reduced to 2.7 billion yuan (U.S. $1.56 billion) from 12.7 billion yuan in 1980 and 17 billion in 1979. This was an encouraging trend, even though in February Vice-Premier Yao Yilin had projected a balanced budget for 1981. Zhao also said that the goals of the 1981 economic plan were likely to be met, with the gross value of industrial and agricultural output rising 3 percent. The premier also reported that the volume of agricultural production for 1981 was expected to be the second largest in China's history, approaching the 332 million tons of 1979, despite floods and drought in many parts of the country during the year. During the protracted readjustment period, priority is to be given to the development of such sectors as energy, building materials, transportation, and communications, as well as light industry.

Zhao said that government organs are to be reduced in size in order to overcome bureaucracy and to raise efficiency. The reform will begin with departments under the State Council. There is to be a "fairly large organizational reduction or amalgamation of these departments, a maximum reduction of the staff, and a fairly big shuffle of leading members." Also, beginning in January 1982, "large numbers of cadres from central and local departments will be sent down to various enterprises to help them improve management."

The NPC listened to a report by Minister of Finance Wang Bingqian on the state's final accounts for 1980 and the implementation of the estimated accounts for 1981. Peng Zhen, vice-chairman of the Committee for Amendment of the Constitution, proposed to the NPC that the time limit for the completion of the work of constitutional revision be extended. NPC Vice-Chairman Yang Shangkun reported on the work of the NPC Standing Committee and explained several draft laws, including the PRC Law of Economic Contracts, the Law on Income Tax of Foreign Enterprises, and the PRC Civil Law Procedure. Supreme People's Court President Jiang Hua and Chief Procurator Huang Huoqing gave reports. Minister of Forestry Yong Wentao reported on a draft bill for a voluntary mass movement for all ablebodied persons above the age of eleven to plant trees.

International Views and Positions. China continued to maintain its active united front foreign policy in 1981. Premier Zhao Ziyang was especially active, visiting Burma and Thailand (26 January–2 February); Pakistan, Nepal, and Bangladesh (1–8 June); and the Philippines, Malaysia, and Singapore (9–13 August). He also attended the North-South Summit conference at Cancún, Mexico, in October. Vice-Premier and Foreign Minister Huang Hua visited India in June and Venezuela and Colombia in August. The India visit resulted in a renewal of Sino-Indian border talks in December.

Relations with the Soviet Union were slightly less acerbic. The two nations exchanged proposals for border talks, and Chinese and Soviets met at social gatherings and conferences. Relations with the United States remained warm, although the Chinese repeatedly registered concern over U.S. policy toward Taiwan, particularly over a possible sale of advanced military aircraft to that government. As if to emphasize the point, the PRC downgraded its diplomatic relations with the Netherlands following its sale of submarines to Taiwan. Secretary Haig's June visit suggested the beginning of a new phase in relations, with the revelation of a decision to sell U.S. arms to China. Relations with Vietnam remained tense, with reports of border skirmishes at times during the year; China continued to support Pol Pot's Khmer Rouge in its difficult struggle against the Heng Samrin regime and Vietnamese occupation forces in Kampuchea. Relations with Japan remained relatively good as both Chinese and Japanese sought ways to make the best of China's economic readjustment program, with its concomitant suspension or postponement of a number of lucrative contracts.

In his December economic report to the NPC, Premier Zhao said that China should discard the notion of total self-sufficiency. Instead, it should advance into the world market and increase exports (including some of its surplus labor), as well as other economic ties, with foreign countries. Foreign companies were welcome, according to Zhao, to invest in joint ventures in mining, manufacturing, and other areas. He urged the Guangdong and Fujian special economic zones to take bold measures to introduce advanced technology and systems of management and to employ foreign capital. A major area of economic cooperation with foreigners is the development of offshore oil resources, and China is expected to take exploration bids in early 1982 from foreign petroleum companies. The NPC also passed a taxation law for foreign companies in China. (*Asian Wall Street Journal*, 1 December.)

Relations with the USSR. Mutual polemics continued, although these did not appear to be particularly strident. Chinese commentators stressed their concern over alleged Soviet global ambitions, particularly as evidenced by Soviet activities in Indochina and Afghanistan, but there did not seem to be undue apprehension about a direct threat from across the Soviet border. In fact, one article in the military newspaper *Liberation Army Daily* commented that Soviet strength failed to match its ambitions and listed various Soviet weaknesses (*Jiefangjun Bao*, 22 June; *FBIS*, 23 June).

Chinese comments on Leonid Brezhnev's speech at the Soviet party congress on 23 February noted that "he once again attacked China's foreign policy, yet he said, 'the Soviet Union has never wanted, nor does it now want, any confrontation with the People's Republic of China' and that the Soviet Union 'would like to build our ties with that country on a good-neighbor basis.' " They also mentioned Brezhnev's proposals to eliminate the threat of war and reinforce international security, including the statement: "The Soviet Union would be prepared to hold concrete negotiations on confidence-building measures in the Far East with all interested countries." (NCNA, Moscow, 23 February; *FBIS*, 24 February.)

On 20 May, *People's Daily* published an article entitled "Does the Soviet Union Have a Global Strategy?"—a major issue "of vital importance to the whole world." The article asserted "that whether the Soviet Union has a global strategy should not be judged on the grounds of a Kremlin-produced 'timetable showing when and where expansion would be carried out,' but . . . on the grounds of serious and comprehensive studies based on evidence. As long as we carefully study the words and deeds of the Soviet leaders and as long as we observe the objective reality, it will not be difficult for us to realize that the Soviet Union really has a global strategy to dominate the world." (*FBIS*, 21 May.)

Within hours of the completion of Secretary of State Alexander Haig's three-day visit to China in June, the Chinese called for negotiations with the Soviet Union to settle the border dispute. There was speculation that the message was directed as much to Washington as it was to Moscow, as a warning that China had other options to consider as long as the United States continued to talk about upgrading relations with Taiwan (*WP*, 18 June). However, nothing appears to have come of the gesture to Moscow, probably because the proposal contained preconditions known to be objectionable to the Soviets.

Furthermore, the gesture to Moscow was accompanied by publication in the *People's Daily* of a lengthy article accusing the Soviets of reneging on an earlier agreement on border talks. The author, Li Huichuan, is director of the Institute of International Studies in Beijing and was a deputy chief of the original Chinese negotiating team. Li claimed that the Chinese and Soviet premiers had reached an understanding during their meeting in Beijing on 11 September 1969 that was to have been a foundation and starting point for reopening boundary negotiations that same year. However, Li said that the Soviet side had refused to proceed according to the understanding and instead created new, major obstacles to the negotiations. (*FBIS*, 18 June; text also available in *Beijing Review* 27 July, 3 August.)

Nevertheless, there were instances of Sino-Soviet cooperation and at least cautiously friendly contact. The twenty-third regular meeting of the Sino-Soviet Joint Commission for Boundary Rivers' Navigation was held at Blagoveshchensk (Hailanpao) from 16 February to 9 March (NCNA, Beijing, 9 March; *FBIS*, 11 March). In Moscow, Vasili V. Kuznetsov, first deputy chairman of the Presidium of the Supreme Soviet, and other Soviet leaders visited the Chinese Embassy on 1 June to offer condolences over the death of Soong Ching Ling (NCNA, Moscow, 1 June; *FBIS*, 2 June). On 16 June in Moscow, China and the Soviet Union signed an agreement on goods exchange and payments for 1981. A delegation from the PRC attended an international meeting in Kiev on nonlinear vibration on 6 September (NCNA, Moscow, 6 September; *FBIS*, 8 September).

The Resolution on Certain Questions in the History of Our Party Since the Founding of the People's Republic of China shed little light on Sino-Soviet differences, but neither did it add much to the polemic. The document acknowledged Soviet help in the 1950s and merely listed Soviet cancellation of aid in 1960 among other reasons for the grave economic setback of that period. It recalled that at the time China "stood up to the pressure of the Soviet leading clique and repaid all the debts owed to the Soviet Union, which were chiefly incurred through purchasing Soviet arms during the movement to resist U.S. aggression and aid Korea." According to the document, "Soviet leaders started a polemic between China and the Soviet Union, and turned the arguments between the two Parties on matters of principle into a conflict between the two nations, bringing enormous pressure to bear upon

China politically, economically and militarily. So we were forced to wage a just struggle against the big-nation chauvinism of the Soviet Union." It was under these circumstances that "a campaign to prevent and combat revisionism inside the country was launched, which spread the error of broadening the scope of class struggle in the Party, so that normal differences among comrades inside the Party came to be regarded as manifestations of the revisionist line or of the struggle between the two lines." The Resolution also criticized a much earlier historical phenomenon: "The erroneous tendency of making Marxism a dogma and deifying Comintern resolutions and the experience of the Soviet Union prevailed in the international communist movement and in our Party mainly in the late 1920s and early 1930s and this tendency pushed the Chinese revolution to the brink of total failure." (*Beijing Review*, 6 July.)

On 20 October, the Chinese government announced that the Soviet Union had proposed a resumption of talks on the disputed Sino-Soviet border and that the proposal was currently being studied (AFP, Hong Kong and Beijing, 20 October; *FBIS*, 20 October).

Relations with the United States. The year 1981 saw a continuation of the growing relationship between the two countries. A new stage was inaugurated with the controversial announcement by Secretary of State Alexander Haig during his June visit to Beijing that the United States would loosen controls over arms sales to China. Haig asserted that the talks had been among the most productive he had ever held in any country and claimed to have dispelled Chinese misapprehensions about the Reagan administration. The Chinese appraisal of the talks was more guarded. Nevertheless, the visit apparently provided for closer consultation and coordination between the two countries regarding actions in certain global trouble spots, created the basis for further high-level visits, including one by President Reagan at some point, and gave the Chinese a better understanding of Reagan foreign policy. (*CSM*, 17 June.) It was reported in mid-June that two secret monitoring stations for detecting Soviet missile tests set up in China with American equipment and Chinese personnel during the Carter administration were continuing to receive support under the Reagan administration (*WP*, 18 June).

On 5 September in Beijing, China and the United States signed an agreement on cultural exchanges covering 1982–1983. This was done amid some controversy over imbalances in the relationship. Some six thousand Chinese were studying in the United States without restrictions, while the fewer than three hundred U.S. students in China were routinely subjected to various restrictions (*NYT*, 6 September). New restrictions were imposed early in 1981; visiting anthropologists and social economists were told to limit field research to three weeks (*WP*, 31 July).

On 18 September, the new American ambassador to China, Arthur Hummel, arrived in Beijing, filling a post vacant for seven months. Hummel is an experienced diplomat who is knowledgeable about China, and his appointment to this position was generally applauded.

Much attention was devoted to the Reagan administration's policy toward Taiwan during the year. Chinese authorities were exercised in particular over the possibility of the sale of advanced F-5 or F-16 fighter planes to Taiwan, as well as over suggestions that official U.S. relations with Taiwan might be upgraded. While nothing definitive was concluded, toward the end of the year it appeared as though the U.S. government had decided to shelve the question of arms sales to Taiwan, while the Chinese appeared resigned to live with the present situation (*CSM*, 20 November). Nevertheless, Chinese leaders continued to voice occasional critical comments, including references to the United States as another "hegemonist" power.

On 11 December, the U.S. Senate ratified an agreement, submitted by President Carter the day before his term of office concluded, establishing normal consular relationships with the PRC. The consular convention had been signed on 17 September 1980.

Publications. The official and most authoritative publication of the CCP is the newspaper *Renmin Ribao* (People's daily), published in Beijing. The theoretical journal of the Central Committee,

Hongqi (Red flag), is published approximately once a month. The daily paper of the PLA is *Jie-fangzhun Bao* (Liberation army daily). The weekly *Beijing Review*, published in English and several other languages, carries translations of important articles, editorials, and documents from these three publications and from other sources. *China Daily*, the first English-language national newspaper in the PRC, officially began publication on 1 June in Beijing and Hong Kong. The official news agency of the party and government is the New China News Agency (Xinhua; NCNA).

University of Hawaii   Stephen Uhalley, Jr.

India

The Indian communist movement is in flux. For the first time since the split in the communist party in 1964, the two major successor groups are cooperating politically. Major differences over domestic and foreign policy issues still divide the pro-Moscow Communist Party of India (CPI) and the independent and Stalinist Communist Party–Marxist (CPM), but a re-evaluation is taking place.

The communist movement in India is a potentially potent force. Communist parties attract some 10 percent of the vote in parliamentary elections and control the governments of some large states. The Communists are probably the most efficiently organized political force in India. Linked to the various parties are front groups capable of mobilizing massive numbers of workers, students, and farmers. The Communists' trade unions claim about half the organized work force, their student affiliates have a sizable following throughout the country, and they are increasingly successful in mobilizing rural support.

Yet, the Communists have been unable to translate these considerable assets into political power, in large part because of their differences. However, events over the past year have brought the Communists closer together than at any time since the 1964 split. Both parties are scheduled to hold congresses for the first time since 1978, and the question of cooperation will surely be a major issue on the agenda. The CPM congress is scheduled for January 1982 and the CPI meeting for March 1982.

Prime Minister Indira Gandhi's Congress (I) Party won two-thirds of the parliamentary seats in the 1980 general elections and shortly captured control of most state governments. Her hold on the political system grew even stronger during 1981. In June 1981 by-elections, the Congress won five of the six contested parliamentary seats, again demonstrating the opposition's inability to cooperate in the electoral arena.

The Communists, however, showed that they had a strong base of support in the state of West Bengal, where they won six of the eight contested assembly seats and the lone contested parliamentary seat. Just a month earlier, they had won in 68 of the 87 municipalities holding elections in the state. When elections were last held in these municipalities, the Communists captured only 22, underscoring the growth of significant grass-roots support. The CPI and the CPM cooperated closely in these elections. The outcome not only demonstrated the dividends of cooperation, but also underscored the regional orientation of the Communists.

While Prime Minister Gandhi faced no credible political challenge to her position in 1981, she had to deal with such problems as escalating labor unrest, ethnic and caste conflicts, and a relatively stagnating economy. She moved through parliament an Essential Services Maintenance Act that places severe restrictions on strikes and offered greater scope to private enterprise to get the economy moving.

Meanwhile, farmers began to organize massive protests against what they perceived to be an unfair exchange between cities and the countryside. In addition, the growing politicization of those at the bottom of the social hierarchy resulted in continued clashes between the police and the Muslims and "untouchables." The Communists attacked the government for its rightward drift, clearly hoping to capitalize on the discontent. Gandhi, in turn, launched a campaign to discredit and weaken the communist movement.

On the international front, India faces a potential superpower confrontation on the subcontinent—the Soviets in Afghanistan and a Pakistan with a developing arms relationship with the United States. Gandhi is caught in a delicate position as she tries to maintain a nonaligned position while the situation in Southwest and Southeast Asia continues to deteriorate. The Communists have lobbied to get her to align more closely with Soviet policies. However, the CPI and CPM are divided over questions that involve China. The CPI argues that China has aligned with "imperialism," while the CPM, though concerned by the drift in Beijing's foreign policy, still accepts China as a legitimate member of the international communist movement.

Communist Party–Marxist: *Organization and Strategy.* The CPM's Tenth Congress in 1978 left the party's aging leadership largely intact. E. M. S. Namboodiripad was retained as general secretary as were all sitting members of the Politburo, the party's chief executive body. The Politburo now has eleven members and the Central Committee 43. Five of the Politburo members are from West Bengal and Kerala, the two states where the CPM has its greatest strength. The Central Committee deliberately has a broader regional representation because the party hopes to expand its base. Only 12 of the 43 Central Committee members are from West Bengal or Kerala. The party is sorely in need of new blood at the top. Only one of the Politburo members is younger than 55, and all but six of the Central Committee members are 55 or older.

Reports have appeared that Namboodiripad would like to retire, in part because of his conflicts with the powerful West Bengal unit of the party. A likely successor is M. Basavapunniah, a Politburo member and increasingly the spokesman for the central leadership.

The CPM has made a major effort to expand its membership base, which hovered around 100,000 throughout the 1970s. It now is over 250,000. Membership is concentrated in Kerala (100,000), West Bengal (80,000), and Bihar (11,000), with much smaller contingents in Tamil Nadu, Andhra Pradesh, Uttar Pradesh, and Assam. For the first time, the party has been unable to recruit a significant number of members in the strategically important Hindi-speaking heartland of India.

Attached to the party are the Centre of Indian Trade Unions (1,000,000 members), the Students' Federation (160,000 members), and a peasant front, the All India Kisan Sabha (1,100,000).

The CPM won 6.1 percent of the vote and 36 parliamentary seats in the 1980 general elections, its largest representation since it first ran candidates in 1967. This is a significant improvement over 1977, when it won 22 seats and 4.3 percent of the vote. The CPM is the dominant partner in the left-front governments of West Bengal and Tripura, where elections are scheduled for 1982, and was the dominant partner in the Kerala state government, which resigned in late 1981 because of infighting among the coalition partners.

The CPM's "revolution from below" line put the party on a collision course with Gandhi during the 1960s and 1970s. The party condemned her as a representative of the "bourgeoisie-landlords" class. During the 1975–1979 state of emergency, the party's activities were severely restricted. A lesson it drew from the experience was the need for political allies. At the party's Tenth Congress, the CPM proposed building a "left alternative" and adopted a parallel policy of cooperating with Gandhi's non-leftist political opponents to prevent her return to power.

The CPM and the CPI cooperated in the 1980 general elections, and their parliamentary representation reached a post-independence high. In mid-1980, regular consultations between the two began, although there is considerable suspicion that the CPI will revert to its united front strategy with Gandhi, and a considerable segment of the CPI do, in fact, support such a policy. The CPI's expulsion in April 1981 of S. A. Dange, its chairman, was reassuring since Dange led the faction favoring the united front strategy.

There was, however, a significant tactical difference between the CPI and CPM over cooperation with the Hindu revivalist Bharatiya Janata Party (BJP) against Gandhi. For the CPM, Gandhi is still the major political problem, and it is willing to work with the BJP, probably the best organized noncommunist opposition party, to fight "authoritarianism." Reflecting fears of Gandhi, the CPM Central Committee at a February meeting stated that the Congress (I) government was "authoritarian" and that there was a "danger of a coup against democracy" (*Hindu*, 13 February). Three months later, the Central Committee went even further and stated that the prime minister wanted to establish a "personal dictatorship" (*Link*, 12 July).

The question of cooperating with the BJP became a lively issue in July, when the opposition parties gathered in New Delhi to discuss electoral reforms, following Mrs. Gandhi's 1981 by-election victories. The CPI refused to attend the conclave because the BJP had been invited. At the meeting, the participants agreed to an all-out "antiauthority unity" line. Reacting to the CPM involvement in this decision, CPI General Secretary C. Rajeswara Rao warned the CPM that this line could impede left unity (*New Age*, 30 August). In late August, the CPI National Council directly attacked the CPM for cooperating with the BJP (ibid., 13 September). Basavapunniah responded that the CPI seriously underestimated the danger of Gandhi and hinted darkly of forces within the CPI that wanted to revert to the united front line by cooperating with the Congress Party (*People's Democracy*, 13 September). There appears to be serious disagreements within the CPM over which parties it should work with. Press accounts note that this question prevented the Politburo from writing a draft political resolution for the 1982 party congress (*Times of India*, 12 October).

Despite the CPI-CPM differences over cooperating with the BJP, the two communist parties significantly stepped up the level of cooperation during 1981, holding regular liaison meetings during the year. This cooperation was underscored by the CPM's decision in early September to accept the CPI as a partner in the left-front government of West Bengal.

Domestic and International Positions. On the domestic scene, the CPM concentrated its attention on forestalling central intervention in the communist-ruled states of Kerala, West Bengal, and Tripura and opposing the rightward drift of Gandhi's economic policies.

The CPM charged that the central government discriminated against communist states in the allocation of development funds. In addition, the CPM called for devolution of authority in the areas of taxation and resource allocation. But the most important concern was to prevent the fall of the communist state governments, particularly in Kerala, which was ruled by a fragile coalition of Communists and noncommunists. Gandhi's Congress (I) Kerala organized a United Democratic Front pledged to "struggle for liberation" against repression in Kerala (ibid., 16 July). In fact, an intensification of social cleavages in the state spilled over into the political arena, leading to a large number of political assassinations. The deteriorating situation in mid-1981 led to a defection of the noncommunist coalition parties and ultimately the resignation of the 21-month-old E. K. Nayanar government. In contrast, the Communists have a solid majority in West Bengal and Tripura, and because they would probably win any fair election, they are likely to serve out their full term in these two states. They are worried, however, about the center's imposing its control on the states near the end of their terms, giving Gandhi time to orient the state bureaucracy in favor of her party before elections are held.

The Gandhi government's efforts to curb strikes, first through an executive order and then through the Essential Services Maintenance Act, met stout resistance from the CPM. Trade union affiliates of the opposition parties, including CPI and BJP affiliates, joined together to hold demonstrations culminating in 17 August, Black Day protest marches. On other issues, the CPM Central Committee at its February meeting catalogued a long list of domestic grievances: corruption, inefficient management of public enterprises, "brutal repression" of peasants, workers, and students, an influx of petrodollars and multinationals, and the growth of large business houses (*Hindu*, 13 February). In March, the CPM took a leading role, along with the CPI, in organizing a million-strong peasant rally in New Delhi, one of the largest rallies ever held in the capital. Similar rallies were held in several state capitals. The success of these rallies demonstrates what the Communists can achieve if they combine their resources.

The post-Afghanistan scene in Asia has created a major quandary for the CPM, for events have tended to polarize the pro-Chinese and pro-Russian elements in the party. (The former are strongly represented in the powerful West Bengal unit and the latter in the central Politburo). The destabilizing developments along Asia's southern tier have aroused old antagonisms between the CPI and the CPM, particularly given the latter's open mind regarding China and the former's closed approach to Beijing.

China has adopted foreign policies, particularly the increasingly close relations between Beijing and Washington, that CPM leaders, especially those at the center, claim will assist "imperialism." In addition, the CPM officially condemned the Chinese invasion of Vietnam and recognized the Vietnamese-installed Heng Samrin regime in Kampuchea. The CPM also lined up with the Soviet party (and against the Chinese) in condemning Eurocommunism, the Solidarity movement in Poland, and the Western naval buildup in the northwest Indian Ocean.

While the CPM tilted toward the foreign policy stands of the Soviet Union in 1981, the CPM continues to criticize the Soviets for not trying to reduce the disunity within the international communist movement. Refusing to read the PRC out of the communist movement, M. Basavapunniah wrote in the official CPM journal that post-Mao China was making "internal corrections of policy" (presumably toward a "correct" Stalinist policy) and such changes had to be "taken due note of." Moreover, he took the CPI to task for linking Sino-Indian relations to China's internal and external policies and asked whether these policies are "the correct Marxist Leninist line." (*People's Democracy*, 24 May.)

The CPM's effort to remain aloof from the Sino-Soviet split reduces the dangers that tensions between the pro-Soviet and pro-Chinese factions will rip the party apart. Politburo General Secretary Namboodiripad has repeatedly reconfirmed the CPM's neutral stance by emphasizing that the CPM is in neither camp.

This neutrality is further underscored by CPM's refusal to sanction party-to-party relations with either the Soviet or the Chinese party. The two communist giants have begun to woo the CPM, by far the more vital of the two Indian communist parties. Jyoti Basu, West Bengal's chief minister, was invited to the USSR in mid-1980, and a high-level team was invited to Hanoi in early 1981. Both invitations were accepted. On the other hand, several CPM leaders have accepted invitations to visit China. The Chinese, according to CPM Politburo member H. S. Surjeet, have extended "feelers" for party-to-party relations. (*Problems of Communism*, July–August.) If true, the Chinese are offering more to the CPM than are the Soviets, who are still committed only to a dialogue.

Communist Party of India: *Organization and Strategy.* The CPI's decision at its Eleventh Congress to replace the united front strategy with a "left and democratic" line set off a lively internal party debate. Those opposed to the shift in emphasis from the united front line, led by Party Chairman S. A. Dange, began to establish a separate political structure in 1980. The split was formalized in 1981. The new party called itself the All-India Communist Party (AICP). The CPI's membership loss to the AICP is uncertain, although published CPI materials maintain that there are now 460,000 members, a drop of 80,000 from figures reported for the late 1970s. The CPI claims that only a few thousand switched to the AICP. (*New Age*, 2 August.) It is also not yet clear how many of the 8-person Central Secretariat (the highest decision-making body), the 29-person Central Executive Committee, or the 118-member National Council have defected. The extent of the loss should become clearer when the CPI holds its congress in March 1982.

The larger part of the membership loss to date is likely the result of the demoralization that set in after the CPI's 1977 electoral drubbing. The party's percentage of the popular vote plummeted from 4.73 percent in the last pre-emergency vote to 2.82 percent in 1977, and it dropped again to 2.6 percent in 1980. The party did manage to increase its parliamentary representation from seven in 1977 to eleven in 1980, partly because of the electoral alliances with the larger CPM.

Another area where losses could occur are among the CPI front groups. The largest of the undivided front groups are the All-India Trade Union Congress (2.5 million members in 26 labor federations), the All-India Students' Federation (140,000 members), and the All-India Kisa Samiti (175,000 members). The most likely group to fragment is the trade union congress. Dange was re-elected its president at its October 1981 session; and he has a large labor following in the western state of Maharashtra. However, loyalist CPI members were elected general secretary and treasurer.

The CPI, like the CPM, has an aging leadership drawn largely from the few states where the party has a substantial following. Six of the eight members of the Central Secretariat are from West Bengal, Kerala, and Andhra Pradesh, as are 12 of the 29 members of the Central Executive Committee, and 27 of the 118 members of the National Council. The party will have to select a new chairman to replace Dange at the next party congress, and a strong contender is likely to be General Secretary C. Rajeswara Rao.

The CPI's decision to shift its emphasis to a "left and democratic front" line was vigorously opposed by a large number of party cadres, perhaps as many as one-fourth, who believe that a united front with the "progressive bourgeoisie" (that is, with Indira Gandhi's Congress Party) is necessary at this stage of India's political and social development. This faction became more outspoken after Indira Gandhi's spectacular electoral victory in 1980. Spokesmen argued that the new strategy consigned the CPI to political impotence. Gandhi's close relations with the Soviet Union provided them added ammunition.

The AICP began to take shape in mid-1980 under the leadership of Dange's daughter, Roza Deshpande. The new party held its first conference at Meerut, Uttar Pradesh, in March 1981, and Deshpande handed over the top executive position to her father. It now has its own official publication, *National Democracy*.

At an April 1981 meeting, the CPI National Council expelled Dange. The charge sheet against Dange attacked him for welcoming the election of Gandhi in 1980, condemned him for not recognizing that Gandhi is pursuing a "pro-monopoly policy," and for not understanding that Gandhi is curtailing "democratic rights and liberties," as well as undermining the democratic system itself. The party drew his attention to the October 1980 National Council policy statement calling for the left to become an "alternative force" in Indian politics. (*New Age*, 19 April.)

Domestic and International Positions. The CPI has no difficulty finding fault with Gandhi's domestic policies and does so loudly and frequently. But it is in something of a quandary over her foreign policies. The Soviet Union has praised Gandhi, and during a late 1980 visit to India, President Brezhnev spoke highly of the prime minister. This praise must surely have induced a certain caution toward Indian foreign policy and even toward Gandhi herself. The question that the CPI seems to be asking is if the international situation demands toning down its criticism of Gandhi for the sake of its international "obligations" to the USSR. The August 1981 National Council meeting apparently signaled a movement in this direction. For example, the council stated that the party's national and international tasks "are so closely interrelated that both have to be taken up for defending the interests of the people." It went on to state that the purpose of the CPI is "not simply to fight against the anti-people and anti-democratic policies of the Congress (I), but also to fight the imperialist warmongers and their allies who are endangering world peace and security of our own country." The council even praised Gandhi for pursuing a "progressive" foreign policy. (*Patriot*, 30 August.)

Nevertheless, the CPI continues to point out "vacillations" in Gandhi's foreign policies. Among such "errors" are India's refusal to endorse the Soviet occupation of Afghanistan, New Delhi's decision to hold high-level political talks with the Chinese, continued reliance on loans from the International Monetary Fund, and India's virtual noncelebration of the tenth anniversary of the Indo-Soviet Treaty of Friendship. Yet, these "vacillations" seem to have received less attention since the August National Council meeting.

Gandhi, for her part, has launched a major propaganda attack against India's Communists, and the focus of her attention seems to be the CPI. That effort shifted into high gear this year. Congress (I) Party supporters in West Bengal and Kerala have clashed with the Communists in an effort to embarrass the state governments and to underscore charges that the state government cannot maintain law and order. The collapse of the 21-month-old left-front government in Kerala, which included both the CPI and the CPM, occurred largely because of tensions among the ideologically divided coalition partners, although Gandhi's efforts to destabilize it probably exacerbated these tensions. The Communists charge, moreover, that their supporters have been dismissed from important executive positions in India's educational and cultural institutions.

To deprive the CPI of any benefits it might gain from improved Indo-Soviet relations, Gandhi in May orchestrated the establishment of the Friends of the Soviet Union (FSU) in direct competition with the Indo-Soviet Cultural Society (ISCUS), an influential CPI front group. She simultaneously ordered her party members not to participate in the activities of the ISCUS and other CPI front groups. In her inaugural address to the FSU on 27 May, Gandhi attacked "professional friends" who act as "self-appointed custodians" of Indo-Soviet friendship." Nurual Hasan, chairman of the FSU, went even further and insinuated that the Communists were cooperating with unnamed "forces of destabilization." The Soviet ambassador and a delegation from Moscow were in the audience.

Just two weeks before this onslaught against the CPI, the Central Secretariat of the CPI issued a stinging rebuke against Gandhi's rule, claiming that she had failed to fulfill one of her electoral promises. Among the government's shortcomings, it listed continued inflation, unemployment, "atrocities" against untouchables and women, communal unrest, the "collapse" of law and order, and concessions to monopolists and multinational corporations. (*New Age*, 24 May.) An article in the official *New Age* (7 June) under the by-line of "Vijay" attacked Rajiv Gandhi, the prime minister's elder son, who has replaced his late brother Sanjay as the prime minister's closest political confidant. Vijay claimed that Rajiv is a "version" of Sanjay, an "ardent supporter" of private business interests, and a potential center of "extra-constitutional authority."

The AICP has echoed many of the criticisms of the CPI against Gandhi's domestic policies, but in much milder terms. Its Central Committee placed the blame for such policies on "wrong advice," thus shifting the focus from Gandhi to various subordinate political figures (*Link*, 27 September).

Marxist-Leninists. The radical Maoist communist movement, relatively quiescent since the central government cracked down on it in the early 1970s, is showing some signs of activity again in Kerala, West Bengal, and Andhra Pradesh. Press reports indicate that some of the groups are trying to establish contact with various secessionist tribal groups in northeastern India. The much-splintered radicals (sometimes referred to as "Naxalites" after a district in West Bengal where they were active in the late 1960s) are more ideologically divided than before, in part because of policy shifts in post-Mao China. Some of the groups now look to Albania as the center of communist orthodoxy (for example, the Communist Ghadar Group); a few have taken an independent Maoist line (the pro–Lin Biao faction); but most are still pro-Chinese.

The S. N. Singh group claims a relatively large following. There are even some who have shifted emphasis from revolutionary activity to building a mass base (for example, the C. P. Reddy group). While the two larger communist parties have no official dealings with the radicals, a considerable part of the left wing of the CPM sympathizes with their revolutionary ideology.

The communist move towards cooperation has also affected the Naxalites. Thirteen groups met early in 1981 in Kerala to discuss "reunification" of the Naxalites, although few concrete results seem to have emerged from this meeting. The participants did identify the USSR as a greater threat to world peace than the United States. (Ibid., 26 April.)

Arlington, Virginia   Walter K. Andersen

Indonesia

Communism in Indonesia is of negligible significance. The Indonesian Communist Party (PKI) has been officially proscribed since 1966 and is split into two small pro-Beijing and pro-Moscow factions operating mainly in exile. Even the onetime frequent warnings by the Suharto government that the underground still constitutes a "latent" threat to national security were rarely heard in 1981. Former PKI Politburo member Jusuf Adjitorop leads the party's pro-Beijing faction of some two hundred members and sympathizers, most of whom live in China. The Chinese faction's publications, *Indonesian Tribune* and *API,* originally published in Tirana, have become steadily less frequent as a result of cooling Sino-Albanian relations. Beijing does not appear to encourage their publication. There are some fifty members and sympathizers of the pro-Soviet PKI faction, mostly living in Moscow and other East European capitals, as well as a few in India and Sri Lanka. Spokesmen for this faction's "leadership group" are Satiyadjaya Sudiman and Tomas Sinuraya, whose statements and opinions occasionally appear in *World Marxist Review.*

Domestic Developments. The aftermath of the problem of the *tapols* (from *tahanan politik* or "political prisoner") is now the main focus of domestic attention paid to the communist question in Indonesia (see *YICA,* 1981, pp. 149–50). The status and living conditions of released tapols, who were suspected of involvement in the abortive 1965 coup by Communists and military dissidents, continues to arouse controversy. At the close of 1979, some 30,000 tapols were released, according to Indonesian officials, leaving only 23 so-called Class A offenders, who were accused of the most serious crimes, including murder. In all but one of the 23 cases, court action had been completed by the end of 1980, according to government sources. The number of Class A prisoners still incarcerated is controversial, however, because of uncertain statistics and different estimates of the number released in 1979. It is generally conceded that released tapols have found it difficult to find employment since they continue to face suspicion from many prospective employers and are barred from positions in political life, the civil service, the armed forces, or "vital industries." All domestic travel by tapols requires a report to authorities and travel abroad requires special permission. Community hostility toward returning tapols has made for further adjustment difficulties. (*Asiaweek,* 7 August; *Country Reports on Human Rights Practices: Report Submitted to the Committee on Foreign Relations, U.S. Senate, and Committee on Foreign Affairs, U.S. House of Representatives,* Washington, D.C.: Government Printing Office, 2 February 1981, pp. 600–603.) The overwhelming majority of the 750,000 tapols held by the government were never tried.

On 23 July Defense Minister Gen. M. Panggabean stated that all former tapols, among them those Class B prisoners suspected of strong communist sympathies and/or involvement in the 1965 coup, would be entitled to vote in the forthcoming 1982 elections, as would released Class A tapols. In the 1977 elections most former tapols had been barred from voting. However, Panggabean's announcement involved only a limited restoration of political rights: former tapols would still be barred from holding public office. (Antara, Djakarta, 23 July; *FBIS,* 24 July; *Asiaweek,* 7 August.) The problems of rehabilitation of released tapols were highlighted on 29 May, when Indonesian Attorney General Ismael Saleh banned two books by the well-known Indonesian novelist Pramudya Ananta Tur, a former Class B tapol released in December 1979, on the grounds that the books contained "Marxist-Leninist propaganda" and were a "threat to security and order." The ban aroused international protests.

Tensions between ethnic Chinese and indigenous Indonesians, long endemic in the country, erupted again into a new wave of riots, which Indonesian officials attributed this time to "certain groups" committed to "a revolution" designed to bring down the government. A fight between a Chinese and an Indonesian student in the central Java city of Surakarta on 19 November quickly grew into an extensive anti-Chinese riot. The anti-Chinese riots spread to other areas, including the towns of Bojolali and Semarang in central Java, Garut in western Java, and Madiun and Ngawi in eastern Java. Home Affairs Minister Amir Mahmud, as well as Admiral Sudomo, the deputy commander of Kopkamtib (Command for the Restoration and Security), the government's chief internal security and intelligence bureau, termed the riots part of a revolutionary plot to overthrow the government and sabotage the forthcoming 1982 elections. According to Sudomo, the riots were an attempt to "ignite a revolution, beginning in central Java, by fanning the flames of anti-Chinese sentiment and racialism," utilizing students for that purpose. But just what group or movement, or what ideology, was behind this "revolution," neither Sudomo nor any other Indonesian official subsequently explained. (AFP, Djakarta, 21 and 27 November, 11 December 1980; *FBIS,* 21 and 28 November, 12 December 1980; *Far Eastern Economic Review,* 5 and 12 December 1980; *Asian Wall Street Journal,* 8 December 1980.)

In connection with the PKI's sixtieth anniversary on 23 May 1980, the editors of the PKI Moscow faction's infrequent journal, *Tekad Rakyat* (Will of the people), issued a belated policy statement. It declared that what had done the Indonesian Communists the "greatest harm" had been the "crude interference of the Mao Zedong group in our internal affairs." But since the 1970s, when a Marxist-Leninist Central Committee of the PKI had been "reconstituted underground," work had proceeded on "rooting out Maoist influence" and on rehabilitating the PKI's organization. The PKI, according to the anniversary statement, remained committed to the freeing of all tapols, including those convicted "in unlawful trials" in recent years, and to the restoration of complete political and civil rights to the tapols. In pursuit of its basic, long-term aim—establishment of "a truly free, democratic, prosperous, and progressive socialist Indonesia"—the PKI would also continue to demand the formation of a broad "National Unity Front representing the interests of the entire people," for the purpose of common action by "Communists, Nationalists, and all other patriots." Only a government reflecting such a united front would be able to undertake "urgent social transformation," provide Indonesians with "food, clothing, land, and work," return to them their basic political freedoms, and restore Indonesia to an honored place in the world community. (*IB,* 1980, no. 19.) Unlike previous *Tekad Rakyat* commemorative messages and statements, this pronouncement did not mention the Suharto government by name as the specific target of Indonesian communist action.

International Aspects. The lack of specific criticism of Suharto's regime can also be noted in current Soviet policy statements on Indonesia. This reflects the Soviets' perception of Indonesia as a nation that is much more concerned about the long-term threat of China in the region and, hence, is more inclined than other states in the area to seek an accommodation with Soviet-backed Vietnam over the Kampuchean question.

Indonesia's relations with China remained uncertain. Djakarta is still suspicious of China's long-term foreign policy intentions, and there was no indication of a normalization of diplomatic relations between the two countries (suspended since 1967). In late November 1980, after Singapore Premier Lee Kuan Yew had declared that China might be rethinking its traditional support for Southeast Asian Communists, Indonesian Foreign Minister Mochtar Kusumaatmadja said that it was doubtful that Beijing would break its ties with communist parties in Southeast Asia. According to Mochtar Kusumaatmadja, it was impossible for the Chinese to announce such a break without "grave political consequences" for themselves. Subsequently, the Indonesian foreign minister reiterated his belief that China "needs a long time" to drop its aid to the Southeast Asian communist underground. (*Indonesian Observer,* Djarkarta, 28 November 1980; *Straits Times,* Singapore, 12 December 1980.)

University of Bridgeport   Justus M. van der Kroef

Japan

The Japan Communist Party (Nihon Kyosanto; JCP), founded in 1922, is one of the largest nonruling communist parties in the world. The party was illegal in the prewar period, and membership did not exceed one thousand. However, it expanded rapidly in the postwar era, especially after Miyamoto Kenji became party leader in 1958. The platform adopted by the Eighth Congress in 1961, with some minor amendments, has guided the party's subsequent activities.

In the 1974 national elections, the JCP won 6.4 million votes (12 percent) and 20 of the 252 seats in the House of Councillors. In the 1975 local elections, the party won 3,165 of the 76,216 seats in prefectural, municipal, town, and village assemblies. In 1975, however, the JCP seemed to have reached its zenith. In the 1976 elections, the JCP lost half of its seats in the House of Representatives.

This performance was repeated the next year in the House of Councillors elections. In 1979, the JCP resigned the seats it had lost in the House of Representatives and increased its popularity somewhat in the popular vote column. In 1980, in national elections for both houses of the Diet, the party lost 12 seats in the more important House of Representatives and 4 seats in the House of Councillors. Its present strength is 29 of 511 seats in the former and 12 seats of 252 in the latter.

In 1981, JCP membership was put at 440,000 out of a population of 117 million. This makes the party the third largest nonruling communist party in the world. During the year, the party gained seats in the Tokyo Metropolitan Assembly elections. However, subscriptions to the party's main publication, *Akahata*, were declining, and a membership drive was having little success.

Leadership and Internal Affairs. In 1980, the Fifteenth JCP Congress reconfirmed 72-year-old Miyamoto Kenji as chairman of the Presidium and leader of the party. Miyamoto's leadership was unchallenged during 1981, although he was hospitalized in mid-April, giving rise to some speculation about a successor. The official cause of his hospitalization was bronchitis, although there was some speculation that he may have cancer. In late May he appeared in public and appeared physically fit.

During Miyamoto's hospitalization, observers spoke of Secretary General Fuwa Tetsuzo as a possible successor. Fuwa, who is sometimes called the "prince" because of his good looks, education, and background, has been considered the next JCP leader for some time.

In March, the party held a four-day conference of prefectural and district committee chairmen in Tokyo, the seventh since August 1977, when such meetings began. The meeting was held to present the party line to local JCP leaders, assess present problems, and exchange experiences. Topics included the antinuclear movement, U.S.-Japan relations, the national budget, revision of the public officers election law, relations with the Communist Party of the Soviet Union, and difficulties in dealing with other opposition parties.

The JCP held a Central Committee plenum on 9–10 June in Tokyo. Central Committee Chairman Nosaka Sanzo presided and Presidium Chairman Miyamoto gave the introductory speech. Miyamoto cited the situation since the U.S.-Japan summit talks, the three nonnuclear principles (no manufacture, no possession, no entry), contradictions in the positions of the anticommunist opposition parties, and the significance of the National Forum for Progressive Unity as important party issues. He also reviewed the causes of strained relations with the Soviet Union, the situations in Afghanistan and Poland, and the task of party building. Miyamoto revealed that a party "peace program" would soon be made public and noted that *Akahata* subscriptions had increased markedly since the beginning of the year.

Another plenum was held on 28–30 June, following the Tokyo Metropolitan Assembly elections. It was ostensibly called to assess the party's electoral performance and to discuss issues not covered at the previous meeting due to the party's preoccupation with these elections. Despite Miyamoto's previous optimism about *Akahata* subscriptions, this was presented as an issue of concern at this meeting. It was noted that falling subscriptions had precipitated a financial crisis since the party depends on sales of the newspaper for a large portion of its funds. Also, concern was expressed regarding the unfulfilled party membership goals. (*FBIS,* 3 August.)

Domestic Attitudes and Activities. The JCP took stands on a number of issues during 1981. The most important related to Japan's security policy, particularly the issues of nuclear weapons and Japan's defense relationship with the United States. Several JCP spokesmen, writing in the March issue of the party publication *Zen'ei*, expressed grave concern about government decisions on rearming Japan. JCP leaders noted that the other opposition parties were moving in the direction of accepting the views of "ruling classes" in the United States and Japan regarding Japan's defense.

The JCP advocated security policies paralleling the party's general line; independence, peace, democracy, and neutrality. Specifically, party leaders called for legislating the three nonnuclear principles, retaining the constitution in its present form—saying that altering it would lead to outlawing the peace movement and would threaten peace—opposing the secrets preservation law, and condemning revision of the criminal code (which the party sees as tantamount to enacting public security legislation).

JCP spokesmen criticized the other opposition parties for "moving to the right" and for becoming "second conservative parties" or "tributary parties" and scored the media for subservience to the government, noting that this accounted for the people's increasing distrust of the press. JCP leaders seemed to be differentiating the party from the other opposition parties and attempting to appeal to those dissatisfied with many aspects of Japanese politics.

As in the past, the JCP continued to criticize "money politics" and "money is everything campaigns." In this connection it advocated a ban on enterprise donations to politicians and parties. The JCP also criticized the policies of the big unions and equated efforts to end the freedom of the workshop with moves to change the constitution.

Early in the year, JCP Diet members complained of the government's security "collusion" with South Korea and opined that the handling of the Kim Dae-jung case in Seoul reflected a U.S. effort to tie South Korean's security to Japan's (*Zen'ei*, March). Earlier, Miyamoto had claimed in an address in the House of Councillors to have official U.S. documents proving that the United States had nuclear weapons at Iwakuni, a U.S. Marine air station in western Japan (*Japan Times*, 1 February). Along this same line, the party newspaper, *Akahata*, accused the Japanese government of linking the Association of Southeast Asian Nations' security concerns to those of the West and thereby serving the United States (*FBIS*, 13 January). The party paper also assailed the administration of Suzuki Zenko over the use of the term "alliance" when speaking of the U.S.-Japan Security Treaty—an issue the press had already played up (ibid., 14 May). Party leaders similarly made an issue of a U.S. submarine's sinking of a Japanese fishing boat, killing a number of Japanese crew members. JCP Diet members called for testimony by the survivors and the captains of the ships that found them (*Japan Times*, 18 April).

In June, shortly after a comment by Edwin Reischauer, former U.S. ambassador to Japan, that the United States regularly had nuclear weapons on its bases in Japan and on ships using bases in Japan aroused a public controversy, Miyamoto announced the JCP's platform for world peace: self-determination for all peoples, a total ban on nuclear weapons, a sharp reduction in conventional weapons, removal of foreign bases, withdrawal of foreign troops, and dismantling of military blocs. He declared that the U.S.-Japan military alliance should be scrapped and chided the Reagan administration for a "new cold war policy" and the Soviet Union for its "social-imperialist mistake" in invading Afghanistan. (*Akahata Commentary Edition*, 6 July.) In August, party spokesmen took issue with the United States for its decision on the neutron bomb and argued that the Suzuki administration had given its tacit approval. (*FBIS*, 14 August.) The JCP's stand on the nuclear issue mirrored the considerable public concern about nuclear weapons, especially in the context of Japanese rearmament and Reischauer's statement. On the other hand, polls showed public support for the U.S.-Japan security treaty.

In June, the party participated in a large protest demonstration demanding that the U.S. aircraft carrier *Midway* be barred from its home port of Yokosuka until it was established that it carried no nuclear weapons. Nearly 700 of the 2,500 demonstrators represented the JCP and its affiliate organizations. (*Japan Times*, 6 June.)

The most important domestic activities for the party during the year were two elections: local assembly elections in January and the Tokyo Metropolitan Assembly election in June. The latter was particularly important since it was regarded as a bellwether of future party performance, particularly since there is no national election scheduled before 1983.

In the local assembly elections, which involved only a small number of assemblies, the JCP won a total of eighteen seats for a gain of two. Although the numbers suggest a JCP victory, there was some concern among party leaders because the gains were in less populated areas and the JCP experienced a net loss in the large cities. This was not a good sign since the JCP's strength is in the large urban areas and there ultimately seems little hope of gaining widespread support in rural areas. On the other hand, these elections were too few in number to be representative.

In the Tokyo Metropolitan Assembly election the party went all out to help JCP candidates. The party's main issue was former Prime Minister Tanaka Kakuei's role in the election. Tanaka is awaiting trial for bribery in the Lockheed case and was trying to strengthen his own faction in the Liberal Democratic Party during the election—according to JCP leaders, so that he could better influence the trial. JCP leaders also made an issue of the Tokyo governor's "Tokyo, my town" projects to improve the city, which they alleged helped only big business. (Ibid., 27 June.)

In the election the JCP marked up a victory—along with the Komei Party, the only other party to make gains. The party won 16 of the 127 seats, for a gain of 5 over its previous position. Since the Tokyo governor is sponsored by a coalition of the Liberal Democratic Party, the Democratic Socialist Party, and the Komei Party and since the JCP won more seats than the main opposition party, the Japan Socialist Party, it became the largest opposition party. However, the JCP had 24 seats in the Tokyo Metropolitan Assembly two elections ago and, together with the Japan Socialist Party, sponsored the winning candidate for governor.

Although the JCP's victory was a good sign for future elections, one of the reasons for its victory was the low voter turnout, and the JCP's better party discipline (*Far Eastern Economic Review*, 10 July). Likewise, the JCP failed to exploit national issues in the election, such as the nuclear issue and U.S.-Japan relations, and was unsuccessful in its effort to make the Tokyo governor's handling of the city's financial problems an issue (*Japan Times*, 8 July).

International Views and Contacts. On 19 January, *Akahata* recapitulated the JCP's position on the Soviet Union's invasion of Afghanistan, which the party had openly and formally condemned a year earlier. It repeated the reports, written by its on-the-spot correspondent when the invasion occurred, that the Soviet Union had not just helped overthrow the regime of Hafizullah Amin, but had, in fact, carried out the coup. It charged that Babrak Karmal, the alleged leader of the coup, was not even in the country at the time. *Akahata* also summed up dispatches from its New York correspondent, who had interviewed Afghan officials in exile, and who substantiated the JCP's interpretation of events there.

The JCP also remained at odds with Moscow over the Northern Territories issue. In February, JCP spokesmen refuted the Soviet Union's interpretation of the Portsmouth peace conference following the Russo-Japanese War of 1904–5. The Soviet position was that the Portsmouth agreement had invalidated the Russo-Japanese friendship treaty of 1855, thereby making Japan's ownership of the northern islands a prize of war that had simply been reversed at Yalta. The JCP argued that there had been no such cancellation of earlier agreements at Portsmouth. (*FBIS*, 6 February.)

Bad feelings toward the Soviet Union did not deter the party from sending a delegation to the Soviet party congress in February, the first delegation to a Soviet congress since 1971—interpreted as a quid pro quo for Soviet participation in the JCP's Fifteenth Congress in 1980 (*Japan Times*, 13 February). On the other hand, the leader of the JCP delegation, Kaneko Mitsuhiro, deputy head of the Secretariat, criticized Soviet foreign policy during his speech to the congress. He quoted at length from the joint communiqué signed between the JCP and the Soviet party in December 1979, just before Moscow's invasion of Afghanistan. The communique—to the obvious embarrassment of Soviet leaders—mentioned both sides' support of peaceful coexistence, mutual respect for sovereignty and territorial integrity, the rights of nations to independence and freedom, the inadmissibility of special rights hegemony, and observance of the principle of the resolution of conflicts by negotiations. Kaneko further rejected the Brezhnev Doctrine, mentioning Afghanistan and implicitly referring to Poland. He concluded by calling for the dissolution of all military blocs and the withdrawal of all foreign troops everywhere. Surprisingly *Pravda* published most of his remarks. (*Radio Free Europe*, 5 March.)

At almost the same time, the JCP circulated a letter to other communist parties throughout the world criticizing the policies of the *World Marxist Review*, a magazine edited in Prague and distributed in 145 nations. JCP criticism centered on the USSR's monopolization of the post of editor in chief, calling this "incompatible with the democratic composition of the editorial board." (Ibid., 3 February.) The JCP also made an issue of a planned series of articles that it said would outrage the Chinese Communist Party. The JCP claimed that it had made its dissatisfactions known to the magazine, but that since nothing had been done, it went public with its complaints.

In June, the JCP went even further in its polemics with Moscow. It sent an open letter to the Soviet party demanding an end to its interference in Poland's internal affairs. The letter attributed Soviet interference in Czechoslovakia, Afghanistan, and Poland to a "deep-rooted ideal of yourselves as the 'vanguard' or 'center' of the international communist movement" (*Japan Press Service*, 15 June). This was shortly followed by another letter asserting that "you take the attitude that everything you are doing on the Polish, Afghan, and other issues is right, and . . . permit no criticism of your attitude" (ibid., 4 July).

On 30 July, the Soviet party responded with a long letter accusing the JCP of "anti-Sovietism" and "distortions" of Soviet foreign policy. The letter stated that "American imperialism" had used the Afghan and Polish situations as an excuse to escalate the arms race and that the JCP had been duped by an "international campaign to give false reports leading to erroneous judgments." (Radio Moscow, 8 August.)

Meanwhile, some observers believed that the JCP and the Chinese Communist Party might be seeking a reconciliation. On 15 January, the *People's Daily*, the official organ of the Chinese party, carried two articles from *Akahata* condemning the Soviet Union's invasion of Afghanistan. It also mentioned that two other Japanese newspapers, *Asahi* and *Mainichi*, had cited the JCP's position. This, together with the JCP's protest of the *World Marxist Review*'s plans to carry an anti-Chinese story, were evidence of a thaw between the two parties. In June, however, JCP Chairman Miyamoto told the press that he believed China "still had a long way to go in restoring a true communist policy line" and that China was in a period of transition (*FBIS*, 30 June). A few months later, the JCP accused China of "still harboring interventionism" after the *People's Daily* carried a report about the possible establishment of a pro-Beijing communist party in Japan composed of former JCP members (ibid., 21 October).

In addition to its interactions with the Soviet and Chinese parties, JCP officials met with a number of other leaders of communist parties. In May, Miyamoto met with East German communist party leader Erich Honecker, who was visiting Japan. The two discussed the situation in Poland. (*Japan Times*, 18 May.) The same month, a JCP leader traveled to Hungary on an official visit. In July, Vice-Chairman Nishizawa Tomio attended the Tenth Congress of the Spanish Communist Party in Madrid, and in August, he visited Romania.

Publications. In April, *Akahata* carried the headline "An Appeal for the Defense of *Akahata*," noting the paper's very grave financial difficulties and appealing to readers for support. The article cited increases in printing and delivery costs, in addition to increases in rebates given to branch bureaus. According to some observers, rebates to branch bureaus, given the paper's previous practice of relying on volunteers, were a bad sign. Circulation dropped from about 3.5 million in March 1980 to 3 million in mid-1981, and the prefectures registering a decline in subscriptions were primarily urban, signifying that the party's base of support was eroding or at least shifting. (Ibid., 7 May.)

For a list of JCP publications, see previous issues of this yearbook.

Southwestern at Memphis   John F. Copper

Kampuchea

During 1981, the Vietnamese-supported regime in Phnom Penh publicly acknowledged that it was run by a communist party known as the Kampuchea People's Revolutionary Party (KPRP). The KPRP is closely allied with the Vietnamese Communist Party (if, indeed, they are not in some respects intended to serve as one party). Their common enemy is Pol Pot's Khmer Communist Party (KCP), which continues to conduct guerrilla operations with the support of China against Vietnamese armed forces in Kampuchea. During the year, the KPRP regime also sought to legitimize itself by holding elections and promulgating a new constitution. These acts may have increased the self-confidence of the regime's leaders, but they brought them no closer to the goal of occupying the seat reserved for Kampuchea at the United Nations.

The Phnom Penh regime also appeared to seek a degree of independence from its discreet but omnipresent Vietnamese backers—mainly by entering into a more direct dialogue with Moscow on matters such as economic aid. KPRP leaders seemed willing to take limited advantage of strains in the Moscow-Hanoi relationship. However, they expressed no desire to face Pol Pot's guerrillas alone, and there was no basis for predicting that they would follow Pol Pot's example of turning against Hanoi and seeking the support of its enemies.

Pen Sovan replaced Heng Samrin as the regime's leader in June and seemed to have Moscow's support, doubtless because Samrin was such a poor international salesman for the regime. Pen Sovan led the Khmer delegation to the Soviet congress in March, although he was then only vice-president of the Kampuchea People's Revolutionary Council. When the council became a party in May, Pen Sovan became secretary general of the party and prime minister of the government. In September, he visited Moscow and had a one-hour meeting with Brezhnev. The number of Soviet advisers in Kampuchea grew from about forty in 1980 to four hundred in 1981. Moscow's willingness to engage in more direct relations with the Phnom Penh regime and even to compete with its Vietnamese client in giving advice and support to the Khmers probably reflects the Soviets' growing interest in countering China's influence in Southeast Asia. In December, Heng Samrin replaced Pen Sovan as secretary general of the KPRP, apparently at Vietnam's insistence. (Pen Sovan's abrupt removal, on grounds of illness, may signal an important change in Vietnam's plans for Kampuchea—or perhaps reflects Hanoi's irritation with Pen Sovan's pro-Soviet statements.) Defense Minister Chan Si was named acting prime minister in the December shake-up.

Leadership and Organization. The Kampuchea People's Revolutionary Council held its Fourth Congress in May and adopted the name Kampuchea People's Revolutionary Party. In a newly drafted constitution, the KPRP was described as the leading force in the political life of Kampuchea, although in fact the Vietnamese Army remained the chief source of politico-military advice and support for its client regime. In June, Pen Sovan was named secretary general of the party and chairman (prime minister) of the Council of Ministers of the People's Republic of Kampuchea (PRK). He appeared to be the most powerful figure in the regime, upstaging the less forceful Heng Samrin. Pen Sovan, a vigorous, 45-year-old cadre, lived in Vietnam for 25 years, returning only in 1979. He is married to a Vietnamese and speaks the language fluently.

Heng Samrin, a Khmer Rouge army major who deserted to Vietnam in the late 1970s, publicly represented the Phnom Penh regime from December 1978 until early in 1981. After the 1981 reorganization, he retained his post as head of state (chairman of the PRK Council of State). Samrin was also one of eight people elected to the KPRP Central Committee's Politburo, but he was not initially named to the more exclusive seven-member Secretariat. The Secretariat (as constituted in May) included Pen Sovan, Say Phuthang, Bou Thang, Hun Sen, Chea Soth, Chan Si, and Chan Phin. Most of these men were in their forties and had lived for a number of years in Vietnam, returning to Kampuchea at the time of the Vietnamese invasion in December 1978–January 1979. One exception was Foreign Minister Hun Sen, who was in his early thirties and was believed to have spent little time in Vietnam.

The Politburo members in May were Pen Sovan, Heng Samrin, Say Phuthang, Chea Sim, Bou Thang, Hun Sen, Chea Soth, and Chan Si. Since six Politburo members also served on the seven-member Secretariat, the main reason for the existence of two bodies may have been Pen Sovan's desire to exclude his rival, Heng Samrin, from the Secretariat and thus gain the secretary generalship, which was reserved for a member of the Secretariat.

The Central Committee in May had 21 members: Pen Sovan, Say Phuthang, Heng Samrin, Chea Sim, Bou Thang, Hun Sen, Chea Soth, Chan Si, Chan Phin, Lim Nai, Chey Saphon, Mat Ly, Soy Keo, Khang Sarin, Heng Sam Kai, Rung Thiam Kaisan, Lay Samon, Sim Ka, Chan Seng, Ms. Mean Saman, and Kim Yin. The last two were listed as alternates. (The order in which the members of these party bodies are cited above follows that given by Radio Phnom Penh; it appears to indicate their relative importance.) Following Pen Sovan's ouster, the leading party and government members, in order of importance, appeared to be Heng Samrin, Chan Si, Say Phuthang, Chea Sim, Bou Thang, Hun Sen, Chea Soth, Chan Phin, Mat Ly, Soy Keo, Ms. Mean Saman, and Ms. Mey Samedi (whose position in the party is unknown). Say Phuthang is chairman of the Central Organizational Committee and Bou Thang heads the Propaganda and Education Committee.

In addition to party posts, many KPRP leaders hold posts in the PRK. Chan Si is acting chairman of the Council of Ministers and minister of defense; Say Phuthang, vice-chairman of the Council of State; Chea Sim, chairman of the National Assembly and of the Kampuchea Front for National Construction; Hun Sen, foreign minister and vice-chairman of the Council of Ministers; Mat Ly, vice-chairman of the National Assembly; Soy Keo, vice-minister of defense; and Mey Samedi, vice-minister of health. Bou Thang, Chea Soth, and Chan Phin apparently hold no governmental position. Mean Saman is head of the Kampuchean Women's Association.

In an interview with a foreign journalist shortly after the 1981 party congress, a senior KPRP official acknowledged that the KPRP was still in an early stage of recruiting and training cadres. Asked if membership was a high as five thousand, he replied, "Much less." Reportedly, the party started a political course for "137 cadres of division, brigade, provincial, and battalion units," with the goal of increasing "the cadres' ability and their knowledge of the KPRP's current political lines, which stress stronger and more effective national defense duties" (*FBIS,* 25 August). Present at the opening ceremony were Chan Si and Soy Keo, Meas Kroch (deputy chief of the General Political Department of the Defense Ministry), other officials of the ministry, and "Vietnamese military experts." This suggests that the KPRP and the Kampuchean Army are being built up simultaneously as overlapping institutions, with many cadres having dual party and military functions.

Since its founding in Vietnam in December 1978, the KPRP regime has sought to include a number of prominent Khmer personalities to give itself an air of legitimacy both at home and abroad. A number of senior officials of the PRK, including the heads of several ministries, were not listed as members of the KPRP Central Committee, although some of them may be party members. This suggests that party membership (or at least a senior party post) is not a requirement for holding key government positions, as long as the individual has personal prestige or technical skills.

The Chinese-supported KCP, led by Pol Pot, Khieu Samphan, and Ieng Sary, controlled all of Kampuchea from April 1975 to January 1979. In December 1981, the KCP announced its own abolition, presumably to facilitate the formation of an anti-Vietnamese coalition with Prince Sihanouk and Son Sann, the two main noncommunist Khmer leaders. Diplomatic observers tended to view the KCP's dissolution as cosmetic. Although universally believed to have murdered enormous numbers of Khmers while in power, the KCP retains a number of political and military assets: an army of 40,000 fairly well trained and armed guerrillas, the seat reserved for Kampuchea in the United Nations, the grudging diplomatic support of the Association of Southeast Asian Nations (ASEAN), and the willing support of China. The KCP also has a clandestine radio station (located in China or Thailand) and perhaps a degree of political support among some peasants because of its anti-Vietnamese stance and reputation for extreme ruthlessness. The leadership and organization of the KCP appeared to remain fairly stable during 1981. Pol Pot remained the key leader, despite having handed over the prime ministership in his exile government to Khieu Samphan, who enjoyed a slightly less tarnished international image (even though he provided the primary ideology on which Pol Pot's reign of terror was based). Pol Pot's brother-in-law and U.N. representative, Ieng Sary, acknowledged the regime's crimes in interviews during the year and tried to place some distance between himself and Pol Pot, perhaps in anticipation of creating a coalition with noncommunist exile groups.

Auxiliary and Mass Organizations. The KPRP regime claims to have the support of mass organizations with large or growing memberships, including the Kampuchean Women's Association and organizations of male and female youth, Buddhist clergy, workers, and peasants. Radio Phnom Penh regularly reports exchanges of visits and messages between these groups and those of friendly nations.

In December 1978, the proto-regime announced the creation, in Vietnam, of an umbrella organization called the Kampuchea National Union for National Salvation (KNUFNS), which subsequently held two or more congresses in Phnom Penh designed to enhance the legitimacy of the Vietnamese-supported regime. Several prominent Khmer survivors of the horrors of earlier years were linked to the KNUFNS and hence to the regime. During 1981, the election of a National Assembly, reorganization of the government, emergence of the KPRP, and promulgation of a constitution were all designed to enhance the regime's legitimacy at home and abroad. This was necessitated by intensive diplomatic efforts, led by China and ASEAN, to expel the Vietnamese and their Khmer clients from Kampuchea—an effort that made it difficult but perhaps not impossible for the Phnom Penh regime to "emerge" and strengthen its position in dealing with the Khmer people and with its Vietnamese and Soviet protectors. Under these circumstances, the KNUFNS was relegated to a secondary role. At some point during 1980 or 1981, the KNUFNS was renamed the Kampuchea Front for National

Construction. Its leadership did not change, and occasionally Radio Phnom Penh reported the group's activities in consolidating support for the regime.

Domestic Party Affairs. There has been some international and press speculation that Pen Sovan and Heng Samrin may be not only personal rivals but also competitors on ideological or policy grounds. For example, some reports suggest that Pen Sovan, for all his deep association with Vietnam, may be more willing than Samrin to press for a measure of independence from Hanoi. The Soviet Union's open support for Pen Sovan, the gradual deterioration of Moscow-Hanoi relations, and the intensive global and regional competition between the Soviet Union and China favor a Khmer policy of playing the Soviets against the Vietnamese (without breaking ties with either).

International Views and Politics. As noted above, 1981 was marked by widespread, intensive diplomatic activity on behalf of the Phnom Penh regime and its Khmer opponents, both communist and noncommunist. On one level, it was proxy diplomatic and guerrilla warfare between Beijing and Moscow for control of territory on Vietnam's western and ASEAN's eastern flank. However, many other interests were at stake, including the viability of Vietnam's political and economic programs, the unity and diplomatic orientation of the ASEAN states, the tone and substance of North-South relations in the Asian-Pacific region, and ultimately the Pacific, and perhaps the global, balance of power.

Judging from the July U.N. meeting on Kampuchea, most nations seem to want to limit the hostilities in Indochina and to help the ASEAN countries in their search for a political solution in Kampuchea. The September U.N. vote on Khmer representation showed only minor changes from the previous years' strong support for ASEAN's position—that seating Pol Pot's KCP representative was the lesser of two evils. By an even larger majority than in 1980, the U.N. General Assembly supported an ASEAN resolution calling for the withdrawal of unnamed "foreign forces" from Kampuchea.

Publications. Radio remained by far the most important medium for the propaganda duel between the KPRP and the KCP. The KPRP continued to broadcast extensively (in Khmer and French) over the Voice of the People of Kampuchea for domestic and foreign consumption. The KCP also made extensive use of its clandestine transmitter, Voice of Democratic Kampuchea, whose coverage also included alleged activities of guerrilla forces in Laos and Vietnam. Publications included a government-controlled newspaper in Phnom Penh called *Kampuchea* and the paper of the KPRP Army, *Revolutionary Army.*

Old Dominion University   Peter A. Poole

Korea: Democratic People's Republic of Korea

Leadership and Organization. The Democratic People's Republic of Korea (DPRK) has a typical communist administrative structure. The center of decision making is in the Korean Workers' Party (Choson Nodong-dang; KWP), and the government merely executes party policy. All important leaders hold concurrent positions in the party and government. Party membership is currently estimated at two million. The population of the DPRK is about nineteen million.

The cult of the North Korean chieftain and his family members continued unabated in 1981. North Korean media constantly stressed that loyalty to Kim Il-song and his ideology of *chuche* ("self-" or "national identity") should continue from generation to generation; the program of perpetuating his ideology and policies was given further institutional muscle.

On 25 January, North Korea started making preparations for the commemoration of President Kim's seventieth birthday anniversary, which falls on 15 April next year, by announcing a contest for literary, musical, and photographic prizes. The ten themes set for works in the competition included Kim's "wise leadership and his noble personality" and the happy life enjoyed by children and students under Kim's care.

In his New Year's message, Kim Il-song said that 1981 was the year in which North Koreans would start their march for implementing the decisions made at the Sixth KWP Congress of October 1980, the most important of which was the designation of his 40-year-old son, Kim Chong-il, as his future political successor.

During 1981, the DPRK zealously promoted the personality cult of Kim Chong-il. An article in *Nodong Sinmun*, the KWP newspaper, on 18 June, for example, depicted the "glorious Party Center" (a North Korean code word for Kim Chong-il) as a "great luminary brightening the world with his brilliant wisdom." Bent on revealing the "greatness and virtue" of Kim Chong-il, North Korean broadcasting stations focused their reports on world reaction to the "leadership of Comrade Kim Chong-il." During the first year following the Sixth Congress, Kim Chong-il made seven public appearances. (On one occasion in mid-October, he appeared together with his father at the Seventh Convention of the Socialist Young Workers' League in Pyongyang.)

The cult of Kim Jung-sook, Kim Il-song's deceased first wife and Kim Chong-il's mother, intensified during 1981. On 17 August, for example, North Korea renamed two administrative units and two schools after her. Calling her an "imperishable woman hero of the anti-Japanese struggle and a communist revolutionary fighter," the announcements of this action said that it was the noble duty of the North Korean people to glorify her "brilliant revolutionary achievements."

North Korea's concern with the post–Kim Il-song era was evident in a *Nodong Sinmun* article on 1 July saying that "we should prevent any kind of unwholesome thought from infiltrating into and perching in our society by opposing exchange of all kinds of impure thought, including flunkyism, doctrinism, and revisionism . . . No force can block the grand march of our people, who are guided by the revolutionary banner of the *chuche* idea."

On 28 May, Shim Chang-wan, a member of the KWP Central Committee and chief of the Political Bureau of the Ministry of Public Security, died of heart failure.

During the first ten months of 1981, the DPRK reshuffled two party leaders, appointed five new deputy premiers, and replaced six ministers, while establishing one new ministry and merging four ministries into two. In the party reshuffle, Kang Hui-won, who ranked seventy-fifth in the Central Committee elected in October 1980, earned candidate membership in the 34-man KWP Politburo. Kang also became responsible secretary of the party committee in the provincial-level Chongjin City, replacing Hyon Mu-Kwang. It has yet to be confirmed whether Kang's appointment to the Politburo increased its membership or whom he replaced if there was no change in the membership. The party reshuffle also replaced Hong Si-hak with Hyon Mu-kwang as party secretary. Hyon is a candidate member of the Politburo of the Central Committee. Hong Si-hak, who had ranked thirty-fifth in the Central Committee, was appointed deputy premier in April.

In the government reshuffle, So Kwan-hui replaced Chang Kuk-chan as chairman of the ministry-level Agricultural Commission; Sin Tae-rok, Kim Tu-yong as coal mining industry minister; Choe Chae-u, Kim Yun-hyok as metal industry minister; Cho Chol-chun, Pak Im-tae as construction minister; Kim Chong-song, Kim Nam-yun as construction material industry minister; and Choe Tae-pok, Kim Il-tae as chairman of the ministry-level Education Commission. (Two of the six new members, So Kwan-hui and Choe Chae-u, were also deputy premiers.)

Hong Song-yong, Hong Si-hak, Choe Kwang, Choe Chae-u, and Kim Hoe-il were appointed deputy premiers during 1981. Their appointment brought the total number of deputy premiers to fourteen. The others were Kye Ung-tae, Kang Song-san, Ho Tam, Cho Se-ung, Kong Chin-tae, Chong Chun-ki, So Kwan-hui, Kim Tu-yong, and Kim Kyong-yon. Yi Kun-mo recently returned to his old position as responsible secretary of the party committee in Nampo City from the office of deputy premier he had held for several months.

Elections were held on 5 March for local people's assemblies, indicating that North Korea will elect the Seventh Supreme People's Assembly in the near future to reshuffle the government. North Korea watchers in Seoul now center their concern on whether Kim Chong-il will become a vice-president in the post-election government reshuffle.

On 28–29 January, the Korean Democratic Party, one of the two minor political parties permitted to exist under tight KWP control to present a facade of representative government, held its Sixth Congress. It renamed itself Korean Social Democratic Party and announced that it would play a stronger role in support of the KWP. The meeting retained Vice-President Kang Yang-uk as chairman of the Central Committee. "The change of the party's name is aimed at establishing ties with socialist parties of the noncommunist world," said a South Korean expert on North Korean affairs. In point of fact, the leader of the French Socialist Party and president of France, François Mitterrand, made a two-day visit to Pyongyang in mid-February.

Domestic Attitudes and Activities. A plenum of the KWP Central Committee held on 1–2 April in Pyongyang urged North Koreans to increase industrial production through maximum utilization of the existing facilities and equipment. At another plenum on 4–6 October, Kim Il-song called for a massive drive to reclaim tideland along the west coast to surpass the target of 300,000 *jongbo* set at the 1980 KWP congress. (One *jongbo* is equivalent to 2.45 acres.)

North Korea fixed its budget for fiscal 1981 at 20.5 billion *won* or U.S. $11.6 billion at a session of the Supreme People's Assembly on 6–8 April. It called for a 7 percent increase in income and 8.7 percent rise in spending over 1980. The share of military outlay in the total budget was 14.7 percent.

The actual defense expenditure is no doubt higher because Pyongyang hides defense expenditures in other sectors.

According to a spokesman for the London Morgan Grenfell Bank, in 1981 North Korea defaulted again on trade debts to Western and Japanese creditors.

South Korea. North Korea's relations with South Korea continued to deteriorate. During 1981, North and South Korean soldiers had six minor border clashes along the 1953 armistice line.

North Korea stepped up its harsh propaganda attacks on the Seoul government under President Chun Doo-hwan, calling him the head of a "mangy fascist clique." On 24 April, for example, Pyongyang's anti-Seoul propaganda radio urged South Korean students, laborers, farmers, intellectuals, and soldiers to participate actively in a "holy war" against their government.

The DPRK rejected South Korean President Chun's repeated calls for a Seoul-Pyongyang summit conference to discuss reunification of the divided Korean peninsula. In its stead, Pyongyang kept repeating its own proposal for a Confederal Democratic Republic of Korea or an intra-Korean "national unification promotion convention" at the nongovernmental level. Neither is acceptable to the South Korean government.

International Views and Positions. During 1981, Pyongyang mounted an intensive diplomatic offensive against South Korea to undermine the international position of the Seoul regime and to develop world support for its own unification policy. Parliamentary, trade, and other goodwill missions were dispatched abroad or invited to North Korea. Moreover, numerous friendly diplomatic gestures were made, especially to Third World countries, which increasingly dominate the United Nations. In particular, the DPRK sought to prevent recognition of "the two Koreas" concept by the world community; to isolate South Korea from the Third World, the communist bloc, and even the Western world; and to drum up diplomatic support for its demand for the removal of U.S. forces from South Korea.

On 3 April, North Korea and St. Vincent agreed to establish diplomatic relations. St. Vincent, a former British dominion in the Caribbean, was the one hundred fifth country with which Pyongyang has diplomatic ties. (Of the 105 countries, 5 have severed diplomatic relations with North Korea: Argentina, Australia, Chile, Iraq, and Mauritania.)

During 1981, several leaders of Third World countries visited North Korea: Khieu Samphan, premier of the exiled government of Democratic Kampuchea under Pol Pot (March); Julius K. Nyerere, president of Tanzania (March); Akba Hashemi-Rafsanjani, speaker of the Iranian parliament (September); Gnassingbe Eyadema, president of Togo (September); Yassir Arafat, head of the Palestine Liberation Organization (PLO, October); and José Eduardo dos Santos, president of Angola (October). North Korea decorated the PLO leader with the title Hero of the DPRK and awarded him a medal of gold star and the National Order, first degree; Kim Il-song pledged 7,000 tons of corn to President Nyerere as a gift; and Eyadema and Kim Il-song signed a treaty of amity and an agreement on economic and technical cooperation between the two countries.

On 9 October, the DPRK dispatched a government mission led by Vice-President Pak Song-chol to Cairo to attend funeral services for Egyptian President Anwar Sadat.

The *Asahi Shimbun* (Tokyo) reported on 5 March that, along with the Soviet Union, Cuba, Vietnam, Bulgaria, and South Yemen, North Korea had dispatched five hundred combat troops to Afghanistan. Over a hundred North Korean military advisers arrived in Zimbabwe in August to train a brigade of five thousand Zimbabwean troops. According to Jack Anderson (*WP*, 8 March), North Korea recently supplied long-range rockets and artillery to the PLO.

In mid-June, the DPRK hosted the second three-day conference on the nonaligned nations' food and agricultural affairs. This meeting, held in Pyongyang, was also attended by representatives of the U.N. Food and Agriculture Organization. The conference discussed questions of economic and technical cooperation in agricultural development among the nonaligned nations. A six-day international symposium of the nonaligned and other developing countries on increasing food and agricultural production convened in Pyongyang on 26 August. The meeting was also attended by representatives of fourteen international organizations, including the U.N. Food and Agriculture Organization, the U.N. Development Program, and the World Health Organization, in addition to delegations from 77 countries. The meeting produced the Pyongyang Declaration, which called for self-reliance in food as a means of achieving political independence, a new international economic order, and promotion of economic and technical cooperation and exchange among the nonaligned nations and other developing countries.

For North Korean Communists, these international gatherings offered an opportunity to propagandize the "great leadership" of Kim Il-song and his son and to solicit the participants' support for Pyongyang's unification policy.

The Soviet Union and China. During 1981, Pyongyang continued to maintain its middle-of-the-road position in the Sino-Soviet dispute, despite its displeasure with recent political developments in post-Mao China. Moscow and Beijing gave verbal and material support in an attempt to gratify North Korea and to draw it closer to each of their sides. The Soviet Union and China both urged the prompt withdrawal of American troops from South Korea and supported Pyongyang's stand on direct U.S.-North Korean contact to settle the problems of the divided Korean peninsula and the North Korean proposal for reunification.

Premier Yi Chong-ok visited Beijing in January and Moscow in February, apparently seeking Chinese and Soviet loans to fund the DPRK's current seven-year (1978–1984) economic plan.

Chinese Premier Zhao Ziyang visited North Korea for three days from 20 December apparently with the aims of discussing economic issues and of driving a wedge between Pyongyang and Moscow.

Radio Moscow revealed on 9 April that the Soviet Union had been using the port of Najin in northeastern Korea to export its goods to Pacific countries, including Vietnam and Kampuchea. It was the first report to be made on the Soviet use of the port for exports of Soviet goods since North Korea and the Soviet Union signed a protocol on expansion of the port on 31 December 1978.

During 1980, trade between North Korea and the Soviet Union totaled 572 million rubles (U.S. $900 million), an increase of 450 percent over 1960, according to Radio Moscow (1 July 1981). The figure represented one-third of the DPRK's total trade during 1980.

Nodong Sinmun (1 July) carried a lengthy article praising President Kim Il-song and his *chuche* idea, implying Pyongyang's distaste for recent moderate developments in post-Mao China, The article, entitled "Firm Establishment of *Chuche* Is a Definite Guarantee for Splendid Achievement of Revolutionary Tasks," was published one day after the Chinese Communist Party made its first public criticism of Mao. The article expressed North Korea's distaste for China's post-Mao domestic policies: "As shown in the long history of the communist movement, all kinds of class enemies and turncoats of revolution viciously plot to slander and distort the leader's revolutionary thought in an effort to deny revolution."

In a congratulatory message to new Chinese Communist Party Chairman Hu Yaobang on 30 June, Kim Il-song expressed hope for Chinese "adherence to Marxism-Leninism and Mao Zedong Thought." Pyongyang sent Kim Song-kol, director of the North Korean Central News Agency, instead of a KWP mission, to convey President Kim's good wishes to Hu, according to Radio Beijing (7 July).

Japan. Relations between the DPRK and Japan have never been cordial. In Pyongyang's view, Japan is excessively partial to Seoul and pursues a policy of "two Koreas" and hostility toward North Korea, as exemplified by the Japanese government's strong opposition to a drastic reduction of U.S. ground forces in South Korea. North Korean media continued to denounce growing Japanese "imperialism" in South Korea and the alleged collusion of Tokyo and Washington to preserve their mutual "colonial interests" in the Korean peninsula.

The Japanese government has never conducted political or diplomatic exchanges with the DPRK regime, limiting itself to cultural, sports, and economic exchanges. Due to the combined pressures from Japan's business and trade interests and left-wing political and labor groups, however, contacts at the nongovernmental level between North Korea and Japan during the early 1980s are expected to continue to increase, although official exchanges between Pyongyang and Tokyo do not appear likely.

During 1981, two North Korean parliamentary missions and Kim Pong-chu, head of the North Korean General Federation of Trade Unions, visited Japan to promote friendly relations between Tokyo and Pyongyang by expanding private-level bilateral relations between the two countries. The ruling Liberal Democratic government in Tokyo approved their visits on condition that they would not engage in political activities.

A nine-man delegation of the Japan Socialist Party flew to Pyongyang on 13 March to sign an agreement with North Korea on the establishment of a nuclear-free peace zone in Northeast Asia.

North Korea failed to repay 3.0 billion yen in trade debts to Japan. It had promised to pay the sum by the end of June. (*Mainichi Shimbun*, Tokyo, 9 July.)

The United States. During 1981, the DPRK continued its hostility toward the United States. Between June and July, North Korea launched its annual one-month anti-American campaign. Throughout the year, Pyongyang condemned the United States for supporting Chun Doo-hwan's "fascist" regime in Seoul and repeatedly urged Washington to withdraw all American troops and lethal weapons "immediately and totally" from South Korea.

North Korea, in its first comment on the Reagan administration, said on 22 January that it expected President Reagan to pursue "a more vicious Korean policy."

On 4 February, the DPRK harshly denounced the Seoul-Washington joint communiqué released at the end of Chun Doo-hwan's talks with President Reagan in Washington. The reaction came in a lengthy article in *Nodong Sinmun*, entitled "An Abominable Case of Collusion Between the Master and His Faithful Hound." The article, full of invectives against Reagan and Chun, called the joint statement "a filthy criminal document, a document for invasion and war, and a document for selling out the country." Branding President Reagan as "the most belligerent of U.S. presidents" and President Chun as "the most notorious betrayer among the South Korean rulers," the article attacked the nullification of the U.S. troop pullout plan, U.S. support for President Chun's 12 January bid for an exchange of visits by South and North Korea's top leaders, and the U.S. plan to augment South Korea's military capability.

On 28 August, North Korea dismissed as groundless slander American charges that DPRK forces tried to shoot down a U.S. SR-71 reconnaissance plane flying in what the Pentagon called "South Korean and international airspace."

During 1981, Professors Donald S. Zagoria and Gregory Henderson, a delegation of Harvard University professors led by Terry MacDougal, and a number of Korean-Americans visited North Korea.

United Nations. As in the preceding years, the Korean question was absent from the agenda of the annual session of the U.N. General Assembly in 1981. Neither Seoul nor Pyongyang proposed it.

Publications. The KWP publishes a daily, *Nodong Sinmun*, and a journal, *Kulloja*. The DPRK government publishes *Minju Choson*, the organ of the Supreme People's Assembly and the cabinet. The *Pyongyang Times*, *People's Korea*, and *Korea Today* are English-language weeklies. The official news agency is the Korean Central News Agency (KCNA).

Washington College   Tai Sung An

Laos

The leaders of Laos unveiled the details of the country's First Five-Year Plan (1981–1985) during 1981; it provides for gradual collectivization of agriculture as the means of achieving self-sufficiency in food. Meanwhile, tension continued to prevail along the borders with Thailand and China.

The country's governing party, the Lao People's Revolutionary Party (Phak Pasason Lao; PPPL) has an estimated membership of 15,000 persons. The population of Laos is about 3.7 million.

Leadership and Organization. No significant change was reported in 1981 in the membership of the PPPL's Central Committee or Politburo (see *YICA*, 1981, pp. 173–74). The sixtieth birthday of PPPL General Secretary and Lao People's Democratic Republic Premier Kaysone Phomvihan was made the occasion for official celebrations on 12 December 1980.

Auxiliary and Mass Organizations. The Central Committee of the Lao Front for National Construction, the principal mass organization, held its annual congress in 1981 under the chairmanship of Souphanouvong, head of state and leader of the Supreme People's Council and of the front's Central Committee (Radio Vientiane, 10 January; *FBIS*, 13 January).

Domestic Attitudes and Activities. In a report to the annual plenum of the Supreme People's Council on 6 January, Kaysone claimed that in 1980, due to his government's policies, for the first time in history Laos harvested more than one million tons of rice. The government's emphasis on expanding the area irrigated was partly credited with this achievement; the farming area served by irrigation systems was placed at 114,200 hectares (Radio Vientiane, 16 January; *FBIS*, 26 January). If true, this represents a major achievement, especially considering the disruption that various resistance activities reportedly continue to wreak on the Lao economy, and it may be a reflection of the government's 1979 decision to proceed slowly with the establishment of agricultural cooperatives and to relax restrictions on local trade.

Also in 1981, the government decided to confer ranks on officers of the Lao People's Liberation Army.

International Views and Policies. Numerous border incidents with Thailand, including exchanges of gunfire, continued to be reported during 1981. Mortar shelling incidents were also the subject of a Lao protest note to the Chinese chargé d'affaires in Vientiane, reflecting the continuing bad relations between Laos and China (KPL, 15 May; *FBIS*, 15 May).

On the whole, Laos continued to follow Hanoi's line in international affairs, particularly Vietnamese views on neighboring Kampuchea. A typical commentary in *Siang Pasason* (10 March) denounced what it called "the Sihanouk anti-Vietnam comedy act," referring to the unified leadership of the resistance to the Heng Samrin regime (*FBIS*, 11 March).

International Activities and Contacts. Lao party leaders were in evidence at Soviet bloc party congresses. Kaysone went to Moscow for the Soviet congress in February (Radio Vientiane, 26 February; *FBIS,* 26 February), and Politburo member Phoumi Vongvichit attended party congresses in Bulgaria, Czechoslovakia, and East Germany (Radio Vientiane, 29 April; *FBIS,* 29 April.)

Visits of Latin American delegations were highlighted in 1981. A delegation headed by Humberto Ortega and representing the Sandinist Front for National Liberation and the government of Nicaragua visited Vientiane in March (KPL, 19 March; *FBIS,* 20 March), and a Cuban party-government delegation arrived in September (Radio Vientiane, 15 September; *FBIS,* 18 September).

In January, a delegation of the Communist Party of India–Marxist visited Vientiane and was received by Kaysone (Radio Vientiane, 27 January; *FBIS,* 29 January).

In the context of the "special relationship" that has bound Laos and Vietnam since 1975, 1981 was a banner year in terms of honoring each other's top leaders. A Vietnamese delegation headed by Gen. Vo Nguyen Giap officiated at a ceremony in Vientiane on 1 May to present Kaysone with Vietnam's highest order, the Golden Star Order. In a speech on the occasion, Giap referred not only to Kaysone's "indomitability and firm revolutionary perseverance," but also the "wholehearted support and assistance" given by Kaysone to the Vietnamese revolution (Radio Vientiane, 1 May; *FBIS,* 4 May). Not to be outdone, Laos reciprocated on 17 July by deciding to confer its highest order, the National Gold Order, on Vietnamese Communist Party General Secretary Le Duan (Radio Vientiane, 20 July; *FBIS,* 22 July).

In September, Kaysone was again in Moscow, this time to receive the Order of Lenin from Leonid Brezhnev, an event that was said to have been learned with "the utmost elation" by the entire Lao people (Radio Vientiane, 16 September; *FBIS,* 17 September).

Publications. The central organ of the PPPL is the newspaper *Siang Pasason* (Voice of the people), published in Vientiane. There is also an army newspaper. Official news is released by the Pathet Lao News Agency (Khaosan Pathet Lao; KPL). Radio Vientiane broadcasts 22 hours a day. Laos signed an agreement with the Soviet Union for assistance in constructing a 150-kilowatt radio station, and construction began on 29 August in Vientiane province (Radio Vientiane, 31 August; *FBIS,* 2 September).

Bethesda, Maryland   Arthur J. Dommen

Malaysia

There are four communist parties in Malaysia, but only two, the Communist Party of Malaya (CPM), whose three thousand members are concentrated mainly along the Thai-Malaysian border, and the North Kalimantan Communist Party (NKCP), whose two hundred members operate primarily in the state of Sarawak in eastern Malaysia, were active during the year, although the latter functioned at a much reduced rate. (For the birth and development of the two small splinter communist parties, see *YICA*, 1976, pp. 334–36.)

Domestic Developments. As in previous years, various Malaysian officials continued to stress the persistent danger of communist subversion. On 15 February the outgoing chief of police of the state of Perak declared that since Malaysian Communists had been thwarted in their guerrilla and military activities, they would revive and intensify their united front and parliamentary tactics, utilizing "various organizations and parties as fronts." In addition to publications and broadcasts, the Communists would likely "let loose among the population secret party members to sow the seeds of discord that would make the situation fertile for communism to breed." He stressed the importance of psychological warfare, "civic courses" for community leaders, and traditional rural mutual assistance projects to bring the people and the authorities closer together and so reduce popular susceptibility to "communist overtures." (Bernama, Kuala Lumpur, 15 February.)

In conjunction with the Malaysian government's discovery that the political secretary of the deputy premier had been recruited as a secret agent by Soviet embassy personnel in Kuala Lumpur (see below), Malaysian Home Affairs Minister Tan Sri Ghazali Shafie warned on 17 July that the CPM was stepping up its subversive activities and was "making a major effort to subvert and win over officials and Malay political parties and organizations," especially in the states of Kelantan and Trengganu along the Thai border. Shafie added that the acceleration of CPM activity came as a result of "instructions from the Chinese Communist Party," which was anxious to counteract what it perceived to be increased Soviet efforts in recruiting Malays. Shafie alleged that in recent months the China-based CPM transmitter, Suara Revolusi Malaya (Voice of the Malayan Revolution; VOMR), had augmented its broadcasts in Malay, and he underscored the strategic importance of Kelantan because, he said, it was only through that state that the CPM was able to "infiltrate communist terrorist groups from South Thailand" in order to supply "the small Communist terrorist groups currently located in the jungles of Perak, Kelantan and Pahang." (*Straits Times*, Singapore, 18 July.)

Despite official warnings of rising communist activity, the frequency and intensity of clashes with insurgents did not notably increase compared with 1980. Indeed, in mid-January, the chief of the state of Perak's Special Branch (intelligence) declared that communist terrorists were retreating deeper into the jungle "in order to avoid contact with government forces" and that the "small number" of insurgents killed (three) in 1980 in Perak reflected the Communists' realization that they could not sustain the losses of previous years (ibid., 16 January).

Different estimates of insurgent activity came from two other sources. According to an unidentified senior Thai security officer interviewed in Yala in southern Thailand in February, the CPM had grown from 2,500 to 3,000 members during the year and operated mainly along the Thai-Malaysian border in the so-called Betong salient of Yala province, the Weng district of Narithiwat province, and the Sadao district of Songkhla province. According to Thai intelligence sources, recent CPM recruits were local people from southern Thailand, and the guerrillas were "fully equipped with modern weapons" and were being supported by local people from whom "protection money" was being collected during the rice harvest. (*Sarawak Tribune,* Kuching, 22 February.) The clandestine CPM transmitter reported that in mid-March a major ambush had inflicted "more than 30 casualties on the enemy" (VOMR, 11 April; *FBIS,* 17 April). The ambush, the VOMR said, came because the "enraged masses" had demanded it since the government had been spreading slanderous anti-CPM propaganda in connection with the surrender of former CPM Chairman Musa Ahmad, announced by the government on 5 January (see below).

Malaysian officials asserted in mid-July that the CPM, in connection with its renewed tactical emphasis on developing various front organizations, had formed "yet another paper organization," the Malay Nationalist Revolutionary Party of Malaya (MNRPM). The MNRPM would supplement the activities of the CPM's two other fronts, the Islamic Unity Party (Paperi) and the Malayan Peasants' Front (BTM), according to the Malaysian government (*Straits Times,* 18 July). An 11 June VOMR broadcast had announced the founding of the MNRPM on 24 May, and depicted the MNRPM as a vehicle for radical nationalist Malay aspirations. The MNRPM declared its policy to be "to unite with Communists, socialists, Nationalists, and religious groups" and to reflect the ideals of the early radical Malay nationalist Dr. Burhanuddin al-Helmi, leader of the Malay Nationalist Party. In its action program, the MNRPM urged all Malays to unite and to build an "anti-imperialist national united front" of different ethnic groups and social strata. Land distribution, wage increases, development of patriotic spirit among Muslims, development of a spirit of "mutual respect" between Malays and other ethnic groups, support for the "just struggles" of the peoples of Afghanistan and Kampuchea aganist Soviet and Vietnamese domination, and a promise to "make efforts to achieve the reunification of Singapore with the (Malayan) peninsula through negotiations" were the other main elements in the MNRPM program. (VOMR, 11 June; *FBIS,* 18 June.)

The Malaysian government views groups like the MNRPM as a danger to the purity of Islam. In December 1980, Deputy Federal Territory Minister Abdullah Haji Ahmad said that "deviant Islamic teachings" were being spread by a new, unidentified "united communist front" group and the Communists knew that "Malays can deal with problems calmly except in matters concerning Islam." The new communist tactic, he implied, was designed to heighten communal tensions. (*Straits Times,* 8 December 1980.)

The NKCP in Sarawak, faction-ridden, driven deeply underground and harassed by repeated government security drives in recent years, attracted little notice, and no significant clashes or capture of insurgents were reported. At the close of 1980, two small NKCP fronts, the North Kalimantan National Liberation League (NKNLL) and the North Kalimantan Iban Brotherhood Party (NKIBP), broadcast statements over the VOMR protesting the fall in prices of such smallholders' products as rubber, pepper, copra, and sago. The statement called on the people to "struggle to secure reasonable prices for local products and to decide their own future." (VOMR, 4 December 1980; *FBIS,* 9 December 1980.) Both the NKNLL and NKIBP are little more than paper organizations, and their influence must be considered negligible at the moment.

There were some significant CPM policy pronouncements during the year. On 25 June the CPM Central Committee adopted the draft of a new party statement on the different ethnic minorities and nationality groups in Malaya. It asserted that the three major ethnic groups—Malays, Chinese, and Indians (Tamils)—as well as the indigenous minorities (Orang Aseli) and other groups such as the Thais and Eurasians, "are the oppressed and the exploited, sharing the same destiny and waging a common struggle." They also were said to "live in harmony, friendship, and mutual cooperation." The CPM, according to the new program, leads the broad masses of all population groups against the present "reactionary cliques" (not further identified) that seek to exploit ethnic identity by demanding special privileges for certain groups: "The reactionary cliques have noisily clamored about the so-called Malay special privileges not only to set apart the Chinese, Indians, and other minority na-tionalities, but to fool, oppress, and exploit the broad laboring Malay masses in a cruel manner . . . The reactionary policy carried out by the reactionary clique in our country was inherited from their British imperialist masters. They have played up the concept of bumiputra [indigenous people] and non-bumiputra by deciding the bumiputras should own 30 percent of industrial and commercial shares. In this way they have incited racial feelings and undermined national unity for the purpose of maintain-ing their reactionary rule." (VOMR, 30 June; *FBIS,* 7 July.)

Basing itself on "Marxism-Leninism-Mao Zedong thought," the CPM advocates a ten-point pro-gram on the nationalities question in Malaya: (1) respect for all nationalities, their cultural charac-teristics, and their customs; (2) promotion of patriotism, democracy, and "cultural exchange" among nationalities; (3) a guarantee of "completely equal political and economic rights" for all nationalities and the right of each nationality to use its own language; (4) recognition that all nationalities have "the right of residence, the right to work, and the right to own land" and that a hard struggle must be waged to eradicate poverty in rural Malay; (5) imposition of severe limits on the operation of foreign capital investment, along with encouragement of small-and medium-size Malay enterprises, including protection for such enterprises run by Chinese or Indians; (6) making Malay the lingua franca among the various nationalities and "the language medium in communication with other countries," while guaranteeing the existence and development of Chinese and Indian schools; (7) respect for Islam and support for the "just struggle of the Muslims," along with encouragement to believers of different faiths to live harmoniously with each other; (8) guarantees of equal treatment for aboriginal ethnic minorities and other population groups and assistance for their educational and economic develop-ment; (9) upholding the "unification" of the nation and the realization "through consultations" of the unification of Peninsular Malaysia with the now independent republic of Singapore; and (10) recogni-tion of the right of the North Kalimantan people to "national selfdetermination" (VOMR, 30 June; *FBIS,* 7 July).

The last two points reaffirm the CPM's traditional position that the creation of the Malaysian federation in 1963 was illegal and that the party speaks only for Malay (Peninsular Malaysia) and Singapore, whose secession from Malaysia in 1965 it also considers illegitimate. The CPM's position has been that incorporation of the Borneo states of Sabah and Sarawak into Malaysia in 1963 also was unlawful and that they have the right to independence—the aim of the NKCP. (Note that although the CPM nationalities program criticizes the nationalities policies of the British colonial and the pres-ent national government, the CPM similarly distinguishes the major Malaysian ethnic groups and their needs.)

CPM statements continue to reflect a high degree of militancy. In a 1981 New Year's Day broad-cast, the VOMR inveighed sharply against alleged "aggression" by "Soviet socialist imperialism" and against "Soviet-Vietnamese hegemonism and its lackeys." The "contradiction" between the latter and "the people of all nationalities of various levels in our country" could become the "principal contradic-tion in our country." This appeared to be a reference to alleged pro-Soviet tendencies in the small CPM offshoots. The statement added that "during the past year the revolutionary army and people recorded new achievements through their united action." Moreover, "the workers, peasants, other rural laborers, urban poor, low paid employees, youths, students, intellectuals, small and middle indus-trialists and businessmen, as well as religious leaders, have launched various kinds of action to oppose exploitation and persecution and defend their own immediate interests and basic rights." The state-ment acknowledged, however, that because both the Malaysian and Singaporean governments were "clinging to anti-Communist and anti-popular policies," the implementation of the CPM's program "remains difficult." (VOMR, 1 January; *FBIS,* 5 January.)

A 31 January VOMR broadcast, on the occasion of the thirty-second anniversary of the founding of the CPM's fighting arm, the Malayan National Liberation Army (MNLA), declared that the latter had gained the complete support of all nationalities in the country. Over the decades, "prolonged attacks" against the MNLA by colonial troops in the past or "reactionary local forces" today had all "come to naught." Unlike statements in previous years, the message did not recapitulate significant skirmishes or raids carried out by the MNLA during the year. Instead, the message referred to attempts by the superpowers, including "Soviet social imperialists," to infiltrate the nation. The same message accused Ghazali Shafie "and company" of in effect being "the agents of Soviet-Vietnamese hegemonism." Without the MNLA, the expansion of these "agents" would "certainly be more rampant." (VOMR, 31 January; *FBIS,* 4 February.) It is apparent that in the CPM's current political demonology, "Soviet-Vietnamese hegemonists" have replaced the United States as the main imperialist danger. This reflects the current warming trend in U.S.-Chinese relations, as the CPM faithfully continues to orient itself ideologically and tactically on Beijing.

As is its custom, the Paperi took the occasion of Mohammad's birthday to attack the Malaysian government's Islamic policies and win support among ethnic Malays. A Paperi Central Committee message asserted that the Malaysian government, in fact, had "ridiculed Islam." The statement attacked the Soviet intervention in Afghanistan and said that it revealed Moscow's plan to "enslave Muslims and rule the world." (VOMR, 17 January; *FBIS,* 27 January.)

A serious blow to the CPM's prestige came with the 5 January announcement by Ghazali Shafie that during the previous November former CPM Chairman Musa bin Ahmad and his wife Zainab had surrendered to Malaysian authorities. The following day, in a lengthy television-radio interview, Musa disclosed that in 1956, he and his wife, a CPM district committee member, had been sent to China on instructions of CPM Secretary General Chin Peng. Although an experienced guerrilla fighter and eventual commander of the MNLA's 10th Regiment, Musa was compelled to remain in China until 1980. He made repeated but fruitless efforts to persuade Chinese authorities to allow him to leave. Only by means of "a secret operation" and with the aid of Malaysian officials did he succeed in returning to his own country in November 1980. His appointment as CPM chairman in 1956 by the party Central Committee appears to have been largely honorary since Chin Peng held all power.

According to Musa, there had been regular meetings between Communist Party of China and CPM representatives, and the Chinese had promised the latter moral and material support. When asked whether any credibility could be given to recent speculation that China might end its aid to communist groups abroad, Musa replied that this was "only a possibility as a short-term political tactic" for the purpose of improving the CPM's presently unfavorable image as Beijing's stooge and in order to win sympathy for China in its struggle with Moscow. Subsequently, Ghazali Shafie declared that there had never been any collaboration between Malaysian and Chinese officials to get Musa out of China. (*Straits Times,* 7 January; *Asia Record,* February; *Malaysian Digest,* Kuala Lumpur, 31 January, 15 April.)

Musa's return provoked bitter attacks on him and on the veracity of his allegations from the CPM Central Committee, CPM fronts, and VOMR. Because of these and other "conspiratorial antiparty activities," Musa was dismissed as CPM chairman, even though the party hoped he would realize his errors and "turn over a new leaf" (VOMR, 15 January; *FBIS,* 21 January).

Subsequent VOMR commentaries ridiculed Musa's allegations of Chinese influence in the CPM, claiming that Ghazali Shafie had orchestrated Musa's statement in order "to curry favor with the Soviet-Vietnamese hegemonists" (VOMR, 28 February, 7 March; *FBIS,* 3 and 12 March). The BTM charged Musa with serving "Soviet-Vietnamese hegemonist aggression" and betraying "the Malayan people of all nationalities, especially of the Malay peasant movement." The BTM statement termed

Musa's allegation of Chinese influence in the CPM a "sheer fabrication." (VOMR, 7 March, 4 April; *FBIS*, 12 March, 13 April.)

Musa's surrender was but one aspect of domestic Malaysian security developments that focused national attention on the problem of communist subversion. Another notable surrender came on 24 June, when Chong Wai Hean (alias Chong Fong), commander of an MNLA "armed work force," gave himself up to Malaysian officials in Perak state. He and his followers had been operating in the Ipoh area. (*Asiaweek*, 10 July.)

On 13 July, Malaysian Premier Datuk Mahathir Mohamad announced that his political secretary, Siddig Mohamed Ghouse, had been exposed as a Soviet agent and had been arrested and that three Soviet embassy officials in Kuala Lumpur had been identified as the agents who had recruited Siddig. The officials were expelled immediately.

The Siddig case silenced for a while the critics of recent amendments to the Malaysian Societies Act and the Malaysian constitution. These amendments, passed on 9 and 22 April by the Malaysian parliament and swiftly signed into law, gave extensive authority to the government's Registrar of Societies to withdraw recognition and thus render unlawful any organization or to remove its officers if their activities were considered "not in accordance with or beneficial for the fulfillment of and adherence to the federal and state constitutions" (*Malaysian Digest*, 30 April). An amendment to Article 150 of the Malaysian constitution gave the head of state authority to declare a national emergency in case of a threat to national security (AFP, 8 April; *FBIS*, 8 April). Questions continued to be raised, however, whether the government's anticommunist measures are not excessively harsh (*Asia Record*, May; *Asiaweek*, 24 April).

International Aspects. Thai-Malaysian relations were strained by the influx of some three thousand Thai Muslims from the Betong area of Thailand's Yala province into Malaysia's Kedah and Perak states between March and November. The refugees were escaping from difficult living conditions resulting from violent altercations between CPM units and the Thai Muslim secessionist Pattani United Liberation Organization (PULO) in their area. PULO seeks independence for the four southern Thai provinces of Pattani, Yala, Songkhla, and Satun and has sympathizers among devout Muslim Malays across the border. A Thai military drive against PULO and CPM elements seeking refuge in the Betong salient added to the tension. According to Thai sources, however, the exodus was caused by unnamed "instigators" spreading tales among border villagers of PULO-CPM fights and communist plans for revenge. The instigators allegedly urged the refugees to "tell Malaysian authorities that they were being harassed by communist terrorists and Thai officials." (*Asiaweek*, 8 May.) Malaysian Home Affairs Minister Ghazali Shafie asserted that the exodus of Thai refugees had been sparked by a "vengeance streak" among the CPM resulting from the return of former CPM Chairman Musa bin Ahmad (*Sarawak Tribune*, 11 April). Substantiation that the Thai Muslim refugees had fled because of harassment both by Thai troops and CPM forces came from independent news sources, however (AFP, Kroh, Perak, 11 April; *FBIS*, 14 April).

For its part, the CPM has disavowed any responsibility for the refugee exodus, claiming that the problem was wholly caused by the instigations of a "few rightist ringleaders of PULO in collaboration with the Malay reactionaries" (VOMR, 28 April; *FBIS*, 30 April). Behind the whole refugee problem is apparently an intensifying struggle between the CPM and PULO over control of the Betong district (long a major CPM recruiting and foraging base) and Kuala Lumpur's long-standing concern not to arouse orthodox Muslims in Malaysia itself by cooperating too forcefully with the Thais against PULO. Moreover, PULO's relative strength (it claims a membership of 20,000, a considerably exaggerated figure) is appreciated in Kuala Lumpur as a local counterweight to the CPM (*Far Eastern Economic Review*, 1 May). Before the refugee problem erupted, there was evidence of a further growth in Thai-Malaysian cooperation in securing their common border against the CPM.

On 9 August, Chinese Premier Zhao Ziyang began a three-day visit to Malaysia. Before his arrival a Malaysian spokesman had announced that Malaysia intended once again to voice to Zhao its objection to and concern over China's support of the CPM. During his stay, Zhao sidestepped discussion of Chinese support for the CPM, choosing instead to emphasize Beijing's endorsement of the plan of the Association of Southeast Asian Nations (ASEAN) to establish a "zone of peace, freedom, and neutrality" in Southeast Asia and to praise ASEAN for its regional economic and social cooperation. Zhao's evident refusal during his visit to disavow the CPM and Beijing's continuing distinction between its dealings on a "government-to-government" and on a "party-to-party" basis evidently remained unacceptable to the Malaysians. (Radio Kuala Lumpur, 7, 9, 11, and 13 August; *FBIS,* 7, 10, 12, and 19 August.)

Malaysian suspicions about Beijing's policies remained strong because of a radio transmitter called the Voice of Malayan Democracy (VOMD), that began broadcasting on 1 July. The previous day, VOMR had suddenly announced that it was stopping its transmissions "to suit the new situation." From the start VOMD broadcasts adopted a hostile tone toward the governments of Malaysia and Singapore. It later became evident, however, that in its broadcasts, the VOMD seeks to create an image of being more authentically and nationalistically Malay than the VOMR had been and to separate itself from formal Chinese influence, in an apparent effort to win greater Malay support. Malaysian monitors discovered that the VOMD is broadcasting from an as yet unspecified location in southern Thailand, not from southern China as originally thought (*Asiaweek,* 14 August). Malaysian officials still believe that Beijing is behind the VOMD, not the least because the CPM itself has not ceased following a China-oriented ideological line. The surrender of Musa bin Ahmad, as well as the attitude of Premier Zhao Ziyang, confirmed Malaysian suspicions that Beijing had not really changed its policy of support for the CPM.

University of Bridgeport   Justus M. van der Kroef

Mongolia

A fusion of two revolutionary groups produced the Mongolian People's Party in 1921. The party held its First Congress in March of that year at Kyakhta, in Soviet territory. It became known as the Mongolian People's Revolutionary Party (MPRP) in 1924, but Russian dominance had already been established in 1921. In 1924, the party's Third Congress and the Great Khural (the equivalent of the USSR's Supreme Soviet) renamed the country the Mongolian People's Republic (MPR) and announced a noncapitalist and anti-bourgeois line.

In 1981, the MPRP claimed 76,000 members, an increase of 9,000 over the total in 1976. The population of the MPR is slightly over 1.7 million.

In 1981, the MPRP held its Eighteenth Party Congress, celebrated its anniversary, adopted its Seventh Five-Year Plan, and welcomed back to earth Mongolia's very own cosmonaut. Mongolia continued close military, political, and economic cooperation with the USSR and condemned almost every move of China. It supported unconditionally the Soviet position in Afghanistan and the Vietnamese position in Kampuchea.

Organization and Leadership. Two longtime candidates of the Politburo advanced to full membership, enhancing their already long-recognized political leadership status. Altangerel has served as first secretary of the Ulan Bator party organization since 1963; Gombojav was commercial counselor at the MPR embassy in Moscow in 1959 and represented his country before the Council for Mutual Economic Assistance between 1966 and 1977. They replaced two twenty-year veterans: Jagvaral and Luvsanravdan. Jagvaral, now reduced to Politburo candidate membership, served many years as minister of agriculture and twenty years ago articulated the official position that nomadism and the yurt were doomed, that socialism meant fixed settlements and permanent living quarters. Luvsanravdan, for many years head of the Party Control Commission, was replaced in that position by Lieutenant General Dejid, former minister of public security and newly appointed candidate member of the Politburo. Choijilsuren became minister of public security.

M. Dash, a newly appointed secretary of the Central Committee, is another veteran in Mongolian politics. He submitted a dissertation in Moscow in 1954 and for many years was minister of agriculture and chairman of the Administration of Collective Farms. He had seemed on his way out in 1976, when he was demoted from full to candidate membership on the Central Committee, replaced as minister of agriculture, and named MPR ambassador to West Germany. But in 1981, Sodnomdorj was named minister of agriculture, replacing L. Rinchin, who was demoted to candidate member of the Central Committee and named ambassador to Yugoslavia. Ts. Molom was appointed new head of the People's Control Committee, replacing Damdinjav, who was demoted to candidate member of the Central Committee and named ambassador to Kampuchea.

The new head of the Institute of Party History, Lkhamsuren, had been a Politburo member in 1954–1957 and 1962–1973. His position thus becomes analogous to that of Shirendyb, head of the Mongolian Academy of Sciences, who also had been a full member of the Politburo and was removed in a genteel purge. In Mongolia the political losers write the history, but at the direction of the winners.

The Central Committee of the party now numbers 91 full members and 71 candidate members, including 21 new full and 45 new candidate members. In celebration of International Women's Day (6 March), the Mongolian wife of Prime Minister Batmonkh was cited in the press instead of the usual reference to Party Secretary Tsedenbal's Russian wife.

Domestic Attitudes and Activities. Mongolian economic planning is closely monitored by the USSR. It was announced that "development and distribution of the productive forces of the MPR for the period till 1990 have been jointly elaborated by corresponding organizations of Mongolia and the Soviet Union." The twenty-first session of the Mongolian-Soviet Committee on Economic, Scientific, and Technical Cooperation met on 9–15 June; participating Mongols included two Politburo members, two party secretaries, and two deputy prime ministers.

The total of 24.2 million head of livestock indicated that the de facto 25 million head ceiling has yet to be overcome. Five million head are privately owned, and the rest are owned by producers' collective associations and state farms. The government attempted to ease the rural manpower shortage by reassigning 15,200 young people who had completed the eighth or tenth grade of general education.

The Soviet Union supplies managerial personnel and skilled laborers for the Erdenet copper-molybdenum mine; Russians comprised 80 percent of the construction workers who built the new town at Erdenet and represent two-thirds of the factory workers involved in mineral refining and processing.

All output goes to the USSR. The 52,000 people of the other comparatively new city in northern Mongolia, Darkhan, are 30 percent Russian. In Ulan Bator, Russians live in their own section of the city, attend Russian schools, shop in Russian stores, and ride Russian busses to work. (*Le Monde*, Paris, 7–9 August.)

May was declared Nature Protection Month and special attention was directed to erosion, drought, forestry, and the environment generally.

International Views and Contacts. Mongolia's relations with the USSR and China are inextricably mixed in domestic and international affairs. Mongolia copies the Soviet Union and follows its example as a wise and experienced "elder brother"; the MPR deals with the USSR on government-to-government and party-to-party levels. Local and regional transborder connections are important as well.

The Soviet military newspaper reported particularly close cooperation between the Sukhe Bator Military Academy in the MPR and the Novosibirsk Military-Political Academy and noted that most of the administrators and staff personnel of the Mongolian military academy had received advanced professional training in the USSR (*Krasnaya Zvezda*, 25 August). The Mongolian armed forces consist of 28,000 men, 130 tanks, 18,000 border guards, a surface-to-air missile battalion, and 2,000 air force personnel (*Le Monde*, 7–9 August). Soviet Army divisions continue to be stationed on the MPR border with China.

First Deputy Minister of Defense Lieutenant General Tsog, visited the USSR in March and was received by Defense Minister Dimitri Ustinov, among others. At the same time, a Soviet military delegation, including the commander of the Transbaikal and Far Eastern military districts and the commander in chief, Soviet Far Eastern Forces, visited Ulan Bator. On 8–12 June, a high-level Soviet delegation that included Soviet Defense Minister Dimitri Ustinov, the head of the Political Administration of USSR Armed Forces, and the chief of the Soviet general staff, as well as an air force marshal and the marshal in charge of billeting and barracks construction, reviewed Soviet and Mongolian military units in eastern Mongolia.

In March, J. Gurragcha became the MPR's first cosmonaut. The commander of the Soviet spaceship was a native of Soviet Central Asia.

Tsedenbal, Batmonkh, and Jalan-ajav attended the Soviet party congress in February. Tsedenbal visited Brezhnev in the Crimea in August.

USSR-MPR electric power transmission began after recent completion of the Darkhan–Ulan Bator section, permitting direct connection of the East Siberian power grid to the Mongolian capital.

Two hundred Mongols went to Irkutsk in August for a joint Komsomol-Revsomol (the Mongolian youth organization) festival.

Non-Soviet connections reinforce the predominant orientation to the USSR more than they provide alternatives. Trade with Eastern Europe comprises 12 percent and with the USSR 80 percent of Mongolia's foreign trade. An Afghanistan delegation visited the MPR at the end of December 1980; the Afghan ambassador in Ulan Bator called attention to Mongolia's "pioneer transition from feudalism to socialism." The Mongolian ambassador in Kabul, Shagdarsuren (b.1918), is exceptionally experienced, having served as minister of foreign affairs (1959–1963), and as director of international relations for the party's Central Committee (1963–1972).

Laotian Politburo member Souphanouvong was in Mongolia for a week in October 1980; Altangerel led an MPR delegation to Laos in December 1980; Politburo member Phoumi Vongvichit headed the Laotian delegation to the Mongolian congress in May. Vietnamese Foreign Minister Nguyen Co Thach visited Ulan Bator in July.

Several well-known communists came to Mongolia for the sixtieth anniversary celebrations: Rodney Arismendi of Uruguay, Alvaro Cunhal of Portugal, and Henry Winston of the United States. Representatives of the Front for the Liberation of Mozambique, the Sandinistas, and the Palestine

Liberation Organization also attended. Jagvaral led a Mongolian delegation to Cuba in December 1980.

A Soviet filter appears to have been interposed even between the MPR and the United Nations. The former permanent representative of U.N. Development Programs in the MPR reappeared in Ulan Bator in July as Lt. Gen. I. S. Bogatyrev, Soviet deputy minister of internal affairs.

A small remnant ethnic Chinese community, perhaps five thousand in number, has been of little political or even economic significance for decades, but the MPR regime in August virulently attacked them. The improbable charges included involvement in speculation, prostitution, damaging state property, espionage, drug smuggling, and gambling. Several Chinese were expelled.

The MPR regime charged in January that Beijing wanted to annex Mongolia to China and that the Chinese were deliberately liquidating the Mongols of Inner Mongolia. In November, however, it was noted that the Chinese had resumed the study of Mongolian language and literature. The Ulan Bator government also charged that China was assimilating Tibetans and developing Tibet as a platform for launching aggression against India.

Ninety-one countries, not including the United States, maintain diplomatic relations with the MPR.

Publications and Communications. Television reception was greatly extended with completion of a cable from the capital to the western part of the country. Intersputnik satellite broadcast coverage directly to MPR sets of the party congress and the sixtieth anniversary celebrations directly to viewers in the USSR, as well as coverage of the Mongolian cosmonaut's successful return. A new radio station at Khubsugul significantly improved reception in northern Mongolia.

Publication in Mongolian, Russian, Chinese, and English continued. The party newspaper *Unen*, the army newspaper, *Ulan Od* (Red Star), and the trade union paper, *Hodolmor*, remain leading publications. Chinese-language efforts include a magazine, *Mongolyn Mede*, and a newspaper, *Menggu Xiaoxibao*. A new scientific-technical journal, *Molodoi Konstruktor*, began publication in May. The Mongolian news agency, Montsame, celebrated its sixtieth anniversary.

University of North Carolina at Chapel Hill   Robert A. Rupen

Nepal

The Communist Party of Nepal (CPN) was quite active in connection with Nepal's first general elections in 22 years, although the party's various factions took divergent positions toward the balloting. CPN membership is estimated at four thousand and Nepal's population at fourteen million.

Leadership and Organization. Bishnu Bahadur Manandhar remains general secretary of the CPN's moderate wing. Keshar Jung Raimajhi is CPN president. There was reportedly serious conflict between the two, however, over participation in the elections. Man Mohan Adhikari still appears dominant among the extremist elements.

Domestic Attitudes and Activities. The major political event in 1981 was the 9 May elections to the National Panchayat, the first held on the basis of universal franchise since 1959. Over one thousand candidates contested 112 seats in the legislature. (The remaining 28 seats are filled by nomination by the king.) (*NYT*, 22 March, 9 May.)

A December 1980 constitutional amendment provided that no political groups would be barred from the elections. The Raimajhi faction of the CPN participated. However, two major opposition leaders—former Premier B. P. Koirala of the Nepali Congress Party and Man Mohan Adhikari—decided to boycott the elections, asserting that recent constitutional changes were an impediment to healthy growth of the democratic system. (*Far Eastern Economic Review*, 5 June.) A Nepali Congress spokesman later claimed the boycott was successful because the voter turnout of 52 percent was lower than in the 1980 national referendum on the partyless Panchayat system.

A substantial number of newcomers pledging to eliminate corruption, improve the economy, and reduce unemployment won, but a large number of official candidates, including Prime Minister S. B. Thapa, were also re-elected. The Raimajhi faction fielded roughly fifty candidates; none successfully. Raimajhi's decision to participate indicated his continuing tactical support for the present regime. Subsequently, the weekly pro-Soviet *Samiksha*, which reflects views of the Raimajhi faction of the CPN, attacked the Nepali Congress and Adhikari for opposing the Panchayat system. Although Adhikari had called for a boycott, a small number of supporters of other extremist factions or pro-Chinese sympathizers won seats. (Ibid.)

The pro-Chinese All Nepal Nationalist Independent Students Union continued to be active in protests and demonstrations during the year. In September university student union elections, it made major gains against the pro-Nepali Congress Nepal Students Union, celebrating its victory with slogans critical of the Panchayat system, the USSR, the United States, and India.

International Views and Policies. During the summer, Nepalese and Indian newspapers reported extensively on the USSR's activities in Nepal and suspicions of Soviet intentions there. The Soviet embassy in Katmandu was allowed to import electronic equipment. One paper alleged the Soviets planned to establish an intelligence center. Some foreign diplomats saw the ease with which the equipment was imported as an indication of pro-Soviet sympathies on the part of the Thapa government. (Ibid., 10 July.)

Probably reacting to these stories and heightened concern over Soviet influence, *Samiksha* asserted there was no record of Soviet interference in Nepal's internal affairs. A week later, the paper observed that "anti-Soviet feelings based on the view that Nepal faces its main threat from the Soviet Union had been intensified" since the fall of Afghanistan's king. (*Samiksha*, 24 and 31 July.)

Among other issues *Samiksha* addressed during the year was Poland, opining that "socialism and the Warsaw Treaty must be safeguarded today in Poland by all means" (ibid., 26 June). Pro-Soviet publications also strongly attacked the U.S. decision to resume work on the neutron bomb.

Publications. The weekly *Samiksha* reflects views of the Raimajhi CPN.

Earlysville, Virginia   Barbara Reid

New Zealand

The Communist Party of New Zealand (CPNZ) was formed in Wellington in 1921. It was thus sixty years old in 1981, and this anniversary was celebrated at meetings and in historical articles by the several successor parties that operate today. Besides the CPNZ, there are the Socialist Unity Party (SUP), which was formed in 1966; the Preparatory Committee for the Formation of the Communist Party of New Zealand (Marxist-Leninist), set up in 1978; and the Workers Communist League (WCL), which dates from 1980. The major Trotskyist group in New Zealand is the Socialist Action League (SAL), founded in 1969.

These groups all function legally, although the WCL claims to be "principally a secret organization" that "combines overt and covert work, legal and illegal work, parliamentary and non-parliamentary work" (WCL Manifesto, 1980). None of the parties publishes membership figures, but a regional conference of the SUP in August was told of "problems associated with the party's rapid growth over the past 12 months" (*New Zealand Tribune,* 7 September). Their combined strength is probably in the vicinity of 600, with 200 for the SUP, up to 150 for the SAL, and up to 100 each for the WCL and CPNZ. The total population of New Zealand is 3.1 million.

The CPNZ was one of the few original communist parties that broke with the Soviet Union in the mid-1960s and took the side of China. After the fall of the Gang of Four, the CPNZ severed its links with China and now aligns itself internationally with Albania. The head office of the party is in Auckland and, apart from a small branch in Christchurch, its support is confined virtually to Auckland province. SUP leader G. H. Andersen describes the CPNZ as "an impotent rump of slogan shouters and banner wavers" (ibid., 6 April), while the WCL dismisses it as "a tiny bureaucratic sect" (*Unity,* 6 May). CPNZ influence on the public life of New Zealand is negligible.

To New Zealanders, the SUP is the communist party. Formed by Communists who refused to follow the CPNZ into the Chinese fold, it has maintained close links with the Soviet Union throughout its fifteen-year history. It is by far the most important of the local communist groups, and despite its small numerical strength and its tiny electoral support, it has gained significant influence in the trade union movement. An SUP leader, K. G. Douglas, is secretary-treasurer of the central union organization, the Federation of Labour, which has some 440,000 members. In August, G. H. Andersen was elected to the National Executive of the federation. This gives the SUP two of the eleven seats on the executive board, but Andersen is also president of the Auckland District Council of the Federation of Labour, which contains a quarter of its total membership.

The SUP is governed by a National Committee of ten members elected at its triennial conference. This committee in turn elects from among its members a National Executive of five, which is located in Auckland, meets weekly, and is the real seat of power in the party. Ella Ayo is vice-president and G. E. Jackson is secretary of the party. The party has thirteen branches throughout New Zealand, five of them in Auckland. There are regional committees in Auckland and Wellington.

The SUP released its party program, "Our Country, Our Future," in June. It decided to contest a few seats in the parliamentary elections on 28 November but to support the opposition Labour Party in other districts and to work for the election of a Labour government. It also stressed the need to build a mass peace movement through the agency of the New Zealand Council for World Peace and expressed support for a Mongolian proposal for a nonaggression pact covering Asian and Pacific countries.

The party has close ties with the Young Workers Alliance and the Union of New Zealand Women. A national conference of SUP women members met for the first time in October to discuss a draft women's program. The two top leaders, Andersen and Jackson, attended the Soviet party congress in Moscow in February. Jackson also attended party congresses in Bulgaria, Czechoslovakia, and the German Democratic Republic.

The WCL and the Preparatory Committee both proclaim their adherence to Marxism–Leninism–Mao Zedong Thought, but while the Preparatory Committee is totally committed to the support of Chinese policies, the WCL has adopted a more independent stand. Both groups regard "Soviet social-imperialism" as the main enemy. The Preparatory Committee has even denounced revolutionary propaganda as diversionary because it interferes with the building of a national anti-Soviet front. The Preparatory Committee stresses the need to develop an arms industry to produce weapons for the defense of New Zealand, and its new journal, *Advance,* reprinted at length a speech on the Soviet naval threat in the Pacific by the chief of staff of the New Zealand Navy.

The WCL is based in Wellington but has members in Auckland and elsewhere. It has support in the universities and has succeeded in gaining a foothold in the trade unions. In October a WCL member was elected secretary of the Wellington District Council of the Federation of Labour, in a contest with an SUP member. The WCL was also active in the antiapartheid movement, which organized mass protests in August and September against the tour of South Africa's Springbok rugby team. On 25 August the prime minister released a Security Intelligence Service report that named several WCL members and claimed that they were exploiting the anti-Springbok tour movement for their own political ends. The report described the WCL as "a revolutionary communist party dedicated to the violent overthrow of the state."

The WCL decided to support the Labour Party in the parliamentary elections as the only alternative to the present National government. At the same time, it stressed the need to "discredit the Labour Party's ideology and to smash it as a political party to achieve socialism" (ibid., 14 October).

The SAL also decided to support the Labour Party in the elections and not to contest seats on its own. The CPNZ, on the other hand, continued its boycott of parliamentary elections on the grounds that "the people's interests . . . are served only by the people's own struggles outside Parliament" (*People's Voice,* 26 October). The parliamentary elections ended in a return of the National Government, but with a reduced majority over the opposition Labour Party. The five SUP candidates polled better than in 1978 but only one of them, G. H. Andersen, gained more than a hundred votes. Their combined share was less than 0.5 percent of the total vote in the five seats contested.

Publications. The different communist groups each have a regular journal. The CPNZ publishes the weekly *People's Voice,* the SUP the fortnightly *New Zealand Tribune,* and the WCL the fortnightly *Unity.* The SAL organ, *Socialist Action,* normally appears fortnightly, but appeared weekly in the two months preceding the elections. The Preparatory Committee launched *Advance* in February; it claims to be not only a Marxist-Leninist paper but also a patriotic New Zealand paper. Circulation figures are kept secret, but *Socialist Action* probably has the largest circulation (about 2,500 copies). Two groups also have theoretical journals: the SUP publishes *Socialist Politics* quarterly, and the Preparatory Committee publishes *Struggle.* The CPNZ theoretical organ *N.Z. Communist Review,* which had appeared under different names since 1943, ceased publication at the end of 1980 without explanation.

University of Auckland   H. Roth

Pakistan

The Communist Party of Pakistan (CPP) was banned in 1954, and no formal communist party has functioned since that time. However, pro-Chinese and pro-Soviet leftists have established a number of political groupings, none very large, or worked through larger political parties, student groups, and trade unions. Although the various leftist parties represent no present threat to the government of President Mohammad Zia ul Haq, they are a certain nuisance to his regime. Their leaders urge leftists within the country's largest dissident political organization, the People's Party of Pakistan (PPP), to take more radical action against the government, and their cadres will take to the streets to exploit any signs of popular discontent.

During 1981, President Zia's martial law regime was confronted with its most serious challenge since the 1977 military coup against the late President Zulfikar Ali Bhutto. In late 1980, leftist student groups won a number of student union elections, emboldening many students to take direct action to express grievances. In addition, leaders of nine opposition parties met in early February to organize the Movement to Restore Democracy (MRD). The MRD planned to stage a number of protest demonstrations that would force the government to call for elections.

On 10 February, students at Multan in the Punjab, the most populous province, set off a round of protests nationwide by organizing demonstrations against an increase in bus fares. The disorder quickly spread to campuses in other cities. However, the movement failed to elicit support from a broader segment of the population. The government moved quickly to quash this protest movement by shutting down campuses and detaining student activists, as well as some political figures. The 2 March hijacking of a Pakistan International Airways (PIA) plane to Kabul broke the momentum of protest, and the unfolding of post-hijacking events significantly strengthened Zia's political position. His political standing was also boosted by the relatively good performance of the economy, by fears generated by the Soviet invasion of Afghanistan, and by his adroit handling of crises.

By the late summer, the government felt sufficiently self-confident to release most of the political detainees that had been rounded up at the time of the hijacking and at the time the MRD was formed. It had already reopened many colleges and universities.

The hijackers were members of the al-Zulfikar organization, a revolutionary terrorist group led by Murtaza Bhutto, son of the late President Zulfikar Ali Bhutto. The PIA plane was ordered to fly to Kabul, where Murtaza had established the headquarters of al-Zulfikar. The hospitality accorded to the hijackers both during and after the event by the Soviet-installed government in Kabul aroused fears of a Soviet threat to Pakistan and created the impression of a link between the hijackers and the PPP (which both sides, however, deny). The killing of a Pakistani diplomat by the hijackers lost them popular sympathy. Indeed, the moderate parties of the MRD pulled back from a direct confrontation with the government in the wake of the hijacking and even criticized the PPP for not sufficiently condemning the hijackers. In addition, the fissures between the moderate and leftist elements of the PPP were further widened. At the close of the year, the MRD was relatively moribund and seriously divided.

The leftist parties are all small and played a minor role in the political events of 1981. The more active among them are the National Liberation Front, led by Mairaj Mohammed Khan; the National Progressive Party, led by Azaz Nasir; and the Kisan Mazdoor Party, led by Afzal Bangash. The first has the largest following, primarily among labor and student circles in Karachi. The second is the orthodox core of the old pro-Soviet CPP. The last was formerly pro-Chinese, but seems to be shifting to a pro-Soviet stand. The Kisan Mazdoor's following is concentrated in the North-West Frontier province. All three groups have tried to associate with leftists in the PPP and have urged the PPP to take a more confrontational stance toward the government. On the domestic front, they also advocate greater governmental control over the economy and a substantial devolution of power to the country's four provinces. Internationally, they tend to side with the USSR and oppose the United States.

Still another group of leftists are in the Baluchi Student Organization (BSO) and the Baluchi People's Liberation Front (BPLF). The more radical factions of the BSO favor independence for Baluchistan, while the moderates tend to favor some degree of autonomy. The BPLF, which contains a Marxist element, calls for complete independence. The BSO has a small number of activists, although it has widespread support among the student community of Baluchistan. The BPLF, some of whose activists are in Afghanistan, has little appeal. Neither group was able to instigate demonstrations against the government during the year. Even the execution of former BSO leader Hamid Balouch in mid-1981 did not trigger outbreaks of violence on college campuses.

The most influential figures in the PPP are the late Zulfikar Ali Bhutto's wife, Nusrat, and his daughter, Benezir. On domestic matters, the two tend to line up with the moderates of the party and on foreign policy issues with the leftists. They advocate some sort of accommodation with the Soviets on the Afghan question.

The government of President Zia wants to preserve its recently acquired nonaligned credentials and maintains correct, if often cool, relations with the USSR. The relationship lacks much political or economic substance. The major bilateral issue during 1981 was the ongoing Afghan civil war against the Soviet-installed regime of Babrak Karmal, which has had a direct impact on Pakistan. Since the start of the civil war, over 2.4 million Afghan refugees have fled to Pakistan. Pakistan has introduced resolutions at the United Nations calling for a withdrawal of foreign troops from Afghanistan. Pakistan also wants a political dialogue to resolve the fighting, but the various proposals to date have foundered because the involved parties could not agree on such issues as a Soviet troop withdrawal and the participants in the talks. On the first issue, for example, the Pakistanis, backed by the moral support of the Islamic Conference and the United Nations, want a withdrawal to precede the talks. The Soviets (and the Afghans) want a political dialogue, but have refused to consider the question of troop withdrawal because such a discussion would constitute "interference" in the domestic affairs of Afghanistan.

Pakistan's relations with China are very cordial. Beijing has been Pakistan's major supplier of sophisticated military equipment for over a decade, and it is a significant trading partner. In 1981, Premier Zhao Ziyang visited Pakistan, the first visit by a Chinese premier in fifteen years. Zhao used the occasion to criticize the Soviet invasion of Afghanistan and to praise Pakistan. Yang Dezhi, chief of the General Staff of the People's Liberation Army of China, visited Pakistan in November in a visit intended to underscore the good bilateral relationship.

The Soviets have used a carrot-and-stick approach toward Pakistan on the Afghan question. On the one hand, Soviet media have periodically blasted Pakistan for assisting the insurgency in Afghanistan. On 8 October, *Izvestiia*, for example, charged that Pakistan is not interested in a serious political dialogue with Afghanistan because Islamabad really wants a stronger military relationship with Washington. There have also been periodic cross-border incidents, most recently in late November, which may have been orchestrated by the USSR to exert pressure on Pakistan. At the same time, the USSR continues to provide economic and technical assistance on such projects as the $2 billion Karachi steel plant, the first segment of which was completed with much fanfare in early September, and the Guddu power station in Sind. Deputy Soviet Minister of Foreign Affairs Nikolai Firyubin also visited Pakistan in late August 1981, and both sides worked hard to create the impression of cordiality.

Arlington, Virginia   Walter K. Andersen

The Philippines

Communism in the Philippines centers around the guerrilla insurgency of the four thousand–man New People's Army (NPA), the fighting arm of the Beijing-oriented Communist Party of the Philippines–Marxist-Leninist (CPP-ML). Membership in the two organizations heavily overlaps, although the CPP-ML has an independent, nonguerrilla cadre and provincial leadership structure. A National Democratic Front (NDF), of some ten thousand active sympathizers and supporters, is a loose federation of radical, usually Marxist groups, among them the National Youth (Kabataang Makabayan; KM), Christians for National Liberation, Union of Nationalist Urban Poor, and Masaka (a peasants' association). The NDF is believed to be infiltrated and largely directed by CPP-ML cadres. All communist activity is proscribed under Philippine law. However, the older, two hundred–member Moscow-oriented Philippine Communist Party (Partido Komunista ng Pilipinas; PKP), currently adopts a critical but more moderate and nonviolent posture toward the Marcos government, and some of its leaders enjoy a semilegitimacy and freedom of movement. Both communist parties operate in a political environment of widespread, though faction-ridden and thus far ineffectual, dissatisfaction with and opposition to the Marcos government.

Party Organization, Tactics, and Programs. In mid-November 1980, Philippine authorities revealed details of the new central CPP-ML leadership, which had been in relative disarray since the 1977 capture of party founder José M. Sison. Rodolfo Salas ("Commander Bilog"), onetime KM activist and former University of the Philippines chemical engineering student, is reported to be the new CPP-ML chairman. Horacio ("Boy") Morales, originally believed to have succeeded Sison, remains in the party Politburo, along with Antonio Zumel, a former news editor of the daily Manila *Bulletin*, and Ed Jopson, another KM leader and youth movement activist. Described as the chief NPA leader as well as CPP-ML vice-chairman is Juanito Rivera ("Commander Juaning"), a young but seasoned guerrilla fighter. (AFP, 14 November 1980; *FBIS*, 14 November 1980; *Asiaweek*, 11 September.)

At about the same time, the Philippine government disclosed the existence of a new anti-Marcos opposition group, called the Catholic Liberation Army (CLA). The CLA's antecedents are obscure; some observers see it as an offshoot of the 6 April Liberation Movement, an urban guerrilla group responsible for a recent chain of bombings and other street violence in Manila. (AFP, Manila, 20 November 1980; *FBIS*, 21 November 1980.) However, other authoritative sources, including some in the government, have described the CLA as a CPP-ML "splinter group," intent on winning direction of various, scattered urban guerrilla bands. The CPP-ML itself has denounced all Catholic-based terrorist organizations, identifying them with the minuscule, underground anti-Marcos Social Democratic Party (SDP), which, according to the CPP-ML, is "American imperialism's Trojan Horse" in the Philippines (AFP, Manila, 24 November 1980; *FBIS*, 24 November 1980).

The CLA, SDP, 6 April Liberation Movement, and similar groups suggest a growing involvement of younger Filipino clergy and prominent laymen in guerrilla-style resistance. In mid-January, Deputy Defense Minister Carmelo Barbero appealed to Catholic church leaders to persuade four clergymen who reportedly had deserted their parishes in northern Abra province in order to join the NPA to return and surrender. Other government spokesmen claimed that captured NPA documents disclosed that "hundreds of church elements," Roman Catholic as well as Protestant, were among the CPP-ML's sympathizers (*Asia Record*, February). Subsequently, the four priests issued a joint statement saying that they had, in fact, joined the NPA. They urged all Filipinos to overthrow the "U.S.-Marcos dictatorship" and asserted that only "an armed struggle" could bring down the Marcos regime (AFP, Manila, 1 April; *FBIS*, 2 April).

According to the military, eight priests have joined the NPA throughout the Philippines, and at least two hold leadership positions (AFP, 12 July; *FBIS*, 13 July). The extent to which clergy are engaged in the anti-Marcos opposition is difficult to gauge since government sources, seeking to rebut long-standing criticism by religious leaders, may well have a stake in exaggerating clerical involvement. The interaction of younger clergy and their followers with the NPA remains, however, of growing importance to the operations of the CPP-ML in terms of winning wider support. The political radicalization of the religious community in the Philippines and its interaction with the NPA through various campaigns of violent anti-Marcos resistance appear to be not only an increasingly significant tactical and organizational asset to Philippine communism but also a challenge to party leadership and control.

In December 1980, the Executive Committee of the CPP-ML Central Committee issued a statement commemorating the party's twelfth anniversary. The statement reaffirmed the party's established line of "smashing the U.S.-Marcos dictatorship through the armed democratic revolution" and of building an "anti-fascist, anti-feudal, and anti-imperial mass movement" in the country. It claimed that a "broad and vigorous" mass movement has developed in the Philippine countryside, involving "several hundreds of thousands of peasants." Actions against landlords have resulted in reductions by fifty percent "or more" of land rent paid by tenants, in wages increases for agricultural workers, and in lowered interest rates on loans to peasants. In the cities, the report claimed that the rising mass movement has expressed itself in strikes, marches, rallies, and petition drives; besides workers, peasants, students, and "other progressive sections of the petty bourgeoisie" were being drawn into the popular struggle. According to the statement, the NPA now has "27 guerrilla fronts" covering "more than 400 municipalities in 43 provinces." While the statement conceded that the capture of Sison had put the party to a "severe test," nevertheless, since 1977, "party membership increased fivefold" with new branches in "barrios, factories, schools, communities and offices." ("Twelfth Anniversary Statement of the Communist Party of the Philippines," *Philippine Liberation Courier*, Oakland, Calif., June.)

The same statement assessed the relative value of cooperation with other dissident groups in the Philippines and noted that in the main, party links with these other dissidents have been strengthened in recent years. The insurgents of the Moro National Liberation Front (MNLF)—who seek "self-determination" for Philippine Muslims, in effect through an independent Muslim state in Mindanao and other adjacent southern Philippine islands—do hold "differing views on a few important questions," but there has been a "growing frequency" of discussions and "several joint actions" with the group. Elements within the PKP were said to be dissatisfied with the policies of "collaboration" with the Marcos government pursued by PKP Secretary General Felicisimo Macapagal. These elements, along with other groups led by prominent religious, professional, and civil rights figures, promote the development of a broad "anti-fascist, anti-imperialist and anti-feudal movement" in the Philippines. Rifts within the ruling Marcos clique and mounting economic difficulties resulting, among other causes, from the "never ending convenience and gains demanded by big foreign and local capitalists" make the general condition of the country "very favorable for the advance to a higher stage of the revolutionary struggle." (Ibid.)

CPP-ML leaders claim that there has been "a qualitative and quantitative expansion of the illegal opposition" in the Philippines (*Far Eastern Economic Review*, 21 August). According to the Beijing-supported Voice of the People of Burma (2 January), the clandestine transmitter of the Burmese Communist Party, various "revolutionary organizations" throughout the Philippines (presumably not just the CPP-ML) "have a strength of 80,000" (*FBIS*, 9 January). NPA sources claim success with their tactic of widening the operations of NPA-controlled village "guerrilla fronts" into "preparation zones" (areas not yet secured by the insurgents). Weapons captured from Philippine security forces are said to be the main source of the guerrillas' arms. Armed NPA indoctrination and propaganda teams reinforce a continuous communist presence in villagers' minds. According to the CPP-ML, existing inequities in land tenure and the promise of more effective land reform than that being undertaken by the government continue to be major sources of communist appeal. Susceptible peasants are drawn into local CPP-ML NDF committees and participate in boycotts and demonstrations until ready for full-scale insurgent action. Guerrilla torture and killings of government officials, Philippine police, and of civilian informers revealed by the NPA's "social investigation" process to be a threat to insurgent operations are matched by similar brutalities committed by government security forces, thus further polarizing political and social relations in the NPA operational areas. (Sheilah Ocampo, "The Communists' Growth Strategy," *Far Eastern Economic Review*, 21 August.)

The PKP prefers a policy of quiet infiltration of trade unions, public services, and schools, eschewing overt violence. Though officially led by Secretary General Felicisimo Macapagal with the aid of a small Central Committee, there are at least two other, as yet uncrystallized, factional groups within the PKP. It has been reported that the PKP is receiving "limited funds" from the Soviet Union (*Far Eastern Economic Review*, 7 August). In a comment on the announced lifting of martial law by President Marcos, Macapagal stressed that this would not benefit the Philippines much unless other restrictions on "democratic rights" were also eliminated. The PKP leader noted the promulgation of new presidential decrees, at the same time as the lifting of martial law, that provided for preventive detention and a ban on "subversive" publications. Macapagal also noted the deep inroads into the Philippine economy made by "foreign monopoly capital" and the alleged transformation of "our financial institutions" into "conduits of the World Bank." He urged Filipinos to continue to struggle for a "genuine" return of civil and political rights. (*IB*, March.)

Domestic Developments. The lifting, after eight years, of martial law provisions by President Marcos on 17 January, Marcos's landslide victory in a referendum on 7 April allowing him in effect to run for a new presidential term, far-reaching constitutional amendments, and Marcos's overwhelming re-election on 6 June to another six-year term as president did not change in the slightest the recent pattern of scattered clashes with NPA insurgents, periodic government warnings about the danger of communist subversion, and announcements of amnesties and releases of political prisoners, including "rehabilitated" NPA insurgents. Toward the close of 1980, Marcos reportedly granted amnesty to 375 members of the CPP-ML and the NPA, but major party figures like José Sison and NPA commander Bernabe Buscayno ("Commander Dante") continued to be held because of their "major crimes against the state." Additional prisoner releases involved several hundred former MNLF adherents and those arrested for offenses such as illegal possession of firearms and other minor transgressions. (Far Eastern Broadcasting Company, Manila, 22 December 1980; *FBIS*, 22 December 1980.)

The Marcos government continues to be criticized, however, for torture, summary executions, and maltreatment of prisoners. The Association of Religious Superiors of the Philippines (AMRSP) reported that in 1980, 106 persons had been "salvaged," a term used to designate illegal arrest and killing after interrogation by Philippine security forces (*Country Reports on Human Rights Practices: Report Submitted to the Committee on Foreign Relations, U.S. Senate, and Committee on Foreign Affairs, U.S. House of Representatives*, Washington, D.C.: Government Printing Office, 2 February 1981, pp. 679–80). Philippine security officials have denied that such operations take place, but the AMRSP's Task Force on Detainees of the Philippines has continued to record the practice. In June 1981 it reported that there were some seven hundred political prisoners in 101 jails and prisons throughout the country (*Asia Record*, June).

Questions have also been raised about the government's counterterrorist tactics in combatting the NPA and MNLF. The use by the Philippine security forces of fanatical anticommunist religious groups and renegade former members of the armed forces (little more than bandits who operate against the NPA under the name, The Lost Command) has aroused criticism. In the early months of 1981 more came to be known of a pro-Marcos terrorist group known as the Rural Reformist Movement (RRM), led by Kumander Alitaptap (Commander Firefly). The RRM has been operating in Davao del Norte province, where scores of villagers reportedly have been shot, beheaded, or forced to flee by the RRM band. In a vehemently worded manifesto, Alitaptap accused the NPA of abusing villagers and demanded the NPA's liquidation, declaring that the RRM's main objective was "to support" the "Marcos program for good government." There have been reports that RRM is controlled by the National Intelligence and Security Authority, the Marcos government's major counterintelligence and counterinsurgency center. The Sandigan (Pillar) unit of the urban 6 April Liberation Movement appears to be encouraged to a limited degree by the government as a counterweight to NPA activities. (*Far Eastern Economic Review*, 24 April.)

Even as Marcos keeps warning that labor, student, and other organizations are being used as communist fronts, the government claims notable success in its antisubversion campaign. In November 1980, Philippine Defense Minister Juan Ponce Enrile declared that no fewer than 485 organizations controlled by subversives had been neutralized by the military, citing in particular the capture of key CPP-ML, NPA, and Light A Fire Movement leaders. (AFP, 6 November 1980; *FBIS*, 10 November 1980.) Yet clashes with the NPA continued throughout 1981 in such varied areas as Samar, Bataan, Quezon, Nueva Ecija, Bicol, Sultan Kudarat, Pampanga, and Batangas provinces.

In connection with the 7 April constitutional referendum, there was an upsurge of NPA activity. Insurgents attacked several polling places throughout the country. In two Samar towns, NPA guerrillas seized ballot boxes at gunpoint and told voters that the referendum was a "Marcos gimmick" to "institutionalize an illegal government." Similar NPA seizures occurred in Cagayan, Davao del Norte, and Zamboanga del Sur provinces. (AFP, Manila, 8 and 9 April; *FBIS*, 8 and 9 April.)

All such NPA activity and alleged instances of overreaction to it by the armed forces produced a spate of government warnings and revelations of communist activity during the year. Defense Minister Juan Ponce Enrile announced that he had ordered the Philippine armed forces to intensify their operations against the NPA, but reports also continued of alleged new NPA plots to start a "reign of terror" in Olocos Sur province and elsewhere. Even the Manila area became the scene of a well-publicized government raid on a "subversive printing plant," during which four prominent CPP-ML cadres, as well as quantities of party propaganda, including its official organ, *Ang Bayan* (The nation), were seized. (Far Eastern Broadcast Corporation, Manila, 1 May, 19 June; *FBIS*, 4 May, 23 June; Baguio Mountain Province Broadcasting Corporation, 11 July; *FBIS*, 14 July.)

Subsequently Marcos told the visiting foreign policy adviser of U.S. Senator Edward Kennedy that communist attempts to infiltrate Philippine labor and student organizations were continuing (*FBIS*, 20 August). Defense Minister Enrile has claimed on several occasions that the NPA is engaging in a "campaign of deception" to persuade the MNLF to supply the Communists with arms. According to Enrile, the NPA badly needs weapons because of the effectiveness of the government's counterinsurgency operations. He denied the NPA's claim that it has managed to fight the government's security forces to a "strategic stalemate." (AFP, Manila, 7 August; *FBIS*, 7 August.) On 26 September, Philippine authorities announced the capture of 51 communist guerrillas at Cotabato City, among them some provincial leaders of the NPA, and the formal surrender of 1,204 "NPA members and sympathizers," who had been active in the Arakan valley area in northern Cotabato province (AFP, Cotabato City, 26 September; *FBIS*, 30 September).

Philippine counterinsurgency efforts against the scattered and weakened Muslim secessionist guerrillas of the MNLF continued. According to past government statements, there has been tactical collaboration between the MNLF and NPA. The extent of that collaboration remains controversial, however. Former NPA leader Bernabe Buscayno declared that during his period of activity in the 1960s and up to his capture in 1976, he was unaware of any link between the NPA and the MNLF (*Asiaweek*, 11 September). The most notable incident involving a possible MNLF-NPA link was the allegation by the government on 1 June that MNLF terrorists had devised an extensive plot, codenamed June Bride, involving the assassination of Marcos and top officials and bombings throughout the country in an attempt to disrupt the 16 June presidential elections. According to the government, the plot resulted from a meeting "somewhere in the Middle East" between MNLF Chairman Nur Misuari, who has received Libyan support in the past, and one of Marcos' principal political opponents, former Senator Benigno Aquino. The plot came to light during an investigation of a bomb explosion at a house in the Marikina section of Manila. (Far Eastern Broadcasting Corporation, Manila, 2 and 6 June; *FBIS*, 3 and 8 June.) But according to other reports, the June Bride conspiracy was discovered with the arrest of two would-be conspirators on 23 May near the Presidential Palace in Manila and involved not just the MNLF but also the NPA and the Palestine Liberation Organization. Details of this collaboration have not been disclosed, however. (*Asiaweek*, 19 June.)

NPA activities in the southern areas that have long been the site of MNLF operations have strengthened official suspicions of the existence of a tactical bond between the two organizations. On 2 July, Defense Minister Enrile disclosed that the MNLF and the NPA had formed "an operational alliance to overthrow the government," adding that this was "the first time" that his ministry could officially "confirm" the "much-rumored" link between the Muslim and communist insurgent groups (*Straits Times*, Singapore, 3 July; Baguio Mountain Province Broadcasting Corporation, 2 July; *FBIS*, 2 July). Enrile's revelation produced some surprise, for on 5 May he had asserted that there was "no concrete evidence" of an MNLF-NPA alliance, although he conceded that such a link was possible.

Despite Philippine government reports of a weakening MNLF and of Libyan disenchantment with MNLF Chairman Nur Misuari (see *FBIS*, 21 February), the Muslim insurgency has persisted. With a more active NPA alliance to support it, assuming Enrile's allegation is correct, Muslim unrest in the southern Philippine provinces is likely to be reinvigorated, adding to the general pattern of anti-Marcos opposition.

It is of great importance to the CPP-ML and the NPA that significant segments of Philippine society automatically perceive all presidential reforms, whatever their intent or nature, as "farcical" or as a mere "perpetuation of the dictatorship"and that voting fraud is assumed in all elections. By early May, major opposition groups, including labor and student organizations, had decided to launch a steady, mass civil disobedience campaign against Marcos. (*Economist*, London, 18 April; AFP, Manila, 7 April; *FBIS*, 7 April; *NYT*, 12 May.) Marcos continued to warn the labor movement against being used as a tool of subversion and assured unions that he would support a new measure restoring the right to strike (Far Eastern Broadcasting Corporation, Manila, 1 May; *FBIS*, 4 May). Despite the prohibition against strikes, however, work stoppages, slowdowns, and labor unrest have been common. Because of what he termed continuing "restlessness," President Marcos threatened on 30 September to reimpose martial law. He charged that government policies to improve the welfare of rural people were being endangered by "subversives," who were particularly "infiltrating labor and student groups." "Let them not test wills," Marcos said, "because if I have to go back to 1972 [the year martial law was proclaimed], I'll go back to 1972" (*NYT*, 1 October).

A 1980 World Bank report noted the regime's growing reliance on the military and discounted the NPA. Unlike the Indochinese communist insurgents of the past, the NPA had "no immediately available nearby sanctuary or source of supply" nor a leader "of the stature of Ho Chi Minh" nor a capacity "of engaging the armed forces in full-scale land warfare." Moreover, most Filipinos apparently "remain staunch anti-Communists," although the report conceded that the NPA "could appear" as the government's main opposition "if things fall apart dramatically after Marcos." (*Asia Record*, December 1980.)

International Aspects. On 13 September, the Philippine Foreign Ministry, in the course of a fisheries conference held in Manila, warned against possible Soviet espionage activities in the Philippines and assistance to local communist (ideological leaning unspecified) rebels. The ministry said that it was possible that transport vessels of the Odessa Shipping Company of the USSR, which are allowed in Philippine waters for fishing purposes, could be in touch with local communist guerrillas through sophisticated electronic equipment. The Foreign Ministry also asserted that the Soviet ships were making soundings of Philippine waters that might facilitate Soviet communication networks and possibly endanger the movement of U.S. naval vessels. After the Soviet embassy sharply denied these allegations, other Philippine Foreign Ministry spokesmen said they had "disauthorized the report" of possible Soviet spying. (Far Eastern Broadcast Corporation, Manila, 14 September; AFP, Manila, 16 September; *FBIS*, 18 September.)

University of Bridgeport   Justus M. van der Kroef

Singapore

Singapore has no distinctive communist party of its own. The Communist Party of Malaya (CPM) and its front groups (see Malaysia) claim jurisdiction over communist activity in Singapore since the CPM continues to reject the legitimacy of the formation of Malaysia in 1963 and Singapore's secession from it as an independent republic in 1965. The ruling People's Action Party (PAP) government of Singapore, especially in the 1960s and early 1970s, regarded the Barisan Sosialis Malaya (Malayan Socialist Front), as communist infiltrated and/or a CPM front. The Barisan denied such allegations, but its program over the years has been notably congruent to that of the CPM. The Barisan is a legal party in Singapore, though severely circumscribed in its activity, and it has perhaps a cadre core of no more than fifty. All communist activity is prohibited under Singapore's internal security laws. In any case it is quickly rendered ineffective by the island republic's efficient police and intelligence services.

Domestic Developments. The PAP's complete control of Singapore's government and politics continued when it won all 75 parliamentary seats and 75.55 percent of the vote in general elections on 23 December 1980. Barisan Sosialis Chairman Lee Siew Choh charged that "the PAP never gives adequate campaigning time for the opposition." Dr. Lee, who lost a close contest against the PAP candidate in Boon Teck constituency, alleged that the electorate was afraid to vote for opposition candidates because the serial numbers of ballot papers enabled the government to trace the identity of voters. The government denied the charge. (*Asiaweek*, 9 January; *Asian Wall Street Weekly*, 8 December 1980; *Economist*, London, 20 December 1980.)

In his election platform, Lee Siew Choh stressed four major points. First, he noted the "lack of human rights" under the PAP regime and the "atmosphere of fear" and the "undemocratic" character of the Lee Kuan Yew government. Second, he alleged that the country suffered from inflation and a high cost of living under PAP policies, for example, rising taxes and utility rates. Third, there was an "overdependence on multinational corporations" at the expense of the Singaporean working force; foreign firms were given incentives such as low utility rates while "penal rates" were being set for "small domestic consumers." Finally, there was a need for closer cooperation with Malaysia "and eventually reunification" in the event "the peoples of the two sides come to understand" why such a merger would be desirable. According to the Barisan chairman, the PAP had done "a lot of damage" to Singaporean-Malaysian relations, and any reunification in future should not make Singapore subordinate to Malaysia but be for the "mutual benefit" of both. (*Straits Times*, 18 December 1980.)

The CPM's transmitter, Voice of the Malayan Revolution (VOMR), in a commentary entitled "General Election Without Freedom" accused the PAP of using general elections to spread "fear and uncertainty" among voters in order to stay in power and of not informing the opposition of the dates of elections until "the very last moment." Because the PAP government had raised the election deposit from $500 to $1,200, exclusive of other election expenses, a political party "would need an enormous sum of money" to contest all 75 electoral constituencies. Since only the ruling PAP seemed able to meet such costs, the opposition to the government was forced to field only a few candidates at each election. The misfortunes faced by Singapore today, according to VOMR, are the result of the PAP government's tying "Singapore's economy to the apron strings of the crisis-ridden capitalist countries." (VOMR, 4 December 1980; *FBIS*, 16 December 1980.) The VOMR did not endorse the Barisan or any other specific opposition party, however.

Despite the continuing appeal among Singapore's electorate of Premier Lee Kuan Yew's "don't rock the boat" political program, there is continuing evidence, as in past elections, of considerable disenchantment among growing numbers of younger, middle-class, and English language–educated voters. Lee Siew Choh conceded that it was precisely the younger, English–educated voter that his party is failing to attract and that the Barisan remains essentially a "Chinese-based" party. This, Lee conceded, did not bode well for the future of the Barisan because Singaporeans were becoming increasingly English-educated. (*Straits Times*, 18 December 1980.)

Accusations of political repression as a result of stringent domestic and foreign anticommunist policies have continued to surround the Lee Kuan Yew government. In June, three detainees, held without trial for more than ten years, were released. One was Lee Tze Tong, an active member of the Barisan Sosialis arrested in 1963, three weeks after his election to the Singaporean parliament. (*Asia Record*, July.)

A U.S. State Department report estimated that there were approximately 35 detainees being held by the Singaporean government at the close of 1980 under its Internal Security Act. The same report asserted that there was a "hardcore Communist cadre of several hundred," either in Singapore itself or in the adjacent Malayan state of Johore. Additionally, there were "several hundred more Communist sympathizers in Singapore." (*Country Reports on Human Rights Practices: Report Submitted to the Committee on Foreign Relations, U.S. Senate, and Committee on Foreign Affairs, U.S. House of Representatives,* Washington, D.C.: Government Printing Office, 2 February 1981, p. 693.) Given the unreliability of Malaysian and Singaporean security and intelligence services, these estimates may well be too large by half.

International Aspects. On 8 November 1980, Premier Lee Kuan Yew visited China for two weeks and had discussions with Premier Zhao Ziyang and other Chinese officials. Lee said that if China ceased supporting various communist organizations in Southeast Asia, Beijing's relations with the Association of Southeast Asian Nations would improve. Lee later remarked that he thought the Chinese were rethinking their traditional support for foreign communist parties. (*Asia Record*, December 1980.) Three months later, Singaporean Foreign Minister Suppiah Dhanabalan declared that "Chinese leaders have probably now come to the conclusion that it is not in their interest to continue supporting Communist groups in this part of the world" (*Asiaweek*, 13 February).

University of Bridgeport   Justus M. van der Kroef

Sri Lanka

Sri Lanka's leftists remain divided, but in 1981 gained representation in parliament for the first time in four years. Communist party membership is estimated at six thousand, with the pro-Soviet Sri Lanka Communist Party (SLCP) accounting for most of it. The country's estimated population is 14.7 million.

Leadership and Organization. Deputy President and SLCP moderate Pieter Keuneman was appointed president following the recent death of S. A. Wickremasinghe. The leadership issue may not yet be settled, however, since the party's moderate and militant factions are still at odds and there is no indication yet that the dominance of the hard-line faction has been affected.

Domestic Attitudes and Activities. The SLCP has returned to the legislature, the first leftist representation since the 1977 general elections. SLCP Political Bureau member Sarath Muttetuwegama won a January by-election. All the major opposition parties supported him, but the ruling United National Party (UNP) did not put up its own candidate. (*Far Eastern Economic Review*, 23 January.)

Although serious differences persist among the various leftist parties, there were instances of cooperation during the year, such as the by-election. In August, Colvin de Silva of the Trotskyist Lanka Sama Samaja Party (LSSP) said that there is growing recognition in the leftist camp of the pressing need to unite (ibid., 16 October). The LSSP has worked with pro-Chinese Communists (and with noncommunists).

The divisions, however, were apparent during the May Day rallies. The LSSP and Maoist Communist Party rallied with former Prime Minister Sirimavo Bandaranaike's Sri Lanka Freedom Party (SLFP) and the Tamil United Liberation Front. At its own meeting, the SLCP denounced the LSSP-SLFP association and called for a united left to oust the UNP. The militant Janatha Vimukthi Peramuna (JVP) in turn attacked the pro-Soviet party.

The leftists also took differing positions on the 4 June District Development Council elections intended to provide some local autonomy. The SLCP called the elections a farce that would not threaten UNP control (ibid., 10 April). The SLFP and LSSP also boycotted the poll, which resulted in UNP victories in three-fourths of the 24 councils. A much lower voter turnout than usual, however, may have indicated some popular unhappiness with the governing party. The Tamil Front won most of the remaining districts. Rohan Wijeweera's JVP obtained representation in a local authority for the first time by winning sixteen seats in 6 councils. (*FBIS*, 6 June.)

An area of continuing communist activity is among students. Here, too, the SLCP, the JVP, which has significant influence in the universities, and other leftist groups compete. In late 1980, SLCP Political Bureau member Leslie Gunawardena described his party's perspective and its efforts to gain influence in the student movement. He saw a steady polarization of forces, with left-wing student elements gaining the upper hand over right-wing groups. The left would become the dominant force if united, however; he pointed to nearly a score of left-wing organizations in Sri Lanka's higher schools. (*WMR*, November 1980.)

Gunawardena claimed the SLCP had strengthened its position among students during the previous couple of years, and party organizations, including both teachers and students, were operating in all higher schools. In its "struggle for the hearts and minds of the young generation," SLCP members participated in student debates, spreading party views; organized rallies and demonstrations; and supported the student movement's demand for democratization of education, including greater representation in decision making. (Ibid.)

One of the most significant political developments in Sri Lanka has been the bitter struggle that has split the Bandaranaike family and the SLFP, the only viable alternative to the UNP. Mrs. Bandaranaike's expulsion from parliament and disenfranchisement in October 1980 for misuse of power led to a dispute within the party over who would fill her seat. Even after a compromise was reached, the split worsened. Mrs. Bandaranaike, who remains SLFP president, was opposed by a group of thirteen dissidents, including her son and the party's deputy leader. By October, the dissidents had been suspended from the party, the rival groups were fighting over possession of party headquarters, and dual lists of officers had been announced. (*FBIS*, 4, 19, and 20 August; *Far Eastern Economic Review*, 4 September, 9 October.) The SLFP will remain weakened even if a reconciliation is achieved. In the absence of an SLFP democratic alternative to the UNP, the left, and perhaps the more radical elements in particular, would probably benefit.

International Views and Policies. The SLCP and LSSP mounted an active anti-U.S. campaign. The pro-Soviet SLCP berated the United States for opposing an international conference in Colombo to discuss an Indian Ocean zone of peace, which would thwart alleged American designs to dominate the region. In contrast, the party defended the Soviet military presence in the area as understandable and "peaceable" and supported Brezhnev's proposal concerning the Persian Gulf. The SLCP statement concluded by appealing for mass action by Indian Ocean nations and others to achieve a zone of peace. (*WMR*, July.)

Attacks on U.S. actions appeared frequently in SLCP and LSSP publications. *Aththa* and *Janadina* alleged that the United States planned to use the Sri Lankan port of Trincomalee for military purposes; *Aththa* also called for a public protest against American oil installations at the port. The Chinese foreign minister's visit during the summer was portrayed as an attempt to involve Sri Lanka in a Sino-American conspiracy in Asia. *Aththa* also criticized President Reagan's statement on protecting South Asia from a revolutionary threat. (*Aththa*, 3 June, 19 August, 7 and 17 October; *Janadina*, 21 August, 14 October.)

Publications. The SLCP publishes *Aththa*, *Mawbima*, *Deshabimani*, and *Forward*.

Earlysville, Virginia   Barbara Reid

Thailand

The Communist Party of Thailand (CPT) suffered further reverses in 1981, continuing the downward slide in the party's fortunes that began in 1979 when the CPT sided with China in criticizing Vietnam's invasion of Kampuchea and thereby lost its guerrilla sanctuaries, training camps, and supply routes in both Kampuchea and Laos (*Bangkok Post* [*BP*], 28 February). Moreover, China began to reduce its own support for CPT insurgents in order to obtain the Thai government's cooperation in allowing Chinese weaponry and other supplies to reach Pol Pot's guerrillas, who are fighting Vietnamese troops in portions of Kampuchea (*Far Eastern Economic Review* [*FEER*], 14 August). By 1980, China was urging the CPT to negotiate a truce with the Thai government and then collaborate with the latter in resisting possible Vietnamese aggression against Thailand. These developments had a demoralizing effect on CPT insurgents. When combined with a growing uneasiness among some lower-level cadres and nonparty members of the CPT's front organization, the Committee for Coordinating Patriotic Forces (CCPDF), regarding prospects for successfully conducting a purely rural-based insurgency in Thailand, the developments caused disarray within insurgent ranks and precipitated a sizable number of defections. Indeed, nearly 1,500 insurgents defected both in 1979 and in 1980, reducing the total number of insurgents to slightly under 10,000 by the end of 1980 from an all-time high of nearly 13,000 in 1978 (*BP*, 28 February; *FBIS*, 10 June).

During 1981 discord within the CPT and in the CCPDF grew, leading to additional defections and the withdrawal of Socialist Party support for the CPT (*FBIS*, 15 June). In the first six months of 1981, more than eight hundred insurgents defected (ibid., 4 August). Some were former peasants from the countryside, but most were intellectuals, former left-wing politicians, labor leaders, and student activists who had fled Bangkok and joined the CPT insurgency after the military coup of 1976. They included such prominent persons as Thirayuth Boonmee, a leading student organizer during the three years after the student revolt in 1973 that toppled the regime of Thanom Kittakachorn; Kriangkamon Laohaphairot, former secretary general of the National Students' Center of Thailand; Anut Aphaphirom, a former leftist writer; Yuthaphong Purisamban, a former radio announcer with the now closed CPT radio station—Voice of the People of Thailand; Sukanya Phattanaphaibun, a former reporter for *Athipat,* a defunct radical newspaper; Sathian Chanthimathon, a former left-wing writer and journalist; and Chamni Chakdiset and Sombon Suwannaphai, the first former secretary general and the second a former Central Committee member of the Socialist Party of Thailand. The vast majority defected from CPT jungle camps inside Thailand, but others returned from China, especially from Kunming, where about one hundred former activists had been based while helping operate the CPT radio station (ibid., 4 June).

Thai authorities break the returnees down into three categories. The first consists of those whose love for revolutionary practice has soured and who wish to be fully reintegrated into Thai society. The second encompasses those who became disillusioned with the authoritarian nature of the CPT, their failure to be admitted to positions of responsibility in the party, the Chinese (and more particularly the Maoist) orientation of top CPT leaders, and the insurgency strategy of the CPT. However, they remain committed to the idea that necessary changes in Thailand can be brought about only through revolution. The third category consists of those who find it impossible, or at least extremely difficult, to continue the armed struggle in the countryside at this time given the lack of external support, shortage of supplies, discord among the insurgents, and mounting pressure applied by government security forces. This group is still faithful to the CPT and its policies and probably would be willing to take up arms again if conditions become more propitious. (*Asiaweek,* 14 August.) In fact, Thai authorities suspect that many in this third group have hidden weapons in the forest until such time as they can resume their activities. Fragmentary evidence that may support this suspicion has been uncovered. For example, a CPT informer led government forces to a large cache of weapons hidden in the jungles of southern Thailand by insurgents before they surrendered. (*BP,* 4 July.)

In April 1981, the insurgents suffered another blow when Damri Ruangsuthan, a member of the seven-man CPT Politburo, was captured in Surat Thani province in southern Thailand while reportedly on a fact-finding mission that involved meeting with regional CPT leaders (*FBIS,* 12 June). He had joined the CPT in 1947, studied Marxism-Leninism in Beijing from 1954 to 1956, been named to the Central Committee of the CPT in 1961 and later to the Politburo, was based in Nan province of northern Thailand in 1964, and crossed the Thai-Lao border frequently in recent years while in charge of insurgency activities in Loei, Phitsanulok, and Petchabun provinces. He was last reported in Tak province in northern Thailand toward the end of 1980 (ibid., 20 May).

With the loss of supply routes through Kampuchea and Laos, the remaining insurgents in 1981 showed that they are becoming increasingly dependent on either capturing weapons from Thai police stations in rural and small semiurban areas on the fringes of the forest or on purchasing and storing weapons in the cities. In July, Thai authorities discovered and seized a large, secret arsenal of weapons (including claymore mines) in Bangkok, apparently intended for CPT insurgents in northen Thailand (ibid., 31 July).

China went a step further in 1981 in reducing its verbal support for CPT insurgents. Even after it had stopped providing weapons and other supplies and had closed down the CPT radio station in Kunming, China took the position that the Chinese Communist Party (CCP) would continue to back the CPT and the insurgency politically. However, in February 1981, Premier Zhao Ziyang of China visited Bangkok and in effect lessened such public backing by announcing that China would not allow relations between the CCP and the CPT to harm relations between the two countries (*NYT,* 2 February).

Furthermore, in 1981 China continued its earlier effort to get the CPT to reach an accommodation with the Thai government whereby the two would collaborate against Vietnamese expansionism (*FBIS,* 15 June). Accordingly, the CPT reportedly made further informal overtures to the Thai government (through intermediaries) proposing truce negotiations and an agreement to join in resisting the Vietnamese (ibid., 16 June). The first response of Thai authorities apparently was one of refusing to enter into official negotiations with the CPT since this would imply recognition of the latter. Subsequently these authorities agreed to talk with CPT representatives if the insurgents first laid down their arms (*FEER*, 14 August). It would appear that the informal exchanges of views continued sporadically during the first six months of 1981. These exchanges apparently ceased after Surachai Sae Dan, a former political activist and reputed insurgent leader in Surat Thani province, was captured in early July. Surachai claimed, and his claim initially was supported by the governor of Surat Thani, that he had come to the provincial seat to discuss possible measures to reduce fighting between government forces and CPT insurgents in the province. Security forces learned of his presence and arrested him. Later, the government officially denied that he had been a representative of the CPT. (*FBIS*, 2 July.) Whatever the truth, the CPT claimed that the government had acted in bad faith when it seized him.

Abortive Coup. An abortive coup attempt was made in early April by elements in the Thai Army. A group of so-called Young Turks (army colonels) persuaded Gen. Sant Chitpatima, deputy commander of the army, to head the coup effort. Troops seized control of Bangkok, but the prime minister, Gen. Prem Tinsulanond, escaped to the northeast where he began to organize resistance. When General Prem's troops moved on Bangkok, and after it was clear that other military units would not join the coup group, the attempt collapsed without serious fighting. The prime minister and royal family then returned to Bangkok, and parliamentary government was restored (*NYT*, 5 April; *FEER*, 19 June).

The suddenness of the coup effort and its equally sudden collapse took the CPT by surprise, preventing it from taking advantage of the temporary confusion and launching widespread attacks against government positions. One exception occurred in Wang Sam More district in Udon Thani province in the northeast, where a group of insurgents attacked and seized a rural police station while the policemen were listening to radio reports of the coup attempt (*BP*, 5 April).

Organization and Strategy. The CPT still was unable to hold its long-delayed Fourth Party Congress. In part this was due to difficulty in finding a secure site within Thailand as well as the reluctance of China to permit the congress to be held on its soil and thereby risk antagonizing the Thai government. Also it partly reflected disagreement within the CPT over ideology and strategy.

The top leaders of the CPT remained locked into a view of Thailand as a "semifeudal, semicolonial" society, while some lower-level CPT leaders and the few intellectuals who have remained in the CCPDF tentatively proposed a "semicapitalist, semifeudal dependency" as a more appropriate working definition. Moreover, top leaders continued to emphasize peasant mobilization and a corresponding military strategy of "jungle surrounds villages, villages surround cities." In contrast, some of the insurgents complained about the futility of trying to organize peasants by talking to them about landlord exploitation of the peasantry, particularly in those areas of Thailand where there is relatively little farm tenancy. Still others stressed the need to build a strong united front among sympathetic elements in the cities and then add a meaningful urban dimension to the insurgency. In the face of these differing views, an informal accommodation appears to have been reached. Some CPT provincial committees approved a "three-zone-strategy" under which the political-military focus is to be distributed more evenly among the cities, villages, and jungle. Among other things, this means placing new emphasis on underground work in the cities. Also, the strategic significance of the jungle is to be de-emphasized except as it serves as a purely military base for a hard-core regular force and as a site to train villagers as support personnel. These and other support personnel are encouraged to return to their home villages to aid regulars when required. (*Asiaweek*, 14 August.)

The Politburo apparently has not officially recognized this new strategy. Some observers suggested that the Politburo permitted these local variations with its official ideology and military strategy in order to pacify critics within the CPT and the remaining intellectuals in the CCPDF, but that it remains committed to emphasizing the countryside (*BP,* 28 February, 13 April). Whatever the case, it is evident that neither the Politburo nor the CPT committees have accepted the idea that revolutionary change is more likely to begin in Bangkok and radiate outward than vice versa—an argument made by some of the CCPDF defectors as well as by analysts in Bangkok (ibid., 10 August).

Defectors reported that a new communist party had been formed in Laos—the Pak Mai ("new party"). Apparently it leans toward the USSR and Vietnam. (*FBIS,* 17 August.) Very little is known about its activities thus far, or even whether it indeed has the status of a communist party. Nor is it clear if this organization differs from the Northeast Thai Liberation Movement reportedly established in Laos in 1979. It is believed that both organizations were formed by former Thai activists based in Laos who broke away from CCPDF.

Insurgency. Except for undertaking a few small-scale guerrilla strikes against government targets, CPT insurgents were placed on the defensive during 1981. They were badly hurt by the lack of adequate logistical support, the increasingly friendly posture of China toward the Thai government, massive defections, and internal discord. Moreover, the Thai government prosecuted its counterinsurgency campaign more vigorously and effectively than in past years. Government security forces were active in seizing and destroying a number of CPT jungle camps, some of which had served as provincial or even regional headquarters for insurgents. One CPT base area in the north, heretofore considered almost impregnable, was overrun by government forces after bitter fighting. Military operations against insurgents were conducted throughout the year rather than just during the dry season. (Ibid., 20 October.) The number of volunteers in the National Defense Volunteer Program grew considerably; there were 540,000 in the northeast alone. Greater priority was given to providing security for villagers, and a new strategy was devised of "homes encircling the forest" in which the government tried to involve the rural population in efforts to isolate the insurgents politically, economically, and militarily. At the same time, the government tried to win over as many of the insurgents as possible by asking them to surrender, be rehabilitated into Thai society, and then join in national development efforts. The government's extremely lenient treatment of most of those who have defected thus far was adduced as evidence of its good faith in this regard. (*BP,* 5 March, 24–26 June.)

The CPT suffered another major blow when Thai security forces overran an insurgent stronghold in the north and seized radio transmission equipment intended for a new radio station. This station would have had the capacity to beam broadcasts to all of Thailand and would have replaced the station in China closed in mid-1979. (*FBIS,* 4 and 11 August.)

Despite its problems, however, the CPT insurgency continues to pose a potential threat to Thailand. Most of the remaining insurgents are hard-core, experienced fighters who, while forced to reduce their operations, are unlikely to give up the armed struggle soon. One Thai observer noted that if they can hold on long enough and if either China or Vietnam resumes its support, the insurgents once again could seriously jeopardize Thailand's political stability (*BP,* 27 June).

The Northeast. For all practical purposes, CPT insurgents are no longer active in the section of Thailand adjacent to the Kampuchean border. One reason is the presence of a sizable number of Thai troops, stationed near the border in order to control the Kampuchean refugees and to protect against incursions by Vietnamese soldiers. Another reason is that the Chinese do not want the CPT to conduct insurgency activities in that area since these activities could disrupt the process by which Chinese supplies reach Pol Pot's guerrillas.

In other parts of the Northeast, an estimated 2,000–2,500 CPT insurgents remained active but at a reduced level. Fewer strikes were undertaken than in previous years, and most of these attacks were by small bands of guerrillas: small units seized a village defense post in Kalasin province, killing one policeman and four volunteers, burned down a rural police station and wounded five policemen in Udon Thani province, attacked government offices and killed three persons at a government-sponsored land settlement in Khon Koen province, and burned down a rural police station and seventeen houses in Nakhon Phanom province, as well as eight government buildings, including a district office and police headquarters, in Sakhon Nakhon province.

In late December 1980, government forces dealt a stunning blow to the insurgents when they seized the northeastern headquarters of the CPT and overran a chain of more than fifty smaller insurgent camps built around the headquarters. These headquarters, known as the Directorate of Petchaburi, were located on a mountain straddling Kalasin, Nakhon Phanom, and Sakhon Nakhon provinces. For eleven years, the headquarters had served as the main center for directing insurgency activities in sixteen provinces of the northeast (*FBIS*, 23 December 1980). During 1981, less dramatic but still impressive gains were made by government forces in the region. For instance, Thai forces captured ten CPT bases in Nakhon Phanom province during an intensive drive from 21 to 25 January (*BP*, 27 January), and government forces captured 36 CPT outposts in Khon Khaen province during a two-week period in March (*FBIS*, 22 March). Fifteen insurgents were killed and ten surrendered when government forces attacked and seized a stronghold on a small mountain in Loei province in February (*BP*, 17 February). The loss of camp facilities and regional headquarters as well as casualties suffered by the insurgents, plus the unusually large number of defections in the northeast, have seriously weakened the CPT insurgency in this area.

The North. Perhaps the largest number of armed CPT insurgents—some three to four thousand—are now found in the North. Yet they, too, have significantly scaled down their military activities. Most of their attacks in 1981 were against road construction crews, guards, and equipment, with the goal of preventing the construction of roads in remote areas where the insurgents are based. One example was the numerous attacks on crews building the strategic Huay Lak–Ban Phak Huak road in Nau province. Other guerrilla activities were more or less confined to small-scale attacks on isolated police posts or to punishing villages suspected of harboring informants.

The government launched several large-scale attacks on insurgent strongholds. The largest and most intensive military effort was directed against a major fortified stronghold located in the highlands of Petchahun province (*FEER*, 8 May). A government force of some two thousand troops and rangers supported by seventeen helicopters and a variety of aircraft attacked this CPT stronghold. The main target was a 50 sq. km. highland covered with corn and rice fields as well as forest lying between the Khao Kho and Khao Ya mountains. It was defended by three hundred regular insurgents and hundreds of armed insurgent militia. Most of the target was captured after bitter fighting that lasted from February through October. While most of the regular insurgents and many of the armed militia were either killed, captured, or escaped, about one hundred were still resisting as late as October. (*FBIS*, 25 February, 20 October.) Some two thousand CPT supporters were driven out of the target area or forced to surrender to government authorities (*BP*, 25 May).

The South. The CPT was estimated to have almost three thousand armed guerrillas in southern Thailand as of October 1981. Most were concentrated in five provinces: approximately one thousand were in Surat Thani, eight hundred in Nakorn Sri Thammarat, and another eight hundred in Pattalong-Trang-Satun (*FEER*, 9 October). Defections took a heavy toll, with the result that several guerrilla units were seriously under strength. The CPT's operational zone in Songkhla province was dissolved because more than half of the two hundred insurgents in that zone had surrendered to government authorities (ibid.). Also, insurgents resisted weakly if at all on the several occasions when government forces attacked insurgent camps in the forest (*FBIS,* 18 August). Moreover, insurgent attacks were carried out by small bands only and most of these attacks were against government property. There were a few small-scale attacks as well on government security forces and other personnel. At least some of the attacks, particularly those on property, were attributed by the insurgents as retribution for what they considered to be a breach of good faith on the part of the government when it seized Surachai Sae Dan.

Government forces seized several small CPT guerrilla groups during the year. They also overran, after considerable fighting, a CPT stronghold in Krabi province. The seizure of this stronghold forced many of the surviving insurgents to flee to Surat Thani and Chumpon provinces. (*BP,* 8 and 11 January.) Government forces also seized a major CPT stronghold in Surat Thani (ibid., 22 February). This camp had served as headquarters of one of the six CPT operational zones in the south, and its loss was a bitter blow to the insurgents. Later in the year, other attacks were launched against insurgent camps in Surat Thani; in parts of that province a curfew was imposed and strict control imposed over the sale of rice and medicine (ibid., 6 August). (See profile on Malaysia for a discussion of the activities in southern Thailand of guerrillas belonging to the Communist Party of Malaya.)

Northern Illinois University M. Ladd Thomas

Vietnam

For the people of the Socialist Republic of Vietnam (SRV) and the ruling Vietnamese Communist Party (VCP), 1980 passed uneventfully, but bleakly. Radio Hanoi began 1981 with a bluntly depressing evaluation of the year just past: "The year 1980 was a year of extreme difficulties. Vietnam was confronted by the possibility of war [with China] . . . Severe weather destroyed hundreds of thousands of hectares of rice . . . The economic sector was beset by poor management, cadre shortages, material shortages, and technical weaknesses . . . [We were] plagued by negative phenomena, such as embezzlement, black marketing, speculation . . . and counterrevolutionary activity." (VNA, 1 January.) There were no significant improvements during 1981, and the year ended much as it began. If there was good news to be found in this for the average Vietnamese, it was that life did not appreciably worsen in 1981.

Party Leadership and Organization. There was speculation early in the year that dramatic developments were imminent in the upper levels of the party, particularly in the Politburo. It was expected that these would come at the Fifth Party Congress, originally set for late 1980 but twice postponed and then rescheduled for spring 1982.

The SRV government underwent considerable institutional change during 1981. Major events included the unveiling of the long-delayed new constitution, communist Vietnam's third, National Assembly elections, and the promulgation of legislation establishing the new government.

The Third Constitution is said to resemble the Soviet model, much as the Second Constitution was said to emulate the Chinese way of government and the First Constitution to have drawn some of its philosophic underpinnings from the U.S. Constitution or at least the writings of Thomas Jefferson. In each instance, the parallel is somewhat forced.

To appreciate and interpret the meaning of the changes effected by the new constitution, it is necessary to understand the political process in Vietnam, that is, Sinic factionalism institutionalized in a state-party mechanism. For a graphic representation of this process—and the way policymaking and decision making are separated from political (and factional) infighting and government administration—visualize two pyramids, one inside the other. The outer pyramid is the state or government. It can be sliced thrice horizontally from top to bottom: national government (Hanoi, cabinet offices, the National Assembly); regional government (interzonal, zonal, provincial); and local government (city ward, village, and hamlet people's councils). Within this broad-based pyramid, rising from base to apex, is a thinner pyramid that is the party. At each level of government are found party elements that are both part of and separate from the respective government level. The party effects control, not puppet-like or through Olympian orders from the Politburo, but locally from the inside out. Political activity is managed, even staged, within the horizontal slices of the broader pyramid and is largely symbolic. Political activity within the party, chiefly in the form of factional infighting and entourage politics, does not exist officially.

The party reserves for itself two main functions—making basic policy and monitoring state activities and bureaucratic behavior to assure that policy is carried out as intended. In recent years the party has assumed additional state administrative tasks. This has immersed party cadres in routine bureaucratic activity, something the leadership does not like, but it often finds that either something is done by party cadres or it is not done at all. For a period in the late 1970s, the leadership tried to free party cadres from routine activity by pushing such work onto military officers and personnel, but they now are fully occupied in Kampuchea and along the China border.

Within this scheme of things, the National Assembly—working with the chief mass organization, the Fatherland Front—exists mainly to mobilize and harness political energies within the society. The process seeks to motivate and activate the population indirectly through a host of overlapping social movements. This task is more central and fundamental to the National Assembly than are such formal functions as approving legislation. The National Assembly is not directly involved either in debate over policy or in legislative activity that might improve governmental administration. This is one reason why the system does not work well. The new constitution seeks to change this, not by granting the National Assembly increased decision-making authority but by reorganizing both the assembly and the state. The Third Constitution creates a "collective" leadership in the form of a more powerful steering committee of the National Assembly, called a Council of State, which in effect is a mini- or semi-legislature permanently in session. This institutionalizes what has been the philosophic concept for the state since the death of Ho Chi Minh in 1979 and for the party since its founding in 1930.

The new National Assembly chairman is the longtime chairman of the now-defunct National Liberation Front (or Viet Cong), Nguyen Huu Tho, a man without significant power. Under him are nine vice-chairmen and seven standing committees. The National Assembly usually meets twice a year for a week each time. In the interim, affairs are in the hands of the newly formed Council of State, headed by Truong Chinh, age 76, chief ideologue (formerly something of a Maoist in his thinking), whose appointment appears to be a promotion, but also a choice designed not to upset the present power balance. The Council of State under Truong Chinh has four vice-chairmen, seven members, and a secretary general. Three of the thirteen are Politburo members (Truong Chinh, Le Thanh Nghi, and Gen. Chu Huy Man).

The National Assembly is the flywheel of a highly effective machine that mobilizes and energizes the population. Its major responsibility is to see that the system does not disintegrate. Improvement of its performance will largely determine the future continuity and stability of the regime. Dumped on Truong Chinh's aging shoulders is the unenviable task of reducing or at least keeping manageable the level of popular discontent.

The remainder of the new national-level state structure, announced on 4 July, consists of the Council of Ministers, a sort of super-cabinet ("the highest administrative organ of the state") headed by Prime Minister Pham Van Dong, age 75, with eight vice-chairmen and a secretary general. The vice-chairmen are To Huu, Pham Hung, Vo Nguyen Giap, Huynh Tan Phat, Vo Chi Cong, Do Muoi, Nguyen Lam, and Tran Quynh. The secretary general is Dang Thi. Parallel to the Council of Ministers is the all-powerful National Defense Council, supreme military authority in Hanoi, chaired by Truong Chinh with Vice-Chairman Pham Van Dong and three members: Pham Hung, Van Tien Dung, and To Huu. Also parallel to the Council of Ministers but with less political power are the Supreme People's Court, headed by Chief Justice Pham Hung (not to be confused with the Politburo's Pham Hung), and the Supreme People's Organ of Control, under Chief Procurator Tran Le. These two organizations head the judicial hierarchy. Finally, as a political gesture to ethnic minorities in Vietnam (about 5 percent of the population), there is the five-person Nationalities Council. Under the Council of Ministers are 26 cabinet officers and ministries and eight state commissions. These remain essentially unchanged from past years.

Within this state apparatus, there is a good deal of overlap of top-level personnel. For example, Minister of Defense Pham Hung holds three posts, and Gen. Van Tien Dung, Truong Chinh, To Huu, and Xuan Thuy hold two each.

Also, there is considerable permeation of the party in this state apparatus, the pyramid within a pyramid at work. All the dual posts noted above are held by Politburo members. The thirteen-man Council of State includes three Politburo and five Central Committee members. All five men on the National Defense Council are Politburo members; of the ten members of the Council of Ministers, only one is not a Politburo or Central Committee member. Of the 84 top positions, 58 percent are held by Politburo or Central Committee members. Not one of these powerholders is a woman.

When these changes in the state structure were under way early in the year, word filtered out of Hanoi that they were to be accompanied by major changes in the party structure, that there were to be retirements and replacements in the Politburo, with Gen. Vo Nguyen Giap and Prime Minister Pham Van Dong departing. Probably such changes—in what would amount to the start of the long-delayed generational transfer of power—had been the intent of the leadership. The stage for announcing these changes apparently was to be the Fifth Party Congress, originally set for February 1981, then postponed. Once again, it appears that the aging Politburo moved to begin reconstituting the highest level of party leadership, only to draw back, fearful of what would happen to the factional balance of power if this Pandora's box were opened. Thus, the leadership grew a year older—the average age of the Politburo is now 67, of the Central Committee about 64. The Politburo must soon take action to overhaul and invigorate the leadership.

Personnel changes in modest numbers did take place in the state and party during the year, but these were technical reshuffles or minor adjustments of power. Truong Chinh was considered to have solidified his political position, if not enhanced his status, as a result of the National Assembly restructuring. To Huu was judged to have strengthened his political position since he and Le Duan were coequals in the delegation that visited Moscow to discuss foreign aid with Soviet officials in September and he delivered the prestigious National Day address the same month.

At 61, To Huu is the Politburo's youngest member. In the factional division between the ideologues and the pragmatists, he is considered to belong with the former, allied with if not a protégé of Truong Chinh. In part this image may be because of his work, over the years, in agitprop activities and in training and retaining party cadres in the special party school system, not because he has particularly stressed doctrine in policy determination. His political constituency, to the extent that he has one, is found among younger (that is, 40- to 50-year-old) party cadres. To Huu has a gentry background, was well-educated (by the French in Hue), and is considered to be a poet of some power. He was not regarded as a heavyweight in Politburo politics in the past; rather, he had the reputation of a patient, nonshrill manager of the elite communication system. Indeed, this may be why his star is rising—an essential lack of offensiveness.

Actions to complete the creation of the new government continued throughout the remainder of the year. National Assembly elections on 26 April filled 538 seats, of which only 75 were contested. The new Seventh National Assembly met on 25 June, approved the slate of its new officials, promulgated the laws establishing the new government, and ordered elections from September through November to choose members for village- and ward-level peoples' councils. The delegates heard a distinctly optimistic address from Le Duan, who described the preceding five years as "a period of great successes" and put the best possible face on recent events. Among the successes he listed were "adding a glorious new page to the fatherland's epic heroic struggle," raising the Vietnamese revolution "to a new strategic posture," and improving Vietnam's ability to defend itself against the Chinese—accomplishments that seem more properly characterized as survival rather than success. Of the measures proposed by various speakers at the National Assembly session—increasing food production, generating more hard currency through stepped-up exports, additional capital construction in key economic sectors, and achieving better management of the economy—none was new, and all were short on specifics and long on moral exhortation.

Party activity during the year centered around anticorruption emulation campaigns, tightening of the ideological screws in the south, and pressing on with what has become a semipermanent purge of party undesirables. The mechanism for this housecleaning continues to be the issuance of new party cards. The Politburo issued strict orders to screen all party members carefully and weed out those who did not meet high criteria of performance and behavior, but these instructions frequently were sabotaged by lower-level officials who "tried to delay the issuance of party membership cards in order to avoid removing unqualified persons from the party. Meanwhile such an unhealthy phenomenon as refusing to issue party membership cards to good persons because of private motives, and such wrong and harmful practices as retaining in the party incapable or degenerate persons—including those holding leading positions—were also reported in certain localities." (Ibid., 12 May.)

Recruiting efforts continued in the ranks of the Ho Chi Minh Youth Union under Dan Quoc Bao, while the Ho Chi Minh Young Pioneers—a force of five million—observed its fortieth anniversary on 15 May.

On 14 July, the VCP Central Committee Secretariat issued a directive ordering basic-level elections in October to choose delegates for the Fifth Party Congress, indicating that the congress would be held in November or December. As of November, the Fifth Party Congress was scheduled for March 1982.

Domestic Activities and Attitudes. The socioeconomic malaise that has afflicted Vietnam in recent years continued during 1981, although the decline that gave rise to this malaise now appears to be somewhat less steep. This is a difficult matter to measure in any objective way since it involves two causal agents and the interaction of each on the other.

The first major source of Vietnam's malaise is economic hard times, or plain poverty, exacerbated by the demonstrated inability of the system to raise material living standards or even maintain present inadequate ones. By any economic index, Vietnam today is in worse economic shape than it was during the darkest days of the war. The worst aspect of this is on the farm and commune, important not only as the source of food but because 85 percent of all economic activity involves food production and food distribution. The grain shortfall this year will be at least 12 percent, possibly as high as 15 percent—this even to meet the 1,500 calories a day considered to be subsistence level. The crop this year is expected to be an improvement over the 15–20 percent shortfall of the past seven years, but even so, Vietnam cannot feed itself and has no prospect of doing so in the near future. Other economic activity was equally discouraging. Vietnam is on the socialist world dole and will remain there, for food, oil, fertilizer, raw materials, and, of course, weapons and military hardware.

During the year, Hanoi was subjected to punitive economic measures by outsiders, including the United States. Washington pressured the World Bank and the Asian Development Bank into canceling some $200 million in development loans, arguing that such aid indirectly funded the Vietnamese war in Kampuchea. France, Japan, Australia, and New Zealand all terminated plans for future aid projects, a loss of some $150 million. Sweden continued its assistance. The U.N. Development Program did grant the SRV $118 million in June, despite U.S. objections, to be used in the agricultural sector.

These losses were only the final installments of cuts that began in 1978 and, while discouraging, they could not have much meaning in economic terms since they simply are not of sufficient magnitude. The SRV needs about $11 billion a year to keep going—that is its national budget—half of which must go to the armed forces. This rock-bottom figure cannot be generated locally, and the deficit must be made up by the USSR.

Exactly how much money the USSR put into Vietnam during the year has been, unlike past years, a matter of considerable debate among Hanoi watchers. Previously they had generally agreed that the SRV's annual aid bill to Moscow was about $2 billion, divided evenly between military and economic spending. Estimates by various observers in 1981 produced a wider spread. The range in economic aid was fixed at $1 to $2 billion while the military aid estimate was even wider, from $250 million to $2 billion. Probably it is a safe estimate that the total for 1981 was about $2 billion, two-thirds economic and one-third military. Projections for 1982 are even more risky. There does, however, seem to be a trend of more economic aid and less military aid.

Some eighteen months ago, the party launched a new economic bootstraps effort, centered around Politburo Resolution Six and now commonly called the Resolution Six program. It sought to loosen economic controls and offer new economic incentives to farmers and food distributors of the economy. In the subsequent three harvests, rice production did increase somewhat—credit for which has been given to the Resolution Six program. There has also been greater efficiency demonstrated in the distribution sector. The Resolution Six campaign may eventually succeed in reversing the Vietnamese economic decline. The reading of most Hanoi watchers at the end of 1981, however, was that it is still too soon to tell how successful it will be.

In mid-1981, as part of the Resolution Six program, Hanoi launched another fiscal campaign against the exporting of gold, diamonds, hard currency, and other valuables. An estimated $1 billion has left the country illegally since 1975, most of it carried out by refugees. In a somewhat innovative move, the Vietnam State Bank began issuing "dollar script," a special paper currency resembling U.S. banknotes (which quickly came to be called "Vietnamese dollars") for use exclusively by foreigners in Vietnam. This amounted to a crackdown on the holding of foreign currency by Vietnamese, and since it was interpreted as meaning that in the future such currency would be harder to come by, the black market in U.S. dollars skyrocketed.

Vietnam indeed is poverty-ridden today, but blame for this—some, if not most—lies with the seventeen men of the Politburo. It is not malicious outsiders or vindictive foreigners but a failure in leadership that has driven Vietnam to its present economic plight. Most of the worst conditions—the drop in rice production, the decrease in per capita income, the ruin of the domestic trade sector, the decrease in industrial plant capacity (due to a shortage of raw materials), and the sharp reduction in transport capability (due to a lack of spare parts for trucks)—have developed since the end of the war and principally because of bad judgments by the Politburo. But these men seem unable to recognize any shortcoming on their part and remain content to blame others—China, the Association of Southeast Asian Nations (ASEAN), the United States. Obviously this economic condition can never be corrected as long as the Politburo's analysis of its cause is faulty.

The second major source of Vietnam's national malaise is sociological. It is a postwar ennui, a nearly universal national loss of spirit. Since 1976, when postwar plans were so confidently first unveiled, Vietnam has been pummeled by one catastrophe after another, mostly self-induced. Hopes and expectations have been constantly dashed. Leadership promises have gone unfulfilled. This has caused a steady erosion of public confidence in the state and party, as well as an erosion of self-confidence among party cadres and members.

Of the many manifestations of this, the foremost has been the extraordinary exodus of Vietnamese, overland and by boat, legally and illegally. To date some 600,000 have fled Vietnam, a third of them Chinese. The departure rate in 1981 averaged about 6,000 a month, peaking at 15,000 in May. The total for the year was expected to be about 75,000, down slightly from the 1980 figure of 76,000. There is no end in sight to the exodus.

Another manifestation has been the continued intolerance and harshness exhibited by Hanoi toward the south. Vengeance in 1975 was understandable if not excusable, but in 1981 it was not. At least 30,000 southerners continue to be held in re-education camps, some for the seventh year; the New Economic Zone is maintained even in uninhabitable areas; one "cultural purity" campaign follows another, ostensibly aimed against "decadence," but often directed at traditional indigenous southern culture. The Politburo still thinks of the south as the enemy and apparently can think of it in no other way.

Finally, the party's loss of moral authority and the state's loss of prestige destroy faith in the system's ability to improve things. From this follows a general indifference to the party-state effort. The psychological effect becomes circuitous. The more the economy declines and remedies fail, the more certain party cadres and the public are that no rectification is possible. To all this despair, the Politburo blandly replies that it is entirely the fault of China and the imperialists. The leadership can count itself fortunate that the malaise among the Vietnamese people manifests itself in lethargic resignation, not in some more volatile expression.

International Developments and Views. The dominant external concern for the Vietnamese leadership during the year remained the war in Kampuchea. The Vietnamese invasion, launched in late 1978, failed to meet its original timetable of six months to break the back of Pol Pot's Democratic Kampuchea (DK). Optimism persisted, however, until early this year when the realization finally settled in that Vietnam was in a long tunnel of protracted conflict in Kampuchea. Throughout the year, adjustments were made accordingly.

The Vietnamese face two tasks in Kampuchea—to end the military resistance, or pacify the country in their terminology; and to create a viable political and governmental entity out of the Heng Samrin regime, which also involves building an effective Khmer communist movement from scratch. The first of these is more easily accomplished than the second. Given sufficient time and effort, Hanoi may be able to reduce the level of guerrilla resistance to a tolerable level, but unless it is willing to make concessions to Khmer nationalism, it will never create a viable government out of the People's Republic of Kampuchea (PRK).

None of the three forces in the field in Kampuchea—the DK, the PRK, and the so-called third force—can prevail in the near future. Obviously what is required under such circumstances is some new governing structure acceptable to all three, and to interested outsiders. Until this is achieved—and prospects are dim—Kampuchea will continue to be the main destabilizing force in Southeast Asia.

Finding themselves on the defensive in Kampuchea in political terms, Vietnamese diplomats took to the offensive during the year. Especially within the region, they conducted a spirited campaign in the name of peace in Indochina. The tone was set at an Indochina foreign ministers' conference in Ho Chi Minh City in late January. Kampuchea, the foreign ministers declared, was the fault of China, although the ASEAN countries and the United States shared some of the blame; Vietnam stood for peace and stability, but constantly was being thwarted in its efforts to achieve this. The solution, they declared, was a tandem conference to negotiate a new arrangement; first would come a "regional" conference, meaning the Indochinese states of Vietnam, Laos, Kampuchea (the PRK) and the ASEAN countries, but not China (apparently not considered part of the region); then would come an "enlarged international conference" to put the world community's stamp of approval on whatever had been decided at the first conference. The statement was short on specifics. Hanoi did intimate, and continued to do so throughout the year, that with respect to ASEAN's chief concern—continued Vietnamese military occupation of Kampuchea—it would be willing to withdraw at least some troops from Kampuchea if Thailand first ceased giving sanctuary to Khmer guerrillas, a proposal tantamount to suggesting that Thailand and Vietnam join forces in war against the Khmer insurgents. Vietnam is bogged down in Kampuchea and apparently would like to extricate itself, but under conditions that would permit continued major influence over Phnom Phenh's decisions.

During the year, in tacit acknowledgment of the stalemate, the leaders of the People's Army of Vietnam (PAVN) sought to reduce the strain of war by redeploying their troops in Kampuchea (estimated at 200,000) into less aggressive, more tenable positions. Apparently they also ordered shifts in Laos; PAVN strength in Laos is estimated by Americans to be about 20,000 (the Lao Army numbers 30,000), but the Chinese insist it is closer to 60,000. There are some six thousand Vietnamese civilian "advisers" in Lao governmental offices.

The general characteristic of Vietnamese operations in Kampuchea during 1981 was military operations designed to cut losses and reduce the strain of the war on Vietnam. There were more road patrols and fewer military sweeps into the risky Cardamom Mountains, more static guarding of towns and less guerrilla bashing. Emphasis was on keeping open the major lines of communication, and the remote backwater areas were ignored. The campaign in Kampuchea deliberately was drawn out in time.

Basic deployment of forces at year's end consisted of six PAVN divisions (the 4th, 57th, 72d, 75th, 339th, and 431st); two Marine units (the 950th Brigade and the 126th Corps); and a headquarters unit (called the 479th Front HQ). With the exception of the headquarters unit at Siem Reap and the 339th Division guarding Phnom Penh, all of these units were deployed no further than 50 kilometers from the Thai border and Gulf of Siam. Most of the strength was concentrated in the northwestern part of Kampuchea, with marine units stationed in the south chiefly to protect Kompong Som and the southern waterways. Meanwhile, guerrilla activity was reportedly ubiquitous, common even east of the Mekong, consisting of raids designed chiefly to advertise the cause rather than to have military meaning. Although it was clear that the PAVN in the near future would not destroy the coherence of the insurgent movement, no serious observer believed that in the same period, the insurgents could prevail or even force some sort of major change of war policy. If there was such a change—for instance, partial Vietnamese disengagement or negotiations to establish some new coalition government arrangement—it would be because of developments in Hanoi, not because of guerrilla activity in Kampuchea.

Vietnam's other external affairs, to the extent that they existed, continued to be dominated by the USSR during 1981, a dominance born of Vietnamese dependence on Moscow for food, oil, and weaponry. The linking of Moscow and Hanoi, in geopolitical terms, has now become a military alliance in all but name. It is both cause and effect of the cold war between Vietnam and China and will last at least as long as the dependence continues. To date, the USSR has been fairly restrained in taking advantage of Vietnamese dependency. In military terms, it is using Vietnam as a surveillance base headquarters and as port of call for the Soviet Navy.

There was much Vietnamese-Soviet public intimacy during the year. Le Duan led a party delegation to Moscow in March for the Soviet party congress and, with To Huu as cochairman, returned with a delegation in September. In June and July, the SRV and the USSR signed a series of economic and trade agreements that had the net effect of integrating the Vietnamese economy further into the socialist world system. Specifically, four agreements were signed: the SRV-USSR Economic, Scientific, and Technical Cooperation Agreement, for economic aid (24 July); the SRV-USSR 1981–1985 Trade Agreement (30 July); Agreement to Coordinate National Economic Planning, 1981–1985 (9 July); and the Joint SRV-USSR Continental Shelf Oil-Gas Exploration and Exploitation Enterprise Agreement (19 June). The first two of these supplemented aid and trade agreements signed in November 1978.

The new agreements closely integrate Vietnamese and Soviet economic planning. They call for completion of 100 current Soviet aid projects and for the launching of 40 new ones. Although short of food, Vietnam agreed to increase its shipments of fruit and vegetables to Soviet Asia. The September talks in Moscow, involving Leonid Brezhnev at one point, appear to have dealt chiefly with aid and economic matters since SRV State Planning Commission Vice-Chairman Dau Ngoc Xuan played a prominent part. At the time, there were rumors in Moscow that the USSR was pressing Vietnam to take a more conciliatory position on Kampuchea, such as a token withdrawal of PAVN troops. Le Duan's public statements during the visit skirted the issue, taking note of virtually every topic except a Kampuchean settlement.

The Hanoi foreign relations event of the year—at least its media event—was the U.N. Conference on Kampuchea in New York on 13–18 July, attended by 93 nations (79 delegates, 14 observers), but not by the SRV or the USSR. As expected, the conference accomplished nothing concrete. On balance, it was something of a diplomatic coup for China and, to some extent, the ASEAN nations. If it did not enhance DK prestige, it solidified its international position (although U.S. Secretary of State Alexander Haig walked out when the DK representative rose to speak).

Before the conference was a response to the Vietnamese proposal on Kampuchea, largely drafted by the ASEAN nations. It called for disarmament of all warring factions in Kampuchea, the simultaneous withdrawal of all Vietnamese military forces, and the establishment of a temporary governing arrangement with the eventual formation of a new government through free and supervised elections. This was not acceptable to the Chinese, who wanted the Vietnamese troop withdrawal to precede all other changes. Their position was fairly candid. It amounted to the argument that bloody-handed as he was, Pol Pot represented the most effective opposition to the Vietnamese now in the field, and nothing must be done to diminish the pressure he could put on the PAVN. The counter-argument was that Pol Pot and the DK were an anathema and that it was both a moral and strategic error to associate with such butchers. Morality versus realism in foreign affairs collided head on in New York, and morality lost. In any event, the conference had no significant effect on the war in Kampuchea.

In other foreign affairs during the year, Hanoi unrelentingly continued its cold-war confrontation with China. There were repeated border incidents during the year, some with casualties, according to the Vietnamese. Verbal assaults continued. As part of its campaign, Hanoi pressed Beijing to reopen the bilateral talks broken off in 1979 (originally opened following the border war of February–March 1978). A formal note to this effect went to China on 13 June and was rejected. The Hanoi press periodically carried reports on Chinese border incursions and other provocations, portraying Vietnam as patient and long suffering, the Chinese as totally unreasonable.

Vietnam continued its on-again, off-again campaign of diplomatic maneuvers against the ASEAN countries, wooing some, threatening some, and attempting to divide them. The war of nerves against

Thailand continued, but at a lower level of intensity. In all of this activity there was much motion, but little movement.

In what was intended to be a friendly gesture to the United States, Hanoi returned three bodies said to be Americans who had died in communist territory during the Vietnam war, but which proved on examination at the U.S. Army's laboratory in Honolulu to be Asians—apparently an unintended mix-up in Hanoi. There were certain other tentative gestures and indications during the year that indicated the two sides might at least be moving towards a new round of discussions, but little beyond that seemed likely. In a 24 June interview with Agence France Presse, Foreign Minister Nguyen Co Thach said, "We are still prepared to normalize our relations with the United States. This is in the interest of our two nations." He added that there was no indication this would take place in the near future, the same judgment arrived at in Washington. General press treatment of the new Reagan administration was restrained and only mildly hostile during the year. Typical was the comment of the PAVN newspaper, *Quan Doi Chan Dan*, that "Reagan is hardly better than Carter" (30 December 1980).

On balance, 1981 brought no changes in Vietnamese foreign relations; Vietnam is still isolated and virtually friendless. Within the region, there is no one it can trust or depend on. Even within the socialist world, only Cuba seems genuinely friendly. The USSR increasingly exhibits indications that it has come to regard Vietnam as another cross it must bear, along with Poland and Afghanistan.

Publications. No new periodicals were begun during the year. For a list of current periodicals, see *YICA*, 1978, p. 330.

University of California at Berkeley   Douglas Pike

WESTERN EUROPE

Introduction

The most significant development in Western Europe during the year was the election of French Socialist François Mitterrand as president of France and the inclusion of four communist ministers in his cabinet. In Western Europe as a whole, two general themes characterized communist party domestic and foreign policy positions during 1981: unity among leftist parties and support for the "peace movement."

For the past several years, communist party activities have emphasized the importance of these two goals. Their endorsement as laudatory political objectives has allowed Western Europe's communist parties to assert the existence of "unity" among communist and other leftist organizations that oppose "capitalism," nuclear power, the "arms race," multinational corporations, the Common Market, and NATO, and leftist unanimity regarding democratic government, disarmament, and world peace. As a result, support of these views found expression throughout the year in the domestic and foreign policy positions of Western Europe's communist parties.

Public concern in Europe was directed toward international crises in, for example, Poland, Afghanistan, and Iran, as well as toward the efforts of the new U.S. government to strengthen the defense capability of NATO. In this latter area, the last three months of the year saw major demonstrations in a number of West European cities in support of nuclear disarmament and a reduction of conventional weapons and forces stationed in Europe. While generally peaceful, the demonstrations had thousands of participants and received virtually unanimous support from the communist parties of Western Europe. At the end of the year, it seemed clear that the emphasis placed on these demonstrations would continue during 1982 and that the "peace movement" would seek to unify as many Western Europeans as possible to oppose increased defense expenditures for NATO forces, whose conventional and nuclear capabilities were far inferior to those of the Soviet Union.

While emphasis on the peace movement illustrated the ability of the left to mobilize in support of an admirable goal, the results achieved by those communist parties participating in national elections illustrated their relative weakness as viable political forces at the polls. Poor electoral performance also illustrated a gradual change in Western European politics: namely, increasing support for socialist parties in Europe. Thus, world attention during the year focused less on the activities of individual communist parties and to a much greater degree on the electoral gains of Western Europe's socialist parties.

With the certainty of presidential elections in France and the possibility of legislative elections, 1981 was of crucial significance not only for the left in general, but for the French Communist Party (PCF) in particular. The triumph of the left, with the election of François Mitterrand as the new French president and with the decisive victory of French Socialists in the ensuing legislative elections, clearly established the dominance of the Socialist Party (PS) as the most powerful political party in the country. The setback of the PCF in both elections signaled a fundamental and significant loss of PCF prestige, if not influence—particularly because every aspect of PCF activity had focused on the elections.

In the legislative elections, the PS won an absolute majority of 269 seats in the 491-seat National Assembly. The PCF, in its most serious defeat since 1945, won 16.17 percent of the vote and 44 seats, compared with 20.55 percent and 86 seats in the previous elections of March 1978. The PCF was given four ministerial posts in President Mitterrand's new government: Transport, Civil Service, Administrative Reform, and Professional Training. While all four positions have a significant bearing on the development of domestic policy, these appointments were made in conjunction with an agreement between the PS and PCF on 23 June that pledged the "entire solidarity" of the PCF at all levels of government.

It is unlikely, however, that the PCF will become a docile party. On the contrary, the PCF remains strong at the local government level and effectively controls the most powerful labor union in France, the Confédération générale du travail. In addition, France is the most powerful West European country to include communist ministers in its government, a development that could serve as a precedent for Italy and Spain. Indeed, the Soviet press endorsed it as "an historic event for France and all Western Europe" (*Guardian*, 5 July).

Despite the electoral defeat of the PCF, this conclusion is not insignificant. As French political analyst Jean-François Revel observed in the autumn: "That the Communists had become weak, yet were responsible for the victory of the Left, seems a paradox. In reality, it is not . . . The rejection of the Left had been based on the rejection of Communism; from the moment Communism appeared weak, there was no longer any reason to reject the Left." What this development meant, Revel concluded, was that "Marxism has won" and that government by ideology has returned to France: "In all . . . party documents and in Mitterrand's own books one finds the same basic theme: the evil is capitalism, private enterprise, the marketplace; the remedy is collective appropriation of the means of production, nationalization, and the suppression of profit." (*Public Opinion*, August/September, pp. 2–4.)

One can predict that 1982 will undoubtedly see a PCF effort to exercise a greater voice in French politics. Although French voters made a clear distinction between the PCF and the PS in the national elections, it is uncertain what differences will divide and unite the two parties as the new year develops and to what extent they will receive popular support.

Of equal significance will be the effect of the French elections on the future of communist party strength elsewhere in Western Europe. In 1981, 14 of Western Europe's 24 parties were represented in their respective parliaments. These countries were Belgium, Cyprus, Finland, France, Greece, Iceland, Italy, Luxembourg, Netherlands, Portugal, San Marino, Spain, Sweden, and Switzerland (the communist party is not represented in the legislatures of Austria, Denmark, Faroe Islands, Federal Republic of Germany, West Berlin, Great Britain, Ireland, Malta, Norway, and Turkey). Party members hold three cabinet posts in both Finland and Iceland. In San Marino the communist party holds four of ten cabinet posts (Interior and Justice, Social Security and Health, Industry and Trade, Education and Culture).

National elections were held during the year in nine West European countries (two were held in 1980). With the exception of France, no significant communist party electoral victories or defeats were registered. Communist party representation continued to be largest in Italy, where the party holds slightly less than one-third of the parliamentary seats (201 of 630). Of the parties with parliamentary representation, Cyprus had the highest percentage of seats (34.3 percent), followed by Italy (31.9 percent), San Marino (26.7 percent), Iceland (18.3 percent), Finland (17.5 percent), and Portugal (16.4 percent). The remaining parties held between 0.94 percent (Belgium) and 8.96 percent (France) of their respective parliamentary seats.

The parliamentary strength of the communist movement in Europe did not play a decisive role during the year. The victory of the PS in France clearly detracted from attention that might otherwise have been devoted to communist party activities on the continent. The recovery of the communist movement during 1982 is questionable. It is clear, however, that much attention will be devoted to the ability of the PCF to influence French politics in 1982, as well as to the role the communist parties of Western Europe will play in the developing peace movement.

The only country in Western Europe in which the communist party is the largest left-wing party is Italy, and thus political observers will look to Italy for "the possibly infectious consequences of the French Communists' entry into government" (*Economist*, 4 July). Whether such consequences will be discernible is uncertain. The PCI continues to struggle with the dilemma of a large parliamentary representation and an inability to exercise a readily apparent and positive impact on Italian politics.

During the year, the Italian Communist Party (PCI) devoted considerable attention to criticism of the Italian government and to efforts to form, with Italy's Socialist Party (PSI), an alliance described as the "democratic alternative." Possibly reflecting the position of other socialist parties in Western Europe, the PSI was unreceptive to such proposals. As the year ended, the two parties were no closer to an alliance than they had been in January; PCI statements, however, indicated that it would continue efforts to form a coalition in 1982.

The PCI, together with the Spanish Communist Party, took the leading role in the Eurocommunist movement during the 1970s. In 1980 and 1981, the PCI continued to advocate independence from the Soviet Union as well as the prerogative of criticizing Soviet policy openly. It was joined in this position by many of Western Europe's smaller communist parties, in addition to that of Spain. In a number of Western European countries this has resulted in the decision of "hardline pro-Soviet elements to split off and form rival factions to the established party." (ibid.).

The PCI's position vis-à-vis the policies of the Soviet government continued to reflect the deterioration of its relationship with the Communist Party of the Soviet Union, which was very close at one time. The PCI was openly critical of the Soviet invasion of Afghanistan, expressed support for dissident movements in communist countries, advocated a policy of rapprochement with China, and emphasized the leading role it played in the creation of Eurocommunism. On repeated occasions, the PCI warned that an invasion of Poland "would have disastrous effects not only for that country but for the very idea of socialism" (*L'Unità*, 10 December 1980). This elicited the Soviet response that the PCI had made "concentrated attacks against the foundations of socialism in Poland" (ANSA, 18 February). On the subject of Western Europe's defense, PCI General Secretary Enrico Berlinguer supported Italy's membership in NATO, but opposed the entry of Spain, which he believed would represent a "unilateral" alteration of the balance of power in Europe. The party also supported arms limitation negotiations and urged the Soviet government to restore the military balance in Europe by reducing deployment of its SS-20 missiles.

The Communist Party of Spain (PCE), legalized in 1977, emerged as a major advocate of Eurocommunism between 1977 and 1981, emphasizing its independence from Moscow and respect for parliamentary democracy. As in Italy, the secretary general of the PCE, Santiago Carrillo, was unsuccessful in forming a political alliance with Spain's Socialist Workers' Party (PSOE). Within his own party, Carrillo continued to be opposed by "hard-core Stalinists" for his strong "anti-Soviet" position. Dissension within the PCE became publicly apparent at the party's Tenth Congress in July. Carrillo was re-elected secretary general, but a group, comprising 26 percent of the delegates and called "Eurocommunists for Renewal," unsuccessfully sought to limit his responsibilities and subordinate his position to a "collegial secretariat." As a consequence, and in an effort to consolidate party leadership, the Central Committee was reduced in size from 160 to 104 members, the majority of whom strongly support Carrillo's leadership.

National elections are not scheduled in Spain until 1983. Therefore, the new year is likely to see a continuation of the party's efforts to create some form of political alliance with the PSOE. There is, however, every indication that Carrillo will have to place his first priority on maintaining the strength of his own leadership within the PCE in an effort to end the divisive intraparty strife that continued throughout 1981.

For the past two years, the views and positions of the communist parties of France, Italy, and Spain have warranted careful analysis, for the dynamics of change within Western Europe's communist movement have been located primarily within these three parties. During 1982 these parties will almost certainly continue to provide the strongest voices of communism in Western Europe. This is not to say that the activities of the remaining parties do not demand careful analysis, but their significance during the coming year is difficult to estimate.

This conclusion continues to apply to Portugal. The Portuguese Communist Party (PCP) received 16.7 percent of the vote in the 1980 national elections and holds 41 of the 250 parliamentary seats. Party Secretary General Alvaro Cunhal is strongly in control of the PCP, which is pro-Soviet in orientation. As in other Western European countries, the PCP sought to maintain "unity of the left" and urged new parliamentary elections in 1981 in an effort to "prove" that the "reactionary" government did not represent the popular will.

The major dilemma facing the PCP is its strong pro-Soviet position at a time when Soviet advocacy of the peace movement contrasted with Soviet occupation of Afghanistan and the threat to Poland presents a glaring contradiction, which is reflected in declining support for the party among the Portuguese. New elections were not held during the year, and Cunhal repeatedly found the PCP in direct opposition to the Portuguese Socialist Party, which sought to establish a clear distinction between the two parties. At the end of the year, the PCP was developing plans for its Tenth Party Congress, which will be devoted to an analysis of the changes in the country's political life since 1974.

In Cyprus, Greece, Turkey, and Malta, communist party activities did not exert significant influence on political life. In Turkey the party remains proscribed, and in Malta the party, founded in 1969, exercises little impact. The Cypriot party (AKEL) receives its major support from the Greek majority, which constitutes about 80 percent of the island's estimated 657,000 population. Among nonruling communist parties, the proportion of party members to national adult population probably ranks AKEL second only to its Italian counterpart. Despite its overall size, AKEL has played a minimal role in the politics of Cyprus. In the May 1981 Greek Cypriot elections, AKEL made its strongest showing in history, however, by winning the largest number of votes of any party (32.78 percent) and 12 of the 35 seats in the House of Representatives. A national election for president of the republic is scheduled for 1983, but whether AKEL will be able to claim a leading role in Cypriot politics during 1982 is doubtful based on its performance thus far and on the complexities of the Cyprus question as a whole.

In Greece the party remains split into pro-Soviet and Eurocommunist factions. In the October 1981 parliamentary elections, the pro-Soviet Communist Party of Greece (KKE) emerged as the third largest party, but the Eurocommunist faction failed to elect a single candidate to the Greek legislature. The KKE received 10.92 percent of the vote and 13 seats in the 300-seat legislature. The major beneficiary of the leftist, anti-American shift since the end of the military government in 1974 has been the Panhellenic Socialist Movement (PASOK). Led by Andreas Papandreou, the Marxist-oriented PASOK received 48.06 percent of the vote, electing 172 deputies to the Greek legislature and forming the first socialist government in Greek history. PASOK is likely to advocate Greek withdrawal from the integrated NATO command as well as to propose a referendum on Greece's membership in the European Economic Community, both of which the country joined on 1 January 1981. These positions illustrate two issues on which the KKE and PASOK basically agree. Because PASOK does not require a legislative alliance with the KKE, however, the party will encounter difficulty in asserting independent views and positions during 1982.

In Great Britain and Ireland, the Communist parties have not played an important role in electoral politics in many years. The Communist Party of Great Britain (CPGB) has not been represented in the House of Commons since 1950, although one member, Lord Milford, is a member of the House of Lords. The most significant forum for party activities is provided by trade union organizations. Two party members serve on the 38-member General Council of the Trade Union Congress, and numerous contacts exist with members of the British Labour Party. The CPGB does not, however, enjoy a broad base of support among the British populace. As a consequence, party General Secretary Gordon McLennan stressed during the year the need to maintain and further develop the party's influence within the labor movement and to increase "the struggle for peace and disarmament." This effort is, however, unlikely to be any more successful in the future than in the past. Indeed, the CPGB will most certainly suffer a loss of support as a consequence of the creation of a new party during 1981, the Social Democratic Party of Great Britain.

Within the parties of Belgium, Denmark, the Netherlands, and Luxembourg, no new developments of major significance were recorded. In Belgium the party lost two of its four seats in national elections in November, and in national elections held in the Netherlands the party was able to increase its parliamentary representation from two to three seats. No elections were held in Luxembourg, and in the Danish elections, held on 8 December, the communist party failed to win representation. In the Nordic countries of Iceland, Norway, Sweden, and Finland, no significant developments were registered. In Norway the Marxist left continues to be divided into three competing factions; as a result communist influence on Norwegian politics is minor. The September 1981 national elections, however, produced the first conservative government to rule Norway in more than half a century.

In Iceland, on the contrary, the party holds 11 of 60 parliamentary seats and participates in the three-party coalition governing the country. The ministerial posts of Finance, Industry, and Social Affairs are held by communist party members. In Finland the communist-dominated Finnish People's Democratic League (SKDL) received 17.9 percent of the vote in the most recent national elections (March 1979) and holds 35 of 200 parliamentary seats. Factional strife has characterized the Finnish party throughout its history and nearly split the party in 1981. The party served in the four-party coalition governing Finland throughout the year, and party members held three cabinet posts (Labor, Education, and Transportation and Communications). National elections are scheduled for January 1982.

In Sweden, the communist party (VPK) concentrated its efforts on criticism of a wide range of government policies, including opposition to nuclear power and "capitalist" economic policies, and strong support for the peace movement and disarmament, advocating a reduction in existing Swedish military capability, an increase in civil defense expenditures, and creation of a "nuclear free zone" for Scandinavia. In 1982 the Swedish parliament is scheduled to approve the country's defense policy for the current decade, and the VPK is consequently urging adoption of a program that would eventually eliminate Sweden's defense system. At the party's Twenty-sixth Congress, held in November, it was noted that it had failed "to become a mass party." The VPK stressed the importance of new efforts to recruit party members and increase the party's popularity (an October 1981 poll indicated that the VPK was supported by only 4 percent of the populace). Party activities in 1982 will focus on preparations for the national elections scheduled for September. The VPK's popularity, however, will be difficult to increase, especially in view of an unprecedented violation of Swedish territorial waters in October when a Soviet submarine, apparently carrying nuclear weapons, ran aground close to the Karlskrona naval base in southeastern Sweden.

The influence of the communist parties of Austria and Switzerland has continued to diminish following defeats suffered by both parties in national elections held in 1979 (neither party gained more than 1.5 percent of the vote). The communist party of West Berlin (SEW) did not experience any significant leadership or organizational changes at its Sixth Congress in May. The SEW is not represented in the city's parliament and received only 0.7 percent of the vote cast in May municipal elections (compared with 1.1 percent in 1979). For all practical purposes, the SEW is a mirror image of and completely dependent on the East German Party and competes for support with a number of leftist groups in West Berlin.

No national elections were held in the Federal Republic of Germany during the year. The German Communist Party (DKP) elected 12 new members to its 92-member Executive Committee at its Sixth Congress in May, but recorded no significant changes in leadership. During the year the party's major focus of attention was directed to mobilizing support for the "peace movement" (*Friedensbewegung*), which resulted in a demonstration in Bonn on 10 October by an estimated 250,000 persons. Consistent with this emphasis, the party congress was described as the "anti-nuclear-missile congress." It was attended by 57 delegations from fraternal parties and "anti-imperialist" liberation movements. Party Chairman Herbert Mies stressed at the congress that "the peace movement . . . is at present a movement of a new dimension, a movement of many forces, a movement with immense effect. This is the result of the activities of all forces that have been engaged for a long time in peace committees and peace organizations; this is a result of the activities of us Communists." (*Deutscher Informationsdienst*, 30 June.) This effort to achieve "unity of action" among Social Democrats, Free Democrats, secular and religious pacifists, trade unionists, and members of the DKP was unusually successful and presaged a dramatic increase in attention devoted to the peace movement during 1982.

Hoover Institution   Dennis L. Bark

Austria

The Communist Party of Austria (Kommunistische Partei Österreichs; KPO), founded on 3 November 1918, has been a legal party throughout Austria's history as a liberal democracy (until 1933 and since 1945). Before 1933, the party was held to insignificant strength by the Austro-Marxism of Otto Bauer's left wing of the Social Democratic Party. In 1945, the party leadership (under Johann Koplenig) returned from the Soviet Union and entered the antifascist concentration government of Karl Renner as an equal partner, assuming such portfolios as interior and education. The KPO's taste of power came to a sudden end when, after agreeing to free elections before the end of 1945, it found itself with 5 percent of the vote (only marginally higher in the Soviet zone of occupation). The extreme unpopularity of the Soviet occupation of northeastern Austria (till 1955) helped keep the party insignificant. Soviet action against the Hungarian uprising of 1956 depressed the KPO's vote share from 5 to 3 percent and ended its parliamentary representation. Since the invasion of Czechoslovakia in 1968, the KPO's vote share has hovered around the 1 percent mark.

The party has about 25,000 members. Except for a brief ideological split after Czechoslovakia, it has been united in its strict and unimaginative adherence to Moscow's line. Despite its weakness, the KPO maintains a clear primacy among Austrian communist groups.

The year under review shows a glaring contrast between words and achievement. The address of

Party Chairman Franz Muhri at the Twenty-Fourth Party Congress (6–8 December 1980) had more than the usual share of criticism of Austria's internal politics under Bruno Kreisky's Socialist government, and it formed the framework for discussion during 1981 of a new party program. On the other hand, the party's electoral performance was extremely weak. It was unable to draw any benefit from the first serious crack in Austria's unprecedented postwar prosperity. Despite the weakness of the nationalized steel industry, especially the part located in the province of Styria, the KPO lost votes in both the Styrian and the steel industry elections in 1981.

The election to the Styrian provincial diet on 4 October was Austria's only public election in 1981. The KPO, which garnered 9,876 votes (1.3 percent) in 1978, gained exactly 21 votes (*Arbeiter-Zeitung*, 5 October). Later in October, this poor showing was duplicated in elections of shop stewards in Austria's steel industry.

The VEW, Austria's most troubled steelworks, held shop steward elections in all of its five plants. The KPO elected two shop stewards, a loss of four, and its share of the vote declined from 6.6 to 3 percent. In Austria's largest steelworks, VOEST, the number of KPO shop stewards declined from twenty to seventeen, and the KPO's vote share was reduced from 10.7 to 9 percent. (Ibid., 7 and 9 October.)

The only other significant election during the year was the spring election of representatives of university students. The Communist Student Union (KSV) obtained 3.8 percent of the vote nationwide and 3.6 percent at the University of Vienna. The Trotskyist Revolutionary Marxist Group, with 3 percent of the overall vote, had 4.3 percent of the vote in Vienna. Although this gave both groups a handful of seats, the KSV, as the only list in the Vienna faculty elections, failed to obtain a single seat on faculty committees. (*uni aktuell*, Vienna, n.d.)

On 4 July, the *Economist* (London) published an article entitled "Where Red Could Also Follow Pink." The article, quite appropriately, did not mention the Austrian Communists. Austria's first, though minor, economic crisis since 1945 has done nothing for the electoral fortunes of the KPO. If anything, the elections of 1981 have shown that, in adversity, workers reinforce their bonds with the governing, democratic, and anticommunist Socialist Party.

Leadership and Organization. The KPO's Twenty-Fourth Congress met in Vienna on 6–8 December 1980. The 68 members of the Central Committee were elected by secret ballot. Franz Muhri, the party's veteran leader, remained party chairman, Erwin Scharf secretary of the Central Committee, and Hans Kalt editor of the daily *Volksstimme*. In addition to these three, the Politburo includes Michael Graber, Franz Hager, Anton Hofer, Hans Karger, Karl Reiter, Irma Schwager, Walter Silbermayr, and Ernst Wimmer. Josef Progsch and Karl Zenker left the Politburo. (*Wiener Zeitung*, 10 December 1980.)

Party Internal Affairs. Muhri's report to the congress was entitled "For Unified Action Against the Right! For Democracy, Peace, and Socialism!" Three pages were devoted to international and five to domestic policy matters. The last four pages dealt with party affairs. After calling for united action in the workplace and for communist participation in citizens' and renters' initiatives, Muhri proclaimed the preparation of a new party program. Written by the Central Committee, the program was to "be subjected to a wide discussion" by "all forces of the left, all Austrians who worry about the future, who seek an alternative to the dominant profit system, and who are of the opinion that basic societal changes are necessary. Only after these discussions is the project of the party program to be edited; early in 1982 it will be submitted to an extraordinary party congress for discussion and decision." Muhri called for socialism "in Austrian colors. . . . There is no universally valid model of socialism, either a Soviet one or one of 'Eurocommunism.' " Austria's revolution, Muhri claimed, cannot be imported, but must arise from the crisis of the Austrian exploitative order.

Muhri called for a number of organizational changes: more discipline, more emphasis on youth, more of a two-way information flow within the party, better public relations, more regular weekly meetings, better preparations for shop steward elections (with emphasis on the railroads), and more emphasis on municipal politics. Especially important is the struggle, on the part of both sexes, for truly equal rights for women. Party unity, Muhri said, had been re-established after the 1968–1970 crisis, but it constantly needs securing and firming up.

Domestic Attitudes and Activities. In his speech to the congress, Muhri pointed to four peculiarities of the economic crisis of 1980: (1) the state lacks the funds for effective intervention, despite heavy wage and sales taxes; (2) rapid technological change threatens the labor market; (3) ties with the European Economic Community enable foreign monopolies to penetrate Austria; and (4) a sector of the labor force has lost faith in the government and is ready to fight it. Muhri pointed out that communist workers had twice thwarted plant closings. He demanded the creation of 300,000 new industrial jobs. Austria must import less and produce more. The nationalized banks must sacrifice their huge profits and make cheap credit available. Muhri demanded economic redistribution in favor of workers and shorter hours. The purchasing power of workers, employees, and pensioners must rise.

Muhri also called for the democratization of Austrian society, the trade unions, and the educational system. Austria's national minorities must be given equal rights. He warned against the rise of privileges in public life, citing the case of then Vice-Chancellor Hannes Androsch (who subsequently resigned because of a conflict of interest). Muhri also demanded the dissemination of communist views "as representative of the greatest intellectual stream of our time" by the Austrian broadcasting system. He closed the part of his speech dealing with domestic affairs with a call for united action against neofascism.

International Views and Positions. Muhri's speech to the congress began with remarks on foreign affairs. He warned against the "threat" of Ronald Reagan and welcomed the defeat, in the German elections, of Franz-Josef Strauss. He criticized the Austrian media for supporting strikes and economic demands in Poland. In pleading for closer economic relations with the Soviet bloc, he ascribed Austria's independence and neutrality to the strength and international authority of the Soviet Union. He found words of appreciation for the Kreisky government for having hosted the head of the East German communist party, Erich Honecker, and for recognizing the Palestine Liberation Organization.

On 7 March, *Sovetskaia Rossiia* reprinted a *Volksstimme* story alleging that Polish groups behind the Solidarity movement had links with the Central Intelligence Agency. On 18 August, *Volksstimme* reported that two young Communists had chained themselves to lampposts in front of Vienna's *Amerika-Haus* to protest the "irresponsible course of the U.S. Government, which in effect amounts to preparation for a nuclear war."

International Activities and Party Contacts. While on an official visit to Chancellor Kreisky during the second week of April, Nikolai Tikhonov, chairman of the USSR Council of Ministers, found time to meet with Muhri, Scharf, Kalt, and Hans Steiner, head of the KPO Central Committee's Foreign Relations Department (*Volksstimme*, 10 April). Significantly, Tikhonov invited Muhri to a reception he gave for Kreisky (Tass, 8 April).

The KPO's year of international visits began with Muhri's visit to Bucharest, where he had a conversation with Nicolae Ceauşescu (*FBIS*, 8 January). In mid-February, Muhri visited János Kádár in Budapest (ibid., 18 February). In March, Hans Kalt attended the Soviet party congress. While in Moscow, he gave a radio interview. (Ibid., 3 March.)

In late May, Lubomír Štrougal, the prime minister of Czechoslovakia, came to Vienna on a brief official visit. Like Tikhonov before him, he found time for a talk with Muhri (*Volksstimme*, 26 May).

In a telegram to the Ninth Congress of the Polish communist party, the KPO said that it identified "with the hard and complicated struggle that is being waged by your country's Communists to overcome the present economic and political difficulties" (ibid., 15 July).

Publications. The KPO continues to publish the daily *Volksstimme* and the theoretical monthly *Weg und Ziel.*

University of Alberta   Frederick C. Englemann

Belgium

The Communist Party of Belgium (Parti communiste de Belgique/Kommunistische Partij van België; PCB/KPB) celebrated its sixtieth anniversary in 1981. It has a membership of only ten thousand in a population of 9.9 million, and compared to other far-left groups, it is not particularly militant. The political influence of the PCB/KPB has always been limited, except between 1945 and 1947, when it participated in postwar coalition governments. In the 1946 elections, the party obtained a record 12.7 percent of the vote and sent 23 deputies to the House of Representatives. Since then, its electoral representation has continuously decreased.

In the elections of 8 November, the PCB/KPB obtained 139,000 votes (2.3 percent), 40,000 fewer than in 1978 (3.25 percent). But the loss was, in fact, heavier since 900,000 additional voters cast ballots in 1981, following the enfranchisement of young people between the ages of 18 and 21. In the 212-member House of Representatives, the PCB/KPB now only holds two seats, compared with four in the previous parliament. But in the Senate (181 seats, of which 106 are elective), it has one directly elected member, a loss of one from the previous parliament.

None of the previous communist deputies in parliament were re-elected, including National Chairman Louis Van Geyt. The two new communist deputies are Jacques Nagels (44), professor of political economy at the Free University of Brussels and a member of the Central Committee, and Daniel Fedrigo (31), a language teacher in Huy (near Liège) and a member of the party since 1977. The new communist senator is Jules Vercaigne (41), a railwayman from Mons, who belongs to the Eurocommunist tendency of the PCB.

The party remains stronger in Wallonia, in the old industrial centers, than in Flanders (the communist members of parliament are Walloons). The Belgian Communists do not have their own trade union organization. They exercise a minor influence within the Walloon-dominated Belgian General Confederation of Workers, which is linked to the French-speaking Socialist Party and the Flemish Socialist Party.

Leadership and Organization. In contrast to the Socialists, the Social Christians, and the Liberals, which are split into Flemish- and French-speaking parties, the PCB/KPB has remained united. It has three regional councils: one Flemish (Dutch-speaking), headed by Jef Turf; one Walloon (French-speaking), headed by Claude Renard; and one for Brussels (bilingual), headed by Rosine Lewin. Louis Van Geyt is the national chairman.

The Central Committee met several times to examine documents prior to the Twenty-Fourth Congress, which will be held in February or March 1982 (the last congress met in April 1979). After examining the drafts of the new statutes of the party, the Central Committee declared its continued support for "democratic centralism" (*Le Drapeau rouge*, 16 June).

Three organizations are linked with the PCB/KPB: the Communist Youth of Belgium (dynamic despite its small number of activists), the National Union of Communist Students (whose influence in the universities is insignificant), and the children's Union of Belgian Pioneers. The two most active front organizations are the Belgian Union for the Defense of Peace (its secretary, Jean Du Bosch, a conspicuous Eurocommunist, is a member of the Central Committee of the party) and the Belgian Association of Democratic Lawyers. The Belgian Union for the Defense of Peace condemned the Soviet intervention in Afghanistan, while the PCB merely "regretted" it (see *YICA*, 1981, p. 359).

The Belgian Association of Democratic Lawyers suspended its contacts with the Union of Czech Lawyers, which "instead of defending democratic freedom and socialist legality, is covering up its violation" (*Le Drapeau rouge*, 5 June). Cannon Goor, a winner of the Lenin Peace Prize, is the driving force behind the International Committee for Security and European Cooperation. Also allied with the PCB is a small agricultural association, the Union of Family Farmers.

Domestic Attitudes and Activities. In 1981, two Belgian prime ministers resigned in less than six months: Wilfried Martens on 31 March and Mark Eyskens on 25 September. Both were Social Christians, and both directed a coalition government of the Social Christians and the Socialists from the two parts of the country. The second political crisis of 1981 led to the decision to hold elections in November. The rupture had become inevitable when the coalition partners did not support the Walloon Socialists in demanding urgent financial aid to Wallonia's ailing steel industry.

When the most recent political crisis erupted, Louis Van Geyt declared: "We consider that it marks the failure of the policy followed by the outgoing coalition to face up to worsening economic, social, and institutional problems without harming the powers and privileges of financial groups" (ibid., 23 September).

The "anticrisis" plan of the PCB/KPB proposes nationalization of private banks, the steel industry, manufacturing concerns, and the electric utilities. This proposal would not necessarily imply state possession of these key industries (ibid., 26 September). The pro-Soviet federation of Liège favors nationalization and has recommended the organization of a general strike, an idea that the majority of the party has refused to adopt (ibid., 1 June).

The PCB/KPB continues to defend points of view that are sometimes close to those of the ecological movements (for example, it opposes the construction of new nuclear power plants in Chooz, France, at the Belgian border, although the French Communist Party favors the project). It also supports the struggles of urban community movements and demonstrations in favor of the legalization of abortion.

International Views and Positions. The PCB/KPB continues to pursue its campaign against the proposed installation of Pershing II rockets and cruise missiles in Belgium. Although agreeing on 12 December 1979 to the installation of new American nuclear arms in Western Europe, the Belgian government deferred its decision on their installation in Belgium in order to explore the possibility of negotiations with the USSR.

Of all Belgian parties, the PCB contributed most, proportionally, to the success of a demonstration held in Brussels on 25 October, which rallied 200,000 people supporting the National Action

Committee for Peace and Development (the two Socialist parties—particularly the Flemish one—also supported the demonstration). The committee included many youth and Third World aid organizations.

The demonstrators opposed the installation of the new Euromissiles and demanded the dismantling of Soviet SS-20 missiles. Nevertheless, for Belgian Communists, "the Pershing and the cruise missiles have nothing to do with the SS-20" (see *YICA*, 1981, p. 358). The party maintains that the deployment of the SS-20s has created a balance of power in Europe (*Le Soir*, 30 October). Susa Nudelhole, the Central Committee's expert on foreign policy, declared in May that "the battle against the missiles is of the greatest importance in the action of Belgian Communists in the field of international politics" (*Le Drapeau rouge*, 30–31 May).

The situation in Poland poses difficulties for Belgian Communists. The leaders of the party, wishing to promote democratization, continue to declare that Polish problems must be solved by the Poles themselves. On the occasion of the Ninth Extraordinary Congress of the Polish United Workers' Party (PUWP) in July, the PCB/KPB assured its Polish comrades: "We join you in your efforts to find a Polish solution to the problems that have arisen in your country, a solution that should come from the Polish workers themselves and should be based on a constructive dialogue with all the working forces of the Polish nation" (ibid., 14 July). A month earlier, the Political Bureau of the PCB, analyzing the situation in Poland, had concluded that "the forces of socialist renewal inside the PUWP are confronted with the opposition of conservative elements whose points of view are encouraged from the outside" (ibid., 12 June).

International Activities and Party Contacts. In March, the visit to Paris by a Belgian communist delegation was not followed by the customary communiqué. It was, perhaps, an indication of disagreement between the two parties, provoked by the French party's opposition to immigrant workers.

At the beginning of October, Louis Van Geyt, in the name of the Political Bureau, sent a letter to the Communist Party of Czechoslovakia announcing that the new political trials in Czechoslovakia were "arousing a revival of emotion among the democratic forces of our country." Van Geyt added that his party "disapproved of everything that constituted a repression of a nonconformist opinion." (Ibid., 8 October.)

The first foreign trip was the visit to Romania by Jan Debrouwere, a member of the Political Bureau, who was received by Nicolae Ceauşescu, secretary general of the Communist Party of Romania and president of the republic. The two parties reaffirmed their conviction that "the PUWP, the working classes, and the Polish people could solve by themselves the difficulties that had arisen in the country" (ibid., 14 January).

A delegation composed of Jan Debrouwere and Paul Van Praag, a member of the Central Committee and chairman of the Commission of Party Affairs, visited the Soviet Union from 13 to 17 January. The exchange of views with the Soviet delegation, directed by Boris Ponomarev, Central Committee secretary in charge of relations with nonruling parties, took place in "an atmosphere of frankness and cordiality" (ibid., 20 January). At the end of January, representatives of the Israeli Communist Party, including the mayor of Nazareth, Tawfiq Zayyad, and attorney Felicia Langer, as well as representatives of the Communist Party of Jordan, were received by the PCB/KPB (ibid., 26 January). Belgian communist leaders also received, almost at the same time, Giorgio Napolitano, a member of the Italian party's Directorate (*L'Unità*, 27 January; *FBIS*, 3 February).

In February, a delegation composed of Jan Debrouwere and Jacques Nagels, a member of the Central Committee, went to Poland to express the party's support for "the efforts undertaken by the PUWP to pursue the process of socialist renewal" (*Le Drapeau rouge*, 21–22 February). In July, the PCB/KPB had contacts with the French party, in Paris, and with the Italian party, in Brussels, on the matter of Euromissiles and the prospects opened in Europe by the victory of the left in France (ibid.,

14 July). A delegation of the Japanese Communist Party, led by Vice-Chairman Tomio Nishizawa, visited Belgium from 31 August to 3 September. The Belgian and Japanese Communists have agreed to "develop excellent relations based on the principles of equality, independence, and noninterference" (ibid., 4 September).

Publications. Like all Belgian dailies, *Le Drapeau rouge*, the French-language daily of the PCB/KPB, receives a government subsidy. Its circulation is under ten thousand, of which an estimated two thousand copies are sent to subscribers registered in countries of the "socialist camp." The Flemish Communists publish the weekly *De Rode Vaan*. The French-language ideological review, *Les Cahiers marxistes*, is a monthly, while its Flemish counterpart, *Vlaams Marxistisch Tijdschrift*, appears quarterly. The French-language version is published by the Jacquemotte Foundation and the Flemish version by the Masereel Foundation.

The Far-Left. The most important organization of the extreme left remains the Party of Labor of Belgium (PTB/PVDA). In the November elections, it obtained 46,000 votes, a third of the votes received by the PCB. But unlike the PCB/KPB, the PTB/PVDA is more deeply rooted in Flanders; in many places, for example in Antwerp, it obtained more votes than the PCB. The PTB/PVDA is pro-Beijing in orientation, but it is not officially recognized by the Chinese Communist Party. The PTB/PVDA publishes two weeklies, *Konkreet* in Flemish and *Concret* in French.

The Marxist-Leninist Communist Party of Belgium (PCMLB), which is officially recognized by Beijing, has only a few dozen members. It did not take part in the last elections. The PCMLB publishes the fortnightly *La Voix communiste*.

The Worker's Revolutionnary League (LRT/RAL), the Belgian section of the Trotskyist Fourth International, has several hundred members. It obtained only 12,000 votes in the November elections. The LRT/RAL publishes two weeklies, *La Gauche* in French and *Rood* in Flemish.

The New Left publication *Pour*, which has become independent of any political organization, is the most influential weekly of both the left and the extreme left. Its style remains more professional than that of any other militant weekly, and its editorial staff intends to start a daily newspaper.

Brussels   Willy Estersohn

Cyprus

The original Communist Party of Cyprus (Kommonistikon Komma Kiprou) was secretly founded in 1922 by Greek Cypriot cadres trained in mainland Greece. Four years later the party openly held its first congress after the island became a British crown colony. Outlawed in 1933, the Communists survived underground into the next decade when the party's successor appeared in April 1941 under the name Progressive Party of the Working People (Anorthotikon Komma Ergazomenou Laou;

AKEL). The party was again proscribed by the British in 1955, along with all political organizations during the insurgency by the Greek Cypriot militant group known as EOKA. The AKEL took no part in that four-year struggle for independence and has continually suffered criticism for preventing its followers from engaging in that "anti-imperialist" campaign. Still, AKEL leaders insist that they were "a loud voice against an exploitative labor system in colonial days" and their decision not to take up arms "provided a non-violent alternative to EOKA terrorism in the independence struggle" (*Baltimore Sun*, 18 July 1980). Since the establishment of the Republic of Cyprus in 1960, the AKEL has enjoyed legal status.

As the oldest and best-organized political party existing in the island of Cyprus, the AKEL commands a following far in excess of its estimated 12,000 card-carrying members (*Cyprus Mail*, 26 May 1978). Most of its support comes from the Greek Cypriot community in the island, which constitutes about 80 percent of the estimated population of 640,000. AKEL leaders admit to maintaining "close collaboration" with the illegal Turkish Communist Party, as well as having persons in the Turkish-controlled north of Cyprus with whom they are normally on "friendly terms" (*Tercuman*, Istanbul, 1 April).

The proportion of communist party members to national adult population probably ranks AKEL second only to its Italian counterpart among nonruling communist parties. Despite its overall size, prior to 1981 the AKEL had played down its strength in parliamentary and presidential elections. No party member has held a cabinet post. The parliamentary elections in May 1981 were the first to be held under a proportional representation system. The electorate voted for parties rather than for individuals, as previously done. In the Greek Cypriot elections for 35 House of Representative seats, the AKEL made its strongest showing in history by winning the largest number of votes of any party (32.8 percent) and taking 12 seats, 3 more than in the previous parliament (*Cyprus Bulletin*, 30 May).

Since the Turkish invasion and subsequent occupation of about a third of the northern part of the island in July 1974, the sociopolitical setting in Cyprus has been a fragile calm. After the first outbreak of intercommunal fighting in 1963, the Cypriot Turks withdrew from the central government and have since held separate elections in their community. Pending a final resolution of current constitutional problems in the Republic of Cyprus, the Cypriot Turks in 1975 formed the Turkish Federated State of Cyprus (TFSC) and have continued to operate as a quasi-autonomous entity with help from mainland Turkey. In June, the Cypriot Turks also held elections for president and the 40-member Federal Assembly of the TFSC. The party of President Rauf Denktas won re-election but only 18 seats and are now in power with a slim 21-seat coalition with a minor party. There was no overt communist participation in the TFSC elections, but there were numerous unsubstantiated charges by the Denktas forces that "Maoist elements" were in control of the opposition (*Halkin Sesi*, 13 March).

In the 1978 election for president of the Republic of Cyprus, the AKEL preserved the Greek Cypriot parliamentary coalition majority and backed the incumbent, Spyros Kyprianou, who won without difficulty. While intentionally never seeking the presidency in the past, AKEL leaders nonetheless boasted that they could have "put forward an able presidential candidate" (*IB*, 15 March 1978). The AKEL later found reason for "dissociating" itself from its previous support of Kyprianou due to "weakness, errors, and omissions" in his administration (*Cyprus Mail*, 24 June 1980). During 1981, the AKEL found it convenient to drift back toward support of the president and did not denounce Kyprianou publicly. However, it has remained silent about its plans to run a communist candidate for president in the 1983 elections (ibid., 5 April).

The AKEL was a consistent supporter of the late president of the republic, Archbishop Makarios, who tolerated the Communists because they were almost all Greek Cypriots and moderates. Referring to themselves as "serious and responsible," AKEL leaders claim they never hesitate to face "the people's problems" (*Kharavyi*, 11 September). After the elections in May, AKEL General Secretary Ezekias Papaioannou stated that "a one-party government cannot carry the burden of the struggle"

(Nicosia Domestic Service, 14 September). He called for "a politically representative government, or if this is not acceptable, at least a government approved by all parties, which will agree on a minimum program and which will undertake to implement it" (ibid.). The Communists believe that for the present "not only general democratic but also socialist goals can be reached by democratic means and parliamentary activity" (*WMR*, June 1978). While this statement was made in 1978, the AKEL has given no indication of a change of position. In 1974, the AKEL initially put forward its demand for "a coalition government of anti-imperialist parties and a seat in the Cabinet of Ministers" (ibid.). Unable to achieve the latter objective, even after its plurality in the 1981 parliamentary elections, the AKEL settled on being "the good old party," trying to "reassure people in every way and to gather its ranks— the politically and socially undifferentiated masses—around a platform of reasonable, partial, quantitative demands" (*Andi*, Athens, 16 January). In fact, the leader of the extreme-right Democratic Rally, Glavkos Kliridis, has given the AKEL a "certificate of good standing" and does not regard it as a party of the extreme left. According to Kliridis, the AKEL "does not promote Marxism in Cyprus and does not conduct a class struggle; it does not even seek social change. It simply follows a foreign policy in line with that of Moscow." (Ibid.)

In the past, the AKEL played down its differences with the Greek Orthodox church in Cyprus, particularly during the life of Archbishop Makarios. However, during the 1981 election campaign, General Secretary Papaioannou said that the Communists "would press for State land, church and monastery land to be given to landless peasants" (*Cyprus Mail*, 8 April). In the campaign the AKEL did give priority to economic issues and demands that relate to the standard of living in line with its earlier call for increases in "the incomes of the peasants, middle sections and all other working people" (*WMR*, September 1979). The families of party members reportedly attend Greek Orthodox church services, and the Communists avoid the issue of the influence of the church in secular politics. The AKEL has learned from bitter experience that it cannot appeal to the Greek Cypriot masses—or to the Turkish Cypriots for that matter—by attacking their religious beliefs.

The AKEL has competition on the left from an extremist militant group of young people, as well as from an established socialist party, the United Democratic Union of the Center (EDEK). Reportedly, the extreme left is loosely made up of "a few hundred" college students and intellectuals who are "centered around two bookstores, a periodical, cultural activities, and some efforts to politicize women's problems" (*Andi*, 16 January). This group has organized some public demonstrations to call attention to "a serious question of democratic freedom" in Cyprus. To date, this group has not registered as a political party, nor has it published a manifesto under a specific label.

In contrast, the EDEK (founded in 1969 by Dr. Vassos Lyssarides, a former member of AKEL and personal physician and adviser to Archbishop Makarios) believes without deviation in the idea of an independent and nonaligned Cyprus without the presence of foreign military bases on the island. The EDEK has significant connections in the Third World, especially with the Palestinians, the Afro-Asian Peoples' Solidarity Organization, and fraternal ties with the Panhellenic Socialist Movement, which won control of the government of Greece following elections in October. Until 1978, EDEK and AKEL referred to one another as "the progressive forces"in Cyprus, but a dispute over tactics surfaced in 1979. Since then the two parties have been engaged in open feuding, with EDEK the apparent loser. In the 1981 parliamentary elections, EDEK garnered 8.2 percent of the popular vote and ended up with three seats, one fewer than previously. The EDEK's opponents "consider it a utopian and dogmatic party that will never be able to expand its influence" (ibid.). Nonetheless, given its support from its fraternal party now in power in mainland Greece, EDEK should not be dismissed as a factor in the future domestic and international politics of the island.

Leadership and Organization. According to party rules, the supreme authority in the AKEL hierarchy is its Congress, which is convened every four years. The party's Fourteenth Congress was held

25–28 May 1978, and elected the current Central Committee and the Central Control Commission. Between congresses, the Central Committee directs all party activities and, from its members, elects the Politburo and the Secretariat. The Politburo serves as AKEL's policymaking body between periodic plenums of the Central Committee. The Secretariat is the executive arm of the Central Committee and supervises the work of the party. The Central Control Commission maintains internal discipline and serves as the arbiter of intraparty disputes. The lower levels of the AKEL organization have similar functional bodies, whose distribution of power is based upon the principle of democratic centralism. Each unit, from primary cell to district committee, elects its own executive officers, who are accountable to local members. As is typical in communist party organizations, decisions of higher bodies in the AKEL are binding upon lower echelons.

There were no changes in the leadership of the AKEL in 1981. The leading personalities are General Secretary Ezekias Papaioannou, who has held office since 1949, and his deputy Andreas Fantis. Party leaders are careerists noted for their stability, loyalty, and advanced age. Most are well over sixty, a stark contrast to leaders of the other political parties, some of whom were teenage fighters during the 1955–1959 independence struggle against the British. Papaioannou is 72 years old and has been a party functionary for over half a century. The succession to the current leadership will certainly be a critical problem for Cypriot Communists in the near future. (For names of key AKEL officials, see *YICA*, 1979, p. 123.)

Party Internal Affairs. The AKEL is reputed to be a tightly controlled apparatus from the top to the grass-roots level. Few internal disagreements are ever aired in public, although the right-wing press occasionally reports dissension. For example, *I Simerini*, the newspaper of Glavkos Kliridis and his Democratic Rally party, editorialized (12 March) that AKEL members "no longer obey the stupidity and political madness of their leaders." Rank-and-file members now "assume a critical attitude; they do not accept lightly the absurdities this leadership serves them; they are concerned; they ask, learn, doubt." If true, such reports might explain the emergence of a small radical group of youthful left-wing extremists for whom the AKEL claims no responsibility.

At the 1978 party congress, AKEL leaders were able to report to the delegates that the "goal of winning hundreds of new members, especially young men and women, had been realized. The report claimed that 67 percent of party members were industrial workers; 20 percent came from the peasantry and the middle sections; 24 percent were women; and 30 percent of new members were under the age of 30. There had also been a marked increase among AKEL members of young scientists, whose number had nearly doubled since the last congress. (*WMR*, July 1979.)

Each September, the AKEL holds "a fund-raising drive to provide money for the party's normal activity" and to demonstrate "a symbolic expression of mass support for the party." Even in 1974, the year of the right-wing putsch in Cyprus, the AKEL raised "18,000 Cypriot pounds, but in 1977 the figure was already 80,200 pounds or 30,000 more than in 1973" (ibid.). Additional operating capital for the AKEL is generated "from activities under the indirect but tight control of the party in entire branches of the production and distribution of goods (cooperatives, retail stores, financing enterprises, tourist agencies, export-import enterprises)." As a result of these activities, the AKEL has "become probably the major employer on the island" (*Andi*, 16 January). The two best-known communist-controlled enterprises are the Popular Distiller's Company of Limassol, which produces wines and brandies for the domestic market and export, and the People's Coffee Grinding Company in Nicosia.

Auxiliary and Mass Organizations. Total membership of all elements within the AKEL apparatus, including various front groups, may be indicated by 95,302 votes that the Communists received in the

May elections. The most influential front is the island's largest labor union, the Pan-Cypriot Workers' Confederation (PEO), to which about 45 percent of the 100,000 organized Greek Cypriot workers belong. It is an affiliate of the World Federation of Trade Unions (WFTU), which is a major communist front. Andreas Ziartidhes, a labor leader for over forty years, is the PEO's general secretary; his deputy is Pavlos Dinglis. Both men are influential in AKEL affairs, and both are members of the House of Representatives. The PEO also maintains relations with the Turkish Cypriot left-wing union, Dev-Is, also a member of the WFTU (*Kharavyi*, 12 July 1979).

The AKEL-sponsored United Democratic Youth Organization (EDON) claims to have over ten thousand members in Cyprus and maintains a branch in London, where 125,000 Cypriots live. The EDON has a council seat on the World Federation of Democratic Youth, a communist front headquartered in Budapest. EDON, through a secondary school organization called PEOM, extends its influence to over three times its stated membership. Other communist fronts in Cyprus include the Confederation of Women's Organizations; the Pan-Cyprian Peace Council, a member of the World Peace Council; a farmer's union (EKA); and a number of friendship clubs sponsored by Eastern European embassies. The "London branch of AKEL," or the Union of Greek Cypriots in England, has about 1,200 members (ibid., 24 July 1979). Another major communist front is the Pan-Cyprian Federation of Students and Young Professionals, which is a member of the International Union of Students. About 8 percent of Cypriot students studying abroad receive scholarships to attend Eastern bloc universities.

The AKEL claims it is "a people's party, a party of Greek and Turkish working people" (*WMR*, September 1979). While the AKEL is officially banned on the Turkish side of Cyprus, the Communists have never stopped trying to appeal to the minority population in the island. Speaking at a gathering of EDON members, Papaioannou stated "that the Cypriot youth, Greeks and Turks, had the utmost interest in understanding and uniting with each other in a joint struggle against the common enemy of foreign occupation and imperialism" (Nicosia Domestic Service, 8 February). The Federation of Turkish Cypriot Students and Youth, as well as the Revolutionary Youth Organization in the TFSC, attended an International Union of Students conference held in Nicosia in December 1978, but there have not been any reports of open contacts since. While the Greek Cypriots as a rule are denied entrance into the Turkish side, the AKEL claims that meetings with its sympathizers are held on unspecified "neutral ground" (*Kharavyi*, 12 July 1979).

Domestic Attitudes and Activities. The two major domestic events of the year in Cyprus were the elections in May and the resumption of the intercommunal talks aimed at solving the internal aspects of the Cyprus problem. During the campaign, AKEL candidates found ample opportunity to present their views on domestic issues. General Secretary Papaioannou said that AKEL's domestic policy "aims at radical change." "The party supports a purge and cleansing of the state apparatus and the security forces; an investigation of economic scandals and exemplary punishment of those guilty; protection of trade unionism; the conduct of municipal and communal elections as well as elections for school committees and school boards . . . a public investigation based on the declaration of the origin of personal income; a more just distribution of taxation burdens and the national income; a free education; free medical and medicinal assistance; and the establishment of a university" (Nicosia Domestic Service, 21 March). The communist leader also supported reduction of the voting age to eighteen since "the forthcoming parliamentary elections had particular importance for youth" (ibid., 8 February). He also repeated his claim that the AKEL "is not aiming at the assumption of power and transformation of society to the socialist pattern while the country is still under occupation." The AKEL leader reasserted his "party's stand of readiness to cooperate after the elections with all the 'patriotic forces' which agree with the policy line agreed at the National Council during the lifetime of President Makarios" (*Cyprus Mail*, 5 April). The last statement might indicate that the AKEL was trying to pass itself off as the "intellectual" if not "faithful and legitimate heir of Makarios" (*Andi*, 16 January).

The election results gave the AKEL the largest number of votes among the seven competing parties and the same number of seats as its right-wing rival. The AKEL Politburo hailed the vote as "a resplendent victory of the working people for the achievement of which our party has played a most decisive role" (*Kharavyi*, 27 May).

The twelve AKEL winners, their age, and their constituency are Pavlos Dinglis, 50, Nicosia; Andreas Fantis, 63, Famagusta; Kiriakos Khristou, 66, Limassol; Dinos Konstandinou, 56, Nicosia; Khristos Kourlellaris, 62, Kyrenia; Nikos Mavronikolas, 72, Paphos; Khambis Mikhailidhis, 61, Famagusta; Ezekias Papaioannou, 73, Limassol; Khristos Petas, 59, Nicosia; Mikhail Poumbouris, 62, Famagusta; Yeoryios Savvidhis, 61, Nicosia; and Andreas Ziartidhes, 62, Larnaca. All twelve are long-standing members of the "old guard" leadership, and most hold posts in the party's hierarchy. The AKEL Politburo assured party supporters that "the AKEL–left-wing House members will prove worthy of their confidence" and that "with their work and struggle, inside and outside the House, will honor the fresh contract of honor with the people" (ibid., 3 June).

The editor of *I Simerini* (30 May), which speaks for Glavkos Kliridis's party, dismissed the AKEL as a "party that represents only one-third of the people. Therefore, Papaioannou's enthusiastic statements are useless and politically imprudent since every intelligent and earnest AKEL member has ascertained that he has been a victim of mockery and deception." AKEL leaders responded to this criticism with characteristic fervor: "In view of this attack by the warmongering imperialist circles on an international scale and of their local organs in Cyprus, the unity of all the patriotic democratic forces of our people assumes new dimensions. Such a unity will become the breakwater that will repulse all the activities of the U.S.-NATO circles, and of their local organs, for deviation and anomaly and for the final implementation of their plans to enslave and to partition Cyprus." (*Kharavyi*, 28 June.)

AKEL has consistently supported the intercommunal talks on the territorial aspects of the Cyprus problem as "the only correct procedure for the solution of the internal aspects of the Cyprus problem" (Radio Moscow, 19 May). The AKEL repeated its belief that Cyprus should become "a true federation and not a confederation" with 22 percent of a "bizonal" Cyprus under Turkish Cypriot administration and "participation of the two communities in central organs" based on the original constitutional proportion of 70:30, with the Greek Cypriots in majority (*Kharavyi*, 11 September). The AKEL is not opposed to the continued efforts of the United Nations to bring the two sides together. Thus, "the party's insistence on substantive and constructive talks in no way excludes a parallel preparation for an appeal to the United Nations" presented at the "suitable moment" (Nicosia Domestic Service, 5 September). The Communists in Cyprus have always felt that their own interests in the future of the island's government would be better protected in an international forum, such as the United Nations, rather than through a solution imposed by the United States under NATO's "allied framework" (ibid., 13 March). In AKEL's view, domestic aspects of the Cyprus problem will be solved "with the support and solidarity of all our peaceloving friends who are none other than the socialist and nonaligned countries and all the liberal and peaceloving peoples of the world" (ibid., 11 September). The AKEL still maintains that the international aspects of the Cyprus issue must be solved "in an international conference within the framework of the United Nations" (ibid.).

International Views and Positions. At a gathering of party cadres in September, Papaioannou stated AKEL's position on the international situation: "We are going through a period in grave danger of a world thermonuclear holocaust breaking out. This danger arises from the incendiary and warlike policy implemented by the hawks of the U.S. Pentagon headed by President Reagan. It is expressed through the installation of "cruise" and "Pershing" missiles in Europe, production of the neutron bomb, U.S. refusal to ratify the SALT II agreement, violation of Libyan territorial waters and airspace by the U.S. Sixth Fleet, and the shooting down of two Libyan aircraft by U.S. fighters." (Ibid., 11 September.) He continued to attack U.S. policies around the world, such as "aid" to the "bloodthirsty fascist" regimes in El Salvador, Israel, and South Africa, and criticized "the U.S. decision to sell arms to the Chinese leaders, who have fully conformed to imperialism." Finally, he accused the United States of "financing and encouraging antirevolutionary elements in the People's Republic of Poland," as well as the "arming of counterrevolutionary elements in Afghanistan." Papaioannou concluded by predicting that the "exceedingly incendiary and warlike policy" of U.S. imperialism could result in "the annihilation of the U.S. people in a thermonuclear war."

On the other hand, the AKEL leader noted, "there is the socialist camp headed by the almighty Soviet Union, which will never allow imperialism to gain military supremacy in order to speak from a position of strength... The world balance of power is in favor of socialism, national independence, democracy, international détente, and peace." The AKEL general secretary tied this conclusion to the current situation in Cyprus: the people of Cyprus "are fighting for the abolition of the British and other bases on their territory, for the withdrawal of the Turkish occupation and all other foreign troops, for cessation of the manufacture of the neutron bomb, for détente, for control of strategic weapons and total disarmament, for the independence, sovereignty, territorial integrity, nonaligned character of their foreign policy, and the full demilitarization of Cyprus." Papaioannou favors "the abolition of British and other bases on Cypriot territory," as well as "the withdrawal of the U.S. Sixth Fleet from the Mediterranean." He advocates "the conversion of the Mediterranean into a sea of peace and a bridge of peaceful cooperation between the three continents of Europe, Asia, and Africa." (Ibid.)

Greek Cypriot Communists have continually been embarrassed by the Soviet Union's friendly relations with Turkey, particularly its silence on the Turkish invasion of Cyprus. In partial explanation of these unpopular policies, Papaioannou stated: "Brezhnev's recent speech to the [Soviet party] congress stressed that the Soviet Union wants to develop closer relations with Greece, Cyprus, and Turkey. This is natural because Soviet policy is based on the policy of peace and good neighborliness with various countries and it has no aggressive goals... However, the Soviet Union bears in mind that the West, headed by the United States, is encouraging and breeding Turkish intransigence; and it is precisely for this reason that the Soviet Union has repeatedly proposed to the United States that they jointly cooperate in order to implement the U.N. resolutions on Cyprus." (Ibid., 7 April.) In line with the communist policy of trying to move the island away from "the influence of the West," Papaioannou also said that his party would "strive for the severance of Cyprus's association with the European Economic Community and press for a trade policy in line with the nonaligned character of the country" (*Cyprus Mail*, 8 April).

International Activities and Party Contacts. The AKEL is known to maintain frequent and extensive relations with both ruling and nonruling communist parties, as well as with all the various international front groups. In February, Papaioannou and another member of the AKEL Politburo attended the Soviet party congress in Moscow (Nicosia Domestic Service, 20 February). At the same time, a Bulgarian parliamentary delegation, headed by the chairman of the National Assembly, paid an official visit to Cyprus (ibid., 22 February). In March, Cuban Foreign Minister Isidoro Malmierca arrived for a three-day visit at the invitation of his Cypriot counterpart (ibid., 8 March). In April, Dhonis Khristofinis, Politburo alternate member, visited South Yemen to participate in the Thirteenth Afro-Asian People's Solidarity Organization Congress. During July, Papaioannou went to Bulgaria at the invitation of Todor Zhivkov to "exchange views on the Cyprus issue and other international problems" (Nicosia Domestic Service, 19 July). Another "comradely meeting" between Boris Ponomarev, secretary of the Soviet Central Committee, and Papaioannou took place in Moscow during the first week of

August. In September, an AKEL delegation attended a conference in Prague on questions of the eastern Mediterranean and Middle East. The delegation also visited Budapest and met with leaders of both the Czechoslovak and Hungarian communist parties.

Publications. The AKEL has always given special attention to the "ideological front," including education, agitation, and propaganda. Due to their well-trained technicians, writers, and editors, the Communists have long enjoyed an inordinate influence in Cypriot press circles. The AKEL's central publication is *Kharavyi* (Dawn), which enjoys the largest circulation of any daily newspaper in Cyprus. In addition, the Communists seem to have sympathizers on most of the island's other periodicals. The AKEL also publishes the weekly newspaper *Demokratia* (Democracy) and the magazine *Neoi Kairoi* (New times). Its scholarly journal is an occasional publication entitled *Theoritikos Demokratis* (Theoretical democrat). The PEO labor union publishes a weekly named *Ergatiko Vima* (Workers' stride), while the communist-controlled youth organization, EDON, has a weekly called *Neolaia* (Youth). Cypriot Communists in London have published a Greek-language weekly called *Ta Vima* (The stride) for the past forty years.

Washington, D.C.   T. W. Adams

Denmark

The Communist Party of Denmark (Danmarks Kommunistiske Parti; DKP) arose from the left-wing faction of the Social Democratic Party (Socialdemokratiet; SD) in the turbulent aftermath of World War I. The DKP was organized on 9 November 1919, and except for the German occupation during World War II, it has always been a legal party.

The DKP has traditionally drawn most of its support from among urban industrial workers, seamen, and some leftist intellectuals. Membership edged upward during the 1970s after a decade of stagnation. Before the internal party turmoil of the fall of 1979, party membership was estimated at around eight thousand. The population of Denmark is about 5.1 million.

The past two years have been most disappointing. After nearly a decade of revival, in late 1979 the DKP lost all seven of its parliamentary seats and was forced to expel one of its most influential members. The Soviet invasion of Afghanistan and the fading of European détente further diminished the party's prestige. The sudden reverses were quite unexpected; during 1979 the party had seen its support of the anti-European Economic Community (EEC) movement crowned with electoral success in the first direct elections to the EEC Parliament. The DKP had done well in the 1978 local elections, and its standing in public opinion polls had been stable. Such instant reverses of political fortune have characterized Danish politics since the first protest election of December 1973. Elections have recurred with unprecedented frequency: 1975, 1977, 1979, and another sudden election on 8 December 1981.

Thirteen parties contested the Folketing's (parliament) 175 seats (Greenland and the Faeroe Islands each elect two members in separate elections). Despite the frequency of elections, the SD has been the governing party except for just over a year in 1974–1975 when the Liberal Party (Venstre) was in power. The SD's practice has been to seek a parliamentary majority on an issue-by-issue basis, usually with the several small center parties. It was the failure to secure such support for tax changes in November that led veteran Premier Anker Jorgensen to dissolve parliament and call elections. Although the prospect is occasionally discussed in the political press, the SD has not tried to revive its occasional informal cooperation with one or more parties to its left, such as the arrangement with the Socialist People's Party (Socialistisk Folkeparti; SF) between 1971 and 1973. As a consequence of the December election, in which the SD won 59 seats (the next largest number, 26, was received by the Conservative Party), it is possible that a minority SD government will be formed.

The October 1979 elections were a disaster for the DKP; its share of the vote was halved. Receiving only 1.9 percent of the votes (a loss of 1.8 percent over February 1977), the party fell below the 2 percent barrier necessary for a party to receive representation in parliament. All seven DKP representatives lost their seats.

The DKP's placing in frequent public opinion polls during 1981 hovered around the crucial 2 percent mark, but the party received only 1.1 percent of the vote in the December elections and won no parliamentary seats. The municipal and county elections held in November had not augured well for the DKP. It generally lost support in urban areas, where most of its strength lies. Particularly in Copenhagen, where the DPK had joined the SD in a coalition during the past three and a half years, its support declined. Some suggested that the Soviet submarine incident in Sweden hit the DKP hard. Normally, many local factors influence municipal and county elections.

The DKP was only one of five socialist parties to the left of the reformist SD to contest the 1981 elections. The Left Socialists (Venstresocialisterne; VS), founded as a splinter from the SF in 1967, were absent from parliament between 1971 and 1975. In the 1975, 1977, and 1979 elections, they made modest gains, winning six mandates (3.6 percent of the vote) in October 1979. The party made noticeable gains in the November local elections, particularly in Copenhagen. The SF won ten seats in 1979 (5.9 percent of the vote), a gain of three. Since the SF's purge of moderates in 1976, the party has made steady gains, including in the November local elections. In the December elections, the SF was the big winner, receiving 21 seats (11.3 percent of the vote). The VS lost ground (five seats and 2.6 percent of the vote).

The Communist Workers' Party (Kommunistisk Arbejderparti; KAP), formerly the Communist League of Marxist-Leninists (Kommunistforbund Marxister-Leninister) appeared on the ballot for the first time in 1979. It received only 0.4 percent of the vote. Its performance in the December parliamentary elections was equally dismal (0.1 percent). For those voters demanding more variety in the leftist smorgasbord, still another faction made its electoral debut in December. The Socialist Workers' Party (Socialistisk Arbejderparti; SAP), the country's branch of the Troskyist Fourth International, gathered enough signatures (18,000) to appear on the ballot, but received negligible support in the elections.

After the elections, the Jorgensen government resigned to open the way for a new coalition. The modest gains of some center and right parties (the Center Democrats and the Conservatives) were less than expected. There was talk of a possible government based on the SF, SD, and the small left-center Radicals; but negotiations broke down just before Christmas, and a new SD minority government was formed under Jorgensen. Whatever the outcome, Danish politics will probably remain unstable. Despite the 2 percent swing to the nonsocialist parties, the leftist parties won 15.2 percent of the vote, their highest total yet (Radio Denmark, 17 November, 8 December).

Leadership and Organization. Supreme party authority is the DKP's triennial congress, which held its twenty-sixth meeting in April 1980. It received the report of the Central Committee, adopted the party program and rules, and elected the governing bodies—the Central Committee (41 members, 11 alternates), the Control Commission (5 members), and two auditors. The Central Committee in turn elected the party chairman, the Executive Committee (15 members), and the Secretariat (5 members).

Jorgen Jensen was elected party chairman by the Central Committee in December 1977, following the unexpected death of longtime DKP Chairman Knud Jespersen. Jensen, 62, is a veteran of many years of party activity and has been a Central Committee member since 1952. Long active in trade union affairs, he is a member of the Danish Metalworkers' Union's Executive Committee, even though the union is controlled by the SD. He has also been chairman of a union local near Copenhagen. Ib Norlund, who was briefly acting DKP chairman during Jespersen's illness, was the party's parliamentary leader until October 1979. He remains the party's chief theoretician. Paul Emanuel is party secretary.

Until 1979, the DKP seemed unique among the several Marxist parties in Denmark for its lack of personality conflicts and policy differences. In late 1977, however, the party criticized Central Committee member Preben Moller Hansen for his autocratic behavior as chairman of the communist-dominated Seamen's Union (*Berlingske Tidende*, 28 November 1977). By 1979 this argument became public, and Hansen, along with two close supporters, resigned from the DKP Central Committee. A bitter flurry of recriminations ensued, and Hansen left the DKP altogether, threatening to take some of the 2,700 members of the DKP's maritime division with him (*Aktuelt*, 30 October 1979; *Berlingske Weekendavisen*, 2 November 1979). It is likely that these internal struggles contributed significantly to the party's poor electoral showing, especially in the Copenhagen region. Others have felt that Jensen lacks his predecessor's personal popularity and political skills.

Not much is known about party finances other than that they seem to be adequate and that there are frequent collection campaigns for the party's daily newspaper, *Land og Folk*. Until it lost its parliamentary representation, the DKP, like all parliamentary parties, received a monthly subvention from the public treasury.

Despite these setbacks, the DKP exuded optimism at its triennial congress in April 1980. Over four hundred delegates participated. There was a 40 percent turnover in the party's Central Committee membership, but little competition for places. Total DKP membership, as reported to the Twenty-Sixth Congress, was approximately nine thousand, with the average age of members just over 40 (*Kristeligt Dagblad*, 8 April).

The party's two main auxiliary organizations are the Communist Youth of Denmark (Danmarks Kommunistiske Ungdom; DKU), led by Gerda Kristensen, and the Communist Students of Denmark (Danmarks Kommunistiske Studenter; KS) chaired by Frank Aaen. Aaen was elected to the DKP Central Committee at the April 1980 congress. Founded in 1974, the KS held its Fourth Congress in Copenhagen in November 1978. In 1980, KS activist Bent Thaarup won the chairmanship of the leftist-dominated National Union of Danish Students (Danske Studenters Faellesraad). This reflects the KS's effective organization on many Danish university campuses. Although student activism in Denmark has declined in recent years, Communists and other leftists control many student organizations and sit on university councils.

An autonomous Faeroese Communist Party, headed by Egon Thomsen, appeared in 1975. Little has been heard from it recently. It failed to gather the few hundred signatures necessary to qualify for the ballot in 1978, nor was it visible during the 1981 local elections. It must be considered defunct, but given current economic problems on the Faeroes, a resurgence of radical forces cannot be excluded. The DKP is not directly active in Greenland, which received home rule in 1979. The leftist Siumut

(Forward) Party, which won control of the Greenlandic legislature, is loosely allied with the SF. It is active in the campaign to withdraw from the EEC.

Domestic Activities and Attitudes. High energy and labor costs plus record interest rates contributed to the continuing stagnation of the Danish economy in 1981. Since the initial "oil shock" of 1973–1974, Denmark has suffered from high unemployment, particularly among young and female unskilled workers, large deficits in trade and in the state budget, and modest growth. Until defeated in November over proposals to place special taxes on pension and insurance funds, the SD governed as a minority and relied on several small center parties for parliamentary support. Premier Jorgensen's policy of seeking broad coalitions on an issue-by-issue basis brought heavy criticism from the parties to the left of the SD as well as from the left wing of the SD itself. The DKP has been unable to protest in parliament, but SF and VS spokesmen denounced the SD government regularly during 1981. The two leftist parties regularly join the parties of the right in voting against the SD and its allies. It was such a vote that toppled the SD minority government in November and caused the sudden elections of 8 December.

Because of its parliamentary setback in 1979, the DKP has emphasized local government policies. From 1978 to 1981, it supported the SD municipal government in Copenhagen and held one of the city council's "portfolios." Its compromises on the overburdened city budget brought criticism from other leftist parties, especially the VS. As noted, the DKP suffered a substantial loss of votes in the November municipal elections.

The DKP's domestic program has not changed significantly in recent years. A recent publication entitled *Hvor laenge endnu?* (How much longer?) focused on the steadily increasing unemployment (240,000 or over 8 percent of the labor force). The DKP would attack the problem through greatly increased investment in new and rehabilitated housing, public works, increased educational opportunities, prolonged maternity leave, and a reduction of the standard workweek to 35 hours (presumably with no reduction in pay). The party claims that the net cost of such measures would amount to about four billion kroner (about U.S. $560 million). Even without such measures, the SD budget proposal submitted just prior to the dissolution forecast a deficit of forty billion *kroner.* The local and parliamentary election campaigns saw a variety of proposals from the various parties.

The DKP was not able to win political points from Danish labor problems in 1981. In March 1981, for the first time in nearly a decade, the basic collective bargaining agreements were reached without parliamentary action or widespread labor unrest, except among printers and journalists. Widespread stoppages and lockouts continued in these areas until early summer. (*Nordisk Kontakt,* nos. 4 and 9.) The DKP has long been stronger in the trade union movement than in electoral politics. Although the national labor federation (Landsorganisationen) is firmly controlled by unionists loyal to the SD (though they have recently been openly critical of its policies), some Communists and other Marxist activists are prominent in union locals. Communist strength in the Metalworkers' Union was evident at the union's congress in September, but support for the union's SD officers remained strong. Until the split with the maverick Preben Moller Hansen, the Communists were in command of the Seamen's Union. The past years of economic stagnation have tested union patience, but have not caused radicalization. The DKP-sponsored leftist opposition in key unions (the so-called shop-steward movement) remained quiet during 1981.

Energy policy has been another area of leftist activism in recent Danish politics. The question of nuclear power (Denmark currently has no reactors, nor are any under construction) and the promising North Sea oil and gas finds remained the principal issues. Protracted negotiations with the private holders of North Sea concessions have provoked calls for nationalization from the DKP as well as from the VS and SF (ibid., no. 4). Until 1979, the DKP had been staunchly pronuclear, but two weeks after the Three Mile Island incident, the DKP joined the antinuclear forces (*Information*, 10 April 1979).

The events of 1981 demonstrated the difficulty the DKP has in projecting a distinctive profile. Although polls in March gave the DKP 4 percent of the potential vote (similar to its pre-1979 strength), its fortunes sank during the following months. The setback in the November local elections presaged the poor showing in the December elections.

International Views and Positions. International issues were prominent in Danish politics in 1981. The DKP made its views known, but there was no variation in the party's position: unswerving support for Soviet foreign policy and unaltered opposition to Denmark's two main links with other Western nations—NATO and the EEC. As international tensions continued to increase, the focus of Danish foreign policy debates moved marginally away from the EEC and distant global issues and centered on the country's own exposed position.

Although public opinion polls indicated record strong support for Denmark's membership in NATO, there was nevertheless considerable debate over Denmark's role in the alliance and over revitalizing détente. Foreign criticism of Denmark's modest defense efforts (the so-called Denmarkization issue) brought sharp retorts from the left and the SD. Denmark's consideration of expanding NATO supply depots ("prepositioning") on its territory (no foreign troops are currently stationed in Denmark proper, but there are important installations in Greenland) attracted vigorous comment from the DKP and other foes of Danish links with the West. In addition, an organized peace campaign quickly gained momentum. In conjunction with similar forces in other Nordic countries, plans for a peace march to Paris were made at a meeting in Aalborg in May (ibid., no. 10). Although the DKP supports these developments, it was not especially visible. In November, there was considerable turmoil when Danish authorities arrested a prominent writer, Arne Herlov Petersen, on charges of espionage and expelled a Soviet diplomat. The charges cited Soviet agents and Petersen for funding various anti–nuclear weapons advertisements in the Danish press (*Jyllands-Posten*, 6 November). The Danish peace movement has plenty of spontaneous support, but Soviet strategy has been to minimize the role played by Denmark, Norway, and Iceland in NATO and to encourage their withdrawal. The weakness of the DKP may have encouraged Soviet agents to try a variety of approaches (see Trond Gilberg et al., "The Soviet Union and Northern Europe," *Problems of Communism*, 30, March–April).

The discovery in October of a Soviet submarine in restricted Swedish waters indirectly influenced Danish discussions. Preben Moller Hansen publicly doubted DKP Chairman Jensen's "regrets" over the incident and predicted that the DKP would suffer an electoral backlash (*Information*, 2 November). The VS and SF were more outspoken in their criticism of the Soviet violation of Swedish neutrality. SF Chairman Gert Petersen has been consistently critical of both the United States and the Soviet Union for the demise of détente. The violation of Swedish neutrality made adoption of the SF's long-standing proposal for similar neutrality for Denmark even more unlikely (*Nordisk Kontakt*, no. 11).

Communists continued to be active and prominent in the Popular Movement Against the EEC (Folkebevaegelsen imod EF), which was formed in the early 1970s as a nonpartisan alliance. The movement did very well in the first direct elections to the European Parliament in 1979. Although the VS and SF ran alternative anti-EEC lists, the movement received 20.7 percent of the vote and elected four candidates, including the communist editor of the anti-EEC weekly *Det Ny Notat* (The new notice), Jens Peter Bonde. The DKP holds 6 of the 21 seats on the movement's Executive Committee.

International Activities and Party Contacts. Trips to Eastern Europe and elsewhere are a regular activity of DKP leaders. In April, Jensen visited East Germany and issued the usual communiqué extolling fraternity (ADN, 15 April). A larger delegation from the DKP, headed by Executive Committee member Margrit Hansen, paid a visit to the USSR from 30 June to 12 July. In addition to talks with Soviet party officials in Moscow, the Danes visited Uzbekistan. The concluding communiqué reaffirmed DKP support for the USSR and the Soviet party (*Pravda*, 12 July). In September, Ib Norlund led a DKP delegation to Romania for visits to various party and trade union facilities. The independent line of Nicolae Ceauşescu and the Romanian party was not mentioned in the final communiqué (Agerpres, 10 September). Reverse hospitality was accorded a visiting East German delegation headed by Politburo member Erich Mückenberger in July. The delegation met with Jensen and other prominent party activists, as well as with noncommunist politicians (ADN, 31 July).

Publications. The daily *Land og Folk* (Nation and people) is the central DKP organ. Its circulation of some 10,500 increases on weekends to about 14,000. In contrast to 1980 (and to many other Danish newspapers), *Land og Folk* was not involved in the various labor conflicts that shut down much of the Danish press for prolonged periods in 1981. Typographers' costly demands on the communist paper require a subsidy of at least 6 million kroner ($850,000). *Tiden-Verden Rund* (Times around the world) is the party's theoretical monthly journal. The DKU publishes *Fremad* (Forward).

Other Marxist Groups. Ever since the DKP lost its parliamentary seats, more attention has accrued to the VS and SF, which compete with the DKP for left-socialist support. In domestic politics, both parties maintain an independent profile, but in practice their differences are in nuance. Both have been sharply critical of the governing SD, which has looked to the center for political support. Although SF Chairman Petersen has suggested the possibility of left-wing support for more radical SD measures, there has been no response from the SD. Since 1959, when it was formed by purged DKP Chairman Aksel Larsen, the SF has been the most pragmatic of the various leftist groups. In 1966–1967 and 1971–1973, it provided parliamentary support for minority SD governments in domestic matters. This pragmatism caused several splits, and since 1977 the SF has presented a more radical profile. Chairman Gert Petersen has been a prominent SF parliamentarian and theorist since 1961. Although suspicious of DKP dominance in the anti-EEC Movement, the SF is also opposed to Danish membership and elected one member to the EEC parliament. The SF has long been a vocal critic of NATO, U.S. foreign policy, and Danish defense efforts and advocates unilateral disarmament (*Information*, 4–5 October 1980). Although the SF is a purely Danish party, it has close ties to an analogous party in Norway, the Sosialistisk Venstreparti, and expresses enthusiasm for Yugoslavia and other advocates of Eurocommunism.

The VS is also a native party without institutional ties to foreign movements. At its Eleventh Congress (closed to the public) in December 1980, the party reaffirmed its commitment to "extra-parliamentary tactics"—demonstrations, strikes, and occupations. The congress reflected the continuing division within the VS between a "moderate" wing led by VS Chairman Preben Wilhjelm and several more "revolutionary" factions. There was controversy over the party's public criticism of Soviet domestic and foreign policies, but no deviation from its traditional strong criticism of the United States, NATO, and the EEC. The party's tendency to purge members continued (*Berlingske Tidende*, 5 December 1980).

In addition to these established parties, a myriad of "parties," cultural groups, and publications reflect various Marxist viewpoints. The KAP, headed by Copenhagen University lecturer Benito Scocozza, elected a new Central Committee in January and produced a platform. Although presumably still loyal to China, the party has made fewer references to Beijing in recent years. It has also been active in student protest movements and in the most radical union factions (*Arbejderavisen*, 14–20 January). The Trotskyists, currently organized in the SAP, have some two hundred adherents. They remain critical of all foreign powers and domestic competitors.

Among the many non-DKP leftist publications are the SF's financially ailing *Socialistisk Dagblad* (Socialist daily); the KAP's *Arbejderavisen* (Workers' news); the SAP's *Klassekampen* (Class struggle); and the independent and radical socialist *Politisk Revy* (Political review).

University of Massachusetts   Eric S. Einhorn
Amherst

Finland

The Finnish Communist Party (Suomen Kommunistienen Puole; SKP) is one of Western Europe's most important parties in relative size and political influence. Its front party, the Finnish People's Democratic League (Suomen Kansan Demokraatienen Liitto; SKDL), which it almost completely dominates, has since World War II been one of Finland's four leading parties, attracting from 16 to 23 percent of the vote. It won 17.9 percent in 1979, in the last parliamentary elections, and holds 35 of the 200 seats in the Eduskunta. The SKDL has served in seven governments, including the present one.

The SKP was founded on 29 August 1918 at a meeting near Moscow by a group of Social Democrats, who had fled Finland after the "reds" lost the Finnish Civil War. Headquartered in the USSR until World War II, it operated through various front organizations fairly effectively, except for the early and mid-1930s, and dominated the principal trade union federation during much of the 1920s. The wartime record of Communists in the armed forces during the 1939–1940 and 1941–1944 wars between Finland and the USSR gave the movement a reputation of patriotic loyalty, despite the efforts of SKP leaders to incite desertion and opposition to the wars. Under the terms of the armistice with the USSR, the SKP was legalized in 1944 and has since operated openly in Finland.

Factional strife has characterized the SKP throughout its history and nearly split the party in 1981. Following the election of a moderate, Aarne Saarinen, as chairman in 1966, the SKP at its Fifteenth Congress in 1969 adopted a more reformist program. The hard-line, Stalinist (sometimes called "Taistoists" after its leader, Taisto Sinisalo) wing walked out and formed separate organizational units. Under Moscow's pressure, the party has not formally split, despite the intransigence of the two sides. An extraordinary congress in 1970 adopted a formula giving the Stalinists about one-third of the leadership posts, but they have failed to live up to their agreement to dissolve their organizational units and newspapers. (See Seija Spring and D. W. Spring, "The Finnish Communist Party: Two Parties in One," in David Childs, ed., *The Changing Face of Western Communism*, New York: St. Martin's Press, 1980, pp. 172–204.)

Part of the disagreement concerns the role of the SKDL; the Stalinists would like to end what little independence it has. Started in 1944 as an electoral coalition of the SKP and left-wing socialist associations, it has developed a nationwide organization of its own and a separate program, more moderate than that of the SKP. Although it has never attracted many noncommunist groups and over two-thirds of its parliamentary representation (29 out of 35) are SKP members, its chairman has always been a left-wing noncommunist. (Ibid.) The current chairman, Kalevi Kivistö, like his predecessor, Ele Alenius, has considerable prestige among noncommunists.

The SKP has an estimated membership of 47,000 to 48,000 out of a population of 4,784,000. While its principal support is among workers in the industrial centers of the south, the SKP has historically attracted support in the northern rural areas. In fact, the SKDL receives its largest percentage of electoral district votes in the northern and eastern districts of Finland. Much of the communist support springs from the civil war heritage. The SKP has never received the support of many intellectuals. (Ibid.) Recently, as the party has sought to adjust to the decrease in the number of farmers and blue-collar workers relative to white-collar workers in Finnish society, the number of better-paid workers in the party has increased, and the reformist wing of the party has started attracting more intellectuals.

Nineteen eighty-one was a turbulent year politically. The power balance in Prime Minister Mauno Koivisto's coalition government shifted toward his party, the Social Democrats, as a result of the local elections of 1980, which confirmed the declining electoral base of the Center Party and the SKDL (the fourth coalition partner is the small Swedish People's Party). Public opinion polls indicated that the SKDL continued to lose support in 1981, while the opposition National Coalition (Conservative) Party picked up enough additional support over its gains in the 1980 election to threaten the position of the Social Democrats as the largest party. Since President Urho Kekkonen's age—he is 81—and poor health made it unlikely that he would run again for re-election, potential candidates of the various parties started jockeying for position. Kekkonen's Center Party in particular sought to counter the growing popularity of Koivisto. The stage for crisis was thus set, when controversy among the governing parties arose in early April over the terms of an incomes policy that government economists thought necessary to contain inflation and maintain economic prosperity. The Center Party and the SKDL disliked a compromise program considered by the government, and the SKDL's intransigent position produced a stalemate. Koivisto met the challenge by threatening to dissolve the coalition, and the two parties backed down, fearing that a new government might include the Conservatives. Koivisto emerged from the crisis with increased prestige. (*Nordisk Kontakt*, nos. 4–9.)

Although bickering over budget proposals continued in the fall, the coalition survived the year, making its tenure—31 months in December—one of the longest in recent times. The SKDL continued to hold three cabinet posts, two by SKP moderates and one by SKDL Chairman Kivistö. On 18 March, Arvo Aalto resigned his position of minister of labor to devote full time, in his capacity as SKP secretary general, to the party's effort to recoup losses among the electorate and to prepare for the upcoming SKP congress. He was replaced by a relatively unknown moderate SKP economist, Jouko Kajanoja. Kivistö remained vice-minister for education and Veikko Saarto minister of transportation and communications.

In August, President Kekkonen's health deteriorated sharply during a visit to Iceland, making a special presidential election likely in the near future. Because of the president's power—Kekkonen has dominated Finnish politics for over two decades—the succession question overshadowed all other issues. Koivisto was named acting president, giving him a preferred position in the presidential race. On 27 October, Kekkonen announced his resignation, and elections to the Electoral College were set for 17–18 January 1982. The college is to meet 26 January. Special nominating conventions or party councils were held in November to select party candidates. The Social Democrats chose Koivisto, as expected. In a surprise upset, the Center Party convention did not accept the recommendation of party Chairman Paavo Väyrynen that former Prime Minister Ahti Karjalainen be its nominee; instead, it named former party Chairman Johannes Virolainen. The Conservatives selected Harry Holkeri and the Swedish People's Party the editor of *Huvudstadsbladet*, Jans Magnus Jannson, a possible compromise coalition candidate for nonsocialist forces. After much controversy, the SKP Central Committee concurred with an SKDL decision that its 40-year-old chairman, Kalevi Kivistö, would be its candidate.

Leadership and Organization. The SKP's Nineteenth Party Congress of 22–24 May opened with an unprecedented situation. Because of a revolt against factional feuding among many of the elected delegates, there was no prior agreement on election of party leaders. Resistance to the re-election of Chairman Aarne Saarinen, leader of the moderate faction (sometimes referred to as liberals or Eurocommunists), and of Vice-Chairman Taisto Sinisalo, head of the hard-line, Stalinist group, continued throughout the congress. Because the dissidents could not find a leader, Saarinen and Sinisalo were re-elected by the new Central Committee after the congress adjourned, on the proviso that a new congress could be called in a year's time if the two leaders did not reunite the party. (The Central Committee or six party districts can call an extraordinary congress, such as that held in 1970.) A woman, Maija-Liisa Halonen of the Metalworkers' Union, replaced retiring Olavi Hänninen as the second vice-chairman; she was considered a moderate but a potential leader of a "third force." In response to grass-roots pressure, four members of the Secretariat were ousted from the Politburo and the Central Committee. Over one-half of the members of the Central Committee were replaced (32 of 50 full members and fifteen deputies), partly as a result of the efforts of those seeking to reunify the party but mainly because of a generational shift. The average age of Central Committee members is now 44.

Nevertheless, the new members also fell at least to some extent into the old categories of majority moderates and minority Stalinists and the same proportion was kept: 29 to 21. The number of members of the Executive Committee (Politburo), also selected by the Central Committee from among its own membership, was increased from fifteen to sixteen; nine of the incumbents were replaced, and the new proportion of the majority and minority factions was ten to six. Members of the new Politburo were Saarinen, Halonen, Aalto, Kajanoja, Hänninen, Inger Hirvelä, Erkki Kauppila, Aarne Aitamurto, Arvo Kemppainen, and Tutta Tallgren of the majority faction and Sinisalo, Urho Jokinen, Marjatta Stenius-Kaukonen, Esko-Juhani Tennilä, Seppo Toiviainen, and Pentti Salo from the minority. (*Huvudstadsgladet*, 25 May; *Nordisk Kontakt*, no. 10.)

Party Internal Affairs. The SKDL's electoral decline in the 1980 local elections, when its share of the vote was only 16.7 percent, fanned factional strife and subsequently caused a reaction among party followers to that strife. Each of the factions blamed the other for the controversy and the electoral losses (*Kansan Uutiset*, 22 October 1980; *Tiedonantaja*, 22 October 1980). Earlier in 1980, Saarinen and Sinisalo had challenged each other openly and set out their main points of conflict on the pages of the chief party paper, *Kansan Uutiset*. Saarinen pointed out that the party must adapt to changing conditions, particularly to the decline of its traditional support among small farmers and forest workers and to the improvement in the working and living conditions of workers in general. He expressed his belief that sectarian and unbending adherence to Marxist-Leninist doctrines was costing the party the support of workers. He went so far as to assert that the actions of some party members lent credence to bourgeois charges that the SKDL represented a foreign power and constituted a fifth column. Sinisalo responded angrily that Leninism was not dead. Socialism could not be attained under conditions controlled by bourgeois democracy, he insisted, and class interests should be placed above national interests. The policies that the SKP had adopted in cooperating with bourgeois parties in the government coalition had caused the party not only to abandon the historic battle against capitalism, but also actually to help implement government measures favoring capitalism. (*Kansan Uutiset*, 26 and 27 February 1980.) A running battle between the two leaders continued until the eve of the congress.

The revolt against both leaders started in early 1980 in the Lappland party district, the party's largest, among party members who were weary of the strife and believed that it was a principal cause for the party's declining support (*Nordisk Kontakt*, no. 10). Jorma Wahlström, head of the SKDL parliamentary group, suggested in an article in a northern Finland SKDL newspaper that both

Saarinen and Sinisalo should be replaced. Lappland was joined by the Oulu and Kainu districts in the north, and the movement spread throughout the country, particularly among the newer party members (ibid., no 3). Attention centered on Secretary General Aalto as the replacement for Saarinen, despite Sinisalo's attack on Aalto for advocating a "historic compromise" line (*Kansan Uutiset*, 27 February 1980). The minority faction became convinced that the object of the revolt was to force Sinisalo out and united behind him (*Huvudstadsbladet*, 25 May).

The Nineteenth Congress started with the moderates holding a commanding majority—296 of the 522 delegates, compared with 226 for the Stalinists. However, the moderate delegation was not under the control of Saarinen or other top leaders. Although Saarinen and Sinisalo recognized the need to end factional strife in their opening statements, the debate over whether to replace the two monopolized the congress's attention. Seeking a consensus, the Elections Committee met almost continuously until the morning of the congress's last day, when it gave up after selecting nominees for the new Central Committee. At that point, the majority faction caucused under the chairmanship of parliamentary Deputy Arvo Ramppainen of Oulu and again voted to replace Saarinen, 183 to 95. However, the dissidents were frustrated by Aalto's and Vice-Chairman Olavi Hänninen's refusals to stand for the chairmanship as long as Saarinen would not voluntarily resign, despite the efforts of dissident leaders to persuade them. An attempt to recruit Aarne Aitomurto, chairman of the Construction Workers' Union, also failed.

The majority rump, led by Aalto and the Helsinki delegation, then rallied behind Saarinen. It, together with the minority Stalinist faction, which unanimously chose to support Saarinen in order to secure Sinisalo's re-election, outnumbered the dissidents. In another unprecedented action, the congress, whose proceedings were already delayed, adjourned without electing the top leadership, leaving the decision to the Central Committee. (Ibid., 25 May; *Nordisk Kontakt*, no. 10.)

The dissidents dropped their opposition and the Central Committee, meeting immediately after the adjournment, unanimously re-elected Saarinen and Sinisalo. The two leaders pledged to work for party unity. Saarinen, 67 years old, stated his intention of resigning before the next congress in favor of Aalto, a statement he repeated in later interviews with newspapers. (*Nordisk Kontakt*, no. 10; *Helsingin Sanomat*, 31 May; *Huvudstadsbladet*, 2 June; *FBIS*, 8 June.) An important factor working to prevent a complete split was the attitude of the Soviet delegation to the congress; its leader, Soviet Politburo member and party secretary of the Leningrad district Grigori Romanov, expressed in his address to the congress the Soviet desire that the SKP strive to reach unity (*Pravda*, 24 May; *FBIS*, 2 June). One Finnish magazine claimed that the Soviet delegation worked behind the scenes to save the SKP's dual leadership (*Suomen Kuvalehti*, 5 June).

On political and organizational issues, except for unanimous adoption of a "political document" stating general attitudes toward international issues (*IB*, July, pp. 7–8), the moderates united and forced through the majority's program proposals. Besides the leadership struggle, the major issues concerned the policies the party should follow in its relation with the other parties in the government coalition and whether *Kansan Uutiset* should continue to be the principal party organ. Sinisalo, who opened the congress, repeated his attacks on the SKP's government policies. Saarinen, in his report as chairman to the congress, defended them, pointing out that compromise was necessary and warned of the threat the Conservative Party posed to the government coalition. A proposal by the minority faction that the SKDL withdraw from the coalition was defeated, and the congress then endorsed continued participation in a government with the Social Democrats and the Center Party. A call was issued for order within the SKP and for obedience to party decisions; the majority and minority factions were instructed to appear united in parliament and in other state and municipal agencies. A minority proposal that the SKP reject a compromise agreement between the coalition partners on the taxing of social benefits, one aspect of an anti-inflationary package of economic and social legislation, was voted down by a closer margin, 252–232, after an understanding that the SKDL parliamentary delegation would seek improvement of the whole package was reached. (*Huvudstadsbladet*, 25 May; *Nordisk Kontakt*, no. 10.)

The congress's decisions left the party organization and functions in an uncertain state. One of the decisions forbade the holding of caucuses before Central Committee and Politburo meetings. The effect was described by a leader of the dissident moderates who had been named to the Politburo, Arvo Kemppainen, in an interview with *Kansan Uutiset* (15 August). Kemppainen said that discussions of the Politburo and the Central Committee were general in nature because of the lack of prior decisions and planning. This, in turn, affected the work of district organizations and the enthusiasm of party activists. He disclosed that the Central Committee was forming a work group to "clarify the position of the party machinery from the Central Committee to the district level."

Domestic Attitudes and Activities. Factional strife complicated the SKDL's cooperation with the Social Democrats and the Center Party in the coalition and was a prime factor in the government crisis in the spring. Although, at the end of 1980, the Finnish economy was still thriving compared with other West European economies, government and business economists feared that rising inflation (then running at about 14 percent) would threaten the competitiveness of Finnish exports on international markets. When talks between trade unions and employers' associations on nationwide wage contracts broke down at the beginning of the year, the government intervened. Differences among the coalition parties made a solution difficult, and the government appointed an arbiter acceptable to all interested parties—Matti Pekkanen, managing director of the Central Association of Forest Industries—to prepare a national incomes policy. His two-year package, dubbed the Pekkanen Plan, called for a voluntary price freeze, nominal wage increases, a limited indexing of wages, subsidies to agricultural producers, some tax decreases, and a lowering of government spending, including social welfare benefits. This package was accepted by the employers' organizations, agricultural organizations, and most of the trade unions—those that the Social Democrats controlled—but was opposed by many Communists for not favoring low-income groups and workers more. The Center Party had some reservations because of its desire to secure more benefits for the agricultural sector. SKP and SKDL leaders had great difficulty in gaining general communist acceptance of the package. They hesitated to exert discipline because the SKP was preparing for its congress and the Stalinists were ardently opposed to the agreement. The proposed tax on social welfare benefits was the chief sticking point.

In early April, the issue came to a head when Koivisto threatened to resign if the governing parties would not accept the package without major changes. At that point, Saarinen claimed in a statement to the press after talking with President Kekkonen, that the president wanted Koivisto to resign and the coalition reformed under another prime minister. Koivisto responded publicly that only parliament could dismiss him. Kivistö took the lead in resolving the crisis by expressing confidence in Koivisto, while Saarinen remained silent. In the interests of preserving the coalition, the SKDL and the Center Party retreated, and the package was sent to parliament with the understanding that only minor changes would be made in it. (*Huvudstadsbladet*, 12 April; *Nordisk Kontakt*, nos. 4–9.)

In his address to the party congress, Saarinen laid out the party's stand toward the government's budget and fiscal policy: subsidies for housing, national health services, day-care benefits, and expenditures for education and culture should be increased, not decreased as the Minister of Finance Ahti Pekkala (a Center Party representative) had asked; a proposal to increase defense spending should be dropped; and business taxes should be kept at the same level, not decreased as planned. (*Huvudstadsbladet*, 23 May).

Opposition to the Pekkanen Plan also created struggles in the trade unions. While the Social Democrats control 23 of the 28 trade unions within the Finnish Confederation of Trade Unions (SAK), the Communists have a large following in nearly all unions. They control one-third of the leadership of the SAK, including the vice-chairmanship. They dominate the powerful Construction Workers' Union and the smaller Rubber and Leather Workers' and Building Maintenance Workers' unions. Their greatest influence is in the largest and most powerful union, the metalworkers, where they command the support of about 47 percent of the members, compared to some 50 percent for the Social Democrats. (Spring and Spring, "The Finnish Communist Party," p. 172.) A majority of the metalworkers voted against the Pekkanen Plan, and the Communists, especially in those unions where the Stalinists have influence, threatened to use their potential to embarrass the anti-inflation program, mainly through wildcat strikes. They were not able, however, to thwart passage of the plan.

The question of who would succeed President Kekkonen was important for the Communists because of its implications for Finland's relations with the USSR and for their own role in Finnish government and society. Despite the general belief that Soviet leaders favored former Prime Minister Ahti Karjalainen of the Center Party, Saarinen indicated in statements to the press an unwillingness to support him. Sinisalo took sharp exception to Saarinen's position and said Saarinen should remain quiet on the issue (*Uusi Suomi*, 22 January). Saarinen first maintained distance from Koivisto, despite the fact that polls showed he was favored by many Communists, but later softened his position. At the party congress, Sinisalo agreed with Saarinen that the SKP should play an independent role and that the SKDL should run its own candidate (*Huvudstadsbladet*, 23 May).

After Kekkonen's breakdown in health in the early fall heightened the succession issue, the SKP quandary grew. Since an SKDL candidate would have little or no chance, the question arose as to whether the SKDL should combine with other parties on a joint candidate on the second round of voting in the Electoral College (patterned on that of the United States, except that the electors are released from supporting their party's candidate after the first vote; only the two top candidates can be considered in the third vote). Speculation arose that if neither the Conservatives nor the Center Party would support Koivisto, the Communists might play a key role in the final selection, as they had in Kekkonen's election in 1956.

In order to prevent a right-wing candidate from being elected, the best alternative for the SKP would be to join with the Social Democrats. In articles in *Kommunisti* and *Kansan Uutiset*, Aalto reportedly proposed that the SKDL and the Social Democrats enter into negotiations on establishment of common goals and on the possibility of presenting a common presidential candidate (*Helsingin Sanomat*, 21 August). Most acceptable to the Communists was Social Democratic Party Chairman Kalevi Sorsa, who was thought to be the Soviets' second choice (*Huvudstadsbladet*, 7 February, 19 September). Stalinist attacks on Koivisto grew; in October, Sinisalo said that Karjalainen or Sorsa would be preferable to Koivisto. When Kivistö retorted that he preferred Koivisto to Karjalainen, *Tiedjonanta* made an oblique attack on Kivistö by stating that the SKDL "has no eastern relations," meaning that it lacked favor with Moscow. Saarinen then entered the fray, accusing *Tiedjonanta* of being divisive and the minority of a "contemptible" attempt to prevent Kivistö from being the SKDL candidate. (*Suomenmaa*, 3 October; *Kansan Uutiset*, 6 and 11 October; *Huvudstadsbladet*, 8 October.) Saarinen later said that he had earlier expressed some doubts about Koivisto but he believed now that Koivisto, if elected, would follow the foreign policy line of Kekkonen and his predecessor, Juho Paasikivi (*Huvudstadsbladet*, 16 October).

International Views and Positions. The SKP's principal effort in the international field in 1981 was to try to ensure the maintenance and strengthening of ties with the USSR as the presidential election drew near. The SKP had stood solidly behind the Paasikivi-Kekkonen line of placing top priority on reassuring Moscow that Finnish authorities would adopt no policies constituting a threat to Soviet security. The two party factions united on this point, although the Stalinists were more ardent in their support of Moscow views. In his report to the Congress, Saarinen said that strengthening the forces that supported the present foreign policy would be the central theme for the Communists in the presidential election (ibid., 23 May).

Most attention was given to securing greater allegiance of all Finnish party leaders to the 1948 Treaty of Friendship, Cooperation, and Mutual Assistance with the USSR. SKP leaders adhered to the Soviet view that Finland's first obligation was to that treaty's provisions for creating a common defense against any threat from Germany or its allies, rather than to Finland's neutrality policy. In what was interpreted as a warning to the Finnish presidential candidates, an unsigned article in *Pravda* on 13 March attacked "right-wing tendencies" in Finland as threats to the Paasikivi-Kekkonen line.

Debate on this issue resumed in the late spring when the internal discussions of a parliamentary defense committee commissioned to examine the 1948 treaty leaked to the press. Keijo Korhonen of the Center Party reportedly wanted a sentence placed in the committee report stating that Soviet assistance to Finland would come only after an attack on Finland had taken place. A moderate SKP committee member, Jorma Hentila, said the Korhonen initiative had the potential to create trouble in Finnish-Soviet relations. A Stalinist member, Matti Viialainen, wrote a reservation to the committee report asserting that Finnish-Soviet military cooperation would "strengthen considerably the preventive significance" of the treaty, but Hentila would not join him in such an unpopular position and Viialainen stood alone in support of his reservation (*Dagens Nyheter*, 23 May).

In an apparent attempt to reassure Soviet leaders that no change in foreign policy would take place under a new president, all four major parties, including the Conservatives, had stated by the summer that they favored extending the 1948 pact as presently written. The pact runs until 1990. (*Huvudstadsbladet*, 15 June.)

The closeness of relations between the Finnish and Soviet communist parties and an outline of SKP attitudes toward international issues were reflected in the joint statements issued during a major meeting of delegations of the two parties in Moscow on 27–28 April. Chief emphasis was placed on "maintaining and strengthening" détente, "curbing" the arms race, and finding "effective" measures of disarmament. Attention was also focused on the "militaristic course" of the new U.S. administration and its "plans" to deploy "new types" of nuclear missiles in Western Europe, thereby "imperiling" the future of the continent. President Kekkonen's nuclear weapons–free zone proposal for Scandinavia was praised, and support was given to a "constructive outcome" of the Helsinki review conference in Madrid (Tass, 29 April; *FBIS*, 30 April). These themes were repeated in the "political document" adopted by the party congress (*IB*, July, pp. 7–8). However, while the SKP continued to defend Soviet activities in Afghanistan, it criticized Soviet policies toward Poland. Early in the year, Saarinen stated in an interview with *Suomen Sosialdemokraatti* (16 January) that he agreed with a Hungarian delegation visiting Finland that each communist party must determine its own issues. "Outside intervention will not help but complicate the situation," he said, adding that noninterference was the "only way to avoid conflicts and maintain effective ties in the international communist movement."

Considerable SKP effort was devoted to criticizing the United States and NATO over NATO's plans to modernize its long-range theater nuclear force and deploy newer weapons in Western Europe. The argument was made that this action would upset the strategic balance in favor of the United States and that arms negotiations should be comprehensive and include all nuclear weapons (*Kansan Uutiset*, 1 June, 1 July). Communist propaganda activity on this issue increased when the new U.S. administration decided to build the enhanced radiation weapon, or neutron bomb, a development that caused considerable popular reaction in Finland. The SKDL Executive Committee and SKP Secretary General Aalto issued statements criticizing the decision. The SKP Political Committee met to discuss the matter and arranged a public demonstration to express opposition to the new weapon. (Ibid., 11–13 August; *Tiedonantaja*, 14 August; *Huvudstadsbladet*, 14 August.)

The SKP also sought to encourage support of a Nordic nuclear weapons–free zone. SKP leaders criticized Finnish government officials for not taking more initiative on the matter following Norwegian Prime Minister Odvar Nordli's endorsement, in a New Year's address, of such a zone if it were part of a wider security arrangement in Europe and included territory outside Scandinavia. Although Soviet commentators immediately sought to encourage Scandinavian creation of a zone (*Pravda*, 22 January), the Finnish government, while still supporting the 1963 Kekkonen Proposal for a Scandinavian zone, stood apart from the Norwegian initiative and took no action to start negotiations. Leonid Brezhnev attempted to encourage support for the concept in a written response to questions of the Finnish newspaper *Suomen Sosialidemokraatti*, published on 26 June. Brezhnev said the USSR was "prepared to commit itself to not using nuclear weapons against those Nordic countries that participate in the nuclear-free zone and, consequently, refuse to manufacture, acquire, or deploy nuclear weapons on their territory." In an effort to counter criticism that the USSR would not consider removing its nuclear weapons located near the Nordic countries, he said that the USSR did not "exclude the possibility of considering the question of some other actions that involve our own territory in the region bordering on the Nordic nuclear-free zone. The Soviet Union is prepared to discuss this matter with countries that are interested." (Finnish News Agency, 27 June.) The stranding of a Soviet submarine within a restricted Swedish military zone in late October aroused strong reaction throughout Scandinavia and ended Scandinavian and Finnish interest in pursuing the nuclear weapons–free zone theme.

The Communists continued to criticize the "close relations" between the United States and China and accused the two of cooperating against the USSR, other socialist countries, and "liberation" movements (*Tiedonantaja*, 26 June). Secretary of State Alexander Haig's visit to China in June was also looked on with disfavor (*Kansan Uutiset*, 11 June).

In the international economic field, the Communists were very pleased with the continued high level of Finnish trade with the USSR. The first yearly trade agreement under the 1981–1985 agreement between the two countries was signed in Moscow on 29 January. It projected record trade, 11 percent over 1980; the main items were Soviet fuel to Finland and Finnish metal and forestry products to the USSR. This trade has become very important for Finnish prosperity; in 1980, the USSR was Finland's largest trade partner. Twenty-one percent of Finnish exports and 18 percent of its imports were involved. Agreements were also reached on Finnish participation in the construction of a railway car repair yard in Leningrad, a deep-water port in Tallinn, and a hydroelectric plant in Soviet Karelia. In the fall, one of the largest orders a Finnish shipyard has ever received was placed by the USSR. Thirteen vessels are to be delivered to the USSR in 1983–1984 (*Huvudstadsbladet*, 16 August).

International Party Contacts. SKP contacts with its fraternal parties in the Soviet bloc were at a high level in 1981, largely because of the SKP's congress but also because of the turbulent international and Finnish political scene. On the other hand, Finnish-Soviet government contacts slowed, because of Kekkonen's health. Kekkonen's 12–17 November 1980 visit to the USSR was his last. In late January, Soviet Minister of Culture, Petr Denishev, made an official five-day visit to Helsinki, and in May, Soviet Deputy Chairman Ivan Arkhipov visited Finland, where he was the guest of Prime Minister Koivisto. On 27–30 May, General L. Sutela, commander in chief of the Finnish Defense Forces, was the host of Marshal Nikolai Ogarkov, Soviet chief of the general staff. Sutela returned the visit on 21 September. At the beginning of the year, Ahti Karjalainen, a director of the Bank of Finland, led a Finnish delegation to Moscow to participate in a Soviet-Finnish Economic Cooperation Committee meeting.

There were three important exchanges between the Finnish and the Soviet communist parties: the Romanov-led Soviet delegation to the SKP congress discussed above, and two SKP visits to Moscow. On 27–28 February, a Finnish delegation attended the Soviet party congress. Led by Saarinen, it included Sinisalo, Aalto, International Secretary Olavi Poikolainen, and Stalinist Politburo member Urho Jokinen. The delegation met Mikhail Suslov, Politburo member and secretary of the Soviet

Central Committee; Boris Ponomarev and Mikhail Zimianin, secretaries of the Central Committee; and Vitali Shaposhnikov, deputy head of Soviet party's International Department. Reportedly, the two delegations discussed SKP factional strife, SKP leaders' plans for the upcoming SKP congress, and the Polish situation (*Helsingin Sanomat*, 28 April; *Frankfurter Allgemeine Zeitung*, 22 May). On 8–15 June, after the SKP congress, Sinisalo led a delegation to Moscow made up of the new members of the SKP's Politburo and Central Committee as well as "active" SKP rank-and-file members to attend a seminar series set up by the Soviet party. Radio Moscow (16 June) reported that they met with Soviet "scientists and theoreticians" to discuss international issues, the state of the international communist movement, and decisions "taken in the light of the 26th CPSU [Soviet] Congress on the theoretical and practical problems of developed socialism" (*FBIS*, 22 June).

Exchanges with East European parties were numerous. The Hungarians led the way with several visits in the early part of the year, and nearly every East European party was represented at the SKP congress. Visits with West European parties were less frequent. In fact, dissident moderate leader Arvo Kemppainen complained in the interview with *Kansan Uutiset* (15 August) that ties should be developed with the Scandinavian, French, Italian, Spanish, and Portuguese parties. The last meeting with the Danish, Norwegian, and Swedish parties was in Oslo on 26–27 June 1980. Its communiqué called for cooperation in fighting the NATO decision to produce and deploy new U.S. nuclear weapons in Europe and for joint action to foster security talks between NATO and the Warsaw Pact on medium-range missiles and to encourage mutual force reductions through the Vienna talks. Other goals were "concrete" results for European peace and security at the talks in Madrid, a post-Madrid conference on military détente and disarmament in Europe, and an international effort to combat hunger and poverty. (*IB*, 1980, nos. 17–18.)

Other Marxist Parties. Finland is unique among the Nordic countries in having no significant leftist organizations outside the SKP and SKDL. There is the small pro-Chinese Marxist-Leninist Group of Finland. Its members have visited Beijing and occasionally demonstrate against Soviet "social imperialism," but it has achieved no political influence.

Publications. The editors of the two major SKP papers, *Kansan Uutiset* for the majority faction and *Tiedonantaja* for the minority, feuded strenuously during 1981. At the party congress, the minority demanded that a new organ be established for the party. *Tiedonantaja*'s chief editor, Urho Jokinen, a member of the Politburo, accused *Kansan Uutiset* of propagating non-Marxist as well as Marxist ideas. In a straightforward factional division, the congress voted to keep *Kansan Uutiset* as the main party organ. Efforts to get *Tiedonantaja* to follow the official party line or cease publication failed, and the press problem remained one of the most intractable for the party.

Kommunisti is the SKP's monthly journal, and *Folktidningen* is the weekly newspaper for the party's small Swedish-speaking minority. There are several smaller, local newspapers for each of the factions. Finnish Maoists circulate several violently anti-Soviet publications.

U.S. Department of State   Finis Herbert Capps
Washington, D.C.

(Note: Views expressed in this article are the author's own and do not represent those of the State Department.)

France

The French Communist Party (Parti communiste français; PCF) was founded in December 1920, when the majority of delegates to the Socialist Congress at Tours voted to join Lenin's Third International. The PCF remained a marginal force in French politics until the formation of the Popular Front in 1935. The PCF supported the program of the Popular Front, participated in its electoral success in 1936, but refused to accept ministerial responsibility in that government.

Despite its illegality from 1939 to 1944, the PCF emerged as a powerful postwar force due to its role in the resistance. The PCF participated in the immediate postwar governments until May 1947. Until the adoption of the Common Program of Government in June 1972, the PCF remained a relatively stable, but isolated party of the left. The Left Alliance of the PCF, the Socialists (Parti socialiste; PS) and the Radicals (Mouvement des radicaux de gauche) fundamentally altered French political patterns. Despite defeats in both the presidential elections in 1974 and the legislative elections in 1978, when the left alliance broke down, the evolution of the parties of the left continued. The year 1981, with the certainty of presidential elections and the possibility of legislative elections, thus became crucial not only for the left in general but for the PCF in particular.

The triumph of the left, in the person of François Mitterrand (PS) in the presidential elections and the PS in the ensuing legislative elections, decisively established the PS as the most powerful political party in France. The simultaneous setback of the PCF in both elections signaled a fundamental and significant decline of the PCF on all levels.

The 1981 Elections. Every aspect of PCF activity in 1981 was centered on the presidential and legislative elections. In anticipation of the elections, the PCF made two decisions that subsequently shaped its electoral policies and tested its strength. The first decision led to the independent candidacy of Georges Marchais, the secretary general of the PCF, for the presidency of the republic. This decision, in turn, made the first round of the presidential elections on 26 April 1981 a test of the relative strength of the PCF and the PS, whose respective candidates vied directly for electoral support. The results of the first round of presidential voting decisively demonstrated the dominance of the PS and Mitterrand over the PCF and Marchais. Mitterrand received 7.5 million votes (25.84 percent) as opposed to 4.5 million (15.34 percent) for Marchais.

The electoral decline of the PCF was massive and undeniable. The PCF had polled 20.55 percent in the first round of the March 1978 legislative elections, 22.46 percent in the March 1979 cantonal elections, and 20.57 percent in the June 1980 European Parliament elections. The vote in the presidential elections signified a loss of approximately 25 percent of the PCF's electoral strength. Marchais explained the defeat mainly in terms of the "useful vote" factor: "Communist voters had voted for Mitterrand because they were manipulated by opinion polls suggesting that there was a danger of having two right-wing candidates in the second round" (*L'Humanité*, 29 April). In light of precipitous declines even in such PCF strongholds as Le Havre (down 20 percent) and Seine–Saint Denis (down 10 percent), political analysts, as well as critics within the PCF itself, found this explanation inadequate and questioned the present direction and future course of the PCF.

The second major decision that shaped the electoral strategy of the PCF was its unqualified support of Mitterrand in the second round of the presidential elections on 10 May. This decision, adopted by the Central Committee on 28 April greatly enhanced Mitterrand's candidacy, but involved no concessions on the part of the PS. In the second round, Mitterrand triumphed with 15.7 million votes (51.75 percent) to incumbent Valéry Giscard d'Estaing's 14.6 million (48.25 percent). In a statement following Mitterrand's victory, the PCF Politburo made two key assertions. First, the 10 May victory could not have been won without the Communists. Second, the PCF was ready to assume its responsibilities in the government and on all levels of national life. Despite the undeniable importance of PCF support in the Mitterrand victory, the PS made no offer of ministerial posts at that time. On 22 May, in his first full day in office, Mitterrand dissolved the National Assembly and set 14 and 21 June as the dates for new legislative elections.

The results of the legislative elections further demonstrated the decline of the PCF, which polled 4.1 million votes (16.17 percent) in the first round and won 44 seats in the new Assembly, compared with 5.9 million (20.55 percent) and 86 seats in the previous legislative elections of March 1978. The victorious PS polled 9.4 million votes (37.51 percent) in the first round and won an absolute majority of 269 seats in the new 491-seat Assembly. The large number of abstentions (29.64 percent) in the first round and the PS-PCF agreement of second-round withdrawal in favor of the stronger candidate of the left could not conceal the disastrous PCF performance. Despite Marchais's claim of a joint victory, the PCF had suffered its worst electoral defeat since World War II.

Leadership and Organization. In accordance with PCF custom, party congresses decide major organizational questions. The organizational structure established at the Twenty-Third PCF Congress in May 1978 remains, therefore, intact, with its expanded Central Committee of 145 members, its Political Bureau of 21 members, and the Secretariat of the Central Committee of 7 members. Georges Marchais continues as secretary general. In light of severe criticism of both the leadership and the direction of the PCF in 1981, especially in the wake of the crushing electoral setbacks, the Twenty-Fourth Congress, now scheduled for February 1982, will undoubtedly effect significant changes in both leadership and organization.

In a probing article, Guy Koponicki has examined the socio-professional stratum beneath the official, publicly acknowledged leadership of the PCF (*Le Matin Magazine*, 17–18 January, pp. 15–17). It is this "real party," as opposed to militants in the regular party organizations, that has access to decision making and the circulation of information within the PCF. In his description of this real party, Koponicki perceptively analyzes the inner workings of the PCF and its leadership.

> The camouflage of a certain number of facts is a party rule. Meetings of the Secretariat, the Political Bureau, and the Central Committee are held behind closed doors, and members have the right to only expurgated reports on them. They are never given an exact accounting of finances, personnel, and party property. There is naturally a financial report at congresses, but it does not include the balance sheet of *L'Humanité* or of the various party enterprises. The activity of several sections of the Central Committee leads to no public report: the treasury, the handling of party property, foreign policy. Mandates are not limited in time, and no one ever knows for how long one elects a federal secretary, a member of the Central Committee, much less the secretary general of the party. Terms are renewed at each congress but have no limitation. There is no rule on holding several offices at once, and many communist cadres, in addition to their responsibilities in the party, hold two or three elective offices. The secretary general sets the example here. This set of factors makes the members of the caste solitary, not only vis-à-vis the outside, but vis-à-vis the rest of the party. They know all or part of the secrets, know the "explanation to be given". Their power has increased in recent years, but they must handle new contradictions.

No official statement of PCF membership was published in 1981. However, Marchais, in a report to the Central Committee on 25 June, claimed 700,000 members. More conservative estimates place actual membership at under 590,000, based on a loss of 10 percent of an estimated 650,000 in 1980. (*National Review*, 26 June.) However, this attrition must be balanced against new memberships and be interpreted in light of the PCF's history as a *parti-passoire*.

Party Internal Affairs. During 1981, Marchais's presidential candidacy and PCF electoral tactics heightened tensions and dissensions already existing within the PCF concerning Soviet involvement in Afghanistan, the Solidarity movement in Poland, and the absence of democratic debate within the party itself. Relationships between the PCF and the intellectual community were especially strained in 1981. Several intellectuals, artists, and journalists quit the party, most notably the poet, Eugène Guillevic. Despite previous pledges of no more expulsions from the PCF, a few dissidents were expelled, including writer and former party official Jean Elleinstein. The response of PCF leaders to the flight of the intellectuals was a massive counterappeal for support for Marchais's presidential candidacy, signed eventually by 1,200 faithful communist intellectuals. However, several prominent communist intellectuals and artists refused to sign the appeal. Marchais's apparent indifference to the flight of traditional intellectuals is directly related to the PCF's intensified efforts to recruit adherents from the nearly four million members of a new class of intellectuals—engineers, technicians, and executives (ingenieurs, techniciens, et cadres; ITC). "A tangible expression of this orientation is a top-level reform of the Intellectuals and Executives Department, henceforth split up into two departments: the intellectuals coming under Guy Hermier, and the ITC under Charles Fiterman and Jean Colpin. The whole thing is symbolized by the entry into the Politburo of an engineer who is responsible for CGT [General Confederation of Labor] executives, René Le Guen." (*Le Point*, 5 January, pp. 30–31.) This orientation has led to increased PCF discipline over the journalists and editors of *L'Humanité* and the scholars of the Institute for Marxist Research.

Intellectual dissent and criticism, following various individual and group protests, culminated in the founding of an organization called Communist Encounters, which aims to "promote discussion among Communists on all current issues without avoiding the most burning and controversial issues" (*Le Monde*, 15 May). On 15 May, this group began publishing a weekly newspaper, *Rencontres communistes*, which is openly critical of the revival of neo-Stalinism in the PCF. On 2 October, in the biggest purge since World War II, the PCF declared that the 30 founding members of the group had put themselves "outside of the party," a euphemism for expulsion. Included in the group was its leader, Henri Fizbin, who resigned from the Central Committee of the Paris Federation, but still considers himself a Communist.

Auxiliary and Mass Organizations. In 1981, disaffection erupted publicly in two crucial spheres of party influence and activity—labor and youth. The dominance of the PCF in the General Confederation of Labor (Confédération générale du travail; CGT)—strained by the growing demand for a unified labor movement, declining CGT membership, increased agitation for closer cooperation between the PCF and the PS, and strong worker support for the Solidarity movement in Poland—met new opposition. Defections of workers from the PCF were especially evident in 1981 electoral patterns. Much more sensational were the 14 October resignations from the Secretariat of the governing Confederal Bureau of the CGT of two PCF members, Christiane Gilles and Jean-Louis Moynot. Their resignations, preceded by similar action by seven PS secretaries of the Confederal Bureau, were protests against the increasing PCF control of the direction of the CGT. That direction, in turn, has stifled labor movement unity, democratic discussion, and syndical autonomy within the CGT. (Ibid., 16 October.)

Among youth, the growing dissatisfaction with the PCF was reflected in the relatively uneventful year of the Communist Youth Movement (Mouvement de la jeunesse communiste de France). In contrast, the Revolutionary Communist Youth (Trotskyist) continued its rapid growth (*International Press*, 26 January).

Domestic Views and Activities. The key to understanding the often confusing positions taken by the PCF in 1981 is its twofold electoral strategy: the defeat of Giscard d'Estaing and the right and maximum PCF strength vis-à-vis the PS. This strategy required that the PCF appear as the champion of a united left and yet minimize the appeal of the PS.

The platform of the PCF was embodied in 131 proposals advanced by Marchais in November 1980. These 131 proposals were broken down into four objectives (jobs for all, with humane working conditions; a juster society; a free, responsible life in a fraternal society; and a society open to youth), to be achieved by three means (development of France, emphasis on French sovereignty both at home and abroad, and major democratic reforms). Specifically, the proposals called for such programs as the creation of a half million new jobs each year, the building of five million new units of low-cost housing, increased emphasis on law and order, and an immediate halt to the entry of new immigrant workers. (*Le Monde*, 22 November 1980.)

The law-and-order emphasis and the opposition to new immigrant workers combined to produce two major problems for the PCF. On 24 December 1980, PCF Mayor Paul Mercieca led a group of fifty persons in an attack on a dormitory housing three hundred immigrant workers from Mali in the "red belt" Paris suburb of Vitry-sur-Seine. To the astonishment of countless Frenchmen, including many PCF members, this action was approved both personally by Marchais and editorially by *L'Humanité*. Similarly motivated but less vicious attacks on immigrant workers subsequently occurred in other PCF-dominated municipalities. (*Times*, London, 12 February.) On 1 February, PCF Mayor Robert Hué led a demonstration in the Paris suburb of Montigny-les-Corneilles under the windows of a Moroccan family accused in local party leaflets of being drug dealers, despite the lack of any police evidence (*WP*, 10 February). Such PCF tactics further alienated many intellectuals as well as workers and lent an air of desperation to the PCF campaign.

The stunning success of the PS in both the presidential and legislative elections confirmed the decline of the PCF. The electoral conduct of the PCF demonstrably lost voters to the PS on the left and won voters previously fearful of too close a tie between the PCF and the PS to the latter from the center and even the right. The size of the PS victories enabled President Mitterrand to delay any decision on PCF participation in the new government until after the second round of the legislative elections. The PS was able to work out a statement of unity with the PCF, in which the PCF had to accept PS terms on all matters, including a pledge of "entire solidarity" on all levels of government as well as foreign policy (see below). This agreement, reached on 23 June, was a humiliating acknowledgment of the PCF's reduced importance. Four PCF ministers serve in the Mitterrand cabinet: Politburo member Charles Fiterman (transport), PCF Senator Anicet Le Pors (civil service), Jack Ralite of *L'Humanité* (administration reform), and agricultural expert Marcel Rigout (professional training).

International Views and Positions. The PCF has consistently been outspoken in matters of foreign policy, usually presenting itself as the champion of peace, national liberation of subject peoples, anti-imperialism, and French sovereignty. The PCF is consistently pro-Soviet and anti-American in foreign policy matters. On European matters, the PCF has come to a reluctant acceptance of the European Economic Community (EEC), but insists on the protection of French interests, even to the use of the right of veto for this purpose. The French franc must be restored to balance against the West German mark, and French products must be protected against unfair competition from imports. Accordingly, the PCF strongly opposes the entry of Spain and Portugal into the EEC. On European defense, the PCF, consistent with its general pro-Soviet orientation, is opposed to NATO, sees no specific threat posed by Soviet deployment of SS-20 missiles, and fears West German revanchism, fostered by U.S. imperialism.

On the crucial questions of Afghanistan and Poland, the PCF continued to espouse pro-Soviet positions throughout the electoral campaign, despite the political consequences of these unpopular policies among all sectors of the French electorate, especially intellectuals and workers. The PCF reasserted its positions that the Soviet involvement in Afghanistan was not an invasion, but a response to a call for help and that there would be no Soviet intervention in Poland because the Poles must settle their own affairs. The continued support of these pro-Soviet policies made the PCF's subsequent joint statement with the PS on 23 June appear as an abandonment of principle to party hard-liners and an admission of error to its critics. In the joint PS-PCF statement, the PCF agreed to active support of the EEC, Israel's right to existence and security, a homeland for the Palestinians, and, most significantly, Soviet withdrawal from Afghanistan and noninterference in the independent, successful conduct of the economic, social, and democratic reform under way in Poland.

Other matters on which the PCF took public positions in foreign affairs included opposition to France's sale of Mirage jets to Iraq, support of revolutionary movements in El Salvador and Nicaragua, opposition to an attempted coup against the Mauritanian government allegedly backed by Morocco, and support of Lebanon against Israel. Foreign policy positions further complicated the functioning of the PCF because insistence on support of these unpopular positions, especially in reference to Afghanistan and Poland, required increased pressure on militants at precisely the same time intensified demands for democratic discussion within the party were being advanced. Ironically, the foreign policy positions most challenged and criticized within the PCF were the very policies later modified in the PS-PCF joint statement.

International Activities and Party Contacts. During 1981, the PCF maintained frequent contact with communist parties abroad and with Third World organizations. The PCF welcomed to its Paris headquarters party delegations from abroad, most notably an official delegation from Yugoslavia's neutral communist party (20 January). Representatives were likewise received from many Third World organizations, most notably the Sandinista National Liberation Front of El Salvador (30 January) and the Palestine Liberation Organization (6 July). PCF delegates, in turn, visited the Bulgarian Communist Party (18 February) and the Socialist Unity Party of East Germany (2 July). Significantly, the PCF was represented at the Twenty-Sixth Congress of the Communist Party of the Soviet Union (CPSU) in Moscow by Politburo member Gaston Plissonnier, who had represented the PCF in 1976 at the Twenty-Fifth Congress. In 1976, the participation of Plissonnier and the absence of Marchais was interpreted as a conscious effort by the PCF to establish some distance between itself and the CPSU without boycotting the congress. In the 1981 election year, that interpretation was still more plausible.

The Extreme Left. In its efforts to secure as strong a position as possible on the left in the 1981 elections, the PCF had to pay close attention to the extreme left and its varied electoral strategies, activities, and criticisms. Charges of racism were raised against the PCF, especially after the attack on Malian workers, by the French Revolutionary Communist League (LCR) in its weekly journal, *Rouge* (3–9 January). The LCR also vehemently criticized the PCF for its refusal to allow PCF members to sign nomination papers for the LCR candidate, Alain Krivine, and further requiring PCF regulars who had already signed to remove their signatures. The apparent pettiness of the PCF in such matters received extensive publicity (*Intercontinental Press*, 6 April, p. 344). The PCF, in turn, denounced a campaign by "various Trotskyist organizations" that called for an immediate union of the PS and PCF in order to guarantee the defeat of Giscard d'Estaing and the triumph of the left. One new publication on the extreme left, the pro-Albanian biweekly *La Forge*, attracted increased attention this year.

Publications. The principal publications of the PCF are the national daily *L'Humanité*, the weekly *L'Humanité-dimanche*, and three provincial dailies. The regular party press includes the monthly theoretical journal *Cahiers du communisme*, the weekly magazine *France nouvelle*, and a host of smaller, more specialized journals (see *YICA*, 1979, pp. 145–46). The PCF also maintains its own publishing houses, most notably Editions sociales.

Boston College   Francis J. Murphy

Germany:
Federal Republic of Germany

The predecessor of the pro-Moscow German Communist Party (Deutsche Kommunistische Partei; DKP) was the Communist Party of Germany (Kommunistische Partei Deutschlands; KPD), founded on 31 December 1918. The Moscow-controlled KPD, the third largest political party in the Weimar Republic, contributed greatly to the destruction of the post–World War I German democratic system. Following the rise to power of Hitler in January 1933, the KPD was outlawed and reduced to an ineffective underground party. Many thousands of its members fell victim to Nazi suppression, including the party's longtime head, Ernst Thälmann, who was murdered in a Nazi concentration camp.

During the Allied occupation, the KPD was reactivated. In the first national elections in the Federal Republic of Germany (FRG) in 1949, the KPD obtained 5.7 percent of the vote and fifteen seats in the Bundestag. The communist vote decreased in the next elections in 1953 to 2.2 percent, below the 5 percent required by the German electoral law for representation in the federal legislature.

In August 1956, the Federal Constitutional Court outlawed the KPD because the court found that the party pursued objectives in violation of the FRG's Basic Law. The KPD continued as an underground organization directed from East Berlin, where its leader, Max Reimann, resided. The party's influence and membership declined during the illegal period despite massive financial and operational support provided by the Socialist Unity Party of Germany (Socialistische Einheitspartei Deutschlands; SED) of the German Democratic Republic (GDR).

In September 1968, the DKP was founded, recruiting its leaders from the underground KPD, which at that time had about seven thousand members. In 1971, the Federal Security Service stated that as the successor of the KPD, the DKP could be outlawed by decree of the federal minister of interior. The DKP has repeatedly declared that it is a part of the international communist movement and the only legitimate political heir to well-known former leaders of the KPD.

At the Sixth Party Congress of the DKP (29–31 May), membership was reported as 48,856. This figure indicates an increase of 2,376 members since the Fifth Party Congress (October 1978).

Leadership and Organization. The Sixth Congress elected 91 persons to the DKP Executive (Parteivorstand), dropping ten former members and adding twelve new ones. The Executive, in turn, elected a seventeen-member Presidium (Herbert Mies, Hermann Gautier, Jupp Angenfort, Kurt Bachmann, Martha Buschmann, Werner Cieslak, Gerd Deumlich, Kurt Fritsch, Willi Gerns, Erich Mayer, Ludwig Müller, Georg Polikeit, Rolf Priemer, Max Schäfer, Karl Heinz Schröder, Werner Stürmann, and Ellen Weber) and an eleven-member Secretariat (Herbert Mies, Hermann Gautier, Vera Achenbach, Jupp Angenfort, Gerd Deumlich, Kurt Fritsch, Willi Gerns, Josef Mayer, Ludwig Müller, Karl Heinz Schröder, and Wilhelm Sprenger). The Presidium re-elected Herbert Mies as chairman and Hermann Gautier as deputy chairman. The Central Arbitration Commission, elected by the party congress, selected Otto Hans as its chairman. Willi Mohn became the chairman of the Central Auditing Commission and Erich Mayer treasurer of the Presidium. (*Deutscher Informationsdienst* [*DI*], 22 June, pp. 13–15.)

Willi Mohn reported at the party congress that in 1980 the DKP collected DM 5.5 million from its members. Reportedly the DKP has obtained DM 638,642 from party members in the form of inheritance pledges. (Ibid., pp. 6–7.) Mohn denied the accusation that the party receives financial support from the SED.

The organizational structure of the DKP follows the typical communist party model. Some 1,400 primary party organizations in factories, neighborhoods, and universities are subordinated to the 187 county *(Kreis)* organizations, which in turn are directed by twelve district *(Bezirk)* organizations.

The most important affiliates of the DKP are the 15,000-member German Workers' Youth (SDAJ), the 6,000-member Marxist Student Union–Spartakus (MSB-Spartakus), and the Young Pioneers (JP), with some 3,000 children between the ages of six and fourteen (ibid., 19 February, p. 9, 25 May, p. 6).

The DKP makes effective use of a number of communist-led organizations in order to expand its influence among various groups, particularly in the peace and ecological movements, and to obtain support for various "unity of action" programs. The Committee for Peace, Disarmament, and Cooperation (KFAZ) is the most successful of the DKP-led groups. Founded in 1974, the KFAZ has succeeded in organizing numerous demonstrations, meetings, and campaigns for the collection of signatures on peace manifestos that propagate the Soviet version of peace and disarmament policies. Most KFAZ officials are connected with the Soviet-controlled World Peace Council or are members of the DKP leadership.

The German Peace Union (DFU), founded in 1960, is another organization that the DKP has utilized to expand its influence among various peace groups and members of the two political parties (the Social Democrats and the Free Democrats) forming the present governing coalition in the FRG. The DFU, for example, organized a meeting of prominent opponents of the NATO decision of December 1979 to modernize NATO's medium-range missile systems in Europe and station 572 Pershing II and cruise missiles on West German territory as a counterbalance to the Soviet SS-20 missiles. Communist control is secured because party members occupy key positions in the DFU's Directorate and Federal Presidium. (Ibid., 15 July, pp. 6–7.) The "Krefelder Appell" (Krefeld appeal), demanding that the government rescind its agreement to the NATO decision, obtained over one million signatures. It also was the common denominator for numerous antiwar demonstrations throughout the FRG; the largest took place in Bonn on 10 October where about 250,000 persons protested the FRG's security policy and NATO commitment. The DKP and its affiliated organizations made the collection of signatures for the Krefeld appeal one of their main activities in 1981. (*Pravda*, 1 June; *FBIS*, 4 June.) Quotas were assigned to party organizations (*Frankfurter Allgemeine Zeitung* [FAZ], 1 June).

Communists also occupy leading positions in the German Peace Society/United War Service Resisters (DFG/VK), Association of Victims of the Nazi Regime/League of Antifascists, Association of Democratic Jurists, and Democratic Women's Initiative and in numerous so-called citizens' initiatives against *Berufsverbot* (the practice of denying government employment to political extremists), nuclear power plants, and the alleged fascist revival.

Party Internal Affairs. The most important internal party event was the Sixth Party Congress, held in Hanover (29–31 May). Boris N. Ponomarev, candidate member of the Soviet Politburo, secretary of the Soviet Central Committee, and head of the Soviet delegation attending the congress, expressed satisfaction that the DKP referred to the congress as an "anti-nuclear-missile party congress" (ibid., 1 June). Of the 677 official delegates and 137 guest delegates, 768 belonged to trade unions and 338 to the SDAJ, MSB-Spartakus, or JP (some delegates were members of both categories), indicating the emphasis party leaders place on close relations with trade unions and the party's affiliated organizations. Delegations came from 57 fraternal parties and "anti-imperialist" liberation movements. Even though the DKP is relatively insignificant in terms of membership and electoral potential, its value to the Soviet Union and GDR lies in its usefulness for pro-Soviet and anti-Western propaganda. That value was demonstrated by the fact that the Soviet delegation was headed by Boris N. Ponomarev, accompanied by the first deputy head of the International Department of the Central Committee, Vadim V. Zagladin, Central Committee member Pavel Leonov, and the Soviet ambassador to the FRG, Vladimir Semenov. The East German delegation was led by SED Politburo member Kurt Hagen. (Radio Free Europe, *Background Report*, no. 162, 5 June; ADN, East Berlin, 29 May; *FBIS*, 3 June.)

Party Chairman Herbert Mies delivered the DKP Executive's report. He emphasized the party's fight for peace and its support of united action of the working class, democratic alliances, and joint actions of left-wing forces. (ADN, East Berlin, 31 May; *FBIS*, 3 June.) He stressed that "the peace movement in the Federal Republic of Germany is at present a movement of a new dimension, a movement of many forces, a movement with immense effect. This is the result of the activities of all forces that were engaged for a long time in peace committees and peace organizations, this is a result of the activities of us Communists." (*DI*, 30 June, p. 4.) Other important topics of the congress were new forms of work among the masses and the organization of alliances with other political forces and movements, including the possibility of "an organized parliamentary merger of various democratic and left-wing forces" (ibid., pp. 14 and 21).

The congress attempted to give the impression that the party was solidly behind the leadership and that the discontent apparent during 1980 had been eliminated. A number of dissidents have either left the party or been expelled. (See *YICA*, 1981, pp. 394–95.) Presidium member Kurt Fritsch strongly rejected the accusation originating with the "class enemy" that the DKP lacks intraparty democracy. He emphasized that party unity is based on "convincing talks" within the membership. (*FAZ*, 1 June.)

In conjunction with the MSB-Spartakus, the SDAJ held the third annual Festival of Youth in Dortmund (19–20 June). In addition to the entertainment portion of the festival, several seminars dealt with "peace" and "anti-NATO" issues. *Unsere Zeit* (*UZ*, 19 June), the official organ of the DKP, claimed 210,000 participants and guests from 52 countries.

The MSB-Spartakus held its Seventh Federal Congress on 3–4 October in Bremen. The main topics were the "fight for peace," "the role of the student movement in the struggle for peace," and "new phenomena of the extra-parliamentary opposition." (*DI*, 18 August, p. 6.)

As in previous years, party members were asked to enroll in the ideological courses offered by the DKP's educational institutions (see *YICA*, 1981, p. 394).

Domestic Attitudes and Activities. The "anti–NATO missile campaign," the collection of signatures for the Krefeld Appeal, and the support of the "peace demonstration" on 10 October in Bonn were probably the most successful communist attempts to achieve unity of action among Social Democrats, Free Democrats, secular and religious pacifists, and trade unionists. The demonstration in Bonn obtained the support of over 560 groups and organizations—among them the Christian Peace Conference, Protestant student organizations, Young Socialists (the youth organization of the Social Democrats), Young Democrats (the youth organization of the Free Democrats), the Greens (an ecological party strongly infiltrated by left-wing elements), trade union locals, various citizens' initiatives, and all communist-affiliated organizations. (*DI*, 18 August, p. 7, 28 September, pp. 5–9.) The peace demonstration, the largest post–World War II demonstration in the FRG, obtained respectability and thus influence as a result of the support of over sixty Social Democratic and Free Democratic members of the Bundestag and the public address given by Social Democratic Presidium member Erhard Eppler (*FAZ*, 9 and 11 October). Klaus Thüsing, a Social Democratic member of the Bundestag, even demanded the transformation of the peace movement into a broad "people's movement" in the FRG (*UZ*, 12 June). Another demonstration on behalf of the Krefeld Appeal was planned for 21 November in Dortmund. It was supposed to be the high point of the "hot fall" announced by various peace organizations. The objective was to collect two million signatures by that date for the Krefeld Appeal. (*DI*, 18 August, p. 11.)

The DKP continued to employ issues used in unity of actions in previous years, such as opposition to *Berufsverbot*, nuclear power plants, neo-Nazism, and the outlawing of the KPD, to broaden its influence (ibid., 19 February, pp. 5–6, 23 March, p. 17, 30 June, pp. 20–21, and 7 September, p. 2). The DKP succeeded on numerous occasions in organizing and participating in popular front activities, such as the peace initiative in Münster in which about fifty groups and organizations took part (ibid., 9 May, pp. 2–3) or the demonstration in April in Bonn protesting a meeting of the NATO Nuclear Planning Group (*FAZ*, 4 April).

Concern about DKP infiltration of trade unions was expressed by the trade union association's (DGB) chairman, Heinz Oskar Vetter, at the Fourth Special DGB Congress in Düsseldorf (March). It was recommended that the new basic program of the DGB should make provisions to forestall growing communist influence. However, representatives from the Metalworkers' Union and the deputy chairman of the Young Socialists, Klaus Peter Wolf, favored a program that would assure the continuing influence of Communists. The youth organizations of the trade unions are among the main target groups of communist propaganda. (Ibid., 14 March, 28 April.)

The DKP also provides moral support to the occupiers of vacant houses by emphasizing *"Wohnen ist ein Recht"* ("housing is a right"). The practice of occupying houses and a number of subsequent forced evictions have led to violent street demonstrations in many German cities. At a national congress of home occupiers, held in Münster on 28–29 March, speakers referred to the de facto alliance of Social Democrats, Communists, and Greens. The DKP and its affiliates strongly supported the congress, which decided on decentralized actions throughout the FRG. (Ibid., 30 March.) The DKP and other left-extremist elements believe that "the struggles over houses" should be coordinated actions against the state and its institutions.

International Views and Party Contacts. As in previous years, all DKP statements on international issues are virtually identical with those expressed in Moscow and East Berlin. One of the DKP's main propaganda activities during 1981 was in support of the "peace program" advanced by Leonid Brezhnev at the Soviet party congress in February (*UZ*, 27 February). The Soviet party's message of greetings to the Sixth DKP Congress emphasized the importance of the DKP's support for the Soviet peace program (*Pravda*, 30 May; *FBIS*, 5 June).

The DKP echoed Moscow's assertion that the United States is the main imperialist power and is trying to achieve world domination (*Pravda*, 4 June; *FBIS*, 4 June). DKP Chairman Mies pledged his party's commitment to proletarian internationalism and unconditional solidarity with the Soviets in dealing with the "counterrevolution" in Poland (ADN, East Berlin, 31 May; *FBIS*, 3 June). "When we hear from People's Poland voices that defame socialism and glorify the so-called free market, when labor unions arise that are far from the tradition of the revolutionary workers' movement, and even boast of the support of antisocialist forces from abroad—then it is clear to us that imperialist centers of subversion and domestic counterrevolutionary forces are exploiting serious mistakes of the PUWP [Polish United Workers' Party] to create a situation in which the socialist order is seriously threatened." (Radio Free Europe, *Background Report*, no. 162, 5 June, p. 3.) *Unsere Zeit* (28 April) repeated the unanimous view of the leaders of the Warsaw Pact meeting in Moscow on 5 December 1980 that "Poland is a socialist state, a strong link in the family of socialist countries, so it is and so it will remain."

The German Communists declared their solidarity with "fighters" against imperialism in South Africa, the Middle East, Turkey, and South and Central America (*UZ*, 19 June; *DI*, 30 June, p. 7). A delegation from the Democratic Front for the Liberation of Palestine (DFLP) led by DFLP Central Committee member S. Fahed visited the DKP Party Directorate (*DI*, December 1980, p. 4). *Unsere Zeit* (30 January) published an interview with Shafik Jorge Handal, a leader of "Farabundo Marti" Liberation Front in El Salvador and secretary general of the Communist Party of El Salvador.

International party contacts included the attendance of DKP Chairman Herbert Mies at the Soviet party congress and numerous delegations from fraternal parties at the DKP party congress. In line with DKP support of house occupiers, the party sponsored an international conference on *Wohnungsnot* ("distress caused by the housing shortage") on 19 March in Munich. Invitations were sent to thirteen European communist and workers' parties. (*DI*, 23 March, p. 4.)

Publications. No major changes were reported in DKP publications during 1981. The production of factory newspapers continued to receive high priority. The 36 DKP-controlled collective bookshops belong to the Association of Socialist Publishers and Bookdealers, an organization founded by the DKP. Seventeen publishers belong to the association. Erich Mayer, a member of the DKP Presidium, is chairman. (*DI*, 23 March, pp. 2–3.)

Other Leftist Groups. The New Left comprises all groups opposed to the pro-Moscow "orthodox" communist organizations. It includes an ever-changing array of organizations and splinter groups, each claiming to be the one true Marxist-Leninist revolutionary organization. The spectrum of the New Left covers the various Maoist (dogmatic) K-groups, as well as antidogmatic and anarchistic views. Membership in these organizations has declined since 1978 primarily because of their lack of success and the high demands they make on their members. However, the growth of the antinuclear and peace movements and the housing issue provided the left-extremists with increased opportunities and led to frequent violence and severe clashes with the police. A report from the security service of Schleswig-Holstein on the influence of left-extremist organizations, especially in the anti–nuclear power plant movement, indicated that the leadership of the militant antinuclear movement was no longer supplied by the K-groups, but was directed by the antidogmatic left-extremists, in particular by the autonomous groups pursuing anarchist objectives (ibid., 9 April, pp. 10–11). Activities of left-extremists are directed against the state and its institutions in the belief that resistance to the state authorities will eventually create the conditions required for the desired revolution.

The dogmatic K-groups, whose membership totals about seven thousand, have undergone a continuous process of reorientation since 1977 because of the changing policies of Beijing. One formerly large group, the Communist Party of Germany (KPD—not to be mistaken for the pro-Soviet underground KPD), decided in 1980 to dissolve and to discontinue its activities. The Maoist-oriented Communist League of West Germany (Kommunistischer Bund Westdeutschlands; KBW) was successful, until recently, in keeping its members committed to the revolutionary cause. However, ideological controversies within the DKW led to a split in the party; in September 1980, about five hundred KBW members, or one-fourth of the total membership, founded the League of West German Communists. (Ibid., 19 January, pp. 10–13.) Other KBW followers joined various antidogmatic groups. Dissension among the remaining members of the KBW continued, and its dissolution appears to be only a matter of time. A struggle over the DM 15 million in the KBW treasury has already started. First Secretary of the KBW Central Committee Hans Gerhard Schmierer sought to keep the party and treasury together, while others have proposed making the money available to Third World liberation organizations. Despite the KBW's uncertain future, party leaders invested millions of marks in procuring printing machines for its newspaper, *Kommunistische Volkszeitung*. (*FAZ*, 18 September.)

The Communist Party of Germany–Marxist-Leninist (KPD-ML), a pro-Albanian splinter group, founded the Communist Student Association in 1981. Its youth organization, the Communist Youth of Germany, held its Second Congress in Essen, surrounded by secrecy. The congress reportedly elected a new leadership and ratified new statutes and an action program. The congress was attended by delegations from Albania, Canada, Denmark, France, England, Portugal, Spain, and Turkey. (*DI*, 25 May, p. 2.) Chairman Ernst August led a KPD-ML delegation to Tirana and pledged that his party would pursue policies in the spirit of Marxist-Leninist unity and proletarian internationalism (Tirana Domestic Service, 14 May; *FBIS*, 16 March). The KPD-ML emphasizes the antimilitaristic struggle and work within trade unions. The Revolutionary Trade Union Opposition (RGO) held its Second Congress, with 170 "elected delegates" in attendance. Delegations from several Maoist (Albanian)–oriented trade unions attended the congress. RGO Chairman Thomas Scheffler was re-elected. In its report on the congress, *Rote Morgen*, the official organ of the KPD-ML, tried to create the impression that trade unions belonging to the DGB were represented in violation of the DGB's rule forbidding its members to belong to left-extremist organizations except the DKP. (*DI*, 2 February, p. 8.)

The Communist League (KB), another K-group, also experienced a decline in membership. The KB succeeded, however, in utilizing the home occupiers' movement, recognizing it as a new field for action against the sociopolitical system of the FRG (*FAZ*, 9 March). The KB was one of seventeen organizations participating in the 13 June anti-NATO demonstration in Heidelberg. Unity of action was achieved with, among others, the Popular Front Heidelberg (an affiliate of the KPD-ML), the communist-controlled DFG/VK, the Antiwar Committee Heidelberg, the Anti-Imperialist Collective Heidelberg, and a number of gay organizations. (*DI*, 25 May, p. 4.)

Socialists and Communists belonging to different Marxist organizations such as the Socialist Buro, KBW, DKP, and KB, as well as former members of the dissolved KPD, established a new joint publication, *Moderne Zeiten* (Modern times), in summer 1981. The publication opposes the Marxists Rudolf Bahro and Andre Gorz, who emphasize ecological issues and the danger of a new world war. (*FAZ*, 18 September.)

Another feeble joint effort was the Second Socialist Conference, held in Marburg in February. Followers of the Socialist Buro, KBW, former members of the KPD, the Group "Z" (a recent splinter group of the KB), and the Marxist Group failed to arrive at a common ideological denominator and basis for common action. (Ibid., 20 February.)

Combined membership in the numerous antidogmatic groups is estimated at about 3,200 (ibid., 20 March). An anarchist group in Hamburg founded Black-Red Aid, an aid society for arrested "revolutionaries." (*DI*, 2 February, p. 6).

Next to the Red Army Faction (RAF), the Revolutionary Cells (RZ) have been responsible for most of the terrorist incidents in the FRG. The RZs are concerned primarily with "preparation of the armed struggle" carried out by "autonomous groups," aimed at the involvement of the masses (ibid., 23 March, p. 16, 7 September, p. 6). The *Düsseldorf Stadtpost*, a publication of the RZ, lists addresses of U.S. installations and of city and police offices and offers detailed instruction on manufacturing bombs and incendiaries (ibid., 7 September, pp. 4–5).

A statement of jailed RAF terrorists, published in the KB organ *Arbeiterkampf* (Workers' struggle), demanded that RAF prisoners be confined together with "social revolutionaries," that is, convicted house occupiers (ibid., 19 February, p. 7). The RAF claimed responsibility for a number of terrorist attacks against U.S. personnel and installations (*Calgary Herald*, 13 April).

It appears that as a result of organizational and personnel weaknesses, the various groups and organizations of the New Left are increasingly willing to participate in "popular front" alliances and even to collaborate with the DKP (*DI*, 23 March, pp. 15–16).

The Young Socialists (JUSOS), the official youth organization of the governing Social Democrats, though generally not perceived as a left-radical organization, shares many objectives with the extreme left. For example, the JUSOS strongly opposes NATO, especially the NATO decision of December 1979, and is noted for its outspoken anti-American attitudes. The organization maintains many contacts with communist youth organizations in communist-ruled countries and demands basic changes in the German economy and social structure. Both the JUSOS and the Young Democrats (the Free Democrats' youth organization) have participated on numerous occasions in unity of actions with left-extremists and thereby have given substantial support to left-radical objectives. (*FAZ*, 29 June.)

Another example of JUSOS support of the extreme left occurred in the municipal elections in Lower Saxony (27 September). The youth wing of the Social Democrats refused to campaign for the party in the city of Oldenburg and was regarded as tacitly backing the Communists, who won 12.5 percent of the vote, chiefly at the expense of the SPD. (*NYT*, 29 September.)

WEST BERLIN

The United States, Britain, and France still "occupy" West Berlin. The 1971 Quadripartite Agreement concerning Berlin confirms that the former German capital is not part of the FRG and has a "special status" based on agreements concluded in 1944 and 1945. The GDR, supported by the Soviet Union, has incorporated the Soviet sector and made East Berlin its capital. The Western powers have encouraged the FRG to maintain close ties with West Berlin. Since 1959 the population of West Berlin has declined from 2.3 to 2.0 million.

The special occupation status of Berlin allowed the SED to organize a West Berlin subsidiary. In 1962, the name of the party was changed from Socialist Unity Party of Germany–West Berlin to Socialist Unity Party of West Berlin (Sozialistische Einheitspartei Westberlin; SEW) to give the illusion that the SEW was an indigenous party.

The SEW, like the DKP, is absolutely loyal to Moscow and holds the same ideological and political views as the East German and Soviet parties. The party has about seven thousand members (*DI*, 19 February, p. 9). In elections for the city's House of Representatives on 10 May, the party obtained 8,216 votes, or 0.7 percent of the valid votes cast, compared with 1.1 percent in 1979.

The SEW held its Sixth Party Congress on 15–17 May. It was attended by 425 delegates and representatives from sixteen fraternal parties (DPA, 17 May; *FBIS*, 20 May). Party Chairman Horst Schmitt and his two deputy chairmen, Dietmar Ahrens and Inge Kopp, were re-elected. The party congress adopted new Basic Principles and Objectives, replacing those of 1969. The SEW avowed loyalty to the "proven principles of democratic centralism and proletarian internationalism." Following the example set by the SED, which remained the primary source of party funds, all references to German reunification and to a common German national culture were eliminated from the new Basic Principles and Objectives. (*FAZ*, 18 and 19 May.) The congress also adopted a document entitled "The SEW and the Tasks for the 1980s," which defines the work of the Communists of West Berlin in their "struggle for peace, security, and social progress" (Tass, 15 May; *FBIS*, 19 May). Schmitt claimed that the influence of the SEW and its policy is greater than that reflected in its vote share (ADN, East Berlin, 15 May; *FBIS*, 20 May). He also reported that in the preceding four years the number of SEW primary organizations at enterprises had increased and 1,328 people had joined the party (*Pravda*, 16 May; *FBIS*, 28 May). No figures were given for those who had resigned or been expelled.

West Berlin witnessed numerous demonstrations marked by violent clashes with the police. Many of these demonstrations were in support of house occupiers. (At one time over 170 houses were illegally occupied.) Antiwar and anti–nuclear armament protests, including a demonstration against U.S. Secretary of State Alexander Haig, were typical unity of actions with socialists and left-extremists.

Hans Mahle, editor in chief of the official organ of the SEW, *Die Wahrheit*, resigned for age and health reasons. Mahle emigrated in 1933 to the Soviet Union and belonged to the Group Ulrich that returned in 1945 to create a communist East Germany by order of Moscow. His successor is Heinz Grünberg, former deputy editor in chief. (*FAZ*, 16 October.)

The University of Calgary   Eric Waldman

Great Britain

The Communist Party of Great Britain (CPBG), founded in 1920, is significant primarily because of its influence in the trade union movement. It does not operate in Northern Ireland. Although the CPGB is a recognized party, it consistently polls badly in both local and national elections. The party has never had more than two representatives in the House of Commons, and none at all since 1950. One aging party member, Lord Milford, continues to sit in the House of Lords. The party has about eight councillors at various levels of local government. Officially membership is given at 18,500, out of a British population of 56 million.

Leadership and Organization. The CPGB is organized in four levels: the National Congress, the Executive Committee and its departments, districts, and various local and factory branches. Constitutionally, the biennial National Congress is the supreme authority of the party, but in reality it serves as a rubber stamp for the party leadership. Responsibility for party activities on specific issues lies with the 42-member Executive Committee, which meets every two months. The Executive Committee selects members of special committees, full-time heads of departments, and the 16-member Political Committee, the party's effective controlling body. The leading officers of the Political Committee are Gordon McLennan (general secretary) and Mick Costello (industrial organizer), who is expected to become the next head of the CPGB. Other leading officers are Gerry Pocock (international department), Dave Cook (organization), George Mathews (press), and Jean Styles (women).

The CPGB exercises considerable influence through the trade union movement. Although the CPGB does not control any individual union, it has played a prominent role in nearly all union-government confrontations of recent years. The CPGB is the only effective organization seeking to control the outcome of trade union elections. Its success, due partly to low turnouts in most union elections, has been outstanding, and nearly every union executive in Great Britain contains a party member, with the notable exception of the electricians. The 38-member General Council of the Trade Union Congress has two communist members: George Guy of the National Union of Sheet Metal Workers and Ken Gill of the Technical and Supervisory Section of the Amalgamated Union of Engineering Workers.

Communist influence is not restricted to labor relations. The trade unions dominate the Labour Party through their overwhelming financial support and the system of bloc voting. In 1981, the Labour Party adopted a new electoral college system. Votes on important party issues are apportioned equally among constituency parties, trade unionists, and Labour MPs. In practice, this means that a few trade union executives, some of whom are CPGB members, can decisively affect key elections. This is a highly controversial issue within the Labour Party, but since Labour's substantial left wing supports the procedure, it is unlikely to be changed in the near future.

The CPGB has a small youth wing, the Young Communist League (YCL), which is active in many youth groups, such as the Anti-Nazi League and the Campaign Against Youth Unemployment. However, it is forced to the margins of political activity by other ultra-left groups.

Party Internal Affairs. Party membership continues to decline. The 1981 figure of 18,500 represents a drop of 2,000 since 1979. The picture is even bleaker in the YCL, which in 1981 had a mere 954 members. The YCL loses about 10 percent of its membership every year. The most striking loss in 1981 was the defection of Sue Slipman, the first woman president of the National Union of Students, to the new Social Democratic Party because she preferred the intellectual freedom prevailing there. The picture of decline is highlighted by the serious difficulties of the party's daily newspaper, the *Morning Star.* Daily sales are well under 30,000, and the paper is kept afloat only by East European purchases of about 15,000 copies daily.

Finance remains a critical area for the party, although it still conducts a considerable level of business. Party membership fees are rarely paid on time, and members are urged to pay in advance and, when possible, more than the obligatory minimum. The party's business interests include Central Books, Lawrence and Wishart Publishers, Farleigh Press and London Caledonian Printers, Rodell Properties, the Labour Research Department, and the Marx Memorial Library.

The decline in party membership is partly due to advances made by non-Moscow-aligned far-left parties and to the success of the far left in capturing many key posts in the Labour Party. In recent years, several communist activists have defected to the Labour Party, where they feel they can exercise a greater influence. It is doubtful that their principles have changed. The most notable are Jimmy Reid of Scotland's Upper Clyde Shipworkers and Arthur Scargill, who was elected head of the powerful National Union of Mineworkers in December 1981.

Not surprisingly, affiliation with the Labour Party was a critical issue at the party's Thirty-Seventh Congress, held in London in November 1981. General Secretary McLennan called for the development of links between the CPGB and the Labour Party's left wing. He stressed the similarity of views between the two groups, particularly on nuclear disarmament, withdrawal from the European Economic Community, and an alternative economic strategy. Development of the link was essential, McLennan claimed, to ensure a left-wing victory in the next general elections. In the long run, he wished to establish a formal link between the CPGB and the Labour Party (a link formally proscribed under existing Labour Party regulations). The congress, however, rejected the affiliation proposal by a vote of two to one. A CPGB spokesman said that although affiliation was a long-term objective, the general feeling among the delegates was that it was not a key issue at the moment.

Domestic Attitudes and Activities. Communist activity remained centered on two targets: the Conservative government and what remains of the Labour Party's right wing in that party's leadership. The rapid growth in unemployment, public expenditure cuts, and new trade union legislation furnished the party with considerable propaganda material in 1981. By December unemployment in the United Kingdom stood at 2,940,700 and was expected to rise to 3,000,000 in January 1982 and to 3,250,000 by the end of the year. The CPGB cites the ruling Conservative Party's tight monetarist policy as the chief cause of the problem. An outbreak of serious social unrest in many of England's older inner-city areas compounded the problem. Brixton in London and Toxteth in Liverpool were particularly badly hit. Although various factors were at work, including race and political agitation, unemployment was widely believed to be a cause of the unrest. The CPGB was active in protest marches and demonstrations against unemployment.

In the autumn, the secretary of state for employment announced new measures on trade union reform, including a new law making trade unions liable for breach of contract. The unions indicated their intention to try to block this legislation, even if it meant resorting to a general strike. Communist unionists were in the forefront of this campaign.

The CPGB continues to agitate for the Labour Party to implement its more radical policies. Although few of the advances made by the left within the Labour Party can be attributed to communist party activity, there is a clear affinity between CPGB proposals and the more extreme Labour ideas. The CPGB wants a price freeze, a tax on corporate profits, the abolition of the value-added tax, a reduction in interest rates, a ban on nuclear and chemical weapons, and an immediate reduction of £ 1 billion in defense spending. The party also favors national assemblies in Scotland and Wales and withdrawal from Northern Ireland. The "British Road to Socialism," the party program adopted in 1977, commits the party to parliamentary socialism (although it conceives strikes and demonstrations as a vital element in the party's bid for power) and to loose association with organizations not necessarily convinced of the CPGB's long-term aims, including feminist, minority, and community groups. In practice, the party is being outdistanced by more vigorous organizations.

The party congress reaffirmed the CPGB's support for proportional representation in both national and local elections. In other actions, it instructed the Executive Committee to initiate detailed studies of the police and armed forces and called for a public campaign for unionization of the armed forces and full political rights for members of the police and armed services. Most resolutions were in line with traditional party policies (commitment to full employment, increased trade with the Eastern bloc, more money for the socially disadvantaged, withdrawal from Ireland), but the wording of some was revealing. In a resolution against racism, the CPGB admitted that it had few nonwhites among its members. By a huge majority, the congress made its immediate electoral aim the defeat of the Conservatives and the return of a Labour government "with as strong a left presence as possible." The NATO decision to deploy medium-range theater nuclear missiles in Great Britain reinvigorated the Campaign for Nuclear Disarmament, in which the CPGB has been active. The campaign reached its peak on 24 October, when over 150,000 demonstrated in London against nuclear weapons.

International Views and Party Contacts. Easily the most striking development in 1981 was the party's condemnation of the Soviet invasion of Afghanistan. The party muddled the issue, however, by refusing to call for the withdrawal of Soviet troops. The congress endorsed the executive's view that the party "disagreed with the intervention as an interference in the internal affairs of Afghanistan and urged the withdrawal of Soviet troops," but an amendment sponsored by some fifty branches and backing the invasion but calling for the "earliest withdrawal" of troops was defeated 157 to 115. A party spokesman attempted to reconcile the CPGB's dissident view with Moscow's by claiming that the decision was in accordance with the international communist movement's policy of noninterference in the domestic affairs of nations. McLennan, speaking in Moscow on 1 March at the Soviet party congress, publicly criticized the Soviet intervention. Tass omitted the key passages from what it claimed was the "full" text of McLennan's speech. In December, the party condemned the introduction of martial law in Poland.

Despite these actions and the CPGB's Eurocommunist orientation, its criticisms of the Soviet Union remain muted. More typical of party stances was the speech of Executive Committee member Mrs. Pat Milligan during the congress's debate on peace, which praised the Soviet Union for its "readiness to create the basis for meaningful talks to lessen international tensions." Generally the CPGB's views mirror those of the Soviet party. In particular, the CPGB stresses solidarity with Vietnam, Angola, and revolutionary forces in South Africa, Chile, and the Middle East.

The CPGB hosted party delegations from Chile, Cyprus, Ireland, and South Africa and representatives of several national liberation movements, including the African National Congress (South Africa), the Palestine Liberation Organization, the Popular Front for the Liberation of Angola, the Democratic Revolutionary Front (El Salvador), and the South-West African People's Organization.

Publications. The *Morning Star* is the CPGB's daily organ. The CPGB's liveliest magazine is the fortnightly *Comment*, which contains all major Executive Committee statements and regular reports on party activities. *Marxism Today* is a theoretical monthly and occasionally carries articles of genuinely original research. *Challenge*, now published in a more attractive format, is the YCL journal.

In addition, the party publishes several journals of more specialized interest. *Link* is a feminist paper. *Economic Bulletin* appears twice yearly. *Education Today and Tomorrow* appears five times a year. *Science Bulletin* is a quarterly concerned with the relationship between science and socialism. *Euro-Red*, another quarterly, is a regular commentary on political developments in Western Europe. *Our History Journal* focuses on party history. Irregular journals include *Red Letters*, a cultural magazine; *Socialist Europe*, on East European affairs; *Music and Life*; and *Medicine in Society*, which serves as a discussion forum for communist health workers. Several local party branches produce their own information bulletins, which sometimes contain sizable articles.

Other Marxist Groups. In addition to the CPGB, there are several small but zealous Trotskyist groups whose roots date to the student revolt of 1968. Membership is small, but most have a high turnover rate, suggesting a larger degree of latent support. Great Britain is in a serious state of recession with widespread factory closures, unemployment running near three million, and occasional instances of racial violence. Although not as rigid as during the Great Depression, the present mood of labor is hardening and there is probably a greater sense of relative deprivation. Britain's Trotskyist groups are particularly active in areas that could lead to violence. All of the major groups are anxious to promote factory occupations as a model of resistance. Several helped foment the serious rioting that afflicted Britain in the summer of 1981, most notably the Militant Tendency and the Revolutionary Communist Party. Since the disturbances, many more ultra-left cadres are attempting to capitalize on the discontent, particularly among the nonwhite community. Further violent flare-ups can be expected in 1982.

Several Trotskyist groups practice "entryism" —the tactic of penetrating larger moderate socialist parties. The most important of these is the Militant Tendency in the Labour Party, which derives its name from its paper, the *Militant*. About two thousand strong, Militant now holds all seats on the Executive Council of the Labour Party's Young Socialists and controls about fifty Labour constituencies. Two other Trotskyist entryist movements are the Worker's Socialist League, led by Alan Thornett, and the Socialist Campaign for Labour Victory (deliberately named to be easily confused with the official Campaign for Labour Victory), which is run by the Trotskyist Workers' Action.

The evidence in support of the accusation that the Militant Tendency is a party within a party contrary to the Labour Party's constitution was so substantial that Labour Party leader Michael Foot finally persuaded his party's Organization Committee to instigate a complete and thorough investigation of Militant. Within hours of the decision, the Militant Tendency announced an unprecedented campaign through the rank and file of the Labour Party—and over the heads of the national executive—to fight the expulsion of its supporters from the party. The evidence that the Militant Tendency does recruit and has a highly organized membership is overwhelming.

The largest Trotskyist organization, the Socialist Workers' Party (SWP), claims groups of militants in the auto industry, the docks, the railways, the National Union of Mineworkers, the National Union of Teachers, and the National and Local Government Officers' Association. Despite the SWP's efforts, its base in the working class is limited. More successful have been the party's efforts among immigrants. An SWP section called Chingari (Spark) produces papers in several Indian languages. The SWP is also associated with Women's Voice, a socialist feminist organization, and Flame, a black group. The SWP is, however, a sectarian body disinclined to cooperate with other groups. The party is particularly active in backing the Anti-Nazi League, a fertile source of new recruits in the past but of dubious long-term utility given the low level of neo-fascist activity.

The SWP's 40-member National Committee, elected at its annual conference, elects the full-time 10-member Executive Committee. Jim Nichol is national secretary, Steve Jeffery industrial organizer, and Lindsey German organizer of women. The SWP has numerous branches and 70 district committees. It runs "fractions" in the civil service, local government, railways, the postal service, and British Telecom. One of the SWP's many bookstores was destroyed in an arson attack in early 1981. The SWP claims its greatest support in the north of England and in Glasgow. Duncan Hallas is SWP chairman, but its best-known personalities are its theoretician Tony Cliff (pseudonym of Ygael Gluckstein) and the polemical journalist Paul Foot, nephew of the Labour Party leader. The party's organ, the weekly *Socialist Worker*, claims a circulation over 20,000. Pluto Press, a left-wing publishing house, is closely associated with the SWP.

Despite the violent tone of its propaganda, the SWP seems to have had little to do with the summer's rioting. SWP leaders regretted the party's failure to gain control and organize the rioting. The party made strenuous efforts to capitalize on the discontent and turn it into a revolutionary form. "The riots and looting have been fantastic," commented Tony Cliff, "but they have not gone far enough. Because they have not been organized, the kids attacked shops when they should have been attacking factories. We must teach them to take the bakery, not just the bread."

The next most important and probably more militant Trotskyist party is the International Marxist Group (IMG), the British section of the United Secretariat of the Fourth International. The IMG has about 1,500 members. The party's national secretary is Bob Penington, but Tariq Ali is a much better known figure. Robin Blackburn, former lecturer at the London School of Economics, and Norman Gervas are its chief theorists. The group has a weak industrial base, but is trying to galvanize support from popular single-issue campaigns, such as the Campaign Against Youth Unemployment and the Campaign for Nuclear Disarmament. In the past, it was concerned with promoting unity among the disparate ultra-left groups in the Socialist Unity Party. The party was active in the campaign to secure the election of far-left candidate Tony Benn as deputy leader of the Labour Party.

Another significant Trotskyist group is the Workers' Revolutionary Party (WRP), an affiliate of the Fourth International (International Secretariate). Its daily newspaper, *Newsline*, claims sales of three thousand. The WPR's youth section, the Young Socialists, is comparatively large, with significant participation among black youths. The WRP is secretive, but is known to have groups of militants in the docks, engineering, mining, the theater, and the auto industry. Its best-known personalities are actors Ken Loach, Tony Garnett, and Corin and Vanessa Redgrave. The WRP held its Fifth Congress from 31 January to 3 February. Decisions were passed unanimously with no real debate. The WRP wants to occupy factories and workplaces threatened with closure with committees consisting of representatives of workers, staff, and technical and supervisory personnel. "The committees would constitute a preparatory step towards the conquest of political and industrial power and the nationwide administration of industry by a Workers' Revolutionary Government." Acting parallel to these would be community councils, front organizations acting under the cloak of defending local interests. Ultimately, a workers' militia would be created from among the Young Socialists and "revolutionary youth centers." To this end, the WRP has established a "youth training" scheme intended to develop young people's "opposition to the capitalist system and all it stands for."

The main strength of the New Communist Party (NCP), a hard-line pro-Soviet splinter from the CPGB formed in 1977, is among industrial workers in Yorkshire, particularly Rotherham. It has a membership of about a thousand and employs twelve full-time officials. Among the claimed backers of its weekly newspaper, the *New Worker*, were two Labour MPs.

Through its slavish backing of Moscow, the NCP has succeeded in winning some East European backing. Party officials have negotiated a lucrative and exclusive contract with the Czechoslovak Orbis Publishing House to publish and distribute its material in Britain.

The party printed a polemical attack entitled *Quo Vadis Poland* on the Solidarity movement, which claimed that the Polish union was manipulated by persons addicted to "reactionary nationalism, chauvinism or Zionism." Two leading members of the party had to be expelled in November, however, because of their refusal to endorse the party's harsh stance toward Solidarity. Many members are considering joining the Labour Party.

London   Richard Sim

Greece

The Communist Party of Greece (Kommunistikon Komma Ellados; KKE) was founded in 1921. During the 1920s, the party remained small and weak, suffering a series of internal splits. In 1931, it was reorganized under a Comintern-imposed Stalinist group. Five years later, it was forced underground by the Metaxas regime. The party gained extensive influence during the Nazi occupation through its resistance organization, the National Liberation Front, and its military arm, ELAS. An attempt in December 1944 to seize power by force in newly liberated Greece was put down by the British. A guerrilla campaign (1946–1949), supported mainly by Yugoslavia, was eventually crushed by the Greek Army. The party remained outlawed between 1947 and 1974. From 1952 to 1967, the communist left was represented by the United Democratic Left (EDA). During the military dictatorship (1967–1974), the party split into two factions, one loyal to Moscow and another (labeled KKE/Interior; KKE/I) espousing a more independent, moderate, Eurocommunist orientation.

In the 18 October parliamentary elections, the pro-Moscow KKE emerged as the third largest party in Greece, receiving 13 seats in the 300-seat legislature. The KKE/I failed to win a single seat. Overall support for the communist left did not change substantially. Compared with the November 1977 elections, when the KKE received 9.29 percent, and the KKE/I and its allies including EDA 2.72 percent for a total of 12.01 percent, the KKE received 10.88 percent and the KKE/I 1.35 percent for a combined total of 12.23. The EDA did not enter any candidates this time. One of its principal leaders, Manolis Glezos, was elected under the Panhellenic Socialist Movement (PASOK) banner.

Membership in the KKE is estimated at 33,500 and in the KKE/I at 4,800.

Leadership and Organization. The KKE is organized along traditional communist party lines. Party cells are located in factories or other "collectives." Major cities such as Athens have a city party organization. There are also departmental and regional committees. A party congress meets approximately every four years. There is a 70-member Central Committee, as well as a Politburo assisted by a Secretariat. The present Politburo is composed of Secretary General Kharilaos Florakis, Nikos Kaloudhis, Andonis Ambatielos, Grigoris Farakos, Mina Giannou, Roula Koukoulou, Kostas Loules, Kostas Tsolakis, Loula Logara, Dimitrios Gondikas, and Stratis Tsambis.

The party's youth organization (KNE) is directed by a Central Council. Spyros Khalvatzis is the current KNE secretary. The KNE held a congress in September, attended by several foreign Communists, including Gus Hall of the Communist Party, U.S.A.

Party Internal Affairs. The major event for the KKE during 1981 was its emergence in the October elections as the only communist party represented in the legislature. The election results spelled the virtual elimination of the KKE/I and the EDA as political forces in the future.

The continuing anti-NATO, anti-American sentiment in Greece—inspired primarily by the widely accepted notions that the United States and NATO allowed Turkey to invade Cyprus in 1974 and supported the military regime—did not benefit the communist party as much as its leaders had expected. The major beneficiary was PASOK, formed in September 1974 by Andreas Papandreou, a former economics professor at the University of California at Berkeley and son of late liberal Premier George Papandreou. In the October elections, PASOK received 48.06 percent of the popular vote, elected 172 deputies to the Greek legislature, and formed the first socialist government in Greek history. To expand its popular base, PASOK had to tone down its Marxist rhetoric considerably during the months preceding the election.

Domestic and International Views and Positions. A KKE Central Committee plenum in February 1981 set the stage for the forthcoming elections. The plenum reaffirmed the party's familiar positions on major international issues and called for mobilization and common action by the "broadest" possible coalition of "patriotic-democratic" forces against "the imperialist cold war offensive waged by the new American administration," the withdrawal of all nuclear weapons from Greece, the removal of the four American/NATO bases, and Greek withdrawal from NATO. The party again attacked Greece's membership in the European Economic Community (EEC) as detrimental to Greek workers and farmers.

Domestically, the KKE declared that it was prepared to support PASOK to form a government after the elections. It insisted, however, that *Alaghi* (the sociopolitical change advocated by PASOK) could not be realized without the KKE's active participation.

PASOK, for its part, began to moderate its views during the year, distancing itself from its more extremist, avowedly Marxist positions of the past. In July, the party's Central Committee approved a series of policy statements outlining in great detail the policies PASOK planned to implement once in power. PASOK indicated that it would not unilaterally or precipitously take Greece out of NATO. "Our strategic orientation," the foreign policy plank read, "is the dissolution of both cold war blocs, NATO and the Warsaw Pact. Our country's withdrawal from NATO falls within this strategy." PASOK's position on the American bases was moderated from outright rejection to a plan for annual evaluation and renegotiation of their status.

As the governing party, PASOK is now obligated to recognize that Turkey's claims in the Aegean and the continuing presence of Turkish occupation forces on Cyprus require a strong defensive capability on the part of Greece, a capability that depends on weapons systems available to Greece primarily through NATO and the United States. The Papandreou government also realizes that disassociation from NATO will increase Turkey's leverage at Greece's expense. In his first major statement to the outside world ("Issues and Answers," ABC, 25 October), Papandreou indicated that he was not planning a unilateral withdrawal from NATO. However, in a major policy address to the Greek parliament in mid-November, he announced that his government intended to set "a timetable for the removal of American bases" and would also consider possible withdrawal from the "military wing" of NATO (*San Francisco Chronicle*, 23 November).

Papandreou may not approach another critical issue, Greece's membership in the EEC, with the urgency implied in earlier statements. Papandreou had repeatedly stated in the past that he intends to put the question of EEC membership to a public referendum. As premier, he appears more likely to negotiate revisions favorable to Greece before proceeding with a referendum.

In spite of its Marxist elements, especially among leading cadres, the PASOK government is not likely to follow a pro-Soviet foreign policy. Neither is it likely to take Greece into the ranks of the nonaligned. Nevertheless, on a number of issues, the PASOK government will express views and take positions opposing American objectives. Characteristically, Papandreou met representatives of the five members of the Arab Steadfastness and Confrontation Front, Syria, Algeria, Iraq, Libya, and the Palestine Liberation Organization (PLO), before meeting any other diplomatic representatives in his capacity as premier. One of the first steps of the Papandreou government was to elevate the diplomatic status of the PLO representative in Athens.

With regard to domestic affairs, PASOK has toned down its previous rhetoric about a new socialist constitution and a communal organization in agriculture. Currently, it retains its objective of socializing the banks, the large shipyards, steel mills, mining companies, insurance companies, and pharmaceutical firms. Many of these concerns are already either government owned or under some form of government control.

PASOK does not need the KKE's votes in the legislature to enact its program, which reduces the KKE's leverage. Nevertheless, KKE deputies in the legislature will have many opportunities to exploit any popular dissatisfaction with PASOK's policies. Before the October elections, both PASOK and the KKE were in the opposition, and both exploited popular disaffection with the New Democracy government. With PASOK in power, however, the KKE becomes the principal spokesman of left-wing opposition. This may improve the KKE's appeal in the future. The KKE's major handicap, however, is and will continue to be its subservience to Moscow and the popular perception that it is a foreign-controlled party.

International Party Contacts. The KKE continued its contacts with foreign communist parties during the year. In February, Kharilaos Florakis visited Moscow for the Soviet party congress. Shortly before departing for Moscow, Florakis had met with a delegation of the Syrian Communist Party. Not unexpectedly, the two parties condemned "Zionist and imperialist forces," which are "aided in their plans by the Beijing leadership." In April a KKE delegation composed of Mina Yiannou and Yiannis Palavos visited the German Democratic Republic and met cadres of the Socialist Unity Party of Germany. In June, a delegation of the French Communist Party met in Athens with Florakis, Andonis Ambatielos, and Orestis Kolozov, the chief of the KKE's International Section. In August, Ambatielos visited Budapest at the invitation of the Hungarian Central Committee. In September, a delegation of the Cuban Communist Party Central Committee visited Athens at the invitation of the KKE. Also in September, Communist Party, U.S.A., Secretary General Gus Hall visited Athens at the invitation of the KKE's Central Committee.

The KKE/I was not as active. Its contacts were mostly with Yugoslav and Romanian Communists and with European Eurocommunist parties. In February, Secretary Bambis Dhrakopoulos of the party's Central Committee visited Belgrade at the invitation of the League of Communists of Yugoslavia. Also in February, Lefteris Voutas, a member of the Executive Bureau, visited Bucharest. In March, Dhrakopoulos, accompanied by Nikolas Vouvelis of the party's International Relations

Committee, visited Algeria and participated in an international conference on the reunification of Korea.

PASOK leader Andreas Papandreou continued his close contacts with the European socialist parties, especially the French Socialist Party. At the same time, he expanded the party's contacts with Eastern Europe and the Soviet Union. Following a formal invitation from the Soviet government, a PASOK delegation composed of three members of its Executive Bureau and two members of its International Relations Committee visited Moscow in May. The delegation had talks with Boris N. Ponomarev, Soviet Politburo candidate member and secretary in charge of relations with nonruling communist parties, and Vadim V. Zagladin, Central Committee member and first deputy chief of the Soviet party's International Department. In late April, Papandreou visited Bulgaria at the invitation of Bulgarian President Todor Zhivkov. During the visit, Papandreou signed a cooperative agreement between PASOK and the Fatherland Front. In May Papandreou visited Bucharest at the invitation of Romanian President Nicolae Ceauşescu.

Other Marxist-Leninist Organizations. The October parliamentary elections revealed that the more extremist leftist groups enjoy minimal public support. The Revolutionary Communist Party (EKKE) in an alliance with the other pro-Chinese group, the Marxist-Leninist–KKE (ML-KKE), managed to gather 4,536 votes, or 0.08 percent. A Trotskyist organization, EDE-Trotskists, fared even worse; it received only 0.03 percent. Another organization, the Revolutionary Left, received 0.11 percent.

Publications. The KKE's official organ is the 61-year-old daily *Rizospastis*. The KKE also publishes the long-established monthly theoretical review *Kommunistiki Epitheorisi*. The KKE/I and EDA relied during the year on the daily *Avgi*. Other organizations publish sporadic tabloids such as *Laikoi Agones* (EKKE) and *Laikos Dromos* (ML-KKE). The political influence of these publications is minimal.

More important is the continuing publication of translations of books by Marxists or other leftist authors and the frequent publication of anti-American, anti-NATO articles and comments by noncommunist newspapers and periodicals such as the wide-circulation *Ta Nea, Eleutherotypia, Ethnos, Exormisi* (affiliated with PASOK), and *Andi*.

Howard University   D. G. Kousoulas

Iceland

The People's Alliance (Althydubandalagid; AB), heir to the Icelandic Communist Party, has evolved into a broad, left-socialist party with some communist influence in its leadership. It has wider support than the Social Democrats and participates in the present coalition government. The communist movement in Iceland developed around the issue of Iceland's independence from Denmark and has always been nationalist in orientation, little influenced by the international communist movement.

The Icelandic Communist Party (Kommunistaflokkur Islands) was formed in 1930 by a left-wing group that had broken off the Labor Party (Althyduflokkurin) after the latter had joined the Second International in 1926. The Labor Party had been formed in 1918, when Iceland gained home rule from Denmark, by the socialist trade union movement and was both a political party and a trade union federation. After the Communists left, the Labor Party took the name of Social Democrats. In 1938, another left-wing group splintered from the Social Democrats, mainly because the latter would not form a popular front with the Communists. It joined with the Communists to create a new party, the United People's Party–Socialist Party (Sameiningar flokkur althydu–Sosialista flokkurinn; UPP-SP). Patterned on the Norwegian Labor Party, the UPP-SP based its ideology on "scientific socialism–Marxism" but with no organizational ties with Moscow. It declared its sympathy with and interest in the realization of socialism in the USSR and generally had the same viewpoints on international affairs as Moscow. It was an uncompromising advocate of Iceland's complete independence from Denmark. By the time independence was achieved in 1944, the other parties had accepted it as a responsible democratic party, and the conservative Independence Party and the Social Democrats agreed to enter a coalition with it.

In 1956, the UPP-SP formed an electoral alliance with still another group of left-wing Social Democrats, led by a former Social Democratic Party chairman, Hannibal Valdimarsson, and the small, isolationist National Preservation Party. It assumed the name People's Alliance and later became the present party. Led by Valdimarsson, the AB enabled the UPP-SP to regain control of the Icelandic Federation of Labor, by then called the Althydusambad Islands (ASI); the UPP-SP had previously controlled the ASI between 1942 and 1948. The UPP-SP absorbed the National Preservation Party, whose platform to oust the U.S.-NATO base at Keflavik had cut severely into the UPP-SP's electoral support, and in 1968 dissolved itself into the AB, which then formed itself into a national Marxist party.

The AB has an estimated 2,200 members out of a total population of about 229,000 and is the largest labor party. It received 19.7 percent of the vote in 1979, the most recent parliamentary elections, and controls 11 of the 60 Althing seats. It attracts more workers than the Social Democrats, and intellectuals make up an important and growing segment of the party. Geographically, the AB has traditionally had its center in the eastern and, to a lesser extent, northern fjords. There the party is supported by a cross-section of the population—workers, businessmen, farmers, and fishermen. Recently, however, the center has shifted more to Reykjavik and to the intellectual wing, headed by Ragnar Arnalds, Olafur Ragnar Grimsson, and Kjartan Olafsson. The replacement of Ludvig Josepsson, an Eastfjords businessman, as party leader by Svavar Gestsson symbolized this shift. The labor wing's most prominent leaders are Gudmundur J. Gudmunsson, Benedikt Davidsson, and Asmundur Stefansson, chairman of the ASI. The AB's success in becoming the third largest party, behind the Independence Party and the basically rural Progressives, is due to its clever and dynamic leadership, to divisions among the Social Democrats, and above all to its effective exploitation of Iceland's strong nationalism. It has emphasized social and economic reform over broad visions of revolutionary change. It has well-disciplined and effective action corps in all sectors of the society and has been the only party to consistently oppose association with the United States and membership in NATO. It has also been the most bellicose in seeking extension of Iceland's right to control fishing off its shores, particularly during the "cod wars" with Great Britain.

In 1981, Icelandic political developments were hectic. The coalition under Prime Minister Gunner Thoroddsen, which had been formed in February 1980 and consisted of maverick members of the Independence Party, the Progressives, and the AB, continued throughout the year, despite its razor-thin parliamentary majority and difficult national issues. The three AB cabinet members continued in office: Svavar Gestsson as minster of social and health affairs, Ragnar Arnalds as finance minister, and Hjörleifur Guttormsson as minister of industry. All three had served in the previous three-party center-left coalition under Olafur Johannesson, the former chairman of the Progressive Party and foreign minister in the current coalition.

Economic problems, especially Iceland's extraordinarily high inflation rate, dominated the government's attention. At the beginning of the year, Thoroddsen presented an overall economic program whose goal was to stabilize and expand the economy, but differences over it almost caused defections among the AB's parliamentary delegation and threatened the government's viability. AB leaders had to walk a difficult path to keep their followers' support, especially among the trade unions, while compromising sufficiently with their coalition partners to stay in the government.

The same situation prevailed in the field of foreign and defense policy. Johannesson tried to gain parliamentary support for construction of a new air terminal so that civilian and military activities at the Keflavik base could be separated. AB leaders opposed him, even to the point of threatening to bring the government down.

The opposition Independence and Social Democratic parties were frustrated by the political situation. They supported the government's efforts to stabilize and expand the economy, while believing that the measures taken were insufficient. They defended NATO membership and continuation of the Keflavik base against AB attacks and fought the delay in construction of the planned air terminal.

Leadership and Organization. At its biennial congress on 20–23 November 1980, the AB replaced its chairman and vice-chairman. This change was chiefly the result of a generational shift and did not affect party policies. Ludvig Josepsson, a long-time Communist from the eastern fjords, was replaced as chairman by 36-year-old Minister of Social and Health Affairs Svavar Gestsson. Although identified with the Reykjavik intellectual wing of the party, Gestsson is popular in all party groups, including trade unionists. A teacher who had studied in East Germany and a journalist for the AB's principal newspaper, *Thjodviljinn*, from 1968 to 1978, he had served as minister of commerce in the Johannesson government (*Visir*, 17 October).

Kjartan Olafsson, longtime editor of *Thjodviljinn*, was elected vice-chairman. He is also identified with the Reykjavik intellectual wing of the party (*Nordisk Kontakt*, no. 16, 1980; *Morgunbladid*, 22 and 25 November 1980). Gudrun Helgadottir was elected secretary and Tryggvi Adalsteinsson treasurer. These four constitute the Executive Committee and are automatically members of the 48-member Central Committee, as are the three AB cabinet ministers. Since Gestsson is also a cabinet minister, the number of ex officio members is six. The remaining 42 members were selected by the party congress.

The Party Council, whose members are elected mainly by local party units, is the most powerful party organ between congresses. The Council met on 20–22 November and elected a new Central Committee. Sixteen members of the former committee were replaced.

Party Internal Affairs. Although there was little evidence of factional battling during the party congress, dissatisfaction with the coalition government and the AB's role in it was prominent. Charges were made that the party should have been more militant against NATO and the Keflavik base and should have had a greater effect on government policies toward them.

The congress endorsed national industrial development but only if ownership was entirely Icelandic. Fear of foreign control of Icelandic industry and economic concerns was stressed, as was support for actions to prevent environmental pollution and to secure greater social benefits for lower-income groups. (*Morgunbladid*, 22 November 1980.)

At a press conference immediately after the congress, Gestsson said that the AB would not accept projects that would enlarge the Keflavik base and would have to leave the government if it approved them. He explained that the party did not favor expansion of the base's oil storage capacity and wanted to prevent any pollution from the present storage facility. He would not give any specific recommendations for government action. He also said that Icelanders should be in charge of the country's labor affairs and rejected "foreign heavy industry." (Ibid., 26 November 1980.)

Throughout 1981, the opposition press reported disputes and divisions among AB leaders, but these seldom broke out in the open and did not seem to affect party activities. On 31 December 1980, a statement of Gudrun Helgadottir that she could no longer support the government's economic program, together with a similar statement of a maverick Independence Party parliamentary deputy who had formerly supported the government, threatened a government crisis (*Nordisk Kontakt*, no. 1).

Domestic Attitudes and Activities. Iceland's inflation rate of about 60 percent at the beginning of 1981, its narrow industrial base, and the declining international economy threatened the Icelandic economy with stagnation and declining exports. Its gross national product rose only 2 percent in 1980, and the outlook for 1981 was zero growth and no decline in the inflation rate. On 31 December 1980, the Thoroddsen government proposed a temporary price freeze, a onetime reduction in the indexing of wage increases, stabilization of the foreign exchange rate of the Icelandic krona, and special financing arrangements for producers of export goods (ibid., no. 1).

The proposal to hold wage increases to less than the rise in the cost of living, which would actually reduce real wages, presented a difficult problem for the AB. Gudrun Helgadottir's opposition to the program contributed to a stalemate in the Althing over the passage of necessary legislation to give the program legal standing. Thoroddsen was forced to put the program into effect by adopting "provisional legislation" while awaiting Althing action. (Ibid.) In justifying the new measures, which were at variance with the AB congress's program, Finance Minister Arnalds maintained that it would bring the inflation rate down to 40 to 50 percent; otherwise it would rise to over 70 percent (*Morgunbladid*, 6 January). He continued to insist that the measures were sufficient to bring inflation to the 40 percent level, despite the judgment of economists to the contrary.

When the Progressive Party wanted to take additional anti-inflationary measures in late April, citing the Icelandic Economic Institute's claim that the government's program would lower inflation to 50 percent at best, the AB objected and won its way (*Nordisk Kontakt*, no. 2). On 1 May, the government softened the program by restoring full indexing of wages. It announced guidelines for price increases, while giving the Price Control Board the power to roll back prices. Inflation had not risen much beyond the 50 percent level by July, however, because of sluggish economic activity. In the fall, price controls and heavy debt burdens hit almost all manufacturing enterprises that sold on the domestic market, while international competition was hurting export industries.

The ASI canceled its wage agreements as of 1 November, and its wage negotiations committee called for wage increases of 13–17 percent. The Employers' Federation calculated that, together with fringe benefits and quarterly bonuses, this would mean a rise of wage costs by 30–40 percent, a level that would cause a further increase in the inflationary spiral. The AB was in a difficult position, caught between the government's need to restrain inflation and increase economic activity on the one hand and the demands of workers for increases in real wages on the other.

The AB had difficulty adapting to the government's industrial expansion policy because of its opposition to foreign capital. AB Minister of Industry Guttormsson argued, when debate occurred over the creation of sea chemical, steel, and rock-wool industries, that the plants should be small in size and primarily Iceland-owned. The AB argument that Icelandic control over new industries was necessary received wide support and was a condition stated in proposals the government put forward on 1 May for expansion of existing hydroelectric plants and the building of five new ones. This plan to expand energy production aroused strong opposition from the Social Democrats and the Independence Party because of the lack of decision on how the energy was to be used and on priorities for construction. The chief stumbling block was AB insistence that the capital come mainly from Icelandic sources. (Ibid., no. 10.)

International Views and Positions. The AB's major goal in the international field in 1981 was to stop any increase in the strength or activities of the Icelandic Defense Force, which consisted entirely of U.S. military personnel, stationed at the Keflavik base. Although Olafur Ragnar Grimsson led the party's hard-core antibase group, Gestsson took personal charge of this campaign. Opposition to the base and Iceland's membership in NATO and criticism of the United States were themes that all factions of the party endorsed. By stressing them, the leadership could unite the party, particularly at a time when workers were being asked to make sacrifices to fight inflation. At his press conference after the AB congress, Gestsson laid out the party's basic policy: it could not accept any projects that would enlarge the base.

Attempts to carry out this policy created increased friction with the other government parties as party leaders became aware of growing Soviet military strength and endorsed NATO efforts to meet that threat. Former Social Democratic leader Benedikt Gröndal, in articles in *Morgunbladid* (5 and 6 February), sought to convince Icelanders of the danger and inform them of NATO's efforts to meet it, arguing that newer and more powerful aircraft should be brought into Iceland. Geir Hallgrimsson, Independence Party leader, joined Gröndal in this effort.

On 15 March, the state radio announced a list of projects planned by the base. In addition to construction of an air terminal and modernization of oil storage facilities, attention centered on construction of protective aircraft and munition storage shelters and new radar units.

During a major foreign policy debate in the Althing on 11 May, Foreign Minister Johannesson said that there was more reason than ever to be in NATO, and Gröndal and Hallgrimsson accused the AB of conducting a scare campaign through its charges that the base was aggressive not defensive in orientation and that there were nuclear weapons on the base. Gestsson countered by asserting that a "foreign power" had forced the defense arrangement on Iceland and, by pressure on the Progressives, had kept the AB's predecessor, the UPP-SP, out of the government. He also said that the AB and its allies had prevented the Americans from gaining a "further foothold in the country" after 1951, but that the base had become an important "control station" in the U.S. nuclear weapons system. This offensive policy had disrupted the "balance of terror" and exposed Iceland to danger; he maintained that it was just as relevant today as previously to get the troops out and to resign from NATO. (*Morgunbladid*, 12 May; *Nordisk Kontakt*, no. 9.)

Belief grew that there was a secret government agreement giving the AB a veto over major base construction. In answer to questions in the Althing on 17 March, Progressive Party Chairman

Steingrimur Hermansson replied that there was no written agreement but that the ministers followed "certain" rules. The prime minister and Gestsson were silent. On 29 March, the state radio said that authoritative sources had revealed that there was a secret agreement. *Morgunbladid* (31 March) then reported that Gestsson had announced the agreement in an internal AB newsletter. The newsletter reportedly said that since the AB could not carry out its own policy under the circumstances, it sought to maintain the status quo at the base.

On another thorny base issue, however, AB leaders decided to compromise rather than force a government crisis. They had adamantly opposed a proposal to build new oil storage tanks with larger capacities at Helguvik to replace aging ones that threatened pollution of the area. Olafur Ragnar Grimsson voted in the Foreign Relations Committee to authorize the foreign minister to expedite the search for solutions to the difficulties involved. But both Gestsson and Grimsson said they were still opposed to building the tanks at Helguvik or with any greater capacity. (*Morgunbladid*, 21 May; *Nordisk Kontakt*, no. 10.)

The USSR did not escape AB criticism. *Thjodviljinn* (4 and 5 December) sharply attacked Moscow on the Polish issue at the end of 1980: "Socialism that cannot live unless protected by Soviet tanks is much worse than no socialism at all." It compared the situation to the Warsaw Pact invasion of Czechoslovakia in 1968: "The Kremlin rulers showed in an explicit way by invading Czechoslovakia that they will stop at nothing . . . the invasion of Afghanistan is proof of that." Vice-Chairman Olafsson returned to the attack in September, asking "what right do the old men in the Kremlin have to silence the Poles . . . What would people here say if the United States demanded that the Icelandic government stop all anti-American activity?" Gestsson told a newspaper that the AB opposed stationing of forces of either superpower in any small country, whether it be Afghanistan, Czechoslovakia, or Iceland (*Visir*, 17 October).

One of the AB's principal propaganda efforts centered around Grimsson's attendance in late September at a disarmament meeting in London sponsored by European Nuclear Disarmament and the Committee on Nuclear Disarmament. Grimsson spoke at the meeting and was interviewed by *Thjodviljinn* on his return. *Thjodviljinn* (1–4 and 6 October) followed this by a series of articles and editorials praising the British Labour Party's policies on disarmament, particularly its call for the removal of all nuclear weapons from British soil.

Much of the AB's attempts to stir up pacifist and neutralist sentiment was carried out through the Organization of Base Opponents (OBO), which also draws support from other leftist and some centrist groups. Although the OBO has not been able to attract much attention in recent years, in 1981 it sought to capitalize on the rising fear of nuclear weapons. On 7 May, for example, it protested the presence of the base in a demonstration before the U.S. Embassy on the thirtieth anniversary of the arrival of U.S. military forces under the 1951 bilateral defense agreement. When the "peace" movement in Europe generated interest among Icelanders later in the year, the OBO became more active. On 1 September, it adopted a resolution protesting the U.S. decision to produce the neutron bomb, stressing that it would be used outside the United States in case of conflict (*Thjodviljinn*, 1 September).

The AB sought unsuccessfully to arouse interest in the Norwegian proposal for a Nordic nuclear weapons–free zone as part of a wider disarmament measure. When Leonid Brezhnev indicated to a Finnish newspaper that Moscow would be willing to help create such a zone, Gestsson told *Morgunbladid* that he thought an effort should be made to discover what Brezhnev meant. "It is dangerous," Gestsson asserted, "for Iceland to be excluded [from such a zone]; it could increase the pressure for us to take nuclear weapons here or to change our position on nuclear weapons." He also said that "opinions vary as to whether the Scandinavian countries are free of nuclear weapons or not," a reference to AB accusations that nuclear weapons were stored at the Keflavik base. (Ibid., 5 July.) During an interview with the Norwegian newspaper *Ny Tid* (8 July), Arnalds also expressed annoyance at the failure of the other Scandinavian nations to consider inclusion of Iceland in a Nordic zone.

Grimsson and *Thjodviljinn* editor Einar Karl Haraldsson attended a peace conference in Finland at the end of June, and Grimsson told the conference that Iceland, Greenland, and the Faeroe Islands wanted to be included in a nuclear-free zone (*Thjodviljinn*, 2 July). *Thjodviljinn* continued to call for a Nordic nuclear weapons–free zone throughout the year. However, when a Soviet submarine possibly carrying nuclear weapons became stranded within a restricted Swedish military zone in late October, the AB criticized Soviet policy sharply. *Thjodviljinn* (6 November) headlined a report "The Hideous Duplicity of the Soviet Union: There Are Nuclear Weapons on Board the Stranded Submarine," and AB Vice-Chairman Kjartan Olafsson said "the Soviet Union holds a world record in one field only; namely, hypocrisy and dissimulation" because it has "pretended to be more pacifist than most other people." He urged that "the nations of Europe, from Poland to Portugal, from Greece to Iceland, should jointly demand that the Soviet Union withdraw its SS-20 missiles immediately and that medium-range NATO missiles not be deployed in Western Europe." He condemned the World Peace Council, an international front organization, for not criticizing the Soviet action. (Ibid., 10 November.)

International Party Contacts. Despite its championing of many of the international themes stressed by Western European communist parties and Moscow, the AB has made a distinct effort to disassociate itself from the international communist movement and especially from Moscow. Its policy is not to participate in international communist affairs; and after the Warsaw Pact invasion of Czechoslovakia in 1968, it threatened to expel any AB member supporting Soviet "imperialist activities." It did not attend any international communist meetings, including the Soviet party's congress in February, nor did it have any formal ties with the Soviet or any communist party. Instead, the AB sought to identify with the British Labour Party and the French Socialist Party after François Mitterrand's victory (ibid., 3–4 October).

Publications. The AB's principal paper is the Reykjavik daily *Thjodviljinn* (Will of the nation). The party also publishes at least two weeklies outside the capital: *Verkamadhurinn* in Akureyri and *Mjolnir* in Siglufjördhur.

Other Marxist Groups. There is a sprinkling of small Marxist groups, all politically insignificant. The tiny (thirty-member) Communist Organization of Marxists-Leninists (Kommunista Samtokin), consists of several splinter groups. Formed in April 1976, it claims to be the rightful heir to the original Icelandic Communist Party, but has close ties with the Chinese Communist Party. Its chairman is Ari T. Gudmundsson. In the fall of 1981, it reportedly considered seeking to join the Social Democratic Party (*Dagbladid*, 16 September). Its publication, *Verkalydsbladid*, appears irregularly. The Trotskyite Revolutionary League has about two hundred members but no chairman. Its publication, *Neisti* (The spark), also comes out irregularly.

U.S. Department of State   Finis Herbert Capps
Washington, D.C.

(Note: Views expressed in this article are the author's own and do not represent those of the State Department.)

Ireland

The Communist Party of Ireland (CPI) was founded on 14 October 1921 when the Socialist Party of Ireland expelled dissident members and joined the Comintern. However, the party's initial existence was short-lived and conditioned by the civil war. The CPI was refounded in June 1933, the date now accepted by Irish Communists for its origin. The organizational structure of the CPI was disrupted during World War II, largely because of the belligerent status of Northern Ireland and the neutrality of the south. In 1948, southern Communists founded the Irish Workers' Party and those in the north the Communist Party of Northern Ireland. At a "unity congress" in Belfast on 15 March 1970, the two groups reunited, forming a united party.

The CPI has about five hundred members and has its main support among northern Protestants; Catholic Marxists in the south usually join Sinn Fein—the Workers' Party (SFWP), the Provisional Sinn Fein, the Socialist Labour Party, or any one of about twenty ultra-left parties. The population of the Republic of Ireland is 3,364,881 and that of Northern Ireland 1,536,065.

Leadership and Organization. The CPI is divided into two area branches, north and south, corresponding to the political division of the island. The Congress is the supreme constitutional authority of the party but in practice simply endorses the decisions of the national executive. The innermost controlling body is the National Political Committee, which includes Andrew Barr (chairman), Michael O'Riordan (general secretary), Tom Redmond (vice-chairman), Johnny Nolan (national treasurer), James Stewart (assistant general secretary), Joseph Bowers, Madge Davison, and Fergal Costello.

The CPI holds no seats in any significant legislative assembly in either north or south and has little prospect of doing so. It has one local councillor in the south. The Communists do, however, have some influence in the trade unions and in the Northern Ireland Civil Rights Association (NICRA). The CPI also controls a small youth organization, the Connolly Youth Movement.

Domestic Attitudes and Activities. The CPI's domestic policies divide into two spheres. In the north, the Communists condemn all violence but implicitly hold the British responsible for the conflict. The party seeks a phased British withdrawal from the province. First, troops should be withdrawn to barracks, and then a bill of rights as advocated by NICRA should be introduced. This would ensure protection for the Catholic community. Finally, British forces should be withdrawn and massive British financial aid pumped into the province. Secular education should be introduced. Although hostile to the Irish Republican Army (IRA), the Communists want convicted IRA prisoners to be granted the status of political prisoners. In 1981 this issue was very much to the fore: IRA prisoners, convicted on terrorist charges, launched a hunger strike campaign at Northern Ireland's Maze Prison. The action, which began in March, did not end until 3 October, when it had to be called off because an increasing number were abandoning their fasts as they approached death. The CPI, while by no means supporting the IRA, continued to campaign for the IRA prisoners.

The CPI itself, however, eschews violence and is therefore opposed to all sectarian tendencies, preferring to seek a broadly based, trade union–oriented front embracing both Catholics and Protestants. It is accordingly antipathetic to the Provisional IRA, which it considers a promoter of sectarian strife. The party is adamant on this issue. "The military campaign of the Provisionals . . . is absolutely and unequivocally wrong" (*Irish Socialist*, October 1981). Similarly, the CPI believes the Protestant paramilitary forces to be inherently anti–working class and spawned by bigotry.

The CPI seeks the immediate implementation of a bill of rights to guarantee fundamental liberties. In addition, it endorses the program of the Northern Ireland Committee of the Irish Congress of Trade Unions. The objectives of this campaign are sixfold: security of employment and well-paid work, the right to live free from threats of intimidation, free association to secure peaceful change, good housing, equal educational opportunity, and adequate social services to protect the socially deprived.

In the south, the CPI's policy statements differed little from previous years. It continues its campaign of opposition to the government on most issues, including state ownership, education, health, women's rights, civil liberties, and unemployment. The CPI continues to base its hopes on a broad left-wing alliance, although it acknowledges that it has no popular support for its policies. The CPI's economic proposals include the establishment of a national development corporation and state oil and mineral companies and public ownership of banks.

The general elections of 11 June were inconclusive. Neither of the major parties, Fianna Fail or Fine Gael, won an overall majority. The Labour Party lost heavily; yet Garret Fitzgerald, leader of the minority Fine Gael Party, managed to form a new administration. The CPI contested seats in Dublin but polled only a few votes. The Communists campaigned incessantly for the remainder of the year against Fitzgerald's government. In general, the CPI's policies remained unchanged from previous years, but in the context of a deepening recession, the party paid more attention to unemployment and opposed taxation increases or cuts in public expenditures.

International Views. The CPI's complete subservience to Moscow is perhaps the most distinctive feature of party policies. It continues to support the Soviet Union's intervention in Afghanistan and favors repression in Poland and Czechoslovakia. The party is committed to supporting Ireland's withdrawal from the European Economic Community. Favored single-issue campaigns are solidarity with the "liberation" movements of Chile, South Africa, and Namibia.

Other Marxist Groups. Of the many small Marxist groups in Ireland, the most notable is the SFWP, the political wing of the official IRA. It is pro-Moscow and publishes the monthly *United Irishman*. Other groups include the Irish Republican Socialist Party and a Eurocommunist CPI splinter group, the Irish Marxist Society. There is also a small Maoist organization, the Communist Party of Ireland–Marxist-Leninist.

Also important is the Provisional Irish Republican Party (PIRA) and its political front, the Provisional Sinn Fein. The movement is now often referred to simply as the IRA. It was formed in 1969 by IRA members dissatisfied with that organization's Marxist leadership. The PIRA has about 350 active terrorists. In recent years, the PIRA has been taken over by Marxist militants, although its grass-roots membership is motivated more by Irish nationalism.

The main campaign of the year was the attempt to gain political status for convicted PIRA prisoners in Northern Ireland. It centered on a hunger strike in Northern Ireland's Maze Prison and was a brilliant propaganda success. After 216 days and the death of ten hunger strikers, the PIRA ended its campaign on 3 October because an increasing number were abandoning the hunger strike, thanks to the intervention of their families or because of clinical complications.

The campaign undoubtedly aroused sympathy abroad and, in the United States, increased the flow of donations. Even more ominous was the increase in recruitments by paramilitary organizations on both sides of the religious divide. A total of 64 people were killed during the period, a sharp rise over earlier figures. Also, because more police had to be deployed on antiterrorist duties, crime rose. Three days after the PIRA abandoned its fast, the new secretary for Northern Ireland announced concessions to the Maze prisoners. Although denounced by Protestant leaders, the concessions fell short of granting political status.

London   Richard Sim

Italy

The Italian Communist Party (PCI) celebrated its sixtieth anniversary in 1981. The party was formed in January 1921, when a radical faction of the Italian Socialist Party (PSI) led by Amedeo Bordiga, Antonio Gramsci, Palmiro Togliatti, and others seceded from the PSI and formed the Partito Communista d'Italia, later renamed Partito Communista Italiano. Declared illegal under the fascist regime, the PCI reappeared openly on the political scene in 1944 and participated in governmental coalitions in the early postwar years. Excluded from office in 1947, it remained in opposition at the national level until the mid-1970s. In the parliamentary elections of 1976, the PCI received 34.4 percent of the vote, seven percentage points more than it had received in 1972. Partly because of this, the PCI came to play a major role in national politics between the summer of 1976 and January 1979 as part of the governmental majority, but without holding cabinet posts. In the parliamentary elections of June 1979, the communist share of the vote dropped to 30.4 percent with a corresponding loss of 26 seats in the lower house and 7 seats in the upper. After the end of the experiment with a coalition of "national solidarity" in January 1979, the PCI returned to the opposition.

At the local level, the PCI has been in power in a number of municipalities since the beginning of the postwar period, particularly in the regions of Emilia-Romagna, Tuscany, and Umbria. Following the municipal and regional elections of 1975, the PCI gained control of an even larger number of local governments. Popular support for the communist party declined somewhat in the regional elections of 1980 and in the municipal elections of 1980 and 1981. However, the PCI continues to govern the major urban centers of the country, generally in coalition with the Socialists and other parties. The cities of Rome, Naples, Turin, and Bologna have communist mayors.

Leadership and Organization. Since the death of party Chairman Luigi Longo in October 1980, the position of chairman has not been filled. The general secretary of the party, confirmed at the last national party congress (April 1979), is Enrico Berlinguer. The national organization includes a Central Committee (169 members), a Central Control Commission (55 members), a Directorate (32 members), and a Secretariat (7 members). The office of head of the party parliamentary group is also an important position. Ferdinando Di Giulio, who had occupied this office, died in summer 1981 and Secretariat member Giorgio Napolitano was chosen to replace him.

Following a reorganization in September 1981, the members of the Secretariat are Enrico Berlinguer, Mario Birardi, Gerardo Chiaromonte, Adalberto Minucci, Alessandro Natta, Adriana Seroni, and Alfredo Reichlin. In addition to the party organs mentioned above, there are several bureaus staffed by experts in different areas. The most important of these are International Affairs (Giancarlo Pajetta), Party Problems (Adriana Seroni), Propaganda and Information (Adalberto Minucci), Cultural Activities (Aldo Tortorella), Economic and Social Problems (Gerardo Chiaromonte), Women (Lalla Tropia), Regional and Local Governments (Armando Cossutta), Problems of the State (Pietro Ingrao), and Education (Achille Occhetto).

The basic unit of party organization is the section. The smaller units that existed in the past (cells) no longer function. Party members belong to one of the 11,000 sections organized in neighborhoods, villages, or places of work. Activities of the sections are coordinated through plant, town, and area committees. Sections are grouped into federations, which usually coincide with the area of a province. In turn, federations are grouped into regional committees. Indications of a decline in the quantity and quality of party activities at the section level became visible in 1981. One party member reported that in the south, "our sections are getting empty and even the comrades are getting fed up" (*Rinascita*, 9 January).

Reporting to the Central Committee on the issue of party mobilization, Giorgio Napolitano referred to "present difficulties of the sections," adding that "the repetitiveness of the meetings, the prolixity, and generality . . . the abstruseness of jargon . . . discourage many forces from becoming involved in party life and even party membership and prevent us from using skilled energies." He urged "a determined regeneration of working habits and leadership methods . . . and the elimination of stifling forms of ritualism and bureaucratism." As part of an effort to revitalize the organization, the same meeting of the Central Committee proposed that "a campaign be waged to make section meetings end with an approval of brief documents to be examined by area committees and federations, which in turn would pass on the positions and the proposals to the central party organs. While acknowledging the need for the Directorate and the Central Committee to adopt without delay resolutions on matters of pressing nature, we propose that in other cases a special form of consultation be instituted through special meetings of all the federation committees." (*L'Unità*, 8 January.)

The number of party members claimed at the end of 1978 was 1.8 million. Membership appears to have declined slightly since then because the number of new members (about 70,000 in 1981) was insufficient to compensate losses due to attrition. Membership in 1981 was said to be 1,715,890 (ANSA, 10 October). The figure includes members of the Youth Federation (Marco Fumagalli, secretary). The social composition of party membership in 1978 was laborers, 40 percent; retirees and housewives, 28 percent; white-collar workers, small businessmen, artisans, and professionals, 18 percent; farmhands and small farmers, 11 percent; students, 3 percent.

The PCI's budget for 1980 showed expenditures of 70.9 billion lire, 12 billion more than in 1979 (*L'Unità*, 30 January). In 1980, the PCI posted a deficit of 5.1 billion lire. Fifty-five percent of all expenditures went for grants by the national party headquarters to local branches and organizations. Information and propaganda activities absorbed another 23 percent. An additional 3.8 billion (or 5.4 percent) was spent to cover the cost of the campaign for the municipal elections of 1981. The cost of publishing the party daily, *L'Unità*, came to 9.7 billion, including capital expenses for renovation of the physical plant. Annual membership fees continued to be the single most important source of revenue (22.1 billion or 31 percent of the total). The average annual contribution of card-carrying members was 10,811 lire (about U.S. $10). Funds collected through various activities sponsored by the party, such as *Unità* festivals, netted almost 25 billion lire. The balance of the revenues (20.2 billion) was obtained through public financing of the parties as provided by a 1974 law. Noting that the funds received through this source accounted for less than 30 percent of the total, PCI officials stressed "the need for a revision of the legislation dealing with public financing of parties," an issue that the Italian parliament discussed later in the year (ibid.).

It is widely believed that in addition to its own resources, the PCI benefits indirectly from the activities of the National League of Cooperatives. Some 15,000 firms operating under the umbrella of the league employ 260,000 people in a variety of economic sectors (travel, construction, insurance, agriculture). Some of the companies affiliated with the league are active in foreign trade, especially with Eastern European countries.

Domestic Views and Activities. During most of the 1970s, the strategic line pursued by the PCI was known as the "historic compromise." This policy endorsed a collaboration involving the two largest parties, the Christian Democratic Party (DC) and the PCI, as well as other political groups. This experiment, the coalition of national solidarity, was inaugurated in summer 1976 and lasted until January 1979, when the agreement dissolved over the issue of communist participation in the cabinet. Although the experiment had been unsuccessful, PCI leaders advocated this position throughout 1979 and most of 1980. The policy was reaffirmed as late as 5 November 1980 at a meeting of the Central Committee. On that occasion, Berlinguer stated: "The goal of a government of democratic unity with the participation of the PCI ... is not to be changed unless another clearly defined goal of great significance can be defined and accepted by the party" (ibid., 7 November 1980). Three weeks later, however, a special meeting of the PCI Directorate was called, and a sudden change in policy was announced. The PCI would no longer pursue an alliance with the DC, but would rather strive to bring about a "democratic alternative"; that is, a government without the Christian Democrats (ibid., 28 November 1980). Even though some party leaders attempted to explain that the decision represented a "development" of the previous strategy rather than a "shift," there is little doubt the PCI move implied a new posture, not only toward the DC but also toward other parties (Socialists, Republicans). The willingness of these groups to collaborate with the PCI was crucial to the success of the democratic alternative.

The new strategy of the PCI, known as the "Salerno shift," from the name of the city in which Berlinguer made a major speech explaining the new line, was very much in evidence during 1981. Communist leaders, free from the constraints of the historic compromise strategy, increased their attacks on the Christian Democrats. They criticized the policies of the Arnaldo Forlani cabinet in dealing with terrorism and the economy and repeatedly asked for the resignation of the government. In March, Berlinguer stated "the single preliminary and irrevocable condition for constructive dealings between the Communists and other parties is that this government leave office" (ANSA, 28 March).

Additional ammunition for the communist attacks on the cabinet was provided by the publication of a list of politicians and high-level officials said to be members of a secret and illegal Masonic association known as the P2. The Forlani cabinet eventually resigned in late May. During the negotiations for the formation of a new government, the PCI expressed its appreciation that for the first time in the postwar period the premier-designate was not a Christian Democrat (*L'Unità*, 12 June). However, when the new cabinet headed by Republican Giovanni Spadolini asked for a vote of confidence, the PCI parliamentary group cast a negative vote. PCI leaders explained that "the government's structure and composition fall significantly short of intentions and expectations and reduce the importance of the change. Indeed, there is no sign of the innovations that Senator Spadolini had promised." (Ibid., 12 July.)

PCI attitudes toward and relationships with the PSI were also affected by the party's new strategy. The ultimate goal of the PCI is to convince the Socialists to join the Communists in the democratic alternative alliance. This goal remains unattainable as long as PSI leaders prefer a strategy of cooperation with the DC. In this respect, the deliberations of the PSI congress, held in Palermo in April, could not but dash PCI's hopes that the democratic alternative would soon become a reality. Throughout the year, the PCI alternated efforts to lure the PSI away from its alignment with the DC with criticism of the official line of the PSI and its role in the Spadolini cabinet. PSI Deputy Secretary Claudio Martelli and Socialist Minister of Defense Lallo Lagorio were often the targets of PCI attacks. Lagorio came under heavy criticism when the government announced its decisions to make an air base in Sicily available for the deployment of NATO missiles and to contribute Italian troops to the peacekeeping force in the Sinai region (*Corriere della Sera*, 2 November). Communist accusations that the Socialists' stance was ambiguous continued throughout the year. There were also frequent polemics between local representatives of both parties.

International Views and Positions. In the latter part of the 1970s, the relationship between the PCI and the Communist Party of the Soviet Union (CPSU) became increasingly tense. A number of events and stands taken by the PCI in international affairs has contributed to the deterioration of a relationship that in earlier times was very friendly. Among these were the critical views voiced by PCI leaders on the shortcomings of the regimes of Eastern Europe, strong PCI support for dissident movements in communist countries, the PCI policy of rapprochement with the Chinese Communist Party, the condemnation of the Soviet invasion of Afghanistan, the leading role played by the PCI in the creation of Eurocommunism, and the emphasis of PCI leaders on autonomy and independence. This trend toward cooler PCI-CPSU relationships continued in 1981.

Events in Poland and the position taken by the Italian Communists intensified the controversy in the latter part of 1980. On 10 December, the PCI official party organ stated that "foreign intervention and acts of force would have disastrous effects not only for that country but for the very idea of socialism, for the fate of democratic forces, for the prospects of international détente and cooperation" (*L'Unità*, 10 December). A PCI communiqué stressed "the danger represented by external interference and the very serious consequences that a military intervention would face" (*Le Matin*, Paris, 11 December 1980). Some communist leaders voiced their concern in strong terms. Napolitano hinted at the possibility of a total breakdown of the relationship when he said "any intervention would have irreparable consequences." It was also confirmed that a letter summarizing the PCI's official views on the Polish situation had been sent to the communist parties of the USSR, Bulgaria, East Germany, Hungary, Czechoslovakia, and Poland. (*Radio Free Europe Research*, 19 December 1980.) The CPSU's response (sent in December 1980 but made public only at a later date) accused the PCI of "having made concentrated attacks against the foundations of socialism in Poland" (ANSA, 18 February).

Given this state of affairs, it is understandable that Berlinguer's decision not to attend the CPSU congress in Moscow was received with the "deepest irritation" (ibid., 10 February). Moreover, the choice of Giancarlo Pajetta as head of the Italian delegation was not designed to please the CPSU, given Soviet leaders' criticism of Pajetta for his role in the rapprochement between the PCI and the Chinese Communist Party (*Radio Free Europe Research*, 27 February). Matters did not improve during the CPSU congress. Initially, the Italian delegation was barred from presenting its message to the delegates. Having seen the text in advance, the CPSU reportedly asked that Italian officials change parts of the address that spoke out in favor of the independent trade union movement and against the Soviet intervention in Afghanistan. But the PCI delegates "refused to alter a word" (ibid.). Pajetta was finally able to give the speech, but he had to deliver it in the Hall of Columns to a meeting of Moscow Communists chaired by Moscow party chief Viktor Grishin and not to the congress delegates assembled within the Kremlin. Reporting on these events, Pajetta said: "It could not be up to us to decide when and where to speak, but it was not up to anyone else to decide on or even influence the content of our speech" (*L'Unità*, 28 February). Eventually *Pravda* did publish the text in full and with a faithful translation, after a meeting of Pajetta and PCI Directorate member Paolo Bufalini with Secretary of the CPSU Central Committee Boris Ponomarev. Before returning to Italy, Bufalini gave a speech at the Moscow Social Science Institute in which he stated that the Italian delegation "failed to understand and was surprised" at the decision not to allow them to speak from the official rostrum of the Congress (ibid., 3 March).

Polemical exchanges between the two parties did not end with this episode. Yuri Zhukov, Moscow's best-known political commentator, published a long article in *Pravda* dealing with relationships among communist parties and stated that "Eurocommunism is incompatible with Marxism-Leninism and it has no future." To this *L'Unità* (3 March) responded: "An incomprehensible point is the joy with which Zhukov states his conviction of an imminent failure of Eurocommunism. What makes him so happy? What does he believe could be built on the hoped-for ruins of this or that party? He can be sure that the beneficiary of such a defeat would not be Marxism-Leninism." In June, in an article appearing in *Novoe Vremya*, Y. Samailov sharply rejected the accusation of Soviet interference in Poland voiced in the PCI weekly *Rinascita*. "Regrettably," he wrote, "this is not the first time that Italian comrades have judged developments before they have occurred and documents before they have read them" (Tass, 24 June).

One month later, *Pravda* published an article by Vadim Zagladin in which he suggested the need for "closing ranks," for reducing polemics between communist parties. The PCI saw this as an attempt to force unanimity, and a prompt response appeared in an unsigned article in *L'Unità* (25 July). "What is unacceptable in Zagladin's article is the definition of a limit beyond which communists who think differently from the CPSU play into the hands of imperialist propaganda. Are those who think differently from the CPSU on the intervention in Afghanistan playing into the imperialists' hands? What would Zagladin say if in the future the CPSU were to acknowledge that it was a mistake?"

The PCI had other opportunities to point out its evaluation of the situation in Eastern Europe. In August, the Czechoslovakia party daily, *Rudé Právo* commemorated the thirteenth anniversary of the "new course" in Czechoslovakia and stated: "The events of 1968 and the lessons drawn from them have an international validity that is acknowledged by many communist and workers' parties." *L'Unità* (27 August) responded that "the parties referred to by *Rudé Právo* do not include the PCI, which since 1968 has never ceased repeating its assessment of the new course and of the Soviet military intervention." On 30 December, *L'Unità* published a blast of unprecedented ferocity against the Soviet system in connection with events in Poland.

During the year, the PCI made known its positions on a number of international issues. The party's view of NATO remained unchanged. Asked whether there was a contradiction between the PCI's acceptance of that alliance and the party's negative stand on Spain's proposed entry into NATO, Berlinguer replied: "Our position in favor of maintaining Italian membership in the Atlantic pact is no act of faith but an act of political realism that takes into account the fact that a balance has been created between the blocs and that any unilateral alteration could upset it" (ibid., 1 July).

PCI criticisms of the foreign policy of the Reagan administration became stronger as the months passed. In February, a commentary by Giuseppe Boffa stated: "Reagan's only messenger to Europe so far has been a high-ranking diplomat sent to explain that what is happening in El Salvador is the fault of the USSR and of Cuba. Since not even the Latin American governments take such remarks seriously, it is not surprising that the envoy was received only with cold courtesy on this side of the Atlantic" (ibid., 2 February). In April, some concerns were expressed over the potential military uses of the U.S. space shuttle (ibid., 18 April). On 7 May, after a NATO meeting in Rome, the PCI organ stated: "We must remember that we are members of the Atlantic alliance but not aircraft carriers for U.S. missiles or auxiliary troops."

During the summer and early fall, the attention of PCI leaders turned more and more toward the issue of the arms race between the superpowers: "We have urged immediate negotiations to achieve a balance at the lowest possible level. This remains our position. The aim must be both to dismantle the number of SS-20 missiles that constitute an imbalance and to halt the deployment of the Euromissiles, as the first step toward liberation of the whole of Europe from nuclear weapons . . . But it is necessary to want and to facilitate negotiations both by adopting a political strategy aimed at peaceful coexistence and cooperation among states with differing social systems and by abandoning all objectives of supremacy . . . But the Reagan administration is doing the opposite. Its strategy is summed up in the following objective: a United States that is stronger than anyone and that dominates everyone else." (Ibid., 26 July.) A few weeks later, Secretariat member Adalberto Minucci added: "The decision by the president of the United States to give the go-ahead for production of the neutron bomb casts an ominous shadow over the entire world situation . . . The fact that Reagan is now overturning Carter's decision . . . constitutes an outright provocation and indicates the direction in which the new U.S. administration is moving." (Ibid., 19 August.)

International Party Contacts. As in previous years, extensive international contacts were undertaken by PCI officials in the last months of 1980 and during 1981. In November 1980, Directorate member Giancarlo Pajetta and Foreign Section Chief Antonio Rubbi received in Rome Miloš Minić, chairman of the Presidium of the League of Communists of Yugoslavia and deputy director of its International Relations Department. In January 1981, Herbert Haeber, heading a delegation of the East German communist party (SED), visited PCI headquarters and was received by Giorgio Napolitano. This was followed a few days later by the arrival of a delegation of the Brazilian Workers' Party, which was received by Berlinguer.

In February, PCI officials welcomed a delegation of the Nicaraguan Sandinista Front. On 21 March, Faruq Qaddumi, chief of the Political Department of the Palestinian Liberation Organization, was received by Pajetta who confirmed the PCI's "full solidarity with the Palestinian people" (ibid., 21 March). In April, Berlinguer held talks with Walid Jumblatt of Lebanon, and a delegation representing the Commission to Organize the Working People of Ethiopia visited Italy at the PCI's invitation. In the same month Petru Enache of the Romanian party met with Pajetta, and Mieczyslaw Wotczak, Culture Section chief of the Polish United Workers' Party, was received by his counterpart in the PCI, Aldo Tortorella.

Other visits of foreign delegations to PCI headquarters in Rome included an important meeting between Santiago Carrillo of the Spanish Communist Party and Berlinguer. This was followed in mid-July by a visit of a Chinese delegation headed by Peng Chong, member of the Politburo and the Secretariat of the Chinese Communist Party.

During 1981, PCI officials traveled abroad extensively. In February, Giorgio Napolitano headed a PCI delegation to Belgrade. In March, Nilde Jotti, member of the Central Committee and speaker of the lower house of the Italian Parliament, visited Romania and met with President Nicolae Ceauşescu and other officials. In April, Gianni Cervetti attended the SED Congress in East Berlin. In June, Ugo Pecchioli met in Belgrade with Yugoslavian Presidium member Stane Dolanc and discussed "relations within the international workers' movement" (ibid., 11 June). During the same period, a delegation of PCI members visited the Soviet Union. According to *Pravda* (5 June), "the Italian comrades gave a positive appraisal of the achievements of the USSR and declared their support for the peace initiatives advanced by Brezhnev."

In July, Rodolfo Mechini, deputy head of the PCI's Foreign Affairs Section, visited Budapest at the invitation of the Hungarian Socialist Workers' Party. In the same month, Franco Raparelli of the Central Committee visited East Berlin, and Paolo Bufalini and Gianni Cervetti conducted talks with

Boris Ponomarev in Moscow. In August, two PCI provincial leaders, Antonio Bassolino and Giuseppe Trippa, met in Bulgaria with Dimitur Stanishev of the Central Committee of the Bulgarian Communist Party, a delegation of PCI federation secretaries headed by G. Quercini of the Central Committee visited the USSR, Giancarlo Pajetta held talks with Romanian party leaders.

In September, Berlinguer traveled to Belgrade for talks with Yugoslav party President Lazar Mojsov. Later in the month, a PCI delegation headed by Giuseppe Dama visited Hungary at the invitation of the Hungarian party. At the end of September, it was reported that Giancarlo Pajetta had spent three weeks in China, where he had met with Peng Chong (ANSA, 24 September). In October, Berlinguer undertook a trip to Central America. After spending four days in Cuba, where he talked with Fidel Castro, the PCI secretary briefly visited Mexico and Nicaragua. On returning to Italy, Berlinguer declared that he had been invited to the United States by universities and research institutes but that he had not accepted these invitations "because it was not the right moment for a visit" (*Corriere della Sera*, 26 October).

Publications. The official party newspaper, *L'Unità*, is published daily in both Milan and Rome. In the summer, *L'Unità* editor Alfredo Reichlin became a member of the Secretariat, and the position of editor was given to Claudio Petruccioli. Another daily published in Rome, *Paese Sera* (although formally independent), is considered to be close to the PCI and was reported to be in poor financial condition in 1981. The PCI weekly, *Rinascita*, edited by economics expert Luciano Barca, is a cultural journal that attracts primarily an intellectual audience. The theoretical journal of the party is *Critica Marxista*, edited by Aldo Tortorella. Other specialized journals deal with history (*Studi storici*), international affairs (*La nuova rivista internazionale*), and economics (*Politica ed economia*). The popular periodical *Donne e politica* is addressed to women. The International Affairs Department of the PCI publishes a bulletin in four languages, featuring texts of important speeches by prominent leaders. The publishing house of the party (Editori Riuniti) produces a large number of volumes in a wide variety of fields.

Other Communist Groups. The Party of Proletarian Unity for Communism (PDUP) and Proletarian Democracy (DP) compete with the PCI. In the parliamentary elections of 1979 the PDUP obtained six seats in the lower house. The DP is not represented in parliament but has one representative in the European Parliament. Both parties are also represented in a number of municipal and regional assemblies. In some cases, these groups are part of left-wing coalitions at the municipal level.

Terrorist Groups. A number of self-styled "real communist" groups have been operating underground for a decade and have claimed responsibility for many acts of political violence aimed at politicians, business executives, newspapermen, prison guards, policemen, and members of the judiciary. Although many terrorists have been arrested, political kidnappings, bombings, and assassinations were carried out in 1981 by members of the Red Brigades and other groups, including Front Line, Brigades for Communism, and Communist Combatant Formations. Information provided by arrested terrorists indicates that Italian terrorists have extensive international contacts and support and that a number of nations (Yemen, Libya, Cuba, and some Eastern European states) have provided financial assistance, weapons, and training facilities (*L'Espresso*, 8 February).

San Marino

The Communist Party of San Marino (CPS) was established in February 1921 as a section of the Italian Communist Party, which had been created a month before. Although in June 1941 this section became an independent party, CPS positions over the years have been influenced by the presence and the policies of its larger Italian counterpart. This is not surprising since San Marino is located in the Red Belt of Italy and the small republic is surrounded by Italian communities in which leftist parties, especially the communist party, have traditionally been strong.

Following World War II, the CPS formed a coalition government with the San Marino Socialist Party and was in power for well over a decade. Excluded from office in 1957, the CPS remained in the opposition for twenty years. In 1977, following the breakdown of a center-left coalition, the CPS attempted to form a government of "national solidarity" similar to the formula being employed in Italy at the same period. It would have included Communists, Socialists, and Christian Democrats, that is, all the large political groups. The attempt failed, and the electorate was called to the polls in May 1978 to resolve the impasse. The returns gave the CPS 25 percent of the vote, a slight increase over the 23.7 percent obtained in the 1974 elections. In the Grand and General Council, the legislative assembly of 60 seats, the CPS retained its 16 representatives. Following the 1978 elections, the CPS returned to power in coalition with the Socialists and the left-oriented Socialist Unity Party. In the Congress of State, San Marino's cabinet, CPS representatives hold four of the ten portfolios: interior and justice, social security and health, industry and trade, and education and culture. Moreover, since 1978 one of the two positions of captains-regent, who act as heads of state for six-month terms, has been given to a CPS cabinet member.

At its Tenth Congress in 1980, the CPS reaffirmed the policy of collaboration with the other parties of the left. It reconfirmed Ermenegildo Gasperoni as party chairman and Umberto Barulli as general secretary. It was reported that since the Ninth Congress (1976), CPS membership had grown by 15 percent, with particular increases in the number of woman and young members. According to Barulli, the CPS attaches "much importance to the development of contacts with craftsmen, business-men and small entrepreneurs ... the 10th congress set the task of invigorating the policy of alliance between the working class and the middle classes." With respect to the international communist move-ment, Barulli stated: "The Communists of San Marino believe in the vivifying power of proletarian international solidarity. Starting from the principle that each party is independent ... we have been strengthening our ties with the fraternal communist and workers' parties." (*WMR*, April.)

The CPS maintains contacts with a number of other communist parties. The Chinese foreign minister visited San Marino in 1979. In January 1981, a delegation from the East German party held talks with CPS officials in San Marino. In September, Barulli traveled to Bucharest at the invitation of the Romanian Central Committee (Agerpres, 9 September).

The periodical *La Scintilla* is the official organ of the CPS.

Ohio State University

Giacomo Sani

Luxembourg

The Communist Party of Luxembourg (PCL) was founded in January 1921. Before World War II, it played an insignificant role in Luxembourg politics. Following the war, the party increased its influence to some extent, partly because of the enhanced prestige of the Soviet Union. Since 1945, the PCL has been represented in parliament and in the town councils of Luxembourg City and several industrial centers of the south. From 1945 to 1947, the cabinet included one communist minister. The party's influence subsequently decreased but increased again following the elections of 1964. It reached a new climax in the elections of 1968 and decreased again in the elections of 1974 and 1979. In municipal elections in October 1981, the PCL received 7.2 percent of the votes, compared with 16 percent in 1975.

Since the last elections, the communist presence in the legislative assembly has been almost insignificant. With only two representatives, the PCL cannot form a party fraction of its own, and no other splinter party is willing to cooperate with it. Party membership is estimated at six hundred. The population of the Grand Duchy is about 365,000 (1980).

Party leadership is dominated by the Urbany family. René Urbany, party chairman, and his father, Dominique Urbany, are apparently the only active members of the three-member Secretariat. Joseph Ruckert, who replaced Arthur Useldinger as central party treasurer, may have only nominal responsibilities. Members of the Urbany family occupy other key positions. René Urbany remains director of the party press. The organization of former resistance fighters, the Réveil de la résistance, is directed by François Frisch, brother-in-law of René Urbany and member of the Central Committee. He is also active as secretary of the Luxembourg Committee for European Security and Cooperation. René Urbany's sister, Yvonne Frisch-Urbany, leads the Soviet-sponsored Pushkin Cultural Center; his father-in-law, Jacques Hoffmann, is a member of the Central Committee and the Executive Committee. He is also a member of the executive board of the communist printing company Coopérative ouvrière de presse et d'édition (COPE). The board of directors of COPE includes Joseph Grandgenet (president); René Urbany (administrator-director); François Frisch, Jacques Hoffmann, Théo Bastian, and Camille Muller (administrators); and Dominique Urbany (auditor).

The PCL remains unswervingly loyal to the Soviet Union, and it follows Soviet foreign policy positions faithfully, favoring disarmament and opposing the rearmament of the country by the establishment of a supply base for U.S. armed forces in Luxembourg.

In August 1981, PCL Chairman René Urbany stated in an editorial in the party paper "that the formation of a broad and active peace movement could not be delayed any longer in the Grand Duchy." He appealed to all "progressive" forces in the country "to put aside ideological and political differences and to start together a campaign against nuclear escalation and for the salvation of peace." A committee was founded to direct the activities of the so-called Movement for Peace.

Leaders of the PCL often visit the USSR and other East European countries. Aeroflot, the Soviet national airline, links Luxembourg with, among other destinations, Moscow and Havana. The USSR embassy in Luxembourg is better equipped than is necessary for diplomatic representation in a small country. Under the leadership of Ambassador K. B. Oudoumian, of Armenian origin, there are seventeen legal representatives and one temporary Soviet employee associated with embassy duties.

Publications. The party organ, *Zeitung vum Lëtzeburger Vollek*, has a daily distribution of between 1,000 and 1,500 copies. The party's publishing company, COPE, publishes this paper, as well as the French edition of the *World Marxist Review*, and also distributes foreign communist publications. The PCL distributes its publications periodically to households and also participates in the political programs of Radio Luxembourg.

The PCL's new party headquarters houses the party's printing company and the offices of the party's publications, with technical equipment and production capacity greatly exceeding the needs of the PCL. Publications from these installations are supplied to other communist parties and organizations beyond the Grand Duchy.

Malta

The Communist Party of Malta (CPM) was founded in 1969 during a secret congress in Gwardamangia. Its secretary general and founder is Anthony Vassallo, who is assisted by Paul Agius. The CPM has been legal since its establishment, and describes itself as a "voluntary organisation made up of the most politically conscious members of the workers' class, together with others who are exploited by the Capitalist system, who are determined to found a Socialist Malta" (*Proletarjat*, no. 1).

The CPM's current strength is estimated at 150. This figure does not include members of CPM front organizations. The CPM maintains close associations with disgruntled followers of Dom Mintoff's ruling Malta Labour Party (MLP). In fact, a substantial number of CPM members are MLP members, notwithstanding a circular issued by MLP officials warning against such action. In addition, a number of CPM members have infiltrated the government-controlled General Workers' Union (GWU). The GWU is the largest trade union in Malta, and its numbers comprise more than 50 percent of organized workers in the country.

Leadership and Organization. The CPM is run by a Central Committee, elected at the triennial congresses. Representatives from affiliated organizations, including the Malta-USSR Friendship and Cultural Society, the Malta Peace Council, and the Communist Youth League (CYL), also sit on the Central Committee.

The Central Committee elected during the Second CPM Congress, held in Valletta (16–18 February 1979), consists of Chairman Anthony Baldacchino (a shipwright and GWU shop steward at the Malta Drydocks), Secretary General Anthony Vassallo, International Secretary Paul Agius (also vice-president of the Malta-USSR Friendship and Cultural Society, and secretary general of the Malta Peace Council), Education and Propaganda Secretary Mario Vella Macina (former secretary general of the CYL and an economist at the government-operated Malta Development Corporation), Documentation Secretary Lilian Sciberras (former international secretary of the CYL and assistant librarian at the University of Malta), John Agius, Philip Bugeja, Renald Galea, Mario Mifsud, John Muscat, and Paul Muscat.

During the early 1970s, the CPM established the League for Social Justice (Xirka ghall–Gustizzja Socjali; XGS) to garner support among university students. Very few students have joined the XGS, however, and most are socialists rather than communists. The attempt to have a communist organization at the university has not succeded, but the CPM has recruited a small number of students.

The headquarters of CPM is located in Valletta. It forms part of the offices of the Progressive Bookshop and Progressive Tours, Ltd., both officially owned by Paul Agius. These commercial enterprises represent East European publishers as well as East European airlines and are the main source of CPM funds.

Domestic Activities. The front normally used for domestic activities by the CPM is the Malta-USSR Friendship and Cultural Society. The wives of Czech doctors serving on the island used to teach Russian at the society's headquarters, which is situated within the CPM offices. The society has also sent a number of Maltese students to Soviet universities. Currently there are approximately ten Maltese students in the Soviet Union. The first student sent to a Soviet university has now returned fully equipped to serve the interests of his sponsors. Guzeppi Schembri was graduated in international law from Kiev University in early 1981. On his return, he was employed by Malta's Foreign Office and placed in charge of the Moscow desk.

During 1981, a number of agreements were signed between Malta and the Soviet Union. The CPM was heavily involved, and at times this was publicly acknowledged. In 1981, the Soviet Union was granted, for the first time, the right to have an embassy in Malta (there will be some twenty Russian families resident on the island). The first Soviet ambassador was Viktor N. Smirnov, who served in Australia between 1970 and 1976, where he met Paul Agius, then an immigrant in Australia. (Agius returned to Malta in early 1973.) Agius undertook several diplomatic pilgrimages to Moscow during the year.

The establishment of the embassy resulted in additional agreements. The first, concluded in January, gave the Soviet Union the use of facilities at Has-Saptan for oil storage. These facilities were constructed and used by NATO until the early 1970s, when NATO forces were ordered out by Prime Minister Mintoff. It is estimated that by December 1981 some 150 Soviet ships had used the facilities.

Paul Agius was also responsible for the visit to Malta in October of Nikolai Talyzin, deputy chairman of the USSR Council of Ministers. This visit ended with the signing of two agreements by Talyzin and Mintoff. The first emphasized the neutrality of Malta, and the second resulted in a trade agreement between Malta and the USSR. The first agreement is the most important. In it, the USSR expressed "its readiness to consult with the Government of the Republic of Malta on questions directly affecting the interests of the two countries, including the neutral status of Malta, and in case of situations arising which create a threat to peace and security, or to the violation of international peace, will also be prepared, as necessary, and at the request of the Government of the Republic of Malta . . . to enter into contact with it so as to remove the threat or to establish peace."

During its 1979 congress the CPM declared its intent to contest the next elections. These were held 12 December 1981, but no CPM candidate ran.

International Views. The CPM generally supports the MLP's nonaligned foreign policy. However, it considers that it is "foul and reprehensible to ignore the distinction between the USSR and the USA." The CPM views the presence of the Soviet fleet in the Mediterranean as a major deterrent to any aggressive ambitions of "imperialism's strike force." The CPM considers that military bases ought to be removed from the Mediterranean, which should be converted into a nuclear-free zone. The CPM calls for Israel's withdrawal from all occupied Arab territories, as well as the formation of a sovereign and independent state for the people of Palestine. Likewise, the CPM insists that the Cyprus problem must be settled in accordance with U.N. resolutions. (*WMR*, August.)

Publications. The CPM published *Proletarjat*, a mimeographed bilingual journal, between October 1977 and April 1979, when publication was suspended with issue number 13. In May 1980, the CPM began publishing a monthly newspaper in Maltese, *Zminijietna* (Our times), aimed at factory workers, in contrast to the former publication, which was aimed primarily at the party faithful. The last issue of *Zminijietna* (no. 5) was published in January 1981. The CYL published *Spartakus* in 1977, a mimeographed bilingual journal that was issued only thrice between November 1977 and September 1978. During 1981, the CYL began publishing another mimeographed journal, *Il-Bandiera l-Hamra* (Red flag).

Netherlands

The Communist Party of the Netherlands (Communistische Partij van Nederland; CPN) was founded as the Communist Party of Holland in 1918, but the official founding date is that of affiliation with the Comintern, 10 April 1919. The present name dates from December 1935. The party has always been legal except during World War II.

For over a decade, the CPN's policy was based on the "new orientation" proclaimed at its 1964 congress. This program stressed domestic political goals and subordinated relations with international communism to the goal of creating a domestic united front in which Communists and Socialists would play the leading role. After 1975, however, increasing involvement in the international communist movement and the normalization of relations with the Communist Party of the Soviet Union (CPSU) spelled the end of the new orientation policy.

Between 1959 (when the party split) and 1972, the CPN share in elections increased from 2.4 to 4.5 percent of the vote. Elections for the lower house of parliament in May 1977 brought a considerable loss. Compared with 1972, the CPN vote declined from 329,973 to 143,420 (1.73 percent). The number of CPN seats in the 150-member lower house dropped from 7 to 2. Provincial and municipal elections in the spring of 1978 confirmed this decline. The number of CPN seats in provincial governing bodies dropped from 19 to 5 and in municipal governing bodies from 129 to 85. Elections for the lower house of parliament in May 1981, however, brought a small gain. Compared to 1977, the CPN got 178,147 votes (2.05 percent) and won 3 seats.

CPN membership has increased from 10,000 to 13,000 in the past few years. Members are scattered throughout the country, with centers of activity in the provinces of North Holland and Groningen. The social composition of the party has broadened to include university intellectuals and workers in the service sector. The population of the Netherlands is about fourteen million.

Leadership and Organization. The CPN's Twenty-Seventh Congress (June 1980) elected a new Central Committee of 73 members, including 15 new members of whom 7 were women—a considerable increase in female participation. Among the new members were people with experience on executive boards and political action committees.

The Central Committee selected a sixteen-member Executive Committee, the principal policymaking body; Henk Hoekstra is the chairman. The CPN parliamentary delegation consists of Marcus Bakker, chairman of the CPN faction in parliament; Joop Wolff; and the new member, a woman in her early thirties, Ina Brouwer. Bakker and Wolff are members of the Executive Committee, and Brouwer is on the Central Committee. The Secretariat, consisting of three members of the Executive Committee and one general member of the Central Committee, is the organizational and administrative center of the party.

The most active of CPN front organizations is the General Netherlands Youth Organization (Algemeen Nederlands Jeugd Verbond; ANJV). The Netherlands Women's Movement (Nederlandse Vrouwen Beweging; NVB), like the ANJV, works to support CPN demands.

Party Internal Affairs. The Twenty-Seventh Congress reconfirmed the new coalition policy, which had been approved by the Twenty-Sixth Congress in 1978. The goal of this policy is a CPN-influenced leftist majority.

The 1978 congress also approved changes in the constitution of the CPN. An article allowing religious believers to be party members was dropped, as was an article forbidding propaganda against the ideological foundations of the party. The purpose of these changes was to make the party more attractive to outsiders and to prevent criticism.

Party leaders make a special effort to show that the CPN is a democratic party by allowing free discussion on various subjects. This has encouraged the emergence of a group of dissidents in the CPN, who criticize the attitude of the leadership toward democratization of the party. Working particularly in the universities, they believe that democratization should be accelerated. The existence of this group became known through a conference it held in August 1980. The main subject was CPN internal democracy. The fear was expressed that all essential criticism would receive no hearing because of the leadership's interpretation of democratic centralism. On the other hand, the dissidents made it clear that they were not trying to form a faction within the party. Although CPN leaders oppose this group and more or less regard it as a faction, they refrain from expressing this publicly. The image of the CPN as an increasingly open party could be seriously damaged by drastic measures against the opposition. CPN leaders have chosen a more indirect way of denouncing the demands of the dissidents. When asked about this point, CPN leaders minimize the objections of the group by calling it a marginal force.

Domestic Attitudes and Activities. The CPN election campaign demanded that buying power be strengthened and employment and a peace policy be promoted. The main policy of the new government should be to reduce corporate and military power. The CPN should participate in this new government, based on a progressive majority, as a driving force.

The results of the elections were disappointing for the CPN. Its gain of one seat was much less than expected. First, opinion polls had predicted four to six CPN seats. Second, the noncommunist media devoted much more attention to the CPN than in previous years, stressing the new course of the party and its increasingly open character. Third, the party put so much effort into the campaign in terms of volume and intensity that the results must be regarded as negligible. This point, however, was not publicly admitted. Moreover, the two other small, left-wing parties gained as well, particularly the Pacifist Socialist Party, which picked up two seats (from one to three).

During the months following the elections, the CPN concentrated on its main success in the past:

the peace campaign. In 1980, following the government's late 1979 decision to postpone stationing theater nuclear weapons on Dutch soil until the end of 1981, the CPN did not pursue its campaign to stop the nuclear arms race in general and the neutron bomb in particular. Criticism of the Soviet invasion of Afghanistan and the exile of Andrei Sakharov no doubt played a role in this attitude. However, at the end of 1980, the CPN decided to take up the peace issue again. On 22 and 23 November 1980, an international meeting was organized in Amsterdam with the theme: What can we do against the nuclear arms race? The idea was to bring together representatives from Eastern and Western Europe to discuss the role that smaller countries, like the Netherlands, could play in the disarmament process. Several West European countries sent delegations, primarily communist party representatives. All East European countries sent delegations, and the Soviet Union sent a particularly strong delegation. The conference was a success for the CPN, both internationally and domestically, and included the participation of noncommunist Dutch representatives from parliament, the universities, and the churches.

Since this conference, the CPN has strengthened its efforts to step up the peace campaign. Such an opportunity came in August 1981, when the U.S. government decided to start production of the neutron bomb. The CPN took the lead in a number of strong protests against this decision. One special activity of an autumn campaign was a boat trip through the Netherlands with the theme: "Cruise against the cruise [missile]." Originally meant to be directed against the deployment of medium-range nuclear weapons, it later came to include the neutron bomb.

International Views and Party Contacts. The CPN's involvement in international communism, which resumed during the late 1970s, continued in 1981. Compared with previous years, however, a certain reserve was noticeable—not so much because of disagreements over principles as because of tactical considerations. Under its new coalition policy, it is essential for the CPN to cooperate with other groups. It wants to avoid damaging those relations by being overly acquiescent toward the international communist movement and the foreign policy of the Soviet Union.

While maintaining its ambiguous attitude toward the Soviet intervention in Afghanistan, the CPN increasingly defended the position of Polish workers. The CPN feels that Poland should solve its own problems without interference from others. The Soviet Union should not exert pressure on Poland, but should analyze critically its own responsibility in regard to the present situation in Poland.

This latter attitude was attacked in the Soviet, East German, and Czechoslovak press. The 2 March issue of *Pravda* stated that "certain communist parties" were attacked because of their views on the situation in Poland. The CPN was not mentioned, but it reacted in *De Waarheid* by justifying its views. During the congress of the Communist Party of Czechoslovakia in April 1981, the Dutch CPN representative, Joop IJsberg, was recalled by the CPN to protest the aggressive behavior of Czechoslovakan party leader Gustav Husák, who compared the present Polish situation with the situation in the East Germany in 1953, Hungary in 1957, and in his own country in 1968.

The CPN delegation to the Twenty-Sixth CPSU Congress during the last week of February 1981 consisted of CPN Chairman Henk Hoekstra and a representative from the Amsterdam area. The CPSU's reservations toward the CPN were illustrated by two facts: the statement on communist parties maintaining good relations with the CPSU did not cite the CPN; and Hoekstra's speech was presented at one of the secondary meetings.

The reputation of the CPN, however, concerning its ability to organize successful peace campaigns remained intact in the international communist world. Soon after the international conference in Amsterdam in November 1980, Joop Wolff traveled to the Soviet Union to exchange ideas on intensifying the anti–nuclear weapons campaign in the Netherlands. One of the main discussants was Vadim V. Zagladin, candidate member of the CPSU Central Committee and first deputy chief of the CPSU Central Committee's International Department.

Although the actual effect of the "cruise against the cruise" action was limited, much international interest, particularly from the Soviet Union and East European countries, emerged from it. During the campaign, Y. E. Kornilov, a prominent Tass representative, was present. In September, a CPN–led delegation of eight members visited Moscow on the invitation of the Soviet Peace Committee.

The CPN was heavily involved in all the protest meetings against nuclear weapons that marked the latter part of 1981, either through direct participation or through CPN-led delegations. It participated in a meeting in Bonn on 27 August, which discussed the possibilities of international coordination, as well as in all the protest meetings in the capitals of the major West European countries during the last quarter of 1981.

Publications. The CPN daily, *De Waarheid* (The truth), has a circulation of about 20,000. The theoretical bimonthly *Politiek en Cultuur* is used for training purposes. The ANJV and NVB publish monthly newspapers. The CPN's Instituut voor Politiek en Sociaal Onderzoek issues a quarterly, *Komma*, which, as a discussion forum, seeks to contribute to the further development of the theory and strategy of the socialist movement in the Netherlands. The CPN maintains its own publishing house and bookshop, Pegasus, and operates two commercial printing plants, one for *De Waarheid* and one for other printed matter.

Pro-Chinese Groups. Recent developments in China have embarrassed pro-Chinese groups in the West who still worship Mao Zedong. The same is true for the three pro-Chinese groups in the Netherlands. However, they have been cautious not to express themselves too openly against new developments in China. After the trial of the Gang of Four, who played an important role in the Chinese Cultural Revolution, representatives of these groups have been more critical of China.

The Netherlands Communist Unity Movement–Marxist-Leninist criticizes the Chinese Communist Party for its treatment of the Gang of Four. It believes that although the Cultural Revolution was far from perfect and even made serious mistakes, its adherents cannot be condemned as criminals. This attitude is clearly expressed in the group's paper, *De Rode Tribune* (The red tribune).

The Communist Workers' Organization, Marxist-Leninist takes a different view. Its paper, *De Rode Vlag* (The red flag), has compared the trial of the Gang of Four with the trials in Moscow in the 1930s, with the difference, however, that the accusations now are true. This group tends to condemn the Cultural Revolution as a degeneration of Marxism-Leninism.

The Group Marxists-Leninists takes a stand between the other two groups. In its paper *Rode Morgen* (Red morning), it has expressed its belief that the Cultural Revolution was originally a positive movement, but that some leaders created abuses. The political significance of the Cultural Revolution should be studied and lessons drawn from it.

International Documentation and Information Centre   C. C. van den Heuvel

Norway

The Norwegian Communist Party (Norges Kommunistiske Parti; NKP) has been among the weakest in Western Europe since its decision in 1975 not to merge with several left-socialist parties and factions. This decision split the party and caused its then chairman, Reidar T. Larsen, and several other leaders to leave the NKP for the new Socialist Left Party (Sosialistisk Venstreparti; SV). The SV is now the strongest and the NKP the weakest of three Marxist parties to the left of the Norwegian Labor Party (Det Norske Arbeiderparti; DNA), which is a reformist social-democratic movement. The DNA has been the main governing party in Norway since 1945, and despite an electoral setback in 1981, it remains the country's largest political party. The third active Marxist party is the Maoist Workers' Communist Party (Arbeidernes Kommunistiske Parti; AKP), which has run in the last three parliamentary elections as the Red Electoral Alliance (Rod Valgallians; RV). Although still sympathetic to China, its enthusiasm for the Chinese model has waned since 1976.

The NKP was organized on 4 November 1923 by radical politicians and trade unionists who split from the DNA, as the latter was ending its brief membership in the Third International. The NKP first demonstrated electoral strength in 1945, when it won 11 of the 150 Storting (parliament) seats, thanks to communist participation during World War II in the Norwegian resistance movement and the Soviet liberation of northern Norway. The cold war quickly eroded NKP strength, and by 1957 the Communists held only a single seat in parliament. In 1961, dissident members of the DNA started the Socialist People's Party (Sosialistisk Folkeparti; SF), and the NKP lost its last mandate. Not until the formation of the Socialist Electoral Alliance (Sosialistisk Valgforbund—a forerunner of the SV) in 1973 by the SF, NKP, and dissident left Laborites did Communists once again sit in the Storting. Standing alone in the 1977 elections, the NKP received only 0.4 percent of the vote, far short of winning a parliamentary seat. The decline continued in the 1979 local elections. In the September 1981 parliamentary elections, the NKP received only 7,025 votes (0.3 percent). No national party did worse.

Although exact membership figures for the NKP are not available, there are surely considerably fewer members than the two thousand to five thousand estimated before the 1975 schism. In 1980, divisions within the party over Soviet policy in Afghanistan may have led to further resignations. The population of Norway is just over 4.1 million.

Although the SV was initially an electoral alliance of the left under a common platform, the 1975 decision to merge the three factions has not created a stronger left-socialist bloc. Despite the spectacular initial showing in the 1973 parliamentary elections (11.2 percent of the vote, 16 out of 155 seats), the party quickly lost strength in ensuing local and national elections. In September 1981, the SV gained marginally in the Storting elections, raising its share of the vote to 4.9 percent (a gain of 0.8 percent from 1977) and its mandates to four (a gain of two) (*Nordisk Kontakt*, no. 12). Most of the new SV votes presumably came at the expense of the DNA, but the SV did not live up to earlier public opinion polls or to Chairman Berge Furre's hopes of 10 percent of the votes (*Arbeiderbladet*, 12

March). The elections reflected a strong swing to the right, with the conservative Right Party (Høyre) winning 31.6 percent of the vote and 54 seats. With the parliamentary backing of the Center and Christian People's parties, the conservatives formed the first conservative government to rule Norway in more than half a century.

The third Marxist party, the AKP, ran in the 1981 parliamentary elections under its usual RV banner and drew 17,593 votes (0.7 percent). This was about the same strength shown in the 1979 municipal and county elections and is far short of the vote necessary to win a seat. Nevertheless, the RV outpaced the NKP, which is now clearly the weakest Marxist party in popular support.

The 1973 upsurge of leftist strength, particularly around the SV, resulted from an emotional campaign against Norwegian membership in the expanded European Economic Community (EEC). Supported by both socialist and nonsocialist political groups, the National Movement Against the EEC achieved a narrow victory in the September 1972 EEC referendum after more than a year of vigorous activity. Parliamentary elections a year later showed severe losses for those parties (especially the DNA) that had supported EEC membership. By 1975, however, the issue had faded, and surveys showed that the SV had lost strength because of opposition to its anti-NATO line and the internal turmoil connected with the merger efforts.

The 1977 parliamentary elections reduced the Norwegian leftist parties to their pre-EEC fringe position. With the waning of détente and the increase in East-West tensions in Europe in 1980, there were signs that Norwegian leftists were seeking to capitalize on the ensuing fears of a new European cold war. Proposals for increased defense spending and the stockpiling (called "prepositioning") of military equipment on Norwegian territory were vigorously opposed by the left, including elements in the DNA. Revival of the peace and anti–nuclear weapons campaign suggested the possibility of a new "national movement" analogous to the EEC campaign. A U.S.-Norwegian agreement on weapons prepositioning was approved by the Storting by a wide margin (95–13) in January. Public opinion polls indicate strong support for NATO membership despite anxiety about renewed international tensions (*Nordisk Kontakt*, no. 2).

The victory of the conservatives in the 1981 elections and the formation of a conservative government under Kaare Willoch will reduce the influence of the SV further. SV votes were occasionally essential for the DNA government during the 1977–1981 period. These votes were not significant on foreign and security policy issues where a Labor-nonsocialist consensus has prevailed for more than thirty years.

Leadership and Organization. Personalities are important in a small democracy, and there has been considerable continuity among the three left-socialist parties. Current NKP Chairman Martin Gunnar Knutsen emerged as leader of the rump-NKP after the party's divisive Fifteenth Congress (November 1975), which voted 117 to 30 against merger with the SV. Knutsen was unanimously re-elected chairman at the NKP's harmonious Sixteenth Congress in April 1978, as were Rolf Nettum, organizational vice-chairman; Hans Kleven, political vice-chairman; and Arne Jorgensen, editor of the party's twice-weekly *Friheten*. There have been no leadership changes at the party's annual conferences since the congress. The Norwegian Communist Youth League (Kommunistisk Ungdom; KU) is the party's most important affiliate.

The Soviet invasion of Afghanistan produced an unusual amount of intraparty strife in 1980. Five of the NKP Central Committee's thirteen members protested the action, and the debate spilled over into the noncommunist press. The Central Committee of the KU also objected to NKP support for Soviet policy in Afghanistan (*Arbeiderbladet*, 12 January 1980). Although the NKP leadership contained the dissent, this latest uproar is thought to have cost the party both members and votes.

The SV can be regarded as a descendant of the SF party, which was formed by anti-NATO Laborites in the early 1960s. In a 1979 radio interview, SV chairman and Tromso University historian

Berge Furre was asked whether the SV was not merely the SF resurrected. Furre stressed the broader scope of the SV, the merger of several leftist groups in 1975, and the party's commitment to far-reaching social and economic reforms. These themes were echoed at the party's most recent congress, held in Oslo in March. The congress re-elected Furre as the party's chairman and Hilde Bojer and Torbjorn Dahl as vice-chairmen. Erik Solheim, former chairman of the youth organization, was elected secretary. Steinar Hansson was re-elected editor of *Ny Tid*. The new female political secretary is Arna Egesvik, and the new trade union chairman is Tor Harald Skaug.

Between congresses, the SV's main policymaking body is its Executive Committee. At present, it consists of Furre, Kari Loftsnes, Ellen Hartmann, Asbjorn Wikestad, Bitte Vatvedt, Adolf Larsen, Irene Iversen, Lasse Jahnsen, and Bjorg Ofstad. Deputy representatives are Kjell Roland, Maja Arnestad, Finn Gustavsen, Aud Gustad, Bjorgulv Froyn, and Gunhild Emanuelsen. Gustavsen founded the SF in 1961 and played a large role in the organization of the SV. Although he retired from parliamentary politics in 1977, he is the SV's "grand old man" and a frequent party spokesman to the press (ibid., 16 March).

The SV congress was attended by some 250 delegates and emphasized two main themes: the party's traditional anti-NATO and antidefense line and its willingness to cooperate with the DNA after the elections. There was some dissatisfaction with the party's modest influence in the trade union movement and with the party's weekly, *Ny Tid*. Commentators noted the relative tranquility of the congress and the party's growing homogeneity. For example, none of the ex-Communists who switched to the SV in 1975 remain in positions of influence (*Aftenposten*, 13 March).

Less is known about the internal organization of the AKP, which made marginal gains in the 1981 parliamentary elections. An amalgam of various Maoist groups that arose in the late 1960s, mainly as splinter groups from the SF and NKP youth organizations, the AKP was formally organized in late 1972. Paal Steigan has been the party's only chairman. Ideologically, politically, and presumably organizationally and financially, the AKP has maintained very close ties to the Chinese Communist Party. In recent years, however, enthusiasm for China has declined, especially following the purge of the Gang of Four and new Chinese foreign and domestic policies.

The "defection" (that is, resignation) of one of the AKP's former inner-core members, Helge Ogrim, possibly sheds some light on the AKP's unusual internal practices. Ogrim claimed the party exercises rigid Stalinist discipline over its members, including internal informers, direction of career and studies, and obligatory "self-criticism." Such tactics may explain in part the ability of the AKP to infiltrate various organizations such as the venerable Norwegian Students' Association (Det Norske Studentersamfunnet). Only some 1,400 out of the roughly 20,000 students at Oslo University currently belong to the association (ibid., 14 May 1979). The AKP runs candidates under the RV electoral front and also has a youth affiliate, Red Youth (Rød Ungdom) (*Arbeiderbladet*, 23 April; *Klassekampen*, 22 May).

Domestic Attitudes and Activities. Parliamentary elections in September encouraged all political parties to produce detailed programs. The elections occurred at a time of changing economic prospects. Norway's economy has been among the strongest in the West because of the growing production of oil and gas in the North Sea. Economic performance in 1981 has been less vigorous than in the previous two-year period. Inflation was running at about 11–12 percent, and economic growth was expected to be a minimal 0.5 percent. Unemployment remained quite low by international comparison, just over 2 percent (*Nordisk Kontakt*, no. 9). Nevertheless, outside of the oil sector, Norwegian industry felt strong competitive pressures, and oil revenues now account for over 25 percent of state revenues (ibid., no. 13).

Petroleum's growing economic importance was reflected in the domestic political debate. Both the SV and NKP were critical of the decision to pursue promising oil finds north of 62° latitude, but such prospecting continued. Similarly, the SV believes that the pace of petroleum production should be reduced. Neither position influenced public policy significantly, and the new conservative government will continue to develop the country's important energy resources.

Another domestic issue that provoked controversy was the Labor government's plans to develop hydroelectric resources in northern Norway—the Alta-Kautokeino hydro project in Lappland. Because the project would infringe on traditional resources of the Lapp population, protesters have sought on several occasions to block construction. Sit-ins led to clashes with police. The SV defended the protesters and warned of "North Irish or Basque conditions" if the government sought to continue the project (ibid., no. 2). Once again, the new government intends to continue existing plans, which have made concessions to the local population.

Both the SV and NKP presented detailed electoral programs for the 1981 parliamentary election campaign. The NKP program remained true to the program adopted in 1973 before the party schism. Among the main points were increased state subsidies for collective housing construction, price controls, higher social security payments, longer paid vacations, shorter working hours, and additional efforts to increase employee control over management. Tax reform is stressed, with heavier taxes on higher incomes to replace taxes on low incomes and a value-added tax on necessities. These proposals do not differ significantly from either the SV's or RV's, and they highlight the NKP's problem in projecting a distinctive profile. As noted below, foreign and security policy are the principal areas of nuance among the Marxist left. This was also clear from an NKP Central Committee meeting on 26–27 September following the conservative electoral victory. Foreign and defense issues were highlighted, but the NKP also called for a common front against the new government's expected domestic policies.

Because of its representation in parliament, the SV has been better able to project its views on domestic politics. The March SV congress adopted an electoral program with little variation from earlier platforms. The six-hour workday and greater support for local social programs were stressed. Environmental issues were less prominent than earlier. The country's oil revenues were no longer ridiculed and were now the *deus ex machina* for the SV's redistribution and Socialism in Norway programs (*Arbeiderbladet*, 16 March).

The AKP's election front, RV, adopted its electoral program at a national conference on 4–5 April. Though stressing that the RV does not base its plans for a socialist Norway on any foreign models, its domestic program differs little from either the NKP's or SV's.

The larger trade unions, as well as the Norwegian Trade Union Confederation (Landsorganisasjonen; LO), are firmly controlled by Laborites. Both the AKP and SV claim to have gained some local support in the labor movement, but this has not been significant. The NKP has traditionally been stronger in the trade union movement than in electoral politics, and a larger proportion of its members are industrial workers than is the case with the SV or AKP. The DNA-LO link remains unchallenged. Radical groups are most common in the Construction Workers' Union (unemployment in the construction industry has risen since mid-1980). Radicals are also found in the metal, wood, and electrochemical fields, particularly in the older industrial cities of the east and north-central parts of the country.

International Views and Positions. There has been little variation in the international views of the NKP, SV, and AKP during recent years. The NKP leadership regularly reconfirms its unswerving loyalty to the principles of "proletarian internationalism" and Soviet foreign policy. Accordingly the NKP regularly attacks Norwegian membership in NATO and its defense cooperation with the United States and West Germany. Recent proposals for strengthening NATO through the deployment of theater nuclear forces (cruise missiles), development of the neutron bomb, and the prepositioning of NATO supplies in Norway have been bitterly attacked. In July 1980, these views were summarized in a joint statement with the communist parties of Sweden, Finland, and Denmark (*Friheten*, 1 July 1980; *IB*, 1980, nos. 17–18).

Soviet-Norwegian relations have been strained in a number of areas in recent years, including the demarcation of territorial limits in the Barents Sea, Soviet activities on Svalbard, and occasional Soviet violations of Norwegian waters and airspace. The NKP downplays such issues, as well as Soviet activities in Afghanistan. In 1981, limited progress was made on bilateral Soviet-Norwegian issues. Since the 1975 schism, the NKP dropped its earlier "nonaligned" orientation and became one of the most consistently pro-Soviet of the European communist parties. Several of the current NKP leaders, such as Vice-Chairman Hans Kleven, have written in support of Soviet military intervention in Eastern Europe. Following the 1981 elections, the NKP leadership called for broad public support for the "Scandinavian nuclear free zone." The NKP proposal included only the territory of the five Nordic countries.

The SV has continued to make its anti-NATO, antimilitary, and anti-EEC position a central plank of its party platform. These issues were central to the origins of the SV and its predecessor, the SF. It was therefore not surprising that the SV vigorously opposed the U.S.-Norwegian agreement on storing weapons at Norwegian sites for use by NATO reinforcements during a crisis. As noted above, the agreement was approved in January, and in addition to the two SV deputies, nine Laborites and two Liberals voted against the agreement (*Nordisk Kontakt*, no. 2). Despite this setback, the SV threw its weight behind the rapidly growing "peace movement," which has been evident in most of Western Europe. It denounced the Reagan administration with a new vehemence. The "nuclear free zone" attracted considerable support from within the DNA and among many nonsocialists. Premier Odvar Nordli noted in January that the Nordic countries were already free of nuclear weapons, but that the region included the heavily armed Kola peninsula of the Soviet Union. He suggested that a nuclear free zone could best be achieved in a European context.

Soviet response to these proposals has been ambivalent. Although rejecting the application of such zones to Soviet territory, Soviet commentators have supported those statements of the peace movement directed against NATO. Soviet agents are thought to be giving the movement more than moral aid. With the Soviet submarine incident in October (the discovery of a Soviet sub within restricted Swedish waters and the probability that it carried nuclear weapons), the Scandinavian peace campaign, particularly its anti-NATO dimension, suffered a real setback. It is unlikely, however, that such events will change the traditional position of the SV on international issues.

The AKP continues to be critical of both "superpowers," but reserves most of its criticism for the Soviet Union. In its electoral program, the AKP was critical of Norwegian NATO membership and urged a defense strategy based on Maoist "people's war" tactics and a strong civil defense. In other areas, the AKP's foreign policy views remain close to those of Beijing.

International Party Contacts. The international position of the NKP is reflected in its close ties to the communist parties of Eastern Europe and the Soviet Union. In August, NKP Chairman Knutsen paid his annual visit to Moscow and met with several high Soviet party officials, including Boris Ponomarev. The ensuing communiqué stressed the congruence of views and strongly emphasized the need to oppose U.S. foreign and defense policy views, particularly NATO force modernization plans (Tass, 7 August).

Representatives of nine foreign communist parties attended the Sixteenth NKP Congress in 1978. The Soviet delegation was headed by Gennadi Sizov, which, together with the relatively small number of international representatives, reflects the NKP's limited importance (*Arbeiderbladet*, 15 April 1978).

Official NKP statements on the topic of Eurocommunism have usually been ambivalent. While stressing that different national circumstances dictate varying tactics, the NKP has been critical of the moderate line on specific issues expressed in the past by French and especially Italian communist leaders. While the NKP does not directly criticize foreign communist parties, it underlines the example of the Soviet experience (*WMR*, November 1978). A wider view is unlikely to emerge following the visit of NKP editor Jorgensen to Poland in February despite a visit to Solidarity headquarters in Gdansk (PAP, 6 February).

The SV remains outside of any formal network of international ties, but it maintains close informal ties with the Socialist People's Party in Denmark, the Left Party–Communists in Sweden, and the People's Alliance in Iceland. On several occasions, the SV has expressed enthusiasm for Eurocommunism, especially as evidenced by the Italian Communist Party.

The AKP continues to look toward China for international support and inspiration. In recent years, this tie has become more discreet as less radical forces have emerged in China. The AKP has frequently declared its support for the Albanian and North Korean parties.

Publications. The main NKP organ is *Friheten* (Freedom), first published as an underground paper during World War II. Dwindling circulation caused its transition from a daily to a weekly publication in 1967. Fund raising to keep the paper going is a continuous NKP preoccupation. During the fall of 1977, *Friheten* increased publication to twice a week. In line with Norwegian policy, the NKP Press Office receives 25,000 Norwegian kroner (about U.S. $5,000) in public support. The KU publishes a youth bulletin, *Fremad* (Forward). The SV newspaper is *Ny Tid* (New Times), which was intended to absorb the readership of the SF publication *Orientering*. The latter was highly regarded in the 1950s and 1960s by many readers outside the SF. *Ny Tid* has been plagued by continuing financial and editorial difficulties, in addition to an "espionage" scandal in 1977. During the 1981 SV congress, the paper was once again subject to criticism. Finally, there is the AKP weekly *Klassekampen* (Class struggle), which also enjoys a small public subvention. The AKP's theoretical journal is *Rød Fane* (Red flag).

University of Massachusetts   Eric S. Einhorn
Amherst

Portugal

The 60-year-old Portuguese Communist Party (Partido Comunista Português; PCP) is one of Western Europe's largest communist parties and the area's staunchest pro-Soviet organization. Within Portugal, it is the largest and most influential communist group. Between 1974, when the party was legalized, and 1980, membership grew from 15,000 to 187,000. Party leaders assert that this trend has continued despite a loss of votes in the 1980 parliamentary elections. The PCP claims more card-carrying members than any other political party in the country; the Socialists are said to have 100,000 and the government coalition 85,000. Even so, the 1980 returns gave the communists just under 17 percent of the vote and 41 of the 250 seats in parliament. Some leftist votes were attracted to a communist front organization, the Popular Democratic Movement (Movimento Democrático Popular). The population of Portugal is estimated at 9.9 million. (*Expresso*, Lisbon, 17 April; *Guardian*, London, 7 May.)

The PCP controls 50 of the 305 town councils. There is leftist, and perhaps some communist, influence in the Council of the Revolution, a military advisory group to the president and self-designated guardian of the socialist constitution. The greatest communist impact is felt in the labor movement and in the farm worker collectives in southern Portugal. Most labor unions are affiliated with the communist-controlled General Confederation of Portuguese Workers (Confederação Geral de Trabalhadores Portugueses–Intersindical Nacional). PCP power in these two sectors has been diminished by the government's continued dismantling of the collectives and by the inability of low-paid industrial workers to sustain long strikes. (*Guardian*, 7 May.)

The numerous far-left radical groups that flourished following the 1974 revolution have languished in recent years. The most active survivors regrouped in 1980 to form the Popular Unity Front (Frente de Unidade Popular) under the leadership of former presidential candidate Maj. Otelo Saraiva do Carvalho. Little has been heard from a guerrilla organization, the Popular Forces of 25 April (Fôrças Populares do 25 de Abril), which was launched with fanfare and a bank robbery in April 1980 (see *YICA*, 1981, p. 439).

Leadership and Organization. Despite the PCP's declining influence in national affairs, there are no outward signs of internal discontent over the leadership of Alvaro Cunhal, secretary general since 1961. He heads a 72-member Central Committee, One party member commented that Cunhal's "excellent physical and political form" would permit him to last a long time in his post. It is anticipated that the sole purpose of the Tenth Congress, scheduled for 1982, will be to evaluate the change in the country's political life, which the PCP considers reversible. (*Expresso*, 18 October 1980.) No deviation from the party's Marxist-Leninist ideology is expected. To outside critics of the party's "dogmatism and immobility," Cunhal responds that the PCP's ideology is not a "petrified body of concepts" but a "living theory" that allows the party to learn from and adapt to new situations (*Avante!*, 12 March).

Domestic Attitudes and Activities. Struggling against a conservative tide in Portugal, the PCP pressed in vain during the year for parliamentary elections. The PCP's aim was to "prove" that the "reactionary" government did not represent the popular will. The party claimed repeatedly that the mandate of the Democratic Alliance (Aliança Democrática; AD) had been invalidated by numerous illegalities in the October 1980 parliamentary elections as well as by the AD's "clamorous" defeat in the December 1980 presidential elections (see *YICA*, 1981, pp. 437–38). The AD's legitimacy was further vitiated, said the PCP, by its daily violations of the constitution, its wrecking of the economy, and its "proclaimed" intention of liquidating the democratic system (*Diário de Notícias*, 17 February; Lisbon Domestic Radio, 6 September).

The Communists declared that the convincing re-election of President Ramalho Eanes had checked the reactionary offensive and prevented, for the time being, the wave of repression, lawlessness, and persecutions that could have been unleashed (*IB*, March). Alvaro Cunhal cautioned all the same against complaisance as well as against the "whitewashing" of the new AD prime minister, Francisco Pinto Balsemão. The latter was said to be more moderate than his predecessor, the late Francisco Sá Carneiro. The PCP leader acknowledged that the two were "not the same," but Balsemão had not "fallen from heaven . . . uninvolved in the AD's subversive plan." (*Avante!*, 31 December 1980.)

On taking office in January, Pinto Balsemão fulfilled Cunhal's expectations by pledging to "liberate civil society" from the Marxist legacy of the 1974 revolution. At the same time, he promised to "respect" the Socialists and Communists in parliament. Together, the two opposition parties hold a nine-seat majority. (*NYT*, 10 January.) Actually, the real challenge to the prime minister came from the right wing of his own party, which opposed his "excessively soft line" toward President Eanes (ibid., 23 February). The besieged Balsemão resigned in August but was invited to return after his critics were unable to produce a credible alternative (ibid., 29 August). Cunhal dismissed the new cabinet as a "vulcanization" job: "The bigger the job, the louder the bang when the tire blows out." He promised that the Communists would do their utmost to provoke a new crisis. (Lisbon Domestic Radio, 6 September.)

Cunhal was especially critical of the Socialists for having thrown a life buoy to the AD "just as it was beginning to go down." Had the parties of the left united when the government coalition was in crisis, he said, a "democratic turnabout" could have been achieved; however, it was evident that the Socialists "preferred capital to the world of labor." The Socialists had allied themselves with the AD in many municipal councils to thwart achievements of communist majorities, the PCP leader alleged, and they sabotaged the labor movement with scab trade unions and other divisive activity. (Ibid.; *Expresso*, 17 April; *Avante!*, 2 July.)

The PCP continued to denounce the AD's "subversive" plan to revise the constitution by unconstitutional means, that is, through a referendum instead of by a two-thirds majority of parliament. Actually, Balsemão pledged not to overstep the limits of his office, thereby implying he would not seek a referendum. What most alarmed the Communists was the proposal to desocialize the constitution totally and to abolish the Council of the Revolution, the military watchdog of socialist gains. The PCP acknowledged that the council's dissolution was inevitable, but said it hoped to prevent "government control and partisan manipulation" of the armed forces; their administration was "a task for the military alone" in the present stage of Portugal's democratic evolution. (Lisbon Domestic Radio, 18 January; *Visión*, New York, 26 January; *Expresso*, 17 April; *Avante!*, 28 May.) President Eanes withdrew early in the year as chief of staff of the armed forces and said in July that there was no further need for intervention by the army "as sole interpreter" of the people's will. In the same month, the council vetoed, as it had the previous year, a parliamentary bill allowing the return of nationalized banks and insurance companies to the private sector. (*CSM*, 19 January, 28 July; *NYT*, 19 July.)

Communist attacks also focused on the AD government's economic program and on the "somber" prospects facing Portuguese workers. The PCP cited declining real wages, growing unemployment, and an offensive by employers against labor and against trade union activists. (Lisbon Domestic Radio, 17 July; *IB*, March.) Cunhal charged that employers were receiving help from the government, which was resorting to "fascist-style" methods through increased use of intelligence services and coordinated police forces (*Avante!*, 28 May). The Socialists and Communists opposed antiterrorist legislation approved in June on the grounds that it would result in persecution of the left but not the right. The law fixed heavy penalties for sabotage, assassination attempts, and recruitment of mercenaries. (*NYT*, 10 June.)

Cunhal promised an intensified "popular mass struggle" to defend the vital interests of the Portuguese (*Avante!*, 22 January). Later in the year, ports, dairies, and slaughterhouses were briefly paralyzed by striking civil servants demanding 22 percent pay raises (*NYT*, 15 April). The government limited increases for public employees to the rate of inflation—16 percent (ibid., 2 April). When AD deputies voted themselves a 100 percent pay raise "to reinforce parliament's prestige," the Communists protested and voted against this increase for a "privileged class of professional parasites" (*CSM*, 7 July).

The Communists held an agrarian reform congress in June to celebrate the "surprising and extraordinary" survival of more than four hundred agrarian cooperatives. It was noted that five years of "theft and plunder" by successive governments had halved the agrarian reform acreage by December 1980, but that the remaining cooperatives were thriving with twice as many machines per hectare as in the early days of the revolution. (*Avante!*, 4 June.)

International Views and Positions. The PCP raised a "storm of protest" over the possibility of new Portuguese commitments to NATO, including naval base facilities within Portugal and on the Atlantic island of Porto Santo, off Morocco. The fear was that nuclear-armed aircraft carriers would be allowed to establish home ports in Portugal. The PCP alleged that tentative suggestions had been made that nuclear dumps be constructed within the country. Cunhal declared that it was necessary to prevent Portugal from being transformed into "a springboard for the Pentagon's aggressive policy." Also taking part in the left-wing campaign to prevent the stationing of nuclear arms in Portugal was Lt. Col. Ernesto Melo Antunes, a prominent member of the Council of the Revolution, foreign minister in 1975, and a proponent of nonalignment. (*Komsomolskaia Pravda*, 6 March; *CSM*, 26 March; *Avante!*, 28 May.)

The PCP denounced the United States' "criminal military intervention" in El Salvador and its stifling of the popular struggle there. The party noted the "profound hyprocrisy" of U.S. support for fascist dictatorships in Central America in contrast to the "imperialists' systematic anticommunist campaigns, especially those orchestrated around events in Afghanistan and Poland." (*Avante!*, 22 January.) The latter were not victims of Soviet "expansionism" or "interference," it was claimed; carrying out a revolution and building a new society required mobilization of "an entire people." The PCP expressed its solidarity with efforts of the Polish party "to correct mistakes and shortcomings" and "to isolate and defeat the antisocialist forces." Cunhal predicted that there would be no Soviet invasion of Poland and that Soviet troops would soon be withdrawn from Afghanistan. (*O Jornal*, Lisbon, 12–18 December 1980; *Guardian*, 7 May; *Avante!*, 2 and 16 July.)

International Activities and Party Contacts. While attending the Soviet party congress in Moscow in February, Cunhal warmly reaffirmed the PCP's fraternal solidarity with the Soviet Union. He scoffed at "propaganda" that a communist party can be independent only when it keeps aloof from the Soviet Union or participates in an anti-Soviet campaign. The truth is, he said, the independence of a party that yields in that way to anti-Soviet pressures is questionable. He was especially scornful of Eurocommunism, "a transient vogue." (Tass, 25 February, 8 March; *Komsomolskaia Pravda*, 6 March.) Other PCP visitors to Moscow during the year studied Soviet experiences in socialist economic integration and environmental conservation. In Mongolia, Cunhal was presented the Sukhe Bator Order for his "outstanding" contribution to the anti-imperialist struggle and to the consolidation of communist unity (Montsame, Ulan Bator, 13 July).

During visits of PCP delegations to Bulgaria and Czechoslovakia and during a visit to Lisbon of some Cuban Communists, party leaders stressed the need for communist cohesion on the basis of Marxism-Leninism and proletarian internationalism. A joint statement issued on the occasion of a visit to Greece by Cunhal expressed solidarity with the Afghan and Polish regimes, the Turkish "democratic organization," and advocated the withdrawal of all warships from the Mediterranean (*FBIS*, 28 January). There were also "visits of friendship" to Romania, Hungary, Yugoslavia, Cuba, and Guinea-Bissau. In January, a PCP group attended the World Forum of Youth and Students for Peace, Demilitarization, and Disarmament in Helsinki. The PCP met in Lisbon with delegations from the Yemen Socialist Party, the Commission to Organize the Party of the Working People of Ethiopia, the Communist Party of Cuba, and the Popular Movement for the Liberation of Angola. The Cuban and Portuguese Communists condemned South Africa's "criminal aggression" against Angola (*Avante!*, 17 September).

Publications. PCP organs include the weekly *Avante!* and the theoretical journal *O Militante.* A semiofficial PCP newspaper is the daily *Diário de Notícias.*

Other Far-Left Organizations. Imprisoned leader Carlos Antunes of the now extinct radical-left Proletarian Revolutionary Party reportedly began a hunger strike in June, demanding that he and 22 other militants be released as "political prisoners" under the 1975 amnesty law. They were jailed nearly three years ago for bomb attacks and armed robbery. (*FBIS,* 25 June.)

University of the Pacific   H. Leslie Robinson

Spain

The Communist Party of Spain (Partido Comunista de España; PCE) is the largest, most influential, and most moderate of the various leftist organizations in Spain. A hard-line, pro-Soviet force for many years after it was founded in 1920, the party became highly critical of Moscow following the 1968 invasion of Czechoslovakia. Subsequently, it developed a Eurocommunist strategy of following a "democratic path" to socialism and altered its self-description from "Marxist-Leninist" to "Marxist, revolutionary, and democratic." PCE membership mushroomed from 15,000 at Franco's death to over 200,000 in 1977, when the party was legalized. Since then its strength has declined sharply to 140,-000, although estimates range to as low as 70,000 (*Intercontinental Press,* 9 February). The population of Spain is estimated at 37.7 million.

In the 1979 national elections, the PCE became Spain's third-largest party but with only 10 percent of the vote and 23 seats in the 250-member parliament. The Communists' major influence has been in the labor movement, but in recent years their Workers' Commissions (Comisiones Obreros; CC OO) have been losing members and becoming less influential than the Socialist-controlled unions. In 1980 factory elections, the CC OO won almost a third of the delegates, down 2 percent from 1978, while the Socialist unions almost equaled CC OO strength with a gain of 9 percent (*Actualidad Económica,* Madrid, 25 December 1980; *NYT,* 9 February; *Radio Free Europe Research,* 12 August). In the Basque area, a regionalist trade union has outstripped both the CC OO and the Socialist unions (*Times,* London, 24 January). Increasing exclusion of the Communists from labor pacts and from various political negotiations has strengthened the impression that the party is becoming a marginal force in Spain (*Radio Free Europe Research,* 14 August).

The principal far-left terrorist organization is the Basque Homeland and Liberty (ETA) separatist movement. Organized in 1952 to oppose Franco's police state, it split several years later into a military wing (ETA-Militar), which wages a continual campaign of disruptive bombings and assassinations, and a less violent "political-military" faction (ETA-Politico-Militar). Both groups demand independence from Spain for a Marxist Basque republic, although the moderate group is willing to accept a gradual approach. ETA guerrillas have contacts with the Soviet Union and have received training in South Yemen and Cuba (*NYT*, 11 May). Legal political parties with ties to the underground Basque groups are Herri Batasuna (United People), associated with ETA-Militar, and Euskadiko Esquerra, linked with ETA-Político-Militar.

The October First Antifascist Resistance Group (Grupo de Resistencia Antifascista Primero de Octubre; GRAPO), a more erratic group also dedicated to violence, operates primarily in Madrid and Barcelona. Its name commemorates the killing of four policemen in Madrid on 1 October 1975. It is thought to be connected with the Communist Party of Spain, Reconstituted (Partido Comunista de España, Reconstituido; PCE-R), although the suspicion that right-wing infiltrators use it as a justification to provoke a military coup is widespread. GRAPO tends to kill liberals and moderates; the ETA targets right-wing authorities (*CSM*, 8 May). Some 350 persons were killed in Spain, primarily by ETA and GRAPO, between 1978 and 1980 (*Visión*, New York, 11 January).

Occasional acts of violence are carried out by a few minor left-wing extremist organizations, such as a Catalan separatist band called Terra Lliure, and some anarchist groups. The various tiny Trotskyist, Marxist-Leninist, and anarchist parties have little impact in Spain. The three principal ones are the PCE-R; the pro-Soviet Unified Communist Party of Spain (Partido Comunista de España Unificado), a medium for Enrique Líster's anti-PCE fulminations; and the pro-Albanian Spanish Communist Party, Marxist-Leninist (Partido Comunista de España, Marxista-Leninista), which was legalized in February. China has reportedly quietly abandoned the splinter Maoist parties it had earlier promoted (*Los Angeles Times*, 4 December 1980).

Organization. In July, the dissension-ridden PCE held its Tenth Congress, the second since the party was legalized in 1977. A key issue, as it had been at the Ninth Congress in 1978 (see *YICA*, 1979, p. 199), was the leadership of 66-year-old Santiago Carrillo. His easy re-election as secretary general was unsurprising, but the open opposition of a third of the 1,214 delegates revealed the continuing erosion in his support. Fourteen other officials were elected to the Central Committee with more votes than he received, including Dolores Ibarruri, who was also re-elected president, and Nicolás Sartorius, Carrillo's deputy and possible successor. (*NYT*, 2 August; *Radio Free Europe Research*, 14 August.)

A factional uproar at the gathering climaxed months of rumbling over the PCE's loss of members, especially among intellectuals, and over the party's declining impact on labor and political developments. Typical expressions of the malaise were manifestos issued in January and May by communist lawyers and officeholders. Most faulted by them for the "discouragement and confusion in our ranks" and for the party's reduced credibility with the public was "an increasing gap between the political formulations of the PCE and its internal reality." (*Radio Free Europe Research*, 12 August.)

Taking part in maneuvers to discredit and unseat Carrillo were pro-Soviet hard-liners (called "dogmatists" and "Afghans"); they, however, represented only 6 percent of the delegates. The real challenge came from a larger minority—the "Eurocommunists for renewal," who constitute 26 percent of the membership. Demanding the retirement of veteran leaders, they proposed that the secretary general should be a mere "coordinator," subordinate to a "collegial secretariat." They also sought more internal debate, more lower-level involvement in decision-making, and more independence for regional party organizations. (Ibid.)

The most significant affront to Carrillo had come earlier in the year from dissidents of the Unified Socialist Party of Catalonia (Partido Socialista Unificado de Cataluña; PSUC). The PCE's largest regional branch, it accounts for a fifth of the party's membership and for 13 of the PCE's 23 seats in parliament. Chafing at Carrillo's iron grip on the party, the dominant "Leninist" faction—previously a supporter of Eurocommunism—allied itself with the pro-Soviet "Afghans" at a January regional congress and dropped the PSUC's commitment to Eurocommunism. Carrillo was quick to note that the two factions were ideologically incompatible. Some PCE leaders in Madrid said there was evidence that the Soviet embassy had helped pack and finance the congress. Even if that was true, it later became evident that the Leninists' action was simply a ploy to discomfit Carrillo and to acquire negotiating leverage. The Catalans immediately offered to hold talks with the PCE leadership to "rebuild internal unity." At a PSUC Central Committee plenum in May—following a visit by Carrillo—the Leninists changed allegiance and voted in favor of a reaffirmation of Eurocommunism. Some thought this reversal, so soon after the January shift, was influenced by a perceived need for leftist unity following the abortive right-wing military coup in February. Even so, the Catalans arrived at the PCE congress in July in a combative mood. (*NYT*, 26 October 1980; *WP*, 7 January 1981; *Radio Free Europe Research*, 12 August 1981.)

Carrillo sought to disarm his critics by posing as the champion of rejuvenation and democratization. What communist party, he asked rhetorically, has ever held such a free congress? What could not be tolerated, the secretary general insisted, were organized factions. In this connection, between the Ninth and the Tenth congresses, the PCE expelled 86 members for "factionalist activity" or for "indiscipline." (*El Correo Catalán*, Barcelona, 2 August; *Radio Free Europe Research*, 12 and 14 August.)

Carrillo supporters overwhelmingly dominate the new Central Committee, which was reduced from 160 to 104 members, as well as the Executive Committee, which dropped from 45 to 24 members. Of the latter, eleven are members of the Secretariat, which is in charge of the day-to-day operations of the party. There are only seventeen "renewalists" in the Central Committee (16 percent of its membership), some of them influential party figures, while the crucial Secretariat is solidly pro-Carrillo. (*FBIS*, 11 August; *Radio Free Europe Research*, 14 August.)

Those holding membership on both the Executive Committee and the Secretariat are Leopoldo Alcaraz, Jaime Ballesteros, Santiago Carrillo, Enrique Curiel, Anselmo Hoyos, Ignacio Latierro, Juan Francisco Pla, Adolfo Pinedo, Francisco Romero Marín, Simón Sánchez Montero, and Nicolás Sartorius. Other members of the Executive Committee are Felipe Alcaraz, Julián Ariza, Manuel Azcárate, Marcelino Camacho, Francisco Frutos, Ignacio Gallego, Juan Galán, José María González Jerez, Angel Guerreiro, Antonio Gutiérrez Díaz, Gerardo Iglesias, Robert Lertxundi, and Jordi Sole Turax. (*Mundo Obrero*, 14–20 August.)

Domestic Attitudes and Activities. The 23 February attempt to overthrow the Spanish government intimidated the PCE and other major parties into assuming a more cautious political stance during 1981. Communist and Socialist leaders of the trade unions contributed to the new mood by calling for "moderation [in wage demands] to save democracy" (*CSM*, 25 March). Even so, a climate of wrangling and political instability—one of the major sources of concern to the military—bred repeated rumors about fresh plotting (ibid., 6 November).

Santiago Carrillo warmly applauded King Juan Carlos for his pivotal role in persuading army commanders not to support the assault on parliament by paramilitary Civil Guards. At the same time, the communist leader assented to the monarch's plea to politicians for a restrained posture toward the military. Carrillo had words of praise for the Army as a whole and urged punishment, "to the full extent of the law," only for the minority involved in holding legislators and government ministers hostage for eighteen hours. (*NYT*, 26 February; *WP*, 27 February; *El Pais*, Madrid, 6 March.) Carrillo and right-wing politician Manuel Fraga Iribarne marched arm-in-arm in a huge demonstration in Madrid to celebrate the survival of democracy (*CSM*, 2 March).

Carrillo warned that in the absence of a united "left-wing strategy" against the prevailing power structure and big finance, 23 February could be a "dress rehearsal for something much more disastrous." The country needed a leadership that, albeit with the necessary prudence, would "sever the roots of putschism in the Army and the police force." (*L'Unità*, Rome, 1 March.) The communist deputy welcomed the "overdue" resignation of Prime Minister Adolfo Suárez in January, but said his replacement by conservative Leopoldo Calvo Sotelo was no solution; unable to act decisively, his "discredited" minority government would have to make concessions to whatever parliamentary group was needed to shore up a precarious power base. (Madrid Domestic Radio, 29 January; *El País*, 6 March.)

Convinced that the Calvo Sotelo cabinet could not last more than five months—certainly not until the scheduled 1983 elections—Carrillo vowed to "make life impossible" for it with "radical" opposition in parliament and in the streets (*Visión*, 9 and 23 March). A fundamental change in policy could be made, he said, only by a government with a "broad-based majority," that is, a coalition of Calvo Sotelo's Union of the Democratic Center (Unión del Centro Democrático; UCD) and the Spanish Socialist Workers' Party (Partido Socialista Obrero Español; PSOE). According to Carrillo, this could be achieved through the existing parliament; early elections would be "foolish." (Madrid Domestic Radio, 29 January, 25 February.) The only role sought by the Communists in this arrangement was as one of the negotiators of a political program based on a genuine consensus (*El País*, 20 January).

The UCD paid no heed to PSOE leader Felipe González's intimation that he might be willing to serve in a coalition government. Many observers felt that the "23 February syndrome" among the military amounted to a permanent veto on any possibility of leftist participation in the government. (*NYT*, 2 February, 10 May.) Carrillo's response was that the Army would be reassured by a decisive government that actually produced political results (*El País*, 6 March). (A private poll in early March concluded that a majority of Spaniards preferred González as prime minister. Calvo Sotelo was in third place after Fraga Iribarne. Carrillo was supported by only 3 percent of those polled. [*Visión*, 9 March.])

Uneasiness about the armed forces' reaction elicited from the PCE frequent denunciations of terrorist acts as "intolerable" attempts to blackmail democracy. Carrillo recommended a study of antiterrorist experiences abroad, as in Italy, to learn more efficient techniques of combatting violence. He suggested that Herri Batasuna, the legal political arm of the more violent wing of ETA, should be outlawed. A further restraint on ETA, he said, could be assured by strengthening Basque autonomy, though not to the extent of "dismantling" Spain. (*El País*, 6 March; Madrid Domestic Radio, 23 May.) The PCE was concerned that the "proliferation of regional banners" was leading to excesses and that the increasing number of small regional parties in the Cortes was likely to "distort the political game" (*Le Monde*, Paris, 5 March). This was also a common concern to the UCD and the PSOE; all three major parties saw their political strength eroding in regional elections (*NYT*, 10 May). They were therefore not dismayed when the government began slowing the pace of decentralization. This deceleration was evidently designed primarily to appease a military distressed over the fragmentation of Spain. (*CSM*, 25 March; *NYT*, 10 May.)

The UCD, PSOE, and PCE also lost strength in the Galician elections for a regional parliament in October. However, they were opposed there not so much by regional parties as by the right-wing Popular Alliance (Alianza Popular). No PCE candidate was elected, but two local Marxist parties gained four seats. These groups favor absolute independence for Galicia and had called for a negative vote in the home-rule referendum of December 1980. Of the 26 percent of the Galician population that bothered to cast ballots at that time, 21 percent voted against the measure. (*NYT*, 23 December 1980, 22 October 1981.)

International Views and Positions. The PCE and PSOE pressed for a national referendum on the issue of Spanish membership in NATO in the face of the government's determination to seek only parliamentary approval by a simple majority vote. Polls indicated that the measure, although it aroused little public concern, would be rebuffed in a popular vote. The two parties said that a renewal of the defense treaty with the United States would provide a sufficient guarantee of Spain's security and that the existing East-West balance should not be disrupted by expanding NATO. Carrillo complained that the only things Spain had to offer NATO were targets for atomic weapons. He continued to express particular concern that Spain's special ties to the Arab world and Latin America would be harmed. Some observers felt that opposition, at least by the Socialists, was somewhat muted following the February coup attempt for fear of further agitating the military. (*NYT*, 22 March, 3 June, 9 September; *Mundo Obrero*, 1–7 May.) Carrillo said in September that his party had gathered half a million signatures in favor of a referendum; a month later, parliament approved a formal government petition for entry into NATO (*NYT*, 28 September, 30 October).

As U.S. Secretary of State Alexander Haig prepared to visit Spain in early April, Communists said that he would need "many efforts at seduction" to counter the effects of reports that the U.S. embassy knew in advance about the February coup plans and that the American base at Torrejón was in a state of alert at the time. There was widespread criticism of Haig in Spain when, during a brief stopover in Madrid while the coup was under way, he "insensitively" refused comment on Spanish "internal affairs." Many thought this indicated a lack of support for democracy. (*Mundo Obrero*, 27 March–2 April.) The PCE also denounced President Reagan's decision to make the neutron bomb available to Europe since this could only promote escalation of the arms race (Madrid Domestic Radio, 11 August).

Communists deplored the "lack" of an international policy, which led the Spanish government to act "by isolated steps," following guidelines set by Ronald Reagan. A PCE spokesman regretted Spain's "neglect of the North-South dialogue." The nation should have been represented, he said, at the October Cancún meeting in Mexico since for historical and cultural reasons, Spain was in a privileged position to contribute to the colloquy with the Third World. Calvo Sotelo's "indifference" was attributed to his announced policy of limiting the government's foreign concerns to those directly bearing on Spain. (NOTIMEX, Mexico City, 8 August.)

International Activities and Party Contacts. The reconciliation between the Spanish and Chinese communist parties, after two decades of frigid relations, was consolidated during a visit to Beijing by Santiago Carrillo in November 1980. He returned to Beijing in August 1981, and a Chinese delegation attended the Tenth Congress of the PCE in July. The agreement of the two parties to respect each other's independence and to tolerate differences represented an indirect slap at the Soviet Union's self-image as the pilot of international communism. Carrillo said that the 59-year-old Chinese Communist Party and the 60-year-old PCE "are now mature enough to think with our own brains." The accord represented a turnaround, moreover, for the Chinese, who were seen to be abandoning their own past dogmatism and recognizing that their "imperfect" brand of communism was not necessarily a model for the rest of the world. Recanting previous assertions that Eurocommunism was not true Marxism, they averred that such an innovative approach might well prove the proper one for socialism, at least in Western Europe. (*Mundo Obrero*, 14–20 November 1980; *Los Angeles Times*, 4 December 1980.)

The Chinese opening to Western communist parties and the labor crisis in Poland were presumably among the "changes" that, according to the PCE, will give East Europeans important new chances to establish their independence" (*Los Angeles Times*, 4 December 1980). The Soviets reacted with a sharp warning in their foreign affairs weekly, *New Times*, against any strengthening of ties with the Chinese, who were said to be "changing tactics" in their attempt to split the world communist movement (*Times*, London, 18 December 1980). At the Soviet Union's February congress, to which the PCE sent only a low-level delegation, Eurocommunist criticisms that "distorted socialist reality" were denounced as damaging to the world revolutionary process and as aiding imperialist propaganda. The PCE was not included in a list of foreign parties with which Moscow said it had good relations. (Ibid., 25 February.)

Pravda was encouraged in January by a "marked swing" against Eurocommunist positions as seemingly evidenced by the Catalan Communists' anti-Carrillo attitude (*IB*, 18 January). Following the July PCE congress, the same newspaper (1 August) pointedly highlighted the delegates' criticism of Carrillo and said that the secretary general had forgotten to mention in his report anything about the PCE's loss of 60,000 members during the previous three years. *Pravda* took Carrillo to task for his "superficial comments" about allegedly insufficient democracy in "existing models of socialism." A message delivered by a Bulgarian Communist Party delegation discreetly reminded the delegates of the need for "unity of the socialist community," based on the principles of Marxism-Leninism and proletarian internationalism (BTA, Sofia, 28 July). Communist parties from 75 countries attended the congress.

In visits to Romania and Yugoslavia during the year, Carrillo and his hosts repeatedly stressed the need for autonomy for each party and noninterference from abroad. In numerous statements throughout the year, in Spain and abroad, the PCE leader continued to insist that the Poles should be allowed to resolve their problems by themselves; he also reaffirmed his condemnation of the 1980 Soviet invasion of Afghanistan. Otherwise, he asked, "with what moral authority are we going to ask Reagan to take his hands off El Salvador?" (*La Vanguardia*, Barcelona, 15 March.)

Publications. The principal PCE publications are the weekly *Mundo Obrero* and the bimonthly ideological journal *Nuestra Bandera*.

Other Far-Left Organizations. Political terrorism appeared to be on the wane early in 1981 but soon surged anew. It was clearly decisive in provoking the attempted overthrow of the government in February and was subsequently intensified with the apparent aim of teasing the Army to try again (*NYT*, 6 March; *CSM*, 23 April). The principal murder victims continued to be Civil Guards and army officers. One gravely wounded victim was a senior military aide to King Juan Carlos, who had at one time been in charge of democratic reforms in the Spanish armed forces after the death of Francisco Franco (*NYT*, 5 and 8 May; *CSM*, 8 May). An abducted engineer was killed in February when authorities refused an ETA demand that a nuclear power plant be dismantled (*NYT*, 8 February). The manager of the Spanish branch of a French company was assassinated in April, possibly as a warning to French authorities not to accede to Spanish demands for the extradition of Basque terrorists living in southern France (ibid., 15 April).

Responsibility for the assassinations and bombings was claimed by the hard-line military branch of ETA and by the nebulous GRAPO. The February kidnappings of three foreign consuls by the more moderate political-military wing of ETA also incensed the police and military. The release of the victims was promised on condition that newspapers publish an Amnesty International report on torture in Spain and that the state-run television transmit color photos of a dead victim of police torture. The demands were not met, but the victims were soon released unharmed following the abortive coup. A Basque industrialist was also released three months after his January abduction. (Ibid., 1 March, 15 April.)

Frustrated by an inability to contain the illegal ETA activists, who are hidden by sympathetic Basques or take refuge in southern France, police detained and charged scores of Herri Batasuna radicals with aiding the ETA (ibid., 20 May). Later in the year, two radical feminists and a professor with alleged ties to the PCE were also arrested for helping the terrorists (ibid., 23 October). On 23 March, the government agreed to deploy a limited number of army troops in the Basque region, especially along the French border, to reinforce police efforts against the terrorists (ibid., 24 March). Legislation was approved in April authorizing use of states of emergency if necessary (*CSM*, 5 May). A "parallel police" group, allegedly far-right French terrorists in the employ of Spanish police, was said to be tracking down ETA militants in French Basque towns. They were reportedly successful in assassinating one ETA leader in late December 1980. (Ibid., 31 December 1980.) Two others were killed in October by Spanish police as they were apparently fleeing to the border (*NYT*, 23 October). The police killing of a GRAPO leader left one "last dangerous" member of that group at large (ibid., 6 September). An imprisoned GRAPO militant died in June following a three-month hunger strike (*FBIS*, 22 June).

Dovetailing with the stepped-up antiterrorist campaign was a government decision to protest publicly Spanish terrorist links with unspecified foreign countries. Privately, such countries were identified as the Soviet Union and its satellites, including Cuba, Libya, and Algeria. The presumed aim of this aid was to precipitate a military coup that would make Spain unacceptable to NATO. (Ibid., 9 and 11 May; *WP*, 13 May.) It was supposedly to curtail such outside "manipulation" that the Spanish government decided to reduce sharply the Soviet Union's heavy diplomatic representation in Spain (*NYT*, 14 April).

The Basque population grew increasingly restive over the antics of the ETA "fascist fanatics," as a PSOE leader called them. Basques were outraged when Herri Batasuna representatives interrupted King Juan Carlos's February visit to the Basque legislature with an insulting demonstration (ibid., 5 February). The assassination of a civilian that month sparked one of the biggest public protests against terrorism—a one-day general strike—ever seen in northern Spain. The anti-ETA momentum was partially set back a few days later, however, with the revelation of the death of a reputedly tortured Basque terrorist suspect in police custody. A second general strike was called during which thousands protested this "brutal murder." An investigation of those involved in the incident provoked the indignation of conservative military and Civil Guard leaders and helped to precipitate the aborted putsch in February. (Ibid., 27 February.) There was speculation that the military's discontent over Prime Minister Suárez's failure to crack down harder on terrorists was a major factor in the latter's resignation in January. The Army was especially angered over his proposal that the king, during a visit to the Basque country, offer amnesty to some 120 ETA members. (*WP*, 30 January; *CSM*, 2 February.)

In reaction to the coup attempt, the political-military branch of ETA declared an "unconditional cease-fire" and called on the violent military wing to halt its campaign of killing. A continued armed struggle, it insisted, would "multiply the evils of militarism" and isolate ETA in the Basque region. On the other hand, it said it would reconsider the cease-fire if there were a successful coup d'etat. (*NYT*, 1 March.) Spanish police intelligence reported afterward that several intransigent members of the organization had deserted to the military wing, which decided on an accelerated campaign of assassinations (ibid., 23 March). A spokesman for Euskadiko Ezkerra, the political party associated with the moderate wing of ETA, said the attempted coup had strengthened "the determination to take the guns away from ETA." He said there was now little popular reaction to arrests or to the dispatching of army troops to the Basque area. (Ibid., 20 May.)

The mainstream Basque Nationalist Party was also said to be more sympathetic than previously to the notion of cooperating with police in identifying and locating ETA gunmen (ibid., 23 March). Party leaders continued to stress, however, that the solution to terrorism lay more in political than in security measures—that is, Basques should be given more autonomy to deal with the problem themselves. The Madrid government did agree to an all-Basque police force to replace what Basques call the "occupation force" of police and Civil Guards, but the complete changeover was expected to take up to five years since recruits must be trained. (*CSM*, 23 April.) Declining support for the ETA may have contributed to a three-month lull in violence after July, but when Basque politicians became angered over moves in Madrid to curtail home rule—an apparent concession to the disgruntled military—the terrorists felt encouraged to resume their "armed struggle" (*NYT*, 18 October).

Terrorism exacerbated the economic crisis of the region. There was a steady exodus of small businessmen to escape payment of "revolutionary taxes" extorted by terrorists. Tourists and foreign investors continued to be frightened away, although tourism in other parts of Spain was booming.

Unemployment approached 20 percent early in the year, compared with 12 percent for the rest of Spain. (*CSM*, 23 April.)

Publications. *Egin*, mouthpiece of ETA-Militar, is a daily published outside San Sebastián, believed to be financed by robberies and "revolutionary taxes" collected by ETA from Basque businessmen (*NYT*, 20 March).

University of the Pacific   H. Leslie Robinson

Sweden

The forerunner of Sweden's communist party (Sveriges Kommunistiska Parti; SKP) was founded in May 1917 and joined the Comintern in July 1919. Inner tensions plagued the SKP from the 1920s to the advent of World War II. Following a period of relative insignificance during the 1950s, the party profited from the rise of the New Left in the 1960s. In 1967, it absorbed new groups from the radical left and changed its name to Left Party–Communists (Vänsterpartiet Kommunisterna; VPK). A large minority within the party criticized the VPK for being "reformist" and founded the Communist League, Marxist-Leninist (Kommunistiska Förbundet Marxist-Leninisterna; KFML), which was pro-Chinese in orientation. In 1973, the KFML changed its name to SKP.

From 1970 to 1976, the VPK exerted an influence on Swedish politics disproportionate to its parliamentary strength. After the 1970 elections, Prime Minister Olof Palme and the Social Democratic Party (SDP), with 163 seats in the 350-seat parliament, relied on the VPK to form a majority. During no other period in Sweden's postwar history has the communist party exerted such influence on parliamentary life. Between 1970 and 1973, it participated in such important parliamentary committees as defense and taxation. Following the 1973 elections, however, Palme frequently compromised with the Liberal Party, weakening VPK participation in Swedish parliamentary life. The fall of the Social Democratic government in 1976 marked the beginning once more of political insignificance for the VPK.

In October 1978, the nonsocialist coalition government (Conservative, Liberal, and Center parties) resigned after failing to reach agreement on Sweden's nuclear policy, and Liberal Party leader Ola Ullsten formed a minority government. After the September 1979 elections, the nonsocialist parties returned to power with a slim majority. The VPK gained 3 seats in parliament for a total of 23 but was excluded from the parliamentary committees by the nonsocialist majority. The VPK, however, came to play an important role outside parliament in the winter of 1979–80, and the strength of the party in the opinion polls grew.

One of the main reasons was the VPK's participation in the People's Campaign Against Nuclear Power in the Swedish referendum on nuclear power held on 23 March 1980. During the referendum campaign, VPK ideologues repeatedly stressed the importance of using the antinuclear and environmental movements for tactical purposes. By means of support received for Alternative 3 in the referendum, in partnership with the Center Party, VPK became an equal partner with a nonsocialist party and with a number of dissident Social Democrats who also supported Alternative 3. At the time of the referendum, the VPK stood out as a party that could attract a large number of voters from the center. However, the nuclear issue became moot after the referendum. The debate disappeared almost overnight, as voters lost interest. In early 1980, opinion polls showed the VPK having more supporters between 18 and 24 years than, for example, the Liberal Party did (11.5 percent versus 9.5 percent). Among students, the VPK had the second largest following (15 percent), larger than that enjoyed by the Social Democrats, the Center Party, or the Liberal Party, and the Social Democrats were losing youth support to the VPK (*Svenska Dagbladet*, 3 March). In early 1980, the VPK had the support of 10 percent of the voters in Sweden's two largest cities, Stockholm and Göteborg and had a good chance of reaching 10 percent in the whole country. But the loss of interest in the nuclear issue and the party's continuing lack of influence in Swedish politics changed the situation for the VPK.

December 1980 polls showed the VPK holding its 1979 strength and in general indicated growing support for the socialist parties, especially the SDP, which had gained voters both in Stockholm and in the countryside. The polls showed 54.6 percent of the electorate favoring the socialist bloc and 43.6 percent the nonsocialist bloc. The VPK received 5.4 percent, indicating no change over the 1979 election results.

Opinion polls in 1981 have indicated a steady decline. In October, the VPK was supported by only 4 percent and was in danger of losing its representation in parliament. On 27 October, a Soviet submarine carrying nuclear weapons was stranded on a rock in the southeastern archipelago of Sweden. The resultant shock to the majority of Sweden's voters is very likely to hurt the VPK. This will weaken the VPK even more, although the SDP will probably provide the VPK indirect support to secure parliamentary seats in the September 1982 elections. In addition, the newly established Environmental Party may take votes away from the VPK next year. The VPK claims 18,000 members. The population of Sweden is about 8.4 million.

Leadership and Organization. The party congress is theoretically the highest organ of the VPK. It elects a 35-member central committee, known since 1964 as the Party Board. The board in turn selects an 8-member Executive Committee, which directs party work. There are 28 party districts, corresponding to Sweden's electoral districts, and 395 local organizations. The Communist Youth (Kommunistisk Ungdom) is the party youth organization. Party chairman is Lars Werner.

Domestic Attitudes and Activities. The declining role of the VPK in Swedish national politics has been reflected in the opinion polls. During a visit to Finland in April 1981, Lars Werner commented that "the VPK's main task is to govern Sweden ... the party, with its 23 seats, has no chance of getting anything through the Riksdag [parliament] on its own, but its great strength lies in its ability to function as an intermediary for opinion coming from the grass roots to the Riksdag ... Even if we do not get our motions passed, it can happen that others pick them up and carry them further ... The main thing is for opinion to be transmitted." (*Huvudstadsbladet,* Helsinki, 21 April.)

To Werner, the most important political question in Sweden was solving the economic crisis. He attacked the government for reducing food subsidies, for refraining from increased price monitoring, and for believing that market forces would bring about a solution. One of the main points in the VPK's political program is the abolition of the value-added tax on food. The party collected 150,000 signatures in favor of this move and Werner was confident of the support of farmers on this question. Werner also claimed to be confident of a socialist majority after the 1982 elections. His ideal government would be "a coalition consisting of the Social Democrats, the VPK, and forces from the trade unions and the TCO [Central Organization of Salaried Employees]—but on a basis of a policy that contained a minimum of what could be agreed on where concrete questions were concerned." (Ibid.)

Recently more women have joined the VPK, which Werner regarded as a positive trend. He hoped that the party leadership will eventually reflect the membership structure, which would mean a 33 percent representation for women. (Ibid.)

The fall of the Swedish government in May did not affect the VPK. The Conservative Party left the twenty-month-old three-party coalition, charging that its two allied coalition partners, the Center and Liberal parties, had not fulfilled their promise of sweeping tax reforms to aid economic recovery. The other parties had also accepted the SDP demand that any tax change be delayed until 1983. A nonsocialist minority government of the Center and Liberal parties was formed with Center Party leader Thorbjörn Fälldin as prime minister. The VPK remained in opposition as before.

As for the economic crisis in Sweden, VPK continues to direct propaganda efforts toward immigrants. The immigration of workers to Sweden, 50 percent of whom come from Finland, is (according to VPK ideologues) proof of "imperialist exploitation by Swedish capitalists . . . The immigrants are needed to raise access to labor and to check demands for higher wages . . . The immigrants are the 'fuel' the companies need to develop and retain the market economy in Sweden . . . Through the use of the immigrants, the capitalists believe that they can diminish the strength of the working class; that is, the immigrants are economically, socially, and politically isolated. It is therefore in the interests of the whole working population to guard the economic, social, and political rights of immigrants. It is necessary to counter the attempts of the capitalists to deprive a part of the working class of its elementary social rights." (*Socialistisk Debatt,* no. 1.) The article claims that immigrants now constitute 15 percent of the Swedish working class.

During 1981, the VPK used the growing peace movement in Sweden for political purposes. Just as the SDP, and its leader, Olof Palme, has given the peace movement its support, so has the VPK. The party advocates support for the People's Defense for Peace and National Independence campaign and stresses the following points:

1. A foreign and commercial policy for Sweden that promotes "peace, disarmament, and national independence." The VPK wants Sweden to join the Movement of Nonaligned Nations and to support peace activities with government funds. Advocacy of a nuclear-free zone in Scandinavia is a focal point, as are activities to stop the modernization of NATO's nuclear forces in Western Europe. Sweden should resign from all international economic organs of cooperation that "strengthen imperialism," such as the World Bank. Sweden's exports should be oriented toward the Third World, and no import or export of weapons should be permitted.

2. A major goal is to achieve complete popular support for peace and disarmament. The VPK believes in state support for peace activities in trade unions and in political and interest group organizations. Support should also be given to international cooperation between peace organizations and national and international initiatives for "peace, disarmament, and peaceful cooperation across borders." The VPK also advocates school education on "peace and disarmament questions."

3. Civil defense should be strengthened with funds taken from the conventional defense budget. The protection of the population should be given first priority.

4. Economic defense should concentrate on self-sufficiency and a decentralized energy system.

5. The VPK seeks gradual unilateral disarmament of Sweden's defense forces, beginning with the Air Force, which should acquire no new airplanes. The Navy should also be dissolved, and Sweden should retain only coastal patrol boats. Air defense, tanks, and artillery should also be eliminated from Sweden's defense forces. The army should be reorganized into a militia and organized at the local level. All psychological defense efforts should be abolished.

Support for a "popular campaign for peace" is envisioned. Tactically this effort should concentrate on establishing a Scandinavian nuclear-free zone. A committee for "a nuclear-free Scandinavia" is to be created with members drawn from trade unions, political parties, youth organizations, sports organizations, etc. The demand for a nuclear-free zone in Scandinavia should become the basis for demands to abolish all nuclear weapons and to dissolve military pacts.

The second tactical line is creation of the People's Defense for Peace and Disarmament. The purpose of this front should be to eliminate Sweden's conventional defense in 1982, when the Swedish parliament is to decide on defense policy for the 1980s. The VPK is seeking one single, large popular front to direct all peace activities. VPK members are to play a leading role in this effort.

In a series of articles, VPK ideologues discussed the strategy and tactics of the party in the wake of the Twenty-Sixth Congress in November 1981. One of the main problems has been low support for the party among workers. Only 5–6 percent of Sweden's workers support the VPK. A stronger labor vote, according to the VPK, would serve as an "ideological motor" in the trade unions and radicalize the unions. To achieve this, party leaders should "give priority much more than before to national campaigns." Consequently, VPK policy should be presented "in an easily understandable way . . . The party is in reality in a very troublesome position. We have failed to become a mass party. We have a sagging recruitment . . . in the working class." One leading Stockholm VPK member, author Per Kågesson, demanded a Marxist analysis of the situation in the Soviet Union and Eastern Europe. "The result of such an analysis can only be a breaking off of relations with the Communist Party of the Soviet Union and other parties that deny real power to working people over the economy and society." (Ibid., no. 4.) The debate clearly showed strong Eurocommunist currents in the party.

The stranding of the Soviet submarine close to the Karlskrona naval base in southeastern Sweden was a hard blow both to VPK and the peace movement in Sweden. It was a blatant show of Soviet disregard for the sovereignty of a small, neutral country bordering the Soviet empire. Werner's comments indicated that it would take time for the party to make the public forget "mistakes we made in uncritically accepting what the Soviet Union said . . . It is mainly the parties to the right of us that try to link VPK with the Soviet Union." (*Svenska Dagbladet*, 9 November).

International Views and Positions. In an article on strategy in *Socialistisk Debatt* (nos. 2–3), the theoretical organ of the VPK, one of Sweden's leading Marxist theoreticians, Göran Therborn, criticized the Soviet Union: "Soviet policy is taking more and more brutal forms, in the war in Afghanistan, in pressures in Poland, in the strangulation of internal opposition. China is playing a growing negative role in the world, from the constant threat to Vietnam to the support of Pol Pot and the junta in El Salvador . . . The international policy of VP must be . . . a close watch over what is happening in the Euroleft both in Eastern and Western Europe and the Central American rural revolution for democracy and socialism."

The VPK has charged the United States and NATO with seeking "a first-strike capablility of their own." Western supremacy would be used, according to the VPK, to exert political pressure in international relations, in an effort to secure strategic raw materials and therefore halt "national liberation movements" in the Third World. NATO and the United States threaten world peace, not the Soviet Union and the Warsaw Pact.

In July, Werner urged the Swedish government to work actively for a conference on a nuclear-free zone in Scandinavia. Quoting Leonid Brezhnev that the "Soviet Union is ready to guarantee that nuclear arms will not be used against the countries in a Nordic nuclear-free zone," Werner exhorted the Swedish government to "act quickly with an initiative now, break out of passivity, send out invitations to a conference and direct talks on the establishment of a Nordic nuclear-free zone" (*Dagens Nyheter*, 4 July).

International Activities and Party Contacts. On 22 January 1981, a VPK delegation visited Bucharest at the invitation of the Romanian Communist Party. Lars Werner and Bo Hammar were the leading VPK participants in the delegation. On 23 January, the delegation was received by Romanian leader Nicolae Ceaușescu. The two parties stated their "determination to diversify relations, to develop solidarity between them, based on the principles of full equality, observance of independence and noninterference in internal affairs, of every party's right to independently develop its revolutionary tactics and strategy according to the historical, social, and political conditions in its own country" (*Agerpres*, Bucharest, in English, 23 January).

In May, East German Foreign Minister Oskar Fischer visited Sweden and met with Lars Werner. Both "underlined the necessity of increasing the struggle for maintaining peace and against the deployment of new U.S. medium-range missiles in Western Europe and against the plans for neutron weapons" (*Neues Deutschland*, East Berlin, 7 May).

Rival Communist Organizations. There are a large number of extreme-left groups in Sweden. The leading pro-Chinese group is the SKP. It grew, as noted earlier, out of the KFML and is officially recognized by Beijing. The Party Board is the leading body. Its Third Congress in December 1980 reelected Roland Pettersson chairman. The party platform took an anti-Soviet and pro-defense stand: "SKP policy must take as a starting point the fact that the Soviet Union has the ability to gain control of Western Europe militarily and is conducting its aggressive policy in the name of socialism and Marxism-Leninism . . . the defense of Sweden as an industrial nation, the fight for self-preservation, and an independant supply of energy, in addition to a defense policy and international solidarity work with Afghanistan and Poland, for example, are all objectives" (*Klassekampen*, Oslo, 13 December 1980).

The party claims a membership of two to three thousand. The submarine incident occasioned sharp SKP attacks on the Soviet Union. In a speech at a demonstration outside the Soviet Embassy in Stockholm, leading SKP figure Jan Myrdal, son of Gunnar Myrdal, claimed that the Soviets had political reasons for their activities. "It is Soviet policy coldly and deliberately carried out through a demonstration of military strength. The armored fist must be seen close under our nose. And we must be made to realize that we are a small and militarily weak nation, a border state. This military policy can be compared to the peace agitation about the Sea of Peace and nuclear-free zones and peace and friendship between people." (*M-L Gnistan*, 6 November.) Myrdal also attacked the Swedish peace movement in the same speech. "The peace movement is not a peace movement. It is a paralyzing fear of war that itself constitutes a drawing of war over our country." The leaders of the peace movement are all "acting just like the fifth column that Hitler used. They are drawing us into war." (Ibid.) In an article commenting on the submarine incident, the SKP paper wrote: "Those peace activists who are hoping that the Soviet Union will create an atmosphere of détente and who have demanded unilateral Swedish disarmament must have been given something to think about" (ibid., 6 November).

In October 1980, *M-L Gnistan* reported a merger between the SKP and the Marxist-Leninist Front after ten years of discussion. The secretary general of SKP, Ingemar Eriksson, commented of the merger: "It is a break with our tradition. The tradition on the left is, of course, to split apart." (Ibid., 24–30 October 1980.)

In May 1981, the magazine *Opinion* published a booklet on SKP influence on illegal strikes and trade unions. A number of secret documents showing SKP involvement in a number of illegal strikes during the latter part of the 1970s were presented. Most SKP members are members of the Metalworkers' Union. The Kindergarten Teachers' Union also has many SKP members. The SKP has heavily infiltrated such unions as the Swedish Student Nurses' Union, Vocational Students' Union, and

Social Service Students' Union. The National Tenants' Association is an important target of SKP-infiltration.

A special service was formed during the 1970s by the SKP to enable its members to move around the country to seek jobs. An internal information bulletin of 1975 stated: "To make it possible for the party to get a hold within the working class, the party cannot leave the question of choice of profession and housing to chance and each member's personal wish" (*SKP Avslöjat,* Stockholm, 1981, p. 76).

The Communist Party of Marxist-Leninist Revolutionaries (Kommunistiska Partiet Marxist-Leninisterna [revolutionärerna]; KPML [r]) grew out of an association of the same name that broke away from the KFML in 1970. Party chairman is Frank Baude. The KPML(r) has a Central Committee with at least fifteen members and five deputy members and is governed by a Politburo. The main center of party strength is in Sweden's second largest city, Göteborg. The party is, according to its own information, active in some ninety localities throughout the country. Membership is believed to be about 1,500. Recently the KPML(r) has criticized China and supported Albania.

The Communist Workers' Party (Arbetarpartiet Kommunisterna; APK) broke away from the VPK in 1977. It is a small, pro-Moscow party, not represented in parliament, with its main strength in northernmost Sweden and in Stockholm. In February 1981, Rolf Hagel, APK party chairman, attended the Soviet party congress in Moscow. In a speech there, Hagel gave the following description of the situation in Sweden: "In our country, as in all highly developed capitalist countries, the situation is characterized by an ever-deeper economic crisis. Plant shutdowns and growing unemployment are becoming ever more common phenomena for the people of our country. The reactionary forces are stepping up their activity ... Sweden is an example of the inability of reformism to free the working class from oppression and impoverishment." (Radio Moscow, in Swedish, 26 February.)

The APK organ *Norrskensflamman*'s comments (30 October) on the submarine incident were pro-Soviet: "The Soviet Union has no reason whatsoever ... to take any action to impair relations between our two countries. The submarine had technical problems, which led to a regrettable mistake in navigation ... Those who are delighted over what has happened have other interests at heart than those of Sweden's. The fierce campaign going on now should be condemned by every friend of peace because it is only serving the interests of confrontational politics."

The Swedish section of the Trotskyist Fourth International is the Communist Workers' League (Kommunistiska Arbetareförbundet; KAF). It is directed by the Executive Committee of the International. Main centers of KAF strength are in the larger cities. The organizational backbone of the party is the "revolutionary activist" cell. Important recruiting centers are the universities, labor market training centers, industry, and large hospitals. The names of the KAF Central Committee's 39 members and the number of the members on the Politburo are secret.

Publications. *Ny Dag* (New day), the VPK central organ, is published twice weekly. The main organ of APK is the daily newspaper *Norrskensflamman* (Northern lights), published in Luleå. The theoretical organ of the VPK is *Socialistisk Debatt* (Socialist debate). The SKP's central organ is *M-L Gnistan* (Spark). The KPML(r) publishes the weekly *Proletären* (Proletarian). The main organ of the KAF is *Internationalen* (International).

Helsingborg, Sweden   Bertil Häggman

Switzerland

The oldest communist party in Switzerland is the Swiss Labor Party (Partei der Arbeit/Parti du travail/Partito del Lavoro; PdA). Founded on 5 March 1921 as the Swiss Communist Party, banned in 1940, then re-formed under its present name on 14 October 1944, it is pro-Soviet. Membership is estimated at five thousand. The population of Switzerland is 6.3 million.

The PdA has been joined in the lower house (Nationalrat) by two newer left-wing parties: the Progressive Organizations Switzerland (Progressive Organisationen Schweiz; POCH) and the Autonomous Socialist Party (Partito Socialista Autonomo/Parti socialiste autonome/Autonome Sozialistische Partei; PSA). One left-wing deputy from the new canton of Jura (established in 1978, first participation in national elections was in November 1979) successfully campaigned as an independent at the behest of the POCH and PSA to draw more votes.

The POCH was founded in 1972 by students critical of elderly PdA leaders and described itself as "communist" and pro-Soviet. In June 1979, the POCH announced that it was no longer part of the worldwide communist movement, but represented "newly emerging forces." It concentrates on local "underdog" issues taking stands to the left of the PdA, but votes with the PdA nationally and in parliament. It draws an irregular and sometimes considerable number of votes among discontented leftists in larger industrial cities. Membership is estimated at just under a thousand.

The PSA originated as a result of cantonal dissatisfaction with the Socialists (2nd International) in Ticino in 1969 (and in Berne in the late 1970s). It is more militantly leftist than the PdA and tries occasionally to undercut the older party on local issues. Membership is estimated at seven hundred.

The PdA, POCH, and PSA coordinated their strategy during the 1979 national elections and are registered in parliament as a fraction of seven members—with the one independent voting with them. They have no seats in the 46-member upper house (Ständerat).

Three other parties of the extreme left also warrant mention: the Socialist Workers' Party (Sozialistische Arbeiterpartei/Parti ouvrier socialiste; SAP), the Communist Party, Switzerland (Kommunistische Partei, Schweiz; KPS), and the Communist Party, Switzerland, Marxist/Leninist (KPS/ML). SAP is a new name, adopted in October 1980 for cosmetic reasons, for what was formerly the Marxist Revolutionary League (LMR). The LMR had been founded in 1969 by one hundred young intellectuals disappointed by PdA political maneuvering in parliament. The LMR sought to re-establish a pure revolutionary party of elitist cadres and joined the Fourth International (Trotskyist). The party concentrates on revolutionary cadre work and has no elected representatives in any cantonal or federal political body. The LMR claims approximately five hundred members.

The KPS (estimated membership one hundred) claims to be Marxist, but not Leninist; the KPS/ML (estimated membership two hundred) is pro-Chinese. Neither has elected representatives in cantonal or federal political bodies. Both parties represent a movement that appeared in 1980 and captured headlines during the first half of 1981 as the "chaotists" (German: *Chaoten,* or "people advocating chaos"). They turned street protests into destructive violence in cities, beginning in Zurich and spreading to Bern, Basel, and occasionally Lausanne, but not to Geneva. Usually functioning as well-organized groups with painted faces or wearing masks, they are led by a hard core of several hundred, many of whom are foreigners. They are linked with the West European squatter movement (Amsterdam, Berlin) as well as with the "green" (environmentalist) and antinuclear movements. They participate, marginally or centrally, in violent demonstrations; their avowed aim is to keep society and the state from functioning.

Leadership and Organization. The PdA is governed by a 50-member Central Committee with representatives from all linguistic areas of Switzerland. The 14-member Politburo has a 5-member Secretariat headed by Armand Magnin (Geneva, age 61). The Twelfth Congress of the PdA was held on 26–27 May 1979. It adopted a sixteen-point program stressing such familiar points as equal rights for women, increased welfare, and decreased working hours.

The POCH consists of cantonal sections that send delegates to irregularly scheduled national conventions and other gatherings. An extraordinary assembly in June 1979 decided on ideological divorce from the communist movement. A seminar in September 1981 was held under the heading "Reviving the General Debate." A party committee of some fifty members elects two full-time members of the Central Secretariat; one of them is Secretary Eduard Hafner. There are sections in eight cantons: Bern, Basel-Land, Basel-Stadt, Jura, Lucerne, Schaffhausen, Solothurn, and Zurich. Other cantons have informal organizations.

The SAP has a tighter organization than the POCH does. It refuses to divulge names of members or their number. It has a Politburo that operates collectively. Members are obligated to contribute substantial parts of their income to the party. Its Fifth National Congress in October 1980 (convened as an LMR congress) adopted the party's new name. A leading member is Peter Siegerist, head of the Bern office.

Domestic Attitudes and Activities. While parties and groups of the extreme left were trying to regroup or invigorate their programs, the main conflict raged within the Socialist Party (see *YICA*, 1980, p. 214). Its left wing, a minority, but better organized than more moderate members, almost voted the party out of Switzerland's traditional governing coalition (two Liberal-Conservatives, two Catholics, two Socialists, one Popular Party member in the government's Executive Cabinet). At its national convention on 17–18 October in Interlaken, the vote to continue the coalition was 232 to 231. Party Chairman Helmut Hubacher and Finance Minister Willy Ritschard attacked party leftists in major speeches. With the narrow decision to remain in the government, the party will begin 1982 divided and apprehensive.

Discontent with Soviet actions in Afghanistan and Poland was masked by a policy of increased criticism directed against "big powers" in general. As a consequence, both the United States and the Soviet Union were singled out for criticism at different times during the year.

There were no national elections in 1981, but there were several national votes. In April, an initiative to grant foreign workers practically the same rights as their Swiss counterparts was defeated 1,304,000 to 252,000 (almost 40 percent of those entitled to vote went to the polls). In June, initiatives proposing equal rights for women (797,000 to 525,000) and better protection for consumers (858,000 to 450,000) were successful. Voter participation in June was 33.9 percent.

In cantonal elections, the POCH gained one seat in Basel-Stadt in June and two in Solothurn, while the PdA lost one in Basel-Stadt. Elections for the cantonal government in Geneva in October and for communal authorities in Vaud, one week later, saw a defeat of the PdA, which lost six of its sixteen seats in Geneva and most of its strength in Vaud. In Lausanne, the PdA retained only seven of its thirteen seats in the 100-member municipal legislature. Altogether, the PdA lost forty seats in the sixteen biggest cities.

During the year opposition to a new nuclear power plant in Kaiseraugst (near Basel) abated somewhat. It is, however, expected to regain strength in 1982 because the Swiss government has confirmed the need for further nuclear plants in the 1990s. Immediately after this decision in October, security around government buildings was increased; even visits to the Swiss parliament (Bundeshaus), a tradition for students and tourists, were curtailed temporarily.

Publications. Circulation figures (in parentheses) are uncertified claims of publishing organizations. The PdA publishes the daily *Voix ouvrière* in Geneva (7,000); the weekly *Vorwärts* in Basel (6,000); the German-language *Emanizipation*, a weekly for women; the weekly *Tribune ouvrière* (3,000); and the monthly *Positionen*, in German. The SAP publishes the bimonthlies *Bresche* in German and *La Brèche* in French. The KPS/ML's *Offensiv* appears at irregular intervals. Originally antimilitaristic, it has followed Chinese government policy since 1979 and urges a stronger national defense against the Soviet Union. The KPS/ML also publishes the monthly *Oktober*, which appears in French and Italian editions (*Octobre*, *Ottobre*). The KPS publication *Rote Fahne* ceased publication in 1980. *Tell,* named after Swiss national hero William Tell, resulted from a merger of *Focus*, a monthly that claimed a circulation of 10,000 in 1979, and *Leserzeitung*, an unsuccessful ideological periodical in Basel (the illustrated monthly aimed at a circulation of 20,000 when it was founded in 1979). The new publication has released no circulation figures. A new weekly, *Wochen Zeitung*, published by left-wing students, appeared in October.

Bern, Switzerland   Swiss Eastern Institute

Turkey

Turkey was under the rule of a five-man military junta (the National Security Council) during all of 1981. The junta assumed power in an efficiently executed coup on 12 September 1980. Of the three tasks it set itself at the outset (ending political violence, stabilizing the economy, and paving the way for a return to stable parliamentary rule), the junta appeared to make excellent progress on the first two. Organized violence was not a social or political problem during 1981, despite occasional incidents. The junta did not shrink from taking draconian measures to bring violent groups under control and rarely missed an opportunity to publicize the seizure of illicit arms caches or the arrest of alleged terrorist cadres. Tens of thousands were detained, thousands were indicted. A large number of death sentences were demanded by military prosecutors (over two thousand, according to one estimate), and a significant number of these were confirmed. Almost all of these cases were directly linked with terrorism. One outstanding exception was the case of 52 leaders of the Confederation of Revolutionary Trade Unions (DISK) who were accused not of violence or terrorism but of belonging to a "Marxist-Leninist organization" whose aim was to establish a "proletarian dictatorship based on the worker classes" (*FBIS*, June 30; *NYT*, 25 December). Given the relatively bloodless political history of Turkey, at least since 1925, this regime seems prepared to establish an unenviable record in terms of the number of executions carried out under its aegis.

Although most of the individuals affected by these authoritarian measures were leftists, the extreme right did not escape unscathed. One of the most massive cases involved Alparslan Turkes, former deputy prime minister and leader of the fascist Nationalist Action Party (NAP), and several hundred of his supporters (including former members of parliament). The 950-page indictment confirmed the general impression that this group formed the vanguard of right-wing violence, including the sectarian massacres in the cities of Kahramanmaras and Corum in late 1978 and mid-1980, respectively. The prosecution called for capital punishment for Turkes and 219 of his cohorts. Mehmet Ali Agca, convicted of the near-fatal attack on Pope John Paul II in May 1981, was also linked with this group. Despite suspicions of organized international support for Agca, no conclusive evidence was made public either before or during his trial. Agca, however, passed through Soviet bloc countries during his extensive travels, and the possibility of Soviet collusion cannot be discounted. Nor was it clear whether Agca spoke only for himself in citing fundamentalist religious motivations for his attack. The NAP and its leader often exploited religious piety as well as ethnic divisions among villagers and townspeople in Turkey, and Agca may well have been at once a victim and an agent of this explosive political tactic. Despite such undercurrents, religious fundamentalism was not a dominant theme in Turkish politics either before the 1980 coup or thereafter. Had there been no coup, however, such a trend might well have emerged.

The governing junta used the attack on the pope to emphasize its antiterrorist campaign and to demand cooperation from such European governments as those of Italy and especially West Germany. Political extremists active among the hundreds of thousands of Turkish workers in the latter country constitute both potential and actual sources of continued subversion and polarization, and they are beyond the legal reach of the Turkish government. Turkish spokesmen faulted German security officials for an alleged lack of diligence or competence in pursuing fugitives from Turkish justice as well as perpetrators of violent crimes against Turkish residents in Germany. Privately, some in Turkey attributed this perceived failure to pro-rightist proclivities of members of the German security organization with Nazi backgrounds. Be that as it may, Turkish officials, including the head of the government, Gen. Kenan Evren, urged Bonn as well as other European governments to adopt a more cooperative attitude toward the Turkish effort to stamp out terrorism.

The junta's commitment to a return to parliamentary government became the subject of increasing skepticism during 1981, especially on the part of Turkey's European allies. As promised, a "consultative assembly" was formed and held its opening session in late October. However, the mode of selection of its members, the character of those selected, and their limited powers underlined the junta's determination to control the political process. The junta reserved to itself the power to appoint one-fourth of the members directly. The remainder were appointed by the junta from a list of nominees submitted by the governors of the 67 provinces (themselves junta appointees). The junta also reserved the right to veto actions of the assembly. The membership of the assembly was characterized by at least one observer as "very right wing" (*Financial Times*, London, 16 October). With one exception (the aged ex–Prime Minister Sadi Irmak), the members did not include any well-known names or anyone with significant national political experience. Nevertheless, as one of its first acts, the assembly challenged the junta's narrow definition of its powers.

The conservative and authoritarian tendencies of the junta were manifested in other ways as well. On the same day the formation of the consultative assembly was announced, all political parties were banned, including the venerable Republican People's Party (RPP), founded by Ataturk in 1923, and their assets confiscated. In a televised address announcing these actions, General Evren excoriated the leaders of these parties. When Bulent Ecevit, former prime minister and immediate past chairman of the RPP, tried to defend himself publicly against these charges, he was indicted for violation of an earlier decree banning political statements by former members of parliament and subsequently sentenced to four months imprisonment. This action prompted the European Economic Community to postpone a $650 million aid package and threw a dark cloud over Turkey's relations with Western Europe (though, significantly, not with the United States) (*Chicago Tribune*, 5 December).

In another case, a politically conservative newspaper columnist was sentenced to nine months imprisonment for "defaming" a court in 1977 (*NYT*, 16 December); the case may have been related to this columnist's criticisms of the junta's restrictions on the new consultative assembly and of the secrecy surrounding the formation of the assembly (*FBIS*, 30 July). The earlier sentencing of a former RPP minister of public works for "Kurdish and separatist propaganda" reflected the junta's extreme sensitivity and concern with the issue; nearly 2,500 persons were arrested on similar charges (*Facts on File*, 10 April, p. 244). In another case, a leftist newspaper editor was sentenced to seven and one-half years in prison for "propagating communism" (ibid.). By its first anniversary in power, the junta had charged more than a score of Turkish journalists, including the editors of the largest daily newspaper. Though not all of them were found guilty or sentenced, the impact clearly was to impose a straitjacket of self-censorship on the press. Even foreign correspondents were not immune: on 25 August, a BBC reporter was summoned by the authorities on unspecified charges (ibid., 11 September, p. 659); although the case was dropped a week later, the implications cannot have been lost on others.

Finally, the junta's determination to restructure Turkey's social institutions was signified by the promulgation of a new and rather restrictive labor code in the spring and a far-reaching new law of higher education on 6 November. The former was criticized by the centrist and relatively apolitical labor federation, which had otherwise evinced general support of the junta. The latter aroused sharp criticism and even consternation in higher education circles, for it virtually abolished autonomy for the universities. This measure evoked fears of a major new brain drain from the universities and even from the country. As with the labor code, the criticism came from among supporters of the junta whose political leanings could hardly be questioned (*NYT*, 29 November).

Amid all this, the charges brought against the former leader of the National Salvation Party (NSP), Necmettin Erbakan, and 33 of his supporters (including former members of parliament) seemed almost incidental, although in historical context the case assumed considerable significance. The group was charged with violating the principle of secularism by trying to establish an Islamic regime in Turkey. The government demanded sentences of 14 to 36 years. (*Facts on File*, 10 April, p. 244.) It should be recalled that many of those attending a rally held by the NSP a few days prior to the 1980 coup wore brimless headgear (still outlawed) and refused to stand during the playing of the national anthem. In the wake of the coup, there was considerable speculation that this incident had been an extreme provocation to military commanders, for whom Ataturk's advocacy of secularism holds major symbolic importance.

In the face of these political developments, the illegal Turkish Communist Party (TCP) maintained a drumfire of opposition and criticism over its clandestine transmitters in Eastern Europe and the Soviet Union. Its position was spelled out in some detail in an extensive report to a party plenum by TCP Secretary General Ismail Bilen, which was broadcast over the Voice of the Turkish Communist Party during September (*FBIS*, 11–30 September). Neither the place nor the date of the plenum meeting was announced, although Bilen frequently referred to the grave difficulties under which the meeting occurred, due to the restrictions imposed by the junta.

While conceding that the military junta had ended the "chaos created by fascist and Maoist leftist terrorism," Bilen roundly denounced Turkey's current government on a variety of domestic and foreign policy issues. On the question of terrorism, for instance, he accused the government of detaining, at one time or another, over 100,000 Turkish citizens and of condoning if not encouraging, systematic torture to elicit information and confessions to be used in ferreting out others and formulating indictments against, among others, peaceful and progressive members of the communist party. Bilen was unable to deny that the junta had moved forcefully against the most fanatic right-wing and religious reactionaries (Turkes and Erbakan), but he nevertheless accused it of otherwise vacillating between reaction and reform. He called on the junta to stop suppressing Kurdish nationalist and revolutionary democrats, whose desire for separate identity within the boundaries of the Turkish republic he regarded as perfectly legitimate.

In general, Bilen characterized the junta as a tool of monopoly capitalist interests in Turkey and of international imperialism as directed from the United States. This, according to Bilen, explained the junta's decision to enforce the program of economic austerity inaugurated in January 1980 by the government of Suleyman Demirel, even to the point of keeping the architect of that program, Turgut Ozal, in office as deputy prime minister. He clearly viewed the austerity program as putting the entire burden of economic recovery on the working classes. Although the junta served the interests of the ruling class, Bilen cautioned that it was not simply the blind tool of that class. Nevertheless, the junta was willing to associate Turkey with the confrontationist policy of the Reagan administration, whose plans, among other things, called for the establishment of a base for the Rapid Deployment Force in Turkish-controlled northern Cyprus.

Bilen reiterated that true Marxism-Leninism abhorred terrorism and specifically denounced the splinter group that publishes the *Workers' Voice* for portraying terror as the armed uprising of the masses. This, he averred, confuses marginal elements with the "real revolutionary vanguards of the whole of the proletariat."

The secretary general dwelt at some length on Kemalist ideology and those who espouse it. Noting that it was in its origins "the ideology of the national bourgeoisie" and that it had an "anti-imperialistic essence," he granted that it was populist to a degree and that its role in history was progressive, as is typical of national bourgeois movements. However, he was quick to point out that the Kemalist movement had failed to abolish feudalism. Moreover, in more recent years, the national bourgeoisie began to disintegrate, part of it becoming monopoly capitalists while the bulk was pushed toward the urban proletariat.

Contemporary Kemalism took several forms, according to Bilen. In the hands of the junta, it had become the official ideology. The junta was adapting it to serve the ruling classes by robbing it of its anti-imperialist character and reducing it to "the liberal tendencies of the monopolies." A second form of Kemalism was that of the RPP under Ecevit. This was linked with social democracy and was a hesitant and vacillating position. Finally, there was revolutionary and democratic Kemalism as espoused by the proletarianized urban middle class.

As for the party's tactics and goals for the future, Bilen predicted the eventual establishment of a "temporary revolutionary government" that would "ensure democratic freedoms, start deep anti-imperialist, anti-monopolistic and agricultural reversals and hold elections for a democratic constituent assembly." For the more immediate future, he reiterated the party's commitment to a united front with other democratic revolutionary elements, such as the Turkish Labor Party, the Turkish Socialist Workers' Party, leftist elements in the RPP, progressive elements among teachers and labor unions (represented, respectively, by the so-called TOB-DER and DISK, both closed down and hounded by the junta's prosecutors), and progressive, anti-imperialist Kurdish and Turkish youth. Under the harsh conditions imposed by military rule, the secretary general admonished the party to learn from its past mistakes and to immerse itself in "daily work" among the masses of workers and peasants.

The timing of Bilen's analysis of Kemalism was interesting, for it occurred in the midst of the Turkish government's concerted efforts to set forth its version of the great national hero's reform program as an ideological alternative to the extremes of fascism and communism. This effort was carried out as part of a yearlong celebration of the centenary of the birth of Mustafa Kemal Ataturk. The motivation of the current Turkish leaders may be beyond question. Unfortunately, given the increasingly frequent manifestations of authoritarian rigidity that characterize the regime, as well as the recent history of ideological and political fragmentation and polarization, it is difficult to be optimistic about the political stability of the country in the future.

University of Illinois at Chicago   Frank Tachau

EASTERN EUROPE AND THE SOVIET UNION

Introduction

The plethora of events that took place in the Soviet Union and Eastern Europe in 1981—some of them unprecedented—dictates the purpose and scope of this introduction. It will refer only to major or trend-indicating occurrences in the region (scrutinized in detail in the *Yearbook*'s individual profiles), while pointing out the general problems of our time for which 1981 was an essential gestational historical phase.

Soviet Union. *Domestic Issues.* In the Soviet Union, many signs suggested that the 1980s will be stormy at both the domestic and the international level as the long-lasting period of stability of leadership and politics under Leonid Brezhnev approaches an end. This was perceptible at the outwardly placid Twenty-Sixth Congress of the Communist Party of the Soviet Union (CPSU) and gained momentum throughout the year. The congress took place in Moscow between 23 February and 3 March, and in a formal sense it essentially affirmed the domestic status quo. No one hinted at the succession problem, and the Politburo and Secretariat were re-elected without a single change, an event unprecedented in party history. Brezhnev's main report to the congress (shrewd on the issues of international politics; see below) was rather subdued and missing the dynamic satisfaction of his address to the previous congress in 1976 when dealing with domestic matters.

A double-faced approach characterized public reports and behavior of CPSU chiefs. On one hand, they exuded, or tried to exude, self-confidence. Main party ideologist Mikhail A. Suslov called the Twenty-Sixth Congress "the congress of creators," and both he and Brezhnev spoke of the "new Soviet man" administering "mature socialism" of a "homogenized" and progressively "classless" Soviet society. On the other hand, party leaders bluntly and pervasively criticized Soviet deficiencies. Brezhnev and Suslov insisted on the necessity of improving ideological and organizational work within the party. According to Suslov, "the remodeling of political, educational, and propaganda work" was moving slowly, and there was a "lack of vigor in overcoming the essential existing shortcomings." Among these, Suslov enumerated "philistine mentality, avidity, and money grubbing." (*Partiinaia zhizn*, no. 8, April.) Brezhnev, too, in his report recognized, in Prof. Leonard Schapiro's words, "the darker sides of Soviet life" such as "drunkenness, corruption, anti-semitism (as well as Zionism), bribery, speculation, absenteeism from work, inefficient production, or dull party propaganda" ("Political and Social Aspects of the 26th CPSU Congress," *World Today*, London, May). Pursuing the same line of argument, an American scholar wrote about the deterioration of the quality of Soviet life and made the following list: "Increasing infant mortality, shortening of life expectancy for males, emerging imbalances in the supply of labor, and the growth of black markets and economic corruption." The same author made a particularly startling statement: "The high mortality from acute alcohol poisoning in the Soviet Union is significant since it is completely outside the range of world experience." (*Wall Street Journal*, 10 November.)

A leading U.S. sovietologist, Prof. Seweryn Bialer, after carefully examining these and other factors shaping and shocking Soviet society, concluded that the 1980s will be a harsh decade for the USSR and that "the difference between the optimistic and pessimistic scenarios [is] the difference between a difficult situation and a deep crisis" (*Foreign Affairs*, Summer). The Soviet economy in 1981 combined difficulties with crises. Its two quintessential problems were *food* and *capital* shortages, the first affecting primarily the domestic situation and the second the international.

The USSR has suffered three serious crop failures in a row. In 1981, instead of a projected 236 million metric tons of grain, the harvest was only 175 million tons. Fully aware of the seriousness of lagging food production, Brezhnev stated in a 16 November speech to the CPSU Central Committee that "the food problem is, economically and politically, the central problem of the five-year plan" (*CSM*, 19 November). Such a candid remark should be viewed in connection with Prof. Marshall I. Goldman's assertion that the Soviet economy has been "plagued during the last two years by an unusual number of labor disputes and public protests in such places as Kiev, Odessa, Togliatti, Gorky, and Donetsk. Most of these outbursts have been linked to complaints about food supplies." ("The Kremlin's Grain Disaster," *NYT*, 9 September.) Significantly, Soviet automotive officials belatedly conceded that in the spring of 1980 a labor dispute had occurred in Togliatti at the country's largest car plant (*Wall Street Journal*, 18 November).

A corollary of the grain shortfall was the imperative of large wheat and corn imports and the consequent increases in the Soviet hard-currency burden. Food shortages, however, encompassed other basic necessities of life, such as meat, milk, and eggs, leading to de facto rationing in Moscow and a handful of other "favored centers, islands of sufficiency in a sea of undersupply" and to a formal rationing, by coupon, in many places outside the capital. The food privileges of the Soviet elite, whose special stores are well stocked with food, and of workers on key projects, such as military plants and hydroelectric power facilities, is certainly not seen with approval by the bulk of the population. "There is open grumbling everywhere, and now and then a report from some distant place of a flare-up of discontent" (*NYT*, 15 January 1982; see also *Economist*, London, 19 September).

Despite these and similar economic deficiencies—in a report to the Twenty-Sixth Congress, Prime Minister Nikolai A. Tikhonov mentioned low labor productivity, slow development of individual branches of the economy, and dispersion of investments—Soviet leaders refrained from making substantive changes in economic priorities. The Tenth Five-Year Plan (1976–1980) was seriously underfulfilled in the key fields of national income and industrial and agricultural production. The new five-year plan (1981–1985), adopted at the party congress, is more modest than the previous one, but it still "looks over-optimistic—*unless* major changes bring about a sharp decline in waste and a substantial improvement in productivity" (Alec Nove, "The New Soviet Five-Year Plan," *World Today*, May). Professor Nove does not expect any improvement and concludes that the present "ageing conservative leadership [is] unable to imagine new ways of overcoming increasingly serious problems . . . Stability has now become immobility, or even petrification . . . While there is yet no catastrophe, the economy is certainly in a mess." In fact, to use the terminology of Roy A. Medvedev, the "four different Soviet economic systems"—military, heavy industry, consumer, and agricultural—each keeping in decreasing order the best people, the best supplies, and the best equipment both for men and for projects and enjoying in that order the attention of the authorities, were maintained by the congress. The only change—a slight one—was the official encouragement given to private plots, especially to private livestock raising. (Medvedev was interviewed in Moscow by a U.S. journalist; see "Why the Russians Can't Grow Grain," *NYT*, 1 November).

The problem of Soviet capital shortages assumed a particular importance in 1981. With the communist world's total borrowing from the West estimated at $80 billion and a general deterioration in the credit-worthiness of the Soviet bloc, the USSR found itself in a precarious financial situation. Record prices for imported grain, disappointing oil revenues, a marked worsening in the balance of payments (with a deficit estimated at $8 billion in 1981, compared with a modest surplus in 1980), and the sharp increase in aid to Poland led to a decline in Soviet currency holdings. This explains the simultaneous drop in the Soviets' foreign banking reserves (from about $9 billion in 1980 to $5.5 billion in February 1981 to $3.6 billion in June 1981) and their heavy sales of gold—to earn hard currencies—in the second half of the year. (*Business Week*, 12 October; *Wall Street Journal*, 12 November; *NYT*, 5, 7, and 8 January 1982.)

Pointing out that in the 1980s capital will be in short supply and that the Soviet Union can easily circumvent a grain embargo, Felix G. Rohatyn, chairman of the Municipal Assistance Corporation (credited with saving New York City from bankruptcy in 1975), offered some thoughts on East-West relations that merit ample quotation (*NYT*, 11 January 1982). Under the significant title, "We Cannot Create a 'Municipal Assistance Corporation' for Poland: Let It Go Bankrupt," Rohatyn argued that the Western banking system will not collapse with the bankruptcy of Poland, but the capital requirements of Soviet bloc countries, together with the domestic requirements of the Soviet Union, might make the Soviets tractable on other issues. "In our constant competitive struggle with the Soviet Union, capital can be as potent a weapon as intercontinental ballistic missiles. Why should the West supply the Soviet Union with such a weapon . . . The West has been relieving the Soviet Union of what may be its greatest shortage—capital—at the cost of making bad loans while pretending to oppose Communism. That is bad business, bad policy, bad morality . . . We should put the economic burden of the satellite states squarely on the Soviet Union and point up the bankruptcy of the Communist system by declaring bankrupt one of its largest units. When the economic burdens grow sufficiently heavy, the Soviet Union may become more accommodating and, together with the United States, may find it in its self-interest to reduce drastically defense budgets that neither country can really afford . . . It might turn out to be our only effective way, in the long run, of bringing about change behind the Iron Curtain."

While the Soviet economy in 1981 failed to meet production targets (with the exception of natural gas and oil), Soviet leaders and planners saw a bright energy and economic future a few years hence. Moving Siberian natural gas from the largest field in the world through a pipeline system to the European part of the USSR, Eastern Europe, and Western Europe would bring major benefits to the Soviet Union. It would satisfy domestic energy needs, bolster the economies of the member-states of the Council for Mutual Economic Assistance (CMEA) and—through lucrative sales in Western Europe—earn hard currencies. According to U.S. experts, the Soviet Union should realize $23 billion from the sale of oil and natural gas to Western European countries in 1985 (when the pipeline structure is to become operative), allowing it to buy needed Western technology (ibid., 3 September). In early December, in Bonn, representatives of the Soviet government and of many Western European companies, headed by the Germans, the most persistent advocates of the "pipeline-for-gas swap," signed what was called the biggest East-West deal ever. Its essential features were a 3,000-mile gas pipeline (estimated cost—$15 billion) and a 25-year agreement for the annual purchase of 10.5 billion cubic meters of Soviet gas (*Time*, 7 December). One political dividend of the Bonn agreement for the Soviet Union was Washington's failure to convince Western Europeans to reject the deal on the grounds that it could make them economically dependent on the Soviet Union and subject to blackmail by gas cutoffs. Also in the field of energy, the USSR and Czechoslovakia (especially the latter) were engaged in developing nuclear plants (*Wall Street Journal*, 6 October).

Nothing of an exceptional nature happened in 1981 in the always touchy and potentially explosive field of non-Russian nationalities. There was, however, a significant downturn in Jewish emigration from the Soviet Union. In 1979, a record number of 51,320 Jews were allowed to leave; in 1981, the number plummeted to 9,447. Exit is still denied to another 500,000 Jews who have asked to emigrate (*NYT*, 26 January 1982).

As for dissent, Gen. Semyon K. Tsvigun, the top career officer of the KGB, the Soviet security and intelligence organization, asserted in the September issue of the official party organ *Kommunist* that the KGB has succeeded in crushing political dissidence in the Soviet Union (ibid., 7 October). The continuing appearance of underground material suggested that the claim of the KGB chief was exaggerated. The special case of the most famous Soviet dissident, Andrei Sakharov, showed that despite a publicly announced negative decision, Soviet authorities could "capitulate" under given circumstances. The case involved an official refusal to issue a visa to Sakharov's daughter-in-law so that she could join her husband in the United States. A seventeen-day hunger strike by Sakharov and his wife protesting the decision created an international uproar unknown since the 1948 hunger strike of Mahatma Gandhi. Realizing that their global peace policy could suffer, the Soviets reversed the decision, and the point was made that even in a closed society top officials were sensitive to the pressure of world opinion.

Foreign Relations. In 1981 the USSR demonstrated as it has in the past—though with more intensity and anxiety—the two constants and one flexible element that have characterized its global role as a superpower. The two constants were its advocacy of peace and its military might; flexibility consisted in multifaceted and diverse political struggles corresponding to Soviet interests and adjusted to specific conditions in various countries or regions.

Leonid Brezhnev was the standard-bearer of the 1981 Soviet peace offensive. In his report to the Twenty-Sixth Congress of the CPSU in February, he extolled Soviet efforts to "remove the threat of war and to preserve and deepen détente [while acting] to expand mutually beneficial cooperation with the most countries of the world" (*Socialism: Theory and Practice*, Moscow, no. 3, p. 7). In a letter to President Reagan, dated 25 May but made known only six months later (*NYT*, 21 November), Brezhnev wrote that "the USSR wishes peace, cooperation, a sense of mutual trust and benevolence [between our two countries] . . . as well as a search for mutually acceptable solutions of practically all major questions existing between us." Finally, in an interview given to the German weekly *Der Spiegel* in early November (*Pravda*, 3 November), the Soviet leader stated that Soviet military doctrine was defensive in nature, that there existed an approximate balance between Soviet and Western medium-range missiles in Europe, and that the Soviet Union was looking forward to Soviet-American negotiations to limit nuclear arms in Europe. Each of these peace appeals interspersed with attacks blamed the United States for increasing international tension by weakening détente and pursuing a reckless nuclear policy. As Leonard Schapiro stated in the study mentioned earlier, Brezhnev's report "was intended for those in Europe, in the Third World and elsewhere, who either take up a neutral attitude between the United States and the Soviet Union or are outright hostile to the United States." In the November interview, Brezhnev emphasized that Western Europe and specifically West Germany faced "decisions of a fundamental order," the choice being a continuation of détente, which would lead to more trade and larger deals like the proposed pipeline from the Siberian gas fields, or "fruitless and dangerous confrontations," possibly involving a limited nuclear exchange in Europe.

While the peace offensive served the Soviet Union at the levels of diplomacy and propaganda, Soviet military might was its strongest argument. One of the most hotly debated issues of 1981 was the problem of Soviet military strength and U.S. efforts to counter it. Late in the year, a "battle of military booklets" occurred. In early October, the U.S. Defense Department published a booklet entitled *Soviet Military Power*. According to Secretary of Defense Caspar Weinberger, "The Soviet Armed Forces today number more than 4.8 million men . . . All elements of the Soviet Armed

Forces—the Strategic Rocket Forces, the Ground Forces of the Army, the Air Forces, the Navy and the Air Defense Forces—continue to modernize with an unending flow of new weapon systems, tanks, missiles, ships, artillery and aircraft. The Soviet defense budget continues to grow to fund this force buildup, to fund the projection of Soviet power far from Soviet shores and to fund Soviet use of proxy forces to support revolutionary factions and conflict in an increasing threat to international stability."

On 20 November, the Soviet Committee for European Security and Cooperation issued a booklet entitled *The Threat to Europe.* The Soviet pamphlet asserted that nuclear war, including a limited nuclear war in Europe or elsewhere, would be a universal disaster; whatever Soviet strategic thinking in the 1960s about offensive action may have been, it was not valid today when Soviet military thinking is "of a purely defensive nature"; failure to deploy SS-20 missiles would have tilted the security balance in favor of the United States; it is the United States, not the Soviet Union, that is seeking a first-strike capability; numerical superiority of Soviet forces is necessary because of the huge territory the army must defend, the overall length of Soviet frontiers, and the nature of the potential dangers [both the United States and China were lumped together here, and the possibility of a blockade of Soviet territory was mentioned]. Finally, "during the first roughly 20 years after the war, the United States had a strategic nuclear advantage over the U.S.S.R. At the turn of the 70's, the defensive efforts of the Soviet Union ended this superiority. Since then, there has been military strategic equilibrium." (*NYT*, 21 November and 6 December.) The Soviet pamphlet was written before President Reagan's 18 November proposal to curb missiles in Europe, and in early December another booklet, entitled "Whence the Threat to Peace?" was published in Moscow. Much of it was a repetition of the previous pamphlet, with sharper attacks against the military policies of the Reagan administration. According to the Soviets, the traditional American military doctrine emphasizing offensive measures has been accentuated. President Reagan plans to increase U.S. nuclear potential by using the space shuttle as "a space attack system" and installing "an in-depth anti-missile system" (prohibited under a 1972 Soviet-American treaty). Given the military equality between the two countries, there is no need for the United States to rearm. "Rearmament on the pretext of achieving parity is in actual fact a drive for military superiority." (Ibid., 17 January 1982.) In the same vein, Soviet Defense Minister and Politburo member Marshal Dimitri P. Ustinov, speaking on the anniversary of the Bolshevik Revolution, denounced U.S. and Chinese "lunatic imperialist reaction," confirmed that the USSR paid "unremitting attention to its defenses," and, while asserting that the Soviet Union was not seeking military superiority over others, warned that "we will not allow such superiority to be created over us" (ibid., 8 November).

This battle of words should now be placed in a different setting—Soviet flexibility. The United States and Western Europe became the most significant theaters of these confrontations.

Ronald Reagan's incumbency did not look promising to the Soviet leaders, although during the last year of the Carter administration Soviet-U.S. relations were anything but cordial and cooperative. Known for his conviction that overt and covert Soviet actions were the source of most troubles in the world, the new U.S. president stated a few days before his inauguration that "the Soviet empire should know that there will be no further concessions from us unless there is a concession in return . . . I believe in legitimate negotiations that are aimed at reducing the strategic nuclear weapons in the world." (*Time*, 5 January.) Specifically, SALT II, already buried under Carter, would be subordinated to the requirements of a stronger national defense. On 29 January, President Reagan accused Soviet leaders of reserving "the right to commit any crime, to lie, to cheat" in order to attain their goal of world domination and disclosed a tough U.S. message warning of dire consequences for East-West relations if Soviet troops invaded Poland. The day before, the new secretary of state, Alexander Haig, had expressed Washington's unhappiness with Soviet press statements that the United States was using the hostage issue as a pretext for planning an invasion of Iran. Haig asserted that "Moscow was involved in conscious policies, in programs which foster, support and expand [international terrorism], which is hemorrhaging in many respects throughout the world today" (*NYT*, 30 January).

Overall in its dealings with the Soviet Union, the new administration suffered from other handicaps that Soviet policymakers tried to exploit. The president himself concentrated until late into the summer on getting his tax and spending cuts through Congress. Moreover, disinclined to handle the complexities of foreign affairs personally, he essentially left those matters to his secretaries of state and defense, men of incompatible characters and occasionally divergent views. Perhaps worse—better from the Soviet angle—there emerged the impression that the administration was hesitant about what new weapons to build and their emplacement. Domestic critics, and even some loyal Reaganites, complained that the administration had failed to develop a coherent, global American strategy and that Washington was reacting to events rather than shaping them. Influential critics in the media denounced the "militaristic" nature of the administration's foreign policy, pointing to its obsession with new weaponry, rejection of détente, and procrastination in beginning the talks on arms limitations that Brezhnev was constantly calling for. Against this backdrop, two commentators concluded that "Soviet leadership seems convinced of American hostility but uncertain of American willpower" (*Wall Street Journal*, 18 September).

Whatever critics said, the president remained highly popular, and the public responded favorably to some strongly worded denunciations of Soviet behavior. A four-page document issued by the State Department in early October charged that the Soviet Union was using forgery, blackmail, "disinformation" (a term more and more frequently used by critics of the Soviet Union), and political-influence operations in an elaborate effort to discredit and weaken the United States (AP, 8 October). Likewise, the FBI claimed that more Soviet spies than ever were working in the United States (ibid., 16 November). Well-documented books, pamphlets, and articles explored the murky field of international terrorism and hinted at the sophisticated and clandestine jobs performed in that field by organs of the Soviet secret services (see Claire Sterling, *The Terror Network: The Secret War of International Terrorism*, New York: Holt, Rinehart & Winston, 1981). The State Department began a particularly intensive campaign in September over the "yellow rain"—Soviet-produced chemical weapons used against anticommunist insurgents in Southeast Asia and Afghanistan. An editorial in the *Wall Street Journal* (8 October) summed it up by denouncing "the Soviet-backed campaign of terror and destabilization that is under way across the globe today."

Soviet media vehemently denied all allegations and in turn informed their audiences about the mischiefs perpetrated by U.S. imperialists around the world. (For a subject-by-subject, area-by-area, and country-by-country analysis of Soviet attitudes on world developments, based on Soviet and non-Soviet sources, see the quarterly *World Affairs Report*, published by the California Institute of International Studies, Stanford, and edited by Prof. Ronald Hilton.) More important, however, the Soviet government found a potentially promising means of promoting its peace offensive and splitting NATO: an unprecedented mass movement in Western Europe to block the deployment of new U.S. missiles.

Two million people demonstrated in October and November in major European cities against nuclear weapons, specifically against deployment of a new generation of U.S.-built nuclear missiles in Western Europe starting in late 1983, a fact of utmost importance to Soviet policymakers. The USSR has systematically built up its own military strength for the past fifteen years—in contrast to the intermittent rearmament efforts of the West. If deployment of new U.S. weapons, especially the cruise missile that particularly worries Soviet military experts, is blocked, the Soviets will in practical terms, even without an invasion, dominate Europe. The latter, unable or unwilling to defend itself militarily, has become increasingly frightened that any nuclear exchange between the weakened NATO forces and the superior forces of the Warsaw Pact will lead to European annihilation. Out of that fear has grown the temptation of accommodation at nearly any price with Europe's strong and determined

Eastern neighbor. In the words of Irving Kristol, " 'Appeasement' leading to 'Finlandization' is the implicit foreign policy of the nuclear movement in Europe" (*Wall Street Journal*, 15 July).

On the political level, the Kremlin was favored in 1981 by a serious crisis in NATO, which the London *Economist* (6 June) described as "the early stages of what could be a terminal illness." Melvyn Lasky, coeditor of the London-based monthly *Encounter*, lamented about the "specter of 'self-Finlandization' haunting the Rhine, from Bonn to Rotterdam" (*Wall Street Journal*, 21 October), and Josef Joffe, a senior editor of the prestigious German weekly *Die Zeit*, wondered whether the Federal Republic of Germany (FRG), "America's staunchest ally, [has] finally succumbed to that dread disease variously known as 'Hollandittis' or 'self-Finlandization'?" (ibid., 14 October). Concomitantly, neo-isolationism, with its essential ingredient of the withdrawal of U.S. troops from Europe, became a hotly debated issue on the pages of U.S. newspapers (*NYT*, 7 December), while a militant antinuclear movement was spreading on U.S. campuses, within churches, and among action-prone radical groups (ibid., 21 November; *San Francisco Chronicle*, 23 November; *Newsweek*, 11 January 1982).

The FRG is the centerpiece of Soviet interests in Europe for military, political, and economic reasons. In practical terms the growing closeness between Moscow and Bonn was particularly gratifying for the Kremlin, while provoking criticism and distrust in other European capitals as well as in Washington. Brezhnev chose Bonn for his first official visit (22–25 November) to a nonbloc state since the Soviet invasion of Afghanistan. The place was appropriate from the Soviet standpoint—some 400,000 antinuclear demonstrators had rallied in the German capital on 10 October. (Only 40,000 came to Bonn on 22 November to demonstrate for human rights.) Chancellor Helmut Schmidt, who persisted in his balancing act between his proclaimed loyalty to NATO and the pursuance of an active *Ostpolitik*, established a new and direct relationship with Brezhnev during his visit. Schmidt's assumption of the role of middleman or interpreter between the Soviet Union and the United States contributed to making West Germany "a new 'power' among the superpowers" (*CSM*, 27 November).

Enhanced economic cooperation with the FRG was of a paramount importance to the ailing Soviet economy. Bonn's rejection of Washington's pleas to cancel the Siberian natural gas pipeline project was most welcome in Moscow. Bonn, in turn, explained that economic transactions with the USSR and the Soviet bloc benefited West Germany, which was facing its highest unemployment rate since the end of World War II. Other Western European governments and business and banking concerns eagerly followed the German example of resisting U.S. pressure and promoting local interests by trading with the USSR.

Soviet satisfaction with the course of events in Western Europe epitomized by the disarray within NATO received at least a temporary blow on 18 November. President Reagan, with considerable domestic and foreign media exposure, offered the Soviet Union a four-point program of arms reduction for discussion at the Geneva arms limitation talks in late November. Even in the briefest form the program was comprehensive and attention catching: (1) the United States would agree not to deploy 572 new Pershing II and cruise missiles in five NATO countries, if the USSR agreed to dismantle 600 SS-20, SS-4, and SS-5 missiles in the Soviet Union; (2) Moscow and Washington would begin talks to achieve "substantial reductions in strategic nuclear weapons which would result in levels that are equal and verifiable" (the negotiations would be called START—Strategic Arms Reduction Talks); (3) a reduction of conventional forces in Europe would also be discussed; and (4) an international conference would be held to reduce the risks of a "surprise attack and the chance of war arising out of uncertainty or miscalculation" (*San Francisco Chronicle*, 19 November).

This was the U.S. president's first major foreign policy speech. Although it obtained the immediate approval of both houses of Congress and the enthusiastic endorsement of NATO's highest representatives, it had some characteristics that were certainly not to Moscow's liking. First, the address did not come out of the blue, but had been discussed in advance with the United States' European partners; it might be said that Reagan had heeded their advice by delivering it. Second, the articulation of sentiments that Europeans did not expect to hear from Reagan ("I believe the time is right to move forward on arms control and the resolution of critical regional disputes at the conference table. Nothing will have a higher priority for me and for the American people over the coming months and years"; *NYT*, 19 November) was aimed at confuting the conviction of the president's neutralist critics abroad that Ronald Reagan was "a shoot-from-the-hip zealot, hell-bent on provoking nuclear war" (*Time*, 30 November). For the same reason, Reagan's phrase "zero option," by which his program became best known, was intentionally taken from slogans occasionally used by German antinuclear groups (*CSM*, 30 November). Third, by choosing to make his proposal a few days before the arrival of Leonid Brezhnev in Bonn, President Reagan made the latter event anticlimactic and put both the Soviet leader and West European nuclear opponents on the defensive.

The Soviet reaction was predictable, though not fully coordinated during the first few days. In a dispatch from Washington, only hours after the president's speech, a Tass correspondent called it "a ploy to scuttle disarmament talks and to blunt the antinuclear movement in Western Europe." He then advanced two arguments (to become standard Soviet criticisms) to refute the president's claims: Reagan had deliberately overlooked U.S. submarine-based missiles, the so-called forward-based missiles, weapons borne by bombers based in Western Europe or on carriers off Europe, and French and British nuclear weapons; and Reagan's contention that the Soviet Union had a superiority of six to one in medium-range missiles was a "groundless allegation" based on "absolutely fantastic figures" (*NYT*, 19 November). The next day Soviet media attacks widened. The director of Tass, Sergei A. Losev, writing in *Izvestiia*, expressed amazement that Reagan's proposal had attracted favorable attention in Western Europe and dismissed the address as "sheer demagoguery." A different reaction was heard during a press conference given on 20 November by Vadim V. Zagladin, a member of the CPSU Central Committee and an influential adviser to Brezhnev, who expressed coolness to the American proposal, but found in it "a welcome change": "Since entering the White House, Reagan has spoken in a very bellicose way, always calling for new bombers, new submarines, and the rockets. If in fact he now wants to be a peacemaker, then we can welcome this as a turn to the better." (*NYT*, 21 November.) *Pravda* (21 November) adopted a tougher approach, asserting that the aim of Reagan's address was to "hoodwink West Europe on arms," while he was in fact maneuvering to regain "nuclear superiority in Europe." But it was left to Leonid Brezhnev to formulate the official Soviet attitude. At a dinner speech in Bonn on 23 November, he both denounced the Reagan proposal and offered his own. The unacceptable part of the "zero option" was that it "demanded of us that we disarm unilaterally." The USSR proposed a freeze on the deployment of new medium-range nuclear missiles in Europe pending talks with the United States on more reductions. As a gesture of goodwill, the USSR offered to reduce unilaterally the number of nuclear weapons in the European area of the USSR (*NYT*, 24 November). What weakened the attractiveness of Brezhnev's proposals was that they contained nothing new, being similar to points he had made in a speech in East Berlin in October 1979. During the next few days, until the formal opening of negotiations in Geneva on 30 November, attacks on the Reagan proposals softened, with the assurance that the Soviet side would present its case with straightforwardness and in detail behind the closed doors of the Swiss city's conference hall.

The 18 November U.S. proposal certainly represented a setback for the main Soviet goal of splitting NATO. However, it was far from a real defeat for the Kremlin. "When you look at these negotiations in classic terms, the Soviets hold all the cards," said a U.S. expert on NATO. "Their missiles are already deployed; ours aren't. In the Soviet Union marshals decide military matters; the public doesn't. And in Western Europe, the Soviets have gotten a lot of mileage out of the rhetoric of moderation." (*Wall Street Journal*, 24 November.)

Only days after the Geneva conference started—in an apparently cordial atmosphere and with an agreement to maintain the confidentiality of the negotiations—two interrelated events risked ending everything. The imposition on 13 December of martial law in Poland, with an army Council of National Salvation assuming full powers over the state administration and presided over by Gen. Wojciech Jaruzelski, already prime minister as well as defense minister and secretary general of the communist party, put the Soviet and U.S. governments at loggerheads. A Tass statement issued on 14 December called the Polish crackdown "an internal matter" imposed to save the country from the "mortal danger" of counterrevolution. President Reagan viewed it differently and accused the Soviet Union of heavy and direct responsibility for the repression in Poland. On 23 and 29 December, the U.S. government imposed economic sanctions against both the Polish and Soviet governments. The latter was to be punished for engineering the Polish coup and persecutions through a domestic proxy. The Soviets reacted furiously. Tass described the sanctions as "a deliberate striving of the U.S. leadership to worsen the international situation even further, to hurl the world back to the dark times of the cold war and to give U.S. imperialism a free hand in pursuing a military policy aimed at achieving world domination" (*NYT*, 31 December). •

At the same time, the Soviet government could feel satisfied—at least for now. The sanctions were basically mild and economically of limited effectiveness, and their imposition left the United States isolated within NATO. The West European allies made it clear that short of a direct invasion of Poland, they were not willing to participate in anti-Soviet measures. Moreover, despite the principle of linking U.S. diplomacy to Soviet behavior, Washington opted to continue the Geneva conference, causing at the beginning of 1982 a heated domestic controversy about the alleged softening of U.S. foreign policy under Secretary Haig. The Geneva talks resumed on 13 January 1982.

Within the general context of its peace offensive, Soviet foreign policy suffered two setbacks that negatively affected Western public opinion and governments. The grounding of a Soviet submarine armed with nuclear weapons off the Swedish coast in October and November diminished the attractiveness of Soviet appeals for a Nordic nuclear-free zone. Second, even though some West European governments refused to follow the United States in blaming the Soviet Union directly for the 13 December coup in Poland, the relentless Soviet pressure throughout the year on the Polish government to stifle the process of democratization and particularly to crack down on Solidarity revealed to many the discrepancy between the USSR's support for peace in one part of Europe and its advocacy of repression in the other.

Since Soviet strategists concluded that Western Europe was the most promising field for their peace offensive in 1981, they soft-pedaled overt militancy in other regions. The point was to persuade West Europeans and the peoples of the Third World that Moscow, not Washington, was the peace-loving superpower. Still, the Soviet global presence was perfectly visible even if relatively inconspicuous. The Kremlin pursued a cautious policy in the Middle East, supporting radical Arab regimes and Palestinian liberation movements and encouraging the pro-Moscow Communist Party of Iran (Tudeh) to cooperate with the Tehran regime. The USSR's grip over African countries under its or its proxies' (Cuban and East European, especially East German) control did not diminish, even though problems with some Afro-Marxist governments and movements became marginally bothersome. Moscow continued and even intensified military aid to Cuba, making the U.S. government uncertain how to react. Ties with the revolutionary government in Nicaragua were keen though discreet, and Soviet interest in helping the insurgents in El Salvador was manifest but again extremely prudent, especially with regard to the delivery of weapons. In Asia, the Chinese proved to be as recalcitrant as ever, and even the Vietnamese were less tractable than in the past.

Finally, and paradoxically enough, within the Soviet imperial domain, the satellite states of East Central Europe, trouble—real or potential—was on the agenda. Poland was a constant nightmare, and the spread of its revolutionary workers' "democracy virus" threatened all people's democracies, including the Soviet Union itself. The 13 December solution was certainly ingenious, but was the military takeover (even if Jaruzelski was an extremely politicized general) the proper formula for replacing a Marxist-Leninist, civilian-headed party?

To sum up, 1981 was an unequal year for Soviet foreign policy. Measured by the yardstick of correlation of forces, expected to work in the Soviets' favor in the confrontation with capitalism, there were pluses (especially in Western Europe), successes and question marks elsewhere, and dubious victories (Poland) and liabilities closer to home. Impressive military strength (though even in Afghanistan, the Red Army could not achieve victory after two years of exertion) could not compensate for domestic ideological and economic failures—important ingredients for the pursuit of a fully effective foreign policy. This is perhaps what Leonid Brezhnev had in mind when, in his report to the Twenty-Sixth Congress of the CPSU, he spoke of a "rough and complicated" world.

Eastern Europe. For all the countries of the Soviet bloc, as well as for nonaligned Yugoslavia, 1981 was in both symbolic and practical terms the year of Poland. In a general sense, all of the problems that led to the emergence of Solidarity—a failing economy, a remote and inflexible government, a bureaucracy that was unresponsive and corrupt—affected the countries of Eastern Europe as surely as they did Poland. With some variations, East European countries were saddled with "declining growth rates, chronic shortages of food and consumer goods, mountainous foreign debts and a cowed but sullen population" (ibid., 10 January 1982; see also *Wall Street Journal*, 22 December 1981).

Even before the crisis in Poland, East European countries were suffering from systemic economic difficulties. According to the latest figures issued by the International Monetary Fund, overall growth of the European members of the CMEA declined from an average 5.7 percent in 1976 to 1.2 percent in 1980 (*NYT*, 8 January 1982). The Polish economic catastrophe in 1981 worsened the global situation and demonstrated that the CMEA, despite its promising plans for economic integration in the future, was presently not in a position to help its member-states. A high-level CMEA meeting in Sofia in July failed to coordinate the members' national economic plans for 1981–1985 because of uncertainty over Poland. With their centrally planned economies, sudden cutbacks or irregularities in delivery of vital raw materials and other commodities—coal, sulphur, industrial goods, and food—caused a series of problems. With bottlenecks building up quickly, the CMEA countries were forced to use their scarce hard-currency resources to buy from the West what they urgently needed and at the same time (prompted by Moscow) to help Poland in its economic predicament. The drastic drop in Polish coal exports to its CMEA partners (from 20 million tons in 1979 to 12 million in 1980 to only 4 million in 1981) darkened the energy picture even more. The regional pattern of years past—the Soviet Union supplying energy and raw materials in return for machinery and consumer goods—encountered greater difficulties in 1981 (see George Blazyca, "Comecon and the Polish Crisis," *World Today*, October).

Growing Soviet consumption, increasing amounts of oil exports reserved for hard-currency sales, and the heavy burden of aid to Poland (in 1981 a more expensive ally than Cuba, which receives $3 billion a year) are hurting East European economies. Facing a probable 10 percent cut in energy shipments from the USSR (*CSM*, 15 January 1982) and unable to afford OPEC oil prices, Eastern Europe has been forced to impose hard austerity measures, with all the risks that implies, especially given the existing food crisis. The latter results from the bureaucratic inefficiency of collectivized agriculture, faulty pricing policies, and, in the short run, three exceptionally bad harvests (*Economist*, 26 December). An essential point is that the better-off countries have for some time experimented with market mechanisms (Hungary), given incentives to the agricultural sector (Hungary, Bulgaria), or rationalized production and saved energy and raw materials (East Germany).

All this has led to a basic dilemma: reform the regimes in order to avoid a repetition of the Polish disturbances or maintain established economic practices and ways of life of the entrenched ruling class. This is the promise or the danger of Polish "contamination." Even the most politically apathetic industrial workers in Eastern Europe could not remain indifferent to the news of an emerging new order in Poland, with truly independent trade unions, having a legal right to strike, and with the workers actually beginning to manage their shops and factories. The excitement was higher among professionals, who watched Polish society expanding the limits of its autonomy at the expense of the state. But those most interested in the Polish maelstrom were the intellectuals (including nondissidents), who were fascinated with the explosion of free creativity in Poland. It was indeed unbelievable that probably the most antiregime film ever made in a communist-ruled country, Andrzej Vajda's *Man of Iron*, passed the official censorship, was rushed abroad as the Polish entry at the Cannes festival, won the Golden Palm prize as the best foreign film, and was seen by hundreds of thousands in Warsaw a few weeks before the 13 December crackdown. Another illustration of the interest created by the events in Poland was the reaction of participants at a large international conference of Marxist theoreticians in mid-September at an Adriatic spa in Yugoslavia. They discussed—and totally disagreed about—the brand of socialism having the correct answers to present scientific, technological, and developmental questions. At the end of a day of debate "came the moment that testifies about the unity of theory and practice in today's socialism: everyone, regardless of differences, with unhidden anxiety, was expecting news from Poland" (from a report entitled "Before the Challenge of the Future," published in the prominent Belgrade weekly, *NIN*, 27 September).

The determination of the keepers of "real socialism" in the Soviet Union to put an end to the creeping Polish "counterrevolution" symbolized by the Solidarity phenomenon was understandable. Realizing that a direct invasion of Poland by the Red Army or Warsaw Pact units would be politically and militarily counterproductive, they arranged (or at least approved in advance) for the Polish Army, particularly the highly trained and superiorly equipped units of special security forces, to throttle—immediately following the proclamation of martial law on 13 December—the still inchoate Polish democracy. One cannot judge so close to the event how effective General Jaruzelski's coup was and what will happen in the future. One thing is certain: Soviet leaders were resolutely determined not to allow the social pluralization of their imperial domain. Communist party leaders in Eastern Europe enthusiastically endorsed the crackdown in Warsaw, but might not some of them be looking behind their backs uneasily for a general to emerge and establish law and order?

If 1981 was for Eastern Europe the year of Poland, for Poland 1981 was the year of Solidarity. An editorial in the London *Economist* (12 September) explained the situation in two sentences: "Solidarity is not just a union. It is the Polish nation." This striking formula illuminates, however, only one aspect of the problem. Solidarity represented both qualitatively and quantitatively the best that a nation could offer at a given moment of history—it was, in French terminology, "the real country." But there was another country—"the legal country," the anti-Solidarity country—and it succeeded at the end of the year in gaining the upper hand.

At its zenith, Solidarity incarnated an exceptional reality of modern revolution and a matchless performance of social uplifting. According to the perceptive correspondent of the *New York Times* in Poland, John Darnton, "A revolution is taking place [in Poland]—one of those moments in history when a majority of a society is seized with the inspiration to overrun the existing order—and . . . so far the revolution has been bloodless because its backing is so incredibly strong and disciplined" (*NYT*, 6 June). Stefan Nowak, professor of sociology at the University of Warsaw, credited Solidarity with "the reintegration of our atomized society . . . the elimination of the feeling of powerlessness and . . . the restoration of people's dignity" (*Scientific American*, July).

From another angle of observation—Solidarity's place within Polish society—the extraordinarily complex and turbulent conditions under which it had to act and its weaknesses are immediately apparent. The mention of two adverse factors will suffice: the antagonism of the totalitarian formal and legal structure to all of Solidarity's aspirations, and the constitutionally guaranteed leading role of the communist party (officially called the Polish United Workers' Party; PUWP). Though enormously weakened, the PUWP still had hundreds of thousands of members, many in positions of power, for whom

Solidarity was the enemy. As for Solidarity itself, its very success was also a source of vulnerability. Solidarity was inexperienced in every sense of the word: both its leaders and members had been accustomed for decades to obeying and listening to PUWP dictates. The post–31 August 1980 freedoms and rights were intoxicating but also trying. How do you organize a free trade union? Who decides about launching a strike? Should national organization be centralized or founded on local or regional levels? How do you negotiate with the government? How do you implement your program, especially since Solidarity's first national convention (in Gdansk, September–October) elaborated and accepted a detailed economic and political program—not a trade union charter but a plan to reorder the entire society? And how do you do all this when you are deprived of all the levers of power, when you confront a centralized information media, a state administration including the police, an entrenched bureaucratic apparatus, from factory directors to top economic planners, when the enemy watches your every step, when the economic situation worsens hourly, when you know that the big neighbor to the East wants your destruction?

Solidarity was fortunate to be led by Lech Walesa. The charismatic former worker knew how to handle the masses and negotiate with state and party leaders and was, like Lenin, at the same time a man of deepest convictions and a political maneuverer of exceptional intuition and dexterity. He was in turn enormously helped by the elevation of Karol Cardinal Wojtila of Krakow to the position of pope and by his closeness with the late primate of the Polish Catholic church, Stefan Cardinal Wyszynski, another man with unusual qualities of moral firmness and political ability (Oriana Fallaci's interview with Walesa, published in the *Washington Post* on 8 March, reveals Walesa's ideas and personality more thoroughly than any other interview or speech of his). But the case of Walesa, especially during the second part of 1981, confirms Solidarity's difficulties. His more impatient colleagues accused him of being too prone to compromise with the authorities, he was often unable to stop an unnecessary strike, he knew that officialdom never negotiated in good faith, and he had no power to stop the economic debacle. He remained popular with the rank and file of Solidarity and with millions of Poles outside the movement or the church, but in the end he became a victim of a system that he despised but dealt with for the benefit of an independent Poland.

Poland's economic predicament is another key element in evaluating events in the country in 1981. The sinking economy was one of the heaviest stones around Solidarity's neck: "I fear the economic crisis could lead to such social despair that the whole revolution will be jeopardized," said a Warsaw citizen in the early fall (*CSM*, 4 September). And the calamity was of monumental proportions. "The queues," observed a U.S. economist, "are the visible manifestation of the worst economic disaster to befall any European country since the devastation of World War II" (*Fortune*, 7 September). In a particularly penetrating article, Prof. Seweryn Bialer stated that by the late 1970s "Poland faced nothing less than the collapse of its planning and management system and the total bankruptcy of its economy" (*Foreign Affairs*, no. 3). In 1981 things turned even worse, but while Solidarity accused the government and the party of being the source of the economic tragedy and being unwilling or unable to find a way out, they blamed Solidarity's strikes and social actions for creating chaos in the country and preventing economic recovery.

As for the PUWP, it was totally discredited in the eyes of the people, irreformable because excessively factionalized. Unprepared to assault Solidarity frontally and the despair of Moscow, the PUWP still had a hard core ready to fight if a proper formula could be devised. And one was. It consisted in charging the best-known official in the country, General Jaruzelski, with the leadership of the *Military Council of National Salvation* on 13 December. Using essentially patriotic phraseology, Jaruzelski opened his speech to the country by saying: "I address you today as a soldier." He knew that a member of the army, credited during the bloody fighting in Gdansk in 1970 with saying, "Polish troops will not fire on Polish workers," had a chance of being listened to. In a survey of the public's confidence in social institutions published by the Warsaw weekly *Kultura* in early June, the church topped the poll,

Solidarity was second, the army third. The police and the PUWP figured thirteenth and fourteenth, respectively (AP and UPI, in *San Francisco Chronicle*, 22 June). But the real work that started when the general stopped talking was done not by regular army units but by specially trained internal security forces. Three of them—the Motorized Police Units (ZOMO), a part of the regular police force; the WSW, which is subordinate to the head of military counterintelligence; and the KBW, the Internal Security Force and border units—capable of mobilizing about 250,000 people, were superbly armed with everything necessary to crush any organized resistance among the civilian population (see *NYT*, 5, 6, and 10 January 1982). They were extraordinarily effective in isolating Poland from the rest of the world (by cutting all telephone, telegraph, and telex lines as well as all means of travel) and in separating Polish citizens from each other. Within hours nearly the entire leadership of Solidarity, including Lech Walesa, was arrested, making any organized nationwide strike or resistance movement impossible. The courage of those who engaged in strikes or civic resistance was more a mark of their spirit than of a movement that could successfully oppose special forces under the orders of General Jaruzelski and his discreet Soviet KGB advisers. The coup of 13 December proved how illusory was the hope of one of the most intelligent Polish dissenters and an adviser to Solidarity, Adam Michnik, who at one time believed that "a hybrid system is conceivable, one where totalitarian organization of the state will coexist with democratic institutions of society" (*Biuletyn Informacyjny*, no. 60, 1980). Much closer to the mark was one of the sharpest European correspondents in Warsaw, Bernard Guetta of *Le Monde* in Paris, who, while reporting Solidarity's fall convention, concluded and repeated the argument several times: "The game is close. It may end once more, after very hard tensions, with a false compromise—the result of coming within a hair's breadth of a catastrophe. But the war is well and truly declared, for what is at stake now is nothing else but power, not formal but real." (*Le Monde*, 6–7, 10, and 22 September.)

Compared with the Polish cataclysm, everything else that happened in Eastern Europe in 1981 appeared trivial, even if it had significance from the local standpoint. Romania followed the Polish example of a poorly managed economy. Its failing agricultural policy led to the first food shortages in decades (*NYT*, 26 January 1982). The country became the second in East Europe (after Poland) to introduce food rationing and the first to ration bread. On 9 October, the hoarding of foodstuffs was made punishable by imprisonment for up to five years (*Economist*, 24 October). Popular dissatisfaction led in October to several violent protests against the government, especially in the largest coalfield (ibid., 21 November). These events led to the erosion of the "personality cult" of state and communist party chief Nicolae Ceauşescu, who showed signs of nervousness throughout the year by shuffling ministers and officials in a continuous search for answers to Romania's economic woes. The 1981–1985 plan reduced industrial growth in favor of investments in agriculture, and farmers were encouraged to cultivate private plots. Romania's large foreign debt (estimated at $8.4–12 billion) turned Ceauşescu toward both the CMEA and the USSR for economic relief—with less than promising results. A vociferous critic of Solidarity, Ceauşescu felt less threatened because free trade unions were strictly prohibited, intellectual dissent was minimal, and the Orthodox church well controlled. The repressive apparatus of the regime, still Stalinist in many respects, was well prepared to handle troublemakers. In his complex political game with the USSR, Ceauşescu ordered huge peace and antinuclear demonstrations in various Romanian cities, with the largest in Bucharest on 5 December. Some 300,000 marchers shouted in favor of the removal of all nuclear weapons from Europe ("from the Pyrenees to the Carpathians"), and Ceauşescu proposed that other European states take an active part in the Geneva negotiations (*NYT*, 6 December). Ceauşescu criticized the U.S. government's economic sanctions against Poland following the imposition of martial law and on 26 December stated that "nobody should interfere in the internal affairs of Poland" (AP, 26 December).

Czechoslovakia also experienced economic difficulties. Addressing a meeting on 30 October of the communist party Central Committee, Prime Minister Lubomír Štrougal explored causes and aspects of the economic slump. Shortfalls in the domestic production of coal (compounded by the failure in deliveries of Polish coal, copper, sulfur, and other raw materials) caused delays in production and forced electricity and heating reductions in the winter months. The energy sector was also hit by the cuts in Soviet exports of crude oil, while the country's shortage of convertible currency negatively affected compensatory transactions elsewhere. Agriculture was another weak point, with the grain harvest 1.6 million tons below forecasts. Imports from abroad, implying Western suppliers, had to be purchased in hard currency (*NYT*, 8 November). Although there were no food shortages in 1981, officials indicated that for the first time since the 1950s, the regime was preparing to announce an increase in meat prices, a politically difficult step in view of Poland's experiences in the past (ibid., 8 January 1982). Throughout 1981, the Czechoslovak regime was extremely sensitive to the events in Poland, with the media unremittingly criticizing both Solidarity and "revisionist" elements within the PUWP. The domestic crackdown on dissent was intense, especially in the second part of the year. Relations with the Catholic church were tense, although foreign observers were impressed by what seems to be a religious revival among young people, who are flocking to both Catholic and Protestant churches (ibid., 26 September, 4 October; *WP*, 9 September). Czechoslovak media greeted the imposition of martial law in Poland in the most approving terms. Western radio stations, especially Radio Free Europe, were vehemently attacked for broadcasting misinformation about the events in Poland, while the U.S. government was accused of being the main supporter of counterrevolution in Poland.

In contrast to Romania and Czechoslovakia, Hungary was in 1981 the showcase of prosperity in Eastern Europe. Its shops were full of foodstuffs and other consumer goods. Its experiment with greater reliance on market forces, private enterprises operating on the profit principle, and liberalization of foreign trade made progress during the year despite opposition from the bureaucracy overseeing the running of the economy. Despite its relatively high foreign debt (estimated to be between $7.0 and $8.5 billion), Hungary did not have problems in obtaining foreign credits. On 4 November (five days before Poland), Hungary applied for membership in the International Monetary Fund. It planned to make its currency, the forint, convertible on 1 January 1982. It was in the field of agriculture that the most positive results were registered. Brezhnev, in his report to the Twenty-Sixth Congress of the CPSU, complimented the skillful operations of Hungarian agricultural cooperatives and enterprises. Surpassing industry in export drives, "agriculture is not only an important dollar (and rouble) earner; it is also a guarantor of domestic political stability in its role as the supplier of the domestic market" (K. F. Cviic, "Hungary's Reforming Role," *World Today*, October). Despite the economic successes of Hungary's "goulash communism," the country experienced other problems. Speeches made at the 27 March meeting of the communist party Central Committee revealed that "unjust privileges" persisted, that the intelligentsia was full of an "abstract anti-power feeling," and (in János Kádár's words) "egotism, acquisitiveness, and the chasing of status symbols" have become widespread. "Youth had been allowed to have 'amusement' as its main concern." Kádár also admitted that "what happens in Poland compromises the socialist system and is sad and bitter for the cause of socialism." The Central Committee decided to take a tougher stand, including stricter censorship, against negative phenomena (*Guardian*, London, 4 July). In September, the party warned a group of dissenters that there was no place for hostile opinions in Hungary (AFP, 9 September). "Freedom to conform and consume" is what Hungary offers, according to one foreign visitor (*NYT*, 22 December). Economic experimentation, nonexistent in any other country of the Soviet bloc, was compensated by Hungary's total alignment with the Soviet Union's foreign policy. Unwilling to antagonize the Soviets, the government squashed the Hungarian trade union federation's attempt to establish contact with Solidarity. Both the higher state authorities and the Hungarian media fully approved the proclamation of martial law in Poland, but with less stridency than those of other bloc states.

While Hungary maintained a low profile in 1981, the German Democratic Republic (GDR) and its spearhead, the Socialist Unity Party (SED), projected an image of dynamism and self-assertion both within the Soviet bloc and outside it. SED General Secretary Erich Honecker was the best known communist leader in Eastern Europe. Some Western commentators considered that the GDR had become "a principal surrogate [of the Soviet Union]. The Russians hope to make use of [its] appeal to German nationalism, its growing industrial prowess, and its international role as a trading partner." (*Business Week*, 12 October.) In the field of intra-German affairs, the GDR was anxious to maintain intensive and beneficial trade relations with the FRG. At the same time, it persisted in its drive to be recognized by West Germany as a foreign country. A massive cultural campaign launched during the summer aimed at a reappraisal of Prussia, with the goal of presenting the GDR as a socialist state and the true Germany in contrast to a flabby, cosmopolitan, demoralized FRG searching for an identity of its own. While retaining the system of full economic planning, the GDR was the only country in the Soviet bloc that did not lower economic growth targets for the 1981–1985 period. Despite high foreign indebtedness (around $10.3 billion), it engaged heavily in international trade (Mexico, Canada, and Japan), leading some Western experts to see a danger in further economic expansion (*Wall Street Journal*, 11 December). The GDR actively promoted the Soviet peace offensive in the FRG and contributed to the complications in Bonn-Washington relations. Honecker tried to exploit his mid-December visit with the chancellor of the FRG, Helmut Schmidt, by asserting in press conferences well covered by the Western media that "there cannot be anything more important in the world than maintaining peace." He criticized U.S. policies ("the world does not need long-term re-armament programs, neutron weapons decisions or concepts for limited nuclear war") and warned Schmidt that the FRG should not tie its fate to the installation of nuclear weapons on West German territory. (*NYT*, 13 December; *WP*, 13 December.) At the same time, the GDR continued, alongside the USSR and Cuba, to pursue an active policy in Africa and the Middle East, especially in South Yemen, where its experts, including military and police advisers, played important roles (see John M. Starrels, *East Germany: Marxist Mission in Africa*, 1981). Developments in Poland were uppermost in the minds of East German leaders in 1981. In a stern article, the SED's theoretical journal *Einheit* (May/April) explained why true socialism was incompatible with social pluralism and why the concept of free trade unions was alien to Marxism-Leninism. Solidarity was a constant object of attacks, as was the weakness of the PUWP's leadership. The SED fully approved the threatening 5 June letter of the CPSU's Central Committee calling for action against counterrevolution in Poland. Irregular deliveries of Polish coal were an irritant to GDR industry. Units of the GDR's army were regular companions of the Red Army in frequent maneuvers around Poland, which East German media covered in detail. Rumors in the FRG press (see *Der Spiegel*, 2 August) that leaflets in East Berlin asked for liberalization along the lines of Poland and that there were strikes in isolated factories and clashes between workers and police in some cities were dismissed by the official GDR news agency as "deceitful tricks" (*NYT*, 3 August). GDR leaders were very sensitive to Polish developments, especially because millions of East Germans kept well informed about events in Poland by tuning in FRG broadcasts. East German media enthusiastically endorsed the introduction of martial law in Poland and strongly condemned U.S. attitudes. A *Neues Deutschland*'s article (23 December; *FBIS*, 28 December) assured a PUWP regional leader that German Communists would "a thousand times over" stand alongside the Polish people and the PUWP.

The Bulgarian government was sensitive lest economic mishandling lead to situations like those in Poland and Romania. While maintaining a Soviet-like system of centralized planning and fully collectivized agriculture, the Bulgarian government gave workers special incentives for improvements in quality and increases in production and encouraged peasants to develop private plots. There was no shortage of food in the country (*NYT*, 9 November; *Economist*, 21 November). The Bulgarian government also tolerated greater freedom of expression in the cultural area, with displays of avant-garde art in the museums and easy access to Western publications. Lyudmila Zhivkova, the British-educated daughter of durable Bulgarian party leader Todor Zhivkov, died this summer at the age of 39. As

Bulgaria's culture minister, she was credited with the budding Bulgarian "Westernization," certainly unpalatable to the Soviet Union (*NYT*, 11 December). As in the case of Hungary's nonorthodoxy in economic matters, Moscow tolerated Bulgarian cultural liberalization because Todor Zhivkov's foreign policy remained unswervingly pro-Soviet. The celebration of the thirteen hundredth anniversary of the foundation of the Bulgarian state was the main public event of the year. Ceremonies and meetings were held frequently throughout the entire country. A strong sense of Bulgarian nationalism was systematically fostered during these functions. Relations with Yugoslavia were outwardly friendly, but quarrels about Macedonia remained acerbic as in the past. As in other Eastern European countries, official reaction to the introduction of martial law in Poland was uniformly positive.

Albania remained politically isolated and ideologically intransigent. It is the only country in Eastern Europe whose party (at its congress in early November) has attacked private plots as capitalist and therefore prohibited. The rebellion of ethnic Albanians in early spring in Kosovo, an autonomous province of the Republic of Serbia, received full support in Tirana and led to tensions between Albania and Yugoslavia. Addressing the congress, Enver Hoxha urged Yugoslavia to elevate Kosovo's status to that of a constituent republic and denied that Albania was making territorial claims on the troubled province. Hoxha charged that Yugoslavia had set up a "reign of terror" in Kosovo and that "jails are packed with young men and women ... Instead of being reasonable, the Serbian and Yugoslav chiefs sent in tanks and shed people's blood" (AP, Vienna, 1 November). A mystery enveloped the suicide on 17 December of Albanian Prime Minister Mehmet Shehu, long considered Hoxha's closest political friend and his heir apparent. According to the official version, Shehu committed suicide "in a moment of nervous distress." The other, and apparently more plausible, version is that Shehu was killed or forced to kill himself following a dispute over future policy at a meeting of the Albanian Central Committee. At stake was the problem of opening Albania to the outside world, a position that Shehu allegedly advocated, while Hoxha opposed it. (*NIN*, 3 January 1982; *NYT*, 3 January 1982; Reuters, Vienna, 20 January 1982.)

Nonaligned Yugoslavia had, after Poland, the most internal troubles in 1981. The rioting in Kosovo shook both the party and government and ordinary citizens. It was the most serious internal crisis since the Communists seized power after the war, as well as a blow to one of the basic tenets of Titoism: *bratstvo-jedinstvo* ("fraternity-unity") among all nationalities of Yugoslavia. Collective leaders of both the State Presidency and the Presidium of the Central Committee of the League of Communists of Yugoslavia (LCY), who have so far succeeded in maintaining their political homogeneity, refused to grant to Kosovo the status of a republic. They argued that this would encourage nationalist tendencies elsewhere and lead to a disintegration of Yugoslavia. The leaders disagreed, however, among themselves how to pacify Kosovo, which was still simmering with dissatisfaction at the end of 1981.

The LCY, with over two million members, was shaken by a sharp conflict between two tendencies: techno-burocrats (as their enemies called them) favoring political recentralization and a strictly business-like management of enterprises, and partisans of the genuine concept and practice of workers' self-management (as they called themselves), which although a basic law of the land was still far from being implemented. This conflict went to the heart of the Yugoslav dilemma: Should the six republics and the two autonomous provinces behave as quasi-sovereign states dedicated to local interests (a tendency strengthened in 1981) or as cooperative, equal units of a healthy, federalist, socialist community? A leading Serbian Marxist theoretician diagnosed the basic problem in these terms: "[The deep world crisis] affects the most sensitive fabric of our society, the unity of the country, its commonality. Tendencies pulling in the direction of disunity and disintegration are gaining broad and dangerous dimensions" (*NIN*, 10 January 1982).

The process of de-Titoization became perceptible in 1981. Formally, Tito was still venerated in the media, and crowds filed past his tomb in Belgrade. But some of the highest LCY leaders hinted in speeches and interviews that some of the worst problems of the country had their origins under Tito and that they were less and less willing to be the scapegoat for current popular dissatisfaction.

Cultural pluralization was an undisputable fact of life in 1981—tolerated as long as it did not assume a politically oppositional character. Intellectuals and simple citizens accused of subversive activities against the state and of contacts with the "fascist" emigration encountered stiff repression. A sudden deterioration took place in relations between the state and the major religious denominations—especially the Catholic church in Croatia. "Clerico-nationalism," a new term used by the highest LCY functionaries to assail militant and basically antistate activities, allegedly exists in all churches.

Economic performance was highly unsatisfactory. The rate of inflation was 43 percent; foreign indebtedness reached $21.2 billion; imports far exceeded exports; labor productivity reached only 33 percent of that in other middle to highly developed countries; the overall situation in agriculture was negative, necessitating imports of cereal grains; the rate of unemployment was 14 percent; and real personal income of the employed fell 7 percent. There were compensatory factors, however, including income from tourism and remittances from workers abroad, as well as a widespread "underground" economy. "If the Yugoslavs are not rebelling—like the Poles—it is because many can draw on savings made in the previous decade of ever-increasing income" (CSM, 28 December). The highest state functionaries in charge of the economy often sounded like irate opposition leaders.

Relations with the Soviet Union were outwardly cordial and economically significant. Unable to compete on Western markets, Yugoslavs found eager importers among CMEA members, especially the USSR. The Yugoslav-Soviet trade agreement for 1981–1985 called for an 80 percent growth over the previous five-year plan. Yugoslavia also obtained a large credit for the purchase of Soviet goods. The Yugoslav federal secretary for foreign trade declared in June that Yugoslavia does not have such developed economic relations with any other country of the world—a fact that worried experts in the West lest such economic closeness lead to political dependency. Events in Poland were followed with utmost interest in Yugoslavia. The LCY was never sympathetic to Solidarity and hoped that a rejuvenated PUWP would find valid socialist solutions for a socialist Poland. A Soviet invasion was dreaded. Top party leaders received the imposition of martial law and the unprecedented assumption of supreme power by a general (even if an old party member) with mixed emotions. One of them vented his apprehension in public. Some Yugoslav generals felt differently. They let Yugoslav politicians know that they were not satisfied with the handling of the Kosovo question.

Hoover Institution   Milorad M. Drachkovitch

Albania

The Albanian Communist Party was established on 8 November 1941 in Tirana on the initiative of Josip Broz Tito and the Comintern. Two Yugoslav emissaries, Miladin Popović and Dušan Mugoša, acting on instructions of the Central Committee of the Yugoslav Communist Party, managed to unite the three existing factions of Albanian Communists under a centralized organization and a provisional leadership headed by Enver Hoxha as provisional secretary. The First Congress of the party (1 November 1948) changed the organization's name to Albanian Party of Labor (Partia e Punës e Shqipërisë; APL) and purged its ranks of "Titoist-revisionist" elements.

Party members continue to hold all key governmental, military, security, and mass organization positions. Similarly, they control the leadership and activities of the Democratic Front, the mass organization that fields candidates for the National Assembly and to which all eligible voters (except those convicted and imprisoned for political crimes) must belong as a patriotic duty. The APL's pre-eminence was formally established by the 1976 Albanian constitution, which declared it the sole leading political force.

Ideologically the APL remains isolated from the major groupings of ruling communist parties. Since the Sino-Albanian break in 1978, it has fancied itself the "leading center" of the "true Marxist-Leninist" movement and has expanded its links with splinter groups in Europe and the Third World, including known terrorist groups. Twenty-four "Marxist-Leninist" parties were invited to participate in the Eighth APL Congress (1–8 November 1981) (*Zëri i Popullit*, 9 November). Among the traditional parties, only the Vietnamese Communist Party was invited. It was represented by Central Committee Secretary Song Hao, who used the opportunity to attack "hegemonists" (ibid., 4 November).

At the congress it was announced that the party had 122,000 members and 24,363 candidate members. The membership of the APL has remained almost constant in relation to the population. Only 4.5 percent of the Albanian people belong to the party, a mere 0.3 percent increase over the membership in 1976. The social composition of the APL has changed slightly since 1976. Nearly 38 percent of the members are classified as workers; 29.4 percent as cooperativists (peasants), and 32.6 percent as office workers. Women make up 30 percent of the party membership. The composition of the candidate members shows higher percentages of workers (42.40 percent) and cooperativists (40.47 percent); only 17.7 percent are classified as office workers. Women constitute 40.47 percent of the total number of candidate members. (Enver Hoxha, *Report Submitted to the 8th Congress of the Party of Labour of Albania,* Tirana, 1981, p. 84.)

The new emphasis on workers, women, and peasants indicates the steps taken by the party to counter what has been called a "problem of excessive party bureaucratization." In his report to the congress, Hoxha explained the new orientation of party membership as reflective of a need to bring into the party people "from the sphere of production, especially the main fronts." (*Zëri i Popullit*, 8 November.)

According to the most recent statistics, the population of Albania in mid-1981 stood at 2,761,000 (*Ylli*, May, p. 4). This figure reflects an annual growth rate of 2.3 percent or approximately three to four times higher than the growth rate of other European countries. Current projections are that the population of Albania will reach 3,340,000 by 1990. The average age of the Albanian population is 25.7 years, making it the youngest in Europe. Despite party emphasis on industrialization and mechanization of agricultural production, the majority of Albanians still live in rural areas (66.5 percent). The past two decades have witnessed only a minor increase in urban population.

Leadership and Organization. Several significant changes were introduced in the APL at the congress. Most were predictable since throughout the year there had been criticism of the lack of enthusiasm among party members and cadres and their frequent refusal to assume duties in the countryside and production (*Zëri i Popullit*, 8 November). High-ranking APL members often complained of excessive bureaucratization (see *Rruga e Partisë*, February, pp. 77–87).

The changes introduced at the congress involved all high organs of the party. First, the Central Committee, which was increased from 79 to 81 full members, has 17 new faces. Among the 39 alternate members of the Central Committee, 22 are new (*Zëri i Popullit*, 8 November.)

The Politburo, too, added several new faces. The highest policymaking body now consists of thirteen full members (as compared with twelve in 1976) and five alternates. The additions in the Politburo are two former candidate members—Lenka Çuko, the only woman in the highest party body, and Simon Stefani—former Central Committee member Muho Asllani, and district party worker Hajredin Çeliku.

Dropped from membership in the Politburo were two party stalwarts, Spiro Koleka and Haki Toska. Pilo Peristeri lost his position as a Politburo candidate member, but retains his job as chairman of the Central Control and Auditing Commission. However, Peristeri was given two vice-chairmen for the latter job, Gaqo Nesho (first secretary of the Tirana APL district), who was also elevated to full Central Committee membership, and Mihal Bisha, a newcomer to high party organs.

Enver Hoxha sought to explain the changes as "nonpolitical" in nature. In his concluding remarks to the congress, he offered three criteria to justify the recomposition of the party leadership: first, the need to "rejuvenate" the party; second, the need to facilitate a graceful exit for those who, for health or age reasons, can no longer carry out their duties; and third, the need to remove those who "despite the assistance given them by the party in their work and struggle, have not justified themselves as members of the leadership" (ibid.). The recomposition of the Central Committee lowered its median age to 49 years (compared with 51 in 1976). The percentage of Central Committee members who hold higher degrees from state and party institutions increased to 32 percent of the total.

Obviously, the big losers were Koleka and Peristeri, both of whom had been considered close Hoxha confidants. Koleka retains his position as deputy chairman of the Council of Ministers. Perhaps both of them were replaced for age or health reasons, but neither was known for bad health. Toska, however, was known to be in good health. Prokop Murra, former deputy chairman of the State Planning Commission and minister of energy, was dropped from the Secretariat, reducing its membership to four. Murra was appointed a candidate member of the Politburo.

The chief beneficiary seems to be Simon Stefani, one of the younger members of the Politburo. Stefani was born in the village of Liari (Gjirokastër) in 1920 and has been a protégé of Hoxha, who also comes from the same region. He has been a member of parliament since 1962 and a regular contributor of theoretical articles to both *Zëri i Popullit* and the *Rruga e Partisë*. In 1976, he was elected a full member of the Central Committee and as an alternate member of the Politburo. Elevated to full Politburo membership at the congress, he joins Enver Hoxha (first secretary), Ramiz

Alia, and Hekuran Isai in the Secretariat. Although Stefani is younger than both Hoxha and Prime Minister Mehmet Shehu, he is old enough to have participated in the resistance, making him a member of the revolutionary guard, which has ruled Albania since the end of the war.

Lenka Çuko, party secretary of the Lushnje district and alternate member of the Politburo, was also elevated to full membership in the Politburo. Although she is prominently mentioned in the party-controlled press, it is highly unlikely that she will play a significant role in the party.

Auxiliary and Mass Organizations. All mass organizations and trade unions have been absorbed with the party's demands for increased productivity and the introduction of "socialist discipline" in all ranks of Albanian society. The Central Council of the United Trade Unions of Albania (UTUA) convened a special meeting on 23 April to discuss and analyze the activities of the largest labor organization and to "take measures" to assure the success of the Seventh Five-Year Plan. Apparently, there is serious dissatisfaction with the work of UTUA and the inability of its leadership to "mobilize" the masses. Rita Marko, who spoke at the special meeting, underscored the need for higher productivity and "honest work." (Ibid., 28 April.) However, more serious criticism for the lack of mass motivation was expressed by UTUA Secretary General Idriz Dhrami, who gave the keynote speech at the meeting.

One area of increased trade union activity was foreign contacts. UTUA delegations visited Canada and West Germany to augment their knowledge of the work of similar organizations. In both instances the invitation came from splinter Marxist groups. Similarly, several foreign delegations visited Tirana and were hosted by party officials and Rita Marko. (Ibid., 9 and 15 January, 2 May.)

Some UTUA member-associations were singled out for thorough examination and criticism of their work. Qirjako Mihali and Simon Stefani were critical of the work of construction unions and the lack of zeal on the part of grass-root party organizations in that field (ibid., 2 January; *Rruga e Partisë*, February, pp. 77–87).

The Seventh Five-Year Plan has been uppermost in the concerns of the Central Committee of the Union of Albania Labor Youth (UALY). A Central Committee plenum on 20 June heard Etemije Zenela, a high official of UALY, criticize the inadequate performance of youth organizations in persuading their members to "work where the party wants them to" (*Zëri i Popullit*, 21 June). This was in reference to recurring complaints that Albanian young people are reluctant to return to the countryside or to perform manual tasks in the cities. Like similar mass organizations, the UALY entered the intense national debate over the events in Kosovo. In a major editorial on 9 August, *Zëri i Rinisë* (Voice of youth) demanded an "end to the oppression" of Albanian youth in Kosovo and offered its full support.

The Albanian Writers' Union and its chairman, Dritero Argoli, were active during the entire year, first in promoting cultural cooperation between Albania and Kosovo and after the Kosovo events, in defending the Albanian position vis-à-vis Yugoslavia (which after considerable analysis of Albanian-Yugoslav cultural links abrogated several agreements as one-sided). Argoli defended the "mutual benefit" of such agreements and attacked "big-Serb" cultural chauvinism (ibid., 7 June).

On numerous occasions, the APL expressed displeasure over the inadequate work done by cadres in various spheres of activity. Among other criticisms aimed at them were inadequate supervision of industrial projects and corruption. In a rather revealing article, *Rruga e Partisë* (April) criticized the practice of "cheating" with statistics and "registering more work than actually has been done." Problems with mass organizations and cadres were the subject of several articles in *Zëri i Popullit*. Among other matters, the party organ implored cadres in factories and on farms to be vigilant against inadequate "control over the controllers" (*Zëri i Popullit*, 16 and 20 May).

Internal Party Affairs. The APL Central Committee occupied itself with the deteriorating economic situation in the country and sought to place some of the blame on inadequate leadership and lack of proletarian spirit among cadres and the mass organizations. Several major editorials in *Zëri i Popullit* zeroed in on the UALY and district party organizations. The absence of proletarian discipline among workers in general was noted in similar articles. Finally, the shortcomings of party cadres were pointed out on several occasions. (See ibid., 5 July.)

The ninth plenum of the Central Committee (15–16 June) discussed problems with the work of cadres. During the same session, it approved rather ambitious draft directives for the Seventh Five-Year Plan "for the promotion of the economy and culture of Albania for the 1981–1985 period" (ibid., 17 July).

The draft directives, presented by Petro Dode, chairman of the State Planning Commission, sought to overcome the failure of the previous five-year plan. The Seventh Five-Year Plan, the first to be undertaken without foreign assistance, projects a growth in collective productivity of 22–24 percent over 1980 and a 34–36 percent growth in overall industrial production. Investment for the five-year period is to grow by 23–25 percent over 1980, while state receipts from all sources are expected to increase by 34–36 percent. (Ibid.)

It is apparent from the activities of the Central Committee that the APL still aspires to be the "center of true Marxism-Leninism." Numerous delegations of splinter parties from all parts of the world were invited to Albania during 1981, including delegations from West Germany, Iran, and New Zealand. Similarly, the APL dispatched delegations to meetings of splinter parties, such as the Third Annual Conference of the Portuguese Communist Party, Reconstituted. Twenty-four Marxist-Leninist parties (that is, those who do not follow either Moscow or Beijing) were invited to the Eighth Congress (ibid., 9 November).

The wives of both Shehu and Hoxha were quite active in party affairs during 1981. Nexhmije Hoxha was awarded the Order of Socialist Labor by the Politburo on her sixtieth birthday, and Fiqret Shehu continued to direct the Party School, which this year graduated 652 party cadres (ibid., 9 February, 14 July).

Enver Hoxha maintained a low profile throughout the year and spent most of his time writing his memoirs (volumes 32–34 were published) and attending cultural events (ibid., 3 October). He missed the celebration of the founding of the People's Republic of Albania, but was present and received the salute of the participants during the May Day parade, in which several foreign delegations were present (ibid., 2 May). Mehmet Shehu, on the other hand, was quite active in receiving foreign visitors, thus dispelling rumors of poor health and reduced power (*Baltimore Sun*, 16 December 1980). The prime minister, who during 1980 had been relieved of his duties as minister of defense, also commenced the writing of his memoirs. The first volume, dealing with the 1942–1944 period came off the press, with the imprimatur of the Central Committee (*Zëri i Popullit*, 21 May).

Although Shehu appeared to be emerging as the "elder statesman" and Hoxha's successor, available documentation suggests that he was under conflicting pressures throughout the year, and his suicide on 18 December remained a mystery. His problems increased following the Eighth APL Congress, with the removal from the Politburo of Spiro Koleka and the demotion of Pilo Peristery, his two key supporters. His death remained mysterious because of the existence of two mutually exclusive versions. On 19 December, the Albanian press agency quoted a joint party and government statement saying that Shehu committed suicide "at a moment of nervous breakdown." This was followed by a brief obituary. (Reuters, 19 December; *NYT*, 2 January 1982.) The second version, stemming from Belgrade and some Western sources, affirmed that Shehu had been killed or forced to kill himself following a stormy all-night session of the Central Committee after a dispute with Enver Hoxha. The subject of the dispute was the opening of Albania to the outside world, with Shehu defending such a course and Hoxha opposing it. Several arguments were invoked in support of the thesis that Shehu was the victim of a fierce settlement of accounts. A few days before his death, Shehu had met with high Greek and Romanian officials who saw nothing abnormal in the Albanian prime minister's behavior; his obituary was extremely short and dry, and no state funeral and national mourning were declared for him. This was in marked contrast to the ceremonies following the death in 1979 of Hysni Kapo, one of Albania's ruling triumvirate, who was given a state funeral and buried in the Martyrs' Cemetery in the center of Tirana. In a vehement statement, Albanian diplomats in Vienna denied that the Central Committee had met on the night Shehu committed suicide. No national mourning was extended to him because the party considered the suicide a disgraceful act. Finally, Shehu had allegedly been seriously ill for a long time, and the nervous breakdown could have been the result of his illness. (*NIN*, 3 January 1982; *NYT*, 3 January 1982; Reuters, Vienna, 17 January 1982.) A rumor that Shehu had wounded Hoxha was dispelled when Hoxha appeared before parliament in Tirana on 14 January 1982 to vote for the election of Shehu's successor as prime minister, Adil Carcany. Carcany's first move was to dismiss four ministers considered to be Shehu's political protégés. (AP, 14 January 1982.) All this suggests that another major purge of higher party bodies was under way at the beginning of 1982.

Following long-established procedure, all district party organizations held regional congresses to elect executive organs in preparation for the congress. With the exception of the chief of the Gramsh region, all regional first secretaries were re-elected (*Zëri i Popullit*, 24 September). However, there appeared to be problems with party organizations in the armed forces. This was reflected in, among other ways, several rather cryptic news items in the party-controlled press. According to one such item, "some important problems confronting [a unit's] party organization, as well as their instruments" were exposed (*FBIS*, 21 September). Petro Dode, a Central Committee member and chairman of the State Planning Commission, also alluded to problems within the armed forces in a speech commemorating the founding of the Albanian Army (*Zëri i Popullit*, 11 July).

Domestic and Political Developments. As in 1980, several changes were made in the composition of the cabinet and central and regional party organs. Ostensibly, most of these changes were necessitated by the poor performance of industry and agriculture and the determination of the Hoxha regime to place the entire economy on an independent, totally self-reliant footing.

The Ministry of Industry and Mining was split into two entities, creating a separate Ministry of Energy. Prokop Murra was named minister of engergy and Llambi Gjegprifti took over the truncated Ministry of Industry and Mining. These changes, which were announced by Simon Stefani at the sixth session of the Ninth Legislature, aimed at spurring greater productivity in the industrial sector, but they also had a political dimension. Obviously, Murra was the loser, while Gjegprifti, a younger party leader, assumed greater responsibility in the government. The Ministry of Agriculture, too, came under criticism for lagging productivity, and new directives aimed at curbing the emergence of petit-bourgeois attitudes in the countryside were issued (ibid., 28 March).

The sixth session was called into session on 26 March with a rather routine agenda. It dealt with the "report of the Council of Ministers on the fulfillment of the 1980 plan"; approved a bill for economic and cultural development for fiscal 1981; received and approved the 1981 budget; reorganized the office of prosecutor general, adding more powers to it; ratified decrees issued by the Presidium of the People's Assembly; and introduced several reforms in the penal code and a new bill for pardoning of offenses (ibid., 27 March).

The state budget foresees income of 7.75 billion leks (5 leks equals U.S. $1) and expenditures of 7.48 billion leks, leaving a 27 million lek surplus (*Gazeta Zyrtare e RSPSH*, no. 2, p. 27). The defense portion of the budget is set at 940 million leks. The budget for the 26 provinces is set at 2.75 billion leks, with Tirana receiving the largest share.

In a report to the assembly, Dode confirmed earlier information that several sectors of the economy, including agriculture, foreign trade, and the tool industry had fallen short of the goals and that "assurances had been taken" to correct shortcomings. Among such measures were the creation of the Ministry of Energy and unspecified instructions to the Ministry of Agriculture. (*Zëri i Popullit*, 27 March.)

The Economy. As in 1980, the economy continues to suffer the consequences of insufficient trained personnel to run the industrial complexes and a chronic shortage of machinery and spare parts. Dode pointed to these and similar problems in his report and budget proposals to the National Assembly on 27 March. He assured the deputies that "specific measures" were being taken to overcome shortcomings in the work of several ministries and to "guarantee the success" of the Seventh Five-Year Plan. Yet it appears that the problems are too complex to be resolved by "special measures." Dode singled out several key ministries for "deficiencies," including Agriculture, Communal Property, Internal Trade, Foreign Trade, and Industry and Mining. (Ibid.)

Dode outlined three "basic problems" affecting the economy and promised an intensified campaign to "correct them": first, he confirmed that there was a low level of appreciation of "scientific methods of management"—that is, a shortgage of skilled personnel to run major industrial units. Second, he noted the emergence of "petit-bourgeois and bureaucratic manifestations" throughout the economy, which required "new measures" to correct. Finally, there was a lack of emphasis on quality, which explains the difficulties faced by the Ministry of Foreign Trade in meeting export goals. (Ibid.)

The emergence of petit-bourgeois attitudes was the target of criticism by party organs. Hoxha brought it to the attention of the congress as a "serious problem." In his report, Hoxha implored his colleagues to emphasize "true socialism" and scientific management of the economy. (Hoxha, *Report*, pp. 59–66.) He also underlined the "need" to further restrict "private plots" in order to "strengthen the organization and management of production" (ibid., p. 17).

The "private plot" and the "contradictions that it presents" for an orthodox Stalinist economy were the subject of criticism for several months prior to the congress. *Rruga e Partisë* (February) decried petit-bourgeois tendencies among the inhabitants of several Greek-occupied areas in the Gjirokastër region, described as "incorrect attitudes toward work and communal property, fed by feelings of private ownership and narrow personal interests."

Party bureaucrats also attacked private ownership of livestock. Dode and Hoxha demanded that in the interest of corporative spirit, the small number of privately owned household animals must be herded together (*Zëri i Popullit*, 27 March, 22 September).

Suggesting corruption in production, *Rruga e Partisë* (April) alluded to the practice of "registering more work than actually done." Similarly, a signed article in *Zëri i Popullit* (16 May) strongly implied deficiencies in controlling quality and quantity.

Social and Cultural Developments. The regime's efforts to uproot outmoded customs and practices continued without much evidence that it has attained its goal of creating the new socialist man. "Harmful practices" are obvious in "attitudes toward work and property" (Hoxha, *Report*, p. 127). The inability of the party and mass organizations to change regressive attitudes is attributed to inadequate work by cadres and district party organizations, some members of "whom also fall prey to old traditions" (*Rruga e Partisë*, February, p. 78). The problems created by the persistence of old beliefs and foreign ideas were seen as responsible for the lack of appreciation among youth for "scientific work" and for the low level of knowledge of the meaning of laws and the functions of state organs (*Bashkimi*, 20 May). The family, too, remains far from being socialist. Conservativism continues to find expression in arranged marriages, in failures to respect the principle of complete equality within the family, and "in camouflaged forms of buying and selling brides" (*Shqipëria e Re*, June, pp. 8–9).

Although no specific statistics were given, "bride transactions" appear quite common among the Gheg population of northern Albania.

The persistence of old or alien customs apparently has affected the Albanian military as well. According to party critics, "foreign military concepts" have found their way into Albanian military doctrine. A basic problem in the military has been the emergence of elitism "where cadres remain apart from the masses of soldiers and do not hear their voices as they should" (*Rruga e Partisë*, July, p. 58). Even more disappointing to the party and state is the pervasiveness of the feeling of "private ownership," which, in their view, remains a serious contradiction in a socialist economy. Some of the blame for such manifestations was placed on the "deep-rooted" feelings of the Albanian people toward "ownership"; most of it is, however, attributed to the infiltration of foreign ideas and concepts. Postulating a direct link between the "private plot" and social development, Professor Hekuran Mara foresees efforts to "gradually limit it with the aim of eventually achieving its complete removal" (*Zëri i Popullit*, 17 March).

Foreign Policy. During 1981, the People's Socialist Republic of Albania established diplomatic relations with Malaysia, thus increasing the total number of countries with which it maintains relations to 95. Agreements for trade and economic relations with 55 countries are also in effect.

With the exception of Yugoslavia, with which relations have deteriorated to the level of polemics, Albanian foreign policy continued the course set in the 1970s of strictly separating formal relations from any meaningful opening of the borders to foreign culture, ideas, or persons. Albanian spokesmen, however, continued their more or less intellectual exercise of presenting Albania as a full participant in the world community, which insists on maintaining its independence from major blocs and avoiding dependence on foreign sources for economic and cultural development.

At the APL congress, Hoxha and Shehu gave some indications of Albanian flexibility concerning relations with Great Britain and West Germany. Hoxha pointed to a single issue that has prevented resumption of formal relations with Great Britain, broken since 1946; namely, its refusal to return to Tirana the Albanian gold ("plus interest"), taken at the end of World War II. As for West Germany, Hoxha simply declared that "there are no insurmountable difficulties to the establishment of diplomatic relations" and "with understanding by both parties over certain questions, this can be achieved." (Hoxha, *Report*, p. 220.)

Tirana excluded the possibility of improvement of relations with either of the two superpowers or with Israel and "racist regimes" in Africa, but reaffirmed its interest in further improvement of "formal relations" with East and West European countries.

Albania continued to offer its support to the Afghan people fighting against Soviet social imperialism and saw the Iranian revolution as essentially "anti-imperialist." The Afghanistan invasion, in particular, received wide press coverage. The Iran-Iraqi war is still interpreted as the result of Western imperialist machinations—to justify expansion of U.S. military presence in the Persian Gulf. (*Zëri i Popullit*, 20 and 28 June, 5 August.)

Numerous delegations from Third World and European countries visited Tirana as official guests of the Albanian state and party in 1981. By and large, they represented splinter Marxist groups and known pro-Albanian individuals. Delegations from West Germany (1 May), Algeria (1 May), Iran (16 February), Denmark (28 June), and Turkey (26 June) visited Tirana and other Albanian cities.

Albanian-Yugoslav Relations. Relations between Tirana and Belgrade started off quite promising at the beginning of 1981. Commercial and cultural agreements were signed in Tirana between delegations from the Yugoslav district of Kosovo and the Albanian government (ibid., 27 February). The chairman of the Kosovo Executive Council, Riza Sapundzhia, visited Tirana and was welcomed by

Petro Dode, and a delegation of the Kosovo Academy of Sciences was hosted by the Tirana Academy of Science (ibid., 3 February; *Rilindja*, 2 February).

Characteristic of Albanian-Yugoslav relations was Tirana's emphasis on cultivating closer bonds between Albanians in Kosovo and Albania proper, thus feeding an always present Albanian nationalism within the Yugoslav federation.

Following an uprising of students and workers in April in Priština and other Albanian-dominated cities in Kosovo, the Tirana regime reversed its policy of cautious cooperation with Belgrade, which was induced by its fear of the Soviets, and commenced a campaign of anti-Serbianism. Tirana's initial reaction to the events in Kosovo was simply to "report" them either directly or through quotations from the "world press" (*Zëri i Popullit*, 3 March). However, the official neutrality was broken on 8 April, when *Zëri i Popullit* published a major editorial entitled "Why Were Police Violence and Tanks Used Against the Albanians in Kosovo?" Claiming exploitation of the Albanians in Kosovo by Great Serbian chauvinists, *Zëri i Popullit* demanded a "solution to be found in the deeper causes of the unrest" rather than with force or by blaming it on external forces. This was followed by a second editorial on 23 April, which accused Yugoslavia of deliberate genocide against Albanians in Kosovo and of a policy of expelling them from their place of birth. Citing Albanians forced to emigrate to Turkey, the party organ accused Yugoslavia of double standards in its treatment of national groups. Finally, a third editorial on 17 May reiterated Tirana's accusations against Belgrade and demanded republic status for the Kosovo area.

Complicating matters further were two additional elements. On 23 May, two bombs exploded on the terrace of the Yugoslav Embassy in Tirana. The Albanian police report strongly implied that the devices had been planted by embassy personnel (ibid., 3 and 15 June). The Yugoslav government protested the incident, both in Tirana and Belgrade. In both instances, Tirana rejected the protests. Second, on 6 June, the respected Athens daily *Kathimerini* published a map (it was traced to Albanian émigrés) that showed the Epirus region of Greece and Kosovo as parts of a Greater Albania. In addition, the paper quoted Albanian sources that confirmed the claims indicated on the map. Both the article and the map were reprinted in the Yugoslav press, escalating the conflict and dragging Greece into it. Subsequently, the Greek parliament debated the issue of the Greek minority in Albania, which according to one deputy, "suffers far and beyond what the Albanians in Yugoslavia suffer" (*Ellinikos Voras*, Salonika, 8 June).

On 15–16 June, the ninth plenum of the APL Central Committee took up the issue of Kosovo and demanded "republic status" for the province. At the APL congress, Hoxha reiterated the same demand, declaring that Albania has no territorial claims on any of its neighbors. At the same time, he decried Belgrade's decision to abrogate its cultural treaties with Tirana. Apparently, the suspension cut off the one-way flow of literature reaching Kosovo. To compensate, the Tirana regime established a radio and television station close to the Yugoslav border and began beaming propaganda and news to its compatriots across the borders (*Zëri i Popullit*, 10 June, 1 July). In the course of anti-Yugoslav polemics, the Hoxha regime brought into the picture Soviet social imperialism, whose hand it sees behind Great Serbian chauvinism. Finally, Hoxha and Shehu (who was suspected to be the author of the 17 May editorial) revealed that in 1946 Tito had promised to return Kosovo to Albania. Hoxha repeated this "historical" revelation at the Eighth Congress (Hoxha, *Report*, p. 208).

While its relations with Yugoslavia deteriorated, Tirana sought to improve relations with Athens. Several editorial comments praised the "warm relations" between the two countries, and Hoxha declared in his report to the congress that "no one will be able to disturb them" (ibid., p. 216). Yet the Greek press continues to publish extensive accounts of conditions in Albanian prisons and the proportionately large number of Greek prisoners. Finally, the synod of Greek bishops unanimously passed a resolution at its October meeting denouncing the continuous persecution of people for religious reasons, long after the official abolition of the church in 1967 (*Estia*, Athens, 23 October).

Albanian-Polish Relations. The Albanian press gave extensive coverage to events in Poland, but continued to maintain the line enunciated a year earlier; namely, that Poland's problems result from the "revisionist policy followed by its party" and several other factors, including the Vatican, the Polish church, Western imperialism, and the absence of any "organized political force" in the country to deal with its pressing problems (*Zëri i Popullit*, 13 February; Hoxha, *Report*, pp. 185–86). The way out of the impasse, in the view of APL leaders, is for "the working class to find its Leninist way" and to topple the Polish regime. However, although the Albanians decried the state of affairs in Poland, they expressed serious concern over its implications. The fear of Soviet intervention was apparent in the Albanian press, and on numerous occasions Tirana denounced military maneuvers around Poland and Warsaw Pact Commander in Chief and Soviet Marshal Viktor Kulikov's "tightening of the screws" on other satellites. Similarly, the Soviet Central Committee's letter to its Polish counterpart was denounced as arrogant and typical of "Soviet social imperialists" (*FBIS*, 15 June).

Albanian-Chinese Relations. China and Albania maintain diplomatic relations, but all economic ties between the two countries have ended. The Hoxha regime holds the Chinese fully responsible for the failure of Albania's Sixth Five-Year Plan and for the so-called blockade against socialist Albania "imposed by revisionists, imperialists, and social imperialists." In his speech to the National Assembly, Petro Dode called Chinese behavior toward his country "treacherous" and harmful to the socialist cause (*Zëri i Popullit*, 27 March).

The Albanian press kept a close watch on U.S.-Chinese relations and as usual condemned the post-Mao leadership for leading China to capitalism (ibid., 18 June). The trial of the Gang of Four received attention in the Albanian press, and in one instance it was described as "not a trial of the living, but of the dead" (ibid., 3 February). *Zëri i Popullit* viewed the post-Mao leadership conflicts in China as the inevitable result of Mao's thought, which is anti-Marxist and "has been and remains the ideology of all groups and factions" (ibid.). Hoxha's denunciation of China's new leadership during his eight-hour speech at the APL congress was equally harsh (Hoxha, *Report*, pp. 248–55). In fact, he branded China an ally of Western imperialism.

Albanian-Soviet Relations. The Albanian position on the Soviet Union remained unchanged throughout the year. Hoxha again denounced the "Soviet revisionists" and "socialist imperialists" for the harm they have caused to the "international communist movement" and priased the "leadership of Stalin" and his contribution to communism (*Zëri i Popullit*, 15 March). The Soviet party congress was throughly criticized in a major *Zëri i Popullit* editorial (28 March), which saw it as an "attempt to develop an ideological justification to enslave the peoples" of Eastern Europe. Soviet policy toward Eastern Europe in general and Poland in particular, as enunciated by Brezhnev in his address to the Soviet congress, was seen by the paper as an ineffective attempt to furnish an ideological basis for the Kremlin's "revisionist policy of the integration and merger of East European countries into the Soviet Empire."

The Soviet invasion of Afghanistan was a recurring theme in the Albanian press, and photographs of Afghan guerrilla fighters were often published in Tirana dailies. Also, the Soviets were described as conspiring with the United States to "undermine the Iranian revolution" in order to divide the area into spheres of influence (ibid., 8 March). Soviet intentions against Poland were a major topic of the Albanian press, even though its view of the Polish leadership does not differ much from that of Soviet media.

Relations with Eastern Europe. Ties with Eastern European countries continued to be based on a pragmatic approach, with no sign of a desire to improve party-to-party relations. In his report to the APL congress, Hoxha reaffirmed that "the profound disagreements" between the APL and the parties of Eastern Europe remain. But while not abandoning the "struggle against modern revisionism" (which includes all East European countries), he said, "we are for normal relations, for trade exchanges on the basis of equality and reciprocal benefits with Romania, Czechoslovakia, Poland, and the German Democratic Republic." (Hoxha, *Report*, p. 220.) Several low-level missions from East European countries visited Tirana to sign trade agreements.

Relations with Western Europe and the United States. Tirana greeted Ronald Reagan's inauguration with virulent anti-American tirades. *Zëri i Popullit* (22 January) decried his policies as evidence of a coming "threat to world peace" and attempts to support counterrevolution in Third World countries. President Reagan's inaugural speech was seen in Tirana as intimating "new Vietnams and new Koreas . . . a criminal path of imposing Pax Americana with tanks, aircraft, and missiles (*FBIS*, 22 January).

The proposed U.S. budget, too, was also seen as a promise of new American militarism. The increased presence of the United States in the Middle East and the Persian Gulf was especially criticized and interpreted as American collusion with Israel against the Arabs. Visits by U.S. senators and congressmen in the area were monitored and reported. In a few words, relations between the United States and Albania remained frozen during the year.

Albanian ties with other Western European powers were "correct" and similar to those it has with some East European countries. The election of Socialist François Miterrand in France was greeted rather warmly by Haxhi Leshi, president of the republic, as was the election of Greek Socialist leader Andreas Papandreou (ibid., 13 May; *Zëri i Popullit*, 19 October). Trade agreements were signed with several Western European countries, and a Swedish firm contracted with Tirana to buy all of Albania's ferrochromium output (*JPRS*, 23 June). Relations with Portugal, Switzerland, Austria, Denmark, Norway, and the Netherlands were praised as "sincere" and beneficial by Hoxha. Furthermore, Albania developed "excellent relations with Turkey," a country with which it shares a "cultural heritage" (Hoxha, *Report*, pp. 218–19).

International Party Contacts. Party contacts were limited almost exclusively to pro-Tirana, splinter Marxist-Leninist groups. Only one "traditional" party was represented at the APL congress, the Vietnamese Communist Party. The remaining foreign delegations were splinter groups from Brazil, West Germany, Spain, Portugal, Ecuador, Canada, Denmark, Iran, France, Japan, Togo, New Zealand, Dominican Republic, India, Britain, Indonesia, Dahomey, Iraq, Sweden, and Chile (*Zëri i Popullit*, 9 November).

Publications. The APL paper, the daily *Zëri i Popullit*, has the largest circulation in Albania. The party's theoretical journal, *Rruga e Partisë*, is published monthly. *Bashkimi*, the daily organ of the Democratic Front, claims a circulation of 45,000 copies. The UALY organ *Zëri i Rinisë* and the UTUA organ *Puna* appear twice weekly. *Laiko Vema*, organ of the Greek minority, is published twice a week in Gjirokastër. Fifty-six national periodicals and newspapers, including trade journals, and thirteen local journals are published in Albania. The official Albanian news agency is the Albanian Telegraphic Agency (ATA).

Howard University   Nikolaos A. Stavrou

Bulgaria

The Bulgarian Communist Party (Bulgarska komunisticheska partiya; BCP) dates its separate existence from 1903 when the Bulgarian Social Democratic Party, founded in 1891, split into "broad" and "narrow" factions. The latter took the name Bulgarian Communist Party and became a charter member of the Comintern in 1919. Outlawed in 1924, the party re-emerged in 1927 as the Workers' Party, changing its name again in 1934 to Bulgarian Workers' Party (Communist). The BCP designation was restored in 1948 after the party was firmly in power. Its best-known leader was Georgi Dimitrov, secretary general of the Comintern from 1935 to 1943 and premier of Bulgaria from 1946 to his death in 1949.

Although the BCP commanded the support of nearly one-fifth of the Bulgarian electorate in the early 1920s, a combination of inept leadership and government repression reduced its membership to about 15,000 by World War II. The party's resistance efforts during the war, although real, were neither extensive nor significant in bringing it to power. On 5 September 1944, the Soviet Union declared war on Bulgaria, and three days later the Red Army entered the country unopposed. During the night of 8–9 September, the communist-inspired Fatherland Front coalition seized power from the week-old, pro-Western government of Konstantin Muraviev. Following the coup d'etat, the BCP employed tactics that included force and violence to consolidate its hold on the country. The trial and execution of opposition leader Nikola Petkov for treason in 1948 marked the end of organized internal resistance to communization. Stalinist purges, including the trial and execution of the party's general secretary, Traycho Kostov, for Titoism in 1949, turned the party into an obedient Soviet tool. Todor Zhivkov, the most durable of Soviet bloc leaders, became the party's first secretary in 1954 and increased his authority during the period of de-Stalinization. Since 1962 he has combined state and party leadership, maintaining a firm hold on power with obvious Soviet backing. Domestically, Zhivkov's regime has seen a significant improvement in the material standard of living and, in recent years, a gradual and limited liberalization of cultural life. Zhivkov's foreign policy has been marked by consistent loyalty to the Soviet Union.

At the opening of the BCP's Twelfth Congress on 31 March, Zhivkov reported that party membership stood at 825,876 (*Otchet na Tsentralniya komitet na BKP pred XII kongres*, Sofia, 1981, p. 113). As of 1 January, the population of Bulgaria was about 8.9 million (BTA, 16 January; *FBIS*, 19 January).

Leadership and Organization. The structure of the BCP is modeled on that of the Communist Party of the Soviet Union (CPSU). As is common in such systems, no clear distinction can be made between state and party leadership. The most powerful body in the country is the BCP Politburo, whose members also hold other leadership positions in the party, state, and important social organizations.

Zhivkov and the Politburo. Nineteen eighty-one was expected to be a banner year for Zhivkov. As he entered his twenty-seventh year as party leader, he appeared confident and in vigorous health. During the year, he presided over a number of events, both symbolic and substantive, that demonstrated his continuing pre-eminence. Yet these events were overshadowed by the sudden, unexpected death of his daughter Lyudmila, so that when he responded to the birthday greetings of well-wishers on 7 September, it was in subdued tones and with a reference to the cruelty of fate.

The Twelfth Congress recreated for Zhivkov the post of secretary general of the Central Committee, a position that had not existed since the death of Georgi Dimitrov in 1949. In elevating Zhivkov from first secretary to secretary general, the congress placed him on the same formal level as the party leaders of Czechoslovakia, the German Democratic Republic, and the Soviet Union. The press and Zhivkov's colleagues, both at the congress and after, referred effusively to his achievements and "personal merits," and the party issued a new biography of him, an album of photographs dealing with his life, and a film biography, *A Man of the People.* He also received the title Hero of the People's Republic of Bulgaria, the Order of Lenin from the USSR, and many other awards from foreign governments. (Radio Free Europe, *Background Report*, 12 May; Radio Free Europe, *Situation Report*, 10 September, item 1.)

On a more substantive level, Zhivkov downgraded the status of Stanko Todorov, one of the few remaining influential party veterans whose career he had not entirely shaped. In the National Assembly session of 16 June, Todorov, who had held the post of chairman of the Council of Ministers since 1971, was not returned to that office, but was relegated to the less significant post of chairman of the National Assembly. It was also reported that his wife, Sonya Bakish, had lost her position as editor of the popular magazine *Zhenata dnes* (Woman today). There were rumors that Todorov's demotion had been opposed by the Soviet Union, and this may have influenced the choice of his successor, Grisha Filipov. A Politburo member since 1974, Filipov was born and raised in the USSR and still speaks Bulgarian with a distinct Russian accent. He has a stronger background in technology and economic administration than Todorov, and this, too, may have been a reason for the change. (Sofia Domestic Service, 16 June: *FBIS*, 17 June; *NYT*, 17 June.)

On 21 July, it was announced that Lyudmila Zhivkova had died following a cerebral hemorrhage suffered the preceding day (BTA, 22 July; *FBIS*, 23 July). She was five days short of her thirty-ninth birthday. Since her appointment to the Politburo in 1979 (see *YICA*, 1980, p. 12, 1981, pp. 224, 227–28, for further biographical information), she had become one of the most powerful people in the country, assuming the direction of nearly all aspects of cultural and educational life. She was generally given credit for giving Bulgarian culture a greater degree of freedom and a more Western orientation, and for bringing younger, innovative people into the higher levels of government. She also emphasized the theme of Bulgarian national consciousness, demonstrated this year in her organization of the thirteen hundredth anniversary celebration and sponsorship of events and exhibitions devoted to Bulgarian history and culture all over the world. There were reports that her nationalism and interest in non-Marxist ideologies had recently led to difficulties in her relationship with Soviet leaders. Because Zhivkov had clearly come to depend heavily upon her and because her death was the first major political event in Bulgaria in over a decade that Zhivkov had not orchestrated, his reaction and the role of Zhivkova's protégés will be closely watched as indicators of Bulgaria's political future.

The Twelfth Congress re-elected the previous Politburo with the exception of Tano Tsolov and Gen. Ivan Mikhailov. Tsolov's retirement was generally expected since he had not been seen in public for two years and had been dropped from various other positions during that time. A member of the Politburo since 1966, he is believed to have suffered a stroke or some other debilitating illness (*YICA*, 1981, p. 224). Mikhailov, while still active, was 84 at the time of the congress and a 27-year veteran on the Politburo. During recent years he seems to have played a largely ceremonial role in politics, devoting himself to the study of traditional Bulgarian folk medicine, a subject that has become something of a craze in the country and on which he has written a book and several articles. (Radio Free Europe, *Background Report*, 12 May.) There had been some speculation that 82-year-old Tsola Dragoycheva might also retire at the Twelfth Congress. However, Dragoycheva's memoirs have been the subject of bitter polemics with the Yugoslavs (see *YICA*, 1980, 16–17, and below), and her retirement might have been interpreted as a concession to Yugoslav criticism. Moreover, she is popularly regarded with some affection. Her three-volume memoir, which dealt with her personal as well as political life, was a genuine best-seller and in 1981 was made into a film, which she narrated. She is a useful symbol of the present leadership's links to the party and national past, a theme that has been heavily emphasized recently, especially in this year of anniversaries.

The Twelfth Congress dropped three candidate Politburo members and added one. The new member is Petur Dyulgerov, the new chairman of the Central Council of Trade Unions. It soon became apparent that the dropping of Todor Stoychev, a candidate member since 1974, was just the first step toward his complete removal from power. Drazha Vulcheva, who had also become a candidate member in 1974, apparently suffered from her poor performance as minister of education, a post that had been turned over to Alexander Fol, one of Zhivkova's associates, at the end of 1979. Finally, the downfall of Krustiu Trichkov, a candidate member since 1966, was clearly associated with his removal as head of the Committee for State and People's Control, which he had led since 1971.

Following the changes made at the Twelfth Congress and the death of Lyudmila Zhivkova, the Politburo now consists of eleven full and three candidate members. The full members, together with their most significant positions are Todor Zhivkov (secretary general of the BCP's Central Committee, chairman of the State Council), Todor Bozhinov (first deputy prime minister), Ognyan Doynov (BCP Central Committee secretary, member of the State Council), Tsola Dragoycheva (member of the State Council, honorary chairman of the Bulgarian-Soviet Friendship Society), Gen. Dobri Dzhurov (minister of national defense), Grisha Filipov (BCP Central Committee secretary, prime minister), Pencho Kubadinski (member of the State Council, chairman of the Fatherland Front), Alexander Lilov (BCP Central Committee secretary, member of the State Council), Petur Mladenov (minister of foreign affairs), Peko Takov (deputy chairman of the State Council, chairman of the Bulgarian Tourist Union), and Stanko Todorov (chairman of the National Assembly). The three candidate members are Petur Dyulgerov, Andrey Lukanov, and Georgi Yordanov. The last two are both deputy prime ministers.

The Central Committee and Secretariat. Of the 166 full members of the BCP Central Committee on the eve of the Twelfth Congress, 147 were re-elected. Fifty new members were elected, 30 of whom were promoted from the ranks of candidate members, bringing the total to 197. There were no surprising demotions in this group. Of the nineteen who were not re-elected, several were considerably advanced in years and probably ready for retirement, and the rest had already suffered demotions in state or party posts. The average age of the full members at the time of the congress was 57.5 years; only 45 were under 50. One hundred twenty-two are known to have higher education. These include 21 with training in law, 25 philosophy-philology, 16 economics, 24 engineering, 8 agronomy, and 15 military. By profession they are overwhelmingly officials in the government (79), party (70), or mass organizations (13). There are only nine workers, one industrial manager, and one agricultural manager. Women, with only eleven members, are strongly underrepresented, as are most of the national minorities (three Jews, one Turk, one Bulgarian Muslim, no Gypsies). Fresh blood was brought into the party leadership at the candidate member level. Here, of the 139 candidate members elected, 97 were new. Less information is available about this group, but it is known that nineteen of them are women, five are Turks, and there are no Jews or Gypsies.

Of the nine Central Committee secretaries on the eve of the Twelfth Congress, only Petur Dyulgerov was not re-elected. Two new ones were added: Vasil Tsanov (age 59), who was promoted from his post as chairman of the National Agroindustrial Union (that is, minister of agriculture), and

Chudomir Alexandrov (45), the fast-rising first secretary of the Sofia city party committee (see ibid., 1981, p. 224). The eight re-elected secretaries include Politburo members Lilov, Filipov, and Doynov and Dimitur Stanishev, Georgi Atanasov, Stoyan Mikhailov, Milko Balev, and Misho Mishev. (Radio Free Europe, *Background Report*, 12 May.)

District Party Committees. Although all 28 first secretaries and all but a handful of the approximately 125 secretaries were re-elected during the "accountability election conferences" held between 5 and 16 March, two major shake-ups occurred. On 10 March, six days before the scheduled election, Todor Zhivkov and Central Committee Secretary Georgi Atanasov attended a plenum of the Veliko Turnovo committee at which First Secretary Nikola Vasilev and "other cadres" were dismissed. No direct explanation was given, although there was circumstantial evidence indicating that corruption was the cause. Vasilev had been first secretary since 1973 and was also a candidate member of the Central Committee, a position to which he was not re-elected at the Twelfth Congress. He was replaced by Nikolay Tsonev (born 1935), who also became a candidate member of the Central Committee. (Ibid., 30 April, item 2.)

At the beginning of 1981, Todor Stoychev (age 60) was the dean of district party leaders, having been first secretary of the Varna party committee since 1959, as well as a candidate member of the Politburo and a member of the State Council. The Twelfth Congress, however, removed him from the Politburo, and in a governmental reorganization in June, he was also dropped from the State Council. On 3 July, Zhivkov and Alexander Lilov descended on a plenum of the Varna committee that removed Stoychev from his last stronghold. He was replaced by Dimitur Popov (born 1935), who had been head of the Varna people's council. Moreover, an outsider, Georgi Georgiev of Sofia, was brought in as "second secretary" in charge of organization and cadres. (Ibid., 25 June, item 2.) No reason was given for these changes, but it may be assumed, particularly in view of the Georgiev appointment, that Zhivkov intended to purge the deeply entrenched "old guard" that Stoychev had built up during his 21 years in charge.

Auxiliary and Mass Organizations. Bulgaria possesses a number of organizations whose functions are to relay the decisions of the BCP to major social groups and to maintain contact with their foreign counterparts, either directly or through international organizations. Among the more important are the Central Council of Trade Unions (CCTU, about four million members), the Komsomol, or Dimitrov Communist Youth League (1.4 million), whose first secretary is Georgi Tanov, and the Civil Defense Organization, directed by Col. Gen. Tencho Papazov, which provides mass training in paramilitary tactics and disaster relief. A Committee on Bulgarian Women, whose chairman is State Council member Elena Lagadinova, has been in existence since 1944, but has no real significance.

During the year, perhaps in response to developments in Poland, the leadership took a critical look at the trade unions. They were reportedly criticized for automatically deducting dues from a worker's salary (membership in the unions is "voluntary," and dues are supposed to be collected directly by union representatives) and for failing to invest sufficiently in the construction of social and recreational facilities. On the eve of the Twelfth Congress, the CCTU held a plenum (23 March) to effect a change of leadership. Misho Mishev, chairman of the CCTU since 1974, was released to devote his full energies to work as a BCP Central Committee secretary, a position he had held since July 1979 and to which he was promptly re-elected at the Twelfth Congress. Mishev, who was 69 at the time of the plenum, came to the CCTU from the army, where he held the rank of lieutenant general and headed the Political Department. While no official criticism appeared in the press, it was rumored that Mishev's lack of vigor and innovation was the cause of his removal. Certainly his replacement, Petur Dyulgerov, born in 1929, is much younger and has a reputation for energy and efficiency. At the Twelfth Congress one week later, Dyulgerov was named a candidate member of the Politburo, a position that has usually gone with the CCTU chairmanship but Mishev had not held. (Ibid., 30 April, item 1; Sofia Press Agency, *Information, Documents, Commentaries*, no. 73, August.) In a speech to the Twelfth Congress, Zhivkov called for trade union democracy to be raised to a higher level and for union leaders to listen carefully to the members and to organize state support for projects born in the labor collectives (*Otchet*, p. 107). In a speech to "outstanding workers" (29 April), Zhivkov called on the unions to wage war on "the ugly phenomena of our reality and on manifestations of lack of discipline, waste, squandering, embezzlement, and theft of socialist property" (*Rabotnichesko delo* [*RD*], 30 April; *FBIS*, 5 May).

A special place is occupied by the Bulgarian Agrarian National Union (BANU), whose "fraternal cooperation" with the BCP in the government of the country is explicitly recognized in the constitution. Agrarians hold 99 of the 400 National Assembly seats, 4 of the 27 portfolios in the State Council (justice, public health, communications, and forestry), and about one-fifth of the seats in local people's councils. BANU leader Petur Tanchev, whose post as first deputy chairman of the State Council makes him Zhivkov's nominal successor as head of state, frequently represents Bulgaria on visits to foreign countries or acts as host to visiting noncommunist political figures. Membership in BANU has stood at 120,000 (apparently a quota) for several years. On 18–20 May the BANU held its Thirty-fourth Congress; 1,195 delegates and 112 foreign delegations from 74 countries attended. Tanchev confirmed the union's fidelity to BCP leadership and pledged to cooperate wholeheartedly in achieving the goals established by the Twelfth BCP Congress seven weeks earlier. (Sofia Press Agency, *Information, Documents, Commentaries*, no. 71, June; Sofia Domestic Service, 18 May; *FBIS*, 19 May; Radio Free Europe, *Situation Report*, 25 June, items 1–3.) On 21–22 May, the BANU hosted an international meeting of noncommunist, left-wing parties on the subject of "Détente, Peace, and Social Progress." Zhivkov delivered a speech blaming the United States for undermining détente and endangering world peace (*RD*, 22 May).

Most mass organizations are collective members of the Fatherland Front (about five million members). Led by Politburo member Pencho Kubadinski, the front's main function is to stimulate patriotism and enthusiasm for party goals.

Party Internal Affairs. At the end of 1980 or early in 1981, Zhivkov reportedly circulated a letter to district party committees and people's councils on the significance of the events in Poland. He stated that while Bulgaria faced no immediate threat from internal, antisocialist elements, poor performance in some sectors of the economy and abuses of power by party, state, and economic officials had had a bad effect on the population. He called for a shift in economic priorities and for a number of measures to reduce popular resentment. The Council of Ministers and the BCP Central Committee responded by ordering sharp cuts in administrative budgets for official travel and entertainment and by adopting new regulations on the use of state automobiles. In the future only members of the Politburo, the BCP Central Committee, and the Council of Ministers may use Mercedes; deputy ministers may use Volgas; and lower-ranking officials must use Ladas. District party committees may have only three official cars, one Volga and two Ladas, and only the first secretary may use the Volga. It was also ordered that senior officials in government and economic enterprises receive instruction in "the legal rights of ordinary citizens."

As the Twelfth Party Congress (31 March–4 April) approached, the government and the press inaugurated a campaign emphasizing the close ties between party and people. The draft theses were published more than two months in advance of the congress, and public comment was invited. Moreover, citizens were encouraged to come forward with grievances, and for several weeks numerous complaints about shortages of goods and inefficiency and dishonesty among party and government officials appeared in the press. To demonstrate the regime's responsiveness, several middle-level officials in the Ministries of Transportation and Communications and in the National Agroindustrial

Union were reprimanded or otherwise punished. (Sofia Domestic Service, 9 and 18 February; *FBIS*, 10 and 19 February; *RD*, 11 February; *FBIS*, 19 February.) Speeches of party leaders and reports in the press also emphasized that 1981 was the twenty-fifth anniversary of the historic "April plenum" that marked the beginning of de-Stalinization in Bulgaria and has since been promoted as a symbol of party democracy and reform.

The draft theses and Zhivkov's report to the congress provided a certain amount of information about the evolution of the party since the preceding congress in 1976. Zhivkov stated that as a result of the exchange of party cards begun in 1978, 38,452 individuals had "lost the right to call themselves communists" because of "political, professional, or moral shortcomings." Since 1976, 108,065 new members had been added, bringing total party membership to 825,876. Zhivkov also stated that industrial workers, "the backbone of the party," constituted 42.7 percent of the membership, but did not give the relative shares of white-collar or agricultural workers. (*Otchet*, pp. 112–13; *RD*, 10 April; *JPRS, East European Report*, no. 1874, 29 April.)

The draft theses for the congress were divided into five sections: foreign policy; economic development (the Eighth Five-Year Plan); science, culture, education, and the mass media; economic management, government, and society; and the party's leading role. After Zhivkov's opening address and messages of support and greetings from distinguished foreign guests, the congress broke up into five working groups, one devoted to each section. This device permitted over 230 speakers to be heard, compared with about 35 at the Eleventh Congress. Most of the speeches dwelt on the achievements of the preceding five years and very generally on the tasks ahead. There was no criticism of the draft theses, which were adopted almost verbatim. Zhivkov's report and the theses called for continued emphasis on the need for rejuvenation of the party by constant recruitment of young people. Zhivkov called it "a great achievement of our cadre policy" that over half of district party secretaries and over two-thirds of local party secretaries are under 45 (*Otchet*, p. 116). The theses also called for the greater development of internal party democracy, but without explaining how it was to be achieved. They stated that "broad democracy and freedom of opinion in the discussion of any matter ... are inseparable from the observance of iron discipline ... while meticulously implementing the decisions and instructions of superior party organs" (*RD*, 10 April; *JPRS, East European Report*, no. 1874, 29 April).

Domestic Affairs: *Elections, Governmental Changes, Legislation.* Elections for the Eighth National Assembly were held on 7 June. According to the official report, 6,519,674 of the 6,524,086 votes cast went to the candidates nominated by the Fatherland Front, who were all victorious. Todor Zhivkov was returned to the assembly from Sofia's electoral district by a vote of 20,483 to 0 (Sofia Domestic Service, 7 June; *FBIS*, 8 June). Of the 400 deputies elected, 271 belonged to the BCP, 99 to the BANU, and 30 had no party affiliation, although 20 of these were Komsomols. Eighty-seven deputies, including all 20 of the Komsomols, were women. Eighty-three deputies were said to be industrial or agricultural workers.

Elections for members of people's councils, mayors, judges, and jurors were held concurrently. Only a few isolated votes were cast against the Fatherland Front list or declared invalid. Statistics on the 53,712 people's councillors elected indicated that 57.9 percent were BCP members, 17 percent were BANU members, and the rest were nonparty, including 12.2 percent Komsomols. Women constituted 33.8 percent and industrial or agricultural workers 54.4 percent. Of the 3,960 mayors elected, 88.4 percent were men, 89.5 percent were BCP members, 4.9 percent were BANU members, the rest were nonparty, including 3.0 percent Komsomols. (*RD*, 9 June.)

At its first session, 16–17 June, the National Assembly approved a number of personnel and organizational changes in government bodies that were submitted by a plenum of the BCP Central

Committee. Vladimir Bonev retired from the position of chairman of the National Assembly. He was replaced by Stanko Todorov, who yielded his position as chairman of the Council of Ministers to Grisha Filipov. Most of the Council of Ministers remained intact, although there were a few minor changes. Stanish Bonev, a close associate of Grisha Filipov and head of the Central Committee's Planning and Economic Department, was made a deputy prime minister, and Drazha Vulcheva and Krustiu Trichkov were both dropped as deputy prime ministers. The Ministry of Electronics and Electrotechnology was merged with the Ministry of Machine Building, and the Ministry of Supplies and State Reserves was abolished.

Todor Zhivkov was re-elected chairman of the State Council, and Petur Tanchev was re-elected first deputy chairman. The number of deputy chairmen was increased from three to five. The two newcomers were Yaroslav Radev, a lawyer and chairman of the National Assembly's Legislative Commission, and Georgi Atanasov, a former Komsomol leader who was also named chairman of the watchdog Committee on State and People's Control, replacing Krustiu Trichkov. This committee was transfered from the jurisdiction of the Council of Ministers to that of the State Council. Eight members of the State Council were replaced. Ivan Mikhailov retired from this body as he did from the Politburo. For three others, Yaroslav Radev, Grisha Filipov, and Misho Mishev, their replacement was due to promotion or transfer to another important position. The remaining four, Boris Velchev, purged from the Politburo and BCP Central Committee in 1977, Todor Stoychev, Lalyu Ganchev of the BANU, and Evgeni Mateyev, had already suffered serious demotion or were in the process of doing so. The new members included two district party first secretaries, Ivan Panev of Plovdiv and Nikolay Zhishev of Burgas, Politburo member Ognyan Doynov, Komsomol Central Committee Secretary Stanka Shopova, BANU member Angel Dimitrov, and Petur Dyulgerov. For the remaining two, Vladimir Bonev and Krustiu Trichkov, election to the State Council was probably intended as compensation for the loss of more important positions. (Radio Free Europe, *Situation Report*, 25 June, items 1–3.)

At its second session on 7 July, the National Assembly adopted a new amnesty law presented by Zhivkov. In his speech, Zhivkov connected this law to the thirteen hundredth anniversary of the Bulgarian state and claimed that it was proof of the regime's "profound humanity." The new law provides amnesty for citizens convicted of crimes, the maximum sentence for which is less than three years imprisonment. Moreover, Bulgarians who left the country illegally or who left it legally but failed to return will be amnestied if they return before 31 December 1983. (Ibid., 29 July, item 3.)

Economy. In response to a request from Zhivkov, the launching of new heavy industrial projects was postponed for at least six months, and work currently proceding on several others was cut back or halted. This released labor and funds for increased housing construction and consumer goods production and importation. These measures apparently had the desired results; by midyear there were numerous reports that Bulgarian shops held an unusually large variety and quantity of goods and that queues had virtually disappeared (ibid., 10 September, item 2). It has not yet become clear, however, if this concern for consumer welfare was aimed at creating a favorable impression during the year of the party congress and anniversary celebration or if it marked a long-term change of policy.

Kiril Zarev, chairman of the State Planning Committee, published his report on the results of the 1980 plan on 30 January. In most categories the actual increases were slightly below those called for in the plan, but overall results still showed substantial growth. The principal failure was in agriculture, where poor weather brought an actual decline in output. On the other hand, Bulgaria's foreign trade grew by 14.1 percent as opposed to the 7.5 percent envisaged in the plan. Moreover, for the third straight year, Bulgaria showed a favorable balance of trade with nonsocialist countries, allowing the large debt accumulated in the mid-1970s to be reduced from $3.7 billion to $3.4 billion. (*RD*, 30 January.)

The plan adopted for 1981 showed a slight scaling down of expectations. Planned increases in the major categories were national income 5.1 percent, labor productivity 4.8 percent, industrial production 5.6 percent, agricultural production 4.7 percent, real per capita income 3.1 percent and foreign trade 8.3 percent (Radio Free Europe, *Situation Report*, 5 February, item 3). According to an interim progress report, the plan was being met 108 percent at midyear, but no details were given (BTA, 26 July; *FBIS*, 27 July).

A broader perspective on Bulgaria's economic development was given at the Twelfth Congress. The report on the achievements of the Seventh Five-Year Plan confirmed that Bulgaria's economic performance fell well short of the original targets. National income had been projected to grow by 45 percent, but actually increased by about 35 percent. Industrial production grew 35 percent (target 55 percent), agricultural production 12 percent (target 20 percent), and real income 12.7 percent (target 20 percent). Reasons for these shortfalls were said to be rising prices of imported raw materials, fuel, and machinery; adverse climatic conditions; and organizational and planning shortcomings and failures. Goals for 1985, and, in some areas, for 1990 showed more modest expectations and reflected the fact, confirmed during the Council for Mutual Economic Assistance (CMEA) session in July (Sofia Domestic Service, 2 July; BTA, 4 July; *FBIS*, 7 and 8 July), that Soviet energy deliveries for the foreseeable future would not rise above the 1980 level. According to the theses on economic development discussed at the congress, national income should increase by 25–30 percent during the Eighth Five-Year Plan and by 20–25 percent during the Ninth. It was stated that consumer industry would grow at about the same rate as heavy industry. Agricultural production is supposed to grow by 20–22 percent and real income by 16–18 percent. (*RD*, 10 April; *JPRS*, *East European Report*, no. 1874, 29 April.)

Although the "new economic mechanism" (see *YICA*, 1980, p. 14) was highly praised at the congress, there were signs during the year that its application in agriculture was encountering difficulties. It was supposed to require agroindustrial complexes to adapt to market demand and to become economically self-sufficient. However, at the beginning of the year and again in October, it was announced that owing to increased costs of production, the government would raise procurement prices paid for most crops without passing the price increases on to consumers. This seems to indicate a return to the subsidy system that the new economic mechanism was intended to eliminate. (Sofia Domestic Service, 27 October; *FBIS*, 28 October.)

Social and Cultural Events. Bulgaria's cultural life was dominated by the thirteen hundredth anniversary of the founding of the first Bulgarian state. Organized by Lyudmila Zhivkova, and probably conceived by her as well, this yearlong celebration was both national and international in scope. Jubilee committees were set up in most countries with which Bulgaria has relations, and hundreds of exhibits, performances by Bulgarian artists, and scholarly meetings were organized around the world in order to gain goodwill and recognition of Bulgaria's cultural heritage. Within Bulgaria there was a continuing series of events aimed at building Bulgarians' self-esteem and sense of international importance. Some of these, such as the First International Conference of Bulgarian Studies, which brought over six hundred foreign scholars to Sofia, were highly successful. Others, such as an international gathering of first ladies, attended by only one invitee, were less so. Todor Zhivkov delivered the closing speech of the jubilee to the National Assembly on 20 October. In a rousing, patriotic address, he stated that the primary characteristics of the Bulgarian people were a fierce democratic and independent spirit, perseverance, and ardent patriotism combined with socialist internationalism. Although a highly emotional survey of Bulgaria's history and national heroes, Zhivkov's speech was not belligerent, and he avoided mentioning any of the past grievances against Bulgaria's neighbors. (Sofia Domestic Service, 20 October; *FBIS*, 21 October.)

Zhivkov also presided over the ninetieth anniversary of the BCP on the slopes of Mt. Buzludzha, where the party was founded. After Grisha Filipov delivered the principal address, Zhivkov dedicated a monument, a BCP pantheon, surmounted by a 70-meter pylon on which rested an illuminated red star, 12 meters in diameter and said to be the largest of its kind in the world. (Radio Free Europe, *Situation Report*, 27 August, item 1.)

A lasting memorial to Lyudmila Zhivkova's influence on Bulgarian culture, particularly to the substantial material resources she was able to make available, is the magnificent Palace of Culture, which was opened for the Twelfth Congress. Built in only two years, at a reported cost of $500 million, this impressive structure provides a setting for the performing arts worthy of any European capital.

There was little original in the Twelfth Congress's theses on science, culture, education, and the mass media. Calling generally for "improvements" and couched in the formulas that Lyudmila Zhivkova had introduced, they are likely to have far less an impact on Bulgaria's cultural life than will the death of Zhivkova.

Foreign Affairs: *The Soviet Union.* As in the past, Bulgarian leaders continued to emphasize their loyalty to the Soviet Union and to support Soviet positions on all major international questions. The theses on international affairs adopted by the Twelfth Congress called friendship with the Soviet Union the "cornerstone" of Bulgaria's foreign policy and stated that "the further strengthening of unity, unity of action, and fraternal alliance with the members of the socialist community and, above all, with the great Soviet Union will remain the basic direction of the foreign policy of our party and state" (*RD*, 16 February). Zhivkov visited the Soviet Union on 21 February–3 March to attend the Twenty-Sixth CPSU Congress, which he called "the most important political event in the world" (Sofia Domestic Service, 24 February; *FBIS*, 25 February). On 6–7 August, he made his annual visit to Brezhnev in the Crimea. According to the official report, the two leaders discussed the results of their respective party congresses and the development of even more extensive economic relations. Bulgaria will expand both agricultural and industrial exports to the USSR, while the Soviet Union will aid in the construction of a third major metallurgical center, to be built near Burgas. Brezhnev and Zhivkov were also reported to have endorsed the idea of a nuclear-free zone in the Balkans and "shared a complete unanimity of views" on other international questions. (BTA, 7 August; *FBIS*, 10 August; Radio Free Europe, *Situation Report*, 14 August, item 1.) Immediately after Zhivkov's visit, the USSR launched a satellite equipped with Bulgarian instruments—"Intercosmos: Bulgaria 1300"—to mark Bulgaria's anniversary. A tracking station to receive data from the satellite was set up near Stara Zagora, and Politburo member Ognyan Doynov led a Bulgarian delegation to the USSR to observe the launch. In addition to collecting data about certain processes in the ionosphere and magnetosphere, the satellite will survey a number of Bulgarian archeological sites to detect the most promising ones for further exploration. (BTA, 3, 7 and 8 August; *FBIS*, 11 August; Sofia Press Agency, *Information, Documents, Commentaries*, no. 72, July.)

Zhivkov gave particularly strong backing during the year to the Soviet call for the restoration of détente, and he condemned the NATO decision to deploy medium-range nuclear weapons as an attempt by "war-loving circles" to upset the military balance. He also consistently defended the Soviet intervention in Afghanistan, calling it in his speech to the Twelfth Congress "fraternal internationalist aid" (*Otchet*, p. 156).

Other East European and Balkan Countries. During the year, Bulgaria maintained a relatively moderate position on developments in Poland. The harshest comment came from Defense Minister Dobri Dzhurov in an address to the Fourteenth All-Army Party Conference on 11 March, shortly after the CPSU congress. Dzhurov directly compared the situation in Poland with those in Hungary in 1956 and Czechoslovakia in 1968. He added that Poland would not be "relinquished" to the imperialists, just as Hungary and Czechoslovakia had not been earlier. (*Narodna armiya*, 12 March; *FBIS*, 18 March.) Authoritative articles in the press, believed to express the opinion of the Politburo, directed attention to manifestations of anti-Sovietism and antisocialism and called on the Polish communist party not just to condemn them, but to take steps to eradicate them (*RD*, 31 May, 3 and 7 July; *FBIS*, 3 June, 6 and 13 July). On the other hand, the Bulgarian press and Zhivkov himself consistently expressed confidence in the ability of the Polish party and other "healthy forces" in the country to resolve the crisis and restore stability (*Otchet*, p. 144). During the first three months of the year, Bulgaria also delivered approximately $16 million worth of food to Poland, deferring payment until after 1983 (Radio Free Europe, *Background Report*, 15 July).

Bulgaria has always stressed its loyal and active participation in the Warsaw Pact and CMEA. On 2–4 July, Sofia hosted the thirty-fifth CMEA Council session. Grisha Filipov, speaking in Russian, made the opening address, and Zhivkov held a reception for the delegates at which he stressed the CMEA's past accomplishments. (Sofia Domestic Service, 2 July; *FBIS*, 7 July; BTA, 4 July; *FBIS*, 8 July.) Bulgaria's relations with the other Warsaw Pact and CMEA states are generally good. Hungarian Prime Minister György Lázár visited Bulgaria 12–13 February to sign a new trade agreement. Bilateral trade is to expand 50 percent over the next five years. Hungary will send Bulgaria computers, precision engineering equipment, pharmaceuticals, farm machinery, and buses, and Bulgaria will export 10,000 electric trucks as well as loading equipment and soda ash. (Sofia Domestic Service, 13 February; *FBIS*, 17 February.) Relations with Romania remained good, although Bulgaria's shift in economic priorities apparently has caused a postponement or slowdown in the Nikopol–Turnu Magurele hydroelectric project that had begun in 1978. Romanian leader Nicolae Ceauşescu met with Zhivkov in Ruse on 21 January (Sofia Domestic Service, 21 January; *FBIS*, 22 January), after which it was reported that work on the Bulgarian side of the Danube had been halted. Zhivkov was expected to pay a return visit to Romania in the winter or late fall.

Foreign Minister Petur Mladenov met with his Turkish counterpart in Ankara on 22 April. The two ministers reached an agreement on expanding economic cooperation and reported progress on the resolution of a minor boundary dispute along the Rezovska river. (BTA, 22 April; *FBIS*, 23 April.) On 31 August–1 September, four members of the Turkish left-wing Dev-Sol who had hijacked a Turkish domestic flight and forced it to land in Burgas were brought to trial in Sofia. The minimum sentences, three years imprisonment, and Bulgaria's rejection of a Turkish extradition request reportedly provoked resentment in Ankara. (Radio Free Europe, *Situation Report*, 10 September, item 3.)

Annual meetings between Bulgarian and Greek leaders have been held since 1975. This year Zhivkov met with President Constantine Karamanlis on 27–30 May in the Greek islands. The two leaders reported that they shared "similar views on a number of international issues" and were encouraged by the progress of economic and cultural exchanges. There were indications, however, that Bulgarian-Greek trade declined sharply this year in the wake of Greece's entry into the European Economic Community. Zhivkov agreed to participate in further bilateral projects and in multilateral cooperation in limited, technical areas. (*RD*, 31 May; *FBIS*, 3 June.) Bulgaria particularly welcomed the victory of Andreas Papandreou's Panhellenic Socialist Movement (PASOK) in the Greek elections in October. On a visit to Bulgaria on 28–30 April at the invitation of the Fatherland Front, Papandreou was received by Zhivkov and signed an extension of a PASOK–Fatherland Front friendship and cooperation agreement made in 1979 for the 1981–1985 period. (BTA, 29 April; *FBIS*, 30 April.)

It may have been expectation of a Papandreou victory in Greece that prompted Zhivkov to raise the idea of a nuclear-free zone in the Balkans. Although not new—it has been advocated by Romania since 1957—the proposal received a fresh impetus after Zhivkov's meeting with Brezhnev in August. After that time it began to appear regularly in Zhivkov's speeches and in reports of his meetings with foreign leaders. Immediately after the PASOK victory, Zhivkov concluded a speech to the National

Assembly on Bulgaria's anniversary with a call for a Balkan summit to be held in Sofia sometime in 1982 to discuss making the region a nuclear-free zone (Sofia Domestic Service, 20 October; *FBIS*, 21 October). Although the reaction of other Balkan leaders has not yet become apparent, the announcement by Papandreou on 11 November (*WP*, 12 November) that he would seek the removal of American nuclear weapons from Greek soil seemed to foreshadow a favorable Greek response.

The improvement in relations with Yugoslavia that was marked by an exchange of visits between Yugoslav Foreign Minister Josip Vrhovec and Alexander Lilov at the end of 1980 seemed to gain momentum in the first months of 1981. Milan Potrč, chairman of Yugoslavia's Trade Union Council, visited Bulgaria 9–12 February, toured a number of industrial sites, spoke warmly of improving relations, and called for expanded trade (BTA, 11 February; *FBIS*, 12 February). On 19–28 April a Bulgarian commercial and industrial exhibition held in Belgrade produced trade agreements worth $175 million (BTA, 28 April; *FBIS*, 11 March). Polemics over the Macedonian question, however, soon overshadowed these hopeful developments. Yugoslav journalists called attention to an article in a minor Bulgarian historical journal that referred to Tito's World War II Macedonian policy as "hegemonistic and nationalistic" and spoke of Macedonian nationality as "an artificial creation." Yugoslav commentators argued that this demonstrated that Bulgaria had not abandoned its territorial pretensions and suggested that the Soviet Union was manipulating Bulgarian historians. (Radio Free Europe, *Situation Report*, 20 February, item 1.) A reply in the Bulgarian newspaper *Otechestven front* (18 March) stated that Bulgaria's policy toward Yugoslavia was well known and consistent and referred to Zhivkov's standing offer to sign at any time a treaty guaranteeing the inviolability of borders. It also accused the Yugoslavs of stirring up "a psychosis of tension and confrontation." Yugoslavia then announced that it would not participate in any events connected with Bulgaria's anniversary because Lyudmila Zhivkova and historian-academician Khristo Khristov had publicly referred to the 1903 St. Elias Day uprising in Macedonia as an event in *Bulgarian* history and because the committee formed to organize the anniversary celebration included Macedonian-born Venko Markovski, a "Yugoslav émigré." On the eve of the Twelfth BCP Congress, Politburo member Tsola Dragoycheva, whose memoirs have been banned in Yugoslavia, reissued a collection of excerpts from them dealing with Macedonia with a new introduction attacking Yugoslavia's "anti-Bulgarian campaign" and "disinformation" (*Takava e istinata*, Sofia, 1981, pp. 3–11). At the Twelfth Congress, Zhivkov noted that Bulgarian-Yugoslav relations were "not all that they should be," but he expressed optimism that they would get better (*Otchet*, p. 148). Later in the year an article in the Yugoslav newspaper *Borba* (24 September) accused Bulgaria of encouraging national separatist movements in Yugoslavia by allying with "notorious fascist" anti-Yugoslav figures. This accusation, however, was based on a misleading article that appeared in the Croatian émigré press (*Nova Hrvatka*, 14 June) and seemed to be without substance. Bulgarian leaders and the press maintained almost complete silence on the rioting among Albanians in Kosovo and its aftermath. By the late fall, hostilities seemed to diminish in spite of a border shooting incident in which one Bulgarian was killed. On 24–25 October, Yugoslav Foreign Trade Secretary Metod Rotar visited Bulgaria to conclude a new agreement on trade and joint construction projects (Tanjug, 25 October; *FBIS*, 27 October).

The introduction on 13 December of martial law in Poland was amply covered in Bulgarian media. In its 16 December issue, *Rabotnichesko delo* (*FBIS*, 21 December) hailed "the incredibly difficult and responsible mission which the Military Council for National Salvation led by Army Gen. W. Jaruzelski has undertaken" and expressed the hope that the Council is "finding more secure support among the people." On the same day, a commentator for the official news agency (BTA) reviewed Western reactions to the events in Poland. He found a division existing between realists who thought that their countries should not interfere in Poland's internal affairs (the French and British foreign ministers and the Austrian chancellor were put in this category) and others—such as the United States—who still supported Solidarity and its hopes for "power-seizing and for liquidation of socialism" (ibid., 17 December). The Bulgarian trade union daily, *Trud*, wrote on 18 December that the entire Bulgarian people favored martial law but distinguished two kinds of Solidarity members. The official leadership was nothing but "a reliable shield of the reaction which [did] its destructive acts under the mask of a trade union." There were, however, the "misled Solidarity members [who] can and will surely find their place in the struggle for getting out of the political and economic crisis." (Ibid., 23 December). *Rabotnichesko delo* (26 December; *FBIS*, 28 December) branded President Reagan's Christmas speech announcing sanctions against Poland as reflecting "the incredibly hysterical and unrestrained campaign against the Soviet Union and Poland." Commenting on U.S. sanctions against the USSR, Radio Sofia called them "a gross violation of international law" and a "policy of overt confrontation with the socialist community countries." (*FBIS*, 30 December.)

The Third World. Following up Todor Zhivkov's visit to Syria last year (see *YICA*, 1981, pp. 230–31), Politburo member Todor Bozhinov led a Bulgarian delegation to Damascus on 19–22 January, where he met with President Hafiz al-Asad. At the end of the visit an agreement was signed covering Bulgarian-Syrian cooperation on electrification, irrigation, transport, power generation, and industrial construction projects (BTA, 23 January; *FBIS*, 23 January). On 26–29 October, Asad paid a return visit to Bulgaria. According to the official report on his meetings with Zhivkov, the two leaders were in general agreement on the world situation. Asad endorsed the idea of a Balkan nuclear-free zone, and a trade protocol was signed covering the period 1982–1985. (Damascus Domestic Service, 29 October; *FBIS*, 2 November.)

After the Soviet Union and the German Democratic Republic, Libya ranks third among Bulgaria's trade partners. On 26–27 April Moammur Khadafy met with Zhivkov in Sofia, returning a visit the Bulgarian leader had made to Tripoli last year (see *YICA*, 1981, p. 230). Little information on their meeting, which apparently was a brief one, beyond the usual denunciations of imperialism and Zionism was published (*RD*, 28 April; *FBIS*, 1 May). Shortly before Khadafy's visit, an article on Bulgarian-Libyan cooperation in the field of health services revealed that two thousand Bulgarian medical personnel, including six hundred physicians, were working in Libya and approximately three hundred Libyan medical students come to Bulgaria for training every year (BTA, 13 April; *FBIS*, 16 April).

Another Middle Eastern head of state, 'Ali Nasir Muhammad al-Hassani of the People's Democratic Republic of Yemen, visited Bulgaria during the year. His visit was described as a "holiday," and no information about it was published except for his date of departure, 1 October (Sofia Domestic Service, 30 September; *FBIS*, 1 October). It is widely believed that in addition to rendering economic support, Bulgaria is a significant supplier of arms to South Yemen.

During the year, visits by two Palestine Liberation Organization (PLO) delegations, 3–5 May and 21–28 June, provided the Bulgarian government with the opportunity to reaffirm its "complete support" for the PLO (BTA, 4 May; *FBIS*, 5 May; *RD*, 30 June, *FBIS*, 7 July). A Bulgarian-Palestinian Friendship Society, headed by Kiril Ignatov, a member of the BCP's Central Committee, was established (BTA, 14 January; *FBIS*, 23 January). Bulgarian press commentary on the assassination of Anwar Sadat took the position that the Egyptian leader did not reflect the views or interests of his people and that Egypt ought now to rejoin the "anti-imperialist front" of Arab states (BTA, 7 October; *FBIS*, 8 October).

Bulgaria continued to pursue a vigorous African policy, particularly with those African states oriented toward the Soviet bloc. African heads of state who visited Bulgaria and met with Zhivkov during the year included Denis Sassou-Nguesso of the Congo (17–18 May), Chadli Benjedid of Algeria (10–11 June), Samora Machel of Mozambique (18–19 August), and José Eduardo dos Santos of Angola (2–6 October). Bulgaria signed a trade protocol with Algeria covering cooperation on finance, tourism, the training of agricultural specialists, and water conservation (BTA, 19 February; *FBIS*, 22

February). Other agreements on economic, scientific, and technological cooperation were signed with Benin and Nigeria (BTA, 24 June; *FBIS*, 25 June) and with Mozambique (BTA, 28 May; *FBIS*, 29 May). Lieutenant General Abdallah Twalipo, Tanzanian minister of defense, met with Grisha Filipov and Defense Minister Dobri Dzhurov in Sofia on 15–17 October, after which an agreement intensifying cooperation between the Bulgarian and Tanzanian armed forces was signed (Sofia Domestic Service, 15 October; BTA, 17 October; *FBIS* 16 and 19 October). Lieutenant General Alberto Chipande, defense minister of Mozambique, began talks with Dzhurov in Sofia on 28 October, but no further information about them was released (Sofia Domestic Service, 28 October; *FBIS*, 30 October).

Although Bulgaria maintains diplomatic relations with the People's Republic of China, Bulgarian leaders consistently echo Soviet criticism of Beijing's "hegemonistic" ambitions. In addressing the Twelfth Congress, Zhivkov spoke of positive developments in China following the liquidation of Mao's cult of personality, and he expressed the desire to improve relations if the Chinese would play a constructive role in the world communist movement. However, at the present moment the anti-Soviet policies of Chinese leaders made China an ally of imperialism and reaction. (*Otchet*, pp. 140–41.) Bulgaria signed a trade agreement with Bangladesh to cover the period through 1986 (Sofia Domestic Service, 11 February; *FBIS*, 12 February), and an agreement on scientific and industrial cooperation with India (BTA, 28 May; *FBIS*, 29 May). Phoun Sipaseut, foreign minister of Laos, visited Bulgaria on 12–15 October and met with Mladenov and Grisha Filipov (*RD*, 13 October; *FBIS*, 16 October). Hun Sen, foreign minister of Kampuchea, visited Bulgaria on 15–17 July (BTA, 15 July; *FBIS*, 16 July), as did Kampuchean Prime Minister Pen Sovan on 21–23 October (BTA, 23 October; *FBIS*, 27 October). On each of these occasions, communiqués were issued condemning "American imperialists" and "Beijing hegemonists."

Bayardo Arce Castaño, a member of the Sandinista National Liberation Front Directorate, visited Bulgaria to attend the anniversary celebration. It was reported that he met with Zhivkov, who pledged Bulgarian support for Nicaragua's national reconstruction (Radio Sandino, Managua, 23 October; *FBIS*, 27 October).

Western Europe and the United States. In speaking to the Twelfth Congress, Zhivkov stated that Bulgaria seeks to expand its relations with the developed capitalist states on the bases of peaceful coexistence and mutual advantage and that in recent years meetings between political leaders and with Western business circles had led to positive results (*Otchet*, p. 152). Bulgaria enjoys generally correct relations with West European countries, most of which made at least token gestures toward the celebration of Bulgaria's anniversary. A visit by Austrian Foreign Minister Willibald Pahr on 26–28 January prepared the way for a state visit by Chancellor Bruno Kreisky on 12–15 May. Both Zhivkov and Kreisky praised the Austrian-Bulgarian relationship, which Zhivkov has often called a model for states with differing social systems. The joint communiqué stressed their intention to further expand economic cooperation and their mutual desire for a restoration of détente between East and West. During a lecture at Sofia University, Kreisky stated that Poland must be allowed to solve its problems on its own and that outside interference would inevitably end détente for a long time. (BTA, 28 January, 16 May; *Arbeiter Zeitung*, Vienna, 15 May; *FBIS*, 2 February, 18 and 19 May.) Later in the year it was announced that Austria would grant Bulgaria a two billion schilling loan to finance construction in the tourist industry (*Die Presse*, Vienna, 20 October; *FBIS*, 23 October).

West German Foreign Minister Hans-Dietrich Genscher visited Bulgaria on 8–11 July, meeting with Zhivkov and Foreign Minister Mladenov. While Genscher characterized his country's relations with Bulgaria as "friendly," he sharply criticized the buildup of Soviet military forces and the Soviet intervention in Afghanistan, defended NATO's plans to deploy medium-range missiles, and warned against intervention in Poland. His remarks, probably intended for transmission to Moscow, were presented only in heavily edited form in the Bulgarian press. (Radio Free Europe, *Situation Report*, 29

July, item 4.) On 23 October, Danish Foreign Minister Kjeld Olesen held talks with Mladenov in Sofia. Although both foreign ministers deplored the worsening of East-West relations, they did not agree on the causes. They endorsed the idea of nuclear-free zones in the Balkans and in Scandinavia. They characterized relations between Denmark and Bulgaria as "very good" but admitted that much needed to be done to improve trade. (BTA, 23 October; *FBIS*, 27 October.)

Statements by the press and public figures on the United States reflected the continuing deterioration of East-West relations. On several occasions Zhivkov accused the United States of unilaterally ending détente and introducing a new arms race. Direct dealings between Bulgaria and the United States remained businesslike, however, and cultural and scholarly exchanges continued. In February a three-year agreement covering commercial navigation and maritime affairs was signed, and at the same time an agreement with Dow Chemical for trade and joint industrial production was completed (BTA, 19 February; *FBIS*, 20 February). Annual bilateral negotiations, begun in 1979, were continued with a visit by Assistant Secretary of State Lawrence Eagleburger to Sofia on 28 October, where he met with his counterpart, Deputy Foreign Minister Marii Ivanov. The granting of most-favored-nation status to Bulgaria remained blocked by Bulgaria's insistence that the assurances required by the Jackson-Vanik legislation constitute an unacceptable infringement on its sovereignty.

Bulgaria's major disappointment lay in the failure of Western business to respond to the joint venture legislation introduced in 1980 (*YICA*, 1980, p. 15). In an effort to invigorate this form of cooperation, the Bulgarian Chamber of Trade and Industry organized a conference on economic relations with developed capitalist countries attended by representatives of fifty companies from Europe and the United States (BTA, 10 June; *FBIS*, 15 June), and in July the Ministry of Finance announced that it would provide financing for joint ventures at less than the U.S. prime rate (*Wall Street Journal*, 13 July).

International Party Contacts. Nearly all the world's communist parties and movements—with the notable exceptions of the Chinese and Albanian—were represented among the 126 foreign delegations at the BCP's Twelfth Congress. During the year, high-level Bulgarian delegations represented the BCP at party congresses or other important party events in Cuba, the German Federal Republic, Greece, Israel, Kampuchea, Mongolia, Nicaragua, Portugal, Spain, and Switzerland.

For several years Zhivkov has invited communist party leaders to visit Bulgaria's Black Sea resorts for summer vacation. This year his invitation was accepted by the party leaders of Chile, Cyprus, France, Iraq, Laos, Lebanon, Martinique, Morocco, Norway, Portugal, and Syria. Many of them participated in the ceremonies marking the BCP's ninetieth anniversary in August. At other times during the year Bulgaria was also visited by the party leaders of Lebanon, Mozambique, the United States, and the German Federal Republic. Zhivkov met personally with most of these leaders, after which the usual statements on peace, solidarity, and cooperation were issued. An Italian delegation also spent a week studying the BCP's methods of training party cadres.

Perhaps in anticipation of the post-Brezhnev era, Zhivkov accelerated the awarding of honors to high Soviet officials. This year's recipients of the Order of Georgi Dimitrov included five Soviets: Nikolai Baibakov, Konstantin Chernenko, Vasili Kuznetsov, Nikolai Tikhonov, and Col. Gen. Khachik Ambaryan, the Warsaw Pact representative to the Bulgarian Army. The award was also given to Gus Hall of the Communist Party, U.S.A., and to Polish President Henryk Jablonski.

Publications. The official daily of the BCP is *Rabotnichesko delo* (Workers' cause), its monthly is *Partien zhivot* (Party life), and its theoretical journal is *Novo vreme* (New times). Government legislation and decrees are published in *Durzhaven vestnik* (State newspaper). The mass Fatherland Front organization publishes the newspaper *Otechestven front*, and the Agrarian Union, *Zemedelsko zname* (Agrarian banner). The Komsomol publishes the newspaper *Narodna mladezh* (National youth), the monthly journal *Mladezh* (Youth), and the fortnightly literary journal *Puls* (Pulse). Significant publications emanating from the government are *Narodna armiya* (National army) from the Ministry of Defense, *Kooperativno selo* (Cooperative village) from the National Agroindustrial Union, *Narodna prosveta* (National education) from the Ministry of Education, and *Planovo stopanstvo* (Planned economy) from the State Planning Committee. Economic events are surveyed in *Ikonomicheski Zhivot* (Economic life), and cultural ones in the weekly *Literaturen front* (Literary front) and the monthly *Septemuri* (September), both published by the Bulgarian Writers' Union, and in *Narodna kultura* (National Culture), the weekly journal of the Committee on Culture. The Sofia Press Agency publishes an English-language weekly, *Sofia News*, and the series *Bulgaria: Information, Documents, Commentaries*. The official news agency is Bulgarska telegrafna agentsiya (BTA).

University of Maryland Baltimore County   John D. Bell

Czechoslovakia

The Communist Party of Czechoslovakia (Komunistická strana Československa; KSČ) emerged, like most of its fraternal parties, out of the turbulent differentiation process affecting the socialist movement after World War I. In Czechoslovakia, this process was concluded relatively late. The KSČ was constituted only in September 1921, at a merger congress in Prague, by a number of radical groups organized along ethnic divisions. Of these the left wing of the Czechoslovak Social Democratic Party was the most important. After the rise of fascist regimes in Central and Eastern Europe in the 1930s, the KSČ remained the only legal communist party east of the Rhine. Following the German takeover of Czechoslovakia on the eve of World War II, the party became illegal. It was reconstituted after the liberation and in February 1948, it seized absolute power in a coup d'etat that ended a long-standing pluralist political order. In the current legislature and government, the KSČ always controls at least two-thirds of all seats and posts. The three highest political functions in the country are filled by KSČ members: Gustav Husák, secretary general of the KSČ, is president of the republic, and Lubomír Štrougal and Alois Indra, both KSČ Presidium members, hold the posts of federal prime minister and the chairman of the Federal Assembly, respectively.

Since 1968, Czechoslovakia has been a federation of two ethnic units: the Czech Socialist Republic and the Slovak Socialist Republic. The 1968 constitutional reform was introduced by the short-lived liberal government headed by Alexander Dubček, later removed from power by the Soviet-led invasion. The brief era of reform is often referred to as the Prague Spring or Socialism with a Human Face. Since the Soviet military intervention in August 1968, which considerably undermined popular perceptions of the legitimacy of party leaders, KSČ policy has been one of so-called normalization. The goal is to recreate the conditions that prevailed before the Dubček period. In the course of normalization, the plans to reorganize the party along federal lines were scrapped. The Slovak party section, the Communist Party of Slovakia (Komunistická strana Slovenska; KSS), founded before the war as an autonomous regional body, has no counterpart in the Czech-inhabited provinces, where only sections of the national organization exist. This inconsistency produced "asymmetric centralism"—the paradox of a federalized nation ruled by a centralist communist party.

Organization and Leadership. Both of the KSČ's two supreme governing bodies, the Central Committee and the Presidium, were newly elected at the Sixteenth Party Congress in April 1981, but there were no significant changes in membership and functions. The leadership in control since April 1969 was, on the whole, returned to power. The next congress will meet in 1986.

The Sixteenth Party Congress elected a Central Committee of 123 members, an increase of 2 over the previous body. The number of candidate members grew from 52 to 55. Sixteen full and 18 candidate members are women. The Presidium has 12 members and 1 candidate member. The Secretariat consists of a secretary general, eight secretaries, and two Secretariat members. (*Rudě právo*, 11 April.)

Organization of the KSS is similar to that of the KSČ. It held its congress in March (KSS congresses are not numbered). A Central Committee of 91 full members and 31 candidates was elected. The KSS Presidium has 11 members. The top executive official of the KSS, who, in contrast to his KSČ counterpart, bears the title of first secretary, is Jozef Lenárt (*Pravda*, Bratislava, 23 March).

Membership. Since the end of World War II, the KSČ has ranked among the largest communist parties of the world per capita of population. Despite several major purges, the most recent in 1970, the party has retained its mass character. According to Secretary General Husák's opening speech at the Sixteenth Congress, there were on 1 January 1981, 1,538,179 members and candidates to membership, organized in 45,564 local units. In the five years since the Fifteenth Congress, 321,000 applicants were admitted into the party, and 12,814 members were expelled. Membership grew by some 11 percent. Among the new admissions, 61 percent were industrial workers, 7.8 percent members of agricultural cooperatives, and 22.1 intellectuals (a category without precise definition in the report). Over 90 percent of the new members were under 35 years. (*WMR*, May.) The Slovak party organization represented about 25 percent of the total national membership, although the Slovak ethnic group represents almost a third of Czechoslovakia's population. Sixty-four percent of KSS cardholders were industrial workers (*Pravda*, Bratislava, 21 March). On 30 June 1981, Czechoslovakia had 15.3 million inhabitants, of whom 5.0 million were Slovaks (*Rudé právo*, 29 July.)

Party Internal Affairs. The congresses of the KSČ and the KSS were the two most important events in Czechoslovak communism during 1981. The KSS congress in Bratislava (20–22 March) was attended by 732 voting delegates and 36 delegates with advisory status. It did not introduce any important changes in the membership of the KSS's leading bodies. Jozef Lenárt was re-elected to his second term as first secretary. No changes were made in the composition of the KSS Secretariat and Presidium. (*Pravda*, Bratislava, 23 March.) The congress of the national party organization opened in Prague on 6 April and closed on 10 April. In attendance were 1,451 elected delegates. No important personnel changes were effected; all Presidium and Secretariat members retained their seats, while the faces in the Central Committee changed mostly for reasons of death or retirement. (*Rudé právo*, 11 April.)

The KSČ congress attracted attention from foreign observers because of circumstances that were not directly related to the congress agenda. The unexpected presence at the opening ceremony on 6 April of Soviet party boss Leonid Brezhnev induced some commentators to speculate about a possible communist summit in Prague to discuss the situation in Poland. These speculations proved unfounded.

No officials of comparable rank arrived from other communist countries, and Brezhnev delivered a relatively moderate speech as far as the Polish events were concerned (Radio Moscow, 7 April). It appeared particularly moderate compared with the opening address given by Gustav Husák the same day. Husák stressed the concern of other communist parties in Eastern Europe over the preservation of the "socialist character" of the Polish system, as well as their right and willingness to stop developments "hostile to socialism." In brief, Husák's was the strongest restatement of the Brezhnev Doctrine made until then outside the Soviet Union.

Besides this sharp condemnation of the Polish workers' movement, Husák also criticized domestic economic performance, particularly its "failure to reach the turning point for the better." This failure, along with international difficulties beyond Czechoslovakia's control, necessitated "a fundamental change in thinking." Considerably greater savings and cuts in expenditures and more strenuous work were indispensable. Husák devoted much of his speech to the current state of the party. Recalling that 1981 was the sixtieth anniversary of the party, he reviewed the more recent history of the KSČ and praised its faithfulness to the Leninist line, despite "revisionist interruptions," such as occurred in 1968. He further emphasized the need to educate the people toward "class-based vigilance and implacability vis-à-vis bourgeois ideology." In this educational process, an important role fell to atheistic propaganda. Husák endorsed the Soviet position on every international issue and approved the idea, promoted by Moscow, of coordinating foreign policies by means of regular international communist conferences. (*WMR*, May.)

Neither in the secretary general's address nor in any other presentation by KSČ officials at the congress was there any extensive reference to the experiment with new methods of industrial management introduced in 1978 in 140 selected enterprises and justified as a measure to improve the efficiency of production and the quality of products. It seemed that this project has been given a lower priority.

On 11 June, at the third session of the new Central Committee, Gustav Husák submitted a report evaluating the 5–6 June general elections, the internal situation in the KSČ, and the domestic economy. He pointed out that the reformist period of 1968—which Husák and his associates call "the crisis development in the party and the nation"—had necessitated more careful selection of party members and candidates and a more thorough, all-around political education of all Communists. Commenting on economic conditions, he warned committee members that much better work discipline and a greater sense of responsibility in the workplace were needed to overcome present and future economic problems. (Radio Prague, 11 June.)

Mass Organizations. Against the background of the dramatic developments in neighboring Poland, party leaders appeared to realize better the importance of labor unions and the risks involved for the regime in letting worker discontent be articulated through unofficial channels. Signs of such discontent were not absent in Czechoslovakia. Sporadic hints in the media suggested that the Polish example may have had an impact on Czechoslovak workers. As early as fall 1980, party spokesmen admitted that protests against unsatisfactory working conditions and occasional wildcat strikes had occurred in some industrial regions, especially Ostrava and North Bohemia (*Rudé právo*, 10 and 13 October 1980). At about the same time, Husák went to Ostrava and held talks with workers and union officials about grievances over the harsh demands of the economic plan (*Czechoslovak Situation Report*, no. 28, 28 November 1980). Husák's participation indicated the KSČ's worry that the mood of Polish workers might "infect" their Czech and Slovak colleagues. The talks were continued, in February 1981 in Prague, between the government and the Presidium of the Central Trade Union Council. On this occasion, a catalogue of workers' grievances was published in a joint communiqué, and a pledge was made to "widen socialist democracy, working people's participation in production management, implementation of the unions' legal rights at factory level and higher levels, and to unions' greater share in key decision making with regard to the standard of living and people's social security" (*Rudé právo*, 12 February). Worker discontent and the unsatisfactory performance of the unions were also topics of discussion at the KSČ congress in April. Karel Hoffmann, chairman of the Central Trade Union Council, conceded in his report that Czechoslovak workers had followed events in Poland with far greater interest than union officials would like to admit (ibid., 9 April). This concession, of course, did not imply Hoffmann's sympathy for Solidarity. At a joint session of the Czech and the Slovak trade union councils in Prague on 12 May, Hoffmann promised support to "truly class-oriented and socialist trade unions in the Polish People's Republic," obviously meaning the official, party-controlled organization. He also announced the participation of the Czechoslovak unions in the forthcoming Tenth World Trade Union Congress, to be held in Cuba in February 1982. After the congress, Hoffmann called for "a broad propaganda campaign among Czechoslovak working people, with the purpose of clarifying the Trade Union Council's principles and aims." (*Práce*, 12 May.)

Domestic Affairs. The Polish crisis made party leaders apprehensive not only about the mood among workers but also about the stability of the regime. It seemed that in 1981 the KSČ sought, with greater resolve than ever, to broaden the basis of public consensus and thus to help legitimate its rule. A reference in a speech by Husák on New Year's eve to the 35 years that had elapsed "since the beginning of a new and free life of the people" placed the most important event of postwar history in the 1945 liberation, which ushered in a three-year era of pluralist politics, and not in the February 1948 coup d'etat that brought the KSČ to power. Until recently, official pronouncements have identified the latter as the "beginning of a new life in Czechoslovakia." (Czechoslovak Television, 1 January.) This desire to reach audiences and elicit support beyond the confines of the communist party organization was also evident in the secretary general's May Day address (Radio Prague, 1 May). In the eyes of KSČ leaders, the search for more universal approval of communist policies, however, was in no way incompatible with unreserved obedience to their Soviet sponsors. A few days after the May Day speech, Husák in his capacity as supreme commander of armed forces issued an army order to remember the anniversary of the liberation. In this proclamation, he reminded army personnel and the nation that in the opinion of present party leaders, Czechoslovakia owed everything, including its very existence, to the Soviet Union and therefore was bound to its great ally forever by ties of unqualified loyalty and obedience. (*Rudé právo*, 11 May.)

General elections were held in Czechoslovakia on 5 and 6 June, with the expected but hardly credible results of 99.96 percent of the vote cast for the National Front, set up and presented by the KSČ (ČETEKA, in English, 7 June). The elections were preceded by an election campaign in which one of the main arguments adduced for the correctness of current policies was the standard of living. It was pointed out that although leaving much to be desired, this standard of living was better than that presently enjoyed by the Poles—an argument that tried to serve the double purpose of making the regime more palatable to the voters and reducing the attractiveness of the Polish social movement. This line was also adopted by hard-liner Vasil Bil'ák, a Presidium member, in a campaign speech in the East Slovak town of Prešov (*Rudé právo*, 26 May).

Culture and Religion. Several statements and comments made by party representatives during 1981 indicated that popular support was falling far short, even 33 years after the KSČ's accession to absolute power, of what the party wished or what the election results would suggest. Also, the re-education of the populace in a communist spirit showed little success; the "new socialist man" was slow in coming. Religiosity, especially among the young, continued to worry party ideologists. At the start of the new year, the KSČ philosophical review, *Nová Mysl* (no. 2), devoted an unusual amount of space to an attack on emigré Slovak Catholic organizations who allegedly conduct an anticommunist campaign in the guise of concern about improvement and liberalization of socialism. Actually, the author of the article feared less the activities of what he termed the "clerical emigration" in the United States and Canada than the revival of a movement that included Catholics and had brought the reformist leadership to power in 1968. The phenomenon of increasing rather than decreasing religiosity was in itself disturbing enough, as regime spokesmen had to admit. In an interview with journalists in the fall, Karel Hrůza, head of the State Secretariate for Religious Affairs, mentioned an important change among practicing church members. Previously, he said, churchgoers had been mostly old women; today, there were many young people, too. Asked about possible causes of the religious revival, Hrůza mentioned the search by the young for meaning in life and for something that could counteract the materialism of the consumer society—neither of which, obviously, the communist system could provide. (*NYT*, 4 October.) Faced with this situation, the regime stepped up its antireligious drive, relying heavily on coercion. In September, three Catholic priests and four laymen in Bohemia and Moravia were sentenced to prison for allegedly engaging in "illegal undertakings"—that is, for holding services without official permission or printing and distributing religious literature (AFP, 30 September).

Catechisms and translations of papal encyclicals were not the only clandestine publications the communist police were looking for and confiscating in 1981. Equally offensive to the regime was the unofficial reproduction of works rejected by publishing houses for political reasons. Underground literature has not been a Czechoslovak specialty; it developed first in the Soviet Union—hence the term *samizdat*, the Czech version of which is *edice-petlice* (meaning something like "publications from under padlock"). A recent analysis published in Canada revealed that there have been, during the last two years, no fewer than four hundred writers in Czechoslovakia whose works were not allowed to be published and who had to resort to samizdat or smuggle their manuscripts to the West (*Knihy 1980– 1981*, Toronto). The authorities seemed to pay more attention to samizdat activities in 1981 than in previous years. Following Western newspaper reports, the police questioned well-known Czech writer and Dubček supporter Ludvík Vaculík for 48 hours in January and confiscated his manuscripts, typewriters, and other supplies (*Le Monde*, Paris, 25 February).

Dissidence. Circulation of unofficial publications has been only one manifestation of dissent in Czechoslovakia. Dissent continued to take more overt forms. The two groups whose aim has been to protect human and civil rights—Charter 77 and VONS (Výbor pro obranu nespravedlivě stíhaných, Committe for the Defense of Unjustly Prosecuted Persons)—protested on several occasions and often made headlines in the Western press. The leadership of Charter 77 was reconstituted in January. The group's representatives, Marie Hromádková and Miloš Rejchrt, after completing one year in their functions, stepped down and were replaced by Václav Malý, a Roman Catholic priest, and Bedřich Placák, a heart surgeon (Reuters, Vienna, 14 January). In May, the Chartists sent an open letter of tribute and sympathy to Andrei Sakharov, Soviet physicist and Nobel laureate, exiled by the Soviet government to Gorki. They commended him for his "courageous fight for a dignified life for his fellow citizens" and assured him that his example was a source of inspiration to civil rights defenders in Czechoslovakia. (AFP, Paris, 8 May.)

Repression of dissident groups also continued. The measures taken by the authorities in 1981 seemed to indicate a determination to stamp out dissidence altogether or at least to deal a crippling blow to its visible symbols. Police searched the homes of VONS members Jan Litomský, Stanislav Adámek, Pavel Roubal, Josef Brychta, and Marie Bolubcová (*Le Monde*, 25 February). Shortly before the KSČ congress in April, a number of Charter 77 spokesmen and signatories were detained by the police or put under house arrest for the duration of the congress (AFP, Paris, 3 April). Later in the year, signs multiplied that the regime may have decided on a systematic operation with the help of the judiciary to eliminate dissident groups. The placing of former Charter representative and onetime Minister of Foreign Affairs Jiří Hájek and ten other Charter supporters in "provisional custody" was seen by foreign observers as the opening move in this operation (ibid., 7 May). It was believed to be in connection with the arrest made at the Czechoslovak border, shortly before, of two young French citizens, Françoise Anis and Gilles Thonon, on charges of having "transported documents and money for Czechoslovak citizens devoting themselves to subversive activities in Prague, Brno, and Bratislava" (ČETEKA, 29 April). Immediately afterwards, seven known civil rights workers, Jan Bednář, Jan Ruml, Jiří Ruml, Karen Kynclová, Zbyněk Fišera, Ivan Havel, and Olga Havlová, were apprehended (*Die Presse*, Vienna, 8 May). This made a total of 18 dissidents under arrest, but some Western sources put the number as high as 24 (AFP, Prague, 8 May). Charter spokesmen protested against these detentions in an open letter sent to Federal Premier Štrougal and the Federal Assembly. They called the police action "illegal repression and an attempt to frighten the defenders of human rights" (ibid., Paris, 8 May).

Later in May, two arrested Charter activists were released, but the regime did not change its plan of silencing or discrediting leaders of the dissident movement. Carefully orchestrated attacks in the media against the Chartists in custody suggested that a mass trial, patterned after the model of Stalin's political trials, was in the making; the charge was to be "subversive activities in collusion with a foreign power" (*Rudé právo*, 30 June, 13 August), an ominous indictment although difficult to uphold on the basis of available facts. The names that appeared most often in the press and radio incriminations were those of poet Jaromír Hořec, sociologist Jiřina Šiklová, university professor and writer Milan Šimečka, mathematician Ivan Havel, and former Foreign Minister and member of the KSČ Central Committee Jiří Hájek. Foreign correspondents in Prague expected the trial to take place in late August, but it was repeatedly postponed. It was assumed that the delay was due to the regime's wish not to complicate relations with Western nations, especially Austria, which Husák was to visit. Originally scheduled for September, this visit, too, was postponed. If this hypothesis is correct, the KSČ may not be completely insensitive to world opinion. Meanwhile, the courts of appeal have in two cases quashed sentences imposed on dissidents who already had been condemned but whose prison terms the authorities wanted to extend. The two defendants were Charter activist Petr Cibulka and sociologist Rudolf Battěk. It was interesting that in the case of Battěk, the lower court, in passing the additional sentence that later was annulled, justified the verdict by citing the "deteriorating situation abroad and in Poland" (UPI, 28 July), thus revealing one of the most important motives behind the current persecution of dissidents in Czechoslovakia.

Economy. In 1981, Czechoslovakia shared all the major economic problems of Soviet bloc countries. Although difficulties were much less acute than in Poland, two chronic ailments continued: the shortage or high cost of energy and raw materials and a balance of payments deficit. The latter improved in 1981, but a sizable deficit remained, with both socialist and nonsocialist trading partners. The deficit totaled more than 2 billion Kčs (about U.S. $375 million at the official rate of exchange). However, exports grew 7.9 percent and imports only 4.6 percent during the first six months of 1981 (*Rudé právo*, 29 July).

The 1981 performance of the Czechoslovak economy was rather mixed. Industrial sectors based on domestic raw materials, such as paper, timber, glass, and ceramics, seemed to perform satisfactorily, but results in the building industry and capital construction were only mediocre. Although a general growth of 2 percent had been planned, the volume of work performed in these two categories was 2.7 and 2.6 percent lower than in 1980; labor productivity declined by 2.3 percent while wages increased. In the housing sector, 25,661 units were completed during the first half of 1981, only 23.4 percent of the plan target. The progress of scientific research and technological innovations also left much to be desired; the latter, for example, reached only 90 percent of the plan figure. This put in doubt the attainment of the goal, set by Czechoslovakia and other Council for Mutual Economic Assistance (CMEA) countries, of relying more on homegrown know-how and reducing dependence on

Western technology. (Ibid., 6 July.) The shortcomings of the economy were more significant than ever in 1981, as it was the first year of the Seventh Five-Year Plan. These failures necessitated a scaling down of the target figures in comparison with the more ambitious (but also only partly fulfilled) objectives of the Sixth Five-Year Plan. The reductions were drastic: on the average, targets were about half of those of the previous plan, but some were cut as much as 66 percent (ČETEKA, in English, 28 February). Observers of the Czechoslovak economy were interested in the progress of the industrial management reform introduced in 1980, but there was little to be learned from official sources on this subject. Party congress documents, for example, ignored the subject.

In addition to the steady increase in the price of Soviet oil, on which Czechoslovakia depends for the overwhelming part of its consumption, two additional circumstances adversely influenced the Czechoslovak economy: the 1981 harvest was an average one, which will necessitate larger grain imports in 1982; and trade with Poland, Czechoslovakia's third largest trading partner, dropped because of the political and social upheaval in that country. The balance of payments with Poland was positive in the first half of 1981, but the volume of exchanged goods and services dropped approximately 15 percent over the previous six months (*Statistické přehledy*, September). The current five-year plan calls for the value of trade with Poland and other CMEA countries to continue to grow, but at a much slower pace; exchanges with the USSR, for example, which almost doubled during the Sixth Five-Year Plan, are expected to increase only 36 percent (Czechoslovak Television, 19 February). These figures do not include any increase in the price of Soviet oil, which would force Czechoslovakia to further augment the volume of exports to the USSR unless it is prepared to accept a sizable payments deficit. The price of Soviet oil increased by 50 percent from 1976 to 1979, and the steepest rise (40 percent) came in 1980. In 1982, Czechoslovakia is to buy Soviet crude and oil products worth 1.1 billion rubles or 9.1 billion Kčs (Radio Prague, 25 January). The overall prospects of the Czechoslovak economy do not seem too rosy, as discussions at the Sixteenth Party Congress and various statements made by KSČ leaders in 1981 revealed. The causes of this situation lie partly outside the country's control, but they are also partly due to the regime's unimaginative and rigid policies.

Foreign Affairs. In foreign policy, Czechoslovakia was a model Soviet satellite. Official media zealously contrasted Western—and especially American—warmongering and saber-rattling with the selfless peace efforts of the Soviet Union (*Rudé právo*, 14 February). This line of argument was somewhat difficult to sustain in view of the continuing Soviet occupation of Afghanistan and frequent reassertion of the Brezhnev Doctrine on limited sovereignty of communist states, which amounted to a poorly veiled threat of a Soviet military intervention in Poland. Czechoslovak party and government spokesmen justified the presence of Soviet troops in Afghanistan as a necessity for the preservation of peace and security in that area. This was particularly stressed during the visit to Prague of Afghan communist leader Babrak Karmal, who headed a delegation of the Revolutionary Council of Afghanistan. The two states signed a treaty of friendship and cooperation valid for 25 years that resembled the treaties with Czechoslovakia's most important communist partners, such as the USSR. This gives it a great symbolic value, further emphasized by the presence at the ceremony of virtually the entire party Presidium and Secretariat and many Central Committee members (Radio Prague, in English, 24 June).

As for other countries with communist regimes or under Soviet influence, Czechoslovakia in 1981 cultivated contacts with Ethiopia, Libya, and South Yemen, all three of which Husák, accompanied by an impressive array of top party and state officials, visited in September (Radio Hvězda, 7 September). Treaties of friendship and cooperation were signed with Ethiopia and South Yemen, while an agreement on economic and technological cooperation was concluded with Libya (*Rudé právo*, 15 September). Before Husák's trip to Africa, visits from, and agreements with, other African countries whose regimes the KSČ considers progressive, took place. In February, the minister of foreign affairs of Mozambique, Joaquim Chissano, visited Prague, and a mixed Czechoslovak-Mozambican commission on cooperation was established (ibid., 5 February). A month later, diplomatic relations with Zimbabwe were established (ČETEKA, 26 March). In May, a two-year program of cooperation in education, information, and health care was finalized in Brazzaville between Czechoslovakia and the People's Republic of the Congo (Rudé právo, 12 May). A trade and payments agreement was concluded with the People's Republic of China in the spring (ČETEKA, 11 May). Economic and trade talks to broaden cooperation were also initiated with Mexico (NOTIMEX, Mexico City, 30 March).

Czechoslovak spokesmen and mass media also lent unreserved support to the Soviet line on such issues as the U.S. hostages crisis and the American embargo on grain shipments to the USSR. Regime commentators acknowledged that the Iranian radicals who took U.S. diplomatic personnel hostage had violated international law, but lectured the United States about the "lesson to be drawn from this undoubtedly regrettable affair." The United States, they counseled, should realize the risks involved in systematic meddling in the internal affairs of other states—a rather unthinking statement from those who experienced a Soviet military intervention and must have witnessed continual Soviet interference ever since in the internal affairs of their own country (Rudé právo, 22 January). Czechoslovak media registered with satisfaction President Reagan's lifting of the grain embargo as proof of a more realistic approach than that shown by his predecessor. According to official Czechoslovak sources, the embargo had no effect (Radio Prague, in English, 25 April). The Czechoslovak press gave wide coverage to the speech of Soviet Deputy Minister of Foreign Affairs Semen Kozyrev at the U.N. Conference on the Law of the Sea and declared that his criticism of the U.S. position was "crushing" (Rudé právo, 19 March).

Soviet leaders compensated their model satellite in kind. When Italian President Alessandro Pertini remarked that Czechoslovakia may be one source of support for international terrorism, Soviet Minister of Foreign Affairs Andrei Gromyko summoned the Italian ambassador and protested (Radio Prague, 27 January). Although to official Czechoslovak commentators this action may have appeared as an example of international proletarian solidarity, it only underscored the semicolonial status of postinvasion Czechoslovakia.

On the other hand, the Czechoslovak government showed an unusual sensitivity to possible or often only imaginary interference whenever Western diplomats or private individuals were involved. In February, two French diplomats in Prague were ordered to leave the country on short notice. The charge was espionage, but there were indications that the two may have had contacts with Czechoslovak citizens classified as "subversive" (WP, 17 February). A few days later, a West German political science professor, Konrad Loew, was arrested and deported for allegedly having "spread fascist philosophy in public." He was supposed to have made these "provocative utterances" at a symposium of the Czechoslovak Academy of Sciences. Some observers believed that Loew's public statements, which were critical of the Soviet Union, were less the cause of his deportation than his informal contacts with some nonconformist Czechoslovak intellectuals (Le Monde, 25 February). The regime's treatment of dissidents clouded relations with other European states. Uncertainty over the state's intentions toward arrested Charter activists was one of the main reasons for the postponement of a long-planned official visit to Austria by Husák. The visit was prepared in talks between Štrougal and Austrian authorities in June. However, in September the Austrian government announced that Husák's visit had been postponed indefinitely. In addition to the indignation of Austrians over persecution of Chartists, the revelation by Czechoslovak Television that a Czechoslovak intelligence agent, Josef Hodič, had been spying on Czechoslovak exiles in Austria for several years further complicated relations. Hodič had posed as a refugee and obtained Austrian nationality before returning to Czechoslovakia (Rudé právo, 2 July). Austria also watched with apprehension the building of three nuclear reactors in Czechoslovakia, not far from the Austrian border (Reuters, 3 September). Later in the year, new negotiations about Husák's visit were opened, but by late 1981 no definite date had been set. Czechoslovak media reacted to the postponement by vehemently attacking the "provocative activity of exiles" in Austria and charged "malevolent and hostile sorties" on the part of the Austrian press (*Rudé právo*, 12 September). The sensitivity of the Czechoslovak regime in these matters was illustrated by its demonstrative cancellation of a performance of the Slovak Philharmonic Orchestra in Vienna after the Vienna municipal theater staged a play by Václav Havel, a prominent Czechoslovak dissident now in prison (*Die Presse*, 8 May).

As for contacts on state level with the USSR and other communist countries in Eastern Europe, 1981 saw the signing of a document on economic cooperation with the Soviet Union. In March, Foreign Minister Bohuslav Chňoupek spent five days in the USSR and talked to his Soviet counterpart, Andrei Gromyko. "Full identity of views on all questions discussed" was reported (Radio Prague, 18 March). A long-term trade agreement for the duration of the Seventh Five-Year Plan was signed with East Germany at the beginning of the year (ČETEKA, in English, 13 January). In September, Czechoslovakia and Poland approved a trade protocol envisaging exchanges in 1982 of goods and services worth 1.5 billion rubles (U.S. $2.25 billion) (ibid., 2 September).

Reaction to Polish Events. The position of KSČ leaders on the developments in Poland, negative from the start, did not change in 1981. Czechoslovak Communists had recognized, as early as August 1980, what was at stake: the power monopoly, or—to use vocabulary of party ideologists—the leading role of the party. Being themselves the Soviet-appointed guardians of this role in Czechoslovakia, the ruling team headed by Husák had to reject all ideas of sharing responsibilities for political decision making. This view was articulated clearly at the turn of the year in an editorial by Václav Hora in the party theoretical weekly *Tribuna* (24 December 1980), entitled " 'Independent' Unions in the Plans of Antisocialist Forces." The quotation marks around "independent" indicated what the KSČ found most objectionable about Solidarity. Hora linked Solidarity to "foreign anticommunist centers," declared that it was constituted by "false friends of the Polish people," and denied it the right to represent workers. Hostile coverage of the Polish crisis continued throughout the year. Articles and television programs depicted Solidarity as a provocateur, an imperialist Trojan horse, and a fifth column of capitalism (*Rudé právo*, 26 January; 21 March; *Tribuna*, 22 April). The new Polish trade union was also linked to the AFL-CIO and the German neo-Nazi movement (*Rudé právo*, 13 January; ČETEKA, in English, 16 January).

A new element in the Czechoslovak media campaign against the process of social and political differentiation in Poland was the initially covert but eventually explicit criticism of Polish party leaders for tolerating the union movement or even negotiating with Solidarity. The previously assumed ability of the Polish party to deal with the crisis gradually became doubted. Karel Pomajzl, writing in the KSČ weekly *Tvorba* (16 September), challenged the Polish party's concern about the preservation of national unity. He argued that such concern could only open the door to "false unity with reactionary Polish exiles" and ultimately lead to the restoration of capitalism. After Stanislaw Kania's dismissal in October, the wave of criticism subsided a little, probably due to a wait-and-see attitude toward new party boss Wojciech Jaruzelski.

Critical commentary on Poland was not left to mass media and party theoreticians alone. Leading KSČ officials frequently expressed their worries over events to the north. Several Presidium members addressed the topic at the pre-congress local and regional party organizations meetings (Radio Hvězda; 7 March; *Rudé právo*, 9 March). Secretary General Husák included an extensive and very critical passage on Poland in his opening speech to the congress (ibid., 7 April). These statements included a claim, sometimes indirect, sometimes direct, that other communist parties and states in the Soviet orbit had the right to intervene in the Polish crisis if necessary. Even as military intervention became less likely, Czechoslovak party leaders never missed an opportunity to publicly restate this position. Attempts were undertaken, too, by KSČ leaders to boost the morale of what they called the "healthy forces in Poland." Karel Hoffmann, chairman of the Central Trade Union Council, went to Warsaw to visit officials of the party-controlled unions, reduced to insignificance by Solidarity (ČETEKA, 15 March). Czechoslovak radio also broadcast special programs in Polish warning the Poles of the possibility of a "counterrevolution" like that in Czechoslovakia in 1968 (Radio Prague, 18 April). The impact of these "fraternal counsels" is not known, but the Polish-language programs did not become a regular feature.

Czechoslovak authorities also took specific measures to contain the influence of the Polish reform movement on Czechs and Slovaks. Early in 1981, some border crossing points to Poland were closed. Travel formalities for tourist traffic with Poland, until then relatively liberal, were stiffened. The maximum amount of Polish currency that could be exchanged was cut considerably. Restrictions were also imposed on Polish persons traveling to Czechoslovakia. (*Rudé právo*, 13 February.) In April, Western agencies reported from Prague that a number of "exile Poles in Czechoslovakia"—a category not closely defined and difficult to imagine—were arrested and expelled because they had printed and distributed in North Moravia Czech-language tracts on the Polish crisis (AFP, Prague, 30 April).

Even before the imposition on 13 December of martial law in Poland, Czechoslovak media strongly attacked activities of antisocialist forces in Poland, especially Solidarity "provocations." On 14 December, *Rudé právo* greeted the establishment of the Military Council of National Salvation as "an act of urgent self-defense" and stated that "Polish communists and the government of People's Poland are showing the way out of the all-social crisis . . . They have our sympathies and can rely on our all-out support" (*FBIS*, 17 December). On 15 December, the trade union organ *Práce* justified the declaration of the state of emergency in Poland as "the logical response of the state leadership to the deepening disruption and to the risk of the civil war" (ibid., 16 December). That same day, Prague television bitterly attacked the leaders of the Italian Communist Party for their condemnation of the measures adopted by the Polish government and compared them with "the people of the Franz-Josef Strauss type" (ibid.). The Spanish and British parties were also criticized in the Czechoslovak press for the same reason. Radio Prague admitted on 21 December that tension existed in the mines of Katowice and that production had stopped in the shipyards of the Baltic coast. It also spoke of the continuous purge of those Polish party members who had committed harmful acts. It assailed the White House for "assuming patronage of the antisocialist forces" and scolded Washington for provoking "a wave of anti-Soviet hysteria while talking about an alleged intervention [in Poland] planned by Moscow." (Ibid., 23 December.) The 23 December decision of the U.S. government to take economic sanctions against Poland was characterized by a vehement article in *Rudé právo* as a measure taken to prevent "the current normalization process" in Poland. It stated that the government of General Jaruzelski enjoyed the support of an overwhelming majority of Polish society. (Ibid., 30 December.)

International Party Contacts. The relations of the KSČ with many chapters of the world communist movement, burdened by the legacy of the Soviet intervention, which most communist parties outside the Soviet orbit condemn but the Husák leadership continues to justify, have become even more complicated since the Polish crisis. The Czechoslovak party line on Poland produced an additional cleavage within the communist camp since only a few parties advocate a military intervention against the Polish workers. These differences came to light at the Sixteenth Party Congress. Twenty delegates of foreign communist parties addressed the issue of Poland in their speeches; a majority took a position similar to that expressed by Mireille Bertrand, the representative of the Communist Party of France, who declared a Soviet intervention "unthinkable" (*Rudé právo*, 16 April).

Consistent with the Brezhnev Doctrine, an article of faith with present KSČ leaders, is the rejection by Husák and his associates of the idea of a more independent course for communist parties operating in the West. This stand has brought relations with the Communist Party of Italy, among others, to a new low. Although an Italian delegation was in attendance, this most important chapter of the world communist movement in Western Europe did not address the KSČ congress (ibid., 17 April). In view of the fundamental hostility of the KSČ toward emancipation trends within the West European fraternal parties, it came as no surprise that Spanish Communists were represented in Prague by a splinter, Moscow-oriented party called the Unified Communist Party of Spain, instead of the Communist Party of Spain (ibid., 8 April). The boss of the latter, Santiago Carrillo, theoretician and promoter of the policies of Eurocommunism, is anathema to the Husák team, which sees the salvation of communism in unqualified subservience of all parties to the Soviet party. For the same reason, Czechoslovak media provided an extensive coverage of the formation in Barcelona of the Catalan branch of the Unified Communist Party in Spain whose numerical importance appears to be even more negligible than that of the parent body (ibid., 9 January).

Disregarding the unsatisfactory state of its relations with many communist parties, the Husák team continued to support the USSR unreservedly on all matters concerning international communist affairs. Czechoslovak press and radio criticized China for harming the Albanian economy by discontinuing trade relations in 1978. The usual criticism of Albanian leaders for rejecting current Soviet policies was not spelled out this time (ibid., 23 January). As another anti-Chinese gesture, and a token of support for the Soviet position, the KSČ represented by Miroslav Čapka, chairman of the Control and Auditing Commission of the Central Committee, congratulated the Kampuchean People's Revolutionary Party (KPRK) for its political and social accomplishments and assured it of "fraternal friendship." Čapka addressed the KPRP in Phnom Penh in May on the occasion of its Fourth congress. He recalled the "disinterested internationalist assistance given to the KPRP by the Soviet Union, Vietnam, and other socialist countries." (SPK, in French, Phnom Penh, 30 May.) By giving precedence to the Soviet Union over Vietnam, which actually carried out the military intervention that ousted Pol Pot, Čapka implied Soviet initiative in an operation that reduced Chinese influence in Indochina considerably.

An interparty contact in 1981 that received attention from many observers was the meeting in February between Secretary General Husák and Polish party leader Stanislaw Kania in Prague. No mention was made in the final communiqué of the crisis in Poland, much less of any role for the KSČ in its resolution, but it was believed that these points had been discussed (Radio Prague, 15 February). That same month, Husák led the Czechoslovak delegation to the Twenty-Sixth Congress of the Communist Party of the Soviet Union in Moscow. In his address to the congress, Husák emphasized that the five-year period between the Fifteenth and the Sixteenth congresses of the KSČ had been a successful one, but that the years to come would not be easy, especially in the economic area (ibid., 24 February). On his return trip, Husák spoke to a Czechoslovak-Soviet friendship meeting in the Latvian capital, Riga. Here he stressed Soviet help in the technological progress of Czechoslovakia as exemplified by the construction of the Prague subway and the nuclear plant at Jaslovské Bohunice (ibid., 2 March). Soviet media reciprocated these eulogies by providing unusually detailed coverage of the KSČ's congress in April, thus upgrading this event, which had already been put into the limelight by the presence of Brezhnev (Radio Moscow, 9 April; 14 April).

In May, Romanian Secretary General Nicolae Ceauşescu arrived in Czechoslovakia for a three-day visit and was received with great pomp. In no speech or communiqué was it recalled that Romania not only had failed to participate in the 1968 military intervention but also had vehemently condemned the Soviet action. In the final protocol of the visit, the Czechoslovaks adroitly placed the usual Romanian call for respect of national sovereignty and noninterference in the affairs of other states into a passage condemning imperialism and neocolonialism, although it has not been in this context that Romanian leaders have stated and restated this principle (*Rudé právo*, 23 May). Husák had his annual meeting with Brezhnev in the Crimea in the summer. The KSČ Central Committee, in appraising the results of these talks, scored the "aggressive forces of imperialism" for "threatening the peaceful life of the peoples and enhancing the danger of an outbreak of a new war," but failed to mention Poland (ibid., 22 August). Observers concluded that this topic may not have been discussed at all. If true, this would indicate less imminence of a Soviet intervention.

Publications. The central press organ of the KSČ is the daily *Rudé právo*, published in Czech in Prague. The main daily of the Slovak communist party is *Pravda*, appearing in Bratislava. Questions of general party policy and theory are addressed in the Czech weekly *Tribuna* or its Slovak counterpart, *Predvoj*. Issues of party organization and day-to-day activities are dealt with in the fortnightly *Život strany*. The Trade Union Council publishes the Czech daily *Práce* and the Slovak daily *Práca*. The Socialist Youth Union publishes the Czech daily *Mladá fronta* and the Slovak-language *Smena*. The weekly *Tvorba*, originally a theoretical review, now features analyses and comments on questions of international politics, economics, and culture. The official press agency is Československá tisková kancelář, abbreviated ČTK or, more commonly, ČETEKA.

University of Pittsburgh   Zdeněk Suda

Germany:
German Democratic Republic

The German Communist Party (KPD) developed into one of the world's largest communist parties within a few years of its formation in 1918. The process of bolshevization and Stalinization that the KPD underwent starting in the early 1920s, however, stripped it of all independence. Turned into a pliant tool of Soviet communism, the KPD was repeatedly compelled to pursue policies beneficial to Soviet state interests but inimical to its own viability. Forced to flee Germany when Hitler assumed power, many top KPD functionaries were brought to the Soviet Union, where, working with their Russian counterparts during the 1930s and 1940s, they fashioned plans for a "democratic republic" in postwar Germany. In 1945–1949, they implemented many of these plans, adapted and modified to fit changing circumstances, in the Soviet Zone of Occupation (SBZ). Backed by Soviet occupation authorities, German Communists forced Social Democrats in the SBZ to "unite" their party with the KPD in 1946. The resulting Socialist Unity Party (SED) has ruled the German Democratic Republic (GDR) ever since.

Leadership and Organization. Neither the Central Committee elected at the Tenth Party Congress (11–16 April) nor the Politburo chosen by the new Central Committee showed any significant changes over those elected in 1976. Erich Honecker's re-election as general secretary was a surprise to no one. The number of Politburo members dropped from nineteen (in 1976) to seventeen. Gerhard Grüneberg, Central Committee secretary of agriculture, died on the eve of the congress and was not replaced in the Politburo (Werner Felfe, already a Politburo member, took over the post of secretary of agriculture). Party veteran Albert Norden was not re-elected to the Politburo and lost his seat on the Central Committee as well. Though rumored to be seriously ill, Norden's dismissal occurred abruptly, considering that sickness or age has not generally been a criterion for dropping someone of Norden's stature from a top party post. Norden's retirement was not reported in the press until a few weeks later, when he was awarded the Karl Marx Medal. (*Neues Deutschland* [*ND*], 30 April). The number of Politburo candidates fell from nine in 1976 to eight. Two former candidates, Joachim Herrmann and Horst Dohlus, had been promoted in the interim to full membership; only one new candidate, the chief editor of *Neues Deutschland*, Günter Schabowski, was appointed. Changes in the Central Committee were more numerous, although they offered no surprises. The number of full members rose from 145 in 1976 to 156, of whom 126 had belonged to the previous group. The number of Central Committee members is now at its highest level in history, due in part to the increase in SED members and candidates from 2,043,413 in 1976 to 2,172,110 at the latest congress. (The population of East Germany is 16.7 million). The number of high military officers in the Central Committee jumped markedly. Previously, Gen. Heinz Hoffmann, minister of defense and Politburo member, and Gen. Horst Stechbarth enjoyed full Central Committee membership, and Lt. Gen. Horst Brünner was a candidate. In the new Central Committee, Col. Gen. Fritz Streletz is now a full member, and Lt. Gen. Klaus-Dieter Baumgarten, Adm. Wilhelm Ehm, and Col. Gen. Wolfgang Reinhold are candidates. The number of state security officers has also increased. State security chief Erich Mielke (also a Politburo member) and his deputy, Col. Gen. Bruno Beater, both longtime Central Committee members, are now joined by Maj. Gen. Horst Felber, who replaced Gen. Gerhard Heidenreich. Deputy Minister of State Security Lt. Gen. Rudolf Mittig is a newly elected candidate. (*Frankfurter Allgemeine Zeitung* [*FAZ*], 18 April; *Deutschland Archiv* [*DA*], no. 5, pp. 449–52, no. 7, pp. 715–18; *Informationen*, no. 9, pp. 7–9.)

Prompted by headlines such as "Those Who Favor Peace Cast Their Votes on 14 June for the Candidates of the National Front of the GDR" (*ND*, 13/14 June), East Germans "went folding," as the saying goes, approving the National Front's "common electoral ballot" of 679 members to the People's Chamber by folding the ballot containing the *Einheitsliste* ("unity list") and dropping it into the box. The yes vote for the new People's Chamber of 500 delegates and 179 deputy delegates was 99.86 percent, the same as in 1976. Only 16,645 voted no, the effort requiring, after all, a public demonstration of disapproval. (Ibid., 15 June.) The composition of the People's Chamber, which met for its constituent assembly on 25 June, remains unaffected by any election: the SED receives 127 seats; 52 go to each of the four other parties; the Free German Trade Union Federation is allotted 68; the Free German Youth get 40; the Democratic Women's League has 35; and 22 belong to the Cultural League. These fractions have remained the same since 1963. This year's elections were important because they marked the first direct elections of East Berlin's delegates to the People's Chamber, a clear violation of the Quadripartite Agreement of 1971. (*FAZ*, 16 June.) Western protests were ignored (*Informationen*, no. 3, p. 3); objections raised by West Berlin Governor Richard von Weizsäcker were dismissed with the words: "Evidently Mr. Weizsäcker . . . is still not aware that since the formation of the GDR, Berlin has been its capital" (*FAZ*, 26 June).

Auxiliary and Mass Organizations. The Free German Youth (FDJ), one of the GDR's two largest and most influential mass organizations, held its Eleventh Parliament from 2 to 5 June. Attended by some 3,359 delegates and 131 foreign delegations, the parliament matched the Tenth Party Congress in its uneventful ritualism. Egon Krenz, 44, since 1974 first secretary of the FDJ Central Council (and since 1976 an SED Politburo candidate), was re-elected. Confirmed as second secretary (a post he has held since December 1980) was Eberhard Aurich, 36. His advancement to SED Central Committee membership at the party congress in April gave rise to speculation that Aurich would soon replace the older Krenz as head of the FDJ. (*DA*, no. 7, pp. 682–86; *FAZ*, 3 June.) According to Krenz, the FDJ now has 2.3 million members (72,000 more "young workers" than five years ago [*ND*, 3 June]). Erich Honecker and Krenz gave major speeches at the Eleventh Parliament. A keynote of Honecker's address was his criticism of the NATO decision to deploy medium-range missiles in Europe; Honecker referred to the growing West European protests against the stationing of Pershing II and cruise missiles in Europe and demanded an end to the arms race and the start of negotiations to control the spread of armaments. In reference to West Germany (FRG), he said: "It is not enough that representatives of both German states declare that a war shall never again emanate from German soil. Rather, it is imperative to prevent the FRG from being transformed into a starting ramp for new U.S. missiles, into a powder keg." (Ibid., 6/7 June.) Krenz's address hit on the same theme, combined with general diatribes against imperialism and praise of "our socialist fatherland, the German Democratic Republic" (ibid., 3 June). Other remarks pointed toward concern over Poland: "Our enemies never tire of explaining that Marxism-Leninism does not show youth reality as it is. But such talk from the mouths of anticommunists, revisionists, or so-called renewers has long since been exposed as a maneuver to separate the young generation from the historical mission of the working class" (ibid.). Another passage revealed more clearly that Poland was troubling Krenz; he promised "the bonds of solidarity to all fighters against the counterrevolution in our neighboring country" (*DA*, no. 7, p. 683). The irony in his choice of words was unintentional. Following the tactics of the SED's Tenth Party Congress, the strongest expression of concern came not from a prominent party personality but from a common delegate who protested manifestations of anti-Sovietism in Poland and hoped that "the many Communists whom I have gotten to know in the People's Republic of Poland will have the strength to put an end to these machinations." (Ibid.)

Inevitably, leaders of the Free German Trade Union Federation (FDGB), the other of the GDR's two largest mass organizations, felt particularly affected by the events in Poland and responded accordingly in speeches and articles. Harry Tisch, a member of the SED Politburo and chairman of the FDGB, elaborated in an article published in the official party monthly, *Einheit* (no. 4/5, pp. 354–61), on the "close, trusting relation between the party and the trade unions" in the GDR as a cornerstone of the political power of workers and peasants. As for unions under socialism, he explained that "the party exercises its leading role in the trade unions mainly through the work of the Communists active in them, through their doing exemplary trade union work." But the party knew of "no tutelage or regimentation," said Tisch, adding: "In its trade union policy, the SED always proceeds from the consideration that the trade unions operate as independent organizations under their own responsibility." After all, the FDGB was "free and independent since, according to the principles of our constitution, no one may confine or obstruct their [the unions'] activity." He also lashed out at "the eager efforts by reaction to return to the agenda the slogan of 'free' trade unions, 'independent' of the working class party and the proletarian state." At the thirteenth session of the FDGB's National Executive Committee, Tisch came out even more forcefully against the "distortion" by imperialism of "the position of trade unions in socialism."

Tisch remarked that anticommunist agitation prejudiced the cause of normal international relations among trade union organizations and alleged reactionary intrigues by leaders of the American AFL-CIO trade unions. After having obstructed normal relations with trade unions in socialist countries for many years, they now acted as if they had discovered that their heart was on the side of socialism. Through considerable financial and material aid to Lech Walesa's trade union in Poland, they were interfering in the affairs of that socialist country with the intention of establishing a counterforce against the Polish United Workers' Party (PUWP) and further escalating the confrontation with the socialist state. Tisch expressed the hope and expectation that Poland's Communists and patriots would succeed in turning back all counterrevolutionary attacks, claiming that Poland has been, is, and will remain socialist. (*Tribüne*, 23 April; *JPRS*, 21 May.)

Party Internal Affairs. The SED's Tenth Party Congress met from 11 to 16 April. Forty-nine speakers addressed some 2,678 delegates, who signified their preprogrammed approval of the uneventful proceedings with the standard show of enthusiasm for the "historic" event. The congress proceeded strictly according to script, confirmed past and present party policies, and contrasted the SED—by intention—with the erratic performance of the Polish party. Mikhail Suslov, chief Soviet ideologue and representative to the congress, left direct references to Poland to the Bulgarian and Hungarian representatives. But Suslov did say that "the situation on the continent is being aggravated by attempts by reaction to erode our community, to undermine the basis of socialism by means of interference in the domestic affairs of socialist countries and by ideological subversion and provocations and by psychological warfare" (Moscow Domestic Service, 12 April; *FBIS*, 13 April). Honecker, in his Central Committee report to the congress, spoke of the "severe difficulties" confronting the PUWP and assured Polish Communists and "all Polish patriots" of the SED's "fraternal solidarity." Echoing Suslov, who had noted that "only the consistent and strict realization of the Marxist-Leninist doctrine" guaranteed the "triumph of socialist ideals" and that deviation from that revolutionary teaching had always brought about dire consequences (*FAZ*, 14 April), Honecker stated: " 'Models' for so-called 'renewed' socialism, from wherever they might emanate, have proved totally unsound every time." (*ND*, 12 April.)

Domestic Affairs: *Dissent and Repression.* In midsummer the GDR began preparations for a massive twentieth-anniversary celebration of the building of the Berlin Wall. On 13 August, "Working-class militia," units of the National People's Army, border troops, and people's police (some 10,000 strong watched by 120,000 spectators, according to East German figures) marched past a reviewing stand under the watchful eyes of Erich Honecker and other leading state and party dignitaries. The rationales given this year for the "securing of the GDR's state border" deviated little from past excuses and fell into two categories: the "actions of 13 August" successfully "thwarted an imperialist attack" by NATO and ended the "unscrupulous" misuse of an open border to "bleed the GDR to death economically" (ibid., 13 August). According to one commentator, by the early 1960s, the GDR had assumed a sufficiently high degree of control over the means of production to enable socialism to develop. Specialized workers, technicians, scholars, scientists, doctors, and so on, however, were constantly being lured away to the West with the goal of undermining the economy of the GDR and saving West German monopolies "gigantic sums" in training expenses. (Ibid., 1/2 August.)

Would the wall ever come down? Answering Japanese journalists during a visit to Japan, Honecker said: "Of course, when all of the preconditions that led to the construction of the antifascist protective wall are no longer operative, then one could imagine entertaining thoughts about the border security installations around [West] Berlin" (*DA*, no. 8, p. 785).

On the eve of the celebration, an incident made-to-order for the East German press occurred at the border. An East German guard attempting to escape was stopped by his partner, whom the fleeing guard shot to death. While the GDR was demanding the return of the soldier (the West Germans refused), the dead guard was posthumously promoted and buried with high military honors. (*FAZ*, 4 and 6 August; *ND*, 13 August.) The incident was characterized in *Neues Deutschland* (4 August) as a "grave attack" on the GDR state border; only by reading between the lines was it obvious that the "perpetrator" was also an East German. Readers were likewise left to guess that the case involved an escaping border guard. The mentality of those who make "fleeing the republic" a criminal act of aggression against the state was similarly evident in the description of the dead guard's commitment to "protecting the border" and "safeguarding socialist achievements" (*ND*, 13 August).

The West German Ministry of the Interior announced that in 1980 51 persons escaped across the border; in 155 other cases, West German guards observed the arrest of East Germans attempting to escape. Three persons were injured by automatic weapons systems or by border-guard machineguns.

In the border region, the East Germans continue to replace less effective minefields with automatic firing systems. (*Informationen*, no. 8, p. 4.)

At the SED's Tenth Party Congress, Honecker contended that "thirty years of the GDR confirm the truth: never before have literature and art been able to develop on German soil so freely as in our socialist GDR" (*ND*, 12 April). In the words of writer Frank-Wolf Matthies, however, "the republic is leaking out like rusty gasoline cans" (*DA*, no. 7, p. 767). The past year brought the departure to the West of Matthies (who voiced his disinclination to "vomit [his] Weltschmerz into the poetry albums of decreed opinion" any longer [*Der Spiegel*, 26 January]) and Thomas Erwin (*FAZ*, 19 January, 23 February). The next to leave were two older, well-known writers, Erich Loest and Karl-Heinz Jakobs (ibid., 17 March, 25 April). Deputy Minister of Culture Klaus Höpcke said that the state would continue to allow "authors who liked to travel" to leave (ibid., 17 March).

In early 1981, an Amnesty International report strongly criticized the GDR for violations of human rights and called on the country to bring its penal code into conformity with international norms. According to Amnesty International, some 200 persons are arrested yearly on political charges in the GDR, and between 3,000 and 7,000 political prisoners are behind bars. (Ibid., 5 February.) Another report listed a total of 55,000 prisoners, among whom some 4,500 are political. GDR Justice Minister Hans-Joachim Heusinger dismissed the charge as "significantly exaggerated" (ibid., 20 June). Asked about the Amnesty International report, Honecker took the tack that has become standard in the last decade; namely, organizations and groups antagonistic to the GDR or "socialism" are financed by Western secret services.

In early February, the East German Ministry of State Security celebrated its thirty-first anniversary and received a message of congratulations from the SED Central Committee. Signed by Honecker, the ministry was complimented for having lived up to the "political and operational" demands placed on it "under the conditions of the aggravated international situation" by safeguarding the security of the GDR and foiling "all subversive machinations of the enemy" (*ND*, 7/8 February). Also in February, Minister of State Security Erich Mielke, revealing his unease over the situation in Poland, warned against contacts with Westerners: "The activity of [our] Chekists is, above all, to aim at thwarting the insidious and seditious activity directed against our republic and other socialist states" (*FAZ*, 24 February).

According to the "working group '13 August,'" the Federal Republic of Germany (FRG) has spent two billion marks since 1964 to buy the freedom of East German political prisoners. Up to 1,200 prisoners annually have been expelled to West Germany through their "purchase"; in December 1980–January 1981, 300 prisoners reportedly arrived in the West. (*Die Welt*, 16 June.)

Economy. On 17 January, *Neues Deutschland* claimed that the economic goals of 1980 had actually been overfulfilled. However, the GDR's equivalent of gross national product grew by only 4.2 percent in 1980, the last year of the 1976–1980 five-year plan. Although the figure was not an embarrassment, especially in contrast to the economic stagnation in other Warsaw Pact states, it was short of the planned 4.8 percent. In fact, the plan was underfulfilled in each of the past five years (1976: 3.7 percent [target 5.3]; 1977: 5.2 [5.5]; 1978: 3.8 [5.2]; 1979: 4.0 [5.3]). Nor can the average yearly growth from 1976 to 1980 of 4.2 percent be favorably compared with the 5.2 percent reached in 1966–1970 and the 5.4 percent in 1971–1975. Foreign trade in 1980 increased by 10 percent, two percentage points short of the plan; exports to developing countries and Western industrial states grew by 36 and 27 percent, respectively, compared with the preceding year. A promising sign was the GDR's success at rationalizing its use of energy and raw materials (which must be purchased with hard currency on the world market) by 5 percent, without seriously affecting the rate of growth. (*FAZ*, 19 January; *Informationen*, no. 3, pp. 10–13.) German-German trade, which grew by 12 percent in 1979, expanded again in 1980 by 18.7 percent (*Informationen*, no. 6, pp. 8–9, 13–14). In the first half of 1981, however, trade between the two Germanies grew by only 4 percent compared with the first six months of 1980 (ibid., no. 17, p. 16).

The introduction of the new five-year plan (1981–1985) at the SED's Tenth Party Congress was surrounded by the customary rhetoric. Said Honecker, "Safeguarding what we have achieved . . . as well as expanding upon it demands an unprecedented rise in economic achievement" (*ND*, 12 April). But the goals disclosed at the congress made no allowance for such a dramatic upswing in the GDR's economic output. In fact, the objectives are virtually identical with the past plan, calling for 28–30 percent growth by 1985, an average of 5.6–6.0 percent annually. The plan surprised some Western observers because Honecker had admitted in February that in view of the worldwide economic picture, he would not regard it as a "tragedy" if the annual growth rate up to 1985 fell short of 4 percent. If the new plan nonetheless aims for a wholly unrealistic 5.6–6.0 percent rate (compared, incidentally, with Soviet hopes for 3.6–4.0 percent and a Czechoslovak goal of 2.8–3.2), the reasons are not grounded in the GDR's economic reality; rather, political and ideological thinking dictates optimism. Honecker's policy of continued low rents and low prices for basic consumer goods is in real jeopardy because of the effect of higher prices on the world market and increased defense expenditures unless the economy expands at the rate called for in the new plan. Realistic expectations, however, point toward a growth rate of 3.0–3.5 percent over the next five years, insufficient to maintain the present standard of living. Domestic stability is at stake, and the SED knows it. The party's continual trumpeting of the contrast between crisis-ridden capitalism and stable, economically vibrant, and forward-moving socialism has tied the party's claim to legitimacy as an agent of economic laws and historical progress to an ongoing improvement in the people's standard of living possible only through economic growth. The SED cannot come out with a realistic economic assessment without risking popular discontent, although by hiding the truth the SED merely postpones the day of reckoning. Already at the Tenth Party Congress a discussion of economic failures during 1976–1980 was circumvented (Willi Stoph spoke only of the future, ignoring the preceding five-year plan); moreover, the new "directives" for 1981–1985 came out only *after* the congress, preventing the "broad popular discussion" about the new plan that had occurred over the four months preceding the 1976 congress. The SED has backed itself into a corner. As yet, the relatively stable economy (compared with other members of the Council for Mutual Economic Assistance) has served to retard any rise in popular discontent and, in fact, provoked a significant amount of anti-Polish sentiment among East Germans, who fear that events in Poland may yet negatively affect their standard of living. But decisions will have to be made eventually. One observer sees only three possibilities for the SED. First, growth can be continued for a while longer and the standard of living maintained, but only at the cost of taking out more foreign loans that enable the GDR to keep pace with higher prices for raw materials (the GDR, with a population of 17 million, owes the West $10 billion; Poland, with 35 million, has a foreign debt of $23 billion). Second, growth is allowed to come to a standstill, and the GDR standard of living slides. Or third, fundamental economic reforms entailing changes in the political structure and political policy of the SED are introduced in order to raise production. Sooner or later, the SED will have to settle on a specific course of action, with all of the consequences that that entails. (See *DA*, no. 7, pp. 729–33, no. 9, pp. 931–37.)

The 18–19 July issue of *Neues Deutschland* published the economic indicators ("the results of diligent work") for the first half of 1981. Although the statistics were generally favorable, the SED also continued its practice of presenting vital information in a manner that makes productive comparisons difficult. In any case, the statistics claim that gross national product had risen 5 percent, the same rate of growth reached last year during the first six months. As promising as the figure was, foreign trade was discouraging. The goal was 16 percent increase, but only 12 percent was attained (the slowdown in trade with Poland was, of course, a contributing factor). A key part of the five-year plan requires the export of more goods to procure hard currency, but imports instead outpaced its exports.

The hitch here is that increased industrial production does not necessarily guarantee a hard-currency market for GDR products. (*FAZ*, 21 July; *Informationen*, no. 16, pp. 8–10; *DA*, no. 9, pp. 938–40.)

Military. In March, the National People's Army (NVA) celebrated its twenty-fifth anniversary, which was commemorated in a slew of articles, many in *Einheit*. Defense Minister Heinz Hoffmann said that the NVA "is ready and in the position to fight under any conditions; work together on a high level with the most modern and strongest socialist defense power, the glorious Soviet Army, and with the other allied armed forces; tame, jointly with them, the imperialist aggressors; and defeat, by all the rules of warfare, anyone who would dare to attack the achievements of socialism and communism" (*Einheit*, no. 2, pp. 141–48). Another high-level NVA officer, Col. Gen. Herbert Scheibe, concerned himself with the ideological preparedness of the NVA, explaining that still more attention ought to be paid to the "education and training of our officers on the basis of the Marxist-Leninist world outlook" (ibid., pp. 149–55). In an allusion to Poland, Col. Gen. Heinz Kessler (deputy minister of defense and head of the main political administration of the NVA) pleaded in favor of a more clearly delineated "image of the enemy" in the minds of NVA soldiers, who needed to be shown that in the class struggle imperialism applied various measures and methods against socialism, "from creeping and cleverly camouflaged counterrevolution up to open military aggression" (*FAZ*, 7 May). Oblique references to the Polish situation showed up now and then in other stories carried by *Neues Deutschland*. Kessler, for example, in a speech to "party cadres" in Berlin, said: "To do everything necessary, in an unshakable fighting alliance with the USSR and other fraternal states, for the reliable military defense of the socialist achievements of fraternal peoples . . . is and shall remain of the utmost concern in the SED's military policy in the aftermath of the Tenth Party Congress" (ibid., 12 June).

Relations Between Church and State. The events in Poland cast their shadow on church-state matters as well. Relations between the SED and East German Protestants had been relatively cordial since the meeting in March 1978 between Bishop Albrecht Schönherr and Honecker, but the Polish summer of 1980 brought about a definite relapse. The SED is worried, of course, that the Evangelical church might become a locus for opposition to state policies, and church protests against the increase in required exchanges of hard currency for Western visitors, objections to extensive GDR press coverage of Warsaw Pact military maneuvers, and unhappiness over the quasi-voluntary military affairs courses in GDR schools did nothing to alleviate the party's fears. The SED responded with censorship of church newspapers, travel restrictions on Western journalists and church representatives wishing to attend high-level church convocations in the GDR, and a number of blunt warnings by various SED functionaries to Protestant leaders. Klaus Gysi, the GDR's secretary for church affairs, spelled out the party's position: "We proceed from the assumption that the separation and independence of churches in our republic vis-à-vis churches in the FRG and that the time-tested separation of church and state—that is, the noninterference of the state in church matters and the noninterference of the church in state business—is . . . in the interest of everyone and, not least of all, in the well-understood interest of the churches themselves." The churches' refusal to respond to the SED's policy of demarcation with West Germany by loosening ties with West German Protestants prompted a warning "in no uncertain terms" from Politburo member Paul Verner to Schönherr that "all-German machinations" were to cease. (*Der Spiegel*, 4 May, pp. 62–63, 66; *FAZ*, 23 February, 22 and 30 March; *DA*, no. 4, pp. 345–47.)

Catholics in the GDR (who comprise a scant 8 percent of the population) also demanded to be heard in 1981. Unlike its Protestant counterpart, the Catholic church had long followed a much stricter policy of disassociation from the state. But in early 1981, a pastoral letter read to congregations throughout the GDR raised three unusually contentious questions, discussing them in pessimistic terms: 1. "As Christians do we still have a chance in our country?" 2. "What will become of the

Christian faith of our children and young people?" 3. "Do we find in the diaspora church the community we need?" (*FAZ*, 25 March; *DA*, no. 5, pp. 459–62.)

Foreign Affairs: *Relations with the West.* The GDR's relations with Western Europe and the
United States reflect the SED's unqualified acceptance of Soviet policies. The year 1981 brought no
change in that allegiance. Virtually every issue of *Neues Deutschland* published stories about the
peace movement in the West; statements by prominent Westerners opposed to the stationing of a new
breed of medium-range missiles in Europe, development of the neutron bomb, and so on are immediately seized upon. The reports all drive home a number of related themes; namely, NATO has em-
barked on a "policy of confrontation," NATO and the United States are striving for military
superiority over the Soviet Union and the Warsaw Pact nations, and the Western "legend about the
'danger from the East' " serves merely as an "alibi" for Western military expansion. This "lie" serves
as a tool to manipulate public opinion, dampen the resistance movement to NATO's arms buildup, and
wage "psychological warfare" against the socialist states. (Cf. *ND*, 13 May.) No mention is ever made
of the invasion of Afghanistan, the attempt to intimidate Poland, or the deployment of Soviet SS-20
missiles. *Neues Deutschland* (19 November) responded to Reagan's offer not to station medium-range
missiles in Western Europe in return for the removal of Soviet SS-20 missiles by quoting from various
Western newspapers sympathetic to the Soviet position—all under the heading "Representatives of
the Peace Movement: A Broadly Conceived Diversion."

German-German Relations. Relations between the two Germanies have recovered only to a limited extent from the low point reached in fall 1980, when rising tensions between the United States
and the Soviet Union and the escalating Polish crisis reduced GDR-FRG efforts to shield their relations from the superpower conflict to a shambles. By midyear efforts were again under way to set up a
meeting between Honecker and West German Chancellor Helmut Schmidt, who had spoken of his
willingness to meet with the SED chief "at any time" (*FAZ*, 15 June). A month later, the West German government made a firm offer to arrange talks between the two German leaders with no preconditions, that is, with no demand that changes first be effected in the GDR's policy on border exchanges
of hard currency. In mid-August news that Schmidt had written Honecker a letter leaked out, and on
21 August, Schmidt said that he could envisage a meeting with Honecker in the near future (*Informationen*, no. 17, pp. 3–4). In early August, the East Germans sent out a signal when Honecker and
Brezhnev, meeting in the Crimea, voiced the opinion that "in the current complicated situation large-
scale international exchanges, along with effective political contacts between statesmen representing
countries with differing social systems, are especially valuable and necessary" (ibid., no. 16, p. 5).
Later in the month, *Neues Deutschland* (31 August) announced that Honecker would answer
Schmidt's letter presently and that he anticipated a "positive development in German-German talks
at the highest level." The paper also quoted an Associated Press dispatch that spoke of the West
German offer of talks with no preconditions and referred to hopes in Bonn that a summit between
Schmidt and Honecker might be arranged following Brezhnev's visit. Shortly after, Honecker re-
sponded to Schmidt's letter and expressed his desire for a meeting to take place after Brezhnev's visit
(*Der Spiegel*, 7 September, p. 30).

In early December, with little advance warning, the meeting was set for the middle of the month,
and on 11 December Schmidt arrived in East Berlin. He and his entourage were driven immediately to
a hunting lodge (formerly belonging to Ulbricht) at Werbelinsee. The two leaders discussed a wide
range of issues in an apparently cordial atmosphere that held up until 14 December, when news of the
crackdown in Poland began arriving. The summit resulted in no new agreements or treaties; the results, said Schmidt, would become evident during the coming year. Some specific issues, of course,

were dealt with. FRG Minister of the Economy Otto Lambsdorff announced that an agreement extending SWING credits to the GDR at the annual rate of 850 million marks until 30 June 1982 would be signed shortly; in the meantime, a new agreement would be negotiated. He stressed, however, that such an accord would be linked to progress in such matters as the minimum hard-currency exchange for visitors from the West and eased travel regulations. In another matter, whereas the GDR press spokesman referred to the necessity of eliminating "long outdated doctrines" (that is, West German refusal to recognize a GDR nationality), Schmidt pointed out that the Federal Republic was bound by its constitution, the Four-Power Agreement, and the basic treaty governing relations between the two Germanies (see below). Although everyone attempted to assess the talks favorably, some members of the West German delegation revealed that nothing new or substantive had come of them; Honecker supposedly repeated everything he had been saying since fall 1980 and on the subject of German-German relations merely rehashed his Gera speech in less harsh language. (*FAZ*, 12 and 14 December.) The speeches given by the two leaders highlighted the differences between the two countries on a broader political level. For Honecker the eyes of the world were fixed on Geneva and the Soviet-U.S. negotiations there: "But the beginning of negotiations is no guarantee in itself of a favorable outcome. It would be imprudent to assume otherwise because the U.S. offer of a 'zero solution,' when examined closely, comes down to a minus solution at the cost of the Soviet Union and our defense alliance . . . Good-neighborly relations cannot prosper in the shadow of new U.S. atomic missiles." Schmidt responded by saying that "we note with grave concern the change in the military balance of power between East and West caused by the new Soviet medium-range missiles capable of carrying three warheads each. We are convinced that it is possible to re-establish parity even without Western modernization—by means of limiting the production of weapons and by disarmament. For that reason the United States of America proposed for the negotiations just beginning in Geneva that both sides forgo the stationing of medium-range missiles." (*ND*, 14 December.)

Other discussions and polemics between the two countries revolved around two main questions: the obligatory exchange of hard currency for Western visitors to the GDR and the West German refusal to recognize GDR citizenship. Honecker contended that purely economic considerations had dictated the "resetting" of the minimum exchange rate and that in the GDR the reason "for all the noise" in the West about the new policy was "incomprehensible" and blamed inflation in the West. The East German wire service later called the present rate "too low as it is" (*FAZ*, 13 May). The number of visits by West Germans and West Berliners to the GDR has fallen to its lowest level since the Quadripartite Agreement and related accords signed in 1971 and 1972 (ibid., 4 July).

Honecker also hammered away at the question of a GDR citizenship:

> The issue of state citizenship plays a role in relations between the GDR and the FRG only because, in complete violation of international law, the FRG still insists on a law covering citizenship that dates to the time of Wilhelm II and pursues a policy that discriminates against GDR citizens . . So it is high time for the FRG to recognize fully the existence of two sovereign German states that are independent of each other. The *idée fixe* of the "continuation of the German Reich in the borders of 1937" has no place in today's world anyway, and certainly it cannot be the basis for making policy. The sooner this is taken into account in Bonn, the better it will be for the further normalization of relations between the GDR and the FRG. (*ND*, 12 February.)

Helmut Schmidt brought up many of the same problems in an April address on the state of the nation, explaining the West German stance on the issue of citizenship: "All Germans who come to us—from whatever part of the world—shall receive the basic guarantee of rights . . . offered under the constitution. We are aware that since 1967 the GDR has its own law regarding state citizenship. But the GDR needs to recognize that its legislation concerning citizenship has nothing to do with German citizenship as defined in our constitution or in our laws." (*Informationen*, no. 8, p. 18.)

The speech brought the expected reaction from the GDR. *Neues Deutschland* pointed out the "obvious discrepancy" between expressions of hope for an improvement in East-West relations and a lack of willingness to "recognize facts." The paper criticized West Germany for violating international law in refusing to recognize a GDR citizenship and for keeping alive the notion of "national unity." This was, according to *Neues Deutschland*, an attempt to challenge the sovereignty of the GDR and interfere in its internal affairs, in other words, a violation of the Helsinki accords. (*FAZ*, 11 April.)

Still, the pitch of speeches at the Tenth Party Congress on German-German relations was not unduly high, although most speakers raised the same points. The paramount issue, however, remains West Germany's support of NATO's program of rearmament. The GDR was interested in the development of "normal, good-neighborly relations," said Honecker, but this was not a matter divorced from the international situation: "Those who persist in pushing forward NATO's high level of armaments, those who are affecting the military and strategic balance of power in Europe with new atomic missiles produce a state of affairs that runs counter to the further normalization of relations between the two German states and endanger what has already been achieved" (*ND*, 12 April). In a passage not carried in the printed version of his speech, Honecker brought up the issue of citizenship again (*FAZ*, 13 April), and Politburo member Konrad Naumann drove home the same point in his speech (*Informationen*, no. 8, p. 6). Later, at the constituent assembly of the People's Council, Willi Stoph (head of the Council of Ministers) and Paul Verner repeated the argument. Stoph quoted Honecker almost verbatim when he noted that "a heightened arms buildup" and "adherence to a revanchist doctrine of the 'continuation of the German Reich in the borders of 1937' are facts that hinder further progress . . . and even endanger what has already been achieved." Verner added that "good-neighborly relations" could scarcely thrive "in the shadow of Pershing II missiles." (Ibid., no. 14, p. 3.)

Honecker was the cause of controversy of a different sort early in the year when he raised the question of German reunification for the first time in years. He said in a speech at the Berlin SED regional delegates' conference: "When certain people in the West today spout all-German slogans and pretend that the unification of the two German states means more to them than their wallet, we have this to say to them: Beware! Socialism will come knocking at your door some day, too, and when the day is at hand for West German working people to tackle the socialist transformation of the Federal Republic, then the question of the reunification of both German states will be an entirely different matter. There shall be little doubt about the direction of our decision then." (*ND*, 16 February.) The remark caused a commotion in West Germany among some politicians who chose to read more into the comment than Honecker probably intended (*FAZ*, 14 March). Nor was there any reason for papers in the West to speak of an abandonment of a ten-year policy holding that Germany's division was irreconcilable, as the *Washington Post* (17 February) wrote. Egon Franke, FRG minister of internal German affairs, put things in the proper perspective. The SED had never renounced the idea of unification under communist conditions, he said, and it would be a mistake to interpret the remarks positively or optimistically. "Between our concept of national unity and the communist perspective that Honecker has conjured up there is a world of difference . . . If the GDR chooses to enhance its daily policy of demarcation with the prospect of a unified communist Germany, this is neither something entirely new nor does it justify hopes here in the Federal Republic of Germany." (*Informationen*, no. 5, p. 14.) Assuming that Honecker's remarks were not accidental, Helmut Schmidt's speculation about Honecker's reason for raising the possibility of reunification may be correct. Schmidt suggested indirectly that Germans in the GDR longed to identify with a German nation, the GDR being for most a poor substitute, and that the SED sought to still this longing by resurrecting hopes of some sort of unity in the hazy future (ibid., no. 8, p. 18).

Poland. East German press coverage of developments in Poland was exhaustive and reflected the SED's deep concern over the course of events. Early in the year, there was a noticeable tendency to let "extremist members" of Solidarity bear the brunt of criticism for allowing the crisis to get out of hand and for refusing to "concentrate on trade union matters" (*ND*, 20 May, reporting on the contents of an article in *Izvestiia*). Later on, however, the GDR press rarely bothered to distinguish between "certain leaders" and Solidarity as an organization. A keynote in East German reporting concerned the intrusion of Western imperialism into Polish internal affairs. On 24 June, *Neues Deutschland* published a *Pravda* commentary: "Every day brings forth new evidence for imperialist intereference in Poland . . . Under the guise of 'defending' Poland against 'external interference,' the United States and some other NATO partners are attempting to spread fear and distrust and to incite certain elements in Poland to anti-Soviet actions and attacks against the country's ties of alliance in the form of the Warsaw Pact." An article by Gus Hall, secretary general of the Communist Party, U.S.A., was used to make the same point: "Directives go out from Washington to Bonn, London, Paris, and Rome explaining how to exploit the difficulties in Poland" (ibid., 9 July). Hall's major charge, however, was that the Central Intelligence Agency lurked behind the events in Poland. This theme was later repeated both in GDR reporting on Soviet editorials as well as in East German editorials and dispatches from correspondents in Warsaw. *Neues Deutschland* (23 September) quoted a Tass story that attributed encouragement of the Solidarity leadership to "centers of subversion and secret services of the West." The paper's Warsaw correspondent, Horst Iffländer, echoed the same theme: "In Poland . . . not a day passes without some new Solidarnosc provocation [the East Germans steadfastly refuse to call Solidarity by its German name] . . . It is apparent to all that these antisocialist attacks are steered according to an imperialist scenario worked out by the secret services of the NATO nations. The extremist groups who are preparing for the takeover of power are accorded the 'broad material and political assistance' of imperialist agencies." (Ibid., 27 August.) The 3/4 October issue of *Neues Deutschland* quoted Polish press reports on contacts between Solidarity leaders with "Western diversionary and spy centers" and added: "The AFL-CIO formed a 'relief fund for Polish workers.' The funds in this bank account are at the disposal of the head of the European division of the AFL-CIO, Irving Brown, a CIA agent." Yet another article, by Paul Weinreich (who reports frequently from Poland), pointed out that "certain counterrevolutionary forces are already working with the BND [the West German intelligence agency] and other Western secret services." Weinreich then touched on a favorite East German theme: the Polish events are being misused and manipulated by those whose eyes are fixed on Poland's western territories. Such people, who dream of a "Germany in the borders of 1937," overlook the existence of one of Poland's closest allies, "the socialist German Democratic Republic," which recognizes the Oder-Neisse line as Poland's western boundary. "Whereas revanchism, the revision of the results of postwar development, has been elevated to official policy in the FRG, the GDR today is one of the guarantors of the western borders of popular-democratic Poland." (Ibid., 6 July.) Numerous other accounts made the same point (see ibid., 5 May, 6 October), which fits in nicely, of course, with the general SED propaganda line against West Germany.

An article in *Neues Deutschland* brought something of a respite from the normal invective. After months of abuse, the paper's editorial staff evidently decided it was worth trying to reason with the Poles and published a piece that explained the nature of the ties between "popular-democratic Poland and the GDR" and the threat posed by the current crisis to their mutually beneficial bonds of friendship. All this led up to a contrast between East German–Polish relations (the GDR's acceptance of the Oder-Neisse "peace border") and West Germany's "dreams of a new division of Poland." In the GDR "we know too well . . . what solidarity means," the article continued (the irony in the use of the word "solidarity" again being unintentional); during the "imperialist blockade against the GDR" and its struggle for international recognition, the GDR had also experienced the power of solidarity. These sentiments were then coupled with the question of when the party and state leadership would get control of the situation.

Early East German reporting on the situation in Poland still contained references to past mistakes made by party and state in setting economic policy, but this appraisal soon yielded to the tendency to make Solidarity solely responsible for the chaotic economic conditions. Iffländer's article in *Neues Deutschland* (21 May) marked a transition: "As justified as it is to look back into the past, it is just as true that Solidarnosc and the elements behind it are responsible for what has occurred in Poland since August 1980." The same issue of the paper carried an article by Weinreich, who explained: "The general 'downturn' is continuing at an alarming pace because of the destructive actions of Solidarnosc." Both articles spoke of Solidarity's "true ambition." "Solidarnosc Prides Itself In Its 'Struggle' for Power' " was the headline of Iffländer's article; Weinreich referred to the "dyarchy" (*Doppelherrschaft*) in Poland that, in part, could no longer even be called by that term.

The East Germans reserved their most abusive language for their surprisingly extensive coverage of Solidarity's strikes. One article painted a bleak picture of economic conditions, referring in several detailed paragraphs to the scarcity of "meat, butter, sugar, flour, rice, and other basic food commodities" and mentioning the rationing that provided the "normal consumer" with only small amounts of necessary food items monthly. "This is an expression of the misery to which the rule of Solidarnosc has led popular-democratic Poland." (Ibid., 11/12 July.) Other stories contained detailed reports of various strike actions, such as the use of busses, trucks, and autos to block traffic in downtown Warsaw in early August "in order to incite further the present unrest and to provoke the state organs" (ibid., 5 August). A few days later, *Neues Deutschland*, quoting the Polish news agency, again charged "Solidarnosc" with sole responsibility for the chaotic conditions in the country (ibid., 7 August) and followed that story with a report that "counterrevolutionary forces want to hinder the stabilization of the situation" (ibid., 10 August). Broad coverage of the printers' strike in late August was also provided; the words "terror" and "terrorist physical abuse" came up often in reference to Solidarity's supposed intimidation of printers who wished to show up for work (ibid., 19, 20, and 21 August). In early November, ADN "quoted" a local Solidarity representative who called for the "murder of party and state officials" (ibid., 3 November).

The East German press covered the major party plenums and congresses in Poland extensively, although the reporting on the PUWP's eleventh plenum, needless to say, was selective; Polish leader Stanislaw Kania's address to the plenum, for instance, was rendered in indirect discourse (ibid., 12 June). The letter written by the Central Committee of the Soviet communist party to its Polish counterpart was printed verbatim next to the resolutions of the plenum and commented on thoroughly (ibid., 13/14 June). The PUWP's Ninth Party Congress in mid-July was likewise accorded wide coverage, although the only speech printed intact was Werner Felfe's (Felfe was the SED's representative to the congress). He reiterated the theme of "revanchist forces" in West Germany dreaming of the German Reich in "the borders of 1937" (ibid., 16 July). Kania's address was again paraphrased; deleted were his positive remarks about Solidarity, his insistence that party functionaries should issue statements about their private holdings, his praise of the church's role in mediating between the union and the party, and his expression of commitment to the accords of August and September 1980 (*FAZ*, 18 July). *Neues Deutschland* also hid the fact at first that the Polish party head would be elected by secret ballot cast by all delegates for various candidates, rather than by the Central Committee (ibid., 17 July). After *Pravda* finally reported that Kania had been elected by "secret ballot" (though no mention of several candidates was made; ibid., 20 July), the GDR press also informed its readers that Kania had defeated another candidate, Kazimierz Barcikowski, in a secret ballot cast by all delegates (ibid., 21 July).

Solidarity's Gdansk congress and—not surprisingly—its "Appeal to the Peoples of Eastern Europe" infuriated the East Germans. *Neues Deutschland* (12/13 September) published a Tass dispatch that set the tone:

The first stage of the Solidarnosc congress, which the extremist circles of that organization have transformed into an antisocialist and anti-Soviet orgy, has concluded. The speeches and the documents passed by the congress dispel any doubt about the true goals of the organizers and inspirers of the Gdansk riot ... The so-called Appeal to the Peoples of Eastern Europe passed at Gdansk, which calls for a struggle against the socialist order ... is a brazen, unabashed provocation with respect to the socialist countries ... In their efforts to serve imperialist subversive centers, these miserable, worthless politicians have mounted an attack on the socialist order in Poland's neighboring states.

Neues Deutschland went on to comment that an entire conglomeration of counterrevolutionaries (including agents of imperialist secret services and all those who "hate socialism and the people's power in Poland") were conspiring to undermine the foundations of the socialist Polish state. The *Neues Deutschland* report on the Tass story concluded: "The 'Solidarnosc' congress in Gdansk was ... a review of those forces that are preparing to assume power. These gentlemen have gotten so entirely out of control that they are incapable of seeing the extent to which their adventuresome acts of provocation, which are exacerbating an already complicated situation in Poland, prompt anger and outrage." "Outraged" reactions to the congress and the appeal printed in *Rabotnitchesko delo* (Sofia) and *Rudé Právo* (Prague) were also republished in *Neues Deutschland* (21 September).

In the fall, the tone of the stories grew even harsher. *Neues Deutschland* (18 September) published a Polish Central Committee statement warning Solidarity against formulating a program of political opposition, for this would result in a confrontation "that would make the shedding of blood a real possibility." The next day, the paper printed the Polish party's statement that "in the case of extreme necessity, the use of all the means at the party's disposal would be employed" (ibid., 19/20 September). Soon after, Weinreich compared Solidarity's "militia" with Hitler's storm troopers. Referring to the beginning of a new, decisive phase in the Polish situation, Weinreich "quoted" Walesa, who was said to have called on Solidarity to use "all possible means" for furthering counterrevolutionary efforts. Weinreich then lamented the weakness of "party and state organs," who "must not retreat one single step more before the frontal attack of the counterrevolution, but, rather, must finally go over to the offensive. We can no longer accept the lack of a serious defense by state authorities." Weinreich added that responsibility for the "catastrophic economic situation" in the country had long been attributed to the " 'mistakes of the past,' " but it was now clear that Solidarity and those who continued to back away from the never-ending threats of the union were responsible for the catastrophe. Weinreich concluded with a call for "decisive measures" to end the counterrevolution. (Ibid., 22 September.) A day later, Iffländer added that the political atmosphere in Poland was becoming explosive because the "counterrevolution is engaged in a frontal attack upon the socialist state power," openly aiming at a takeover. The contention that the situation in Poland had been brought about by mistakes of the past had been exposed as a legend concocted and disseminated by counterrevolutionary demagogy. "When," Iffländer asked, "will the leadership of the land finally take the lead in a consistent struggle against the counterrevolutionary danger and for socialism in popular-democratic Poland?" (Ibid., 23 September.) In early October, Weinreich added that Solidarity had divested itself of its disguise by formulating its "program of counterrevolution" (ibid., 3/4 October). On 14 October, *Neues Deutschland* printed a *Pravda* article that characterized the safeguarding of "the revolutionary achievements of the Polish people" as not just their internal affair. "It is a matter of the vital interests of all peoples and states that have chosen the road of socialism. This imparts to the Polish workers and to the party and state leadership of the country a special responsibility. Recognition of this responsibility must ... be demonstrated in an effective repudiation of the counterrevolution and its imperialist wire-pullers as well as in the strengthening of the positions of socialism in Poland." The same day, *Neues Deutschland* quoted a story in *Trybuna luda* (Warsaw) referring to "political terror" and citing the opinion of "many PUWP members" that it was necessary to "put an end to anarchy and destruction."

The replacement on 18 October of Stanislaw Kania by Gen. Wojciech Jaruzelski as first secretary of the PUWP was briefly noted by *Neues Deutschland* (19 October). Otherwise, there were no East German comments on the change. *Neues Deutschland*, however, carried the news on the introduction of martial law in Poland on 13 December on the front page opposite a story on the Schmidt-Honecker summit. Jaruzelski's speech was translated in full, and the proclamation issued by the Military Council for National Salvation was paraphased at length. Other news items reported the various measures enacted by the government; for instance, the closing of borders, control of radio and television channels, the prohibition of all union activity, and so on. Accounts of the reaction from abroad emphasized that the imposition of martial law represented an internal Polish affair. No attempt was made to hide the gravity of the situation, and the reports made it clear that the measures had been necessary to deal with massive unrest.

Subsequently, the ADN and other media concentrated on describing the large amounts of aid (foodstuffs, medical supplies, clothing, Christmas parcels for Polish children) that were delivered by convoys to Poland. On 20 December, the ADN reported the gradual stabilizing of economic and public life in Poland (*FBIS*, 21 December). On 23 December, the day the U.S. government announced the imposition of economic sanctions on Poland, *Neues Deutschland* printed a violent article against Solidarity and the "counterrevolution" in Poland. It assailed "the old [German] revanchists" who under Hilter marched and spilled Polish blood and who now rejoiced when political organizations allied with Solidarity "offered them fraternity." The article hailed "the upright communists, the soldiers of the Polish Army, the militiamen, and the workers [with whom] the Soviet Union and the other states of our family of peoples are fraternally bound" (ibid., 28 December).

Relations with the Third World. In 1979, Erich Honecker paid visits to a number of Third World countries important to the SED's foreign policy (see *YICA*, 1981, pp. 255–57, on the scope of the GDR's activity in these countries). This year some of the leaders of these countries came to the GDR. High-level talks took place, for instance, between Honecker and the president of Angola, José Eduardo dos Santos, who spent three days in the GDR in October. The Angolan foreign minister had preceded him in May (ibid., 16/17 May). The two leaders signed a variety of accords, among them one between the ruling parties of both nations on cooperation from 1981 to 1985, and a treaty on legal assistance in civil, labor, and criminal matters (ibid., 13 and 15 October).

A month later Honecker had a similar meeting (with a similar outcome) with 'Ali Nasir Muhammad al-Hasani, head of party and state in South Yemen. A number of accords were signed for the purpose of "deepening ties" between the two countries. (Ibid., 10 November.) On 1 September, *Neues Deutschland* published several reports on the visit to South Yemen of an NVA delegation headed by Col. Gen. Heinz Kessler. The closest the stories came to mentioning the GDR military presence in the country was a reference by a Defense Ministry official to the "aid and support of the socialist countries, above all the Soviet Union." Another account mentioned Yemeni Defense Minister Saleh Musleh Qassem's expression of appreciation for the "assistance rendered by the GDR" (ibid., 3 September). A story on South Yemen published in October referred to the help of East German scientists and experts in "the state apparatus" (ibid., 14 October). Incidentally, Erich Honecker was asked by Japanese journalists whether NVA troops were active in other countries. He said that, as chairman of the National Defense Council, he was "unaware" of East German troops outside the GDR, apart from those on maneuver in other Warsaw Pact states (*Informationen*, no. 12, p. 10). In other matters pertaining to the presence of NVA troops in Africa, the ADN published the statement of the GDR press attaché in Nigeria denying that the GDR was rendering assistance to the Libyan army. Reports to the contrary were intended to "slander" the GDR policy of solidarity and support for the struggles of the African peoples for freedom and national independence, to "complicate the situation in Chad, and cause tension among neighboring African states." (*FAZ*, 10 March.) Libyan leader

Moammar Khadafy also denied that East German or Cuban military advisers were present in Libya (ibid., 18 March).

For unexplained reasons, *Neues Deutschland* came out in July, August, and September with a number of small stories and other news reports about Afghanistan, after mostly ignoring the topic for months. They were not particularly noteworthy, reporting on various GDR flights carrying "solidarity goods" (ibid., 21 July) or "solidarity donations" (ibid., 1/2 August) and expressing Afghan gratitude for these manifestations of solidarity (ibid., 23, 25/26 July). The various reports were interesting, however, inasmuch as they mentioned fighting in Afghanistan, or, in *Neues Deutschland*'s parlance, "the concerted efforts" in Afghanistan to safeguard the achievements of the national democratic revolution (ibid., 25/26 July). Now and then other references to the fighting cropped up, for instance in a brief ADN dispatch about a "successful operation" of Afghan forces against "counterrevolutionary elements" who had disrupted the "peaceful life of the population in the region through unceasing attacks" (ibid., 27 July). Honecker, in a telegram to Babrak Karmal, spoke of the constant need for the "young people's power" to defend itself against the "backhanded attacks of counterrevolution and external reaction" (ibid., 19 August). A lengthy story in September told how Afghanistan's "working people" were coming to terms with the counterrevolution (ibid., 19/20 September). In July, the *Frankfurter Allgemeine Zeitung* (23 July) reported that East German advisers were present in Afghanistan, working in field hospitals or mobile hospital units. According to the report, an unknown number of East German experts were working jointly with Soviet specialists in building up the Afghan news agency as well as—an East German speciality—an Afghan secret police.

Following the visit to East Berlin in March 1980 by a Kampuchean delegation headed by Heng Samrin (at which a friendship and cooperation treaty as well as other accords were signed), GDR-Kampuchean relations were developed further when the Kampuchean foreign minister spent two days in the GDR. The talks appear to have been general, and no new agreements were signed. (*ND*, 9 and 10 July.) His visit was followed a few weeks later by the arrival in East Berlin of a Kampuchean military delegation headed by the defense minister (ibid., 27, 28, and 30 July).

In June, the Nicaraguan foreign minister spent five days in the GDR (*Aussenpolitische Korrespondenz*, 26 June, pp. 201–3). An agreement on cultural and scientific cooperation for 1981 and 1982 and one on cooperation between the foreign ministries of both countries for 1982 and 1983 were signed (ibid., 17 June). But the high point of the year for GDR foreign policy in the region was Honecker's five-day trip to Mexico in mid-September. Honecker was well received and held a round of talks with President José López Portillo that concluded in a number of agreements and arrangements meant to complement and expand upon the previous accords on trade and scientific and technical cooperation. (Ibid., 10, 11, and 12/13 September.) On his return home, Honecker stopped off in Cuba for a brief meeting with Fidel Castro (ibid., 14 and 15 September).

International Contacts and Party Conferences. Meetings and consultations between party and state officials and representatives of various other communist or sympathetic states continued at the usual pace in 1981; none of these generally routine talks was especially noteworthy. Nor were the speeches given by SED officials at the Twenty-Sixth Party Congress of the Communist Party of the Soviet Union (CPSU). Honecker's contribution to Brezhnev's personality cult is symptomatic: "We are very impressed and inspired by the significant report of the Central Committee to the Twenty-Sixth Party Congress made by the general secretary of the CPSU, our friend and comrade, Leonid Ilich Brezhnev. . . We have particular regard for and praise the untiring work, rich in initiative, done by the outstanding continuer of the cause of Lenin, the great pioneer for peace and social progress, the consistent Marxist-Leninist, our friend and comrade, Leonid Ilich Brezhnev." (East Berlin Voice of the GDR, 24 February; FBIS, 25 February.) SED Politburo member Hermann Axen later referred to the congress as an "event of global significance" that "inspires new ideas and deeds in preparation of the SED Tenth Congress" (*Einheit*, no. 4/5, pp. 331–39; *JPRS*, 23 June). The pilgrimage by East European communist party heads to the Crimea to meet with Brezhnev during his summer vacation has become a yearly ritual. Honecker held talks with Brezhnev this year, too, and *Neues Deutschland* (4 August) carried banner headlines about the "friendly meeting." Although the communiqué was couched in the usual innocuous language, important policy matters do come up for discussion at these meetings. For instance, a speech given in May 1981 by the "ruling ambassador" in East Berlin (as he is sarcastically referred to by East Germans) appeared to hint that last year's meeting included talks on the subject of the sudden change in GDR policy toward West Germany that occurred two months later (*FAZ*, 8 May). This year, Brezhnev seems to have prodded Honecker into an expression of willingness to meet with Helmut Schmidt, talks that Soviet leaders hope to use, of course, within the context of their opposition to NATO's planned stationing of new theater nuclear weapons in Western Europe and especially in West Germany (cf. ibid., 5 August).

Publications. The official organ of the SED, the daily *Neues Deutschland*, has a circulation of over one million copies. All major cities publish a party daily, with East Berlin having two: *Berliner Zeitung* and *BZ am Abend*. The SED Central Committee brings out two monthly magazines: *Einheit*, a theoretical review, and *Neuer Weg*, which treats problems of party life. The FDJ publishes the daily *Junge Welt*, and the FDGB the daily *Tribüne*. All four noncommunist parties have press organs. Allgemeiner Deutscher Nachrichtendienst (ADN) is the GDR's official press agency.

University of North Carolina (Chapel Hill)   David Pike

Hungary

Hungarian Communists formed a party in November 1918 and were the dominant force in the Hungarian Soviet Republic, which lasted from March to August 1919. Thereafter the party functioned as a minute and faction-ridden movement in domestic illegality and in exile. With the Soviet occupation at the end of World War II, the Hungarian Communist Party emerged as a partner in the coalition government, exercised an influence disproportionate to its modest electoral support, and gained effective control of the country in 1947. In 1948, it absorbed left-wing Social Democrats into the newly named Hungarian Workers' Party. On 1 November 1956, during the popular revolt that momentarily restored a multiparty government, the name was changed to Hungarian Socialist Workers' Party (Magyar Szocialista Munkáspárt; HSWP).

The HSWP rules unchallenged as the sole political party, firmly aligned with the Soviet Union. Its exclusive status is confirmed in the revised state constitution of 1972: "The Marxist-Leninist party of the working class is the leading force in society." Party membership is 812,000 out of a population of 10.7 million (1980).

Leadership and Organization. The party is led by János Kádár, 69, who has held the post of first secretary since November 1956. Other members of the Secretariat are András Gyenes (the foreign and interparty affairs specialist), Ferenc Havasi, Mihály Korom, Károly Németh, and Miklós Óvári. The Politburo includes Kádár as well as György Aczél (a deputy prime minister and cultural overseer), Valéria Benke, Sándor Gáspár (secretary general of the National Council of Trade Unions), Ferenc Havasi (chairman of the Central Committee's Economic Policy Committee), Mihály Korom (party, mass organization, and military affairs, and chairman of the Central Committee's Physical Training and Sports Committee), György Lázár (prime minister), Pál Losonczi (head of state), László Maróthy, Lajos Méhes, Károly Németh (chairman of the Youth Committee and of the Party Building Team), Miklós Óvári (chairman of the Agitprop Committee and of the Cultural Policy Team), and István Sarlós (secretary general of the Patriotic People's Front). János Brutyó is chairman of the Central Control Committee.

Following the Central Committee's plenum of 2 December 1980, Lajos Méhes was named to head the new Ministry of Industry (combining three former ministries). Méhes, 54, was originally a toolmaker who joined the party in 1945 and became a full-time activist. He served as first secretary of the Communist Youth League (KISZ) from 1964 to 1970, then as secretary general of the metalworkers' union, and most recently as first secretary of the Budapest municipal party committee. He was replaced in that last job by László Maróthy, former first secretary of the KISZ. That position, in turn, has been filled by György Fejti, who previously worked in both the party's and the KISZ's Central Committee offices.

Apart from Prime Minister Lázár, the Council of Ministers consists of four deputy prime ministers, Aczél, János Borbándi, Lajos Faluvégi (also chairman of the National Planning Office), and József Marjai, as well as Jenö Vancsa (agriculture and food), Imre Pozsgay (culture and education), Lajos Czinege (defense), István Hetényi (finance), Frigyes Puja (foreign affairs), Péter Veress (foreign trade), Méhes, István Horváth (interior), Vilmos Sághy (internal trade), Imre Markoja (justice), Kálmán Abraham (public construction and urban development), Emil Schultheisz (public health), and Árpád Pullai (transport and telecommunications).

Auxiliary and Mass Organizations. Following the HSWP's Twelfth Congress (March 1980) and parliamentary and local council elections (June 1980), three mass organizations held congresses: the trade unions, the Patriotic People's Front, and the Communist Youth League.

The preparations for the trade union congress began in the spring of 1980 when 4.5 million workers elected 380,000 stewards in 7,500 union organizations. In September, the Budapest and county union councils held their congresses, followed by the congresses of the nineteen industrial branch trade unions. Debates at these meetings revolved around wages, the cost of living, the inadequacy of managers, and the need to protect groups and individuals.

The Polish events prompted some direct as well as indirect reactions from Hungarian union leaders. Sándor Gáspár felt the need to explain that in a workers' state the government and the unions have the same objectives and that in such circumstances opposition to the established workers' power would endanger the interests of the working class. "The strike is not an instrument for the building of socialism," argued Gáspár. Strikes were neither allowed nor prohibited in Hungarian law, they were simply unnecessary, although it had to be admitted that the occasional spontaneous work stoppage did occur (*Népszabadság*, 19 October 1980). Hungarian unions do, in fact, enjoy certain prerogatives, but these fall far short of genuine autonomy. In recent years the role of the elected union stewards has been expanded. The council of union stewards deals with enterprise management on a variety of issues, and it must be consulted on managerial appointments.

The Twenty-Fourth Congress of Trade Unions was held 12–14 December 1980, with 774 Hungarian delegates as well as foreign representatives. The Polish delegation did not include a representative of Solidarity. Secretary General Gáspár referred in a mild statement to the "regrettable Polish events" and the need for a "socialist solution." He stressed that in Hungary unions played a key role and were not supervised by the state. Enterprise democracy had to be developed further, he affirmed, but strikes could "only make us poorer, not richer." In an address to the congress, Kádár observed that the relative independence of enterprise managers in the Hungarian economic system meant that the trade unions also had to be prepared for "independent action." Labor Minister Ferenc Trethon assured the congress that the five-day workweek would be gradually introduced, but not at the cost of a loss in enterprise income. (In fact, possibly under the impetus of the Polish crisis, the five-day workweek was introduced in a number of enterprises on 1 July 1981, with the rest to follow in 1982, earlier than originally planned.) The congress re-elected Gáspár secretary general and elected 211 members to the National Council of Trade Unions (NCTU).

The Patriotic People's Front (PPF) is the most broadly based agent of political mobilization. It is used by the HSWP to implement the policy of alliance with nonparty groups and masses. The PPF held its Seventh Congress in Budapest on 14–15 March. In an address to the 1,100 delegates, Kádár deplored the stalling of détente by the imperialists. He noted that opponents of socialism had become more active recently in Hungary and forewarned those who might "desire to create a stir." Positive debates were acceptable, but destructive attacks on the achievements of socialism were not. Domestic affairs were open to critical debate, averred Kádár, and he noted that for the first time the draft of the five-year plan had been submitted to various bodies for discussion. Kádár emphasized that relations between church and state were normal and settled. László Cardinal Lékai, in turn, spoke to the congress of the importance of the family in modern society and of the need for unhindered religious education.

The PPF congress re-elected party veteran Gyula Kállay as president and István Sarlós as secretary general. The newly elected National Council has 271 members (previously 251); there are now seven (eleven) deputy presidents; the Presidium of the National Council has 45 members (25), with four secretaries (three). A new body is the National Secretariat, with fourteen members, including the secretary general and the four secretaries. The PPF also has sixteen working groups concentrating on such areas as constitutional law, international relations, the problems of the aged, and regional development. Among its other activities is the organization of unpaid "social" work projects. The front does not have individual members; it consists of 4,500 local committees with 98,000 members. In the midst of economic difficulties and regional as well as East-West tensions, HSWP leaders cling to the alliance policy as the guarantee of domestic stability. Shortly after the PPF congress, the Central Committee declared that it "highly values its nonparty allies' contribution to the attainment of our national objectives." (Ibid., 28 March.)

The Tenth Congress of the KISZ was held 31 May–2 June. By all accounts the organization is in disarray. It appears no more relevant to young workers seeking housing than to university students eager for uninhibited debate. Membership reportedly rose from 800,000 in 1976 to 874,000 in 1981. However, the proportion of young workers who are members of the KISZ has fallen from 31 to 21.9 percent, and the proportion of university students who belong is also down. The congress heard routine speeches acknowledging that young people are impatient and want, according to György Fejti, "more consistent implementation of our policies." The problems of KISZ were summed up by György Aczél in an interview with a Western newspaper: "The young are distrustful. They do not give us a calm moment. They disregard our history and our foreign political situation." (*Dagens Nyheter*, 23 May.) On the other hand, a survey of high school seniors showed low historical knowledge and patriotic feeling among Hungarians compared with their French counterparts (*Mozgó Világ*, no. 2).

Economic Affairs. The general thrust of the party's economic policy for the 1980s is to overcome the severe imbalances of recent years by improving productivity by every means possible, including some that strain the bounds of ideological orthodoxy. The Sixth Five-Year Plan (1981–1985) was introduced as a framework that "serves to outline our fundamental economic policy objectives, but is designed so as not to limit management's flexibility in working out the operational details" (*Népszabadság*, 4 October 1980). Numerous organizations were given the opportunity to discuss the draft, including the PPF Presidium, the Council of Hungarian Women, the Hungarian Economics Society, the Academy of Sciences, and the NCTU Presidium. The plan ultimately approved by the Central Committee and the government anticipates that over the five years national income will grow 14–17 percent, industrial production 19–22 percent, the building industry 11–14 percent, agriculture 12–15 percent, and real per capita income 6–7 percent. These targets are lower than the levels achieved in the previous plan period, and lower still than the preceding targets. Publicity surrounding the plan stressed that great efforts will be required just to maintain the standard of living.

The more productive utilization of labor and capital was the purpose of a series of new regulations regarding the economic structure. Effective 1 January, state enterprises were permitted to contract out the operation of shops and services having no more than five employees (twelve in catering). As a result, some five hundred small shops and restaurants (catering mainly to tourists, but so far not showing adequate profits) were put up for lease to the highest bidder. The manager of a leased business may dispose freely of the profits after paying the annual rent and other expenses. This alters the former leasing system, which afforded less independence and less risk to the manager. In a related measure, the government has reduced taxes for private artisans.

The trend toward consolidation of industry through mergers has brought the number of state industrial enterprises down from 1,368 in 1960 to 702 in 1979. The government is now seeking to reverse this trend in the expectation that smaller enterprises will be more flexible in adapting to changing market demands. A new decree to take effect 1 January 1982 provides new models and incentives for small-scale enterprises. It allows for small cooperatives (minimum 15, maximum 100 members), open to pensioners and other part-timers as well, mainly for service and repair work; for industrial and service groups (minimum 5 members) to be formed as subsidiaries of existing cooperatives; for improved social benefits for private artisans; and for regularization of the status of "economic working associations" (minimum 2, maximum 30 members), to be authorized by the local councils primarily for tourist services. Decentralization to improve flexibility in production as well as in use of manpower is also the purpose of a new provision for the rental of enterprise facilities by private artisans.

The ancillary activities of agricultural cooperatives multiplied in the early years of the New Economic Mechanism, then were subjected to restrictions. Here, too, permissiveness is the new rule; a decree reduced the number of prohibited types of production, provided incentives for import substitution, and removed the prohibition on sideline activities near urban areas. The importance of household plots and small private farms, which cover 14 percent of agricultural land but produce 35 percent of agricultural output, was also recognized in the setting of higher prices for some produce and in easier credit. The party newspaper has noted opposition among "dogmatic purists" to the measures favoring privatization and moonlighting (ibid., 25 January).

Consumer prices were projected to rise by 4.5–5.0 percent in 1981. Price increases in January and February affected some food items, detergents, gasoline, fertilizer, pesticides, building materials, and postal rates. At the end of June, meat prices were increased by 10 percent. Canteen prices in factories and schools were not altered, and the lowest pensions were increased; these concessions were reportedly granted on the recommendation of the trade unions (*Népszava*, 28 June). A new wage scale, introduced 1 January, allows for greater differentiation by raising the brackets for the most qualified, productive workers and for those working under exceptionally difficult circumstances.

The price increases are part of an economic strategy aimed at gradually bringing prices in line with real production costs. Limited convertibility of the forint is a related objective, and a step toward that goal was the unification of the commercial and noncommercial (tourist and personal) exchange rates on 1 October. The Hungarian National Bank had been closing the gap between the two rates since 1973. In the future, the rate will be fixed weekly rather than monthly. The balance of trade in the first half of 1981 showed some improvement, the deficit in hard currency being less than half that of the corresponding period a year earlier. This improvement was due, however, not to an improved balance of trade with nonsocialist countries but rather to a hard-currency surplus in trade with the socialist bloc. Trade over and above the planned amounts in that sector is frequently settled in hard currency, and Hungary's agricultural exports had soared thanks to a very productive 1980 and strong demand within the Council for Mutual Economic Assistance.

The new Ministry of Industry was established in order to reduce ministerial intervention in enterprise management while improving central guidance. The ministry is to develop a unified industrial policy in cooperation with the newly reformed Chamber of Commerce, the stress being on the profitability of each enterprise, large and small. The ministry supervises the operation of over a thousand enterprises employing 1.3 million workers and producing almost half the national income. A related change is the expansion in the role of the Chamber of Commerce, which will now be called on to mediate in interenterprise disputes that were hitherto resolved administratively by the relevant ministry. Another institutional change was the dissolution on 30 September of the Ministry of Labor and its replacement by a State Wage and Labor Office. The change was presented as part of the modernization of the state's economic administration, in this case to simplify administration and reduce staff (from 240 to 80 by July 1982). The new office assumes the tasks of developing the wage system, labor legislation, and manpower policies, but does not inherit the ministry's responsibility for coordinating social policy. Another new institution is the Wage and Labor Council, which consists of representatives of the relevant ministries, the NCTU, the National Association of Trading Cooperatives, and the Chamber of Commerce; it is attached to the Council of Ministers.

Dissent and Society. The incidence and nature of political dissent have undergone some change in recent months. There is still little evidence of dissent outside intellectual circles, but within the latter the distribution of samizdat publications, the holding of impromptu "flying universities," and student demands for a greater say in university curriculum all indicate a growing inclination to test the regime's tolerance.

A group of sociologists and other intellectuals formed a Foundation for Aid to the Poor in late 1979, and a year later organized an exhibition of artists' work to collect money for the poor. These initiatives clearly embarrassed the regime, which barely tolerated them but then decided to address the issue. In April, the Hungarian Sociological Society organized a conference on the problems of the poor. Leading party and other experts debated definitions of poverty and agreed on the need for further study of social problems and social policy. The conference brought out that one-tenth of the population had an income lower than half the national average; that overcrowded housing was a widespread phenomenon; that 9 percent of children and adolescents needed supervision by social workers; that nearly one million aged people needed help; and that alcoholics, criminals, and other social deviants were nurtured in circumstances of acute poverty (*Társadalmi Szemle*, June).

A collection of essays dedicated to the memory of István Bibó created an even bigger stir in party and intellectual circles. Bibó was a leading political thinker and scholar who had advocated a "third road" between East and West for Hungary in the immediate postwar period, served as a minister in Imre Nagy's revolutionary government in 1956, was subsequently imprisoned, and died in 1979. His writings were published abroad. The thousand-page manuscript, with contributions from 76 authors, was submitted to a Budapest publisher in the fall of 1980 and was rejected. In December, the Politburo commissioned a report on this challenge of the intellectuals, and the resulting confidential document, written under the authority of Mihály Kornidesz, head of the Central Committee's Science, Public Education, and Culture Department, was leaked. The attempt to publish the manuscript was characterized as a provocative act on the part of a new, broadly based alliance of intellectuals. The latter included known dissidents such as the party veteran and Nagy supporter Ferenc Donáth and the distinguished writers Gyula Illyés and György Konrád, but for many others this was their first act of defiance. The essays were generally critical in tone, questioning the legitimacy of the communist regime, characterizing the 1956 events as a genuine and positive revolution, addressing the question of Soviet domination, in some cases even criticizing Bibó for having entertained illusions regarding the possibility of cooperation with the Communists, and generally advocating pluralism and a multiparty system. The party report noted that the successes of the Polish opposition have radicalized Hungarian intellectuals and recommended that the authorities try to exploit their differences and divide them and counterattack by publishing the more acceptable works of Bibó. (*Frankfurter Allgemeine Zeitung*, 26 June.)

In March, the Hungarian Writers' Union disbanded the Attila József Circle. The latter can be traced back to a conference of young writers in 1969 and was officially established in 1973 to serve the special needs of young writers through meetings and publication. The circle had fostered much debate, and its demise may have owed much to young writers' distaste for the self-censorship expected of them. The monthly magazine *Mozgó Világ* (World in motion) had served as an outlet for the radical and avant-garde writings of the circle's members and other young intellectuals, and its publication was suspended for three months. Formerly sponsored by the KISZ, it reappeared as an independent publication with a new and more prudent editorial staff.

In the September issue of the HSWP organ *Pártélet* (Party life), Kornidesz exhorted the party's cultural activists to fight anti-Marxists, a "narrow group of intellectuals who have come under the strong influence of various bourgeois ideologies" and who exaggerated the importance of their role in society. He called for greater vigilance in the areas of publishing and literary criticism against anti-Marxist denigration of the prevailing order and its achievements, particularly in provincial centers where there has been greater laxity in cultural and ideological control.

Compulsory military service was reduced on 1 January from 24 to 18 months. Passport regulations were simplified effective 1 July for travel to Bulgaria, Czechoslovakia, East Germany, Poland, and Romania. The first retirement home for Catholic laymen, administered by the church, was opened in July in Budapest.

The Polish Crisis. Official attitudes regarding the events in Poland since the creation of Solidarity became progressively more critical as tensions grew, but Budapest's hostility was less intense than that evident in Prague and East Berlin, or even Moscow. The Hungarian media, particularly in the earlier stages of the crisis, eschewed commentary and used official Polish sources, thereby relaying both the positive and negative pronouncements of the Warsaw regime concerning Solidarity.

In an address to the trade union congress in December 1980, Kádár stressed Hungary's historical links and current ties, notably economic, with Poland. He voiced support for the Polish party in meeting its commitments to its socialist allies and in solving its domestic problems. Polish party leader Stanislaw Kania visited Budapest on 19 March, and later that month the Hungarian Central Committee and the media denounced the strikes and the political objectives of Solidarity's "extremist circles." At the East German party's congress in April, Károly Németh observed that "hostile and anarchistic forces threaten the historic achievements of the Polish people and the basis of socialist order." In a more tolerant vein, the Central Committee's Foreign Affairs Department head, János Berecz, allowed on a radio program that socialist institutions are capable of change and new institutions (such as Solidarity) could be integrated as long as they were not hostile to the system.

By May, criticism was harsher. *Magyar Hirlap* (29 May) charged that Solidarity had created an intolerable situation, challenging the state's authority. It was reactionary and hostile to the Soviet Union and heading for counterrevolution. This critical view was strengthened by "our own experiences of a quarter century ago that have not been and cannot be forgotten." Hungarian radio covered the Polish Central Committee's June plenum, and *Népszabadság* (12 June) published the Soviet letter to Polish leaders. The party newspaper saw antisocialist elements in Poland in league with the imperialists "pushing the country toward an abyss" and implicitly called the Polish party to task for not correcting the errors and renewing socialism (*Népszabadság*, 14 June). Berecz led an HSWP delegation to confer with Kania on 22 June (coinciding with a visit from the Bulgarian party). The joint statement noted that the concerns in the Soviet Central Committee's letter of 12 June were shared by the Polish party and that the Polish situation could threaten the entire socialist community. Kádár had reportedly sent a similar letter to Kania as well as to Todor Zhivkov and Gustav Husák (*Le Figaro*, 26 June).

The Hungarians followed the Warsaw regime's lead in trying to differentiate between Solidarity as an acceptable labor movement and political radicalism. Thus *Népszabadság* (28 June) accused the Polish intellectual group KSS "KOR" of subverting Solidarity. On the occasion of the Solidarity congress, the paper charged that "the extremist element of the Solidarity organization is consciously aiming at aggravating social tension and . . . has threatened to paralyze the system" (6 September). The appeal to East European workers issued by Solidarity after the first session of its congress was denounced by *Népszabadság* (11 September) as well as at staged mass meetings. Meanwhile, the regime took pains to appease Hungarians, particularly as the twenty-fifth anniversary of the revolution approached. On the occasion of a visit to Miskolc, Kádár asserted that "friend and foe alike recognize that Hungary's domestic situation is solid" (ibid., 2 July).

Events following the introduction on 13 December of martial law in Poland received full attention in Hungary. The organ of the NCTU, *Népszava*, hailed on 15 December the establishment of the Military Council of National Salvation, approved the "smashing blow" it had given to enemies of socialism in Poland, and expressed solidarity with Polish Communists (*FBIS*, 16 December). On the same day, *Népszabadzág* expressed "complete understanding" and offered "sincere sympathy" to the government headed by General Jaruzelski and stated that what had happened in Poland was "an internal affair of the country" (ibid.). In a speech given on 18 December before the National Assembly, Minister of Foreign Affairs Puja hailed socialist Poland as "a firm member of the Warsaw Pact," with whom Hungary will pursue "fraternal relations on the basis of the principle of proletarian internationalism" (ibid., 29 December). In its continuous coverage of Polish developments, *Népszava* on 20 December assailed Solidarity leaders for betraying their original principles and becoming a subversive political force. The paper also attacked Radio Free Europe for spreading misinformation on the events in Poland, a method already used at the time of the 1956 "counterrevolution" in Hungary. Describing the clashes between miners and police forces, *Népszava* blamed Western instigators for the bloodshed in Poland (*FBIS*, 23 December). The introduction of economic sanctions against Poland announced by the U.S. government on 23 December was characterized by Radio Budapest as "a savage onslaught against Poland and the USSR" (ibid., 24 December). Radio Budapest admitted on 27 December that the "very tough measures" [of the Polish government] have not yet met with full sympathy in the whole of Polish society" (ibid., 28 December). As for the economic sanctions against the USSR announced on 29 December, Radio Budapest observed that even U.S. commentators found the measures of "negligible practical significance" (ibid., 30 December).

Interparty Relations. The Hungarian delegation to the Soviet party congress in February was led by Kádár and included Lázár, Gyenes, Berecz, and the ambassador to Moscow, András Szuros. Union chief Sándor Gáspár also attended the congress as a guest. In his address, Brezhnev praised the "expert organization" of Hungary's agricultural collectives and enterprises, a reference that was widely reported in Hungary to indicate Soviet approval of the country's market-oriented economic system. Noting that "our enemies count on the position of socialism becoming weaker," Kádár voiced support for the "fraternal Polish party and the proponents of socialism in Poland. We believe that the Polish people, guided by the PUWP [Polish United Workers' Party], will find a socialist way out of the complicated situation. As the Polish comrades themselves have put it, Poland was, is, and will remain a member of the family of socialist countries." Kádár also visited Brezhnev in the Crimea on 27 July, in the context of a regular series of annual bilateral meetings. The official report on the meeting referred to ideological cooperation to combat anticommunism and to expansion of trade.

Kádár and Czechoslovak party leader Husák had an unannounced and brief meeting at Bratislava on 12 November 1980; their communiqué contained the usual faintly threatening expression of confidence in the Polish party's ability to ward off imperialist meddling and resolve Poland's domestic problems in accordance with socialist principles. Czechoslovak Premier Lubomír Štrougal visited Budapest in the spring.

Lazar Mojsov, the then president of the Presidium of the League of Communists of Yugoslavia, paid an official visit to Budapest on 3–5 June. He and Kádár met "in an atmosphere of full openness, comradeship, and friendship." The communiqué hailed the "continuity of the Yugoslav-Hungarian summit dialogue, which had been conducted so happily for decades between Josip Broz Tito and János Kádár." As usual, the right of communist parties to determine their policies independently, according to their particular circumstances, was reiterated, and the positive role of the two countries' minorities was hailed.

The less than comfortable position of the Hungarian minority in Romania was once again exposed in a petition addressed to Kádár by the Intracounty Workers' Committee for the Realization of a Transylvanian Hungarian Television. Charging that Romanian authorities systematically hamper the cultural life of Hungarians in that country, the petition asked Kádár to secure Hungarian-Romanian collaboration for the installation of relay stations to allow Hungarians in Transylvania to watch telecasts from Hungary. The appeal was not acknowledged publicly in Hungary.

In May, the HSWP Central Committee and the periodical *Peace and Socialism* organized an international theoretical conference entitled "The Dialectic Relationship of Nationalism and Internationalism in the Workers' Movement." Forty-seven parties were represented (*Pártélet*, August).

An NCTU delegation attended the first congress of the Central Council of Afghan Trade Unions in March. The following month a Hungarian-Afghan technical and scientific cooperation agreement was signed; under its terms, Hungarian technical and health specialists will be sent to Afghanistan, while the latter will send students to Hungary. An HSWP delegation attended the congress of the Kampuchean People's Revolutionary Party in Phnom Penh in May. In June, a Hungarian-Vietnamese working plan on scientific, educational, and cultural cooperation was signed in Budapest. András Gyenes led a delegation to Sweden in January at the invitation of Sweden's Left Party–Communists.

General Foreign Policy. In addressing the Soviet congress, Kádár summed up Hungary's foreign policy line in terms that as usual did not depart from the Soviet version. The unconcealed aims of extremist imperialist forces, he observed, had halted the process of détente. Anti-Soviet and anticommunist pressures had intensified, aided by the policies of Chinese leaders. Hungary's principal foreign policy objectives were to halt the arms race and reduce tensions, particularly in Europe, by a successful conclusion to the Madrid talks. Hungary fully endorses the Soviet proposal for negotiations on medium-range nuclear weapons in Europe as well as the European disarmament conference proposal under discussion at Madrid. Also at Madrid, Hungary and Finland introduced a resolution calling for aid for the dissemination of the cultural products of relatively isolated language groups.

With regard to the Third World, Hungary follows the Soviet line as well. The communiqué arising from the state visit of Nigerian President Alhaji Shehu Shagari denounced South African military aggression and called for an independent Namibia, an Indian Ocean "peace zone," the restitution of the Palestinians' national rights, and for Israeli evacuation of all occupied Arab territories, including Jerusalem.

Publications. The HSWP's principal daily newspaper is *Népszabadság* (People's freedom), edited by Péter Várkonyi. The theoretical monthly *Társadalmi Szemle* (Social review) is edited by Valéria Benke, the monthly organizational journal *Pártélet* (Party life) by Vera Lajtai. Other major newspapers are *Magyar Hirlap*, the "government" daily; *Magyar Nemzet*, published under the auspices of the PPF; and *Népszava*, the NCTU organ. The official news agency is Magyar Távirati Iroda (Hungarian Telegraphic Agency; MTI).

University of Toronto Bennett Kovrig

Poland

The communist movement in Poland began with the formation in December 1918 of the Communist Workers' Party of Poland, subsequently renamed the Communist Party of Poland in 1925. The Comintern dissolved the party in 1938 but revived it in 1942 as the Polish Workers' Party. This party seized power after the war and consolidated control by gradually eliminating its potential competitors. In December 1948, the Communists forced a merger with the Polish Socialist Party and established the Polish United Workers' Party (PUWP), which has since maintained a dominant position in the country's political and economic institutions. The PUWP's leading role was formalized in 1976 through a constitutional amendment. Two other existing political organizations, the Democratic Party (DP) and the United Peasant Party (UPP), are restricted to supportive functions.

The PUWP has always maintained control over elective state bodies, the Sejm (parliament) and local people's councils, and public institutions. The main instrument for coordinating electoral activity has been the Front of National Unity (FNU), a formal coalition of established social and political groups, which has been dominated by the party and chaired since February 1976 by PUWP Politburo member Henryk Jablonski. The FNU has been the only organization empowered to present candidates for elections. In the last national elections (March 1980), FNU candidates received 99.52 percent of the vote, with 98.87 percent of eligible voters taking part in the exercise (*Trybuna ludu*, 25–26 March 1980). The communist party won 261 of the 460 parliamentary seats (56.7 percent), the UPP obtained 113 seats (24.6 percent), and the DP got 37 seats (8 percent). The remaining 49 seats were filled by nonparty deputies, including thirteen from various Catholic groups. The results of the elections were identical with those held in March 1976. They were denounced by dissident groups as "fictitious" and without "any significance" since there had been "no social control over the outcome of the voting" (Reuters, 28 March 1980).

The party's control over public institutions has been ensured through the practice of *nomen-*

klatura, a process whereby appointments to decision-making positions at all levels of state administra-tion are either made or supervised by PUWP officials. A comprehensive list of these positions is periodically prepared by the PUWP Central Committee (for a recent list, see *Revue française de sociologie,* no. 2, April–June 1979).

Leadership and Organization. The highest authority within the party is the congress, which is convened at least every five years. During 14–20 July, the PUWP held a special, extraordinary con-gress to account for changes since the last regular congress (February 1980). The extraordinary con-gress elected the new Central Committee, composed of 200 full and 70 deputy members, the Central Control Commission (90 members), and the Central Audit Commission (70 members). It also elected, by a precedent-setting direct vote, Stanislaw Kania as the party's first secretary. Subsequently, the Central Committee chose, by a secret ballot but upon Kania's recommendation, members of the party's top executive bodies, the Politburo and the Secretariat. The Politburo is charged with pol-icymaking functions between Central Committee plenums; the Secretariat supervises all aspects of party work.

There was a continuing turnover in the compositon of party leadership at all levels during 1981. Following the series of changes that had occurred in 1980 and led to a removal of Edward Gierek as well as most of his associates from positions of power in the Politburo and the Secretariat (*YICA,* 1981, pp. 268–70), major transformations again affected the PUWP central leadership in 1981.

On 30 April, the Central Committee removed Jozef Pinkowski from the Politburo and released Emil Wojtaszek, a deputy member of the Politburo and Central Committee secretary, as well as Jerzy Wojtecki, a Central Committee secretary, and Zbigniew Zielinski, a member of the Secretariat, from their functions. At the same time, the committee elected two manual workers, Gerard Gabrys and Zygmunt Wronski, as full members of the Politburo, as well as two professional party staffers, Jozef Masny and Kazimierz Cypryniak, as deputy Politburo member and Central Committee secretary, re-spectively.

The next change in the composition of the central leadership occurred in connection with the extraordinary congress. The most important initial aspect of that change was a thorough purge of the incumbent members of PUWP executive bodies. The purge was conducted in two stages: first, during the election campaign for delegates to the congress; and second, in the election to the Central Com-mittee at the congress itself. In order to be chosen either to the Politburo or the Secretariat, candidates had to be elected first to the Central Committee, the prerequisite of which was election as a delegate to the congress.

Four top party officials failed to win a mandate as a delegate. They were two full members of the Politburo, Gabrys and Wronski, and two deputy members, Masny and Jerzy Waszczuk, the latter also losing his position as a Central Committee secretary. Their departure from the leadership, forced by a rank-and-file vote, merely signaled the beginning of a purge process. A more comprehensive cleansing of the party elite was to take place during the election to the Central Committee.

Balloting for the Central Committee took place on 17 July, after three days of debate largely consumed by procedural wranglings and disagreements. The vote was secret, and the delegates chose from a list of candidates that was substantially larger than the number of seats (275 for 200); the list was prepared by combining an official slate of candidates proposed by the congress's nominating com-mission with nominations from the floor. Delegates expressed their preferences by crossing out the names of specific candidates they did not wish to vote for.

The results of the vote amounted to a massive vote of no confidence in the leadership and the party's establishment. Five Politburo members (Tadeusz Grabski, Henryk Jablonski, Mieczyslaw Ja-gielski, Mieczyslaw Moczar, and Andrzej Zabinski), three deputy members (Tadeusz Fiszbach, Wladyslaw Kruk, and Roman Ney) as well as four Central Committee secretaries (Stanislaw

Gabrielski, Grabski, Zdzislaw Kurowski, and Ney) failed in their bid for re-election. Only four incumbent members of the party's central leadership preserved their seat in the Central Committee: Kazimierz Barcikowski, Wojciech Jaruzelski, Stanislaw Kania, and Stefan Olszowski.

The purge of the executive leadership was accompanied by an equally thorough change in the composition of the Central Committee. Only 16 out of 143 full members elected in February 1980 were re-elected; only 2 former deputy members and 1 full member of the Central Control Commission were promoted to full Central Committee membership, while 181 members (90.5 percent) were total newcomers. Among the deputy members, only 5 out of the 70 were re-elected, 2 came from the former Central Control and Audit Commissions, while 63 (90 percent) were new. More important, the new Central Committee was politically a much different body from the previous one. It included a large group of industrial workers and technicians (82, or 41 percent) as well as several peasants and farm managers (37 or 18.5 percent), while the party and state officials were reduced to a mere 38 seats. The old Central Committee was dominated by the party and state establishment (85 out of 143 seats), and industrial and agricultural groups had only 40 representatives.

Following the election of Stanislaw Kania by the entire congress as the party's first secretary, the Central Committee chose, on Kania's recommendation, the following individuals as members of the Politburo: Kazimierz Barcikowski (re-elected), Tadeusz Czechowicz, Jozef Czyrek, Zofia Grzyb, Wojciech Jaruzelski (re-elected), Hieronim Kubiak, Jan Labecki, Zbigniew Messner, Miroslaw Milewski, Stefan Olszowski (re-elected), Stanislaw Opalko, Tadeusz Porebski, Jerzy Romanik, and Albin Siwak. In addition, two deputy members of the Politburo were also elected: Jan Glowczyk and Wlodzimierz Mokrzyszczak. The new Secretariat consisted of Barcikowski (re-elected), Czyrek, Kubiak, Zbigniew Michalek, Milewski, Olszowski (re-elected), and Marian Wozniak. Kania, as the party's first secretary, obtained seats in both the Politburo and the Secretariat on the strength of the congress's vote.

The selection of a new leadership at the congress did not end the process of change. On 18 October, during a plenum of the Central Committee, Kania suddenly submitted his resignation as first secretary. The reasons for this action are unclear. It has been speculated that Kania initially conceived resignation as a tactical move, intended to force the committee to reject the offer and thus provide him with a clear indication of political support for his policies. (*Le Monde*, Paris, 19 October). The Central Committee, however, accepted the resignation, without debate, by a vote of 104 to 79. Then, it elected Gen. Wojciech Jaruzelski as the new first secretary (a biography of Jaruzelski follows this profile). He was the only candidate for the position, winning 180 of the 184 votes cast. (PAP, 18 October.) Kania was automatically removed from both the Politburo and the Secretariat.

In many respects, Kania was a tragic figure. A veteran party politician (he had been a Politburo member since 1971 and a Central Committee secretary since 1975), Kania became the party's first secretary on 5 September 1980. Replacing the thoroughly discredited Edward Gierek, Kania was immediately burdened with the task of rebuilding the morale of the profoundly disillusioned communist organization and defending its self-asserted leading role. To make matters worse, Kania was forced by circumstances not only to deal with an increasingly disgruntled party membership and to face mounting social pressures for political and institutional change, but also to ensure for himself and his policies the support of Poland's communist neighbors, particularly the Soviet Union.

By early 1980, Kania had come forward with an outline of a comprehensive strategy to deal with the situation (*YICA*, 1980, pp. 275–76). This strategy combined acceptance of wide-ranging operational changes within the system, particularly in the areas of economic management and state administration, with insistence on the political and institutional continuity that would preserve the party's domination over all organized aspects of public life. Promoted as a "strategy of socialist renewal," it was to be implemented through a series of agreements—that is, by peaceful means. Accepted by the party's top-level leadership and receiving a qualified endorsement from Soviet leaders, this strategy provided the party's political guidelines throughout 1981.

The implementation of that strategy encountered, however, growing obstacles. In part, this was because a movement of self-organization engulfed the entire society, with an increasing number of groups claiming the right to institutional autonomy. It became obvious that the task of preserving the party's monopoly over decision making was not only difficult but perhaps impossible. Another obstacle was growing criticism of the strategy within the party itself. For conservative elements within the party and large sectors of the administrative establishment, the very acceptance of operational changes appeared to endanger their vested interests. For those who were inclined to accept broad innovations in the party's operations, on the one hand, the strategy seemed merely to represent a narrow and ineffective attempt to preserve the status quo. Finally, the failure of party leaders to impose their policies on the public provoked angry outbursts of impatience from Poland's communist neighbors. Their complaints and threats, although effective in influencing the behavior of party groups and members, proved ineffective in pacifying or arresting the aspirations of the newly emerging social forces. The net result was a political stalemate, in which the scope of activities of various social organizations expanded, though without any explicit institutional recognition, while the party preserved its formal position but failed to regain authority.

Kania's departure from power signified that for the majority of Central Committee members, a continuation of that stalemate had become unacceptable. By consenting to his resignation, they seemed to express their frustration and anger that so little had been achieved and so little had been done to restore the party. By the same token, however, by electing Jaruzelski, who had been Kania's close associate, the Central Committee indicated its hesitation to embark on a new road.

Indeed, Jaruzelski himself made it clear in his inaugural speech that he was determined to follow the principles of socialist renewal. Furthermore, he clearly established a bond of continuity between himself and his predecessor. Describing Kania as his "very close friend of many years," Jaruzelski affirmed that both he and Kania had "shared the same road, characterized by accomplishments as well as failures." Admitting joint responsibility with Kania for what the leadership had done throughout the year, Jaruzelski pledged to "continue on the same general course," though promising "to do everything to make [this course] more effective" (*Trybuna ludu*, 19 October).

The choice of Jaruzelski was promptly endorsed by the Soviet leadership, which expressed "confidence" that the new PUWP leader would "use [his] great prestige to rally the ranks of the PUWP on the basis of the principles of Marxism-Leninism, in the interest of defending the socialist gains of the Polish working class and all the working people of Poland against encroachments by counterrevolution and of overcoming the political and economic crisis" (ibid., 20 October). Similar messages were also sent to Jaruzelski by leaders of other communist parties.

The removal of Kania was not followed by any major transformation in the composition of the leadership. Commenting on the apparent decision to preserve the leading group's continuity in office, Jaruzelski said that "changes [in leadership] do not constitute an act; they reflect a process" and added that the party "finds itself under particularly strong fire from its enemies, and in such conditions one does not undertake any broad maneuvers." Even so, Jaruzelski recommended, and the Central Committee approved on 28 October, the election of Gen. Florian Siwicki as a deputy member of the Politburo. At the same time, the committee elected Wlodzimierz Mokrzyszczak, already a deputy member of the Politburo, and Marian Orzechowski as secretaries of the Central Committee. It was assumed that Siwicki, a Soviet-educated military officer who has been chief of staff of Poland's armed forces and a deputy minister of national defense since 1973, would be concerned with military matters. Orzechowski, a university professor from Wroclaw, was put in charge of ideological matters. Mokrzyszczak became involved with organizational problems of the party.

On 28 October, the Central Committee expanded the structure of party's central professional staff. Little information was provided on the nature of the change. The only element of considerable political importance was the appointment of Gen. Tadeusz Dziekan, an officer with long experience in the military department of the Central Committee, the Main Political Administration of the armed forces, as head of the Cadre Department. In that position, Dziekan would be responsible for appointments to sensitive positions in the party's regional and local bodies.

Changes at the central level of leadership were accompanied by even greater transformations in the regional and local bodies of the party. Most of these changes took place during the election campaign preceding the extraordinary congress. During the campaign, party members elected about 600,000 new officers in basic party bodies, including some 100,000 first secretaries. More than 50 percent were newcomers. A similar turnover occurred in elections to 2,359 local and regional committees; here the percentage of newcomers reached 52 percent. (*Nowe Drogi*, August, p. 60.)

There is no information on the size of PUWP membership. In February 1980, the party claimed over 3.04 million members. From mid-1980 until June 1981, however, about 300,000 members left the party, including some 186,000 who formally resigned (ibid., p. 90); there are reasons to believe that the membership decline continued throughout 1981. Indeed, one could estimate that at the end of 1981, PUWP membership might have oscillated around 2.0 to 2.5 million. The population of Poland is 35.7 million.

Auxiliary and Mass Organizations. The PUWP's relation with society has been traditionally rooted in the principle of the party's control over all organized political and social activities. The primary function of the many existing public organizations, such as political parties, labor and social unions, or youth movements, has been to relay the party's policies to specific social groups and help the PUWP in its goal of integrating the country's population into a community permanently directed and managed by the party itself.

The emergence of Solidarity, which developed during the autumn months of 1980 from a protest movement into a mass organization and gained official recognition as an independent labor union in November 1980, has severely undermined and weakened the position of existing organizations in Poland's public life. This process continued during 1981, marked by a progressive and increasingly evident organizational disarray within some of the institutionalized bodies, massive losses of membership in others, and occasional changes in political orientation among quite a few of the once reliable supporters of the political establishment. Even so, despite a clear decline in importance suffered by these organizations, none has either folded or attempted to redefine its traditional functions. At the end of 1981, they still formed part of an institutional system ensuring a semblance of political continuity.

This was particularly evident with regard to the two minor political parties, the DP and the UPP, traditionally allied with the PUWP. The DP held a national congress on 14–18 March, which led to a thorough renovation of its leadership (only three incumbents of the 119-member Central Committee were re-elected) and adoption of a new program professing an enhancement of internal democracy within the organization. At the same time, however, the DP reiterated its long-standing acceptance of the socialist party and the PUWP's leading role in Poland's public life (*Trybuna ludu*, 16 and 17 March).

The situation in the UPP, an organization claiming to represent peasants, was even more complicated. The party's leaders, who had been formally elected at the UPP's national congress in December 1980, were forced to resign on 7 May following allegations by regional bodies that they had failed to respond to the new political and social situation in the country. Their successors also failed to pacify the ferment within the party, and a new purge of leading officers was conducted at a special plenum on 5–6 November. Whether those changes could bring about a measure of stability within the organization remained problematical; indeed, the party announced plans to hold an extraordinary congress in the near future to decide on changes to be introduced in the structure and the programs of the organization.

These personnel changes in the leaderships of the two parties had no apparent impact on either their policies toward the PUWP or their functions within state institutions. Both groups remained strongly supportive of the PUWP's dominant role in policymaking and actively participated in the state's institutional life. Indeed, as if to indicate the relative political insignificance of the leadership changes, none of the dismissed officials, although formally discredited in their own party, lost their position in the state administrative hierarchy (former DP leader Tadeusz Mlynczak continued as a deputy chairman of the Council of State, and the UPP's former head, Stanislaw Gucwa, is still exercising the important function of Sejm speaker.) In early 1980, the DP claimed 110,000 and the UPP 458,000 members. It is likely that the membership in both organizations declined during 1981.

Throughout 1981 there was a continuing, and perhaps growing, fragmentation of Poland's labor organizations. While in mid-1980, a single and centrally directed labor organization had claimed control of the activity of some 23 branch unions with a combined membership of more than 13.6 million, at the end of 1981 there were about a hundred separate labor organizations operating in the country.

Before the December declaration of martial law, the largest and most influential labor organization was Solidarity (9.5 million members). It operated a network of 38 territorial chapters and thousands of local units; there was a Solidarity unit in almost every factory, office, and institution. Each unit enjoyed considerable autonomy in setting its own tasks and defining methods of activity. The same could be said about regional chapters, many of which published journals, in additon to a large number of internal bulletins and other periodicals. Solidarity's national leadership, which was elected at the organization's first national congress held in two stages (5–10 September and 26 September–7 October), consisted of the 107-member National Commission and 21-member Audit Commission. The work of the National Commission, which was the main policy-setting body, was coordinated by a 13-member Presidium. The chairman of Solidarity, Lech Walesa, who had chaired the organization's National Coordinating Commission since September 1980, was elected by the congress as the national leader. Claiming organizational and political independence of the state authorities, Solidarity was financially self-sufficient and supported itself from membership dues. All other mass organizations are subsidized by the state.

Another labor institution, organizationally and politically seperate from Solidarity, unites some 23 branch trade unions. Claiming a membership of about 3.5 million, the branch trade unions are the remnant of the old centralized labor movement. Although they adopted the name of independent and self-governing trade unions and formed a loose body, the National Consultative Commission, to coordinate their activities, the branch unions preserved strong continuity in their organizational features and political outlook; indeed, they continued to act as an agency of the state and party and voiced official policy in the name of the working people.

Besides these two major labor institutions, about seventy or more so-called autonomous labor unions were operating before mid-December. They were composed mainly of small professional groups in specific local enterprises, such as jewelers, insurance workers, customs officials, or civil aviation technicians. Their influence was negligible in the country's major industries, and the bulk of their membership consisted of white-collar workers. Some twenty autonomous unions joined together in 1981 to form the Confederation of Autonomous Trade Unions; this confederation claimed a combined membership of about one million.

An important development, indicative of the progressive fragmentation of the institutional system, was the establishment of a separate labor union of individual farmers. The organization was formally registered by a Warsaw court as the Independent Self-Governing Labor Union for Individual Farmers—Solidarity on 12 May. This decision by the state authorities culminated several months of peasant agitation and occasional demonstrations and strikes. The main goals of the union were described as defending the interests of the peasants in the areas of prices, free-market sales, and the distribution of scarce means of production, primarily of machinery and fodder (Radio Warsaw, 12 May). More important, however, was the implication arising from the emergence of Rural Solidarity that the authorities were unable to prevent the formation of an autonomous organization in the countryside in the face of a determined pressure from the peasants. At the time of its establishment, Rural Solidarity claimed a membership of about 2.5 million or over 70 percent of Poland's private farmers (AP, 12 May).

To neutralize the political impact of that development, the authorities formally established on 12 May the Agricultural Circles and Rural Organizations Trade Union. This organization was little more, however, than a continuation, under a different name, of a long-existing group controlled and directed by party and state authorities. There was no indication that the newly refurbished official union would be substantially different from its predecessor.

The process of fragmentation was not limited to industrial and rural organizations. Similar tendencies were also clear in the youth movement. They were already noticeable during the last months of 1980, when the three major youth organizations—Union of Polish Socialist Youth, Socialist Union of Polish Students, and Union of Polish Scouts—decided to abandon the centralistic coordinating umbrella of the Federation of Socialist Unions of Polish Youth. The trend away from centralism and toward separateness increased during 1981 with the formation, and the official recognition, of such new youth organizations as the Union of Rural Youth, the Union of Democratic Youth, and the Independent Student Association.

Even long-established and traditionally loyalist organizations were not immune to the spontaneous fervor of social self-assertion. The Union of Fighters for Freedom and Democracy, a veterans' group dominated by conservative communist politicians, lost some of its membership to a newly formed veterans' movement associated with Solidarity. There was also ferment in the League of Women, with several regional chapters of that organization demanding the convocation of a special national congress to change the league's leadership and policies. Indeed, at the end of 1981, it seemed that no sector of Poland's society, and no institution or organization, was left unaffected by the general and widespread pluralistic pressures; there were separate organizations of consumers and producers, of artists and journalists, of workers and peasants. Even policemen attempted to set up an occupational union to defend their interests. While the party was still able to control and supervise the activity of some of these groups, more and more claimed, or at least aspired to, independence from the party's management.

Party Internal Affairs. During 14–20 July, the PUWP held an extraordinary national congress, its ninth congress since 1948. In almost any circumstances, such a special gathering of party activists would mark the high point of internal politics, providing a possible watershed in the organization's history. It did not, however, although the event temporarily captured the attention of both domestic and foreign observers. Instead, the most important development for the party during 1981 was a continuing process of organizational disintegration, combined with equally significant changes in ideological posture among the membership and in the party's relation with the population.

The congress's tasks were threefold: to select a new party leadership, to introduce lasting changes in the organizational structures and proceedings so as to make the party more democratic, and to adopt a new program of action for the future that would ensure public support for the party's policies and revitalize its position in society. It succeeded in only one of these tasks—the election of a new leadership. As for internal organizational changes, the 1,955 delegates were unable to prepare an acceptable set of rules and left that task to a special commission. The commission reportedly completed its work during 1981, but the results remained unpublished by the end of the year. One of the two programmatic documents, a resolution on current policies, was issued some weeks after the congress ended and had little or no immediate impact on the party's behavior. The other, an outline of long-term intentions, was to be prepared later by a special commission of the Central Committee.

Even so, there is no doubt that the congress played an important role in the party's politics and perhaps made a lasting imprint on its history. Above all, it served as a landmark of democratic procedures. It set a precedent by adopting such provisions as the election of party leaders by secret ballot from among multiple candidates. More important, the congress allowed for both the definition and the adoption of these procedures through open discussion by the delegates themselves. As a result, the congress became a lively affair. It featured long procedural disputes and spirited debates replete with contradictory statements and declarations; it was both genuinely exciting and relatively unpredictable.

The congress ended with an appeal to the nation for a common and concerted effort "to pull the country out of the crisis . . . that endangers the existence and the future of the state." The responsibility for the crisis was put "not so much on the socialist system . . . as on the [former] party and state leaders who betrayed its ideals." The appeal further stated that "no one to whom the future of the socialist fatherland is dear should abandon us [the party] in this moment of historical trial." (*Trybuna ludu*, 21 July.)

This element of institutional continuity was also present in the concluding address of Stanislaw Kania, who was re-elected as the party's first secretary by the congress. Asserting that the congress had contributed to the emergence of popular "goodwill that would remove doubts and bring back confidence in our capacity" to rule, Kania said that "this congress dispelled all doubts about the party's willingness and determination to ensure that Poland remains and will continue to be a reliable ally of the Soviet Union and a firm link in the socialist community." Kania also said, with respect to the domestic situation, that his leadership would "strengthen the role of labor unions as both the representatives of workers' interests operating independently of the administration and the partners [of the party] in finding an agreement on ways to overcome the continuing crisis." In this context, he affirmed the leadership's acceptance of the "active role played in public life by Catholic and Christian organizations as well as the cooperation between the church and the state." Kania saw the main domestic issue "in establishing lawful order in the state and condemning and struggling against alien forces that [both] foster tension and, by using demagogy and 'disinformation,' try to set up [a separate system of] authority besides and against the existing one." (Ibid.)

Yet the congress was soon to be almost forgotten and disregarded, as the party proved unable to overcome its many internal difficulties and new troubles continued to emerge. Perhaps the most important and nagging problem was the progressive organizational disarray. This became apparent from the beginning of 1981 with the emergence and subsequent expansion of the so-called "horizontal structures" within the organization. These structures were formed through largely informal efforts by large numbers of local party activists to set up permanent links among separate party bodies within cities, provinces, or even factories and educational institutions so they could prepare their own operational network to facilitate elaboration of coordinated positions on specific issues of the day.

The immediate objective of this movement was to replace those occupying positions of authority within the party. To achieve that goal, several tactics were used. In some cases, a direct vote was taken to remove incumbents within basic party bodies, and new people were elected to replace them (*Polityka*, 11 April). In others, pressure was put on the central leadership to remove specific individuals (*Trybuna robotnicza*, 11 February). More serious still, and difficult for the leadership to contain, were growing demands by numerous local organizations, particularly in large industrial centers, for secret elections to all party offices at all levels of the party's operations.

The high point in the development of the "horizontal structures" was a conference held on 15 April in the city of Torun. Attended by some 750 delegates representing numerous party bodies from 14 of Poland's 49 provinces, the conference was organized by rank-and-file members, without previous authorization from the party hierarchy. It served as a forum for a wide-ranging debate on ways to improve the quality of political work within the organization, introduce greater democracy in its internal operations, and revise the concept of the party's role in public life in order to make it compatible with current social and political realities. The main theme of the debate was the need to institutionalize the "horizontal" links in the statutes of the party and, in this way, to ensure a lasting change in the organization itself. (*Trybuna ludu*, 16 April.)

To counter the growing influence of the horizontal movement, the leadership employed different strategies. One was to acquiesce in some of the reformist demands, particularly new electoral procedures, but on the condition that they would be only temporary and would have to be legitimized through eventual statutory changes. The other was to create a countermovement within the party itself. This was exemplified by the emergence, in May, of the so-called Katowice Forum, a firmly orthodox group of activists from the Silesian city of Katowice. Although ostensibly separate from the party's organizational hierarchy, the group was provided quarters by the local party committee, headed by then Politburo member Andrzej Zabinski; the committee also facilitated the group's publishing activity (*Glos Wybrzeza*, 1 June). In May, the forum issued a manifesto strongly criticizing the political situation in the country and condemning both the movement of social self-organization and the reformist ferment in the party (*Sztandar Mlodych*, 28 May). Similar groups soon emerged in other cities throughout the country; their activities received considerable publicity in the domestic press as well as abroad, particularly in other communist countries.

None of these efforts deterred party reformers. Indeed, there were indications that proponents of change in the party's structures and operations could have succeeded in their plans, particularly through electing their candidates as delegates to the party congress. The reformist momentum was effectively checked, however, following publication of a special letter from Soviet leaders to members of the PUWP's Central Committee (*Trybuna ludu*, 11 June). The letter, while repeating Moscow's approval of the party's program for "socialist renewal," was sharply critical of the PUWP leadership's failure to implement that program in a way that would reassert the party's leading role in public life, condemned reformist trends in the organization, and called upon "all honest Communists" to rally together. Significantly, the letter contained an implication that both Kania and Jaruzelski "as well as other Polish comrades" had failed to heed earlier warnings from Moscow about the dangers that might result from the continuing crisis. Nonetheless, the letter stopped short of calling for their resignations. (Text of the letter follows this profile.)

There was a tendency then to assume that the Soviet criticism might reflect Moscow's disenchantment with the performance of Polish leaders. In retrospect, however, it seems more likely that Soviet support for conservative groups in Poland was intended to intimidate the reformers. Indeed, the immediate result of the letter was a marked increase in the power and prestige of both Kania and Jaruzelski. Kania was re-elected party leader at the congress, a development formally endorsed by Moscow. Jaruzelski's assumption of power in October was also supported by the Soviet leadership. In the aftermath of the Soviet letter, the horizontal movement lost political influence and effectively disappeared.

Success in removing the reformist disease was not, however, synonymous with improvement in organizational discipline. Indeed, the disarray only intensified, with the expansion of conservative and ultraorthodox trends. Following the congress, various forums merely changed their names to "Marxist-Leninist seminars," "workers' discussion clubs," and the like and continued their activities. The new leadership made no attempt to stop this trend. Actually, as a result of the direct personal intervention of Politburo member and Central Committee secretary in charge of propaganda matters Stefan Olszowski, a network of new conservative clubs emerged under the name of "Reality." These clubs, in close cooperation with an already existing group, Warsaw 1980, received permission to publish a mass-oriented weekly, *Rzeczywistosc*. This weekly soon established a new standard of orthodox propaganda, openly attacking Solidarity and other autonomous social organizations and calling for decisive action by the party to quell social unrest.

By the end of the year, there were no reliable figures for membership in the various conservative organizations within the party. It was clear, however, that they had failed to strengthen internal discipline. In addition, they contributed to the deterioration of relations between the party and society. This process developed in two forms. One was a decline in rank-and-file involvement in party work, with increasingly limited attendance at party meetings and functions and massive resignations. The other was a growing movement, initiated by local Solidarity bodies in factories and supported by the workers, to remove the party from workplaces. Such a movement was, perhaps, unavoidable in view of the widely held sentiment that since the party was responsible for leading the country and the country suffered from major economic and social setbacks, those connected with party operations were responsible for the problems. A corollary to this feeling was the conviction that the removal of the party from active participation in economic decisions was a prerequisite for improvement. First practical steps in that direction were taken in mid-November, when workers from a large factory in Zywiec voted by an overwhelming majority (970 for to 79 against, with only 77 abstentions) to deprive the local party body of financial support from the factory and oblige it to hold meetings after working hours. In addition, the workers imposed a requirement on factory management to cease any consultations related to factory operations with party authorities (Radio Warsaw, 23 and 24 November). Similar actions were reported in factories in more than twenty provinces.

More important, these proletarian measures against the self-proclaimed "workers' organization" were supported by many rank-and-file members of the party itself. Indeed, commenting on the situation in the party during a Central Committee plenum at the end of November, Central Committee secretary in charge of organizational matters Wlodzimierz Mokrzyszczak said that "the main source of weakness of some of the party organizations is their ideological and political emasculation. There are considerable breaches in the form of violation of political and organizational discipline and there are instances of incorrectly interpreting the principles of democratic centralism. Ideological pluralism is being introduced in the life of the party. The consequence of these tendencies is the internal disintegration of part of the party rank and file. Certain party organizations—and sometimes the authorities as well—become incapable of active work. Threats coming from the opponents of socialism are not seen. The possibility of basing the party's activities on principles different from those of Marxism-Leninism and the basic requirements of the party statutes is being tolerated." He then added that "in struggling for the unity of the party, we must reject the illusory slogans of social solidarity, we must resolutely oppose right-wing, opportunist, revisionist, and also sectarian-conservative views. Any attempt to create informal structures harms the party." (*Trybuna ludu*, 28–29 November.) At the end of 1981, however, there was little or no chance that the communist organization would soon reunify.

Domestic Affairs. Political tension and conflicts between the authorities and the population intensified throughout 1981. At the heart of the problem was the unresolved issue of who should govern the country. The party and its leaders remained determined to preserve their traditional exclusive supervision of all organized social activity. They also insisted on their self-asserted right to set the direction of social and political evolution. Numerous social groups, including the powerful worker and peasant Solidarities as well as a growing number of other public associations and unions, believed the party incapable of coping with economic and social difficulties. The net result of the continuing infighting was a permanent stalemate, which merely solidified the deep-seated stagnation of the system's operations and intensified the general crisis. The situation changed abruptly on 13 December, when the authorities imposed a state of emergency.

One can distinguish three stages in the evolution of Polish politics during the year. The first, extending through the first three months of 1981, was dominated by a series of assertive actions by Solidarity and repeated attempts by the party and the government to restrict the labor movement's influence among the workers. This stage ended with a major conflict between the two sides over an incident in which several members of the movement were physically mistreated by the police. Solidarity countered by a general warning strike, and the government was forced to enter formal negotiations with the movement's representatives. The second stage centered on the party's attempts to develop a position on the social and political changes that would provide it with a modicum of public support. The third stage began with a national congress of Solidarity, a congress that provided the movement with a long-range program of action and institutionalized its structures, and ended with the imposition of the state of emergency, an act that terminated normal political life.

The First Stage. Serious conflict between the authorities and Solidarity started at the very beginning of 1981. The movement's leadership demanded, on 7 January, a shortening of the workweek from 46 to 40 hours by declaring all Saturdays free. The government countered by proposing 42.5 hours. The movement refused, and the dispute rapidly developed into a major political issue. As numerous strikes were staged by workers in factories and institutions throughout the country in support of the movement's leadership while repeated attempts to solve the problem by negotiations failed, it became a testing point of the relative influence of the government and the labor movement. The conflict was eventually resolved by a compromise reached on 31 January: the five-day, 40-hour week was accepted by the government "in principle." For 1981, however, both sides agreed that every fourth Saturday would be a working day in view of the "persistent economic problems." The final determination of when the shorter week would be introduced—Solidarity insisted that it should be by 1982—was to be done through Sejm legislative action (PAP, 31 January). By the end of 1981, no action on the matter had been taken.

Concurrently with the "free Saturday" conflict, and partly as a result of what workers perceived as official attempts to avoid resolution of that issue, new strikes and protests broke out against other aspects of government social and economic policies. Most of them were localized and dealt with specific grievances. Taken together, however, they were politically significant; these activities underscored official corruption and institutional inefficiency while forcing the party and government establishment to attempt to appease the protesters. Among the most publicized protests were a strike in Bielsko-Biala (to remove local administrators accused of corruption), a strike in Jelenia Gora province (to remove officials and turn a party vacation center into a hospital), a peasant strike in Ustrzyki Dolne (to force the authorities to recognize a peasant union), and student strikes in Lodz to secure official recognition of a new student organization. Each of these strikes, and many others as well, entailed protracted negotiations with representatives of the government. More important, almost all proved successful, in the sense of wresting concessions from the authorities. Although most of these concessions were not implemented, the very fact that the political establishment was forced to talk with the protesters and accede to their demands both weakened the position of the authorities and provided the strikers, real and prospective, with a feeling of confidence and power.

Clearly aware of the long-term implications of this development, political leaders attempted to adopt a tougher and more decisive approach to sociopolitical matters. On 9 February, the party's Central Committee replaced Jozef Pinkowski with Gen. Wojciech Jaruzelski as head of the government; this decision was formally ratified by the Sejm on 11 February.

Presenting his political views to the nation, Jaruzelski, a career military officer and a Politburo member since 1971, said in his inaugural address to the Sejm that "the time has come to arrest the creeping process that has undermined the stability of the country's life. There is no room for two [systems of] authority in the state. Such a situation would inevitably lead to a collision, with disastrous consequences for the country and the nation." (*Trybuna ludu*, 13 February.) Furthermore, Jaruzelski decried the "numerous attempts to penetrate and use social organizations, particularly some bodies within Solidarity, by evil and hostile forces that [want] to steer them in false, anarchistic, and anti-socialist directions." He then warned that unless those activities were stopped, "they would bring about not only economic ruin but also a breakdown in social relations, eventually resulting in the most terrible fratricidal conflict." Urging the rapid "normalization" of sociopolitical relations, Jaruzelski then called for "a three-month, 90-day moratorium on strikes . . . so we can use that time to put order into the most fundamental problems of our economy, to take account of both positive and negative aspects [of public life], to undertake the most urgent social programs, to take the first steps toward the introduction of a program of economic stability, and to prepare for wide-ranging economic reforms."

Although the appointment of Jaruzelski was clearly meant to take advantage of the image of firmness usually associated with the military profession, there was no indication that his political ascendancy would entail changes in official policies. That much was implicitly confirmed by Kania, who, speaking in the Sejm in support of Jaruzelski's appointment, said that "the government of Prime Minister Jaruzelski will be a government motivated by the same objectives as [the one directed by Jozef Pinkowski], but at the same time, it will use new, more effective methods to achieve their implementation" (ibid., 12 February).

Even so, Solidarity welcomed the Jaruzelski government. Its official spokesman, Karol Modzelewski, said in a press interview that "the establishment of a new government . . . creates real opportunities to turn back the dangerous course of events that became particularly visible during the last weeks" (*Zycie Warszawy*, 16 February). He also explained the position of the labor movement by affirming that "it . . . does not constitute a second authority" and merely "wants to become a recognized and respected social partner [of the authorities]. This is the only way out of the crisis."

There was no indication, however, that the authorities were willing to acquiesce in Solidarity's objectives. Although on 17 February the government registered the new Independent Student Union, thus ending the long process of strikes and protests at colleges and universities, no progress was made on the issue of an independent organization for peasants. There was also no move by the government to change industrial policies and administrative relations between the authorities and labor organizations in factories. The net result was the persistence of tension in public life as workers, frustrated by official procrastination in implementing earlier agreements, continued to stage local strikes or proclaim strike alerts in many parts of the country.

It was against this background that a new major crisis in relations between the authorities and Solidarity broke out in March. The crisis arose from an incident in the city of Bydgoszcz on 19 March. Some members of the local city council as well as a group of Solidarity representatives invited to take part in the council's deliberations were evicted by force from the council building by the police. Several Solidarity activists were physically abused, and three were hospitalized with serious injuries.

The crisis quickly escalated to a test of power between the two sides. First, a hastily convoked meeting on 22 March between Solidarity leader Lech Walesa and Deputy Prime Minister Mieczyslaw F. Rakowski brought about a sharp exchange of views, but no solution to the conflict. On the same day, the Politburo issued a statement asserting that the "action by the law and order bodies [in Bydgoszcz], conducted under the orders of competent authorities, was in accordance with the law" and accusing Solidarity of "politicizing its activities and taking illegally upon itself functions of constitutionally established representatives and executive bodies, thus creating a state of anarchy" (*Trybuna ludu*, 23 March). Also on 22 March, Poland's Catholic primate, Stefan Cardinal Wyszynski, publicly appealed to both authorities and citizens to refrain from any action that could heighten tension. "The state authorities," the cardinal said, "must realize that they serve society and its rights to social freedom and that they must fulfill its needs in accordance with the requirement of safeguarding the physical and spiritual well-being of each citizen. The authorities must take into consideration the consequences of each irresponsible step taken by the agencies of public order." To citizens, he pointed out that "everyone who strives to achieve the legitimate goal of social self-organization, as well as that of economic justice, must know that to fulfill those aspirations, there is a need for a great time interval, patience, and functional opportunities." (Radio Warsaw, 22 March.)

On 24 March, the leadership of Solidarity decided to stage a warning strike on 27 March to protest the official failure to punish those responsible for the incident in Bydgoszcz. At the same time, union leaders decided to call on all their members to prepare for a general strike on 31 March unless the government entered into serious negotiations on the matter with Solidarity representatives. Instructions were sent immediately to all chapters of the organization; they included detailed information on how to stage the strike, how to defend against police attacks, and how to prepare for a possible takeover by union activists of all administrative responsibilities in all areas of the economy. Union leaders demanded the punishment of those responsible for Bydgoszcz, permission for peasants to form their own union, security for union members in their activities as well as their right to reply to any media criticism, payment of workers for the duration of strikes, and termination of all pending cases against people arrested for political opposition to government policies. (Radio Warsaw, 25 March; *Le Monde*, 25 March.)

The negotiations between Solidarity and the government started on 25 March. No progress was registered, however, as the two sides merely exchanged mutual accusations and recriminations. Further talks were postponed until 27 March. In the meantime, Cardinal Wyszynski met Jaruzelski and Kania on 26 March; no communiqué on the talks was issued. On 27 March, Solidarity staged a successful nationwide warning strike to protest official procrastination. This action appeared instrumental in forcing more serious negotiations, particularly after it became obvious that many party members had taken part despite the party's instruction that all party members refrain from any participation in the strike. On 29 March, the Central Committee met in a plenary session and, following an unusually stormy debate during which two reputed hard-line leaders, Stefan Olszowski and Tadeusz Grabski, offered their resignations from the Politburo, issued a declaration that "obliged the Politburo and the government to explain the incident in Bydgoszcz in full and to draw the full consequences from that development" (*Trybuna ludu*, 31 March).

On 30 March, several hours after the conclusion of the Central Committee's session and shortly before the scheduled beginning of the strike, Solidarity and the government reached an agreement on settling their immediate differences. The agreement included the government's admission that the police action in Bydgoszcz "was clearly against the rule of solving conflicts through political means" (ibid., 31 March). It also included official "guarantees for the [unhampered] activity of the labor unions" as well as a promise, undertaken by both sides, "to do everything possible to eliminate conflicts over the issue of peasant self-organization." Furthermore, the government undertook to take up the issue of "free expression in public and professional life" through parliamentary action and proposed that both sides "start new negotiations on the general scope of relations [between the authorities and Solidarity] so that future conflicts could be resolved without arousing the entire nation." This was supported by an official pledge to pay full wages to those workers who had taken part in the warning strike on 27 March, providing that the general strike was called off; it was. For its part, Solidarity declared that "a speedy fulfillment by the government of its earlier promises would create the conditions for the unification of the entire society, which constitutes an indispensable requirement for pulling the country out of its current social and economic crisis."

The Second Stage. The March conflict had a profound impact on Poland's domestic politics, affecting the attitudes of both the authorities and the labor movement in the subsequent months. For the authorities, it demonstrated that their ability to control activities by social groups or even rank-and-file party members was extremely tenuous. Furthermore, it indicated that any attempt to use strong-arm tactics in dealing with Solidarity would backfire and, unless they could be implemented nationwide, would only strengthen the labor movement. For Solidarity, the conflict provided testimony of widespread social support. More important, it may have given union leaders the feeling of actual power matching, if not exceeding, that of the government itself.

The immediate consequence of the conflict was an alleviation of the political crisis, but this did not mean that progress was made toward its resolution. The government's tactics became more cautious. On 10 April, Jaruzelski formally asked the Sejm "to suspend the workers' right to strike for a period of two months" (Radio Warsaw, 10 April). That request presented the Sejm with a legislative dilemma since there was no law covering the right to strike (the issue had been settled merely through various agreements between the workers and the government and was still subject to final determination by the legislature). It was resolved through a parliamentary declaration calling for "the suspension of strikes and the threat of strikes for the duration of two months" (*Trybuna ludu*, 11 April).

Solidarity neither supported nor rejected the resolution. Instead, Walesa, in a nationally broadcast television interview on 13 April, said that Solidarity would voluntarily refrain from any strikes if the government adopted policies aimed at a lasting resolution of the economic and social crisis. "The government will have to cope with something," he said, "with an initiative; it must come up with . . . a gesture [of its own] that is not forced [upon it] by us, that is not [merely a fulfillment of] a promise made to us earlier. Then we will believe that a renewal is taking place, a renewal that we would like to see. For the time being, however, there are only words."

No action that would change the structural characteristics of the system in a lasting fashion, however, and no new innovative policies were made. Although the Sejm approved on 6 May a law providing for the official registration of independent peasant labor (they registered on 10 May), an action long demanded by Solidarity, the legislators made it clear that the law was only "provisional in character" and the final determination of the institutional aspects of the existing labor movement would have to be achieved through "a general law on labor unions" (ibid., 7 May). Moreover, despite the continuation of negotiations between the authorities and Solidarity since the beginning of April on different aspects of their mutual relationship, no progress was made, and agreements on specific matters (access to the media, for example) were not implemented. Even so, there were no strikes in the country until early July.

The authorities' attention centered on preparations for the party's extraordinary congress. Although the pre-congress electoral campaign was marked by anti-Solidarity declarations by various party politicians, union leaders made no response. Conversely, the authorities did not interfere with Solidarity's commemorations of past worker struggles against the communist party. Mass celebrations of the workers' rebellions in Poznan in 1956 and in Radom in 1976 took place in those cities in June.

On 2 July, the government presented at a Sejm session an outline of some aspects of its economic policy. It proposed to stabilize the economy through increased support for agriculture, conservation of natural resources, and budget cuts. These were to be temporary measures, however, since the resolution of economic problems would have to await the adoption of "economic reforms that . . . should reinforce the strategic functions of central planning and provide for effective operation of enterprises, based on the principle of self-financing and self-management" (ibid., 3 July). In a related action, the government presented its proposal on the organization of state enterprises and self-management at the enterprise level. The proposal was ambiguous, including provisions for direct government intervention in the work of enterprises, but failing to define when such interference was permissible.

On 8 and 9 July, labor troubles again surfaced in several areas of the country in the form of brief (two- to four-hour) warning strikes by longshoremen, transportation workers, and airline personnel. The causes were localized, relating to either administrative or narrowly economic grievances. But the underlying problem was growing worker frustration with the apparent inability or unwillingness of the authorities to fulfill their earlier promises. This was clearly indicated by Lech Walesa. Speaking to a mass meeting in Gdynia on 9 July, he reportedly remarked that although "some 640 agreements have already been negotiated with the government . . . the most important problem remains to implement them" (Radio Warsaw, 9 and 11 July).

This frustration led to growing pressure within Solidarity to adopt by itself measures that would streamline administrative and economic operations. On 8 July, at a meeting attended by representatives of some key industrial enterprises as well as delegates from several hundred other factories, comprehensive proposals on the establishment of an effective self-management system in factories were presented for discussion within the union. Those proposals defined the enterprise as "a socially owned institution" in which decisions should be made by workers themselves. In addition, the proposals envisioned that the self-management bodies should both appoint and recall enterprise directors, set economic plans, and determine the financial bases for all factory operations. (*Dziennik Baltycki*, 17–18 June.) The proposals ran counter to the officially approved drafts for legislative action on the matter.

The workers' initiative provoked sharp attacks by party leaders, especially by Stanislaw Kania, during the PUWP's congress. The authorities took a formal stand on the issue during a Central Committee meeting on 2–3 September. Presented in terms of the party's economic policy and its political prerogatives, it amounted to a major strategic statement announcing the party's determination to change the existing economic system. The process would be conducted gradually by introducing specific measures, all of which were to be proposed by the party and the government and approved by the Sejm. The most important immediate element, which was likely to determine the success of the entire operation, was to settle the issue of self-management in state enterprises. The authorities had already presented a draft proposal to the Sejm and regarded acceptance of that proposal by the Sejm and the population as vital, despite existing opposition to some of its crucial features. Acceptance would constitute a key condition for any future changes in the economic system and would have profound political significance in terms of stabilizing political and social relations.

Underlying the party's position was the conviction that the self-management scheme advocated by Solidarity would have political consequences. It would undercut the party's control over the economy without enhancing the effectiveness of factory management. Stanislaw Kania, commenting on the union's proposal on appointing and recalling enterprise directors, said that "the party would never abandon its right to [conduct] recruitment policy for state bodies. [This right] resulted from the party's historical responsibility for the development of the country, for its socialist character. It also flows from the constitutional rules that clearly give the party its leading role . . . The party as a whole cannot be pushed out to a position of marginal importance because the party is the leading force of the working class and the nation, a force that carries a historical responsibility for the country's destiny" (*Trybuna ludu*, 4 September).

Even so, party leaders failed to push their views through the legislative process. Having been provided with formally defined proposals for legislation on the self-management issue by both the government and Solidarity, the Sejm prepared a compromise version of the law that envisaged a sharing of responsibility for the selection of directors between the government and local self-management bodies. Solidarity leaders approved the compromise. It was formally enacted by the Sejm on 25 September, despite a last-minute attempt by party leaders to change the text of the law in the government's favor. This fact alone must have dealt a serious blow to the already deteriorating authority of the party and its leaders. A further, and more serious, danger to their power arose from the progressive institutionalization of the labor movement and its increasingly political aspirations.

The Third Stage. On 5 September, Solidarity opened its national congress in Gdansk. The gathering, which spanned two separate sessions and lasted a total of eighteen days (5–10 September and 26 September–7 October), provided the mass labor movement with a comprehensive program and elected its national leadership. The congress was an event of great significance for Poland and its people. At no time during the history of the communist regime had a public movement that claimed organizational autonomy and political independence of the state authorities been able to hold a formal gathering to debate its role and function within the system. The congress was an important landmark, breaking, at least symbolically, a long-existing pattern of restrictions and authoritarian constraints.

The first session of the congress was taken up by a prolonged discussion on the leadership's report on the movement's activities during the preceding year and culminated in the adoption of some thirty programmatic resolutions. The report painted an impressive picture of Solidarity's development: "In all regions of the country there are now union authorities that have been elected democratically . . . In the course of the past year, the union has transformed itself from a loose federation of interfactory committees, linked together by acceptance of the principle of solidarity, into a strong organization of more than 9,500,000 members . . . Solidarity, as the great force, creates the possibility for social equilibrium in which the public will be protected and the authorities will be effectively controlled" . . . "It is not an exaggeration to say that a revolution is taking place in Poland and the main force behind that revolution has been Solidarity." (*Glos Pracy*, 7 September.)

The resolutions, ranging from political appeals for democratic changes in the country to specific recommendations for statutory improvement in the union's charter, had a provisional character—all of them were to be presented to the rank and file for final approval, which was to be done during the second session. Probably the most controversial and politically explosive was the resolution explaining Solidarity's activities to the workers of Eastern Europe. It conveyed "greetings" to the working masses of all Eastern European countries and "all nationalities in the Soviet Union" and stated that "contrary to the lies spread [about Solidarity] in your countries, we are an authentic . . . representative of the working people, emerged from the workers' strikes . . . We support those of you who have decided to enter the difficult road of struggle for a free and independent labor movement." (Radio Warsaw, 9 September.) Following the conclusion of the congress's first session, this resolution was uniformly condemned by both the Polish media and those of the communist countries of Eastern Europe. Particularly harsh attacks were made in the Soviet press.

The second session centered on two crucial issues: the election of the union's national leadership and the adoption of a program of activity for the future. On 2 October, Lech Walesa was elected chairman of Solidarity. He outpolled three other contenders, drawing 462 votes (55 percent) of the 844 ballots cast. The congress also elected the 107 members of the National Commission, the union's policymaking body, and 21 members of the Audit Commission, an internal control agency. The members of the National Commission subsequently elected from among themselves the 13 members of the Presidium, the top executive body.

At the end of the session, the congress adopted a comprehensive program for the organization. It defined Solidarity as "social" rather than merely "a labor movement" and defined its goals in terms of work for "justice, democracy, truth, legality, freedom of opinion, and the renewal of the state" as well as for an improvement in economic conditions. More specifically, the program described the role of Solidarity in Poland's public life as that of "the only guarantor for society [of change in social and economic areas] charged with a basic duty to take all possible short- and long-term steps to salvage Poland from ruin and society from poverty, despondency, and self-destruction. There is no other way to attain this goal but to restructure the state and the economy on the basis of democracy and all-around social initiative." (*Tygodnik Solidarnosc*, 16 October.) As for current political issues, the program declared that "no support for the government's program of stabilization of the economy would be possible" unless "social control" were extended over all economic activities and "individuals commanding social and professional respect were placed in directing positions in the economy." In this context, the program recommended the creation of a Social Council for the Economy to act as a public supervisory agency on economic matters. With respect to international relations, the program reiterated Solidarity's determination not to "violate Poland's international alliances," but also included a reminder that "Poland can serve as a valuable partner only if it defines by itself, and in full consciousness, its own obligations."

The main significance of the congress, aside from its political novelty, was in outlining and reinforcing the line separating the mass social movement and the political establishment. That separation has obviously been perceived by both sides for a long time, having clearly emerged at the time of the Gdansk agreements in August 1980. The congress, by providing a formal organizational underpinning to the movement and defining for it a conceptual program of action, turned those perceptions into institutional reality.

Relations between the authorities and Solidarity deteriorated after the movement's congress, and the government's attitudes hardened perceptibly. On 13 October, the government invited *all* labor organizations to engage in negotiations on economic reforms, with the subject and forms of the talks to be proposed by the authorities. When Solidarity responded with a counterproposal for a *bilateral* meeting, arguing that other labor unions remained insignificant, the government agreed but maintained its intention to set up a mixed body for future talks. When the talks started on 15 October, with Solidarity representatives pointing to the urgent need to establish a social council to supervise the economy, the authorities formally accused the union of attempting to "undermine the state structures and to overthrow the existing constitutional order and the principles of people's power . . . as well as to set up a totalitarian dictatorship" (Radio Warsaw, 16 October). Predictably, the talks led nowhere.

Since the conclusion of the congress, numerous strikes had been staged in factories throughout the country. Most of those were of short duration and were related to mounting dissatisfaction over continuing shortages of food and other basic consumer products. The strikes were peaceful, but there were some incidents in which police assaulted Solidarity activists attempting to publicize the movement's policies. In at least two incidents, in Katowice and in Wroclaw, clashes occurred between workers and police.

On 17 October, Jaruzelski replaced Kania as first secretary of the party, and the Central Committee of the PUWP adopted a tough resolution blaming Solidarity for the economic crisis and calling on all party members who were members of Solidarity "to define their political positions in a clear way" (*Trybuna ludu*, 19 October). Within a few days, it was announced that several party members involved in independent social organizations (for example, the chairman of the Journalists' Union, Stefan Bratkowski, and prominent Solidarity activist Bogdan Lis) were expelled from the communist organization. Tough measures were also undertaken to restrict the freedom of the press, with several editors removed from their positions.

On 23 October, the government announced the formation of special military "operational groups" that were sent to the countryside to "ensure the flow of supply between the towns and the countryside" as well as to "observe the mechanism of food supply" (ibid., 24 October). The groups were also to streamline the work of local administrators. In view of subsequent developments, it is more than probable that their true task was to prepare contingency plans for the establishment of military control over the country. On 24 November, similar groups were sent to big factories and large cities.

On 28 October, Solidarity staged a successful general strike to protest the authorities' "refusal to provide society with the right to control official activities" in the economy and to signal public disapproval of a centrally directed "campaign of propaganda and repression against the union's activists" (Radio Warsaw, 28 October). The strike was brief, lasting only one hour, but affected the entire country. Within hours of its conclusion, the party's Central Committee met in Warsaw in a plenary session. No resolution from the session was published, and only a few speakers were reported to have taken the floor. In retrospect, perhaps the most important speech was delivered by Politburo member Kazimierz Barcikowski, who said that "if Solidarity's conduct remains unchanged, other far-reaching decisions designed to protect the vital interests of the nation and the state will become unavoidable" (*Trybuna ludu*, 29 October).

On 31 October, the Sejm passed a resolution calling for an immediate end to strikes. The resolution was adopted in response to Prime Minister Jaruzelski's proposal to provide the government with the right to use "extraordinary means of action for the protection of the citizens and the state" but stopped short of accepting that proposal. Indeed, it was not clear what Jaruzelski's proposal would have entailed. In any case, the resolution had little effect on the workers; sporadic and localized strikes continued unabated even while Solidarity's national leadership repeatedly appealed for peace.

The political atmosphere in the country improved somewhat at the beginning of November as Poland's primate, Archbishop Jozef Glemp, met with Jaruzelski and Walesa on 4 November to "exchange views on ways to overcome the crisis . . . and on the possibility of forming a front of national accord" (ibid., 5 November). Aside from the symbolic importance of the meeting, the first encounter of its kind, the only tangible result was a resumption of talks between Solidarity and the government. The talks, proposed by Solidarity, started on 18 November, following delays caused by the government's procrastination, and were to resolve differences between the authorities and the labor movement over approaches to economic and social problems. The talks marked the third attempt in 1981 to reconcile those differences.

It was obvious from the outset of the talks that no agreement was possible. The resulting deadlock on each issue offered for discussion—the character of national accord (the government wanted to define its main features, and Solidarity wished to establish some form of partnership), the economy (Solidarity wanted to establish social control over economic activities, and the government refused to accept this), the union's access to broadcast media (the government refused to give to Solidarity even a degree of control over the content of its programs)—only reinforced the frustration of Solidarity activists and their impatience for some form of action to end the prevailing uncertainty.

On 23 November, the police raided the apartment of Jacek Kuron, a former leader of the dissolved dissident Committee for Social Self-Defense KOR and an adviser to Solidarity's national leadership. The raid was staged to prevent the formation of a new organization, Clubs for a Self-Governing Republic: Freedom, Justice, Independence (ibid., 23 November). Several dozen participants in the would-be meeting went to another location, however, and set up the organization. Its purpose was to establish a network of "new ideological and political bodies," separate from Solidarity as a labor movement, to "provide the foundation for future political parties" (AP and UPI, 23 November). The initial form of these bodies would be discussion clubs in different cities.

On 28 November, the party's Central Committee adopted a formal declaration calling for contingency legislation to provide the government with extraordinary powers to deal with social and economic problems. Stopping short of outlining those powers, the declaration said that they should guarantee "effective counteraction to destructive actions that are destroying the country and its economy and threatening the socialist state, law and order, and public security" (*Trybuna ludu*, 30 November).

If nothing else, the declaration contributed greatly to the heightening of tension in the country, which had already been affected by long strikes at colleges and universities to protest the government's delays in introducing new legislation on higher education. Even so, no industrial strikes took place during the last weeks of November and the beginning of December, although strike alerts were declared in separate factories. It was clear, however, that the authorities had already adopted a policy of toughness toward all real or presumed manifestations of social activism.

On 2 December, a thousand riot police assaulted a building of the Firefighter Officers' Academy in Warsaw, evicting three hundred striking students. The students were protesting official plans to put the school under the exclusive jurisdiction of the Ministry of Internal Affairs. The successful eviction was described by hard-liner Stefan Olszowski as a "demonstration of force" on the part of the authorities. Speaking to a gathering of party activists in a tractor factory near Warsaw, Olszowski attacked Solidarity's actions as "reactionary" and charged that they amounted to an "open counter-revolution," adding that "there will be a clash about that . . . there will be a war in Poland about that" (Radio Warsaw, 3 December). During the discussion that followed his speech, Olszowski was asked if the authorities envisaged the possibility of introducing a state of emergency. He replied that this would be done if necessary. (*Sztandar Mlodych*, 4–6 December.)

Meeting on 3 December, the day after Olszowski's speech, Solidarity's national leaders adopted a position sharply critical of the authorities' behavior. According to excerpts of speeches by union leaders surreptitiously taped by the authorities and then extensively publicized by the official media, the tenor of the meeting was combative and politically radical. Most speakers, including Lech Walesa, agreed that a confrontation between Solidarity and the authorities was inevitable and urged the union to prepare itself for a sudden attack. In a formal statement issued at the conclusion of the meeting, Solidarity leaders said that any legal action to provide the government with extraordinary powers would amount to "an attempt to eliminate the workers' and civil rights." They also warned that acceptance by the Sejm of the party's request would provoke a 24-hour general strike throughout the country, while any attempt to implement such legislation would be countered by a general strike of unlimited duration (*Tygodnik Solidarnosc*, 11 December). The meeting also issued a list of demands "fundamental to the goal of reaching a national accord," including a halt to anti-Solidarity harassment, acceptance by the Sejm of a new law on trade unions, free elections to people's councils, acceptance of Solidarity's participation in economic policymaking, and access to the media by the union and other social organizations.

There was no response from the authorities. Indeed, it was clear that relations between the authorities and the labor movement had deteriorated to such a degree that no single act would mitigate the hostility. Archbishop Glemp attempted to mediate the growing conflict by sending separate letters to Walesa and Jaruzelski with appeals for another trilateral meeting. Glemp sent a separate letter on 7 December, urging the Sejm not to grant special powers to the government (AFP, 8 December). No response was registered.

On 11–12 December, Solidarity's National Commission met in Gdansk to decide the movement's strategy for action. After hearing reports on the negotiations with the government, the commission concluded that further talks would be futile since the government refused to compromise on any issues. Determined to developed its own program to resolve economic and social problems but recognizing official opposition to their implementation, the commission decided to appeal to the movement's rank and file to put additional pressure on the authorities and force them to change policies. Among the proposals made during the meeting were calls for the establishment of a permanent body within the movement capable of defining economic policies for the entire country, free and democratic elections to both the people's councils and the Sejm, and a nationwide referendum on the performance of the Jaruzelski government by 15 January 1982, unless the authorities undertook serious negotiations with the union on the economic problems. It is not clear whether any of these resolutions was adopted; the meeting was adjourned in the late hours of 12 December as all communication links between Gdansk and the rest of the country were severed. As the participants in the meeting went to their hotels for the night, they were still not aware that a major political change had taken place in the country and that a state of emergency had been declared.

The State of War. The state of emergency was introduced at midnight, 12–13 December, when armed troops of the riot police and the military seized Solidarity offices in different parts of the country, arrested thousands of activists and leaders, and confiscated documents and equipment. At the same time, all internal communications links as well as international telephone and telex lines were cut. Police and army troops appeared on the streets, imposing control over all social activities. Six hours after the military and police operations started, Jaruzelski announced in a nationwide radio and television broadcast the "introduction, by a decision of the Council of State, of a state of war" throughout the country (Radio Warsaw, 13 December). "State of war" is Polish legal parlance for "state of emergency."

Jaruzelski told the nation that the highest political authority had been placed in the hands of a Military Council of National Salvation, a body of twenty high military officers and chaired by Jaruzelski himself. While stressing that the imposition of the state of emergency was not a "military coup d'etat," Jaruzelski stopped short of saying when military control would be terminated. "The military council will be dissolved when the rule of law returns to the country's public life and when conditions emerge for the normal operations of both administrative and legislative bodies." He also announced that "a group of people who endanger the security of the state" had been detained, but was quick to add that the military council "counted upon the trust and aid of all patriotic and progressive groups in society" to help it fulfill its self-defined task of "ensuring internal peace and security in the country." (The text of Jaruzelski's speech follows this profile.)

Jaruzelski's announcement was amplified by a long series of proclamations, announcements, and instructions outlining the rules of the state of emergency. Repeatedly broadcast by the media, the rules included a ban on public meetings (with the exception of religious services), a ban on all artistic and sports events, far-reaching restrictions on public transportation between different localities, closing of all border points, and an imposition of a nighttime curfew. They also included a reimposition of censorship, closing of almost all newspapers and periodicals, and a limitation of radio and television programming to a single, centrally controlled program. The activities of all major social organizations, including labor unions, Catholic associations, youth movements, and professional groups, were suspended.

The clear purpose of these instructions was to create a psychological impact on the public, which, overwhelmed by the gravity of the situation and the imposition of unending restrictions, would accept the changes as not only inevitable but also inescapable. Obviously long-planned and prepared, they conveyed the impression of official toughness and determination.

It was apparent, however, that the success of the military measures hinged on their public acceptance, or at least public resignation. To secure such compliance, the authorities organized a mass police and military dragnet aimed at arresting all real and potential critics and opponents. Reportedly numbering in the tens of thousands (official figures put the number of detainees at over five thousand), the arrests affected all sectors of the population, with particular emphasis on Solidarity leaders and activists. To magnify the impact of these measures, the results of the police actions were repeatedly announced in nationwide broadcasts. The unmistakable message was that anyone even contemplating opposition to the authorities would be promptly and severely punished.

This image of authority was undermined, however, by repeated demonstrations of social unrest, admitted by the media only partially. Immediately following the imposition of the state of emergency, there were persistent reports of widespread strikes in factories and mines, of street demonstrations, and of other instances of protest. On 16 December, police and military troops killed seven workers while storming the Wujek mine near Katowice; many more workers as well as numerous policemen were reportedly seriously injured. On 16 and 17 December, there were major street demonstrations in Gdansk and in Warsaw; in Gdansk some 330 people were reported to have been wounded and one person killed. Violence was said to have occurred in numerous other cities, where the forces of order attacked factories, universities, and other institutions.

On 16 December, the Catholic episcopate prepared a statement decrying the situation of "terror imposed upon the entire nation by military force." The statement supported Solidarity's role and activity and demanded "the freeing of prisoners [and] the revival of the labor movement." (*WP*, 17 December.) The statement, which followed an initial appeal for social peace by Archbishop Glemp on 13 December, was not released, however, perhaps owing to pressure from the authorities.

Violence and open protests gradually subsided within a week or so of the imposition of the state of emergency, only to give way to widespread work slowdowns and passive resistance. There was no evidence, however, that the avowed objectives of the current regime would be rapidly achieved. These objectives were twofold: first, to reinvigorate the communist system through the strengthening of its basic institutions, the government and the party; second, to destroy the recent movement of social self-organization that included Solidarity as well as other groups and associatons that had acquired an autonomous status during the months following the August 1980 strikes and the subsequent establishment of an independent labor movement.

As the year closed, there was no evidence that the party could resume its self-proclaimed position of the leading force in the country. On the contrary, the communist organization appeared more disorganized than ever, its membership depleted and its reputation thoroughly discredited. The authority of the government, never fully established and recognized, was even further undermined by the imposition of military controls. Solidarity, while forced into submission and deprived of its leadership (most of its leaders, including Lech Walesa, were interned), continued to present a major danger to the new rulers. Indeed, the imposition of the state of emergency did not reverse the evolution of Poland's politics; it merely halted it.

The Economy. The Polish economic situation deteriorated considerably during 1981 even in comparison with 1980, which had been much worse than previous years. According to preliminary estimates, Poland's national income in 1981 was almost 15 percent lower than that of 1980. In socialized industry, sales were down 13 percent over 1980 for the majority of basic industrial goods. Output in the construction and machinery industries dropped by nearly 20 percent. Coal production during 1981 was about 163 million tons, comparable to the production level of 1974 and a decline of some 37 million tons over 1979 (the 1979 production figures may have been artificially boosted through statistical manipulation).

There was some improvement during 1981 in agricultural production. Total farm production rose by almost 4 percent. Particularly high growth was noted in grain production (almost 20 percent). Production of meat, milk, and eggs, however, declined by 14 percent; livestock sales fell by over 25 percent, milk sales by almost 8 percent, and eggs by nearly 1 percent.

There was a growing imbalance between supply and demand in the consumer sector during the year. Deliveries of consumer goods, calculated in constant prices, declined by about 10 percent in comparison to 1980, while wages increased by 25 percent. This only contributed to the massive inflationary pressure. (All data from official PAP report, 3–4 January 1982.)

The official media frequently alleged that the economic downtrend was essentially due to strikes and social agitation. Officially prepared estimates provided a different picture. During the first nine months of the year, for example, abstentions due to strikes amounted to a mere 1.7 percent of all abstentions from work (*Tygodnik Solidarnosc*, 11 December). In view of this figure, it could be argued that losses caused by mismanagement, transportation problems, and lack of proper equipment and spare parts were certainly much higher than those prompted by strikes.

To a large extent, Poland's economic problems resulted from the country's troubles in foreign trade relations. Exports during 1981 declined by some 14 percent and imports by 7 percent. To make matters worse, Poland's indebtedness, particularly with Western banking institutions and Western governments, increased dramatically, creating a serious danger of default. At the end of August, Poland's indebtedness to Western lenders totaled U.S. $27 billion.

Throughout the year, intermittent talks were held between representatives of Western banks and Polish officials on a possible rescheduling of the debts. Little progress was achieved. At the end of the year, Poland's financial position seemed likely to deteriorate even further as the state of emergency affected work in both industry and agriculture; no figures were available, however, to provide even the most tentative estimate of economic losses caused by that operation.

The Catholic Church. Continuing the practice of past years, the Catholic church was deeply involved in Poland's social and political life throughout 1981. This involvement was particularly visible in the church's continuing support for Solidarity. The movement's leaders periodically conferred with religious officials, numerous priests engaged directly in Solidarity's social activities, and Catholic publications provided a broad forum for dissemination of the union's views and programs. The church extended similar support to other independent social bodies, such as autonomous peasants' unions (church officials consistently argued for their recognition by the authorities), youth movements, and various professional associations. The church hierarchy also maintained close contacts with the authorities. These contacts were largely channeled through a joint government-episcopate commission, which dealt with current problems in church-state relations, but included sporadic meetings between the church and party government leaders.

The main objective behind the church's activities in the public arena was its desire to play a mediating role in conflicts separating the authorities and various social organizations. Church officials intervened, for example, in a conflict at the beginning of February in the town of Bielsko-Biala, where they helped to negotiate an end to a strike. They also intervened indirectly in resolving the March crisis. Primate Glemp was instrumental in setting up a meeting between Walesa and Jaruzelski in November, and he also intervened to ease the conflict over the issue of extraordinary powers for the government in early December. After the establishment of the state of emergency, church leaders led a campaign for a release of detained Solidarity officials as well as other individuals.

Perhaps the most important development affecting the church during 1981 was the death of Stefan Cardinal Wyszynski. The cardinal, who had headed the Polish church since his appointment as primate in 1949 and had been seen by both the Poles and others as not only a towering religious figure but also a true national hero, died in Warsaw on 28 May. The venerable cleric and charismatic statesman led the church through a particularly difficult period in the institution's history, during which the church was frequently exposed to official persecution—Wyszynski himself was imprisoned between 1953 and 1956—but finally emerged as the most vital religious community in any country of Eastern Europe. Widely recognized by the Poles as a symbol of the highest spiritual and patriotic qualities, Cardinal Wyszynski was a respected father figure trusted by generations of his compatriots. His international prestige was greatly enhanced when in 1978, his pupil, Karol Cardinal Wojtyla, was elected to the throne of Saint Peter as Pope John Paul II.

Following Wyszynski's ceremonious funeral, attended by some 250,000 mourners as well as by numerous visitors from abroad and high-ranking representatives of the Polish communist authorities, the pope appointed Archbishop Jozef Glemp as Wyszynski's successor on 7 July. Glemp promptly pledged to continue the policies of his predecessor. In particular, he declared his determination to pursue "dialogue and cooperation" with the authorities, but also asserted the need for "renewal" in social relations (*Zycie Warszawy*, 10 July). In this last respect, especially important was Glemp's declaration on relations between the church and Solidarity. Made shortly before his appointment as head of the church, the declaration indicated that the church would be "prepared to act in Solidarity's defense when human rights are violated. It will advise these independent . . . labor unions to act wisely in situations of conflict. The church wants . . . to approach its contacts with Solidarity primarily in a pastoral spirit, but it refuses to be drawn into politics and will continue to do so in the future." (*Tygodnik Powszechny*, 21 June.) This declaration gained added importance during the state of emergency, when the human and civil rights of the union members were clearly violated.

Institutional and Governmental Changes. The most important institutional development during 1981 was the official recognition of numerous social organizations, such as peasants' labor unions as well as youth and professional associations, as public bodies autonomous of direct control and supervision by the government. These organizations were recognized through a legal process of court registration. Even so, the recognition was essentially provisional since final determination of their status remained dependent on legislative action; the Sejm did not act during the year, and the activities of these organizations were suspended following the introduction of the state of emergency. By the end of the year, no judgment could be made on their future existence.

Numerous major changes were made during the year in the composition of the government. The most important was the replacement of Jozef Pinkowski by Wojciech Jaruzelski as prime minister on 11 February. About thirty ministries also changed hands. The general trend, particularly visible during the second half of the year, was toward militarization of the civilian administration. By the end of 1981, at least five ministries were headed by military officers, and many other posts, both at the central and the local levels, were taken over by army personnel.

The most important legislative act was the adoption of a law on censorship. Passed by the Sejm on 31 July and enacted on 1 October, the law retained the principle of prior censorship but made its execution dependent on clearly defined areas of "national interest" and provided authors and publishers with the formal right to defend themselves against any unjustified interference with their work. Furthermore, the law exempted from censorship several categories of publications, including internal information bulletins printed by social organizations (that is, labor unions) "as long as their contents are in keeping with the organizations' statutory aims" (*Gazeta Krakowska*, 3 August). Other important laws included a law on organization of enterprises and self-management that was passed by the Sejm on 25 September. All these laws were suspended during the state of emergency; their future remained uncertain.

Foreign Affairs. The existence and activities of Solidarity added a new dimension to Poland's foreign relations in 1981. They created new factors that directly and indirectly opened up new opportunities for the country to stimulate international attention to its problems as well as to accumulate goodwill and understanding for its difficulties. At the same time, they complicated established relations and links between the Polish government and its traditional partners.

Throughout the year, the labor movement conducted varied and intensive activities abroad. Lech Walesa made five foreign trips: to Italy (January), Japan (May), Sweden (May), Switzerland (June, to attend a session of the International Organization), and France (October). Each time he led a Solidarity delegation, and each time, he and members of his group met with foreign officials, politicians, and journalists. The purpose of these trips was to represent the labor movement and explain its actions and objectives. Yet Walesa also talked with his hosts about broader, national problems and goals. Formally approved and sanctioned by the government, the trips served, in effect, an important supportive role for the country's interests. In addition, many other officials of the union visited foreign countries and held talks with representatives of labor and political organizations. The tangible results of these contacts were expressed through repeated manifestations of international support for Solidarity, support demonstrated by donations of money and equipment by other labor organizations as well as numerous assurances of solidarity with its goals and objectives. At no time during the year was there any evidence that Solidarity's international operations affected the national interests of Poland or its government.

These operations, however, involved relations with Western countries and Western organizations. No Solidarity delegation either visited or was invited to any East European countries. The implicit, and sometimes explicit, hostility of East European political and labor establishments was dramatically illustrated on the occasion of Solidarity's congress, which was attended by numerous labor delegations from the West but none from the Soviet bloc. Indeed, the Polish movement encountered a continuing barrage of hostile press propaganda and repeated criticism. Only once, in September, was a tentative gesture toward possible cooperation made. The Hungarian trade union organization wanted to establish contact with Solidarity, but this initiative was hastily squelched by Hungarian political leaders.

The government's main preoccupation in the area of foreign policy during 1981 was, as in previous years, Poland's relationship with the Soviet Union. This relationship was complex, but its dominant feature was continuing Soviet concern about developments in Poland. Evidence of that concern was amply demonstrated through numerous and repeated Soviet press warnings and criticisms. It was also projected through sporadic, but pointed, official statements by the Soviet leaders. At the same time, there was no firm evidence that the Soviet leadership had ceased to rely on Polish party leaders to put their house in order, although Moscow gave frequent advice on how this should be done and most likely provided its own services.

The fundamental statement defining the Soviet attitude toward Polish internal developments (fully approved by Polish party and government leaders, thus providing a basis for mutual relations) was included in a communiqué from a meeting held by both sides on 4 March, immediately after the Twenty-Sixth Congress of the Soviet party. It said that Soviet leaders remained convinced that "Polish Communists have both the opportunity and the strength to reverse the course of events and to eliminate the peril looming over the socialist achievements of the Polish nation" (PAP, 4 March). That conviction must have wavered at times, but Soviet doubts seemed to be related to unexpected developments in Poland—such as the disintegrative trends within the party and Solidarity's capability to mobilize massive public support for its actions—rather than any fears about the will of the Polish leaders to "reverse the course of events."

Soviet concern over the growth of Solidarity and, even more so, over the volatile situation in the Polish party came to the fore during a visit of Soviet Politburo member Mikhail Suslov to Warsaw in April. During the talks with Suslov, Polish leaders emphasized "the significance of the unity of all patriotic forces of the nation in order to remove the danger to the gains of socialism in Poland and to counteract the attempts to sow anarchy as well as to undermine the socialist state." Suslov assured the Poles that the Soviet party maintained "solidarity with the efforts of the PUWP to stabilize the social and economic situation, to strengthen the party on the ideological basis of Marxism-Leninism, and to defend the fundamental values of socialism." (*Trybuna ludu*, April.) On 25 April, barely a day after Suslov's return to Moscow, the Soviet press agency attacked "revisionist elements" active in the ranks of the PUWP, charging that they were striving to "paralyze the party of Polish Communists as the leading force in society" (Tass, 25 April).

At the beginning of June, in the midst of the electoral campaign for the PUWP's extraordinary congress, Soviet leaders sent a letter to members of the Polish party's Central Committee (see above). The letter was initially seen as an indication of Moscow's disenchantment with the performance of Polish leaders, especially Kania and Jaruzelski. In retrospect, however, it appears that Soviet intentions were not so much to undercut Kania and Jaruzelski as to provide them with an opportunity to serve as a rallying point for those groups in the party that might have been influenced by reformist tendencies but were to develop second thoughts in the face of a threat from Moscow of direct intervention in the party's affairs. Indeed, the issue of internal party problems was not raised during the visit of Soviet Foreign Minister Andrei Gromyko to Warsaw during 3–5 July. Neither was it mentioned in a speech delivered by the Soviet representative at the PUWP congress, Politburo member Viktor Grishin, although he pointedly reminded the gathering that the Soviet Union would "never abandon" its communist allies in a time of troubles and difficulties (*Trybuna ludu*, 15 July). Both Kania and Jaruzelski were easily re-elected to top leadership positions. The two men went to the Crimea on 14 August to talk with Leonid Brezhnev; the meeting was said to be "friendly" and was devoted to a discusson of "broad, all-around cooperation between Poland and the Soviet Union" (Tass, 15 August).

From 5 till 12 September, the Soviet Union mounted massive military exercises around Poland's northern and eastern borders involving more than 100,000 troops as well as numerous naval units. Other exercises, staged on Polish soil, took place during March. During both maneuvers, there were several high-level meetings between the military officers of both armies; there were also several meetings between top Polish political leaders and Soviet military commanders. In mid-September, the Soviet leadership sent a letter to Polish leaders complaining about "the growth of anti-Sovietism in Poland" and demanding "resolute action" to halt such activities (Radio Warsaw, 18 September).

The frequency of contacts between Polish officials and Soviet military officers increased after the replacement of Kania by Jaruzelski as PUWP first secretary on 17 October. On 3 and 4 November, an ideological conference of Central Committee secretaries was held in Moscow. Poland was represented by a delegation headed by Stefan Olszowski. On 4 November Polish Foreign Minister Jozef Czyrek met in Moscow with Andrei Gromyko; no details on their conversation were published aside from a note that it took place in "a warm, comradely atmosphere." On 24 November, Marshal Viktor Kulikov, commander in chief of Warsaw Pact forces, arrived in Poland for a visit of several days. While in Warsaw, Kulikov and Soviet General Anatoli Gribkov met with Jaruzelski and several other Polish generals (*Pravda*, 126 November); no communiqué was published. Kulikov reportedly returned to Poland at the beginning of December and stayed there until at least 17 December; there was no formal confirmation of his presence in Poland, however. Following the imposition of the state of emergency, the Soviet press published several reports that, while cautious in their comments, clearly approved of the unfolding developments.

Poland's relations with other East European countries remained unchanged during the year, as their activities largely mirrored those of the Soviet Union. The media of these countries, particularly those of Czechoslovakia and the German Democratic Republic, maintained a steady flow of criticism of Poland's internal situation.

Relations with Western countries were essentially friendly and cooperative, with the Polish authorities concentrating their activities on improving economic rather than political contacts. French Premier Pierre Mauroy's scheduled visit to Poland in December was postponed at the request of the Polish government on 11 December. Following the imposition of the state of emergency, France took a sharply critical position toward the Polish authorities.

An even more decisive stand against the state of emergency was taken by the United States. The U.S. government announced several economic sanctions against Poland, while allowing private aid, primarily food shipments, to continue. The U.S. sanctions were likely to affect some aspects of Poland's economic operations. Washington's position encountered some opposition from various West European countries, particularly West Germany. The Federal Republic of Germany was, during 1981, Poland's largest Western trade partner; the future of this relationship is unclear.

Publications. The official organ of the PUWP is the daily *Trybuna ludu*; the party also has daily newspapers in all 49 provinces. The party sponsors an important specialized daily, *Zolnierz Wolnosci*, published by the Main Political Administration of the armed forces, the military department of the Central Committee. Two biweeklies, *Zycie partii* and *Zagadnienia i materialy*, are for party activists. Another biweekly, *Chlopska droga*, is for rural readers; the monthly *Ideologia i polityka* is aimed at the general public.

Among other important publications in 1981 was *Tygodnik Solidarnosc*, a national weekly sponsored by Solidarity, which also operated ten regional weeklies as well as numerous internal bulletins and periodicals. The most important Catholic paper is *Tygodnik Powszechny*. All papers, with the exception of Solidarity's internal bulletins, were censored; the scope and the rigidity of censorship, however, declined considerably in 1981. The official Polish news agency is Polska Agencja Prasowa (PAP).

Radio Free Europe   Jan B. de Weydenthal
Munich, Germany

Biography. *Wojciech Jaruzelski.* Born on 6 July 1923 in Kurow, Lublin voivodship (district) in southeastern Poland. Official biographies state only that his family belonged to the intelligentsia. Independent research indicates, however, that it was a landowning family, that his father was an officer in the Polish cavalry, and that the young Wojciech attended a Jesuit boarding school. While, again, according to the official version, "he spent some time in the Soviet Union after the outbreak of World War II," the Jaruzelski family was most probably among the some 900,000 people transported to the Soviet Union after the Red Army occupied the eastern part of Poland in the fall of 1939.

In the latter part of the war, Jaruzelski, still a teenager, was employed as a worker and in 1943 joined the Polish army formed on Soviet territory. He was sent to a Soviet officers' infantry school in Ryazan, where he specialized in intelligence. He followed the battle route of the Polish First Army, including the liberation of Warsaw in January 1945 and the Soviet drive to take Berlin. During the years 1945–1947, he took part in mop-up operations against the armed underground ("the forest bands")—the remnants of the Polish nationalist anti-Nazi resistance who refused to surrender their weapons and continued an anticommunist partisan war.

Jaruzelski advanced swiftly in both his professional military career and through the ranks of the PUWP. Before 1960, he headed different military schools and commanded army units. From June 1960 to February 1965, he was chief political commissar of the armed forces. In 1961, he became a member of the Sejm. From 1962 until April 1968, he was vice-minister of national defense. In 1965, he was promoted to the rank of general, making him at age 33 the youngest general in the Polish army. The same year he was nominated chief of staff of the army. In 1968, he became minister of national defense, a position he still holds. As for his party career, he became a member in 1947. He was elected to the party's Central Committee in April 1964; in December 1970, he became a candidate member of the Politburo, and a year later a full member (another position he still holds). After dismissals of three prime ministers within one year, Gen. Jaruzelski assumed that post on 12 February 1981. On 18 October 1981, he was named to succeed Stanislaw Kania as first secretary of the communist party. Finally, on 13 December he proclaimed the state of emergency and became the head of the all-powerful Army Council for National Salvation. With the accumulation of all these top functions—minister of national defense, prime minister, head of the communist party, and now chief of the military junta—Gen. Jaruzelski occupies an unprecedented position in the postwar history of East Central Europe. (Sources: *Trybuna ludu*, 21–22 July; Radio Warsaw, 18 October; *FBIS*, 19 October; *New York Times*, 19 October; *Time*, 28 December).

Hoover Institution   Milorad M. Drachkovitch

LETTER OF THE CENTRAL COMMITTEE OF THE CPSU*

Dear Comrades,

The Central Committee of the Communist Party of the Soviet Union is sending this letter to you with a feeling of deep anxiety for the fate of socialism in Poland, for Poland as a free and independent country.

Our action is motivated by the interest we have as members of the CPSU in the affairs of the party of Polish Communists, in the whole of the Polish sister nation and of socialist Poland, which is an integral part of the Warsaw Pact and of the Council for Mutual Economic Assistance. Soviet and Polish Communists have acted together shoulder to shoulder all the years since the war. Our party and all the Soviet people have helped their Polish comrades in the construction of a new life. And we cannot but be anxious about the mortal danger that at present hangs over the revolutionary achievements of the Polish nation.

We say openly: certain tendencies in the development of People's Poland, in particular in the field of ideology, and in the economic policy of its previous leaderships, have caused us great anxiety for

---

*Text of letter, dated 5 June, sent to the Central Committee of the Polish United Workers' Party.

many years past. In complete agreement with the spirit of the relations existing between the CPSU and the PUWP, we had already spoken about this with that leadership during talks at the very highest level and at other meetings. Unfortunately, these friendly warnings, as well as the deeply critical statements expressed in the PUWP itself, were not taken into account and were even ignored. As a result, a profound crisis broke out in Poland that extended to the whole economic and political life of the country.

The change in the entire leadership of the PUWP, the effort of the party to overcome the serious errors and violations of the rules of the construction of socialism, to regain the confidence of the masses and above all of the entire working class in the party, and to reinforce socialist democracy, have been entirely understood by us. From the first days of the crisis, we considered it important that the party should firmly oppose the attempts of the enemies of socialism to take advantage of the difficulties that have arisen for their long-term aims. But this was not done. The continual concessions to the antisocialist forces and their demands have lead to a situation in which the PUWP has retreated step by step under the pressure of the internal counterrevolution, which is supported by foreign centers of imperialist diversion.

At the present time, the situation is not only dangerous, but it has led the country into a critical situation. It is not possible to arrive at any other conclusion. The enemies of socialist Poland do not conceal this, nor do they conceal their intentions. They are carrying out a struggle for power and are already winning it. They are taking control of one position after another. Counterrevolution is using the extremist wing of Solidarity as a striking force. It has tricked workers who have joined this trade union, to drag them into a criminal plot against the people's power. A wave of anticommunism and anti-Sovietism is being developed. The imperialist forces are undertaking ever more audacious attempts to interfere in the internal affairs of Poland.

The serious danger that hangs over socialism in Poland also constitutes a threat to the very existence of an independent Polish state. If the worst happened and the enemies of socialism came to power, if Poland no longer enjoyed the defense of the socialist countries, then the hungry hands of imperialism would fasten themselves upon her. Who could then guarantee the independence, the sovereignty, the frontiers of Poland as a state? No one.

You remember, comrades, the meeting of the leaders of the fraternal parties of the socialist community that took place in Moscow on 5 December 1980. On 4 March 1981, there took place talks between the Soviet leadership and the PUWP delegation to the Twenty-Sixth Congress of the CPSU. On 23 April this year, a delegation of the CPSU met the entire Polish party leadership. During these meetings, as well as in the course of other contacts, we voiced our growing anxiety regarding the activities of the counterrevolutionary forces in Poland. We spoke of the need to overcome the confusion in the ranks of the PUWP, to defend party cadres decisively against enemy attacks, and to defend people's power.

We called particular attention to the fact that the enemy had gained control of the mass information media, which, for the greater part, had become instruments of antisocialist activities and which were being used to undermine socialism and disorganize the party. Attention was drawn to the fact that the battle for the party would not be won while the press, radio, and television were working, not for the PUWP, but for its enemies.

We vigorously pointed out the need to reinforce the authority of the organs of public order and the army and to strengthen them against the ambitions of the counterrevolutionary forces. When a free hand is given to those who malign and attempt to disorganize the security organs, the militia, and even the army, this, in practice, implies the disarming of the socialist state and abandoning it to the class enemy.

We wish to underline the fact that on all the questions discussed, Stanislaw Kania, Wojciech Jaruzelski, and the other Polish comrades expressed their agreement with our points of view. But in fact nothing changed. Nor was there any change in the policy of concessions and compromise. One position after another was surrendered without taking into account the documents of our last Central Committee plenum, drawing attention to the counterrevolutionary threat. Up till now, not a single measure has been taken in practice to counter this threat, nor have the organizers of the counterrevolution been directly mentioned.

In the past period the situation inside the PUWP itself has become a subject of particular concern. Little more than a month remains before the party congress. Despite this, it is the forces hostile to socialism who are more and more setting the pace in the campaign for the election of the delegates and of the leadership bodies. It is not unusual for people chosen at random, and who openly preach opportunist points of view, to get into local party organizations and to be included as delegates to conferences and to the congress. This fact cannot but cause anxiety. The result of the many manipulations by the revisionists and opportunist enemies of the PUWP is that experienced militants completely devoted to the cause of the party and with an irreproachable reputation, are put on one side.

The fact that among the delegates elected to the forthcoming congress there are only a very small number of Communists of working class origin is also a cause for profound anxiety. The process of preparation for the congress is complicated by the so-called horizontal movement, which constitutes an instrument for dismantling the party to the advantage of the opportunists to bring to the congress people who are indispensable to them. Nor can the possibility be excluded that, during the congress itself, an attempt could be made to deliver a decisive blow to the Marxist-Leninist forces in the party so as to liquidate them.

We wish to say in particular that during the past months the forces of counterrevolution have been carrying out all sorts of anti-Soviet activity aimed at wiping out the results of the activity of our two parties and to revive nationalist and anti-Soviet feelings in various sections of Polish society. These slanderers and liars do not stop at anything. They claim that the Soviet Union allegedly "plunders Poland"—and this is being said without taking into account that the Soviet Union has given, and is giving, enormous extra material aid in this difficult period. This is being said of a country that, by its deliveries of oil, gas, minerals, and cotton at prices up to half world prices, is actually supplying the main branches of Polish industry.

Dear comrades, in addressing ourselves to you through this letter, we have in mind not only our anxiety for Poland, for the future perspective for Soviet-Polish cooperation. We, as well as the brother parties, are no less concerned at the fact that the offensive of the antisocialist forces, enemies of People's Poland, threaten the interests of our entire community, its cohesion, its integrity, and the security of its frontiers. Yes, our joint security. Imperialist reaction is supporting and stimulating Polish counterrevolution and does not conceal its hopes to change the balance of forces in Europe and the world in its favor.

Imperialism is actively using the Polish crisis to denigrate the economic system, the ideals, and principles of socialism. It is being used for new attacks against the international communist movement.

Thus the PUWP has not only the historic responsibility for the fate of its own country, its independence and its progress, for the cause of socialism in Poland. You, comrades, also carry an enormous responsibility for the joint interests of the socialist community.

We consider that it is still possible to avoid the worst and a national catastrophe. In the PUWP there are many honest and determined Communists who are ready to fight for the ideals of Marxism-Leninism, for independent Poland. In Poland there are many people devoted to the cause of socialism. The working class, even workers who have been tricked by the enemies' machinations, will after full reflection, follow the party.

It is now necessary to mobilize all the healthy elements of society, to counter the class enemy and combat counterrevolution. This requires in the first place a revolutionary will on the part of the party, its militants, and its leadership. Yes, its leadership. Time is running out. The party can and must find in itself the forces to reverse the course of events and channel them in the right direction even before the congress.

We would like to believe that the Central Committee of our sister Polish party will rise to its historic responsibilities.

We wish to assure you, dear comrades, that in these difficult days, as in the past, the Central Committee of the CPSU, all Soviet Communists, and all the Soviet people are in solidarity with your struggle. Our point of view was succinctly expressed by Comrade Brezhnev at the Twenty-Sixth Congress of the CPSU: "We will not abandon fraternal, socialist Poland in its hour of need; we will stand by it."

Central Committee, Communist Party of the Soviet Union

ADDRESS TO THE POLISH NATION*

Citizens of the Polish People's Republic: I turn to you today as a soldier and as the head of the Polish Government. I turn to you in matters of supreme importance. Our country has found itself at the edge of an abyss. The achievements of many generations, the house erected from Polish ashes, is being ruined. The structures of the state are ceasing to function. New blows are being struck every day at the dying economy. Our living conditions are imposing on people an increasingly greater burden. Lines of painful division are running through many Polish homes. The atmosphere of endless conflicts, of misunderstandings and of hatred is sowing psychological devastation and injuring the traditions of tolerance. Strikes, strike readiness and protest actions have become the norm. Even schoolchildren are being dragged into it.

Yesterday evening many public buildings were occupied. Exhortations for a physical settling of accounts with the "reds," with people who hold different views, are being made. Acts of terrorism, of threats, of mob trials and also of direct coercion abound. The wave of impudent crimes, of assaults and break-ins is sweeping the country. Fortunes amounting to millions are being accrued by economic underground sharks and are growing. Chaos and demoralization have assumed the proportions of a disaster.

The nation has come to the end of its psychological endurance. Many people are beginning to despair. Now it is not days but hours that separate us from a national catastrophe. Honesty compels one to ask the question: Did things have to come to this?

In assuming the office of chairman of the Council of Ministers, I believed that we could lift ourselves up. Have we thus done everything to stop the spiral of the crisis? History will assess our activities. There have been errors, and we are drawing conclusions from them. Above all, however, the past months have been a busy time for the government, a time of wrestling with enormous difficulties.

Unfortunately, however, the national economy has been turned into an arena for political struggle. A deliberate torpedoing of government activities has brought about a situation in which results are not commensurate with the work put in, with our efforts. We cannot be said to lack good will, moderation and patience. Sometimes there has been, perhaps, even too much of it. One cannot fail to notice the respect for social agreements displayed by the government. We have gone even further. The initiative of the great national accord won the support of millions of Poles. It created an opportunity for the democratic system to become more deeply rooted and for the range of reforms to be broadened. These hopes have been frustrated.

The Solidarity leadership was not present at the common table. The words uttered in Radom and

---

*Delivered by Premier Wojciech Jaruzelski on 13 December.

at the session in Gdansk have completely unmasked the true intentions of its leading bodies. These intentions are confirmed on a mass scale by everyday practice, by mounting aggressiveness by extremists, by an open striving for a complete partition of the socialist Polish state. How long can one wait for a sobering up? How long can a hand stretched out toward accord meet with a closed fist? I say this with a heavy heart, with immense bitterness. Things could have been different in our country; they should be different. The continuation of the current state could inevitably lead to a catastrophe, to complete chaos, to poverty and famine. Severe winter conditions could multiply losses and engulf numerous victims, especially among the weakest, whom we want to protect most. In this situation idleness would be a crime against the nation. It is necessary to say "enough," to block the path to confrontation which Solidarity leaders have openly announced. We must make it clear today as the date approaches for the mass political demonstrations, including in the center of Warsaw, which have been called in connection with the anniversary of the December events—that tragedy must not recur. One must not—we have no right to—allow the announced demonstrations to become a spark which sets the entire country alight.

The self-preservation instinct of the nation must be heard. Adventurists must have their hands tied before they push the homeland into the abyss of fratricide.

Citizens, great is the burden of responsibility which falls on me at this dramatic moment in Polish history. It is my duty to take this responsibility. Poland's future is at stake; the future for which my generation fought and for which it gave the best years of its life.

I announce that today a Military Council for National Salvation (Wojskowa Rada Ocalenia Narodowego) has been established. The Council of State, in accordance with the Constitution, introduced today at midnight martial law (*stan wojenny*) throughout the country. I want everyone to understand the motives and the aims of our action. We are not striving for a military coup, a military dictatorship. The nation has enough strength, enough wisdom in itself to develop an efficient democratic system of socialist rule. In such a system the armed forces will be able to remain where they belong—in the barracks. No Polish problem can, in the long run, be solved through force. The Military Council for National Salvation is not replacing constitutional organs of power. Its sole task is the protection of legal order in the country and the creation of executive guarantees that will make it possible to restore order and discipline. This is the last path we can take to initiate the extrication of the country from the crisis, to save the country from disintegration. The Committee for National Defense (Komitet Obrony Narodowej) has appointed plenipotentiaries, military commissars, at all levels of state administration and in some economic units. The plenipotentiary commissars have been granted the right to supervise the activity of organs of state administration from ministries to parishes. The proclamation of the Military Council for National Salvation and the decrees published today define in detail the norms of public order for the period of the duration of martial law.

The Military Council will be dissolved when the rule of law once again reigns supreme, when conditions permit the normal functioning of civil administration and of representative bodies.

Let no one, however, count on weakness or vacillation.

In the name of national interest a group of people presenting a threat to the safety of the state has been interned (*internmowac*) as a precautionary measure. This group contains extremist Solidarity activists and activists of illegal antistate organizations. On the orders of the Military Council, several dozen people who are personally responsible for bringing about a profound state of crisis in the 1970s and who abused posts for personal gain have also been interned. These people include: [former first secretary] Edward Gierek, [and former Politburo members] Piotr Jaroszewicz, Zdzislaw Grudzien, Jerzy Lukaszewicz, Jan Szydlak, Tadeusz Wrzaszcyzk [see *YICA*, 1981, pp. 268–69] and others. A full list will be published. We shall consistently purge Polish life of evil, irrespective of from where it is generated.

The Military Council will ensure conditions for a ruthless stepping up of struggle against crime. The activities of criminal gangs will be dealt with by the courts by way of summary proceedings. Persons who engage in large-scale speculation, benefiting from illegal profits, violating the norms of social co-existence will be pursued and brought to book with all severity. Fortunes amassed illegally will be confiscated. Persons occupying leading posts who are guilty of negligence on duty, waste, pursuing their own narrow interests (*partykularyzm*), abuse of power and an unfeeling attitude towards the concerns of the citizens will, at the suggestion of the plenipotentiaries and military commissars, be relieved of their posts after disciplinary procedures have been followed.

Respect must be restored for human work. Respect must be ensured for law and order. Personal safety must be guaranteed for everyone who wants to live and work in peace. Provisions of the special decree provide for forgiveness and leniency for certain crimes and offenses against the interests of the state committed prior to 13 December this year. We are not looking for vengeance. Those who, without ill will, allowed themselves to be carried away by emotions and yielded to false inspirations can avail themselves of this chance. Citizens, the Polish soldier has faithfully served and serves the fatherland. He has always been in the forefront, always there when needed by society. Today, too, he will discharge his duty with honor.

Our soldiers have clean hands. Private interests are alien to him; difficult service is not. He has no goal other than the good of the nation.

The fact that we have resorted to the help of the army can only have, and only has, a temporary nature, an extraordinary nature. The army will not act outside the normal mechanisms of socialist democracy. Democracy, however, can be practiced and developed only in a strong state, ruled by law.

Anarchy is a negation, an enemy of democracy. We are but a drop in the stream of Polish history. It is composed not just of proud pages but also dark ones: the liberum veto [right of any single individual to veto anything], the pursuit of private interests, quarrels. As a result we had a decline, a fall and disaster. This vicious circle must be broken at some stage. We cannot afford to have history repeat itself. We want a great Poland—great by its achievements, its culture, its form of social life, its position in Europe. Socialism, accepted by society and constantly enriched by life's experiences, is the only path. It is such a Poland that we will build, it is such a Poland that we will defend. Party people have a special role to play in this cause. Despite mistakes that have been made, despite bitter reverses, the party, as far as the process of historical changes is concerned, continues to be an active and creative force. In order to efficiently discharge its primary mission, to cooperate fruitfully with allied forces, it must lean on people who are honest, modest and courageous, on people who in any milieu will deserve the name of fighters for social justice, for the good of the country.

It is this above all that will decide the party's authority in society—this is its prospect. We shall cleanse the always active sources of our ideas of deformations and distortions and we shall protect the universal values of socialism, enriching them all the time with national elements and traditions. On this path, socialist ideals will become closer to the bigger part of the nation, to working people who are not party members, to the young generation and also to the healthy trend in Solidarity, specially the working class trend which, with its own forces and in its own interest will push away from itself the prophets of confrontation and counterrevolution.

In this way we understand the idea of national accord. We support it. We respect a multiplicity of views. We recognize the church's patriotic attitude. There exists a superior goal, uniting all thinking and responsible Poles: love for the fatherland, the need to strengthen independence, fought for and gained with such difficulties, and also respect for our own state. This is the strongest foundation of a genuine agreement. Citizens, just as there is no turning back from socialism, so there is no turning back to the erroneous methods and practices of pre–August 1980. Steps taken today serve to preserve the fundamental premises of the socialist renewal. All important reforms will be continued in conditions of order, businesslike discussion and discipline. This also applies to economic reform. I do not wish to make promises. We are facing a difficult period.

In order that tomorrow may be better, we must recognize the hard realities of today. We must understand the necessity of making sacrifices. I would like to attain one thing: calm. This is the fundamental condition from which a better future should begin. We are a sovereign country. From this crisis we must, therefore, emerge on our own. It is with our own hands that we must remove the threat. If this chance were to be wasted, history would not forgive the present generation.

We must put an end to the further degradation of our state's international position. A country of 36 million inhabitants, situated in the heart of Europe, cannot remain indefinitely in the humiliating role of petitioner. We cannot fail to notice that today derisory opinions about our republic, supposedly ruled by anarchy, spring to life again. Everything possible must be done to ensure that such opinions are thrown into the rubbish heap of history.

In this difficult moment I address myself to our socialist allies and friends. We greatly value their trust and constant aid. The Polish-Soviet alliance is, and will remain, the cornerstone of the Polish raison d'état, the guarantee of the inviolability of our borders.

Poland is, and will remain, a lasting link in the Warsaw treaty, an unfailing member of the socialist community of nations.

I address myself as well to our partners in other countries with which we wish to develop good, friendly relations. I address myself to the entire world public: We appeal for understanding for the extraordinary conditions that have arisen in Poland, for the extraordinary measures that have turned out to be essential.

Our measures do not threaten anyone. They have but one goal: to remove the internal threats, thereby preventing the threat to peace and international cooperation. We intend to observe treaties and agreements to which we are a party. We want the word "Poland" always to give rise to respect and sympathy in the world.

Poles, brothers and sisters, I address myself to you as a soldier who remembers well the horrors of war. Let not a single additional drop of Polish blood be spilled in this tormented country which has experienced so many reverses and sufferings already!

Let us jointly remove for good the specter of civil war. Let us not erect barricades where bridges are needed. I address myself to you, Polish workers: Give up, for the fatherland, your inalienable right to strike, for such period as may turn out to be necessary to overcome the gravest difficulties. We must do all we can so that the fruits of your hard work are not wasted.

I address myself to you, brother peasants: Do not allow your fellow countrymen to go hungry! Show concern for the Polish land, so that it may feed us all!

I address myself to you, citizens of older generations: save from forgetfulness the truth about the war years, about the difficult time of reconstruction. Hand it down to your sons and grandsons. Hand down to them your ardent patriotism, your readiness to make sacrifices, for the good of your native country. I address myself to you, Polish mothers, wives and sisters: Spare no effort so that no more tears are shed in Polish families. I address myself to young Poles: Show civic maturity, deep reflection on your own future, the future of the fatherland. I address myself to you, teachers, creators of science and culture, engineers, doctors, writers: Let reason get the upper hand over inflamed emotions on this dangerous turn in our history! Let the intellectual function of patriotism win over illusory myths!

I appeal to you, my comrades-in-arms, soldiers of the Polish Army on active duty and in the reserve: Be faithful to the oath you made to the fatherland for better or for worse. It is on your attitude today that the fate of the country depends. I appeal to you, functionaries of the Citizens' Militia and security service: Guard the state against the enemy and guard working people against lawlessness and violence.

I appeal to all citizens: An hour of difficult trial has come. We must prove equal to this trial. We must prove we are worthy of Poland.

Fellow countrymen, for the entire Polish nation and all the world to hear, I wish to repeat these immortal words: "Poland has not perished so long as we are alive!" [The first words of the Polish national anthem.]

SOURCE: Radio Warsaw, 13 December; *FBIS*, 2, no. 239, pp. G13–17.

Romania

The Communist Party of Romania (*Partidul Comunist Roman*; CPR) was founded on 8 May 1921. Throughout most of the interwar period, the CPR was outlawed. Factionalized and controlled by the Soviet-dominated Comintern, the party had little popular support. The Soviet occupation of Romania in 1944 ensured the emergence of a people's republic headed by the party, which was renamed the Romanian Workers' Party (*Partidul Muncitoresc Romin*) in 1948. Under the leadership of Gheorghe Gheorghiu-Dej, the party gradually initiated, in the 1960s, a more nationalistic internal course and a more autonomous foreign policy. This orientation has been continued by Nicolae Ceauşescu, who succeeded Dej on the latter's death in 1965. In that same year, the party's Ninth Congress proclaimed Romania a socialist republic, and the party reverted to its original name. Since 1948, the CPR has been the only party in Romania.

Party membership, as of 31 December 1980, totaled 3,004,336 according to a report of the CPR's Central Committee (*Scînteia*, 28 March). This contrasts with a membership of 2.9 million at the time of the CPR's Twelfth Congress in November 1979, when Ceauşescu reported that the party members were 90 percent Romanian, 8 percent Hungarian, and 2 percent German and other nationalities—an approximation of the ethnic composition of the country. The CPR is the largest communist party in Europe relative to population; an exchange of party membership cards in 1980 resulted in a purge of 30,000 members who were deemed unworthy of such status (ibid., 26 March). The Romanian population, as of 31 December 1980, totaled 22.3 million.

Organization and Leadership. The CPR is organized into committees (8,500) and basic units (64,200) at the various local working places and into organizations at the communal (2,705), town and municipal (241), county (40), and national levels (ibid., 28 March). Every five years the 40 county organizations (a new county was created in 1981) and the Bucharest party organization elect deputies to a national party congress, which, according to party statutes, is the supreme authority of the CPR. In practice, though, congresses have merely ratified decisions made by other party bodies: the Central Committee, the Secretariat, the Political Executive Committee, and the Permanent Bureau. The CPR's last congress was held 19–23 November 1979. Supplementing the work of these ongoing bodies is the National Conference of the CPR, which meets between congresses to review the implementation of party decisions. The last conference occurred 7–9 December 1977.

Despite the plethora of party leadership bodies and other party organiations, meetings, and conferences, political power has been highly centralized in the hands of the CPR's secretary general, Nicolae Ceauşescu, and increasingly his wife, Elena. In addition to membership in leading party bodies, she reputedly exercises considerable control over party and governmental personnel assignments. She also has assumed governmental leadership positions, including that of first deputy prime minister. Other of the Ceauşescus' relatives are in mid-level positions throughout the party and state apparats, and their youngest son, Nicu, has continued his gradual emergence in political life.

Unlike most other communist parties, the CPR does not have a politburo. Decision making is centered in two bodies: the 47-member Political Executive Committee and the 15-member Permanent Bureau. There is also a 10-member Secretariat. However, with the increasing personalization of power by the Ceauşescus and their constant leadership reshuffles ("cadre rotation"), formal lines of authority have become somewhat blurred and the power of party bodies reduced.

Ceauşescu continued his leadership rotations in 1981. Many of the changes reflected his growing concern over Romania's economic troubles. The first set of changes occurred in February and March. The Central Committee (ibid., 13 February) removed Vasile Marin from the Secretariat, where he was responsible for agriculture, and appointed longtime Ceauşescu adviser Emil Bobu in his stead. Bobu was released from his posts as minister of labor and head of the Central Council of the General Federation of Trade Unions. The Central Committee "recommended" that onetime Minister of the Interior Cornel Onescu be assigned to the latter position. A few days later, Bobu was appointed to head the new National Agricultural Council, which apparently has replaced the National Council of Agriculture.

Additional CPR changes (ibid., 26 March) saw four candidate members added to the Political Executive Committee—including the minister of defense and the new head of the trade union organization—and a tenth person, Petru Enache, assigned to the Secretariat. The party changes were followed by a governmental shake-up (ibid., 27 March) that involved nine ministerial changes, including new chiefs for labor, state planning, and finance. In the process CPR notable Paul Niculescu lost his leading governmental positions as deputy prime minister and minister of finance and was subsequently dropped from the Permanent Bureau. His place there was taken by the new chairman of the State Planning Commission, Emilian Dobrescu.

A second leadership change took place in August and September. An 18 August meeting of the Political Executive Committee "accepted" the resignation of Leonte Rautu, a longtime CPR leader who headed the party's elite Stefan Gheorghiu Academy. The Political Executive Committee, noting that some of Rautu's close family members wanted to leave Romania permanently, asserted that such behavior reflected negatively on a high party official and was thus "incompatible" with his official status. Rautu's resignation was widely interpreted as having been more or less forced by Ceauşescu as part of his intensified campaign against the large numbers of Romanians seeking to emigrate or defecting to the West. (*Wall Street Journal*, 8 September.)

Ceauşescu's presidential decrees of 8 September and 19 September rearranged the leadership of two troubled economic areas—energy and agriculture. As a result, the Ministry of Machine Building was split in two; the Ministry of Mining, Oil, and Geology was split into three ministries, and energy chief Virgil Trofin was removed from his leading governmental positions; Angelo Miculescu was removed as minister of agriculture; and Ilie Radulescu was appointed to head Romanian Radio and Television (leaving his status as CPR secretary unclear).

A final set of personnel changes occurred at the 25–26 November joint plenum of the CPR's Central Committee and the Supreme Council for Socioeconomic Development. Virgil Trofin, recently fired as minister of mines, was purged from the party's Central Committee, thus ending the political career of a onetime CPR luminary. Along with several other officials, he was held responsible for malfeasance at a major mining combine. At the same session, it was also announced that Ilie Radulescu and Dumitru Popescu had been dropped from and Marin Enache appointed to the Secretariat. Popescu assumed Leonte Rautu's old position as head of the party's Stefan Gheorghiu Academy.

In a speech to the joint plenum, Ceauşescu leveled an unprecedented blast at all of the party and government leadership bodies, as well as at the usual collection of deficient ministries and ministers. He charged the bodies with "serious shortcomings" in the implementation of decisions and berated them for their inadequacies. (*Scînteia*, 26 November; *FBIS*, 7 December.) Ceauşescu's increasing vindictiveness toward his own inner circle did not presage any change in Romanian policies. Rather, it reflected his growing frustration and penchant for scapegoating in the face of mounting internal problems.

Mass and Auxiliary Organizations. The CPR has a large number of mass organizations, councils, conferences, and congresses covering nearly all major groups and activities in the society so as to integrate them with the policies of the party. The CPR's conception of democracy revolves around building up the membership of the mass organizations, which usually meet in plenary session at least once every few years. Most sessions have a keynote speech in which Ceauşescu outlines the problems and prospects for the group's activities.

The major mass meetings in 1981 took place against the backdrop of the Polish crisis and in the midst of Romania's own economic dilemmas. Ceauşescu presided over the Second Agricultural Congress (19–21 February), the Romanian Trade Unions Congress (6–8 April), and the Second Congress of Working People's Councils (24–26 June). His remarks at the last meeting were typical Ceauşescu rhetoric about democratic participation: "This congress is being attended by over 11,000 representatives of the workers' class and other categories of working people, being thus the most representative and the broadest democratic forum of mass participation in leading our socialist society. The congress conclusively reflects the leading role of the workers in Romanian society." (Bucharest Domestic Service, 24 June; *FBIS*, 25 June.)

In a similar vein, Ceauşescu told the congress of the General Union of Romanian Trade Unions that it had growing leadership responsibilities. The congress itself issued a program declaring that the union was to "unite and mobilize" Romanian workers in fulfilling the decisions of the Twelfth CPR Congress and Ceauşescu's declarations. (*Scînteia*, 14 April.) The only noteworthy change in the operation of the trade union was at the leadership level where Ceauşescu assigned the positions of minister of labor and chairman of the General Union of Romanian Trade Unions to different individuals—rather than to one person as had been the case since 1977. This apparently was designed to give the union a semblance of greater institutional autonomy from the government.

Another organization used by the CPR to project an image of popular political participation is Romania's mass front, the Socialist Democracy and Unity Front, which has over 2.5 million members and 32,000 local organizations. Also of some significance is the Union of Communist Youth, a vehicle for advancing the careers of young party activists. Nicu Ceauşescu is a secretary of the group's Central Committee. Due to his Romanian youth group activities, he became in 1981 the chairman of the U.N. Consultative Committee for the International Youth Year, which enabled him to visit several foreign countries.

Internal Party Affairs. Some of the problems that plagued the CPR in 1980 deepened in 1981. Economic difficulties—food shortages, foreign debts, declining growth rates—fed a mood of disillusionment within the party and the country. The continuation of the Polish crisis heightened Ceauşescu's concern over Romania's difficulties, although there seemed to be only marginal spillover from events in Poland. Nevertheless, Ceauşescu was extremely wary about the future impact of Poland on his own rigid approach to communism, even though his foreign policy principles forced him, on balance, to argue for Poland's right to independence.

Ceauşescu's approach to internal problems was his usual attempt to inspire popular support by nationalistic proclamations and ideological exhortations. Party members were called on to manifest greater rectitude and responsibility in solving problems and dealing with the masses. Ceauşescu also continued his bitter attacks on "retrograde" ideas and persons wishing to emigrate. At the same time, he tried to project an image of the CPR as being innovative and responsive to Romanian domestic problems.

The Romanian leader used the occasion of the sixtieth anniversary of the CPR on 8 May to reiterate nationalistic themes and to sketch the party's ties to Romania's noncommunist past. He seemed particularly concerned to argue—in another riposte to those Hungarian historians who claim that Magyars preceded Romanians as inhabitants of Transylvania—that the "successors of the Dacians and Romans" (that is, the Romanians) have always lived in the geographical territory of Romania. Advised Ceauşescu: "Perhaps some historians in certain neighboring countries would do better to point out what our common forefathers have done to develop friendship between our neighboring countries" (Bucharest Domestic Service, 8 May; *FBIS*, 12 May). He also asserted that the Austro-Hungarian empire had "oppressed a large number of peoples in Central Europe, including a part of the Romanian people" (in Transylvania).

Ceauşescu's criticisms were directed not only at Hungary, but also—and more obliquely—at the Soviet Union. He stated that the CPR had raised a number of questions within the Comintern about the party's "right to independently draft its political line, in accordance with historical conditions in Romania," noting that Romania's participation in the Comintern did not give the latter a right "to interfere in our party's life." Such themes are not new, but Ceauşescu resurrected them in an attempt to reassert his claim as the protector of Romanian national interests.

Although Ceauşescu did not directly mention Poland in his speech commemorating the party's sixtieth anniversary, some parts of it were seemingly aimed at claiming that Polish-type problems had not and would not emerge in Romania. The Romanian leader declared that Romanian Communists had already dealt with violations of socialist legality and that party members "do not and may not have special rights or privileges." He also warned that "certain contradictions" continue under socialism, but that party alertness would prevent them from becoming "grave social disturbances." But, at the same time, the "party's leading political role means not to give orders but to convince and ensure the proper functioning of the democratic bodies."

His rhetorical attempt to reconceptualize the role of the CPR emerged in other speeches as well. Ceauşescu told a 25 March Central Committee plenum that since the party numbered over three million members, "it would be difficult to talk of a party of professional revolutionaries . . . Even the notion of 'vanguard party' must be reconsidered to a certain extent." (*Scînteia*, 26 March; *FBIS*, 1 April.) In a parallel proclamation, he asserted that the "concept of proletarian dictatorship no longer corresponds to current social and historical realities in Romania" and suggested its replacement by the "concept of workers' democracy or state of workers' democracy."

In reality, though, the primary political fact of life within the CPR remained the overwhelming political control of Nicolae and Elena Ceauşescu. Their personality cults continued to flourish. Elena Ceauşescu's birthday on 7 January provided the opportunity for a flow of media praise. She was depicted as the ideal role model for Romanian women and a world-famous scientist (see *Scînteia*, 7 January). Praise for Nicolae Ceauşescu on his sixty-third birthday on 26 January was even more profuse than in earlier years, continuing for several days. Articles, poems, and paintings stressed a complete identification between Ceauşescu the person and Romania the nation. His "thought" and leadership were once again posited as the source of all contemporary Romanian achievements.

Domestic Affairs. Economic crisis and sporadic unrest dominated Romanian life in 1981. The gravity of the country's economic situation was reflected in a host of negative economic indicators. Romania's balance of payments deficit was approximately $2.4 billion, and its total hard-currency trade debt had grown to over $9 billion by mid-1981 (*Wall Street Journal*, 20 October). Food shortages, which were a serious problem in 1980, worsened in 1981, compelling the regime to announce criminal penalties for "hoarding" of basic foodstuffs and a rationing system for bread, flour, and cornmeal (*Scînteia*, 10 and 17 October). The 1980 economic plan results showed a continued slowdown in Romania's economic growth rate with one sector, agriculture, registering a 5 percent decline in the value of production (ibid., 30 January). The overall economic crisis led Ceauşescu to question, if only momentarily, his priority of rapid industrialization, and the deteriorating Romanian standard of living contributed to worker and consumer discontent.

The country's most pressing economic problem concerned its escalating foreign debt. The problem had become so acute by late 1981 that a Romanian finance official said that Romania was seeking to delay repayment of its short-term debts because of a "temporary payments incapacity" (*Financial Times*, London, 24 September). There were also reports that Romania was asking Western firms to postpone demands for repayments so that hard currency could be diverted to meet obligations to Western banks—and thus avert default and/or the need to reschedule (Reuters, Bucharest, 3 November). It was symptomatic of the country's economic difficulties that a mid-June International Monetary Fund emergency standby facility of $1.5 billion for Romania, to help it meet its balance of payments deficit, was insufficient to cope with the situation by the fall.

The primary cause of Romania's foreign debt problems was its increasing dependence on imported oil to offset declining domestic production. Romania's oil output peaked in 1976 at 14.7 million metric tons, declining to 11.5 million tons in 1980. While oil imports represented only 3.3 percent of consumption in 1976, they represented over 40 percent by 1981 (*Wall Street Journal*, 31 August). With the fall of the Shah of Iran and the Iran-Iraqi war, Romania's traditional sources of oil imports became problematic, forcing it into the more expensive spot market at a time when interest rates were reaching new highs. The price of imported oil increased so much that Romania had to cut back its refining and resale of petroleum, its chief hard-currency earner, because such exports were no longer lucrative. (Ibid., 22 January.) The party daily, *Scînteia* (10 July), complained bitterly that the basic causes of international instability were the "eruptions of the price of some raw materials, especially oil" and the manipulation of interest rates by Western banks, which was "transforming credit into a new form of exploitation and subjugation of developing countries." The paper also pointed out that price increases and credit costs forced Romania to pay almost $2 billion more in 1980 than in 1979 for imported oil.

The second most pressing problem was agriculture, long a stepchild to the country's strategy of rapid industrialization. The drop in agricultural output in 1980, combined with continuing food exports and increasingly chaotic agricultural administration, contributed to severe domestic food shortages. The regime refused to admit that there was a scarcity of food per se and asserted that a host of other factors—hoarding, careless harvesting and storage, profiteering, poor distribution—had created a supply imbalance at the marketplace. A propaganda campaign revolving around these charges dominated the media in early October as a prelude to the imposition of partial food rationing.

A governmental decree on 10 October (*FBIS*, 13 October) established criminal penalties of six months to five years imprisonment for "hoarding of quantities—in excess of the needs of a family for 1 month—of edible oil, sugar, flour, corn flour, rice, coffee and other food stuffs" and prohibited their use as animal fodder. The decree also specified that sugar and edible oil could be sold only to people who lived and worked in their respective localities. A second decree, published 17 October (ibid., 19 October), asserted that in order to "ensure proper supplies" and to "secure a rational consumption" on the basis of "regional self-management" (that is, with each county responsible for securing its own food supplies), each person would be allocated during 1981–82 "an average of bread, flour, flour products and cornmeal . . . equaling up to 150 kilograms of wheat and up to 30 kilograms of corn." Ceauşescu later complained that Romanian consumption of grain products was much too high—higher even than in Western Europe—and that such rationing would actually result in a healthier populace. He also indicated that the rationing should not be applied rigidly, but adjusted to meet needs based on the nature of each person's work and age. (Bucharest Domestic Service, 5 November; *FBIS*, 6 November.)

The rationing decrees culminated months of criticism by Ceauşescu of Romanian agriculture. At the beginning of 1981, he complained that "in 1980, along with not too favorable weather conditions, many of the shortcomings in agricultural production were due to organizational shortcomings and to the manner in which action was taken to carry out agricultural work, to lack of responsibility on the part of agricultural bodies, People's Councils and, certainly, due to the lack of responsibility of party organizations and bodies. We must state that in the fall of 1980 the agricultural activity was carried out inappropriately both as regards crop harvesting and sowing." (*Scînteia*, 16 January; *FBIS*, 21 January.) Such complaints were reiterated by Ceauşescu throughout the year.

At one point Ceauşescu even questioned the wisdom of his economic priorities. Speaking to the Second Agricultural Congress, he said: "In light of the socialist construction experience in our country, it becomes obvious that the thesis of priority industrial development to the detriment of agricultural development and modernization was responsible for neglecting the importance of increasing agricultural production. Application of that concept brought about disproportions in the general socioeconomic development and had a negative impact on the people's living standard." (Bucharest Domestic Service, 19 February; *FBIS*, 23 February.) While Ceauşescu called for a "new agricultural revolution," it soon became apparent that his unprecedented critique did not presage any change in existing economic priorities. Indeed, the 1981–1985 plan posits continued emphasis on industrialization, even while there is much official rhetoric about the importance of agriculture and raw materials.

The food and energy crises were the most serious causes of the general decline in growth rates that has characterized the Romanian economy since the late 1970s. The 1980 economic plan results (*Scînteia*, 30 January) indicated that national income grew by 2.5 percent (as opposed to the planned 8.8 percent). Industrial production increased by 6.5 percent (as opposed to the planned 11.4 percent). Agricultural production registered a 5 percent decrease (instead of the planned 4.7–6.0 percent increase). Although it was not definitively shown in the 1980 plan results, the Romanian standard of living, already the second lowest in Eastern Europe (next to Albania's), suffered a sharp setback.

As a result of the gloomy economic situation, Romanian consumers and workers evidenced a greater willingness to vent their grievances. Reports of sporadic work stoppages and demonstrations began to reach the West (Reuters, Bucharest, 19 February; *NYT*, 9 March). Romanian restiveness seemed to be more acute by the end of the year, following the antihoarding and rationing measures. Some reports indicated that antigovernment demonstrations had erupted in Romania's mining region—the scene of a major coal miners' strike in 1977. Violent outbursts were also reported in several other parts of the country, although they appeared to be readily contained by the authorities. The most serious disturbances, however, seemed to be centered in the mining area around Motru, where people reportedly engaged in street demonstrations and occupied local party headquarters. (*Daily Telegraph*, London, 13 November; AFP, 17 November.)

Another indication of the discontent within Romania was the rising pressure to emigrate, either legally or illegally. This situation was highly embarrassing to Ceauşescu, who once again reacted angrily to the idea of leaving the country to settle in the West. Said Ceauşescu in a speech marking the fiftieth anniversary of the party's newspaper: "An uncompromising attitude must be adopted against all those who, snared by foreign propaganda and by the empty illusion that an easier life could perhaps be had elsewhere, are ready to leave their country, the fatherland which their parents and ancestors fought to develop and for which they secured a free and independent future . . . We must clearly show that we are the only ones that can solve our difficulties, through united work and led by our Communist Party ... We must make all our people, our young people understand that a better life cannot be had outside, in the search for a bit more money, but here, in our own country, by working and struggling to overcome difficulties." (*Scînteia*, 16 August; *FBIS*, 18 August.)

International Affairs. The accumulation of domestic problems, the foreign trade liquidity crisis, and the continuing Polish upheavals operated as constraints on Romania's foreign policy activity in 1981. Ceauşescu, usually an inveterate world traveler, stayed close to home. Romania continued to cultivate ties with the United States, Western Europe, China, and the Third World as counterbalances to the Soviet Union, but it also struck a generally less abrasive tone in its approach to the USSR, the Council for Mutual Economic Assistance (CMEA), and the Warsaw Pact. The restrained mood of Romanian foreign policy during most of the year led some Western media to speculate that Romania's resolve to be independent was eroding in the face of internal and external problems (see *Wall Street Journal*, 20 October). Ceauşescu may have been seeking to rebut such speculation when in October and November he launched a Romanian "zero option" proposal regarding U.S. and Soviet medium-range missiles in Europe—a stance that went beyond anything the Soviet Union or the Warsaw Pact had offered.

Relations with the United States and the West. Romania moved quickly to establish contacts with the newly elected Reagan administration and to receive assurances of continuing U.S. support for Romania. Secretary of State Alexander Haig met with Romanian Foreign Minister Stefan Andrei three times: 15 May (Washington); 17 June (Beijing, where both were making official visits); and 29 September (New York). The Haig-Andrei discussions in May and Andrei's brief meeting with President Reagan occurred at the same time U.S. Secretary of Commerce Malcolm Baldridge was in Bucharest to meet Ceauşescu and head up the U.S. delegation to the U.S.-Romanian Joint Economic Commission meeting. The Romanian media hailed these visits as part of "the constant evolution of Romanian-American relations, reaching natural and favorable conclusions" (*Lumea*, 21 May). Agerpres (16 May), the Romanian news agency, described the first Haig-Andrei meeting as taking place in an "atmosphere of cordiality, sincerity, and mutual understanding," which would "intensify the Romanian-American contacts and consultations at all levels." The Reagan administration subsequently supported renewal of Romania's most-favored-nation trade status, which has contributed to a bilateral trade turnover of $1 billion and made Romania the United States' leading export market in Eastern Europe (*Business America*, 5 October).

Romania's relations with Western Europe, at least as measured by state visits, lagged behind previous years. Prime Minister Ilie Verdet visited the United Kingdom (13–16 May), and Ceauşescu traveled to Austria (9–12 June). West German President Karl Carstens visited Romania (27–30 October) for talks with Ceauşescu and a tour of the country. The Romanian authorities initially tried to preclude him from mingling with the population, but they relented somewhat after he complained. The incident marred his visit, at least as it was covered by the West German media (DPA, Hamburg, 28 and 29 October).

The Conference on Security and Cooperation in Europe (CSCE) review meeting in Madrid, a forum Bucharest has looked toward to diminish bloc divisions in Europe, was criticized by Ceauşescu for its lack of results. He urged the Madrid meeting to set the stage for a Conference on Confidence and Disarmament in Europe, and he again offered to host the next CSCE review meeting. Ceauşescu asserted that Romania "is prepared to and will guarantee all conditions necessary for a favorable course of that meeting" (*Frankfurter Rundschau*, 27 October).

Relations with the Third World. Romania, a "guest" in the nonaligned movement and a member of the Group of 77, continued to promote its ties with the Third World. The Romanian deputy foreign minister attended the meeting of nonaligned foreign ministers in New Delhi (9–13 February). Major Third World leaders visiting Romania included Syrian President Hafiz al-Asad (5–7 February); South-West African People's Organization leader Sam Nujoma (5–7 March); Palestine Liberation Organization leader Yassir Arafat (25 May and 16–17 December); the emir of Kuwait (12–14 September); Libyan President Moammur Khadafy (24–26 September); Indian Prime Minister Indira Gandhi (18–20 October); and Zimbabwe Prime Minister Robert Mugabe (13–16 November). Mugabe had been a frequent visitor to Bucharest in the years before Zimbabwe (Rhodesia's) independence; Romania was the only Warsaw Pact state to back Mugabe's guerrilla and political faction. His first visit to Romania as prime minister provided another opportunity for both sides to demonstrate their political affinity. Mugabe thanked Ceauşescu for Romania's earlier support, which, he said, "was given on all conceivable fronts of the struggle" (Agerpres, 14 November). The two states signed a friendship treaty.

The Middle East was a particular focal point of Romania's Third World involvement. Unlike previous years, however, Ceauşescu seemed less preoccupied with launching diplomatic initiatives aimed at resolving the Middle East crisis. His main accent was on finding oil supplies, preferably through barter arrangements, to compensate for Romania's own declining oil production. Romanian economic delegations and personal emissaries from Ceauşescu frenetically roamed the Middle East looking for favorable trade and aid. The most significant progress may have been made vis-à-vis Iraq, although few details were announced. Since the outbreak of the Iran-Iraqi war, Bucharest had evinced a tilt toward Iraq, which prompted some speculation that Romania might be trading military supplies and food for oil. In any event, while relations with Iran seemed to languish, those with Iraq were quite active. Romanian Foreign Trade Minister Cornel Burtica delivered a message from Ceauşescu to Iraqi President Saddam Husayn (February), while Ceauşescu received a high-level Iraqi military (July) and a political and economic delegation (September). Prime Minister Verdet visited Iraq on 8–11 December and held high-level talks centering on the expansion of bilateral economic relations.

On the Middle East political front, the assassination of Egyptian President Anwar Sadat was a blow to Ceauşescu, who had developed strong political relations with the Egyptian leader. Romania, as the only Warsaw Pact state with diplomatic ties to Israel and the Arab world, had been an active backer of Israeli-Egyptian rapprochement and had supported the Camp David peace process. Ceauşescu called the assassination a "murderous criminal act" against a "close friend" of Romania (Bucharest Domestic Service, 6 October; *FBIS*, 7 October); he led a major party-state delegation to the Egyptian Embassy to express condolences, and the government declared 9–10 October to be days of national mourning. A Romanian delegation, led by Political Executive Committee member Gheorghe Radulescu, attended the Sadat funeral. In the course of Romania's long involvement with Sadat's Egypt, Ceauşescu had met many times with his successor, Muhammed Hosni Mubarak—which will probably contribute to further development of Egyptian-Romanian relations.

Relations with Independent Communist Parties and States. Romania has been an active political partner of the Eurocommunist parties, China, and Yugoslavia in attempting to thwart Soviet control over international communism. Those ties remained in force in 1981, although they did not have the prominence of recent years. Ceauşescu received Spanish Communist Party leader Santiago Carrillo on 2 January. Both urged that differences among communist parties be solved through discussions and stressed that the problems in Poland should "be resolved only by the Polish people themselves" (Bucharest Domestic Service, 2 January; *FBIS*, 5 January).

Romanian-Chinese relations were highlighted by Foreign Minister Andrei's visit to Beijing. The Romanian minister met leading Chinese officials for a review of bilateral and international issues. Chinese Premier Zhao Ziyang praised the "Romanian people's brilliant successes in safeguarding their national independence and dignity" (NCNA, Beijing, 16 June; *FBIS*, 17 June). Various Chinese and Romanian delegations continued to exchange visits.

Ceauşescu and the post-Tito Yugoslav leadership maintained the traditional pattern of regular meetings established under Tito. Ceauşescu hosted Yugoslav President Cvijetin Mijatović on 1–2 February in Timisoara, an occasion on which "both parties' will was reaffirmed, to amplify and intensify the political dialogue, the collaboration on multiple planes" (Agerpres, 2 February). Romanian Prime Minister Verdet visited Belgrade on 20–22 April at the invitation of Yugoslav Prime Minister Veselin Djuranović; both sides pledged to "eliminate from international relations the policy of force, all forms of pressure, intervention and interference in internal affairs" (Tanjug, Belgrade, 22 April; *FBIS*, 23 April). Similar themes were sounded during the 9–10 November meetings in Bucharest of Ceauşescu and Sergej Kraigher, the new Yugoslav president. In a broadcast before the Kraigher visit, an authoritative Yugoslav political commentator said: "The only right policy leading out of the present crisis is the policy of noninterference, of not resorting to force or to threats with force and of blunting the sharp edge of intrabloc rivalry and conflict. Though a member of the Warsaw Pact, our neighbor Romania and President Ceauşescu personally operate in the same way." (Zagreb Domestic Service, 8 November; *FBIS*, 9 November.)

The Polish Crisis. Poland continued to pose challenges for the Ceauşescu regime. Ceauşescu's independent foreign policy necessitated Romanian support for the Polish party's right to handle its own affairs without Warsaw Pact or Soviet threats. But, at the same time, Polish political developments contravened Ceauşescu's brand of communism and were particularly troubling in light of Romania's own political and economic problems. Ceauşescu had to juggle the Polish crisis in terms somewhat compatible with Romania's foreign policy principles, while also making clear to Romanians that Polish-type developments would not be tolerated by his regime. While this juggling did not always lead to a consistent stance, Romania was more supportive of Poland than was any other Warsaw Pact member.

The Romanian media covered Polish developments very sporadically and selectively—focusing primarily on the Polish party's statements, emphasizing the economic and social chaos, and generally ignoring Solidarity. The CPR itself, in a Central Committee resolution of 26 March, asserted its "support for the surmounting of the hardships . . . without any outside interference" (Agerpres, 26 March; *FBIS*, 27 March). Ceauşescu reiterated this point during his trip to Austria. He said that the "Polish United Workers' Party, the Polish government and people can surpass on their own the problems facing them" (Agerpres, 12 June; *FBIS*, 17 June).

Following the 5 June Soviet "warning letter" to the Polish party (generally interpreted in the West as a gambit aimed at forcing the Polish party to remove Stanislaw Kania and/or postpone the party's Ninth Extraordinary Congress), Romania appeared to strengthen its support for Polish party autonomy. *Scînteia*, in a lengthy editorial, endorsed the forthcoming congress as an "event meant to strengthen the party's unity, increase its force and to improve its combat capacity" and said that it might "mark the conclusion of the clarification process in the party and society as regards the way to be followed, may become a starting point for the passing to a practical, nationwide solution to the problems" (*FBIS*, 15 June). Two weeks later Ceauşescu gave the Romanian imprimatur to Kania and his program of "socialist renewal." Ceauşescu told the concluding session of the Congress of Working People's Councils that while "concerned over certain states of affairs in friendly Poland . . . we want to express complete solidarity with the PZPR [the Polish party] and we fully support the position held at the last PZPR Central Committee plenum by Comrade Kania, who outlined the road to Poland's renewal and for Poland's socialist development." (Bucharest Domestic Service, 26 June; *FBIS*, 30 June.) No other East European leader backed Kania so explicitly.

However, Solidarity's own congress in September, which included an appeal to East European workers to follow the path of free trade unions, clearly agitated the CPR, which had suppressed a Romanian free trade union effort in 1979. The party paper berated "antisocialist elements who dominated the Solidarity congress" and their attempt "to formulate an antiworker, counterrevolutionary policy designed to curb the process of socialist renewal in Poland, to gravely impair socioeconomic life."

> The interests of the Polish people dictate that all reactionary elements who take advantage of the current difficulties to harm the interests of socialism in Poland should be dealt with most firmly ... Similarly, in order to establish a healthy social climate in Poland, it is decisively important to unswervingly implement and enforce the laws of the country, to safeguard socialist legality, and to forcefully deal with any attempt to weaken state order and discipline in Poland, to bring in arbitrariness and anarchy, and to cause social and political instability. There should not be the slightest hesitation or tolerance in dealing with those who mock the law and the norms of social life and socialist behavior. (*Scînteia*, 22 September; *FBIS*, 24 September.)

Such critiques of another communist party's internal affairs are rare. The statement reflected Bucharest's exasperation at the radicalization of Solidarity, as well as the inability of the Polish party to bring matters under control. While Romania still expressed the belief that the Polish party "will know how to act to defeat reactionary forces," its support for the Polish party seemed strained in the fall of 1981.

Following the Jaruzelski government's martial law crackdown, Romania expressed its understanding that the "exceptional measures" were necessary to avert civil war and to counter the growing "antisocialist forces" (*Scînteia*, 15 and 26 December; *FBIS*, 15 and 28 December). At the same time, Romania reiterated that Poland "must be left to solve its problems by itself without any outside interference." *Scînteia* also criticized, albeit indirectly, U.S. economic sanctions against Poland in the wake of the crackdown, claiming that Romania was "puzzled" by such actions as they would create more problems for the country.

Relations with the Soviet Union and Eastern Europe. For most of 1981, Romania's approach to the Soviet Union and Eastern Europe was marked by tactical restraint. Ceauşescu visited Bulgaria (January) and Czechoslovakia (May), and Prime Minister Verdet visited East Germany (March). Ceauşescu, in the course of his trips to Eastern European countries, as well as the Soviet Union, did not retreat from the main lines of his earlier nonconformist foreign policy positions. But neither did he, at least until later in the year, stake out new ones. This appeared designed to improve Romania's prospects for economic interactions with nearby socialist states, particularly in terms of obtaining more Soviet oil.

The less combative tone was apparent in Ceauşescu's 24 February speech to the Soviet party congress. The Romanian leader spoke of the "upward course of relations of close friendship and solidarity" between the two parties and asserted that "we pay particular attention to cooperation with our great neighbor and friend, the Soviet Union." Ceauşescu also spoke positively about Romania's cooperation with the CMEA and with the Warsaw Pact so as "to defend ourselves against any kind of imperialist aggression." (Bucharest Domestic Service, 24 February.) Ceauşescu's visit to Moscow had been preceded by Romanian Foreign Minister Andrei's 17 February meeting with Soviet Foreign Minister Andrei Gromyko—described as "businesslike and comradely"—which may have been designed to set the ground rules for Ceauşescu's attendance at the congress.

Prime Minister Verdet led a high-level delegation to Moscow on 22 June for talks with Soviet Prime Minister Nikolai Tikhonov. Described as taking place in a "friendly, businesslike atmosphere," the discussions evidently centered on issues of economic cooperation (Bucharest Domestic Service, 22 June; *FBIS*, 23 June). Verdet returned to Moscow on 21 August to open a Romanian exhibit. He again met with Tikhonov in a "warm and friendly atmosphere" and discussed "further extension and strengthening of Soviet-Romanian relations." (Moscow Domestic Service, 21 August; *FBIS*, 24 August.) The Romanian desire to promote bilateral economic relations was further highlighted during Ceauşescu's short trip to the Crimea for discussions with Brezhnev on 31 July. The meeting, described in slightly cooler terms than the previous year—"friendly and frank"—apparently included a discussion of Romanian investments in the Soviet Union that would enable it to receive "additional amounts of gas, electricity and other products. The possibility of oil deliveries by the Soviet Union was also discussed." (Tass, 31 July; *FBIS*, 3 August.) The noncommittal reference to oil deliveries—Romania obtained some 10 percent of its oil imports from the USSR in 1980—indicated that Moscow was not rushing to help Romania with its economic crisis.

Soviet hedging on future oil deliveries to Romania paralleled Romania's inability to make headway within the CMEA on greater energy and raw materials cooperation. Prime Minister Verdet, in a 2 July speech to the CMEA heads of government meeting, reiterated Romania's newfound interest in cooperating more with CMEA, but he also pointed out that there had been little reciprocity. On energy, Verdet said:

> Another essential problem on which we are focusing is securing a greater volume of fuel, energy and raw materials through mutual cooperation . . . In dealing with this problem we proceed from the fact that, in the first decade of implementation of [CMEA's] comprehensive program, the volume of fuel, raw materials, minerals, and metals secured by Romania on the basis of mutual cooperation dropped from 47 percent of total imports in 1970 to 21 percent in 1980. As a result, we currently import most of our fuel, raw materials and metals from third countries and pay for them in freely convertible currency. This of course limits the scope of Romania's general cooperation within CMEA. (*Scînteia*, 7 July; *FBIS*, 14 July.)

Romania's economic courting of the Soviet Union and the CMEA, together with its more restrained foreign policy, prompted some Western speculation that Ceauşescu might not be able to sustain his independent course. This speculation received something of a setback, however, when Ceauşescu launched a major Romanian European "peace offensive" in October and November. He began to push European arms control proposals that went beyond Soviet policy at the time. On the controversial question of U.S. and Soviet medium-range missiles in Europe, Ceauşescu told the West German newspaper *Frankfurter Rundschau* (27 October): "We advocate the view that above everything else it is necessary to make every effort to halt the deployment and development of new medium-range missiles as well as all nuclear missiles in Europe. This applies to the discontinuation of the deployment of the U.S.-made missiles just as it applies to the withdrawal of Soviet missiles." Ceauşescu subsequently expanded this to advocate the "nondeployment, withdrawal and reduction—by both sides—of medium-range missiles as a first step toward completely eliminating and eradicating them." (Bucharest Domestic Service, 4 November; *FBIS*, 5 November.)

Ceauşescu's proposals amounted to a variation on Western "zero option" formulations that Moscow had pointedly rejected. The Soviets had offered to reduce some of their SS-20s targeted on Europe in return for nondeployment by the United States and NATO of its Pershing II and cruise missiles. Ceauşescu, in calling for concurrent Western nondeployment and Soviet withdrawal, leading to eradication of the SS-20s, seemed to stake out a position closer to President Reagan's November arms control proposal than to Brezhnev's. Thus, Ceauşescu alone among Warsaw Pact leaders asserted that President Reagan's initiative was "important" and deserved to be "considered and analyzed"—although he was careful to balance this by saying that Brezhnev's proposals deserved the same serious consideration. (Interview with Dutch TV, 21 November; *FBIS*, 23 November.) This was his first new break with a major Soviet foreign policy position since the indirect Romanian criticism of the Soviet invasion of Afghanistan.

Although Ceauşescu did not push his views to the point of disrupting the Warsaw Pact foreign ministers' meeting in Bucharest on 1–2 December, Soviet Foreign Minister Andrei Gromyko evidently deemed it necessary to remain in Bucharest for talks with the Romanian leader. The discussions, which involved an "exchange of opinions" on several international problems, were characterized as "comradely"—an indication that disagreements remained. (Tass, 3 December; *FBIS*, 4 December.)

Publications. *Scînteia* is the daily newspaper of the CPR, and *Era Socialista* is its theoretical journal. *Romania Libera* is the other major daily paper. *Lumea* is the weekly foreign affairs journal. *Revista Economica* is the major periodical devoted to economic policy. The two most important historical journals are *Anale de Istorie* and *Magazin Istoric*. Agerpres is the Romanian news agency.

Washington, D.C.   Robert L. Farlow

Union of Soviet Socialist Republics

The Communist Party of the Soviet Union (Kommunisticheskaia Partiia Sovetskogo Souizu; CPSU) traces its origins to the founding of the Russian Social Democratic Labor Party in 1898. The party split into Bolshevik (claiming majority) and Menshevik (alleged by the Bolsheviks to be the minority) factions at the Second Congress, held at Brussels and London in 1903. The Bolshevik faction, led by Vladimir I. Lenin, was actually a minority after 1904. Unable to regain the policymaking dominance attained at the Second Congress, the Bolsheviks broke away from the Mensheviks in 1912 at the Prague Conference to form a separate party. In March 1919, after the seizure of power, the party was renamed the All-Russian Communist Party (Bolsheviks). When Union of Soviet Socialist Republics was adopted as the name of the country in 1924, the party's designation was changed to All-Union Communist Party (Bolsheviks). The present name was adopted in 1952. The CPSU is the only legal political party in the USSR.

Total membership of the CPSU was reported to be 17,480,000 at the time of the Twenty-Sixth Congress in February. Since the last congress, the party had added 1,800,000 new members and expelled 300,000. Of the newly admitted members, 59 percent were classified as working class and over 10 percent as collective farmers. (*Pravda*, 24 February.) On 1 April 1980, party membership had been 17,193,376 (ibid., 24 June 1980). Party membership has grown in absolute terms during the Brezhnev era, but the rate of increase has slowed, dropping from an average rise of 6.0 percent in the years 1961–1966 to a low of less than 1.25 percent in 1978. After a temporary upsurge in 1979, with a rise of approximately 4.2 percent over the previous year, the rate of growth fell again in 1980, although not to the low level of 1978. Membership reports at the Twenty-Sixth Congress indicated a rate of growth for 1980 of somewhat less than 2.5 percent. Present party membership is about 9.3 percent of the adult population and 6.5 percent of the total USSR population of 266,754,000.

Some 70 percent of new candidate members are drawn from the ranks of Komsomol. Women account for slightly less than one-fourth of total party membership. More than half of all males over

30 with a higher education are party members; the corresponding figure for women is around 15 percent. Around 45 percent of party members are aged 40 to 60, some 37 percent are between 25 and 40, and less than 6 percent are under 25.

Although in recent years the party has pursued a policy aimed at achieving a distribution by nationality corresponding to the general population mix within particular regions, Great Russians retain their numerical preponderance, accounting for roughly 60 percent of total membership. Ukrainians make up about 16 percent, Belorussians more than 3.5 percent, and other nationalities around 20 percent. Notably, recent increases in the Central Asian republics have been at best slightly higher than the general average for the party, despite rapid population growth.

In terms of social composition, the party remains somewhat unrepresentative of the population. The peasantry is markedly underrepresented, with collective farmers accounting for only 12.8 percent of membership. The remainder consists of professional and white-collar personnel and members of the military forces. (Ibid., 24 February.)

Organization and Leadership. The CPSU's structure parallels the administrative organization of the Soviet state. There are 414,000 primary party organizations (ibid.), some 2,900 rural *raion* committees, 815 city committees, 10 *okrug* (area) committees, 149 *oblast* (district) committees, 6 *krai* (territorial) committees, and 14 union-republic committees. There is no separate organization for the Russian republic (RSFSR), the largest constituent unit of the country; regional and city committees in the RSFSR are supervised directly by the CPSU Central Committee. Two city committees, those of Moscow and Kiev, are accorded special status, being separate from and equal to the *oblast* committees.

The All-Union Congress is, according to party rules, the supreme policymaking body. The Congress elects the Central Committee and the Central Auditing Commission. The Twenty-Fourth Congress (1971) set the maximum interval between congresses at five years. In the interim, the highest representative organ is the Central Committee. Actual power is concentrated in the Politburo, the Secretariat, and the 22 departments of the Central Committee.

The Twenty-Sixth Congress of the CPSU was held in Moscow, 23 February–4 March 1981. Of the 5,002 delegates to the congress, 3,572, or 71.4 percent, were elected for the first time. According to the report delivered by Ivan V. Kapitonov, party cadres secretary and chairman of the credentials commission, the delegates included 1,370 industrial workers, 877 agricultural workers, 269 representatives of the arts, sciences, and professions, and 115 members of the USSR Academy of Sciences and other academies (Moscow Domestic Service, 25 February; *FBIS*, 26 February). Attending as observers were 123 delegations from 109 countries (*Izvestiia*, 7 March).

The congress elected a new Central Committee of 319 full members and 151 candidate members, compared with 287 full members and 139 candidate members elected by the Twenty-Fifth Congress in 1976. Only about ten percent of sitting full members failed to obtain re-election. Gennadi F. Sizov was re-elected chairman of the Central Auditing Commission, which was reduced from 85 to 75 members. (*Pravda*, 4 March.)

The first plenum of the new Central Committee unanimously re-elected the fourteen full Politburo members, the eight candidate members, and the ten secretaries of the Central Committee (*NYT*, 4 March). This marked the first time in more than fifty years that a party congress had not changed the Politburo or Secretariat. The second Central Committee plenum of the year, in November, also made no changes in the party leadership (ibid., 17 November). The November plenum featured a report by Brezhnev on the economy. The general secretary endorsed a comprehensive program to revamp the farm economy and defended as necessary severe cuts in investment outlays under the Eleventh Five-Year Plan (*Pravda* and *Izvestiia*, 17 November).

The most recent elections for the Supreme Soviet were held on 4 March 1979. Approximately three-fourths of the 1,500 members of the bicameral Supreme Soviet are members of the CPSU, and all deputies are officially designated by the party. The 1981 summer session of the Supreme Soviet, 23–24 June, recorded no major changes of policy or personnel. Its major business was the adoption of a resolution supporting President Brezhnev's appeal to Western nations for prompt negotiations on arms control (*Pravda*, 24 June). The fall session of the Supreme Soviet, 17–19 November, gave official approval to the new five-year plan (*Izvestiia*, 20 November).

The current composition of the Politburo is as follows:

Members	**Other Positions**
Brezhnev, Leonid I.	General Secretary, CPSU Central Committee; Chairman, Presidium of the USSR Supreme Soviet
Suslov, Mikhail A.	Secretary, CPSU Central Committee
Kirilenko, Andrei P.	Secretary, CPSU Central Committee
Tikhonov, Nikolai A.	Chairman, USSR Council of Ministers
Pelshe, Arvid I.	Chairman, Party Control Commission
Chernenko, Konstantin U.	Secretary, CPSU Central Committee
Grishin, Viktor V.	First Secretary, Moscow City Party Committee
Kunaev, Dinmukhamed A.	First Secretary, Kazakh Central Committee
Shcherbitsky, Vladimir V.	First Secretary, Ukrainian Central Committee
Andropov, Yuri V.	Chairman, Committee of State Security (KGB)
Gromyko, Andrei A.	Minister of Foreign Affairs
Romanov, Grigori V.	First Secretary, Leningrad *Oblast* Party Committee
Ustinov, Dimitri F.	Minister of Defense
Gorbachev, Mikhail S.	Secretary, CPSU Central Committee

Candidate Members

Demichev, Piotr N.	Minister of Culture
Rashidov, Sharaf R.	First Secretary, Uzbek Central Committee
Solomentsev, Mikhail S.	Chairman, RSFSR Council of Ministers
Ponomarev, Boris N.	Secretary, CPSU Central Committee
Aliev, Geidar A.	First Secretary, Azerbaidjan Central Committee
Kuznetsov, Vasili V.	First Deputy Chairman, Presidium of the USSR Supreme Soviet
Shevardnadze, Eduard A.	First Secretary, Georgian Central Committee
Kiselev, Tikhon Y.	First Secretary, Belorussian Central Commiteee

The present Central Committee Secretariat is composed of ten men: Brezhnev (general secretary), Kirilenko (organizational affairs), Suslov (ideology), Chernenko (Politburo staff work), Ponomarev (nonruling communist parties), Gorbachev (agriculture), Vladimir I. Dolgikh (heavy industry), Kapitonov (cadres), Konstantin V. Rusakov (ruling communist parties), and Mikhail V. Zimianin (culture).

Republic first secretaries are Karen S. Demichyan (Armenia), Geidar A. Aliev (Azerbaidjan), Tikhon Y. Kiselev (Belorussia), Karl G. Vaino (Estonia), Eduard A. Shevardnadze (Georgia), Dinmukhamed A. Kunaev (Kazakhstan), Turdakun V. Usbaliev (Kirgizia), August E. Voss (Latvia), Piatras P. Griskiavicus (Lithuania), Semen Grossu (Moldavia), Dzhabar R. Rasulov (Tadzhikistan), Mukhamednazar G. Gapurov (Turkmenia), Vladimir V. Shcherbitsky (Ukraine), and Sharaf R. Rashidov (Uzbekistan).

Auxiliary and Mass Organizations. The most important of the many "voluntary" organizations allied with the CPSU is the Communist Youth League (Kommunisticheskii Soyuz Molodezhi; Komsomol), headed by 48-year-old Boris N. Pastukhov. The Komsomol has over 40 million members (*Pravda*, 24 February).

Other large organizations include the All-Union Central Council of Trade Unions, headed by Aleksei I. Shibaev, with a claimed membership of more than 129 million (ibid., 1 March); the Voluntary Society for the Promotion of the Army, Air Force, and Navy, whose members seek to "instill patriotism and pride" in the armed forces; the Union of Soviet Societies for Friendship and Cultural Relations with Foreign Countries; and the Soviet Committee of Women.

Party Internal Affairs. The first seven weeks of the year featured preparations for the Twenty-Sixth CPSU Congress, particularly the usual organizational meetings at all levels. After the congress, party organizations devoted major attention to implementing decisions reached at the February conclave and publicizing the main outlines of the new five-year plan. The congress itself was a rather humdrum affair, filled with speeches praising the leadership's course in foreign and domestic affairs. Some criticisms were voiced about particular deficiencies, but in general the congress failed to confront the serious problems affecting Soviet society. The leadership held fast to its positions, the only important personnel changes being a mild, restricted turnover of Central Committee ranks, marked by further increases in the number of security personnel and Brezhnev clients. "Stability of cadres" appears to have degenerated into virtual total immobility as the aged hierarchs cling tenaciously to power, postponing as long as possible the inevitable generational transfer. Taking their cue from the congress, party ideologists in 1981 emphasized the concept of "developed" or "mature" socialism and the leading role of the party in the "scientific-technical revolution."

Party Congress. The Twenty-Sixth CPSU Congress convened in Moscow on 23 February, during a period of escalating crisis in Poland, rising East-West tensions, severe domestic economic problems, and continuing disarray in the world communist movement. These concerns found expression in major speeches.

The composition of leading party bodies resulting from the congress reflected the aims of stabilization and entrenchment. All 24 officials at the pinnacle of power, in the Politburo and Secretariat, were reconfirmed in their posts (see above). The increase in the size of the Central Committee accentuated prevailing gerontocratic tendencies in the leadership. Additions and deletions lowered the average age (64 in 1980) only slightly; by the Twenty-Seventh Congress in 1986, the average age of full Central Committee members should be close to 70. Prominent new full members included Georgi A. Arbatov, head of the Institute of the U.S.A. and Canada; Georgi M. Kornienko, first deputy minister of foreign affairs; Nikolai V. Talyzin, a deputy prime minister since 1980; and Anatoly G. Yegorov, head of the Institute of Marxism-Leninism (ibid., 4 March). A number of old Brezhnev foes who had lost key party or state positions during the 1970s were dropped from membership: former USSR President Nikolai V. Podgorny, former First Deputy Prime Minister Kiril T. Mazurov, Ambassador to Japan Dimitri S. Polyansky, and former Leningrad party leader Vasili S. Tolstikov. Also missing were former Agriculture Minister Vladimir V. Matskevich; Mikhail A. Lesechko, who "retired" as a deputy prime minister in 1980; and Georgi A. Titov, first deputy head of Gosplan, the State Planning Commission. Most other deletions from membership were "token" workers and women, who usually serve only one term.

Several members of Brezhnev's personal political clique were promoted. His chief foreign policy adviser, Andrei M. Alexandrov-Agentov, was elected a full member of the Central Committee; his aide Anatoly I. Blatov was named a candidate member. His son, Yuri L. Brezhnev, first deputy minister of foreign trade, also attained the rank of candidate member. Most notable was Brezhnev's tightening hold over security organs. Promoted to full membership were three close Brezhnev associates: Semyon K. Tsvigun, first deputy head of the KGB and Brezhnev's brother-in-law, and deputy heads of the KGB Victor M. Chebrikov and Georgi K. Tsinev (*Valeurs actuelles*, Paris, 16 March). Chebrikov is a former first secretary of the city party committee in Dnepropetrovsk, Brezhnev's home base, and Tsinev is a 1934 graduate of the Dnepropetrovsk metallurgical institute. Brezhnev's son-in-law, Lt. Gen. Yuri M. Churbanov, first deputy head of the Ministry of the Interior, was named a candidate member of the Central Committee (*NYT*, 4 March).

The armed forces are also well represented on the new Central Committee. Twenty-three marshals and generals are included among full and candidate members, in addition to several "political" officials of the armed forces and heads of technical services. Armaments Minister P. V. Finogenov, who supervises the activities of twelve other ministries, was elected a full member (*Valeurs actuelles*, 16 March).

The congress was attended by delegations from 109 countries, 13 more than in 1976. Notable absentees included French party leader Georges Marchais, who was campaigning for the presidency of France, and the Italian party's secretary general, Enrico Berlinguer. Berlinguer, but not Marchais, had attended the Twenty-Fifth Congress in 1976. The French party was represented by party secretary and Politburo member Gaston Plissonnier, who told the congress that his party hoped for further development of relations with the CPSU on the "new basis" established during Marchais's visit to Moscow in January 1980 (*Pravda*, 26 February; see also *YICA*, 1981, pp. 386–87). Berlinguer was represented by his deputy Giancarlo Pajetta, who was not allowed to address the congress. At a meeting of parties in the Hall of Columns, chaired by Moscow party chief Viktor V. Grishin, Pajetta questioned Soviet policies on both Afghanistan and Poland and called for a solution in Poland that would respect its "independence and autonomy" and ensure "socialist development, renewal and the national independence for which that people has borne so many sacrifices" (*NYT*, 1 March).

Aside from Plissonnier, the only leaders from nonruling European parties to address the congress were those of Portugal, West Germany, Great Britain, Greece, and Finland (*Pravda*, 25 and 26 February; Tass, 27 February). Among the nonruling parties, only the delegates from Portugal and Ecuador explicitly endorsed the Soviet positions on both Poland and Afghanistan.

In a brief speech to the congress, Cuban party leader Fidel Castro sharply criticized the United States and attributed the difficulties in Poland to a failure to "respect Leninist norms" (*Pravda*, 25 February). Yugoslavia's chief delegate, Dušan Dragosavac, gave a conciliatory speech stressing Tito's friendship with Brezhnev (ibid., 26 February).

The congress was obviously stage-managed to avoid a confrontation with the Eurocommunists and to promote an image of harmony within the world movement. But the CPSU's insistence on Moscow's leadership and "proletarian internationalism" was evident in several speeches, notably that of Vladimir V. Shcherbitsky, long an outspoken critic of Eurocommunism: "History and the laws of class struggle convincingly teach that any attempt to distance oneself from the experience of real socialism, to cast doubt on the international character of Leninism, inevitably leads to a loss of class orientation and, in the last analysis, does tremendous harm to the people of one's country, the world revolutionary process, and the cause of the struggle for peace" (ibid., 24 February).

Brezhnev also reaffirmed the CPSU's opposition to deviations from the Moscow line: "Our party proceeds from the fact that differences of opinion between Communists can be overcome, provided of course that they are not differences of principle—differences between revolutionaries and reformists, between creative Marxism and dogmatic sectarianism or ultra-leftist adventurism. Here of course there can be no compromises." (Tass, 23 February.)

Brezhnev's keynote address was, as usual, the most highly publicized event of the congress. The party leader spoke for only a few minutes and then turned over to an assistant the task of reading the speech (*NYT*, 24 February). The lengthy address was composed of four main sections: "The International Policy of the CPSU"; "The Economic Policy of the CPSU in the Period of Developed Socialism"; "Soviet Society's Socio-Political and Cultural Development and the Tasks of the Party"; and "The Party-Vanguard of the Soviet Political System" (for text, see *Pravda*, 24 February).

Brezhnev maintained that integration of the world socialist system had progressed over the previous five years but acknowledged difficulties: "Far be it from us, comrades, to paint the picture of the present-day socialist world in exclusively radiant colors. Complications, too, occur in the development of our countries." In the past ten years, according to Brezhnev, the economic growth rates of countries belonging to the Council for Mutual Economic Assistance have been twice those of the developed capitalist countries. On the other hand, he admitted that "the past few years have not been among the most favorable for the national economies of some socialist states."

The party leader promised continued support for the defense of the regime in Poland, which was threatened by "opponents of socialism supported by outside forces," and indicated that the crisis in that country was largely due to deficiencies in party leadership: "The events in Poland show once again how important it is for the party, for the strengthening of its leading role, to pay close heed to the voice of the masses, to combat all signs of bureaucratic routine and voluntarism resolutely, to develop socialist democracy actively, and to conduct a considered and realistic policy in foreign economic relations."

In regard to China, Brezhnev concluded that "unfortunately, there are no grounds yet to speak of any changes for the better in Beijing's foreign policy." But, he said, "if Soviet-Chinese relations are still frozen, the reason for this has nothing to do with our position." On Afghanistan, Brezhnev defended the Soviet intervention and praised the Babrak Karmal government. The USSR would be prepared to withdraw its military forces, he said, only when adequate guarantees were obtained against the "infiltration of counterrevolutionary gangs into Afghanistan."

Although voicing standard accusations against "imperialism," Brezhnev appeared to take a relatively low-key approach toward the Third World. In regard to arms control, he reiterated earlier Soviet proposals but offered to extend the "conference zone" (the area in which notification of troop movements is required under the Helsinki agreement) to the entire European part of the USSR in exchange for a corresponding move by NATO. He also presented a revamped proposal for a moratorium on deployment of new medium-range nuclear missiles in Europe and a freeze on existing systems and indicated a willingness to meet with U.S. President Ronald Reagan.

Brezhnev acknowledged domestic economic problems; resolution of these problems, according to Brezhnev, depends mainly on increased productivity. Energy was singled out as a special concern. Already "absorbing the lion's share of capital investments," the demands of the extractive industries would increase during the 1980s. In agriculture, Brezhnev called for increases in forage crops and better support facilities for collective farm production. While "the collective and state farms were and continue to be the mainstay of socialist agriculture," further development of private plot farming was also emphasized. The general secretary also called for the correction of deficiencies in housing construction, production of consumer goods, and quality of products.

The section of the keynote speech devoted to domestic social development was organized around the concepts of "mature socialism" and the "homogenization" of Soviet society. Brezhnev acknowledged that the intelligentsia is the fastest growing social sector but maintained that a process of fusion is taking place between manual and mental labor. He claimed substantial progress in movement toward the classless society: "In evaluating the experience of our society's development over the past few decades, I think we can assume that a classless society will take shape mainly within the historical framework of mature socialism." The most important immediate task in the processes of social homogenization was the lessening of "social distinctions" between different sections of the country. This involves, among other things, the touchy nationalities issue. Brezhnev noted the growth of the non-Russian population and called for respect for "national sensibilities and national dignity." At the same time, he warned against the "artificial inflation" of nationalism and spoke of the "party's sacrosanct duty to educate the people in a spirit of Soviet patriotism and socialist internationalism, to foster a sense of pride in belonging to the integral great Soviet Union."

Presumably influenced by events in Poland, Brezhnev criticized the trade unions for sometimes lacking "initiative" and reacting "inadequately" to breaches of labor law. In the ideological field, Brezhnev returned to a theme emphasized at the second Central Committee plenum of 1978, scoring the use of "hackneyed expressions and ready-made formulas" by the media. The Komsomol also came in for criticism; Brezhnev said that it should devote more attention to "labor training, moral upbringing, and ideological and political education."

Party congresses are timed to coincide with the inception of five-year plans. The congress approved the general outlines of the next plan (*Pravda* and *Izvestiia*, 3 March) but left detailed consideration to the fall session of the Supreme Soviet. Under the Eleventh Five-Year Plan, national income was scheduled to increase by 18–20 percent, industrial production by 26–28 percent, and agricultural production by 12–14 percent (*Izvestiia*, 24 February).

Prime Minister Nikolai A. Tikhonov delivered the major economic report to the congress. He claimed an increase of around 16 percent in personal income (26 percent rise for collective farmers) during the Tenth Five-Year Plan. He also reported that over 50 million people had received improved housing. However, he noted important shortcomings: low labor productivity, slow development of individual branches of the economy, and dispersion of investment. The main reason for these shortcomings, Tikhonov said, is that "we have not done away with the force of inertia and the traditions and habits left over from the period when the accent was placed not so much on quality as on quantity." (Ibid., 28 February.)

The party first secretaries of Kazakhstan, Uzbekistan, and Turkmenia all called for rapid implementation of the project to divert part of the flow of some Siberian rivers southward for irrigation purposes. Dinmukhamed A. Kunaev said that one of the main issues of Kazakhstan's economy is the problem of water supply and urged completion of the preparatory work for the diversion project (Tass, 24 February; *FBIS*, 25 February). However, Brezhnev and Tikhonov made no reference to this key project in their speeches.

The congress adopted a resolution calling for the preparation of a new party program to be presented at the Twenty-Seventh CPSU Congress in 1986; this will replace the program adopted at the Twenty-Second Congress in 1961. That document, drafted at the behest of Khrushchev, had predicted that the USSR would surpass the United States in all major areas of production by 1980. A front-page *Izvestiia* editorial (7 March) attributed this proposal to the "great deal of experience of socialist and communist building" accumulated over the past twenty years and to "new changes and processes" that "have occurred in the international arena" during that period.

Organizational Matters. Lower-level party organizations held follow-up meetings concerning implementation of the congress's decisions, notably those related to the Eleventh Five-Year Plan and to ideological work. Typical was the June plenum of the Moscow committee, which passed a resolution promising to "persistently improve ideological and political education work" and "actively assist in implementation of the tasks of the next stage of construction of communism" (*Pravda*, 4 June).

In August, the Central Committee published a resolution entitled "On the Further Improvement of Party Studies in Light of the Decisions of the Twenty-Sixth CPSU Congress." The resolution provided for the reorganization and upgrading of party schools "in line with the demands of developed socialism" and instructed that propagandists should not be "overloaded with other assignments" (ibid., 11 August).

Another August resolution of the Central Committee dealt with the monitoring and verification of performance in party organizations. The Central Committee criticized tendencies toward a "pro forma approach to the organization and monitoring of performance," the forwarding of unnecessary resolutions, and the substitution of conferences, reports, and briefing papers for real organizational work (ibid., 16 August).

Evidently reflecting a widespread organizational problem, *Pravda* (4 June) published an article in June denouncing nonpayment of party dues. The author, V. Leshchinsky, an administrator of the Moldavian Central Committee, cited instances in which communists avoided proper dues by failing to declare all their earnings.

Ideology. Mikhail A. Suslov, Central Committee secretary for ideology and Politburo member, published a lengthy article in April on "developed socialism," interpreting the decisions of the Twenty-Sixth CPSU Congress in relation to that concept (*Partiinaia zhizn*, no. 8, April). Suslov stressed "the steadily increasing role of the party in our life" under "developed socialism" and the elimination of social distinctions. Whereas Brezhnev, at the party congress, had emphasized territorial disparities, Suslov played up the "distinctions between the town and the countryside." The Twenty-Sixth CPSU Congress, called by Suslov the "Congress of the Creators," had set the course for solution of this and other problems.

Suslov said that the "new man" was progressively changing from "an ideal of a remote future into an object of the party's actual concern." In this connection, it was necessary to combat "philistine mentality, avidity, and money-grubbing" and "indifferent attitudes" and to promote ideological, political, and educational work. Here Suslov delivered a sharp criticism of his own sector of the party apparatus: "The remodeling of political, educational, and propaganda work is going on slowly and there is a lack of vigor in overcoming the existing essential shortcomings."

The Soviet media reaffirmed the party's adhesion to "proletarian internationalism" and its opposition to revisionism, reformism, and Eurocommunism expressed in the late 1970s by such spokesmen as Konstantin I. Zarodov (the Kremlin's leading exponent of revolutionary violence) and Vladimir Shcherbitsky. Several articles appearing in the first half of 1981 denounced the concept of "new internationalism," put forward by the Italian party to replace the doctrine of "proletarian internationalism" and to describe its relations with East and West European communist parties and with noncommunist organizations in Western Europe (Radio Liberty, 1 July). Boris N. Ponomarev, head of the Central Committee's International Department, denied that "proletarian internationalism" was obsolete and that there was a need "to replace it by some kind of new internationalism" (*Kommunist*, no. 5, March). Vadim V. Zagladin, deputy head of the International Department, wrote: "The appeal of the supporters of the "new internationalism" to replace the class solidarity of the communist parties by a diffuse alliance with all forces struggling for general democratic goals within the framework of the existing system is absolutely unacceptable" (*Mirovaia ekonomika i mezhdunarodne otnosheniia*, no. 4). Yuri Krasin, an official of the Academy of Social Sciences, agreed that the "new internationalism" meant a jettisoning of the class approach and added: "The Marxist-Leninists are opposed to the dissolution of the communist movement in some sort of boundless and amorphous internationalism" (*Novoe vremia*, no. 7, February).

Domestic Policies. The primary domestic concern of the CPSU during the year was again the economy. Sluggish economic performance and low productivity constituted major worries for the leadership, but no fundamental reforms to cope with long-standing, underlying problems were envisioned. In agriculture, the collective farm system headed for its third straight year of poor harvests. On the energy front, long-term prospects appeared brighter than previously believed in the West, but there were transitional difficulties in adjusting to the changed requirements of the 1980s. Meanwhile, the security organs continued their relentless repression of dissent amid indications of growing tensions among minorities in Georgia, Central Asia, and the Baltic republics.

Economy. First-quarter economic reports for 1981 showed disappointing results at the outset of the Eleventh Five-Year Plan. Average daily industrial production reportedly increased by 4.2 percent and labor productivity by 2.3 percent. However, production declined in a number of industries, notably coal, steel pipes, petroleum apparatus, chemical equipment, timber, and motor vehicles. Labor productivity was down in the power and electrification, petroleum, coal, and metallurgy industries. Overall production increases were modest in most republics, and Moldavia recorded a decline. (*Ekonomicheskaia gazeta*, 26 May.)

In a May interview, N. Rogovsky, chief of the Gosplan Labor Department, candidly admitted failures in labor productivity and cautioned against "naive" overconfidence in the goals set under the new plan. Most important, according to Rogovsky, is the introduction of labor-saving equipment, which is to account for at least 60 percent of the total increase in labor productivity over the next five years, and the provision of added incentives by tying wage increases more closely to increases in labor productivity (*Sotsialisticheskaia industriia*, 17 May).

In May, the U.S. Central Intelligence Agency revised its 1977 forecasts concerning Soviet oil production in the 1980s. Analysts had predicted that the USSR would have to import as much as 3.5 million barrels of oil a day by 1985, with domestic production limited to 8–10 million barrels per day. The May estimate placed 1985 Soviet daily production at 10–11 million barrels. Some U.S. State Department officials said the new projection may prove to be an underestimate. The Eleventh Five-Year Plan calls for oil production of 12.4–12.9 million barrels per day in 1985. (*NYT*, 18 May.)

Natural gas production was one of the few major areas in which the Soviet economy met its targets for 1980 (*CSM*, 8 June). However, in January it was announced that natural gas deliveries to West Germany and Austria in the first quarter of the year would be cut by one-third due to technical problems in the Soviet distribution system (*NYT*, 10 January). In August, the new minister of the gas industry, Vasili A. Dinkov, announced a shift in natural-gas strategy designed to save a billion rubles in development costs. The Yamburg arctic gas field was to have been a major supplier of West Germany and other European countries; under revised plans, the Soviets will concentrate on the Urengoi field, 150 miles to the south of Yamburg (*Sovetskaia rossiia*, 1 August). In the current five-year plan, investment in the gas industry, most of it in Siberia, is to be 20 billion rubles, twice the amount invested in 1976–1980 (*NYT*, 21 August).

Soviet spokesmen habitually claim that the USSR is immune to the inflation that plagues Western economies. However, in September the government announced major price increases, including a doubling of gasoline prices and a 17–25 percent rise in tobacco and vodka prices (ibid., 20 September).

Gosplan head Nikolai K. Baibakov told the Supreme Soviet in November that goals for 1981 would not be met in the coal, iron, and steel industries, but did not specify the extent of the shortfalls. At the same time, Baibakov announced a downward revision of planned growth in capital investment during the period of the new five-year plan. In March, growth in capital investment had been projected at 12 to 15 percent; Baibakov estimated the growth rate at 10.4 percent. (*Pravda* and *Izvestiia*, 18 November.)

Following poor grain harvests of 179 million tons in 1979 and 189 million tons in 1980, the Soviet Union appeared headed for another poor harvest in 1981. In early September, the U.S. Department of Agriculture estimated the Soviet harvest at 185 million tons, some 20 percent below the official target of 236 million. Soviet agricultural specialists were said to have told Western diplomats that the yield would be somewhat better than 185 million tons (*NYT*, 1 September). A 28 August article in *Izvestiia* appeared to set the stage for forthcoming bad news. The article dealt with serious problems affecting wheat, feed grain, and oil seed production and noted that soil moisture in most areas had been only 75 percent of normal. Continuing food shortages were indicated by first-quarter figures that showed production of butter and vegetable oil both at 93 percent and meat and sausage products both at 99 percent of output for the corresponding period in 1980 (*Ekonomicheskaia gazeta*, 11 May).

The Central Committee and the Supreme Soviet were told in November that food production was down, but no exact figures were given. Meanwhile, the U.S. Department of Agriculture reduced its estimate of the Soviet grain harvest to 175 million tons. Soviet grain imports, 28 million tons in 1981, were expected to rise to 43 million tons in 1982, half of this from the United States. (*NYT*, 17 November.)

At the fall plenum of the Central Committee, Brezhnev unveiled a comprehensive program for revamping the farm economy. The proposals called for decentralization of decision-making processes, incentives to encourage local initiative, more storage facilities, and fuller use of private plots. On the same occasion, Brezhnev made a statement that attracted attention in the Western press: "The food problem is, economically and politically, the central problem of the five-year plan." (*Pravda*, 17 November.)

Dissent. Andrei Sakharov, banished to internal exile in Gorky in 1980, remained the acknowledged leader of the dwindling dissident community, but the KGB has reportedly tightened the conditions of his house arrest. Statements by Sakharov on such matters as the Polish strikes and Western human rights policies were smuggled out of the USSR by his wife, Yelena Bonner. In May, Mrs. Sakharov reported that Soviet authorities had reacted to the worldwide campaign for her husband's release by harassing the fiancée of his stepson, who now lives in the United States. Liza Alexeyeva had been refused permission to emigrate and had been questioned by the KGB (*Times*, London, 22 May). During the summer, the couple were married by proxy in Montana, a ceremony that the USSR does not recognize. On 22 November, Sakharov and his wife began a hunger strike to protest the refusal of Soviet authorities to permit Liza Alexeyeva's emigration to the United States (AP, 25 November). On 4 December, the Sakharovs were hospitalized on government orders to "prevent any complications in the state of their health" (*NYT*, 5 December). An official statement called the fast "a fresh provocation calculated to attract the attention of the West to Sakharov's anti-Soviet views" (*Izvestiia*, 4 December). A day after the forced hospitalization of the Sakharovs, Liza Alexeyeva was reportedly picked up by the KGB, threatened, and released (AP, 5 December). In the meantime, a huge movement in support of the Sakharovs and against the policy of the Soviet government was organized around the world. A prominent French weekly wrote that the Soviets did not dare let Sakharov die: "For he had the entire world behind him, Mitterrand, Reagan, the pope, scores of Nobel prize winners. Never, since the disappearance of Gandhi in 1948, did a hunger strike provoke such emotion. Suddenly the Soviet apparatus had to give up and to reverse its decision" (*l'Express*, Paris, 18 December). Liza Alexeyeva was informed on 8 December that she would receive an exit visa; simultaneously, after seventeen days, the Sakharovs, exhausted but triumphant, ended their hunger strike.

A rally at U.N. headquarters in May in support of Jews prevented from emigrating from the USSR was attended by an estimated 150,000 people. Guests of honor included the wife of imprisoned human rights activist Anatoly Shcharansky and Iosif Mendelevich, freed in February after serving a prison term for an attempted airplane hijacking in Leningrad in 1970. Major speakers at the rally included New York City Mayor Edward Koch, Jane Fonda, and President Reagan's national security adviser, Richard V. Allen (*NYT*, 1 June).

The son and grandson of the late Soviet composer Dimitri Shostakovich defected to the West in April (ibid., 13 April). Maxim Shostakovich, conductor of the Soviet Radio Symphony Orchestra, and his son Dimitri, pianist for the orchestra, defected while on tour in West Germany and were granted political asylum in the United States (ibid., 15 April). The Soviet media waited more than three weeks to announce the defection, then denounced Maxim Shostakovich as a "conceited egotist" and a "parasite" (*Literaturnaia gazeta*, 9 May).

Two Estonian dissidents were sentenced to labor camps in January on charges of "anti-Soviet agitation" (AP, 9 January). Mart Niklus, 46, was sentenced to ten years in a labor camp and five years of internal exile for signing documents that included an appeal for autonomy of the Baltic republics. Yuri Kukk, 40, received a two-year term. In March, it was reported that Kukk had died in a labor camp near Murmansk (*NYT*, 28 March).

The security organs maintained the drive to silence the few remaining prominent members of the major human rights activist groups. Members of the "Helsinki monitoring groups" sentenced to labor camps or internal exile included Aleksandr Lavut (December 1980), Malva Landa (March 1981), and Tatiana Osipova (April 1981). Two members of the Commission for the Study of the Use of Psychiatry for Political Ends were arrested in early 1981, Feliks Serebrov in January and Anatoly Koriagin in February. "Free trade union" movement leader Aleksei Nikitin was confined to a psychiatric hospital in December 1980, and Mark Morozov of the same group was sentenced to labor camp in January 1981. The samizdat magazine *Poiski* (Research) was finally silenced with the sentencing of the last of its editors, Viktor Sorokin. Three other leading dissident writers, Vladimir Voinovich, Vasili Aksionov, and Lev Kopelev, were expelled from the USSR in December 1980. (*La Croix*, Paris, 15 April.) One of the veterans of the human rights movement, Genrikh O. Altunyan, was sentenced in March, after a trial in Kharkov, to seven years in strict-regime labor camps and five years of internal exile (UPI, 2 April; Radio Liberty, 12 May).

Despite severe pressures from the authorities, dissident activity continued. The main samizdat journal, *Chronicle of Current Events*, was still publishing, although on a highly irregular schedule. Two documents of the Lithuanian Helsinki Monitoring Group appeared in February, charging gross violations of the human rights of dissidents in Lithuania and Estonia (Radio Liberty, 22 May).

Nationalities. Emigration of Jews from the Soviet Union declined in 1980. More than 50,000 Jews had been allowed to leave in 1979; in 1980, coinciding with the freeze in U.S.-Soviet relations, the figure was down to 21,471 (*NYT*, 4 January). There was a temporary upsurge on the eve of the Twenty-Sixth CPSU Congress, but by late March emigration had declined to a monthly average of about a thousand, and police were reportedly dispersing crowds of applicants outside the visa office in Moscow (*Baltimore Sun*, 19 March).

There were strong indications of growing uneasiness about the security and stability of predominantly Muslim areas of the USSR. In December 1980, an article by Maj. Gen. Ziya M. Yusif-Zade, head of the Azerbaidjan state security police, and a speech by Geidar A. Aliev, Azerbaidjan party first secretary, called for "increased vigilance" of citizens and "heightened effectiveness" and coordination of security organs to cope with threats of subversion (*Bakinsky rabochi*, 19 and 25 December 1980; *NYT*, 8 January). The prime minister of Kirghizia was murdered on 4 December 1980; according to some reports, Muslim nationalists were responsible. The presidium of the Supreme Soviet, meeting on 6 January, included in its agenda a discussion of local efforts in Kirghizia and the Kursk region to "strengthen law and order and increase the struggle against violation of the law" (*Pravda*, 7 January).

Two major demonstrations related to nationalities policy occurred in Georgia's capital city Tbilisi in March. On 23 March, about one thousand students protested against the dismissal from Tbilisi University of literary critic Akaki Bakhradze, who was subsequently reinstated. On 30 March, some one thousand intellectuals demonstrated in front of the Supreme Soviet building in Tbilisi, demanding that Georgian history be included in the curricula of the republic's schools and colleges and protesting against trials of Georgians living in the Abkhaz Autonomous Republic, where strong protests have been lodged in recent years against Georgian domination (AFP, 4 April; FBIS, 6 April).

Several nationalist demonstrations were reported in Estonia in September and October 1980. In a report to the Estonian party congress in January, party chief Karl G. Vaino complained about "particularly glaring manifestations of blinkered national attitudes on the part of ideologically and politically immature people" (Sovetskaia Estonia, 29 January). However, speaking at the Twenty-Sixth CPSU Congress, he attributed the nationalist discontent to "anti-Soviet propaganda" from Western "bourgeois propaganda centers" (Pravda, 27 February).

International Views and Policies. Soviet foreign policy during the year was preoccupied with the crisis in Poland, the dramatically altered context of relations with the United States, and questions of arms reductions and the nuclear balance. All of these concerns were linked in the Soviet search for a strategy that would preserve the gains in the world power balance the USSR achieved during the 1960s and 1970s and at minimal cost. Geographically, this meant concentration on Western and Central Europe, with an apparent downgrading for the near future of the Soviet goal of a rapid "restructuring of international relations" keyed primarily to the Third World.

The USSR had scored significant gains during the 1970s by using proxies in Africa and Asia and building up its nuclear and conventional armaments at a steady pace during a period of Western military retrenchment. Skillfully exploiting the aura of détente, the Soviets advanced their global interests and put forward realistic claims concerning a decisive change in their favor of the world "correlation of forces." But the era of cheap victories ended abruptly with the December 1980 invasion of Afghanistan. During 1980, the Soviets appeared to accept the end of détente grudgingly, while leaving options open for the future and attempting to cope with critical situations in Poland and Afghanistan. During 1981, the outlines of a broad strategy to meet the international turnabout of 1979–1980 began to emerge, although major ambiguities remained. Soviet spokesmen continued to affirm their favorable position in the world correlation of forces, but it was clear that dangers posed by bloc incohesion and a newly activist American foreign policy had brought into question the optimistic assessments regularly advanced by the Soviets in recent years.

The year was marked by numerous charges and countercharges between Washington and Moscow, enhancing the acrimonious "cold war" atmosphere in superpower relations. But vehement propaganda blasts against the United States were accompanied by the blandishments of a new Soviet "peace offensive." The Soviets stoutly rejected "linkage" of superpower negotiations with restraint by the USSR in its international behavior, as envisioned by American leaders, and issued calls for renewed talks to prevent a spiraling arms race. Continuing the campaign to stop deployment of Pershing and cruise missiles in Western Europe, Moscow welcomed the upsurge of pacifist and neutralist sentiment in Western Europe, which culminated in massive demonstrations in Bonn, London, and Rome in October. While pursuing its "peace offensive," the USSR continued to deploy the SS-20 intermediate range missiles, which had inspired the NATO plans for a modernization of Western strategic arms. By July, the Soviets had reportedly installed 160 of the SS-20 missiles, with deployment proceeding at the rate of one per week (Los Angeles Times, 24 June).

At the Twenty-Sixth Congress, Brezhnev offered to meet with President Reagan (Tass, 23 February). This appeal evoked only a lukewarm response from Washington, and Brezhnev tried again in early summer. On three occasions in June, he accused the United States of avoiding arms talks. At the Supreme Soviet meeting, Brezhnev blamed the United States for starting an "unprecedented" arms race that was raising the risk of nuclear conflict and called on Western nations to press for prompt negotiations (*Pravda*, 24 June).

Both sides faced political and economic pressures prompting efforts to curb a new round of escalation of armaments. In September it was announced that the United States and the Soviet Union would begin negotiations in Geneva on 30 November on the reduction of nuclear arms in Europe (AP, 24 September). Essentially, there was an implicit agreement that both countries would proceed with plans for deployment while their representatives talked. Negotiations on the control of intercontinental missiles were expected to begin in early 1982, according to Reagan administration officials (ibid., 25 October).

Poland continued to be a major irritant in Soviet-U.S. relations. The disastrous condition of the Polish economy created enormous burdens for the entire Soviet bloc; the USSR pledged assistance, but its own economic woes precluded a unilateral salvage operation for Poland, which is virtually bankrupt and unable to service its huge debts to West European countries. Meanwhile, the forces pressing for internal democratization in Poland, led by the Solidarity labor union, attenuated communist control of that country and posed the danger of spillover effects in other bloc countries, including the Soviet Union itself. Soviet military intervention seemed the most obvious answer to the problem. But Soviet military forces were already heavily committed in Afghanistan, and an invasion of Poland would almost guarantee Western economic reprisals and accelerated rearmament. Such a move might also trigger guerrilla warfare in Poland; some military estimates placed the personnel requirements for such an operation at one million men. Reluctant to incur the heavy liabilities that an invasion would entail, the USSR used its political, economic, and military power to exert relentless psychological pressure on Polish leaders and Polish dissidents.

Moscow sought to keep its hand in the tumultuous Middle Eastern arena by forging closer relations with Syria, reaffirming support for the Palestinians, and repeating calls for a general settlement of conflicts in the region through an international conference that would include the Soviet Union. The Soviets scored a diplomatic success in May when Jordan's King Hussein visited Moscow and endorsed the Soviet proposal for an international conference (Tass, 26 May). Moscow reacted with formal coolness to the assassination of Egyptian President Anwar Sadat in October but responded sharply to subsequent American initiatives to contain Libya. In late October, Brezhnev soundly condemned U.S. "interference" in the region directed against Libya and renewed his call for an international peace conference (*Pravda*, 28 October).

Soviet-U.S. Relations. Soviet leaders assumed a somewhat conciliatory stance toward Ronald Reagan following his election as president in November 1980. Early in the new year, the Soviets appeared to maintain a wait-and-see attitude, hoping that, like former President Nixon, his reputation as an anticommunist would not be sustained under the pressures of the presidency. If the Kremlin entertained hopes of defusing Reagan's militant opposition to Soviet objectives, some circles were evidently not so sanguine; at the beginning of the year, the armed forces newspaper published a sharply critical article (*Krasnaia zvezda*, 4 January). Nevertheless, in line with the apparent overriding priorities of preventing Western redress of the arms imbalance and stabilizing Central Europe, the Kremlin tentatively offered a bit of olive branch on the eve of Reagan's inauguration. Foreign Minister Gromyko published an article in which he hinted at a softening of the Soviet stance on negotiations for both general arms limitations and missiles in Europe (*Kommunist*, no. 2, January).

Although wary of Reagan, the Soviets were apparently quite unprepared for the unprecedented barrage of anti-Soviet rhetoric that issued from Washington's highest levels in the first days of the new administration. Reagan, at his first press conference, said that Soviet leaders used any methods, including lies, cheating, and crimes, to pursue their expansionist aims (*NYT*, 1 February). Alexander Haig, at his first press conference as secretary of state, accused the Soviets of being the primary supporter of international terrorism (AP, 30 January). The Soviet media replied with personal attacks on Reagan and a long statement charging that the United States, not the Soviet Union, was the center of international terrorism (Tass, 1 February).

Charges and countercharges continued during February, but Brezhnev was not deterred by the tense atmosphere; at the Twenty-Sixth CPSU Congress, he fired the first major shot of Moscow's 1981 "peace offensive." Presenting an eight-point peace program that was largely a rehash of old Soviet proposals, he attracted most attention by suggesting a summit meeting with President Reagan (ibid., 23 February). At first, Secretary Haig expressed U.S. interest in Brezhnev's proposals but shortly reverted to the theme of "linkage." He called for a "climate of greater reciprocity and restraint" and dashed hopes for an early summit meeting: "It should not be undertaken unless the prospects for success and the outcome of such summitry is promising" (AP, 27 February).

The summit turndown was probably not unexpected. Subsequently the Soviets continued to press for negotiations, with the expressed aim of freezing the status quo in Europe. In the absence of such talks, the Soviets proceeded feverishly with installation of their SS-20 missiles in Eastern Europe, projected an image of flexibility presumably designed to at least delay West European adhesion to NATO rearmament plans, and encouraged the pacifism burgeoning in West European countries by depicting those countries as the arena of nuclear war if U.S. strategy were to be implemented. Meanwhile, Soviet analysts presented a consistent line regarding NATO missile plans: nuclear symmetry or balance characterized existing deployments; the United States was seeking to upset the balance in a vain search for nuclear superiority; consequently, the United States, not the USSR, was the source of a "nuclear threat" and the instigator of an accelerated arms race.

Georgi A. Arbatov, director of the Institute of the U.S.A. and Canada, summarized the Soviet position in an authoritative article in the party's theoretical journal in late April. Arbatov viewed recent American strategic pronouncements as simply a reflection of the consistent aim, extending over three or four U.S. administrations, to secure nuclear superiority over the USSR. Whenever the United States contemplated a new weapons system, according to Arbatov, its military circles attributed to the Soviet Union the nuclear superiority that they wished to obtain for the United States. As for the present situation, he claimed existence of an overall balance between the superpowers: "The existing disproportion between the USSR and the United States in terms of land-based strategic missiles reflects the objective, historically established difference in the military-technological development of the two powers and their geographic position, and . . . the particular advantages of the Soviet Union are counterbalanced, in a general relation of strategic forces, by other factors favorable for the United States." The stability of this nuclear balance was threatened, according to Arbatov, not by the USSR but by the United States, with a series of technological breakthroughs, including MIRV, the MX, Trident 1 and 2, and the cruise missile. "The continuous shift of the world alignment of forces throughout the seventies," this analyst continued, prompted attempts by the imperialists "to replay détente in their favor if not scuttle it altogether" and to embark on a new quest for military supremacy. If the United States persisted in pushing the arms race, Arbatov said, the USSR would accept the challenge: "In the USSR economy, science and technology are at such a high level that we can develop in a very short time any type of weapons on which the enemies of peace would like to make a stake. . . The Soviet Union did not let, and will not let, anyone talk to it in language of threats and blackmail. . . Equally futile are the plans for the 'economic exhaustion' of the USSR by an unrestricted arms race." (*Kommunist*, no. 6, April.)

In May, Lt. Gen. Nikolai Chervov of the Soviet General Staff claimed that NATO held a superiority of about 1.5 to 1 in nuclear explosive power of medium-range missiles in Europe. The USSR, Chervov said, had actually decreased both the number and the total destructive power of its medium-range missiles (DPA, Hamburg, 14 May; *FBIS*, 15 May). In the same week, *Krasnaia zvezda* (10 May) charged that the U.S. strategy was to delay or prolong arms talks "until the moment when all 572 American missiles are set up in position and targeted on the Soviet Union." Reporting on the Mutual and Balanced Force Reduction talks in Vienna, Tass claimed that the USSR had withdrawn 20,000 of its troops from Central Europe while U.S. forces in West Germany had increased by 31,000 over four years. The Soviet delegation at Vienna renewed Brezhnev's call for a freeze on the existing quantitative and qualitative level of nuclear weapons in Europe (Tass, 29 May; *FBIS*, 1 June).

In a June interview, Moscow television political analyst Valentin Zorin maintained that Western discussions of a "balance" are distorted by failure to include American weapons deployed in a forward position. When these are included, he said, there exists "an equilibrium in every sense in Europe." Further, "the deployment of the 600 new American missiles is an attempt to upset the balance in favor of the West, the United States, and NATO" (Budapest Domestic Service, 23 June; *FBIS*, 25 June). At the Madrid session of the Conference on Security and Cooperation in Europe, Soviet Deputy Foreign Minister Leonid F. Ilyichev chided the NATO countries for failure to respond to Brezhnev's proposal on extension of the "confidence zone" (*Izvestiia*, 18 June).

The views expressed by these analysts and officials were definitely confirmed as Soviet policy in several public statements by Brezhnev. Speaking in Kiev in May, the Soviet leader said that the USSR favored a "broad dialogue" with the West on arms limitations but was ready to respond to any military challenge (*Pravda*, 10 May). In June, Brezhnev charged that Washington was "using all sorts of pretexts" to delay the start of arms control talks and that the new U.S. administration had taken "no real steps" to begin discussions on strategic arms limitations and medium-range missiles in Europe (ibid., 10 June). In a speech to the Supreme Soviet in late June, Brezhnev again accused the United States of evading arms control talks and called on Western legislatures to press Washington for prompt negotiations. He blamed the United States for starting an "unprecedented" arms race and said that "launching pads are being prepared for hundreds more nuclear missiles in Western Europe" (ibid., 24 June).

After President Reagan decided to proceed with production of the neutron bomb (*NYT*, 7 August), the campaign against the American arms buildup accelerated. The Reagan decision was denounced as an "aggravation of the threat of nuclear war," as "monstrous," and as "an extremely dangerous act of playing with fire" (*Pravda*, 10 and 11 August; *Izvestiia*, 11 August). Meanwhile, Moscow encouraged the growth of pacifist opposition to the projected NATO missile deployments in West European countries, usually spearheaded by left-wing elements in the social-democratic parties. Typically, Western opponents of the NATO plans mildly criticized the USSR for deployment of the SS-20 but concentrated their protests upon the United States. In October, a huge rally in Bonn attended by large numbers of Social Democratic Party (SPD) deputies protested against the NATO deployments; two weeks later, massive demonstrations were held in London, Rome, Paris, Brussels, and Oslo (*NYT*, 10 and 26 October).

While posing as the champion of peace, Moscow also brandished the stick of its military power. In March, the USSR successfully tested a satellite-killer missile; in the autumn, reports circulated in the West that this missile was now operational. Soviet spokesmen repeatedly stressed that the USSR would match any Western buildup. In July, Moscow emphasized this threat in an article by Nikolai V. Ogarkov, army chief of staff and first deputy defense minister. Ogarkov said that the USSR had begun to strengthen its strategic nuclear arsenal to counter increased U.S. military spending: "Special attention is being given to those forces and weapons that ensure the highest degree of might in the Army and Navy. The first component of this might in modern conditions is the strategic nuclear force, which serves as the basic factor to deter an aggressor." (*Kommunist*, no. 10, July.)

Despite the heated polemics, U.S. and Soviet diplomats made progress in getting arms limitations negotiations back on course. In June, Secretary Haig announced that he would meet USSR Foreign

Minister Gromyko at the United Nations in September to set a date for formal negotiations on limiting new nuclear missiles in Europe (*NYT*, 7 June). When Gromyko addressed the United Nations in September, he denounced the United States on the issues of Poland, El Salvador, Cuba, and Libya, but said that his country desires "normal business-like relations with the United States" (ibid., 23 September). As Gromyko spoke, Washington announced that President Reagan had dispatched a letter to Brezhnev offering to discuss "the entire range of issues dividing the two countries" and saying that the United States is prepared to "establish a framework of mutual respect" with the Soviet Union (AP, 22 September). Following the meeting between Haig and Gromyko, a joint U.S.-Soviet communiqué announced that negotiations on control of nuclear weapons in Europe would begin on 30 November in Geneva (*NYT*, 25 September). American officials later indicated that talks on controlling international missiles were expected to begin in early 1982 (AP, 25 October).

On the eve of Brezhnev's scheduled visit to Bonn in November, Reagan offered not to deploy new American missiles in Europe if the Soviets would dismantle their forward missiles targeted at Western Europe (*NYT*, 19 November). Following talks with West German Chancellor Helmut Schmidt in Bonn, Brezhnev rejected Reagan's proposal and reiterated the USSR's call for a moratorium on missile deployment. If the United States accepted such a freeze, Brezhnev said, as "a gesture of goodwill" the Soviets would "unilaterally" reduce the number of medium-range nuclear weapons in the European part of the USSR (ibid., 24 November). The Geneva talks began as scheduled on 30 November, with initial bargaining positions evidently set by Brezhnev's and Reagan's public statements. However, the talks began in an apparently cordial atmosphere. The two sides agreed to meet twice a week and to maintain the confidentiality of the negotiations (AP, 2 December). Following the establishment on 13 December of martial law and the military regime in Poland, which the U.S. government believed was preplanned and manipulated by the Soviet Union, there were speculations that as a measure of retaliation President Reagan might suspend the Geneva talks. It did not happen during the remaining part of the year.

Arms limitations had been one "functional area" identified by Secretary Haig in late February as "linked" to "greater reciprocity and restraint"; other such "functional areas" included trade, credits, technology transfers, and agricultural supports (ibid., 27 February). Soviet spokesman Leonid M. Zamyatin, head of the Foreign Information Department of the CPSU Central Committee, claimed in a press conference at the party congress that this "linkage" relating to trade was hurting the United States because "we can get similar types of goods in other countries." Zamyatin charged that "certain elements in the U.S. who aren't interested in détente are seeking to use trade with the Soviet Union for political ends" (*Wall Street Journal*, 2 March). After the United States imposed a partial grain embargo and increased restrictions on high-technology exports, U.S.-Soviet trade dropped 56 percent in 1980, to a five-year low of $1.96 billion (ibid).

Fulfilling a campaign pledge, the Reagan administration lifted the grain embargo in April (*NYT*, 25 April). This move raised serious questions about the proclaimed strategy of linkage since the Soviets were maintaining the intervention in Afghanistan, which had inspired the embargo and were threatening Poland. Lifting of the embargo was followed by an agreement allowing the Soviet Union to purchase up to nine million metric tons of additional U.S. wheat and corn. However, at the same time, the United States made sales of surplus butter to other countries contingent on assurances that none would be resold to the Soviet Union (*WP*, 10 June.)

However uncertain the application of linkage by the United States, it seemed clear that Washington's criteria for measuring Soviet "restraint" had little to do with Soviet internal politics. Instead of the Carter administration's emphasis upon "human rights," the Reagan leadership spotlighted Soviet military expansionism and support for "national liberation movements." If U.S. pressure had a restraining effect in such trouble spots as Afghanistan, Poland, and the Middle East, it was obviously only one of many factors in the calculations of a Soviet leadership burdened by a plethora of commitments and crises. In one particular geographical area, Central America, U.S. charges drew vehement Soviet denials.

At a February press conference, Reagan said that the Soviet role in arming the rebels in El Salvador "would be one of the things that should be straightened out" prior to a summit meeting (AP, 24 February). Speaking for Soviet leaders, Leonid Zamyatin denied that the USSR had shipped arms to El Salvador and said that "the President is absolutely incorrect" (*NYT*, 26 February). This and subsequent denials failed to impress the new American administration, which continued to insist that Soviet involvement in the region, both directly and through Cuban proxies, was increasing. In July, Secretary Haig said that the State Department had noted "with increasing concern" the shipment of sophisticated armaments to Nicaragua from the Soviet Union, Libya, and Cuba (ibid., 3 June).

Poland. At the outset of the year, many Western analysts anticipated an imminent Soviet military intervention in Poland. The Kremlin was confronted with the gravest threat to bloc cohesion since the Prague Spring of 1968. Indeed, given the existence of a mixed economy in Poland, toleration for the Catholic church, and the growing power of the independent labor union Solidarity, deviation from Soviet norms had by far exceeded that of the Prague Spring. But departure from a Moscow-approved model of socialism was probably less important than the threat to the Soviets' military dominance of the road to Germany. With Poland virtually surrounded by Warsaw Pact forces and with these forces in motion much of the year, it seemed only a matter of time before Soviet forces moved in. Nevertheless, through the spring and summer, as the Polish economic crisis intensified and communist political control in the country weakened, Moscow resisted the temptation, evidently wary of the heavy costs that an intervention would entail. Instead, the Soviet leadership maintained intense pressure on the PUWP and the Polish government to bring the situation under control.

Both Solidarity and the Warsaw regime's toleration of that dissident organization drew scathing criticism from Moscow throughout the year. In January, when the five-day workweek was the immediate issue raised by Solidarity, the Soviet media depicted the economic issue as a cover for the political aim of replacing the socialist regime; Solidarity was attacked as a counterrevolutionary organization opposed to the communist party (*Izvestiia*, 9 January; *Pravda*, 10 January; Tass, 1 11, and 25 January). *Pravda* (8 January) denounced Adam Michnik, a leading theoretician of the free trade-union movement and a close associate of Solidarity leader Lech Walesa, as one of those "renegades who seek to speak on behalf of the Polish people" in an attempt to attract support for "hostile and subversive outbursts against the socialist state."

Indications that the U.S. government considered Poland crucial to the developing linkage strategy and open support for Solidarity by American trade unions predictably aroused Moscow's ire. Soviet spokesmen charged that the United States was attempting to detach Poland from the socialist system and the Warsaw Treaty Organization (WTO) (Tass, 20 and 24 January; *Krasnaia zvezda*, 28 January).

At the Twenty-Sixth Congress, the Soviets set the pattern for their rhetorical approach to the Polish crisis. Several bilateral and international conferences involving Polish leaders during the year were marked by words of encouragement from Soviet representatives or their proxies and expressions of confidence that the Poles could solve their own problems, combined with criticisms of past "mistakes" by the Warsaw regime. Invariably, such meetings were followed by an intensification of the Soviet media campaign against dissent and its toleration in Poland. At the congress, Brezhnev attributed the Polish crisis to "imperialist subversive activity combined with mistakes and miscalculations in domestic policy." But, he said, "we will not abandon fraternal, socialist Poland in its hour of need; we will stand by it." (*Pravda*, 24 February.) While Brezhnev appeared anxious to bolster the Kania leadership, he made it clear that Moscow expected a more vigorous domestic policy from the Polish communists.

Kania assured the congress that Poland remained an "unbreakable link" in the socialist system and expressed thanks for the confidence shown in Poland's ability to solve its own problems. Kania promised that his government would stop the "counterrevolutionary forces" trying to "sow anarchy" in Poland (*NYT*, 25 February). Shortly after the congress, Kania returned to Moscow with Prime Minister Wojciech Jaruzelski for talks with Brezhnev and other Soviet leaders. The conference communiqué stressed the need to overcome the anarchy and disorder threatening socialism in Poland (*Pravda*, 5 March).

Following the meetings in Moscow, the Soviets stepped up pressures on Warsaw; Soviet troop concentrations around Poland increased tensions. Nine days after returning from the Soviet capital, Kania asserted that "Poland is and will be an ally of the Soviet Union" (*NYT*, 15 March). In March, 60,000 troops reportedly took part in the Soyuz 81 maneuvers in Poland, Czechoslovakia, East Germany, and the USSR. Ignoring Western protests that the maneuvers were designed to pressure Poland, the Soviet media avoided coverage of the exercises, except for one brief press notice that gave no details (Tass, 22 March). If the maneuvers were intended as a means of exerting pressure on Poles, they seemed to have little effect on the volatile situation. American television reporters noted that the Poles seemed much less concerned about a possible Soviet intervention than were Western political leaders. Nevertheless, Soviet military power remained Moscow's ultimate weapon against Polish dissent if all else failed. Western observers viewed Soviet naval maneuvers in the Baltic during August and September as a further attempt by Moscow to exert military pressure. In early August, the U.S. Defense Department reported that 17 major Soviet ships and 52 to 54 smaller ships were taking part in naval exercises in the Baltic Sea (*NYT*, 7 August). Additional military maneuvers held in Belorussia in September under the personal command of Defense Minister Dimitri F. Ustinov and involving 100,000 troops took place while a Solidarity convention was meeting in Gdansk. In October, the U.S. delegate to the European security conference in Madrid, Max Kampelman, accused the USSR of failing to give notification of Soyuz 81 and the Baltic maneuvers as required by the 1975 Helsinki accords (AP, 30 October).

While exerting military pressure on the Poles, Moscow escalated its attacks in the media. On the eve of Brezhnev's departure for the Czechoslovak party congress, *Pravda* (2 April) delivered a vitriolic attack against an "antisocialist" meeting at Warsaw University and sharply criticized Polish communist authorities for failing to respond to it. At the Prague congress, the CPSU leader reaffirmed the Brezhnev Doctrine and offered "fraternal aid" to Poland (*NYT*, 8 April).

The next major step in Moscow's "war of nerves" against Poland was a 24-hour visit by Mikhail A. Suslov, CPSU ideological secretary and Politburo member, on 23–24 April to confer with Polish leaders (*Pravda*, 25 April). Immediately after Suslov's return to Moscow, the CPSU issued a statement charging that "revisionist elements" in the ranks of the PUWP were trying "to paralyze the party of Communists" in carrying out its role "as the leading force in society" (Tass, 25 April; *Pravda*, 26 April).

The criticism of "revisionist" elements within the PUWP and "antisocialist" elements outside it continued, culminating in a CPSU Central Committee letter to the Polish party on 5 June calling on the PUWP to check the activities of "anticommunist" and "anti-Soviet" forces in Poland. The letter pointedly noted that Kania and Jaruzelski had agreed to "our point of view" in meetings between Soviet and Polish leaders, "but, in fact, nothing changed and there was no correction to the policy of concessions and compromise. . . . It is now necessary to mobilize all healthy forces to confront the class enemy and fight the counterrevolution. This calls for a revolutionary will of the party, of its militants, and of its leadership. Yes, of its leadership. Time does not wait. The party can and should find within itself forces to reverse the course of events and put things into order, in goodwill, even before the congress." (*WP*, 10 June.)

Soviet patience with what Moscow regarded as temporizing leadership in Warsaw seemed nearly exhausted; indeed, there were reports that the Soviets had sought to unseat Kania at the PUWP

Central Committee plenum in June. Kania had survived that trial, but the PUWP congress, set for July, raised new questions. Secret balloting for congress delegates evoked the prospect of a runaway anti-Soviet meeting, with the possibility of the emergence of a new leadership far more unfavorable to Moscow than was Kania. Plainly concerned, the Soviets utilized indirect pressure to try to secure a postponement. The Czechoslovak Central Committee sent a letter to the PUWP Central Committee warning that counterrevolutionary forces were taking over the Polish party and suggesting that the Poles postpone their party congress (*NYT*, 3 July). Some Western observers saw the congress as so threatening to Moscow that the Soviets might finally initiate a military intervention to prevent it. Foreign Minister Gromyko was dispatched to Warsaw for a two-day visit in early July (*Pravda*, 5 July). The specific purpose of the Gromyko mission was not clear, but when he left Poland, the Soviets had apparently reluctantly acceded to the convening of the PUWP Congress.

The congress met as scheduled on 14 July. Moscow city First Secretary Viktor V. Grishin headed the Soviet delegation, which also included Belorussian First Secretary Tikhon Y. Kiselev and the Central Committee's secretary for ruling communist parties, Konstantin V. Rusakov (ibid., 14 July).

Grishin told the PUWP congress that "we have believed and continue to believe that it is the job of the Polish Communists themselves and the working people of people's Poland to extricate their country from the crisis." He noted mistakes of previous leaders in economic matters and ideological-political work that had resulted in "the isolation of the vanguard from the masses." The primary condition for overcoming the crisis, Grishin concluded, was "the restoration of the PUWP's fighting efficiency and the strengthening of its solidarity on a principled Marxist-Leninist basis" (ibid., 15 July).

Kania was re-elected first secretary (*NYT*, 19 July), becoming the first European communist party leader ever elected by secret ballot. Brezhnev sent congratulations to Kania (*Pravda*, 20 July), and the Soviet delegation met with Kania and Jaruzelski before returning to Moscow. The official communiqué described the meeting as taking place in a "warm, friendly atmosphere" (Tass, 20 July; *Pravda*, 21 July).

R. I. Kosolapov, editor of *Kommunist* and a candidate member of the CPSU Central Committee, reiterated Grishin's Warsaw remarks about ideological shortcomings in a *Pravda* article (31 July): the "lowering of class consciousness" among some Polish workers was "due to a number of circumstances, including not only the extreme weakness of ideological-political work among the masses but also the completely unsubstantiated and utopian nature of a number of the social and economic tasks set by the previous Polish leadership during the 1970s."

When Kania and Jaruzelski met with Brezhnev for the usual August meeting in the Crimea, they were able to report a respite in the hectic situation in Poland. Solidarity leaders had urged their followers to call off strikes and demonstrations and had agreed to a temporary revival of Saturday as a workday. The Soviets responded by allowing Poland to defer debt repayments until 1985 and by pledging substantial economic aid (Tass, 15 August).

The good news from the Crimean summit was not enough to save Kania. Production was down by 17 percent in July over the same period a year earlier and continued to plummet, due partially to strikes in the coal industry, Poland's most important source of exports. Local strikes posed continuing problems, and severe food shortages brought repeated protest demonstrations. In September, Soviet Ambassador Boris Aristov delivered a stern message from the CPSU Central Committee to Polish leaders demanding immediate and "radical" measures to crush "anti-Sovietism" in Poland once and for all (UPI, 17 and 18 September). In October, Kania was ousted and replaced by Jaruzelski. Disorders spread, and Solidarity called a one-hour symbolic general strike. Evidently finally agreeing to the tough line favored by Moscow, Polish leaders sent military forces to outlying regions to assume control of the economy and to maintain order and called on the Polish parliament for extraordinary measures to end the wave of strikes. At the end of October, an estimated quarter million Poles remained on strike.

In November and December, Solidarity and church leaders tried to establish cooperation with the new party leadership in order to calm the country and avoid confrontations. However, the economic situation showed no improvement, and an incident in early December created new tensions. Cadets at a firefighters' school in Warsaw staged a sit-in, demanding removal from the jurisdiction of the Interior Ministry, which could mobilize them as riot police, and were supported by a cheering crowd of some seven thousand people. A thousand riot police moved in, made arrests, and dispersed the crowd (AP, 1 and 2 December). A few days later, on 13 December, Jaruzelski announced in a surprise radio address the establishment of martial law with an army Council of National Salvation assuming full powers over the state administration. Basic civil rights were curtailed, all organizations connected with Solidarity (trade unions and farmers', students', and professional associations) were suspended, and most of their leaders—including Lech Walesa—were detained. Some former PUWP leaders, including Edward Gierek, were also taken into custody. Claiming that his aim was not military dictatorship and promising that socialist renewal measures would be pursued and the progressive reforms of August 1980 preserved, Jaruzelski justified his action by the need to save Poland from chaos and civil war. He then asserted that "the Polish-Soviet alliance is and will be the cornerstone of the Polish raison d'état and the guarantee of inviolability of our borders. Poland is and will be a firm link of the Warsaw Pact, an unfailing member of the socialist community" (*NYT*, 14 December).

A few days before the crackdown, the Soviet press had depicted the situation in Poland in alarmist terms. On 7 and 8 December, Radio Moscow, quoting Warsaw sources, broadcast taped excerpts from a meeting of Solidarity leaders held in the city of Radom on 3 December. The tapes, according to Radio Moscow, proved that counterrevolution was on the rampage in Poland and that Walesa had stated that ways must be found to "make a lightening quick maneuver to seize power." (*Radio Liberty Research*, 9 December.) On 10 December, a Tass dispatch quoted Polish television as saying that local Solidarity officials has begun to set up "commando units" in some factories. "Theft of weapons and explosives from state storehouses had been recorded . . . some Polish clerics were increasingly delivering antigovernment sermons [while] Polish authorities were taking precautionary measures against 'counterrevolution,' including reinforcement of patrols around government and party offices." (*CSM*, 11 December.)

Radio Moscow reported the imposition of martial law in Poland within one hour, but it took more than 24 hours before the first Soviet official commentary was made. A Tass statement issued on 14 December described the events in Poland as "an internal matter," aimed at saving the country from the "mortal danger" of counterrevolution. It added that Soviet leaders "received with a feeling of satisfaction" the affirmations of Poland's links with the USSR and the Warsaw Pact. (*NYT*, 15 December.) Tass assailed President Reagan's assertion in his 17 December press conference that the Polish military acted with Soviet support and charged that "leaders of the counterrevolutionary forces were preparing to carry out their plans with knowledge and encouragement, and even on direct instructions, of the Washington Administration" (ibid., 19 December).

When on 23 December Reagan announced credit and commercial sanctions against Poland, he took the unusual step of revealing intelligence secrets to support his contention that Moscow deserved a major share of blame for the developments in Poland: "The tragic events now occurring in Poland have been precipitated by public and secret pressure from the Soviet Union. It is no coincidence that Soviet Marshal [Viktor G.] Kulikov, chief of the Warsaw Pact forces, and other senior Red Army officers were in Poland while these outrages ('killings, mass arrests and the setting up of concentration camps') were being initiated. And it is no coincidence that the marshal law proclamations imposed in December by the Polish Government were being printed in the Soviet Union in September." (Ibid., 24

December.) Moscow's reaction was predictably harsh. Tass commented that President Reagan's economic sanctions against Poland were an act of "unprecedentedly crude pressure and abominable intervention into strictly internal affairs of a sovereign state" (*WP*, 25 December). Tass described the decision of the U.S. government to punish the Soviet Union directly for the military crackdown in Poland (announced on 29 December and consisting of seven economic measures) as "a deliberate striving of the U.S. leadership to worsen the international situation even further, to hurl the world back to the dark times of the cold war and to give U.S. imperialism a free hand in pursuing a military policy aimed at achieving world domination" (*NYT*, 31 December).

Western commentators observed that the Soviet government had several reasons to be satisfied with its 1981 confrontation with the United States over Poland. Polish security forces appeared successful in breaking the back of Solidarity, without the involvement of the Red Army; the Polish crackdown sharply divided Western European governments from Washington on the degree of Soviet responsibility; and the economic sanctions were generally considered mild and of limited effectiveness (causing, moreover, sharp controversies in the United States), while the United States' NATO allies remained unwilling to join in any sanctions against the Soviets. Finally, in a decision that many interpreted as a break with the U.S. policy of linkage, Washington expressed its readiness to continue the Geneva talks on limiting the number of medium-range nuclear missiles in Europe. (*Wall Street Journal*, 30 December; *NYT*, 2 January 1982; *CSM*, 4 January 1982; *Time*, 11 January 1982).

Afghanistan. Bogged down in a classic guerrilla war, unable to control the countryside, and needing overwhelming numerical superiority to stay even on the battlefront, the USSR gave indications of seeking a face-saving solution to cut its losses. However, Moscow caustically rejected the call of the United States and six other Western nations at the Ottawa conference in July for Soviet withdrawal from Afghanistan (Tass, 18 July). A 5 August *Pravda* article by "A. Petrov" (a pseudonym used for policy statements) described the Ottawa call as a cover for U.S. aggressive designs rather than a positive step toward normalization. Petrov repeated earlier Soviet statements to the effect that only the international aspects of the Afghan problem could be discussed, "not internal Afghan affairs."

Moscow continued to support the peace plan of the Babrak Karmal government, first advanced in May 1980. The Afghan proposals called for bilateral negotiations with Iran and Pakistan to achieve a settlement, with guarantees by third states, including a guarantee by the United States not to engage in "subversive activity against Afghanistan." In August, the Kabul government repeated the essentials of the May 1980 proposals, adding an offer to participate in trilateral negotiations. A *Pravda* commentary by Pavel Demchenko (30 August) warmly endorsed the modified Kabul proposals. Demchenko indicated that acceptance and implementation of the Afghan plan could produce conditions "for withdrawing Soviet troops from Afghanistan."

Reports circulated in late October that Iran was preparing a peace plan that would call for withdrawal of Soviet troops, temporary occupation of Afghanistan by troops from Iran and other neighboring countries, and the setting up of a new government. Some Western observers considered such a solution as possibly acceptable to the USSR since it would enable the Soviets to retire from the costly struggle without yielding Afghanistan to the West (*Newsweek*, 26 October).

On the battlefront, the conflict settled down to a pattern of minor skirmishes between Soviet-Afghan forces and guerrilla bands. In August, Moscow reported that 43 regular Afghan troops had defeated an attack on a Soviet post on the Pakistani border by seven hundred Afghan rebels (Tass, 12 August). In October, the Yuonus Khalis faction of the Islamic Party announced the capture of a Soviet adviser, geologist E. R. Okrimyuk; he was held hostage in support of demands for the release of fifty insurgents imprisoned by the Kabul regime (AP, 23 October).

At the end of the year, the war continued, and Soviet troops were unable to curb the widespread insurgency despite a costly commitment. In the two years that Soviet troops have been in Afghanistan, their numbers increased from the original 85,000 to 110,000 deployed in eleven divisions around the country (*NYT*, 17 December).

Somewhat embarrassing to the USSR was its failure to block a U.N. General Assembly debate on alleged use of lethal chemical weapons in Afghanistan and Kampuchea against rebel forces. By an eighteen to five vote, with two abstentions, the assembly's General Committee put the "yellow rain" issue on the agenda (ibid., 17 September).

Japan. Soviet-Japanese relations continued to be strained over the issue of the territories lost by Japan to the USSR at the end of World War II. An article by Yevgeny Rusakov in *Pravda* (29 August) denounced Japanese "hawks" for acting "contrary to common sense" on the issue. Rusakov charged that the Japanese government had allocated the equivalent of more than U.S. $60 million for fiscal 1982 for "waging a campaign of illegal territorial claims against the USSR"; that the proclamation of 7 February as Northern Territories Day had been used as a pretext for "holding an anti-Soviet orgy"; and that the Japanese Foreign Ministry had demanded of some countries that certain Kurile Islands be shown on maps as Japanese territory. In December, the issue of Japanese rearmament added new frictions. On the fortieth anniversary of the attack on Pearl Harbor, the Soviet Union warned Japan against expansion of its military forces (*Krasnaia zvezda*, 7 December).

India. The USSR continued to maintain especially friendly relations with India. In a long article in August on the tenth anniversary of the Soviet-Indian friendship treaty, Foreign Minister Gromyko described the relationship between the two countries in glowing terms and lavishly praised Indira Gandhi. Gromyko said that Soviet-Indian relations "are a graphic example of the practical embodiment of the principles of the peaceful coexistence of states with different social systems." (*Pravda*, 8 August.) Playing on India's concerns about Pakistan, Gromyko sharply criticized U.S. promises of military aid to the latter country and repeated the Soviet call for a "zone of peace" in the Indian Ocean.

China. Soviet relations with China continued to be strained. Poland added a new subject of controversy between Moscow and Beijing and the Soviets continued to voice fears of encirclement as the United States and China gave fresh evidence of cooperation, despite the change of administrations in Washington. At the Twenty-Sixth Congress, Brezhnev said that "unfortunately, there are no grounds yet to speak of any changes for the better in Beijing's foreign policy." But, he added, "if Soviet-Chinese relations are still frozen, the reason for this has nothing to do with our position." (Ibid., 24 March.) The PRC dismissed Brezhnev's peace proposals at the congress as "old stuff with a new label" (*NYT*, 16 March) and praised the new American stance toward Soviet "hegemonism" (UPI, 15 March).

The Soviet media presented harshly critical reports on the Central Committee plenum of the Chinese Communist Party in June, accusing it of rejecting certain erroneous propositions and Mao's "personality cult" but retaining the general thrust of Maoist policy. The characteristic feature of the PRC's platform was said to be "China's claim to 'exclusiveness,' to a 'special Chinese path' in revolution and the building of a new society—thus, in fact, a disregard for the general laws governing the construction of socialism." Beijing was accused of lying about a "Soviet threat," of pursuing "hegemonistic" claims in Asia, and of supporting the United States in the escalation of the arms race and the aggravation of international tensions. (*Pravda* and *Izvestiia*, 5 July.)

The Soviets also accused China of siding with the "imperialists" on the issue of Poland. An official statement in late June rejected Chinese criticism of the CPSU Central Committee letter to the PUWP (see above) as "irresponsible slander" and said that China was attempting to "blacken" the USSR and drive a wedge between Poland and the Soviet Union. By doing so, the Soviets said, China was "weakening world socialism" and increasing international tension (Tass, 30 June).

In an 8 August article in *Pravda*, Gromyko accused the Chinese of encouraging American support for Afghan rebels and called U.S. Secretary of State Alexander Haig's summer visit to Beijing "the escalation of a reckless policy." Gromyko maintained that "the demonstrative expansion of the military aspects of the Washington-Beijing partnership in the international arena is leading to an increasingly tense situation in the Far East and in the world as a whole."

The ambiguous attitude of the new U.S. administration toward Taiwan did produce some tensions between Beijing and Washington. But instead of turning this to its advantage, Moscow kept blasting away, charging the "Beijing ruling top crust" with foreign policy "adventurism" (Tass, 26 October). The Soviets did propose resumption of the border talks with China that had been suspended for nearly two years but an article in the CPSU's foreign affairs journal indicated no change in the Soviet bargaining position (*Mezhdunarodonaia zhizn*, no. 11, November).

Western Europe. Willy Brandt, SPD and Socialist International chairman, was welcomed to Moscow with much fanfare in late June. Brandt, the original protagonist of *Ostpolitik* and détente, was obviously viewed as a key figure in the controversy over nuclear arms in Europe. Brandt conferred with Brezhnev, Gromyko, and Ponomarev; the official communiqué described the talks as taking place "in a friendly and constructive atmosphere" (*Pravda*, 1 July). However, Moscow subsequently announced that it had rejected Brandt's proposal for removal of nuclear weapons from the Kola Peninsula (Tass, 23 July).

The Soviets took a cautious attitude toward the new socialist-dominated government of François Mitterrand in France. However, a *Pravda* commentary by V. Gunsenkov (1 July) called the "victory of leftist, democratic forces in such a major country as France," an event of "great importance, not only for France but elsewhere as well."

Soviet relations with Sweden were severely strained in October when a Whiskey-class submarine ran aground in Swedish territorial waters. The incident occurred after several months of increased WTO submarine patrol activity in the Baltic; the strategic importance of the area had been emphasized by the early autumn visit to Stockholm of U.S. Defense Secretary Caspar Weinberger. The Swedish government threatened to repel with force any Soviet attempt to free the submarine and rejected as inadequate expressions of regret by the Soviet ambassador. The sub commander was questioned by Swedish officials, who suspected Soviet intelligence-gathering activity directed at the Karlskrona naval base. (*NYT* and UPI, 28 October–3 November.) The episode certainly harmed a Soviet initiative to establish a nuclear-free zone in Scandinavia.

Africa. In May, the USSR concluded a Treaty of Friendship and Cooperation with the People's Republic of the Congo, following negotiations in Moscow. The treaty preamble declared that the two countries were animated by the "ideals of the struggle against imperialism, colonialism, and racism" and the desire for "unity of all progressive forces in the struggle for peace, freedom, independence, and social progress" (*Pravda*, 14 May; *FBIS*, 19 May).

Middle East. Soviet strategy in the region revolved around Brezhnev's proposal at the CPSU congress for a general settlement of Middle East conflicts by means of an international conference including the USSR. The Soviets received a boost in May when Jordan's King Hussein visited Moscow and endorsed the Brezhnev conference plan (Tass, 26 May). However, Hussein subsequently reverted to his usual balancing act, visiting Washington for friendly talks with Reagan (*NYT*, 1 and 2 November). Brezhnev repeated his call for a conference in a major speech in Tbilisi in May; he also warned that a "rash step" in the Middle East could engulf the entire region in war (*NYT*, 23 May). Brezhnev again sounded the call for an international peace conference on the Middle East in October (*Pravda*, 28 October).

The USSR reaffirmed its support for the Palestinians and for "rejectionist" forces on a number of occasions during the year. In April, Vladimir L. Kudryavtsev, chairman of the International Relations Committee of the USSR Supreme Soviet, told the Palestinian parliament in exile that the Soviet Union stood on the side of the Syrians and the Palestinians "in their struggle against American imperialism and Zionism" (Reuters, 12 April). Meanwhile, the Soviets moved even closer to Syria, whose leader, Hafiz al-Asad, had signed a friendship treaty with the USSR in October 1980. There were reports of joint Soviet-Syrian amphibious maneuvers in the eastern Mediterranean, and in April, Israel charged that Soviet advisers were operating with the Syrian Army in Lebanon. Soviet officials heatedly denied the Israeli charge. (*NYT*, 25 and 26 May.)

The Soviets reacted cautiously to the assassination of Egyptian President Anwar Sadat in October. However, when the United States subsequently set in motion diplomatic initiatives aimed at the containment of Libya, Moscow responded with a rhetorical counteroffensive. In late October, Brezhnev condemned U.S. "interference" in the region directed against Libya (*Pravda*, 28 October). Prior to the assassination of Sadat, the Soviet ambassador to Egypt and six other diplomats had been expelled for alleged participation in a plot to overthrow the Egyptian president. Subsequently, 23 more Soviet diplomats and seventeen members of the Soviet military liaison office in Cairo were ordered to leave the country, reducing the Soviet presence in Egypt to a bare minimum. An Egyptian cabinet statement accused the Soviet embassy of ignoring repeated warnings to stop "hostile activities against the regime and the people" (*Daily Telegraph*, London, 16 September).

International Party Contacts. The Twenty-Sixth CPSU Congress provided the arena for the most diversified and most widely publicized contacts between the CPSU and other parties during the year. Soviet congresses are always used to showcase "proletarian internationalism" and the purity of the Soviet party and the world communist movement; this requires the widest possible participation by other communist parties. New records were set for attendance by other parties when the CPSU Congress convened in February, with 123 delegations representing 109 countries (ibid., 20 February). Enrico Berlinguer of Italy and Santiago Carrillo of Spain, Eurocommunist critics of Soviet policies, demonstrated the incohesion of the world movement by their conspicuous absence.

The leaders of ruling parties facing the most critical domestic situations, Stanislaw Kania of Poland and Babrak Karmal of Afghanistan, were accorded prominent exposure at the congress, evidently with the aim of shoring up their images at home. Criticism of Soviet world policies was avoided at the congress sessions, but at a meeting of party delegations in the Hall of Columns chaired by Viktor V. Grishin, the chief Italian delegate, Giancarlo Pajetta, criticized the USSR on the issues of Poland and Afghanistan (see above). At the conclusion of the congress, the CPSU Central Committee held a reception for foreign delegations; speeches were delivered by Brezhnev and by Gustav Husák, first secretary of the Czechoslovak party (ibid., 4 March).

Following the congress, the North Korean delegation, led by Premier and Politburo member Yi Chong-ok, met with Soviet Premier and Politburo member Nikolai A. Tikhonov, CPSU Secretary for Ruling Parties Konstantin V. Rusakov, and other Soviet officials in the Kremlin (ibid., 5 March).

During the first two weeks of August, heads of the ruling East European parties traveled to the Crimea for their usual summer meetings with Brezhnev (ibid., 28 July, 10 and 14, August). Most notable was the conference between the Soviet leader and Kania and Jaruzelski, which resulted in an accord on Soviet economic aid for Poland (ibid., 15 August).

At the Bulgarian party congress, held in Sofia 31 March to 4 April, the CPSU was represented by a delegation led by Vladimir V. Shcherbitsky (ibid., 31 March). Earlier, a Bulgarian delegation led by Lyudmila Zhivkova, a member of the Bulgarian Politburo, had visited Moscow and concluded an agreement on cultural exchanges covering 1981 to 1985 (ibid., 15 January).

Brezhnev led the Soviet delegation to the congress of the Czechoslovakian party in April. The CPSU leader delivered a major address at the Prague meeting in which he promised "fraternal aid" to Poland and reaffirmed the Brezhnev Doctrine (*NYT*, 8 April).

Brezhnev and Tikhonov sent greetings to Fidel Castro on Cuba's Liberation Day, the anniversary of the 1959 revolution (*Pravda*, 1 January). In February, Marshal Nikolai V. Ogarkov, Soviet army chief of staff and CPSU Central Committee member, visited Cuba for talks with Cuban party and government leaders (Tass, 8 February).

The CPSU delegation at the Nineteenth Congress of the Mexican Communist Party, in March, was headed by Vladimir G. Lomonosov, member of the CPSU Central Committee for Labor and Social Questions (*Pravda*, 8 March).

The CPSU Central Committee sent greetings to the Venezuelan Communist Party in March on the occasion of the party's fiftieth anniversary celebration (Tass, 6 March). The CPSU Central Committee also sent greetings to the Italian party when it celebrated its sixtieth anniversary in January (*Pravda*, 21 January). Brezhnev and Tikhonov sent congratulations to Kampuchea's leader, Heng Samrin, on the second anniversary of the communist triumph in that country (ibid., 7 January).

Politburo member and Leningrad First Secretary Grigory V. Romanov represented the CPSU at the Nineteenth Congress of the Finnish Communist Party in May (ibid., 24 May). During an official visit to Austria in April, USSR Prime Minister and CPSU Politburo member Nikolai A. Tikhonov met briefly with Austrian Communist Party leader Franz Muhri (ibid, 10 April). Central Committee secretary and Politburo candidate member Boris N. Ponomarev led the CPSU delegation at the Sixth Congress of the West German Communist Party, held in Hannover in May (ibid, 30 May).

Publications. The main CPSU organs are the daily newspaper *Pravda* (circulation more than 11 million), the theoretical and ideological journal *Kommunist* (appearing eighteen times a year, with a circulation over 1 million), and the semimonthly *Partiinaia zhizn*, a journal of internal party affairs and organizational matters (circulation more than 1.16 million). *Kommunist Vooruzhennikh sil* is the party theoretical journal for the armed forces, and *Agitator* is the same for party propagandists; both appear twice a month. The Komsomol has a newspaper, *Komsomolskaia pravda* (six days a week); a monthly theoretical journal, *Molodoi kommunist*; and a monthly literary journal, *Molodaia gvardia*. Each USSR republic prints similar party newspapers in local languages and usually also in Russian. Specialized publications issued under supervision of the CPSU Central Committee include the newspapers *Sovetskaia rossiia*, *Selskaia zhizn*, *Sotsialisticheskaia industria*, *Sovetskaia kultura*, and *Ekonomicheskaia gazeta* and the journal *Politicheskoye samoobrazovaniie*.

University of New Orleans   R. Judson Mitchell

Yugoslavia

The Communist Party of Yugoslavia (CPY) was created in June 1920, although the Yugoslav Communists date their party to April 1919, when a unification congress in Belgrade established a Socialist Workers' Party of Yugoslavia (Communists), which included both communist and noncommunist elements. This party was disbanded fourteen months later. At the party's Sixth Congress in November 1952, the CPY changed its name to League of Communists of Yugoslavia (Savez komunista Jugoslavije; LCY). As the only political party in the Socialist Federative Republic of Yugoslavia (SFRY), the LCY exercises power through its leading role in the Socialist Alliance of the Working People of Yugoslavia (Socijalistički savez radnog naroda Jugoslavije; SAWPY), a front organization that includes all mass political organizations as well as individuals representing various social groups.

The LCY claims a membership of 2,199,444 (*Borba*, 2 October), or 9.84 percent of the country's total population (*NIN*, 10 May).

Census. The 1981 census—the seventh since 1921 and the fifth in communist Yugoslavia—was carried out between 1 and 15 April. Table 1 indicates the total population, both in Yugoslavia as a whole and in the individual republics and autonomous provinces.

The census revealed that Yugoslavia's three poorest regions (Kosovo, Macedonia, and Montenegro) had the highest birthrates, while two of the most advanced regions (Croatia and Vojvodina)

TABLE 1

Population

	1971	1981	Percentage Increase
Bosnia-Herzegovina	3,746,000	4,116,000	9.8
Montenegro	530,000	583,000	10.0
Croatia	4,426,000	4,576,000	3.3
Macedonia	1,647,000	1,914,000	16.2
Slovenia	1,727,000	1,884,000	9.0
Serbia, total	8,447,000	9,279,000	9.9
Serbia proper	5,250,000	5,666,000	7.9
Kosovo	1,244,000	1,585,000	27.4
Vojvodina	1,953,000	2,028,000	3.8
Total	20,523,000	22,352,000	8.9

SOURCE: *NIN*, 10 May.

registered the lowest. In view of the stormy events in the autonomous province of Kosovo—part of the republic of Serbia—in the spring of 1981 (see below), more detailed data about the ethnic composition of Kosovo should be given. Out of the 1,585,000 inhabitants of Kosovo, 1,227,424 (77.4 percent) were Albanians; 209,792 (13.2 percent) Serbs; 26,875 Montenegrins (1.7 percent); Muslims 58,948 (3.7 percent); Turks 12,575 (0.8 percent); and others 48,946 (3.1 percent). The number of Albanians in Kosovo increased by 311,256 over 1971, while the number of Serbs dropped by 18,472 and of Montenegrins by 4,680. The total population of Albanians in Yugoslavia is unknown since no data were reported from Macedonia and Montenegro, which in 1971 had some 280,000 and 36,000 Albanians, respectively (*Yugoslav Survey*, no. 1, 1 February 1973).

The autonomous province of Vojvodina, also part of the republic of Serbia, had 2,028,000 inhabitants, of whom 54.5 percent were Serbs (17,108 more than in 1971); the province also had 383,820 Hungarians (40,046 fewer than in 1971), 164,880 "Yugoslavs" (117,952 more than in 1971), and 108,630 Croats (29,931 fewer than in 1971). The populations of some other national minorities in Vojvodina also decreased.

Auxiliary and Mass Organizations. The SAWPY claims to have had thirteen million members in June 1979. Its supreme body is the Federal Conference (FC). At a session in Belgrade on 27 May, the FC elected Kolj Široka (b. 1922), an Albanian functionary from Kosovo, as its new president for a one-year term (*Borba*, 28 May). Ištvan Rajčan, a Hungarian from Vojvodina who was elected secretary of the SAWPY Presidium in April 1980, was not replaced but retained his post for another year.

The Confederation of Trade Unions of Yugoslavia (Savez sindikata Jugoslavije; CTUY) had, according to the latest official statistics (1977), 4,782,670 members, or about 95 percent of all those employed (*Socialist Thought and Practice*, no. 4, April). On 20 May, the CTUY Council elected Rade Galeb (b. 1927), a Serb from Bosnia-Herzegovina, its new president for a one-year period, to replace Milan Potrč, a 43-year-old Slovene (*Vjesnik*, 21 May). In an interview, Galeb revealed that only 40.1 percent of workers nationwide were members of various CTUY organs at the communal (42.8 percent), provincial-republican (31.4 percent), and federal level (34 percent), compared with 43.7 percent in 1976. In 1979, workers occupied 51.9 percent of the positions on workers' councils throughout the country, compared with 76.2 percent in 1960. Galeb also said that in the two chambers of the Assembly of the SFRY, only 25 of the 308 members (8.2 percent) were blue-collar workers. (*Večernje novosti*, 6 and 7 July.)

On 24 December 1980, the League of Socialist Youth of Yugoslavia (LSYY) held a Program-Electoral Conference in Belgrade. Miodrag Vuković (b. 1956), a Montenegrin from Titograd, was elected president for one year, and Božo Jovanović (b. 1951), a Montenegrin from Kosovo, was elected secretary, also for a one-year period (*Politika*, 25 December 1980). Vuković replaced the Macedonian Vasil Tupurkovski, 30, who had been elected president of the LSYY in June 1979 "for a one-year period," but retained his post for eighteen months. No explanation was given for such an exception. The LSYY had "more than 3.6 million members" at the beginning of 1980 (*Borba*, 21 February 1980), of whom "more than 650,000" were LCY members, or 29.5 percent of the party's total membership (ibid., 7 June); only 9.8 percent of high school pupils were LSYY members (*Komunist*, 26 June). The official organ of the LSYY is the weekly *Mladost*.

Party Internal Affairs: *Leadership and Organization.* The supreme bodies of the LCY are the 165-member Central Committee and the latter's 23-member Presidium. After Tito's death on 4 May 1980, only four persons were members of both the eight-member Presidency of the SFRY and the Presidium: Dr. Vladimir Bakarić, Petar Stambolić, Stevan Doronjski, and Fadil Hodža. Doronjski died on 13 August and was replaced in the SFRY Presidency by Radovan Vlajković (b. 1922) and in the Presidium by Dušan Alimpić (b. 1921). At a Central Committee session on 30 September, Petar Stambolić resigned from his post in the Presidium and was replaced by Dragoslav Marković (b. 1920), the president of the Assembly of the SFRY.

At a session on 25 May, the Presidium elected Montenegrin party official Dobroslav Ćulafić (b. 1926) a new secretary of the Presidium; his term is to last until the Twelfth LCY Congress in June 1982 (*Politika*, 27 May). Ćulafić replaced Dr. Dušan Dragosavac (b. 1919), who on 20 October was elected president of the Presidium until the party congress. He replaced Lazar Mojsov (b. 1920), whose one-year chairmanship expired at that time (*Borba*, 21 October).

Preparations for the Congress. On 30 September, the Central Committee of the LCY decided to convoke the Twelfth LCY Congress in June 1982. The plenum stipulated one elected delegate for every 2,000 LCY members. This means that 1,100 delegates would be elected in addition to 360 chosen by the six republican parties (60 from each), the 80 from the two provincial parties (40 from each), the 30 from the army, and the 204 members of the LCY Central Committee, Control Commission, and Statutory Commission. This makes a total of 1,774 delegates with voting status. Table 2 shows party membership by republics and provinces as well as the number of delegates to be sent from each of them to the party congress in Belgrade.

TABLE 2

Republican and Provincial Parties

	Total Number of Members	Number of Elected Delegates	Additional Delegates	Total Number of Delegates
Bosnia-Herzegovina	396,192	198	60	258
Montenegro	79,042	39	60	99
Croatia	364,822	182	60	242
Macedonia	147,930	75	60	135
Slovenia	132,408	66	60	126
Serbia proper	618,218	309	60	369
Vojvodina	234,017	117	40	157
Kosovo	95,968	48	40	88
Army	114,962	58	30	88
LCY organization at the federal level	15,885	8	—	8
Total	2,199,444	1,100	470	1,570

SOURCE: *Borba*, 2 October.

Internal Conflicts. Tito's death has left a big gap in Yugoslavia, both at the party and at the state level. In his lifetime, Tito's personality cult and uncontested authority prevented dangerous internal confrontations. Since his death, however, internal conflicts have surfaced, with two major groups fighting each other in the party and in the state. According to Dr. Muhamed Kešetović, a top party theoretician, "For a considerable time, we have been witnessing a potential conflict between two basic currents: one that has never accepted the socialist self-management system as a strategy and lasting assignment but rather as an unobligatory passing tactic, and another current that has firmly believed in self-management. This potential conflict has turned into a real one with potentially fateful consequences. All this has been taking place within the same movement, that is, within the framework of the LCY and even within its forums." (*NIN*, 18 October.)

Not daring to attack Tito and his ideas directly, the "techno-burocrats" (the enemies of self-management) have concentrated their attacks on Edvard Kardelj (1910–1971), once Yugoslavia's number two leader, and his ideas of the "pluralism of self-management interests," blaming "the Kardeljization of the system" for all current difficulties (ibid.). Kardelj's last work, *Roads of Development of the Socialist Self-Management Political System* (for details, see *YICA*, 1978, pp. 94–95, 1979, pp. 98–99), was the basis of the Eleventh LCY Congress in June 1978 (see ibid., 1979, pp. 94–98). Kardelj's main argument was that pluralism of interests had to exist despite the prohibition on the existence of different parties. For him, the only problem was the "forms such political pluralism should take." Without naming names, but implying that techno-burocrats were entrenched at all levels of Yugoslavia's political and economic life, Branko Vukušić, one of Kardelj's close collaborators, claimed that "Some people have been trying 'secretly' to spread about Kardelj false information requesting the "de-Kardeljization of the system" (*NIN*, 8 November). Kešetović had asserted that it was "precisely the technocratic 'de-Kardeljized' practice that has prevented the application and confirmation of the [self-management] system" (ibid., 18 October). Vukušić went even further and revealed that before his death Kardelj had warned that "if we did not radically reorder our situation, we might experience 'the fate of Chile,' in which economic chaos and internal destabilization preceded" the military takeover, especially now "when even the most pessimistic fears of Kardelj have been realized" (ibid., 8 November).

Similarly, Dr. Vladimir Bakarić, the sole survivor of the once-famous Tito-Kardelj-Bakarić triumvirate, complained that in Yugoslavia "no one obeys anyone else" and that necessary changes could not be carried out because "certain places where changes should be introduced are occupied by people who oppose change, who think that things have not been too bad and that our problems could be solved by certain monetary, credit, or similar manipulations" (*Vjesnik*, 19 July). General of the Army Kosta Nadj, the president of Yugoslavia's Veterans' Federation, demanded that "incapable people should either resign their functions or be thrown out; this must become the rule" (ibid., 7 November).

One or Eight Communist Parties? On 1–2 July and 4 November, the LCY Commission for Organizational and Statutory Questions held two important sessions. The main topic of both sessions was the future top party organizational setup, an issue to be resolved at the Twelfth Congress. At the July session, Dr. Prvoslav Ralić of Belgrade, one of Yugoslavia's top party theorists, touched one of the sorest points in the Yugoslav political scene by asking: "Has the LCY been a united organization, or has it been a federation of several parties" (*Komunist*, 24 July)? The problem of whether the LCY was a united organization or a federation of eight parties (six republican and two provincial) existed even in Tito's lifetime, but his authority thwarted all attempts to "federalize" the party.

At the July meeting, several speakers warned against federalization and suggested that some sections of the current party statutes would have to be changed in order to stress "democratic centralism" as the most important principle in party life (*NIN*, 19 July). Other speakers argued that self-management should be applicable not only at the state but also at the party level. Countering that argument at the July meeting, Serbian theorist Prof. Dragomir Drašković said that should self-management principles "be legalized in the party . . . instead of being a united organization, the party might turn into a 'confederation' of republican and provincial parties." He warned the party not to let itself be turned "into a holy alliance of national bureaucracies" (ibid.).

The 4 November session revealed differences over five major issues concerning the party's future organization. The first disagreement concerned the method of electing members of the LCY Central Committee (*Večernje novosti*, 5 November). The second controversy was whether Presidium members should be elected by secret or open ballot. The third issue was the most important: Should a new LCY president be elected, or should a collective leadership, in this case the Presidium, take Tito's place?

The fourth was whether to reduce Presidium membership from the present 23 to 17 in the future. Finally, the fifth issue was a proposal to include in both the new party statutes and the Twelfth Congress's resolution Tito's demand made at the Eleventh Congress in June 1978 "to democratize cadre policy" by proposing more candidates "for all leading bodies." (Ibid.)

Professional Party Functionaries. In 1981, the LCY employed 5,872 persons, of whom 1,514 were party functionaries. Their average monthly personal income amounted to 32,235 dinars (about U.S. $850), compared with 37,536 dinars (about U.S. $1,000) for the highest paid Presidium member and an average monthly income of 7,000–9,000 dinars (U.S. $180–240) for the bulk of Yugoslav workers (ibid., 5 September, 8 November).

Signs of De-Titoization. Although mentions of Tito's life and work in the Yugoslav media continued to bear the customary "cult of personality" marks and crowds filed before his tomb in Belgrade, there were clear signs of a growing "de-Titoization" process as the year progressed. Many people attributed the outbreak of violence in Kosovo to Tito's leniency toward ethnic Albanians. The strident "de-Kardeljization" campaign omitted direct reference to Tito, but self-management was, in fact, closely linked with Tito's ideas and policies. Branko Vukušić argued that "Kardeljization is in reality Titoization" and added that "those who talk about the Kardeljization of the system in a derogatory sense must very well know that Kardelj's work in all its components is to such an extent Titoist that it is impossible to make any distinction between them" (*NIN*, 8 November). High Yugoslav officials, worried by Yugoslavia's poor economic performance and the related popular dissatisfaction and unwilling to be the culprits for so many problems, suggested in public speeches and interviews that the "mistakes" had deeper roots, stemming from the years when Tito was in the saddle. A few days before Lazar Mojsov stepped down from his one-year term as president of the Presidium, he answered the question of an American correspondent about developments in Yugoslavia since Tito's death by saying: "The biggest difference since Tito's death is that we have a more democratic atmosphere than ever. There are so many polemics, criticisms in the press, and more tolerance than ever for it." Mojsov also admitted that Tito's requirement of constant rotation within the leadership, down to the communal government and party levels, had run into a fundamental obstacle. "There are not enough Yugoslavs able or willing to fill the jobs." (*NYT*, 23 October, 15 November.) The lenient term—two years in jail—to which a Belgrade court sentenced on 17 September the noted younger Serbian poet Gojko Djogo for a ferociously contemptuous description of Tito's personal rule would have been unthinkable during Tito's life or immediately after his death.

The man who began reducing Tito to human proportions is none other than his official biographer, Vladimir Dedijer. In the second volume (four are planned) of his best-selling and highly controversial book, *Novi prilozi za biografiju Josipa Broza Tita* (New contributions to the biography of Josip Broz Tito), Dedijer reveals some hitherto "unmentionables" concerning Tito's personal traits. He pays, of course, just dues to the late Yugoslav Caesar, saying in an interview concerning his book that although Tito was "a gigantic figure exceeding all earthly standards—political, cultural, and economic," he also had many "human faults." This is why, Dedijer said, "one does a disservice to such a great personality by writing of him according to protocol as about a pharaoh, extolling him to the sky and hiding his faults." (*Start*, 26 September.)

According to Dedijer, Tito, like all peasants, had a love for "good clothes." "This longing was so great that Tito became a waiter" just for the chance to wear nice clothes. Of course, "one should write of Tito's faults but without going too far. Tito must be described as he really was," a man full of "passions and faults," wrote Dedijer. However, except for describing Tito's approach to "love and women" and his "passion for gambling" (ibid; *NIN*, 8 November), Dedijer failed to mention any of Tito's political errors.

Domestic Affairs: *The State Presidency.* On 15 May, the Slovene Sergej Kraigher was elected president of the State Presidency for a one-year period (May 1981–May 1982), while a Serb from Serbia, Petar Stambolić, was elected vice-president. This means that Stambolić is slated to become the new president in May 1982. The only change in the State Presidency took place after the death of Stevan Doronjski on 13 August; he was replaced by Radovan Vlajković as the representative of Vojvodina. The composition of the nine-member State Presidency at the end of 1981 was Sergej Kraigher (Slovenia), Petar Stambolić (Serbia), Dr. Vladimir Bakarić (Croatia), Cvijetin Mijatović (Bosnia-Herzegovina), Lazar Koliševski (Macedonia), Vidoje Žarković (Montenegro), Radovan Vlajković (Vojvodina), Fadil Hodža (Kosovo), and Dr. Dušan Dragosavac (an ex officio member since he is president of the LCY Presidium until June 1982). Except for Kraigher, who was elected a State Presidency member in 1979 for an eight-year term, and Radovan Vlajković, who was elected in November 1981 under the same conditions, all other members will serve until their second term expires in May 1983. According to the constitution, they cannot be elected for a third time.

Kosovo Riots. On 11 and 26 March and on 1 April, large-scale student demonstrations took place in Priština, the capital of the autonomous province of Kosovo, as well as in the towns of Prizren and Podujevo. The demonstrations started with Albanian students protesting against bad food in the university cafeteria and bad living conditions in the dormitories, but soon turned into riots and violent confrontation with Yugoslav security forces and army units. Since the authorities were caught by surprise by the turmoil and since it was the first major flare-up of ethnic antagonism since Tito's death (in fact since the Yugoslav Communists came to power), some basic information on Kosovo, its past and inhabitants, is in order.

Historical Background. No other geographical concept provokes such emotion among Serbs and Montenegrins as that of Kosovo. In the Middle Ages, Kosovo, a part of the state of Rascia, was the cradle of Serbian national independence and of Serbian cultural and religious life. Kosovo takes its name from the plateau of *Kosovo polje,* in 1389 the scene of a decisive battle between the Serbs (allied with the Bosnians and Albanians) and the Turks. The invading Turks defeated the Serbs and their allies and crushed the last remnants of the Serbian medieval empire. Serbia then came under the suzerainty of the Ottoman Empire. For over five centuries, the idea of avenging Kosovo inspired the Serbs, and in 1912, the Turks were finally driven from the Balkans during the First Balkan War. Emotions linked to Kosovo still remain alive among the Serbs, and no other event in their history has had such a deep and lasting impact.

Under Turkish rule, 65 to 68 percent of the Albanians became Muslims, as did many Serbs and Croats in Bosnia-Herzegovina. The last two groups, however, retained their Slavic characteristics. The Serbs regarded the Albanians as friends of the Turks. The numerical preponderance of Albanians in Kosovo has contributed greatly to the two nations' almost uninterrupted hostility. In the Kingdom of Yugoslavia (1918–1941), the Albanians were generally considered second-class citizens, with no schools teaching their language. Several riots in the early 1920s were crushed by the army. The Yugoslav Communists, headed by Tito, took an opposite stand: the Albanians in Kosovo got not only elementary and secondary schools, but also the third largest university in Yugoslavia (after Belgrade and Zagreb), with some 50,000 students.

Despite all efforts, Kosovo remained Yugoslavia's most underdeveloped province. Its economic backwardness and the psychological atmosphere of hatred and intolerance between the two nations call for the conclusion that the relative progress achieved in Kosovo under communist rule has not led to a rapprochement between the Albanians and Serbs, but rather to an increase in mutual hostility. For some fourteen years (since Aleksandar Ranković's purge in June 1966), Kosovo was Tito's personal domain. Most of the officials ruling in Kosovo were his personal favorites, especially Mahmut Bakalli (b. 1936), the president of the provincial party committee. Yet, according to an American observer

(David Binder, *NYT*, 15 November), the seeds of Yugoslavia's current difficulties in Kosovo were planted in large part by Tito himself. The bloody rebellion took place a little more than a year after Tito had "generously and probably unwisely told [the Albanians] in their own Kosovo region, 'This land is yours.'" Tito's anti-Serbian line encouraged Albanian nationalists in Kosovo and led to a mass exodus of the Serbs from Kosovo. Moreover, the relative prosperity of Yugoslav Albanians compared with their ethnic kin in neighboring Albania did not enhance their loyalty to the Yugoslav state.

Aspects and Impact of the Kosovo Disturbances. In the first detailed official account of the incidents that forced Belgrade to proclaim a state of emergency in Kosovo, LCY Presidium member Stane Dolanc admitted, on 6 April, that party leaders were caught off guard by the Kosovo riots, during which, according to Dolanc, eleven people were killed and 57 wounded. (Western correspondents who visited Kosovo after the event thought these casualty figures extremely low; see ibid., 29 October.) "We and the Communists there were surprised by the violence, intensity, and brutality of these people," Dolanc declared. "It was planned and well organized [and had] nationalist, irredentist, and counterrevolutionary overtones." (*Vjesnik*, 7 April; *NYT*, 7 April.)

The variety of placards and slogans—"Kosovo—a republic"; "We are Albanians, not Yugoslavs"; "We have no rights here"; "We do not want capitalism, we want socialism"; "Marxism-Leninism"; "Down with the bourgeoisie"; "We want a unified Albania" (*NIN*, 12 April)—suggests that the protesters were indeed nationalists but also, at least some of them, extreme political leftists. While the slogan "Kosovo—a republic" was the most frequent and prominent and was considered the most moderate, there emerged a concept of "Albanization," which the Yugoslav press picked up. According to Stipe Šuvar, a leading Croatian Communist, Albanization consists in "the homogenization at any price, especially in the cultural, sociocultural, and sociopsychological fields, of all Albanians irrespective of state boundaries" (ibid., 30 August).

From the outset, Yugoslav leaders rejected the idea of a full-fledged republic of Kosovo; in Dolanc's words, "its establishment would in essence mean the disintegration of Yugoslavia" (*Vjesnik*, 7 April). Dušan Dragosavac went a step further: "There is a real danger now of other nationalisms manifesting themselves here and there in response to the revealed Albanian nationalism" (*NYT*, 6 April). Yugoslav public opinion reacted sharply, even indignantly, to the events in Kosovo (essentially through letters to the editors of dailies and weeklies), castigating the official press for late and inadequate reporting and government officials for unsatisfactory and often contradictory explanations concerning the background and characteristics of the riots. Official statements did not, however, fully answer the public's questions. In general, responsibility for Kosovo was attributed either to domestic weaknesses or to foreign intrigues. The LCY's official organ, *Komunist* (7 August), indulged in bitter self-criticism and stated that the crux of the matter was "the usurpation of power and LCY alienation from the working class. For many years techno-burocratic forces have been the source of usurpation and have unrestrictedly dominated the social life of the province." Stipe Šuvar agreed with this verdict and commented that the basic responsibility was attributable to "our lack of vigilance, our erroneous policy, our inability to correctly devise premises of socialist development in Kosovo, especially within the broader scope of intranational relations" (*NIN*, 30 August). Those higher in the LCY hierarchy preferred to look to conspiratorial domestic and external groups, manipulated by foreign powers, as sources of the upheaval. In a report to LCY Central Committee on 7 May, Lazar Mojsov stated that "counterrevolutionary elements were carefully organized from a foreign-agency center . . . camouflaged under the name Albanian Communist Marxist-Leninist Party in Yugoslavia" (ibid., 10 May). A few days later, Yugoslav Minister of Interior Gen. Franjo Herljević offered a slightly different version. In an interview with the Tanjug news agency, he said that "a pro-Albanian organization called the 'Red Hand' . . . active in accordance with instructions from Tirana [was also linked] with fascist Albanian groups abroad" (*Vjesnik*, 13 May). Speaking at a meeting on the first anniversary of Tito's death, Minister of Defense Gen. Nikola Ljubičić also alleged foreign involvement and attacked "different dark forces in the world hampered by a strong Yugoslavia" (*NIN*, 10 May).

The thesis of an international conspiracy against Yugoslavia focusing on Kosovo was advanced in a series of three articles written by Dušan Janković and published (with obvious official approval) in the most prominent Yugoslav weekly, *NIN* (26 July, 2 and 9 August). According to the author, the aims of the Kosovo counterrevolutionaries corresponded fully to the strategy of the so-called *indirect approach* and their actions to the methods of a *special war* (these phrases soon became routine expressions in the Yugoslav press). Basing his analysis on the Central Committee's evaluations, Janković asserted that by provoking the Kosovo crisis the enemy intended to accomplish a broader destabilization of Yugoslavia. Who was the "enemy"? The big-power blocs. The author remarked that simultaneously with the first demonstrations in Priština, NATO's military committee convened in Rome and reminded his readers that Italy was vitally interested in the "Albanian question" and the "Adriatic door." At the same time, a meeting of the Warsaw Pact's military representatives took place in Sofia. Their deliberations were seen in the light of the importance of the Albanian factor in the policy of Bulgaria. Here too, *NIN*'s readers were reminded that Bulgarian troops had occupied eastern Kosovo during World War II, incorporating it into Bulgaria. Pursuing his argument by quoting some Western books describing the onset of World War III, but insisting that Albania was being used by others, Janković described three phases of "counterrevolutionary conspiracy": preparatory (indoctrination, infiltration, organization), eruptive (violent demonstrations and riots), and armed insurrection, with foreign support if necessary. The first two phases succeeded in Kosovo, while the third failed owing to the effective counteraction of Yugoslavia's armed forces. But the "creeping counterrevolution" continued—the "special war" was going on.

Leaving aside the question of how NATO and the Warsaw Pact could use Enver Hoxha's Albania to destabilize Yugoslavia once order was re-established in Kosovo, Belgrade launched the "differentiation" campaign (another term entering official terminology). It consisted in investigating the culpability or loyalty of the citizens of Kosovo during the disturbances. Leaders of and participants in the riots were arrested, tried, and sentenced to usually heavy jail terms, while state and party officials found lax in the exercise of their duties lost their jobs or were demoted. Thus, at its plenary session on 6 August, the Kosovo provincial party committee purged Mahmut Bakalli, replacing him as president with the veteran Veli Deva (b. 1923). At the same session, four more members were either expelled or resigned. In addition, the provincial Presidium was reduced from nineteen to thirteen members (*Borba*, 7 August). The newly elected Kosovo provincial committee consisted of eight Albanians, four Serbs, and one Muslim. One day earlier, a similar reshuffle had been carried out within the top administrative structures of the province's government. Ali Šukrija (b. 1919), one of the most prominent party and war veterans, was elected president of the Kosovo State Presidency to replace Džavid Nimani (b. 1919), who resigned in July (ibid., 18 July). Finally, and quite surprisingly, Dušan Ristić, a Serb, the president of the Kosovo National Assembly, also resigned (ibid., 6 August).

On 17 November, the LCY Central Committee met in plenary session to discuss the situation in Kosovo nine months after the bloody riots. The major report was delivered by Dobroslav Ćulafić, secretary of the Presidium, who admitted that the main cause of the troubles in Kosovo had been the "erroneous policy" of the past, especially in "vital sectors of social, economic, and cultural life." Dealing with Enver Hoxha's request that Kosovo be given the status of a separate republic within Yugoslavia (*Zëri i Popullit*, 2 November), Ćulafić said that the LCY found the slogan "Kosovo—a republic" the same inside or outside Yugoslavia. As for the emigration of Serbs from Kosovo, Ćulafić stated that it had begun in 1968 and had increased during this year's "counterrevolutionary events." He argued, therefore, that everything must be done to stop the emigration and even make it possible for the Serbs who had emigrated to return (*Večernje novosti*, 18 November).

The ensuing discussion revealed that between 1 March and 6 November 663 persons had been expelled from the party, 373 dropped from its rolls, and eleven party organizations dissolved. In addition, 342 persons had been dismissed from their jobs (including 138 from various schools). A discussant warned that "hostile activities" continued in Kosovo, with unknown persons "writing slogans on walls, spreading leaflets, organizing acts of sabotage, threatening terrorist actions, etc." General Bruno Vuletić complained that army units serving in Kosovo and family members of officers and soldiers were subjected to "unworthy and indecent pressure" by "nationalistic and irredentist elements" trying "to present the soldiers of the Yugoslav army as an occupying force." Vuletić further alleged that "the Communists and commanders in the army wonder why our enemies have not yet been identified; some of them think that the enemies are to be found in our own ranks." He also raised the question of the guilt of the Central Committee of Serbia and even of the Central Committee of Yugoslavia and its Presidium for the Kosovo riots. (Ibid.) General Vuletić's remark can be understood as a warning by the army against Serbian and Yugoslav party leaders who have been trying to put the whole blame on Kosovo party leaders.

In the closing speech, Dušan Dragosavac dealt with the employment problems of "our Albanian comrades" in Kosovo. In his opinion, they should be given jobs and party functions not only in Kosovo, but also elsewhere in Yugoslavia. Dragosavac also touched on the problem of the overly severe sentences handed down in Kosovo against the rioters and said that the Presidium had discussed the problem. (Ibid., 20 November.)

Dragosavac's reference to harsh punishments against the rioters in Kosovo (in August alone the courts of Kosovo passed more than a thousand years of prison sentences against the rioters, many of them teenagers) reflected earlier criticism by Stipe Šuvar and the former prime minister, the Slovenian Mitja Ribičič. While rejecting the Kosovo Albanians' "Greater Albanian" chauvinism, Šuvar warned his Serbian comrades that excessive rigidity toward Kosovo Albanians might worsen the situation in the country as a whole (*NIN*, 30 August). Ribičič said that "the excesses in Kosovo" were "a product of the spirit of nationalist euphoria and are consequences of basing one's own [Kosovo's] development on credits and funds [aid from other republics], rather than on one's own work." He criticized the Kosovo party and state leaders who "did not go beyond the asphalt roads because the 'leading' Mercedeses do not go on macadam roads." Yet, Ribičič said, "I think that an eighteen-year-old boy who, having no education, thinks that the slogan 'We want a republic' means radicalism, that such a boy should not be sentenced to a twelve-year prison term . . . I am against court-administrative proceedings; political methods are more effective" (*Vjesnik*, 19 September).

Despite the repressive measures taken by the authorities, the situation in Kosovo remained tense. Radio Belgrade reported on 10 December "a continuation of hostile activities" at the Priština student center and emphasized the need for more effective differentiation.

The Third Self-Managers' Congress. Between 16 and 18 June, the Third Congress of Yugoslavia's Self-Managers took place in Belgrade. It was attended by 1,743 delegates: 1,405 elected in enterprises, 160 representing the six republics and the two autonomous provinces, 10 representing the army, 10 designated by civilians working in the army, 54 coming from abroad to represent Yugoslav "guest workers" in Western countries, and all 104 members of the Preparation Committee organizing the congress (ibid., 17 June). The first such congress had been held in June 1957 in Belgrade and the second in May 1971 in Sarajevo. The Third Congress was opened by Lazar Mojsov, at the time president of the Presidium. A resolution adopted on 18 June stated that "the fundamental social and economic conditions for workers to gain control over the entire income they generate have been created in Yugoslavia" (*Borba*, 19 June). Yet, it was evident from Mojsov's opening speech, the resolution adopted, and the comments of some speakers at the congress, that after 31 years of workers' self-management, the workers have not yet become "real self-managers." Mika Špiljak, a top CTUY functionary from Croatia, cautioned that "the weaknesses and difficulties perceived do not stem from self-management as such," but rather from "inconsistency and opposition to the implementation of the Yugoslav constitution and the [November 1969] Law on Associated Labor, which provide for the full development of self-management relations and the system of delegation" (ibid.). In a vivid report about the congress entitled "What Was Applauded," a *NIN* correspondent emphasized those speeches that expressed the delegates' criticism of the existing state of affairs. "Powerful applause," for example, greeted a speaker who requested the suppression of "double power," meaning that "decisions made in the name of the working class should be replaced by the self-managing decisions of the working class itself" (28 June).

Intellectual Pluralization and Varieties of Repression. The perception of a growing malaise in post-Tito Yugoslav society, sharpened by echoes of the extraordinary degree of intellectual freedom in Poland, emboldened many Yugoslav writers, intellectuals, university professors, directors of publishing houses, and editors of student papers to express nonconformist views or take actions they would have shunned in the recent past. The defenders of the official Yugoslav version of Marxism, while engaged in a sharp polemic among themselves, realized that ideological orthodoxy was a thing of the past and that the battle should be waged against direct "dissenters," ideological-political opponents of the regime who had to be prevented from reaching wider circles of the public.

Another aspect of pluralization is the appearance of books and articles of a nondissident character, often published by prominent firms or widely read magazines, whose themes are so remote from the official line that their publication would have been unthinkable a few years ago. Three examples will suffice. After being rejected for six years by publishers he had approached, the Slovenian author Branko Hofman found that 22 literary critics had pronounced his novel *Noć do jutra* (Night to morning) the best novel of 1981 and that it would be published soon both in the original Slovenian and in Serbo-Croatian translations. The novel deals with the hitherto taboo topic of the "hellish island" in the Adriatic on which thousands of Cominformists (members of the CPY who remained faithful to Stalin after the outbreak of his conflict with Tito in June 1948) were interned and tortured and on which many died. "Look at that miserable 'Goli otok' [the name of the island]," said Hofman in an interview. "We all knew about it. And we all pretended as if it had never existed." (*NIN*, 10 January 1982.) Second, a Serbian literary critic was asked to evaluate for *NIN* the ten best foreign novels published in Yugoslavia in 1981. He gave places one to four to two Polish writers (Leszek Kolakowski and Czeslaw Milosz), one Russian (Vladimir Voinovich), and one Czechoslovak (Milan Kundera), all of whom live abroad and are known as bitter critics of the regime in their native country. (Ibid.) Finally, again after several years of enforced waiting, a Belgrade publishing company started printing all of Dostoyevski's writings as a publicist and all of his notebooks dealing with philosophical-religious topics and literary criticism—the first endeavor of the kind in the world. The multivolume project will include the most significant works on Dostoyevsky written by prominent Russian religious writers. (Ibid.)

There were new developments throughout 1981 in the fifteen-year-old conflict between the regime and a group of professors at the School of Philosophy of the University of Belgrade who, according to an official claim, have "passed from disagreement over certain historical conceptions to positions that signify outright opposition to everything being done in our country to build socialist self-management" (*Borba*, 18 May). The incriminated professors (the "Belgrade seven") were suspended from their chairs in 1975 because of their affiliation with the Marxist "revisionist" periodical *Praxis*, banned in February of the same year. For years the tenacious professors, with the solid support of many of their colleagues and students, struggled legally and politically to regain their teaching positions. They lost the battle when the revised Serbian Universities Law of 5 June 1980 was applied at the end of that year. On 30 December 1980, the seven professors, including the internationally renowned Mihailo

Marković, Svetozar Stojanović, and Ljubomir Tadić, were dismissed from their positions as "suspended" employees of the university. The seven protested the dismissal as "illegal and anticonstitutional." At an enlarged session on 3 February, the university party committee accused the seven of "hostile activities" (*Vjesnik*, 4 February). Especially sharp attacks were directed against one of them, Professor Ljubomir Tadić, who stated in an interview published in an Austrian periodical that a "general crisis" prevailed in Yugoslavia and that "the old dogmatic practice of Stalinism is in operation," that is, "a dictatorship without a dictator" (*Wiener Tagebuch*, 1 January). In an interview given to a Swedish daily, Tadić said that Tito's successors "have never gotten themselves noticed other than as lackeys in the great charismatic leader's shadow. Now they are alone on the stage and try to derive their authority from the grave. A tragicomic situation! And they are themselves men without qualities, men who never in their lives have accomplished anything original or anything involving their own powers." (*Svenska Dagbladet*, 18 January.)

As a sort of job compensation, the dismissed professors accepted the Serbian government's offer of work in the Social Science Institute, which is attached to Belgrade University (Reuters, 22 March). In May, however, they again came under strong attack. Party officials in Belgrade and Zagreb accused them of "slandering the achievements of Yugoslavia's socialist revolution, of trying to set up an organizational network for the purpose of uniting extreme rightist and extreme leftist oppositional groups in Yugoslavia" (*Vjesnik*, 21 May; *Politika*, 20, 21, and 22 May). This strongly worded denunciation came as a belated reaction to a student meeting held on 23 April at Belgrade University. The meeting initially passed unnoticed by the press because it happened soon after the Kosovo riots. In May, however, the Belgrade weekly *Student* published an editorial devoted to it, which all the major Yugoslav dailies reprinted in full (*Borba*, 18 May). About four hundred students attended the 23 April meeting and expressed the opinion that the documents provided and discussed at the university party committee on 3 February were not complete or informative enough to give clear insight into the whole issue. Therefore, the students unanimously demanded that additional and complete information based on faculty archives should be provided in order to enable students of the philosophy department to see the problem clearly.

The authorities' alarm and utmost displeasure with the results of the 23 April meeting were expressed in *Borba* of 18 May. After regretting the students' "ignorance" and their naiveté in allowing themselves to become a "fertile ground for manipulation," the article drew much more sinister conclusions: "The period following the death of Comrade Tito has been seen by many forces as an opportunity for an attempt, why hide it, to shatter our community. We experienced the strongest manifestations of that with all the dramatics last month in Kosovo. We also see in the events at the School of Philosophy the germ of new attempts at destabilization. Perhaps these are strong words, but they are used advisedly. And the very proximity in time and a certain kind of continuity between the hostile activity in Kosovo and the events at the School of Philosophy are not accidental."

The device of denouncing and threatening oppositional elements, and giving full media exposure to the attacks, was used against other dissidents by the highest members of the LCY hierarchy. (In something that could be called a polemical David versus Goliath syndrome, the attacked usually answered by mimeographed "open letters," distributed in a few hundred copies and occasionally picked up by the Western press or printed in émigré publications, which increased the risk for the dissidents of being accused of contacts with enemies of the state.) In his New Year's message, Gen. Kosta Nadj, president of the partisan veterans' organization, threatened the prominent Serbian writer Dobrica Ćosić (a partisan fighter himself during World War II) and his friends with reprisals because of their "counterrevolutionary activities." In early March, Dr. Fuad Muhić, a top party theoretician from Sarajevo, sharply attacked Ćosić and Prof. Ljubomir Tadić for criticising "Titoism as an anti-Stalinist Stalinism" and scheming to "abolish the LCY as a revolutionary party" (ibid., 3 March). A few days earlier, the president of the Croatian Assembly, Jure Bilić, had berated "counterrevolutionary and nationalistic" groups in Croatia and other parts of Yugoslavia. His attacks on Ćosić and his friends concentrated on the forbidden periodical *Javnost* (see *YICA*, 1981, pp. 332–33). According to Bilić, the *Javnost* group was "treasonous, Great Serbian, and hegemonistic and needed to be unmasked" (*Vjesnik*, 19 February).

In blistering "open letters," Ćosić answered Nadj and Bilić. To the general, he said: "If in this country today people are sentenced to six years imprisonment solely for having begun singing 'nationalistic songs' in their own homes, celebrating the baptism of their baby [an allusion to the case of a Serbian Orthodox priest arrested and sentenced in October 1980], then, General, should your claim prove correct, for the 'nationalistic' and 'purely counterrevolutionary activities' of 'Ćosić's groups,' following the standards of your 'revolutionary justice,' I deserve to be sentenced to at least 66 years of imprisonment" (*Die Welt*, Bonn, 11 March). As for Bilić, Ćosić (with Tadić as a cosigner of the letter) counterattacked and accused the Croatian leader of "legalizing the language and the atmosphere of psychological terror [while the proposed unmasking measures] could represent a fertile ground for legalization of physical terror as well." (The letter was published in the London-based monthly *Naša reč*, May.)

Repressive measures against opposition in Croatia were particularly stern and got stiffer later in 1981. In the first trial of an important dissident since the death of Tito, Dr. Franjo Tudjman, 59, retired army general and former director of the Institute of the History of the Labor Movement, was sentenced on 20 February to three years imprisonment on charges of "maliciously and falsely presenting sociopolitical conditions in Yugoslavia" in interviews with foreign journalists. Tudjman was also accused of insisting that in the Ustashi concentration camp of Jasenovac "60,000 people—Serbs, Croats, Jews, Gypsies, and other antifascists—were exterminated, rather than 600,000 as the official statistics claim"—still a touchy issue in Yugoslavia and among the Yugoslavs abroad. In making this statement, Tudjman allegedly wanted to re-establish historical truth in order to "free the Croatian people from a collective and lasting guilt" (*Vjesnik*, 21 February). According to the Council on the Jasenovac Memorial Area, which for years has compiled figures on war crimes in the Independent State of Croatia during World War II, "around 700,000 victims found their death in the Jasenovac camp, and hundreds of thousands perished elsewhere . . . Only in Jasenovac were discovered 162 mass graves" (*Politika*, 4 April).

In May, a Zagreb University student, Dobroslav Paraga, 21, was sentenced to three years imprisonment for "antistate activities" (ibid., 21 May); in June the Croat writer Vlado Gotovac, 51, was sentenced to two years for the same reason (ibid., 6 June). The sternest sentence was pronounced on 9 September. Dr. Marko Veselica, 45, former professor of political economy at Zagreb University received a sentence of eleven years imprisonment for spreading "false information on conditions in Yugoslavia" to West German media and for maintaining connections with "extremist exiles" (*Borba* and *Vjesnik*, 10 September).

Indications of the extraordinary post-Tito nervousness among the Yugoslav secret police, or at least some of them, were apparent in the bizarre persecutions of Milovan Djilas and Vladimir Dedijer. Djilas has been the target of Yugoslav press invective so long that *Borba*'s attack on his latest biography of Tito, translated into five foreign languages, entitled "Djilas from One Treason to Another," was a routine obloquy (*Borba*, 23 October). What was new and alarming were the death threats Djilas claimed to have received from organs of the Yugoslav regime (see *Die Presse*, Vienna, 2 November; *Die Welt*, Bonn, 6 November). The gist of the threats, contained in letters Djilas received from abroad, was that unless he were ready to disclose all he knew about war crimes in Yugoslavia, his only son, Aleksa, 28, would be killed. (The younger Djilas is presently working on his Ph.D. dissertation at the London School of Economics and has already established an international reputation as an able and prolific publicist critical of the regime in Yugoslavia.) Djilas obviously intended to forewarn public opinion in the West if anything should happen to his son; he added that the episode could also serve as incriminating material in any trial that the regime might organize against him.

Dedijer's case was even stranger, given the success of the second volume of his biography of Tito. MIT Professor Noam Chomsky described Dedijer's present predicament in a letter to the *New York Times* (14 January 1982): "In the past several months . . . Vladimir Dedijer has been subjected to attacks and harassment that must arouse deep concern. He has been harshly denounced in the press. He and his family received death threats, and one of his co-workers was warned that his children would be killed if he continued to assist Dedijer in his work."

On a different level, Yugoslav police and courts were busy throughout the year arresting and sentencing individuals, in practically all parts of the country, for "criminal acts against the state." The common denominator in all the indictments was contact with terrorist exiles and subsequent attempts by the accused to organize local groups with subversive and terrorist aims.

Conflict Between State and Church. A BBC program on 30 July reported that "after several years of a relative calm in the relations between the Church and the Yugoslav state, these relations have suddenly turned to the worse during the last four months." A writer in *NIN* (2 August) asked: "Are our churches really [engaged] in an offensive, or is the state 'nervously' reacting because of the international and domestic situation?" The answer was unequivocal for Presidium member Branko Mikulić. In a candid and militant speech, he reviewed signs of "clerico-nationalism" (a term by now ubiquitous in Yugoslav journalism), in all the main churches in Yugoslavia. According to Mikulić, the churches were mounting a full offensive. In Croatia, for example, a continuation of prewar and wartime clerico-nationalist movements—a present-day "youth Catholic movement"—was being established; Muslim clerico-nationalism was fostering reactionary and counterrevolutionary ideas of Young Islam; Serbian Orthodox clerico-nationalists were building a "God-praying" movement whose main tenet was that all other churches were enemies of Orthodoxy. (Ibid.)

The Roman Catholic church in Croatia had a particularly intensive brush with state/party authorities eager to fight what they perceived as church meddling in politics. Early in the year, Jakov Blažević, Croatia's state president, sharply attacked the Catholic hierarchy, denouncing its alleged oppositional and nationalistic activities, especially in connection with the "cultivation of Alojzij Cardinal Stepinac's memory" (*Večernji list*, 31 January–1 February). (Sentenced in 1946 to sixteen years imprisonment as a "war criminal," Stepinac spent six years in prison and the remainder in detention in his native village, where he died in 1960.) Blažević's attack against the cardinal, who is respected and even revered among many Croats inside and outside the church, caused some seven thousand people to turn up for a special memorial mass for Stepinac in Zagreb Cathedral (*Economist*, 21 March). The most authoritative statement of the church's position was issued by a synod of the Conference of Yugoslav Bishops (Catholic) on 30 April in Zagreb. In five articles, the church's highest representatives clearly formulated their standpoint, proclaiming their loyalty "to our legitimate government" and denying the charge of making political claims. They affirmed their determination, however, to use all permissible means to "defend our believers from the atheization that is being systematically conducted in our society" and protested against government restrictions on some basic church's rights, including freedom of the religious press and exclusion of religion and the church from the news media. As for Cardinal Stepinac, they confidently stated that all testimony concerning his role would one day be re-examined. They concluded by expressing their readiness to cooperate with other churches, while performing their Catholic mission "in full conformity with the Holy See and in the spirit of the Second Vatican Council" (*Glas koncila*, 17 May). In his Easter message, Archbishop Franjo Kuharić of Zagreb, made a list of practical revendications for the Croatian church strikingly similar to those the church in Poland was seeking (*NIN*, 2 August).

During the summer, a "supernatural event" in a small Herzegovinian village escalated the conflict between the regime and the Catholic church. On 24 June, four children, aged eight to twelve, "saw and talked" with the Virgin Mary, who appeared to them over several days (*Svijet*, 13 July). Within days, crowds of up to 40,000 people a day started to arrive from all over the country, fasting, praying, singing religious hymns, and hoping for miraculous cures for the sick and crippled. At first, the church hierarchy maintained a reserved attitude, the press ridiculed the apparitions, and a top party leader dismissed the case as "political manipulation by clerical-nationalists" (*Economist*, 12 September). Soon, however, events took a nastier turn. The police accused the local priest of spreading "antisocialist propaganda and nationalist hatred," especially after he said in one of his sermons that "I, myself, and all of my listeners have been enslaved for the past forty years" (*Glas koncila*, 27 September). He was subsequently jailed and sentenced to three and a half years in prison for spreading "hostile propaganda" (AP and UPI, 22 October). A friar in a neighboring parish was also arrested and at first sentenced to 60 days for "obstructing the police in the exercise of their duties" in connection with the Virgin Mary apparitions, but in November he was sentenced to eight and a half years for "antistate propaganda" (*Vjesnik*, 13 August, 12 November).

Many priests, both Roman Catholic and Serb Orthodox, were arrested and sentenced to sometimes heavy jail terms, especially during the second part of the year. The most frequent charges were "provocation of religious intolerance" and "enemy activities." (*Bulletin*, the organ of the Committee to Aid Democratic Dissidents in Yugoslavia, printed in New York City, surveys the priests' arrests and sentences; see particularly nos. 8 and 9, 30 September and 30 November.)

The Economy. Overall economic performance in 1981 was highly unsatisfactory. As *Forbes* magazine (21 December) commented, "It won't be Soviet tanks threatening Yugoslavia but the world economic crisis compounded by domestic mismanagement" (which should be understood in the light of internal LCY conflicts, discussed earlier). Yugoslavia's problems were admitted and described with extraordinary frankness by the highest officials of the party, not to mention extremely worried economists, sociologists, and political scientists. Thus, the 30 September meeting of the LCY Central Committee drew attention to the gravity of the economic situation, reflected "in high inflation, high balance-of-payments deficit, high foreign indebtedness, excessive spending, and closing into [that is, retreating into] republican and regional boundaries" (Tanjug, 30 September). Two days later, in a speech in Bosnia, the outgoing chairman of the LCY Presidium, Lazar Mojsov, added to the list of economic shortcomings the lack of coordination between the social plan of Yugoslavia and the plans of the republics and provinces, while "the unity of the Yugoslav market is bursting at the regional and republican, provincial seams." After describing the central tenet of the Yugoslav economy—stabilization—as "a noisy slogan," Mojsov (in what must have been an angry speech) denounced such evils as "the habit of living off someone else's work, numerous deformations and disruptions of social values, erosion of morals, bribery, corruption, usurpation and other accompanying negative aspects." (Ibid., 1 October.)

The rate of inflation in 1981 was 43 percent, the highest since the 30 percent mark of 1960 (*NIN*, 10 January 1982). In the first nine months of 1981, Yugoslavia's foreign debt reached $21.2 billion (*Politika ekspres*, Belgrade, 15 October). *Forbes* (21 December) stated that in 1972 Yugoslavia's foreign debt was a manageable $4 billion. Calling the present figure "absurd," the article said that Yugoslavia's per capita indebtedness was higher than those of Poland, Brazil, or Turkey and that the cost of servicing the debt would rise to $4 billion in 1982. From January through September, Yugoslav exports totaled $5.38 billion, or 19 percent more than during the same period of 1980, while imports reached $8.8 billion, 10 percent more than in 1980. Only 61 percent of Yugoslavia's total imports were covered by exports. (*Ekonomska politika*, 5 October.) Some 2,620 enterprises, mainly industrial, lost a total of $8.1 billion, up 84 percent over the first nine months of 1980 (*Borba*, 20 September). According to Zagreb's *Vjesnik* (13 June), Yugoslav labor productivity is only 33 percent of that in other middle to highly developed countries. The overall situation in agriculture was negative; the 1981 wheat crop was 7 percent less than the 1980 crop, and the country had to import $111 million worth of food (*CSM*, 15 December). In a postwar first, the 1981–1985 plan will give priority to agriculture.

There were 5,740,000 persons employed in the socialist sector of the economy (*Borba*, 24 July) and 802,877 unemployed (*Ekonomska politika*, 24 August), a 14 percent rate of unemployment (*Vjesnik*, 23 November; *Die Presse*, 25 November). Discrepancies exist concerning the number of Yugoslav workers employed abroad. The 1981 census put the figure at 577,648; the institute in charge of the labor force listed 452,728; foreign statistics published at the end of 1980 mentioned 706,845 persons; according to the Yugoslav Federal Office of Labor Exchange, some 800,000 Yugoslavs were working abroad, accompanied by 237,246 family members (*Politika ekspres*, 19 October).

The average monthly salary for workers was 7,000–9,000 dinars ($180–240). From January to May, 243,500 million dinars (about $6.5 billion) went for personal wages and salaries, 36 percent more than in the same period in 1980. Since the cost of living jumped by 42 percent, "it appears that the real personal income of the employed was reduced by 7 percent" (*Ekonomska politika*, 13 July).

The Yugoslav economy was not without its strong points. The level of industrial production was within planned limits. About $2 billion was expected as net earnings from tourism (*Večernje novosti*, 17 October). Gross foreign currency remittances from workers abroad should rise to $5.7 billion (Reuters, 15 December). "The country's always active underground economy is showing new signs of growth as mechanics and plumbers and others with marketable skills cut down on their official jobs and increase their moonlighting ... for hard currency" (*Forbes*, 21 December). Finally, as observed in the *Christian Science Monitor* (28 December), "if the Yugoslavs are not rebelling—like the Poles—it is because many can draw on savings made in the previous decade of ever-increasing income."

The sluggish economic performance in 1981 prompted Yugoslav planners to outline more modest goals for the immediate future, while concentrating on the essentials: higher productivity with an emphasis on increased exports, lowering of the rate of inflation, and improvement (or at least a halt in the decrease) of the standard of living.

Foreign Policy: *The Soviet Union.* Soviet-Yugoslav relations in the first year after Tito's death were characterized by efforts on both sides to avoid any deterioration. The Yugoslav press published some critical articles concerning certain aspects of Soviet policies in the past and even the present, but on the official level Tito's successors were anxious to strengthen Yugoslavia's political (party), trade, and military contacts with Moscow.

Party Relations. The LCY delegation at the Twenty-Sixth Soviet Congress in Moscow was headed by Dušan Dragosavac, at that time the secretary of the Presidium. He addressed the congress's 25 February session, praising Lenin and the October Revolution as well as the revolution in Yugoslavia, "which was also a part of the general struggle throughout the world for the liberation of people from exploitation and oppression." He extolled Tito and Yugoslavia's self-management system ("inspired by the teachings of Marx, Engels, and Lenin"). Dragosavac said Yugoslav-Soviet relations were "developing successfully on the principles established in the Belgrade [1955] and Moscow [1956] declarations and in other Yugoslav-Soviet documents adopted during the meetings between Comrades Tito and Brezhnev ... We assessed Comrade Brezhnev's attendance at Tito's funeral [in May 1980] as an expression of respect for Tito and as an expression of readiness to continue developing all-around, equal, and mutually useful Yugoslav-Soviet cooperation, to which the LCY Central Committee attaches great attention." (*Borba*, 26 February.)

On his way to Asia, Yugoslav Foreign Minister Josip Vrhovec met Soviet First Deputy Foreign Minister Viktor Maltsev in Moscow (Tass, 20 May). A week later it was reported in Moscow that the

Soviet Union would honor Tito by naming a new street or a square in Moscow and a street in the Siberian city of Omsk after him. Also a special postage stamp with Tito's portrait was to be issued, and a Soviet merchant ship built in Yugoslavia was to be named after the Yugoslav leader. (Ibid., 28 May.) In July Leonid Brezhnev sent a telegram to Yugoslav leaders on the fortieth anniversary of the "uprising and the socialist revolution in Yugoslavia" praising Yugoslav-Soviet friendship (Tanjug, 3 July). In September, in connection with the tenth anniversary of the Yugoslav-Soviet declaration signed by Tito and Brezhnev in Belgrade, the Soviet press positively appraised the development of Yugoslav-Soviet relations in the past decade (*Pravda*, 26 September).

Trade Relations. The great increase in Yugoslavia's trade with the Soviet Union provoked many comments both in the country and abroad. In explanation, Yugoslav media pointed to the difficulty of selling Yugoslav products in the West and to "consumer expansion" in East Europe. In July, the Yugoslav Chamber of Economy estimated that trade with the Soviet Union might reach U.S. $6 billion in 1981, $250 million over plan. Yugoslav exports to the Soviet Union were expected to be about $3.15 billion and imports about $2.85 billion. In the first five months alone, Yugoslavia and the Soviet Union exchanged $2.55 billion worth of goods, with Yugoslav exports amounting to $1.36 billion. As in the past, oil continued to be Yugoslavia's major import from the Soviet Union; its exports to that country consisted mainly of copper, alloys, aluminum, footwear, textiles, and machinery. (Tanjug, 16 July.)

On 15 June, a Yugoslav-Soviet trade agreement for 1981–1985 was signed in Moscow. It provides for $32 billion in trade, a record 80 percent increase over the previous five-year period (*Vjesnik*, 16 June; *NIN*, 12 July). On the same occasion it was announced that Moscow will offer a ten-year, $450 million credit to Yugoslavia at 4 percent, with no payments for the first two years. Yugoslavia will use the money to buy Soviet goods. Radio Moscow (15 June) quoted the Yugoslav federal secretary for foreign trade as saying that "Soviet-Yugoslav cooperation has not before known such a scale of exchange. Yugoslavia does not have such developed economic relations with any other country of the world." Prominent Western newspapers noted and commented with some alarm on such a trend. The *Wall Street Journal* (2 June) entitled a detailed article, "Tito's Legacy: Yugoslavia, After Years of Economic Neglect, May Have No Choice but to Lift Exports to Russia." The *Christian Science Monitor* (7 January 1982) offered a wealth of statistical data on the same topic, and *Forbes* magazine (21 December) was most explicit: "A loss of economic independence has already set in. In 1970 Communist customers accounted for only 30 percent of Yugoslavia's merchandise exports. By last year the figure had climbed to 46 percent. Russia now provides about 40 percent of Yugoslavia's 16-million-ton-a-year oil consumption and could reduce the economy to chaos with a twist of the valve." Yugoslav officials insisted that their "Eastern connection" (the title of an article published in *NIN* on 12 July) was a matter of necessity and not of a deliberate choice and that Yugoslavia remained faithful to its Titoist nonaligned position in international affairs.

Military Contacts. On 29 June, Sergei G. Gorshkov, commander of the Soviet Navy and admiral of the fleet, arrived in Belgrade at the head of a naval delegation on a six-day "official and friendly visit" as a guest of the Yugoslav armed forces (*Politika*, 30 June). A month earlier, a group of Soviet ships had sailed unofficially into Dubrovnik to visit the cultural and historical sights of the town (Tanjug, 27 May). While in Yugoslavia, Gorshkov had talks with Adm. Branko Mamula, chief of staff of the Yugoslav Army. Gorshkov left Yugoslavia on 4 July.

On 6 July, another top Soviet military personality, Gen. Aleksei A. Yepishev, chief of the Main Political Directorate of the Soviet Army and Navy, arrived in Belgrade as an official guest of the Yugoslav armed forces. Immediately after his arrival, Yepishev was received by Gen. Nikola Ljubičić, Yugoslavia's defense minister. Three days later, Yepishev had talks with Gen. Dane Ćuić, president of the party committee in the Yugoslav People's Army, as well as with Dobroslav Ćulafić, secretary of the

Yugoslav Presidium (*Borba*, 10 July). No details of the visit were published in the press, but according to "informed sources" Yepishev's talks with top Yugoslav military leaders "included negotiations on production under license in Yugoslavia of a version of the Soviet T-72 tank" (Reuters, 10 July). Earlier it was reported that for the first time in fifteen years, the Yugoslav Navy received a new ship from the Soviet Union, a 2,000-ton, rocket-carrying frigate (*Die Welt*, 2 April). In October, a new group of Soviet ships arrived in Dubrovnik for an "unofficial visit" (AP, 8 October).

Polemics. The Zagreb fortnightly *Start* (the Yugoslav equivalent of *Playboy*) published excerpts in a Croatian translation from the book *Razpotja komunizma* [Communism's crossroads] by Slovenian journalist and author Janez Stanič. Stanič made many critical remarks concerning Soviet policies in the past, especially the invasion of Czechoslovakia in August 1968. He also referred unflatteringly to Brezhnev's "personality cult," criticized Moscow's theory of "limited sovereignty," and described the Soviet Union as the "main obstacle" to any real integration of Eastern Europe (*Start*, 30 January). A party monthly also claimed that as long as "closely knit groups" in Eastern Europe, especially in the Soviet Union, insisted that only the Soviet socialist mode was correct, the danger of armed conflict between communist countries would increase day by day (*Socijalizam*, January).

In March, an article in a Belgrade daily criticized both the West and the East for the worsening international situation (*Borba*, 15 March). *Pravda* (19 April) reacted sharply to the article, but its author, Vlado Teslić, retorted that Yugoslavia would continue to defend its independence: "We have never equated the blocs on the basis of the time at which they were established or on the basis of any other characteristics. However, we have always consistently declared [our opposition] to bloc party and foreign domination and to all forms of political and economic hegemony" (*Borba*, 26 April).

The United States. The presidential change in Washington was accepted in Belgrade with relief after U.S. Ambassador to Yugoslavia Lawrence Eagelburger was apointed assistant secretary of state for European affairs (*Stuttgarter Zeitung*, 20 January). But the fear remained that Reagan might become "a reactionary president," although he was rated a "wise politician who demonstrated this characteristic as governor of California" (*Vjesnik*, 20 January). Commenting on President Reagan's inaugural speech, Radio Zagreb (21 January) expressed hope that the new U.S. administration would behave toward Yugoslavia in the same manner as did the previous one. President Reagan's first press conference on 29 January was said to have been "iced" with "cold war tones" (Tanjug, 30 January). Still the hope remained that the U.S. president would "transform" his views (*Borba*, 1 February).

Throughout 1981, Yugoslav-U.S. relations showed elements of both disagreement and cooperation. In February, the Yugoslav Foreign Ministry objected to the U.S. intervention in El Salvador (Tanjug, 23 February). Four days later, the U.S. Navy destroyer *John Hancock* arrived in the north Adriatic port of Rijeka "on an unofficial visit" (ibid., 27 February). In March, Yugoslavia's ambassador to Washington, Budimir Lončar, paid an official visit to Pittsburgh, a center for many Americans of Yugoslav origin (*Politika* 7 March). Two Serbian exiles were sent to jail for ten years on "bombing and conspiracy charges" (AP, 4 February), and five "Croatian terrorists" were convicted on federal charges involving an aborted plot to commit bombings and murder "in order to promote their cause" (*NYT*, 28 March). They were given sentences of 20 to 35 years (ibid., 13 May).

The assassination attempt on President Reagan shocked Yugoslavia (Radio Belgrade, 30 March; Radio Zagreb, 31 March). Yugoslav Foreign Trade Secretary Metod Rotar paid an official visit to the United States at the end of April and beginning of May, and U.S. Agriculture Secretary John Block visited Yugoslavia in late May. From 31 May to 3 June, the traditional gathering of Yugoslav and U.S. economists took place in Dubrovnik. A statement by Lawrence Eagelburger before the Subcommittee for Europe and Middle East of the House of Representatives that Yugoslav-U.S. relations were developing favorably found a positive echo in Belgrade (*Borba*, 12 June).

On 18 and 19 June, U.S. Deputy Secretary of Defense Frank Carlucci had official talks in

Belgrade with Yugoslav Defense Minister Gen. Nikola Ljubičić (*Politika*, 20 June). Several days later, Yugoslav media sharply attacked "President Reagan's anticommunist statements" (*Večernji list*, 23 June). In July, Yugoslav authorities requested the extradition of Andrija Artuković, 81, who as minister of interior for the Nazi-allied Independent State of Croatia during World War II allegedly ordered the death of hundreds of thousands of Serbs and Jews (*NIN*, 12 July).

The most important event of the year was a short stay in Belgrade on 12 and 13 September of U.S. Secretary of State Alexander Haig. He praised Yugoslavia's "strong tradition of freedom and independence" and its "strong leadership role in the nonaligned movement." Haig noted that 1981 marked the hundredth anniversary of diplomatic relations between Belgrade and Washington (Tanjug, 12 September). A joint statement issued on 13 September stressed the need for a continuing dialogue to develop Yugoslav-American relations on the basis of equality and mutual respect. It reaffirmed the principles of independence, sovereignty, equality, and noninterference as the basis for relations between the two countries (Reuters, 13 September). In his toast at a dinner in Belgrade, Secretary Haig said that "we also admire Yugoslavia for its many sons and daughters who have contributed, as Yugoslav Americans, to the richness and diversity of our own country." Turning to Washington's current attitude toward Yugoslavia, Secretary Haig said: "The Reagan administration, like its predecessors, will continue the traditional American policy of strong support for Yugoslavia's independence, territorial integrity, and national unity. We believe that an independent, truly nonaligned Yugoslavia is a positive factor in ensuring both European security and world peace. Our position with regard to Yugoslavia is clear." (Tanjug, 12 September.) Secretary Haig added, however, that the views of the American and Yugoslav governments were not always identical on "all international problems." "It is no secret," Haig said, "that we have had differences and that we will have them in the future."

In October, a group of 35 U.S. company executives, on a fact-finding visit to Yugoslavia, held talks with Premier Veselin Djuranović on ways and means of intensifying bilateral economic cooperation (UPI, 23 October). While in Belgrade, they were received by Petar Stambolić, vice-president of the State Presidency, who told them that "Yugoslavia adheres firmly to Tito's course of safeguarding its full independence and nonalignment in foreign policy, as well as of developing the self-management socialist system and full equality of all nationalities and national minorities in domestic policy" (Tanjug, 24 October).

The U.S.-Yugoslav Economic Council met in New York on 5 December mainly to discuss the "stagnation" in economic relations between the two countries. During the first nine months of 1981, Yugoslav exports to the United States amounted to $195 million and imports to $537 million, a deficit of $342 million (*Indeks*, no. 11, November, p. 32). The American participants in the talks insisted that the greatest obstacle to economic cooperation was the absence of Yugoslav legislation designed to encourage American investment. The American hosts were told that "in the spring of next year" new measures would be adopted (*Politika*, 6 December).

China. Yugoslav-Chinese state and party relations remained friendly, although economic cooperation did not reach the planned level. Throughout the year, Yugoslav media were full of articles and reports concerning changes in China during the five years since Mao's death. The trial and sentencing to death of Mao's widow, Jiang Qing, were depicted as "a trial against a suicidal course, against leftism run amok, which led the Chinese revolution to an absurdity: it began eating itself and waging a war against common sense" (*Komunist*, 30 January). Another comment asserted that Jiang's trial was "one more step in the direction of internal democratization" (Radio Zagreb, 27 January). Hu Yaobang, then general secretary of the Chinese Communist Party, was extolled as a leader "playing an ever more significant role" in China's political life and "a realistic reformer" (*Vjesnik*, 15 February).

After a visit to China, Antun Vratuša, former prime minister of Slovenia, said in an interview that China's most important preoccupation was economic reform. Vratuša stated that favorable conditions existed for the improvement of Yugoslav-Chinese cooperation. In Beijing, he added, a special association with three hundred members was studying the Yugoslav economic system (*Komunist*, 20 March).

On 29 May, Yugoslav Foreign Minister Josip Vrhovec arrived in Beijing for a four-day official visit. During a formal dinner, Ji Pengfei, vice-premier of the State Council and head of the International Liaison Department of the Chinese Central Committee, praised Yugoslavia's "great successes," especially in promoting the socialist self-management system. Vrhovec returned the compliment by hailing "the successes the Chinese people are achieving in their struggle for socialism and well-being" (Tanjug, 29 May). Next day, Chinese Premier Zhao Ziyang received Vrhovec and praised Yugoslavia's role in the nonaligned movement. In a communiqué issued at the end of Vrhovec's visit, it was said that both sides were satisfied with "very fruitful talks," which had especially emphasized the role of nonaligned countries (*Vjesnik*, 3 June).

In early June, a Chinese economic exhibition was organized in Belgrade. That same month Xiong Fu, editor in chief of the Chinese party's theoretical organ, *Red Flag*, was the guest of the LCY's *Komunist*. In an interview, Xiong discussed the problems plaguing the Chinese party, especially since 80 percent of China's one billion inhabitants are peasants. One of the goals soon to be achieved, Xiong said, was the rehabilitation of the old cadres: "During the Cultural Revolution, about 100 million people suffered." Other tasks were the improvement of the political situation ("in the recent past, there were sabotage, unrest, and the like") and the "strengthening and perfecting of the party leadership," with an emphasis on the elimination of overly powerful individuals. Xiong called Mao "a great leader of our revolution," but admitted that Mao had committed many mistakes. (*Komunist*, 26 June.)

Dobroslav Ćulafić headed an LCY delegation to China, where he stayed from 5 to 11 November. On 7 November, Ćulafić met Hu Yaobang, the new chairman of the Chinese Communist Party, who assessed Yugoslav-Chinese relations "very highly" and paid a tribute "to the independent Yugoslav road in internal development and international activities and to the consistent continuation of Tito's policy" (Radio Belgrade, 7 November). On 11 November, Deng Xiaoping, vice-chairman of the Chinese party, met Ćulafić and praised relations between the two parties (NCNA, 11 November). The same day, Ćulafić said that "the LCY and the Chinese Communist Party were determined to continue developing and promoting Yugoslav-Chinese cooperation on the basis of equality and mutual respect and to further strengthen friendship between the peoples of Yugoslavia and China" (Tanjug, 11 November).

The Yugoslavs complained, however, that "economic cooperation has not kept up with the level of development of political cooperation." Both sides tried to justify such a negative trend "by their internal difficulties." Instead of the planned annual trade amounting to a total value of $300 million (in both directions), the actual value of trade in 1980 was around $160 million. (*Borba*, 5 November.) During the first nine months of 1981, Yugoslav exports to China amounted to $13 million, while Yugoslav imports from China amounted to $21 million (*Indeks*, no. 11, November, p. 32).

Poland. In 1981, the Yugoslav ambivalence toward the events in Poland continued: on the one hand, the Yugoslav Communists defended the Poles' right to self-determination; on the other, they were on guard against the spread of the "infection" to Yugoslavia. In a speech before the Kosovo provincial party committee, Dušan Dragosavac stated in mid-January: "As Communists and as a socialist country, we shall, to the best of our ability, extend our moral and material support to the Polish party and state leadership in the resolving of the current situation ... Our sympathy is not directed toward anything that is or could be antisocialist" (*Borba*, 15 January). In this sense, LCY leaders shared the attitude expressed by Mieczyslaw Rakowski, Poland's deputy prime minister, in an interview given while visiting Yugoslavia in June. Rakowski admitted that the Polish United Workers' Party (PUWP) had so far failed "to meet the demands of the time," but he also affirmed that the Polish party would "not share the power with forces that are against it," such as Solidarity (*Komunist*, 26

June). Heading an LCY delegation to the PUWP's extraordinary congress in Warsaw in mid-July, Aleksandar Grličkov, a member of the LCY Presidium, stated in a speech to the congress that Yugoslavia was convinced that the Polish people, "led by the party," would implement socialist renewal and further progress in all fields of Polish national life (Tanjug, 15 July). Stanislaw Kania's reelection as head of the PUWP was highly praised (ibid., 19 July).

Yugoslav officials were aware, of course, of the tremendous impact of Solidarity on Polish workers. They—alone in Eastern Europe—sent a trade union delegation to attend the Solidarity congress in Gdansk in September–October. The head of the delegation, which returned before the end of the meeting, stated that "Yugoslav unions are opposed to all interference and that is why they oppose the Solidarity message to Eastern Europe" inviting official trade unions to establish independent unions following the Polish example (*Rad*, 18 September). Contrary to some Western analysts who saw similarities between the Yugoslav practice of workers' self-management and Solidarity's (very different) program for industrial democracy, LCY leaders made the necessary distinctions. Poland "should follow no model of any kind; not even the Yugoslav model should serve as an example," said Miloš Minić, the member of the LCY Presidium in charge of foreign policy. "The Polish people, the Polish working class, and the PUWP alone are called upon to find a solution for the difficulties that the country has been experiencing and to find the path to further socialist development in Poland—without interference from any quarter whatsoever." (*Politika*, 26 June.) Minić's statement reflected the fear of Yugoslav leaders that a deterioration in the Polish situation could lead to a Soviet military intervention, which they fervently hoped would not take place.

The Yugoslav media covered the events in Poland extensively. Without contradicting the LCY's line of confidence in the PUWP's recuperative powers, the Yugoslav press and Yugoslav correspondents in Poland were much less sanguine on that score. *Borba* (10 March) bluntly stated that "the Polish party is in deep trouble," and Zagreb's *Vjesnik* (30 March) asserted that the "party is divided, irresolute, not yet really determined to implement the policy of renewal." According to the *NIN* correspondent in Warsaw (18 October), the PUWP had lost every confrontation with Solidarity. (*NIN*'s reporting from Poland in 1981 was among the most comprehensive and informative in Europe, East or West.)

Official Yugoslav reaction to the imposition of martial law in Poland on 13 December was predictable. A spokesman for the Federal Secretariat of Foreign Affairs stated on 15 December that what had happened was "an internal affair of Poland" and that "the Polish people, the Polish working class, the PUWP and other Polish political forces are the only ones called upon, within the ambit of that country's sovereignty, to find a way out of the crisis in which Poland has found itself" (Tanjug, 15 December). That same day, the Commission for International Cooperation of the LCY's Presidium expressed its hope that Poland's difficulties would be resolved "by democratic means, through agreements and contracts, and also through implementation of social and economic reforms which much correspond to the needs of the development of Polish society. This, of course, also means the suppression of antisocialist and anticommunist forces." (Ibid., 16 December.) On 18 December, Stane Dolanc briefed Ljubljana's communist activists on Poland and observed that "it was the first time in the history of socialist countries that the army has seized power. With this development, Poland has become an exceptionally dangerous hotbed of crisis, which could have grave consequences within Polish society, in the workers' movement in the world and in international relations in general." (Ibid., 18 December.) On 25 December, the CTUY Council expressed the confidence of Yugoslav trade unionists that "a solution [to the Polish crisis] can be found in a democratic way, through dialogue and agreement among the socialist and other democratic forces in the Polish society" (ibid., 25 December).

The Yugoslav media did not conceal their concerns over the Polish coup. Radio Zagreb commentator Milika Šundić asserted (16 December) that the military crackdown "had been in preparation for a long time" and that Jaruzelski's proclamation "does not represent the end but [rather] the deepening of the existing crisis." The Ljubljana daily *Delo* (16 December) entitled an article: "Poland: The Situation Has Not Eased, Nor Are the People Satisified," and Belgrade's *Politika* (16 December) warned that both "civil war and foreign intervention would be an irreparable tragedy for Poland, a heavy blow against socialism, and a serious danger to peace in Europe."

During the first nine months of 1981, Yugoslavia's exports to Poland amounted to $150 million and imports to $123 million (*Indeks*, no. 11, November, p. 32), compared with $262 million and $275 million, respectively, for all of 1980 (Tanjug, 3 February).

Relations with Neighboring Countries. (See the section dealing with the Kosovo riots for relations with Albania.) Yugoslav-Bulgarian relations in 1981 vacillated between vitriolic polemics over the Macedonian question and exchanges of official delegations discussing ways and means of improving trade and other relations between the two countries. An article published in the Bulgarian historical periodical *Vekove*, for example, was sharply attacked because of its "virulent anti-Yugoslav propaganda" (*Vjesnik*, 12 February), its "forgetting of Bulgaria's fascist past" (Radio Zagreb, 14 February), and its ascription of "the role of liberators to Bulgarian fascist troops who, together with Hitler's Wehrmacht, marched into Yugoslavia early in World War II" (*Borba*, 27 February). At the same time, a CTUY delegation on an official four-day visit to Bulgaria had talks with "Bulgarian colleagues . . . in an open and constructive spirit and in an atmosphere of cordiality and mutual understanding" (Tanjug, 12 February). The memoirs of veteran Bulgarian Communist Tsola Dragoycheva were sharply attacked by Svetozar Vukmanović-Tempo, a veteran Yugoslav communist, as "distorting historical facts and joining the anti-Yugoslav campaign" (*NIN*, 22 February). A few days later, another article in the Bulgarian historical periodical *Istoričeski pregled* was assailed for "being full of falsifications concerning the final war operations for the liberation of Yugoslavia" (*Borba*, 8 March). Dragoycheva's memoirs were again severely criticized for "having intensified the slanders against the Yugoslav communist party" (*Nova Makedonija*, 13 March). The Twelfth Congress of the Bulgarian Communist Party, held in Sofia 31 March to 4 April, was attended by a low-level LCY delegation headed by Svetozar Durutović, an executive secretary of the LCY Presidium. In his speech at the congress, Durutović called for efforts to solve disputes between Yugoslavia and Bulgaria (*Politika*, 2 April). Durutović also spoke in the Bulgarian town of Rousse and called for equal rights for all national minorities (*Borba*, 4 April). During a two-day meeting in Belgrade (9 and 10 April), delegations of the Yugoslav and Bulgarian writers' unions discussed future cooperation between their two organizations (Tanjug, 10 April). Lazar Koliševski, top Macedonian leader and author of *Aspects of the Macedonian Question*, scored Bulgaria for attempting "to deny the Macedonian national identity" (ibid., 15 April). A day later, a protocol on long-term Yugoslav-Bulgarian cooperation in the automobile industry was signed in Sofia (ibid., 16 April).

New attacks against Tsola Dragoycheva appeared in the middle of May. A Skoplje daily alleged that "some circles in Bulgaria have apparently reached the conclusion that the present moment is convenient for the further escalation of Greater Bulgarian nationalistic positions in that country's policy on the 'Macadonian national question' " (*Nova Makedonija*, 16 May). Shortly thereafter, Ivan Stambolić, Serbia's prime minister, received Andrey Lukanov, Bulgarian Politburo member and deputy prime minister; the next day, he was received by Yugoslav Prime Minister Veselin Djuranović (ibid., 19 and 20 May). In September, Yugoslav border guards "shot and killed a Bulgarian citizen" (Radio Sofia, 4 September). The Yugoslavs denied the Bulgarian version of the incident, accusing "three Bulgarian citizens" of trying to infiltrate Yugoslav territory (Tanjug, 7 September). Later that month, Dragoslav Marković, president of the Yugoslav National Assembly, said in a speech that "one of the biggest problems facing the two countries was the rights of the Macedonian minority in Bulgaria" (ibid., 24 September).

During the first nine months of 1981, Yugoslavia's exports to Bulgaria amounted to $52 million and imports to $81 million (*Indeks*, no. 11, November, p. 32). In April, it was reported that the two countries would increase their mutual trade in the period 1981–1985 to $3 billion (*Ekonomska politika*, 11 May), a significant increase over the $1.2 billion total for the 1976–1980 period (Tanjug, 20 April).

Yugoslav-Romanian relations continued to be friendly, as the frequency and cordiality of top-level contacts indicated. Tito used to meet Romanian leader Nicolae Ceauşescu every year. In February, then President of the Yugoslav State Presidency Cvijetin Mijatović paid an offical two-day visit to Romania and had talks with Ceauşescu (*Borba*, 3 February). Several days later, Yugoslavia's deputy prime minister in charge of the economy, Zvone Dragan, arrived in Bucharest to sign a trade protocol covering the 1981–1985 plan. In the period 1976–1980, total trade value reached $2 billion; in 1981–1985, it is to reach $4.01 billion (Tanjug, 14 February).

In April, Romanian Prime Minister Ilie Verdet paid an official three-day visit to Yugoslavia and held talks with Veselin Djuranović centered on intensifying bilateral cooperation in line with the Tito-Ceauşescu accords (*Borba*, 10 April). The volume of trade between the two countries was to reach $740 million in 1981 (*Privredni pregled*, 7 May), although Yugoslav economic sources estimated that it would not exceed $300 million (*Ekonomska politika*, 16 June).

In early July, Yugoslav Defense Minister Nikola Ljubičić visited Romania for talks with his counterpart and also was received by Ceauşescu (*Vjesnik*, 11 July). In September, Romanian Foreign Minister Stefan Andrei paid an official visit to Yugoslavia for talks with Josip Vrhovec. The two ministers urged noninterference in the affairs of other countries and strict respect for the principles of independence, sovereignty, territorial integrity, and equality. (Ibid., 16 September.) In October, Patriarch Justin of the Romanian Orthodox church arrived in Belgrade as a guest of the Serbian Orthodox church (Tanjug, 1 October). On 9 and 10 November, Sergej Kraigher, president of the State Presidency, paid an official visit to Romania, where he had talks with Ceauşescu. According to a joint communiqué, Yugoslavia supported a Romanian proposal to hold a conference in Bucharest in 1982 of experts on multilateral cooperation in the Balkans in the fields of energy and raw materials (ibid., 11 November).

Despite some minor disagreements, Yugoslav-Hungarian relations developed in a friendly way. Of all the members of the socialist camp, Hungary has been considered in Yugoslavia as "the most outstanding example of a successful harmonization between foreign pressure designed to bring about the equalization of socialism throughout the camp and domestic demands to preserve one's own specific features" (*Start*, 28 March). In April, Zvone Dragan arrived in Budapest to discuss questions of collaboration between Hungarian and Yugoslav planning bodies (Radio Budapest, 14 April). In the first nine months of 1981, Yugoslavia's exports to Hungary amounted to $134 million and imports to $145 million (*Indeks*, no. 11, November, p. 32).

At the end of April, Yugoslav media criticized an article in the Hungarian party daily *Népszabadság* for "distorted" reporting about the Kosovo riots (see, for example, *Borba*, 26 April). In June, an LCY delegation headed by then President of the Presidium Lazar Mojsov, paid an official visit to Hungary. In an implicit reference to Poland, the joint communiqué insisted that "communist and workers' parties, and every other progressive movement . . . [must] shape their policy, the road, and means of attaining their historical aims independently and in a sovereign way" (*Vjesnik*, 6 June). Also in June, the Hungarian and Yugoslav defense ministers held talks in Belgrade (*Borba*, 23 June). Several days later, a number of accords providing "for expanded ties between the armies of the two countries" were signed (Radio Budapest, 28 June).

The problem of the Slovene minority in Austria, an irritant in past relations between the two countries, was toned down in 1981, with the Yugoslav insistence that their countrymen in Austria should be treated correctly. Yugoslavia's trade deficit with Austria was very high. During the first nine months of 1981, Yugoslavia's exports to Austria amounted to $111 million and imports to $306 million (*Indeks*, no. 11, November, p. 32). To remedy the situation, the Yugoslav government decided on 5

December to restrict "shopping tourism" with Austria (as well as with Italy). The restriction meant that the amount of goods—mainly coffee and various detergents—that could be imported duty free was reduced from 1,500 dinars (about \$40; \$1 = 38 dinars) to only 200 dinars (about \$5.25) (*Borba*, 7 December).

Giorgio Napolitano, a member of the Italian Communist Party Secretariat, spent two days in Belgrade discussing the international situation, European détente, the nonaligned movement, and the international communist movement with LCY leaders (*L'Unità*, 20 February; *Borba*, 20 February). In March, a Yugoslav army delegation headed by Adm. Branko Manula paid an official visit to Rome (Tanjug, 3 March). Commemorating the sixth anniversary of the Osimo Agreements signed in October 1975 between Yugoslavia and Italy, Yugoslavia media hailed the positive development in Yugoslav-Italian relations (*Vjesnik*, 30 August). In September, Enrico Berlinguer had talks in Belgrade with Yugoslav party and state leaders (*Borba*, 7 September). In October, Josip Vrhovec and Italian Foreign Minister Emilio Colombo formally opened to traffic a new border crossing near Nova Gorica (*Vjesnik*, 19 October).

During the first nine months of 1981, Yugoslav exports to Italy amounted to \$505 million and imports to \$726 million, a trade deficit of \$221 million (*Indeks*, no. 11, November, p. 32). In 1980, the Yugoslav deficit had amounted to \$280 million (*Politika*, 29 January).

Nonalignment. Yugoslavia's role in the nonaligned movement after Tito's death was reduced to keeping alive memories of the pivotal role Tito had played in the movement. In September, the twentieth anniversary of the first nonaligned summit in Belgrade was solemnly commemorated (see *Vjesnik*, 29 August, special supplement). On 9–12 February, at the nonaligned foreign ministers' conference in New Delhi, the Afghanistan issue caused great difficulties, despite Indira Gandhi's plea for unity and cooperation. Initially, Yugoslav leaders were not satisfied with prospects for the New Delhi conference because of "disagreements in the movement in interpreting and implementing the original principle of nonalignment and because some nonaligned countries resort to the use of force" (Radio Zagreb, 7 February). After the conference ended, the Yugoslavs changed their attitude and praised it as "an unqualified success," especially in view of the conference's affirmation of the principles adopted at the sixth nonaligned summit in Havana, including the nonbloc orientation of the movement (*Borba*, 15 February). Yugoslav media hailed the fact that in New Delhi "Belgrade-1961 and Josip Broz Tito were designated as specific symbols of the policy and movement of nonalignment" (ibid., 12 February). According to Yugoslav commentators, the nonaligned movement "has asserted itself as the only international factor able to offer long-term and complete political solutions leading the world out of the political and economic crisis into which it has been pushed by the bloc powers" (*Medjunarodna politika*, March).

Publications. The main publications of the LCY are *Komunist* (weekly) and *Socijalizam* (monthly). The most important weeklies are *NIN* (*Nedeljne informativne novine*; Belgrade) and *Ekonomska politika* (Belgrade). The major daily newspapers are *Borba* (published in Belgrade and Zagreb), *Vjesnik* (Zagreb), *Oslobodjenie* (Sarajevo), *Politika* (Belgrade), *Delo* (Ljubljana), and *Nova Makedonija* (Skoplje). Tanjug is the official news agency.

Radio Free Europe   Slobodan Stanković
Munich, Germany

Council for
Mutual Economic Assistance

In 1981, despite mounting domestic problems, particularly among the East European member-states and increased difficulties with integration, the Council for Mutual Economic Assistance (CMEA) focused much of its concern on developments in Poland. Created in 1949, the CMEA comprises the Soviet Union, Bulgaria, Czechoslovakia, East Germany, Hungary, Poland, Romania, and the non-European states of Cuba, Mongolia, and Vietnam. Whereas all of the member-states suffered from declining economic growth rates, unsatisfactory productivity, inflation, consumer shortages, expensive and/or uncertain energy supplies, and hard-currency indebtedness to the West, in Poland these problems have led that state to the brink of political and economic disaster, deeply affecting the other members.

Structurally, the CMEA rejects the notion of supranationality and appears to conform to the oft-declared principles of national sovereignty and equality of member-states. Unlike the European Economic Community (EEC), it does not have an international legal personality. The CMEA Council is the chief decision-making forum, and its powers are strictly circumscribed. Its recommendations take effect only if member-governments adopt them. The unanimous vote provision incorporated into the charter continues to determine voting practice. In fact, the CMEA suffers from institutional under-development, and it was only in 1971 that the three major committees were created: the Committee for Planning and Cooperation, the Committee for Scientific and Technical Cooperation, and the Committee for Materials and Technical Supply. These committees were given the right to "influence" the work of other CMEA organs and to assign certain priorities.

Despite the principle of equality, the CMEA was and remains a Soviet-controlled organization. Since World War II, Moscow has sought to impose general conformity in domestic and foreign policies in Eastern Europe. Initially, the motivation was largely political, and the idea of economic integration was not compatible with the Soviet and East Central European system of "command economies" revolving around a central plan. Genuine economic integration would involve the creation of a single command economy encompassing all member-states.

The Soviet Union has, however, made significant progress in achieving its goal of greater control over the bloc states and over the newer members outside of Europe. In 1962, Moscow managed to push through the adoption of the "international socialist division of labor," which called for the coordination of member-states' economies and an acceleration of specialization. This attempt failed in large part because of the determined opposition of Romania (with tacit support from some of the other states). Two CMEA banks were also created: in 1964 the International Bank of Economic Cooperation, with the "convertible ruble" as its base currency, and in 1970 the International Investment Bank as a projected multilateral clearing bank. Neither was especially successful, and the ruble continues to have only very limited convertibility. A number of multilateral projects were undertaken, including joint pipelines and joint investments in iron ore extraction. The most significant step toward integration, however, was undertaken in 1971 when the twenty-fifth CMEA Council session adopted the "comprehensive program for economic intergration." This program was amplified in 1975 when the twenty-ninth council session approved a five-year plan for further multilateral economic integration. It envisioned ten large projects, nine of which provided for closer links among the Soviet Union and the bloc states, costing 9 billion transfer rubles (U.S. $12.2 billion) (*Times*, London, 3 January 1976). In 1976, at the thirtieth council session, further coordination and integration were envisioned. This process has continued. The aim has been to set a "complex target program" for coordinating long-term planning to 1990, involving five "target groups": fuel and energy; machine building; agriculture and food supply; consumer goods; and transport (Radio Free Europe–Radio Liberty, *Research*, no. 147, 16 June 1980). To achieve this goal, Soviet Premier Alexei Kosygin urged members at the thirty-second council meeting in 1978 to move decisively toward the overall integration of their individual economies (*Scînteia*, 28 June 1978). In 1979, at the thirty-third session, he stressed the need for joint effort in the energy field (see *YICA*, 1980, p. 108).

Ten years after the introduction of the "comprehensive program for economic integration," the CMEA continues to pursue the goal of socialist integration. Such integration, though perceptible, has been slow. Although deliveries of machinery, for example, rose to 40 percent of intra-CMEA trade from 10 percent in 1971 (*Economic Survey of Europe in 1979*, Geneva, 1980, p. 219), delays in production coordination and a cumbersome, interlocking barter trade system have hindered progress. Attempts to create greater regional self-sufficiency through several long-term target programs resulted in a 1978 decision to focus on fuel, machine building, and agriculture and food production.

The ninety-eighth CMEA Executive Committee session, held in Moscow on 13–15 January 1981, discussed long-range plans for scientific and technical cooperation and on fuel and energy production (*Pravda*, 17 January). Representatives of the ten CMEA members and Yugoslavia's permanent representative to the organization focused on the creation of machine and equipment complexes and the improvement of productivity through greater cooperation. The Executive Committee instructed CMEA organs to draw up proposals on expanding cooperation among member-states in order to meet fuel and energy requirements to 1990 and beyond.

Moscow continued to urge greater integration within the CMEA throughout the year. At the Soviet party congress in February, Leonid Brezhnev urged the socialist states to intensify cooperation in production and in science and technology. He proposed economic coordination, a convergence of economic mechanisms, and direct contacts among state bodies and organizations within the CMEA. But as the economic situation deteriorated in Eastern Europe, such goals became even more difficult to attain. The economic and political quagmire in Poland has greatly complicated joint planning and joint investments. Poland has had difficulties in delivering essential goods to its CMEA partners and has sought additional loans as well as delays in repaying existing loans not only from its Western creditors but also from its CMEA partners. These were some of the most pressing problems confronting the thirty-fifth council session, which met in Sofia on 2–4 July.

Thirty-Fifth CMEA Council Session. In addition to the ten members, Yugoslavia participated in the conference and signed the protocol. The session was attended by invited observers from Angola, Afghanistan, South Yemen, Laos, Mozambique, and Ethiopia. Among other matters, the session was to formulate the Coordinated Plan for Multilateral Integration Measures for the period 1981–1985. Pressure for reform had been building up within the organization, but Poland's difficulties presented extra constraints. Warsaw's inability to restore economic health not only delayed its own five-year national plan but resulted in failures to deliver goods contracted by its partners and to fulfill important joint investment obligations. These reinforced planning uncertainties in the CMEA. Whereas Poland's national income contracted by 4 percent in 1980, some projections coming from Poland itself have suggested a decline of 15 percent for 1981 (*Zycie Gospodarzce*, no. 23; George Blazyca, "Comecon and the Polish Crisis," *World Today*, October, p. 376). Industrial production dropped 10 percent in the first quarter of 1981. In the first four months, machine tool production fell 20 percent, while heavy vehicle production contracted by 14 percent (*Financial Times*, 6 April, 8 July). Poland's failure to deliver contracted goods hit the CMEA particularly hard because of its highly coordinated trading system, which, due to its reliance on long-range economic projections in five-year plans, lacks the flexibility to adjust quickly to new conditions. The drop in Polish machinery exports to the Soviet Union was significant, and Warsaw's failure to deliver about $40 million worth of coal, sulphur, and machinery angered its five East European partners. In 1981, the situation worsened. East European leaders have complained bitterly about Poland's inability to meet its trade commitments and have attributed many shortcomings in their own economies to these trade disruptions. Poland, for its part, came to the thirty-fifth session hoping both for a sympathetic hearing and for aid.

Hopes for the formulation of an effective coordination program were unfulfilled. The communiqué (*Pravda*, 7 July) agreed only in principle on the main guidelines for the five-year plans of member-states. The session approved the Coordinated Plan for Multilateral Integration Measures, but left debate on many crucial details to a summit of party leaders in early 1982 and to the next CMEA Council session, scheduled for Budapest. Moreover, it did not resolve the problem of Poland's inability to contribute to key joint investment projects or to deliver goods. Nor did the participants reach an agreement on multilateral aid to Poland. CMEA Secretary General Nikolai Fadeyev declared on 5 July that although member-states were working independently on the problem, the session had not discussed the question of joint aid (*Facts on File*, 1981, p. 513). In April, the Soviet Union had warned that it would not save a CMEA country from defaulting on loans to Western nations.

The Soviet Union and the other East European members of the CMEA did extend considerable help to Poland. Between August 1980 and June 1981, Moscow gave Poland $4.2 billion in credits including $965 million in convertible currencies (PAP, in Russian, 20 June; Radio Free Europe, *Background Report*, 15 July). Figures from the Bank for International Settlements show that Soviet deposits in Western banks fell $3.05 billion during the first quarter of 1981, while Poland registered a marked decline in its borrowings, which fell from $15.1 billion to $14.7 billion (*Toronto Globe and Mail*, 24 August). These figures suggest that Poland paid some of its debts to Western banks during the first quarter with the help of the Soviet Union. After an informal summit between Brezhnev and Polish party leader Stanislaw Kania and Premier Wojciech Jaruzelski on 14 August, the Soviet Union announced that it would postpone repayment until 1986 of more than $4 billion in credits owed it by Poland (*Toronto Daily Star*, 24 August). Bulgaria, Czechoslovakia, Hungary, East Germany, and Romania provided Poland with additional food and consumer goods during 1981. Repayment for these deliveries, which were worth nearly $100 million at official exchange rates, has been deferred until 1983 to 1989 (PAP, 23 June; Radio Free Europe, *Background Report*, 15 July). Given the magnitude of Poland's problems, such aid may be inadequate. It does, however, show the concern of all East European states over Poland's economic and political stability.

At the July session, the member-states apparently disagreed over machinery, chemicals, and agricultural prices. Unlike the EEC, the CMEA does not have a common agricultural policy. Hungary, Romania, and Bulgaria, the main East European food exporters, argued strongly for higher agricultural prices, but the session could agree only that greater attention would be paid to agriculture in the organization's future plans (*Times*, London, 6 July). Energy cooperation was also an area of disagreement, even though several of the member-states, including Romania, were eager to provide funds, equipment, and labor for joint projects that would assure an expansion of energy supplies from Moscow. Much needed currency reforms were not discussed at all at the meeting, according to Fadeyev (*Facts on File*, 1981, p. 513). The limited convertibility of the ruble has been a significant barrier to trade. The highly developed East European states would benefit most from a fully convertible ruble and have been pressing strongly for such currency reforms, without success.

The few specifics in the session's communiqué dealt with scientific and technological cooperation, for example, in the development of microtechnology and telephone equipment, and measures for promoting economic development in Vietnam, Cuba, and Mongolia. More aid will be given to these countries, including help to increase the production and processing of citrus fruit in Cuba. The communiqué also mentioned the greater cooperation between the CMEA and Yugoslavia in recent years. (*Pravda*, 7 July.)

There was considerable criticism of the session, particularly by Romania. Prime Minister Ilie Verdet expressed his deep disapointment that Romania's suggestion that trade among the member-states should double between 1981 and 1985 was not accepted and that only a 38 percent increase was envisioned (Agerpres, 6 July). His criticism probably reflected Bucharest's frustration over the uncertainty of future energy supplies from the Soviet Union. A Romanian delegate did declare after the meeting that the thirty-fifth session had failed to resolve the "main problem" (*Times*, London, 6 July). There was some more subtle criticism from the other East European member-states as well. For instance, György Lázár, chairman of the Council of Ministers of Hungary, declared at the session that long-term reliable provision of fuels, energy, and raw materials was of strategic importance to Hungary and that existing procedures should be refined further (*Magyar Hirlap*, 3 July).

These problems, however, have not been the only blocks to greater integration in the CMEA. For example, Poland's problems have driven Warsaw to increase its trade with CMEA member-states. In the first four months of 1981, Polish imports from the socialist countries grew by 14.4 percent, while imports from the capitalist countries fell by 17.8 percent (*Zycie Gospodarcze*, no. 22; Blazyca, "Comecon," p. 377). Romania and Yugoslavia also increased their trade with CMEA states. But even though this may have strengthened Soviet leverage over these states, economic problems affecting all of the member-states were key factors in retarding integration. According to the West German Institute of Economic Research (DIW) in 1980 the CMEA turned in its worst economic performance to date (*Financial Times*, 19 June). According to the DIW, the Soviet Union had a growth rate of 2–3 percent, well below target. In 1981, the difficulties faced by the Soviet economy did not abate. The shortfall in agricultural production was especially disastrous (total grain output dipped below 175 million tons).

The combined growth rate of the six East European members of the CMEA was 1.1 percent in 1980, according to the DIW report, with Poland registering a 4 percent contraction in its produced national income (gross national income minus services). Romania has been particularly hard hit by rising energy prices and by the Iran-Iraqi war, which has deprived it of much of the oil that it was able to purchase on a barter basis. Coupled with poor agricultural production, this has led to increasing shortages of consumer goods. As in the case of Poland, food staples, if available, can be had only after long waits. Consequently, Romania introduced rationing and instituted an intensive campaign against hoarding. Due to hard-currency problems, Bucharest has had to turn increasingly to the Soviet bloc for grain. Hungary, one of the more successful economies in the CMEA, has also encountered increasing difficulties, including new inflationary pressures and rising import bills. The national five-year plan for 1981–1985 envisions a moderate 2–3 percent annual growth rate (*Magyar Hirlap*, 3 July). East Germany was the only European CMEA state to improve its produced national income in 1980. Its growth rate rose from 3.6 percent in 1979 to 4.2 percent in 1980, according to DIW figures; however, its "consumer socialism" is being replaced by a new austerity. The regime has conducted an intensive and unsubtle propaganda campaign to turn the resentment of the population against the Poles. Czechoslovakia has also encountered difficulties as its technological edge erodes. Both it and Bulgaria have been turning their trade more toward the Soviet Union.

These problems have led the East European members to implement urgent measures to stave off the type of economic (and political) deterioration that has occurred in Poland. Romanian leader Nicolae Ceaușescu fired several officials, including the finance minister, the planning chief, and the agricultural minister. In February, he began a program of change designed to reduce growth in industry and to allocate more investment to agriculture (*Toronto Globe and Mail*, 2 November). Czechoslovakia, Bulgaria, and even East Germany have shifted resources from investment to consumption. Economic growth rates have slowed throughout the Soviet bloc, and governments are emphasizing qualitative improvements in the economy.

A fundamental flaw in these economies hinders efforts to cope with such problems as the current worldwide inflation, energy shortages, and bad harvests. The problem is that planned economies lack flexibility. Attempts to reform the system have enjoyed only limited success. The Soviet Union has viewed the weakening of centralized control and the introduction of market measures as challenges to the rule of the communist party. Instead, it has opted for an infusion of new technology from the West. With the exceptions of Hungary and now Poland, Soviet bloc states have followed the Soviet model fairly closely. Even Budapest modified its 1968 New Economic Mechanism (NEM) in the early 1970s, when it ran into worker opposition over pay differentials. But massive borrowing of technology and the consequent huge trade deficit with the West have not helped the CMEA states solve their problems.

Measures that indicate a trend toward the decentralization of decision making and an increase in the autonomy of individual enterprises have been introduced in Eastern Europe (*NATO Review*, June 1980, pp. 27–30). The degree of decentralization and the restructuring of price systems in order to reflect supply and demand more closely vary considerably from state to state. They range from minor reforms in Bulgaria and East Germany to a noticeable comeback for the NEM in Hungary. There are inherent obstacles, however, to the type of decentralization and market orientation that may bring about the necessary flexibility. In Romania, Bulgaria, Czechoslovakia, and East Germany, the ruling parties are very sensitive to any potential challenges to their own centralized control. Soviet concern about threats to socialism in Hungary and in Poland work as strong external constraints in addition to the domestic ones that exist. Such limitations have made it difficult to cope with current problems, including the growing energy crisis. The Soviet Union's own statistics show that its CMEA partners can now meet only 65 percent of their energy needs from the communist world. By the end of the decade, the figure, according to some estimates, will fall to 50 percent. (*Economist*, London, 30 August 1980.)

Energy. Before the quantum increase in world oil prices in 1973, the Soviet Union could and was willing to meet the oil needs of the CMEA states. After 1973, Moscow not only increased its prices to the other CMEA members but also restricted the supply. The price increases were large, reaching 130 percent in 1975, for example. A more stable pricing system was devised; adjustments were made on a yearly basis on prices calculated according to the average world levels over the preceding five years. There were indications that the Soviet Union wanted to change the pricing system in 1980 but backed down for the time being because of objections from the other CMEA members. Price discussions, however, are continuing among the CMEA states, and the Soviet Union may move to world prices soon. For the moment, CMEA importers have been enjoying lower than world prices. According to Yugoslav sources, the Soviet Union has been delivering oil to the CMEA states at 25 percent below world prices (Tanjug, 1 March 1980; *FBIS*, 5 March 1980). In July, Moscow claimed that during 1979 Soviet deliveries reduced East Germany's oil bill by 30 to 40 percent and that Poland saved 2.5 billion rubles during 1975–1980 (Tass, 18 July 1980; *FBIS*, 22 July 1980). The eagerness of CMEA countries to have access to Soviet oil, even with the large price increases, is understandable. This, in turn, naturally helped increase Soviet leverage over these states.

The growth rate of Soviet oil production has been declining, however, and some Western sources predict that Moscow may become a net importer of oil. In 1980, the USSR produced 12 million barrels per day, as opposed to the original target of 12.4–12.8 million barrels (*Business Week*, 15 December 1980). The 80 million tons of oil per year that Kosygin promised in June 1980 for the next five years will not meet the requirements of the CMEA states. In 1979, the Soviet Union supplied only 70 million tons of their 120-million-ton requirement (ibid., 3 March 1980). With a current requirement of 150 million tons, the CMEA states must purchase 70 million tons on the world market. Given high world prices and the unreliability of such suppliers as Iran and Iraq, the importance of Soviet oil to CMEA members will increase despite its probable decrease as a proportion of their total oil imports.

Attempts by the East European states to obtain increased imports of Soviet oil have apparently been unsuccessful. In June, there were reports from Moscow that the Soviet Union would deliver more oil, gas, and other raw materials (Moscow World Service, 14 June; *FBIS*, 25 June). Natural gas deliveries to the European CMEA members were to increase by 50 percent and oil deliveries for the 1981–1985 plan period by an estimated 30 million tons (Moscow World Service, in English, 18 June; *FBIS*, 25 June). But at the thirty-fifth session, Secretary General Fadeyev would say only that Moscow would not reduce future exports from the 1980 level of 80 million tons annually (Radio Free Europe, *Situation Report*, 31 July, p. 15). A July statement by Nikolai Tikhonov, chairman of the Council of Ministers of the USSR, suggested that Moscow had not changed its mind (*Times*, London, 6 July). Tikhonov did say, however, that the summit meetings of CMEA heads of state, long sought by the East European members because of their concern with energy supplies, would discuss energy.

In addition to oil, the Soviet Union's continuing ability to supply other energy resources helps increase its control over the CMEA. Moscow has the capacity to increase its exports of natural gas and electricity through intra-CMEA grids and can and does supply nuclear power plants. The Orenburg gas pipeline, a major joint CMEA project, began operations in 1979. Even Romania, which has tried to avoid dependence on the Soviet Union in order to pursue an autonomous foreign policy, now receives a yearly quota of 1.5 billion cubic meters of natural gas through this pipeline (Radio Moscow, 12 July 1980; *FBIS*, 25 July 1980). Hungary is scheduled to receive increased amounts of Soviet electricity through the Ukraine-Hungary intergrid electric transmission line, in addition to natural gas and oil. The Soviet Union and the CMEA states plan to build 150 nuclear plants with a total capacity of 140,000–150,000 megawatts by 1990. Moscow plans to use nuclear power to generate 25 percent of Soviet electricity by 1990, Czechoslovakia 40 percent, Bulgaria 50 percent, and Hungary 25 percent. (*Eastern Economist*, 8 February 1980, p. 227.) The nuclear technology is to come from the Soviet Union (Czechoslovakia is the only CMEA state licensed to build Soviet-designed reactors).

Joint investment in production of electricity from nuclear power is becoming the norm for the European members of CMEA. Massive nuclear power plants are being built or are planned in the Soviet Union to supply electricity to East European states. All of these nations, including Yugoslavia, are involved to some degree. At the thirty-third CMEA Council session of June 1979, the European members and Yugoslavia agreed that more than fifty major industrial enterprises from the signatory countries should participate in a program for the manufacture and delivery of equipment for nuclear power stations (Radio Free Europe, *Background Report*, 20 January). The East European states have invested heavily in the building of these plants. A large nuclear power station is to be completed at Khmelnitskiy by 1984 and another one is planned at Konstantinovka to be completed before 1990 (*Figyelo*, 30 April 1980, p. 4). Czechoslovakia, Hungary, and Poland have joined with the Soviet Union in building the first plant (both have a capacity of 4,000 megawatts of electricity). Warsaw has been by far the largest East European contributor. Romania and apparently Bulgaria and East Germany will participate in the second project (Radio Free Europe, *Background Report*, 20 January). In addition, Poland has contracted to participate in the construction of two larger nuclear power stations in the Soviet Union at Kursk and Smolensk. Poland's inability to provide all the funds it had promised is therefore very disruptive.

Despite some manufacture of parts in Eastern Europe, basic nuclear technology is to come from the Soviet Union. Romania is the only exception. Bucharest has purchased Candu reactors from Canada and intends to build these reactors under license. The Iran-Iraqi war, however, has drastically reduced Romanian barter purchases of Middle Eastern oil, and high prices on the spot market may greatly weaken Romania's ability to buy Western technology. The crisis was significant enough to force

Romanian President Nicolae Ceauşescu to cancel a projected October visit to Canada to sign agreements for additional Candu reactors. In 1981, Romania did secure a $300 million loan from the U.S. Export-Import Bank for a nuclear power plant, but this is a relatively small amount, given the cost of large plants. If the crisis persists, Romania may also have to turn to the Soviet Union for nuclear technology.

Indebtedness to the West. Hard-currency debts pose a continuing problem for the European CMEA states. Purchases of high-technology goods and grain from the West have led to adverse trade balances and ever higher hard-currency debts. The repayment of these debts has become increasingly burdensome. According to a Central Intelligence Agency assessment, the gross debt for the Soviet Union, the East European states, and the CMEA banks totaled $77.1 billion and the net debt came to $64.7 billion at the end of 1979. The study also showed that the 1979 debt service ratio (based on exports to noncommunist states) came to 18 percent for the Soviet Union, 92 percent for Poland, 54 percent for East Germany, 38 percent for Bulgaria, 37 percent for Hungary, and 22 percent for Romania and Czechoslovakia. ("Estimating Soviet and East European Hard Currency Debt," June 1980.) For most of the European CMEA states, the situation deteriorated further in 1980 and 1981. Soviet and East European debts (without the CMEA banks) reached $78.9 billion in 1980 (*NYT*, 27 September). There were increases in Poland, Romania, the Soviet Union, East Germany, and Czechoslovakia. The first two registered the largest increases, with the Polish debt reaching $24.5–27 billion (ibid., 3 July) and that of Romania, $9.4 billion. This huge foreign debt is both symbolic of and to a significant extent responsible for the dire economic straits of Poland. Romania, with a much smaller economy than that of Poland, is also in great difficulty. In the fall of 1981, it obtained a $1.3 billion loan from the International Monetary Fund, but this is still inadequate. It has been desperately trying to reduce its balance of payments deficit from the record $2.4 billion of 1980 to $1.8 billion in 1981 (ibid., 27 September) and to reorient more of its trade toward the socialist bloc. Nevertheless, diplomatic sources have disclosed that Romania has been negotiating with Western companies to allow payment delays, in some cases by as much as six months, in order to avoid the problem of asking Western banks for extensions (*Toronto Globe and Mail*, 5 November). A concerted effort by the Soviet Union and the East European states to reduce imports from the West and to increase their own sales can enjoy only a limited success. Given the bad harvest in the Soviet Union, Moscow has to continue to import vast quantities of grain from hard-currency areas, and all of the CMEA states need to buy Western technology. On the other hand, their manufactured goods are of low quality and encounter great difficulties competing on Western markets. The Soviet Union is in the best position of all the CMEA states since it is able to sell large quantities of gold for hard currency and has reached agreements with West European nations, particularly with West Germany, to supply natural gas and other raw materials in substantial quantities.

As CMEA indebtedness has increased, Western nations have begun to show greater caution in making additional loans. Yet they cannot cut off loans to the CMEA states altogether, for when debts become large enough, the debtor's leverage increases as that of the creditor's decreases. The CMEA states continue to be eager to trade and to seek Western loans although they may be more cautious in the future about getting into greater debt. They face a dilemma: if they do not drastically reform their economies to make them more sensitive to market forces and thereby create the necessary flexibility to deal with crises, they require Western technology and loans as an alternative (if unsuccessful) means of coping with problems. If, on the other hand, they move to introduce significant market-style reforms, they need Western technology to rebuild their outmoded plants.

Romania, in its eagerness for Western trade concessions, broke ranks with the other CMEA states. CMEA policy has been that general treaties should be signed only on an organization-to-organization basis, but on 28 August 1980, Romania signed two agreements with the EEC, which came into force on 1 January 1981. Bucharest's agreement with the EEC assures it of substantially increased access to West European markets. In November, Romanian Deputy Prime Minister Cornel Burtica, during talks with the EEC Commission, asked for an accord on economic cooperation to back up the existing trade pact between his country and the EEC (ibid., 6 November). Poland also felt that its grave economic situation necessitated aid from the West in addition to that from the Soviet Union, and it has made repeated requests to Western nations. In November, it applied for membership in the World Bank and the International Monetary Fund (ibid., 11 November). This could bring increased aid to its economy but also opens it to outside influence. Since the socialist states have contended that the World Bank and the International Monetary Fund are Western-controlled institutions, the Polish move is quite a bold one.

Trade with the West and the large indebtedness of the East European CMEA states should not obscure the Soviet Union's continuing control. Moscow's leverage may even increase as the East European CMEA states become more cautious about borrowing from the West and Western banks become more reluctant to lend additional funds. Although integration has proceeded glacially at best, CMEA trade is increasingly directed toward the Soviet Union as the preponderant trading partner and supplier of vital raw materials and energy. As the economic situation in Eastern Europe deteriorates and the dependence of the non-European CMEA members on foreign aid grows, Soviet dominance of the CMEA can only increase.

University of Toronto   Aurel Braun

Warsaw Treaty Organization

Uncertainly and tension characterized the activities of the Warsaw Treaty Organization (WTO) in 1981. The turmoil in Poland raised fears that the events of 1968 in Czechoslovakia would be repeated. Soviet condemnations, which were parroted by the leaders of most WTO members, and military exercises raised the specter of the imposition of the Brezhnev Doctrine on Poland. This focus on intra-WTO relations obscured somewhat the intensive Soviet and WTO effort to ensure their continued nuclear and conventional superiority in Europe.

Created on 14 May 1955, the WTO was Moscow's response to the decision of the Western allies to include West Germany in NATO. Moscow declared that the WTO's aim was to prevent the remilitarization of West Germany and to help dissolve NATO. Moscow's offer to disband the WTO if NATO is simultaneously liquidated is reiterated every year. In addition to the multilateral WTO, the Soviet Union created a network of bilateral treaties in Eastern Europe after 1955. However, a multilateral treaty provided Moscow with political, military, and juridical benefits that bilateral treaties might not have. Moreover, in certain limited ways, a multilateral forum may be useful for conflict resolution among the member-states and as a safety valve for nationalistic frustrations.

Although the disparities between NATO and the WTO regarding the importance and nature of membership make dissolution of the Western alliance such a prize for Moscow that it would be worth the sacrifice of the WTO, this ultimate and often expressed Soviet goal belies the pact's growing importance. The WTO has become a useful forum for articulating policy agreement and support for Soviet proposals. A multilateral alliance is also an important asset to Moscow in its ideological confrontations with the West and the People's Republic of China. Militarily, a multilateral alliance has enhanced the ability of the Soviet Union to create more effective defensive and offensive forces in Europe. Juridically, the WTO provided a partial legal justification for the 1968 invasion of Czechoslovakia. It is little wonder that by 1971 Brezhnev declared that the WTO was "the main center for coordinating the fraternal countries' foreign policies."

Nominally, the WTO is an organization of sovereign states (East Germany, Poland, Czechoslovakia, Hungary, Romania, Bulgaria, and the Soviet Union). Its top governing body is the Political Consultative Committee (PCC), composed of the first secretaries of communist parties, heads of state, and foreign and defense ministers of the member-states. Day-to-day affairs are handled by the Joint Secretariat, which is chaired by a Soviet official and has a representative from each country. There is also a Permanent Commission (located, as is the Secretariat, in Moscow), which makes foreign policy recommendations for the WTO. Supreme military power is supposed to reside in the Committee of Defense Ministers. Created in 1969, it consists of the defense ministers of the six East European states and the Soviet Union. A second military body, the Joint High Command, is responsible for strengthening the WTO's defense capabilities, preparing military plans in case of war, and deciding the deployment of troops. The command consists of a commander in chief and the Military Council. The council meets under the chairmanship of WTO's commander in chief and includes the chief of staff and permanent military representatives from each of the allied armed forces. There is also a Committee of Military Technology. In 1976, a Committee of Foreign Ministers and a Unified Secretariat were added. Both the commander in chief and the chief of staff have always been Soviet generals. Currently, Marshal Viktor G. Kulikov is commander in chief, and Army Gen. Anatoli I. Gribkov is first deputy commander and chief of staff. Air defense, which has a high priority in WTO and Soviet strategic planning, has always been under a Soviet commander. The Soviet Union continues to provide the bulk of WTO air defense, which consists of early radar warning systems, air defense control centers, a manned interceptor force, and surface-to-air missiles and antiaircraft artillery units. These four elements are under the command of Soviet Marshal of Aviation Aleksandr I. Koldunov, who is also a deputy commander in chief of the WTO. The entire air defense system is integrated with that of the Soviet Union. In addition, there are common fuel pipelines, joint arms and ammunition depots, and continuous joint planning. Militarily, the WTO appears to be very much a Soviet creature. Some Western observers, however, have noted "cracks" in the structure of the WTO, including a calculated Soviet policy of providing obsolete weapons to its partners and resentment on the part of the satellite states of the "Russian superiority complex," which is embodied in rigid rules against unofficial fraternization between Soviet troops and nationals of the host country (*NYT*, 5 September 1980).

Military Developments. In the 1950s, the WTO was largely dormant, with the Soviet Union relying on the geographic benefits of the East European states as a potential defensive or offensive glacis. In the early 1960s, however, Moscow decided to increase the military role of the WTO, and in October 1961 the pact held its first joint maneuvers. Greater roles were assigned to the armed forces of the bloc states, although no WTO military doctrine evolved. Soviet military strategy prevailed, and this helped lead to the evolution of a "tier" system in the bloc. Moscow came to refer to the three countries on the axis of the most likely locus of an East-West conflict—the German Democratic Republic (GDR), Poland, and Czechoslovakia—as the "first strategic echelon" of the WTO. This northern tier continues to receive superior armaments from the Soviet Union and holds Moscow's primary strategic attention. Czechoslovakia's location in this more important tier was a factor in the 1968 invasion. Poland's location in this tier adds an important strategic dimension to Soviet evaluations of the disintegration of socialist rule in that troubled state. The late WTO Chief of Staff Sergei Shtemenko contended in an article published posthumously that a key function of the alliance was the "suppression of counterrevolution" in Eastern Europe (*Za Rubezhom*, 7 May 1976).

The WTO preoccupation with Poland carried over into 1981. The WTO summit meeting held in Moscow on 5 December 1980 gave its full support to the forces "devoted to socialism" in Poland and repeatedly emphasized the need for Poland to remain a firm component of the socialist community (*Keesing's Contemporary Archives*, 1981, p. 30909). At the end of November 1980, Western reports noted concentrations of WTO troops around Poland. There were also unconfirmed reports that large numbers of reservists from the Carpathian region of the Soviet Union (an area close to both Poland and Czechoslovakia and in fact the staging point for the Soviet invasion of Czechoslovakia) had been called up. (*CSM*, 15 January.) There was much doubt throughout 1981 that the grace period offered to Polish party leaders at the December 1980 summit was indefinite.

With every Soviet or WTO military visit, with every Soviet and East European warning of the danger of "counterrevolution" in Poland, with every large-scale military maneuver, fears of intervention ebbed and flowed. Kulikov's visits to Poland and his statements on the situation aroused particular interest. His first visit (accompanied by Gribkov), ostensibly to attend the thirty-sixth anniversary of the Soviet Army's liberation of Warsaw, was widely interpreted as an attempt to pressure Poland. He arrived during several large-scale strikes by farmers attempting to form a rural union and in the wake of a harsh Soviet denunciation of Poland's independent unions (*Pravda*, 8 January). In June, Kulikov claimed that counterrevolutionary forces were trying to "tear the country [Poland] out of the socialist community" and that the WTO armies under his command would defend communist rule in Poland (*Krasnaya Zvezda*, 21 June). His warning coincided with intensive Soviet media pressures on Poland and came just before the warning in *Pravda* (23 June) that any change in Poland's international status would threaten Soviet security interests. Kulikov's fourth visit to Poland (8 August) was noteworthy because it coincided with heightened attacks on Solidarity in the Soviet press (*Pravda*, 7 August). On his arrival, Kulikov met with Gen. Wojciech Jaruzelski, the Polish prime minister and defense minister, the Polish chief of staff, Gen. Florian Sawicki, and Gen. Afanasi S. Shcheglov, but not with Polish party leader Stanislaw Kania. There were reports that Kania was ill or preparing for his meeting with Leonid Brezhnev in the Crimea (*NYT*, 9 August), but Kania's replacement later in the year by Jaruzelski suggests that this visit may well have been an omen.

Many of the statements emanating from the Soviet Union and its WTO allies expressed concern that Poland remain both a socialist state and an alliance member. The timing of several of these statements is significant, particularly in the light of the military activities that took place in and around Poland during 1981. For example, on 28 January, the Soviet Union accused NATO of trying to detach Poland from the WTO (*Krasnaya Zvezda*, 28 January. In early June, a letter from the Soviet Central Committee to its Polish counterpart stressed Soviet interest in a "socialist Poland as a member of the Warsaw Pact and the Council for Mutual Economic Assistance" (*Times*, London, 11 June). With the exception of Romania, the other members of the WTO echoed Soviet worries. In April, during WTO maneuvers, Czechoslovak leader Gustav Husák declared that "history has taught us how important it is to have a good neighbor, a reliable ally" and "that the protection of the socialist system is not only the concern of each socialist state but also the joint concern of the states of the socialist community, which are determined to defend their interest and the socialist achievements of their people" (*NYT*, 7 April). On 13 June, the Czechoslovak party daily, *Rudé Právo*, declared that Polish leaders would have the full support of their Czechoslovak comrades in defending Polish communism and proceeded to compare the situation in Poland to the events that ultimately led to the invasion of

Czechoslovakia in 1968. Denunciations of Solidarity came from other WTO states as well; even Romania, which opposed any outside intervention, condemned what it interpreted as efforts by Solidarity to assume a political role.

Joint maneuvers benefit the Soviet Union in ways other than increasing military preparedness. "Intervention-through-maneuver" helped deprive Czechoslovakia of a better chance to prepare its defenses and aided in disguising Soviet preparations from the West. Other WTO exercises, in 1969 and 1971 for example, functioned in part as attempts to intimidate Romania. Military exercises in 1981, as the rule of the communist party in Poland was increasingly challenged, may thus have had significance beyond their strategic importance.

On 17 March, the Soviet Union and its WTO allies began the first large-scale maneuvers since Brotherhood in Arms '80. Code-named Soyuz 81, they took place in Poland, the GDR, Czechoslovakia, and the western USSR. They were initially described as staff exercises involving no more than 20,000 troops. On 10 March, WTO officials gave the advance notice required by the 1975 Helsinki accords, although not the full 21-day advance notice. These maneuvers eventually involved over 60,000 troops, including air force, reconnaissance, and intelligence units (ibid., 6 April). They were extended several times, and according to the East German news agency, at the beginning of April fresh troops joined the exercises in and around Poland (*Times*, London, 6 April). Forces were brought to the coast by amphibious craft, and fresh reserves were transported "from deep inside home territory" (ibid.). The maneuvers ended on 7 April, making them—at 22 days—one of the longest in WTO history. The extension meant that the exercises continued during Brezhnev's visit to Prague for the Czechoslovak party congress and that thousands of fresh troops joined the maneuvers during his stay.

Western observers believed that there were at least three possible interpretations for the timing, size, and duration of the maneuvers: the Soviet Union may have reversed a decision to invade; the maneuvers were part of a contingency plan involving increased preparedness; or they were part of the psychological pressure that the Soviet Union was bringing to bear on Poland. The psychological warfare dimension is reinforced by statements of Poland's WTO allies. The East German military newspaper declared that the maneuvers demonstrated that WTO forces would defend socialism and commented that participating troops had come to understand that the activities of Solidarity were counterrevolutionary and supported by external forces of imperialism (*Volksarmee*, 7 April; *Facts on File*, 1981, p. 226). On 4 April, the Soviet government newspaper, *Izvestiia*, in an indirect reference to Kania, asserted that the hopes of September 1980 (when Kania came to power) had not been justified. There were unconfirmed reports that some maneuvers had been conducted in Poland without the participation of Polish troops and without notification of the Polish high command.

Smaller joint maneuvers continued during the year. In June, there were reports of joint Soviet-Polish maneuvers in Silesia and movements of Hungarian troops (*NYT*, 27 June). These coincided with renewed Soviet attacks on Solidarity and assertions of a major security threat to the WTO. Fears in the West that maneuvers could become an invasion were rekindled on 3 July when *Krasnaya Zvezda* announced that Soviet and Polish soldiers were conducting "joint tactical maneuvers." The paper did not disclose the location but emphasized the necessity for strong measures by socialist and patriotic forces against counterrevolutionary schemes. It did concede, however, that there was hope that Polish Communists would be able to consolidate their ranks and defend socialism. On 14 July, *Krasnaya Zvezda* announced that the joint field exercises had been completed.

In addition to joint maneuvers, the Soviet Union itself carried out exercises around Poland that could be interpreted as attempts to pressure Poland. In early August, about one hundred Soviet warships, including two aircraft carriers and a 15,000-ton amphibious troop ship, gathered in the Baltic for the West-81 military exercises. West German officials contended that this was the largest concentration of Soviet ships they had observed in the Baltic (*Toronto Daily Star*, 15 August). These exercises came while Poland's top leaders were in the Soviet Union for a "short working visit." In attendance were the defense ministers of Hungary, Vietnam, East Germany, Cuba, Mongolia, Poland, Romania, and Czechoslovakia and the first deputy defense minister of Bulgaria. Even though the declared goal was to work out questions of combat coordination and cooperation in joint military operations involving troops from various branches of the armed forces, the location of the exercises and their scale undoubtedly underlined to Poland Moscow's ability to move quickly and decisively once a decision to intervene has been made.

The WTO's ability to respond to external threats improved in 1981. The Soviet Union has been implementing the largest conventional and nuclear arms buildup in the postwar period. According to a U.S. Defense Department report released on 29 September, the Soviet Union had 180 divisions, 50,000 tanks including T-64s and T-72s, 5,200 helicopters, 1,398 intercontinental ballistic missiles and 950 submarine-launched ballistic missiles (*Soviet Military Power*, Washington, D.C., p. 3). The Reagan administration charged that the Soviet Union was attempting to achieve military superiority. According to the report, the Soviet Union and the WTO deploy 3,500 tactical bombers and fighter aircraft in Eastern Europe. The manpower level of Soviet tank divisions has also risen. According to Gen. Bernard W. Rogers, supreme allied commander, Europe, in 1981 the number of WTO divisions facing NATO increased to 184 divisions (*Aviation Week & Space Technology*, 26 October).

Perhaps even more worrisome has been the qualitative improvement in Soviet and WTO forces. The deployment of new fighter bombers greatly increased the Soviet Union's ability to strike deep behind enemy lines. Moscow has also substantially enhanced its ground-based air defenses through new highly mobile gun systems and surface-to-air missiles. Furthermore, the Soviet Union has deployed large numbers of T-64 tanks, which are superior to the U.S. M-60, and is developing the T-80 tank. In the air, not only do WTO forces deploy over five thousand tactical aircraft (an increase of 25 percent since 1970, with a production rate of more than a thousand fighters a year), which give them a two-to-one numerical superiority over NATO air forces, but training in the use of the newer aircraft has also improved. (Ibid.) The qualitative edge that the Western nations enjoyed was substantially eroded in 1981.

Of the WTO divisions facing west, 53 are non-Soviet. Of these, at least 15 are Polish (*NYT*, 26 September). There have been questions regarding the political reliability of East European forces (Dale R. Herspring and Ivan Volgyes, "Political Reliability in the Eastern European Warsaw Pact Armies," *Armed Forces and Society*, 6, no. 2, Winter 1980, pp. 270–96), but there is a difference between the potential performance of these forces in an offensive operation and their probable behavior in defense of their homeland. The role they would play should not be underestimated. While the Soviet Union has not provided its WTO allies with the latest equipment, the very rapid qualitative buildup of the Soviet armed forces has led to a considerable "trickle down" to East European WTO forces, resulting in substantial qualitative improvements.

Political Developments. The WTO has helped the Soviet Union in the enunciation of "common" policies, despite occasional dissent from Romania. In 1981, the WTO states joined the Soviet Union in condemning Poland's free trade unions and in warning Warsaw that it must maintain socialist control and its position in the "socialist community." Bucharest rejected the notion of intervention, although it condemned the activities of the Polish unions. The Soviet Union also had the support of the WTO states (with some differences in the case of Romania) at security talks in Geneva, Madrid, and Vienna. At the Geneva intermediate-range nuclear weapons talks, the Soviet Union has tried to prevent NATO's deployment of 572 U.S. Pershing II and cruise missiles. Brezhnev rejected Reagan's 18 November "zero option" proposal, which called for the dismantling of the older Soviet SS-4 and SS-5 rockets and the new mobile triple-warhead SS-20 missiles in exchange for a commitment not to deploy the Pershings and cruise missiles (*Toronto Globe and Mail*, 30 November). Brezhnev rejected Reagan's contention that the Soviet Union had a six-to-one superiority and offered to reduce some of the

Soviet Union's medium-range nuclear weapons. The U.S.-Soviet-European arms talks, which began at the end of November in Geneva, commenced with a disagreement on the size of the forces that each side has at its disposal. The WTO nations supported the Soviet position, with Romania suggesting nuclear free zones and the elimination of all nuclear weapons on foreign territories.

Little if any progress has been made at the Mutual and Balanced Force Reduction Negotiations (MBFR) in Vienna. The negotiations have been going on for eight years, without resolution of the problems of data. The Western nations contend that WTO ground and air force personnel number nearly 200,000 more than officially stated by the Eastern side. On 6 July, *Pravda* lashed out at the West for claiming that socialist states had a manpower superiority in Central Europe. *Pravda* claimed that updated figures showed that NATO had more troops in Central Europe than the WTO states did. *Pravda* also condemned the West for its unwillingness to count the 20,000 troops the Soviet Union withdrew from East Germany in 1980. With a new American ambassador to MBFR, efforts at reaching a common ground continue.

The Conference on Security and Cooperation resumed early in 1981 at the Madrid follow-up session. Little progress has been made in trying to resolve such issues as enhancing confidence-building measures and providing increased protection of human rights to the citizens of all participatory states. Western nations have strongly condemned Soviet violations of human rights. The WTO states have rejected such criticism as unacceptable interference in domestic affairs.

Moscow has sustained its control over the WTO, both in the military and the political sphere. Western perceptions of the threat of Soviet and WTO intervention in Poland have fluctuated with the various military maneuvers and statements made by Soviet and WTO leaders. There is little doubt, however, that the Soviet Union has pursued an intensive psychological campaign against Poland. Yugoslav writer Nicola Pejnović argued in May in the Yugoslav monthly *Socijalizam* that as long as the Soviet Union insists that the Soviet road to socialism is the only correct one, the danger of armed conflict between communist countries will continue to increase (*Times*, London, 5 May). Soviet and WTO condemnations of developments in Poland indicate that the Soviet Union may not yet be ready to allow a different road to socialism in a strategically vital state such as Poland.

University of Toronto   Aurel Braun

International Communist Front Organizations

Control and Coordination. The international, Soviet-line communist fronts operating since World War II are counterparts of organizations established by the Comintern after World War I. Their function today is the same as that of the interwar organizations: to unite Communists with persons of other political persuasions to support, and thereby lend strength and respectability to, Soviet foreign policy objectives. Moscow's control over the fronts is evidenced by their faithful adherence to the Soviet policy line as well as by the withdrawal patterns of member-organizations (certain pro-Western groups after the cold war began, Yugoslav affiliates following the Stalin-Tito break, and Chinese and Albanian representatives as the Sino-Soviet split developed).

The Communist Party of the Soviet Union is said to control the fronts through its International Department (ID), presumably through the Soviets serving as full-time Secretariat members at front headquarters (U.S. Congress, *The CIA and the Media*, p. 574). This is the case in eight fronts: the World Peace Council (WPC), the World Federation of Trade Unions (WFTU), the Women's International Democratic Federation (WIDF), the Afro-Asian Peoples' Solidarity Organization (AAPSO), the International Organization of Journalists (IOJ), the Christian Peace Conference (CPC), the International Association of Democratic Lawyers (IADL), and, most recently, the International Union of Students (IUS). Past experience indicates that it may be the Soviet vice-presidents who exercise this function in the two other major front organizations: the World Federation of Democratic Youth (WFDY) and the World Federation of Scientific Workers (WFSW).

In addition to Soviet control of each front through the ID and headquarters personnel, coordination of front activity appears to be effected by the WPC. This makes sense because the Soviets consider the "peace movement" the most important joint action by the "anti-imperialist" forces and the most important of the movements "based on common specific objectives of professional interests" — that is, the front organizations (*Kommunist*, no. 17, November 1972, p. 103, no. 3, February 1974, p. 101). A glance at the nearly two hundred positions on the WPC Presidential Committee reveals that they include, in addition to ID Deputy Chief Vitali S. Shaposhnikov, slots for one or two of the top leaders of each of the ten fronts discussed here except for the IADL. The IADL president is, however, one of the 1,500-plus members of the WPC proper. (WPC, *List of Members, 1980–1983.*)

Policies. Front activities are organized around campaigns corresponding to various Soviet foreign policy objectives. During 1981, the "U.S. threat" to world peace, specifically the projected deployment of Pershing II and cruise missiles in Western Europe and development of the neutron bomb, appeared to be the most important of these campaigns. These specific themes were prominent in the Program for Action of 1981 issued by the WFDY at its annual Executive Committee meeting (Beirut, 18–20 March); in the International Conference Against the Arms Race, in which the WPC played a major role (Stockholm, 6–8 June); in the only broadly interfront meeting during the year, involving all major fronts except the IADL and WFSW (Prague, 12–13 Spetember); and at the WIDF-sponsored World Congress of Women (Prague, 8–13 October). The CPC's Working Committee meeting (Kiev, 29 March–1 April), the IADL's International Antiwar Conference (Moscow, 19–20 June), the WFTU's annual General Council meeting (Budapest, 1–3 July), and the IOJ's Ninth Congress (Moscow, 19–22 October) emphasized "world peace," but in a more general way.

WPC President Romesh Chandra (India) claimed credit in advance for the WPC's "initiative" in staging the late-October West European mass demonstrations protesting U.S. nuclear policies (*Neues Deutschland*, 13 August). When these demonstrations did occur, however, most involved at least some criticism of the *existing* placement of Soviet SS-20 missiles within striking range of Western Europe as well as the *projected* U.S. nuclear defense of the area; this was the almost inevitable result of the broad sociopolitical range of demonstrators enlisted in the effort. On the other hand, more uniformly pro-Soviet participants in more strictly controlled demonstrations also had undesirable results from the Soviet standpoint; for example, the one demonstration in this series most clearly controlled by a WPC affiliate, that in Paris on 25 October, had only one-eighth to one-half the people of its London, Rome, or Brussels counterparts; and it resulted in the further alienation of socialists from the Communists (who were perceived as the controlling element here) (*Daily Telegraph*, London, 26 October).

One month later, Czech communist leader Vasil Bil'ak took note of the problem in an address to a meeting of communist parties called to discuss the activities of the *World Marxist Review:* "This heterogeneous nature of the movement of peace forces will make it sometimes necessary to seek various compromises, which cannot be avoided in a political field concerning matters of such importance as the issue of war and peace ... There are people who, in the interests of 'objectivity,' seem to be looking for guilt on both sides. Succumbing to such views is tantamount to losing judgment and a class-based attitude toward the assessment of developments and to closing one's eyes to historical facts." (*Pravda*, Bratislava, 26 November.)

Related to these antinuclear efforts were relatively minor agitations for "peace" or "atom-free" zones. Most often, this seemed to involve the Indian Ocean (WPC Presidential Committee Bureau meeting in Antananarivo, Madagascar, in January; AAPSO Council session in Aden in March; and WFDY-IUS cosponsored meeting in Trivandrum, India, in August). The formula was also applied to Scandinavia (WPC-sppported meeting in Aalborg, Denmark, in May) and the Pacific (WFTU-supported meeting in Port Villa, Vanuatu, also in May).

The fronts continued to support the Palestinian cause during the year. The WFTU inaugurated a new quarterly, *Solidarity Palestine*, around June, and continued to cooperate with the Organization of African Trade Union Unity, International Confederation of Arab Trade Unions, and General Federation of Palestine Unions in the International Trade Union Committee of Solidarity with Palestine. What was more striking during 1981 was front support for the Lebanese "people" (against both the Israelis and Lebanese rightists). During 16–18 March, the WFDY, along with its Lebanese affiliate, sponsored an International Youth and Student Conference for Solidarity with the Youth and People of Lebanon in Beirut, just prior to the meeting of the organization's Executive Committee in that city. The resolutions coming out of the 22–25 June International Conference of Solidarity with Syria and the Palestine Liberation Organization (PLO), held in Damascus and sponsored by the WPC, supported Palestine and the PLO, the Lebanese people, and Syria, as did the Arab resolution passed by the WFTU General Council meeting in Budapest on 1–3 July. In early August, following the July Israeli raids, the leaders of three fronts led delegations of their respective organizations to Lebanon: President Romesh Chandra of the WPC, Acting Secretary General Ibrahim Zakariya of the WFTU, and President Kaarle Nordenstreng of the IOJ. The IUS also sent a delegation to Lebanon at this time.

In Latin America the front focus appeared to be Nicaragua, with El Salvador taking second place. Just after the WPC Presidential Committee meeting in Havana (19–21 April), President Chandra led a WPC delegation to Nicaragua, where he presented the organization's Ho Chih Minh award to Nicaragua's people and to the ruling Sandinist National Liberation Front. Also in late April, the IOJ, along with the Federation of Latin American Journalists and the Union of Journalists of Nicaragua, sponsored a World Meeting of Journalists in Managua, which appeared to have as its theme the defense of "free Nicaragua." In September, the WFDY and Sandinist Youth Organization sponsored a Latin American and Caribbean Youth meeting, also in Managua and with Nicaragua as its main theme. The one major resolution concerning Latin America coming out of the July WFTU General Council meeting expressed support for the Salvadoran revolutionaries.

Another continuing theme was support to antiregime activities in Namibia and South Africa (at the Aden AAPSO Council session of March, the Havana WPC Presidium meeting of April, and the Budapest WFTU General Council session of July). Other meetings appeared devoted to the support of unstable pro-Soviet regimes (the May AAPSO-sponsored International Conference on Solidarity with the Kampuchean People in Phnom Penh and the November AAPSO Presidium meeting in Kabul, which emphasized support for "revolutionary Afghanistan"). More isolated campaigns were represented by the February International Youth Conference on Ireland, held in Dublin and cosponsored by the WFDY and its Connolly Youth Movement affiliate, and the September Latin American Conference of Solidarity with Haiti, held in Panama with the support of the WPC.

Personnel. The political affiliations and nationalities of the top leaders of the fronts reflect the extent of communist influence. The presidents of both the WPC and WFTU, Romesh Chandra of India and Sándor Gáspár of Hungary, are Politburo-level members of their respective communist parties (*New Age*, 16 April 1978). Both attended the February–March congress of the Communist Party of the Soviet Union in their front capacity (*Pravda*, 23 February). While the WPC's executive secretary, John Benson, is a member of the Australian Labor Party, the acting secretary general of the WFTU, Ibrahim Zakariya, is a member of the Sudanese Communist Party Central Committee (*WMR*, April 1977).

While it is hard to determine the political affiliations of the younger leaders involved in international front activity, the WFDY and IUS have one top leader each from a communist country and one from a noncommunist country: the WFDY's president, Ernesto Ottone, is from Chile, while its secretary general, Miklós Barabás, is from Hungary; IUS President Miroslav Stepan is from Czechoslovakia, while its secretary general, Srinivasan Kunalan, is from India. While it would not do for any CPC leader to be a card-carrying communist, both President Károly Toth and Secretary General Lubomír Mirejovsky are from communist countries (Hungary and Czechoslovakia, respectively). On the other hand, both the WIDF's president, the Australian Freda Brown, and its secretary general, the Finn Mirjam Vire-Tuominen, are fairly prominent members of their country's Soviet-line communist parties (*Socialist*, 21 November 1979; *Times*, London, 9 November 1981). In contrast, neither WFSW Acting President Pierre Biquard nor WFSW Secretary General Jean-Marie Legay (both Frenchmen) is known to be a Communist.

The top officers of the other fronts considered herein follow more or less the pattern noted for the WPC, the WFDY, and the IUS. IADL President Joe Nordmann is a member of the French Communist Party, while IADL Secretary General Amar Bentoumi has no known connection with the Algerian party. IOJ President Kaarle Nordenstreng (Finland) is a noncommunist, while IOJ Secretary General Jiři Kubka is from Czechoslovakia. While AAPSO President Abd-al-Rahman Sharqawi (Egypt) is a noncommunist, the organization's secretary general, Nuri Abd-al-Razzaq Husayn, was reported to be a member of the Iraqi Communist Party Central Committee in 1972 (*Baghdad Observer*, 11 July 1972).

The fronts invariably showed an increase in membership in 1981. The WPC now claims affiliates in "over 135 countries" (WPC, *List of Members, 1980–1983*), up from "over 130 countries" (see *YICA*, 1981, p. 456). The WFTU now claims about 200 million members (*Pravda*, 27 February), up from the 190 million claimed as of last year (see *YICA*, 1981, p. 457). It admitted the Jatio Sramik League of Bangledesh as an affiliate at its July General Council meeting. At the time of the 8 October WIDF congress, the organization was still claiming only the 129 affiliates in 114 countries it had in 1979 (ibid., p. 459), but it appears that new organizations were accepted for membership at that meeting (*Rudé Právo*, 15–16 October). The most spectacular increases appear to have occurred in AAPSO, which at its March Council meeting presumably added organizations in three additional countries to the 84 in which it claimed affiliates in late 1980 (*New Times*, no. 51, 1980, p. 24) and for the first time provided for associate membership for "solidarity committees" in Western Europe and North America in the WFDY, which currently claims over 250 national affiliates in more than 100 countries (*WMR*, December, p. 121); and in the IOJ, which admitted 21 new member-organizations at its 9 October congress and now claims members in more than 120 countries (ibid., p. 122). Less spectacular but still significant was the admission of eight new affiliates to the World Federation of Teachers' Unions, a WFTU trade union international, at its June conference in Budapest. The Transport, Port, and Fishery Workers Trade Union International admitted two new affiliates at its Eighth Conference, which met in Damascus in October; this brought to 26 the number of new affiliates admitted since its last conference in 1977 (*Flashes*, 23 November).

External Relations. All the major fronts have consultative status with the Economic and Social Council (ECOSOC) and the United Nations Educational, Scientific, and Cultural Organization (UNESCO), except AAPSO, which apparently has no such status with the latter. Other relationships exist between the fronts and U.N. specialized agencies, most significantly the WFTU's consultative status with the International Labor Organization. A major setback to such relationships occurred in February, when both the WPC and AAPSO failed in their efforts to upgrade their status with ECOSOC to "Category I" (a status already achieved by the WFDY and the WIDF). This failure was due to British and U.S. initiatives disputing the WPC's and AAPSO's contention that they received no governmental funding and criticizing their policies for being one-sided and, in specific instances, diametrically opposed to those of the United Nations. (*ECOSOC Report*, 16 March.) With UNESCO things went better: IOJ President Kaarle Nordenstreng apparently spent the bulk of the year in Tanzania on a UNESCO exchange (*New Outlook*, no. 26, April–May), and WIDF representative Françoise Lafitte (France) was re-elected chairman of the Non-Governmental Organization–UNESCO Standing Committee in June (*Flashes*, 6 July).

At the other extreme, the *World Marxist Review*, self-styled "theoretical and information journal of [63] communist and workers' parties," continued its relations with the international fronts. The journal's Problems of Peace and Democratic Organizations Commission (under Aleksandr Didusenko) is its point of contact with the fronts. In September 1980, Didusenko attended the WPC-sponsored World Parliament of Peoples for Peace in this capacity. Four top front officers wrote articles for the December issue of *World Marxist Review*: WPC President Romesh Chandra, WFTU Acting Secretary General Ibrahim Zakariya, WIDF President Freda Brown, and CPC President Károly Toth. A link is provided by Bert Ramelson, the Communist Party of Great Britain's current representative to the *WMR*'s fifteen-member Editorial Board and a WPC Presidential Committee member. Links with the WFTU, the IUS, the IOJ, and the CPC should be easily maintained since they, like the *WMR*, are headquartered in Prague.

The WPC's relationship to the new Generals for Peace organization appears to be quite close. Not only did these ex-NATO officers launch their June antimissile campaign in the midst of that started by the WPC, but four of the nine so far identified with the organization are WPC members: Francisco da Costa Gomes of Portugal, Georges Koumanakos of Greece, Nino Pasti of Italy, and Antoine Sanguinetti of France. A fifth, Gert Bastian of West Germany, played a prominent role in the May Nordic Peace Forces Conference.

In contrast, the WFTU's relationship with the Solidarity union in Poland was cool and distant. WFTU Acting Secretary General Zakariya visited Poland in April but made contact with only the official or "old" trade unions, explaining that Solidarity "is not yet a union" (*Trud*, 8 April; *Flashes*, 20 April). Moreover, invitations to Solidarity's September–October congress were ignored by WFTU affiliates in the Soviet bloc countries (Radio Warsaw, 5 September). WFTU President Gáspár explained this behavior by noting that the congress had sent an invitation to "every free worker of Eastern Europe" to form free trade unions (MTI, Budapest, 7 October).

McLean, Virginia   Wallace Spaulding

Select Bibliography, 1980–81

GENERAL ON COMMUNISM

Adelman, Jonathan R., ed. *Communist Armies in Politics: Their Origins and Developments.* Boulder, Colo.: Westview Press, 1981. 175 pp.

Adibekov, Grant M. *Profintern: Politika kommunistov v profsoiuznom dvizhenii.* Moscow: Profizdat, 1981. 238 pp.

Amnesty International, U.S.A. *"Disappearances": A Workbook.* New York: Amnesty International Press, 1981. 168 pp.

Anger, Per. *With Raoul Wallenberg in Budapest.* New York: Holocaust Library, 1981. 191 pp.

Bahro, Rudolph. *Critical Responses.* White Plains, N.Y.: E. M. Sharpe, 1980. 235 pp.

Besançon, Alain. *The Rise of Gulag: Intellectual Origins of Leninism.* New York: Continuum, 1981. 329 pp.

Borg, Olavi. *Katsaus kommunismin syntyyn ja levinneisyyteen aatteena ja poliittisena liikkeenä.* Tampere, Finland: Tampereen yliopisto, Politikaan tutkimuksen laitos, 1980. 38 leaves.

Bottomore, Tom, ed. *Modern Interpretations of Marx.* Oxford: Blackwell, 1981. 218 pp.

Brewer, Anthony. *Marxist Theories of Imperialism: A Critical Theory.* Boston: Routledge & Kegan Paul, 1980. 308 pp.

Brezhnev, Leonid Ilich. *Socialism, Democracy, and Human Rights.* New York: Pergamon Press, 1980. 247 pp.

Cave Brown, Anthony, and Charles B. McDonald. *On a Field of Red: The Communist International and the Coming of World War II.* New York: Putnam, 1981. 718 pp.

Communist Party of the Soviet Union. Central Committee. Institute of Marxism-Leninism. *The Moving Forces of the World Revolutionary Process.* Moscow: Politizdat, 1981. 392 pp.

Conquest, Robert. *We & They.* London: Temple Smith, 1980. 252 pp.

Cornforth, Maurice C. *Communism and Philosophy: Contemporary Dogmas and Revisions of Marxism.* London: Lawrence & Wishart, 1980. 282 pp.

Dawisha, Karen, and Phillip Hanson, eds. *Soviet–East European Dilemmas.* New York: Holmes & Meier, 1981. 226 pp.

De Santis, Hugh. *The Diplomacy of Silence: The American Foreign Service, the Soviet Union, and the Cold War.* Chicago: University of Chicago Press, 1981. 270 pp.

Dlubek, Rolf. *Marx und Engels über die sozialistische und kommunistische Gesellschaft: Die Entwicklung der marxistischen Lehre von der kommunistischen Umgestaltung.* East Berlin: Dietz Verlag, 1981. 542 pp.

Eden, Douglas, and Frederick Short. *Political Change in Europe.* New York: St. Martin's Press, 1981. 163 pp.

Elliot, Charles F., and Carl A. Linden, eds. *Marxism in the Contemporary West.* Boulder, Colo.: Westview Press, 1980. 177 pp.

Entwicklung und Kampf der kommunistischen Bewegung in Asien und Afrika. East Berlin: Dietz Verlag, 1980. 336 pp.

García F., María Luz. *El capitalismo monopolista de estado: Aportes al movimiento comunista internacional.* Cumana, Venezuela: Universidad de Oriente, Dirección de Información Científico Técnica, 1980. 88 pp.

Harding, Neil. *Lenin's Political Thought: Theory and Practice in the Socialist Revolution.* New York: St. Martin's Press, 1981. 337 pp.

Hirszowicz, Maria. *The Bureaucratic Leviathan: A Study in the Sociology of Communism.* Oxford: Robertson, 1980. 208 pp.

Holmes, Leslie. *The Policy Process in Communist States.* Beverly Hills, Calif.: Sage Publications, 1981. 320 pp.

Hunt, Alan, ed. *Marxism and Democracy.* Atlantic Highlands, N.J.: Humanities Press, 1980. 188 pp.

Karatnycky, Adrian; Alexander J. Motyl; and Adolph Sturmthal. *Workers' Rights in Western Democracies and Eastern Europe.* New Brunswick, N.J.: Transaction Books, 1980. 150 pp.

Konstantinov, F. T., et al. *Dialektika internatsionalnogo i natsionalnogo v sotsialisticheskom obshchestve.* Moscow: Nauka, 1981. 366 pp.

Korionov, Vitalii Germanovich. *Muzhaiushchie v bitvakh: Kommunisticheskoe dvizhenie. Uspekhi, problemy, deiateli.* Moscow: Izdatelstvo politicheskoi literatury, 1981. 254 pp.

Krippner, Stanley. *Human Possibilities: Mind Exploration in the USSR and Eastern Europe.* Garden City, N.Y.: Doubleday, Anchor Press, 1980. 348 pp.

Lefebvre, Henri. *Une pensée devenue monde: Faut-il abandonner Marx?* Paris: Fayard, 1980. 263 pp.

Lindsay, Jack. *The Crisis in Marxism.* Totowa, N.J.: Barnes & Noble, 1981. 183 pp.

Lodge, Juliet, ed. *Terrorism: A Challenge to the State.* New York: St. Martin's Press, 1981. 247 pp.

Löw, Konrad. *Warum fasziniert der Kommunismus?: Eine systematische Untersuchung.* Cologne: Deutscher Instituts-Verlag, 1980. 374 pp.

Marx, Karl, and Friedrich Engels. *The Collected Writings in the "New York Daily Tribune."* Edited by A. Thomas Ferguson and Stephen J. O'Neil. New York: Urizen Books, 1980. N.p.

Medvedev, Roy A. *Nikolai Bukharin: The Last Years.* New York: Norton, 1980. 176 pp.

Metodologie marxisticko-leninských sociologických výzkumu: Přispěvky k prohlouben i marxistickoleninské sociologie a ke kritice empirismu. Prague: Horizont, 1980. 148 pp.

Michalski, Wladyslav, ed. *Komunisci a socjaldemokracja: Problemy jednosci ruchu robotniczego.* Warsaw: Wydawnictwo Ministerstwa Obrony Narodowej, 1980. N.p.

Millar, T. B. *The East-West Strategic Balance.* Winchester, Mass.: Allen & Unwin, 1981. 200 pp.

Moore, Stanley W. *Marx on the Choice Between Socialism and Communism.* Cambridge, Mass.: Harvard University Press, 1980. 135 pp.

Musil, Jiri. *Urbanization in Socialist Countries.* White Plains, N.Y.: E. M. Sharpe, 1980. 184 pp.

Naik, J. A., ed. *Russia in Asia and Africa: Documents, 1946–1971.* Kolhapur, India: Avinash Reference Publications, 1979. 664 pp.

Oberg, James E. *Red Star in Orbit.* New York: Random House, 1981. 272 pp.

O'Neill, Bard E.; William R. Heaton; and Donald J. Alberts; eds. *Insurgency in the Modern World.* Boulder, Colo.: Westview Press, 1980. 291 pp.

Pecsi, Kalman. *The Future of Socialist Economic Integration.* Armonk, N.Y.: E. M. Sharpe, 1981. 189 pp.

Pipes, Richard. *U.S.-Soviet Relations in the Era of Détente.* Boulder, Colo.: Westview Press, 1981. 230 pp.

Pla, Alberto J. *La historia y su método.* Barcelona: Fontamara, 1980. 126 pp.

Russell, James. *Marx-Engels Dictionary.* Westport, Conn.: Greenwood Press, 1980. 140 pp.

Schulz, Donald E., and Jan S. Adam, eds. *Political Participation in Communist Systems.* New York: Pergamon Press, 1981. 344 pp.

Shirina, Kirill Kirillovich, and F. I. Firsov, eds. *Chetvertyi kongress Kominterna. Razrabotka kongressom strategii i taktiki kommunisticheskogo dvizheniia v novykh usloviiakh: Politika edinogo fronta.* Moscow: Izdatelstvo politicheskoi literatury, 1980. 519 pp.

Shoup, Paul S. *The East European and Soviet Data Handbook: Political, Social, and Developmental Indicators, 1945–1975.* New York: Columbia University Press, 1981. 482 pp.

Shpil'kova, L. V. *Problemy vneshnei politiki afro-aziatskikh stran: Sbornik nauchnykh trudov.* Moscow: Moskovskii gosudarstvennyi pedagogicheskii institut imeni V. I. Lenina, 1980. 131 pp.

Šik, Ota. *The Communist Power System.* New York: Praeger, 1981. 176 pp.

Sterling, Claire. *The Terror Network: The Secret War of International Terrorism.* New York: Holt, Reinhart & Winston, 1981. 357 pp.

Sternheimer, Stephen. *East-West Technology Transfer: Japan and the Communist Bloc.* Beverly Hills, Calif.: Sage Publications, 1980. 88 pp.

Stojanovic, Svetozar. *In Defense of Democracy in Socialism.* Buffalo, N.Y.: Prometheus Books, 1981. 145 pp.

Stuart, Douglas T., and William T. Tow, eds. *China, the Soviet Union and the West: Strategic and Political Dimensions for the 1980's.* Boulder, Colo.: Westview Press, 1982. 320 pp.

Szajkowski, Bogdan. *Marxist Governments: A World Survey.* 3 volumes. London: Macmillan, 1981.

Tucker, D. F. B. *Marxism and Individualism.* Oxford: Blackwell, 1980. 255 pp.

Turchin, Valentin. *The Inertia of Fear and the Scientific Worldview.* New York: Columbia University Press, 1981. 300 pp.

Ul'ianovskii, Rostislav Aleksandrovich. *Present Day Problems in Asia and Africa: Theory, Politics, Personalities.* Moscow: Progress, 1980. 239 pp.

United States. Central Intelligence Agency. *Communist Aid Activities in Non-Communist Less-Developed Countries, 1979 and 1954–79: A Research Paper.* Washington, D.C.: National Foreign Assessment Center, DOCEX, 1980. 45 pp.

Vajda, Mihaly. *The State and Socialism.* New York: St. Martin's Press, 1981. 150 pp.

Veen, Hans-Joachim. *Is Communism Changing?* Mainz: Hase & Kohler, 1981. 86 pp.

Welsh, William A., ed. *Survey Research and Public Attitudes in Eastern Europe and the Soviet Union.* New York: Pergamon Press, 1981. 536 pp.

Westoby, Adam. *Communism Since World War II.* New York: St. Martin's Press, 1981. 512 pp.

Wolfe, Bertram D. *Revolution and Reality: Essays on the Origin of the Fate of the Soviet System.* Chapel Hill: University of North Carolina Press, 1981. 401 pp.

Zaleski, Eugene, and Helgart Weinert. *Technology Transfer Between East and West.* Paris: Organisation for Economic Cooperation and Development, 1980. 435 pp.

Zavtour, A. A., ed. *Kommunisticheskoe vospitanie trudiashchikhsia sostavnaia chast' stroitel'stva kommunizma: Voprosy nauchnogo kommunizma. Mezhvuzovskii sbornik.* Kishinev: Shtiintsa, 1980. 159 pp.

Ziring, Lawrence. *Iran, Turkey and Afghanistan: The Northern Tier.* New York: Praeger, 1981. 160 pp.

Zivs, S. L. *Human Rights: Continuing the Discussion.* Moscow: Progress, 1980. 187 pp.

AFRICA AND THE MIDDLE EAST

Akhavi, Shahrough. *Religion and Politics in Contemporary Iran.* Albany: State University of New York Press, 1980. 225 pp.

Albert, David H., ed. *Tell the American People: Perspectives on the Iranian Revolution.* Philadelphia: Movement for a New Society, 1980. 212 pp.

Amirsadeghi, Hossein. *The Security of the Persian Gulf.* New York: St. Martin's Press, 1981. 294 pp.

Benson, Ivor. *The Battle for South Africa.* Durban: Dolphin Press, 1979. 121 pp.

Bourquia, Abdeslam, et al. *Essais sur l'histoire du Parti communiste marocain.* Casablanca: n.p., n.d. 82 pp.

Burmistrov, V. N. *Narodnaia demokraticheskaia respublika Iemen.* Moscow: Nauka, 1981. 173 pp.

Chubin, Shahram, ed. *Security in the Persian Gulf.* 2 volumes. Montclair, N.J.: Allanheld (for International Institute for Strategic Studies), 1981.

Cohen, Amnon. *Political Parties on the West Bank Under the Jordanian Regime (1949–1967).* Ithaca, N.Y.: Cornell University Press, 1981. N.p.

Darch, Colin. *Soviet View of Africa: An Annotated Bibliography on Ethiopia, Somali and Djibouti.* Boston: G. K. Hall, 1980. 200 pp.

Flores, Alexander. *Nationalismus und Sozialismus im arabischen Osten: Kommunistische Partei und arabische Nationalbewegung in Palästina, 1919–1948.* Münster: Periferia Verlag, 1980. 357 pp.

Gann, Lewis H., and Peter Duignan. *Africa South of the Sahara: The Challenge to Western Security.* Stanford: Hoover Institution Press, 1981. 238 pp.

Gann, Lewis H., and Thomas H. Henriksen. *The Struggle for Zimbabwe: Battle in the Bush.* New York: Praeger, 1981. 154 pp.

Glagolev, Igor' Sergeevich. *Soviet Aggression in Southern Africa.* Sandton: Southern African Editorial Services, 1980. 15 pp.

Gorman, Robert F. *Political Conflict on the Horn of Africa.* New York: Praeger, 1981. 240 pp.

Gromyko, Anatoly A., ed. *Afrika v 70–80-e gody: Stanovlenie natsional'noi ekonomiki i strategiia razvitiia.* Moscow: Nauka, 1980. 325 pp.

———, ed. *Zarubezhnye kontseptsii ekonomicheskogo razvitiia stran Afriki: Kriticheskii analiz.* Moscow: Nauka, 1980. 271 pp.

Heldman, Dan C. *The USSR and Africa: Foreign Policy Under Khrushchev.* New York: Praeger, 1981. 187 pp.

Helms, Christine Moss. *The Cohesion of Saudi Arabia.* Baltimore: Johns Hopkins University Press, 1981. 313 pp.

Henriksen, Thomas H., ed. *Communist Powers and Sub-Saharan Africa.* Stanford: Hoover Institution Press, 1982. 155 pp.

Hourani, Albert. *The Emergence of the Modern Middle East.* Berkeley: University of California Press, 1981. 243 pp.

Isaac, Rael Jean. *Party and Politics in Israel: Three Visions of a Jewish State.* New York: Longman, 1981. 228 pp.

Jazani, Bizhan. *Capitalism and Revolution in Iran.* London: Zed Press, 1980. 151 pp.

Jureidini, Paul A., and R. D. McLaurin. *Beyond Camp David: Emerging Alignments and Leaders in the Middle East.* Syracuse, N.Y.: Syracuse University Press, 1981. 197 pp.

Katouzian, Homa. *The Political Economy of Modern Iran.* New York: New York University Press, 1981. 389 pp.

Katz, Stephen. *Marxism, Africa, and Social Class: A Critique of Relevant Theories.* Montreal: McGill University, Centre for Developing Area Studies, 1980. 112 pp.

Kazemi, Farhad. *Poverty and Religion in Iran: The Migrant Poor, Urban Marginality and Politics.* New York: New York University Press, 1981. 180 pp.

Keddie, Nikki R. *Iran: Religion, Politics and Society.* London: Cass, 1980. 243 pp.

Klinghoffer, Arthur Jay. *The Angolan War: A Study in Soviet Policy in the Third World.* Boulder, Colo.: Westview Press, 1980. 229 pp.

Kosukhin, Nikolai Dmitrievich. *Formirovanie ideino-politicheskoi strategii v afrikanskikh stranakh sotsialisticheskoi orientatsii: Genezis i razvitie ideologii.* Moscow: Nauka, 1980. 259 pp.

Lefort, René. *Ethiopie: La Révolution hérétique.* Paris: Maspero, 1981. 413 pp.

LeoGrande, William M. *Cuba's Policy in Africa, 1959–1980.* Berkeley: University of California, Institute of International Studies, 1981. 82 pp.

Medvedko, L. I. *K vostoku I zapadu ot Suetsa.* Moscow: Politizdat, 1980. 368 pp.

Merhav, Peretz. *The Israeli Left: History, Problems, Documents.* San Diego: A. S. Barnes, 1980. 397 pp.

Mestiri, Ezzedine. *Les Cubains et l'Afrique.* Paris: Karthala, 1980. 239 pp.

Mohiddin, Ahmed. *African Socialism in Two Countries.* Totowa, N.J.: Barnes & Noble, 1981. 231 pp.

Naumkin, V. V. *Natsional'nyi front v bor'be za nezavisimost' IUzhnogo Iemena i natsional'nuiu demokratiiu.* Moscow: Nauka, 1980. 278 pp.

Nelson, Harold D., and Irving Kaplan, eds. *Ethiopia: A Country Study.* 3rd edition. Washington, D.C.: American University, Foreign Area Studies, 1981. 366 pp.

Nodal, Roberto. *The Cuban Presence in Africa: A Bibliography.* Milwaukee: University of Wisconsin–Milwaukee, Department of Afro-American Studies, 1980. 16 pp.

Novrik, Nimrod, and Joyce Starr, eds. *Challenges in the Middle East: Regional Dynamics and Western Security.* New York: Praeger, 1981. 133 pp.

Ottaway, David, and Marina Ottaway. *Afrocommunism.* New York: Africana Publishing Company, 1981. 237 pp.

Pahlavi, Mohammad Reza. *Answer to History.* Briarcliff Manor, N.Y.: Stein & Day, 1980. 204 pp.

Plascov, Avi. *The Palestinian Refugees in Jordan, 1948–1957.* London: Cass, 1981. 268 pp.

Rabinovich, Itamar. *The Soviet Union and Syria in the 1970's: A Study in Influence.* New York: Praeger, 1981. 200 pp.

Ramet, Pedro. *Sadat and the Kremlin.* Santa Monica, Calif.: California Seminar on International Security and Foreign Policy, 1980. 66 pp.

Rezun, Miron. *The Soviet Union and Iran: Soviet Policy from the Beginnings of the Pahlavi Dynasty Until the Soviet Invasion in 1941.* Leiden: Sijthoff, 1981. 425 pp.

Ro'i, Yaakov. *Soviet Decision-Making in Practice: The USSR and Israel, 1947–1954.* New Brunswick, N.J.: Transaction Books, 1980. 540 pp.

Rothenberg, Morris. *The USSR and Africa: New Dimensions of Soviet Global Power.* Washington, D.C.: Advanced International Studies Institute, 1980. 280 pp.

Sayegh, Raymond. *Le Golfe en ébullition: Le Chah d'Iran, la fin d'une dynastie, Khomeiny et l'après Khomeinisme, le rôle de l'Arabie seoudite, les répercussions régionales.* Paris: Pichon et Durand, 1979. 116 pp.

Sella, Amnon. *Soviet Political and Military Conduct in the Middle East.* London: Macmillan, 1981. 211 pp.

Singh, K. R. *Iran: Quest for Security.* New Delhi: Vikas, 1980. 443 pp.

Smolansky, Oles M. *The Soviet Union and Iraq.* New York: Praeger, 1981. 200 pp.

Tibi, Bassam. *Arab Nationalism.* London: Macmillan, 1981. 286 pp.

Traore, Sekou. *Afrique socialiste.* Paris: Anthropos, 1979. 135 pp.

Wiseman, Henry, and Alistair M. Taylor. *From Rhodesia to Zimbabwe: The Politics of Transition.* New York: Pergamon Press, 1981. 192 pp.

Yodfat, Aryeh Y., and Yuval Arnon-Ohanna. *PLO Strategy and Tactics.* New York: St. Martin's Press, 1981. 222 pp.

THE AMERICAS

Angus, Ian. *Canadian Bolsheviks*. Montreal: Vanguard Publishing, 1981. N.p.

Armstrong, David. *A Trumpet to Arms: Alternative Media in America*. Boston: Houghton Mifflin, 1981. 384 pp.

Booth, John A. *The End of the Beginning: The Nicaraguan Revolution*. Boulder, Colo.: Westview Press, 1981. 225 pp.

Burga, Manuel. *Apogeo y crisis de la república aristocrática: Oligarquía, aprismo y comunismo en el Perú, 1895–1932*. Lima: Ediciones Rikchay Perú, 1980. 235 pp.

Campbell, Leslie K. *Architects of Destruction: The Personal Observations of a Concerned American*. San Juan Capistrano, Calif.: Campbell, 1980. 282 pp.

Chilcote, Ronald H., ed. *Brazil and Its Radical Left: An Annotated Bibliography on the Communist Movement and the Rise of Marxism, 1922–1972*. Millwood, N.Y.: Kraus International Publications, 1980. 455 pp.

Del Picchia, Pedro. *O PCB no quadro atual da política brasileira: Entrevistas com seis membros do Comitê Central*. Rio de Janeiro: Civilização Brasileira, 1980. 85 pp.

Díaz Soto y Gama, Antonio. *Otro holocausto*. Mexico City: Editorial Jus, 1980. 140 pp.

Fournier, Marcel. *Communisme et anticommunisme au Quebec*. Laval, Quebec: Editiones Coopératives Albert Saint-Martin, 1979. 165 pp.

Guarasci, Richard. *The Theory and Practice of American Marxism, 1957–1970*. Lanham, Md.: University Press of America, 1980. 242 pp.

Hall, Gus. *Los trabajadores y su papel esencial en las luchas del pueblo contra los monopolios*. New York: International Publishers, 1980. 127 pp.

Halperin, Maurice. *The Taming of Fidel Castro*. Berkeley: University of California Press, 1981. 345 pp.

Horowitz, Irving L., comp. *Cuban Communism*. 4th edition. New Brunswick, N.J.: Transaction Books, 1981. 688 pp.

Kolesnikov, N. S. *Kuba*. Moscow: Nauka, 1980. 366 pp.

Konder, Leandro. *A democracia e os comunistas no Brasil*. Rio de Janeiro: Graal, 1980. 156 pp.

Kramer-Kaske, Liselotte. *Die kubanische Volksrevolution, 1953–1962*. East Berlin: Deutscher Verlag der Wissenschaft, 1980. 43 pp.

Kuvakin, Valerii Aleksandrovich. *Marksistskaia filosofskaia mysl' v SSha: 70-e gody XX-ogo veka*. Moscow: Izdatelstvo Moskovskogo universiteta, 1980. 168 pp.

Levenstein, Harvey A. *Communism, Anti-communism, and the CIO*. Westport, Conn.: Greenwood Press, 1981. 364 pp.

Liubarskaia, Alla Mikhailovna. *Goras Trobel: Slava i zabvenie*. Leningrad: Nauka, 1980. 258 pp.

Lowy, Michael, ed. *Le Marxisme en Amerique Latine de 1909 a nos jours*. Paris: Maspero, 1980. 445 pp.

MacEwan, Arthur. *Revolution and Economic Development in Cuba*. New York: St. Martin's Press, 1981. 265 pp.

Machado, Gustavo, et al. *La lucha armada: Hablan cinco jefes*. Caracas: Universidad Central de Venezuela, Facultat de Ciencias Económicas y Sociales, División de Publicaciones, 1980. 411 pp.

Márquez, Gabriel García; Gregorio Selser; and Daniel Waksman Schinca. *La batalla de Nicaragua*. Mexico City: Brugera Mexicana de Ediciones, 1979. 451 pp.

Medina, Medofilo. *Historia del Partido Comunista de Colombia*. Bogota: Centro de Estudios de Investigaciones Sociales, 1980. 624 pp.

Mesa-Lago, Carmelo. *The Economy of Socialist Cuba: A Two-Decade Appraisal*. Albuquerque: University of New Mexico Press, 1981. 235 pp.

Mestiri, Ezzedine. *Les Cubains et l'Afrique*. Paris: Karthala, 1980. 238 pp.

Montaner, Carlos Alberto. *Secret Report on the Cuban Revolution*. New Brunswick, N.J.: Transaction Books, 1981. 284 pp.

Navarro, Antonio. *Tocayo*. Westport, Conn.: Sandown/Shamrock, 1981. 270 pp.

Navasky, Victor S. *Naming Names*. New York: Viking, 1980. 482 pp.

Partido Comunista Brasileiro. *PCB, Vinte anos de politica, 1958–1979*. São Paulo: Livraria Editoria Ciências Humanas, 1980. 353 pp.

Partido Comunista de Bolivia. Congreso Nacional. *Por la victoria democrática y el ejercicio de la soberania nacional: Hacia un partido de masas. IV Congreso Nacional*. La Paz: Ediciones "Unidad," 1980. 119 pp.

Partido Comunista del Perú. *La lucha por la construccion del Partido Comunista del Perú*. Lima: Alba, 1980. 56 pp.

Partido comunista en el Uruguay. Dirección Nacional de Relaciones Publicas, 1980. 31 pp.

Payne, Anthony. *The Politics of the Caribbean Community, 1961–79: Regional Integration Among New States*. New York: St. Martin's Press, 1980. 298 pp.

Pereira, Astrojildo. *Construindo o PCB (1922–1924)*. São Paulo: Livraria Editora Ciências Humanas, 1980. 151 pp.

Sandino, Augusto C., and Carlos Fonseca Amador. *Nicaragua: La estrategia de la victoria*. Mexico City: Editorial Nuestra Tiempo, 1980. 350 pp.

Spadafora, Hugo. *Experiencias y pensamiento de un medico guerrillero*. Panama: Centro de Impresion Educativa, 1980. N.p.

Spindel, Arnoldo. *O que é o comunismo*. São Paolo: Editoria Brasiliense, 1980. 86 pp.

Strike at Olin: Test Case for Labor. New Haven: Communist Party of Connecticut, 1980. 31 pp.

United States. Department of State. *Communist Interference in El Salvador: Support of the Salvadoran Insurgency*. Washington, D.C., 1981.

Vogelgesang, Sandy. *American Dream, Global Nightmare: The Dilemma of U.S. Human Rights*. New York: Norton, 1980. 302 pp.

Walker, Thomas W. *Nicaragua: A Profile*. Boulder, Colo.: Westview Press, 1981. 380 pp.

Willetts, Peter. *The Non-Aligned in Havana*. New York: St. Martin's Press, 1981. 283 pp.

ASIA AND THE PACIFIC

Alatas, Hasas Syed. *Bahaya komunis*. Kuala Lumpur: Sarjana Enterprises, 1980. 83 pp.

Amnesty International. *Report of an Amnesty International Mission to the Socialist Republic of Vietnam, 10–21 December 1979*. London: Amnesty International Publications, 1981. 42 pp.

Arnold, Anthony. *Afghanistan and the Soviet Invasion in Perspective*. Stanford: Hoover Institution Press, 1981. 126 pp.

Arunova, M. R., ed. *Demokraticheskaia Respublika Afganistana*. Moscow: Nauka, 1981. 174 pp.

Barnett, A. Doak. *China's Economy in Global Perspective*. Washington, D.C.: Brookings Institution, 1981. 752 pp.

Barth, Ariana, and Tiziano Terzani. *Holocaust in Kambodsha*. Hamburg: Spiegel Verlag, 1980. 220 pp.

Bartke, Wolfgang. *Who's Who in the People's Republic of China*. Armonk, N.Y.: E. M. Sharpe, 1981. 744 pp.

Baum, Richard, ed. *China's Four Modernizations: The New Technological Revolution*. Boulder, Colo.: Westview Press, 1980. 307 pp.

Blecher, Marc J., and Gordon White. *Micropolitics in Contemporary China: A Technical Unit During and After the Cultural Revolution*. White Plains, N.Y.: E. M. Sharpe, 1980. 135 pp.

Brugger, Bill. *China: Liberation and Transformation, 1942–1962.* Totowa, N.J.: Barnes & Noble, 1981. 288 pp.

———. *China: Radicalism to Revisionism, 1962–1979.* Totowa, N.J.: Barnes & Noble, 1981. 275 pp.

Bunge, Frederica M., ed. *Thailand: A Country Study.* 5th edition. Washington, D.C.: Government Printing Office, 1981. 354 pp.

Camilleri, Joseph. *Chinese Foreign Policy: The Maoist Era and Its Aftermath.* Seattle: University of Washington Press, 1980. 286 pp.

Chan, F. Gilbert, ed. *China at the Crossroads: Nationalists and Communists, 1927–1949.* Boulder, Colo.: Westview Press, 1980. 268 pp.

Chang, Ya-chun. *Chinese Communist Activities in Africa.* Taipei: World Anti-Communist League, ROC, 1981. 67 pp.

Chiu, Hungdah, ed. *Agreement of the People's Republic of China, 1966–80: A Calendar of Events.* New York: Praeger, 1981. 329 pp.

Chung, Chong-Shik, and Gahb-chol Kim, eds. *North Korean Communism: A Comparative Analysis.* Seoul: Research Center for Peace and Unification, 1980. 426 pp.

Clague, Peter. *Iron Spearhead: The True Story of a Communist Killer Squad in Singapore.* Singapore: Heinemann Educational Books (Asia), 1980. 153 pp.

Communist Party of India. National Council. *Review of 1980 Mid-Term Lok Sabha Elections and Resolutions Adopted by the National Council of the Communist Party of India.* New Delhi: Communist Party of India, 1980. 79 pp.

Duiker, William J. *The Communist Road to Power in Vietnam.* Boulder, Colo.: Westview Press, 1981. 393 pp.

Elliott, David W. P., ed. *The Third Indochina Conflict.* Boulder, Colo.: Westview Press, 1981. 250 pp.

Garside, Roger. *Coming Alive: China After Mao.* New York: McGraw-Hill, 1981. 458 pp.

Girling, John L. S. *Thailand: Society and Politics.* Ithaca, N.Y.: Cornell University Press, 1981. 306 pp.

Goldman, Merle. *China's Intellectuals: Advice and Dissent.* Cambridge, Mass.: Harvard University Press, 1981. 276 pp.

Garchev, A. S., ed. *The Undeclared War: Imperialism vs. Afghanistan.* Moscow: Progress, 1980. 156 pp.

Greenblatt, Sidney L.; Richard W. Wilson; and Amy Auerbacher Wilson; eds. *Organizational Behavior in Chinese Society.* New York: Praeger, 1981. 288 pp.

———. *Social Interaction in Chinese Society.* New York: Praeger, 1981. 260 pp.

Griffiths, John C. *Afghanistan: Key to a Continent.* Boulder, Colo.: Westview Press, 1981. 225 pp.

Harrison, Selig S. *In Afghanistan's Shadow: Baluch Nationalism and Soviet Temptations.* New York: Carnegie Endowment for International Peace, 1981. 228 pp.

Hsiung, James C., and Samuel S. Kim, eds. *China in the Global Community.* New York: Praeger, 1980. 288 pp.

Hsuan, Mo. *How Do the Chinese Communists Treat the Intellectuals?* Taipei: World Anti-Communist League, ROC, 1980. 71 pp.

Japanese Communist Party. *The 15th Congress of the Japanese Communist Party, Atami, February 26–March 1, 1980.* Tokyo: Japanese Communist Party, Central Committee, 1980. 351 pp.

Kraus, Richard Curt. *Class Conflict in Chinese Socialism.* New York: Columbia University Press, 1981. 250 pp.

Misra, K. P., ed. *Afghanistan in Crisis.* New York: Advent Books, 1981. 150 pp.

Monks, Alfred L. *The Soviet Intervention in Afghanistan, 1979–1980.* Washington, D.C.: American Enterprise Institute, 1981. 60 pp.

Nelsen, Harvey W. *The Chinese Military System: The Organizational Study of the Chinese People's Liberation Army.* 2d revised edition. Boulder, Colo.: Westview Press, 1981. 288 pp.

Newell, Nancy Peabody, and Richard Newell. *The Struggle for Afghanistan.* Ithaca, N.Y.: Cornell University Press, 1981. 236 pp.

Norodom Sihanouk Varman. *War and Hope: The Case of Cambodia.* New York: Pantheon, 1980. 166 pp.

Oxnam, Robert B., and Richard C. Bush, eds. *China Briefing, 1980.* Boulder, Colo.: Westview Press, 1980. 126 pp.

Papp, Daniel S. *Vietnam: The View from Moscow, Peking, Washington.* Jefferson, N.C.: McFarland, 1981. 258 pp.

Parente, William J. *Politics in Indonesia.* New York: Praeger, 1981. 250 pp.

Peng, Shu-tse. *The Chinese Communist Party in Power.* New York: Monad Press, 1980. 508 pp.

Prybyla, Jan S. *Issues in Socialist Economic Modernization.* New York: Praeger, 1980. 140 pp.

Rose, Leo E., and John T. Scholz. *Nepal: Profile of a Himalayan Kingdom.* Boulder, Colo.: Westview Press, 1980. 144 pp.

Sayeed, Khalid B. *Politics in Pakistan: The Nature and Direction of Change.* New York: Praeger, 1980. 206 pp.

Schier, Peter, and Manola Schier-Oum, eds. *Prince Sihanouk on Cambodia: Interviews and Talks with Prince Norodom Sihanouk.* Hamburg: Institut für Asienkunde, 1980. 105 pp.

Seymour, James D., ed. *The Fifth Modernization: China's Human Rights Movement, 1978–1979.* Stanfordville, N.Y.: Human Rights Publishing Group, 1980. 301 pp.

Sinha, Sri Prakash. *Afghanistan im Aufruhr.* Zurich: Hecht Verlag, 1980. 207 pp.

Solomon, Richard H., ed. *The China Factor: Sino-American Relations and the Global Scene.* Englewood Cliffs, N.J.: Prentice-Hall, 1981. 323 pp.

Sun, Kim Il. *The Benevolent Sun: Mt. Paekdu-san Tells.* Pyongyang: Foreign Languages Publishing House, 1980. 470 pp.

Thornton, Richard C. *China: A Political History, 1917–80.* Fully revised and updated. Boulder, Colo.: Westview Press, 1981. 500 pp.

Ting, Wang. *Chairman Hua, Leader of the Chinese Communists.* London: C. Hurst, 1980. 181 pp.

Tiurin, V. A., ed. *Laos: Spravochnik.* Moscow: Nauka, 1980. 263 pp.

Turley, William S., ed. *Vietnamese Communism in Comparative Perspective.* Boulder, Colo.: Westview Press, 1980. 272 pp.

Van der Kroef, Justus M. *Communism in Southeast Asia.* Berkeley: University of California Press, 1980. 342 pp.

Vogel, Heinrich, ed. *Die sowjetische Intervention in Afghanistan: Entstehung und Hintergründe einer weltpolitischen Krise.* Baden-Baden: Nomos Verlag, 1980. 390 pp.

United States. Central Intelligence Agency. National Foreign Assessment Center. *Directory of Officials of the Socialist Republic of Vietnam.* Washington, D.C.: Library of Congress, 1980. 204 pp.

———. Congress. House. Committee on Foreign Affairs. Subcommittee on Asia and Pacific Affairs. *Human Rights in Asia: Communist Countries.* 96th Congress, 2d session, 1 October 1980. Washington, D.C.: Government Printing Office, 1981. 190 pp.

WESTERN EUROPE

Araquistain, Luís. *Marxismo y socialismo en España.* Barcelona: Fontamara, 1980. 268 pp.

Arbeidernes Kommunistparti. *Faglig arbeid: Studiebok.* Oslo: Duplotrykk, 1980. 191 pp.

Are, Giuseppe. *Radiografia di un partito: Il PCI negli anni '70 struttura ed evoluzione.* Milan: Rizzoli, 1980. 344 pp.

Barak, Michel. *Fractures au P.C.F.: Des communistes parlent.* Paris: Karthala, 1980. 269 pp.

Bardavío, Joaquín. *Sabado santo rojo.* Madrid: Uve, 1980. 208 pp.

Becker, Jean-Jacques. *Le Parti communiste veut-il prendre le pouvoir?* Paris: Seuil, 1981. 333 pp.

Bergami, Giancarlo. *Gramsci, comunista critico: Il politico e il pensatore.* Milan: Angeli, 1981. 137 pp.

Berlinguer, Giovanni. *Un eurocomunista in America: Nota di viaggio.* Bari: De Donato, 1980. 114 pp.

Bertone, Franco. *L'Anomalia polacca: I rapporti tra stato e chiesa cattolica.* Rome: Editori Riuniti, 1981. 290 pp.

Boggs, Carl, and David Plotke, eds. *The Politics of Eurocommunism: Socialism in Transition.* Boston: South End Press, 1980. 479 pp.

Bolloten, Burnett. *The Spanish Revolution: The Struggle for Power During the Civil War.* Chapel Hill: University of North Carolina Press, 1980. 664 pp.

Braga de Macedo, Jorge, and Simon Serfaty, eds. *Portugal Since the Revolution: Economic and Political Perspectives.* Boulder, Colo.: Westview Press, 1981. 232 pp.

Butler, David, and Dennis Kavanaugh. *The British General Elections of 1979.* London: Macmillan, 1980. 433 pp.

Capdevielle, Jacques. *France de gauche, vota à droite.* Paris: Presses de la Fondation Nationale des Sciences Politiques, 1981. 355 pp.

Cerny, Philip G., and Martin A. Schain, eds. *French Politics and Public Policy.* New York: St. Martin's Press, 1980. 300 pp.

Chesneaux, Jean. *Le P.F.C., un art de vivre.* Paris: Maurice Nadeau, 1980. 210 pp.

Cohen, Solal; Annie Nizan; and Henriette Nizan. *Paul Nizan: Communiste impossible.* Paris: Grasset, 1980. 284 pp.

Collectif d'Histoire et d'Etudes Marxistes (CHEMA). *La Parti communiste de Belgique (1921–1944).* Brussels: Fondation Joseph Jacquemotte, 1980. 152 pp.

Daix, Pierre. *Les Hérétiques du P.F.C.* Paris: Robert Laffont, 1980. 350 pp.

Dauphin, Raymond. *Le défi d'une nouvelle gauche française ou la France vers le socialisme par le travaillisme.* Paris: La Pensée Universelle, 1980. 277 pp.

Del Noce, Augusto. *Il cattolico comunista.* Milan: Rusconi, 1981. 420 pp.

Drucker, H. M., ed. *Multi-Party Britain.* New York: Praeger, 1980. 256 pp.

Eden, Douglas, and Frederick Short. *Political Change in Europe: The Left and the Future of the Atlantic Alliance.* London: Blackwell, 1981. 163 pp.

Elections législatives de juin 1981: La gauche socialiste obtient la majorité absolue. Paris: Le Monde, 1981. 140 pp.

Elleinstein, Jean. *Ils vous trompent, camarades!* Paris: Pierre Belfond, 1981. 213 pp.

Flechtheim, Ossip K., et al. *Der Marsch der DKP durch die Institutionen.* Frankfurt/Main: Fischer Taschenbuch, 1980. 272 pp.

Füllenbach, Joseph, and Eberhard Schulz, eds. *Entspannung am Ende?* Munich: Oldenbourg, 1980. 381 pp.

Genscher, Hans-Dietrich. *Deutsche Aussenpolitik: Ausgewählte Grundsatzreden, 1975–1980.* Bonn: Aktuell, 1981. 333 pp.

Goulemot, Jean Marie. *Le Clairon de Stalin: De quelques aventures du Parti communist français.* Paris: Sycomore, 1981. 161 pp.

Hellman, Marion F., et al., eds. *Europäische Gewerkschaften.* West Berlin: Verlag Olle & Wolter, 1980. 252 pp.

Hillenbrand, Martin J., ed. *The Future of Berlin.* Montclair, N.J.: Allanheld, Osmun, 1981. 313 pp.

Isenberg, Veronika. *Die kommunisten Spanien und Portugals und die Europäische Gemeinschaft.* Cologne: Bundesinstitut für Ostwissenschaftliche und Internationale Studien, 1980. 97 pp.

Jelen, Christain. *Le P.F.C. sans peine.* Paris: Fayard, 1980. 124 pp.

Jesse, Eckhard, ed. *Bundesrepublik Deutschland und Deutsche Demokratische Republik: Die beiden deutschen Staaten im Vergleich.* Berlin: Colloquium, 1980. 415 pp.

Johnson, R. W. *The Long March of the French Left.* New York: St. Martin's Press, 1981. 354 pp.

Jouvenel, Renaud de. *Confidences d'un ancien sous marin du PCF.* Paris: Juillard, 1981. 201 pp.

Kindersley, Richard, ed. *In Search of Eurocommunism.* New York: St. Martin's Press, 1981. 220 pp.

Kogan, Norman. *The Political History of Postwar Italy.* New York: St. Martin's Press, 1981. 176 pp.

Konopnicki, Guy. *Le P.C.F. ou la momie de Lénine.* Paris: Garnior Frères, 1980. 222 pp.

Krell, Gert. *Nuklearrüstung im Ost-West Konflikt.* Baden-Baden: Nomos Verlag, 1980. 217 pp.

Lacorne, Denis. *Les Notables rouges: La Construction municipale de l'Union de la Gauche.* Paris: Presses de la Fondation Nationale des Sciences Politiques, 1980. 255 pp.

Lamalle, Jacques. *Jean-Baptist Doumeng: Le Milliardaire rouge.* Paris: Jean-Claude Lattes, 1980. 221 pp.

Lange, Peter, and Maurizio Vannicelli, eds. *The Communist Parties of Italy, France and Spain: Post-War Change and Continuity.* Winchester, Mass.: Allen & Unwin, 1981. 385 pp.

Lange, Peter, and Sidney Tarrow, eds. *Italy in Transition: Conflict and Consensus.* Totowa, N.J.: Frank Cass, 1980. 186 pp.

Lavau, Georges. *A quoi sert le Parti communiste français?* Paris: Fayard, 1980. 212 pp.

Lavigne, Raymond. *Je suis un communiste heureux.* Paris: La Table Ronde, 1981. 283 pp.

Liebman, Marcel. *Een geschiedenis van het Belgisch kommunisme, 1921-1945.* Ghent: Masereelfonds, 1980. 154 pp.

Lopez, Raimundo G., and Antonio Gutierrez Diaz. *El PSUC y el Eurocomunismo.* Madrid: Editores Manuel Campo, 1981. 204 pp.

Mallinckrodt, Anita M. *Die Selbst-darstellung der beiden deutschen Staaten in Ausland.* Cologne: Verlag Wissenschaft und Politik, 1980. 391 pp.

Marchais, Georges. *L'Espoir au présent.* Paris: Editions Sociales, 1980. 203 pp.

Meeting of European Communist Workers' Parties for Peace and Disarmament, Paris, 28-29 April, 1980. Moscow: Progress, 1980. 202 pp.

Middlemas, Robert Keith. *Power and the Party: Changing Faces of Communism in Western Europe.* London: Deutsch, 1980. 400 pp.

Morrison, Rodney J. *Portugal: Revolutionary Change in an Open Economy.* Boston: Auburn House, 1981. 200 pp.

Myten om VPKS oberoende. *En dokumentation Vänsterparteit Kommunisternas politiska, ekonomiska och organisatoriska bindingar till utlaendska kommunistregimen.* Stockholm: Tiedens Foerlag, 1980. 47 pp.

Não ao Mercado Comun. Conferência do PCP. Porto 31 de maio de 1980. *Conclusões gerais.* Lisbon: Edições Avante, 1980. 78 pp.

————. *Efeitos globais de adesão a CEE a alternativa.* Lisbon: Edições Avante, 1980. 148 pp.

Napolitano, Giorgio, and Enrico Berlinguer. *Partito di massa negli anni ottanta.* Rome: Editori Riuniti, 1981. 64 pp.

Norlund, Ib. *Internationalisme: Danmarks kommunistiske Parti i den kommunistiske verdensbev-ägelse.* Copenhagen: Tiden, 1980. 380 pp.

O'Ballance, Edgar. *Terror in Ireland: The Heritage of Hate.* Novato, Calif.: Presidio Press, 1981. 287 pp.

Ory, Pascal. *Nizan: Destin d'un revolte, 1905-1940.* Paris: Ramsay, 1980. 330 pp.

Parti Communiste Français. *Les Intellectuels, la culture et la révolution.* Paris: Editions Sociales, 1980. 425 pp.

———. Paris. Group Parlamentaire. *Naissance, contraception, avortement: Les Moyens de décider.* Paris: Editions Sociales, 1980. 179 pp.

Partido Comunista Português. *Programa eleitoral do PCP: Eleiões para a Assembleia de la República.* Lisbon: Edições Avante, 1980. 116 pp.

Partito Comunista Italiano. *I comunisti e la cooperazione: Storia documentaria, 1945–1980.* Bari: De Donato, 1981. 333 pp.

Pellicani, Luciano. *Gramsci: An Alternative Communism?* Translation of *Gramsci e la questione comunista.* Stanford: Hoover Institution Press, 1981. 120 pp.

Penniman, Howard R., ed. *Britain at the Polls, 1979.* Washington, D.C.: American Enterprise Institute, 1981. 345 pp.

———, ed. *Greece at the Polls: The National Elections of 1974 and 1977.* Washington, D.C.: American Enterprise Institute, 1981. 220 pp.

———, ed. *Italy at the Polls, 1979.* Washington, D.C.: American Enterprise Institute, 1981. 335 pp.

Peukert, Detlev. *Die KPD im Widerstand: Verfolgung und Untergrundarbeit an Rhein und Ruhr 1933 bis 1945.* Wuppertal: Peter Hammer Verlag, 1980. 460 pp.

Pridham, Geoffrey. *The Nature of the Italian Party System.* New York: St. Martin's Press, 1981. 240 pp.

Probst, Ulrich. *Die kommunistischen Parteien der Bundesrepublik Deutschland.* Munich: Vögel, 1980. 202 pp.

Quilès, Yvonne. *Sous le PC, les communistes.* Paris: Seuil, 1980. 283 pp.

Richter, Heinz. *Griechenlands Kommunisten und die Europäischen Gemeinschaft.* Cologne: Bundesinstitut für Ostwissenschaftliche und Internationale Studien, 1980. 54 pp.

Robrieux, Philippe. *Histoire intérieure du parti communiste, 1920–1945.* Paris: Fayard, 1980. 581 pp.

Roucaute, Yves. *Le P.F.C. et les sommets de l'état.* Paris: PUF, 1981. 380 pp.

Schlogel, Karl, et al. *Partei kaputt: Das Scheitern der KPD und die Krise der Linken.* Berlin: Olle & Wolter, 1981. 140 pp.

Schuler, Michael. *Die Kommunistische Partei Frankreichs.* Marburg: Verlag Arbeiterbewegung und Gesellschaftswissenschaft, 1980. 242 pp.

Schwab, George. *Eurocommunism: The Ideological and Political Theoretical Foundations.* Westport, Conn.: Greenwood Press, 1981. 325 pp.

Stachura, Peter. *The German Youth Movement, 1900–45.* New York: Macmillan, 1980. 245 pp.

Stehle, Hansjakob. *Eastern Politics of the Vatican, 1917–1979.* Athens: Ohio University Press, 1981. 466 pp.

Stettler, Peter. *Die Kommunistische Partei der Schweiz, 1921–31: Ein Beitrag zur schweizerischen Parteiforschung und zur geschichte der schweizerischen Arbeiterbewegung im Rahmen der Kommunistischen Internationale.* Bern: Francke, 1980. 627 pp.

Tachau, Frank. *Turkey.* New York: Praeger, 1981. 270 pp.

Tandler, Nicholas. *L'Impossible biographie de Georges Marchais.* Paris: Albatros, 1980. 233 pp.

Whetten, Lawrence L. *Germany, East and West: Conflicts, Collaborations and Confrontation.* New York: New York University Press, 1980. 244 pp.

Wilkens, Herbert. *The Two German Economies.* Revised and updated edition. London: Gower, 1981. 180 pp.

EASTERN EUROPE

Andren, Nils, and Karl E. Birnbaum, eds. *Belgrade and Beyond: The CSCE in Perspective.* Rockville, Md.: Sijthoff & Noordhoff, 1980. 180 pp.

Bačić, Hrvoje, et al. *Constitutional System of Yugoslavia.* Belgrade: Jugoslovenska stvarnost, 1980. 133 pp.

Biondi, Lawrence, ed. *Poland's Church-State Relations.* Chicago: Loyola University of Chicago Press, 1981. 73 pp.

Black, Jonathan. *Militärseelsorge in Polen.* Stuttgart: Seewald Verlag, 1981. 173 pp.

Bolz, Klaus, ed. *Die wirtschaftliche Entwicklung in ausgewählten Ländern Osteuropas zu Jahreswende 1979/80.* Hamburg: Verlag Weltarchiv, 1980. 273 pp.

Bornstein, Morris; Zvi Gitelman; and William Zimmerman; eds. *East-West Relations and the Future of Eastern Europe.* London: Allen & Unwin, 1981. 301 pp.

Brey, Thomas. *Der "jugoslawische Weg zum Sozialismus" und die Bundesrepublik Deutschland.* Bochum: Studienverlag Brockmeyer, 1980. 363 pp.

Bulgarska komunisticheska partiia. Kongres (12th: 1981). *Dvanadeseti kongres na Bulgarskata komunisticheska partiia: Dokladi i resheniia.* Sofia: Partizdat, 1981. 283 pp.

Buxhoeveden, Christina von. *Geschichtswissenschaft und Politik der DDR.* Cologne: Verlag Wissenschaft und Politik, 1980. 301 pp.

Çami, Foto. *Constitution of Triumphant Socialism.* Tirana: "8 Nëntori" Publishing House, 1980. 153 pp.

Castellan, Georges. *Dieu garde la Pologne.* Paris: Robert Laffont, 1981. 302 pp.

Ceauşescu, Nicolae. *The People's Welfare: A Major Target of the Policy of the Romanian Communist Party.* Bucharest: Meridiane, 1980. 221 pp.

―――. *The Solving of the National Question in Romania.* Bucharest: Meridiane, 1980. 137 pp.

Croghan, Martin J., and Penelope P. Croghan. *Ideological Training in Communist Education: A Case Study of Romania.* Washington, D.C.: University Press of America, 1980. 201 pp.

Danecki, Jan, ed. *Toward Poland "2000": Problems of Social Development.* Wroclaw: Zaklad Narodowy Imienia Ossollinskich Wydawnictwo Polskiej Akademii Nauk, 1980. 281 pp.

Dejiny československo-bulharských vztahu. Prague: Academia, 1980. 296 pp.

Deutsche Kommunisten über die Partei: Artikel und Reden 1918 bis 1939. East Berlin: Dietz Verlag, 1980. 323 pp.

De Weydenthal, Jan B., et al. *August 1980: The Strikes in Poland.* Munich: Radio Free Europe Research, 1980. 447 pp.

Djordijevich, Dimitrije, and Stephen Fischer-Galati. *The Balkan Revolutionary Tradition.* New York: Columbia University Press, 1981. 271 pp.

Documents on the Policy of the GDR. *Erich Honecker on Current Political Issues.* East Berlin: Panorama, 1981. 30 pp.

―――. *Report by the Central Statistical Office of the GDR on the Fulfillment of the National Economic Plan in the First Half of 1981.* Dresden: Panorama, 1981. 30 pp.

―――. *A Successful Policy Geared to the Needs of the People and the Preservation of Peace: Deliberations of the People's Chamber of the GDR on 25 and 26 June 1981.* East Berlin: Panorama, 1981. 29 pp.

Duverger, Maurice. *Les Orangers du lac Balaton.* Paris: Seuil, 1980. 253 pp.

Ebert, Friedrich. *Einheit der Klasse, Macht der Klasse.* East Berlin: Dietz Verlag, 1979. 480 pp.

Economic Reforms in Eastern Europe and Prospects for the 1980's: Colloquium, 16–18 April 1980, Brussels. New York: Pergamon Press, 1980. 320 pp.

Eidlin, Fred H. *The Logic of "Normalization."* New York: Columbia University Press, 1980. 278 pp.

Experience and the Future Group, comp. *Poland Today: The State of the Republic.* White Plains, N.Y.: E. M. Sharpe, 1981. 231 pp.

Fischer-Galati, Stephen, ed. *Eastern Europe in the 1980s.* Boulder, Colo.: Westview Press, 1981. 291 pp.

Fornaro, Pasquale. *Béla Kun. Professione: rivoluzionario. Scritti e discoursi, 1918–1937.* Soveria Mannelli, Italy: Rubbettino Editore, 1980. 277 pp.

Forster, Thomas M. *The East Germany Army: Second in the Warsaw Pact.* 2d edition. London: Allen & Unwin, 1980. 310 pp.

Freiburg, Arnold. *Kriminalität in der DDR.* Wiesbaden: Westdeutscher Verlag, 1980. 370 pp.

Gatter-Klenk, Jule. *Vielleicht auf Knien, aber vorwärts! Gespräche mit Lech Walesa.* Königstein/Ts.: Athenäum, 1981. 174 pp.

German Democratic Republic. *Directives Issued by the 19th Congress of the SED for the Five Year Plan for the GDR's National Economic Development, 1981–1985.* East Berlin: Verlag Zeit im Bild, 1981. 196 pp.

Ghermani, Dionisie. *Die nationale Souveränitätspolitik der SR Rumänien.* 2 volumes. Munich: Oldenbourg Verlag, 1981.

Golebiowski, Janusza W., and Wladislawa Gora, eds. *Ruch robotniczy w Polsce Ludowej.* Warsaw: Wiedza Powszechna, 1980. 646 pp.

Gradl, J. B. *Anfang unter dem Sowjetstern: Die CDU 1945–1948 in der sowjetischen Besatzungszone Deutschlands.* Cologne: Verlag Wissenschaft und Politik, 1981. 208 pp.

Graham, Lawrence S. *Romania: A Profile.* Boulder, Colo.: Westview Press, 128 pp.

Groschoff, Kurt, ed. *Die Landwirtschaft der DDR.* East Berlin: Dietz Verlag, 1980. 470 pp.

Haase, Herwig E. *Entwicklungstendenzen der DDR: Wirtschaft für die 80er Jahre. Eine prognose der Probleme.* West Berlin: Osteuropa Institut, 1980. 115 pp.

Hacker, Jens, et al. *Die nationale Volksarmee der DDR in Rahmen des Warschauer Paktes.* Munich: Bernard & Graefe Verlag, 1980. 238 pp.

Hajdu, Tibor. *The Hungarian Soviet Republic.* Budapest: Akadémiai Kiadó, 1979. 172 pp.

Hare, Paul; Hugo Radice; and Nigel Swain; eds. *Hungary: A Decade of Economic Reform.* Winchester, Mass.: Allen & Unwin, 1981. 257 pp.

Höcker-Weyard, Christine. *Die Rechtsinstitut und Rechtsinstitutionen des jugoslawischen Selbstverwaltungssystems.* Baden-Baden: Nomos Verlag, 1980. 263 pp.

Höhmann, Hans-Hermann, ed. *Partizipation und Wirtschaftsplanung in Osteuropa und der VR China.* Stuttgart: Kohlhammer, 1980. 284 pp.

Honecker, Erich. *Die nächsten Aufgaben der Partei bei der weiteren Durchfürung der Beschlüsse des IX. Parteitages der SED.* East Berlin: Dietz Verlag, 1980. 94 pp.

———. *From My Life.* New York: Pergamon Press, 1981. 500 pp.

———. *Reden und Aufsätze.* Volume 6. East Berlin: Dietz Verlag, 1980. 671 pp.

———. *Report of the Central Committee of the Socialist Unity Party of Germany to the 10th Congress of the SED.* Dresden: Verlag Zeit im Bild, 1981. 203 pp.

Hoxha, Enver. *Speeches, Conversations and Articles, 1969–1970.* Tirana: "8 Nëntori" Publishing House, 1980. 506 pp.

Institut für Hochschulbildung. *Das Hochschulwesen der DDR: Ein Überblick.* East Berlin: Deutscher Verlag der Wissenschaften, 1980. 259 pp.

Instituto di Studi Storici, Politici e Sociali, Bucharest. *Problemi di storia della Romania.* Milan: Teti, 1980. 414 pp.

Jeffries, Ian. *The Industrial Enterprise in Eastern Europe.* New York: Praeger, 1981. 165 pp.

Jones, Christopher D. *Defending Socialism in Eastern Europe: Political Autonomy, Military Intervention and the Warsaw Pact.* New York: Praeger, 1980. 350 pp.

———. *Soviet Influence in Eastern Europe.* New York: Praeger, 1981. 200 pp.

Kalenichenko, P. M., and V. P. Kolesnik. *Granitsa druzhby i mira.* Lvov: Vishcha Shkola, 1980. 156 pp.

Karatnycky, Adrian. *Workers' Rights, East and West: A Comparative Study of Trade Union and Workers' Rights in Western Democracies and in Eastern Europe.* New Brunswick, N.J.: Transaction Books, 1980. 150 pp.

Kardelj, Edward. *Self-Management and the Political System.* Belgrade: Socialist Thought and Practice, 1980. 287 pp.

———. *Self-Management: One of the Laws in the Development of Socialism.* Belgrade: Socialist Thought and Practice, 1980. 41 pp.

———. *Tito and Socialist Revolution of Yugoslavia.* Belgrade: Socialist Thought and Practice, 1980. 275 pp.

Klein, George, and Milan J. Reban, eds. *The Politics of Ethnicity in Eastern Europe.* New York: Columbia University Press, 1981. 279 pp.

Koliševski, Lazar. *Aspects of the Macedonian Question.* Belgrade: Socialist Thought and Practice, 1980. 250 pp.

Kontos, Joan Fultz. *Red Cross, Black Eagle: A Biography of Albania's American School.* Boulder, Colo.: East European Quarterly, 1981. 217 pp.

Koval'chak, Hryhorii I. *Pol'skaia Narodnaia respublika v sodruzhestve stran-chlenov SEV: Ekonomicheskii ocherk.* Kiev: Naukova dumka, 1980. 197 pp.

Lavigne, Marie, ed. *Stratégies des pays socialistes dans l'échange international.* Paris: Economica, 1980. 333 pp.

Lendvai, Paul. *The Bureaucracy of Truth: How the Communist Governments Manage the News.* Boulder, Colo.: Westview Press, 1981. 285 pp.

Leslie, R. F.; Antony Polonsky; Jan M. Ciechanowski; and Z. A. Pelczynski. *The History of Poland Since 1863.* Cambridge, Eng.: Cambridge University Press, 1980. 494 pp.

Letowski, Janusz, ed. *Administration in People's Poland.* Wroclaw: Zaklad Narodowy Imienia Ossolinskich, 1980. 276 pp.

Lommax, Bill, ed. *Eyewitness in Hungary: The Soviet Invasion of 1956.* Nottingham, Eng.: Spokesman, 1980. 183 pp.

Mamatey, Victor S., and Radomir Luza, eds. *Geschichte Tschechoslovakischen Republik, 1918–1948.* Vienna: Herman Böhlhaus Verlag, 1980. 553 pp.

Moczulski, Leszek. *Revolution Without Revolution: The Anti-Communist Manifesto of 1979.* Published in the underground magazine *Droga*, Warsaw, June 1979. 13 leaves.

Mojsov, Lazo. *Dimensions of Non-Alignment.* Belgrade: Jugoslovenska Stvarnost, 1981. 281 pp.

Moorthy, Krishna K. *After Tito What?* Atlantic Highlands, N.J.: Humanities Press, 1980. 207 pp.

Mynarek, Hubert. *Zwischen Gott und Genossen: Als Priester in Polen.* West Berlin: Ullstein, 1981. 312 pp.

Nelson, Daniel N. *Democratic Centralism in Romania: A Study of Local Communist Politics.* New York: Columbia University Press, 1980. 186 pp.

———, ed. *Romania in the 1980's.* Boulder, Colo.: Westview Press, 1981. 313 pp.

Die Organisation des Warschauer Vertrages. *Dokumente und Materialen, 1955–1980.* East Berlin: Staatsverlag der DDR, 1980. 252 pp.

Osteuropa Institut München. *Yearbook on East-European Economics.* Volume 9, part 1. Munich: Olzog Verlag, 1980. 249 pp.

Party Preferences in Hypothetical Free Elections in Czechoslovakia, Hungary and Poland. Munich: Radio Free Europe/Radio Liberty, 1981. 28 pp.

Paul, David W. *Czechoslovakia: A Profile of a Socialist Republic at the Crossroads of Europe.* Boulder, Colo.: Westview Press, 1981. 186 pp.

Pollo, Stefanaq. *The History of Albania: From Its Origins to the Present Day.* London: Routledge & Kegan Paul, 1981. 322 pp.

Polonsky, Antony, and Boleslaw Drukier, eds. *The Beginnings of Communist Rule in Poland*. Boston: Routledge & Kegan Paul, 1980. 180 pp.

Pölöskei, Ferenc. *Hungary After Two Revolutions*. Budapest: Akadémiai Kiadó, 1980. 148 pp.

Polski sierpień 1980: Reediycja almanachu gdańskich środowisk twórczch "Punkt" nr. 12/80. New York: Biblioteka Pomostu, 1981. 302 pp.

Pomorskii, Andzhei, and Mikhail Nazarov, comps. *Solidarnost'*. Frankfurt/Main: Possev, 1980. 198 pp.

Portes, Richard. *The Polish Crisis: Western Economic Policy Options*. London: Royal Institute of International Affairs, 1981. 58 pp.

Potichnyj, Peter J., ed. *Poland and the Ukraine: Past and Present*. Edmonton and Toronto: Canadian Institute of Ukrainian Studies, 1980. 364 pp.

Radu, Michael. *Eastern Europe and the Third World: East vs. South*. New York: Praeger, 1981. 376 pp.

Razumovsky, Andreas. *Ein Kampf um Belgrad: Tito und die jugoslawische Wirklichkeit*. West Berlin: Ullstein, 1980. 540 pp.

Riege, Gerhard. *Nationalität: Deutsch. Staatsbürgerschaft: DDR*. East Berlin: Staatsverlag der DDR, 1980. 154 pp.

Rupnik, Jacques. *Histoire du Parti communiste tchecoslovaque*. Paris: Presse de la Fondations Nationales des Sciences Politiques, 1981. 287 pp.

Rüster, Lothar. *Die internationale ökonomischen Organisationen der RGW-Länder: Rechtsfragen*. East Berlin: Staatsverlag der DDR, 1980. 157 pp.

Schnitzer, Martin. *U.S. Business Involvement in Eastern Europe*. New York: Praeger, 1981. 155 pp.

Shehu, Mehmet. *Der Kampf um die Befreiung Tiranas*. Tirana: "8 Nentori" Publishing House, 1980. 131 pp.

Simon, Maurice D., and Roger E. Kanet, eds. *Background to Crisis: Policy and Politics in Gierek's Poland*. Boulder, Colo.: Westview Press, 1981. 418 pp.

Singer, Daniel. *The Road to Gdansk: Poland and the USSR*. New York: Monthly Review Press, 1981. 256 pp.

Skilling, Gordon H. *Charter 77 and Human Rights in Czechoslovakia*. Winchester, Mass.: Allen & Unwin, 1981. 363 pp.

Sugar, Peter F., ed. *Ethnic Diversity and Conflict in Eastern Europe*. Santa Barbara, Calif.: ABC-Clio, 1980. 553 pp.

Surpat, Gheorghe, ed. *Romania in anii socialismului, 1948–1978*. Bucharest: Editura Politica, 1980. 467 pp.

Taborsky, Eduard. *President Edvard Beneš Between East and West, 1938–1948*. Stanford: Hoover Institution Press, 1981. 299 pp.

Tito's Historical Decisions, 1941–1945. Belgrade: Narodna armija, 1980. 198 pp.

Topol, Andrzej. *Sojusz przyjazn z ZSRR w programach oraz w dzialalnosci PPR i PZPR*. Katowice: Uniwersytet Slaski, 1979. 252 pp.

Triska, Jan F., and Charles Gati, eds. *Blue-Collar Workers in Eastern Europe*. London: Allen & Unwin, 1981. 302 pp.

Tudjman, Franjo. *Nationalism in Contemporary Europe*. Boulder, Colo.: East European Quarterly, 1981. 293 pp.

Tymowski, Andrzej, ed. *The Strike in Gdansk, August 14–31, 1980*. New Haven, Conn.: Don't Hold Back, 1981. 50 pp.

Tyson, Laura D'Andrea. *The Yugoslav Economic System and Its Performance in the 1970's*. Berkeley: University of California, Institute of International Studies, 1980. 112 pp.

United States. Central Intelligence Agency. National Foreign Assessment Center. *Directory of Offi-*

cials of the Czechoslovak Socialist Republic. Washington, D.C.: Library of Congress, 1980. 175 pp.

———. *Directory of Officials of the Federal Republic of Yugoslavia.* Washington, D.C.: Library of Congress, 1981. 223 pp.

———. *Directory of Officials of the People's Socialist Republic of Albania.* Washington, D.C.: Library of Congress, 1980. 92 pp.

———. *Directory of Officials of the Socialist Republic of Romania.* Washington, D.C.: Library of Congress, 1980. 185 pp.

Varsanyi, Julius, ed. *Quest for a New Central Europe.* Adelaide: Australian Carpathian Federation, n.d. 295 pp.

Vidnyanskiy, S. V. *Konsolidatsiya profsoyuznogo dvizheniya v Chekhoslovakii, 1969–1975.* Kiev: Naukova Dumka, 1979. 212 pp.

Völgyes, Ivan. *Hungary: A Profile.* Boulder, Colo. Westview Press, 1981. 128 pp.

Weber, Hermann. *Kleine Geschichte der DDR.* Cologne: Verlag Wissenschaft und Politik, 1980. 199 pp.

Wehler, Hans-Ulrich. *Nationalitätpolitik in Jugoslavien: Die deutsche Minderheit, 1918–1978.* Göttingen: Vandenhoeck & Ruprecht, 1980. 164 pp.

Westen, Claus; Boris Meissner; and Friedrich Christian Schroeder; eds. *Der Schutz individueller Rechte und Interessen im Recht sozialistischer Staaten.* Baden-Baden: Nomos Verlag, 1980. 248 pp.

Wiedeman, Paul. *Economic Reform in Bulgaria: Coping with "the kj Problem."* Vienna: Wiener Institut für Internationale Wirtschaftsvergleiche, 1980. 34 pp.

Yedlin, Tova, ed. *Women in Eastern Europe and the Soviet Union.* New York: Praeger, 1980. 320 pp.

THE SOVIET UNION

Adelman, Jonathan R. *The Revolutionary Armies: The Historical Development of the Soviet and the Chinese People's Liberation Armies.* Westport, Conn.: Greenwood Press, 1980. 230 pp.

Agurskii, M. *Ideologiia Natsional-bol'shevizma.* Paris: YMCA Press, 1980. 231 pp.

Aktual'nye problemy istorii sovetskogo Kazakhstana: K 60-letiiu Kazakhskoi SSR. Alma-Ata: Nauka, 1980. 341 pp.

Amalrik, Andrei. *Journal d'un provocateur.* Paris: Seuil, 1980. 381 pp.

Andrew, Joe. *Writers and Society During the Rise of Russian Realism.* Atlantic Highlands, N.J.: Humanities Press, 1980. 190 pp.

Antonov-Ovseyenko, Anton. *The Time of Stalin: Portrait of a Tyranny.* New York: Harper & Row, 1981. 374 pp.

Azbel, Mark Y. *Refusenik: Trapped in the Soviet Union.* Boston: Houghton Mifflin, 1981. 513 pp.

Baylis, John, and Gerald Segal, eds. *Soviet Strategy.* London: Croom Helm, 1981. 263 pp.

Bertram, Christoph, ed. *Prospects of Soviet Power in the 1980s.* Hamden, Conn.: Shoe String Press, Archon Books, 1980. 126 pp.

Besemeres, John F. *Socialist Population Politics: The Political Implications of Demographic Trends in the USSR and Eastern Europe.* White Plains, N.Y.: M. E. Sharpe, 1980. 373 pp.

Blekher, Feiga. *The Soviet Woman in the Family and in Society.* New York: Wiley, 1980. 234 pp.

Bornstein, Morris, ed. *The Soviet Economy: Continuity and Change.* Boulder, Colo.: Westview Press, 1981. 379 pp.

Borys, Jurij. *The Sovietization of Ukraine, 1917–1923: The Communist Doctrine and Practice of National Self-Determination.* Revised edition. Edmonton: Canadian Institute of Ukrainian Studies, 1980. 488 pp.

Bourdeaux, Michael, and Michael Rowe, eds. *May One Believe—in Russia? Violations of Religious Liberty in the Soviet Union.* London: Darton, Longman & Todd, 1980. 113 pp.

Brezhnev, Leonid Il'ich. *Otchetnyi doklad Tsentral'nogo Komiteta KPSS XXVI s"ezdu Kommunisticheskoi Partii Sovetskogo Soiuza i ocherednye zadachi partii v oblasti vnutrennei i vneshnei politiki, 23 fevralia 1981 goda.* Moscow: Izdatelstvo politicheskoi literatury, 1981. 110 pp.

Brod, Peter. *Die Antizionismus- und Israelpolitik der UdSSR: Voraussetzungen und Entwicklung bis 1956.* Baden-Baden: Nomos Verlag, 1980. 147 pp.

Buttlar, Walrab von. *Ziele und Zielkonflikte in der sowjetischen Deutschlandpolitik, 1845-1947.* Stuttgart: Klett-Cotta, 1980. 300 pp.

Caldwell, Lawrence T., and William Diebold, Jr. *Soviet-American Relations in the 1980's.* New York: McGraw-Hill, 1981. 314 pp.

Campbell, Robert W. *Soviet Energy Technologies: Planning Policy, Research and Development.* Bloomington: Indiana University Press, 1980. 268 pp.

Carrère d'Encausse, Hélène. *Le Pouvoir confisqué: Gouvernants et gouvernes en U.R.S.S.* Paris: Flammarion, 1980. 328 pp.

Charles, Milene. *The Soviet Union and Africa: The History of the Involvement.* Lanham, Md.: University Press of America, 1980. 237 pp.

Cocks, Paul M. *Science Policy: USA/USSR, Volume 2, Science Policy in the Soviet Union.* Washington, D.C.: National Science Foundation, 1980. 331 pp.

Collins, John M. *U.S.-Soviet Military Balance, 1960-1980.* New York: McGraw-Hill, 1980. 644 pp.

Davies, R. W. *The Socialist Offensive: The Collectivization of Soviet Agriculture, 1929-1930.* Cambridge, Mass.: Harvard University Press, 1980. 452 pp.

Davis, Christopher. *Rising Infant Mortality in the U.S.S.R. in the 1970s.* Washington, D.C.: U.S. Department of Commerce, Bureau of the Census, 1980. 33 pp.

Dellenbrant, Jan Ake. *Soviet Regional Policy: A Quantitative Inquiry into the Social and Political Development of the Soviet Republic.* Atlantic Highlands, N.J.: Humanities Press, 1981. 192 pp.

De Pauw, John W. *Soviet-American Trade Negotiations.* New York: Praeger, 1979. 180 pp.

Desfosses, Helen. *Soviet Population Policy: Conflicts and Constraints.* New York: Pergamon Press, 1981. 209 pp.

Dietz, Raimund. *Price Changes in Soviet Trade with CMEA and the Rest of the World Since 1975.* Vienna: Wiener Institut für Internationale Wirtschaftsvergleiche, 1980. 290 pp.

Diplomacy of Power: Soviet Armed Forces as a Political Instrument. Washington, D.C.: Brookings Institution, 1981. 733 pp.

Donaldson, Robert H., ed. *The Soviet Union in the Third World: Successes and Failures.* Boulder, Colo.: Westview Press, 1981. 458 pp.

Duncan, Raymond W., ed. *Soviet Policy in the Third World.* New York: Pergamon Press, 1980. 322 pp.

Dunmore, Timothy. *The Stalinist Command Economy: The Soviet State Apparatus and Economic Policy, 1945-53.* New York: St. Martin's Press, 1980. 176 pp.

Ericson, Edward E., Jr. *Solzhenitsyn: The Moral Vision.* Grand Rapids, Mich.: William E. Eerdmans, 1980. 230 pp.

Fallenbuchl, Zbigniew M., and Carl H. McMillan, eds. *Partners in East-West Economic Relations: The Determinants of Choice.* New York: Pergamon Press, 1980. 461 pp.

Farmer, Kenneth C. *Ukrainian Nationalism in the Post-Stalin Era.* The Hague: Martinus Nijhoff, 1980. 241 pp.

Ferro, Marc. *Des soviets au communisme bureaucratique: Les Mécanismes d'une subversion.* Paris: Gallimard/Juillard, 1980. 263 pp.

————. *October 1–17: A Social History of the Russian Revolution.* Boston: Routledge & Kegan Paul, 1980. 351 pp.

Feuchtwanger, Edgar J., ed. *The Soviet Union and the Third World.* New York: St. Martin's Press, 1981. 200 pp.

Fisher, Wesley A. *The Soviet Marriage Market: Mate-Selection in Russia and the USSR.* New York: Praeger, 1980. 299 pp.

Gabriel, Richard A. *The New Red Legions: Volume 1, A Survey Data Source Book; Volume 2, An Attitudinal Portrait of the Soviet Soldier.* Westport, Conn.: Greenwood Press, 1980.

Ginzburg, Eugenia. *Within the Whirlwind.* New York: Harcourt Brace Jovanovich, 1981. 448 pp.

Golan, Galia. *The Soviet Union and the Palestine Liberation Organization: An Uneasy Alliance.* New York: Praeger, 1980. 275 pp.

Goldman, Marshall I. *The Enigma of Soviet Petroleum: Half-Full or Half-Empty?* London: Allen & Unwin, 1980. 214 pp.

Grandstaff, Peter J. *Interregional Migration in the USSR: Economic Aspects, 1959–1970.* Durham, N.C.: Duke University Press, 1980. 188 pp.

Gregory, Paul R., and Robert C. Stuart. *Soviet Economic Structure and Performance.* 2d edition. New York: Harper & Row, 1981. 419 pp.

Greenway, Ambrose. *COMECON Merchant Ships.* 4th, revised edition. White Plains, N.Y.: Sheridan House, 1981. 180 pp.

Gromyko, Andrei. *Lenin and the Soviet Peace Policy.* Moscow: Progress, 1980. 495 pp.

Guillain, Robert. *L' Espion qui sauva Moscou: L'Affaire Sorge racontée par un temoin.* Paris: Seuil, 1981. 188 pp.

Hanson, Philip. *Trade and Technology in Soviet-Western Relations.* New York: Columbia University Press, 1981. 259 pp.

Heitman, Sidney. *The Soviet German in the USSR Today.* Cologne: Bundesinstitut für Ostwissenschaftliche und Internationale Studien, 1980. 135 pp.

Henry, Maureen. *The Intoxication of Power: An Analysis of Civil Religion in Relation to Ideology.* Boston: D. Reidel, 1980. 231 pp.

Hill, Ronald J., and Peter Frank. *The Soviet Communist Party.* Winchester, Mass.: Allen & Unwin, 1981. 167 pp.

Huyn, Hans. *Fünf vor Zwölf: Die Welt nach Afghanistan.* Vienna: F. Molden, 1980. 274 pp.

Istrati, Panait. *Vers l'autre flamme: Après seize mois dans l'U.R.S.S., 1927–1928. Confession pour vaincus.* Paris: Fondation Panait Istrati, 1980. 342 pp.

Jacobs, Dan N. *Borodin: Stalin's Man in China.* Cambridge, Mass.: Harvard University Press, 1981. 369 pp.

Jacobsen, C. G. *Sino-Soviet Relations Since Mao: The Chairman's Legacy.* New York: Praeger, 1981. 161 pp.

Kaiser, Robert G. *Russia: From the Inside.* New York: E. P. Dutton, 1980. 186 pp.

Kalin, I. P. *Kommunisticheskie idealy, kak ikh utverdit' i razvit' v cheloveke: Iz opyta Kompartii Moldavii po sovershenstvovaniiu partiinogo rukovodstva vospitatel'nym protsessom.* Moscow: Izdatel'stvo politicheskoi literatury, 1981. 238 pp.

Kaplan, Fred M. *Dubious Specter: A Skeptical Look at the Soviet Nuclear Threat.* 2d revised printing. Washington, D.C.: Institute for Policy Studies, 1980. 930 pp.

Kelman, Jacob M., ed. *Anti-Semitism in the Soviet Union: Its Roots and Consequences.* Volume 2. Jerusalem: Hebrew University of Jerusalem, Centre for Research and Documentation of East-European Jewry, 1980. 371 pp.

Kommunisticheskaia Partiia Sovetskogo Soiuza. S"ezd. (26th: 1981: Moscow, R.S.F.S.R.). *Materialy XXVI s"ezda KPSS.* Moscow: Izdatelstvo politicheskoi literatury, 1981. 223 pp.

Koorna, A. *Economic Strategy of the CPSU in the Tenth Five-Year Plan Period, 1976–1980.* Tallinn: Perioodika, 1980. 101 pp.

Kuznetsov, Edward. *Prison Diaries.* Briarcliff Manor, N.Y.: Stein & Day, 1980. 254 pp.

Lebedev, Nikolai I. *SSSR v mirovoi politike, 1917–1980.* Moscow: Mezhdunarodnye otnosheniia, 1980. 357 pp.

Leibzon, Boris M. *Mezhdunarodnoe edinstvo kommunistov: Istoricheskii opyt, printsipy, problemy.* Moscow: Politizdat, 1980. 251 pp.

Luchterhandt, Otto. *UN-Menschenrechtskonventionen: Sowjetrecht—Sowjetwirklichkeit.* Baden-Baden: Nomos Verlag, 1980. 319 pp.

Malia, Martin. *Comprendre la révolution russe.* Paris: Seuil, 1980. 244 pp.

McAuley, Alistair. *Women's Work and Wages in the Soviet Union.* London: Allen & Unwin, 1981. 228 pp.

Medish, Vadim. *The Soviet Union.* Englewood Cliffs, N.J.: Prentice-Hall, 1981. 367 pp.

Meier, Reinhard, and Kathrin Meier. *Sowjetrealität in der Ära Breschnew.* Stuttgart: Seewald Verlag, 1980. 279 pp.

Mickiewicz, Ellen. *Media and the Russian Public.* New York: Praeger, 1981. 176 pp.

Miftakhov, Z. Z. *Bor'ba kommunistov Tatrii za ukreplenie diktatury proletariata v pervy gody sovetskoi vlasti: Iz opyta raboty kommunistov v sisteme sudebnosledstvennykh uchrezhdenii.* Kazan: Izdatelstvo Kazanskogo universiteta, 1980. 215 pp.

Mochalov, Boris M. *Requirements of Developed Socialist Society.* Moscow: Progress, 1980. 144 pp.

Motyl, Alexander J. *The Turn to the Right: The Ideological Origins and Development of Ukrainian Nationalism, 1919–1929.* Boulder, Colo.: East European Monographs, 1980. 212 pp.

Murphy, Paul J. *Brezhnev: Soviet Politician.* Jefferson, N.C.: McFarland, 1981. 361 pp.

Nogee, Joseph L., and Robert H. Donaldson. *Soviet Foreign Policy Since World War II.* New York: Pergamon Press, 1981. 320 pp.

Nove, Alec. *The Soviet Economic System.* Winchester, Mass.: Allen & Unwin, 1980. 406 pp.

Pajaujis-Javis, Joseph. *Soviet Genocide in Lithuania.* New York: Manyland Books, 1980. 246 pp.

Pallot, Judith, and Denis J. B. Shaw. *Planning in the Soviet Union.* Athens: University of Georgia Press, 1981. 303 pp.

Pankhurst, Jerry, and Michael Paul Sacks, eds. *Contemporary Soviet Society: Sociological Perspectives.* New York: Praeger, 1980. 185 pp.

Parrish, Michael. *The USSR in World War II: An Annotated Bibliography of Books Published in the Soviet Union, 1945–1980, with an Addendum for the Years 1975–1980.* 2 volumes. New York: Garland Publishing, 1981.

Pavlenok, Petr Denisovich. *Stanovlenie i razvitie sotsialnoi odnorodnosti: Zakonomernost' kommunisticheskoi formatsii.* Moscow: Izdatelstvo "Znanie," 1981. 64 pp.

Payne, Samuel B., Jr. *The Soviet Union and SALT.* Cambridge, Mass.: MIT Press, 1981. 377 pp.

Petersen, Phillip A., ed. *Soviet Policy in the Post-Tito Balkans.* Washington, D.C.: U.S. Air Force, n.d. 157 pp.

Penkaitis, Norbert. *Fiskalische Instrumente der sowjetischen Agrarpolitik.* West Berlin: Duncker & Humbolt, 1980. 132 pp.

Podrabinek, Alexander. *Punitive Medicine.* Ann Arbor, Mich.: Karoma Publishers, 1980. 223 pp.

Ponomarev, Boris N., ed. *The International Working Class Movement.* Volume 1. Moscow: Progress, 1980. 674 pp.

Rapport secret au Comité Central sur l'état de l'église en URSS. Paris: Seuil, 1980. 186 pp.

Rigby, T. H.; Archie Brown; and Peter Reddeway; eds. *Authority, Power and Policy in the USSR.* New York: St. Martin's Press, 1980. 207 pp.

Romerstein, Herbert. *Soviet Support for International Terrorism*. Washington, D.C.: Foundation for Democratic Education, 1981. 40 pp.

Rositzke, Harry. *The KGB: The Eyes of the People*. New York: Doubleday, 1981. 294 pp.

Rubinstein, Alvin Z. *Soviet Foreign Policy Since World War II: Imperial and Global*. Cambridge, Mass.: Winthrop, 1981. 295 pp.

Sacks, Michael Paul. *Work and Equality in the Soviet Union: The Division of Labor in Soviet Society*. New York: Praeger, 1981. 271 pp.

Schapiro, Leonard, and Joseph Godson, eds. *The Soviet Worker: Illusion and Realities*. New York: St. Martin's Press, 1981. 291 pp.

Schmidt-Hauer, Christian. *Das sind die Russen: Wie sie wurden, wie sie leben*. Hamburg: Knaus, 1980. 410 pp.

Scott, Harriet Fast, and William F. Scott. *The Armed Forces of the USSR*. Boulder, Colo.: Westview Press, 1981. 439 pp.

Seen, Alfred Erich. *Assassination in Switzerland: The Murder of Vatslav Vorovsky*. Madison: University of Wisconsin Press, 1981. 281 pp.

Shatz, Marshall S. *Soviet Dissent in Historical Perspective*. Cambridge, Eng.: Cambridge University Press, 1980. 214 pp.

Shvets, Igor' A. *Kak stroitsia, zhivet i deistvuet KPSS*. Moscow: Izdatelstvo politicheskoi literatury, 1980. 366 pp.

Simon, William B., ed. *The Soviet Codes of Law*. Alphen aan Rijn: Sijthoff & Noordhoff, 1980. 1239 pp.

Sipols, Vilnis. *Vneshniaia politika Sovetskogo Soiuza: 1933–1935 gg.* Moscow: Nauka, 1980. 390 pp.

Smith, Myron J., Jr. *The Soviet Air and Strategic Rocket Forces, 1939–1980: A Guide to Sources in English*. Santa Barbara, Calif.: ABC-Clio, 1981. 321 pp.

Sonnenfeldt, Helmut. *The Soviet Challenge: A Policy Framework for the 1980s*. New York: Council on Foreign Relations, 1981. 31 pp.

The Soviet Union and Ballistic Missile Defense. Cambridge, Mass.: Institute for Foreign Policy Analysis, 1980. 71 pp.

The Soviet Union, 1978–79: Domestic Policy, The Economy, Foreign Policy. Volume 5. New York: Holmes & Meier, 1980. 297 pp.

Speiss, Kurt. *Peripherie Sowjetwirtschaft: Das Beispiel Russisch-Fernost, 1967–1970*. Zurich: Atlantis, 1980. 200 pp.

Stankovsky, Jan. *Ost-West Handel 1980 and Aussichten 1981*. Vienna: Wiener Institut für Internationale Wirtschaftsvergleiche, 1981. 87 pp.

Suslov, Mikhail A. *Selected Speeches and Writings*. New York: Pergamon Press, 1980. 373 pp.

Tikhonov, N. A. *Izbrannye rechi i stat'i*. Moscow: Izdatelstvo politicheskoi literatury, 1980. 447 pp.

Tomson, Edgar. *Der Ministerrat der UdSSR*. West Berlin: Berlin Verlag, 1980. 295 pp.

United States. Congress. Permanent Select Committee on Intelligence. *Soviet Covert Action: The Forgery Offensive. Hearings*. 96th Congress, 2d session, 6 and 19 February 1980. Washington, D.C.: Government Printing Office, 1980. N.p.

Venner, Dominique. *L'Histoire de l'armée rouge: La Révolution et la guerre civile, 1917–1924*. Paris: Plon, 1981. 298 pp.

Verba, Lesya; Bohdan Yasen; and Osyp Zinkewych, eds. *Helsinki Guarantees for Ukraine Committee. The Human Rights Movement in Ukraine: Documents of the Ukrainian Helsinki Group, 1976–1980*. Baltimore: Smoloskyp Publishers, 1980. 277 pp.

Vienna Institute for Comparative Economic Studies, ed. *COMECON Data, 1979*. London: Macmillan, 1980. 436 pp.

Voine v Afganistane. Frankfurt/Main: Posev Verlag, 1980. 204 pp.

Volten, P. M. E. *Brezhnev's "Peace Program": Success or Failure?* Ph.D. Dissertation. Amsterdam: Vrije Universiteit te Amsterdam, 1981. 462 pp.

Weaver, Kitty. *Russia's Future: The Communist Education of Youth.* New York: Praeger, 1981. 250 pp.

White, Stephen. *Political Culture and Soviet Politics.* New York: St. Martin's Press, 1980. 277 pp.

Wich, Richard. *Sino-Soviet Crisis Politics: A Study of Political Change and Communication.* Cambridge, Mass.: Harvard University, Council on East Asian Studies, 1980. 313 pp.

Yin, John. *Soviet Military Doctrine.* Hong Kong: Asian Research Service, 1980. 196 pp.

————. *The Soviet Views on the Use of Force in International Law.* Hong Kong: Asian Research Service, 1980. 189 pp.

Zajda, Joseph I. *Education in the USSR.* Oxford: Pergamon Press, 1980. 292 pp.

Zorin, Libushe. *Soviet Prisons and Concentration Camps.* Newtonville, Mass.: Oriental Research Partners, 1980. 118 pp.

Zuzanek, Jiri. *Work and Leisure in the USSR: A Time Budget Analysis.* New York: Praeger, 1980. 440 pp.

Index of Biographies

Index of Names